Handbook of Indigenous Education

Elizabeth Ann McKinley
Linda Tuhiwai Smith
Editors

Handbook of Indigenous Education

Volume 1

With 77 Figures and 24 Tables

Editors
Elizabeth Ann McKinley
Melbourne Graduate School of Education
University of Melbourne
Melbourne, VIC, Australia

Linda Tuhiwai Smith
Faculty of Māori and Indigenous Studies
The University of Waikato
Hamilton, Waikato, New Zealand

ISBN 978-981-10-3898-3   ISBN 978-981-10-3899-0 (eBook)
ISBN 978-981-10-3900-3 (print and electronic bundle)
https://doi.org/10.1007/978-981-10-3899-0

Library of Congress Control Number: 2019933556

© Springer Nature Singapore Pte Ltd. 2019
This work is subject to copyright. All rights are reserved by the Publisher, whether the whole or part of the material is concerned, specifically the rights of translation, reprinting, reuse of illustrations, recitation, broadcasting, reproduction on microfilms or in any other physical way, and transmission or information storage and retrieval, electronic adaptation, computer software, or by similar or dissimilar methodology now known or hereafter developed.
The use of general descriptive names, registered names, trademarks, service marks, etc. in this publication does not imply, even in the absence of a specific statement, that such names are exempt from the relevant protective laws and regulations and therefore free for general use.
The publisher, the authors, and the editors are safe to assume that the advice and information in this book are believed to be true and accurate at the date of publication. Neither the publisher nor the authors or the editors give a warranty, express or implied, with respect to the material contained herein or for any errors or omissions that may have been made. The publisher remains neutral with regard to jurisdictional claims in published maps and institutional affiliations.

This Springer imprint is published by the registered company Springer Nature Singapore Pte Ltd.
The registered company address is: 152 Beach Road, #21-01/04 Gateway East, Singapore 189721, Singapore

We would like to dedicate this Handbook to the many people who have brought us to this point and made it all possible: first, to those educators, knowledge holders, and leaders of the past who have kept Indigenous knowledge alive, have nurtured and spoken Indigenous languages, struggled for Indigenous rights, and sought to encourage and sustain Indigenous educational aspirations through the darkest of times. Secondly, we dedicate the Handbook to those who work as Indigenous educators in our communities and schools, who hunger for literature that supports and gives evidence to their work. Finally, we dedicate this Handbook to our early research leaders who have broken through numerous barriers to clear the way for the work that is presented here.

Preface

Indigenous communities across the world traditionally had very sophisticated systems of education that were never static but developed as a result of reflection, collective deliberation, and experimentation. These education systems had no ending: each generation expanded the community's knowledge base. Traditionally, learning occurred as one participated in activities of everyday living and joining in life's ceremonies. While this form of education continues in current times, it is in addition to more structured and formal settings.

The academic field of Indigenous education is a continuation of this journey. Indigenous scholars have been working hard developing space in the academies and writing texts with an aim to expand Indigenous knowledge bases through research. The text draws attention to the fact that every chapter has been led, and largely entirely produced, by Indigenous academics – a feat that would not have been possible even a decade ago.

Over the last four or more decades, the education of Indigenous peoples has become an increasingly central preoccupation in many colonized countries across the globe and for international associations. With Indigenous education systems disrupted and often destroyed by colonial invasion and exploitation, the United Nations Declaration on the Rights of Indigenous Peoples (UNDRIP) has brought to the world's attention our right to teach our histories, languages, philosophies, and literature, to establish and control our own education systems and institutions, to teach in a manner appropriate to cultural methods of teaching and learning, to provide education in our own languages, and for all Indigenous children to have access to an education in their own culture and language. This book addresses all these issues for Indigenous peoples across the globe and in different contexts.

Indigenous education today is a complex, interdisciplinary field of research requiring its Indigenous researchers to straddle disciplines of the academy – a super subject – incorporating subjects such as linguistics, psychology, history, mathematics, astronomy, law, and philosophy, to name but a few, and subjects in the future we have yet to hear about. The Handbook brings together diverse views and strategies from across the world to provide a comprehensive overview of the complexities and nuances of Indigenous peoples' experiences. Indigenous peoples' positioning on education is largely driven by their colonial histories.

The purpose of the *Handbook of Indigenous Education* is to provide a state-of-the-art reference and a comprehensive map of the field to date. It is divided into six major sections based on debates and topics of interest to Indigenous communities, and each section has 10–12 chapters. Each of the six sections is introduced by two section editors who are internationally recognized in the field. All chapters are either led or entirely written by Indigenous academics. We attempted to recruit a wide spread of people from different countries and continents across the globe and achieved this to a large extent; however, we are cognizant there are "gaps." These gaps present a challenge to all of us as we move forward.

The Handbook is available as a print edition and as a fully searchable online version.

Melbourne, Australia Elizabeth Ann McKinley
Hamilton, New Zealand Linda Tuhiwai Smith
March 2019

Acknowledgments

There were a number of challenges in putting together this large edited volume. We needed to access our networks, decide on the section editors, and ask them to choose authors. The entire process required negotiation skills. Communication between the section editors and the editors in chief involved suggestions of authors and topics. Some people approached were not available to write or did not respond to invitations. This is to be expected – Indigenous academics are often overcommitted, trying to satisfy both institutional demands and community obligations. However, books are always the result of a complex web of relationships. This book represents, first and foremost, networks within networks of Indigenous scholars and, secondly, another network of allies who have supported the work of Indigenous scholars in the academy.

We would like to thank those who accepted the challenge and responsibility for being section editors: Leonie Pihama (University of Waikato), Jenny Lee-Morgan (Unitec Institute of Technology), George Sefa Dei (University of Toronto), Jean Paul Restoule (University of Victoria, Canada), Margie Hohepa (University of Waikato), Carl Mika (University of Waikato), Graham Hingangaroa Smith (Massey University), Melinda Webber (University of Auckland), Bryan McKinley Jones Brayboy (Arizona State University), Megan Bang (North Western University), Sharon Nelson-Barber (WestEd), and Zanette Johnson (Intrinsic Impact Consulting). Your knowledge, networks, and commitment to the project have been instrumental to the success of this work. We wish to thank those who opened this work up to Indigenous peoples networks across the globe.

We want to acknowledge the work of all of the authors who have contributed to this book. We wish to thank you all for writing the chapters and spending additional hours on making revisions. It is your contributions that have made this volume possible. The book is a celebration of our collective expertise and the relationships we have with each other. We hope further relationships can be built through this work.

We would like to express our gratitude to the chapter reviewers for both their expertise and their generosity in giving time to provide the feedback necessary to help make this book a quality contribution to education. The number of people required to review this text was extensive, and we are very pleased you shared our vision of the value in this book. We also wish to thank Lilly Brown, who worked tirelessly as our research assistant. We, as editors in chief, were not always as organized as we could have been, but you managed to keep the threads together. And last, but not least, we wish to thank the team at Springer with the production of the book: Springer editor Nick Melchior, for your suggestion that it was timely for such a volume, and the Springer team we dealt with – Rashmi, Neha, and Mokshika and others too numerous to mention – many thanks for your guidance and assistance.

List of Reviewers
Glen Aikenhead, University of Saskatchewan, Saskatoon, Canada
Airini, Thompson Rivers University, Kamloops, Canada
Lilly Brown, University of Melbourne, Melbourne, Australia
Greg Cajete, University of New Mexico, USA
Janepicha Cheva-Isarakul, Victoria University of Wellington, Wellington, Aotearoa New Zealand
Pauline Chinn, University of Hawai'i, Honolulu, USA
Ho-Chia Chueh, National Taiwan University, Taipei, Taiwan
Garrick Cooper, University of Canterbury, Christchurch, Aotearoa New Zealand
Bronwen Cowie, University of Waikato, Hamilton, Aotearoa New Zealand
Rhonda Craven, Australian Catholic University, Sydney, Australia
Ruth De Souza, University of Melbourne, Melbourne, Australia
George Sefa Dei, University of Toronto, Toronto, Canada
Julie Evans, University of Melbourne, Melbourne, Australia
Lesley Farrell, University of Melbourne, Melbourne, Australia
Katie Fitzpatrick, University of Auckland, Auckland, Aotearoa New Zealand
Alicia Flynn, University of Melbourne, Melbourne, Australia
Candace Galla, University of British Columbia, Vancouver, Canada
Lorraine Graham, University of Melbourne, Melbourne, Australia
Sandy Grande, Connecticut College, New London, Connecticut, USA
John Hattie, University of Melbourne, Melbourne, Australia
Camilla Highfield, University of Auckland, Auckland, Aotearoa New Zealand
Margie Hohepa, University of Waikato, Hamilton, Aotearoa New Zealand
Brendan Hokowhitu, University of Waikato, Hamilton, Aotearoa New Zealand
Huia Jahnke, Massey University, Palmerston North, Aotearoa New Zealand
Seu'ula Johansson Fua, University of South Pacific (Tonga Campus), Suva, Fiji
Zanette Johnson, Intrinsic Impact Consulting, Palo Alto, USA
Alison Jones, University of Auckland, Auckland, Aotearoa New Zealand
Te Taka Keegan, University of Waikato, Hamilton, Aotearoa New Zealand
Tahu Kukutai, University of Waikato, Hamilton, Aotearoa New Zealand
Jenny Lee-Morgan, Unitec Institute of Technology, Auckland, New Zealand
Margie Maaka, University of Hawai'i (Manoa), Honolulu, USA
Stephen May, University of Auckland, Auckland, Aotearoa New Zealand
Carl Mika, The University of Waikato, Hamilton, Aotearoa New Zealand
Angus Mcfarlane, University of Canterbury, Christchurch, Aotearoa New Zealand

Acknowledgments

Sonja Mcfarlane, University of Canterbury, Christchurch, Aotearoa New Zealand
Tracy McIntosh, University of Auckland, Auckland, Aotearoa New Zealand
Elizabeth Ann McKinley, Melbourne Graduate School of Education, University of Melbourne, Melbourne, Australia
Julie McLeod, University of Melbourne, Melbourne, Australia
Sue Mentha, University of Melbourne, Melbourne, Australia
Sue Middleton, University of Waikato, Hamilton, Aotearoa New Zealand
Nikki Moodie, University of Melbourne, Melbourne, Australia
Bernadette Murphy, University of Melbourne, Melbourne, Australia
Sharon Nelson-Barber, WestEd, San Francisco, USA
Sophie Nock, University of Waikato, Hamilton, Aotearoa New Zealand
Rachel Nordlinger, University of Melbourne, Melbourne, Australia
Adreanne Ormond, Victoria University of Wellington, Wellington, Aotearoa New Zealand
Leonie Pihama, University of Waikato, Hamilton, Aotearoa New Zealand
Jelena Porsanger, Sami University of Applied Sciences, Kautokeino, Norway
Donn Ratana, University of Waikato, Hamilton, Aotearoa New Zealand
Jean-Paul Restoule, University of Victoria, British Columbia, Canada
Lester-Irabinna Rigney, University of South Australia, Adelaide, Australia
Fazal Rizvi, University of Melbourne, Melbourne, Australia
Raukura Roa, University of Waikato, Hamilton, Aotearoa New Zealand
Christine Rubie-Davies, University of Auckland, Auckland, Aotearoa New Zealand
Sophie Rudolph, University of Melbourne, Melbourne, Australia
Kabini Sanga, Victoria University of Wellington, Wellington, Aotearoa New Zealand
Glenn Savage, University of Western Australia, Perth, Australia
Wee-Tiong Seah, University of Melbourne, Melbourne, Australia
Rae Si'ilata, University of Auckland, Auckland, Aotearoa New Zealand
Naomi Simmons, University of Waikato, Hamilton, Aotearoa New Zealand
Mere Skerrett, Victoria University of Wellington, Aotearoa New Zealand
Christine Sleeter, California State University Monterey Bay, California, USA
Robin Small, University of Melbourne, Melbourne, Australia
Cherryl Waerea-i-te-rangi Smith, Te Atawhai o te Ao, Whanganui, Aotearoa New Zealand
Graham Hingangaroa Smith, Massey University, Palmerston North, New Zealand
Jill Smith, University of Auckland, Auckland, Aotearoa New Zealand
Kylie Smith, University of Melbourne, Melbourne, Australia
Linda Tuhiwai Smith, The University of Waikato, Hamilton, Waikato, New Zealand
R.D. Kekeha Solis, University of Hawai'i (Manoa), Honolulu, USA
Dawn Sutherland, University of Winnipeg, Winnipeg, Canada
Tony Trinick, University of Auckland, Auckland, Aotearoa New Zealand
Malia Villegas, Afognak Native Corporation (Kodiak Island), Alaska, USA
Maggie Walter, University of Tasmania, Hobart, Australia
Te Rina Warren, Massey University, Palmerston North, Aotearoa New Zealand
Melinda Webber, University of Auckland, Auckland, Aotearoa New Zealand

Paul Whitinui, Victoria University, Victoria, Canada
Laiana Wong, University of Hawai'i (Manoa), Honolulu, USA
Lyn Yates, University of Melbourne, Melbourne, Australia
Sarah Young, University of Melbourne, Melbourne, Australia

Editor's Note

All the chapters in the *Handbook of Indigenous Education* have undergone double peer review. Chapters were not given to reviewers "blind" – some reviewers knew the authors, some were known to the reviewers through their work, and others were not known by the reviewers. All reviewers had expertise in the academic subject area. The reviews were returned to chapter authors with the names of their reviewers. We decided on this approach because the field is still small, and authors are well-known and often identifiable due to their topics and the contexts in which they write. Another reason was that because it was the first book of its kind, we wanted constructive feedback to assist authors to make their work stronger, and so we asked the reviewers to read for coverage of the issue, critique/argument or insight, international relevance, structure of the chapter, and readability.

That is, every chapter was independently evaluated by at least two reviewers. This applied to all authors, including section editors and editors in chief who were also chapter contributors. These were deliberately sent to senior academics who would not be intimidated by the seniority of the writers. The section introductions were reviewed by the editors in chief, and the overall introduction to the book was reviewed by section editors and a few senior academics who were chapter reviewers. All the reviewers were chosen for their expertise in the field. As you may note, most of the reviewers are a mix of Indigenous and non-Indigenous academics.

Contents

Volume 1

1 **Towards Self-Determination in Indigenous Education Research: An Introduction** 1
Elizabeth Ann McKinley and Linda Tuhiwai Smith

Part I Colonialism 17
Leonie Pihama and Jenny Lee-Morgan

2 **Colonization, Education, and Indigenous Peoples** 19
Leonie Pihama and Jenny Lee-Morgan

3 **Colonization and the Importation of Ideologies of Race, Gender, and Class in Aotearoa** 29
Leonie Pihama

4 **Colonization, Education, and Kanaka 'Ōiwi Survivance** 49
Nālani Wilson-Hokowhitu and Noelani Goodyear-Ka'ōpua

5 **Mapuchezugun Ka Mapuche Kimün: Confronting Colonization in Chile (Nineteenth and Twentieth Centuries)** 63
Héctor Nahuelpán, Jaime Antimil, and Kathryn Lehman

6 **Truth and Reconciliation in Canada: Indigenous Peoples as Modern Subjects** 85
D. Lyn Daniels

7 **In the End "The Hope of Decolonization"** 101
Moana Jackson

8 **Beyond the Guest Paradigm: Eurocentric Education and Aboriginal Peoples in NSW** 111
Bob Morgan

9 **Liberate the Base: Thoughts Toward an African Language Policy** 129
Ngũgĩ wa Thiong'o

xv

Part II Indigenous Governance: Restoring Control and Responsibility over the Education of Our People 139
George J. Sefa Dei and Jean-Paul Restoule

10 Indigenous Governance: Restoring Control and Responsibility over the Education of Our People 141
George J. Sefa Dei and Jean-Paul Restoule

11 Issues and Prospects of African Indigenous Systems of Governance: Relevance and Implications for Global Understanding 149
Lewis Asimeng-Boahene

12 Indigenous Governance for Africentric School Success 169
George J. Sefa Dei

13 Building Capacity for Indigenous Peoples: Engaging Indigenous Philosophies in School Governance 187
Edward Shizha

14 Indigenous Governance and Education in Belize: Lessons from the Maya Land Rights Struggle and Indigenous Education Initiatives 207
Filiberto Penados

15 Indigenous Leadership: A Complex Consideration 229
Margaret J. Maaka, Kerry Laiana Wong, W. Kekailoa Perry, and Patricia M. G. Johnston

16 Situating Indigenous Knowledges and Governance Within the Academy in Australia 249
Maggie Walter and Wendy Aitken

17 "A World in which [Alaska Natives] Make the Important Decisions": Re-examining Institutional Discourses and Governance in Higher Education 267
Olga Paniik Skinner and Beth Ginondidoy Leonard

18 African Indigenous Governance from a Spiritual Lens 293
Njoki Wane, Rose Ann Torres, and Dionisio Nyaga

19 Mi'kmaw Kina'matnewey and Mi'kmaw Control over Mi'kmaw Education: Using the Master's Tools to Dismantle the Master's House? 309
John Jerome Paul, Lisa Lunney Borden, Jeff Orr, Thomas Orr, and Joanne Tompkins

Part III Language and Culture ... 329
Margie Hohepa and Carl Mika

20 Language-Culture-Education: Problem and
    Potential – An Introduction ... 331
    Margie Hohepa and Carl Mika

21 Aloha ʻĀina-Placed Hoʻomoana ʻŌlelo Hawaiʻi: A Path to
    Language Revitalization ... 339
    Katrina-Ann R. Kapāʻanaokalāokeola Nākoa Oliveira

22 Materials Development for Indigenous Language Learning and
    Teaching: Pedagogy, Praxis, and Possibilities ... 357
    Candace Kaleimamoowahinekapu Galla

23 Still Flourishing: Enacting Indigenizing Language Immersion
    Pedagogies in the Era of US Common Core State Standards ... 377
    Mary Hermes and Erin Dyke

24 Listen to the Voices: Informing, Reforming, and Transforming
    Higher Education for First Nations' Peoples in Australia ... 401
    Jeannie Herbert

25 Maintaining a Cultural Identity While Constructing a
    Mathematical Disposition as a Pāsifika Learner ... 423
    Roberta Hunter and Jodie Hunter

26 Efforts and Concerns for Indigenous Language Education
    in Taiwan ... 443
    Chen-Feng Joy Lin, I-An Grace Gao, and Pi-I Debby Lin

27 Sámi Language for All: Transformed Futures Through
    Mediative Education ... 467
    Erika Katjaana Sarivaara and Pigga Keskitalo

28 Colonialism, Māori Early Childhood, Language, and the
    Curriculum ... 483
    Mere Skerrett

29 Elaboration and Intellectualization of Te Reo Māori: The Role
    of Initial Teacher Education ... 505
    Tony Trinick

30 Ka unuhi a me ka hoʻokē: A Critique of Translation in a
    Language Revitalization Context ... 529
    Kerry Laiana Wong and Ron D. Kekeha Solis

31 A Term's Irruption and a Possibility for Response: A Māori
    Glance at "Epistemology" ... 545
    Carl Mika

Part IV Societal Issues **565**
Bryan McKinley Jones Brayboy and Megan Bang

32 Societal Issues Facing Indigenous Education: Introduction 567
Bryan McKinley Jones Brayboy and Megan Bang

33 Carceral Colonialisms: Schools, Prisons, and Indigenous Youth in the United States 575
Jeremiah A. Chin, Bryan McKinley Jones Brayboy, and Nicholas Bustamante

34 Systems of Support: What Institutions of Higher Education Can Do for Indigenous Communities 605
Jessica A. Solyom, Jeremiah A. Chin, Bryan McKinley Jones Brayboy, Amber Poleviyuma, Sarah Abuwandi, Alexus Richmond, Amanda Tachine, Colin Ben, and Megan Bang

35 "A Future Denied" for Young Indigenous People: From Social Disruption to Possible Futures 631
Emma Elliott-Groves and Stephanie A. Fryberg

36 The Value of Indigenous Knowledge to Education for Sustainable Development and Climate Change Education in the Pacific 651
Timote Masima Vaioleti and Sandra L. Morrison

37 Reclaiming Our People Following Imprisonment 671
Cherryl Waerea-i-te-rangi Smith, Helena Rattray, and Leanne Romana

38 Indigenous Educational Movements in Thailand 695
Prasit Leepreecha and Meixi

39 Yachayninchis (Our Knowledge): Environment, Cultural Practices, and Human Rights Education in the Peruvian Andes ... 725
Elizabeth Sumida Huaman

40 Reflections on the Purpose of Indigenous Environmental Education 767
Kyle Powys Whyte

41 Indigenous Family Engagement: Strong Families, Strong Nations 789
Megan Bang, C. Montaño Nolan, and N. McDaid-Morgan

Volume 2

Part V Transforming Education 811
Graham Hingangaroa Smith and Melinda Webber

42 **Transforming Research and Indigenous Education Struggle** 813
Graham Hingangaroa Smith and Melinda Webber

43 **Envisioning Indigenous Education: Applying Insights from Indigenous Views of Teaching and Learning** 823
Gregory A. Cajete

44 **Psychosocial Analyses and Actions for Promoting Restorative Schools: Indigenous Determinants Connecting Three International Sites** 847
Angus Hikairo Macfarlane, Sonja Macfarlane, Tom Cavanagh, Maria Nieto Angel, Fiona Duckworth, and Letitia Hochstrasser Fickel

45 **Keaomālamalama: Catalysts for Transformative Change in Hawaiian Education** 873
Keiki Kawaiʻaeʻa, Walter K. Kahumoku, Sylvia M. Hussey, Gary Kalehua Krug, Teresa Haunani Makuakāne-Drechsel, Mahinapoepoe Paishon Duarte, and Lisa Watkins-Victorino

46 **The Vaʻatele Framework: Redefining and Transforming Pasifika Education** 907
Rae Siʻilata, Tanya Wendt Samu, and Alexis Siteine

47 **The Age of Reconciliation: Transforming Postsecondary Education** 937
Sheila Cote-Meek

48 **Invisible Light: Using Data to See Native Youth and Families in Policy** 955
Malia Villegas

49 **Building Sámi Language Higher Education: The Case of Sámi University of Applied Sciences** 969
Jelena Porsanger

50 **Diagnosing Elements of Colonization in Indigenous Education: An African Effort to Research and Transform Education for Indigenous Peoples** 997
Kelone Khudu-Petersen and Bagele Chilisa

51 **Refusing the Settler Society of the Spectacle** 1013
Sandy Grande

52 Defining Culturally Responsive Digital Education for
    Classrooms: Writing from Oceania to Build Indigenous
    Pacific Futures 1031
    Lester-Irabinna Rigney

53 The Transformative Role of Iwi Knowledge and Genealogy in
    Māori Student Success 1049
    Melinda Webber and Angus Hikairo Macfarlane

54 Doing Indigenous Work: Decolonizing and Transforming the
    Academy 1075
    Graham Hingangaroa Smith and Linda Tuhiwai Smith

Part VI Case Studies **1103**
Sharon Nelson-Barber and Zanette Johnson

55 Introduction to Case Studies Section 1105
    Sharon Nelson-Barber and Zanette Johnson

56 Raven's Story About Indigenous Teacher Education 1113
    Jo-ann Archibald Q'um Q'um Xiiem

57 We Voyage for the Earth: Cultural Advantage as a Global
    Education Framework 1137
    Shawn Malia Kanaʻiaupuni

58 Ako ki he nofo ʻa Kāinga: A Case Study of Pastoral Care
    Between Wakatū/Kono and Recognised Seasonal Employment
    Workers 1165
    Sandra L. Morrison

59 Ngarrindjeri *Yannarumi*: Educating for Transformation and
    Indigenous Nation (Re)building 1187
    Daryle Rigney, Steve Hemming, Simone Bignall, and Katie Maher

60 Indigenous Knowledge(s) and the Sciences in Global Contexts:
    Bringing Worlds Together 1213
    O. Ripeka Mercier and Beth Ginondidoy Leonard

61 Mā te Rourou: Māori Education and Innovation Through the
    Visual Arts in Aotearoa New Zealand 1243
    Robert H. G. Jahnke and Huia Tomlins Jahnke

62 Te puna wai ora, e tu atu nei e: Stand Up, Stand Strong, and
    Be Proud 1269
    Mere Berryman, Katie Pennicott, and Stan Tiatia

63 Where Indigenous Knowledge Lives: Bringing Indigenous
    Perspectives to Online Learning Environments 1295
    Jean-Paul Restoule

64 Whāia te Ara Whetu: Navigating Change in Mainstream Secondary Schooling for Indigenous Students 1319
Elizabeth Ann McKinley and Melinda Webber

65 Always Alert, Always Agile: The Importance of Locally Researching Innovations and Interventions in Indigenous Learning Communities 1347
Zanette Johnson and Sharon Nelson-Barber

Index 1385

About the Editors

Professor Elizabeth Ann McKinley is a Professor of Indigenous Education at the University of Melbourne. She is known for her work exploring the interaction between science, education, and Indigenous culture. She has a strong research and publication record in the field of Indigenous science education, curriculum, and the capability of mainstream education systems to meet the complex challenges of transforming educational outcomes for Indigenous and other students from underserved communities. Before moving to Melbourne in 2014, she was a Professor of Māori Education and Director of the Starpath Project for Tertiary Participation and Success at the University of Auckland. She is also well known for her capacity building and mentoring work with doctoral students and early career researchers. She has served on a number of panels and committees that have influenced public policy, including the Ministerial Cross Sector Forum on Raising Achievement, and that have assessed research proposals for funding, including New Zealand's Endeavour Fund Impact Panel and Science Challenges Review. She has also served on several panels for the New Zealand Universities Academic Audit Unit. She has received a New Zealand Honour as an Officer to the New Zealand Order of Merit.

Professor Linda Tuhiwai Smith is Professor of Māori and Indigenous Studies at the University of Waikato. Professor Smith has a distinguished career as a researcher and educator who has led many of the developments in Māori and Indigenous research, establishing research centers, building networks, and mentoring researchers. She is known for her work on decolonizing and Indigenous Methodologies and Kaupapa Māori Research. Professor Smith was joint founding Director of Ngā Pae o Te Māramatanga, the Māori Centre of Research Excellence, and former President of the New Zealand Association for Research in Education. Professor Smith is a member of the Waitangi Tribunal. She has received a number of awards including a New Zealand Honor as Companion to the New Zealand Order of Merit. She is a fellow of the Royal Society of New Zealand and of the American Educational Research Association. In 2017, she received the Prime Minister's Lifetime Achievement Award in Education. In 2018, she recently received an Honorary Doctorate of Laws from the University of Winnipeg, Canada, and the Te Puawaitanga Research Excellence Award, the highest honor from the Royal Society of New Zealand for research in Māori and Indigenous knowledge.

About the Section Editors

Leonie Pihama
The University of Waikato
Hamilton, New Zealand

Jenny Lee-Morgan
Unitec Institute of Technology
Auckland, New Zealand

George J. Sefa Dei
OISE, University of Toronto
Toronto, Canada

Jean-Paul Restoule
Department of Indigenous Education, Faculty of Education
University of Victoria
Victoria, BC, Canada

Margie Hohepa
The University of Waikato
Hamilton, New Zealand

Carl Mika
The University of Waikato
Hamilton, New Zealand

Bryan McKinley Jones Brayboy
Arizona State University
Arizona, USA

Megan Bang
Northwestern University
Evanston, IL, USA

Graham Hingangaroa Smith
Massey University
Palmerston North, New Zealand

Melinda Webber
School of Māori and Indigenous Education
The University of Auckland
Auckland, New Zealand

Sharon Nelson-Barber
WestEd
California, USA

Zanette Johnson
Intrinsic Impact Consulting
Palo Alto, USA

Contributors

Sarah Abuwandi Arizona State University, Phoenix, AZ, USA

Wendy Aitken Social Sciences, University of Tasmania, Hobart, Tasmania, Australia

Maria Nieto Angel Doctoral Research, University of Canterbury (UC), Christchurch, New Zealand

Jaime Antimil Villa Wenumapu, Centro de Estudios e Investigaciones Mapuche – Comunidad de Historia Mapuche, Pasaje Llefque, Temuco, Region de la Araucania, Chile

Jo-ann Archibald Q'um Q'um Xiiem Faculty of Education, University of British Columbia, Vancouver, BC, Canada

Lewis Asimeng-Boahene Social Studies Education, Penn State University-Harrisburg, Middletown, PA, USA

Megan Bang Northwestern University, Evanston, IL, USA

Colin Ben Arizona State University, School of Social Transformation, Tempe, AZ, USA

Mere Berryman Te Kura Toi Tangata, Faculty of Education, The University of Waikato, Tauranga, New Zealand

Simone Bignall Office of Indigenous Strategy and Engagement, Flinders University of South Australia, Adelaide, SA, Australia

Bryan McKinley Jones Brayboy Arizona State University, Tempe, AZ, USA

Nicholas Bustamante Arizona State University, Tempe, AZ, USA

Gregory A. Cajete College of Education, Native American Studies, University of New Mexico, Albuquerque, NM, USA

Tom Cavanagh Department of Ethnic Studies in the College of Liberal Arts, Colorado State University, Fort Collins, CO, USA

Bagele Chilisa Department of Educational Foundations, University of Botswana, Gaborone, Botswana

Jeremiah A. Chin Arizona State University, Tempe, AZ, USA

Sheila Cote-Meek Academic and Indigenous Programs, Laurentian University, Sudbury, ON, Canada

D. Lyn Daniels Aborginal Learning, Aboriginal Learning Surrey Schools, Surrey, BC, Canada

Mahinapoepoe Paishon Duarte Kanu o ka 'Āina New Century Public Charter School, Kona, HI, USA

Fiona Duckworth Ministry of Social Development, Wellington, New Zealand

Erin Dyke Oklahoma State University, Stillwater, OK, USA

Emma Elliott-Groves Initiative for Research and Education to Advance Community Health (IREACH), Partnerships for Native Health (P4NH), Washington State University, Seattle, WA, USA

Letitia Hochstrasser Fickel Teacher Education, University of Canterbury (UC), Christchurch, New Zealand

Stephanie A. Fryberg American Indian Studies and Psychology, University of Washington, Seattle, WA, USA

Candace Kaleimamoowahinekapu Galla University of British Columbia, Vancouver, BC, Canada

I-An Grace Gao University of Helsinki, Helsinki, Finland

Noelani Goodyear-Ka'ōpua Department of Political Science, University of Hawai'i at Mānoa, Honolulu, HI, USA

Sandy Grande Education Department, Center for the Comparative Study of Race and Ethnicity, Connecticut College, New London, CT, USA

Steve Hemming Office of Indigenous Strategy and Engagement, Flinders University of South Australia, Adelaide, SA, Australia

Jeannie Herbert Charles Sturt University, Dubbo, NSW, Australia

Mary Hermes College of Education and Human Development, University of Minnesota, Minneapolis, MN, USA

Margie Hohepa The University of Waikato, Hamilton, New Zealand

Jodie Hunter Massey University, Auckland, New Zealand

Roberta Hunter Massey University, Auckland, New Zealand

Sylvia M. Hussey Native Hawaiian Education Council, Honolulu, HI, USA

Moana Jackson Wellington, New Zealand

Huia Tomlins Jahnke Māori and Indigenous Education, Massey University, Wellington, New Zealand

Robert H. G. Jahnke Māori Visual Art, Massey University, Wellington, New Zealand

Zanette Johnson Intrinsic Impact Consulting, Honokaʻa, HI, USA

Patricia M. G. Johnston Te Whare Wānanga o Awanuiārangi, Whakatane, New Zealand

Walter K. Kahumoku University of Hawaiʻi, West Oʻahu Kapolei, HI, USA

Shawn Malia Kanaʻiaupuni Strategy & Innovation Group, Kamehameha Schools, Honolulu, HI, USA

Keiki Kawaiʻaeʻa University of Hawaiʻi, Hilo, HI, USA

Pigga Keskitalo Duodji and Teacher Education, Sámi University of Applied Sciences, Kautokeino, Norway

University of Lapland, Rovaniemi, Finland

Kelone Khudu-Petersen Department of Primary Education, University of Botswana, Gaborone, Botswana

Gary Kalehua Krug Department of Education, Office of Hawaiian Education, Waiʻanae, HI, USA

Jenny Lee-Morgan Unitec Institute of Technology, Auckland, New Zealand

Prasit Leepreecha Department of Social Science and Development, Faculty of Social Sciences, Chiang Mai University, Chiang Mai, Thailand

Kathryn Lehman University of Auckland, Auckland, New Zealand

Beth Ginondidoy Leonard Department of Alaska Native Studies, University of Alaska Anchorage, Anchorage, AK, USA

Chen-Feng Joy Lin National Pingtung University, Pingtung, Taiwan

Pi-I Debby Lin Department of Environmental Health, Harvard T.H. Chan School of Public Health, Boston, MA, USA

Lisa Lunney Borden St. Francis Xavier University, Antigonish, NS, Canada

Margaret J. Maaka University of Hawaiʻi at Mānoa, Honolulu, HI, USA

Angus Hikairo Macfarlane Māori Research, University of Canterbury (UC), Christchurch, New Zealand

Sonja Macfarlane Māori Research, University of Canterbury (UC), Christchurch, New Zealand

Katie Maher Office of Indigenous Strategy and Engagement, Flinders University of South Australia, Adelaide, SA, Australia

Teresa Haunani Makuakāne-Drechsel National Indian Education Association, Honolulu, HI, USA

N. McDaid-Morgan College of Education, University of Washington, Seattle, WA, USA

Elizabeth Ann McKinley Melbourne Graduate School of Education, University of Melbourne, Melbourne, VIC, Australia

Meixi College of Education, University of Washington, Seattle, WA, USA

O. Ripeka Mercier Te Kawa a Māui (School of Māori Studies), Victoria University of Wellington, Wellington, New Zealand

Carl Mika The University of Waikato, Hamilton, New Zealand

C. Montaño Nolan College of Education, University of Washington, Seattle, WA, USA

Bob Morgan The Wollotuka Institute, Indigenous Education and Research, The University of Newcastle, Newcastle, Australia

Sandra L. Morrison School of Māori and Indigenous Studies, University of Waikato, Hamilton, New Zealand

Héctor Nahuelpán Centro de Estudios e Investigaciones Mapuche–Comunidad de Historia Mapuche, Departamento de Ciencias Sociales, Universidad de Los Lagos, Temuco, Region de la Araucania, Chile

Sharon Nelson-Barber WestEd, San Francisco, CA, USA

Dionisio Nyaga Social Justice Education/OISE, University of Toronto/School of Social Work, Ryerson University, Toronto, ON, Canada

Katrina-Ann R. Kapāʻanaokalāokeola Nākoa Oliveira Kawaihuelani Center for Hawaiian Language, University of Hawaiʻi at Mānoa, Honolulu, HI, USA

Jeff Orr St. Francis Xavier University, Antigonish, NS, Canada

Thomas Orr Antigonish, Canada

John Jerome Paul Mi'kmaw Kina'matnewey, Membertou, Canada

Filiberto Penados Center for Engaged Scholarship Abroad, San Ignacio, Cayo, Belize

Katie Pennicott Invercargill Middle School, Invercargill, New Zealand

W. Kekailoa Perry University of Hawaiʻi at Mānoa, Honolulu, HI, USA

Leonie Pihama The University of Waikato, Hamilton, New Zealand

Amber Poleviyuma Hopi-Tewa Women's Coalition to End Abuse, Second Mesa, AZ, USA

Jelena Porsanger Sámi University of Applied Sciences, Kautokeino, Finnmark County, Norway

Helena Rattray Te Atawhai o te Ao, Whanganui, New Zealand

Jean-Paul Restoule Department of Indigenous Education, Faculty of Education, University of Victoria, Victoria, BC, Canada

Alexus Richmond University of Colorado Boulder, Denver, CO, USA

Indian education at Arizona State University, Tempe, AZ, USA

Daryle Rigney Office of Indigenous Strategy and Engagement, Flinders University of South Australia, Adelaide, SA, Australia

Lester-Irabinna Rigney Centre for Research in Education, School of Education, Division of Education, Arts and Social Sciences, University of South Australia, Adelaide, SA, Australia

Leanne Romana Te Atawhai o te Ao, Whanganui, New Zealand

Tanya Wendt Samu Faculty of Education and Social Work, University of Auckland, Auckland, New Zealand

Erika Katjaana Sarivaara Faculty of Education, University of Lapland, Rovaniemi, Finland

George J. Sefa Dei Social Justice Education, OISE, University of Toronto, Toronto, ON, Canada

Edward Shizha Social and Environmental Justice and Youth and Children's Studies, Wilfrid Laurier University, Brantford, ON, Canada

Rae Siʻilata Faculty of Education and Social Work, University of Auckland, Auckland, New Zealand

Alexis Siteine Faculty of Education and Social Work, University of Auckland, Auckland, New Zealand

Mere Skerrett Victoria University of Wellington, Wellington, New Zealand

Olga Paniik Skinner University of Alaska Fairbanks, Fairbanks, AK, USA

Cherryl Waerea-i-te-rangi Smith Te Atawhai o te Ao, Whanganui, New Zealand

Graham Hingangaroa Smith Massey University, Palmerston North, New Zealand

Linda Tuhiwai Smith Faculty of Māori and Indigenous Studies, The University of Waikato, Hamilton, Waikato, New Zealand

Ron D. Kekeha Solis University of Hawaiʻi at Mānoa, Honolulu, HI, USA

Jessica A. Solyom Arizona State University, School of Social Transformation, Tempe, AZ, USA

Elizabeth Sumida Huaman Comparative International Development Education, University of Minnesota, Minneapolis, MN, USA

Amanda Tachine American Indian College Fund, Denver, CO, USA

Ngũgĩ wa Thiong'o University of California, Irvine, CA, USA

Stan Tiatia Invercargill Middle School, Invercargill, New Zealand

Joanne Tompkins St. Francis Xavier University, Antigonish, NS, Canada

Rose Ann Torres Ontario Institute for Studies in Education, University of Toronto, Toronto, ON, Canada

Tony Trinick Te Puna Wānanga, Faculty of Education and Social Work, University of Auckland, Auckland, New Zealand

Timote Masima Vaioleti Faculty of Education, University of Waikato, Hamilton, New Zealand

Malia Villegas Washington, DC, USA

Maggie Walter Social Sciences, University of Tasmania, Hobart, TAS, Australia

Njoki Wane Social Justice Education, University of Toronto, Toronto, ON, Canada

Lisa Watkins-Victorino Office of Hawaiian Affairs, Honolulu, HI, USA

Melinda Webber University of Auckland, Auckland, New Zealand

Kyle Powys Whyte Michigan State University, East Lansing, MI, USA

Nālani Wilson-Hokowhitu Te Kotahi Research Institute, The University of Waikato, Hamilton, New Zealand

Kerry Laiana Wong University of Hawai'i at Mānoa, Honolulu, HI, USA

Towards Self-Determination in Indigenous Education Research: An Introduction

1

Elizabeth Ann McKinley and Linda Tuhiwai Smith

Contents

Being and Becoming a Community of Indigenous Researchers in Education 7
Overview of the Book 9
   Section 1: Colonialism 10
   Section 2: Indigenous Governance 10
   Section 3: Language and Culture 10
   Section 4: Societal Issues 11
   Section 5: Transforming Education 11
   Section 6: Case Studies 12
Cross Themes of the Handbook 12
What Is the Future of Indigenous Education Research? 14
References 15

Abstract

Indigenous education was not always marginalized. Indigenous communities have always maintained and developed complex education systems. However, colonial invasion and exploitation have shattered Indigenous knowledges and ways of knowing, and as a result, the pieces have become scattered – destroyed, hidden, and other parts just waiting to be reconstructed. More recently, Indigenous education has become a collaborative international project with ideas and methods, theories, and examples being drawn upon from diverse Indigenous situations. This chapter lays out the basis of how the editors view Indigenous

---

E. A. McKinley (✉)
Melbourne Graduate School of Education, University of Melbourne, Melbourne, VIC, Australia
e-mail: elizabeth.mckinley@unimelb.edu.au

L. T. Smith (✉)
Faculty of Māori and Indigenous Studies, The University of Waikato, Hamilton, Waikato, New Zealand
e-mail: tuhiwai@waikato.ac.nz

© Springer Nature Singapore Pte Ltd. 2019
E. A. McKinley, L. T. Smith (eds.), *Handbook of Indigenous Education*,
https://doi.org/10.1007/978-981-10-3899-0_77

education – derived from the work that predates the United Nations Declaration of the Rights of Indigenous Peoples (UNDRIP) but is consistent with it. We explore what it means to become and be an Indigenous education researcher by providing an overview of the book. The six sections of the book contain chapters that examine subject matters in relation to a broader understanding of how these ideas resonate internationally. We explore each of the six sections and finally ask questions about the future of Indigenous education research.

Keywords

United Nations Declaration of the Rights of Indigenous Peoples (UNDRIP) · Being and becoming · Future of Indigenous education

When we, the editors, were approached to consider editing the *Handbook of Indigenous Education*, we were excited at the opportunity. We thought it was timely to produce the first large handbook by Indigenous people themselves, partly because for a long time, we have watched others write our story and as a result actively suppress Indigenous knowledges. As the number of Indigenous education academics and researchers increased over the years, largely due to the work of Indigenous academic "pioneers," their allies, and programs established in tertiary institutions, we thought there were enough people who could provide an account of the Indigenous education research journey to date. We also thought it timely to highlight Indigenous education scholarship that is often hidden away in the non-mainstream journals being read only by others who know where to seek it out.

Indigenous education was not always marginalized. Indigenous communities have always maintained and developed complex education systems. For example, traditionally in Māori society in Aotearoa New Zealand, there were institutions of higher learning, students were especially chosen to fulfill special roles in their communities, children were developed, and their particular interests were noted. Learning was elevated above the ordinary pursuits of a community, had spiritual elements to it, and there were rituals and protocols to observe. Colonial invasion and exploitation have shattered Indigenous knowledges and ways of knowing, and as a result the pieces have become scattered – destroyed, hidden, and other parts just waiting to be reconstructed. This Handbook explores the ways in which this has happened to Indigenous communities throughout the world and how the traditions of Indigenous systems of knowledge are now being recovered and remade within the context of their critical engagement with western traditions. However, the Handbook is not only concerned with "recovering" the broken pieces. As educators and researchers, we seek to put the recovered pieces into new places, embrace new technologies, gather new information, and try to make sense of a rapidly changing world with the same confidence as our ancestors had as thinkers and knowledge creators. Indigenous knowledges are not, as Mead (2003) reminds us, "an archive of information" but tools for thinking, organizing information, considering the ethics of knowledge, and informing us about our world and our place in it. These attempts are now "coming of age" in this work.

No matter what the context, Indigenous Peoples have articulated a deep relationship to mother earth, to her lands and waterways, and with that interconnection diverse and relational paradigms of knowing and being. Being of the land gives each of us a unique understanding of the lands in which our ancestors made our homes, enabling us to share a deep sense of place brought about when we live and breathe the land – a land that gives life, shapes our stories, and defines who we are. The relationship to land has also defined the Indigenous experiences of being forcibly removed from land and of being displaced and denied the rights and responsibilities that hold worldviews, meanings, and identities together. It defines the work and the journeys that have gone into putting down ancestral stories and bones into new lands, reservations, and margins where Indigenous Peoples have had to survive. As editors of the Handbook, we wanted to tap into this rich vein of culture, knowledge, and understandings that inform Indigenous approaches to knowledge and education. We have sought to do this by embracing the rich diversity of Indigenous research and by keeping the scope of the sections wide and open and reducing any sense that there is either a homogenous or unitary approach to Indigenous education or indeed a singular definition of education or research.

The United Nations Declaration of the Rights of Indigenous Peoples (UNDRIP), adopted by the General Assembly in 2007 by the majority of 144 members, sets out the internationally agreed-upon rights of Indigenous Peoples to education. While the UNDRIP expresses Indigenous Peoples' historical grievances, contemporary challenges, and socioeconomic, political, and cultural aspirations, Article 14 expresses the keys to the realization of these through education, stating:

1. Indigenous Peoples have the right to establish and control their educational systems and institutions providing education in their own languages, in a manner appropriate to their cultural methods of teaching and learning.
2. Indigenous individuals, particularly children, have the right to all levels and forms of education of the State without discrimination.
3. States shall, in conjunction with Indigenous Peoples, take effective measures, in order for Indigenous individuals, particularly children, including those living outside their communities, to have access, when possible, to an education in their own culture and provided in their own language.

While the UNDRIP enshrines Indigenous education in a rights framework, much of the work in Indigenous education predates the signing of the Declaration and represents decades of education development across different contexts working within the constitutional arrangements of different nation states. The rights to education, schooling, and access to a free primary school education for citizens are recognized in most national constitutions although the recognition of citizenship and entitlements of citizenship for Indigenous Peoples as Indigenous Peoples rather than as an ethnic minority is not always a given. The variable and often marginalized status of Indigenous Peoples and their relationships to the nation-state within which they reside is one of the reasons that the UNDRIP is an important part of the human rights framework as it sets out basic rights and freedoms for Indigenous Peoples. It is also important to recognize that many Indigenous communities are struggling to survive; many Indigenous activists have been assassinated or disappeared, Indigenous LGBTIQ communities are harassed and marginalized, Indigenous women and girls are often the victims of abuse and sexual violence, and Indigenous boys and men are more likely to end up in criminal justice systems. In many situations, identifying as an Indigenous person is still life-threatening. Constitutions and declarations may recognize the rights of Indigenous Peoples, but states and governments must implement policies and infrastructure that protect those rights. Education plays a fundamental role in the survival, security, safety, and well-being of Indigenous communities and ways of knowing and being.

Indigenous educators have advanced Indigenous agendas under all political conditions. While the educational landscape is forever changing, policies for the education of Indigenous Peoples have often remained stuck in old assimilationist frameworks informed by paternalistic ideologies or stymied by a lack of imagination and political will to address the rights of Indigenous Peoples to an education that supports their language, culture, and knowledge. It is often at the local level or with the support of a single forward-thinking official that Indigenous educational initiatives are implemented. These kinds of initiatives can sometimes develop into systemic change (e.g., the Language Nest Kohanga Reo from Aotearoa New Zealand which gave flight to a Māori language education pathway in the Aotearoa New Zealand school system). Too frequently, however, they remain contingent on support and fly under the radar with little official recognition and minimal resourcing. It is still rare to have Indigenous knowledge included in curriculum, to have Indigenous experiences of colonization fully recognized in history, or to have Indigenous perspectives included across curriculum. It is rare to have the full engagement of Indigenous communities in public or private schools, to have governance roles, or to be principals and educational leaders. It is rare to have a critical mass of Indigenous educationalists and researchers, policymakers, and thought leaders operating in one context or jurisdiction. The Handbook brings together an international network of Indigenous researchers who, for the most part, work in quite isolated contexts in their own settings.

Indigenous educators and researchers walk along the interface of multiple knowledge systems, including official and conventional systems, institutions, histories and discourses, communities and knowledge systems, expectations, and accountabilities. For many of the first generation of Indigenous individuals who were well educated, the public or civil service was an immediate career option, while others may have trained for teaching, health-related professions, or the military. Indigenous people "making it" in the system was seen as a successful strategy for assimilation policies – a measure of the system's worth. Following generations have moved beyond public administration of education to leadership roles such as school principals and into specialist areas including teacher education and research. Other successful individuals have become community activists leading educational programs that exist outside official structures and advancing Indigenous knowledge within communities and developing community advocacy for Indigenous focused education. The diverse trajectories for Indigenous educators and researchers are reflected in the varying approaches to Indigenous language revitalization, alternative schooling models, research approaches, and leadership.

There are genuine tensions in this diversity; these are theoretical, political, cultural, disciplinary, and intergenerational. Some of the tensions can be understood best as the politics of decolonization and internal colonization and of differences between those who work for and in communities and those who may be seen as working for and in state structures. Internal colonization acts as an internal control for maintaining the hegemony of colonialism and serves to constantly reinforce the mythologies of Indigenous Peoples being "not good enough," "not intelligent," and "not able to govern themselves." These tensions include the real challenges of choosing priorities, for example, language revitalization priorities, in contexts where there are hundreds of Indigenous languages at risk of extinction. In some contexts, failing to choose is resulting in all the languages disappearing. Other tensions can be understood as cultural-structural approaches that position people along different points of a continuum of change, which engages with how that change can best be effected and how explicit theories of transformation and Indigenous self-determination can be practiced/utilized/executed/employed. For example, some might argue that the only way to attain real transformation is to overturn economic and power structures, and everything else is a waste of effort. Others argue that people have agency to make changes themselves and that culture is a context in which Indigenous Peoples can exercise agency and create transformation. Many tensions are not about opposing political positions but are disciplinary worries about the focus and approach to research, the ontological dimensions of research, the methodologies and theories being used, and the frame and scope of research. Unlike the simplistic binary of qualitative and quantitative methodologies, Indigenous research methodologies tend to grapple with undoing dominant language and definitions, finding ways to use the colonizer's language for decolonial analyses and drawing insights from Indigenous knowledge and values. All these tensions are represented in some way by the work in the Handbook. What holds it together is a basic commitment of authors to the very idea of Indigenous Peoples, to the rights of Indigenous Peoples, and to research by Indigenous people that affirms Indigenous identities and aspirations for self-determination.

There have been too many examples of education policies for Indigenous Peoples by states and governments that have acted in regressive, culturally and socially destructive ways, for example, Residential Schools in Canada, the forced removal of Indigenous children under various welfare provisions, policies that suppress or deny Indigenous knowledge, and language and culture and policies that focus on the presumed deficits of communities and parents. The politics and agenda of dominant non-Indigenous interests which hold sway over education systems where Indigenous Peoples are minorities are always contestable, especially when purported to be "in our best interests." The multidisciplinary, long view of Indigenous education research is concerned with the intergenerational impact of past, current, and future education policies and practices for Indigenous Peoples. The work in this volume builds upon generations of documented Indigenous experiences across multiple education jurisdictions that give testimony to the systematic efforts made by governments to assimilate Indigenous Peoples and by definition destroy their languages, cultures, values, social systems, and practices. More fundamentally, however, the work in this volume provides evidence for the powerful resistance and motivation of Indigenous Peoples to harness the promise and potential of education to advance our aspirations for self-determination and revitalize and strengthen our cultures and languages and our families and communities.

The chapters in the Handbook provide numerous examples of Indigenous educational research being undertaken across the world. Collectively they address system-wide issues, challenges, and opportunities of education, and they span the following diverse themes: from the relationship between societal issues to schooling, from the impact of colonialism to an Indigenous teacher education program, from governance issues to mathematics and the arts curriculum, and from research methodologies to understanding pipelines from school to prison and from prison back to an Indigenous identity. The scope of Indigenous education research is expansive and deep. It is concerned with what happens in formal and informal settings. It is concerned with outcomes and the strategies, policies, pedagogies, and curricula that produce educational outcomes. It questions the taken-for-granted western-centric assumptions, philosophies, discourses, and principles of education and schooling; it challenges what counts, what matters, and how each dimension is defined. For example, Indigenous worldviews value the interconnected relationships of humans within the environment, and so, how does that worldview imagine an education, pedagogically, in curricula, assessment, and teacher education? Indigenous education research is interested in the impact of education on Indigenous well-being and on the survival of Indigenous languages, cultures, and knowledges. Indigenous education research involves building narratives and bodies of knowledge and new terminology about Indigenous education that address the experiences of Indigenous Peoples while simultaneously rewriting the narratives of the nation-state about its identity, history, and relationship to Indigenous Peoples. It is about establishing evidence frameworks that incorporate Indigenous knowledge and paradigms and speak to the practices and challenges of educators working in schools and communities. Indigenous education research maintains a critical gaze on the wider context of education and seeks to identify and address barriers to achieving Indigenous aspirations as well as innovative ways to educate the wider society. Indigenous education research is interested in what works best, how to save a language from extinction, how to nurture an Indigenous child for the future, how to transform higher education institutions, and how to strengthen Indigenous families and young people. And while all these concerns are at play, there is a constant questioning of the role of western knowledge and its tools, of Indigenous knowledge and practices, and of the ethical dimensions and relational principles of being Indigenous while doing Indigenous work. In time this expansive scope may narrow, but at present the energy of Indigenous education research is on rewriting and re-righting the historic archives of Indigenous education that were erased by colonization and on incorporating learnings from the hard-won lessons of Indigenous resistance and survivance. The Handbook represents a state-of-the-art text on

Indigenous education seen through the research lens of Indigenous researchers, but by no means does it represent the entire field of Indigenous educational research.

Being and Becoming a Community of Indigenous Researchers in Education

The Handbook is a reflection of a growing community of Indigenous researchers in education from different places and contexts, trained in diverse disciplines, working with different theories and methodologies, in different languages, and all focusing their attention on the broad field of Indigenous education. This is not an accidental convergence of individual scholars working in isolation but a reflection of the political resurgence of Indigenous Peoples more broadly and of the shared vision for education as a fundamental means, as well as a fundamental right, for self-determination. Indigenous Peoples are critically interested in education and have visions of education as a way to achieve their social, cultural, linguistic, economic, and political well-being as Indigenous nations. Colonial and nation-state education systems, however, were designed, quite deliberately, as a mode for completely assimilating Indigenous Peoples so that they no longer existed. The work of Indigenous researchers in and about education grapples with that tension between transforming education systems designed to destroy and innovating systems that will make things right.

What does it mean to be an Indigenous education researcher? This may seem a self-evident question which naively gestures at Indigenous research in education as if it is just one more approach within the vast multidisciplinary traditions of education research that can be submerged, for example, within quantitative or qualitative research, or from different disciplinary outlooks or from a focus on the big questions being asked about the state of schools in society. It is this sort of simplistic/reductive thinking that casts the identity of the Indigenous researcher in the same category as that of the feminist or that attempts to corral the Indigenous researcher's identity as an ethnic one. Indigenous researchers draw upon a completely different "worldedness" (Mika, 2017) and understandings that situate education in a relational, intergenerational, colonial, and decolonial context. Indigenous concepts and priorities about education may not necessarily be generated from the concerns of our colleagues. The Big Questions about education that often vex researchers often appeal to apparently universal ideas of the dominant group that may not be the big questions from an Indigenous perspective. In fact, even the defining terminology that appeals to ideas of universal application – for example, the term "public education" and the oppositional categories of public/private – has been experienced by Indigenous Peoples as one of the main agencies of colonization. Furthermore, legislative practices reinforced that Indigenous students did not belong in such "public" places. They were not considered full citizens, they were not tax payers, and they still had to undergo prior assimilation by the state before they were deemed ready for school. Indigenous research, not confined to those hegemonies, draws within it understandings about humanness, relationships, ancestors, and metaphysical dynamics; different understandings of the roles of teachers and learners, curriculum, and pedagogy; and a different sense of urgency around language and culture, expectations for governance and leadership, values and ethics, and theories for transforming the way education is conceptualized and organized.

The idea of being and becoming a community of Indigenous researchers in education is deeply entwined with ideas about being Indigenous, being both self-defined and recognized by relations as an Indigenous human being who is part of a collective whose histories and philosophies are connected to place. In one sense being is a constant act of becoming, of constant interaction with the world; at the same time, being is also about just sitting, being still and immersed in a world without trying to act upon it. Being Indigenous is a process and a concept of living in relation to other human and nonhuman beings. It turns on having intimate connections to the earth and the metaphysical elements of the world. But being Indigenous also engages with experiencing the sustained efforts of imperial and colonial powers to deny and redefine the humanness of our being. Being Indigenous in the twenty-first century is political. It is living, it is acting, it is claiming, it is honoring, it is remembering, and it draws upon the genealogies, dreams, lives, histories, creations, and ideas of ancient legacies and ways of being that existed long before European modernity. Being is not only relational but past, present, and future. It is a way to be, a way of being, that crosses time.

Becoming a community of Indigenous researchers of education illuminates the purposeful act of bringing Indigenous researchers from diverse places together to create what Toni Morrison has said is "a shareable language" (Morrison, 1992) for conceptualizing, organizing, practicing, researching, and evaluating the education of Indigenous Peoples. One important vehicle for becoming an Indigenous research community has been the formation of Special Interest Groups and caucuses that have emerged in Education Research Associations. Professor Margie Maaka and Dr. Sharon Nelson Barber played an important role in bringing the two Special Interest Groups of Indigenous Peoples (of the Americas and of the Pacific) together in a preconference to the Annual Meeting of the American Education Research Association. This regular event has facilitated shared conversations about research. Professor Maaka also instigated the Special Interest Group for Indigenous Peoples of the Pacific. These fora have connected researchers, introduced emerging researchers, and fostered collaborations and networks. Other scholars, such as Professor Graham Hingangaroa Smith from Aotearoa New Zealand, Professor Verna Kirkness from Canada, Professor Ray Barnhart and the late Dr. Oscar Kawagley from Alaska, as well as scholars from Sami countries or the Pacific, have traveled afar and introduced young scholars and research to different Indigenous contexts. The World Indigenous Peoples Conferences on Education ("WIPCE") has provided for community and institutional researchers to gather every 2 or 3 years to share knowledge. These are large community hosted conferences that attract Indigenous and non-Indigenous researchers from across the globe. Networks have formed that support collaborations, and educational and research ideas have circulated internationally. New specialist journals have been established or reinvigorated with a consciousness about broadening research to wider Indigenous audience. This in turn has helped create Indigenous Studies as a broad umbrella for studies that focus on Indigenous knowledge and knowledge for Indigenous Peoples that is committed to the sovereignty and self-determination of Indigenous Peoples.

Overview of the Book

In this Handbook, we are trying to address Indigenous approaches to education rather than being directed by the standard disciplinary "gaze" and responding to non-Indigenous Peoples' agendas about what is important in Indigenous education. While many of us as academics are "squeezed" into disciplines, such as anthropology, Indigenous studies, educational psychology, and so on, we decided the book needed to be constructed in a way that reflected Indigenous education issues. Of course, it is nigh impossible to separate our lives in the academy from our lives outside it. All the chapters show our everyday lives are inextricably entwined with our past colonial masters. One of the criteria for the authors was that all chapters needed to be written in English (or at least translated into English). The book is dominated by writers from former colonies of the British Empire (particularly Canada, New Zealand, Australia, and the USA) as well as other countries which have a legacy of English, particularly African countries and the Pacific Islands. One of the chapters was translated from Spanish, and some other authors (not from British colonial countries) had help with their English grammar. There remain a number of challenges for books of this nature. For example, the book only includes Indigenous people who have access to the academy – yet there are many Indigenous Peoples who still remain outside it. Furthermore, another challenge is to become more inclusive of a wider range of Indigenous Peoples from other language groups.

We made the decision to model our Indigenous capacity building ethos by encouraging co-editors for every section – a senior editor with a junior colleague. We tried to make the Editorial teams international, but for very pragmatic reasons, our Section Editors needed to have a close working relationship, and so some of our Section Editors worked in the same institution, and all worked with an editor from their own country. We also encouraged multi-authored chapters led by an Indigenous principal author. It was very important to us that the Handbook became a vehicle for telling our research stories from our Indigenous perspectives and frameworks. There is a vast tract of literature about Indigenous education, authored mostly by non-Indigenous researchers, that is already available, and we wanted to demonstrate the capacity that now exists for Indigenous researchers to be authorities and take leadership of the agenda for Indigenous education research. Many of the teams of collaborating authors, however, are a mix of Indigenous and non-Indigenous researchers.

This book presents a body of research knowledge written by Indigenous scholars about Indigenous education. We have attempted to set a different frame of reference in terms of what has mattered around Indigenous Peoples. The six sections we decided on are the platforms that have enabled us to make sense of our experiences and, simultaneously, to realize the potential to be transformed and meet Indigenous aspirations. However, not all sections were obvious. We debated whether we should have a section on colonialism. The challenge of this section is that the inclusion of colonial histories can come to define Indigenous Peoples, but we realized from the feedback we gathered that we needed to include something. We chose to craft a section that framed colonialism differently by having some commentary by respected elders included to set the section apart from other books. Our sections include:

Section 1: Colonialism

Section editors Leonie Pihama and Jenny Lee-Morgan (both Waikato University, Aotearoa New Zealand) set the scene for Indigenous education in relation to colonialism. This section shows the diversity and similarities in the colonial experiences of Indigenous Peoples as colonizers imported systems of schooling. As the Section Editors say in their Introduction, "While our shared experiences of colonialism have left many of our societies scattered and impoverished, the colonial experience has also been a point of connection for our collective solidarity in survival." While the mechanisms through which schooling contributed to the colonial agendas differed across Indigenous nations, it is evident schooling expedited them – from civilizing the natives through residential schools to supporting the dispossession of lands. In addition to showcasing the multiplicity and complexity of colonial processes and practices, this section also features three respected and well-known decolonizing scholars and activists in their own countries as guest authors to broaden the discussion and provide some insightful analysis.

Section 2: Indigenous Governance

In this section George Dei (University of Toronto, Canada) and Jean-Paul Restoule (University of Victoria, Canada) assert that Indigenous groups had their own systems of governance prior to colonialism. With Indigenous governance, a major topic for Indigenous Peoples from the multi-levels of societal institutions – legal-jurisdictional, political, and economics – to educational institutions, this section explores the conceptualization of Indigenous governance and how such governance is manifested in Indigenous and alternative educational sites. Contributions in the section also examine how such Indigenous Governance offers lessons for re-visioning schooling and education in multiple global and transnational contexts. In their introductory remarks the Section Editors that "Global governance of Indigenous rights is an urgent matter." They have approached the challenge conceptually by "drawing a link between Indigenous Governance and global governance."

Section 3: Language and Culture

Education plays a pivotal role in the regeneration and reconstruction of Indigenous language, culture, and knowledges. This section explores the intricacy of the relationship between language, culture, and education. They argue that neither language nor culture is being "revived/revitalized" as items but is deeply implicated through each other and constitutes Indigenous selves. The Section Editors Margie Hohepa and Carl Mika (both University of Waikato, Aotearoa New Zealand) introduce the authors in this section as ones who "are from communities that are affected by a language-culture-education problem or potential. On their own, any of these separate elements of language, culture, and education complicate a theoretical description of life; in pairs, they produce even more inconsistencies and complexities." Chapters in this section include themes engaging with Indigenous language and cultural knowledge in the curriculum, Indigenous pedagogy inside and outside of colonial-developed institutions, policy leverages for language learning opportunities, the place of Indigenous language and culture in teacher and higher education, and the politics and/or philosophies of language use, translation, and expansion.

Section 4: Societal Issues

Societal issues can impact significantly on the education of Indigenous Peoples. This section presents the reader with a wide range of current, and ongoing, challenges across a variety of Indigenous contexts, including school-prison-community trajectories, human rights violations, and the engagement and support of Indigenous families. The Section Editors, Bryan McKinley Jones Brayboy (Arizona State University, USA) and Megan Bang (Northwestern University, USA), put forward a framework through which to view the narratives of this section that focuses on empowerment, enactment, engage, envision, and enhancement. The Section Editors posit the five Es framework as concepts that "do not place us as 'victims' regarding the impact of wider societal structures but provide a sense of agency (both individual and community) and hope about how to re-capture, re-establish, re-instantiate our nations of peoples." Indigenous communities have dealt with and survived major events and changes in their circumstances and that experience is continuing. It is not accidental that societal issues impact powerfully on Indigenous communities and thereby on educational education. Schools may shield or shelter students from society but can also reproduce the injustices and unfairness of society. Indigenous education has responsibilities to provide safety through knowledge and resiliency through sustaining Indigenous values and agency.

Section 5: Transforming Education

This section, co-edited by Graham Hingangaroa Smith (Te Whare Wānanga o Āwanuiārangi, Aotearoa New Zealand) and Melinda Webber (University of Auckland, Aotearoa New Zealand), focuses on "transforming" both the processes and outcomes of education and schooling to more effectively meet the learning and sociocultural aspirations of Indigenous peoples. The section interrogates the dual concerns related to how education and schooling structures in colonized societies function to reproduce dominant social, cultural, and economic interests on the one hand and in turn maintain outcomes of persisting social, economic, cultural, and learning underdevelopment and marginalization on the other. The dual work covered in this section engages with the need to critically unpack the functioning of schooling in colonized settings and, secondly, with ways to improve schooling and educational outcomes for Indigenous students. The Section Editors view transforming education and schooling as "an important pre-condition to the broader struggle of transforming the social, economic, cultural, and political under-development that reflects the colonized positioning of many Indigenous populations."

Section 6: Case Studies

This final section examines Indigenous experiences across formal and informal learning contexts through case studies. Sharon Nelson-Barber (WestEd, USA) and Zanette Johnson (Intrinsic Impact Consulting, USA) offer the reader a diversity of accounts that First Nations and Indigenous communities have faced – many of them parallel challenges, such as the effects of land loss, colonization, aggressive assimilation, and navigating collective and personal journeys through cultural trauma. The Section Editors ask, "Are our efforts getting results that matter? Are we doing things in ways that reflect our values deeply? Are we relating to one another in the ways our ancestors would have understood and respected? Are our children becoming a next generation who we can trust to carry our cultures forward?" In today's historical moment, this section advances how Indigenous Peoples strategize to meet the challenges of modern local/global Indigenous life. These accounts provide ideas about how to adapt rapidly and survive as peoples and show how our collective efforts can inspire one another to creative solution-building that brings about positive changes.

Indigenous academics, who largely make up this work, are sometimes living and working far from their communities they are writing about. Every chapter is led by an Indigenous author. Again this openly political stand was not without controversy and debate from our writers. But in privileging Indigenous voices, we were not prepared to have one Indigenous person in a writing team named at the end of the line of non-Indigenous writers, nor were we willing to privilege young non-Indigenous academics as part of larger research teams even with an interest and commitment to Indigenous education. This was not what this book was about. Furthermore, we requested our Section Editors, who were involved with choosing authors for their section, to select senior Indigenous academics who would be willing to write alongside junior Indigenous academics, to build the capacity of our community, and many authors responded in kind. More than 40 chapters are written with 2 or more authors.

Cross Themes of the Handbook

It will be clear to readers that, while the Handbook is in sections, there are chapters that could fit in more than one section. There are interrelated and cross-cutting themes, blurred boundaries, and a layering of knowledge and insight across chapters and sections. We want to highlight some of those cross themes here.

Indigenous research in education addresses *a range of contexts* in highly nuanced ways. Attention to context is driven by the specificities of historical, geographical, and political experiences and by the stories that Indigenous communities want to retell and revitalize. Indigenous knowledge and relationships predate colonization, and Indigenous Peoples are more than the story of colonization and devastation. Critically describing contexts is important for reinstalling Indigenous ideas of context into the frame and positioning Indigenous ideas as offering solutions and hope. Indigenous Peoples do not seek to be the perpetual victims of their own stories.

Some of the chapters illustrate a *deep knowledge base* that has been developed over highly specialized Indigenous education areas, such as language revitalization and the inclusion of cultural ideas in curriculum and pedagogy. This expert knowledge is often subsumed in general educational literature as interesting case studies rather than as theory defining examples of the field of language revitalization. Indigenous educators and researchers of language revitalization have profound knowledge of what it means to re-embed Indigenous languages back into communities, families, and cultures.

The chapters examine subject matters in relation to a broader understanding of how these ideas resonate *internationally*. Indigenous education research is an international field with a distinctive literature and networks of knowledge that are shared across borders. In many contexts, Indigenous Peoples are still regarded as being deficient about their own context, let alone the context of others. However, Indigenous education has become a collaborative international project with ideas and methods, theories, and examples being drawn upon from diverse Indigenous situations. Some areas such as research ethics, working in institutions, and culturally informed pedagogies have a rich literature from diverse contexts. Other specific contexts are cited consistently as examples of deep practice informed by 30–40 years of work.

The Handbook provides a rich source for the *diversity of Indigenous methodologies and analyses* for educational research. The chapters demonstrate seamlessly the thoughtful framing of research, attention to what matters from an Indigenous perspective, the critical use of a broad range of education research methodologies, and the incorporation of Indigenous knowledge, languages, and cultural ideas. Indigenous writers have for the most part stopped explaining their cultural frameworks and paradigms for others and have developed diverse ways for generating and applying Indigenous ideas to educational questions.

And finally, the chapters and sections speak to the challenges of *education for marginalized peoples* and have much to contribute to wider educational directions and understandings. Education is seen by Indigenous Peoples as having a powerful potential for the healing and resurgence of Indigenous communities and families. Language is seen as healing, Indigenous knowledge is seen as healing, and Indigenous engagement is seen as healing. Schools and other educational settings should be healing places rather than places of trauma and exclusion. This is a fundamentally different view of education in the twenty-first century that Indigenous Peoples held hundreds of years ago and an equally fundamentally different philosophical understanding of the purpose of education from standard mainstream views of education.

What Is the Future of Indigenous Education Research?

In closing this introductory piece to the Handbook, we wish to ponder on the future. In a recent speech, one of our esteemed elders and author in this book, Dr. Moana Jackson, recounted a story about his granddaughter that sums up the aspirations of Indigenous Peoples:

> I have an eight-year-old granddaughter who is the most beautiful granddaughter in the world, of course. Her first language was our language – the first language learned to speak to read in and to write was Māori and then she began to learn English because it's all around her. We were sitting on the couch one day and she had a book that had a list of English words and she was reading out the words and sometimes she would ask me what they meant. Then at one point she paused for quite a while and then she said to me "[Granddad], what's this word?" and she spelt it to me F - U - T - U - R – E. I said, "That's future" and she said, "What's a future?" Do you know how hard it is to explain to an eight-year-old what a future is? But I did my best and I told a story and then I said, "so the future is when we take all the times of our past, bring them into today, and then we carry them into all of our tomorrows, and the carrying into all of our tomorrows, this is future." She seemed satisfied with that and carried on going through her wordlist.
>
> The next morning I was sitting in the kitchen quite early and she came bustling in, got out the little lunch box that she takes to school and started putting some food in and filled up a water bottle, then bustled outside and stuffed them into the saddlebag on her little bike. While she was doing that, the little Pākehā boy, the little white boy from next door who's two years younger than her - my family called him her shadow because he follows her everywhere - he came through the fence and he said, "What are you doing?" And with that wonderful non-response which children have and which politicians never lose, she said, "Nothing."
>
> Then she got on her bike and started to pedal up the drive and he said, "Where are you going?" She said, "to look for a future." He said, "Can I come?" and she looked over her shoulder and said, "Can you keep up?"
>
> The challenge that faces all countries that have been colonised is that Indigenous Peoples are forging a journey and asking the others in that country, "Will you come with us? Can you keep up?" (Jackson, 2018, pp. 2–3)

The Handbook is an example of some of the current research available in Indigenous education. What is presented here is a significant body of research produced by Indigenous researchers working across diverse contexts. Where does this research take us? Research provides knowledge and insights that help identify the limits and possibilities of education. The challenge for Indigenous research is to have impact at the level of system and structural change. Indigenous education is political and subject to relations of power and the dominant views of nation states. Influencing how education systems should be improved, how schools could be reformed, or how preservice teachers should be educated are challenges for Indigenous education research. Likewise being able to deliver well-being to our communities through the healing and educative powers of an Indigenous education system is a significant aspiration.

In this *Handbook of Indigenous Education*, we too ask the questions Dr. Jackson's granddaughter asks: Will you come with us on this journey to frame our educational institutions in a way that relates to strong Indigenous communities? Can you keep up with us as we forge our paths toward strong and healthy Indigenous communities and families that will benefit everyone?

References

Jackson M (2018) At home on country, at home in the world. Presented at the Dungala Kaiela Oration, Shepparton, Victoria, Australia, 24 July 2018 (Retrieved 18 Sept 2018 from http://www.kaielainstitute.org.au/dungala-kaiela-oration.html)

Mead HM (2003) Tikanga Māori. Huia Publishers, Wellington

Mika C (2017) Indigenous education and the metaphysics of presence: a worlded philosophy. Routledge, London. Retrieved from https://www.routledge.com/

Morrison T (1992) Playing in the dark: whiteness and the literary imagination. Harvard University Press, Cambridge

The United Nations (Adopted by the General Assembly September 2007) The United Nations Declaration on the Rights of Indigenous Peoples (UNDRIPs). The United Nations (Retrieved from https://www.un.org/esa/socdev/unpfii/documents/DRIPS_en.pdf)

Part I

Colonialism

Leonie Pihama and Jenny Lee-Morgan

Colonization, Education, and Indigenous Peoples

2

Leonie Pihama and Jenny Lee-Morgan

Contents

Introduction	20
Colonial Ideologies and Schooling	20
Conclusion	26
References	27

Abstract

The devastation of colonialism has shaped our shared, but different, experiences as Indigenous people. From our natural environment and relational structures that enabled collective wellbeing to our cultural knowledge systems to our languages, and ceremonial practices, colonialism has disrupted and fragmented our ways of being. Education was both a target and tool of colonialism, destroying and diminishing the validity and legitimacy of Indigenous education, while simultaneously replacing and reshaping it with an 'education' complicit with the colonial endeavour. Schooling as a formalised colonial structure served as a vehicle for wider imperialist ideological objectives. This chapter provides a context for understanding the deep connections between colonisation, education and Indigenous peoples, and introduces the chapters in this section that exemplify the ways colonisalim has played out in Aotearoa New Zealand, Australia, Canada, Hawaii, Chile and Africa. Subsequently, the diversity and the similarities in the colonial experiences of Indigenous communities is evident, as imported systems of schooling were deliberately and purposefully imposed upon Indigenous lands and Peoples.

L. Pihama (✉)
The University of Waikato, Hamilton, New Zealand
e-mail: lpihama@waikato.ac.nz

J. Lee-Morgan
Unitec Institute of Technology, Auckland, New Zealand
e-mail: jleemorgan@unitec.ac.nz

© Springer Nature Singapore Pte Ltd. 2019
E. A. McKinley, L. T. Smith (eds.), *Handbook of Indigenous Education*,
https://doi.org/10.1007/978-981-10-3899-0_67

Keywords

Indigenous · Colonisation · Colonial education · Assimilation · Domestication

Introduction

Imperialism, through the destructive reach of colonialism, has had a devastating impact on Indigenous peoples throughout the world. Colonial violence, key to the act of colonialism, has murdered, dehumanized, enslaved, subjugated, and oppressed Indigenous lives, families, and communities, in some cases, for many generations (Dunbar-Oritz 2015; Smith 1999). Each colonial invasion ensured the establishment of power and maximum exploitation of people and resources (Newcomb 2008). Colonial processes, underpinned by an unfettered arrogance and self-asserted superiority, have shaped our shared, but different, experiences as Indigenous people. From our natural environment and relational structures that enabled collective well-being to our cultural knowledge systems to our languages and ceremonial practices, colonialism has sought to explicitly and implicitly disrupt and fragment our ways of being (Walker 1990). Education was both a target and tool of colonialism, destroying and diminishing the validity and legitimacy of Indigenous education, while simultaneously replacing it with an "education" complicit with the colonial endeavor (Hutchings and Lee-Morgan 2016; Smith 1999).

The purpose of this section of the handbook is to set the scene for Indigenous education in relation to colonialism. Here in Aotearoa New Zealand, colonial schooling was established in 1816; however the foundations were set for the imposition of colonial systems of education well before the first mission school opened its doors in Rangihoua in the north (Simon and Smith 2001). This is the case across Indigenous territories. Schooling as a formalized colonial structure served as a vehicle for wider imperialist ideological objectives. What we see in this section is both the diversity and the similarities in the colonial experiences of Indigenous communities as imported systems of schooling were imposed upon Indigenous lands and peoples.

Colonial Ideologies and Schooling

The mechanisms through which schooling contributed to the broader colonial agenda differed across Indigenous nations that ranged from the facilitation of the civilizing intent through the forced removal of Native and Aboriginal children from their nations and their placement into residential boarding schools to the establishment of mission or Native schooling systems in tribal territories (Child 1998; Simon and Smith 2001). Colonial schooling is also seen as a vehicle through which to support the dispossession of Indigenous nations from our lands. It was first and foremost Indigenous lands and resources that imperialism sought to possess (Coulthard 2014; Grande 2015). Indigenous nations living about and caring for those lands were, and continue to be, seen as an impediment to colonial expansionism (Jackson 2007).

Schooling was one vehicle that could expedite the colonial civilization agenda, and in particular the individualization, of Indigenous peoples to enable a deconstruction of collective understandings that informed and maintained tribal resistance to land confiscations and the denial of the sovereignty of Indigenous nations. In America, the residential schools were premised on the ideology advanced by Capt. Richard H. Pratt who established the Carlisle school in 1879. Reflecting on the underpinning ideology of the residential schools system in 1892, he stated:

> A great general has said that the only good Indian is a dead one, and that high sanction of his destruction has been an enormous factor in promoting Indian massacres. In a sense, I agree with the sentiment, but only in this: that all the Indian there is in the race should be dead. Kill the Indian in him, and save the man. (Pratt 1892, p. 46)

Pratt advanced the notion that in order for Native Americans to be fully assimilated into white American colonial society, schools such as Carlisle needed to focus on removing all parts of what it meant to be Indian. Pratt argues, "we make our greatest mistake in feeding our civilization to the Indians instead of feeding the Indians to our civilization" (ibid).

The residential schooling system in Canada not only aligned to the "kill the Indian in him [sic]" ideology they have also been directly implicated in the deaths of many First Nations children and the extreme and inhumane conditions within which many generations of First Nations children resided within. The Truth and Reconciliation Commission of Canada Summary report "Honour The Truth, reconciling for the Future" (2015) documents the genocidal nature of Canadian residential schools stating:

> For the students, education and technical training too often gave way to the drudgery of doing the chores necessary to make the schools self-sustaining. Child neglect was institutionalized, and the lack of supervision created situations where students were prey to sexual and physical abusers. (p. 45)

In Aotearoa New Zealand, Linda Smith (1986) has referred to Native schools system that was located within these communities as a "Trojan horse." Designed to embed assimilatory practices within Indigenous communities, these schools aimed to civilize from within and permeate colonizing ideologies via the children, their families, and tribal communities. The success of imperialist expansion relied upon schooling to fulfill the colonial intentions of Christianizing, civilizing, and the assimilation of Indigenous peoples into roles as domestic laborers. It is clear that the drivers of the historical development of residential and mission schooling systems globally were, at one end of the spectrum, the denial of collective Indigenous identity to enable a full process of assimilation and civilization to be realized and, at the other end, genocidal and ethnocidal practices that sort to exterminate Indigenous nations.

"Colonisation and the importation of ideologies of race, gender and class in Aotearoa" addresses the colonial processes of assimilation employed in the invasion of Indigenous lands and imposed upon Indigenous peoples which are grounded upon the dominant ideologies related to race, class, and gender. This piece by Leonie Pihama examines the underpinning belief systems that provided the rationale for colonization. She argues that these beliefs systems were embedded in the dogma of the Doctrine of Discovery, which provided justification for colonial invasion globally. The imposition of colonial structures of race, gender, and class served to validate acts of oppression and subjugation of Indigenous peoples. These systems of classification, all constructed and imposed by colonial forces, were in essence ways through which colonizers self-legitimized their tyranny over and domination of Indigenous peoples.

In "Mapuchezugun Ka Mapuche Kimün: Confronting Colonisation In Chile (Nineteenth and Twentieth Centuries)," we move closer to the latter end of the spectrum where colonial violence is clearly evident in the case of the Mapuche people the indigenous inhabitants of south-central Chile and southwestern Argentina, including parts of present-day Patagonia. Written by Hector Nahuelpan and Jaime Antimil, and thoughtfully translated from Spanish to English by Kathryn Lehman, this chapter analyzes the process of colonization of the Mapuche as they were forced into the Chilean State and capitalist political economy in the nineteenth and twentieth centuries. The authors utilize archival sources and oral history, to detail the colonial project of dispossession and genocide against the Mapuche people that impacted their language, ontology, and epistemology as well as the political and territorial sovereignty. This included reducing the Mapuche to a minority; the obliteration, eradication, and persecution of the use of Mapuzugun (language of the Mapuche people) and Mapuche kimün (Mapuche knowledge); and racial subordination within the social interactions of subsequent generations, in what they term the "civilizing spaces." Schooling was one of the key "civilizing spaces" that denigrated, in particular, the Mapuche language and knowledge with devastating consequences for the lives of their people. However, Hector Nahuelpan and Jaime Antimil argue that far from being passive subjects, the Mapuche people have displayed diverse forms of resistance, negotiation, and response – a struggle for life facing a project of death represented by colonization.

In ▶ Chap. 6, "Truth and Reconciliation in Canada: Indigenous Peoples as Modern Subjects," Lyn Daniels, who is Cree of the Kawacatoose First Nation in southern Saskatchewan, explores ways in which the Indian Residential schooling are remembered by survivors and the intergenerational impact of those schools. Exploring the role of photographs to record historical narrative related to Residential Schools, Daniels highlights the political intent of these forms of representation to further embed the colonial gaze and in doing so to affirm the wider colonial assimilatory intention of these schooling systems. She argues that "*how educational policies are experienced inter-generationally by the descendants of survivors reveals another dimension of Canadian colonialism*" and draws upon work by fiction writer, W.G. Sebald to ways through which we come to remember and come to know ourselves. Drawing on a range of works of fiction Daniels highlights the centrality of issues of representation and the need for Indigenous Peoples to frame the ways in which histories such as Indian Residential Schools are re-presented. The chapter asserts that moving beyond silence is a process of decolonization. Rememberance is critical to ensuring that current and future generations have a understanding of the history that has impacted upon their ancestors and therefore on their lives. In doing so this chapter considers how the traumatic history of Indian residential schools might be remembered, in particular by inter-generational survivors.

The contribution from Nalani Wilson-Hokowhitu and Noelani Goodyear, "Colonization, Education and Kanaka 'Ōiwi Survivance," provides the reader with an overview of the sustained connection between traditional and contemporary Hawaiian education while traversing a vast expanse of colonial history within Hawaii. It is organized into three main sections that focus on traditional Hawaiian knowledge and learning practices, contact, and the early educational institutions that developed during the nineteenth century, Kamehameha Schools, annexation, and statehood. Kānaka Maoli (Native Hawaiians) from time immemorial have embraced and nourished a deep and growing ontology, epistemology, and axiology. Ka 'imi loa, reaching back through time, our ancestors mapped evolutionary biology extending from the natural world into the spiritual and metaphysical realms with the epic Kumulipo, our most acclaimed creation chant. From the beginnings of creation to the many hālau, or schools, our intellectual capacities encompassed a visual and tactile literacy of reading waves, currents, winds, clouds, weather, animal migration patterns, and celestial bodies. Kanaka developed ahupua'a or land divisions from the mountains to the sea comprising of elaborate hydroponic systems for feeding a nation with kalo (taro) from the land and fishponds at the base of the estuaries. Traditional and contemporary Hawaiian education values aloha 'āina, love and care of our land and waters, as well as the interconnectedness of humans and the natural world, our 'ohana (families), kūpuna (elders and ancestors), and ākua (the spirit realm).

During the nineteenth century, Kanaka faced the multifold threats of European and American imperialism, land alienation, and a dramatic population decline from introduced diseases. In this context the ali'i (chiefly leaders) founded innovative ways to carry out their traditional obligations to care for the well-being of the people. One way they did so was to give their lands in perpetual charitable trusts to support new institutions of care: hospitals, schools, elderly care homes, and service programs for orphaned and destitute children and their communities. The largest of these trusts established and maintains the Kamehameha Schools, founded by Ke Ali'i (the Chief) Bernice Pauahi Bishop. The last section discusses the impact of annexation and statehood while returning the reader to the sustained relationship between traditional and contemporary values for cultural integrity and sovereignty, and the reader is left with the theme of continuity in celebration of the strength and resiliency of the Native Hawaiian people.

While the aforementioned chapters deepen our understanding of the multiplicity, complexity, and diversity of colonial processes and practices in relation to specific countries or ideologies such as race and gender, a feature of this section are three further pieces that speak more broadly to the idea of colonialism. Understanding colonialism is foundational to understanding and being able to work in the context of Indigenous education, in so far that decolonization is a critical part of our reclamation, our regeneration, and, indeed, our survival. Well-respected Indigenous elders in their respective fields, communities, and countries have authored the last part of this section. They are Professor Bob Morgan, a highly respected Indigenous educator from Walgett Western New South Wales (NSW) in Australia; Dr. Moana Jackson who hails from the tribes of Ngāti Porou, Rongomaiwahine, and Ngāti Kahungunu in Aotearoa New Zealand is an Indigenous rights legal scholar and Māori leader; and Kenyan novelist and theorist Professor Ngugi wa Thiong'o, most well-known to us for his work "Decolonising the mind" (1986) where he advocates for linguistic decolonization. All three guest authors are well-respected decolonization scholars and activists in their own countries and well-regarded internationally. Each broadens the discussion about the processes and impact of colonialism, as well as some responses with insightful and inspiring analysis while also grounded in their own contexts, areas of expertise, and experiences.

Professor Morgan is a Gumilaroi man and a highly respected and acknowledged Aboriginal educator/researcher who has worked extensively throughout Australia and internationally in the field of Aboriginal knowledge and learning for over 40 years. In recognition of his commitment and contributions to international Indigenous education rights and freedoms, Professor Morgan has served on numerous Government Commissions and Community Boards and Committees including serving as part of the World Indigenous Nations Higher Education Consortium (WINHEC). In 2007 Professor Morgan was invited to be a keynote speaker to the National Indian Education Association hosted in Hawaii in October 2007. He has also presented at various other international Aboriginal/Indigenous education seminars and conferences. In November 2015, Professor Morgan was honored by being appointed a Distinguished Visiting Professor with Minzu University, School of Education, Beijing, China. Professor Morgan is currently the Managing Director of Bob Morgan Consulting and Chair of the Board of Aboriginal and Torres Strait Islander Studies, Education and Training (BATSIET) with Newcastle University. Professor Morgan also serves as a Professor with the Wollotuka Institute at Newcastle University.

In "Beyond the Guest Paradigm – Colonialism, Cultural Contamination and Eurocentric Education and its impact on Aboriginal Education," Professor Bob Morgan explores early attempts to "educate" Aboriginal students located in and around the new British settlement at Port Jackson (NSW) and how the early education practices and programs remain embedded in contemporary Aboriginal education policies and experiences. The chapter defines core elements of the "Guest Paradigm" that characterizes current Aboriginal education policies and programs and utilizes principles of Aboriginal self-determination, cultural survival, and affirmation to challenge the assimilation and culturally contaminating influences of Eurocentric education on Aboriginal cultural values and traditions and knowledge systems. It concludes with a call to move beyond the guest paradigm by citing examples of scholarly enrichment for Aboriginal peoples, without the sacrifice of culture and traditions, by advocating a strategic disengagement for Aboriginal peoples with Eurocentric education and the development of an authentic model of Aboriginal education.

2 Colonization, Education, and Indigenous Peoples

Dr. Moana Jackson is a highly regarded lawyer, a Treaty of Waitangi expert, an Indigenous rights legal scholar, and a well-respected Māori activist and outspoken leader. Formerly a Director of the Māori Law Commission, in 1993 he was appointed judge on the International Peoples' Tribunal and sat on hearings in Hawaii, Canada, and Mexico. He was appointed Visiting Fellow at the Victoria University Law School in 1995 and was elected Chair of the Indigenous Peoples' Caucus of the United Nations Working Group on the Rights of Indigenous Peoples. In 1988, his analysis of Māori and the criminal justice system in the report He Whaipaanga Hou (Jackson 1988) was pivotal in reframing thinking about Māori law. Since 2011, Dr. Moana Jackson co-chaired a major Working Group on Constitutional Transformation that involved holding more than 300 gatherings throughout Aotearoa New Zealand about the development of a new constitution based on the Treaty of Waitangi. Recognized for his outstanding scholarly contribution to progressing indigenous legal rights and his influential thinking and critical analysis, he has been highly significant for generations of jurists, policymakers, researchers, educators, activists, and Indigenous communities alike. In 2017, Jackson was awarded an Honorary Doctorate of Laws from Victoria University, Wellington.

Dr. Moana Jackson's chapter entitled ► Chap. 7, "In the End "The Hope of Decolonization"" eloquently argues that to embark on the journey of decolonization, it begins with a clear understanding and identification of the work of colonialism. Describing the colonizers as "mythtakers," Jackson creates this term to depict the ways in which untruths were purposefully created to justify processes that enabled the violent theft, rape, and pillage of Indigenous lands, resources, knowledge systems, and of Indigenous peoples themselves. Not limited to a particular region, the devastation of colonialism on Indigenous peoples has maneuvered across the world and has spanned many centuries. Reliant on manufactured myths of racial superiority and doctrines of discovery, Jackson calls out the unwarranted deliberate violence and systematic destruction on Indigenous peoples as the "first global war of terror." He discusses three key dimensions of colonization which continues to form the basis of the colonized legacy in which we still live: the privileging of the colonizers' lives, power as the definitive hunger of colonization, and the colonizers' law as the pretence to reason. In the tradition of many of our elders, Jackson's adept skill in storytelling combined with a wide knowledge and expertise base grounded in lived experience at a tribal community, national and international level, offers a powerful piece that is both deeply troubling as well as encouraging. This chapter is foundational in preparing for any decolonization work, but for those engaging in education as a site of cultural, economic, social, political, and/or spiritual reclamation and development, a commitment to the hope of decolonization is critical.

Lastly, Professor Ngugi wa Thiong'o is an acclaimed Kenyan author, one of the foremost African novelists with a reputation of being a writer of supreme political commitment and who as an adult replaced his Western name with his current Bantu name emphasizing his cultural pride. In 1977, Ngugi publicly announced that he would no longer write in English and campaigned for other African writers to do the same. Since then, he has published most of his novels in Gikuyu, his Native language, before translating them himself for English-speaking audiences abroad.

In 1977 he was imprisoned without trial for a year after the co-authored play with Ngugi wa Mirii, "I Will Marry When I Want," was first performed. The play was highly critical of the inequalities and injustices of Kenyan society. In recent years, he has been considered a front-runner to win the Nobel Prize for Literature. Ngugi currently holds a post as Distinguished Professor in Comparative Literature and English at the University of California, Irvine, USA. In 2004 after a long exile, Ngugi returned to Kenya with his wife. His books have been translated into more than 30 languages and continue to be the subject of further books, critical monographs, and dissertations.

In "Liberate the Base: Thoughts Towards an African Language Policy," Thiong'o begins by drawing attention to the tactical maneuvers of war that centers on protecting one's own base and/or infiltrating the other's through stealth or the willing defectors. Language, of course, is a critical part of the base. He argues that the delegitimization of African languages as credible sources of knowledge, whereby English is presented as the enabler to progress and modernity, is a guise of colonialism. Whereas colonialism was previously articulated through military intervention as a way to pacify African tribal groups, Thiong'o describes this imposition in his chapter as "the linguistic pacification of languages of anarchy and blood." The fundamentalism of monolingualism is premised on the idea that English provides a way of solving the multiplicity of African languages and uniting the continent. Alongside other rationalizations such as globalization, barriers to an effective national African language policy stand in the way to securing African languages. This piece offers ways to think about the concept of relationships of languages, innovative policies that would support that each community has a right to their own language, and inspires visions of our whole and healthy selves with our own languages at the heart.

Conclusion

While our shared experiences of colonialism have left many of our societies scattered and impoverished, the colonial experience has also been a point of connection for our collective solidarity in survival. Similar cultural values and aspirations converge as Indigenous peoples hold hopeful visions for both decolonization and the regeneration of Indigenous knowledge, languages, and cultural ways. Past and present Indigenous scholars (and allies) contribute to a reclaiming, recreation, and reconstruction of knowledge that often extends beyond local communities to an Indigenous academic arena that is not only a "safe" but a reinvigorating place to go. All the chapters in this section focus on providing broad overviews of the ideologies, systems, structures, policies, and practices that have been embedded upon Indigenous lands through colonization as deliberate strategies of colonial imperialist acts of dispossession. What is clear is that in order to challenge, struggle against, and move beyond colonial imperialism, we need to understand its machinery and the ways in which education has systematically been employed to serve the interests of colonial invasion. It is also clear that each of the authors in this section has clear and purposeful aspirations and visions for the future, whereby Indigenous education can be positioned as central to the well-being of our people. To confront and understand the nature of colonialism is a critical part of a decolonizing agenda that posits Indigenous education on the frontline. Indigenous educators are reemerging with colonial critiques and educative frameworks that draw on our own traditions, philosophies, worldviews, rules and rigor, and colonial critiques that bring to the fore issues of self-determination and sovereignty. Our analysis of colonialism reminds us that we are part of a broader political struggle where Indigenous education is a strategic goal.

References

Child B (1998) Boarding school seasons: American Indian families 1900–1940. University of Nebraska Press, Lincoln

Coulthard G (2014) Red skin, white masks: rejecting the colonial politics of recognition. University of Minnesota Press, Minneapolis

Dunbar-Oritz R (2015) An indigenous peoples' history of the United States. Beacon Press, Boston

Grande S (2015) Some of us are Braves: Settler universities and the politics of indigenous refusal. Presentation to the "Public engagement and the politics of evidence in an age of neoliberalism and audit culture" conference, University of Regina, 23–25 July 2015. https://www.youtube.com/watch?v=7nYzYrjN7vI

Hutchings J, Lee-Morgan J (2016) Introduction: Kaupapa Māori in action: education, research and practice. In: Hutchings J, Lee-Morgan J (eds) Decolonisation in Aotearoa: education, research and practice. NZCER Press, Wellington

Jackson M (1988) The Māori and the criminal justice system: He Whaipaanga Hou – a new. Perspective, part 2. Department of Justice, Wellington

Jackson M (2007) Globalisation and the colonising state of mind. In: Bargh M (ed) An indigenous response to neocolonialism. Huia Publishers, Wellington, pp 167–182

Newcomb S (2008) Pagans in the promised land: decoding the doctrine of Christian. Fulcrum Publishing, Colorado

Pratt RH (1892) The advantages of Mingling Indians with Whites. Reprinted in Pratt RH (1973) Americanizing the American Indians: writings by the "Friends of the Indian" 1880–1900. Harvard University Press, Cambridge, MA, pp 260–271

Simon JA, Smith LT (eds) (2001) A civilising mission?: Perceptions and representations of the native schools system. Auckland University Press, Auckland

Smith LT (1986) Is 'Taha Māori' in schools the answer to Māori school failure? In: Smith GH (ed) Ngā Kete Waananga: Māori perspectives of Taha Māori. Auckland College of Education, Auckland

Smith LT (1999) Decolonizing methodologies: research and indigenous peoples. Zed Books, New York

Thiong'o wa N (1986) Decolonising the mind: the politics of language in African literature. Heinemann Educational, London

Truth and Reconciliation Commission of Canada (2015) Honouring the truth, reconciling for the future: summary of the final report of the Truth and Reconciliation Commission of Canada. Retrieved from http://www.trc.ca/websites/trcinstitution/File/2015/Honouring_the_Truth_Reconciling_for_the_Future_July_23_2015.pdf

Walker R (1990) Ka Whawhai Tonu Matou: struggle without end. Penguin Books, Auckland

Colonization and the Importation of Ideologies of Race, Gender, and Class in Aotearoa

3

Leonie Pihama

Contents

Introduction	30
Constructing a Mythology: Race as a Defining Notion	31
Constructing Colonial "Scientific" Justification	34
Constructing Gender: The Myth of a God-Given Order	36
Gender in the Victorian Era	37
Capitalist Oppression: Structuring Class	39
Conclusion	43
References	46

Abstract

The chapter provides a brief discussion of underpinning belief systems of race, gender, and class ideologies that provided the rationale for colonization within Aotearoa. She argues that these belief systems were embedded in the dogma of colonial supremacy, which provided justification for colonial invasion globally. The imposition of colonial structures of race, gender, and class served to validate acts of oppression and subjugation of Indigenous peoples, for the dispossession of Indigenous lands and for the subjugation of the position of women within Indigenous societies. These systems of classification, all constructed and imposed by colonial forces, were in essence ways through which colonizers self-legitimized their tyranny over and domination of Indigenous peoples.

Keywords

Colonial Ideologies · Race · Gender · Class · Indigenous

L. Pihama (✉)
The University of Waikato, Hamilton, New Zealand
e-mail: lpihama@waikato.ac.nz

© Springer Nature Singapore Pte Ltd. 2019
E. A. McKinley, L. T. Smith (eds.), *Handbook of Indigenous Education*,
https://doi.org/10.1007/978-981-10-3899-0_56

Introduction

Within Aotearoa (known in colonial terms as New Zealand), prior to colonial invasion, whānau (extended family grouping), hapū, and iwi (subtribal and tribal groupings) had established a range of educational systems that enabled the intergenerational transmission of knowledge. Learning and teaching within Māori pedagogical processes focused on the well-being of the collective, and the support of individuals within collective relationships, obligations, accountabilities, and responsibilities (Nepe 1991). Many of these relationships and arrangements have been interrupted through our experiences of colonization (Pihama et al. 2014). This chapter explores ideological importations that have contributed to those interruptions; the ideologies of race, gender, and class; and the impact of these colonial ideologies upon Māori as Indigenous Peoples. The definitions explored are those that were imported through a colonial process and, as with all acts of colonial imperialism, such ideologies have no regard for Indigenous knowledge or epistemologies. Rather the ideologies of race, class, and gender that arrived on the shores in Aotearoa were not only alien to our people but were also deliberately intended to ensure our alienation. Colonization has had a traumatic impact upon Indigenous Nations globally through the imposition of colonial power as a dominating and oppressive force (Walker 1990; Smith 1999; Grande 2004). Examining colonial-settler relationships, Coulthard (2014) provides a definition that is of particular relevance to this chapter in that it highlights the centrality, and intersection, of dominant power relations, which are central to the colonizing agenda and process.

> A settler-colonial relationship is one characterized by a particular form of domination; that is, it is a relationship where power – in this case interrelated discursive and non-discursive facets of economic, gendered, racial, and state power – has been structured into a relatively secure or sedimented set of hierarchical social relations that continue to facilitate the dispossession of Indigenous peoples of their lands and self-determining authority. (p. 7)

Acts of colonial invasion have been justified through colonial fictions such as the Doctrine of Discovery, race hierarchies embedded through Darwinian based notions of the "survival of the fittest," class oppression through the imposition of capitalist systems of production, and more recently neoliberal economics. Each of these oppressive acts have been developed, maintained, and reproduced as means for the justification and the ongoing perpetuation of oppressive systems (Jackson 2007). Pākehā (white people) or white men have been instrumental in the instigation and maintenance of power structures in regard to gender with a range of reasoning utilized to justify the positioning of women both as inferior and to be controlled by men (Warner 1976; Davis 1991; Johnston and Pihama 1995). White nations more generally sought to position themselves as superior races and ensure genocide, enslavement, and holocaustic actions against Indigenous, Black, and People of Color around the world. The white bourgeoisie have been at the forefront in the global assertion of capitalist systems of abuse and exploitation (Davis 1991).

This chapter looks specifically at the ideological construction of race, gender, and class as imposed upon Māori through colonization and the ways in which those ideologies manifested in the oppression of our people across our lands. The categorization of race as locating white men, followed closely by white women, at the pinnacle of racial hierarchies is not a surprise to those of us who were positioned in dominant ideologies as being further "down the ladder" in the colonial practices of societal organization. Just as forms of Christianity were used to validate the position of white men in gendered order so to do have they been utilized to legitimize white peoples place in the hierarchy just next to a white male god (Mikaere 2016). In discourses of race it is the "barbaric" "savage" "inferior" "Other" that is racialized, being white is not engaged, rather being white is viewed as the standard from which all other peoples are measured and defined. Adding class to the mix has provided the fundamental economic justification for the foundation and continuance of processes of capitalism that maintain processes of commodification of all things. When value is located solely in terms of capital, those who have been unable to accumulate value take their place in the inferior ranks by virtue of an ideology that is based within monetary systems of greed and exploitation.

Writings related to the history of Māori and schooling have tended toward general discussions of the ways in which the colonial powers established schooling as a vehicle for the "civilizing," and social control, of Māori people, and the complex ways in which these have impacted upon wider societal issues for Māori (Smith 2016). Much of the documentation of the role of colonization in the establishment of British models of schooling has been descriptive, and while providing invaluable description it has tended to be limited in regard to analysis of the wider intersection of colonial ideologies (Barrington and Beaglehole 1974). The complexities of the intersection of colonial invasion, race, and gendered ideologies require investigation for any discussion of the role of Pākehā imposed schooling in Aotearoa. Identifying the construction of race, gender, and class within colonial discourses is a means of understanding underpinning ideologies that exist in the maintenance of unequal power relationships. The importation of these ideologies that are based within Western colonial paradigms has meant the disruption of some fundamental beliefs. This chapter provides a brief overview of historical beliefs related to those constructions in order that we are able to more deeply understand the complexities of the dominant discourses that pervade Māori society. Colonial ideologies encompass those beliefs and ideas that are constituted through the worldviews and knowledge of the colonizer. Blauner (1994) argues that a product of Western colonialism is the development of other means of categorization, which ideologies of race contribute to. Race as a social phenomenon cannot be separated from issues of gender, class, or indigenous struggles.

Constructing a Mythology: Race as a Defining Notion

The concept of race is a colonial importation. Prior to contact between Māori and Pākehā, race did not exist for Māori, rather social organization for whānau, hapū, and iwi was mediated through whakapapa (genealogical connections). Those constructions were based within culturally defined structures. The western notion of race is constructed to ensure colonial interests are served and presented as a taken for granted way of being or considered as a part of a "natural" order. Racially based hierarchies, as they exist in present day Aotearoa, are a historical outcome of colonization. Colonization as a process has been significantly influenced by the ways in which race has been constructed and the embedding of racial discrimination and its contrasting system of white privilege. Race and the development of racial hierarchies have been the justification for, and maintenance of, colonial imperialism around the world (Gould 1981). As Harris (1993) states *"the racialization of identity and the racial subordination of Blacks and Native Americans provided the ideological basis for slavery and conquest"* (p. 1715).

In Aotearoa, there is little talk in wider society about race, even though racial ideologies are a part of the structural arrangements of this country, Māori educationalist, Penetito (2010) states *"New Zealanders are not comfortable talking about race and racism and nowhere is this more obvious than in official educational discourses"* (p. 63). An avoidance of racial issues is a part of maintaining the dominant myth that Aotearoa has "good race relations" (Barnes et al. 2013). There are many organizations that work to maintain a "we are one people" mythology in order to continue the marginalization of Māori (Bell 1996). This idea is not new to Aotearoa. It is in fact a mythology that is perpetuated daily through a colonially imposed system. Barnes et al. (2013) highlight that the colonizing agenda is reproduced in Aotearoa through the *"normalisation of racialised framing and negative stereotypes"* (p. 65). Johnston (1998) states that critical colonial race discussion is imperative in any analysis of Māori issues as race has been a defining notion since early contact. This involves engagement with and critique of the myths that found notions of racial superiority that contribute to the promotion of white supremacist practices (Walker 2016).

Blauner (1994) notes that the term race is problematic because there is such a variance between scientific and commonsense definitions. Goldberg (1990) notes that although the term race has become a contestable notion, most still agree that it continues to impact upon contemporary society. For Davis (1991), race is a key defining element in the stratification of societal hierarchies. Likewise, Anthias and Yuval-Davis (1992) note that where race as criteria for designation has been widely discredited, it remains and continues to impact and therefore cannot be denied. As such the term race cannot be dismissed, as it has a particular place in the way that differences and inequalities have been constructed (Barnes et al. 2013). Added to this is the recognition that racism exists and is experienced painfully by many of our people daily (Harris et al. 2006). What is clear is that race is predominantly defined in ways that legitimate unequal power relations that are based upon dominant notions of race. Race has been presented to us through dominant discourse as biological with the hierarchical structuring of race being presented as inevitable because of the dominant assumption of the "naturalness" of biology (Gould 1981). Western sciences have contributed significantly to the development and maintenance of such ideologies. In Aotearoa, as is the case globally, racial hierarchies were validated through positivist, reductionist approaches to western science that were determined by white men as a means by which to justify their own self-defined "superiority." For example, Century Arthur Thomson, an early medical observer of the Māori, noted

> It was ascertained, by weighing the quantity of millet seed skulls contained and by measurements with tapes and compasses, that New Zealanders [Māori] heads are smaller than the heads of Englishmen, consequently the New Zealanders are inferior to the English in mental capacity. This comparative smallness of the brain is produced by neglecting to exercise the higher faculties of the mind, for as muscles shrunk from want of use, it is only natural that generations of mental indolence should lessen the size of the brains. (Thomson 1859, p. 81)

Outlaw (cited in Goldberg 1990) notes that the notion of race first appeared as a form of categorization in a poem by William Dunbar in 1508. However, we see a range of mechanisms of colonizing classifications within documents such as the Papal Bulls of 1452 and the Doctrine of Discovery of 1493, where Indigenous nations were located as non-Christian and as such provided a broader framework within which race classifications could be positioned. The impact of which is highlighted by Steve Newcomb (1992)

> Under various theological and legal doctrines formulated during and after the Crusades, non-Christians were considered enemies of the Catholic faith and, as such, less than human. Accordingly, in the bull of 1452, Pope Nicholas directed King Alfonso to "capture, vanquish, and subdue the saracens, pagans, and other enemies of Christ," to "put them into perpetual slavery," and "to take all their possessions and property." [Davenport: 20–26] Acting on this papal privilege, Portugal continued to traffic in African slaves, and expanded its royal dominions by making "discoveries" along the western coast of Africa, claiming those lands as Portuguese territory. (p. 18)

Onondaga Nation Faithkeeper Oren Lyons (2009) highlights the Doctrine of Discovery defined Indigenous people as "non-people" through which

> Chistopher Columbus kicked off a frenzy of transatlantic voyages, native lands "discovered" by European explorers were considered "unoccupied" because the people in those uncharted lands were not Christian. (p. B1)

Race as a classification gained increasing authority through the eighteenth century with works that Outlaw describes as "typological thinking," that is, the defining of people as being of certain "types" (Goldberg 1990). This lay a foundation for the next step into classificatory systems of race. Drawing on these western "scientific" explanations, race became quickly legitimated as a colonial tool by which to classify peoples and place groups in relationship to each other through the construction of a "natural" hierarchy. This then legitimated the idea that groups' behaviors could be determined by their positioning in the racial hierarchy. The movement to a hierarchical construction was not, however, immediate but was developed throughout the early nineteenth century. It was in the nineteenth century the term race gained more specific definition related to a process of signifying groups on the basis of biology. The development of this definition of race is linked to a greater need, of Europeans, to classify peoples, particularly given the increased encounters with other peoples.

Jahoda (1999) looking firstly at Western notions of race from within Western societies identifies the construction of the "wild man" as being key in subsequent developments in regard to race. He argues that the images of the "Other" as strange, exotic, and feared have been a constant feature in European history and have its ideological foundations in early Greco-Roman traditions. The conceptualization of difference as foreign and fearful may be seen in ideas about the "monstrous races." The "monstrous races" he argues were believed to have been located in Asia, Africa (then referred to as Ethiopia), and remote parts of Europe. Relating writings by Adam of Breman in the eleventh-century Jahoda (1999, pp. 1–2) identifies clearly that the construction of the "monstrous races" was located very much in notions of the "ferocious barbarian" who were often recorded as being physically misshapen and more often than not referred to as "flesh eaters." What we see in the early writings is the establishment of way in which physicality and beliefs in cannibalism became defining characteristics of the "Other." These were to become increasingly prevalent in the definitions and discourses that developed in relation to Indigenous peoples, where discourses about the "Other" include ideas about physique, sexuality, gender, cannibalistic tendencies, barbarianism, and aggression (Jahoda 1999).

Constructing Colonial "Scientific" Justification

A prominent area of debate throughout the development of race theories was that of the origins of races, in particular surrounding the concepts of monogenesis and polygenesis. Monogenesists believed that all race groups came from a single origin and therefore were also able to reproduce across races. The basis of monogenesis belief was Christianity with the origins deriving from Adam and Eve and a firm belief in eugenesis, of the fertility of people with each other (Bolt 1971; Gould 1981). The polygenesis argument was that races had multiple origins. Gould (1981) notes that the polygenesist debate was considered part of the "American School" of Anthropology, which was not surprising, he advances, given that it was a nation that was practicing slavery and actively dispossessing Native peoples from their lands. Polygenesists argued that sexual relations across races would be unable to reproduce "offspring" and if they did, it would mean a deterioration of the superior race (Benedict 1942; Bolt 1971; Gould 1981). There was a solid belief that any interracial mixing would inevitably mean the deterioration of the superior race, producing what was viewed, by polygenesists, as a "*vicious type of half-breed, useless alike to himself and the world*" (Bolt 1971, p. 10). Sexual relations between races was explained as being an outcome of the "overeager" sexual desires of young white men and the "sexual receptiveness" of Black women.

Monogenesists argued all languages derived from three primary sources, Indo-European, Semitic, and Malay, which then traced to a singular language that had, conveniently, disappeared. Dismissal of this argument was not difficult, particularly given the many varied languages that were supposed to belong to each category. The plurality of languages was more conducive to the idea of plurality of "races," the polygenesis belief. The Darwinian process of evolution was important to the development of ideas regarding race, especially the notion of "species." There is some contention as to how Darwin himself saw the relationship of his studies, of animal and plant species, to people. Lucius Outlaw (cited in Goldberg 1990) notes that Social Darwinism grew from some attempting to relate Darwin's work from the "Origin of the Species" to people. In *The Origin of the Species*, Darwin (1910) consistently infers the inferiority of the "natives." In his observations, on the H.M.S. Beagle, Darwin (1910) refers to the "Indians" as immoral, *"like wild beasts"(p. 208)* and described one group of "Fuegians" as follows:

> These poor wretches were stunted in their growth, their hideous faces bedaubed with white paint, their skins filthy and greasy, their hair entangled, their voices discordant, and their gestures violent. Viewing such men, one can hardly make one's self believe that they are fellow creatures, and inhabitants of the same world. (Darwin 1910, p. 203)

Benedict (1942) contends that there is no doubt that the categorization of people through groupings such as Caucasoid, Mongoloid, and Negroid represent a history of anatomical specialization; however, she argues that people cannot be assigned to a singular category on the basis of biological characteristics. Moreover, she is clear that no one characteristic can determine categorization and that any emphasis on the superiority of one race that is justified through such categorization is highly flawed. Where Benedict (1942) is attempting to place a challenge to the racial superiority notion she continues to accept, if not maintain, the fundamental typologies and has been criticized for that (Anthias and Yubal-Davis 1992).

The movement to identify physical differences between races as a means of determining positioning in the order of things was highlighted even further through processes such as craniometry. Craniometry was utilized in Europe and America as a means by which to determine physical differences as a basis for classification. Gould (1981) challenges the fundamentals that underpin these forms of "science." He provides a depth analysis of a range of measuring tools and their theoretical explanations regarding intelligence. What is most useful is the careful deconstruction of a range of racially based theories in order to reveal both the inadequacies of much of what has been present as valid science and whose interests have been served. As such he has given considerable analysis to reveal the inadequacies of much of what was presented as "pure" science and drawn the connections between works that asserted the racial superiority of white people to acts of oppression and colonization. Research supporting the notion of racial hierarchy have been consistently found to be shaped by a priori racial prejudices and conclusions which influence findings through incorrect calculations or conscious manipulation of data (Gould 1981).

Bolt (1971) argues that the danger of the term race came when it was located beyond a biological concept to one where race and culture were directly linked, and cultural characteristics were used as a means by which to classify divisions of races. This highlights the connection between expressions of the existence of biological race and ideologies of superiority as based on notions of cultural supremacy. The biological sciences pertaining to race gave justification to supremacist ideologies, which in turn spawned the need for the further development of the "sciences" of race. In essence they became one in the same, "science" confirmed the stratification of peoples that in turn legitimated its own existence. There can be no artificial separation as has been indicated by those themselves who participate in such "science," just as there can be no separation of the cultural and political interests of those who control and drive such "sciences." The legitimation of unequal power relationships through the "scientific" premise that some "races" are determined to be inferior and the assertion of white supremacy and colonial dominance continue to justify and reproduce the privilege of colonizing nations (Smith 1999; Newcomb 2008). Such hierarchical assertions also underpin the colonial patriarchal gender relations imported to Aotearoa.

Constructing Gender: The Myth of a God-Given Order

Gender and gender relations are pertinent to this discussion in understanding the ways in which race, class, and gender as forms of social relations and dominant worldviews intersect within the colonizing process. A key process of colonialism is the undermining and fragmentation of existing Indigenous structures and ways of relating including the reconstruction of gender relations (Irwin 1992; Smith 1992; Maracle 1996; Pihama 2001; Bear 2016). As noted in the introduction to this chapter, gender is social constructed and defined within social and cultural contexts. James and Saville-Smith (1989) note the following definition of gender as a social construction:

> The concept of gender refers to qualities, traits and activities collectively deemed to be masculine or feminine in any given society. Although 'things feminine' are associated with females, and 'things masculine' are associated with males, sex and gender are quite distinct. The content of masculinity and femininity does not have an immediate biological foundation, despite the fact that gender defines what it means to be a male or female in a social sense. Gender is a categorization based not on physiological but on social attributes. Sex, that is the categories of 'female' and 'male' is purely physiological. (p. 10)

Conservative notions of gender emphasize that these relations are "ordained by god" and therefore are not only "natural" but is the way "god" planned it. Such arguments are concerned with the conservation of dominant relations between women and men, in order to maintain "traditional" gender relations, e.g., that women's roles are as mothers, wives, and nurturers and men as breadwinners, public figures, and leaders. Conservative explanations also view biological difference as "proof" that traditional gender relations are expected and necessary in order to maintain stability in society. The construction and maintenance of gender hierarchies are dependent upon the acceptance of such ideological assertions as "natural" and necessary. The impact on Indigenous nations, and Indigenous women in particular, has been wide-ranging and extremely destructive (Mikaere 1995; Maracle 1996; Pihama 2001; Bear 2016). Understanding and contexualizing the ways in which gender ideologies maintain oppressive structures is critical, as Bear (2016) states,

> To dismantle and deterritorialize the colonial power structure of racist heteropatriarchy, we must first understand its insidious influence and nature. (p. 164)

Daly (1973) relates the symbolism of "Father God" within Judaeo-Christian beliefs as spawning in the "human imagination" the validity of patriarchy. Simultaneously, societal mechanisms of oppressing women were viewed as "fitting" (Daly 1973, p. 13). Quite simply it is the colonial construction of God as male, God as ruling, God as natural. To which I add, God as white. God as male functions to maintain the subordination of women by man/God, God as white functions to justify the oppression of Indigenous nations. The entrenched notion of male as superior and, in particular, the conceptualization of God as male (and therefore male as God) within Judaeo-Christian beliefs is highlighted by the resistance of any attempt to shift that paradigm. In a system of male monotheism there is an established hierarchical order through which women relate to men as men relate to God (Ruether 1983). The hierarchical God-man-woman ordering then serves to ensure the maintenance and reproduction of processes that subordinate women (Ruether 1983). Gender relations as determined through Christian ideologies provide the justification for the creation of dualisms that reinforce women as inferior to men. Furthermore, male monotheism serves to reinforce patriarchal rule and that women are connected to God not directly but only through men. This order is further intensified with the notion of "evil." Evil is spoken of as "sin." Sin *"implies a perversion or corruption of human nature"* (Ruether 1983, p. 160). The oppositional arrangement of good–evil is directly related to notions of inferior-superior. The notion of "sin" mediates these dualisms in that it provides mechanisms for recognizing "perversion" and imposing judgment. The hierarchical ordering of gender in Judeo-Christianity leads to notions of evil and sin being more directly related to women. This is not to ignore the belief that "sin" is expressed as being a part of "human nature" but recognizes that the patriarchal hierarchy of Christianity has directly associated origins of sin with women. This reinforces the idea that the oppression of women is an outcome of "primordial sin" (Ruether 1983, p. 169). It is through Christianity that Eve was elevated to the status of being the "cause" of the fall of Adam. It was not only Eve's supposed "sin," but it was her mere existence that represented the "fall" of "man" (p. 169).

Gender in the Victorian Era

The notion of the "Victorian" woman comes from an idea that certain values, practices, expectations, and roles of women were derived from the Victorian era. This era relates to the rule of Queen Victoria spanning from 1837 to 1901. This is a particularly relevant period to our history as Māori as within this timeframe colonial invasion was deemed to be in the name of the Crown, who was Queen Victoria. It was also in 1840 that Te Tiriti o Waitangi (Māori Language version of The Treaty of Waitangi) was signed between our people and representatives of the Crown. The Victorian era included the beginning of major expansionism that was a part of the Industrial Revolution.

Prior to the Victorian era, the "domestic industry" incorporated the idea of the family as a productive unit and as *"the unit of production"* (Oakley 1974).

The production process was an integral part of the family operations, with production for family use being a part of the wider goal of production for sale or exchange. Marriage in the seventeenth century was viewed as a taken for granted means of ensuring the well-being of the wider extended family unit. In this marriage form women were expected to contribute economically, there was no idea that women would be dependent on husbands. Such realities in the life of the seventeenth-century English woman was in sharp contrast to the Christian ethic espoused. For example, in Ephesians it was stated *"Wives, submit yourselves unto your husbands ... for the husband is the head of the wife, even as Christ is the head of the church"* (Ephesians 5:23–24 cited in Daly 1973, p. 132). The subjugation of women as preached by the church was legitimated in western "Common law"; however, it has been argued that the impact of this on women's lived realities was minimal up to the Industrial Revolution as economics and production for the family determined relationships (Oakley 1974).

What is clear is that family relationships were altered considerably through industrialization. With industrialization came a shift in the dynamics between work and family. Work became located separate from the family, from the domestic unit. The industry movement outside of the home and the growth of large-scale factory production had brought a "new order" that emphasized not production for the survival of the family unit, but work as a separate activity that was then measured by its monetary return. The family was soon redefined within which there rose the position of "husband as breadwinner," on whom all in the family depended. This was not a rapid change but was a shift that took place between the mid-seventeenth to mid-eighteenth century. Within the Victorian era, industrialization was a critical event that contributed to changes in the roles of English women and the assertion of colonial views of women that were imported to our lands, with the subordination of women as linked directly to Christian doctrine and the subjugation of women by men through the denial of access to an education equal to men (Wollenstonecraft 1985). What is significant in the construction of the Victorian-defined woman is that those ideologies were not limited to expression within that era but extended beyond to reach into the nineteenth and twentieth centuries, creating major changes in the roles of women both in Britain and in the lands colonized by the British (Wollenstonecraft 1985). These shifts are a consequence of patriarchy and capitalism adjusting to each other in the creation of sets of hierarchy that enables domination. The practice of patriarchy in collusion with capitalism, in a British/Victorian context, is a critical point to note.

It may be argued that the influence of the economic shifts through industrialization, combined with Christian discourses, became a potent force in the oppression of women. In order to ensure societies adherence to the dependency of women in the home, the Christian ethic, which was previously marginal because of the economic need for women to produce, gained favor. This was supported by the notions of privatization and domestication. The idea of privatization grew as the separation between work and family increased. Work became identified with the public sphere and home as the private sphere. Because of its separation from the public sphere and the realm of "work," the home became a site within which the various ideologies could be reproduced. The "ideal" Victorian woman was deemed a self-less woman. Her role as "the angel of the house" was maintained through the Christian ethic of woman as virtuous (Coney 1993). To be virtuous was to be a "good" wife and to be following the "naturally ordained" order (Coney 1993, p. 14). These combined ideologies were soon to be imported to Aotearoa as the colonization of this country began to take full force in the late eighteenth century as colonizing countries were seeking expansion to both release their own internal pressures and also to facilitate the expansion of capitalist intentions into the colonies.

Colonial ideologies located women as chattels, the property of men and therefore inferior to them. The espousal of Christian doctrine and biological theories, rather than debunking each other, became a combined force. Women were now both spiritual and biologically devoid. All that remained was the positioning of women as intellectually devoid in order to ensure an holistic argument for the continued subjugation of women. This is further expanded by Fry (1985) who highlights the debate surrounding what was considered as different levels of intelligence of women and men. This development was connected directly to the biological assertions of Darwinism and much of the argument for the intellectual inferiority of women was grounded firmly in a mind-body relationship. That is, biological arguments became the foundation for ideals of intellectual inferiority.

> For many years, there had been fascination with theories concerning the different mental capacities of men and women. The 'cranium theory' which had, through elaborate measurements, set out to prove that women's brains were smaller, lighter and less convoluted than men's were now [1880s] out of date. More fashionable were the gynaecological theories which dwelt on the dangers of upsetting bodily functions in adolescence. (Fry 1985, p. 33)

The broader impact comes through the focus of gender, not solely upon women but in regard to how we come to understand our roles and identities within our societies as Indigenous peoples. Dominant gender definitions based entirely within colonial heteronormative constructions deny the multiple ways that Indigenous nations identify ourselves (Hutchings and Aspin 2007; Bear 2016; Hunt 2016). The undermining of Indigenous knowledge and relationships was systematic and intentional as a part of the process of imposing domesticated units of the nuclear family in order to destroy the fundamental societal building blocks of Māori society (Simmonds and Gabel 2016).

Capitalist Oppression: Structuring Class

Class structures, like the ordering of race and gender, came to Aotearoa as yet another unwelcomed element of Western ideology. This was to be achieved not solely through the expansion of British capitalism but also through "physically transplanting a vertical slice of British Society – economics, politics and ideology" (Bedgood 1980, p. 24). Like other colonizer beliefs, the notion of class and the Western organization of capitalism has assumed a universality that is reflective of the fundamental imperialist belief espoused by colonizing nations that they exist as a superior form. In defining class in relation to the mode of production, Kettle (1963) writes:

> The capitalist class is a class because all who belong to it are owners of productive enterprises who live by exploiting the labour of those they employ. What makes a person a member of the working class is not that he [sic] works or that he is comparatively poor… what makes a worker a worker is that he sells his labour-power for wages. (p. 54)

Social class is related to the economic and social relationships that exist for differing groups in relation to the economic system, the mode of production with the construction of class relations and the notion of class struggle are central (Blackledge and Hunt 1985, Giddens 1986). The capitalist system establishes and maintains itself through the fundamental exploitation of labor-power in order to gain surplus-value or profit (Marx 1971). The mechanisms of capitalistic manipulation have been imposed on Indigenous peoples, as a part of the colonial process, and have their origins not in Aotearoa but in the struggles that have been engaged in Europe. In order to understand the origins of capitalism, and the internal opposing forces of the bourgeoisie and proletariat, Marx and Engels (1913) emphasize that bourgeoisie society grew from the "ruins" of feudalism establishing new classes, new forms of oppressive order, and new forms of struggle.

> By bourgeoisie is meant the class of modern Capitalists, owners of the means of social production and employers of wage-labour. By proletariat, the class of modern wage-labourers who, having no means of production of their own, are reduced to selling their labour-power in order to live. (Marx and Engels 1913, p. 12)

Marx and Engels (1913) identify the fundamental premise of capitalism in its intention to exploit through a process of controlling the means of production and reducing all people to a source of wage labor. The control of the means of production is essential to an ability to control social relations. They state:

> The bourgeoisie cannot exist without constantly revolutionizing the instruments of production, and thereby the relations of production, and with them the whole relations of society. (p. 16)

The proletariat in this equation is thereby reduced to a commodity in the market, which is a critical contribution to the bourgeoisie condition that is the formation and augmentation of capital. Marx (1967a Volume 1) identifies key tenets of capitalist systems, beginning with a discussion of commodity, Marx identifies a commodity as that which value is determined by use, consumption, and through exchange. A commodity therefore has both use-value (that the article fulfills some need or want) and exchange-value, the exchange value being a quantitative relation in value of one article for another. He outlines that exchange value must be able to be expressed in terms of something common, between those things being exchanged, which may be expressed in greater or lesser quantities. It is noted that there are exceptions whereby articles can have use-value and not exchange-value and therefore not be a commodity, also something can be the product of labor and not be a commodity, i.e., if it is for own use. Further to this the exchange-value is reliant upon labor-time or labor-power. The value then of a commodity is determined; Marx (1967a Volume I) writes by *"the amount of labour socially necessary or the labour-time socially necessary for its production" (p. 35).*

Therefore, in simple terms those things that require more labor, for example, by virtue of production or because they are scarce, are considered more valuable. Hence, the social division of labor is constructed through differential value being accorded to differing forms of what is viewed as "useful labor." Marx (1967a Volume I) describes this process of differentiation as including both value of the commodity and use-value:

> All labour is 'expenditure of labour-power' and in its character of identical abstract human labour, it creates and forms the value of commodities. On the other hand, all labour is the expenditure of human labour-power in a special form and with a definite aim and in this, its character of concrete useful labour, it produces 'use-value.' (p. 46)

Full discussion of Marxist theories of class is beyond this chapter; however, the importance of this discussion is to identify the complexities through which capitalism expresses notions of value. What is fundamental to the expression of value, in particular when in search of surplus-value, or profit, is the role of labor-power. Marx argues that in a capitalist system the labor-power of the laborer is exploited in order for the bourgeoisie to gain profit or surplus-value, which is the fundamental intention of a capitalist system in the accumulation of capital (Marx 1967a Volume I, Marx 1971).

In regard to the value of a commodity, there is a process of establishing relative form and equivalent form in determining exchange value, that is, the value of a commodity can be established in its relativity to a commodity of a different kind or in its exchange value to a commodity of a similar kind. Important to this discussion is that it is not money that gives commodities value but it is labor-power that gives value, both use-value and exchange value, which is represented in the form of money. Central to this is the exploitation of labor-power through which commodities, money and capital are accumulated and circulated in particular ways to ensure the interests of the capitalist system are achieved. The fundamental being the accumulation of profit, surplus-value by the capitalist. Bedgood (1980) outlines the notion of class and the complex relationships between value and labor in relation to social relations as follows:

> Class is used in no other sense than to mean relations of production. This is the economic base or infrastructure with a mode of production. It is the base because it is production which creates the material means of subsistence and therefore determines all other forms of social life. It is the base because class relations organise and develop the forces of production and therefore the whole 'progress' of human social evolution. In other words, human labour alone is capable of producing use-values, and the control of the labour process is the basis of the distribution of wealth, power and status. He [sic] who controls labour-power controls the use values of surplus labour and can expropriate the value produced. (p. 11)

Labor power is bought and controlled by the capitalist who it is argued has no care or meaningful relationship with the laborer outside of that which they produce. The need for, and exploitation of, labor-power is a key point of contradiction in the capitalist system of social relations. The contradictory nature of capitalist systems produces the possibility for crisis through which the proletariat can engage in struggle for change. The struggle for change will be driven by the proletariat in becoming conscious of the exploitation of their labor. Class then is both a definition in terms of social relations and how groups are positioned in terms of labor-power and is a potential movement in terms of the potential for class struggle (Thatcher 1998; Wilks-Heeg 1998). The argument being that once the working class identifies the contradictions inherent within, and the exploitative nature of, a capitalist system then class struggle is inevitable. Class struggle is a political struggle, therefore there is always possibility for change, hence the reference to the bourgeoisie as being their own "gravediggers" whereby the victory of the proletariat is deemed inevitable (Marx and Engels 1913).

In seeing class struggles as political acts, the political context as critical in the understanding of class oppression and exploitation. However, fundamental racist and sexist assumptions that dominated the political context are evident through the texts of the *Communist Manifesto* and the volumes of *Capital*. Statements regarding "primitive" societies, references to the "discovery" of the Americas (Marx and Engels 1913, p. 13); descriptions of China and Eastern nations as "barbaric" (p. 17); "half-savage hunting tribes" (Marx 1967b Volume II, p. 110). Kettle (1963) writes that Marx viewed "primitive societies" as not having developed to produce much more than needed, therefore there is no commodity exchange, this is however located as a form of inadequacy in "tribal" communities. In Kettles (1963) interpretation of Marx, there is a "lack" in the "primitive" tribal societies in terms of production, the outcome of which is the need for class-based systems of exploitation which are not a necessity in such societies. The extension of that into racist descriptions of societal structures differs from those of Western capitalist societies. The basis for interpretation of comparison is that of Western understandings, which indicate a eurocentrism that assumes a superiority of the West as argued within social Darwinism and racial ideologies of Western nations.

It is not only issues of race and colonial supremacist constructions within Marxism that gain critical attention. The issue of the gendered nature of the working class is also avoided and therefore falls short of identifying the act of the feminization of labor-power (Game 1998). As such the working classes are constructed as male, when the dominant participants in the working class were in fact European women. The construction of the proletariat as male meant that there was not the interrogation of the role of industrialization in the changing roles and exploitation of women. Where the notion of class systems was evident prior to the invention of capitalism, a particular organization of class is manifested under capitalism that differs from earlier feudal structures. It is this construction of class that was imported and transplanted or immigrated to Aotearoa and had a destructive impact upon the collective nature of Māori society (Bedgood 1980). The intention to destroy Māori societal structures is highlighted in the approach taken by Native Minister C.W. Richmond in regard to the dispossession of lands in Waitara, Sinclair (1990) states:

Richmond wanted to destroy what he called the 'beastly communism' of Māori society by introducing private property in land. 'Chastity, decency, and thrift cannot exist amidst the waste, filth, and moral contamination of the Pahs'. Richmond knew almost nothing about Māori culture or land tenure. He simply believed that it was necessary to 'civilise' the Māori, that is, to lead them to adopt British habits and practices. He had no sympathy for Māori society. He objected to the land purchase officer, Robert Parris, 'hanging about' Māori settlements and wrote, 'It rather lowers the Government to have its Officers running after a pack of contumacious savages'. While Richmond had lived in Taranaki there had been fighting between Māori wishing to sell land and those wishing to keep it. Richmond sympathised completely with the former. Wiremu Kingi Te Rangitake, the leading anti-land-seller was, Richmond considered, 'the bad genius of Taranaki'. Richmond wrote of Kingi, who was living on his tribal land at Waitara, that his attitude was one 'of pure hostility to the interests of the settlement of which he has been occupying a part of the destined site'. A more specifically settler point of view would be hard to conceive. (www.teara.govt.nz)

The confiscation of lands and the reconstruction of lands as commodity, as property and exploitable resource is central to the colonizing capitalist project and is widely documented by Indigenous nations (Waitangi Tribunal 1996; Jackson 2007; Waziyatawin 2008; Dunbar-Ortiz 2014; Manuel and Derrickson 2015). Coulthard (2014) argues that understanding the implications of the birth of capitalist systems in relation to colonial acts of violence and dispossession is critical for Indigenous peoples. In particular, he notes.

Marx's historical excavation of the birth of the capitalist mode of production identifies a host of colonial-like state practices that served to violently strip – through conquest, enslavement, robbery and murder – noncapitalist producers, communities, and societies from their means of production and subsistence. In Capital these formative acts of violent dispossession set the stage for the emergence of capitalist accumulation and the reproduction of capitalist relations of production by tearing Indigenous societies, peasants, and other small-scale self-sufficient agricultural producers from the source of their livelihood – the land. (Coulthard 2014, p. 7)

Such an analysis highlights the insidious ways in which colonization and capitalism collude in the violent invasion of Indigenous lands in order to embed and sustain complex power relationships that construct and maintain oppressive social relations.

Conclusion

This chapter provides a brief overview of some underpinning beliefs in regard to the ideologies of race, gender, and class that were transported to Aotearoa through the act of colonization. An exploration of race, gender, and class explanations prior to colonization is important to understanding the imposition of colonial schooling as they provide the basis for how structures have been developed here by our colonizers. In order to understand more fully the existence of unequal power relationships in education within Aotearoa, there is a need to understand the ideological underpinning those inequalities and the source of the ideologies. It is evident that just as the assertion of the inferiority of some groups is necessary to the maintenance of societal inequalities, so too is there a need to ensure that the privilege of dominant groups, those who benefit, whose interests are served, are concealed. In these paradigms women are measured as inferior to men; Indigenous, Black, and Peoples of Color are positioned as inferior to white; working classes as inferior to the middle and upper classes. These positions of inferiority are not explained in relation to the benefits accrued to the dominant groups but are located within the idea that such inequalities are part of either [white] "god-given forms" or as part of a "natural" order.

The categorization of race as locating white men, followed closely by white women, at the pinnacle of racial hierarchies is not a surprise to those of us located further "down the ladder" in such a process of societal organization. Just as forms of Christianity were used to validate the position of white men in gendered order so to do have they been utilized to legitimize white peoples place in the hierarchy just next to a white male god. In discourses of race it is the "barbaric" "savage" "inferior" "Other" that is racialized, being white is not engaged, rather being white is viewed as the standard from which all other peoples are measured and defined. Adding class to the mix has provided the fundamental economic justification for the foundation and continuance of processes of capitalism that maintain processes of commodification of all things. When value is located solely in terms of capital those who have been unable to accumulate value take their place in the inferior ranks by virtue of an ideology that is based within monetary systems of greed and exploitation.

The importation of such beliefs was a part of the "vertical slice" of British society that was transplanted to Aotearoa (Bedgood 1980). That vertical slice included ideologies that would serve to benefit the colonizing forces and justify their means of operation on Indigenous peoples' lands. In Aotearoa the impact of that ideological transplantation has had immeasurable effect on Māori people and served to provide the foundation for ongoing acts of colonial oppression that continue to this day. The establishment of Mission schooling in 1816 and the legislative change to Native Schooling in 1847 was founded upon the need to entrench these ideological constructions, as a part of the practices of the colonization, assimilation, and christianizing, of our ancestors as "natives."

Historical ethnographic and Native Schools documentation highlights the ways in which colonial impositions came to bear on Māori communities both in the ways in which schooling was constructed as a key vehicle of assimilation and in the ways in which te reo Māori was subjugated, tikanga Māori was marginalized, and Māori knowledge was invalidated upon our own lands (Walker 2016). Schooling is a site where the colonial beliefs pertaining to Māori have been entrenched. The domestication agenda of early schooling was a deliberate move to relocate Māori from positions of rangatiratanga (Māori sovereignty/self-determination) to those of the "subservient native" and was instrumental in the embedding of class structures that form the basis of capitalist complicity with colonialism to ensure the dispossession of Indigenous peoples of our cultural structures and economic base (Newcomb 2008; Mikaere 2016).

Native schooling has been described as a trojan horse of colonization (Smith 1986). Located in the center of Māori communities the modeling of the colonial heteronormative patriarchal nuclear family was a central project of the Native School. The impact of that has been a fundamental disruption to cultural relationships and a reorganization of the basis of Māori society, the whānau. The restructuring of whānau was to work in ways where Māori women were expected to take on board the role of the colonial wife and mother, as well as provide domestic service to Pākehā in their communities. The marginalization of Māori women in Native Schooling occurred at both legislative and curriculum levels and highlights one example of the gendered nature of colonization where the colonial settler government determined that men would provide leadership and decision-making. In terms of the structural developments it was Pākehā men that were deemed in control, at the community level it was deemed, by Pākehā men, that it would be Māori men who would be in control. The misogyny of the colonizers was an inherent value underpinning the curriculum and structures of the Native Schooling system. The importance of a discussion of Native Schools is located in its clear and undisputable presentation of colonial agendas of assimilation as a means of further dispossession. The contribution of Native Schools to a process of individualization is by no means accidental rather it corresponds with the Native Lands Acts that had individualization of land title as a priority. The Native Schools system provided an institutional framework that ensured the colonial agendas of dispossession, erasure of Māori language and culture, undermining whānau, hapū, and iwi structures through reconstructing gender relations, and the positioning of Māori as "barbaric" "uncivilized" and therefore inherently "inferior" were not only realized but were actively pursued.

It is clear that all colonial informed schooling in Aotearoa is driven by these practices and the ideologies that underpin them. Domestication, assimilatory, civilizing beliefs and practices within schooling reflect the intersection of race, gender, and class ideologies and their direct impact upon whānau, hapū, and iwi. Each of the ideological constructions discussed here have clearly been developed, maintained, and reproduced as means for the justification and ongoing perpetuation of oppressive systems. Those systems have been based within constructed categories that have been defined by those most likely to be served by such categorizations. In Western thought, white men have been instrumental in the instigation and maintenance of power structures in regard to gender with a range of reasoning utilized to justify the positioning of women both as inferior, as property and to be controlled by men. White colonizing nations more generally position themselves as superior races and ensure enslavement, genocide, and holocaustic acts around the world. They have also been instrumental in the global assertion of capitalist systems of abuse and exploitation that impact directly upon Indigenous nations. As Arvin et al. (2013, p. 14) remind us it is necessary *"to problematize and theorize the intersections of settler colonialism, heteropatriarchy, and heteropaternalism."* As the neoliberal colonial agenda continues to embed itself within the education system in Aotearoa, it is essential that we maintain an understanding of the constructions of race, gender, class, and the ways that they intersect to maintain dominance over Indigenous peoples. This analysis is critical to our ongoing challenge and disruption of the systemic racism, sexism, homophobia, and classism that continues to be reproduced in the state-driven education system today.

References

Anthias F, Yuval-Davis M (1992) Racialized boundaries: race, nation, gender, colour and class and the anti-racist struggle. Routledge, London

Arvin M, Tuck E, Morrill A (2013) Decolonizing feminism: challenging connections between settler colonialism and Heteropatriarchy. Fem Form 25(1):8–34

Barnes AW, Taiapa K, Borell B, McCreanor T (2013) Māori experiences and response to racism in New Zealand, Auckland. MAI J 2(2):63–77

Barrington JM, Beaglehole TH (1974) Māori schools in a changing society: an historical review. New Zealand Council for Educational Research, Wellington

Bear TL (2016) Power in my blood: corporeal sovereignty through the Praxis of an indigenous eroticanalysis. Unpublished Doctor of Philosophy in English Dissertation, University of Alberta, Edmonton

Bedgood D (1980) Rich and poor in New Zealand. George, Allen & Unwin, Auckland

Bell A (1996) We're just New Zealanders: Pākehā identity politics. In: Spoonley P, Pearson D, MacPherson C (eds) Ngā Patai: racism and ethnic relations in Aotearoa/New Zealand. The Dunmore Press Ltd., Palmerston North

Benedict R (1942) Race and racism. St. Edmundsbury Press, Suffolk

Blackledge D, Hunt B (1985) Sociological interpretations of education. Routledge, USA

Blauner B (1994) Talking past each other. In: Pincus FL, Ehrlich H (eds) Race and ethnic conflict: contending views on prejudice, discrimination and ethnoviolence. Westview Press, Boulder

Bolt C (1971) Victorian attitudes to race. Routledge and Kegan Paul, London

Coney S (1993) Standing in the sunshine: a history of New Zealand women since they won the vote. Penguin Books, Auckland

Coulthard G (2014) Red skin, white masks: rejecting the colonial politics of recognition. University of Minnesota Press, Minneapolis

Daly M (1973) Beyond God the father: toward a philosophy of women's liberation. Beacon Press, Boston

Darwin C (1910) The origin of species by means of natural selection. J. Murray, London

Davis A (1991) Women, race and class. Random House, New York

Dunbar-Oritz R (2014) An indigenous peoples' history of the United States. Beacon Press, Boston

Fry R (1985) It's different for daughters. New Zealand Council for Educational Research, Wellington

Game M (1998) The communist Manifesto: transgendered Proletarians. In: Cowling M (ed) The communist manifesto: new interpretations. New York University Press, New York, pp 132–141

Giddens A (1986) Sociology: a brief but critical introduction, 2nd edn. Macmillan Education, London

Goldberg DT (1990) Anatomy of racism. University of Minnesota Press, Minneapolis

Gould SJ (1981) The mismeasure of man. Penguin Books, New York

Grande S (2004) Red pedagogy: native American social and political thought. Rowman & Littlefield Publishers, London

Harris CI (1993) Whiteness as property. Harv Law Rev 106:1707–1791

Harris R, Tobias M, Jeffreys M, Waldegrave K, Karlsen S, Nazroo J (2006) Racism and health: the relationship between experience of racial discrimination and health in New Zealand. Soc Sci Med 63(2006):1428–1441

Hunt S (2016) An Introduction to the health of two-spirit people: historical, contemporary and emergent issues. National Collaborating Centre for Aboriginal Health, Prince George

Hutchings J, Aspin C (eds) (2007) Sexuality and the stories of indigenous people. Huia Publishers, Wellington

Irwin K (1992) Towards theories of Māori Feminism. In: Du Plessis R, Bunkle P, Irwin K, Laurie A, Middleton S (eds) Feminist voices: women's studies texts for Aotearoa/New Zealand. Oxford University Press, Auckland, pp 1–19

Jackson M (2007) Globalisation and the colonising state of mind. In: Bargh M (ed) Resistance: an indigenous response to neoliberalism. Huia, Wellington, pp 167–182

Jahoda G (1999) Images of Savages: ancients [I.E. Ancient] roots of modern prejudice. In: Western culture. Routledge, London/New York

James B, Saville-Smith K (1989) Gender, culture and power. Oxford University Press, Auckland

Johnston P, Pihama L (1995) What counts as difference and what differences count: gender, race and the politics of difference. In: Irwin K, Ramsden I, Kahukiwa R (eds) Toi Wāhine: the worlds of Māori women. Penguin Books, Auckland, pp 75–86

Johnston PM (1998) He aro rereke: Education policy and māori underachievement: Mechanisms of power and difference, unpublished doctor of philosophy thesis, Auckland: University of Auckland

Kettle A (1963) Karl Marx: founder of modern communism. Weidenfeld & Nicolson (Educational) Ltd., London

Lyons O (2009) 400 years of hostility to native Americans. Albany Times Union on Sunday, 9 Aug 2009, pp B1 and B3. http://www.onondaganation.org/mediafiles/pdfs/un/Doctrine%20of%20Discovery.pdf

Manuel A, Derrickson RM Grand Chief (2015) Unsettling Canada: a national wake-up call. Between The Lines, Toronto

Maracle L (1996) I am woman: a native perspective on sociology and feminism. Press Gang Publishers, Vancouver

Marx K (1967a) Capital: a critique of political economy, volume one: the process of production. International Publishers, New York

Marx K (1967b) Capital: a critique of political economy, volume two: the process of circulation of capital. International Publishers, New York

Marx K (1971) Capital: a critique of political economy, volume three: the process of capitalist production as a whole. Progress Publishers, Moscow

Marx K, Engels F (1913) Communist manifesto. Charles H Kerr & Company, Chicago

Mikaere A (1995) The balance destroyed: the consequences for Māori women of the colonisation of Tikanga Māori. Unpublished Master of Juriprudence thesis, University of Waikato, Hamilton

Mikaere A (2016) Te Harinui: civilising the Māori with school and church. In: Hutchings J, Lee-Morgan J (eds) Decolonisation in Aotearoa: education, research and practice. NZCER Press, Wellington, pp 48–57

Nepe T (1991) Te Toi Huarewa Tipuna: Kaupapa Māori, an educational intervention system. Unpublished Master's thesis, The University of Auckland, Auckland

Newcomb S (1992) Five hundred years of injustice. Shaman's Drum. Fall 1992, pp 18–20

Newcomb S (2008) Pagans in the promised land: decoding the doctrine of Christian. Fulcrum Publishing, Colorado

Oakley A (1974) Housewife. Pelican Books, Great Britain

Penetito W (2010) What's Māori about Māori education. Victoria University Press, Wellington

Pihama L (2001) Tihei mauri ora: Honouring our voices mana wahine as a kaupapa māori theoretical framework, unpublished doctoral thesis, Auckland: University of Auckland.

Pihama L, Te Nana R, Reynolds P, Smith C, Reid J, Smith LT (2014) Positioning historical trauma theory within Aotearoa New Zealand. Altern Int J Indigenous Peoples 10(3):248–262

Ruether R (1983) Sexiam and god-talk: toward a feminist theology. Beacon Press, Boston

Simmonds N, Gabel K (2016) Ūkaipō: decolonisation and Māori maternities. In: Hutchings J, Lee-Morgan J (eds) Decolonisation in Aotearoa: education, research and practice. NZCER Press, Wellington, pp 145–157

Sinclair K (1990) 'Richmond, Christopher William', first published in the Dictionary of New Zealand Biography, vol 1, 1990. Te Ara – the Encyclopedia of New Zealand. https://teara.govt.nz/en/biographies/1r9/richmond-christopher-william. Accessed 13 Aug 2017

Smith LT (1986) Is 'Taha Māori' in schools the answer to Maori school failure? In: Smith GH (ed) Ngā Kete Waananga: Māori perspectives of Taha Māori. Auckland College of Education, Auckland

Smith LT (1992a) Maori women: Discourses, projects and mana wahine. In: Middleton S, Jones A (eds) Women and Education in Aotearoa 2, Wellington: Bridget Williams Books, pp 33–51

Smith LT (1999) Decolonizing methodologies: research and indigenous peoples. Zed Books, New York

Smith LT (2016) Keeping a decolonising agenda to the forefront. In: Hutchings J, Lee-Morgan J (eds) Decolonisation in Aotearoa: education, research and practice. NZCER Press pp ix–x, Wellington

Thatcher ID (1998) Past receptions of the communist manifesto. In: Cowling M (ed) The communist manifesto: new interpretations. New York University Press, New York, pp 63–76

Thomson AS (1859) The story of New Zealand: past and present : savage and civilized. J. Murray, London

Waitangi Tribunal (1996) The taranaki report: Kaupapa tuatahi, muru me te raupatu: The muru and raupatu of the taranaki land and people. Wai 143, Wellington: Government Printer

Walker R (1990) Ka Whawhai Tonu Matou: struggle without end. Penguin Books, Auckland

Walker R (2016) Reclaiming Māori education. In: Hutchings J, Lee-Morgan J (eds) Decolonisation in Aotearoa: education, research and practice. NZCER Press, Wellington

Warner M (1976) Alone of all her sex: the myth and the cult of the Virgin Mary. Picador/Pan Books, London

Waziyatawin (2008) What does justice look like? The struggle for liberation in Dakota homeland. Living Justice Press, St. Paul

Wilks-Heeg S (1998) The communist manifesto and working-class parties in Western Europe. In: Cowling M (ed) The communist manifesto: new interpretations. New York University Press, New York, pp 119–131

Wollenstonecraft M (1985) In: Miriam Brody (ed) Vindication of the rights of woman, Penguin classics. Penguin, London

Colonization, Education, and Kanaka 'Ōiwi Survivance

Nālani Wilson-Hokowhitu and Noelani Goodyear-Ka'ōpua

Contents

Introduction	50
Life, Land, and Language: Kanaka 'Ōiwi Survivance and Settler Colonialism	52
Colonization and Schools of an Independent Kingdom	55
Conclusion	60
References	61

Abstract

This chapter illuminates Kanaka 'Ōiwi resistance and survivance that has prevailed in the face of colonization and Americanization in the Hawaiian Islands. Despite imperialistic invasions, introduced foreign diseases and the aggressive ideological dominance of eurocentrism to our shores, we have remained steadfast. The chapter discusses survivance and futurity in relation to settler colonialism, erasure, and elimination; thus, contextualizing the historical emergence of schooling in Hawai'i, which reveals the complexities of partnerships that evolved between Kānaka, European, and American colonists. Traversing a vast expanse of history in a short space, the purpose of this chapter is to articulate the sustained connection between traditional and contemporary Hawaiian education movements that nurture our futurities, or our ways of thinking about and relating to our futures.

Keywords

Kānaka 'Ōiwi · Colonization · Hawaiian education · Survivance

---

N. Wilson-Hokowhitu (✉)
Te Kotahi Research Institute, The University of Waikato, Hamilton, New Zealand
e-mail: nalani.wilson-hokowhitu@waikato.ac.nz

N. Goodyear-Ka'ōpua
Department of Political Science, University of Hawai'i at Mānoa, Honolulu, HI, USA
e-mail: goodyear@hawaii.edu

© Springer Nature Singapore Pte Ltd. 2019
E. A. McKinley, L. T. Smith (eds.), *Handbook of Indigenous Education*,
https://doi.org/10.1007/978-981-10-3899-0_57

Introduction

I ulu ka lālā i ke kumu. A branch grows from and because of the tree trunk (Pukui 1983, p. 137). This ʻōlelo noʻeau (Hawaiian proverb) uses the word kumu to employ multiple meanings, such as teacher, source, and tree trunk. We use the analogy of a kumu to frame our discussion of education, particularly schooling, and the cultural and political functions it has played over the last few centuries in Hawaiʻi. We intentionally open with the manaʻo (wisdom) of our ancestors as a methodological assertion of our perspectives as Kānaka ʻŌiwi. In particular, we highlight the endemic koa tree (acacia koa) as symbolic of our bravery, fierce survivance, and futurity. The koa has deep taproots to the beginning of Kānaka Maoli existence in our homeland. Like the koa, Kānaka ʻŌiwi are indigenous and genealogically connected to Ka Pae ʻĀina ʻo Hawaiʻi (the Hawaiian archipelago).

Koa trees sustain an equilibrium in Hawaiian rainforests. In relation to this chapter, koa as bravery is what was needed to survive postcontact European invasion to our shores. Survivance is an appropriate term to utilize for Kanaka ʻŌiwi who, in the face of disease, *dis*-ease, and the trauma of having witnessed the exteme loss of life, continue as a people and nation (Silva 2004; Kauanui 2008b). Despite land dispossession and continued forces that work to dislocate our people from their ancestral ahupuaʻa, we have persevered and endured. Regardless of attempts by foreigners to eliminate Kānaka, whether by force at a gunpoint, with "law" that displaced our peoples, or via education and assimilation policies forbidding our language, epistemologies, ontologies, and priorities, we have continued to persist and exist (Kameʻeleihiwa 1992). This is why the metaphor of koa is so befitting. The koa stands strong. The koa is the kumu, the tree, the teacher, and source, from which this branch grows.

Reaching back through time our ancestors mapped evolutionary biology extending from the natural world into the spiritual and metaphysical realms with the epic Kumulipo, our most acclaimed creation chant (Beckwith 1972). From the beginnings of creation to the many hālau, or schools, our intellectual capacities encompassed a visual and tactile literacy of reading waves, currents, winds, clouds, weather, animal migration patterns, and celestial bodies. Kānaka developed an elaborate system of land divisions that included resources from the mountains to the sea, and that utilized sustainable irrigation systems for feeding a nation with kalo (taro), ʻuala (sweet potato) and ʻulu (breadfruit) from the land. Fishponds of various types and sizes enhanced the coastal and nearshore environments, taking advantage of the productivity of estuaries for nurturing fish. Traditional and contemporary Hawaiian education values aloha ʻāina, respect, love, and care of our land and waters, as well as the interconnectedness of humans and the natural world, our ʻohana (families), kūpuna (elders and ancestors), nā ʻaumākua (ancestral guardians), and nā ākua (deities and elements).

Documentation and the importance of education within Kānaka ʻŌiwi culture is exemplified in ʻōlelo noʻeau (proverbs), moʻolelo (narratives), moʻokūʻauhau (genealogies), and mele (songs), which represent merely a few examples of our intellectual heritage. We open and centralize the chapter using ʻōlelo noʻeau, the words of our ancestors, as a political statement of our continuity. Throughout the chapter we perpetuate our intellectual heritage and outline our survivance by integrating ʻōlelo noʻeau, employing moʻolelo to deconstruct dominant discourses and to offer counternarratives of colonization and education in Hawaiʻi from the late 1700s and Western contact to the late 1800s and United States' purported annexation. We present the chapter in honor of our moʻokūʻauhau as Kānaka ʻŌiwi and the mele, songs of past, present, and future.

"Education" as conceived by non-Indigenous peoples ignites epistemologically differing ideologies. Shifting from a predominantly Western worldview and centering Kānaka Maoli ideology of ōlelo noʻeau, moʻolelo, moʻokūʻauhau, and mele reveal enormous material preserved and perpetuated for multiple generations of our people. For example, upon visiting Kānaka scholarly texts such as *Aloha Betrayed* by Noenoe K. Silva (2004), the work of Samuel Manaiakalani Kamakau employs the format of moʻokūʻauhau (genealogies) that chronologically order the Polynesian migrations and multiple arrivals to the Hawaiian Islands prior to Captain James Cook on January 18, 1778. Within the following sections, we traverse over a century of contact between Kānaka and foreigners to our islands, which has severely transmuted Kānaka Maoli culture and life-ways.

Throughout the chapter, we will return to the analogy of Kānaka as koa, referring to bravery, as well as referring to the endangered native tree. Like the use of ʻōlelo noʻeau to open the chapter, our use of metaphor is also epistemologically and methodologically intentional. It is vital to express the complexity and beauty of our survivance as Kānaka ʻŌiwi. Like Kānaka, the koa tree is endemic to the Hawaiian archipelago and thrives in the face of adversity. The seeds of the koa can remain viable in the soil for more than 25 years and to germinate the seeds often need to crack or scar. For Kānaka ʻŌiwi, the seeds of our culture, epistemologies, and ontologies have also experienced a time of existing "underground" waiting for the moment to break through dominant colonial powers to crack and sprout, flourishing into a forest of koa once again. The roots of the koa grow deep into the soil and the branches stretch to the sky connecting Papahānaumoku (Earth) and Wākea (Sky). The koa tree reaches heights of 15–25 m and is instrumental in perpetuating and restoring the native Hawaiian forest. Its canopy protects the growth of other species of trees such as the ʻōhiʻa lehua tree and hāpuʻu ferns. The native forests of Hawaiʻi evolved in symbiosis, where plants, trees, and animals worked together ensuring ecological balance. The word koa in ʻōlelo Hawaiʻi can also mean bold, fearless, and warrior. In alignment with Byran Kamaoli Kuwada's (2015) transformative essay, *We are not warriors, We are a grove of trees*, within the chapter we envisage koa groves as analogous to Kānaka Maoli resistance and survivance from colonization to present.

Colonization and Americanization in the Hawaiian Islands have had devastating effects upon our land and people; yet, Kanaka resistance and survivance have prevailed. Despite imperialistic invasions, introduced foreign diseases and the aggressive ideological dominance of eurocentrism to our shores, we have remained steadfast (Osorio 2002; Silva 2004; Kauanui 2008b). This chapter will offer an overview of colonization by first discussing survivance and futurity in relation to settler colonialism, erasure, and elimination. The following section will examine three central examples of elimination, loss of life, land, and language. It will present dominant discourses surrounding introduced diseases, dislocation, and assimilation in juxtaposition with counternarratives of survivance. This will set the scene for the historical emergence of schooling in Hawai'i, revealing the complexities of partnerships that evolved between Kānaka, European, and American colonists. Contrary to earlier dominant discourses of schooling in Hawai'i, in which scholars have characterized schools as foreign impositions of essentially American design, we argue that the achievements of literacy and the establishment of a public school system in the Hawaiian Kingdom resulted from negotiations between Kānaka and haole (foreigners). By examining this previously misinterpreted historical context we can more fully comprehend the consequences of exclusive haole control over the education system in Hawai'i, as well as Kamehameha Schools, beginning in the 1880s and extending well past the mid-twentieth century. The chapter addresses how a central technique of settler colonial rule was to reframe relationships that have worked to gloss over the ascendance of white businessmen to power over the public education system, Kamehameha Schools and its lands, legitimating the extension of United States empire to the Hawaiian islands.

Despite traversing a vast expanse of history in a short space, the purpose of this chapter is to illuminate the sustained connection between traditional and contemporary Hawaiian education movements that nurture our futurities, or our ways of thinking about and relating to our futures (Recollet 2016; Tuck and Gaztambide-Fernandez 2013). Kānaka Maoli from time immemorial has embraced and nourished our deep and growing ontology, epistemology, and axiology. Schools were not the first educational institutions in the islands. Native educational institutions based on apprenticeship, mastery, and community predated and survived the advent of Western-styled schooling in Hawai'i (Beniamina 2010). When we look deeper into the past in front of us, we extend our reach into futures of our own making. We enhance our capacity to "unsettle" settler colonialisms and ensure space for our futurities, our ways of imagining and producing knowledge about our futures. Indigenous futurities can include forms of knowing and performance, such as sonics, smells, ceremonies, embodied movement, and other ways of jumping settler scales (Recollet 2016, p. 94). Learning and experience are integral aspects of life extending from our origins to our presents and futures, and education has the potential to connect us to or disconnect us from these realms.

Life, Land, and Language: Kanaka 'Ōiwi Survivance and Settler Colonialism

The theoretical framework of this section utilizes the late Patrick Wolfe's (2006) settler colonial analytic and the logic of elimination to better understand Kanaka 'Ōiwi survivance and endurance. The section engages settler colonialism by offering critical counter-narratives in relation to depopulation, land dispossession, and assimilation. Anishinaabe scholar Gerald Robert Vizenor (2008) asserts that Indigenous peoples survivance stories are the renunciations of dominance. To better understand

Indigenity and survivance as an active sense of presence and continuance, it is important to discuss theories of settler colonialism, erasure, and the logic of elimination in relation to colonization in the Hawaiian Islands prior to discussing education.

The nineteenth century was an era in which our people witnessed the near demise of our nation. Beyond the historical and ongoing processes of colonization that have consisted of exploration, exploitation, imperialist militarization, mission schools, and settler colonialism, Kānaka of the nineteenth century simultaneously contended with the diseases that foreigners brought to our islands. European nations fueled and funded exploration in search of natural resources and new lands in which to exploit. European and Euro-American colonists rendered native peoples as inferior to justify their invasion, presumed dominance, and spreading of diseases. Kānaka contended with and negotiated the establishment of political and educational policies in the Hawaiian Islands amongst a debilitating force, disease.

Captain James Cook conservatively estimated that there were approximately 400,000 Native Hawaiians inhabiting the Hawaiian Islands when his crew arrived in 1778, although modern estimates are as high as 800,000 at the time of European contact (Stannard 1989). By 1893, the population of Native Hawaiians was 40,000; meaning that after a century of contact with Europeans 760,000 Hawaiians had died due to the introduction of diseases, such as influenza, sexually transmitted diseases, and small poxes. That is a demise of approximately 90% of the population over 70 years. Depopulation of Kānaka Maoli from foreign diseases meant that the activities of foreigners to our islands, including missionaries in churches and schools, and Christianity took hold of our people at an incredibly vulnerable time (Osorio 2002; Kameʻeleihiwa 1992; Trask 1984).

J. Kēhaulani Kauanui in her book *Hawaiian Blood, Colonialism and the Politics of Sovereignty and Indigeneity* (2008b) analyzes the statistics of depopulation and demise, focusing on life and survivance, rather than death. Dominant discourses of Indigenous demise and depopulation are problematic, not only because they secure a misconception of settler colonial eradication of the first peoples to the lands that European and American European settlers sought to acquire, but also because in the context of Hawaiʻi, the documentation only accounted for full-blooded Hawaiians (Stannard 1989). Kauanui writes, "What is missing in this assessment of the state of the Hawaiian population, which reads like a romantic desire for extinction, is the *increasing* number of Kanaka Maoli (when one accounts for the racially mixed Kānaka Maoli) who make up the vast majority of the Hawaiian population today-all part of the legacy of mass depopulation" (2008b, p. 16). Kauanui (2016) considers the operative logic of settler colonialism articulated by Patrick Wolfe to "eliminate the native" and emphasizes "enduring indigeneity" focusing on existence, persistence, and resistance.

Kanaka Maoli epistemologies and ontologies prioritize moʻokūʻauhau, our genealogies, as expansive and inclusive, extending across Oceania into the cosmos, and are directly connected and rooted to ʻāina (land and that which feeds). Our ideologies of our relationship with place and our cultural identities as Kanaka ʻŌiwi have been severely challenged by European xenophobia and settler colonial racialization.

Kauanui (2008b) addresses the racialization of Kanaka based upon blood quantum and percentage quantification by the United States Congress to undermine Kanaka Maoli sovereignty. She reveals how the exclusionary logic of blood quantum has had legal and cultural effects that have limited land provisions and negated collective entitlement for Kanaka in our homeland. As Wolfe (2006) contends, the settler-colonial logic of elimination is inherently eliminatory, which has also manifested as genocidal. Loss of life in the nineteenth century and racialization is directly related to land dispossession and settler colonialism, which Wolfe (2006) stated "destroys to replace" (Kauanui 2016).

Historian, Jonathan Osorio, argues that "the single most critical dismemberment of Hawaiian society was the Māhele or division of lands and the consequent transformation of 'āina into private property between 1845 and 1850" (2002, p. 44). Rapid depopulation and migration to urban centers led to the abandonment of thriving lo'i (taro fields) and the agricultural communities reliant upon the collective food source. The seemingly unstoppable decline of the Hawaiian population weakened the traditional land tenure system that had sustained our nation for centuries prior to Western contact. The subsistence economy relied on extensive taro cultivation of the upland valleys and labor of the maka'āinana (people of the land). According to Lilikalā Kame'eleihiwa (1992), Western histories define māhele as "to divide," which refers to the shift from communal and collective rights to individual portioning of land. Ka 'ōlelo Hawai'i (the Hawaiian language) is so vital to understanding Kanaka 'Ōiwi worldview. Kame'eleihiwa notes that māhele has another connotation in Hawaiian, which is "to share" (Ibid., p. 9). Until the 1848 Māhele, land "ownership" was not a part of our vocabulary or understanding of our relationship to 'āina. The modern expression for "owner" in Hawaiian is a transliteration, 'ona.

Within a Kanaka worldview, the earth is Papahānaumoku, an Akua (ancestor and god) so the land is regarded with utmost respect. The series of laws that privatized land in Hawai'i not only divided the land into individual allotments for settler colonial acquisition, it also strained the relationship between Papahānaumoku (our first mother) and nā Kānaka o ka 'āina (the people of the land). As Wolfe (2006) contends, settler colonialism dissolves native societies while erecting a new colonial society on expropriated lands. Wolfe states that "settler colonizers come to stay: invasion is a structure not an event" (p. 388).

Among the new colonial structures, language and literacy in both Hawaiian and English became a strategic tool for Kanaka 'Ōiwi resistance to American colonization throughout the nineteenth century. Print media and newspapers, in particular, served as a medium for broad social communication and political organization (Silva 2004). The Hawaiian language newspapers remain, from then until now, a source of our native language and culture, a tangible connection to the wisdom, thoughts, and experiences of our ancestors. Colonization and Americanization in the Hawaiian Islands have had devastating effects upon our land and people; and, yet, the establishment of literacy and Hawaiian language newspapers document the conscious resistance that continues today to strengthen and fuel lāhui Hawai'i (the Hawaiian nation).

In the wake of American Protestant missionary arrival in 1820, early schooling projects were closely tied to developing literacy among Kānaka so that they could be more easily converted to Christianity. The Calvinist missionaries brought imperialistic intentions to civilize and educate our people; thus, their early quest was ideological. Whereas, the first wave of missionaries intended to assimilate and convert Kānaka to Christianity, then leave; many of them and their children found monetary "salvation" through permanent settlement in the islands (Benham and Heck 1998). To this day missionary descendants claim long-term "kamaʻāina" connections to Hawaiʻi (Trask 1999). Returning to the opening ʻōlelo noʻeau, *i ulu ka lālā i ke kumu*, we might liken these missionary families and the networks of economic and political power they developed to the introduced banyan tree, whose pervasive aerial roots consume and entwine the host tree, spreading laterally across the forest until the native koa is consumed and decomposes. In fact, the first banyan tree to take root in Hawaiʻi was planted on the island of Maui in 1873 to commemorate the 50th anniversary of the Protestant mission in Lāhaina, the former capitol of the islands.

American missionaries arrived at the Hawaiian Islands bringing with them Western and Christian values, foreign ontologies, and non-Native epistemologies, that came to influence their early educational institutions and practices in the islands from 1820 to 1840. The missionary schools' intention to civilize the Indigenous peoples of the islands led to the next historical parallel in which social control led to political control. Over the next several decades, this network of missionary families and businessmen generated a growing white supremacist tide. They received backing from the United States in 1898 and usurped control of the lawful Hawaiian government from Queen Liliʻuokalani.

As settler colonialism took fuller root under t US occupation, regimes of the race were imposed upon Kānaka Maoli and other people of color in the islands. Assimilation of Kānaka Maoli via social and political control provided access to land ownership and resource exploitation, yet examples of Indigenous resistance are prevalent in Hawaiian language newspapers (Silva 2004). Kānaka Maoli not only embraced the introduction of written language as a means of extending and communicating their knowledge base and maintaining sovereignty in the Hawaiian language, Kanaka scholars and teachers were active participants in the quest to empower lāhui, which will be discussed further in the following section. Again, this is exemplified in the vast archives of Hawaiian newspapers written in Hawaiian for Hawaiians (Ibid.). In the next section, we turn to the ways that a Kānaka-led school system under the independent Hawaiian Kingdom provides contemporary koa with roots for our survivance.

Colonization and Schools of an Independent Kingdom

Kānaka Maoli are among the few aboriginal nations living under US empire who built a national school system under the laws of a Native-led government in the nineteenth century. Until the end of the 1800s, ʻŌiwi Hawaiʻi also made up a majority of the teachers in the Kingdom. This history has been largely overlooked. Existing histories of schooling in Hawaiʻi have focused almost exclusively on the role of foreigners in teaching Kānaka Maoli and in developing the educational system. These accounts not only suggest public education in Hawai'i was made in the image of American public schooling, but they also ignore the role of Kānaka leaders and teachers in establishing literacy and schooling in the Hawaiian Kingdom. While Americans did influence the Hawaiian Kingdom's school system, missionaries did not simply import and impose schooling upon Hawaiians. Rather, the achievements of literacy and the establishment of a public school system resulted from negotiations between Kānaka and haole, often in struggle, as *hoa* (colleagues or peers) or *hoa paio* (competitors or opponents). Seeing this *hoa* or *hoa paio* relationship destabilizes and provides an alternative to the model that becomes prominent as Americans sought to extinguish Native government.

Kānaka were enamored with the technologies of the printed word. While American missionaries are largely credited with establishing a written form of the indigenous language and then teaching Hawaiians to read, it is clear that the achievements of printing and literacy were a result of the joint efforts of Native Hawaiians and foreigners. The first company of American missionaries who arrived in Hawai'i in 1820 was accompanied by four Kānaka Maoli who had made their way to the east coast of the United States years earlier. These men helped teach the missionaries elements of the Hawaiian language and translated for them upon arrival in the islands. Schutz notes that one of them, Thomas Hopu, was writing letters utilizing spelling that more closely mirrors the modern, standardized Hawaiian orthography well before the American Calvinist mission established its official orthography (Schutz 1994).

Mission station schools became points of access to the new skills of reading and writing, and enrolments grew at an incredibly rapid pace with Kānaka quickly taking on the majority of the teaching roles. Wist (1940) writes that for Hawaiians, "'going to school' was a form of recreation." He recounts that from the mid-1820s-early 1830s, nearly the whole adult population went to schools to learn to read, but he downplays the role of Kānaka in this literacy boom. However, the numbers clearly indicate that it would have been impossible for missionaries alone to have taught all or even most of the Kānaka pupils counted. Only 140 American Protestant missionaries came to Hawai'i between 1820 and 1848. At the height of school enrolments in 1832, when there were more than 53,000 pupils in 900 schools, only 4 missionary companies had arrived in the islands, including just over 50 American men and women, plus 11 Native Hawaiians and Tahitians. Additionally, some missionaries did not stay, so all 52 would not have been in the islands at the same time (Hawaiian Mission Children's Society 1969). They could not have possibly overseen 900 schools or managed a ratio of 1,000 Native students to each missionary. The vast majority of teachers in these schools were 'Ōiwi.

Adult Kānaka came to schools for what they wanted, to learn to read and write, and then they left. Kuykendall writes, "as soon as a bright pupil (and there were many such) had acquired a little facility in reading, he was sent out, or went out on his own initiative, to teach a school of his own" (1938a, p. 106). Only 5 years after the high enrollment of 1832, the number of pupils was down to about 2,000 (Wist 1940). However, Kānaka maintained their passion for reading, writing, and publishing in the following decades, when literacy was used not only as a tool for accessing or creating social capital but also as an important tool of resistance. Within the next two decades, the corpus of Hawaiian schoolbooks and literature amounted to over 80,000,000 pages, as reported by the Hawaiian Kingdom's President of the Board of Education in 1852.

As the number of willing adult pupils in missionary schools waned through the 1830s, the focus shifted toward schooling children as proper national subjects for an evolving nation-state. The codification and institutionalization of public schooling in 1840 was adjunct to the creation of the first Hawaiian constitution under King Kamehameha III, Kauikeaouli, who declared, "He aupuni palapala ko'u." (Mine is a kingdom of education and documents.) Thus, King Kamehameha III established the Kingdom as a constitutional monarchy, transformed by the trappings of modern states including an emergent national public school system. Hawaiian leaders made schooling part of a self-modernizing project, in tension but sometimes articulating with the continuing missionary project of "civilizing" Kānaka. By 1842, elementary level education in reading, writing, geography, and arithmetic was required for anyone to be married or hold high office (Benham and Heck 1998). Hawaiian was the predominant language of instruction in schools, and any attempts to teach English were within the context of a robust literacy within the indigenous language.

For the ali'i class, King Kamehameha III passed a 1840 law establishing a school for chiefly children, in which they would learn English, history, geography, higher level math, and philosophy, among other things. The government did not begin any broader allocation of funds to English-medium schooling until 1851. Throughout the second half of the nineteenth century, the struggle between Hawaiian and English language in government schools and in the law reflected the struggles for power in the Kingdom between 'Ōiwi statesmen and haole businessmen.

'Ōiwi leaders used compulsory schooling as an indispensable part of the production of modern, Hawaiian national subjects, but the two comprehensive historical accounts of public education in the Hawaiian Kingdom overlooked those Kānaka who led the Kingdom's public education system, so it is worth summarizing their contributions here. The Hawaiian Kingdom legislature appointed Hawaiian scholar, author, and ordained minister, David Malo, as the first luna (superintendent) of public instruction for the Kingdom – a post he held for 4 years. Under Malo, they also appointed five kahu kula (school agents or inspectors) who oversaw all government schools on each of the five major islands. All five appointees were Kānaka: John Ii for O'ahu, Papohaku for Kaua'i; Kanakaokai for Moloka'i, David Malo for Maui, and Kanakaahuahu for Hawai'i. They had the power to grant teaching certificates and oversee teachers, to monitor the progress of students, to be the judges of the school law, and to provide for teachers salaries. Malo was a staunch advocate for Native teachers and their adequate compensation.

The educational leadership of Mataio Kekūanāo'a, who led the Kingdom's public school system for 8 years as President of the Board of Education from 1860 until his death in 1868 is similarly overlooked in existing histories. Descended from high chiefs of O'ahu and Hawai'i islands, Kekūanāo'a was an experienced statesman who accompanied King Kamehameha II to London in 1823–1824 to strengthen diplomatic ties between Hawai'i and Britain, and he served as the governor of O'ahu from 1839 to 1863. Kekūanāo'a's predecessor as head of public education, the American Protestant Rev. Richard Armstrong is often credited as bringing stability and developing the "public" character of the educational system, abolishing sectarian schools and introducing a tax-supported economic base. However, the reports of various heads of the Kingdom's Board of Education made to the legislature throughout the Kingdom era (1840–1893) show that it was Kekūanāo'a who articulated the most explicit concern for distancing government schools from church powers and providing an adequate appropriation of public funds to support that separation. For example, in Kekūanāo'a's report of 1866, he spent a significant amount of time talking about his concern for the lack of adequate school facilities resulting from insufficient funding. He advocated moving schools out of churches and mission stations, thus strengthening an inclusive national character, stating "It is necessary to provide as far as possible for *all* the people the advantage of a common school education...the common schools should come to be regarded as strictly neutral ground in religious matters" (Hawaiian Kingdom 1866). Kekūanāō'a further expressed concern with the fact that the poll tax was not providing adequate funding for the common schools and called for increased funding of the schools serving the common people. In addressing the problems of inadequate facilities, Kekūanāō'a proposed that the national Board of Education match the funds of local districts in which parents wanted to build or thoroughly renovate a schoolhouse. This enabled independence from mission and church.

In the debates over language in the schools, Kekūanāo'a firmly articulated the importance of the Hawaiian language in affirming Hawaiian national identity. While advocates for an English-language system of education and government pushed to reduce the status of the Hawaiian language, Kekūanāo'a asserted the importance of government support for Hawaiian-medium education:

> The theory of substituting the English language for the Hawaiian, in order to educate our people, is as dangerous to Hawaiian nationality, as it is useless in promoting the general education of the people. If we wish to preserve the Kingdom of Hawaii for Hawaiians, and to educate our people, we must insist that the Hawaiian language shall be the language of all our National Schools, and the English shall be taught whenever practicable, but only as an important branch of Hawaiian education. (Hawaiian Kingdom 1864)

He urged the legislature to increase funding for schools taught in Hawaiian. It was not until after his administration that enrolment in English-medium schools grew significantly vis a vis the Hawaiian-medium schools.

Unlike Kekūanāo'a, Charles R. Bishop, who served as president of the Board of Education (BOE) throughout the 1870s and early 1880s, significantly increased funding for English-language schools while cutting from Hawaiian-language common schools. In 1876, government funding for the select schools, some of which were also privately supported, amounted to $38,000 for 2,678 pupils, while funding for the common schools was only $13,000 for 4,313 pupils (Hawaiian Kingdom 1878). By the end of Bishop's term in 1883, the select, English-medium schools were receiving more than seven times the funding of the common schools, even though they had far fewer students. Teachers' salaries at English schools – positions filled by non-Natives – were markedly higher, and the availability of teachers in Hawaiian language was curtailed when the courses of study at Lahainaluna Seminary and Hilo Boarding School, which trained many of the native teachers, were changed from Hawaiian to English. While some English-advocates argued that rising enrolments demonstrated that Kānaka wanted to embrace English and move away from their own mother tongue, it is clear that this was no simple matter of abandoning one language for another. As Benham and Heck point out, the choices became unequal as the government increased funding support for English select schools over Hawaiian common schools. For instance, "most of the teacher professional development was conducted for English-speaking education, and many of the texts and materials brought from the United States were not translated for usage in the common schools" (Benham and Heck 1998, p. 93). By 1883, just before Bishop's forced resignation by King Kalākaua, the difference in appropriation was $75,000 for the select schools and $10,000 for the common schools (Hawaiian Kingdom 1884).

This brief history of public education in the Hawaiian Kingdom shows that schooling was not simply a colonial imposition. Kānaka and Haole together engaged in building popular literacy and a national school system. Ali'i and foreigners both folded visions for schooling into competing projects of Hawaiian modernization and nation-building. Sometimes they worked in collaboration as *hoa*, partners and interlocutors embedded in complicated relations of power. At other times, they were clearly *hoa paio*, political opponents articulating and acting on very different visions of how education for Hawaiians should look.

Like the banyan tree that tries to consume its host tree, the colonial patriarchal belief in the inherent superiority of white, Anglo-Saxon Protestants would come to structure the public and private sectors of education in Hawai'i. By the mid-1880s, haole businessmen aimed to usurp governing power and use schools to build a hierarchical plantation society. As previously noted, King Kalākaua was forced to sign an illegitimate Constitution in 1887, which came to be known as the "Bayonet Constitution" because of the armed militia's role in promulgating it. The Bayonet Constitution stripped all Asian people of the right to vote and it disenfranchised Kānaka Maoli through property requirements, while it also severely curtailed the monarch's power.

Queen Lili'uokalani succeeded King Kalākaua, with the intent to replace the Bayonet Constitution. In a coup d'état on January 17, 1893, a small group of white men claimed to establish a provisional government in place of the Queen's. The United States Marines supported the coup and landed troops, which marched directly to the seat of the Kingdom government. Fearing further loss of life of Kānaka Maoli, Queen Lili'ūokalani ordered her forces to stand down, as she would pursue diplomatic rather than military means to seek justice and restitution.

After the illegal overthrow of the Native rule, the white supremacist oligarchy took full control of the government school system, they cut *all* funding for Hawaiian-language education, leaving the vast majority of Kānaka teachers without teaching positions and keiki 'Ōiwi (Native children) without schooling in their ancestral language. Schutz reports that the number of Hawaiian-language medium schools took a dramatic decline, from 150 schools in 1880 to zero in 1902, whereas English-medium schools increased from 60 to 203 in the same period (Schutz 1994, p. 352). This was a direct result of the takeover by white businessmen backed by the US government. Some of them were Kingdom subjects. For instance, Lorrin A. Thurston, a missionary descendant, drafted the Bayonet Constitution and led the 1893 coup d'état. Sanford B. Dole, another missionary descendent and a cousin of James Dole of Dole Pineapple Company, appointed himself President of the Republic of Hawai'i on July 4, 1894. He had been a *hoa*, "friend," advisor, and attorney of King David Kalākaua and Queen Lili'uokalani advocating for Western-isation. The sugar oligarchy's and the US federal government's suppression of education in the Hawaiian language and culture stifled the collective 'Ōiwi ability to define themselves as a nation and people. Dole, Thurston, and their gang eagerly sought to turn Hawai'i into part of the USA through a proposed annexation treaty.

Kānaka, on the other hand, fiercely protested and organized against US annexation of Hawai'i. Noenoe Silva (2004) uncovered the 1897 anti-annexation petitions buried in the United States National Archives and signed by a majority of the Native Hawaiian population at the time. The recovery of these petitions challenges the myth that Kānaka Maoli passively accepted American annexation and affirms the truth that our ancestors stood to demonstrate their opposition to United States political control over our islands and people (Silva 2004). Their efforts were successful in that the US Congress was never able to pass a treaty and to this day, no annexation treaty between the USA and Hawai'i exists. Once the United States entered the Spanish-American and Philippine-American wars in 1898 and 1899 respectively, the USA unilaterally seized Hawai'i for its strategic location for military use. However, the uncovering of our history of competent self-governance and vigorous resistance to colonization sustains a growing independence movement in the islands in the present.

Conclusion

I ulu ka lālā i ke kumu. Returning to our opening 'ōlelo no'eau, a branch grows from and because of its tree trunk, throughout the chapter we have sought to offer an overview of colonization and education in the Hawaiian Islands with special attention to highlighting nā koa aloha 'āina. Bryan Kamaoli Kuwada's essay, *We are not warriors, We are a grove of trees*, honors the continuity and connection between the Kānaka that petitioned against annexation at the turn of the nineteenth century alongside the brave protectors of Mauna a Wākea in 2015, who have gathered together to stand against the development of a 30 m telescope on top of our sacred mountain. Upon considering the colonization of the Hawaiian Islands, resistance and decolonization efforts have happened simultaneously. This is the branch that grows forth from the koa tree, the tree of nā koa aloha 'āina. Contemporary reforestation efforts have shown that if you clear space around a single "mama koa," she will seed and her seedlings will flourish. Likewise, Kānaka remain dedicated to cultural perpetuation and the future health and wellbeing of our islands and people.

References

Beckwith M (1972) The Kumulipo, a Hawaiian creation chant. University of Hawai'i Press, Honolulu
Benham M, Heck R (1998) Culture and educational policy in Hawai'i: the silencing of native voices, Sociocultural, political, and historical studies in education. L. Erlbaum Associates, Mahwah
Beniamina J (2010) Tēnā: a learning lifestyle. Hūlili 6, pp 9–23
Bishop BP (1883) Last will and codicils of the late Hon. Mrs. Bernice P. Bishop. http://www.ksbe.edu/pauahi/will.php
Hawaiian Kingdom (1852) Report of the Minister of Public Instruction read before the King to the Hawaiian Legislature. Report of Richard Armstrong, 14 Apr 1852
Hawaiian Kingdom (1864) Biennial report of the President of the Board of Education to the Hawaiian Legislature of 1864. Report of Mataio Kekuanaoa
Hawaiian Kingdom (1866) Biennial report of the President of the Board of Education to the Hawaiian Legislature of 1866. Report of Mataio Kekuanaoa. Government document
Hawaiian Kingdom (1878) Biennial report of the President of the Board of Education to the Legislature of 1878. Report of Charles R. Bishop, Honolulu
Hawaiian Kingdom (1884) Biennial Report of the President of the Board of Education to the Legislature of 1884. Report of Walter Murray Gibson, Honolulu
Hawaiian Mission Children's Society (1969) Missionary album; portraits and biographical sketches of the American Protestant missionaries to the Hawaiian Islands, 1937th edn. Hawaiian Mission Children's Society, Honolulu
Kame'eleihiwa L (1992) Native land and foreign desires: Pehea La E Pono Ai? Bishop Museum Press, Honolulu
Kauanui K (2008a) Native Hawaiian decolonization and the politics of gender. Am Q 60(2):281–287
Kauanui JK (2008b) Hawaiian blood: colonialism and the politics of sovereignty and indigeneity. Duke University Press, Durham/London
Kauanui JK (2016) "A structure, not an event": settler colonialism and enduring indigeneity. Emergent critical analytics for alternative humanities. Issue 5.1, Spring
Kuwada BK (2015) We are not warriors. We are a grove of trees. In: Hehiale World Press. https://heiale.wordpress.com/2015/07/06/we-are-not-warriors-we-are-a-grove-of-trees/. Accessed 15 Sept 2016
Kuykendall RS (1938a) The Hawaiian Kingdom, vol. 1, Foundation and transformation, vol 1. University of Hawaii Press, Honolulu
Kuykendall RS (1938b) The Hawaiian Kingdom, vol. 2, Twenty critical years (1854–1874). University of Hawaii Press, Honolulu
Osorio J (2002) Dismembering Lahui: a history of the Hawaiian nation to 1887. University of Hawai'i Press, Honolulu
Pukui MK (1983) Ōlelo No'eau: Hawaiian proverbs & poetical sayings, Bernice P. Bishop Museum special publication no. 71. Bishop Museum Press, Honolulu
Recollet K (2016) Gesturing indigenous futurities through the remix. Dance Res J 48(1):91–105. Indigenous Dance Today
Schutz AJ (1994) The voices of Eden: a history of Hawaiian language studies. University of Hawaii Press, Honolulu

Silva NK (2004) Aloha betrayed: native Hawaiian resistance to American colonialism. Duke University Press, Durham
Stannard D (1989) Before the horror: the population of Hawai'i on the eve of Western contact. University of Hawai'i Press, Honolulu
Trask HK (1984) Fighting the battle of double colonization: the view of a Hawaiian feminist. uhmanoa.lib.hawaii.edu. 7008 Library Catalogue
Trask HK (1999) From a native daughter: colonialism and sovereignty in Hawai'i, Revised edn. University of Hawaii Press, Honolulu
Tuck E, Gaztambide-Fernandez R (2013) Curriculum, replacement, and settler futurity. JCT 29(1):72–89 (online); Rochester
Vizenor G (ed) (2008) Survivance: narratives of native presence. University of Nebraska Press, Lincoln
Wist B (1940) A century of public education in Hawaii, October 15, 1840–October 15, 1940. The Hawaii Educational Review, Honolulu
Wolfe P (2006) Settler colonialism and the elimination of the native. J Genocide Res 8(4):387–409

Mapuchezugun Ka Mapuche Kimün: Confronting Colonization in Chile (Nineteenth and Twentieth Centuries)

5

Héctor Nahuelpán, Jaime Antimil, and Kathryn Lehman

Contents

Introduction	64
Pacification as Genocide and Dispossession	65
Civilizing Spaces	69
Concluding Thoughts	79
References	81

Abstract

This chapter analyzes the process of colonization of the Mapuche people as they were forced into the Chilean State and capitalist political economy in the nineteenth and twentieth centuries. Through a critical reading of archival sources and oral history, we review in detail the effects that colonization produced in the context of the political and territorial sovereignty of the Mapuche people, which includes converting them into minorities, the obliteration, eradication, and persecution of the

---

Translated by Kathryn Lehman

H. Nahuelpán (✉)
Centro de Estudios e Investigaciones Mapuche–Comunidad de Historia Mapuche, Departamento de Ciencias Sociales, Universidad de Los Lagos, Temuco, Region de la Araucania, Chile
e-mail: hnahuelpan@gmail.com

J. Antimil
Villa Wenumapu, Centro de Estudios e Investigaciones Mapuche – Comunidad de Historia Mapuche, Pasaje Llefque, Temuco, Region de la Araucania, Chile
e-mail: antimil.kaniupan@gmail.com

K. Lehman
University of Auckland, Auckland, New Zealand
e-mail: k.lehman@auckland.ac.nz

© Springer Nature Singapore Pte Ltd. 2019
E. A. McKinley, L. T. Smith (eds.), *Handbook of Indigenous Education*,
https://doi.org/10.1007/978-981-10-3899-0_24

use of Mapuchezugun (language of the Mapuche people) and Mapuche kimün (Mapuche knowledge), linked to racial subordination within the social interactions of subsequent generations in what we term "civilizing spaces."

The argument developed in this chapter is that colonial violence against the Mapuche people, their language, ontology, and epistemology is part of the historical project of dispossession and genocide against indigenous peoples. Far from being passive subjects, the Mapuche people have displayed diverse forms of resistance, negotiation and response, and a struggle for life facing a project of death represented by colonization.

Keywords

Mapuche people · Chile · Colonialism · Knowledge · Education

Introduction

The region known today as Latin America was divided into nation-states in the nineteenth century following independence from Spain. Although there were many indigenous peoples who lived in their own autonomous territories, the Mapuche people were unique in having their political and territorial sovereignty officially recognized through more than 40 treaties or *parlamentos* with the Spanish colonial government. They exercised sovereignty over an extensive territory located in the American Southern Cone, called Wallmapu (the Mapuche nation), which encompassed two enormous land masses situated on either side of the Andes Mountains: Gülumapu (western lands, now Chile) and Puelmapu (eastern lands, now Argentina).

Despite sovereignty and formal recognition by the Spanish Crown, during the second half of the nineteenth century, the Mapuche people experienced radical change following military campaigns by the Argentinean and Chilean States, grotesquely called "The Pacification of Araucanía" and the "The Conquest of the Desert," respectively. The consequences of both military occupations were enormous because they created colonial relations that continue to the present. Among the greatest repercussions of military invasion have been the loss of most of the territory they controlled until the mid-nineteenth century; the progressive occupation of these lands by Chilean and European settlers who confiscated their lands and plundered resources (currently carried out by national and transnational corporations); the racial subordination of the Mapuche population, their impoverishment, and demographic dispersal through the reduction and forced displacement of their communities; and the creation of a set of civilizing institutions (missions, schools, large landed estates, the army), whose sole purpose has been to "regenerate" Mapuche survivors of these acts of genocide.

In this context, this chapter analyzes the colonization process that forced the Mapuche people to become integrated into both the Chilean State and the capitalist political economy throughout the nineteenth and twentieth centuries. The study of archival sources and oral history enables us to address how Chilean colonial violence and structural racism reduced the Mapuche language (Mapuchezugun) and Mapuche knowledge (Kimün) to minority status, destroying its social network through persecution and subordination of the social interaction of people and families in what we call "civilizing spaces." The latter are the institutions and spaces of social interaction (schools, missions, large landed estates, the army, etc.) introduced through the racial-colonial design and development of the state and society of Chile.

Writing this text has given us a deeper understanding of specific acts of Chilean colonial violence that introduced hierarchies into Mapuche territory, designed to create a world that would replace our own ways of conceiving life and existence. We propose that these strategies were not accidental and instead obeyed a colonial logic and genocidal design that sought to subdue, suppress, and dispossess a territory, its people, and their ways of living.

Pacification as Genocide and Dispossession

When the Chilean Creole elite first moved toward independence from the Spanish Crown in the First National Assembly of 1810, the emerging republic had no control over the enormous territory of the Mapuche people. It required military conquest, initiated in the mid-nineteenth century to occupy and incorporate this land into the state of Chile. Political parties, intellectuals, merchants, and Chilean landowners won the debate over the legitimacy of militarily occupying Mapuche territory south of the Bío Bío River because they saw an opportunity to develop lucrative business and obtain benefits through the appropriation of Mapuche lands, timber, cattle, natural resources, and manual labor. This profoundly colonial project was justified by resorting to a rhetorical discourse on civilization and progress as pathways to eradicate barbarism and savagery, represented by the Mapuche people. This narrative appeared not only in official sources but also in the press, as this quotation from the influential newspaper *El Mercurio* in 1859 suggests:

> The Indian is absolutely incapable of being civilized: nature has spent everything on developing his body, but his intelligence has remained at the level of beasts of prey, whose qualities he possesses in abundance, having never once experienced moral emotion ... How shall men safely approach these wild beasts, how does the peaceful and industrious population enter the forest where ferocity and barbarism find shelter? ... an association of barbarians as barbarous as the Pampas or Araucano Indians is nothing more than a hoard of beasts which urgently begs to be enslaved or destroyed in the interest of humanity and the greater good of civilization. (El Mercurio de Valparaiso 1859)

An influential nineteenth-century Chilean politician gave a similar speech before the House of Representatives on August 10, 1868, in which he stated that:

> Some call upon civilization to benefit the Indian, but what does he do for our progress, for civilization itself? Nothing but act as a contagion of barbarism that has infected our frontier communities, because the conquest of the Indian is essentially what it has been in the United States, the conquest of civilization. It is true that the Indian stands his ground; but he defends it because he hates civilization, he hates the law, the priesthood and education. (Vicuña 1868, 7)

By the mid-nineteenth century, the Chilean elites were united in representing Mapuche territory as an island that divided Chile into two parts, and its inhabitants as barbarism embedded in the middle of the nation that they wanted to build: "on our soil, the Indians form a parenthesis, an interruption, in the midst of civilization's territory" (El Ferrocarril de Santiago 1858). Diverse political, economic, and ideological factors merged to set off a campaign of military invasion into Gülumapu, in official historiography described as the conquest or pacification of the Araucanía (*Araucano* Land). The ideological basis of this genocidal military campaign is found in the colonialist discourse and fantasy of positivism and social Darwinism, which represented the Mapuche people as an *inferior race* who created obstacles for the future of the state and the nation that the Creoles planned to build. The administrative confiscation of Mapuche territory took place through the creation of Arauco Province in 1852, following that was the need to extend the surface of production to escape an economic crisis in 1857. The final cause was the desire for revenge against Mapuche groups who had participated in the revolutions of 1851 and 1859 (Bengoa 1985; Leiva 1984; Pinto 2003).

Two Spanish colonial settlements that had been razed to the ground in a Mapuche uprising in 1598 were "refounded" as Chilean cities in the late nineteenth century: Angol in 1862 and Villarica in 1883. This period marks a rupture in the historical development of Mapuche as a sovereign people when Chilean conquest and military occupation had devastating impacts. Although these events were located geographically in American Southern Cone, they were part of a new historical cycle of global colonialism. This new process forced indigenous territories and peoples to integrate into the nation-state, to consolidate the states' internal frontiers to serve the imperial practices of colonial powers, and to link the production from indigenous territories to the economic centers of the North Atlantic. This economic cycle was generated by the demand for products, spurred by demographic growth, the industrial revolution, and the development of the capitalist mode of production (Nahuelpan 2012). This larger productive enterprise was supported by the ideological influence of positivism and evolutionism that emphasized the existence of "superior races" and "inferior races," which justified colonization, violence, genocide, and the reduction of indigenous peoples as a civilizing act.

Among the episodes of extreme violence unleashed by military troops were the acts that the Chilean colonial government called a war of resources or war of extermination. The strategy was described in an official government document entitled "Discussion of a Plan for the Campaign and Reduction of the Araucanía," which detailed its main objectives:

> Harass the enemy in all areas, pursue them without allowing them any place to plant crops, raise animals or build housing, continue in this way for two consecutive years without listening to promises of peace, and then, if the war is not over, it will be near its end. Then and only then, forced by hunger, illness, poverty and the rigors of war and impotence will they finally be forced to change behavior and offer as many guarantees of safety as are demanded of them. (Ministry of War 1870, 53–54)

The war of resources or extermination employed sporadic incursions by soldiers into lands where the Mapuche people resisted the advance of the army. These armed forces were accompanied by civilians, Chilean settlers, and foreigners clustered into civil squadrons which entered to burn forests, *ruka* (Mapuche houses), sown fields, and to steal large numbers of cattle, textiles, and silver as the spoils of war, and they assassinated and took men hostage, raping women, boys, and girls. In some cases, the children were taken north of the Bío Bío River to serve as manual labor on large landed estates and as domestic service in the landlord's mansions at the border and in the central region of Chile. The destruction and dispossession that the "pacification" produced were not limited to lands, resources, and goods such as cattle, textiles, and silver but included persons, as happened to Mapuche children. These practices were not new: the abduction of boys and girls took place repeatedly during the Spanish colonial cycle, and it returned in the years just before the formal beginning of the pacification campaigns. Mapuche families used forests and mountains as zones of refuge from extermination and abduction, graphically depicted in the words of *Mangil Wenu*, one of the greatest Mapuche resistance leaders of that era, who addressed the following words to the President of the Chilean Republic in 1860:

> Your Provincial Governor (Intendente) Villalón, together with Salbo, ended up with an abundance of animals; but they were not happy with this because they have big bellies; all they did was burn houses and fields, and take families hostage, tearing children away from their mothers' breasts as they ran to hide in the hills, and they commanded that burial grounds be dug up to rob the silver articles buried with the dead according to Indian rituals, murdering even Christian women, as they did with two they caught who went looking for food for their children… Right now, I have a leader, a *cacique* who left the coast because they are fighting him; again, the *caciques* tell me that the first act that the Governor of Arauco carried out was to slit the throat of two Indians and their two little 8 year old daughters, and that they have done the same thing there that they did here. (Mangil Wenu 2008, 319–325)

Along with military invasion, there were other forms of violence such as the expropriation of lands, the creation of a state bureaucracy, the imposition of a new nation-state sociopolitical and juridical structure, and the foundation of forts progressively transformed into intermediary cities. Transportation and communication networks were constructed to exercise control and integrate the territory economically with the rest of the country. Importantly, schools and missions were created as civilizing spaces to lead to the "regeneration" of Mapuche and convert them into productive citizens for the new colonial and racial order.

As soon as the conquest of Gülumapu ended in 1883 with the refounding of Villarica, the historical development of Mapuche society proceeded with a forced transition from political and territorial independence to living under an internal colonialism within the nation-state. One of the most important aspects of this radical change, which forms the context of current conflicts, was the loss of an extensive territory belonging to Mapuche people that became integrated as "federal lands." These were lands that were auctioned off, given as concessions, or assigned to companies and private owners with the intention of establishing private agrarian property. During this time, the Mapuche population was condemned to live in small parcels of land, the so-called reservations or the more familiar Spanish term "reductions" (capitalized to indicate its institutional specificity).

In 1883, the Indigenous Settlement Commission (Comisión Radicadora de Indígenas) was created, and Chilean or foreign settlers recently arriving from Europe acquired a considerable portion of Mapuche lands, while indigenous resettlement was carried out on reservations or reductions, parceled out as "charitable land grants." (The Spanish term *Títulos de Merced* refers to a Christian "grant or title of charity" based on mercy, *merced*.) The demarcation of lands designated as indigenous began in 1884, with areas significantly smaller than those that formed part of their socio-territorial jurisdiction. In order to distribute these land grants, the Mapuche had to prove their effective and continuous possession for at least 1 year, a nonsensical procedure, since the occupation of these lands dated back for centuries. Finally, once the lands were demarcated, the Settlement Commission passed a law that issued a land grant in the name of the republic "for the benefit" of the Mapuche people.

The resettlement process was an eminently colonial practice. As such, it is no coincidence that its terms (Título de Merced, Reducción, Cacique) were the same as those used by the Spanish colonial government in the sixteenth and seventeenth centuries to refer to the reorganization and relocation of the indigenous population in its colonies (Mallon 2009, 157). The state coined the terms "Reservation, Reduction and Charitable Land Grant" because the lands recognized as Mapuche were those that were left over and were reserved after the majority, and best lands were handed over to settlers. Therefore, the notion of reduction denotes the character of agrarian property, which is the territorial dispossession to which Mapuche people were subjected. Likewise, the notion of a charitable land grant expresses an absurd logic as though the process of granting a title was a kind of "gift of charity" granted by the state to the Mapuche people, not the acknowledgment of an older historical occupation (Correa and Mella 2010, 64). The arbitrary nature of the settlement process is clear in descriptions by protectors of indigenous peoples (Protectores de Indígenas) in reports, such as one published by Eulogio Robles in 1912, who stated that:

> Just as the Indigenous were being settled, rural properties for auction were formed, plots of land were offered for rent, pieces of land were donated to settlers and there were enormous land concessions given to individual owners to be colonized.
> What is more, on many occasions, they first auctioned rural properties to be colonized, etc., and on what was left over, Indians were settled. (Robles 1912, 144)

On the other hand, the total surface area of indigenous resettlement was 51,038,667 ha or approximately 6% of the territory controlled by Mapuche up to the mid-nineteenth century. The remaining area, approximately 94%, was designated as federal lands and transferred to Chilean and foreign settlers. Among this last group were merchants, landowners, and military officers who had actively participated in the "pacification" campaigns (González 1986).

As part of the process of reduction, Mapuche people were allowed a minimal territorial space that included the *ruka* (houses) and fields, while the lands used for grazing, timber milling, and food gathering were declared *terra nullius*, federal or "empty lands," which were later offered for auction or delivered without charge to settlers. The reduction ignored relations that Mapuche people had maintained with water (salty versus sweet, potable), the subsoil, specific spaces relevant to spiritual life, or valued because of the presence of *ngen* (protective beings), who remained captive on the landed estates that were being consolidated. They did not respect preexisting rules and forms of occupation, the older demarcations, or sociopolitical and territorial organization based on kinship relations. On the reservations, families who came from different *lof che* (communities) were grouped together or in spaces that these groups had previously occupied, and two or more land grants were distributed, producing conflicts among Mapuche families themselves.

The reduction also forced related groups, who had occupied and used their territories following migratory patterns – which permitted rotation in the use of soil and a diversity of productive activities, into a sedentary life on small areas of land (Vidal 2000). This restricted access to different resources and spaces transformed the Mapuche economy from one based on diversified activities toward self-subsistence, which, in the long term, meant that Mapuche people were subjected to a process that forced them to become *campesinos* (a local form of peasantry based on the European model).

The image of a Mapuche society that was reduced in this way, by being corralled like animals and converted into a minority through "civilization and progress" so loudly proclaimed by the Chilean political elite of that era, is transmitted through writing that feels like an eye-witness account. Lorenzo Kolüman, who lived during the settlement era, communicated to Mankelef y Guevara at the beginning of the twentieth century: "what we have achieved with the civilization they say they gave us is to live cramped like sardines in a can (literally grains of wheat in a sack)" (Kolüman 2002, 43–44).

Civilizing Spaces

The historical process of the colonization of Gülumapu followed clearly defined strategies. Its forced annexation to the Chilean State and the capitalist political economy was not achieved through military conquest and the dispossession of resources alone but was also through mechanisms and instruments that permitted them to take control of the spirit of the people of the land, thereby guaranteeing their submission and the control not only of the body but also of the subjectivity of the Mapuche people. Clear evidence of this project was a report presented by Antonio Varas, a prominent Chilean politician, to the House of Representatives about the "peaceful Reduction of the Araucanian territory." This document, presented in 1848, emphasized a series of strategies that would manage to establish republican sovereignty in a territory that was not yet subject to Chilean law. Varas stated:

> What is the objective? To civilize the Indians, that is, improve their natural condition, enlighten and cultivate their intelligence, develop their good sentiments that are the patrimony of humanity, and elevate their spirit to moral and religious truth. To convert the remains of primitive inhabitants of Chile into useful citizens, to make them participants in the benefits that civilization spreads across all countries, to eliminate from among them the worries or

superstitions that cloud their spirit, to allow their eyes to see the bright light of the Gospel that ennobles man. This is a very dignified enterprise of the Republic... (Varas 1849, 13)

The goals of this republican enterprise would be achieved through the spread of conditions that would eliminate the *mapuche az mongen*, the ways of life of the Mapuche people, conceived as a stumbling block of savagery. From Varas's own words, we can deduce that the conversion he mentions of "these remains of the primitive inhabitants of Chile" referred to their forced conversion into "useful citizens," to regenerate them, moralize them, and civilize them, in other words, to achieve a condition of humanity, from which they were deprived because of their being in a state of barbarism. The conquest enterprise was conceived not only as the taking of a territory but also as a mission of redemption of civilized man in his struggle to expand civilization.

The mechanisms that Varas proposed were clearly articulated. "Missions, schools and commerce with the Spanish population, these are the civilizing means which will allow for the successive integration of the indigenous population into the rest of the nation" (Varas 1849, 27), as stated by this ideologue of Occupation. The labors of conversion and Christianization were to be taken up by the missionary, the primary agent who would manage to "seize the spirit" of the indigenous people. This person's work should focus on the Mapuche population and on one stratum in particular:

> The most promising areas for commitment by the missionary are the children. **Here the good seed will not be smothered by weeds.** It would be vain pretention to civilize the indigenous if we did not make use of the most effective medium to regenerate the people. Take the generation that is growing, prepare it for civilized life, enlighten its understanding, encourage inspiration in its heart for moral and religious sentiments, and after three or four generations, you will have finished with the barbarism that damages them. But it is not just a simple religious teaching the missionary imparts. It must replace the parents, it must have the children completely under its control, educate them, teach them and prepare them for a laborious life as a civilized man. (Varas 1849, 18. Our emphases in bold)

The strategy was clear: boys and girls would be the replacement generation that would allow for a new people to be educated. Macaya (2016, 99) proposes that this system is similar to the concept of the "economy of delayed returns"; in other words, a plan to harvest in the long term, when the seeds that were planted with the precepts of civilization, should render fruit. In this way, missionaries would become the educational and formative reference point for children who would thereby be inculcated with the culture, values, habits, and conception of "civilized man," replacing the educational role of "weeds" or the Mapuche family. Evangelization through the missions would be central, but it would be also accompanied by a process of schooling and work, with the goal of regenerating the people in their totality:

> To civilize or moralize a people without making use of religious influence to me is a fantasy. Let the action of religious missions be joined with other means that similarly approach the same goal; that man should be embraced in his whole being; the task should not be limited to Christianizing them and teaching them to pray, in this way missions will render the fruit expected of them. (Varas 1849, 16)

The year following the presentation of this report, the first Italian missionaries of the Capuchin Order arrived in Mapuche territory, and they established different missionary centers. One of these was set up in *Rulowe* or *Traitraiko mapu*, present-day Puerto Saavedra, at that time called *Bajo Imperial* by the Chilean bureaucracy. Father Constanzo or Constancio de Trisobio arrived and Pascual Coña was one of his first students. The memoires of Coña, as narrated to the priest Ernesto Wilhelm de Moesbach, published in 1930 as "Life and Customs of the Araucanian Indians in the Second Half of the Nineteenth Century" shows the first steps established by the colonization enterprise of the Chilean State to "take control of the spirit" of the Mapuche people (Coña and Moesbach 2010).

The Capuchin priest Sergio Uribe explains that the ministry of his missionary brothers maintained a deeply held conviction whose goals were extolled for "struggling against the evil and error in which the unfaithful, to whom they would preach, were assumed to be lost" (Uribe 1988, 215). This condition made them feel like soldiers in the vanguard. Clearly, Uribe continues; the missionaries as well as the families and farmers who advanced into frontier territory became a "civilizing reconnaissance unit." Aside from their convictions, this religious presence, with all of its ethnocentric and racist implications, was a foundational cornerstone for the destruction of Mapuche ways of life. As soon as the military campaigns of the pacification of the Araucanía were concluded, the spaces of civilization spread out in an organized, systematic fashion. It was the Christian missions under the control of the Capuchin Order and the Anglicans which were specifically designed to convert Mapuche people.

To understand this phenomenon of colonization, authors like Fanon point out that to achieve a colonial regime, the first act is to create the servile condition of the autochthonous population, and to do this, it is necessary to change their system of references: "the cultural panorama is shredded, values ridiculed, erased, emptied" (Fanon 1965, 41). In the same way, he warns that beyond working toward the disappearance of local culture, the colonial regime must condemn the culture of the colonized peoples to an eternal agony. The declarations of the Chilean colonial authorities during the first years of Chilean occupation of Gülumapu followed this line of thinking. For example, a note sent by the Minister of Foreign Relations around 1901 to Gregorio Urrutia, Governor of Cautín, to be distributed to different regions under his control, mandated the following:

> Indigenous customs frequently have ceremonies that our national culture finds sobering, and unfortunately, they produce pernicious effects for the public health of the people who practice them. The Ministry has become aware of the festivals called Machitunes which refer to the Machi doctors curing the sick with Pillantunes or prayers to the Pillan, as in the burial ceremonies for their dead. They celebrate festivals that are actually used as a pretext to become intoxicated and they observe ceremonies that are nothing more than remains of barbarism; it is shameful that they continue to practice these. (...) I draw your attention to this matter so that Your Honor might find whatever means prudent to eradicate these customs and prohibit, in any manner possible, the way that cadavers remain unburied more than the time permitted by Law. (Quoted in Caniuqueo 2006, 261–162)

Not only were the practices and ways of life of Mapuche people considered to be barbarous and savage and deemed to be of an inferior law before the eyes of state agents, but they were also openly declared as practices that must be eradicated, for which the missions and the schools were designed as the principal instruments to achieve this task. The next section will develop this idea in more detail.

The construction of servile and submissive subjects was also achieved through informal spaces and agents, where the colonizing society had an important role. The project of the Arauco Conquest presented in 1861 by Colonel Pedro Godoi to General Manuel García, at that time Minister of War and Navy, offers us a clear idea of this role:

> Let us now rest our gaze on the settlers or European immigrants who were able to arrive and establish new estates. If we are to respect and offer consideration to the savages, how much more do we offer those who bring us commerce, the arts, and civilization? (Godoi 1861, 92)

Something similar was proposed by the same (Varas 1849) in the report cited above. According to him, to achieve true progress in Mapuche lands, they must do more than reduce and civilize the people, since once this goal had been achieved, they would enter into contact with the civilized population of the Chilean "lower class." Therefore, contact would bring about another challenge, since the indigenous – thus civilized and reduced – would naturally adopt the ideas, spirit, and habits of the mestiza (mixed-race) society, whose cultural patterns and ways of life were also contrary to the idea of elite society. To counteract this double problem, the proposal of Varas, like that of Godoi, was designed to promote European immigration:

> Foreign immigration is the only way to wake our people from their indolence; indolence that will be much greater among the civilized indigenous people. Of course, let's keep focused on immigration while taking advantage of the opportunities that civilization of the Indians may offer to reduce their presence in these territories. This is a vow that all those who desire the true advancement of the Republic will undoubtedly take with all their heart. (Varas 1849, 48)

Both Varas and Godoi proposed that to achieve a change of worldview of the colonized population of Gülumapu, whether it would be the Mapuche or the lower class, it was fundamental to have the presence of European settlers. Contact with these new agents of social change, whose cultural schemes seemed similar to the ideals of the Chilean elite, would regenerate both social groups, Mapuche and Chilean settlers, and end the lack of social discipline and low productivity of these groups. In fact, the preference for European settlers enhanced a system of unequal treatment given to Chilean settlers coming from the popular sectors (Pinto 2003, 225). In spite of these differences, both types of settlers saw themselves as a society of occupiers, with alternative visions for life and existence, whose contact was determined by the specific factors of their colonial position, mediated by racism, violence, and the direct or indirect imposition of cultural patterns.

The settlers established themselves in lands stolen from the Mapuche, and they began to create new spaces and institutions: large landed estates, farms, mansions, the city, the market, the military, and other public institutions such as schools, in other words, civilization's spaces. To understand how they occupied these spaces, it is helpful to read the Colonization Charter, drawn up by Nicolás Boloña in 1916. Here one can clearly see how commercial networks became integrated into social behavior among the colonizing society and Mapuche, widely corroborated in a variety of studies (Alonqueo 1985; Mallon 2004; Antimil 2012; Araya and Porma 2012; Nahuelpán 2012).

Large landed estates were one of the major spaces where the hierarchies and subjugation of Mapuche were established. This is where schools were located, along with a very important labor niche for social discipline. The communities were related to each other as racialized servile manual labor: for men, as errand boys, day laborers, farm workers, sharecroppers, tenant farmers, and other forms of work, and for women as domestic workers in the landlord's house. There are many testimonies that narrate the brutality of experiences suffered by these men and women during and after the occupation of Mapuche territory. In a recent publication, Nahuelpán established a dialogue with Manuel, a Mapuche worker who experienced these conditions, which in part explains some of the vicissitudes in this servile regime:

> When I was a boy, they asked me to work on the condition that they give me food, shelter, clothing and an education... I worked as a servant, a gardener, I had to wash, plant, tidy the orchard, take care of hens, clean the henhouse, a lot of things. I had just one tool for cleaning, when it was time to clean it was terrible for me. I had to get up to make fire while it was still dark, so that by 8.00 am the water would be warm. I got up before the bosses, I had to have everything ready. They made their wealth at the expense of Mapuche people, at the expense of errand boys... I had just a few hours to study, in the end really the agreement that we had for my study wasn't respected ... the bosses exploited us like animals and now they don't want us to improve... (Quoted in Nahuelpan 2015, 285)

It is worth noting how this experience reflects ways that the subjugation of Mapuche originated in economies of dispossession and was accelerated through the impoverishment of Mapuche families. However, there are other testimonies that view the lived experience in these spaces through other lenses. For example, Juan speculates that it was some time in the middle of the 1930s that he began to work as an "errand boy" and later as a peon, a sharecropper, and tenant farmer on an estate near his original community. This was the property of a settler of English descent who arrived in Mapuche territory at the beginning of the twentieth century. His testimony is key to understanding the process. He remembered the time he worked as an "errand boy" in the following terms:

> A good person that old man he was. They were all good persons, good people. That's why we were good workers, never drunk, not going around the place kicking up a fuss, nothin' like that's what he said. He raised us like his children, he did. There was one man there, Ramón Ulloga, and he taught me (...) He was there too. That same Mr. Santiago told him "He had to teach his son." He called me his "son". (Juan 2012)

In long conversations with Juan, he pointed out that after being months in the house as a servant "I didn't miss my family any more" and that when he returned to his community "I couldn't wait to go back to the landlord's house" and that "he didn't like the food at his house" or "how they lived so backward." He was so changed that 1 day when he went to his house, he met his aunt *Llanka*, who said to her sister, Juan's mother, that he wasn't like Mapuche any more, he was *wingka* (Chilean or non-Mapuche). The disciplining of Juan by the landlord was fundamental. The settler, transformed into a paternal model, became the educational agent that had a clear influence on the configuration of his *az che* (personal identity), just as Varas had predicted in his report. This is the radical change that Juan had suffered.

The city also merits our attention. There is no doubt that commerce, nothing new for frontier populations, was the first space for socialization, where it was necessary to learn the colonizer's language to carry out trade. Cities also appeared with the other spaces and institutions: courts, military regiments, hospitals, schools, churches, and others. Migration is a phenomenon associated with urban centers, formed by structural features of colonial domination: reduction and the scarcity of land, impoverishment, hunger, and the precariousness of Mapuche families (Antileo 2012). In rural areas, Mapuche migrants were allocated the most precarious and low-wage work: domestic labor, gardening, baking, day labor, and all racialized manual labor (Nahuelpán 2012, 2013; Antileo 2012, 2015). The cities of Temuco, Santiago, and Valparaiso were transformed into centers that offered work, which explains why today, the largest percentage of Mapuche people are living in the peripheral sectors of cities.

The *wariache* – Mapuche who live in the city – had to confront colonial violence as well. Mapuche ways of life such as ceremonies, dress, language, and physical appearance had to be changed to "civilized" ways, to attenuate racial discrimination. This is why Mapuche surnames have changed, as a result of life in the cities and memories of their families. José's testimonial, as a migrant and breadmaker in Santiago City, serves to illustrate this idea:

> Life in Santiago is very hard... **it is like an everyday resistance** ... the people who leave think that in Santiago streets are made of gold, you get handfuls, but it's not like that, I suffered a lot here and in Santiago... in Santiago I did not speak Mapuche, how could I, if it was full of Chileans? And especially if you're Indian, so I didn't speak Mapuche, it was like hiding it because if not, "here comes an Indian", "shitty Indian" "Indian asshole", that's how the people treat you, **but in my mind, I kept it hidden and I was speaking Mapuche.** And when I came back here I began to speak Mapuche again. Over in Santiago I had a friend who I spoke Mapuche with, but hidden, never in front of the bosses or in the street, couldn't do it. (Quoted in Nahuelpán 2015, 280)

The language and Mapuche ways of life were forbidden or eliminated. As José said, they were suppressed, suspended within one's subjectivity, where they continued to live. This has been part of daily resistance before the conquest of subjectivity, of the spirit, and of the body of the people of the land:

> Get rid of Mapuche dress. Being and feeling Mapuche wasn't worth anything, it was not wanted, it was not seen. For that reason, Mapuche ideas, the Mapuche person was hidden far away. Only the power of the *wigka*, their ideas have weight, they are valuable, they are the center of events, while anything related to *mapuche az mogen,* ways of being, was hidden somewhat, it lost all legitimacy and it became invisible. (Quidel 2015, 42)

With these words, Quidel shows us how violence against Mapuche thought and spirituality was practiced as ridicule, since *mapuche az mogen* was hated, viewed as disgusting, ripped out from the roots, expelled, and displaced. For her part, an

80-year-old Mapuche woman who worked from the time she was young in the same conditions offers deep insight into her treatment and life in the house of her bosses:

> I slept in a tiny room, in winter the rain dripped in, I ate a different food from the bosses, I got up before them (...) when I made good food, they celebrated with me, but if I made a mistake they were there always telling me that I was an Indian and all that, my self-esteem was shattered, and so just to get them to stop doing it, you begin to change (...) that happens a lot with the people who go to work as a domestic housekeeper (...) sometimes you don't even realize how you got to believe everything they say. (R.P. Cited in Nahuelpán 2012, 142–143)

Civilizing spaces were constructed – and continue to be constructed today – as instruments of discipline where hierarchies are created and reinforced through ways of knowing, knowledge, habits, customs, languages, and persons (Nahuelpán 2012, 143). These conform to the mechanisms by which the ideology and ways of life of the colonizing society are imposed which introduced discourses about the inferiority of Mapuche people. For this reason, many families began to change their ways of life, hide their practices, and destroy anything associated with their Mapuche roots. From within the Mapuchezugun language, this process is known as *wigkawün* for men and *chiñurawün* for women, becoming changed into a Chilean man or woman. Civilizing spaces functioned as systems of discipline and radical social change, they internalized colonialism through violence; they changed symbolic and cultural systems as well as the conception of Mapuche life itself, forming a support base for the conquest of the people of the land. As a consequence, changes in the paradigms of life of the Mapuche people themselves have not been voluntary decisions: the destruction, exile, suppression, and displacement of these ways were conditioned by an historical project of genocide, and some had greater responsibility than others for this history.

"Reading only comes through bleeding" is a saying referring to violence as an educational method, experienced in the flesh and blood of generations of Mapuche students throughout the twentieth century.

Marta was born in 1994. Like most boys and girls in the Mapuche communities, when she finished eighth grade in a rural school, she enrolled in an educational institution in the city of Temuco. It was summer 2009 when she and probably her family had dreams of "becoming someone in life," a phrase often heard in Mapuche families, who see the education of their daughters and sons as way to escape poverty. Marta had enrolled in the boarding school because of the irregular transport connecting her city or because she would save travel time and could study more easily. With some expectation, hope, and fear, Marta began her life as a student in the city, as many of us did.

"Tie up the pigs, Marta! Put the hen in the cage!" What seemed to be a child's game – for both Mapuche and for Chilean poor country girls – became a living hell: the expectations became disillusionment, hope turned to disappointment, and fear to terror. Night after night, day after day, teasing about her accent grew. It was not funny. One day Andrea, who told us this story, found Marta in tears, hiding. She had spoken only to the girls closest to her so that they would stop this. The teasing continued as did Marta's goals: she exchanged her school notebooks for cheap beer and the classrooms for parties starting in mid-afternoon. She soon had to repeat the course and change schools. Andrea doesn't know what happened to her. She probably gave up and never finished middle school.

At age 14, Martín Alonqueo Piutrín enrolled in National Rural School No 44 in 1923, located on the Santa Carolina estate. His entry into this temple of knowledge was described in the following terms:

> I lived at the school, my grandma came and I was so happy. I was in the central square of the school and right away they came over to bother me, laughing at my grandma's speech and making fun of me. I didn't react, but went to a corner, just stood there looking down and quiet, just watching all the games and hearing songs the girls sang while a group of friends and people I knew surrounded me to talk to me. The bell rang and we went into class with all of my Mapuche friends, speaking in our own language. (...)
>
> During the next break, I was with my friends and neighbors and we were speaking in Mapuche. That's all we did; they told on me to the teacher, but I didn't know the rule about not speaking Mapuche language, just Spanish. After this first accident, I got back with my friends and we continued speaking in Mapuche but whispering (...)
>
> When the bell rang, we went back into class. I paid careful attention to what the teacher taught; but I didn't understand a thing. The bell rang at the end of the day, it was noon. (...) Up to that point, all was going well; but (...) at that point a white child came up to our group, coming toward me speaking to me; but I couldn't answer him because I couldn't make out what he was saying. Since I didn't answer, he began to laugh and say that I was "a horse Indian, who eats horse meat and eats weeds;" you hear this every day, when they talk about Mapuche people.
>
> The ones in that group explained what the expressions he used about me meant. Then, at that moment, I was furious and jumped on him, swearing with this phrase: *"Winka trewa, Winka* dog, what are you saying?" [A very common phrase used by Mapuche people, filled with rage.] Then, a fight broke out and we started punching each other, ... That is what we were doing when they told the teacher, here comes the teacher. I was proud and continued unafraid, but my opponent started to cry as soon as the teacher came up.
>
> The teacher called us and took us to the office, both with our noses bleeding. That's when the teacher interrogated us. I answered the best I could: "This winka, challenged me, miss." That was all I could say, and then I stayed quiet. After that it was my opponent's turn, he defended himself very well, blaming me for everything. I was the guilty one. All the beatings were for me, I took them with resignation because I could not speak enough to defend myself...

Don Martín Alonqueo, after several different jobs, completed his formal studies in the Chilean educational system and began to teaching in March of 1935. Since that time, he has focused on promoting Mapuche culture and defending his "ethnic" brothers and sisters, first as teacher, then in independent groups or as part of Mapuche organizations. Martín Alonqueo was one of the most important Mapuche intellectuals and writers of the twentieth century.

These stories, separated by 90 years, are very similar in content and form. What did Marta do wrong? They spoke Mapuchezugun at home, the Mapuche language, and a form of Spanish influenced by the linguistic structures of her first language. Her Spanish was noticeably different: an absence of connecting phrases, mistakes in gender and number, and so forth, all the influence of bilingualism and speaking two languages. This phenomenon has been studied from different perspectives (Hernández and Ramos 1978; Lagos and Olivera 1988; Contreras 1999), some of which propose the emergence of a contact Spanish different to standard Chilean

Castilian (Olate et al. 2013) which is part of a larger process related to linguistic interactivity (Godenzzi 2007). Like Martín's grandmother, most Mapuche who have lived during the era of Chilean colonialism have been victims, witnesses or victimizers themselves, using social condemnation for this linguistic variation.

Is it Marta's fault that she hates her language and refuses to pass it on to her daughters and sons? Are the girls at the boarding school guilty for having made fun of their classmate? Is the family guilty for having spoken Mapuchezugun and having taught it to Marta? From our point of view, these and other daily normalized practices of discrimination are the consequences of the racism and violence that created colonized Gulumapu society. Quidel expresses it in his own way when he states that:

> It is a way to superimpose one's own way through teaching and arrogance, we were ashamed as Mapuche only for being Mapuche. As the years passed, we Mapuche then reproduced these practices and began to make fun of our own people. We felt very uncomfortable being Mapuche, rejecting everything that was associated with the Mapuche *az mogen*. (The Mapuche world, Quidel 2015, 42)

There is no doubt about the role played by civilizing spaces in this situation. Specifically, the precarious situation of the use and transmission of the Mapuche language has made some think that we are in the presence of a deteriorating language (Gundermann et al. 2011). To arrive at this point, we must understand how the schoolroom has been the major space in which the language has been silenced and prohibited. From its establishment, boys and girls were punished and physically, psychologically, and symbolically assaulted for using the Mapuchezugun language. This had to be replaced by the "civilized" language, Spanish, which has been documented in different research projects (Alonqueo 1985, 158–164; Canales 1998; Quintriqueo 2010, 27–28; Porma 2015; Quidel 2015, 43–46).

Certainly school has been the most important branch of the ideological vanguard of Chilean colonization in Gulumapu. The memoires of the Minister of Foreign Relations, religious instruction, and colonization (Memorias del Ministro de Relaciones Exteriores, Culto y Colonización) presented to the National Congress in 1899 are revealing in this sense:

> (...) The task of their civilization cannot be undertaken with assured success without civilizing the children.
>
> The truth of this statement is demonstrated in the recent experience of founding educational institutions for Indigenous children among some communities in the border region.
>
> They are given education in these places and from their childhood they receive moral advice, lessons appropriate to their social status, examples of virtue, which become deeply impressed on their tender hearts and intelligence, and they carry the generous seed of civilization and morality later to the Reduction and the Indigenous family. (Ministry of Foreign Affairs, Religious Instruction and Colonisation 1899, 20–21)

By 1910, the same ministry reaffirmed the role of schools as a bastion of civilizing work. In the records presented to the National Congress on 1 of June, the following was highlighted:

The solution to the problem is to civilize them, establishing schools throughout the countryside, making military service obligatory for them, motivating them to leave behind their now unacceptable customs of polygamy, while simultaneously getting rid of their practice of having chiefs as leaders (*cacicazgo*). Schools contribute more than anything else to achieving these objectives. (Ministry of Foreign Affairs, Religious Instruction and Colonisation 1910, 470)

The school was supposed to make Mapuche people participants in the "civilized world," introducing them into the new social order that was shaping Gülumapu. However, from the ethnocentric and racist ideas of the Chilean elite, the incorporation of the Mapuche people was to take place by creating second class citizens, servants, subjects, or workers, mixed in with the lowest strata of Chilean national society. In other words, both schooling and discipline of the Mapuche people were designed to make functional subjects for the hegemonic project, as is made explicit in the memoires of the Mayor of Cautín in 1890:

It is necessary to use men who, due to their physical constitution and normal intelligence, are called upon to be easily incorporated into civilized society and to be individuals who are useful to the country as workers and citizens. (Ministro del Interior 1890, 81)

In his writing, Martín Alonqueo highlighted the fulfillment of these objectives, proposed by the colonizing enterprise: the school and the Chilean educational system had served as a "temple of destruction of the Mapuche personality," due to the racist attitude of the teachers toward their Mapuche students, which convinced the latter to feel inferior and "hate themselves" (Alonqueo 1985, 163). Literacy and primary schools in the rural areas turned out to be so inadequate that the only thing they did achieve together was to create "an army of boys and domestic workers, in low wage work, and who were abused" (1985, 176).

... the Mapuche do not speak their language because of the dominant, exclusive system of education; essentially the school and environment destroy Mapuche idiosyncrasy, their way of being and thinking. In this situation, the Mapuche child adapts to the new circumstances and under the enormous influence of his inferiority complex, he acts and operates; the teacher is like his executioner, he disqualifies him with the system of low qualification, which in the end forces him to abandon the halls of education with huge resentment.

As a perverse outcome of this unhealthy system, the Mapuche child refuses to speak his own language, and there are parents whose huge inferiority complex leads them to refuse to teach their language to their children, and they even change their family name (Alonqueo 1989, 12). "Don't speak that pig language" teachers used to tell students who spoke Mapuzungun, "Can't you just speak like people?" (Quidel 2015, 44). In this civilizing process, the "language of the land" or the "language of the People of the Land" was transformed into the "language of the pigs." It was viewed with contempt, as beastial, or in the best of cases considered as a language that had no role in a new era, mostly as an inferior language. Nahuelpán returns to Fanon's idea to refer to this process as internalized colonialism (2013). These ideas were expressed in attempts to eradicate the perception of a different existence and different ways of life. In this regard, different spaces, dimensions, and lives of *Wallontu mapu* – the Mapuche world – have also faced the violence of the colonial mantle, principally through commercialism. According to Jimena Pichinao (2015), we are witnessing a confrontation between civilizing horizons or projected futures, because there is a dissimilar ethical-moral foundation with respect to the conceptualization of the earth, land, human life, and relations with other beings (100). For example, from the *Mapuche Rakizuam* or philosophy of Mapuche life, there is a substantial difference with respect to the concept of property:

> A central idea in this sense is the verification that no space is alone (*kisulelay ta mapu*). Mapuche thought recognizes the existence of multiple lives in the *mapu,* tangible and intangible beings, of which the human being is just one. Places concentrate a series of alterities that are constantly called upon to interact: vegetable species, trees, animals, insects, hills, rivers, lakes, persons forming families, among many others, which give dynamism to ecosystems, and establish modes of inhabiting territory. (Pichinao 2015, 98)

Concluding Thoughts

We have explained how colonial violence against the people of the land, their ontology, epistemology, and language is founded on an historical project based on dispossession and genocide. The first aspect was motivated by a military and civilian campaign of occupation and was euphemistically called the "pacification of the Araucanía." This occupation fulfilled the interests of the Chilean State by appropriating the territory, people, and ways of life to establish sovereignty and integrate them into the capitalist circuits of the political economy. The second aspect of genocide was understood as an historical process legitimated by a racist ideology that alluded to notions of "civilization" and "regeneration," an "extermination" of what was Mapuche and the Mapuche people themselves, which led to a permanent agony. In this context, dispossession and genocide are understood less as a specific historical moment and more as processes that had already begun and are continuing to the present, which include usurpation, appropriation, and the deprivation of the life of the people of the land, now reduced to spaces and conditions of marginality, poverty, exclusion, and subjugation.

Despite the methods applied to silence and eradicate the language, knowledge, and ways of life of Mapuche families and individuals, during most of the twentieth century, they did not remain passive in the face of colonial assault. In general terms, some forms of resistance were maintained in the private sphere of daily and family life and others in a public, collective, and visible sphere. The first of these has allowed for the transmission and maintenance of the language, family, and socio-territorial ceremonies in many places of Gulumapu, practices that reveal a continuum in the *mapuche az mongen* and in the *mapuche rakizuam*, without rejecting the adoption and functional appropriation of tools of colonial society such as formal education in school. The second sphere was oriented toward organizational forms of the state and its Chilean structures. One of these organizations was created in 1910, called Sociedad Caupolicán Defensora de La Araucanía. This organization was created by the first generation of Mapuche teachers who belonged to important lineages before the Occupation. Since that time many other organizations have flourished, among the most notable of which are the *Federación Araucana*, the *Corporación Araucana*, the *Unión Araucana*, and the *Frente Único Araucanao*, or the *Asociación Nacional de Indígenas de Chile*. For more information, see Rolf Foerster and Sonia Montecino, "Organizaciones, Líderes y Contiendas Mapuche. (1900–1970)"). The founders of these organizations have attempted to gain integration and recognition in Chilean society. Their icon has been the struggle for the education and schooling of the Mapuche people. To a great extent, these and other strategies, together with the capacity for agency and resignification of these foreign elements, were largely designed to soften racism, dispossession, and genocide as structuring processes of the Mapuche people's colonization. Clearly, these strategies are part of a repertoire of political actions that continue to our day and also generate responses from the state apparatus.

Over recent decades, a series of state-supported institutional strategies have been introduced. The first is the Intercultural Bilingual Education Program, implemented by Indigenous Law 19.253 (1993), which establishes specific obligations by the Chilean State for the promotion and teaching of indigenous peoples' languages. A related development is the legal recognition of the Mapuche language as a second official language in the Araucanía Region, a process promoted by Mapuche organizations and introduced in two counties, Galvarino (2013) and Padre Las Casas (2014). It is difficult to evaluate the impact of Intercultural Bilingual Program, since there are no quantitative or qualitative studies on it at present. Similarly, to date there are but high expectations for ways the official status of the language will be eventually implemented and developed. Our view is that these are not generous concessions by the state but are instead a clear result of pressure by Mapuche and indigenous movements that have been developed historically, gaining the greatest momentum in the last decade of the twentieth century. For this reason, they do not suggest changes that are dismantling the historical structures of oppression but rather correspond to strategies that may even be understood as counterinsurgency measures to placate Mapuche mobilizations by framing them as multicultural neoliberal policies that several different Latin American states have implemented over the last two decades. In other words, this is not simply a new form of managing cultural difference but is rather a new form of restructuring tutelage and control over the *Indios*.

Despite these developments, as these forms of restructuring by colonial-neoliberal governments were taking place, Mapuche organizations – and their demands – seem to have reached a turning point over the last two decades. This has become evident in the emergence of new forms of political struggle that signal the restitution of "ancient territories" which were not recognized by *Títulos de Merced*, the establishment of de facto autonomous territories and the control of historical Mapuche territory. This type of struggle became visible after the breakdown in negotiations over historical grievances under the Nueva Imperial Agreements during the first post-dictorial government, headed by Patricio Aylwin of the center-left Coalition of Parties for Democracy (Concertación de Partidos por la

Democracia). This breakdown began to be evident when Mapuche communities began a process of occupations of their ancestral lands that came under the control of forestry companies and private owners during the second half of the 1990s. This branch of the current Mapuche movement is best interpreted in the Latin American context of the struggle of resistance by indigenous peoples, who are facing new problems intensified by the neoliberal economic system, specifically those related to the pressure of extractive capital on new territories and social relations.

In the context of these struggles of resistance and the creation of new autonomous regions, we might add others such as those daily forms of resistance mentioned before and those learned in the family sphere, as well as more visible forms, such as first, Mapuche language workshops "Kom kim mapudunguaiñ waria mew," developed by *kimche* – a Mapuche traditional scholar– with Mapuche students and teachers in the University of Chile's Philosophy and Humanities Faculty, and second, the Linguistic Apprenticeships (Internados Lingüísticos) of the Federation of Mapuche Students (Federación Mapuche de Estudiantes, FEMAE). This language immersion process for Mapuche and non-Mapuche takes places for 1 or 2 weeks in the communities where they learn the Mapuche language. These collective actions will surely be analyzed by their protagonists in the medium and long term.

From our point of view, the organizations that base their horizons or projections for struggle on the progression of autonomous regions and territorial recovery, on the *mapuche az mogen* and on *mapuche rakizuam*, represent important spaces of direct and open resistance to dispossession and historical genocide. On one hand, the recovery of territory and autonomy challenges the interests of those who have historically benefited from ownership and maintained their privileged place in the socio-racial order constructed in colonized Gülumapu; this thereby allows communities to recover the dignity taken from them. On the other hand, it is through territorial recovery and autonomy that *mapuche az mogen* and *mapuche rakizuam* y *mapuchezugun* are strengthened, revalued, and transmitted so that its own historical course may continue, being transformed into alternatives for life and existence against the current hegemonic model. In this sense, understanding the confrontation over territory implies uniting those sectorial and dispersed Mapuche movements into a collective, systemic achievement that unites other movements to move forward toward a process of national liberation and decolonization. *Femgechi.*

References

Alonqueo M (1985) Mapuche ayer – hoy. Imprenta y Editorial San Francisco, Padre Las Casas

Alonqueo M (1989) El habla de mi tierra, 2nd edn. Impresos Kolpin, Padre Las Casas

Antileo E (2012) Migración mapuche y continuidad colonial. In: Nahuelpan H et al (eds) Ta iñ fijke xipa rakizuameluwün. Historia, colonialismo y resistencia desde el País Mapuche. Ediciones Comunidad de Historia Mapuche, Temuco, pp 187–208

Antileo E (2015) Trabajo racializado. Una reflexión a partir de datos de población indígena y testimonios de la migración y residencia mapuche en Santiago de Chile. In: Meridional. Revista Chilena de Estudios Latinoamericanos, pp 71–96

Antimil J (2012) Panko ka Tranantúe Mapu ñi Kuifike Zungu. Historia de las comunidades de Panko y Tranantúe desde la segunda mitad del siglo XIX hasta 1950. Tesina para optar al grado de Licenciado en Educación. Universidad de La Frontera, Temuco

Araya D, Porma J (2012) Historia de la Comunidad José Porma, siglo XX. La evolución generacional de la identidad mapuche. Tesina para optar al grado de Licenciado en Educación. Universidad de La Frontera, Temuco

Bengoa J (1985) Historia del Pueblo Mapuche. Ediciones Sur, Santiago de Chile

Canales P (1998) Peyepeyen. Escuelas chilenas en contextos mapuche. In: Revista Última Década: 9, pp 1–15

Caniuqueo S (2006) Siglo XX en Gulumapu: De la fragmentación del Wallmapu a la unidad nacional mapuche. 1888 a 1978. In: Mariman P et al (eds) ¡...Escucha, winka...! Cuatro ensayos de Historia Nacional Mapuche y un epílogo sobre el futuro. LOM Ediciones, Santiago, pp 129–217

Coña P, Moesbach E (2010) Lonco Pascual Coña ñi tuculpazugun. Testimonio de un cacique mapuche, 9th edn. Pehuen Editores, Santiago de Chile

Contreras C (1999) El castellano hablado por mapuches: Rasgos del nivel morfosintáctico. Estudios filológicos 35:83–98

Correa M, Mella E (2010) Las razones del Illkün/enojo. Memoria, despojo y criminalización en el territorio mapuche de Malleco. Lom Ediciones, Santiago de Chile

del Interior M (1890) Memoria ministerial presentada al Congreso Nacional en 1890. Tomo II. Archivo Regional de La Araucanía. Imprenta Nacional, Santiago de Chile

El Ferrocarril de Santiago, 23 Apr 1858

El Mercurio de Valparaiso, 24 May 1859

Fanon F (1965) Racismo y cultura. In: Fanon F (ed) Por la Revolución Africana. Fondo de cultura Económica, México, pp 38–52

Godenzzi J (2007) El español de América y el español de Los Andes: universalización, vernacularización y emergencia. In: Schrader-kniffki M, Morgenthaler L (eds) Romania en interacción: entre contacto, historia y política. Ensayos en homenaje a Klaus Zimmermann. Vervuet- Iberoamericana, Frankfurt, pp 29–50

Godoi P (1861) Proyecto presentado al Supremo Gobierno por el coronel don Pedro Godoi y dedicado al Señor Jeneral don Manuel García, Ministro de Estado en los Departamentos de Guerra y Marina. In: Saavedra C (ed) Documentos relativos a la ocupación de Arauco. Imprenta de la Libertad, Santiago de Chile

González H (1986) Propiedad comunitaria o individual. Las leyes indígenas y el pueblo mapuche. Nütram 3:7–13

Gundermann H, Canihuan J, Clavería A, Faúndez C (2011) El mapuzugun, una lengua en retroceso. Revista Atenea 503:111–131

Hernández A, Ramos N (1978) Rasgos del castellano hablado por escolares rurales mapuches. Estudio de un caso. RLA 16:41–150

Juan (2012) Personal interview with Jaime Antimil

Kolüman L (2002) Kolüman ñi che. Familia Kolüman. In: Guevara T, Manuel M (eds) Kiñe mufü trokiñche ñi piel: Historias de familias/Siglo XIX. CEDM Liwen, Temuco, pp 43–44

Lagos D, Olivera S (1988) Algunas características del español hablado por los escolares mapuches de la comuna de Victoria. Estudios Filológicos 23:89–102

Leiva A (1984) El primer avance a la Araucanía: Angol 1862. Ediciones Universidad de La Frontera, Temuco

Macaya P (2016) Capuchinos italianos en el Wallmapu. La escuela misional: labor y metodología, 1848–1896. In: Canales P (ed) Zuamgenolu. Pueblo Mapuche en contextos de Estado Nacional Chileno, siglos XIX–XXI. (texto en prensa). Ediciones IDEA – USACH, Santiago de Chile

Mallon F (2004) La sangre del copihue. La comunidad Mapuche de Nicolás Ailío y el Estado chileno, 1906–2001. Lom Ediciones, Santiago de Chile

Mallon F (2009) El siglo XX mapuche.Esferas públicas, sueños de autodeterminación y articulaciones internacionales. In: Martinez C, Estrada M (eds) Las disputas por la etnicidad en América Latina: movilizaciones indígenas en Chiapas y Araucanía. USACH, Santiago de Chile, pp 155–190

Ministro de Relaciones Exteriores, Culto y Colonización (1899) Memoria ministerial presentada al Congreso Nacional en 1899. Archivo Regional de La Araucanía. Imprenta Nacional, Santiago de Chile

Ministro de Relaciones Exteriores, Culto y Colonización (1910) Memoria ministerial presentada al Congreso Nacional el 01 de junio de 1910. Archivo Regional de La Araucanía. Imprenta Cervantes, Santiago de Chile

Ministry of War (1870) Fondo Ministerio de Guerra, Correspondencia del Cuartel Jeneral del Ejército de la Frontera. 1869 a 1870, vol 602, fs 53–54

Nahuelpan H (2012) Formación colonial del estado y desposesión en Ngulumapu. In: Nahuelpan H et al (eds) Ta iñ fijke xipa rakizuameluwün. Historia, colonialism y Resistencia desde el País Mapuche. Ediciones Comunidad de Historia Mapuche, Temuco, pp 119–152

Nahuelpan H (2013) Las "zonas grises" de las historias mapuche. Colonialismo internalizado, marginalidad y políticas de la memoria. In: Revista de Historia Social y de las Mentalidades, pp 11–13

Nahuelpan H (2015) "Nos explotaron como animales y ahora quieren que no nos levantemos". Vidas despojables y micropolíticas de resistencia mapuche. In: Antileo E et al (eds) Awükan ka kuxankan zugu Wajmapu mew. Violencias coloniales en Wajmapu. Ediciones Comunidad de Historia Mapuche, Temuco, pp 275–300

Olate A, Alonqueo P, Caniguan J (2013) Interactividad lingüística castellano/mapudungun de una comunidad rural bilingüe. In: Alpha: 37, Osorno, 2013, pp 265–284

Pichinao J (2015) La mercantilización del Mapuche Mapu (tierras mapuche). Hacia la expoliación absoluta. In: Antileo E et al (eds) Awükan ka kuxankan zugu Wajmapu mew. Violencias coloniales en Wajmapu. Ediciones Comunidad de Historia Mapuche, Temuco, pp 87–105

Pinto J (2003) La formación del estado, la nación y el pueblo mapuche: de la inclusión a la exclusión. DIBAM, Santiago de Chile

Porma J (2015) Violencia colonial en la Escuela: el caso de la comunidad José Porma en el siglo XX. In: Antileo E et al (eds) Awükan ka kuxankan zugu Wajmapu mew. Violencias coloniales en Wajmapu. Ediciones Comunidad de Historia Mapuche, Temuco, pp 189–205

Quidel J (2015) Chumgelu ka chumgechi pu mapuche ñi kuxankagepan ka hotukagepan ñi rakizuam ka ñi püjü zugu mew. In: Antileo E et al (eds) Awükan ka kuxankan zugu Wajmapu mew. Violencias coloniales en Wajmapu. Ediciones Comunidad de Historia Mapuche, Temuco, pp 21–55

Quintriqueo S (2010) Implicancias de un modelo curricular monocultural en contexto mapuche. Universidad Católica de Temuco, Temuco

Robles E (1912) Informe del Protector de Indígenas de Cautín. In: Comisión Parlamentaria de Colonización (ed) Informe, proyectos de ley, actas de las sesiones y otros antecedentes. Imprenta y Litografía Universo, Santiago de Chile, pp 131–167

Uribe S (1988) Las misiones capuchinas de Araucanía en la segunda mitad del siglo XIX (1848–1901). In: Pinto J et al (eds) Misioneros en la Araucanía, 1600–1900, un capítulo de historia fronteriza en Chile. Ediciones Universidad de La Frontera, Temuco, pp 199–231

Varas A (1849) Informe presentado a la cámara de diputados por don Antonio Varas, visitador judicial de la república en cumplimiento del acuerdo celebrado en la sesión del 20 de diciembre del año 1848, sobre la reducción pacífica del territorio araucano. In: Saavedra C (ed) Documentos relativos a la ocupación de Arauco. Imprenta de la Libertad, Santiago de Chile

Vicuña B (1868) La conquista de Arauco. Imprenta del Ferrocarril, Santiago de Chile

Vidal A (2000) Conocimiento antropológico sobre los mapuche de Chile. Efectos socioculturales y económicos de su integración forzada a la nación chilena. In: Duran T (ed) Acercamientos metodológicos hacia pueblos indígenas. Una experiencia reflexionada desde la Araucanía (Chile). Universidad Católica de Temuco, Temuco, pp 75–100

Wenu M (2008) Carta al Presidente de la República de Chile, Manuel Montt, Mapu, septiembre 21 de 1860. In: Pavez J (ed) Cartas Mapuche: siglo XIX. CoLibris, Santiago de Chile, pp 319–325

Truth and Reconciliation in Canada: Indigenous Peoples as Modern Subjects

D. Lyn Daniels

Contents

Theoretical Framing	86
Colonial Canadian Policy	87
Colonialism and Photographs of Aboriginal Children	88
Imagined Identities and Haunting Histories	90
Indian Residential School History in Canada	94
Genocide Studies	95
Postmemory and Critical Pedagogy	97
References	98

Abstract

This chapter considers how the traumatic history of Indian residential schools might be remembered, in particular by intergenerational survivors. Photographs that depict this history are notable for displaying the power of the Canadian state to intervene into Indigenous lives at the level of the individual through education policies. These images rely on colonial conceptions of spatial distance understood as time needed for cultural development. Understanding these conceptions is powerful for analyzing photographs of Indigenous peoples, in particular in policy and history texts. How educational policies are experienced intergenerationally by the descendants of survivors reveals another dimension of Canadian colonialism. These themes are explored indirectly, but in depth, by the German born writer, W.G. Sebald (2001) in his fictional writing. A fictional character in his novel, *Austerlitz*, asks: What do we know of ourselves, how do we remember? And what do we find in the end? These questions frame this chapter that discusses memory, history, trauma, and identity in relation to the history and future of education for Indigenous peoples in Canada.

D. L. Daniels (✉)
Aborginal Learning, Aboriginal Learning Surrey Schools, Surrey, BC, Canada
e-mail: daniels_lyn@surreyschools.ca

© Springer Nature Singapore Pte Ltd. 2019
E. A. McKinley, L. T. Smith (eds.), *Handbook of Indigenous Education*,
https://doi.org/10.1007/978-981-10-3899-0_75

> **Keywords**
> History · Identity · Indian residential schools · Memory

The novel, *Austerlitz*, is W.G. Sebald's (2001) compelling project for speaking about the unspeakable wherein an unknown narrator retells his coincidental encounters and life story of the main character, also named Austerlitz, in particular, his efforts to know his history (McCulloh 2003, p. 130). Sebald's novel emphasizes themes of memory, identity, history, trauma, space, repression, and repetition in relation to the genocide of European Jewish peoples. Fictionalizing such an unspeakable subject means that in the character Austerlitz we see the "insidious, if oblique, infliction of harm achieved by the actions of the Nazis" (p. 110) which resulted in the repression of his memories regarding his family history, his nation's history, and therefore his identity. Such themes also emerged from the personal narratives of intergenerational survivors of Indian residential schools, of their school experiences, thereby opening up the possibilities for carrying the memories of a traumatic past to future generations.

Some might be troubled by comparisons of the Holocaust with the history of colonization of Indigenous peoples in Canada; however, I argue that Sebald's novel can be read as an account of the ongoing effects of the increasing intrusion of the state into the lives of individuals, similar to intrusions experienced by Indigenous peoples here. Sebald's novel is inspirational because of his particular theoretical framing and given that there is an absence of similar analyses and approaches embedding these knowledge/power dynamics in the literature on Indigenous experiences of state sanctioned oppression.

Similar to Sebald's other works of fiction, *Austerlitz* has photographs scattered through-out the text. Although photographs can function to reenforce narrative, Sebald's photographs are not accompanied by captions. J.J. Long (2007) argued that the themes in Sebald's novels are linked to colonial power and his use of photographs typically displays these dynamics in relation to an archive: zoos, libraries, and other collections. Long notes their function in depicting the state's power over knowledge, land, animals, and Indigenous peoples. The effects of such power dynamics have material effects intergenerationally for Indigenous peoples in Canada. Such dynamics and ongoing effects are the focus of this inquiry that extends on my doctoral studies research completed in 2016 and my subsequent analysis of both Canada and the province of British Columbia's representations of the history of Indian residential schools and Indigenous peoples in Canada, in curriculum and in policy.

Theoretical Framing

Historical ontology frames this inquiry broadly, as "how our (educational) practices of naming interact with" those "we name" (Hacking 2002, p. 2) and how the practices of naming and being named arise in social, political, and historical conditions.

In using historical ontology (Hacking 2002) to theorize Indigenous memories across time and space, the focus is on the naming practices of policy and the experiences of being named as Aboriginal students, in particular instances where policy practices of constituting identities along the "axes of knowledge, power and ethics" (Hacking 2002, p. 2) are taken up or rejected by the youth. With historical ontology self-identity involves the "truth through which we constitute ourselves as objects of knowledge, the power through which we constitute ourselves as subjects acting on others and the ethics through which we constitute ourselves as moral agents" (p. 2). With "historical ontology" the "ways in which the possibilities for choice, and for being, arise in history" (p. 23) are the focus of investigation. When studies are "intended to show something about our present reality, our present reasoning, our present modes of research. They may ... be called histories of the present" (p. 66).

Linda Tuhiwai Smith (1999) argues that revisiting history requires an understanding that history as a field of thought was framed according to European interpretations. Hence, the history of Indigenous peoples is negated as a colonial practice that justifies post hoc, the imposition of foreign education systems. The Canadian Indian residential school system is a case in point. Smith (1999) calls for theory and research with which we can "engage, understand and then act upon history" (p. 34). As one strategy, Smith reminds us "(t)he need to tell our stories remains the powerful imperative of a powerful form of resistance" (p. 35). Accordingly, this chapter offers a history of some of the present views that Canada and British Columbia hold on Indigenous peoples' identities, their histories and educational needs, and therefore futures as Indigenous peoples. These critical insights were made possible by gaining an understanding of the effects of traumatic history on an individual's identity and their own understanding of their place within history, through the fictional experiences of Austerlitz and through the narration of W.G. Sebald and my subsequent analysis of the use of photography within the colonial policy context.

Colonial Canadian Policy

Imposing by legislation particular ways of being for Indigenous peoples is a historical, Canadian, colonial, "educational," policy practice (Miller 1997). Notably, education policy eras for Indians/Aboriginal peoples in Canada are often referred to by their one-word descriptors: *civilization*, *assimilation*, in the past (Milloy 1999), and today the policy is *reconciliation*. This current policy era purports to bring Indigenous peoples and other Canadians closer together; however, I argue that this naming is in itself a colonial practice designed to disguise the confining features of colonization. For example, during the historical assimilation era, Indian residential schools were supposed to provide education and training for Indigenous peoples to join Canadian social and economic life; however, they ultimately operated as institutions of confinement. Accordingly, policy terms must be interrogated for the presence of such colonial, rhetorical features and is a goal of this chapter.

In writing this account of what Hacking (2002) refers to as "a history of the present" (p. 66), with respect to Aboriginal education policy in BC, in this era of *reconciliation*, my inquiry highlights the roles of memory, "postmemory" (Hirsch 1999), and forgetting in Aboriginal youths' narratives of the effects of colonization and historical Indian and contemporary Aboriginal education policies on their identities. Specifically, I highlight colonial traces in memories of experiences of educational policy and practice and its potential impact on young people attending higher education in BC. These are contrasted with an analysis of the photographic representations of youth in Aboriginal Education Enhancement Agreement policy and representations of Indian residential school history in curricula.

Colonialism and Photographs of Aboriginal Children

Understanding the role of photography in colonial policy practices highlights their continuing use in Canadian policy texts when Aboriginal children are the focus and especially when the history of Indian residential schools has been a topic of national conversation. In my own study of Aboriginal education policies in contemporary British Columbia, known as Aboriginal Education Enhancement Agreements (AEEA), I noted a particular pattern with the function of photographs as they relate to Aboriginal student identity. This aspect of my inquiry relates to how public-school policies construct Aboriginal students and their identities, histories, communities, and futures.

In my analysis, many of the photographs of students in AEEA policies School District #75 (2007), policies that advocate for the teaching of history, show them wearing traditional regalia, making arts and crafts or beside art pieces that readers would likely infer were made by the students themselves or their relatives. These truthful-seeming images support the construction of Aboriginal students as inhabiting a static space. The AEEA policy images position Aboriginal students in a silent, static, anachronistic space outside of time, history, culture, and traditions and therefore as powerless to constitute themselves as knowledgeable, moral agents.

This type of photographic analysis is based on Anne McClintock's (1995) study of colonial photography and is instructive for revisiting historical imperialist notions of time and space. She argues that the use of photography as a colonial technology is related to the imperialist desire to "consume global history at a glance" within a single image conceptualized as "pan-optical time" (p. 36). Colonial photography is the material practice of the "colonial gaze" that displays and disciplines the so-called uncivilized. According to McClintock (1995), the notion of visualizing a culture is "synonymous for understanding it" (p. 122). Such a "point of view – the panoptical stance – is enjoyed by those in privileged positions in the social structure, to whom the world appears as a spectacle, stage, performance" (p. 122). Photography holds the "panoptic" power of collection, display, and discipline, a "technology of surveillance within the context of a developing global economy" (p. 123). McClintock linked the need for "ordering and assembling the myriad world economies into a single commodity culture," with "the need for a universal currency of exchange, through which the world's economic cultures could be subordinated and made docile" (p. 123).

In European colonies, Indigenous peoples were captured in photographs that framed them as further back along a linear progression of cultural development. In this process, Indigenous peoples became objects of the "colonial gaze" where they are seen but are considered to not have the capacity to see. A case in point is the photographic project of Edward Curtis in the early part of the twentieth century, wherein he intended to preserve the so-called primitive cultures of North America by photographing and therefore displaying the historical "truth" of them. I argue that colonial spatial concepts identified by Linda Tuhiwai Smith (1999) of "the line" for establishing boundaries, the concept of "the centre as an orientation to power" and the concept of "the outside" as an "oppositional (and distant) relation to the colonial centre," (p. 53) frame and define such photographs and therefore communicate a colonial and even fictitious construction of Indigenous peoples as "primitive."

In colonial times (mid-1880s onwards), the desire for consuming history at a glance was fulfilled when this conception of history was "collected, assembled and mapped onto a global science of the surface" with the aid of social Darwinism. Anne McClintock (1995) argues that spatial difference is often presented as analogous to cultural development when it comes to Indigenous peoples and that this conception makes its appearance in colonial photography. Separation and distance means that cultures are viewed as measurable and therefore subject to control. When Indigenous cultures are viewed through a spatial lens and then represented back to the West, a process of "colonizing space" is engaged (Smith 1999, p. 51).

As an Indigenous educator working in Aboriginal education I am always cognizant that representations of Indigenous peoples in curriculum, resources, policy, and even in the informal views expressed by educators might be based on unfair, dehumanizing assumptions. Further, as Indigenous peoples had an integral role in creating AEEA policy in BC School District #61 (2005), they are not exempt from perhaps perpetuating unfair characterizations. It might even be the case that with AEEA policies that it was mostly white school district representatives who exercised power relations in reproducing anachronistic images and representations of Indigenous peoples. At the same time, I do not want to assume that Indigenous peoples, in collaboration with school district representatives, adopted a laissez-faire attitude in representing regressive subject positions for Aboriginal students.

One possible explanation is related to what Teresa Strong-Wilson (2013) has noted about photographs of childhood in relation to memoir and autobiography. She notes that they are not only nostalgic but are also inflected with trauma (p. 24). Along these lines I wish to argue that photographs of Indigenous children in traditional regalia in AEEA policy School District #39 (2009) can function as a form of memory. With childhood autobiography, as Strong-Wilson argues, "trauma is often expressed as a longing for that which may not have existed in the first place, compensating for loss 'by supplementing a memory invigorated through absence'" (p. 24). Further, there is an "idealization of the time prior to the trauma" (p. 24). Because accounts of trauma are traceable to childhood, the "body is the primary site for repressed memories in childhood autobiography" (p. 23). Along these lines, we can see an overcompensation in AEEA policy documents School District #43 (2007) that have a goal for teaching history, expressed by the preoccupation with photographs of children's bodies adorned or perhaps protected by traditional regalia and with photographs that perhaps attempt to capture a time before colonization. Strong-Wilson (2013) argues that childhood autobiography photographs are a challenge to "avert the misfortune lying ahead" (p. 24). In that sense, AEEA photographs may also refer to the violence that many Aboriginal peoples have experienced in their youth, in Indian residential schools, in public schools, and in the child welfare system in BC and Canada. When trauma inflects nostalgia, Strong-Wilson (2013) argues that "a longing for change remains trapped, thwarted by actual events. Within this space and time, the body-subject occupies a grey world, shared by living and dead" (p. 25). AEEA policy photographs challenge viewers – that is, educators – to avert the violence that might lie ahead. Or risk having hopes continuously thwarted with more trauma.

During her time at the Shubenacadie Indian Residential School, Isabelle Knockwood (2001) has memories of being the subject of photographs:

> I remember how we used to have to change our prison-style, broad striped blouses for dresses on the day of the photograph. Then we lined up in rows according to height with Wikew (a nun) yelling, "Smile, smile," as the photographer snapped the picture. As students we all knew that a special show was put on whenever the school came into contact with the outside world. The monthly letters home were written in class and anyone who wrote anything critical about the school was punished and made to re-write the letter leaving out the complaints. (p. 143)

Knockwood's use of the phrase "outside world" alludes to Indigenous confinement, while their punishments for their attempts to share their traumatic experiences with their families reveal the high level of surveillance and discipline they were subjected to. Their families are also on the "outside" revealing their distance from the Euro-cultural "center" represented by the school. Knockwood's understanding that there is an "outside world" reveals that her experience is less about *assimilation* with other Canadians and more of one of isolation.

Imagined Identities and Haunting Histories

The title of Isabelle Knockwood's book, *Out of the Depths*, refers to a nun's prayer after a door in the Indian residential school building mysteriously opened. The prayer, "out of the depths I have cried unto thee O Lord. Lord hear my voice" (2001, p. 101), is in a chapter entitled "Ghosts and Hauntings" and recounts the children's experiences with unexplainable occurrences, connected to, in their minds, those who had died at the school. Knockwood explained the choice for the title of her book: "strangely enough, some of the students who were most seriously abused have been able to transform their lives and bring themselves, 'out of the depths'" (p. 158). The depths of misery that Mi'kmaw students experienced inside the Indian residential school building included such punishment as solitary confinement in a dark closet under the dining room stairs with a diet of only bread and water. Knockwood said this was the only room that was left standing after the Indian residential school mysteriously burned down. Few of these buildings exist today; many were ceremoniously destroyed and some Indigenous groups now use them for social and cultural purposes.

Of the six college-age youth I interviewed for this study, only one, Shama (a pseudonym), made a direct comparison of Indian residential school history to the Holocaust. It was a recollection of an exchange between her parents. Her father was Indigenous (now deceased) and her mother is non-Indigenous (from the United Kingdom).

Lyn: Did you ever talk about what it was like in the residential school?
Shama: Yeah, he did. I just remember him saying, like, you know, there's a reason I left. And I don't know whether he meant like circumstance or whether something worse happened, I don't know. But the idea of... he said that a lot of...it was terrible things. Like he would... I remember he said that one of his friends was killed. And I remember my mom like not being able to fathom the whole idea. She knew what a residential school was for the most part but only from what my dad had explained. So, moving here and like seeing those old buildings used as community centres and things like that... on these properties and...
Lyn: Oh yeah, which?
Shama: I'm trying to think. I think it's in Wells (Wells Gray National Park in the BC interior). The residential school there is still standing. And being used as a community centre now and... different things like that. And my mom being like, oh why wouldn't they shut them down? My dad's like, well they didn't tear down the camps, did they? I just... the look on her face. She was mortified because my dad related them to concentration camps. And then she was even more disgusted when she found out those actually existed in BC too. So, it's just the... like, to some degree at least, like the internment camps and stuff. (Personal communication, July 5, 2011).

For another participant, Hudson, his first encounter with the actual Indian residential school buildings proved to be overwhelming. He related his experience researching Indian residential schools for a college course and the difficulty with beginning the writing on the topic. He was reminded of the time he was unknowingly inside a residential school facility when he was enrolled in a course related to his work in the fishing industry:

Hudson: It made me think of everything. And then it also reminded me of how I felt when I was in the Mission school. I despised that place. Could not stand it and I'd ask people, "Why does this building feel this way?" And one of the people there said, "This was a residential school." And it was one of the workers there and she said, "You could feel it?" I said, "Oh it's disgusting. I hate being in here."
Lyn: Yeah. Can you identify what it was that made you feel that way?
Hudson: I just felt sad. Just heavy. Heavy emotions all day. Every time I was in there, to the point where I left... and hit the road. I just felt angry. I felt sad. I was scared. It's the only way I can describe it. And then ...we leave to go to the hotel. Just did not want to be in there.

These memories, of Hudson and Shama, Aboriginal youth, I argue can be viewed as instances where accounts of trauma and oppression are inscribed into the life story of second-generation survivors of historical trauma as postmemories (Hirsch 1999). In Holocaust studies, the term "postmemory" describes the notion that second-generation survivors of the Holocaust identify so strongly with the previous generation's experience of genocide and dehumanization that they begin to constitute memories in their own right (Hirsch 1999).

Linda Tuhiwai Smith (1999) identifies "remembering" as an important Indigenous research project in the context of decolonizing wherein being means being self-determining and taking back control of destinies. Such a project relates to

> the remembering of a painful past and, importantly, people's responses to that pain. While collectively indigenous communities can talk through the history of painful events, there are frequent silences and intervals in the stories about what happened after the event. Often there is no collective remembering, as communities were systematically ripped apart, children were removed for adoption, extended families separated across different reserves and national boundaries. (p. 146)

Along similar lines, Kearney (2004) highlighted Ricoeur's argument that when narratives function as "rememoration" they

> Embody an ethical character quite distinct from the triumphalist commemoration of history's great and powerful. Where the latter tends to legitimate ideologies of conquest, the former moves in the opposite direction, namely, toward a felt reliving of past suffering as if we (readers/listeners/spectators) had actually been there. (p. 102)

In this chapter, framing memories of Aboriginal college students is meant to represent counter-hegemonic narratives of history; thus, they inherit an ethical character "in the service of rememoration" (p. 106). In this view, "(r)ecounting is a way of becoming ... an ethical consciousness" (p. 106). Hudson summed up this important notion thusly,

Lyn: Is that what your quote, "Remember the children"? Is that what that's in reference to? (On his collage). Or what was that quote in reference to?

Hudson: It's there to reach out from now until back then. You have to remember their importance. Because they're who we are in everything we do. It's a big burden to forget them. Like if we stop thinking about residential school then those children suffered for nothing. I think it's important to us to be able to cherish today and move on by constantly being reminded that we had terrible pasts. Atrocities. Countless atrocities. You know, I mean parents weren't even told if their child was dead? (Personal communication, July 6, 2011).

Hudson's reasoning for remembering the past reflects Ricoeur's view on the testimonial role of narratives in terms of an ethical responsibility to the "debt we owe the dead" (Kearney 2004, p. 100) – in particular, he noted the defiant use of

Indigenous languages and efforts for keeping spirits intact. Hudson, a descendent of Indian residential school survivors, positions Indian residential school survivors as moral subjects constituting themselves with knowledge of their language to resist and defy colonial power. Countering silent history with remembrances of atrocities in Indian residential schools in public schools today decolonizes history and highlights the capacity for narratives to "brush history against the grain" as they put the "dominant power in question" (Kearney 2004, p. 110). Hudson's call to "remember the children" is a catchphrase that decolonizes history by "reach[ing] out from now until back then" (personal communication, July 6, 2011) and brings it forward into the present as a way to honor "the debt we owe to the dead" (Kearney 2004, p. 100).

In this investigation, I asked the youth about educational practices that contributed to their Indigenous identities.

Lyn: Yes. That contributed to your identity as a Haida girl. Young woman.
Shama: I think frustration, actually, with a lot of the academics that we were doing…Because it makes me so mad every time. I think that made me want to teach it more and made me want to learn more. I talked to my grandma and she taught me so much and stuff. I think it's what it is. Just frustration with things not being taught the way they should.

Shama was fortunate to have her grandmother to turn to, to learn her history. Regarding identity, Kearney (2004) drew on Ricoeur to argue: "One cannot remain constant over the passage of historical time…Unless one has some minimal remembrance of where one comes from, and how one came to be what one is. For Ricoeur then, identity is a form of memory" (p. 104). This perspective has relevance for Aboriginal youths' understanding of how previous generations of Indigenous peoples experienced colonization and how such history might impact their own education and Indigenous identities. Viewing identity as a form of memory also has implications for Aboriginal education practices today, in particular when the youth have highlighted that this historical knowledge is absent from their education and lives in general. Hudson argued for actively remembering that Indian residential school students mounted active resistance to abusive practices:

Hudson: Yeah. You know, that they found a way to preserve themselves, spiritually among all the nightmares. They managed to hang on to themselves. Then pretend to conform. A lot of them saved their language by speaking it in their head.
Lyn: Right.
Hudson: While they're in bed or prayer or whatever, they're speaking English but in their mind, they were speaking the language, which was very important. It was so important, you know, it showed staying power, who they wanted to be. They didn't lose themselves completely. But they still lost a lot of family values. I mean those were stripped.

Hudson: Parents weren't even allowed to visit. Which, I can only imagine, was extremely hard. (Personal communication, July 6, 2011).

Hudson's understanding of these practices of resistance for survivance illustrates his understanding of the same view that Kearney (2004) holds of the rapport that poetic narratives can have with ethics. In the next section, I discuss how this traumatic history is presented in the recently revised British Columbia (BC) provincial curriculum.

Indian Residential School History in Canada

In British Columbia, one of the newly revised curriculum standards related to the history of Indian residential schools is in the grade five Social Studies topic area of Canadian Issues and Governance. The history of Indian residential schools shows up as a "Sample topic" when you click on the "Content Standard" that indicates, "Past discriminatory government policies and actions, such as the Head Tax, the Komagata Maru incident, residential schools, and internments" (BC Ministry of Education 2018).

Another key feature of the revised curriculum are the suggested activities for students to achieve competencies while engaging in inquiry within each curricular area. An example of such a curricular competency is for students to: "Make ethical judgments about events, decisions, or actions that consider the conditions of a particular time and place, and assess appropriate ways to respond" (BC Ministry of Education 2018). Having studied the traumatic history of Indian residential schools, and given Hudson's call for repaying a debt to those who lost their lives in this genocidal project, I am relieved that the province of BC has provided an option for framing Indian residential school history within an ethical orientation. However, the list of past discriminatory practices is framed toward a multicultural orientation, presenting Indigenous peoples as though they are one of many cultures to be accommodated in Canada and omitting the aspects of the Canadian Constitution that pertain to Aboriginal rights and Aboriginal title to land. Specifically, curricula that is inclusive of the history of Indian residential schools and presented in contrast to the sections of the Canadian Constitution (1982) that acknowledge existing Aboriginal rights to land, resources, language and culture, self-determination, and self-government highlights the historically abusive nature of Canada's relationship to Aboriginal peoples. Beyond, and before, the Calls to Action of the Truth and Reconciliation Commission (TRC), the rationale for teaching the history of Indigenous peoples in Canada, is to honor the *Canada Constitution Act* (1982) and is something all Canadians are compelled to do.

Hacking's (2002) conception of historical ontology as "history of the present" provides a theoretical frame for bringing in memories to understand the history of Indian residential school system as one of genocide; however, there were limitations in theorizing how to act as a moral agent with that knowledge. Kearney's (2004) frameworks on narratives and memory were productive for framing memories as counter-hegemonic history. A significant insight that emerged from this study of memory, history, and policy is that policy can function as a form of collective memory, especially when you consider curriculum as a form of policy. Although policy is not as visible as the cultural institutions of memory that J.J. Long (2007) identified such as museums, archives, newspapers, photography, and historiography (p. 4), policy and curriculum do function as disciplinary technologies in a similar manner as the above-named institutions do.

Within modernity, J.J. Long (2007) argues that memory is no longer a matter of consciousness but now "resides in the material of our social and psychic life" (p. 4). Further, Long argues that modernity did not begin with photography but by abstracting and reconstructing the visual experience. With this type of reconstruction, photography and the archive are understood to be key colonial practices in disciplining viewers to see Indigenous peoples, cultures, and histories as inherently inferior and therefore dispensable. Long (2007) argues that the photograph and the archive function to display the relationship between power and knowledge. Hacking too found that Foucault (1969) defined the "archive" in terms of a "general system of the formation and transformation of statements." Without the multiple views that a decolonizing perspective demands, it is easy to follow the well-worn paths of explanations of this history by simply characterizing it as "assimilation." Taking the decolonizing perspective that I do reveals the rhetorical features of each of the Aboriginal education policy eras deemed to be *assimilation* in the past and *reconciliation*, in contemporary times. By listening to intergenerational memories of Indigenous peoples of Indian residential school history framed by historical ontology and fictional imagination, the possibilities for emerging from this traumatic history are opened. Accordingly, fiction and imagination can step in where memory fails in ensuring our collective identities as Indigenous peoples continue. In the next section, I draw on the scholarship of authors writing in genocide studies to show how their insights are aligned with the history of Indian residential schools.

Genocide Studies

Shoshana Felman (2001, 2009) has noted repetition as a feature of traumatic history. Felman (2009) used fiction, a novella by Tolstoy, to make the argument that when the law is blind to the trauma of a crime, then such traumas will be repeated (particularly through legal trials). Felman (2001) argues that such repetitions are a "legal outcome of traumatic narratives" (p. 29). Felman (2009) also argues that Hannah Arendt's *Eichmann in Jerusalem* is "inhabited by Arendt's mourned and unmourned ghosts" (p. 273), namely, friends that died at the hands of the Nazis. Felman concludes that Arendt did not understand the effects of trauma on the survivors of the Holocaust in her dismissal of dramatic testimonies at Eichmann's trial. Further, Felman (2001, 2009) regards trauma as part of a historical narrative that will be repeated across time if we cannot confront it as sociocultural, that is, embodied in the sociocultural dimensions of indigenous memories of schooling experiences.

That the Canadian state built more than 100 Indian residential school buildings for the production of particular identities for Indigenous children emphasizes how identities are linked to buildings. Such insights were prompted by Sebald's (2001) novel *Austerlitz* where a history of trauma is linked indirectly to the policy stories that buildings tell (Yanow 1995). With respect to his extensive study of train station architecture, Austerlitz, the character confides to the narrator that, he "often found himself in the grip of dangerous and entirely incomprehensible currents of emotion in the Parisian railway stations, which he said, he regarded as places marked by both blissful happiness and profound misfortune" (p. 34). When Austerlitz learns the history of the Liverpool Street train station in London that was adjacent to the historic Bedlam insane asylum, he wonders if traces of the pain and suffering of past inhabitants are left in buildings. This passage alludes to the Nazi's sinister use of buildings, their mistreatment and extermination of the mentally ill and physically challenged, and their use of the European train system to transport victims to the concentration and death camps.

At the Shubenacadie Indian residential school, the students feared becoming sick. "For us the infirmary became the place from which children vanished forever. Sometimes we heard that they had died and sometimes we didn't. To us, it seemed that those sick children just evaporated" (Knockwood 2001, p. 110). Knockwood's collection of survivors' experiences at the Shubenacadie Indian Residential School in Nova Scotia was first published in 1992. The 2001 extended edition includes an additional preface about the author beginning university studies: "I would go down the corridors and I would think that I was going to see a nun or a priest because it reminded me so much of the residential school. I was more oppressed by just the building than I was by anyone there" (p. 166). Accordingly, the emotions evoked by these buildings and the recovered memories associated with them are important themes for Indian residential school survivors and, as documented in previous sections of this chapter, for their descendants as well.

The *Windspeaker* magazine reported on one community's difficulty in determining what to do with the Indian residential school building. The author related the challenge to the fact that 50 of the 60 suits filed by victims of sexual abuse at the school in question, against the federal government, were settled out of court. "Each of the settlements relates to the activities of William Peniston Starr, former director of the school. Starr...was convicted...of 10 counts of sexually assaulting male students when he was administrator... between November 1968 and June1984" (Sutter and Hayes 1997). Further, "...many band members share the victims' anger that the school was demolished last summer and turned into a parking lot at the same time that most of settlements were being offered. This action demonstrated further confirmation that the government wanted the issue over with, with as little fuss and bother as possible." And, "(n)obody has heard our stories or knows the hardships we endured," said a victim. "I would have showed them exactly what happened and where it happened in the school. But now the school is gone" (Sutter 1997). These memories are indicative of the confining choices that Indigenous communities are left with in deciding what to do with the buildings. It shows the "rival claims of memory and forgetting" that was recognized by Ricoeur's discussion of narratives in relation to ethics (Kearney 2004, p. 99) and raises the question, is it possible to forget?

Postmemory and Critical Pedagogy

With the notion of postmemory there is a witness, usually descendants of survivors, to a witness of the Holocaust. Hirsch (1999) argues that acts of remembrance can generate a projection and identification with the memories of the survivors of trauma. Photographs are the media that can connect the generations. Postmemory is the relationship of second-generation children of survivors with the memories of survivors, particularly when the "memories are so strong as to constitute memories in their own right" (p. 8). I position myself in the role of the postmemory witness to the lived experiences of the history of the Indian residential school system, at a personal level, poring over photographs while listening to memories of family members, and at a decolonizing level, relistening to the stories of Indian residential schools. Accordingly, postmemory offers a model of ethical relation to the oppressed or persecuted other and advocates "distance" in order to resist appropriation (Hirsch 1999, p. 9).

Knockwood (2001) positions her own publication as an act of remembrance with the statement that the descendants of those who attended the school "are usually the ones who want to talk to me about it since the book enabled them to understand much of what previously troubled them about their parents and grandparents" (p. 13). Hence Knockwood's collection of memories can be read as a form of "productive remembering" (Strong-Wilson et al. 2013, p. 2) since it has meaning for future generations. They are particularly important for informing my own understanding of this traumatic history. Accordingly, postmemories are not mediated by recollection but by imagination and creativity (Long 2007, p. 59). The implications for critical pedagogy are recognized by Long (2007) when he argues that sufficient material narrative resources are prerequisites for the imaginative and creative investment required for postmemory (p. 60).

According to McCulloh (2003), Sebald's purpose is to ask, "How can one find a compelling way to speak about what is in all its horror and complexity, unspeakable?" (p. 130). Similar to Sebald, Knockwood's (2001) history of Mi'kmaw children in an Indian residential school, as well as other personal narratives, is in consideration of how these memories of a traumatic past might be conveyed to a wider audience. In both approaches, fiction and personal narratives, a history of trauma proves haunting through expressions of its ongoing effects.

In the scene in the novel when Austerlitz is reunited with his former nanny, as part of his research on his family's history, she shows him photographs of his parents and himself as a child. This scene illustrates Hirsch's (1999) notion of postmemory, wherein second-generation survivors of the Holocaust attempt to resolve the previous generations' traumatic history. The nanny, Vera, asks, "What do we know of ourselves? How do we remember? And, what is it we find in the end?" (Sebald 2001, p. 204). These questions are particularly significant for intergenerational survivors of the Indian residential schools, like myself, and the ways in which we might make sense of the traumatic history gathered by the Truth and Reconciliation Commission (2009). The TRC's plans for the collection of this history, in terms of the testimony of survivors, include a national archive to be housed at the University of Manitoba. Similarly, the newly revised British Columbia curriculum, by including this history, is currently being lauded as responding to the TRC's Calls to Action. These moves might be seen as a reappropriation of the history of Indigenous peoples in Canada, thereby placing it in the hands of state-controlled institutions; however, both Sebald and Long might see these moves as renewed attempts to institutionalize Indigenous peoples as modern subjects wherein our histories are not part of our own consciousness but only "resides in the material of our social and psychic life" (p. 4).

In this chapter, my aim, by drawing attention to the "conditions of formation" of the colonial conceptions of Aboriginal/Indian education, as a way to "determine its logical relations and moral connotations" (Hacking 2002, p. 67), was to fulfill my own commitment to "remember the children" by "reaching out from now until back then" (Hudson, Personal Interview, August 18, 2011).

References

Alexie S (2003) The search engine. In: Ten little Indians. Grove Atlantic, New York
BC Ministry of Education (2018) BC's new curriculum. Retrieved from https://curriculum.gov.bc.ca/curriculum/social-studies/5. Last retrieved on 1 Apr 2018
Brooks S (1991) The persistence of native education policy in Canada. In: Friesen JW (ed) The cultural maze: complex questions on native destiny in Western Canada. Detsilig Enterprises, Calgary, pp 163–180
Dieter C (1999) From our mother's arms: the intergenerational impact of residential schools in Saskatchewan. United Church Publishing House, Toronto
Felman S (2001) A ghost in the house of justice: death and the language of the law. Yale J Law and Humanit 13(1):241–282
Felman S (2009) Forms of judicial blindness: traumatic narratives and legal repetitions. In: Sarat A, Kearns TR (eds) History, memory, and the law. University of Michigan Press, Ann Arbor, pp 25–93
Foucault M (1969) The archaeology of knowledge. Routledge, New York
Hacking I (2002) Historical ontology. Harvard University Press, Cambridge
Hirsch M (1999) Projected memory: holocaust photographs in personal and public fantasy. In: Bal M, Crewe JV, Spritzer L (eds) Acts of memory: cultural recall in the present. University Press of New England, Hanover, pp 3–23
Kearney R (2004) Between poetics and ethics. In On Paul Ricoeur: The owl of Minerva, Burlington VT: Ashgate pp 99–114
Knockwood I (2001) (extended edition). Out of the depths: experiences of Mi'kmaw children at the Indian residential school at Shubenacadie, Nova Scotia. Roseway Publishing, Lockeporte/Nova Scotia
Long JJ (2007) W.G. Sebald: image, archive, modernity. Columbia University Press, New York
McClintock A (1995) Imperial leather. Routledge, New York
McCulloh M (2003) Understanding W.G. Sebald. University of SouthCarolina, Columbia
Miller JR (1997) Shingwauk's vision: a history of native residential schools. University of Toronto Press, Toronto
Milloy JS (1999) A national crime: the Canadian government and the residential school system – 1879 to 1986. University of Manitoba Press, Winnipeg/Manitoba

School District #39 (2009) Aboriginal education enhancement agreement. Author, Vancouver. Retrieved from http://www.bced.gov.bc.ca/abed/agreements/sd39.pdf. Last retrieved on 20 Dec 2011

School District #43 (2007) Aboriginal education enhancement agreement. Author, Coquitlam. Retrieved from http://www.bced.gov.bc.ca/abed/agreements/sd43.pdf. Last retrieved on 20 Dec 2011

School District #61 (2005) Aboriginal education enhancement agreement. Author, Victoria. Retrieved from http://www.bced.gov.bc.ca/abed/agreements/sd61.pdf. Last retrieved on 20 Dec 2011

School District #75 (2007) Aboriginal education enhancement agreement. Author, Mission. Retrieved from http://www.bced.gov.bc.ca/abed/agreements/sd75.pdf. Last retrieved on 20 Dec 2011

Sebald WG (2001) Austerlitz. The Modern Library, New York

Smith L (1999) Decolonizing methodologies: research and indigenous peoples. Zed Books, New York

Strong-Wilson T (2013) Waiting in the grey light: nostalgia, trauma and currere in W. G. Sebald's Austerlitz. In: Strong-Wilson T, Mitchell C, Allnutt S, Pithouse-Morgan K (eds) Productive remembering and social agency. Sense Publications, Rotterdam

Sutter T and Hayes RJ (1997). Federal government settles with abuse victims. Windspeaker News

Truth and Reconciliation Commission (2009) Mandate. Retrieved from http://www.trc.ca/websites/trcinstitution/index.php?p=7. Last retrieved on 10 June 2012

Yanow D (1995) Built space as story: the policy story that buildings tell. Policy Stud J 23(3):407–422

In the End "The Hope of Decolonization"

Moana Jackson

Contents

Knowing Colonization	102
The Privileging of the Colonizers' Lives	104
The Privileging of the Colonizers' Power	105
The Privileging of the Colonizers' Law	106
The Difficulty and Hope of Decolonization	108
References	110

Abstract

For hundreds of years, the peoples from Europe who have raped and pillaged their way through Indigenous nations have perfected not just the instruments and practices of dispossession but also a whole archive of doctrines and rewritten histories that purport to justify what they have done. They are in fact what may be termed "mythtakes," deliberately concocted falsehoods to justify a process that is actually unjustifiable. Indigenous Peoples still live with the fact and practice of those mythtakes. To decolonize is to recognize that colonization is a deceptive lie as much as a crushing oppression. However, in the end, decolonization simply means having faith that we can still be brave enough to change an imposed reality. In that quest, there is always hope in knowing that whenever our tīpuna fought or necessarily adapted to survive in the darkest days of oppression, the resistance was never futile and the adaptation was never acquiescence. A first step in rekindling that hope is perhaps to be clear about what colonization was, and is.

Keywords

Decolonization · Colonization · Indigenous law · Law

M. Jackson (✉)
Wellington, New Zealand
e-mail: mjfeb1840@gmail.com

To decolonize is to recognize that colonization is a deceptive lie as much as a crushing oppression. For hundreds of years the peoples from Europe who have raped and pillaged their way through indigenous nations have perfected not just the instruments and practices of dispossession, but also a whole archive of doctrines and rewritten histories that purport to justify what they have done. Sometimes those rationalizations have been debunked or categorized as myths, but they are something far more compulsive and sinister. They are in fact what may be termed "mythtakes," deliberately concocted falsehoods to justify a process that is actually unjustifiable.

Indigenous Peoples still live with the fact and practice of those mythtakes. They have led to what seem like unchallengeable realities of power and expectation, and it always takes a certain courage to contemplate and break free from them. That is certainly the case in Aotearoa, but our people have always been daring even though the colonizers continually try to convince us it is unrealistic (and certainly illegal in their law) to advocate meaningful transformation. However, in the end decolonization simply means having faith that we can still be brave enough to change an imposed reality. In that quest there is always hope in knowing that whenever our tīpuna fought or necessarily adapted to survive in the darkest days of oppression, the resistance was never futile and the adaptation was never acquiescence. A first step in rekindling that hope is perhaps to be clear about what colonization was, and is.

Knowing Colonization

There is an old and often-quoted adage that "the namer of names is the father of all things." Apart from its gendered inappropriateness the adage has a basic truth because whoever assumes the right to name or define something controls its meaning and how others comprehend it. Ever since the colonizers first rampaged through an indigenous land, they have invented confusing definitions of what colonization is. Some have been misleading plays on words which abstract the suffering of its dreadful violence into an almost meaningless ahistoricism or else they have been wrapped in jargon that too often reads like excuses hiding in a thesaurus. Most often the definition is just a rationalization for what they have done (and continue to do), a misremembering of fact or a set of presumptions which position it as a past event rather than a still ongoing process.

Yet colonization was and is a very simple process of brutal dispossession in which States from Europe assumed the right to take over the lands, lives, and power of Indigenous Peoples who had done them no harm. In most indigenous lives it is neither just a past or a memory but a present which links the shock and awe of contemporary international relations to the musings of long dead European philosophers contemplating how to describe human difference and then how to destroy or control those they saw as inferior because they were different.

Decolonization is the process of breaking free from that dispossession and all of the ideas and practices which shaped and were derived from it. It is to interrogate and dismantle all that it has meant and still means to the way we think and live our lives. To Māori in Aotearoa it means knowing a history which did not begin with the

7 In the End "The Hope of Decolonization"

arrival of the first strangers in our land but centuries before in the monasteries, court houses, corporations, and inns in Europe where "ordinary" Europeans came to believe they could and should rule the world.

Indeed when Queen Victoria was crowned in 1838, Britain was merely the latest European country involved in a worldwide surge in colonization. At that time South America was a mess of conflicting interests among different European States while in the north the governments of Canada and the United States were carrying on the suppression of Indigenous Peoples that their English, Spanish, Swedish, Danish, and French forbears had begun. India was seen as the jewel in the colonizing Crown, while China was the unbounded mart for commerce which 2 years after the coronation led Victoria's troops to invade Canton to ensure that Britain could control the opium trade. Other parts of Asia were being fought over as well and many European States were beginning to carve up Africa among themselves like some gigantic birthday cake.

Like every other colonizer the British believed that they were entitled and blessed to rule over those they regarded as racially inferior. If some States such as Sweden and Denmark were no longer active colonizers in the mid-nineteenth century, others continued to dispossess with enthusiasm or diffidence depending upon the costs involved. Indigenous Peoples were being "discovered" in more places than ever before and Europe was hell-bent on dispossessing and destroying them in the first global war of terror.

Colonization permeated every aspect of European and Euro-American society. It provided the vicarious thrill of a marketplace serving up everything from spices and cotton to wool and gold, and it gave them access to everything from the profits of bodies for sale to the raw materials which made their industrial revolution possible. The men pickling indigenous body parts in Edinburgh and the women sipping coffee in Paris may have seen themselves as just scientists or consumers, but their acts were each based upon the same dispossession carried out for the glory of their god and the honor of their sovereign. Colonization was the cleansed-by-distance exotica that titillated their senses and lined their pockets, and they still live on those profits today.

To the millions who left Europe to dispossess Indigenous Peoples colonization was their chance of a lifetime. Many of them may have departed with few belongings and a fear of the unknown but they had learned they were part of a legitimate and civilized endeavor where success and excitement could be theirs for the taking. Among the hordes that left were the usual speculators, bigots, abusers, utopians, and zealots who had been camp followers in the centuries of Europe's internal violence. There were also women oppressed by patriarchy, churchgoers persecuted for their beliefs, peasants who had been removed from their land, slum dwellers crushed by poverty, and others like the Irish who had long been savaged by their neighbors. Colonization for them was an escape. However, in seeking their freedom they also presumed a right to dispossess and thus ended up wielding the same kind of unjust power over Indigenous Peoples that they had once chafed under themselves.

When the Pacific was colonized its diverse islands became early ports of call for Europe's most violent, excitable, and puritanical. Whalers and sealers followed the explorer-colonizers such as James Cook and hunted around for all sorts of prey.

Criminals found the islands a handy bolt-hole to escape the hangman's noose, and speculators liked the combination of tropical weather and easy markets among apparently easy-going and easy to manipulate people. As usual missionaries were particularly keen to take this new earthly paradise and descended with a milliners' wrath demanding that the inhabitants' sinful nakedness be clothed even as many of their own parishioners thought they had swooned into a pornucopia where their wishful thinking might come true. They all tended to paint the people in the racist hues of alarm and desire and classified them in a neat little Pacific chain of being that ranked Pacific peoples in various categories of savagery, with all of them naturally lower than their European superiors. What had already been tried in the Americas and Asia and Africa was easily adapted here. Genocide, and the lies that tried to obscure it, was remarkably transportable.

When it finally descended upon our people, it was underpinned by the same histories that had been lived and mythtakenly justified in all the centuries since Christopher Columbus stumbled into the Caribbean. There are many parts to what may be described as the culture of colonization, but there are three main facts which in a very real sense became the base of the colonizers' power and institutions. They began the process of White privilege and set in place a new race-based reality which privileged their lives over ours.

The Privileging of the Colonizers' Lives

Violence is the systemic reality of colonization. Taking anything without cause is always an act of violence, but doing so with the intention of culturally perpetuating and legitimating the taking is a systemic violence that feeds into everything else the takers wish to do. It can therefore manifest itself in both the obvious violence of war and rape and abuse and the less obvious but equally horrific violence of taking away a people's law or language or faith.

In post-1492 colonization the dualism that divided people into superior and inferior races also divided the world between the privileged who were entitled to live and those whose lives were expendable. Through a vicious circular argument, the colonizers learned that because Indigenous Peoples were less worthy of living their dying was less worthy of lamenting. In the same way that they learned that their will to dispossess was reasonable and legal, they also learned a perverse reality where killing the innocents could be normalized if occasionally regretted. Indeed indigenous death and suffering could be ordered in the dispassionate language of a legal decree or the sterile words of a statute which often gave them a hypocritical moral acceptability which then allowed the colonizers to characterize any retaliatory resistance by Indigenous Peoples as immoral, illegal, and an act of savage rebellion.

The actual instruments of death that the colonizers used are all too familiar. Indigenous Peoples have been speared, shot, bombed, starved, hanged, mutilated, disemboweled, thrown over the sides of ships at sea, burned alive, fed literally to the ravening dogs, and of course scalped for bounty (a practice which the colonizers still mythtakenly blame the victims for). The first bodies dispatched by Columbus established a pattern that was followed with little variation from the ritual gutting of pregnant Mapuche women to the sport of "hooking" young children (catching them on lances and throwing their bodies into walls) and the much later hunting of Tasmanian Aboriginals as game and the targeting of children in massacres and institutions in Aotearoa. Introduced diseases took its toll too of course as did the emotional and spiritual suffering that dispossession necessarily imposed. Indigenous death and trauma was as varied as it was terrible.

Colonization also forced many Indigenous Peoples into a despairing living death, especially when for example colonizers raped indigenous women and children. Such assaults were not rare exceptions but a specific part of the systemic violence of colonization in which the belief that indigenous lands were wasted and "virginal" and therefore "rapeable" was transmuted into a similar presumption that Native bodies were similarly rapeable and able to be wasted and taken. In fact rape and abuse were almost as common as "just wars" and unjust murders except for one important difference: those who were raped were subjected to a lifetime of slow dying, of being shadows slipping into a fear-filled despair because their hurt was also the hurt of those they loved and who loved them. The colonizers still tend to deny that terror or claim it is an exception, but it is recorded in indigenous laments as a recurring reality that is too frequent to be a mere aberration.

The numbers and kinds of dying are reflections of colonization's inhumanity. The concern that was occasionally shown by some individual colonizers did not alter the fact that the millions of people who perished were too often regarded with the same uncaring defiance found in the words of the Bhagavad-Gita "I am become death, the destroyer of worlds" (Swarupananda 1909). In any sense of the word, colonization is a genocide, and as many Jewish people define Hitler's extermination policies as the "Shoah" or great calamity, so surely it was a holocaust.

The Privileging of the Colonizers' Power

Power is the definitive hunger of colonization. The European will to dispossess harnessed power to achieve its ends whether it was the power that came out of the barrel of a gun or the apparent reason of law or the injunctions of a god. Colonization has always been a culturally scripted power game and by its very nature it is a privileging of one form of political power over another.

To achieve that goal the colonizers invented numerous mythtakes to "sell" the imposition of their authority as a response to disorder or a regime change for the better – they were "gifting" something to Indigenous Peoples which they assumed they never had before. Yet every culture formulates a way to power because they realize that social harmony is best maintained if there is some means of ensuring community adherence to shared norms and values. Societies do not function well in a power vacuum and so they all develop a culturally distinctive concept of power, an idea of what it is or should be, and a site of power which is the institution or place where it is actually exercised. Both grow from the stories in a land and both coalesce in constitutions that differ from culture to culture.

Our people had for centuries adapted and defined the concept of power called mana or more recently tino rangatiratanga. Like all concepts of power, it was an expression of independence, but because of our particular ideals of whakapapa and interrelationships, it was also about the interdependence between the different polities of Hapū and Iwi. It was the very Māori expression of the very human desire to be free and to make one's own decisions in one's land. It was a concept of self-determination with a history and associated practice that was handed down through the generations and defiantly protected if the need arose. And because it was an intergenerational responsibility, it was inalienable and could not be ceded or given away to anyone else.

The people of Europe also developed a culturally unique concept of power which they called sovereignty. It reflected their belief that human authority was derived from their Christian God and that it should be structured in a hierarchy similar to that which led upwards to his unquestioned power. Its meaning and extent was argued over throughout the centuries and was then defined within discourses where the same illogical flair that was used to create the inferior indigenous body was also applied to the construction of constitutional chains of being in which sovereignty became the superior and only valid means of understanding and exercising power.

It is therefore no coincidence that the most influential definitions of sovereignty as a somehow "universal" and "civilized" concept of power were devised at the same time that Europe was seeking to destroy the power of Indigenous Peoples. Sometimes its racism was openly expressed as in the view of the French courtier Jean Bodin who argued in 1569 that it marked a hierarchy of progress from societies of apolitical barbarism to those with a civilized constitutional order (Lindfors 2017), or that of Thomas Hobbes who suggested it only came about when nations advanced beyond the primitive "state of nature" (where Indigenous Peoples supposedly lived) to a state of reason (which only the colonizers had) (Williams 2017).

The racialized mythtake of sovereignty and its subsequent imposition on Indigenous Peoples has been the most compelling source of its multi-violence. In Aotearoa, as in other countries, its enforced exercise denied our people the simple human right to maintain our own power and so determine our own future through the political and constitutional institutions which we had always had. It was also necessarily an inherent privileging of the colonizers which ultimately cultivated a sense of powerlessness among our people in which real power and wisdom only seem to come from somewhere other than our own traditions and our own sense of "rightness." It colonized us by closing off our power and constantly trying to close down the hope that we might one day be free and constitutionally independent once again.

The Privileging of the Colonizers' Law

Law is the pretence to reason in colonization. Like the various concepts of power, it is also a unique cultural creation born of every society's recognition that to maintain harmony it is necessary to have agreed values and ideas which people will accept as part of living within their particular social order. Just as societies abhor a power vacuum, so they have always accepted that they cannot live in a "law-less" condition.

Our people have been no different and we developed a rich and complex jurisprudence of law based on the whakapapa or relationships that existed between humans and everything else in the universe. The tikanga or law is based on a relational jurisprudence known as the whakamārama tōtika or the means of explaining rightness. It provided reaffirmation of mana and because of its whakapapa base it also meant that our people lived with the law rather than under it just as one lived with someone else in a relationship.

To the colonizers however, we either did not possess "real" law or had only the rudiments of some primitive "lore" governed by caprice and vengeance rather than reason. When they came to Aotearoa and other parts of the world to colonizes, they therefore presumed that we were not only incapable of being "sovereign," we had no law to guarantee and protect that sovereignty. Their racist arrogance consequently allowed them to proclaim that if an Englishman (always a man) traveled to another white country, he would accept its jurisdiction, but if he traveled to a non-white country such as ours, then he would carry his law with him because primitive lore could not legitimately extend its writ over a civilized colonizer. In fact it needed to be replaced by the civilizing influences of the common law which would then become the "one law for all."

The denial of the Māori law was necessary for the creation of a new legal and political regime in this land. The establishment of the "New Zealand" nation-state in fact required the dismissal of the interwoven legal and political processes of Māori. The rejection of our law was essential to the constitutional subjugation which colonization seeks. However, to mask the dispossession inherent in this process, a new and culturally different symbiosis between politics and law had to be made in which the dispossession itself would be made "legal" in the colonizers' law. By a kind of legal magic the wrong of colonization would become the legitimate base of a new and lawful sovereign State.

This magic provided a veneer of reason in which doing things "in the name of the (ir) law" could countenance everything from the Trail of Tears in the United Sates to the forced confiscation of thousands of acres of land in Aotearoa. It made indigenous dispossession a matter of "domestic" jurisdiction, although it was based on numerous doctrines in what the colonizers soon took to calling "international law" or the law of their civilized nations. Each doctrine was based on racist assumptions and breath-taking gymnastics of illogicality, but they were, and still are, recognized by the colonizers as the jurisdictional rituals which gave legitimacy to whatever they wished to do. They are mythtakes that led to very real and tragic consequences for Indigenous Peoples.

The most famous or infamous is the so-called Doctrine of Discovery which assumed that if a Christian "discovered" a non-Christian indigenous land, the simple act of discovery allowed the land to be taken and occupied. Colonizers from Columbus to Cook waved flags and buried bottles and performed all sorts of theater to announce their "discovery" and with it their self-presumed legal right to the lands and people. No doubt the people themselves were bemused by a strange White man waving a piece of colored rag at them and would only learn later that it signaled the start of a previously unknown violence. In Aotearoa Cook performed rituals of discovery in 1769 which were followed in 1840 by other proclamations issued by Governor Hobson even as he was gathering signatures on Te Tiriti o Waitangi.

Theater always requires a suspension of disbelief of course, and the presumptions of the doctrine of discovery were quickly followed by another ritual denial of Māori independence and law with the implementation of the "doctrine of aboriginal title." Under this doctrine the colonizers agreed to recognize preexisting aboriginal rights, subject to their overarching authority to define what they were as well as extinguish them if they felt it was necessary. The mind-numbing arrogance of the doctrine is that it is still regarded as a mark of the colonizers' benevolence and honor, even though it subordinates any notion of rights as our people had always expressed them in our own land.

The colonizers' law finalized the denial of legal capacity to Māori and other Indigenous Peoples unless that capacity was defined and controlled by the colonizers. It restricted relief or enumeration of indigenous status and rights to the very legal systems and philosophy which were oppressing them. In a very real way it turned once free and independent people into the legal subjects of others – it made them subject to a law and power which was never of this land.

The Difficulty and Hope of Decolonization

In Aotearoa we still live with the legacy of colonization's power and law and violence. We also live with the mind-shifting insouciance of the mythtakes, and especially their belief that colonization here was somehow "better" than anywhere else because of the treaty and a purported honor of the Crown. But the Treaty has always been breached, and the idea of honor in the dishonor of taking someone's lands, lives, and power is a contradiction in terms. No matter how colonization is achieved, it is always a violent genocidal dispossession. To assume, there is some sliding scale of honorable acceptability or a Hit Parade of comparative benevolence in which New Zealand is Number One is one of this country's most misleading lies.

Yet it continues to underpin the power and wealth which Pākehā take for granted as well as the structures and values of the New Zealand State which is now simply characterized as the "reality." Indeed to challenge those realities in any meaningful way, to decolonize their hold over our lives, often leads to allegations that we are being "unrealistic." The result has been that many of our people, and many Indigenous Peoples in other colonized lands, find it hard to imagine any other reality. Many do not even see it as an ongoing oppression because it is all that they know – they may even in some cases be comfortable in their own oppression.

Indeed because of the ongoing exposure to colonized learning and the lack of any meaningful indigenous benchmarks in power and control against which to measure their experiences, many have come to accept for example that a foreign power is legitimate or a foreign law is the law because they do not know their own anymore.

7 In the End "The Hope of Decolonization"

They accept the idea of cultural performance in song and dance and ceremony as the sum total of what it means to be indigenous and lose sight of the fact that such things were once the expression of a proud and effective political independence. There is a sad but understandable "surviving in the now" about such views, but perhaps one of the saddest indicators of how colonization damages the self-perception of those it colonizes is when many Indigenous Peoples now seem to believe that what is happening is due to their own laziness or inadequacy. It is all their own fault. An even sadder one is when they then begin to say that "we are our own worst enemies." To make us believe that is surely the most violent, racist, and ominous power the colonizers have ever wielded.

Linda Smith (2012) has written about "the reach of imperialism into our heads," a reach that many Indigenous Peoples describe as the "colonisation of the mind." The slow overwhelming of what people should think and see as real has not been forced directly at the point of a gun, although that was often the catalyst which first instilled the fear of not conforming to what the colonizers wanted. Rather it has occurred surreptitiously, like a cloud that moves across the sun and takes your shadow without you knowing. And like the sun it has remained a constant reality in indigenous lives. But every reality, and every understanding of reality, is created by humans and can be deconstructed by humans as well. No reality is immutable or beyond change and the centuries of indigenous resistance have always brought change in what seemed unchangeable situations. That history is part of our reality.

And decolonization is not just about challenging and deconstructing the colonized "reality" but having faith once again in our own. To deal with the trauma and wrong that colonization inflicts while creating the hope for something better. There is a moral as well as a political, economic, and constitutional imperative to that reimagining because it is not just about reclaiming long-denied rights but seeking the Māori and indigenous notion of "rightness" in which a sense of relational justice may be restored.

Decolonization takes many forms because there is much to reclaim and every indigenous nation, and every indigenous person, will know best what that means for them. There is however one thing which perhaps we all have in common. We cannot entirely ease the pain of remembering those who suffered and have been killed or abused, and nor should we. But in the very memory of their sacrifice is a decolonizing reaffirmation of their worth, and of ours. To walk the sad trails, to tell the stories of hurt and survival, and to sing the old songs is in its own way to know ourselves. For Māori it is to know with pride as well as a righteous anger that even in the worst days when our people were dying from new diseases or trying to hold onto our dignity in the face of a virulent racism and military invasion, our songs became laments telling of the wrongs that were being done across the land, even against children. They were sad songs but sung in a poetics of fearful protectiveness: "Stay by me little one/there is an anger all around/more fierce than the wind." To reclaim that same fierce protectiveness of who we are is part of decolonizing ourselves.

In Aotearoa one of the most difficult decolonizing projects confronting Māori has always been to reclaim the power taken from us by the colonizers. Our people literally fought to hold on to that mana in the nineteenth century and have continued ever since to debate among ourselves and with others how to achieve that. The starting point for that discourse has always been the 1835 He Whakaputanga (the Declaration of Independence) signed by a number of Hapū and Iwi as a definitive statement of our constitutional reality, and the Treaty of Waitangi signed to allow strangers into our land.

The most recent initiative has been a 5 year process of discussion among a wide cross section of Māori people following a Brief from a National hui to set up a Working Group "To develop and implement a model for an inclusive Constitution for Aotearoa based on tikanga..., He Whakaputanga o te Rangatiratanga o Niu Tireni of 1835, Te Tiriti o Waitangi of 1840, and other indigenous human rights instruments..." (Matike Mai Aotearoa 2015). The Terms of Reference did not ask the Working Group to consider how the Treaty might fit within the imposed colonizing constitutional system but rather to seek advice on a different type of constitutionalism that is *based* upon our own law and He Whakaputanga and Te Tiriti.

The Terms of Reference were themselves therefore a decolonizing statement of intent, and our people responded in over 252 hui and 70 discussion groups held with rangatahi. While there was some consideration given to possible constitutional models, most of the discussion centered on the values which would underpin a non-colonizing constitution, such as the well-being of Mother Earth. There was also a clear recognition that sovereignty was not a Māori concept of power and that our law is fundamental to any new constitutional order.

Our people also accepted that such constitutional transformation would not occur easily or quickly because power unjustly taken is never willingly forfeited. However, a goal was set of achieving substantive change by 2040, 200 years after the signing of the Treaty. Indeed in spite of all that has happened, there is still good will and a belief that the many obstacles to transformation can eventually be overcome and a new constitution established. Our people did not see that as some pious hope but as a legitimate treaty expectation and an essential decolonizing requirement. In the end, it is that willingness to imagine and work toward meaningful change which is our greatest hope for decolonization.

References

Lindfors T (2017) Jean Bodin (c. 1529–1569). Internet Encyclopedia of Philosophy (IEP). Retrieved from: http://iep.utm.edu/bodin/#SSH10bi

Matike Mai Aotearoa (2015) He Whakaaro Here Whakaumu mō Aotearoa: the report of Matike Mai Aotearoa – the independent working group on constitutional transformation. Retrieved from: http://www.converge.org.nz/pma/MatikeMaiAotearoaReport.pdf

Smith LT (2012) Decolonizing methodologies: research and indigenous peoples, 2nd edn. University of Otago Press, Dunedin

Swarupananda S (1909) Srimad-Bhagavad-Gita: English translation and commentary. Retrieved from: http://sacred-texts.com/hin/sbg/index.htm

Williams G (2017) Thomas Hobbes: moral and political philosophy. Internet Encyclopedia of Philosophy (IEP). Retrieved from: http://www.iep.utm.edu/hobmoral/#H7

Beyond the Guest Paradigm: Eurocentric Education and Aboriginal Peoples in NSW

8

Bob Morgan

Contents

Introduction	112
Early Models of Aboriginal Education	113
The Native Institution	114
Education as Cultural Contamination	116
Failed Schooling and Aboriginal Incarceration	117
Disengaged Curricula	118
Teaching as Cultural Production	119
Decolonization Imperatives, Justice, and Self-Determining Education	121
Dreaming a Better Future	122
Hope and Inspiration and Transformational Pathways to Success	123
Conclusion and Future Directions	125
References	126

Abstract

In writing this chapter I hear the voices of brave warriors, male and female, Aboriginal and non-Aboriginal, old and young, individuals who stood against tyranny and oppression and who challenged all of us to dream and to never surrender to injustice. Some of the warriors have passed whilst others continue to dedicate their lives to the cause of justice and the rights and freedoms of Aboriginal peoples and other marginalized and voiceless groups across the globe. This chapter gives voice to their memory, their principled vision and leadership and the ideals for which they stood through examining the impact of

---

Silence is the mother of injustice and oppression in the world and tolerance and inaction is why it is allowed to persist.

B. Morgan (✉)
The Wollotuka Institute, Indigenous Education and Research, The University of Newcastle, Newcastle, Australia
e-mail: murri1949@gmail.com; b.morgan@newcastle.edu.au

colonialism on Aboriginal people in New South Wales (NSW), Australia. The chapter defines core elements of the "Guest Paradigm" that characterises current Aboriginal education policies and programs and utilises principles of Aboriginal self-determination, cultural survival and affirmation to challenge the assimilation and culturally contaminating influences of Eurocentric education on Aboriginal cultural values and traditions and knowledge systems. The chapter concludes with a call to move beyond the guest paradigm by citing examples of scholarly enrichment for Aboriginal peoples, without the sacrifice of culture and traditions, by advocating a strategic disengagement for Aboriginal peoples with Eurocentric education and the development of a authentic model of Aboriginal education.

Keywords
Aboriginal Education · Guest Paradigm · Colonisation · Aboriginal Self-determination

Introduction

In this chapter I set out to examine the impact of colonialism on Aboriginal people in New South Wales (NSW), Australia. Aboriginal Australia is comprised of a multiplicity of cultures and languages, there is no single Aboriginal reality. However, every Aboriginal nation has suffered from the invasion of their lands and the destructive forces of colonialism. In NSW, the site where the first impact of invasion and colonialism was felt and perhaps where the brunt of its debilitating forces has been most profound, the modern struggle for social and restorative justice continues unabated and unresolved. From the earliest days of invasion Aboriginal people have been engaged in the struggle for social and restorative justice, including the right to participate in education. Based on their own longstanding educational traditions, Aboriginal people throughout the continent recognized the value of new knowledge and have taken an active interest in it from first contact until now. What makes the struggle for Aboriginal education equity and justice so perplexing and evasive is the fact that the political landscape upon which the struggle is contested is often defined and constructed by non-Aboriginal people thereby positioning Aboriginal views as reactionary rather than being proactive and emancipatory.

In writing the chapter, I seek to privilege Indigenous knowledge systems and a pedagogy that is informed by narratives and Aboriginal people's connectedness to country and all living things. Narratives, in Aboriginal contexts, reflect what I refer to as the "tethered tangential logic" (Morgan 1993) of Indigenous knowledge creation, sharing, and dissemination. Tethered tangential logic, unlike what some refer to as tangential thinking, which is seen as problematic, acknowledges that at some levels thoughts may appear to "go off track," but because they are "tethered" to an original thought, the writer or communicator eventually returns to the central theme or central message. I also wish to evoke the concept of Dadirri, what Miriam Rose Ungunmerr explains as the "…inner deep listening and quiet, still awareness.

Dadirri recognizes the deep spring that is inside us. We call on it and it calls on us. This is the gift that Australia is thirsting for. It is something like what you [non-Indigenous people] call contemplation" (Ungunmerr Bauman 2002).

Using narratives and this tethered tangential logic method, this chapter argues that Aboriginal education in Australia has been and remains a cleverly constructed and imposed ruse of assimilation and cultural genocide. Eurocentric education for the great majority of Aboriginal people still represents a convoluted and contaminated form of institutionalized injustice that is far removed from what Aboriginal people have historically demanded: an education system that provides culturally affirming learning opportunities and the formal recognition of Aboriginal sovereignty, as well as just restitution for the invasion of a nation and the dispossession of its people.

From the earliest days of colonization, Aboriginal people's participation in Eurocentric education can be best described as an exercise in social engineering and a not-so-veiled form of cultural genocide. Little has changed in Aboriginal education over the years, with most experiences for Aboriginal students being one where they are treated as "guests" in a foreign, Eurocentric, and at times hostile learning environment. Assimilation and the forced separation of Aboriginal children from their families, communities, and country heralded in a process that is described here as the "Guest Paradigm." I coined this phrase to capture my perception, over a lifetime of working in Aboriginal education, of the paradigmatic nature of the problems that I believe emerge when marginalized peoples are compelled to participate in systems, the nature of which they have had little involvement in determining. My use of this term is specific to the Australian Aboriginal context, but links to some extent with Derrida's (2000) concept of a "host-guest paradigm" (pp. 151–155), portraying colonizers as uninvited guests who have taken over their original hosts' property by force, thus assuming the power to relegate the original owners or inhabitants to the dependent status of "guests." The Guest Paradigm in Aboriginal education policy and programming contexts is characterized by the following key elements, which are briefly summarized here as a basis for identifying what needs to be changed in order to establish a new paradigm.

Early Models of Aboriginal Education

Aboriginal people have always respected and valued knowledge and its critical role relative to the development of the skills and knowledge needed to deal with the challenges inherent in living and surviving in an ever-changing world. Since the beginning of the Dreaming, Aboriginal peoples in Australia, and other Indigenous peoples internationally, utilized an epistemological method that sought wisdom from a variety of sources to help define, give meaning to, and celebrate their world. Traditional Aboriginal epistemological systems both intuitively and explicitly recognized the interconnectedness of all things, and this symbiotic relationship helped to create a harmonious coexistence with all living things and the environment.

The traditional epistemological system that sustained Aboriginal nations in Australia for millennia was shattered with the arrival of the British in 1788, and the establishment of their penal colony accelerated a process of dispersal, discrimination, and contamination of Aboriginal culture and traditions. The early years of colonialism in Australia were fraught with brutality and massacre. The clash of cultures and customs burdened by language barriers, coupled with the thirst of the British for new lands, led inevitably to guerrilla warfare, the type that was waged by Aboriginal warriors such as Pemulwuy and others (Willmot 1987). Two decades after the arrival of the British and the appointment of the new Governor Lachlan Macquarie in 1801, deepening tensions and the escalation of violence between the British and the local Eora people increased the frustration levels of Governor Macquarie. This tension and a growing fear of Aboriginal people among the British undoubtedly played a decisive role in Macquarie's support for the establishment of the Native Institution at Blacktown in 1814.

The Native Institution was the brainchild of William Shelley and represents the first attempt by the British to systematically engineer the "civilization" of the "Aboriginal heathens." William Shelley was a missionary who arrived in the new colony after being forced out of Tonga by the local native people. Shelley had made numerous representations to Governor Macquarie, who was increasingly concerned about the failure of the British to pacify Aboriginal people in and around the new settlement.

Other attempts to "educate" and civilize individual Aboriginal people also met with abject failure, with most of those exposed to British education and attempts at civilization eventually rejecting the attempts of the British and reconnecting with their people to whom they were socially, culturally, and spiritually aligned. William Shelley thought that the answer lay in the removal of Aboriginal children from their families, to be educated into a supposedly superior way of life.

The Native Institution

The Native Institution is the earliest experience that Aboriginal people had with Eurocentric and assimilationist education; social engineering served as the fundamental and primary objective of the school. The social engineering imperative is reflected in correspondence between Shelley and Governor Macquarie. In 1814, Shelley wrote:

> in order to effect their improvement and civilisation, let there be a public establishment containing one set of apartments for boys, and another separate set for girls; let them be taught reading, writing, religious education, the boys, manual labour, agriculture, mechanic arts, etc., the girls, sewing, knitting, spinning or such useful employment as suitable for them; let them be married at a suitable age, and settled with steady religious persons over them from the very beginning to see that they continued their employment, so as to be able to support their families, and who had skills sufficient to encourage and stimulate them by proper motives to exertion. (Bridges 1968)

The attempt to socially engineer Aboriginal people so that they would embrace the world of the British was an abject failure. Notwithstanding that some Aboriginal students, according to Commissioner J.T. Bigge (1822), were taught to read and write, the plan to civilize and assimilate Aboriginal students into the social and cultural norms of the British by separating them from their families proved futile.

Following the closure of the Native Institution in the late 1820s, various other attempts to "educate" and assimilate Aboriginal students followed, with early missionaries doing their best to convert the students to Christianity. The social engineering objectives espoused by Governor Macquarie and William Shelley, I would argue, have never really been abandoned by Australian education policy makers, and indeed their toxic influences are embedded in policies and programs that led to the development of pernicious government policies and programs of child removal such as those relating to the "Stolen Generations." The most fundamental learning outcomes for the majority of Aboriginal students enrolled in Eurocentric education systems are failure and assimilation by subterfuge. It is clear from their own historical records that non-Aboriginal authorities have sought to capture the hearts and manipulate the minds of Aboriginal peoples from the earliest days of British colonization, and schooling has been one of their primary tools.

The provision of education services to Aboriginal students in NSW adopted many forms for the remainder of the nineteenth century, including the scattered and solitary enrolment of Aboriginal students in public schools and the emergence of separate Aboriginal schools. The late nineteenth century in NSW also heralded the adoption of the "Clean, Clad and Courteous" policy (Fletcher 1989). There are numerous accounts of Aboriginal students attending public schools in the colony, even though the number of students was relatively small. The "Clean, Clad and Courteous" policy, a colonial form of "dog-whistle politics," dictated that Aboriginal students could attend public school but only if they met strict conditions of being hygienically healthy, appropriately dressed, and respectful. However, this somewhat benevolent policy did not mean that Aboriginal students, or their parents, could necessarily rejoice.

White parents of students who attended schools that also enrolled Aboriginal students frequently complained, leading to the adoption of the practice of excluding Aboriginal students on the basis of these complaints. Often the white parent's complaints involved concerns both for the social well-being of white children and the fear that Aboriginal children would corrupt the morals of white children. The exclusion policy was one of the factors that resulted in the establishment of a number of Aboriginal schools that were scattered throughout NSW, including in the communities at Brewarrina, Foster, (Tobwabba), Cabbage Tree Island, Rolland Plains, Wallaga Lake, Cowra, and Grafton. The schools were poorly resourced and the "curriculum" was structured for the purposes of equipping Aboriginal students with the manual and domestic service skills needed to support white families and society, a form of involuntary and forced slavery. Appallingly, the power of school principals to exclude Aboriginal students upon receiving complaints from white parents was finally removed from the NSW Teachers Handbook only in 1972 (Parbury 1999).

Education as Cultural Contamination

One of the most deleterious impacts of the social engineering objectives of Eurocentric and assimilationist education is the contamination of Aboriginal cultural values and traditions, including the willful destruction of Aboriginal languages. Cultural contamination has led to the emergence of a slow but definite decline of what was once an indomitable Aboriginal spirit, and the sad and tragic emergence of black on black violence and brutality that tragically tears at the social and cultural fabric of contemporary Aboriginal society.

I have sat in meetings and around community circles and have heard the voices of the old ones lamenting the destructive changing of our times, while the voices of the young are filled with despair, frustration, and anger.

Aboriginal parents and carers often lack the confidence in their own knowledge and skills to engage effectively with schools to support their children's learning not because they do not value education, but rather because they were also failed by the education system, and consequently they feel disempowered to positively engage schools to support their children's learning. The young question their place in the overall scheme of events and yet at the same time their words speak, in many respects, of a yearning for a world that respects and values their culture and their identity. Notwithstanding the disillusioned and disaffected state of Aboriginal youth, there is a measure of hope in their voices and their eyes for justice and equality. Their very frustration and anger stems from the deprivation of this birthright. Any study of Aboriginal education must avoid a rush to a deficit model of analysis (Fforde et al. 2013). If deficiency does exist, it resides in the realm of systems and bureaucracies, for it is at this level where Aboriginal students are failed.

Aboriginal people seek to engage and participate in learning experiences that enriches them intellectually, but never at the loss of their cultural identity and the values and traditions that inform their identity. This is not a new phenomenon; it was and remains one of the core expectations in the pursuit of knowledge and the development of skills for Aboriginal people. The authors of the Aboriginal manifesto adopted in 1938 to protest the sesquicentennial of the coming of colonialism to Australia (26 January 1788) argued:

> We do not wish to be regarded with sentimental sympathy, or to be preserved, like the koala bears, as exhibits; but we do ask for your real sympathy and understanding of our plight.
>
> We do not wish to be studied as scientific or anthropological curiosities. All such efforts on your behalf are wasted. We have no desire to go back to the primitive conditions of the Stone Age. We ask you to teach our children to live in the Modern Age, as modern citizens. Our people are very good and quick learners. Why do you deliberately keep us backward? Is it merely to give yourself the pleasure of feeling superior? Give our children the same chances as your own, and they will do as well as your children!
>
> We ask for equal education, equal opportunity, equal wages, equal rights to possess property, or to be our own masters – in two words: equal citizenship.... Give us the same chances as yourselves, and we will prove ourselves to be just as good, if not better, Australians, than you! Keep your charity! We only want justice. (Patten and Ferguson 1938; Horner 1974)

Aboriginal leaders of that era, as have others down through the years, have in fact consistently insisted upon equality without compromising cultural identity and values. The call by Aboriginal people for equal access to the full range of benefits and rights that are available to non-Aboriginal citizens seemingly as their birth right, did not then, nor does it now, means that Aboriginal people aspire to and want to be the same as non-Aboriginal peoples.

The principle that has characterized the struggle for social and political justice for Aboriginal peoples is sovereignty, defined for the purposes of this chapter as: *the social and political rights, freedoms, and resources to make decisions for sociopolitical change and development within the context of cultural survival and celebration.*

Failed Schooling and Aboriginal Incarceration

The Royal Commission into Aboriginal Deaths in Custody conducted between 1987 and 1991 is undoubtedly the most comprehensive study of the various sociopolitical aspects that accompanied colonization, and their impact on Aboriginal life in Australia. Poor levels of education were identified as an underlying factor in the examination of Aboriginal deaths in custody with Commissioner Elliot Johnston QC, in his introduction to Chap. 16 of Vol. 2 of the National Report in highlighting the connection between poor education experiences and incarceration levels of Aboriginal people observed:

> The failure of schooling to provide a meaningful and useful experience for many Aboriginal people interacts with, and is a reflection of, their failure to achieve desired levels of participation in Australian society generally, and to command a level of services in respect of education, health and social justice which is commensurate with the rest of the Australian population. In many of the cases investigated, in hearings conducted into underlying issues, and in numerous submissions, this Commission has heard of the inextricable links between the formal education system, child welfare practices, juvenile justice, health and employment opportunity as factors contributing to the disproportionate representation of Aboriginal people in police and custodial facilities. (Patten and Ferguson 1938, Vol. 2)

The fundamentals of literacy and numeracy mastery are absent in the lives of many Aboriginal people, and the compulsory nature of school attendance coupled with irrelevant or meaningless curriculum content and poor teaching methods renders Aboriginal students powerless and unable to cope with the racism, social marginalization, and poverty that they often encounter.

The pages of Australian history are littered with irrefutable evidence graphically illustrating that the overwhelming number of Aboriginal peoples have been consistently failed by non-Aboriginal education systems. The failure of Australian education systems, particularly at the schooling level of education, to provide culturally appropriate and relevant education, alongside acts of genocide, massacres, racism, and other atrocities suffered by Aboriginal peoples, haunts the Australian psyche and will continue do so until the past is acknowledged and appropriate restitution is made. The events of the past have shaped the present, and the current generation of non-Aboriginal Australians, while not directly responsible for the crimes of their ancestors, is nevertheless the beneficiaries of the policies and practices of their forebears, and they therefore have a moral responsibility if nothing else to remedy the impact and legacies of history.

The consistently poor quality of policies and provisions for Aboriginal education described above has produced predictably poor outcomes for Aboriginal students and their communities. Given the lack of Aboriginal people in education leadership positions, this evidences a failure of non-Aboriginal leadership in the Australian education system. Inspired and innovative educational leadership is critical to achieving positive learning outcomes in Aboriginal education. In a handful of well-documented success stories in Aboriginal education, it is clear that schools that are led by experienced and committed principals set the tone of the school and they inspire and motivate teachers. Innovative and inspirational principals usually assemble a team of senior teachers and administrators who know or who are trained to understand the cultural nuances of the community within which the school is based. At a national level, a striking example of Aboriginal educational leadership was the National Aboriginal Education Committee (NAEC), whose series of over 15 reports and policy documents from 1977 to 1989 laid the foundations for almost every successful initiative in Aboriginal education, from early childhood to tertiary level (Holt 2016).

Disengaged Curricula

Eurocentric education with its irrelevant and meaningless curricula fails to engage Aboriginal students, leading to low self-esteem and poor learning outcomes. The seminal work of the Royal Commission into Aboriginal Deaths in Custody observed:

> For many Aboriginal children, school provides their first significant contact with white society unprotected by their own kin and a known set of social relations. In such circumstances, children can be extremely vulnerable; their sense of themselves as individuals, and as members of a social group, can be easily challenged and undermined. The cases investigated by the Royal Commission suggest that there are at least two possible outcomes to this situation: a sense of powerlessness and inferiority leading to an undermining of self-esteem; or resistance, opposition and alienation from the formal processes of schooling. (Australia, Royal Commission into Aboriginal Deaths in Custody 1991)

Absent from the education process for Aboriginal students is the principle of Dadirri referred to above. This practice of inner deep awareness is the basis for establishing connection with and readiness to incorporate new knowledge. This essential prerequisite for human learning is recognized to some extent in modern cognitive psychology's focus on the importance of past experiences and prior knowledge in making sense of new situations or present experiences, but the "empty vessels" model is still powerfully present in non-Aboriginal education

(Rodriguez 2012). A truly Aboriginal centered learning environment would incorporate Dadirri and other Aboriginal teaching and learning practices in developing a truly appropriate and authentically Aboriginal approach to curriculum and pedagogy (Two highly informative Aboriginal educators' accounts of such practices are: Yunkaporta (2009) and Marika-Munungiritj (1991)).

Teaching as Cultural Production

Government policy approaches to Aboriginal issues, including those relating to education, are often developed in the absence of direct Aboriginal advice and input. One of the consequences of this absence is the tendency for government policies to assume homogeneity of Aboriginal peoples and cultures: an artifact of ethnocentrism that flies in the face of Indigenous multicultural reality. To counter this, education systems must adopt a more local and culturally contextual approach to policy and programming development. In 2012, the NSW Government and its Department of Education announced, with great fanfare, the introduction of the Connected Communities Strategy. Sixty million dollars was allocated to support the program, and 15 schools in NSW with significant Aboriginal student enrolments were identified as participants in the program (NSW Department of Education and Communities 2012). The Centre for Education Statistics and Evaluation (CESE) released its interim report in February 2016 of the Connected Communities Strategy. Even though some progress has been reported in some of the 15 schools, the report clearly shows that very little of any great substance has changed in terms of improving education experiences and outcomes for Aboriginal students in the majority of schools (NSW Government, Centre for Education Statistics and Evaluation 2016).

According to the report, NAPLAN results in the Connected Communities schools remain poor; attendance of students, particularly at high school levels, was problematic; and school/community reference groups were ineffective (NSW Government, Centre for Education Statistics and Evaluation (2016), p. 61 ff. NAPLAN is Australia's controversial National Assessment Program – Literacy and Numeracy, a series of literacy and numeracy tests conducted annually across Australia for all students in Years 3, 5, 7 and 9, and used to create "league tables" of schools, http://www.nap.edu.au/home). The report points to marginal improvements at the primary level of schooling, but little meaningful traction at the secondary level. Research further shows that Aboriginal students tend to disengage from learning and reject their school experience around age 10, or after 5 years of schooling (NSW Aboriginal Education Consultative Group (AECG) and NSW Department of Education and Training (DET) 2004; Bodkin-Andrews et al. 2010). The literacy and numeracy foundations that are laid in early and primary school education are critical to student progression and achievement (As pointed out back in 1989 in the National Aboriginal Education Council's groundbreaking *National Policy Guidelines for Early Childhood Education*. Canberra: Australian Government Publishing Service). Mastery of these critical life enablers demonstrably shapes and influences the life journey of Aboriginal peoples. Schools will continue to struggle to engage effectively with Aboriginal students and the community from which they are drawn, when engagement starts and stops at the front gate of the school, and also while ever Aboriginal students and their communities are viewed and treated as "guests" in an alien and culturally unresponsive learning environment. Shifting and moving beyond this Guest Paradigm must be one of the key objectives of any program, including the NSW Connected Communities program, if it is to generate successful outcomes (For a more successful example, see Malin and Maidment 2003). Governments, of all political persuasions, and their education systems must accept that they have not been able to close the education gap between Aboriginal students and their non-Aboriginal peers. Failure has been the defining characteristic of their attempts, and Aboriginal students and their families are entitled to and deserve better.

Teachers, while often well meaning and committed to the education of the students in their classrooms, are poorly trained by teacher education institutions to teach in Aboriginal contexts and therefore they often teach the curriculum rather than the student. Simply teaching to the curriculum allows teachers to become detached from the lives of their students, particularly Aboriginal students who place so much emphasis on body language and nonverbal communication begin to believe that the teacher is not interested in or concerned about the lives of the students (Sarra 2011). The introduction of high-stakes mass testing compounds this situation, as the financial and reputational risks to schools promote teaching to the test, even above teaching the curriculum, let alone the students (Ford 2013). Most non-Aboriginal teachers who are assigned to schools with significant or large Aboriginal student enrolments are ill prepared for the cultural shock that they encounter in communities of which they have very little understanding (Michie 2011); so they simply teach what they are told to teach, waiting for the first opportunity to transfer to the next school they are assigned to.

Invariably when young teachers and inexperienced principals are assigned to schools with significant Aboriginal enrolments, they "bunker down" and are rarely visible in the local community. They tend to keep to themselves, generating an "enclave mentality," perhaps with the view that "if we stick together then we can survive this ordeal." When teachers move beyond the enclave mentality, they soon develop meaningful relationships with the local community. This in turn signals to the students that the teacher is genuinely interested in them and wants to help students achieve their potential (Michie 2011).

One of the great ironies of failed schooling for Aboriginal students is that many of the students who have been failed by schooling systems find their way into higher education studies, often achieving scholarly excellence leading, in some cases, to distinguished careers in their chosen field of expertise. The success of Aboriginal students at higher and other post-schooling levels of education clearly demonstrates that there is nothing inherently wrong with the capacity of Aboriginal people to deal with the academic depth and rigor that is so valued in the western intellectual domain (Behrendt et al. 2012). Anecdotal data suggest that the post-schooling education experience for Aboriginal people is more amenable to concepts of "cultural diversity and contextual learning," and therefore post-schooling institutions are better able to provide knowledge and skills that enhance the cultural identity and heritage of Aboriginal students rather than diminish it.

Decolonization Imperatives, Justice, and Self-Determining Education

Most Australian schools are Eurocentric in their orientation and focus, including those schools with significant Aboriginal student enrolments. The assimilation imperatives that defined the early colonial attempts to "educate" Aboriginal students still operate beneath superficially modern education policies and practices. The assumption is still that the colonizer society has the power to define non-Aboriginal values and behaviors as inherently desirable, without any need or right of choice, decision-making, or self-determination by Aboriginal people themselves.

Unquestionably, one of the pivotal factors underscoring the failure of non-Aboriginal education systems to meet and accommodate the educational needs and aspirations of the great majority of Aboriginal students is the assimilationist model embedded, both implicitly and explicitly, in successive government policy and programming approaches to Aboriginal education (Hickling-Hudson and Ahlquist 2003).

Whenever Aboriginal people have advocated educational equity, non-Aboriginal people, who are largely responsible for government policy development and implementation, have interpreted this call for equity a call for "sameness." The response has usually been the development and introduction of policies that are designed to facilitate access, a flawed strategic approach that merely opens doors wider to institutions and systems that have historically failed, frustrated, and marginalized Aboriginal peoples. The access model incorporates a "*guest relationship*" wherein non-Aboriginal people create and administer the terms and conditions that regulate Aboriginal involvement and participation in education systems.

What is commonly referred to, as Aboriginal education, is simply a set of access strategies that are designed to facilitate Aboriginal participation in non-Aboriginal systems of education, to equip them for participation in non-Aboriginal economic systems and ways of life. Issues of cultural affirmation, strategies to mitigate racism and social marginalization, as well as the need for social and restorative justice are rarely incorporated into public or private Aboriginal education policies. The limitations of the "access model" are especially evident at the schooling level of education (Lewthwaite et al. 2015).

Increasing access to resources may be desirable, but it implies a passive, consumer role rather than a position of agency and voice. Access does not necessarily lead to empowerment, the "power to make decisions about the future from a position of knowledge, optimism and strength, confident about one's rights, relationships and place in the scheme of things" (Gordon 2015). Moreover, access and empowerment, like inclusion, are conceptualized as beneficial things to be granted, or withheld, by those who hold power over those who do not. Only a model of sovereignty, defined above as "the social and political freedoms and resources to make decisions for socio-political change and development within the context of cultural survival and celebration," can provide a fully adequate basis for success in Aboriginal education.

When the key defining elements (there are others) of the "Guest Paradigm" are effectively addressed in a positive way, the potential for positive learning experiences and outcomes for Aboriginal students are greatly enhanced, enabling Aboriginal students to move beyond the guest paradigm (See also Ockenden 2014). All students, irrespective of race, culture, gender, or faith, are entitled to expect that they will participate in schooling that affirms their identity and equips them with skills and knowledge needed to find their place in modern society. Sadly, schools are failing far too many young Aboriginal people, and tragically, many of these failed young people end up as statistics in juvenile justice centers, and there is no doubt that poor schooling is also a contributing factor to the alarming rate of Aboriginal youth suicide (In comparison with deaths in custody, Australia has been slow to collect data on causes of youth suicide; it would be desirable to see studies here like the Canadian work of Hallet et al. 2007. In Western Australia, where the number of suicide deaths in the Kimberley region alone in 2012 exceeded the Australian Defence Force fatalities in Afghanistan, the WA Mental Health Commission names "poor education outcomes" among the top ten key issues for Aboriginal mental health, and associated suicide rates, http://www.mentalhealth.wa.gov.au/mental_illness_and_health/mh_aboriginal.aspx).

Dreaming a Better Future

This chapter is not about the past. It is about today and the future and argues the need for decisive action if Aboriginal Australia is to move beyond the mere survival that characterizes the contemporary journey of our nations. Aboriginal nations and their leaders must engage in a transformative process to reconceptualize and create a space that is truly liberating, a place where once again Aboriginal nations will be truly self-determining. The transformative process that is advocated is essentially an educative process; all struggles for freedom and human rights are as much evolutionary as they are revolutionary, in that new knowledge and experiences awakens the desire for change, and this awakening creates the need to challenge and reject the Eurocentric teachings of colonialist systems and their assimilationist objectives.

This is not to suggest that elements of the "other" systems have no value: they do, but this argument is more fundamentally concerned with the need for grounded cultural knowledge and affirmation, the need for a culturally focused primacy of place and purpose (See also McCarty and Bia 2002). Aboriginal culture and identity is a complex framework of component parts, the core of which is country (not geography, but a living, relational ecology of place) and the symbiotic kinship structures and relationships that define our identity. Cultural knowledge, traditional values, language, and the interrelatedness of all living things are embedded in the cultural grouping to which we belong (Across the diversity of Indigenous Australia, there is remarkable consensus about the nature of Indigenous culture. Among many similar definitions is this, from Andrews et al. (2006): "... accumulated knowledge which encompasses spiritual relationships, relationships with the natural environment and the sustainable use of natural resources, and relationships between people, which are reflected in language, narratives, social organisation, values, beliefs, and cultural laws and customs..."). Culture, including language which is a transmitter of culture, is a learned behavior, it is not innate or something that we are born with, but rather something into which we are born and over time and teaching we become acculturated. Culture involves knowing whom we are connected to, our country and language and traditions that have sustained Aboriginal peoples in Australia since the beginning of time.

The transformation that must occur requires attention at a variety of important and interrelated levels. The first and most critical level of transformation is at the individual level. Individual Aboriginal people must seek to understand and embrace the core elements of our identity, what makes us different from other cultural groups and what makes us who we are as a people. Schools have a critical role in ensuring that Aboriginal students are affirmed culturally while also providing enhanced academic development opportunities (Hollins 2015). However, for this new knowledge and skills base to be effective, the Eurocentric methods and ways of "knowing and doing" must be rejected and cast aside, or critically evaluated from a position of sovereign choice, to select what is of value and discard what is not. New models of education leadership and advocacy will need to be developed: leadership and advocacy models that are grounded in Aboriginal philosophy and that are firmly and inextricably linked to community, country, and culture.

In the interest of balance, it is only fair to acknowledge that some improvements have been achieved in terms of the participation and retention rates of Aboriginal students in school-based education. However, the fact remains that most Aboriginal students experience failure, setting them up for a range of denials and abuses throughout their lives.

Hope and Inspiration and Transformational Pathways to Success

There are, of course, great examples of creative and innovative models to inspire Aboriginal education leadership; I have had the great privilege to visit with one and to work as a critical friend with another. The first is Dr. Ann Milne, Principal of the Kia Aroha College in Auckland, NZ, and the other is Mr. Brian Debus, now retired, who was the Principal of Menindee Central School in remote NSW during my involvement with the school as a critical friend.

Dr. Milne has been the inspirational leader of Kia Aroha College for many years and has recently announced her retirement. I visited the college in 2011 and I was struck by the creative and innovative approach to learning that permeated the college (Milne 2011). Lasting memories from the visit are of being welcomed by the students in their language and of being taken on a tour of the college where students celebrated their language and culture and embraced the rigor of learning across a number of subjects. One memorable observation was a class that was learning strategies to deal with racism that the students would inevitably encounter in modern New Zealand society. The Menindee experience is somewhat different from that of Kia Aroha College, but inspirational parallels can be drawn between the two schools. Menindee is a work in progress, and during Brian Debus's term it was slowly starting to turn the negative aspects of the school around (McCausland and Vivian 2010). Brian Debus was the first and only white principal that I have known who hosted Aboriginal people into his home for regular social events. Education leaders such as Dr. Milne and Mr. Debus, though non-Aboriginal, are education warriors who inspire and challenge the teachers who they lead to embrace change and to transform the learning experiences of students in their charge. Both Dr. Milne and Mr. Debus epitomize what can be done by working with parents and community to create a positive learning environment for their students.

In the midst of the systemic failure of Aboriginal education described above, there is hope and inspiration. This hope and inspiration can be found in the actions of non-Aboriginal people who are also disenchanted and frustrated with conventional methods of education. Many families, including some Aboriginal families, have opted for home schooling as a means to educate their children. Others have opted to radically transform the way that education is designed and implemented. One such initiative involves the work of Templestowe College, operating within the public education system of Victoria. Many of the principles and education philosophies of Templestowe College resonate because they resemble and are aligned to many of those espoused by Aboriginal people over many years. Addressing the question of what makes Templestowe College different from conventional schools, the College says:

> Well a lot of things actually. Most schools expect the students to fit in with the school, rather than the school trying to adapt to best meet the needs of the individual student. We think very carefully about the direction the school is heading. We want to be leaders and innovators, not followers and we want to inspire these qualities in our students. We believe that the education programs that we are now putting in place will be replicated in many schools in 5 to 10 years' time, simply because the existing model of education does not work for so many students. (The College's educational approach was outlined in Hutton (2014) and on the College website, http://www.templestowec.vic.edu.au/default.aspx)

The college offers a number of innovative and creative learning options for their students, including more than 100 elective subject options; students can make up their own subject; students can "radically accelerate" their learning program, attempting VCE subjects from Year 8; most students complete VCE over 3 or more years; students may take more than 6 years to complete their secondary studies; there are no compulsory subjects after completion of foundation literacy, numeracy, and science; each student has an individual learning plan (ILP); and students complete home learning not homework. The college uses technology extensively to assist students with their learning, and each lesson has its own clear "learning intention" and "reason for learning." The students are provided with teacher feedback on their learning progress every 3 weeks, and students enrolled with the college contribute to the design of the college's curriculum.

Obviously the advent of Templestowe College, and perhaps other similar innovations such as the reported growth in home schooling (Up from 2802 in 2011–12 to 3343 in 2014–15 in NSW. Board of Studies, Teaching and Educational Standards NSW, *Annual Report 2014–15*. Sydney: BOSTES, p. 87, https://www.boardofstudies.nsw.edu.au/about/pdf_doc/bostes-annual-report-2014-15.pdf), demonstrates a level of broader frustration with current Australian education systems for non-Aboriginal students. So there should be no surprise, and even less refuting, the claim that non-Aboriginal education systems continue to fail Aboriginal students by not providing positive and affirming learning experiences.

Conclusion and Future Directions

As argued, sadly schools are failing far too many young Aboriginal people; tragically, many of these failed young people end up as statistics in juvenile justice institutions and undoubtedly poor schooling also contributes to the alarming and unacceptable rate of Aboriginal youth suicide. The challenge in these ever-changing and demanding times is to develop an educative process to engage Aboriginal youth in positive learning experiences and outcomes by utilizing policies and processes that ground them culturally while also allowing them to develop the skills and knowledge for them to enjoy the fullness of life. Every Aboriginal generation will create and live its own journey in its own way. But heritage, a sense of cultural connectedness and purpose, is critical to the enjoyment of a full, culturally affirming and meaningful life journey.

The current model of political advocacy means that Aboriginal people and our communities are rarely in a position to celebrate what it means to be Aboriginal, and results in fatigue, demotivation, and what noted Maori educator Professor Graham Hingangaroa Smith calls "the politics of distraction" (Smith 2009; Regrettably, a number of other recent publications fail to acknowledge Professor Smith, who has been using this term for well over a decade). This politics of distraction cripples our ability to more effectively plan for future generations; the fundamental experience of Aboriginal peoples is limited to survival, not celebration. No genuine and sustainable change is possible until such time as the minds and hearts of Indigenous Australians are freed from this spiritually and culturally debilitating reality.

Colonialism; dispossession; social and political marginalization; the destruction and contamination of cultural values and traditions, including those embedded in Aboriginal education sui generis; the denial of basic human rights and freedoms; and innumerable other abuses have all contributed to the current positioning of Aboriginal peoples in contemporary Australian society. Such positioning generates "war zone" conditions and spawns the social and cultural destruction that many Aboriginal communities are struggling daily to survive. These "war zone" conditions are manifest in far too many Aboriginal communities and are the consequence of weapons of destruction that are more psychological than physical (The phrase "war zone" ironically distracts from the recognition that the colonisers did actually wage a prolonged war of both physical and cultural invasion: a war that arguably continues in the repeated media uses of this phrase to stigmatise Aboriginal communities and sensationalise the consequences of dispossession. One of many such examples is Madigan (2016)). Government public policy and societal attitudes, not to mention the role of the churches, have all contributed, over time, to the creation of these crippling "war zone" conditions. There can be no retreat from this reality.

There is no question that colonialism, across the extent of Indigenous experiences throughout the world, has critically damaged, but has never destroyed, Indigenous peoples and cultures. Assimilationist and Eurocentric education has and continues to be one of the tools that has severely contaminated Indigenous cultures and has served to relegate Indigenous peoples to the margins of modern society. In Australia, white political leaders, and many in mainstream Australia, seem to suffer a form of "collective cognitive dissonance" when it comes to the question of acknowledging the invasion and the murderous brutality that characterized Aboriginal and non-Aboriginal contact. Equally of concern is how some modern Aboriginal politicians seem to have succumbed to the seductive nature of neoliberalism and the politics of distraction defense.

Any system of education that seeks to accommodate and respond to the learning needs and aspirations of Aboriginal students must be structured to allow the opportunity for them to achieve academically while also being proud and grounded in their Aboriginal identity and culture. Increasingly, Indigenous peoples in Australia, New Zealand, Canada, the USA, and other Indigenous contexts are rejecting the assimilation imperatives of Eurocentric education. Culturally informed and responsive systems of education are emerging, systems that provide opportunities for Indigenous peoples to be educated to both compete and survive in modern society while at the same time embracing and celebrating our cultures and identities.

Successive generations of Aboriginal warriors have been entrusted with the responsibility of never allowing the embers from earlier battles to be extinguished and the legacy of resistance and the uncompromised veracity of unceded sovereignty must be the basis upon which a honorable and principled struggle for our rights and freedoms, including those that shape the nature and scope of education, must be based. The virulent and contaminating forces of colonialism are ubiquitous and with modern society's enchantment with materialism and greed Aboriginal people must be more vigilant than ever. We owe it to those who have gone before and it is our legacy to those who follow.

Aboriginal education must serve to enhance Aboriginal identity and culture and provide students with the skills and knowledge to celebrate life in modern society. It must also honor the past in order to capture the future. Nothing more – nothing less.

References

Andrews G, Daylight C, Hunt J (2006) Aboriginal cultural heritage landscape mapping of coastal NSW. Department of Natural Resources, Parramatta

Australia, Royal Commission into Aboriginal Deaths in Custody (1991) Royal Commission into Aboriginal Deaths in Custody national report: volume 2 (Commissioner Elliott Johnson).

Australian Government Publishing Service. AustLII Indigenous Law Resources, Canberra. http://www.austlii.edu.au/au/other/IndigLRes/rciadic/index.html

Behrendt L, Larkin S, Griew R, Kelly P (2012) Review of higher education access and outcomes for aboriginal and Torres Strait Islander people: final report. Department of Industry, Innovation, Science, Research and Tertiary Education, Canberra. https://opus.lib.uts.edu.au/bitstream/10453/31122/1/2013003561OK.pdf

Bigge JT (1822) Report of the commissioner of inquiry into the state of the Colony of New South Wales. House of Commons. State Library of New South Wales, London. http://library.sl.nsw.gov.au/record=b2178938~S2

Bodkin-Andrews GH, Dillon A, Craven RG (2010) Bangawarra'gumada – strengthening the spirit: causal modelling of academic self-concept and patterns of disengagement for indigenous and non-indigenous Australian students. Aust J Indig Educ 39(1):24–39

Bridges BJ (1968) Aboriginal education in eastern Australia (N.S.W.) Aust J Educ 12(3):225–243

Fforde C, Bamblett L, Lovett R, Gorringe S, Fogarty L (2013) Discourse, deficit and identity: aboriginality, the race paradigm and the language of representation in contemporary Australia. Media Int Aust 149:162–173

Fletcher J (1989) Clean, clad and courteous: a history of aboriginal education in New South Wales. JJ Fletcher, Sydney

Ford M (2013) Achievement gaps in Australia: what NAPLAN reveals about education inequality in Australia. Race Ethn Educ 16(1):80–102

Gordon M (2015) The long, hard road to empowering indigenous Australia. Sydney Morning Herald, 28 Mar 2015. http://www.smh.com.au/national/the-long-hard-road-to-empowering-indigenous-australia-20150326-1m8umm.html

Hallet D, Chandler M, Lalonde C (2007) Aboriginal language knowledge and youth suicide. Cogn Dev 22:392–399

Hickling-Hudson A, Ahlquist R (2003) Contesting the curriculum in the schooling of indigenous children in Australia and the USA: from eurocentrism to culturally powerful pedagogies. Comp Educ Rev 47(1):64–89

Hollins ER (2015) Culture in school learning: revealing the deep meaning, 3rd edn. Routledge, New York

Holt L (2016) The development of aboriginal education policy in Australia: voices of the National Aboriginal Education Committee (NAEC). PhD thesis, University of Newcastle

Horner J (1974) Vote Ferguson for aboriginal freedom. Australian and New Zealand Book Co., Sydney

Hutton P (2014) What if students controlled their own learning? TEDx talk, Melbourne, 20 Nov 2014

Lewthwaite B et al (2015) Seeking a pedagogy of difference: what aboriginal students and their parents in North Queensland say about teaching and their learning. Aust J Teach Educ 40(5):132–159

Madigan M (2016) Aurukun: children caught in middle of war zone. The Courier-Mail, 28 May 2016. http://www.couriermail.com.au/news/queensland/aurukun-children-caught-in-middle-of-war-zone/news-story/41996b8483fe711568a71dee5ebadb51

Malin M, Maidment D (2003) Education, indigenous survival and well-being: emerging ideas and programs. Aust J Indig Educ 32:85–100

Marika-Munungiritj R (1991) Some notes on principles for aboriginal pedagogy. Ngoonjook: A J Aust Indig Issues 6:33–34

McCarty TL, Bia F (2002) A place to be Navajo: rough rock and the struggle for self-determination in indigenous schooling. Lawrence Erlbaum, Mahwah

McCausland R, Vivian A (2010) Why do some aboriginal communities have lower crime rates than others? A pilot study. Aust N Z J Criminol 43(2):301–332

Michie M (2011) Identity learning, culture shock and border crossing into effective teaching in indigenous science education. Paper presented at the 42nd annual conference of the Australasian science education research association, Adelaide SA, 29 June–2 July, 2011

Milne A (2011) Colouring in the white spaces: cultural identity and learning in school. Research report. Clover Park Middle School and Te Whānau o Tupuranga, Otara, Manukau

Morgan B (1993) Toward a redefinition of aboriginal education. Opening address at the 1993 world indigenous peoples conference on education (WIPCE), Wollongong

NSW Aboriginal Education Consultative Group (AECG) and NSW Department of Education and Training (DET) (2004) Report of the review of aboriginal education, freeing the spirit: dreaming and equal future. DET, Sydney. https://www.det.nsw.edu.au/media/downloads/reviews/aboriginaledu/report/aer2003_04.pdf

NSW Department of Education and Communities (2012) Connected communities strategy. Department of Education and Communities, Sydney. https://www.det.nsw.edu.au/media/downloads/about-us/news-at-det/announcements/yr2012/connected-communities-strategy.pdf

NSW Government, Centre for Education Statistics and Evaluation (2016) Connected communities strategy: interim evaluation report. CESE, Sydney. https://www.cese.nsw.gov.au/publications-filter/connected-communities-strategy-interim-evaluation-report

Ockenden L (2014) Positive learning environments for indigenous children and young people. Resource sheet no. 33, produced by the Closing the Gap Clearinghouse. Australian Institute of Health and Welfare, Australian Institute of Family Studies, Canberra

Parbury N (1999) Survival: a history of aboriginal life in New South Wales. Ministry of Aboriginal Affairs, Sydney. p 72

Patten J, Ferguson W (1938) Aborigines claim citizen rights! A statement of the case for the aborigines progressive association. Pamphlet. Publicist. National Library of Australia, Sydney. http://nla.gov.au/nla.obj-241787110

Rodriguez V (2012) The teaching brain and the end of the empty vessel. Mind Brain Educ 6(4):177–185

Sarra C (2011) Transforming indigenous education, chapter 7. In: Purdie N, Milgate G, Bell HR (eds) Two way teaching and learning: toward culturally reflective and relevant education. ACER Press, Melbourne

Smith GH (2009) Transforming leadership: a discussion paper, presentation to the 2009 SFU Summer Summer Institute. Simon Fraser University, Vancouver, p 9. https://www2.viu.ca/integratedplanning/documents/DrGrahamSmith.pdf

Ungunmerr Bauman MR (2002) Dadirri: inner deep listening and quiet still awareness. Emmaus productions. Retrieved from http://nextwave.org.au/wp-content/uploads/Dadirri-Inner-Deep-Listening-M-R-Ungunmerr-Bauman-Refl.pdf

Willmot E (1987) Pemulwuy: the rainbow warrior. Weldons, Sydney. Published as an ebook in 2013 as Pemulwuy: the battle for Sydney. Matilda Media

Yunkaporta T (2009) Aboriginal pedagogies at the cultural interface. Professional doctorate (research) thesis, James Cook University

Liberate the Base: Thoughts Toward an African Language Policy

9

Ngũgĩ wa Thiong'o

Abstract

In this chapter Ngũgĩ raises debates and practices evident in many colonized societies which are at the heart of postcolonial theories, that of Indigenous languages, and the knowledges they hold. Ngũgĩ argues there are four perceived barriers to the establishment of an African language policy that form an orthodoxy difficult to shift. However, drawing on the work of language "border communities" and the work of the *Jalada* project, he shows how an African language policy can be developed that reflects current practices that empowers Africa and its peoples and protects its knowledge base.

Keywords

African languages · Language policy · Translation · Multilingualism · *Jalada* project

Recently I published a collection of essays with Seagull Press, under the title, *Secure the Base: Making Africa Visible in the World.* When two armies fight, they protect their own base, while they try to destabilize and even capture their opponent's. Both sides gather intelligence about the other's base through covert and overt means. But suppose the spies sent to the other side are held captives or willingly enjoy the reception, so that instead of sending back what they know, they give away the information about their own base? One side is said to lose a battle when their base

---

This paper is an edited version of that which was presented as the Neville Alexander Memorial Lecture, Harvard, at the Harvard Centre for African Studies, on April 19, 2016

N. w. Thiong'o (✉)
University of California, Irvine, CA, USA
e-mail: ngugi@uci.edu

© Springer Nature Singapore Pte Ltd. 2019
E. A. McKinley, L. T. Smith (eds.), *Handbook of Indigenous Education*,
https://doi.org/10.1007/978-981-10-3899-0_61

is overrun by the enemy forces. If the defeated want to fight back, they try and secure their base. The security of one's base, even when two armies are cooperating to achieve a jointly held tactical or strategic end against a third, is necessary. So either in opposition or in cooperation, fighting units keep their bases secure, and not in disarray.

In the history of conquest, the first thing the victorious conqueror does is to attack people's names and languages. The idea was to deny them the authority of naming self and the world, to delegitimize the history and the knowledge they already possessed, and to delegitimize their own language as a credible source of knowledge and definition of the world, so that the conquestor's language can become the source of the very definition of being. This was with the English conquest of Ireland, Wales, Scotland, or the Japanese conquest of South Korea; Europe's conquest of the Māori and other natives of New Zealand; or the natives of Australia; of South and Northern Native America; or the USA's takeover of Hawaii; or the Norwegian, Swedish and Finnish domination of Saami people; to ban or weaken the languages of the conquered, and then impose by gun, guise or guile, their own language and accord it all the authority of naming the world. It was also done with the enslaved. African languages and names were banned in the plantations and later in the continent as a whole, so much so that African people now accept Europhonity to define their countries and who they are: Francophone, Anglophone, or Lusophone.

I invite you to keep in mind the image of the base and the relationships between bases – hostile or hospitable – as I offer some notes toward an African language policy and the role of inter-African language translation in that process.

Some of course may want to argue that African countries have many languages, hundreds even? But hundreds of languages also mean there are hundreds of communities that use them, and these communities constitute the geographic nation! This linguistic picture confronts policymakers as a nightmare; and they think that if they can ignore the nightmare long enough or frighten it away with more emphasis on European languages, the nightmare will vanish and they will wake up to the bliss of a harmonious European language-speaking African nation. So they engineer a massive transfer of resources from African to European languages. Ninety percent of the resources earmarked for language education goes to European ones and a minuscule percent to African languages, if at all. But reality, however, is stubborn, and they wake up to the same nightmare. European language speakers in any one of the African nations are at most 10% of the population only; the other 90% are African language speakers.

Ironically, in some countries, the colonial period had a more progressive language policy, which ensured basic literacy in mother tongue. That was how I came to learn Gĩkũyũ. But at Independence, the 4 years' elementary education in mother tongue was scrapped. Through and by every means possible, children were immersed in English from kindergarten onward. This resulted in a generation of Kenyans who could barely speak mother tongue, or who could speak it but could not read or write it. Belatedly the state tried to rectify the damage and introduced mother tongue as subject and even produced some texts to meet the need, but these half-hearted efforts were later abandoned. In most schools, the hour earmarked for mother tongue is used for further drilling in English. What began in the colonial era, the delegitimization of African languages as credible sources and basis of knowledge was completed and normalized in the postcolonial era.

Where English was now equated with the gateway to progress and modernity, African languages came to be seen as barriers to this glittering thing called progress and modernity. In Kenya, whenever and wherever a speaker's mother tongue made the speaker not able to pronounce certain English sounds, he was denounced as "shrubbing" English. He had brought bush and darkness to obscure the light and clarity of English. In an article he recently published in the *Jalada* of 15th September 2015 under the title "Writing in African Languages: A question for our times," Mũkoma wa Ngũgĩ tells hilarious stories of African students in Kenya laughing outright at one another for "shrubbing" English.

Clearly this view of African languages as synonymous with the darkness of the bush becomes a big barrier to imagining and therefore crafting a practical language policy. Another barrier is the fundamentalism of monolingualism. A nation is not really a nation without a common language to go with the commonality of territory, economy, and culture. In this context, African languages, because of their huge numbers, are seen as anti-nationhood. Monolingualism is seen as the centripetal answer to the centrifugal anarchy of multiplicity of languages. European languages are seen as coming to the rescue of a cohesive Africa, otherwise threatened by its own languages. It is in the same vein as what colonial military expeditions touted as the pacification of primitive tribes; only now, in the postcolonial era, it is the linguistic pacification of languages of anarchy and blood. The difference is that now it is the African governments and policymakers who are at the head of the linguistic pacification programs. In the colonial era, the slogan behind the pacification was ending tribal wars – Hobbes's war of all against all in a state of nature; now in the postcolonial era, it is ending ethnic wars fueled by African languages. The subtext is that African languages are inherently incapable of relating to each other, but ironically they each can relate to English, especially when Anglophone writing dives into them for a proverb or two to spice their literary offering to a europhone modernity of monolingualism.

In reality, there are very few, if any, monolingual nations in the world. What most have is an officially imposed language as the national language: the language of power. The language of power is a dictatorship of the monolingual on a plurality of languages, and it negates the human right to one's language.

For Africa, and generally the postcolonial state, this dictatorship was first imposed by imperial powers, who put their language at the center of the universe, the source of light. The postcolonial state merely nationalized the already linguistic dictatorship, which in effect means foreign languages assuming the mantle of the identity of the national. In reality, it is simply the borrowed language of the 10% but spreads across the nation. This acquired national language has the double character of being both foreign and elitist. And yet this is what is touted as its advantage: that it is equally accessible to the 10% of each linguistic community and equally inaccessible to all the constituent communities. So its accessibility to the elite, but its inaccessibility to the majority, is therefore what makes it the best language to unify the country. The European language-speaking elite thus sees itself as constituting the nation. European languages become the knight on a horse rescuing the postcolonial state, otherwise trapped within the linguistic House of Babel, by enabling communication across a problematic plurality.

The third barrier arises from fears of being left out of the heaven promised by globalization. This arises from the earlier colonially rooted notion that African languages are not modern enough and that European ones are the only ladders to global heaven. If Africa promotes its languages, the continent will miss the train to heaven. But globalization is a function of finance capital, its dominance in the world, and a logical development of historical capitalism from its mercantile phase, through its industrial, to its present phase where, as finance capital, and aided by technology, it smashes all state barriers to its movement. There must not be any barriers to movement of capital across state borders, but there have to be barriers, even actual physical walls, to prevent the movement of labor across state barriers in pursuit of what that finance capital has stolen from their regions. The result, as I have stated elsewhere in my book *Secure the Base* (Ngũgĩ 2016), are states too weak to interfere with the operation of finance capital but strong enough to police the population, should they dare to do something about it and its negative impact on their lives. For example, in the postcolonial state, police and the military have been used many more times against the population than against any external threat from elsewhere. The joint military exercises, which the Western powers have with the militaries of the postcolonial state, have never been for purposes of a jointly perceived threat from a third country; otherwise, they would also be having joint military exercises on the soil of France, Britain, and America.

But, for some reason, globalization – despite the control of resources by corporate capital from the West – is seen as a good thing, and African languages seem to stand in the way of the elite receiving their share of "global goodies." In my recent book, *Secure the Base* (Ngũgĩ 2016), I have tried to make the distinction between globalism and globalization. Globalization is really "gobblization" of other people's resources by a greedy corporate elite protected by the might of imperial powers. Globalism is a form of social networking of peoples across race, regions, and religions, and it tries to mobilize people against corporate greed and its divisive tactics of divide and conquer.

The fourth barrier to a comprehensive and all-embracing national policy is the conception of the relationship of languages in terms of hierarchy, with the officially sanctioned language, sitting at the top, as the language of power, law, justice, education, administration, and economic exchange. If that language is the former colonial language and they want to replace it, they can only think of choosing one African language among the many to occupy the same position in the hierarchy. The prospect of "the one" becoming the new language of power rings alarm bells in the speakers of other languages.

Hierarchy is not inherent in plurality. The plural can relate either vertically as in steps of a ladder – a hierarchical relation – or horizontally as when people link arms to form a line or a circle, a network. Both are relational, but the hierarchical one means the energy of the higher suffocating the lower, while the network means shared synergy from the contact.

Together, the four barriers form a kind of orthodoxy, with the assumptions behind it normalized as self-evident truth. The orthodoxy becomes an invisible boulder rock that cannot be moved, the very thought of moving it making the mind tired. The prospects of the hopelessness make us not even make a gesture.

Border communities challenge that orthodoxy. These communities that exist on either side of national boundaries speak a variety of languages, but the relationship between the languages is not hierarchical but rather "networkingly." Hierarchy is a question of power. It assumes that some languages are more of a language than other languages, but the notion of a network assumes a give and take, and that there is no language which is more of a language than another language.

Of course border communities do face the challenge of a member of one language group being able to communicate with the member of another. They solve this through multilingualism: most are polyglots. But in addition to that, sometimes there develops a lingua franca among them, but this lingua franca functions differently from the language of power. A language of power assumes that for it to be, other languages must cease to be. It desires to replace or silence all the other languages. But a lingua franca assumes the existence of coequal languages. It simply facilitates communication and dialogue among language equals. The condition of the existence of one is the existence of all. The lingua franca helps facilitate the give and take of a network of languages. It does not replace them. Such a lingua franca is often a distinctive language but known by most other language speakers, in addition to their own.

Translation – a kind of dialogue or conversation among languages – is another challenge to the orthodoxy. The *Jalada* translation project, an instance of that challenge, is unfolding before our very eyes. *Jalada* is an online literary journal run by a Pan African Collective, a group of young people who come from different parts of the continent. *Jalada*'s chief editor, Moses Kilolo, comes from Kenya. *Jalada* itself is an online journal in English, but ironically, what has created the waves is not their English writings but their translation project. In a recent article in the online journal, *Africa is a country*, Mũkoma wa Ngũgi described the effort as a revolution in many tongues. This was very strong praise for their first and, so far, only translation issue. I feel honored that this first translation issue features my own story, *Ituĩka rĩa Mũrũngarũ: Kana Kĩrĩa Gĩtũmaga Andũ Mathiĩ Marũngiĩ*, translatable as The Upright Revolution, or How Humans Began to Walk Upright.

I first wrote the story in Gĩkũyũ for my daughter, Mũmbi, in 2012 as a gift. In my family we have developed a tradition of the gift of stories and poems for birthdays and mother's and father's days, in place of material gifts (or in addition to them). I have found it a much better deal for whereas material gifts perish and are forgotten, the gift of stories, whether published or not, lives on and never loses its luster. Stories are forever. The story, *Ituĩka rĩa Mũrũngarũ*, or How Humans Came to Walk Upright, tells about the competition between the legs and hands to see which pair is more essential to the body. It is a titanic struggle, whose consequences have impacted the course of human history and civilization. It is really a fable. Once delivered as a gift, I put the story aside and forgot all about it until the *Jalada* group, through Mũkoma wa Ngũgĩ, approached me for a contribution to their inaugural translation number. I gave them the only story at hand. The result has been astounding by any measure.

The story was translated into 54 African languages (The story is available in Gĩkũyũ, Amharic, isiNdebele, isiZulu and Xitsonga, Amharic, Dholuo, Kikamba, Lwisukha-Lwidakho, Ikinyarwada, Arabic, Luganda, Kiswahili, Hausa, Meru, Lingala, Igbo, Ibibio, Somali, Nandi, Rukiga, Bamanankan, Lugbarati, Shona, Lubukusu, Kimaragoli, Giriama, Sheng, Ewe, Naija Languej, Marakwet, as well as Afrikaans, English, and French and few others to make 54.), the most translated single story on the continent, according to *The Guardian* that carried the news analysis of the phenomenon. It is indeed rare for the publication of a story to become news, but several newspapers carried reports on the *Jalada* translation feat. Recently a Sunday magazine from Bangalore State in India carried a Kannada or Tamil translation for their three million readers (**From:** Kumar S., the editor in email **Sent:** Tuesday, April 12, 2016: to Moses Kilolo. In the email, thanking the *Jalada* group, he says the story was published on 10th April; *Sunday Magazine* was read by more than 30 lakh people, and it got very good response (NB one lakh is 100 000).) for a story originating in an African language, that in itself is another story. Translations into more languages in and outside Africa continue, and they are hoping to release another issue with the new batch of translations.

Translations as such are not new phenomena in Africa. Of the evening stories that left a mark on me as a child was the one about a father, his son, and their donkey, who, trying to live up to every opinion of neighbors and strangers as to who should carry whom, end up carrying the donkey on their shoulders. Later, when I learnt to read and write, I was very surprised to come across the same story, but with the added pleasure of illustrations. The image of a donkey hanging upside down from a pole supported by the shoulders of the father and son, with the market crowd laughing at their foolishness, still lives within me.

The storyteller in the evening must have oralized the story from its literary source, a process that I have described in my book *Globalectics: Theory and Politics of Knowing*, as the oralization of the literary. It is only last year in Irvine, 70 years after my childhood encounter with it, that I made another discovery, thanks to my YouTube lessons in Spanish. The story was a free translation and adaptation of the Spanish story, *Padre, Hijo, O Caballo* by the medieval Spanish writer, Don Juan Manuel. Only that in the Gĩkũyũ language version, *le Caballo*, the horse, becomes the donkey. Whatever the sequencing, the story, through translation, was now part of my Gĩkũyũ culture.

The Bible in Gĩkũyũ, another part of my culture, was a translation of a series of translations, English, Latin, Greek, Hebrew, and Aramaic all the way back to whatever language that God, Adam, and Eve used in the Garden of Eden. I was very impressed by the fact that Jesus and all the characters in the New and Old Testament spoke Gĩkũyũ! Even God, in the Garden of Eden, spoke Gĩkũyũ!

This inheritance from translation is not unique to Gĩkũyũ or Africa. The Bible in translation similarly had an impact on the growth of many languages in the world. The translation of the Greek and Latin classics into English, French, and German not only aided in the growth of the languages, but the same classics, in their translation, have made an impact on the study and development of drama, poetry, and philosophy in general. It is impossible to imagine Shakespeare without translations. He worked within a culture where translations from other languages into the emerging national tongues were the literary equivalent of piracy for silver and gold on the high seas, a phenomenon I first mentioned in my book on the politics of memory, titled *Something Torn and New: Towards an African Renaissance* (Ngũgĩ 2009).

The *Jalada* translation project then has clearly followed on one of the most consistent threads in world cultures, but similar translation trends in Africa. The East Africa Educational Publishers have brought out Kiswahili translations of most of the classics of African fiction originally written in English, French, and Portuguese. In the article titled "Revolution in Many Tongues," Mũkoma wa Ngũgĩ has detailed other efforts in this direction, citing, for instance, Boubacar Boris Diop of Senegal who has set up a publishing outfit, Ceytu, dedicated to publishing Wolof translations of major classics of African thought, such as Frantz Fanon's *The Wretched of the Earth*. In 2014, SUNY Press bought out a book *Listening to Ourselves: A Multilingual Anthology of African Philosophy*. Brought together and edited by the African-Caribbean-Canadian intellectual Chike Jeffers, this volume carries essays on the different aspects of philosophy but written originally in African languages including Amharic, Dholuo, Gĩkũyũ, Wolof, Yorùbá, and Akan. As far as I know, these essays are among the very first in modern times that have African philosophers philosophizing directly in an African language. The volume does also carry translation into English versions, but it is worth noting this reverses the old order which is translations from the European into the African language.

But the real breakthrough in the *Jalada* project is not just the fact of translation – this has always been done – it is their emphasis on inter-African language translations. This centrality, from one African language to other African languages, is crucial if we are going to change the terms of debate and even the paradigm. In this one issue, more than 30 African languages were in direct conversation, the most in Africa's literary history. But there were also translations into languages outside Africa, that is, English, French, Portuguese, and some of the Indian languages. In short the *Jalada* translation issue, in practical sense, has made the arguments that many of us from Dhlomo and Vilakazi in the South Africa of the 1940s; Cheikh Anta Diop in the 1950s; to my 1984 publication, *Decolonizing the Mind*. And it is simple: that African languages have been and still are legitimate sources of knowledge and that thought can originate in any African language and spread to other African languages and to all the other languages of the world.

But for African languages to occupy their rightful place in Africa and the world, there have to be positive government policies with the political will and financial muscle behind the policies, the publishers and writers too, and the academic institutions as well. It has to be an alliance, including patriotic private capital, and I am glad to see that amidst us is Baila Ly from Guinea Conakry, who, I am told, is a very successful businessman and supports African languages. It was a Kenyan business enterprise that came up with an endowment that helped in the founding of the Mabati-Cornell Kiswahili Prize for African literature. So the entire language enterprise calls for a grand alliance of government, private capital – particularly Africa-based – academies, universities, publishers, writers, translators, interpreters, and readers.

A meaningful and practical policy has to start with the assumption that every language has a right to be, and each community has a right to their own language, or the language of their culture. That means equitable resources for their development as means of knowledge and culture. Such languages will not see other languages as threats to their own being. As in border communities, a language of communication across regions can emerge without threatening the individuality of the other languages. In such a situation, it can only strengthen the linguistic network.

You could have, at the very least, a three-language policy for every child: their mother tongue, the lingua franca, and whatever is the most useful language of global reach, that is, the reach beyond their communities. In the case of East Africa, for instance, this would mean mother tongue plus Kiswahili plus English. But there could be other innovations around such a policy: for instance, the requirement of a fourth, which must be other than the mother tongue, that is, any one of the other several people's languages. In any African country, we can offer rewards for showing additional knowledge of African languages; we could even link promotion to such knowledge. If you have two judges equally qualified fighting for promotion, then the one who demonstrates competence in African languages within the nation gets extra points. This could be extended to the entire civil service and the academic establishment. And certainly nobody in the world should get a job as an expert of things in Africa without them demonstrating a knowledge of one or more African languages spoken within their field of research and expertise. Every interview for such academic positions, in Africa and the world, should include questions like: How many African languages can you read and write? Have you ever published a paper in an African language in the field of your expertise? A combination of some of these tactics and requirements can only result in the empowerment of African languages.

This can help in the complex give and take among languages and cultures. The human cultures should reflect that of nature, where variety and difference are a source of richness in color and nutritional value. Nature thrives on cross-fertilization and the general circle of life. So also the human culture, and it is not an accident that cultures of innovation throve at the crossroads of travel and exchange. Marketplaces of ideas were always the centers of knowledge and innovations. In his book, *Discourse on Colonialism*, Aimé Césaire once said that culture contact was the oxygen of civilization.

Translation, the universal language of languages, can really help in that generation of such oxygen. Translation involves one distinct unit understanding signals from another distinct unit in terms of itself, for instance, within or between biological cells. So, translation is inherent in all systems of communication: natural, social, and even mechanical. Nature is multilingual in a multicultural sense but also interconnected through continuous translation. Translation is an integral part of the everyday in nature and society and has been central to all cultures; but we may not always notice it.

But while it is true that translation is the common language of languages, hierarchies of power and domination distort its full function as our common heritage. In more equitable relations of wealth, power, and values, translation can play a crucial and ultimate role of enabling mutuality of being and becoming even within a plurality of languages.

In the article in which Mũkoma wa Ngũgĩ described the *Jalada* translation issue as ushering a "revolution in many tongues," he also said that "in translation, there are no indigenous, vernacular, native, local, ethnic and tribal languages producing vernacular, native, local, ethnic and tribal literatures, while English and French produce world and global literature. There are only languages and literatures." (Mũkoma wa Ngũgĩ, A Revolution in Many Tongues, in *Africa is a Country*, April 8, 2016.)

I will end with where I began: securing African languages should be part of a whole vision of Africans securing our resources, for as I told the *Jalada* group, when I gave them my story, "*Ituĩka rĩa Mũrũngarũ*":

> The cruel genius of colonialism was to turn normality into abnormality and then make the colonized accept the abnormality as the real norm ... The moment we lost our languages was also the moment we lost our bodies, our gold, diamonds, copper, coffee, tea. The moment we accepted (or being made to accept) that we could not do things with our languages was the moment we accepted that we could not make things with our vast resources.

So our language policies and actions should empower Africa by making Africans own their resources from languages – making dreams with our languages – to other natural resources, making things with them, consuming some, and exchanging some. Then, and only then, can Africa become truly visible in the world under its own terms and from the security its own base.

References

Ngũgĩ (2009) Something torn and new: an African renaissance. Basic Civitas Books, New York
Ngũgĩ (2016) Secure the base: making Africa visible in the globe. Seagull Books, Chicago

Part II

Indigenous Governance: Restoring Control and Responsibility over the Education of Our People

George J. Sefa Dei and Jean-Paul Restoule

Indigenous Governance: Restoring Control and Responsibility over the Education of Our People

10

George J. Sefa Dei and Jean-Paul Restoule

Contents

Indigenous Governance: Towards an Introduction 142
References 148

Abstract

Indigenous Governance has a wide-ranging impact among the Indigenous peoples. The levels of impact are legal-juridical, political, and economic in connection to educational institutions. This section focuses on Indigenous systems of governance with implications for education, learning, and teaching. The chapter conceptualizes Indigenous Governance and its manifestation to Indigenous and alternative educational sites. The legacies of colonialism and colonial settler-hood as well as the urgency for Indigenous self-determination have centralized Indigenous governance in the public domain. This has also been necessitated by the resiliency and agency of Indigenous ways of knowing and praxis. There is an eruption of an antithesis to the dominant conception of governance. It is defined by a rich historical knowledge of Indigenous communities having their own systems of government. Such an indigenous presentation of governance is holistic, open, community based, and liberating. It is an anti-oversimplification of Indigenous peoples' political culture often masked in racist explanations of

G. J. Sefa Dei (✉)
Social Justice Education, OISE, University of Toronto, Toronto, ON, Canada
e-mail: gdei@oise.utoronto.ca; george.dei@utoronto.ca

J.-P. Restoule
Department of Indigenous Education, Faculty of Education, University of Victoria, Victoria, BC, Canada
e-mail: jpr@uvic.ca

© Springer Nature Singapore Pte Ltd. 2019
E. A. McKinley, L. T. Smith (eds.), *Handbook of Indigenous Education*,
https://doi.org/10.1007/978-981-10-3899-0_64

inherent moral and cultural shortcomings of Indigenous communities. At the global level, particularly the Canadian contexts, self-government agreements allow self determination, sovereignty, and upholding of treaty agreements of Indigenous populations. These agreements provide self-control to education, health, social, and economic development. However, the chapter notes that many theorists have critiqued Canada's long history of settler colonialism that never meets or respects the sovereignty of Indigenous groups. Global governance of Indigenous rights is an urgent matter. We approach this question drawing a link between Indigenous Governance and global governance.

Keywords

Indigeneity · Indigenous Governance · Political culture · Colonialism and settler colonialism · Land · Resistance

Indigenous Governance: Towards an Introduction

We begin a discussion of Indigenous Governance recognizing and acknowledging our presence, as well as belongingness on the territory of the Huron-Wendat and Petun First Nations, the Seneca, and most recently, the Mississaugas of the Credit River. Internally, the legal definition of what constitutes as Indigenous has yet to be agreed upon or defined. It is important to note that Indigenous groups had their own system of governance prior to European colonialism, contemporary questions surrounding self-government, and the overall status of Indigenous groups. Indigenous groups have always fought for governance of their own lands. The push for the sovereign recognition of Indigenous groups; this is not a right that Indigenous groups hope to be granted from the nation/colonial state but a desire to return to preexisting conditions prior to European contact. In this discussion we follow Meyer (2012) in defining "Indigenous" groups as those who: "(a) identify themselves as indigenous groups, (b) established their cultures and social institutions prior to European colonialism, and (c) continue to maintain those traditional ways of life to this day" (p. 329).

Indigenous Governance is a major topic for Indigenous peoples from the multilevels of societal institutions from legal-jurisdictional, political, economics to educational institutions. This section focuses on Indigenous systems of governance with implications for education as broadly defined. We conceptualize Indigenous Governance and how such governance is manifested in Indigenous and alternative educational sites outlets. Contributions in the section also examine how such Indigenous Governance offer lessons for re-visioning schooling and education in multiple global and transnational contexts. We bring an international dimension to discussions of "Indigenous" and "Indigenous Governance" by making connections to different orientations of Indigeneity.

The subject of Indigenous Governance has increasingly been very much on public discussions given the legacies of colonialism and colonial settler-hood and the urgency for Indigenous self-determination and sovereignty. There is resurgence in talk of Indigenous Governance given that what is deemed Indigenous is and was never lost. Indigenous is simply being claimed to assist us in positing and pursing a new "politics of futurity." In examining Indigenous Governance there is the imperative and the ontological reality of counter-representations informed by Indigenous cultural epistemes. For Indigenous Governance to be effective, it cannot rest on an understanding of Indigeneity that has and continues to be produced and projected through the colonial imagination. The "Indigenous" resides in bodies, cultural, spiritual and psychic memories, histories, and cultural knowledges and how these can inform counter-visions of society. Discussions about Indigenous Governance attests to the intellectual agency of Indigenous peoples to articulate own lived realities, conditions, and experiences without being interpreted through Eurocentric conceptual frames of thought and Euro-colonial conjectures of modernity. The spiritual is a core axis of articulating an Indigenous Governance. There is the understanding that the spirit and spirit ontologies are relevant in articulating how Indigenous Governance should be valued, validated, and approached. We cannot de-spiritualize Indigenous cultures in the Eurocentric negation of the "spirit/spiritual" as legitimate site of knowing.

The history of development in the Global South has been peppered with critiques of nation state governance denying the rich historical knowledge of Indigenous communities having their own systems of government prior to the advent of European colonization. In Africa today there continues to be the myth that the continent suffers from a shortfall in good governance or that contemporary African development is impeded by bad governance. Such misguided readings undercut the historical evidence and undermine the possibility of history and Indigenous knowledge contributing to "genuine prosperity, economic integrity and fiscal good governance" (Lauer 2007; p. 289).

There has been an oversimplification of Indigenous peoples' political culture often masked in racist explanations of inherent moral and cultural shortcomings of indigenous communities. There is much to be learned from Indigenous publics of governance least of which is the prospects for Indigenous self-determination. We know that Indigenous systems of governance have been developed from the "origins of [Indigenous and ancient] civilizations ...featuring , ... notions of judicial process, third party [cultural] arbitration, executive authority by [Elders and traditional] Councils sanctioned by the impartiality of ancestral power and consensual decision making fuelled by the will to accommodate every viewpoint via compromise rather than will to dominant via the tyranny of the majority opinion" (Lauer 2007, p. 299 citing Wiredu 1988). In thinking through possibilities for the future, Indigenous peoples need to reclaim our ancestral knowledges to confront the continuing "alienation, popularization and corruption of [our] traditions, [cultures] and imagery through ... unauthorized reproduction and commercial exploitation by [non-Indigenous peoples]" (Howes 1996; p. 138). Part of this task is to resist the spurious claims to Indigenous expertise and knowledge by the dominant.

At the global level and, particularly, in Canadian contexts, self-government agreements with Indigenous populations allow for sovereignty and uphold treaty agreements. This agreement allows for more control of education, health, social and economic development, and other control of jurisdictions. Many theorists have critiqued Canada's long history of settler colonialism and not meeting the demands and respecting the sovereignty of Indigenous groups (Manuel 2015; Kulchyski 2007; Lowman and Barker 2015; Regan 2010). One of the central emerging issues stems from many land disputes and the ongoing settler colonial project. Settler colonialism differs from tradition colonialism because of the development of nationalism and the settler's possession of the land.

Global governance of Indigenous rights is an urgent matter. We approach this question drawing a link between Indigenous Governance and global governance. Global governance is a broader term than "government." According to Meyer (2012), there are several dimensions to global governance. Global governance is a theoretical and an analytical concept, global political trends exist (examined through cases studies, empirical data). The role of non-state actors and global civil society also are theorized and explained through the concept of global governance. Therefore, when examining Indigenous rights, these dimensions are all to be examined; in addition, the classification of who is considered Indigenous is also a complex highly political issue.

Indigenous groups have not acted as a monolith. While some bands and indigenous communities have pushed for the recognition of self-government, others have rejected this notion. Globally, neoliberal development policies continue to push Indigenous groups out of their lands. Transnational enterprises have strong economic interests for national resources such as minerals, oil, forests, and other lucrative resources found on Indigenous lands. Conceptually, the right to own their own land is central to Indigenous peoples (Meyer 2012). Globally, Indigenous populations have been demanding the rights to own their ancestral lands; self-determination is also a controversial issue surrounding Indigenous rights. Self-determination is limited and succession groups are not recognized. Full sovereignty is not recognized, only self-rule is recognized or the participation of government matters that pertain to Indigenous groups. In 2007, the United Nations finalized the United Nations Declaration on the Rights of Indigenous Peoples (UNDRIP); it states that it "recognizes that Indigenous peoples, in exercising their right of self-determination, have the right to autonomy or self-government in matters relating to their internal affairs" (Meyer 2012; p. 330). Not all countries adopted the UNDRIP; it was only in 2010 that Canada adopted this policy. Globally, several issues emerged following the implementation of the UNDRIP, firstly the CANZUS groups (includes Canada, Australia, New Zealand, United States), all resisted the UNDRIP (Meyer 2012). Some issues raised included the definition of Indigenous which some African nations argued was problematic; it would be an issue to classify some groups as Indigenous over other groups. There was a push to limit who was considered Indigenous, and the exclusion of certain groups from protection was a central issue in debates about Indigenous governance.

Colonization entails that Indigenous self-determination is commandeered by the colonizer's sovereignty since colonization is not the appropriation of one's land but also of political authority, cultural self-determination, economic capacity, and strategic location (Green et al. 2003; p. 52). Slowey (2001) also argues that an internal division has set in the first nation's communities over the resource development of traditional lands. There are those who do not mind exploiting the land for profit while others refuse to use their natural resources for such financial gain and adhere to their cultural beliefs. This division is a resistance to cultural assimilation, another important part of colonization. Key fragments of colonization are losing hold on Indigenous peoples, with globalization ironically now a tool against colonization due to it loosening the hold of state sovereignty and citizenry over Indigenous people.

In Canada, several generations of Indigenous youth were subject to mandatory residential schooling in an attempt to eradicate our languages, cultures, and existence as Indigenous peoples. A rallying cry and policy that united Indigenous people in opposition to assimilation was a 1972 document called *Indian Control of Indian Education*. On page 1, the goal was straightforward and simply stated: "We want education to give our children the knowledge to understand and be proud of themselves and the knowledge to understand the world around them" (National Indian Brotherhood 1972, p. 1). When education was managed and run from outside our Indigenous communities without parental involvement or consent, many of our people started to forget who they were and many learned to be ashamed of being Indigenous. To take back control of education has meant taking back all elements of control including how it is governed.

Since this landmark document 45 years ago, taking control of how education is managed and run is a key facet of self-determination movements generally, but especially within Indigenous education. Indeed, many years ago, Mohawk educator Diane Longboat (1987) noted that there are many forms of control over education: curricular, human resources, financial, and others. While the federal government of Canada made much of its handing over of control over First Nations education in the 1980s back to First Nations, what was actually happening was a devolution of mere administration and not true control (Longboat 1987). The key points of education control remained with the Crown, whether provincial or federal. Struggles continue to this day to wrest control back, and the more control First Nations and Indigenous peoples have over how education is governed, the more control we will have over what we are able to do to ensure the next generation knows who they are and how to interact with the world around them.

Investigating what it means to have control over governance in education George Dei and Jean-Paul Restoule sought out contributions reflecting on this question in numerous Indigenous contexts globally. The contributors and contributions demonstrate that the linkages between governance and education can be interpreted broadly and liberally and the influence over education depends on a wide range of freedoms including the recognition of Indigenous self-determination and Indigenous knowledge as valid ways and systems of knowing. Governance influences Indigenous student success at every level from K-12 and into postsecondary education and contributes to the vitality of Indigenous cultural and spiritual expression. Looking at diverse global contexts and a wide range of educational applications from within Indigenous communities to changing mainstream institutions, the chapters in this section ultimately emphasize that control of governance leads to greater educational outcomes, stronger Indigenous cultures, and healthier Indigenous bodies, minds, and spirits.

In Lewis Asimeng-Boahene's ▶ Chap. 11, "Issues and Prospects of African Indigenous Systems of Governance: Relevance and Implications for Global Understanding" the author writes about the continuing stigmatization of non-Western, in particular, African, Indigenous knowledge systems. With a number of examples drawn from African Indigenous educational settings, Asimeng-Boahene argues that lessons from African Indigenous knowledge systems can help to re-vision schooling and education in the globalized contexts we find ourselves in today.

George Dei looks at developing governance structures in counter/alternative educational spaces through the lens of the role of Africentric schooling in Ontario and Canada. Asking such questions as how do we conceptualize Indigenous Governance for an Africentric school? How is such governance manifested in Indigenous and alternative educational sites outlets? How do Indigenous systems of governance offer important lessons for re-visioning schooling and education in Euro-American contexts, Dei's discussion is informed by a search for Indigenous philosophies for critical education working with local analytical concepts and ideas to enhance youth learning outside of the conventional school system.

The notion of which cultures are represented within the school council and governance bodies is taken up by Edward Shizha in his ► Chap. 13, "Building Capacity for Indigenous Peoples: Engaging Indigenous Philosophies in School Governance". As he notes, "parental involvement is strongly influenced by ethnic or cultural backgrounds that are different to the school (Berthelsen and Walker 2008; Mansour and Martin 2009). Schools should spend time building positive school-community relationships so that Indigenous peoples get involved in decision-making processes that promote the aims and goals of the school and the aspirations of the students." The tensions inherent in education and schooling come to the fore as we seek to engage more Indigenous parents to participate in running the schools. As schools were set up with a civilizing mission, teaching and reproducing Eurocentric culture, advocating acculturation and assimilation, the space for Indigenous philosophies and governance is contested and necessarily politicizing. Nevertheless, Shizha argues for the need for partnership with the community to create the roles and space where Indigenous parents can run the schools and make the necessary changes to include Indigenous epistemologies to support our youth.

In Filiberto Penados' ► Chap. 14, "Indigenous Governance and Education in Belize: Lessons from the Maya Land Rights Struggle and Indigenous Education Initiatives," we learn about a long-fought struggle affirming the rights to land of the Maya of Southern Belize. Penados discusses the Alcade system of governance that predates colonial administrations and is being co-opted as a means of control. How the Garifuna and Maya have avoided and resisted colonial attempts to control and conquer their education initiatives is an inspiring example of what's possible. Penados engages the question of Indigenous governance's implications for education by examining the role of the Alcades in the Maya land-rights struggle and the Indigenous education initiatives in Belize.

Maaka, Wong, Perry, and Johnston, in their chapter on ► Chap. 15, "Indigenous Leadership: A Complex Consideration," draw heavily from the wisdom of Māori and Hawaiian cultural proverbs to elaborate on how leadership can be represented or fulfilled. They consider what it is that inspires Indigenous people to follow others and in the process arrive at insights on the health of Indigenous leadership, and Indigenous leadership ascension and succession. While many of their examples are rooted in particular cultural contexts, the resulting observations will likely resonate with Indigenous people from many diverse regions around the world.

Shifting focus to postsecondary education reform in Australia and recent calls for the adoption of Indigenous leadership, perspectives, and governance to help improve Indigenous outcomes in the sector, Maggie Walter, and Wendy Aitken outline the potential hazards that come with these positive changes in *Indigenous Governance Within the Academy: Negotiating the Space*. Similarly concerned with avoiding the pitfalls of co-optation and tokenism, the authors warn of the need for university members to be highly aware and make visible the deep cultural assumptions and entrenchment within tertiary education. As the authors state, lessons learned in Australia have salience for the fate of Indigenous Governance within higher education sectors, especially other Anglo-colonized first world nation states.

And Olga Skinner and Beth Leonard use Indigenous spaces theory to offer a critical look at the University of Alaska's attempts to engage with Indigenous knowledge and increase the Indigenous student body. The paper *Indigenous Struggles Within the Colonial Project: Re-envisioning Institutional Discourses and Governance in Higher Education* "examines key public discourses at the University of Alaska Fairbanks (UAF), including strategic governance plans related to the creation and expansion of physical and intellectual landscapes for Indigenous peoples." While there are many good goals and intentions stated within the institution's academic plans, the authors question how well they ultimately encourage a critical consciousness among its members and engage in a pedagogy of place that is situated within Indigenous ways.

Njoki Wane with Rose Ann Torres and Dionisio Nyaga bring a focus to spirituality and its role in Indigenous resistance in their ► Chap. 18, "African Indigenous Governance from a Spiritual Lens." They argue that if spirit is missing in any aspect of people's lives, then there will be an experience of imbalance in the community consequently affecting every aspect of governance. With examples drawn from Kenya, the authors remind us that there is remarkable commonality of Indigenous Governance from different Indigenous groups of the world and that every decision-making practice must incorporate all aspects of human being, the mind, body, and spirit.

John Jerome Paul, Lisa Lunney Borden, Joanne Tompkins, Jeff Orr, and Thomas Orr ask whether the master's tools can dismantle the master's house and come up with a surprising answer. Examining the governance model and achievements of the *Mi'kmaw Kina'matnewey*, a community-based organization that provides intermediary educational services and organizational representation to Nova Scotian Mi'kmaw communities seeking to exercise enhanced self-governance in education, the authors argue that MK has transformed Eurocentric schooling into a decolonizing and transformative force in Mi'kmaw communities. Mi'kmaw culture, language, and identity are thriving under this model, and Indigenous communities around the world can learn from the example.

References

Berthelsen D, Walker S (2008) Parents' involvement in their children's education. Family Matters 79:34–41
Calvano L (2008) Multinational corporations and local communities: a critical analysis of conflict. J Bus Ethics 82:793–805
Dyck N (1989) Aboriginal peoples and nation-states: an introduction to the analytical issues. In: Dyck N (ed) Indigenous peoples and the nation-state: fourth world politics in Canada, Australia and Norway. Institute of Social and Economic Research, Memorial University, St. John's
Green J, Vosko LF, Wallace C (2003) Changing Canada: political economy as transformation: decolonization and recolonization in Canada. McGill-Queen's University Press, Montreal
Harvey D (2007) Neoliberalism as creative destruction. Ann Am Acad Pol Soc Sci 610(1):22–44
Howes D (1996) Cultural appropriation and resistance in the American Southwest: decommodifying Indianness. In: Howes D (ed) Cross-cultural consumption: global markets local realities. Routledge, London/New York, pp 138–160
Keesing RM (1989) Creating the past: custom and identity in the contemporary Pacific. Contemp Pac 1(1/2):19–42
Kulchyski P (2007) The red Indians: an episodic, informal collection of tales from the history of Aboriginal people's struggles in Canada. Arbeiter Ring Press, Winnipeg
Ladner KL (2006) Indigenous governance: questioning the status and the possibilities for reconciliation with Canada's commitment to aboriginal and treaty rights. National Centre for First Nation Governance n. pag. Web. 30 Jan 2017
Lauer H (2007) Depreciating African political culture. J Black Stud 38(2):288–307
Longboat D (1987) First Nations control of education: the path to our survival as nations. In: Barman J, Hebert Y, McCaskill D (eds) Indian education in Canada: volume 2: the challenge. UBC Press, Vancouver
Lowman EB, Barker A (2015) Settler: identity and colonialism in 21st century Canada. Fernwood, Halifax
Mansour M, Martin AJ (2009) Home, parents, and achievement motivation: a study of key home and parental factors that predict student motivation and engagement. Aus Ed and Dev Psych 26(2):111–126
Manuel A (2015) Unsettling Canada: a national wake-up call. Between the Lines Press, Toronto
Meyer WH (2012) Indigenous rights, global governance, and state sovereignty. Hum Rights Rev 13(3):327–347
National Indian Brotherhood (1972) Indian control of Indian education. Policy paper presented to the Minister of Indian Affairs and Northern Development, Ottawa
Orbach A (2011) Rethinking participation, rethinking power: reflections on local autonomy. Can J Dev Stud 32(2):196–209. Worldwide Political Science Abstract
Penikett T (n.d.) Six definitions of aboriginal self- government and the . . .. Web 30 Jan 2017
Rao N (2000) "Neo-colonialism" or "globalization"? postcolonial theory and the demands of political economy. Interdiscip Lit Stud 1:165–184
Regan P (2010) Unsettling the settler within: Indian residential schools, truth telling, and reconciliation in Canada. UBC Press, Vancouver
Slowey GA (2001) Globalization and self-government: impacts and implications for First Nations in Canada. Am Rev Can Stud 31(1–2):265–281
Stavenhagen R (2012) Rights of indigenous peoples: a personal retrospective of Rodolfo Stavenhagen. In: Pioneer on indigenous rights, SpringerBriefs on pioneers in science and practice. Springer, Berlin/Heidelberg, pp 3–12
Wiredu K (1988) The state, civil society and democracy in Africa. Quest 72(1):240–252

Issues and Prospects of African Indigenous Systems of Governance: Relevance and Implications for Global Understanding

11

Lewis Asimeng-Boahene

Contents

Introduction	150
Methodology	151
Conceptual and Theoretical Analysis	152
Contextualizing the Precolonial African Indigenous Systems of Governance	153
Different Types of Indigenous Forms of Governance Structure in Traditional Africa: Precolonial Era	154
Decentralized or Consensus-Based Political System of Governance in the Precolonial Africa	155
Attributes of Centralized or Chieftaincy Political System in the Precolonial Africa	156
The Role of Community Elders in the Centralized and Decentralized Traditional Governance	157
African Traditional Institutions of Governance: Under Colonialism	158
Impact of Colonialism on Decentralized Systems	159
Impact of Colonialism on Centralized Systems	159
African Traditional Institutions: Postcolonial Era	160
Factors Responsible for the Waning Influence of Traditional Rulers in Governance	161
Relevance and Implications for Global Understanding of Indigenous Systems of Governance	162
Conflict Resolution	162
Expansion of Public Services	163
Management of Resource-Based Conflicts (Land-Tenure System)	163
Future Directions	164
Conclusion	166
References	167

L. Asimeng-Boahene (✉)
Social Studies Education, Penn State University-Harrisburg, Middletown, PA, USA
e-mail: lab45@psu.edu

© Springer Nature Singapore Pte Ltd. 2019
E. A. McKinley, L. T. Smith (eds.), *Handbook of Indigenous Education*,
https://doi.org/10.1007/978-981-10-3899-0_25

Abstract

African indigenous systems of governance have remained prey to tradition, Western labeling, colonization, as well as African nostalgia. The overall result has been that African systems of governance have been slurred and reduced to the footnotes of serious academic discourse. The purpose of this chapter is to highlight the traditional architecture of the African indigenous systems of governance and their relevance to modern global schooling and educational systems. As in Renaissance Italy throughout the thirteenth and fourteenth centuries, when a great multiplicity of organizational systems, namely, dictatorship, monarchy, democracy, and theocracy, existed within a fairly small geographical area and often under similar socioeconomic environments, so too in traditional African societies do we find a great variety of political systems within relatively close proximity to one another. It is this very diversity that is of great significance in understanding African political philosophy, which serves as the overarching goal of this paper. The chapter discussion covers the issues and prospects of what African indigenous systems of governance entail in terms of their relevance and implications for global schooling and education. After a discussion of the methodology employed and the conceptual and theoretical analysis for the paper, this chapter addresses precolonial traditional systems of governance, the impact of colonialism on the transformation of African traditional institutions and the status of traditional institutions in the postcolonial era. The next discourse examines the relevance and implications of Indigenous systems of governance for modern-day schooling and political education for global understanding.

Keywords

Indigenous systems of governance · Decentralized: Consensus-based · Stateless · Acephalous · Non-stratified · Centralized: chieftaincy political system

Introduction

African indigenous systems of governance continue to be victims of legends, Western stereotyping, colonization, as well as African Romanticism. The net end product has been that African systems of governance have been denounced and reduced to foot notes of serious academic discourse. Consequently, those observers interested in ascertaining the philosophical bases of African indigenous systems of governance are faced with considerable challenges. On the one hand, the indigenous African political structures that existed before the arrival of the colonizers displayed a multiplicity of structural differences across the continent. On the other hand, when faced with the challenge of examining the political beliefs behind these systems of governance, the researcher of African political thought must rely on a variety of sources including, the evidence written by external visitors to the continent, oral traditions that endured within the societies, archeological and linguistic patterns, and mostly Africa's diverse political structures (Potholm 1979).

Inevitably, African peoples adopted political systems that reflected the political philosophies functioning within their societies. However, the vibrancy and diversity of such sociopolitical heritages continue to be misunderstood and unacknowledged. It is in view of this missing intellectual ore that this paper seeks to highlight the degree to which the structural complexity of Africa mirrors certain basic suppositions about the nature of societal interaction, and connections between power and authority, hence their systems of governance. In Africa, like as in Renaissance Italy in the thirteenth and fourteenth centuries, a great variety of political systems within relatively close proximity to one another existed in traditional African societies. It is this very diversity that is of great significance in embarking on serious attempts at understanding African indigenous governance (Potholm 1979).

Consequently, my vested interest in this chapter is to share with readers, the underlying issues of many African indigenous systems of governance, which explain the persistent political patterns that have occurred in the various parts of the continent, among peoples of diverse linguistic and racial groups with totally varied cultural and historical circumstances. This leads me to begin this chapter by firstly describing the methodological process and the underpinning conceptual framework. This is followed by contextualizing the precolonial indigenous systems of governance. Thirdly, the roles of community elders in the traditional governance are highlighted. This is followed by a critical discussion of traditional governance under colonial and postcolonial settings. The last deliberation focusses on the future directions of indigenous governance in the modern era of globalization.

Methodology

This paper employed a qualitative research method. The qualitative approach was chosen because it allows the researcher to gain insight into the organizational structures and settings, social processes, and poignantly underscores the importance of the personal narratives on the lived experiences of the respondents (Strauss 1994). The inductive properties of flexibility and amenability available in qualitative methodology allow me to discuss the issue through my personal and lived experiences as an African, through my research and scholarly visits to various African countries and through my acquired knowledge about traditional systems of governance. In essence, the paper, which is theoretical in nature, extracts its arguments from documentary sources of data such as legal frameworks and other related policies, journals, textbooks, articles, magazines, dissertations, research reports, and relevant materials and publications from the Internet related to the study. Multiple strategies were employed to ensure the trustworthiness and credibility of the paper. These include, among others, engaging other researchers to critique the script to reduce research bias through triangulation and accounting for personal biases which may have influenced my conclusions (Morse et al. 2002).

Conceptual and Theoretical Analysis

The theoretical framework for this paper is underpinned by two conceptual analyses namely, the debate of whether traditional governance systems are relevant in modern governance and also the theory of political participation.

The Economic Commission for Africa (ECA) (2007) Report identified three different schools of thought about the relevance of African indigenous systems of governance. In the first school are those that believe that traditional institutions belong to historical relics (Fatile 2010). They argue that these institutions not only serve as hindrance to socioeconomic development, but are also divisive and expensive to run. Apart from these, the traditional institutions are viewed as partners to colonial masters who abhorred democracy and as such do not belong to the newly found post-colonial independent state (ECA 2007). Among the arguments advanced by these views are that:

- Chieftaincy has been corrupted by the colonial state and sometimes by the support of the despotic postcolonial state and is, thus, no longer accountable to the populace (Zack-Williams 2002; Kilson 1966).
- Inhabitants under traditional authorities, as in South Africa, live as "subjects" instead of as citizens of the state, and democratic governance would not be achieved while such systems continue to prevail (Mamdani 1996; Ntsebeza 2005).
- Chieftaincy enhances ethnic loyalties as chiefs represent the rallying points of ethnic characteristics (Simwinga, quoted in van Binsbergen 1987, p. 156).
- The hereditary nature of chieftaincy makes it discordant with democratic governance, which entails competitive elections as one of its foundation stone (Ntsebeza 2005).

The second school of thought stresses the areas of potential contribution of traditional institutions of governance. This polar opposite view asserts that traditional institutions are indispensable for political transformation in Africa, as they represent a major part of the continent's history, culture, and political and governance systems. This view attributes the ineffectiveness of the African state in bringing about sustained socioeconomic development to its neglect of traditional institutions and its failure to restore Africa's own history (Davidson 1992). This view is corroborated by Dore (2011) who argues that when policy overlooks history, culture, and social milieu, efforts and resources can be wasted on poorly envisioned policy. However, the ethnic institutions, by themselves, are not an adequate stipulation to empower traditional institutions to ease the transformation of social structures. Contingent on their landscape, traditional institutions, as learned from experience, may alter development and democratic transformation as they undergo constant change (Dore 2011). It is likely, however, that political and economic development would be more effective when widely shared institutions and cultural values are employed (Ejiofo 2004; ECA 2007; Fallers 1955). This school of thought contends that traditional rulers can play better roles in the political process as they have advisory roles to government in administration at both national and subnational levels. Secondly, they play a developmental role by adding to the endeavors of government in mobilizing revenue and resources, sensitizing their subjects to government's program on matters like health issues like immunization and HIV/AIDS campaigns, voter registration, etc. Third is their function in terms of conflict management, as has been acknowledged among traditional rulers (Osakede and Ijimakinwa 2015).

The third school of thought postulates an eclectic argument (Ejiofo 2004). Though it recognizes the limitations of the traditional institutions during the period of colonialism, it emphasizes the fact that "traditional institutions constitute crucial resources that have the potential to promote democratic governance and to facilitate access of rural communities to public services" (ECA 2007, p. 11). Perrot et al. (2003) share this argument when they opine that the destiny of African (traditional) leaders appeared to be sealed just before independence; as they were accused of just serving the colonizers and deemed a useless institution. They further argue that the existence of these traditional leaders was no longer an issue in these days as some of the same government officials, university members, and the literate elite who previously criticized them are now enthroned playing the roles of traditional authority.

This chapter is also conceptually underpinned by the political participation theory, which emphasizes the inevitability of all-embracing political practices and procedures that unite social forces making them the foundations of the democratization practice (Sapru 2008). The theory further argues that traditional rulers in any political society are the lifeblood of the democratic organization through their involvement, contribution and participation in the political process. Thus, conceptualizing different schools of thought about whether traditional governments are germane in modern-day governance and political participation theory as a theoretical framework helps readers to identify, analyze, and transform debate and engage in discussion about the issues and prospects of African traditional governance.

Contextualizing the Precolonial African Indigenous Systems of Governance

"Governance," as a concept, implies those procedures that encompass establishing the rules for the use of power over groups of people living within a certain politicogeographic area and settling conflicts among such people over such rules. Hence, governance can be referred to as the regulation of a wide range of units and engaged in many different ways with no agreement on its latitude when engaged to define the political or community governance. There was significant heterogeneity in political centralization and decentralization across African ethnicities before colonialism. Thus, traditional institutions of governance involve the indigenous political organization where leaders are appointed and installed in conformity with the prerequisites of their local laws and customs (Murdock 1967; Orji and Olali 2010). It should be recognized that prior to colonization, African societies had rich political, economic, and social traditional institutions that oversaw social control, the allocation of resources, and law making. The essence of any governing institution is to preserve the customs and traditions of the people and to manage conflicts arising among or between members of the community by the guiding principles of laws and customs of the people. Traditional institutions are the custodians of the people's norms, cultures, and practices. In most African settings, selection of persons into the offices of traditional institutions is hereditary or by selection or election using traditional methods. The method of selection of the occupants of traditional institutions differs among ethnic groups and communities. Hence, traditional institutions are representations of indigenous people's rights, privileges, laws, customs, and traditions (Khapoya 1998; Potholm 1979).

There are many schools of thought about the types of political systems of governance in Africa, given its size. There were societies in Africa that based the holding of political power on kinship. Some political systems integrated the idea that positions of authority should follow traditional kinship of inheritance, while others insisted that political power should be based on merit. Still others felt that political power should be shared by various interest groups within society. Some African political systems insisted that political power belongs to one group within society – a class, an organization, or even a racial caste. Some African political systems were democratic; others were despotic (Potholm 1979; Reagan 2005).

It is therefore not surprising that contextualizing and resolving conceptual issues about the identity/concepts of African indigenous governance systems is one of the many challenges confronting scholars, philosophers, historians, anthropologists, and educators, as they cannot be pigeon-holed by a single definition. African societies are characterized by fragmentation of various aspects of their political economy including their institutions of governance. The highly contextualized governance systems represent a set of cultural, traditional, and local instruments or mechanisms through which communities organize, manage, and coordinate their activities and consumption of resources. These are passed from generation to generation and currently function in parallel to the modern institutions. The processes and practices that apply will differ greatly given the environment in which they are applied (Ayittey 1991; Khapoya 1998; Potholm 1979; Reagan 2005).

Different Types of Indigenous Forms of Governance Structure in Traditional Africa: Precolonial Era

Since traditional governance systems tend to be culturally defined, there is no universal definition of a traditional governance system. Hence concepts like traditional, nonformal, informal, customary, indigenous, and nonstate governance systems are used interchangeably in different contexts to refer to localized approaches by communities to attain justice within the established system of governance (FIDA-Kenya n.d.). Consequently, not all traditional systems are or were the same. In certain societies and, in particular, large centralized polities, where a traditional leader could rely on his own army or police force, the process resembled more closely that of the formal state system.

Despite their intricate diversity, due to a number of intersecting structures mutual to most traditional systems, much of the modern-day literature classifies African traditional institutions of governance into two types, based on their precolonial forms: (a) the consensus-based systems of the decentralized precolonial political systems, and (b) chieftaincy of the centralized political systems (Ayittey 1991; Khapoya 1998; Potholm 1979; Reagan 2005; Robert 1972). The following discussion helps to clarify the similarities and differences of the two categories.

Decentralized or Consensus-Based Political System of Governance in the Precolonial Africa

Generally, decentralized or consensus-based systems of governance, which are generally also known as egalitarian or nonstratified, acephalous, decentralized, or stateless systems of governance, were political systems without any enduring or established system of power and authority. Decisions were communally made in different circumstances, especially, at informal community meetings. In large parts of Africa, many precolonial political systems were highly decentralized with law making, social control, and allocation of resources carried out by local bodies, such as lineage groupings, village communities, and age sets. Societal power was shared among the local groups. Such societies were ruled by elder members or councils chosen from different lineages of the community. The Nuer of Sudan, the Kikuyu of Kenya, and the Ibo people of Nigeria are examples of decentralized systems. However, their values were not all the same; the Nuer had rigid traditional political structure, and were, therefore, extremely resistant to change, whereas the Kikuyu and the Ibo who were more participatory in their traditional political systems were quite adaptable to change (Ayittey 1991; Khapoya 1998; Potholm 1979; Reagan 2005; Robert 1972).

In these kinds of decentralized societies, social groups like age-sets and secret societies played very strong roles in maintaining order and discipline and harnessing the resources of the community for mutual purposes. These types of systems defended against autocracy and tyranny by eradicating centralized political authority, generally replacing it with strong social and cultural mores and practices related to communal governance. As Williams (1987) commented:

> It was therefore in the societies without chiefs or kings where African democracy was born and where the concept that the people are sovereign was as natural as breathing. And this is why in traditional Africa, the rights of the individual never came before the rights of the community...These self-governing people did not have a Utopian society in any idealistic sense. Theirs was a practical society in every way. Their laws were natural laws, and order and justice prevailed because the society could not otherwise survive. Theirs was, in fact, a government of the people; theirs was, in fact, not a theory, but a government by the people; and it was, in fact, a government for the people. (p. 170)

It should be established that the fundamental principles that guide the consensus-based systems include the lack of concentration of power in an institution or a person and preventing the development of a rigid structure. The settlement of conflicts in such consensual systems consists of a narrowing of differences through negotiations rather than through confrontational processes that produce winners and losers. This system is centered on respect for the rights and views of the individual, as individuals can veto the opinions of the majority. However, individuals are also expected to respect the wishes and interests of the community by accepting compromises, as they can face various forms of community censure, including social isolation, if they fail to do so. This system of accommodation prevents conflicts between minority and majority segments of a community (Legesse 1973).

Another important aspect of this kind of system is that it prevents the existence of political and social gaps between the governed and those who govern, as all eligible members of the community participate in both the creation and enforcement of rules and regulations. Among the well-known examples are the Ibo village assembly in eastern Nigeria, the Eritrean village *baito* (assembly), *the gada* (age-set) system of the Oromo in Ethiopia and Kenya, as well as the council of elders *(kiama)* of Kikuyu in Kenya, Tallensi of Northern Ghana, the Sukuma of Tanzania, and the Nuer of Southern Sudan, where decisions are largely based on consensus (Montagne 1931; Alport 1964).

Attributes of Centralized or Chieftaincy Political System in the Precolonial Africa

A centralized or chieftaincy political system puts the onus of power and decision making on a central authority. Africa has been the place with numerous highly centralized states. Africa has also observed the rise and fall of major empires. Some of these empires were urbanized, economically complex, politically, and culturally sophisticated, and in their era, some were among the most notable civilizations in the world (Reagan 2005). Centralized systems constituted the majority of the diverse indigenous political systems in precolonial Africa and varied extensively in terms of their organizational structure, size, degree of independence, subjugation to other groups, and so on. This form of government, which existed throughout Africa, comprises the Baluba of Zaire, the Asante of Ghana, and the Xhosa in South Africa, the Haya, Alur and Lange of Uganda Hehe and Shanbala in Tanzania, the Bemba in Zambia, and the Oyo in Nigeria (Potholm 1979; Busia 1968; Khapoya 1998).

Population pressures, coupled with other demographic factors, ecological factors, and political factors, often led to the fragmentation of these chiefdoms (Ayittey 1991; Reagan 2005). The level of centralization and concentration of power in the hands of the leaders in these indigenous systems differed from place to place. In some cases, such as Ethiopia and Rwanda, the rulers enjoyed absolute power. In most other cases, the power of the rulers was controlled by various arrangements, including the institution of councils (Beattie 1967). The level of development of the mechanisms of checks and balances also varied from place to place. In some cases, such as the Buganda of Uganda and the Nupe in Nigeria, the formal institutions of checks and balances and accountability of leaders to the population were rather weak (Beattie 1967). In other cases, such as the Asante of Ghana, the Tsana of Botswana, and the Busoga of Uganda, the systems of checks and balances were better defined with constitutional staff to the chiefs to check the power of the leaders and keep them accountable (Busia 1968; Jones 1983; Coplan and Quinlan 1997).

Chiefs played major roles in many areas. They were judges and maintained the rule of law. They served as military leaders and led in wars. They were the custodians of communal ideals and enacted rites and customs that sustained the moral and cultural values of society. In some societies, like the Asante of Ghana, the chiefs were directly responsible for the observance of regulations about the exploitation of nature and the resources of the land, as the traditional worldview postulated a bond between a ruler and the health of the environment (Busia 1968; Brempong 2007).

Common to most of the centralized African kingdoms, unlike the decentralized societies, was the metaphysical view of the king as "the actual embodiment of the kingdom, and [the related idea] that there is a mystical union between the two" (Ayittey 1991, p. 151). In other words, the kingdoms were generally based on a "divine kingship" model. This concept also requires legitimacy based on the popular acceptance of the king. As Kopytoff (quoted in Ayittey 1991) explained:

> The crucial point in Africa was that legitimacy had been conferred by the people by way of the "consent" of their symbols...being the creation of subjects, the African ruler's legitimacy rested on an implicit contract that could be withdrawn...Under a satisfactory ruler, who had lived up to his nurturing obligations, the subjects would present the patrimonial perspective on rulership, in which the ruler is the absolute "owner" of everything. Similarly, the good ruler would state publicly his rule rested on the happiness of the people and on their consent. (p. 152)

Thus, in the centralized systems, there was a central control, leaders gave directions, directives were obeyed quickly, leaders held information, the structure was top down, leaders were ultimately responsible, and reward was according to individual role.

The Role of Community Elders in the Centralized and Decentralized Traditional Governance

Akwakora te ho ansa na wo woo ohene (Asante proverb). To wit "An old man was in the world before a chief was born." This proverb underpins the value that traditional societies place on gerontology, irrespective of the traditional form of governance.

Every society has its cognitive enforcement officers or gatekeepers who together delineate the fundamental cognitive landscape of the people and principally superintend the approved depiction and the defense of the societal norms (Assimeng 2006). Consequently, among the traditional African societies, the above-mentioned policing or gatekeeping role is performed mostly by the adult members through the supposed acquisition of a library of ideas. They are considered to have accumulated the knowledge and wisdom of the society, which is stored in their heads. No wonder then, that, the Akan of Ghana everyday references elders because of their professed wisdom found in wise saying and proverbs, such as "Each time an elderly dies it is as if a library had burned down." In addition to acting as guides to the land and its flora and fauna, the elders convey knowledge to youngsters through moon light tales, and thus watching over their learning process. There is also a reverence of filial piety, the veneration and respect for the elderly which is equated with wisdom. This is nostalgically expressed in the famous African maxim that states "Wo ne panyin a due," woe betides anyone who has no elder person to offer him/her advice (Asimeng-Boahene 2014).

In Ghana, elderly women are much revered due to their supposed knowledge acquired through lived experiences...hence the popular Akan notion of consulting the "old woman": "Yekobisa nana aberewa," (we are going to consult with grandmother) for counsel anytime there is a deadlock or difficulty in making a decision. In addition to their roles in teaching, community elders are also consulted in assessment of judicial matters/processes, such as land-tenure issues and marital affairs in traditional governance system. This type of believed oral knowledge of elders offers diverse ways of understanding the African world and its traditional governance and assumptions that are normally quite different from those seen in Western frames of reference (Asimeng-Boahene 2014).

African Traditional Institutions of Governance: Under Colonialism

The colonial exploitation and manipulation of the African institutions of traditional rule for its imperial reasons is well known (see Brempong and Pavanello 2006). As earlier noted, prior to colonialism, traditional rulers were both the political, social, cultural, and economic administrators of their various localities. They were integral parts of the African culture which made certain of harmony and stability in the society. However, the state of affairs changed when colonial rule was imposed on African societies. It was at this epoch that traditional rulers were subordinated and became instrumental for the attainment of the goals of the indirect rule or direct rule system of the colonialists (Fajonyomi 1997). It was the stretch of the power given to traditional rulers under the native authority system that created some sort of animosity between them and the educated elite in the period toward political sovereignty (Kirk-Greene 1965).

Traditional rule and its systems of succession in the period of independence were undermined by features of colonial governments. Colonial rule meant the abolition of the sovereignty of the traditional states and their subordination to the colonial authorities, represented by the district, Provincial and Chief Commissioners, and the Governor. The colonial government undertook the right of recognition of existing or newly appointed traditional rulers, which destined the right to accept or reject the choices of the king makers. Thus, the practice by the colonial government of the right to enthrone and dethrone traditional rulers undermined the traditional system of government by consent in areas like the Akan of Ghana (Brempong 2007). Hence, African institutions of governance were fundamentally distorted during colonialism and the accompanying fundamental restructuring of African political structures and socioeconomic systems. The colonial state brought the different African political systems under centralized systems.

Impact of Colonialism on Decentralized Systems

In the decentralized traditional systems, social control had been carried out through communal consensus. The colonial state invented chieftaincies to whom they gave some types of authority and imposed hierarchical rule in the system, such as those of the Ibo of eastern Nigeria, the Tonga in Zambia, the Masai in Kenya, and the Savannah areas of Ghana (Brempong and Pavanello 2006). Inevitably, the old system ceased to be the institution known to its people. In some situations, the "invented" chiefs used their power to enrich themselves, and some differentiated themselves from their communities by subverting traditional political values (Tosh 1977). In many other cases, however, the invented chieftaincies were unsuccessful in displacing the consensus-based governance structures (Gartrell 1983). For instance, the warrant chiefs appointed by the British colonial state were unable to replace the traditional system of village council among the Ibo of Nigeria (Uwazie 1994). The Eritrean village *baito* (ruler) also survived colonialism largely in one piece. The district administrators appointed by the colonial state acted principally as tax collectors and the village heads appointed by such administrators largely presided over village assemblies and declared the consensus that came out from an assembly's discussions rather than taking decision making roles.

Impact of Colonialism on Centralized Systems

The impact of colonialism upon authority systems was much greater, as it largely transformed the form and content of governance and, thus, the relations between chiefs and their communities, as Coplan and Quinlan (1997) indicate in the case of Lesotho. The colonial power either demoted or eliminated African leaders who resisted colonization or rebelled after colonization. Leaders who submitted to the British colonial rule were mostly incorporated into the colonial governance structure of indirect rule, which was designed to provide the colonial state with a viable low-cost administrative structure to maintain order, mobilize labor, enforce production of cash crops, and collect taxes. This process of incorporation severely weakened both the formal and informal mechanisms of accountability of traditional leaders to the population by changing the power relations between chiefs and their communities. Under colonialism, chiefs could be removed from power only by the colonial administration. Chiefs were also given control of land, thereby curtailing the ability of ordinary people to shift their allegiance to other chiefs (Busia 1968).

Consequently, the imposition of colonial rule and its legitimization through the various ordinances meant to a great extent the loss of traditional authority. Consequently, colonialism transformed a number of chiefs with some modifications into mere civil servants of the colonial state (Brempong and Pavanello 2006). However, this view is often exaggerated as the roles of Hausa chiefs in Nigeria, for example, were affected differently by colonialism, with the power of those in Niger reduced more severely (Miles 1987). As intermediaries between the colonial state and local people, chiefs were expected to maintain peace and order within their communities. To be effective administrators, chiefs had to maintain their legitimacy with their communities (Coplan and Quinlan 1997).

This required that the chiefs should ease the encumbrance of colonialism by interceding with colonial authorities on behalf of their people and by protecting the interests of their communities. In some cases, chiefs also rebelled against colonialism when unable to persuade colonial administrators to modify some of their policies. For example in the past, the African kings/chiefs and elders were totally relied upon for executive, legislative, and judicial control of the society, Colonialism negatively affected this centuries-old traditional conflict resolution. This was replaced with the establishment of colonial styled courts which practiced colonial laws, foreign pattern of governance, and cultural traits. Finally, colonization shaped the political structure of African colonies to be in line with the needs of the metropolis. It ensured that African economic and political structures both in form and content served the interest of their colonial governments. This, to all intents and purposes was a disservice to Africa as colonization attempted to either eradicate or weaken traditional forms of governance through various ordinances as the way they did with indigenous knowledge systems.

African Traditional Institutions: Postcolonial Era

At independence, most African countries inherited a hybrid and disconnected system in which modern governance systems were superimposed on traditional institutions. Thus, the traditional rule and its systems of succession in the period of sovereignty were also subverted by aspects of Postcolonial governments. The enactments by the colonial and postcolonial governments on traditional rule diminished the customary roles of the traditional rulers. They were, for instance, no longer war leaders, law makers, or law enforcers. The significance of their role as priest chiefs was greatly reduced under the onslaught of Christianity and the exigencies of colonial rule that discouraged traditional activities like annual festivals, for example, as in Asante (Ghana), colonial rule discouraged the major festival of "Odwira" in the fear that it would rekindle what they thought were the dying embers of Asante nationalism (Brempong 2007).

Decolonization represented another landmark in the transformation of African traditional institutions of governance, especially the institution of chieftaincy. The abolishment of the colonial system of indirect rule left in flux the role of the upper echelons of chiefs and their relations with the new African states. Many of the African nationalists, first-generation leaders, such as Houphouet-Boigny (Ivory Coast), Sekou Toure (Guinea), Leopold Senghor (Senegal), and Kwame Nkrumah (Ghana), saw chiefs as functionaries of the colonial system and chieftaincy as an anachronistic vestige of the old Africa that had no place in the postcolonial political landscape. Inevitably, African nationalist leaders, therefore, often pursued policies to Africanize the bureaucracy without indigenizing the institutions of governance. The new political elite, which increasingly grew self-serving and autocratic, also could not tolerate the existence of contending points of power (Economic Commission of Africa (ECA 2005). As they banned opposition parties, they also dispossessed chiefs of the bureaucratic positions they held within the indirect-rule system of the colonial state. Burkina Faso, Guinea, Tanzania, Uganda, Zambia, and Zimbabwe, among others, attempted unsuccessfully to strip chiefs of most of their authority or even abolish chieftaincy altogether. In many cases, in efforts to enhance its own legitimacy, the new elite, especially among the second generation of African leaders, attempted with varying degrees of success to co-opt traditional leaders.

Despite these ambiguous efforts, chieftaincy has continued to operate with large numbers of supporters, especially in rural areas. As an ECA study (2005) notes, chiefs often operate as custodians of customary law and communal assets, especially land. They dispense justice, resolve conflicts, and enforce contracts. They also serve as guardians and symbols of cultural values and practices. Unfortunately, chiefs currently operate largely in an informal setting without clear definitions of their authority. Some countries that have realized the resilience of the institution, such as South Africa and Uganda, are still grappling with how to incorporate chieftaincy and monarchy into their modern governance structure.

Consequently, it could be argued that, to some extent, postcolonial political narratives have, with time, transformed chieftaincy into a vital institution of the modern state due to the idea that the traditional institutions have preserved of their precolonial nature and character. With that, I now turn to the views challenging the relevance of indigenous governance.

Factors Responsible for the Waning Influence of Traditional Rulers in Governance

There are a number of factors that have contributed and are still contributing to the gradual loss of relevance of traditional rulers in governance in recent times. Fatile (2010) posits that some of these factors are self-inflicted by the traditional institutions themselves while others are systemically engendered. Thus, there is no doubt that traditional rulers have gradually witnessed erosion of their power while the power of the elected politicians in the political parties increased. Key issues that have contributed to the waning influence of the traditional rulers include:

- **Diminishing scope of influence**: The creation of new states/regions/provinces and local government areas have further limited the "kingdoms" overseen by the traditional rulers.
- **Social disquiet**: This is attributed to the moral decay in the society, lack of respect for elders, and legally constituted authority including traditional institutions.

- **Misuse of privilege:** The problem of giving chieftaincy titles and honors to less deserving members has created a society with false values and negative role models.
- **Globalization:** This global socioeconomic and political interconnectedness has contributed in the waning influence and interest in monarchies and traditional institutions in the developing world generally.
- **Politics:** Party politics have been and continue to be played in a manner that undermines the influence of traditional rulers over local voters.
- **Conflict of interest:** This is a continuing issue between local government authorities and traditional rulers, about who should do what in local community matters.
- **The economy**: The dwindling economic fortunes affecting traditional rulers have further eroded their influence and authority.
- **Self-inflicted challenges**: Partisanship in politics, lack of integrity by some money-for-chieftaincy policies, in-fighting undermine traditional values, etc.)
- **Socioeconomic and cultural changes:** These changes have resulted in lack of precision about genealogical relationships, while new ideas have generated uncertainties about the constructs of authenticity for rights in succession to stools and skins, as in the case of Ghana (Brempong and Pavanello 2006; Nworah 2007).

Relevance and Implications for Global Understanding of Indigenous Systems of Governance

As already noted, debate over the relevance of traditional institutions in modern-day societies continues to capture headlines. The relevance of traditional institutions, especially chieftaincy, to the transformation of African economies and governance systems for global understanding, schooling, and education is highly disputed in postcolonial writings, especially, among stakeholders, educators, politicians, Africanists, and traditional rulers (Osakede and Ijimakinwa 2015). Despite the declining power of traditional rulers in modern governance, their political systems, to some extent, continue to be relevant in the discharge of certain administrative functions. It is on this basis that this chapter may be timely and necessary to re-examine the relevance of traditional rulers in indigenous systems of governance and educational systems in modern governance structure as there are areas of significance which normally remain unrecognized and unexplained. These include the following:

Conflict Resolution

The African continent remains beleaguered by many internal conflicts that spring from problems of nation-building. One area where the traditional system of governance has shown tremendous success is in conflict resolution. Utilizing the norms of customary laws, disputes such as land, chieftaincy succession, criminal, and civil cases are arbitrated or resolved at the traditional levels. Indigenous methods of conflict resolution include traditional disputes resolution, peace-making, family or community gatherings, and traditional mediation. All these benefit from the traditional methods of resolving problems and to the methods of restoration and reparative justice (Okrah 2003).

Expansion of Public Services

Public-service delivery in Africa is generally poor. An ECA study (2005), for instance, uncovers that less than 31% of the population of the countries in the survey sample voiced approval with the provision of service in their local governments. The lack of political backbone, the inability of the governments, and the absence of local participation in the strategy and distribution of service account for the poor delivery of service. Involving traditional institutions by the states can go a long way toward the improvement of service delivery in various ways. This is suggested because traditional authorities can mobilize local communities for political participation, thereby empowering them to play a part in influencing policy on the distribution of public services. Traditional authorities also have the potential to support the efforts of the government in service delivery by participating in the administration of justice and by mobilizing human and financial resources for expanding educational and health services (ECA 2005). African traditional values, thus, not only converge with modern democratic values, but also have the potential to complement the mechanisms of modern democracy by filling the gaps in the applicability of modern democratic mechanisms. They can also bring overlooked groups of society, including the peasantry, into the political process and improve the chances of gaining entree to public services for such communities.

Management of Resource-Based Conflicts (Land-Tenure System)

Another area of possible contribution of traditional institutions is in the mitigation of resource-based conflicts. The communal land tenure system that is prevalent in much of Africa is the foundation of many of the political structures and democratic values. The communal tenure system opens up access to land for all members of the community. Until economic development creates access to different prospects, the communal tenure system remains a critical instrument for cutting rural unemployment, poverty, and inequality. It also makes the preservation of traditional democratic values and rural self-governance possible. Easing source-based conflicts is likely to require respect for the traditional land rights of local communities and their involvement in decision-making as well as in sharing the benefits of land and other resource allocation (Okrah 2003).

From the above relevant roles played by traditional rulers, it is not surprising that, a growing number of African countries, including some of those that had previously attempted without success to strip chiefs of their power or to completely abolish traditional institutions, have realized the political currency that chiefs possess. For example, Uganda and Zimbabwe have taken measures to reinstate and to integrate chiefs into their governance structure. These two countries have also now conceded to the political risks or opportunity costs involved in abolishing chieftaincy. Chiefs have become "vote-brokers" in rural areas and exercise meaningful informal control over the state's intervention in local affairs (Von Trotha 1996). As vote-brokers, they side themselves with the powers that offer the best chances for upholding their positions and promoting their interests.

The following factors further attest to the relevance of indigenous institutions in modern political times by the chiefs and other traditional leaders. Among others, indigenous institutions continue to play the following important roles:

- **Family assets:** The traditional rulers serve as custodians of family assets including lands, among others.
- **Responsibility to work for the development of the community:** The material advancement of a community and the maintenance of its peace and unity are considered as one of the major duties of a chief or traditional leader.
- **Cultural leadership:** Chiefs and other traditional leaders exemplify and oversee deep-seated cultural values and practices, e.g., fertility of the land, taboos, festivals, etc.
- **Agents of peace:** The traditional leaders provide the assurance upon which new mixed governance structures can be established since chiefs serve as custodians of and advocates for the interests of local peoples within the bigger central political framework.
- **Control over land**: Most of the land holders maintain their lands through forms of "customary tenure"; access to, and use of, land is still controlled or managed in practice (even if not legally) by chiefs, family or family heads.
- **Political representation of the community and community identity:** The role has led to the frequent involvement of chiefs in party politics, either as "brokers" for the mobilization of support, or as powerful actors in their own right (Ayittey 1992; Brempong and Pavanello 2006; Crook 2005; Okrah 2003).

Consequently, notwithstanding the overall minimal knowledge about African traditional systems of governance, the above piece can serve as lessons from African judicial systems of governance for global understanding as it has lighted the various roles the indigenous African systems of governance continue to play in the modern day Africa. This piece has provided information for better understanding of how Africa is combining a modern-day system of governance which is predominantly Western-centric with precolonial indigenous systems of governance. It may be probable to find similar indigenous practices and philosophies in other parts of the world.

Future Directions

The following ideas are recommended for future direction for prospects of African indigenous systems of governance.

There is the need for a paradigm shift. Indigenous institutions must be willing to initiate change as it has become necessary for a renovation of the institution to gain a footprint in this era of globalization. With this approach in mind, there should be a substantive adaptation of traditional approaches on the part of outside development partners toward commitment to indigenous traditional cultures. Thus, there is the need to bolster and rejuvenate traditional institutions of governance by starting to embrace these informal and traditional approaches to issues like conflict management and peace-building among local communities. The involvement of the traditional approaches are not only relevant but sacrosanct to African traditional setting in conflict management and peace-building so that the traditional institutions would regain their nearly lost respect and values in attempt to revive the kind of influence they wielded during the precolonial era.

Consequently, integrating traditional authorities into the modern governance structure should be considered as a way of making African indigenous systems of government more relevant and meaningful for today's schooling and political education for better global understanding of the traditional governance systems. To the extent that African traditional political values and customary laws are essential to the continent's transformation, the role of the authorities who are engaged in the practice and maintenance of those values is indispensable. Chiefs, especially those at the grassroots level, and elders in the decentralized political systems, are the leaders in the practice of those values and they form an integral albeit informal part of the governance structures of rural Africa. As von Trotha (1996) notes, chiefs and village heads under civil chieftaincy constitute a valuable resource in informing the state about the interests of local communities as well as in mobilizing rural populations for active engagement, not only in development activities and the distribution of public services, but also in the national political process.

Unlike government-appointed administrators, lower-level chiefs and village leaders live in conditions largely similar to those of their communities. They share common interests and think like their people. As a result, they are better equipped to represent the interests of their communities than are government-appointed administrators, who are accountable only to the political *elite*. Partnership in development between local traditional leaders and government administrators is also likely to promote cooperative state-society relations that are sorely absent in Africa. However, even though incorporating these leaders has not been controversial, the state has invariably underutilized the traditional leaders at the grassroots level and has not done enough to integrate them into the formal governance structures. This practice needs to be revisited.

Again, in this era of globalization, there should be a study, evaluation, and compilation of "socially desirable" customary laws and usages. This means researchers must unpack the existing stereotypical typology about Africa governance systems to make it possible for outside observers to learn more about the complex characteristics that are lost in its generalizations about Africa. Such insights make it possible for observers to identify the attributes of the various types of traditional institutions that can be used to promote development and democratic governance and those aspects that are incompatible with democratic governance and need to be changed. Without access the true picture of the characteristics and dynamics of traditional institutions, it will be difficult to understand why they have remained resilient and to determine the possible impacts they can make to the fostering of democratic institutions that are harmonious with African authenticities and value systems. This idea is better captured when we recognize the perspective of Basil Davidson (1969) on these issues when he summed up that:

> In the end, it will be a matter of knowing how the civilization of the past can be remade by a new and bold vision. The Africans sorely need their modern revolution: profound and far-reaching in creative stimulus, unleashing fresh energies, opening new freedoms. The world's experience, may help. But the structures that are needed will have to stand on their own soil. Perhaps this is only another way of saying that these new structures, as and when they emerge, will be nourished by the vigour and resilience of native genius, by all the inheritance of self-respect and innovating confidence that has carried these people through past centuries of change and cultural expansion. (p. 317)

The above iterations highlight that the indigenous traditional institutions can become a strong mobilizing metaphor. As already pointed out, the chiefs, among others, can serve as a link for grassroot development schemes in the communities, consequently, making traditional institutions a strong mobilizing force.

Conclusion

Let me conclude. It is heart-warming to reflect and highlight the issues and prospects of African indigenous systems of governance as an educator. In this chapter, I have contextualized the precolonial indigenous systems of governance by discussing the different types of indigenous forms of governance structure in precolonial era and their attributes. I also highlighted the role of community elders in the traditional governance; examined traditional governance under colonialism and post colonialism. Lastly, I focused on the future directions of indigenous governance. I trust the readers will notice that traditional rulers are very important in many traditional settings in Africa. Though some of their powers and vigor in the communities continue to wane in postindependence Africa due to a number of factors, they remain resilient and continuously play a very significant role in terms of cultural leadership by informally managing conflict, control over lands, arranging peacemaking meetings, and political representation of the community and community identity.

Hopefully, in a world so divided along *isms* in terms of race, gender, class, religion, and political ideologies, I hope knowing something about issues and prospects of African indigenous systems of governance can stimulate a debate to serve as a provocation of ideas on current situation of indigenous systems of governance and their potential relevance for better understanding in this era of globalization whereby the world has become increasingly interdependent and interconnected.

Admittedly, in such undertakings, we are likely to raise more issues that we can concretely address about the whole gamut of indigenous governance. However, I see this as an important first step. It may be possible to identify similar indigenous practices and philosophies in other parts of the world that share common realities and, thus, making peoples and nations ostensibly connected in terms of systems of governance. It is this reality that has given me the license to discuss the characteristics of African indigenous governance systems through my personal and lived experiences as an African, through my research and scholarly visits to various African countries, and through my knowledge acquired from various literatures about formal and informal indigenous governance of Africa.

References

Alport EA (1964) The Ammeln. J R Anthropol Inst G B Irel 94(2):160–171

Asimeng-Boahene L (2014) Breaking barriers: African knowledge systems as windows to understanding African childhood in a United States social studies classroom. In: Yenika-Agbaw V, Mhando L (eds) African youth in contemporary literature and popular culture: identity quest. Routledge, New York, pp 148–163

Assimeng M (2006) Understanding society: an introduction to sociology for African students. Woeli, Accra

Ayittey GBN (1991) Indigenous African institutions. Transnational Publishers, New York

Ayittey GBN (1992) Africa betrayed. St. Martin's Press, New York

Beattie J (1967) Checks on the abuse of political power in some African states. Sociologus 11:97–115

Brempong A (2007) Transformation in traditional rule in Ghana (1951–1996). Institute of African Studies, University of Ghana, Accra

Brempong A, Pavanello M (2006) Chiefs in development in Ghana: interviews with four paramount chiefs in Ghana. Institute of Africa Studies, University of Ghana, Accra

Busia KA (1968) The position of the chief in the modern political system of Ashanti: a study of the influence of contemporary social changes on Ashanti political institutions. Frank Cass & Co. Ltd, London

Coplan DB, Quinlan T (1997) A chief by the people: nation versus state in Lesotho. J Int Afr Inst 67(1):27–60

Crook R (2005) The role of traditional institutions in political change and development. CDD/ODI Policy Brief 4:1–5

Davidson B (1969) The African genius: an introduction to African cultural and social history. Atlantic Monthly Press, Boston

Davidson B (1992) Black man's burden: Africa and the curse of nation state. James Currey, London

Dore AO (2011) The impact of traditional institution in modern administration. Lagos, LNG Publishers, Lagos

Economic Commission for Africa (ECA) (2005) ADF IV: governance for a progressing Africa. Economic Commission for Africa, Addis Ababa

Economic Commission for Africa (ECA) (2007) Relevance of African traditional institutions of governance. Economic Commission for Africa, Addis Ababa

Ejiofo P (2004) Chiefs constitutions and policies in Nigeria. West Afr Rev 3(2):30–35

Fadipe NA (1970) The sociology of the Yoruba. Ibadan University Press, Ibadan

Fajonyomi SB (1997) Governing the grassroots. An analysis of decision-making in Nigeria local governments. Olu-Akin Publishers, Ibadan

Fallers L (1955) The predicament of the modern African chief. An instance from Uganda. Am Anthropol 57(2):290–305

Fatile JO (2010) Boundary dispute & communal conflict resolutions. The role of traditional rule. Ziklay Consult Workshop, Lagos

Foundation for International Development Assistance (FIDA-Kenya) (ed) (n.d.) Traditional justice systems in Kenya: a study of communities in coast province. Noel Creative Media Ltd, Nairobi

Gartrell B (1983) British administrators, colonial chiefs, and the comfort of tradition: an example from Uganda. Afr Stud Rev 26(1):1–24

Jones D (1983) Traditional authority and state administration in Botswana. J Mod Afr Stud 21(1): 133–139

Khapoya VB (1998) The African experience: an introduction, 2nd edn. Prentice-Hall, Upper Saddle River

Kilson M (1966) Political change in a West African state: a study of the modernization process in Sierra Leone. Harvard University Press, Cambridge, MA

Kirk-Greene AH (1965) The principles of native administration in Nigeria. Oxford University Press, London

Legesse A (1973) Gada: three approaches to the study of African. Free Press, New York

Mamdani M (1996) Citizen and subject: contemporary Africa and the legacy of late colonialism. David Phillip, Cape Town

Miles W (1987) Partition royalty: the evolution of Hausa chiefs in Nigeria and Niger. J Mod Afr Stud 25(2):233–258

Montagne R (1931) The Berbers: their social and political organization (trans: Seddon D). Frank Cass, London

Morse J, Barrett M, Mayan M et al (2002) Verification strategies for establishing reliability and validity in qualitative research. Int J Qual Inq 1:1–19

Murdock GP (1967) Ethnographic atlas. University of Pittsburg Press, Pittsburg

Ntsebeza L (2005) Democracy compromised: chiefs and the politics of the land in South Africa. Brill, Leiden

Nworah U (2007) Role of traditional rulers in Nigeria. http://www.nathanielturner.com/roleoftraditionalrulers in Nigeria.htm. Accessed 3 Mar 2016

Okrah KA (2003) Toward global conflict resolution. Lessons from the Akan traditional judicial system. J Soc Stud Res 27(2):04–13

Orji KE, Olali ST (2010) Traditional institutions and their dwindling roles in contemporary Nigeria: the Rivers State example. In: Babawale T, Aloa A, Adesoji B (eds) Chieftaincy institutions in Nigeria. Concept Publication Ltd, Lagos, p 402

Osakede KO, Ijimakinwa SO (2015) Traditional institutions and the modern day administration of Nigeria: issues and prospects. J Res Dev 2(9):32–40

Perrot C, Fauvelle H, Francois AX (2003) le retour des rois les autorites iraditionnelles et l'Etaten Afrique contemporaine. Karthala, Paris

Potholm CP (1979) The theory and practice of African politics. Prentice-Hall, Englewood Cliffs

Reagan T (2005) Non-western educational traditions: indigenous approaches to educational thought and practice, 3rd edn. Mahwah, Lawrence Erlbaum Associates, Publishers

Robert S (1972) The survival of the traditional Tswana courts in the national legal system of Botswana. J Afr Law 6(2):103–129

Sapru RK (2008) Administrative theories and management thought. PHI Learning Private Ltd, New Delhi

Strauss AL (1994) Grounded theory methodology: an overview. In: Denzin NK, Lincoln YS (eds) A handbook of qualitative research. SAGE, Thousand Oaks

Tosh J (1977) Colonial chiefs in a stateless society: a case study from Northern Uganda. J Afr Hist 14(3):473–490

Uchendu VC (1965) The Igbo of Southeast Nigeria. Holt, Rinehart, & Winston, New York

Uwazie EE (1994) Modes of indigenous disputing and legal interactions among the Ibos of Eastern Nigeria. J Legal Pluralism 34:87–103

Van Binsbergen W (1987) Chiefs and the state in independent Zambia: exploring the Zambian National Press. J Legal Pluralism 25 & 26:139–201

Von Trotha T (1996) From administrative to civil *chieftaincy*: some problems and prospects of African chieftaincy. J Legal Pluralism 37–37:79–108

Williams C (1987) The destruction of black civilization. Third World Press, Chicago

Zack-Williams T (2002) Introduction: Africa at the millennium. In: Zack-Williams T, Frost D, Thomson A (eds) Africa in crisis: new challenges and possibilities. Plato, London, pp 1–14

Indigenous Governance for Africentric School Success

12

George J. Sefa Dei

Contents

Introduction	170
History and Context: Long Standing Issues of Race, Schooling, and Education	171
Conceptualizing Indigenous Governance	173
Indigenous Governance, Schooling, and Education: The Case of the Africentric School	177
How is Such Governance Manifested in Indigenous and Alternative Educational Sites/Outlets?	180
Conclusion: Indigenous Systems of Governance and the Re-Visioning of Schooling and Education in Euro-American Contexts	182
References	184

Abstract

As a key proponent of the establishment of Africentric schools in Ontario and Canada, my paper will explore the possibilities of enhancing learning outcomes for Black/African, Indigenous, and marginalized youth in counter/alternative educational spaces. The focus is development of a governance structure that takes into account the central tenets of Afrocentric education with parents and local communities as key foundational players in the school's governance. Among key questions for engagement are: how do we conceptualize Indigenous governance for an Africentric school? How such governance is manifested in Indigenous and alternative educational sites outlets? How do Indigenous systems of governance offer important lessons for re-visioning schooling and education in Euro-American contexts? The discussion is informed by a search for Indigenous philosophies for critical education working with local analytical concepts and ideas to enhance youth learning outside of the conventional school system.

G. J. Sefa Dei (✉)
Social Justice Education, OISE, University of Toronto, Toronto, ON, Canada
e-mail: george.dei@utoronto.ca

Keywords

Indigeneity · Indigenous Governance · Community · Leadership · Africentric Schooling · Black/African · Canada

Introduction

The chapter explores Indigenous systems of governance with implications for Africentric schooling and education in Canada. In 2009, after a long community struggle for improvements in Black/African Canadian education, the Toronto District School Board (TDSB) in the province of Ontario opened an Africentric school at Sheppard Public School, Toronto, to cater for junior Kindergarten to grade 6. The School was the first of its kind by a major school board in Canada. The Africentric school is largely viewed as a small-scale pilot study, not set up as a broad model of segregation as its opponents have argued. The School is an optional model of education where students go on voluntary basis and are not forced to be there because of their Black or African identity. Furthermore, the School is open to all students who share in its philosophical principles and ideals, that is, entry to the School is not based on race or ethnicity. Originally the School was primarily intended as an "ameliorative" program to respond to some of the pressing challenge of Black education and academic advancement (see also Lawrence 2009).

Early test results of the school in 2010 revealed some successes: the Africentric school had 81% of its students above the provincial standard of the EQAO tests, well above the 70% across TDSB, and 70% for the province; students of the Africentric school were 8–10 percentage points above the rest of the province in reading and mathematics (Vukets 2011). It is therefore not surprising that in 2014, TDSB opened a second Africentric school, Scarborough's Winston Churchill Collegiate in Toronto at the secondary level. Unfortunately, in later years the Africentric school at Sheppard has faced some growing problems that have impacted its initial success (see James et al. 2015).

It is important to reiterate some of the philosophical principles and the political-intellectual project of an Africentric schooling. Africentric schools are conceptualized as "community institutions" pushing for a special position of the teacher imbued with a decolonizing spirit to "save our children" from mis-education and under education of conventional schooling. The school has close relations and bonding with parents and community Elders. The school teaches about self, identity, culture, history, and heritage, fostering a collective racial pride as critical for enhancing social and academic success of Black/African students in particular. But it is generally understood such pride does not necessarily guarantee academic success for students. Education success, it is understood, entails collective hard work engrained in principles of reciprocity, sharing, responsibility, mutual interdependence, respect for the Elderly, authority, and the power of communal ancestral knowledge. The principles of Africentric schooling are built on the Afrocentric idea of the centeredness of the [African] learner, the promotion of [African] cultures, identities, history, as well as Black agency and resistance (see Asante 1991; Dei and Kempf 2013). Afrocentricity as a guiding principle and philosophical idea is a theory of social change (Mazama 2003; Asante and Mazama 2005, 2010) to advance the social, cultural, emotional, and spiritual development of the African learner. The Africentric school works with the Ubuntu moral philosophy– community, mutual interdependence, sanctity of activity, interconnections, and social responsibility (see Letseka 2014, 2016). For the Africentric learner, there is a groundedness in the community knowledge and African intellectual traditions. The promotion of a strong African identity is upheld as consequential for schooling. This identity is complex and yet firmly African in terms of a social, spiritual, and emotional identification as well as psycho-cultural and political rootedness in African peoples' histories and struggles. There is also a place accorded to African spirituality in learning and the search for Black/African and Indigenous excellence in education.

Even after 6 years it is fair to argue that the Africentric school in Toronto is a "work in progress." Compounding institutional and systemic challenges of funding, leadership, community control, and developing a clear vision and mandate for Black education remain significant challenges. There is also the challenge of how action research (e.g., learning from lessons of the school for mainstream education through partnerships) and success of the school can translate to assist all students in mainstream schools. There is also the problem of developing a truly Afrocentric curriculum and pedagogic initiatives as a cornerstone of the school. The central role of parents, elders, and communities has not always been adhered to leading to conflict and internal strife between school administrators, parents, and the local community. In effect, key issues of vision and leadership have become perennial challenges of the school. Other growing problems and challenges are stakeholders in the school understanding the Afrocentric idea and its principles and what it means to put into practice. There has also been a growing community chorus to go beyond having "just one school" and to set up such schools at the elementary, secondary, university, and other tertiary levels.

The subject of this chapter is not so much a look at this particular school as an examination of some of the basic ideas that propel the Africentric school to be different from the mainstream school. In this context, this chapter examines how Indigenous governance brings some uniqueness to the Africentric schooling idea.

History and Context: Long Standing Issues of Race, Schooling, and Education

Research on minority and Indigenous education on Ontario and Canada has identified the systemic challenges impacting on students' academic success (e.g., representation, knowledge, reframing the "deep curriculum" – Dei et al. 1997, 2000; Solomon 1992; Codjoe 2001; James and Shadd 2001; Kelly 1998). There is the issue of youth disengagement and push-out in schools (e.g., bodies physically present but absent in mind and soul). The salience and silence of race (e.g., the legacy of anti-Black racism) is compounded by colonial settlerhood to deny the dreams and aspirations of many Canadian and Indigenous youth. Compounding these problems are the discursive manipulations of schooling success and educational failures in which schools would take credit for success but then blame and pathologize local families, parents, and communities for "problems." As noted elsewhere (Dei 2008), neoliberalism and its educational agenda has sought a deliberate deployment, interrogation and re-appropriation of the language of education reform (e.g., standards, accountability, excellence, competencies, quality, (human) capital). A very liberal notion of inclusion has depoliticized difference through "standardization recipes" according to Lewin (2000); and what hooks (1989) long ago rightly noted as pursuit of "sameness as provocation that terrorizes" (pp. 22–23).

What critical educational research tells us when it comes to Indigenous, Black, and minority youth education is that we seem to be adding stories to a weak foundation through cosmetic educational changes. We as a society are expecting success while reproducing the status quo that has maintained the systemic impediments to effective schooling for the youth. There is still an on-going search for a level playing field for all youth by addressing the "poverty of school culture" in terms of the processes of educational delivery (teaching, learning, and administration of education). The long standing pioneering research studies by critical scholars such as Apple and Weis (1983), Apple (1999), Ladson-Billings (1994), McCarthy (1990), King (2005), Fine (1991), Gillborn (1995), Giroux (1981), and Willis (1977), Brathwaite and James (1996), James (2000) have all attested to this fact of minority education in Euro-American context.

There are multiple complicities in the making of the perceived "educational crisis." Schools, educators, school boards, policy officials, local communities, parents, and students themselves are all differentially implicated. We have not learned much from international and cross-cultural comparative lessons of promoting educational success. There is an unquestioned faith in integration which has stymied a critical discussion of counter schooling options for different bodies. We have not tapped into wealth of Indigenous cultural knowings about educating learners. It is here that examining Indigenous concepts and conceptions of schooling and the governing of schools may offer some lessons. Such schools are conceptualized and operationalized differently to respond to some of the alienating aspects, including the colonial hierarchies of conventional schooling.

Counter-visioning schooling in North American contexts also requires a theoretical prism for understanding educational challenges and the need for educational change. A decolonial educational praxis that engages antiracism and transgressive pedagogies may have potential for radical educational transformation. Such educational praxis takes into account the question of identity, culture, pedagogy, and politics of schooling. Identity is linked to schooling as inclusive of racial, class, gender, sexual, [dis]abled identities of learners. Education must recognize the saliency of race and social difference (class, gender, sexual, disability, culture, etc.) as consequential in schooling. Students go into schools with their identities as raced, classed, gendered, sexualized, and [dis]abled. A recognition of the relative saliencies of different identities and the situational and contextual variations in intensities of oppression is significant in devising solutions to educational problems facing diverse communities. There is also the severity of issues for certain bodies (e.g., Black, racialized, and Indigenous bodies) to consider.

Conceptualizing Indigenous Governance

In this brief review of the literature, I explore Indigenous governance, while simultaneously providing reasons why colonial governments resist Indigenous governance. I also look at how colonial projects were used to test the relevance and effectiveness of Indigenous governance. I discuss the reasons of acknowledging Indigenous governance, the way forward, as well as critique existing literature of governance.

Indigenous communities worldwide had their form of government before European colonization. Such governance was often built on the premises of love, faith, and commitment to the people and the community. For many Indigenous communities around the world, love is the foundation upon which all relations are built. Love sees beyond the imperfection of the community. It enables leaders to perform their given roles without coercion. Love sees beyond every person's ability and skills. Through love, Indigenous peoples live in a state of harmony. Indigenous life before colonialism revolved around respect, reciprocity, collaboration, and unity. Indigenous peoples see power as a quality that everybody possesses. This way of looking at power was demonstrated among Indigenous peoples through teaching young ones their culture and way of life. Power resides within the local culture and percolates through the community in different measures (Torres and Nyaga 2016). Young ones were taught community values and culture as a way of preparing them for leadership roles. Some of the teachings young ones received involved healing practices. Healing process was a powerful process of governing communities. Power is discussed as part of Indigenous governance in relation to healing the people and the community. Indigenous governance sees power as fluid in that everyone has the capacity to exercising power (Dei 2000; Foucault 1980; Torres and Nyaga 2016). This means that the people chosen to lead the community are guardians of community power.

It is significant to note that in creating a pan-Indigenous identity, we must distinguish between nations and peoples. Leanne Simpson's analysis of Gdoo-naaganinaa provides a specific example of how precolonial nation-to-nation relations on Turtle Island were driven by mutual sustainability, respect, and (possibly) love. As she notes at length, describing Anishinaabe leadership:

> This reciprocity is also reflected in the qualities of traditional leadership. To reproduce the qualities prized in a traditional leader – respect, honesty, truth, wisdom, bravery, love, and humility – our ancestors practiced relationships with children that embodied kindness, gentleness, patience, and love. Children were respected as people, they were encouraged to follow their visions and to realize their full potential while living up to the responsibilities of their families, communities, and nations. This was the key to creating leaders with integrity, creating good governance, and teaching future leaders how to interact in a respectful manner with other human and nonhuman nations. (Simpson 2008, p. 33)

Indigenous governance is an effective and useful tool in solving social issues facing the society (O'Malley 1996; Larson et al. 2008; Njoh 2015). For example, the current form of national government of Canada may be attempting to incorporate some aspects of Indigenous governance. Reed (1999) captures the nature of Indigenous governance in Canada pointing to key principles of sharing, reciprocity, cooperation, generosity, courage, and wisdom:

> Most Aboriginal societies valued individual responsibility and independence, but they also believe in the importance of sharing. Cooperation was key and consensus was a central part of decision making. Indigenous leaders should be responsible to the needs and desires of their people. Among the Siksika (Blackfoot), leaders gained recognition and authority on the basis of their courage, generosity, honesty, and wisdom. They governed only as long as they had the confidence of their people. (Reed p. 10)

Colonial governments realized the importance of working with Indigenous forms of governance for effective administration of communities. It was very clear to colonial administration that as much as Indigenous community leaders were chosen to lead their communities, they had to work in solidarity with other members of the community (see Lauer 2007). Indigenous peoples cherished individual contribution and freedom as embedded in the spirit of community belonging. Ross (2006) discusses the rules guiding Aboriginal and Indigenous peoples' practice, noting among them "the ethic of non-interference, the ethic that anger should not be shown, the ethic respecting praise and gratitude, the conservation-withdrawal tactic, and the notion that the time must be right" (pp. 13–14). Each of these principles plays a great role in Indigenous governance.

How Indigenous governance deals with social issues within communities does not make sense to the colonizer. According to the colonizer, they are irrational and emotional. In fact, colonial governments intimate that these principles of sharing, reciprocity, and generosity are "rigid" and unhelpful to individual freedoms. Nonetheless, Indigenous peoples adore their community and the principles that guide them. They do so because they are involved collectively in creating those principles that serve their communities' best interest. As such they identify with such principles and abide by the rules governing them. Each member of the community has a role to perform. Individual contributions are valued and seen as contributing to the well-being of the community.

The power that exists in this community is not totalizing, in fact, it encourages everybody to work hard for the benefit of all (see O'Malley 1996, p. 318). O'Malley (1996) defines Indigenous governance as "attuned to nomadic existence, reflect[ing] far more fissionable and temporary arrangements and non-corporate forms, in which kinship, age, gender and sacred knowledge and status are central principles" (O'Malley 1996, p. 315 quoting Keen 1989). Other Indigenous scholars have articulated their views of Indigenous governance. Tauli-Corpuz (2006), an Igorot scholar from the Philippines, states that "at a very early age our parents and elders taught us basic values deemed Indigenous values such as respect for nature and ancestors, honesty, and love for Mother Earth" (p. 13). Doxtater (2011) describes the Indigenous governance in Kanataronnon community, noting that:

the well-known model of Indigenous governance is said to have influenced the liberal and socialist nation-states' political philosophy. In the Indigenous model male 'chiefs' perform a judiciary role. Influenced strongly by Indigenous mothers (matrilineal descent), an 'executive' branch includes aides, counselors, mediators, health specialists – any skill or duty used to manage the affairs of the nation. Finally, the right and freedom of the people to govern over their own affairs around 'fires' as special interest groups are 'representative' of the people's will. Consensus building is the central requirement between the judiciary, executive, and representative domains. (390)

Colonization has long been deeply implicated in the erosion of such Indigenous governing processes. One of colonialism's most effective tactics for dismantling Indigenous governance is the construction of the "Indigenous" as something primitive that must be abandoned. For example, Tauli-Corpuz (2006) explains that the people in her Igorot community never considered themselves to be "poor" or "underdeveloped" until they faced globalization. With time, Tauli-Corpuz and her community came to see themselves through the eyes of the colonizer. They were conditioned to believe that the Igorot worldview was an obstacle to development, civilization, and prosperity. By positioning Indigeneity as primitive and Western neoliberalism as progressive, colonial governments are better able to establish hegemonic power.

Ironically, even as the colonizer works to dismantle structures of Indigenous governance, colonial governments take up and appropriate Indigenous ways of governing to address certain social problems (O'Malley 1996; Njoh 2015; Larson 2011). We see this double-edged maneuver – stamping out Indigenous structural power while simultaneously appropriating specific elements of Indigenous governance into colonial systems of power – all over the world. For instance, Australian government tries to appropriate Ngaanyatjarra culture (O'Malley 1996); Japan attempts to ignore Ainu people (Larson 2011); Cameroon exasperates their way of governance through bypassing the people of Meta (Njoh 2015); and the United Nations insists in giving advice to Indigenous People (Tauli-Corpuz 2006). Admittedly, while these examples may not fully present the hypocrisy of simultaneously dismantling and appropriating Indigenous governance, they do point to the acknowledged strengths of such forms of governance in colonial nation states.

How do we account for such development trends? In neoliberal societies, state and national governance is built on principles of power from the top, greed, ownership, fame, individuality, and corruption. In fact, neoliberalism has fostered the spirit of individualism, greed, selfishness through its false praise of individual hard work, personal sacrifice, and meritocracy. At least on paper, leaders are elected with the hope of serving their constituencies and work in between and beyond borders of race, class, ethnicity, gender, ableism, religion, age, and other forms of differences. Leaders in colonial governments are expected to create a space of love and respecting diversity, a space where all community members are welcome to contribute their talents, skills, and time for the benefit of the whole; a space where the notion of racism, classism, ageism, homophobia, and other forms of division, hatred, and prejudice are avoided; most of all, a space where centers, margins, and borders must be eliminated so that there is a continued flow of respect, recognition, and unity to all. We must be thoroughly critical of colonial governance. There is the absurdity of a colonial system that seeks to benefit all while erasing and ignoring social difference. What is on paper is a far cry from what we have witnessed and continue to witness in the supposedly neo-colonial era. But even if this is the case, why have state-run projects and programs aimed at bettering the community so often resulted in alienation, exploitation, and oppression? One needs only look at the tragic consequences of contemporary state governance in a number of African countries (see also Lauer 2007)!

In examining the simultaneous attempts by colonial power to extinguish and appropriate Indigenous governance, we encounter a basic truth: Indigenous governance poses a threat to colonial power. The practice of Indigenous governance, therefore, is a means of both resurgence and resistance (Dei 2000). However, such resistance cannot be effective if it does not consider its relationality to systems of colonial power. For example, O'Malley (1996) examines features of Australian policies of self-determination for Aboriginal peoples, in order to explore systems in which resistance in the form of Indigenous governance can [influence the (?)] establishment of [policy and] regulations. O'Malley discussing contemporary governmentality argues that the approach "privileges official discourses, with the result that it becomes difficult for it to recognize the imbrication of resistance and rule, the contradictions and tensions that this melding generates, and the subterranean practices of government consequently required to stabilize rule" (p. 311). Referencing Foucault (1980), he points to the fact that "power comes from below" and that resistance is never in a position of exteriority in relation to power. Resistance can actually be an essential part of and provider to projects irrespective of success and not just integration into colonial projects. O'Malley (1996) argues that if resistance is viewed and positively incorporated in government, it may result in creating spaces of productivity and cooperation.

O'Malley (1996) further describes liberalism as a system that focuses on technologies and appropriation of Indigenous governance. This appropriation of Indigenous governance creates challenges to colonial governments "…even when the programme is successful in its major goals, liberalism may incorporate alien and contradictory practices and assumptions…such work is subterranean in the sense that to be successfully effected, it must not violate the authenticity of the Indigenous governance in the eyes of the programmers and the programmed" (p. 313). Hence, when a state-run program is built upon appropriated concepts of Indigenous governance, the program will often fail. On the other hand, if Indigenous governance is effectively *incorporated into* (rather than appropriated by) a liberal system of power, "the resultant arrangements…may contribute to liberalism's eclecticism and adaptability through the addition of new concepts, techniques and principles of governance" (O'Malley 1996, pp. 313–314).

To fully understand the relationship between colonial and Indigenous systems of governance, we must also examine the issue of Indigenous self-determination within colonial societies. True self-determination would pose a tremendous threat to colonial power. Liberal governments have traditionally imposed restrictive parameters on Indigenous autonomy and sovereignty, often excluding Aboriginal and Indigenous Peoples in government positions such as managers, teachers, and community advisors (O'Malley 1996). Writing in the Japanese context, Larson et al. (2008) argue that there is a long way to go before Ainu people can fully enjoy and exercise true self-determination: "despite ... [the] international legitimacy [that the Ainu struggle has received], the institutional structures of the Japanese state mediate the effects of international influences and limit Ainu domestic self-determination and participation in governance" (p. 55). Indigenous peoples claim that "domestic policies based on cultural promotion and Ainu welfare provide few points of direct contact between Ainu leaders and the Japanese bureaucracy; further, these points of contact tend to be isolated from the parts of the bureaucracy most subject to international influence" (p. 55). It is contended that, "additionally, actors in the Japanese government exposed to global normative pressures have little direct interaction with Ainu specialists" (p. 56). The Japanese government does not want to recognize Ainu people as Indigenous peoples because their folklore is invisible (see Larson et al. 2008 for further discussion). Similarly, we know the Igorots in the Philippines have not been recognized by the colonial state because it is assumed their practices are outdated, not useful, and therefore invalid (Tauli-Corpuz 2006). This problem is compounded by the erroneous and often racist assertion that Indigenous peoples are "uneducated" and cannot understand the processes of globalization, acculturation, liberalism, as just some examples, and therefore, there is no point of including them in the current governance. We maintain that notwithstanding such negative and problematic views of Indigenous governance, there are projects instituted or that can be instituted that bear true glimpses of what Indigenous governance is and should be about. At a microlevel, we turn to the case of the Afrocentric school in Toronto, Canada.

Indigenous Governance, Schooling, and Education: The Case of the Africentric School

This section of the edited collection concedes school governance to be a major topic for Indigenous peoples with implications for educational institutions and communities. Clearly Indigenous systems of governance have implications for the effective running of schools to ensure educational success as broadly defined. Given that education is pursued in transnational contexts, it is also important for discussions to bring an international dimension to both concepts of "Indigenous" and "Indigenous Governance." In this regard, this chapter applies Indigenous governance to Africentric education and educational leadership within such an institution and particularly, the way Indigenous governance informs and frames school-community structures and relationships.

It is already noted that Indigenous governance is built on the premises of love, faith, and commitment to people and community (Dei et al. 2000). Schooling is about the love of learning. In pursuing this love of learning community comes together to recognize the contributions of everyone to the collective. Beyond the imperfections of learners, the idea of schooling as community ensures that the success of one becomes the success of all. Similarly, one's failure is our failure. It is this principle of community, sharing, reciprocity, love, and caring that undergirds an Africentric school. School governance is built on these principles and teachers, students, staff, and community are expected to be more than the individual and the self. School governance is entrusted in the hands of a collective leadership with assigned roles and responsibilities that ensure collective success. Through love, the members of the Africentric school community live in a harmony. Indigenous life before colonialism revolved around respect, reciprocity, collaboration, and unity.

Exploring the schooling and educational implications of Indigenous governance, we argue that Indigenous governance is bottom up, inclusive, and very holistic. There are no clear lines of demarcating authority and responsibility. This does not mean chaos nor anarchy but a sense of collective decisioning that involves the school and the local community in every sense of a collective partnership. Indigenous governance in Africentric schooling is about collective leadership from local community, parents, educators, and school administrators as well as students. There are chains of accountability even in this style of collective governance since the running of the school, in terms of the delivery of education, teaching, learning, and administration of education is left in the hands of bodies working in collective partnership. Conventional schooling accords much power and authority to school boards and Ministry of Education that usually provide the funding of educational institutions. Even when these funds are taxpayers' money, school rules demarcate these formal institutions as the final arbiters in funding decisions many times relegating the roles of local community and parents as taxpayers and funders of schools into secondary roles. The funding decisions determine broader questions of the "deep curriculum" (Dei et al. 1997) defined to include the culture, climate, and socio-organizational lives of schools, as well as school management, policies, and procedures. The traditional governance structures end up disempowering local communities, parents, students, and to some extent classroom teachers. With the Africentric schooling, funding is provided by local communities as primary taxpayers and not the state. This perception is important since it places communities and parents at the center of school governance.

The school is structured to break down any false separation between "school authorities," "parents and communities," and "students." Indigenous governance of the Africentric school is rather a collective style of governance where the local community (including parents and community workers as Elders) provide guidance and vision for the school, working alongside school administrators, school board officials, teachers, and students to effectively run the school. Each of these bodies has respective and interrelated roles of governance. For example, questions of respect and discipline are handled by Elders, parents, and students, financial governance by school board officials and Council of Elders and parents; school rules and regulations are set by teachers who are guided by school board policies devised collectively with the local communities and parents. Responsibilities of classroom teaching and learning, while left for trained educators and students, will seek to include parents and Elders coming into the school as teachers to impact community communal knowledge and wisdom. School curriculum, classroom instruction, and pedagogy are all matters worked collectively with local communities and parents.

These are not romantic nor utopian ideals but something to guide the operation and governance of the school. It calls for a rethinking outside the proverbial box for a different approach to school governance. School governance is a question of leadership, and specifically collective leadership. It works with Indigenous ideas of community, collective, relations, interconnections, holism, shared vision, shared stakes, social responsibility, and collective accountability.

As argued in another paper (Dei 2017), conventional models of leadership usually tout managerial/bureaucratic leadership, instructional leadership, and transformational leadership, moral/ethical leadership, and participative leadership, situational and contingent leadership as critical skills for social transformation. While these are significant, they do not help us understand the varied conceptions that different communities have of leadership and the fact that in Indigenous and African communities, leadership is less about individual attributes and skills than shared community expectations and roles (see also Portelli and Campbell-Stephenes 2009; Solomon 2002).

Governance as Indigenous leadership is by a "community of leaders." Leadership is principally about equity, centering spirituality, and is community-driven. It is leadership that is bottom-up and emerging. An African/Indigenous centered governance perspective sees leadership as not about a romantic or charismatic persona. Leadership is not about the individual (Brathwaite and James 1996). Such leadership however signifies the heroics of collectivities to resist domination, colonization, and oppression and to ensure that local peoples design their own futures and agenda. It is a leadership based on serving the community rather than the other way around. It is a leadership meant to involve the community, in such a way that power relations are spread out to all. This is manifested in decision-making processes where everyone is considered an important part at the table. It is a kind of leadership where everyone has something to contribute and participate without being victimized (Dei 2017).

African Indigenous governance through collective leadership does not imply any "absolute interiority." Such governance recognizes the agency and power of the Indigene to name what constitutes leadership in cultural contexts (see also Hountondji 1997, p. 18 in a related context). An African conception of leadership is spiritually informed and spiritually based. It is about developing ethical and social responsibility to all humans and nonhumans as sharing the Earth space. It is leadership that is nurtured by the Land and the teachings of Mother Earth. It is leadership that we each live and breathe. It is possessed by all. It is about the ethics of caring for everyone, including the nonhuman. African leadership is about respecting the sanctity of life and developing interpersonal relations that affirm the bond of the individual, group, and the community. Such leadership works with consensus decision making and upholds the integrity of the group. Indigenous African governance embraces African Indigeneity and what local cultural knowledges teach about traditional governance as collective, shared, inspirational, spiritual, and responsibility-laden. It is also governance through traditional styles of collective leadership that cultivates the community's capacity to articulate its own issues and concerns and looks for genuine home grown solutions to problems. This vision of Indigenous African governance through communal leadership identifies local struggles for political, cultural, spiritual, social, and educational liberation as a motivation factor for social and educational change.

How is Such Governance Manifested in Indigenous and Alternative Educational Sites/Outlets?

In articulating a connection between Indigenous governance, schooling, and education, we must begin to think and act anew, that is, something radically different than the conventional practice of educational delivery. The structures and processes of educational delivery such as teaching, learning, and administration of education must be reassessed and reframed in ways that centered Indigenous ideas and philosophies of education and educational governance. It is contended that the "administration of education" as a question of Indigenous governance is critical to counter-visioning schooling and positing a new educational futurity. But, as already noted, school governance in an Indigenous paradigm is not simply about the administration of education. Indigenous governance comprises all the decision-making processes that relate to the socio-organizational lives of schools, as well as the macrosocial and political forces for educational delivery. Clearly, the notion of community and the collective as put forth within a framework of Indigenous governance does not mean doing away with the individual leadership, personal accountability, and self-responsibility. In fact, as noted within the Africentric school, specific personnel can be charged with assigned administrative responsibilities and this certainly can be understood as a personal responsibility. But such responsibility is rendered in the common/community good. Individuals charged with school administrative responsibility have to answer to questions informed by the community welfare. The whole point about school transparency is that assigned formal school leadership, working with educators, students, parents, and the local community are in an alliance or working partnership for effective educational delivery.

I will now give some concrete examples of how Indigenous governance is manifested in counter schooling. The configuration of Indigenous governance in the Africentric school has the wider community as the overall oversight "body" for the school (Brathwaite and James 1996). Elders, parents, and local community groups are responsible for providing vision, guidance, and leadership (Dei et al. 2000). Community and youth leaders identify needs and concerns that schools must address to enhance education and educational outcomes for all learners. Teachers, instructors, and pedagogues are charged with program matters, curricular, and instructional initiatives relating to the broad matters of teaching, learning, and administration of education. Official school bodies such as universities, colleges, school boards, and the Ministry of Education, for instance, take responsibility of much broader administrative, logistical, infrastructural support and structures which go beyond individual schools and classroom educators. The main point is that there is a synergy between these bodies and their responsibilities are not simply shared but connected and intricately linked for the success of educational delivery.

Increasingly one of the challenges faced by contemporary schooling and education is the question of youth discipline (see Dei and Simmons 2016 and many others). Discipline is a governance issue in the sense that it relates to rules and regulations set in school to create conducive learning environments for learners to develop respect for self, peers, group, and society. Discipline is about self and collective comportment for the collective good. Any school that is unruly and full of in-disciplined learners is ungovernable. So discipline is a critical aspect of school governance in any school. In the Africentric school, the emphasis is on teaching discipline rather than enforcing discipline. This marks an important departure from conventional schooling where there is usually too much emphasis on merely enforcing school rules of conduct and behavior to achieve youth compliance. While this is important we believe discipline is more than "laws enforcement." In the Africentric school educators/authorities working within school board guidelines will set the parameters for the official rules and regulations and disciplinary measures appropriate to the traditions of the school (Dei 2017). These rules and regulations are part of the official curriculum. However, these rules are always more than the written code of conduct. There are the official and then the unwritten rules that must be taught to each learner as requirement for being part of a larger collective. While the responsibility is equally placed on the learner to teach herself or himself the official and unofficial rules of social conduct, the responsibility is a social act and contract. They must be taught and learned. Thus, these rules and regulations must always be set in consultation with students, educators, parents, community workers, and local communities to ensure a "buy in" of all parties. Any concerns emanating from disciplinary rules, procedures, and measures must be appropriately dealt with by a committee representative of the different bodies and stakeholders. Community Elders have responsibility to assist educators not only in enforcing discipline, but also in teaching discipline. Teaching discipline includes educating about the local cultural resource knowledge relating to individual and social responsibility, respect for oneself, peers and authority, and the upholding of the traditions of the school for enhancement of learning for the collective success of all. The Indigenous ideals of respect, tolerance, fairness, justice, mutual interdependence, probity, and accountability are all ingrained in local cultural norms and community Elders, parents, and the larger citizenry duly obliged to socialize their youth into the teachings and acceptance of these cultural norms. The adult becomes a parent/guardian and a teacher, not only to their own children but to the children of the larger community as whole.

In the Africentric school, there is a co-creation of school curriculum involving Elders, parents, teachers, and students (Dei 2017). School teachers by virtue of their professional training take leadership on curriculum matters working within Ministry of Education and school board guidelines and official mandates of the curriculum. But the "co-creation" involves prior consultations and involvement of different bodies to develop a sense of collective ownership to the process (James 2010). The curriculum is understood as a way of life for schooling and a path to follow. The curriculum is not a straitjacket to wear literally. Enforcing the curriculum is a governance issue. When all parties do not have buy-in in the process of curriculum construction, it is fraught with challenges and perils. For example, there is the school knowledge and off-school community knowledge. Education must tap into all diverse forms of knowledges (see Banks 1993). The curriculum development must tap into local cultural resource knowledge which are usually embodied in cultural custodians as elders and parents, as well as the "street knowledge" that young learners acquire. The latter knowledge may include popular culture, arts and folk media, and other contemporary forms of media education.

Similarly, classroom pedagogy must ensure that the diversity of lessons is taken into account in delivering education. This may entail using multiple and multifaceted teaching methods. Through an Indigenous governance framework, this approach entails bringing in elders, parents, and community workers as "teachers." Teaching becomes a "pedagogy of community and community knowledges" and the pursuit of Indigenous governance entails the school site is a welcoming place for all with knowledge to share. It is the responsibility of school leadership through Indigenous governance requirements to acknowledge and to make actionable the understanding that everyone counts such that the school becomes a conducive place for learning and sharing of knowledge and ideas. The use of multiple teaching methods as classroom pedagogy also helps in diversifying the school curriculum for multiple learners (James 2010). Indigenous pedagogies which include the application of traditional knowledges and holistic and sustainable approaches to teaching and learning would help support critical understandings of their communities and the teachings of history, culture, identities, etc. As noted elsewhere (Dei and Simmons 2016), diversifying evaluation and assessments methods may include using orality as equal to written text whereby students are given opportunities to attend a community event or participate in organizing an event and have access to other "teachers" as community elders and cultural custodians.

Lastly, funding is a question of school governance. Educational funding has always been a source of tension between schools, school administrators, and local communities (James 2010). Given the centrality of the local community in the Africentric school, the funding question brings some implications of community support and resources. Funding for the Africentric school has community basis, as it is the community which "owns" the school and must therefore contribute to its funding. Such community funding is not simply supported by the idea of Indigenous governance. The principles of Indigenous knowledges justify the place of community in funding matters. Community funding serves to justify a collective governance structure for the school as community members have contributed to sustaining the school.

Conclusion: Indigenous Systems of Governance and the Re-Visioning of Schooling and Education in Euro-American Contexts

It has long been maintained that educational leadership has a direct bearing on academic success and the promotion of effective learning outcomes for youth (see Fullan 2001; Leithwood et al. 1999, 2004; Hargreaves and Fink 2006). Could we also insist that such leadership can be the springboard to put into place countervisions of schooling and education? So what type of education will we have if we place the principles of Indigenous governance at the center of schooling and education? How does Indigenous governance help us to re-imagine our worlds and communities – towards a new vision of schooling and education? The countervisioning schooling and education requires adopting new approaches to educational delivery. This new approach is about teaching, learning, and administration of education. Earlier discussions have emphasized this triplet of teaching, learning, and administration of education as part of the Indigenous governance for the school. In re-visioning schooling and education, we need to break away from the colonial hierarchies of schooling and embrace a sense of collective ownership and undertaking for success for all. The question of leadership and governance as collective is key to educational success. Collective leadership and governance means shared responsibilities and accountability for education success (Hill 1990, 2008). It also means ensuring school authority works for the local community, including the students, parents and other bodies. It means authority as not simply legitimated power but entrusted power with expectation to deliver social success that is broadly defined. It means authority as bestowed with a sense of leadership and vision. Indigenous leadership is also having the foresight to think creatively outside dominant paradigms or the mainstream thinking. It is about working Indigenous knowledge systems that embrace sharing, reciprocity, mutuality, accountability, transparency, and ethics. Authoritarian leadership is about power and the enforcements of rules and regulations not necessary caring about ensuring that all learners have access to the valued goods and services of society that make success happen. Indigenous governance also works with Indigenous principles of community, social responsibility, ethics of caring, mutual interdependence, and reciprocity.

The implication of foregone is calling for a new way of delivering education to learners that breaks away from the competition, individualism, individualized success, as well as the colonial hierarchies and the privileging of some experiences, knowledges, and identities at the expense of others that afflict conventional schooling. In re-visioning schooling and education informed by principles of Indigenous governance, there is a need to return politically, intellectually, culturally, and emotionally to a spiritual base of learning and knowledge production. This is about centering spirituality in schooling and education to connect social identities to schooling, education, and knowledge production (see also Magnusson 2000). Indigenous ontologies highlight a need to challenge and decenter Western epistemologies and to revitalize Indigenous theories and cultural practices, values, and worldviews and to bring accountability and transparency to schooling and education (Nelles and Alcantara 2014). The call for Indigenous governance in schooling is to represent community and community knowledge and to place such cultural knowledges that value relationships, connections and interdependence as the core of schooling and education (see Mila-Schaaf 2008; Smith 1999 in other contexts). Indigenous governance then becomes a springboard and motivator for achieving academic and social success.

For many learners, the academy [like other institutional settings] can be a hostile, unfamiliar place – dismemberment, depersonalization, and becoming intellectual imposters who are not true to authentic selves. There is a need for resistance and healing of selves and bodies to make us whole again. Indigenous governance offers us guiding principles that help bring people into a collective and community and to pursue a more holistic approach to schooling and educational change. The possibilities of Indigenous governance for counter-visions of schooling and education embrace humility, respect, compassion, love, sacredness of activity, and the sanctity of life. Such school governance seeks a connection between the learner, educator, knowledge, and the social community and environments within which learning takes place. This is a far cry from the alienating cultures of conventional schooling which stress individualism, rights, individual academic success over community building, collective responsibility, and social success.

References

Apple M (1999) The absent presence of race in educational reform. Race Ethnicity Educ 2(1):9–16
Apple M, Weiss L (1983) Ideology and practice in schooling: a political and conceptual introduction. Ideology and practice in schooling. Temple University Press, Philadelphia
Asante MK (1991) The afrocentric idea in education. J Negro Educ 60(2):170–180
Asante M, Mazama A (2005) General editors, encyclopedia of black studies. Sage, Thousand Oaks
Asante M, Mazama A (2010) Afrocentric infusion for urban schools: fundamental knowledge for teachers. Ankh, Philadelphia
Banks J (1993) The canon debate, knowledge construction and multicultural education. Educ Res 22(5):4–14
Brathwaite K, James C (eds) (1996) Educating African Canadians. James Lorimer & Co., Toronto
Burrow J (1997) Wampum at Niagara: the royal proclamation, Canada legal history and self-governance. In: Burrows J (ed) Aboriginal treaty rights in Canada: essays on law, equity and respect for difference. University of British Columbia Press, Vancouver, pp 155–175
Codjoe H (2001) Fighting 'Public enemy' of black academic achievement – the persistence of racism and the schooling experiences of black students in Canada. Race Ethn Educ 4(4):343–376
Dei GJS (2000) Rethinking the role of Indigenous knowledges in the Academy. Int J Incl Educ 4(2):111–132
Dei GJS (2008) Racist beware: uncovering racial politics in contemporary society. Sense Publishers, Rotterdam
Dei GJS (2017) An indigenous Africentric perspective on black leadership: the African scholar today. In: Kitossa T, Howard P, Lawson E (eds) Re/visioning African leadership: perspectives on change, continuity and transformation. Toronto, University of Toronto Press
Dei GJS, Kempf A (2013) New perspectives on Africentric schooling in Canada. Canadian Scholars' Press, Toronto
Dei GJS, Simmons M (2016) Citizenship education and embodied ways of knowing: what can be learned from the voices of Ghanaian youth in schooling and education? J Global Citizensh Educ Equity Educ 5(1):1–20
Dei GJS, Mazzuca M, McIsaac E, Zine J (1997) Reconstructing 'Drop-out': a critical ethnography of the dynamics of black students' disengagement from school. University of Toronto Press, Toronto
Dei G, James M, James-Wilson S, Karumanchery L, Zine J (2000) Removing the margins: the challenges and possibilities of inclusive schooling. Canadian Scholars Press, Toronto
Doxtater MT (2011) Putting the theory of Kanataronnon into practice: teaching Indigenous governance. Action Res 9(4):385–404

Fine M (1991) Framing dropouts: notes on the politics of an urban public high school. State University of New York Press, New York
Foucault M (1980) Power/knowledge: selected interviews and other writings, 1972–1977. Pantheon, New York
Fullan M (2001) Leadership in a culture of change. Jossey-Bass, San Francisco
Gillborn D (1995) Racism and anti-racism in real schools. Open University Press, Philadelphia
Giroux H (1981) Ideology and culture and the process of schooling. Temple University Press, Philadelphia
Hargreaves A, Fink D (2006) Sustainable leadership. Jossey-Bass, San Francisco
Hill R (1990) Oral memory of the Haudenosaunee: views of the two row wampum. Northwest Indian Q 7:21–30. 1: 27 2. Ibid., 26. 3
Hill SM (2008) Travelling down the river of life together in peace and friendship, forever: Haudenosaunee land ethics and treaty agreement as the basis for restructuring with the British Crown. In: Simpson L (ed) Lighting the eighth fire: the liberation, resurgence, and protection of indigenous nations. Arbeiter Ring Publishing, Winnipeg, pp 23–45
hooks b (1989) Talking back: thinking feminist, thinking black. South End Press, Boston
Hountondji P (1997) Endogenous knowledge. Research trails. Codesria Book Series, Dakar
James EC (2010) Schooling and the University plans of immigrant black students from an urban neighborhood. In: Milner H, Richard IV (eds) Culture, curriculum and identity in education. Palgrave Macmillan, New York, pp 117–139
James CE, Shadd A (2001) Talking about identity: encounters in race. In: Ethnicity and language. Between the Lines Press, Toronto
James C, Howard PSS, Brown R, Samaroo J (2015) The Africentric Alternative School experience: agency and action. Final report to Toronto District School Board
Keen I (1989) Aboriginal governance. In: Altman J (ed) Emergent inequalities in aboriginal Australia. Oceania Monograph 38, Sydney
Kelly J (1998) Under the gaze: learning to be black in white society. Fernwood Publishing, Halifax
King J (ed) (2005) Black education. A transformative research and action agenda for the new century. Lawrence Erlbaum Associates Publishers, Mahwah
Ladson-Billings G (1994) The dreamkeepers: successful teachers of African American children. Joss-Bass, San Francisco
Larson AM (2011) Forest tenure reform in the age of climate change: lessons for REDD. Global Environ Change 21(2):540–549
Larson E, Johnson Z, Murphy M (2008) Emerging Indigenous governance: Ainu rights at the intersection of global norms and domestic institutions. Alternatives 33:53–82
Lauer H (2007) Depreciating African political culture. J Black Stud 38(2):288–307
Lawrence S (2009) Afrocentric schools and the legal framework of educational equality remarks on the panel: rethinking "Separate but equal": a discussion of equality and Afrocentric schools. Faculty of Law, University of Toronto, March 10
Leithwood K, Jantzi D, Steinbach R (1999) Changing leadership for changing times. Open University Press, Buckingham
Leithwood K, Louis KS, Anderson S, Wahlstrom K (2004) How leadership influences student learning. Wallace Foundation, New York
Letseka M (2014) Ubuntu and justice as fairness. Mediterr J Soc Sci 5(9):544–551
Letseka M (2016) Open distance learning (ODL) through the philosophy of Ubuntu. Nova Science
Lewin KM (2000) New technologies and knowledge acquisition and use in developing countries. Compare 30(3):313–321
Magnusson J (2000) Spiritual discourse and the politics ontology. A proposal for a Roundtable Discussion. OISE, University of Toronto
Mazama A (ed) (2003) The Afrocentric paradigm. Africa World Press, Trenton
McCarthy C (1990) Race and curriculum: social inequality and the theory and politics of difference in contemporary research on schooling. Falmer Press, Basingstoke
Mila-Schaaf K (2008) Workshop report: regional pacific ethics of knowledge production workshop. 2007 Nov 13–15; Tofamamao, Apia, Samoa. UNESCO, Wellington

Nelles J, Alcantara C (2014) Explaining the emergence of Indigenous–local intergovernmental relations in settler societies: a theoretical framework. Urban Aff Rev 50(5):599–622

Njoh AJ (2015) The meta Indigenous politico-administrative system, good governance, and the modern Republican state in Cameroon. J Asian Afr Stud 50(3):305–324

O'Malley P (1996) Indigenous governance. Econ Soc 25(6):310–326

Portelli JP, Campbell-Stephenes R (2009) Leading for equity: the investing in diversity approach. Edphil Books, Toronto

Reed K (1999) Aboriginal peoples building for the future. Oxford University Press, Don Mills

Ross R (2006) Dancing with a ghost: exploring aboriginal reality. Penguin Group, Toronto

Simpson L (2008) Looking after Gdoo-naaganinaa: precolonial Nishnaabeg diplomatic and treaty relationship. Wicazo Sa Rev 23(2):29–42

Smith LT (1999) Decolonizing methodologies: research and indigenous peoples. University of Otago Press, Dunedin

Solomon P (1992) Black resistance in high school: forging a separatist culture. SUNY, New York

Solomon PR (2002) School leaders and anti-racism: overcoming pedagogical and political obstacles. J School Leadersh 12:174–197

Tauli-Corpuz V (2006) Our rights to remain separate and distinct. In: Tauli-Corpuz V, Mander J (eds) Paradigm wars. Sierra Club Books, San Francisco, pp 13–21

Torres RA, Nyaga D (2016) Discussion of power through the eyes of the margins: praxis of postcolonial aeta Indigenous women healers in the Philippines. Int J Asia Pac Stud 12(2):31–56

Vukets C (2011) High school would make students work to pay tuition Toronto star p. GT3

Willis P (1977) Learning to labour. Saxon House, Farnborough

Building Capacity for Indigenous Peoples: Engaging Indigenous Philosophies in School Governance

13

Edward Shizha

Contents

Introduction	188
Unpacking School Governance	189
Postcolonial Theory, Property, and School Governance	191
Indigenous Peoples and School Governance	193
Indigenous Peoples' Participation and the Cultural Deficit Model	194
Parental Engagement as a Community Responsibility	194
What Are Indigenous Philosophies?	195
Community, Peoplehood, and Personhood	195
Participatory Engagement	197
Collectivism	198
Why Indigenous Philosophies in Governance?	200
Recommendations and Conclusion	201
References	203

Abstract

School governance and the involvement of indigenous communities and parents in the affairs of the school contribute significantly to the school performance and educational outcomes of indigenous students. For indigenous peoples and communities, parental involvement is strongly influenced by ethnic or cultural backgrounds that are different to the school culture. There is merit in predicting that parental involvement in school governance increases school enrolments and participation by children from indigenous communities because parental involvement may motivate both parents and students to identify with the school and its programs. Schools should spend time building positive school-community relationships so that indigenous peoples get involved in decision-making processes

---

E. Shizha (✉)
Social and Environmental Justice and Youth and Children's Studies, Wilfrid Laurier University, Brantford, ON, Canada
e-mail: eshizha@wlu.ca

© Springer Nature Singapore Pte Ltd. 2019
E. A. McKinley, L. T. Smith (eds.), *Handbook of Indigenous Education*,
https://doi.org/10.1007/978-981-10-3899-0_31

that promote the aims and goals of the school and the aspirations of indigenous students. This chapter revolves around the assumption that there are very few indigenous peoples who take up positions in school councils or school boards, not because they are not willing to, but because of structural and systemic disadvantages and cultural "impediments." The chapter argues for the establishment of the school-community partnership and the inclusion of indigenous philosophies of school governance within the school in order to build capacity for the local indigenous peoples for them to contribute to the running of the local school. Because schools are institutions within communities, the chapter recommends that effort should be made to facilitate interaction between indigenous communities and school structures through the integration and acknowledgment of indigenous philosophies and epistemologies and rapidly promote indigenous structures and processes of governance.

Keywords

Capital · Collectivism · Indigenous peoples · Parental engagement · Peoplehood and personhood · Postcolonial theory · School-community relations · School governance

Introduction

There is a considerable body of research documenting the poor student and school performance for indigenous students (Hughes and Hughes 2012) resulting from perceived nonparticipation of their parents in school affairs. School governance and the involvement of communities and parents in the affairs of the education of their children contribute significantly to the school performance and educational outcomes of the students. For indigenous peoples and communities, parental involvement is strongly influenced by ethnic or cultural backgrounds that are different to the school culture (Berthelsen and Walker 2008; Mansour and Martin 2009). Schools should spend time building positive school-community relationships so that indigenous peoples get involved in decision-making processes that promote the aims and goals of the school and the aspirations of indigenous students.

This chapter revolves around the assumption that there are very few indigenous peoples who take up positions in school councils or school boards, not because they are not willing to, but because of structural and systemic disadvantages and cultural "impediments." The issue of indigeneity and indigenous governance philosophies in education are fraught with tensions because of the general role played by the schools in reproducing the dominant Eurocentric culture and the acculturation and imagined civilizing role played by the schools. The chapter argues for the establishment of the school-community partnership, the introduction and cementing of indigenous philosophies of school governance, as well as the revision of the leadership roles within the school to build capacity for the local indigenous peoples to contribute to the running of the local school. Indigenous peoples are dynamic and seeking participation in institutions that affect them and their children. Consequently, this reveals their commitment to the construction of democratic governance that transforms them into stakeholders in the local and national polity (Mindiola 2006). Political involvement of indigenous peoples has increased in the past decade in response to the neoliberal development model, which places further emphasis on individual interests, and therefore, as a philosophy, contrasts with indigenous demands for recognition as "peoples" and recognition of their collective rights. This chapter suggests that schools as political systems should generate spaces for dialogue and negotiation among political stakeholders, to achieve broad social consensus or to develop effective school governance actions.

Unpacking School Governance

To start this discussion, it is pertinent to explain governance and school governance. The concept of governance is not new; it has always existed but understood differently in different societies. In Western societies, governance has been concerned with structures, processes, authorities, responsibilities, and accountabilities on how institutions or organizations are run and controlled, while in indigenous communities, it encompasses the flexible collective decision-making process. According to Martin McNeill (2008), governance is about leadership, direction, and control of an organization with its primary functions being to establish the organization's strategic direction and aims; ensure accountability to the public for the organization's performance; and assure that the organization is managed with probity and integrity. Another explanation of governance is derived from the Governance Working Group of the International Institute of Administrative Sciences (1996) which describes governance as the process whereby elements in a society wield power and authority, and influence and enact policies and decisions concerning public life, and economic and social development.

Drawing on from earlier views of Caldwell and Harris (2008, p. 10), school governance may be defined as "the process through which the school builds its intellectual, social, financial and spiritual capital and aligns them to achieve its goals." The issue of school governance is complex. It borders on the questions of leadership, accountability, and responsibility in decision-making. As Plecki et al. (2006) note, education governance opens up debates on the role of stakeholders in the control and management of schools. The debate poses questions such as: "Who is in charge?" "Who is accountable?" "Who is responsible?" (p. 2). In addressing these questions, the importance of governance efficacy as one of the essential drivers for creating an equity context through which school reform occurs should be considered. Governance efficacy is the power of school boards, among others, to change the face of education in their communities through positive and appropriate policymaking, equitable resource allocation, and transparent accountability for all stakeholders (Scott 2009). Accountability involves ownership of management and decision-making processes. As more and more people seek to have their voices heard, and take an increasingly active role in education policy and politics, the picture of who has control of schools becomes obscured. When it comes to school governance, most people confuse it with leadership. Leadership is simply a component of governance as Plecki et al. (2006) argue that governance is about improving education leadership and is not leadership per se. Rather, school governance creates the framework through which high-quality participatory leadership can be exercised.

While governance might have multiple meanings, it may be described as involving different structures, processes, and participants depending on the level of the public educational system and the awareness and conscientization of the local communities to be involved. Duflo et al. (2015) view school governance as a form of school-based management that involves transferring decision-making authority over some school operations to local school-community members through a participatory mechanism. The local school-community members comprises of parents or community leaders, teachers, and heads/principals of the schools. The Organization of Economic Cooperation and Development [OECD] (2014) describes school governance as school management that is directly or indirectly conducted by a public education authority, government agency, or governing board appointed by government or elected by public franchise. From this definition, it can be assumed that if parents or communities are to be involved in school governance, they would be elected by public franchise. According to the OECD, with an increasing variety of education opportunities, programs, and providers, governments are forging new partnerships to mobilize resources for education and to design new policies that allow the different stakeholders to participate more fully and to share costs and benefits more equitably. Again, the involvement of communities is implied in the "different stakeholders" participation. Parents are often expected to be partners with teachers and principals in order to better meet the learning objectives of their children (Zhao and Akiba 2009). Studies conducted by OECD (2014) found that parental involvement in school activities were limited to activities such as volunteering in physical activities, in extracurricular activities, and in the school library or media centers, assisting a teacher in the school, appearing as a guest speaker, or assisting in fundraising for the school. Involvement of parents was not extended to making decisions about hiring of teachers, decisions on tuition and curriculum issues nor financial accountability; issues that were decisions that were made the responsibility of the principals.

Caldwell and Harris (2008) believe that the debate on school governance has focused too loosely on structures, roles, responsibilities, and accountabilities at the exclusion of capitals that exist within these structures and roles. Instead, Caldwell and Harris propose that governance should be seen as "the process through which the school builds its intellectual, social, financial and spiritual capital and aligns them to achieve its goals" (p. 10). While the structures and roles are a necessary element of governance, they are also equally necessary management and leadership processes, which require some form of capital – a type of resource that can be expended to enable the maximization of processes. Looking back at the capitals that schools utilize for governance purposes, intellectual capital is described as the levels of knowledge and skill of all of those who work in or for the school. Reviewing international research, Barber and Mourshed (2007, p. 16) conclude that "the quality of an education system cannot exceed the quality of its teachers." Here I might also add that the quality of parental and community involvement contributes to the quality of the education system. Schools cannot exist outside the communities that surround them. Therefore, communities also provide indigenous intellectual capital that is not usually tapped into by school officials. Social capital is also a very important cog in the function of the school. The term social capital refers to "the strength of formal and informal partnerships and networks involving the school, parents, community, business and industry, indeed all individuals, agencies, organizations and institutions that have the potential to support and be supported by the school" (Caldwell and Harris 2008, p. 59). Indigenous parents and communities contribute immensely to the social capital if the school administrators open their doors to the voices of community leaders and parents. They contribute spiritual capital that can bring sanity and stability in the schools. Spiritual capital is a relatively new concept, which is currently finding its place in economics and business (Zohar and Marshall 2004) as well as in education. Spiritual capital is "the strength of moral purpose and the degree of coherence among values, beliefs and attitudes about life and learning" (Caldwell and Vaughan 2012, p. 178) held by the school and members of the wider community. It involves the ethics and values shared by members of the school and its community. Schools that utilize the services and participation of their communities in school governance are likely to benefit from both the spiritual capital and the social capital that are the backbone of indigenous communities. Unfortunately, school management tends to be concerned more with the monetary resources, or financial capital, than with other forms of capital. However, while monetary resources are important, exclusive reliance on building financial capital in schools and school systems is unlikely to result in significant increases in student performance (Hanushek 2004). The capitals discussed are crucial elements in the interdependence of governance, leadership, and management. These are not separate functions to be exercised by different individuals but complementary approaches to issues that face both communities and school administrators (McNeill 2008). The capitals contribute to governance efficacy, which strengthens school management when power and control are participatory along with the policymaking and proactive support of a school board that take into account parental and community values and ethics (Montecel 2005).

Postcolonial Theory, Property, and School Governance

What is termed "postcolonial" is a very fluid concept defining a historical period, particularly when examining the experiences of indigenous peoples worldwide. While some, for example, in Africa, Asia, and the Caribbean may have attained political independence, there are others in North America, Australia, New Zealand, and South America who are still under colonial oppression. Therefore, in light of these different historical experiences and epochs, Ashcroft et al. (1989) state that:

> We use the term 'post-colonial', however, to cover all the culture affected by the imperial process from the moment of colonization to the present day. This is because there is a

continuity of preoccupations throughout the historical process initiated by European imperial aggression. (p. 2)

In the same vein, Stephen Slemon (1991) acknowledges the multidimensional meanings of the "postcolonial" when he points out that:

> Definitions of the 'post-colonial' of course vary widely, but for me the concept proves most useful not when it is used synonymously with a post-independence historical period in once-colonized nations, but rather when it locates a specifically anti- or *post*colonial *discursive* purchase in culture, one which begins in the moment that colonial power inscribes itself onto the body and space of its Others and which continues as an often occulted tradition into the modern theatre of neo-colonialist international relations. (p. 3)

Postcoloniality denotes a type of condition of societies, peoples, and cultures that went through and continue to experience European imperialism. Postcoloniality defines the relationships between indigenous peoples experiences during colonization and their current experiences within the legacy of Eurocentric social institutions such as experiences with school cultures and the way schools are governed and managed.

In their seminal discourse, *The Fourth World*, Manuel and Posluns (1974) explain the effects of contemporary colonial processes and note that the colonial system is "always a way of gaining control over another people for the sake of what the colonial power has determined to be 'the common good'" (p. 4). People can only become convinced of the colonial common good when their own capacity to imagine ways in which they can govern themselves has been destroyed. The "common good" becomes what is defined by shape-shifting colonial elites (Alfred 2005). Frantz Fanon describes this process as an ongoing dialectic:

> Colonialism is not satisfied merely with holding a people in its grip and emptying the native's brain of all form and content. By a kind of perverted logic, it turns to the past of the oppressed people, and distorts, disfigures, and destroys it. This work of devaluing pre-colonial history takes on a dialectical significance today. (1963, p. 210)

Fanon points out that the most important strength of indigenous resistance, unity, is also constantly under attack as colonial powers erase community histories and senses of place to replace them with doctrines of individualism and predatory capitalism. Postcolonial theorists' formations of power work to disrupt "historical racist views and structural inequities that have emerged through the practices of colonization" (O'Mahoney and Donnelly 2010, p. 443). Recognizing, representing, and creating space for others through participatory engagement requires challenging structural inequalities and adopting a lens that is open to worldviews that vary beyond those typical of Western school elites that see schools as their private property.

Blomley (2004, p. 99) argues that property is a "vector of power" whereby people gain specific entitlements that are shaped and maintained by the ways in which property is defined. These entitlements establish and perpetuate social relations, so that those who benefit from particular property formations have an interest in ensuring that these are preserved. There is thus an inherent school politics that defines schools as working spaces of Western administrative elites. For indigenous peoples, the process of colonization has entailed transformations in the definition of property relations that have challenged both their relationships to property and their understandings of what determines their relationships with other people (cf. Dempsey 2011). Therefore, when it comes to their relationship with the Eurocentric schools and Western administrators, they find themselves marginalized from this "Western property." The exclusion of indigenous peoples from the school space and decision-making tables questions the nature of their relationship to power and control within the school sites. Gombay (2015) raises a very pertinent observation in relation to power and property control. In the encounter between indigenous peoples and the colonial state lies a question about who has the power to determine the social and conceptual practices that establish and maintain school property. Within the social relations and practices of school governance are questions of who owns the school and who has the power to make decisions affecting the running of the school? Is school governance a participatory regime or a question of the elite bulldozing their decisions through the power structures that control the school? It would appear as if the experiences, social relations, and institutions that define how the school and its resources are understood and used are defined from the Eurocentric approaches of colonial powers that render indigenous perspectives invisible by legitimizing the appropriation and silencing of indigenous peoples' cultural heritages regarding participatory consultations and collective decision-making agreements in school governance.

Indigenous Peoples and School Governance

Around the world, indigenous people have been historically marginalized and rendered invisible in most social and economic institutions. Their contributions to school knowledge and decision-making processes are misrecognized, misinterpreted, and misclassified as irrelevant to modernity and scientific jurisdictions (Shizha 2016). However, Paulo Friere and Antonio Faundez (1989) have argued that "...indigenous knowledge is a rich social resource for any justice-related attempt to bring about social change" (cited in Semali and Kincheloe 1999, p. 15). The inclusion of indigenous peoples' voices in school governance is transformative and a form of social change. There are assumptions that parents of indigenous students are not interested in the education of their children and taking part in school functions and activities. Contrary to this assumption, Chenhall et al. (2011, p. 11) argue that the issues of "invisible" parents was an exaggerated problem. They found that many engagement approaches often assume that the invisibility of indigenous parents is associated with an aversion to school institutions and a naiveté of the importance of schooling. Arguably, "invisibility" is not equated to lack of interest in or deficit of schooling culture but it is a consequence of systemic discrimination that promotes the self-interests of Western educators whose control of the education system is defined as having the ability to "get the job done," rendering forthright indigenous peoples' engagement "unnecessary." The participation of parents of indigenous students in school governance is viewed from a Western colonizing Eurocentric perspective that views indigenous people as not having the required cultural capital to get involved. This deficit model theory tends to place indigenous people at a disadvantage and silences their voices (Shizha 2013). The deficit theory masks the colonial mentality of the school elite who view themselves as "experts" who do not need the input of "backward people."

Indigenous Peoples' Participation and the Cultural Deficit Model

Chenhall et al. (2011) warn against indigenous parental engagement strategies being based on a cultural deficit model, which involves an "ideal" parental standard that is based on a Western middle-class parental archetype, which invalidates and delegitimizes different forms of involvement from across plural or diverse ethnic, racial, cultural and socioeconomic backgrounds. The Western middle-class parental archetype reinforces the marginalization of already marginalized parents and fails to promote "higher standards" for their students. Walker and Berthelsen (2010) also argue that schools are biased to represent and to promote more middle-class values, and this places many parents from indigenous backgrounds at a disadvantage. To overcome the cultural deficit model, the inclusion and consultation approach, which takes cognizance of indigenous parents' contribution to school governance, should become the most preferred mode of inclusiveness rather than the integrationist approach that seeks to incorporate indigenous parents into the formal Eurocentric school governance policies, approaches, and philosophies. Integrationism promotes the domination of the oppressed while inclusion and consultation have the effect of emancipatory and empowerment possibilities. The shift should be from the objectives of integration to that of respect for identity of indigenous populations and to promote increased consultation with and participation by parents of indigenous students in the decisions affecting them and their children (Rodríguez-Garavito 2010).

Parental Engagement as a Community Responsibility

Parental engagement also includes advocating or negotiating on behalf of communities. For engagement in the indigenous context, it is important for the school to establish a dialogue within the whole community rather than developing relationships with the individual parents (Emerson et al. 2012). Schools must ask what they can do to make parents feel more confident and comfortable with school involvement and to provide activities and resources that empower communities. The difference between the participation of indigenous and nonindigenous parents in school affairs is "as much, if not more, defined by social class and affluence as by culture" (Chenhall et al. 2011, p. 14). The engagement with schools tends to be associated with the family's level of social capital (Higgins and Morley 2014), financial capital, as well as intellectual capital. More often than not, indigenous people are not defined by their possession of these capitals. While it might be true to some extent that they do not have sufficient financial capital, the same cannot be said about their social capital and intellectual capital. Their social networks as defined by their ability to mobilize their community members have adequate and extensive indigenous intellectual capital that can be tapped into by the school. It is a complex task to define what is meant by parental engagement or involvement (Emerson et al. 2012). However, there is a difference between merely involving parents in school activities and engaging parents in their children's learning. For indigenous peoples, engagement is a shared responsibility of families, schools, and communities that is based on indigenous peoples' philosophies.

What Are Indigenous Philosophies?

An important academic goal is to understand ongoing contestations in knowledge in the search to engage everyday social practices and experiences, as well as the social barriers and approaches to peaceful human coexistence (Dei 2011). Therefore, it makes sense to recognize and acknowledge indigenous knowledges and philosophies as legitimate sources or forms of knowledge that can shape successful and harmonious school governance. This section explores indigenous philosophies that can benefit school governance. This is essential because school spaces and structures are uncontestably occupied and representative of colonizing practices that neglect indigenous peoples' worldviews and ways of knowing and living.

Community, Peoplehood, and Personhood

Community, peoplehood, and personhood are interconnected and inseparable synergies that are deeply rooted in indigenous peoples' worldviews and lived-experiences. Peoplehood models, which discuss the interconnected factors of community, language, and cultural practices, appear to have some promise for discussing the adaptability and resurgence of indigenous peoples and communities (Alfred 2005). Indigenous peoples have long understood their existence as peoples or nations embedded in community and peoplehood expressed in philosophies such as *Unhu* (in ChiShona, a Zimbabwean indigenous language) or *Ubuntu* (in Zulu, a South African indigenous language). Menkiti (2004, p. 324) argues that in Africa "morality demands a point of view best described as one of *beingness-with-others*," while Ramose (2003, p. 382) points out that "the logic of *ubuntu* is towards-ness," a relationship with others, a relationship that exhibits empathy and sympathy towards other humans. Indigenous communities around the world are communal societies, and it is this communalism which defines the peoples' perception of togetherness and being with others as the social whole. The indigenous peoples' philosophy of *Ubuntu* holds that community is essential to intersubjectivity, and that people are incomplete unless they maintain an active connection with others, their society or culture. Intersubjectivity is shared as a mutual understanding of relationships with others and is closer to the notion of the possibility of being in the place where the others are. Thus, in the African context, *ubuntu* is grounded in a traditional African community (Letseka 2013). It is ultimately the lived collective and individual experiences of indigenous peoples that yield the most useful insights for establishing culturally sound strategies to resist colonialism, reclaim (Shizha 2015) and regenerate colonized school spaces and practices. Peoplehood, which is different from personhood, is the cornerstone of the collective and community life of indigenous peoples around the world.

While peoplehood implies the collective, personhood connotes the importance of the individual as a single entity, however, within the collective. Describing the notion of personhood, Gombay (2015) claims that:

> Conceptions of personhood frame the ways in which individuals understand the expectations, responsibilities, and obligations that define their self-perceptions and shape their relations with others. As a person, one is a holder of rights and responsibilities that form the basis of citizenship. Notions of personhood and citizenship, in turn, have reflexive impacts upon the development of peoples' subjectivities, both internally in their understandings of who they are, and externally in their relations with others (p. 13)

What it is to be a person is a social construction founded on collective understandings determined by institutions that are constituted via norms governing peoples' behaviors. While peoplehood "speak of the inseparability and inter-dependence of selves and the collective" (Dei 2011, p. 4), personhood is anchored in colonial philosophies of individuality, individualism, citizenship, and the right to property, which does not emphasize the collective. Colonial administrators around the world had the notion that uprooting the individual from the community would weaken the communities and hence weaken the community's capacities to resist colonial rule and oppression, whittle their resolve, and silence their voices. Therefore, decisions on issues that affected the individual were left to the individual and not the community. This was the essence of the subject formation in the context of settler colonialism (Palmater 2011; Simpson 2014). In this sense, personhood would effectively render the internal arrangements of an indigenous community "opaque" (Riles 2011, p. 35) to external agents because of the looseness of the binding ties when the individual was made more important than the collective. Western jurisprudence conceives of a person as an individual who is a full subject of the law with attendant rights and obligations that determine how s/he participates in the public arena (Poole 1996). This notion of personhood contradicts the community views of *Unhu/Ubuntu* that state that "*umuntu ngumuntu ngabantu*" (A person is a person because of people, or, A person is a person through other persons). This African indigenous peoples' adage reveals compelling truth about what it means to be a "human being" in the African sociocultural context. According to African indigenous teachings, personhood is understood as a process and the product of interconnectedness experienced and or achieved in the context of the community. Communities and the collective have practical consequences that strike at the heart of local politics, including school politics and how the school affairs should be controlled and monitored. When individuals act independent of the community, their voices are not likely to be heard nor are they likely to be effective. The power to channel grievances, ideas, and controlling mechanisms is more effective when it is generated collectively under the ambit of the community rather than at the personhood level. According to Gombay (2015), in colonial school governance, the subject formation underscores how property configurations and the social relations on which these are based conceal looping relations among personhood, citizenship, and the subjectivity that require communities to be conscious of their collectivities. Bewaji (2004, p. 396) contends that:

> The wellspring of morality and ethics in African societies is the pursuit of a balance of individuals with the communal wellbeing. It is not unusual to get the impression that African cultures extol the virtues of community, that moral obligations are primarily social rather than individual.

Participatory Engagement

Community life and peoplehood revolve around participating in community activities and commitment to the virtues of togetherness or *Unhu/Ubuntu* through participatory actions. Participatory and community-based engagement have recently been offered as one solution to address concerns about the politics of gathering, framing, producing, disseminating, and controlling knowledge about indigenous peoples (Shizha 2009). Participatory engagement involves getting involved in decision-making processes in actions that affect people and their communities as well as institutions that serve them. It disengages institutional pressures that work against the development and maintenance of meaningful, accountable, and nonextractive relations with indigenous communities (de Leeuw et al. 2012). It is a collaborative approach that is designed to ensure and establish structures for participation by communities affected by the issues being considered and representatives of institutions, such as schools. The engagement is meant to improve the running of the institutions taking into account the needs and concerns of local or indigenous peoples and their communities. Viswanathan et al. (2004) conclude that indigenous participatory philosophies emphasize co-learning about issues of concern and, within those, the issues that can be solved through reciprocal methods and transfer of expertise; sharing of decision-making power; and mutual ownership of the outcomes and processes of consultations. Following this process, the end result is incorporating the ideas, opinions, and knowledge gained by taking action or effecting social change to improve the well-being of community members and the educational institutions that serve them and their children.

Generally, participatory engagement has the ability to democratize knowledge, decision-making processes, and governance issues to advance community action and social change (Masuda et al. 2011). It reconstitutes power structures in the decision-making process by reinvesting it in the community-school partnership. This process can work to resolve unequal power relations due to differences in class, gender, and ethnicity that may exist between school administrators and indigenous leaders and their communities. Constantly and reflexively, examining how power is manifested in school governance and then acting to make its exercise equitable and beneficial to those who are marginalized and reconstituting power structures aids in the decolonization of school governance and the politics of educational administration. Engaging indigenous peoples and their leaders in school governance can improve educational administration, empower community members, and improve the capacity of local communities. For many indigenous elders and educators, this participatory engagement embraces the notion of taking the best of both indigenous and nonindigenous worlds as knowledge bases and sources for understanding the needs of students and their schools, and as a means for relating sensitively and constructively in an increasingly intercultural world. Governance should, thus, entail a redefinition of the relationship between indigenous and national societies defined in intercultural terms but with a transverse character (i.e., school policies should be designed with the participation of indigenous peoples) (Mindiola 2006). This comes from realizing that there is a transformative power inherent in indigenous philosophies and, furthermore, indigenous ways can be used to foster empowerment and justice in a variety of cultural contexts (Semali and Kincheloe 1999) on the basis of collectivism.

Collectivism

Indigenous peoples rely on collectivism as their philosophy to life in their communities. Collectivism, as with peoplehood, is the idea that the individual's life belongs to the group. According to collectivism, the group is the basic unit of moral concern, and the individual is of value only insofar as serving the group (Biddle 2012). Society cannot escape the fact that human beings are both individuals and part of a collective. In a "collectivist" system, people think of themselves in terms of their affiliation with other people and their community (Yeo 2003) in an interactive dialogic community (Biddle 2012). Individuals in a society exchange ideas and learn from one another. This has always been the hallmark of a collectivist kinship system that exists among indigenous communities. The kinship system is a dynamic and complex social structure that defines how individuals relate to each other in terms of their roles, responsibilities, and obligations. In essence, collectivism refers to cultures in which people are interdependent and interconnected and are other-focused. By contrast, individualism refers to cultures in which people are more independent and self-focused (Beckstein 2014). Individualist ideologies tend to advocate individual rights and freedom from government and from collective controls and restrictions, while collectivist ideologies, on the other hand, endorse the idea of working cooperatively to solve problems. They hold that collective teamwork can accomplish more than individuals and competition can. They stress social harmony and cohesion over competitiveness (cf. Shizha 2009) and emphasize group goals and the common good.

Indigenous peoples, such as the First Nations in Canada (Simpson 2014) and Aboriginal peoples in Australia (Miller 2016), describe their traditional cultures as having a strong sense of the collective. In matters such as land-holding, decision-making, and educating and raising children, many indigenous cultures emphasize thinking and acting collectively to achieve what is best for the common good, collective interest, collective responsibility, and adherence to collective norms. Members of a collectively oriented culture tend to see themselves as at one with other human beings but more importantly with the essence of life (Miller 2016). McIntyre-Mills (2014) refers to "the benefits of balancing individual and collective interests through socio-cultural solidarity and collective action for this generation of life and the next" (p. 46). If society is indeed to develop a "social contract which protects citizens" particularly "those who are voiceless," then "the balance between individual and collective concerns needs to be redressed" (McIntyre-Mills 2014, p. 48–49). Indigenous elders and peoples see their involvement in governing social institutions that affect them and their children, such as schools, as empowering, and as a critical precursor to planning their livelihoods. Thus, indigenous leaders are not simply conduits for the subjectivity-shaping projects of the state and international development groups; nor are they simply acting in their own interest. Rather, they constitute and regulate new types of citizens to ensure the future viability of their organizations and political projects (Erazo 2010).

As pointed earlier in this chapter, parents, as the principal community members, are frequently constructed in deficit terms explicitly by school and educational authority officials. Conversely, parents construct teachers and schools as being in deficit, not knowing or ascribing to indigenous ways of communicating ideas and indigenous governance systems that are inclusive and communal. Sometimes they are likely to express their dissatisfaction by refusing to be coopted into hegemonic school governance that bestows all power and authority onto the heads of schools and other educational administrators while undermining the role of parents and their ways of mobilizing community engagement. Studies in India, for instance, indicate that sometimes parents internalize these deficit constructions of themselves in relation to schooling, which may negatively affect their children's participation in schooling and their own participation in school governance (Balagopalan 2003). Parents may feel that the schools and their top-down hierarchical governance system, where all ideas and information are transmitted from the heads of school to parents, are exclusive and not taking parental and community voices into account. Indigenous parents believe in community mobilization and accountability that provide indigenous societies with solidarity and harmonious coexistence and guarded consensus on social and community issues that affect their lives. The education of their children becomes a social and community issue that affects them, hence the need to be empowered with authority in the decision-making process when it comes to designing policies and programs that affect their community schools.

Research in various African and South Asian contexts has shown how there is unequal access to participation in governance bodies according to socioeconomic status, race, caste, social class, location, political affiliation, and gender (Bush and Heystek 2003; de Grauwe et al. 2005; Rose 2005; Soudien and Sayed 2004). Even when elected onto school committees, some voices are inevitably heard above others. In South Africa, for example, this has been shown to result in skewed participation in important activities such as selecting the medium of instruction and setting school fees (Soudien and Sayed 2004), which might have far-reaching implications for some children's access to and participation in schooling. At the same time, however, some commentators have noted that these participatory bodies have often not been mandated with genuine decision-making powers (Ahmed and Nath 2005; Therkildsen 2000; Watt 2001). Thus, parents and communities are expected to become further involved in schooling in a variety of ways but generally in ways determined by the school, laid down by central and/or regional or local government. Policy literature on community involvement continues to emphasize the need for capacity building within the community to enable them to participate in these ways (Bush and Heystek 2003) without questioning what it is they are being asked to be involved in (Rose 2005). Community participation in schooling has been judged to be working well in the rare instances where there are good understandings and relations between schools, communities, and local educational authorities, operating within a stable social context with a history of community mobilization and a genuine commitment to community decision-making (de Grauwe et al. 2005). However, in most cases, the lived-experiences of indigenous parents and their children are marginalized by the formal organization and procedures embedded in the school culture.

Why Indigenous Philosophies in Governance?

The key to progress toward a relationship between indigenous peoples and the state that is truly postcolonial is recognizing the rights of indigenous peoples to participate in the management of their lands through institutions and processes that reflect their cultural values and economic needs. For example, the United Nation's Draft Declaration on the Rights of Indigenous Peoples stresses in Article 31 that "indigenous peoples, as a specific form of exercising the right to self-determination, have the right to autonomy or self-government in matters relating to their internal and local affairs, including [...] economic activities, land and resources management," and adds in Article 33 that, "indigenous peoples have the right to promote, develop and maintain their institutional structures" (United Nations 1993, p. 50). Schools are institutions with institutional structures that guide and control school governance culture. Henceforth, the declaration provides a justification for the involvement of indigenous peoples in the management and decision-making processes in schools in their communities.

Because schools are institutions within communities, efforts should be made to facilitate interaction between indigenous communities and nonindigenous governments and structures through the inclusion and acknowledgement of indigenous philosophies and epistemologies while remaining as close as possible to indigenous structures and processes of governance. Indigenous peoples have social, intellectual, and spiritual capitals that can impact the school as an institution and the practiced culture of school governance. Higgins and Morley (2014) argue that engaging parents in their children's education improves the children's educational attainment and ongoing engagement in education, while Shizha (2009) claims that participatory engagement of parents and communities in resource usage and decision-making helps to bridge the gap between schools and communities they serve. The involvement of indigenous parents does not only lead to politics of recognition – recognizing the worthiness of indigenous distinctive cultural traditions – but it also ruptures and decolonizes the Eurocentric intellectual capital that negates the tensions between personal (Eurocentric) and collective (Indigenous) identities.

Little is known about the specific ways in which indigenous parental involvement in school governance and decision-making processes socialize their children in positive school-related behaviors or on the various parental engagements that influence children's school-related development. However, there is merit in predicting that parental and community involvement in school governance and management influences increased school enrolments and participation by children from indigenous communities because parental involvement may motivate both parents and students to identify with the school and its programs. The same predictive relationship was acknowledge by Mansour and Martin (2009) who point out that home and parental influences in school affairs have an effect on children's education because they predict student motivation and engagement. Further, Berthelsen and Walker (2008) report that positive parental involvement in their children's schools and schooling, beyond the potential educational outcome benefits for their children, also improved the parents' social and cultural capital. Parents who are involved in school governance are likely to acquire new ways of thinking and viewing the school, not only from their indigenous philosophical perspectives but also from the perspectives of other stakeholders, such as heads of schools and education administrators. Parents and communities that are involved in the governance structures of their schools develop a feeling of ownership and a form of community empowerment – a feeling of being part of the school and its activities.

Recommendations and Conclusion

Collectivism and communal responsibilities should be a philosophy that shapes contemporary school governance. Miller-Grandvaux and Yoder (2002) refer to community schools managed wholly by communities as one way of ensuring that indigenous peoples are empowered. However, there are complex relations between communities and government schools in some countries, leaving aside community involvement in nonstate provision of schooling (see Rose 2005). Even putting aside the questionable assumption that there is such an entity as a school community, there is the question of which community? Another of the problems of government policies is the notion of a school firmly embedded in a particular geographical community, whereas in fact, community members (in terms of school parents, for example) can be drawn from diverse communities, at considerable distance from the schools (Rose 2005; Soudien and Sayed 2004). Much of the policy literature assumes communities to be homogenous, harmonious, and static, whose resources can collectively be mobilized for a perceived collective community good (DeStefano et al. 2007). However, Dunne et al. (2007) argue that communities are multilayered, with their own hierarchies, which are determined to an extent by age, gender, ethnicity, caste, and functions within the community. They are dynamic, as power relations are played out by community members on a daily basis in accommodation and resistance to the hierarchies. There is not just one experience or understanding of community-school relations within a particular community but multiple experiences and understandings, experienced individually and collectively (Dunne et al. 2007).

Schools within indigenous communities should increase community involvement since it is seen to be important in improving their children's enrolment and persistence in school as well as school accountability to the community. One way to mitigate the effect of alienation between communities and schools may be to recruit local teachers and school administrators. Local teachers are likely to be knowledgeable about the indigenous cultures and ways that can be used to mobilize parents into school programs where parental input is required. Local teachers are also important in providing the identity of the school. When parents see most of their own teachers being from their community, they develop a sense of belonging to the school and the school as belonging to them. A sense of identity is vital to creating positive relationships between the parents and the school or educational administrators. Identifying with the school increases political advocacy for greater community "ownership" and involvement in decision-making.

Another factor that can help bring communities closer to schools and empower indigenous peoples and give them a say in how schools function is integrating or teaching in the local language (see Shizha 2009). Indigenous peoples' intellectual capital and spiritual capital are intertwined with their languages. Parents should be given the opportunity to decide on a local language that should be used as a language of teaching and learning. This works effectively in communities where there might be more than one indigenous language spoken. This can also increase the likelihood of parental involvement in school work (DeStefano et al. 2007), which is often assumed to be likely to improve retention and achievement. Another aspect of formal parental involvement in school occurs through participation on governing bodies, school management committees, parent-teacher associations, and community education committees. A search of literature reveals no evidence of the involvement of indigenous peoples in school boards across the Canadian provinces. Structures are needed for the representation of indigenous rights and indigenous interests in school boards and teacher-parent associations. To overcome any cultural disadvantage inherent within education, indigenous parents need to be active and "interfere" with the school culture system to achieve positive outcomes.

This chapter is not based on research evidence collected from field work in schools to examine governance structures. It is a result of examining literature on school governance and indigenous peoples. What is required is to conduct field research that could answer the questions: What is the nature of the relationships between the various actors (local authorities, education offices, communities, and school staff), whose involvement in school governance and management tends to follow Eurocentric models? How are these relationships working with regards to indigenous peoples? How effective is the quality of governance and monitoring of schools that exclude indigenous peoples' contribution and voices? Researchers in education and policy-makers should be involved in gathering and generating data that speaks to the need to build inclusive school governance structures. The challenge for school administrators is to build inclusive schools that are welcoming, flexible, and accessible to all students and parents.

References

Ahmed M, Nath S (2005) Education watch report 2003/4. Quality with equity: the primary education agenda. Campaign for Popular Education (CAMPE), Dhaka

Alfred T (2005) Wasáse: indigenous pathways of action and freedom. Broadview Press, Peterborough

Ashcroft B, Griffiths G, Tiffin H (eds) (1989) The empire writes back: theory and practice in post-colonial literature. Routledge, New York

Balagopalan S (2003) Neither suited for the home nor for the fields': inclusion, formal schooling and the Adivasi child. IDS Bull 34(1):55–62

Barber M, Mourshed M (2007) How the world's best-performing school systems come out on top. McKinsey & Co., London

Beckstein A (2014) Native American subjective happiness: an overview. Indige Policy J 25(2):1–6

Berthelsen D, Walker S (2008) Parents' involvement in their children's education. Fam Matter 79:34–41

Bewaji JAI (2004) Ethics and morality in Yoruba culture. In: Wiredu K (ed) A companion to African philosophy. Blackwell Publishing, Malden, pp 396–403

Biddle C (2012) Individualism vs collectivism: our future, our choice. Object Stand 7(1). Retrieved 3 June 2016 from: https://www.theobjectivestandard.com/issues/2012-spring/individualism-collectivism/

Blomley NK (2004) Unsettling the city: urban land and the politics of property. Routledge, New York

Bush T, Heystek J (2003) School governance in the new South Africa. Compare 33(2):128–137

Caldwell BJ, Harris J (2008) Why not the best schools? ACER Press, Camberwell

Caldwell BJ, Vaughan T (2012) Transforming education through the arts. Routledge, London

Chenhall R, Holmes C, Lea T, Senior K, Wegner A (2011) Parent–school engagement: exploring the concept of 'invisible' indigenous parents in three North Australian school communities. Charles Darwin University, Darwin

de Grauwe A, Lugaz C, Baldé D, Diakhaté C, Dougnon D, Moustapha M, Odushina D (2005) Does decentralization lead to school improvement? Findings and lessons from research in West Africa. J Educ Int Dev, 1(1). Retrieved 20 June 2016 from: www.equip123.net/JEID/articles/1/1-1.pdf

de Leeuw S, Cameron ES, Greenwood ML (2012) Participatory and community-based research, indigenous geographies, and the spaces of friendship: a critical engagement. Can Geogr 56(2):180–194

Dei GJS (ed) (2011) Indigenous philosophies and critical education. Peter Lang, New York

Dempsey J (2011) The politics of nature in BC's Great Bear Rainforest. Geoforum 42:211–221

DeStefano J, Schuh Moore A, Balwanz D, Hartwell A (2007) Reaching the underserved: complementary models of effective schooling. EQUIP2, working papers and issues briefs

Duflo E, Dupas P, Kremer M (2015) School governance, teacher incentives, and pupil–teacher ratios: experimental evidence from Kenyan primary schools. J Public Econ l(123C):92–110

Dunne M, Akyeampong K, Humphreys S (2007) School processes, local governance and community participation: understanding access. Create pathways to access research monograph no 6. University of Sussex, Centre for International Education, Sussex

Emerson L, Fear J, Fox S, Sanders E (2012) Parental engagement in learning and schooling: lessons from research. A report by the Australian Research Alliance for Children and Youth for the Family–School and Community Partnerships Bureau. Family–School and Community Partnerships Bureau, Canberra

Erazo J (2010) Constructing indigenous subjectivities: economic collectivism and identity in the Ecuadorian Amazon. Dev Chang 41(6):1017–1039

Fanon F (1963) The wretched of the earth. Grove Press, New York

Gombay N (2015) "There are mentalities that need changing": constructing personhood, formulating citizenship, and performing subjectivities on a settler colonial frontier. Polit Geogr 48:11–23

Hanushek EA (2004) Some simple analytics of school quality. Invited paper at the making schools better conference of the Melbourne Institute of Applied Economics and Social Research, University of Melbourne, 26–27 Aug 2004

Higgins D, Morley S (2014) Engaging indigenous parents in their children's education. Resource sheet no. 32. Closing the Gap Clearinghouse, Australian Institute of Health and Welfare, Canberra

Hughes H, Hughes M (2012) Indigenous education 2012. CIS policy monograph 129. Centre for Independent Studies, Sydney

International Institute of Administrative Science (1996) Governance: a working definition. Report of the governance working group. Retrieved 21 May 2016 from: http://www.gdrc.org/u-gov/work-def.html

Letseka M (2013) Anchoring ubuntu morality. Mediterr J Soc Sci 4(3):351–359

Mansour M, Martin AJ (2009) Home, parents, and achievement motivation: a study of key home and parental factors that predict student motivation and engagement. Aust Educ Dev Psychol 26(2):111–126

Manuel G, Posluns M (1974) The fourth world: an Indian reality. Collier Macmillan, New York

Masuda JR, Creighton G, Nixon S, Frankish J (2011) Building capacity for community-based participatory research for health disparities in Canada: the case of "partnerships in community health research". Health Promot Pract 12(2):280–292

McIntyre-Mills J (2014) Systemic ethics and non-anthropocentric stewardship: implications for transdisciplinarity and cosmopolitan politics. Springer International Publishing, Cham

McNeill M (2008) What do we mean by governance? Teaching Times. Retrieved 28 May 2016 from: http://www.teachingtimes.com/articles/governance.htm

Menkiti IA (2004) On the normative conception of a person. In: Wiredu K (ed) A companion to African philosophy. Blackwell Publishers, Malden, pp 324–331

Miller K (2016) Balancing individualism and collectivism in an Australian Aboriginal context. Retrieved 7 May 2016 from: http://journals.isss.org/index.php/proceedings59th/article/viewFile/2467/838

Miller-Grandvaux Y, Yoder K (2002) A literature review of community schools in Africa. USAID, Washington, DC

Mindiola O (2006) Indigenous governance and democracy. Focal point: spotlight on the Americas, special edition. Canadian Foundation for the Americas, Ottawa

Montecel RM (2005) A quality schools action framework – framing systems change for student success. IDRA Newsletter (November-December), San Antonio

O'Mahoney JM, Donnelly TT (2010) A postcolonial feminist perspective inquiry into immigrant women's mental health care experiences. Issues Ment Health Nurs 31(7):440–449

Organization of Economic Cooperation and Development [OECD] (2014) Education at a glance 2014: OECD indicators. OECD Publishing, Paris

Palmater PD (2011) Beyond blood: rethinking indigenous identity. Purich Publishing, Saskatoon

Plecki M, McCleery J, Knapp M (2006) Redefining and improving school district governance. Paper commissioned by the Wallace Foundation. University of Washington Center for the Study of Teaching and Policy, Seattle

Poole R (1996) On being a person. Australas J Philos 74(1):38–56

Ramose MB (2003) The ethics of Ubuntu. In: Coetzee PH, Roux APJ (eds) Philosophy from Africa: a text with readings. Routledge, London

Riles A (2011) Too big to fail. In: Edwards J, Petrovic-Steger M (eds) Recasting anthropological knowledge. Cambridge University Press, Cambridge, pp 31–48

Rodríguez-Garavito C (2010) Ethnicity.gov: global governance, indigenous peoples, and the right to prior consultation in social minefields. Indiana J Glob Leg Stud 18(1):1–44

Rose P (2005) Decentralisation and privatisation in Malawi – default or design? Compare 35(2):153–165

Scott B (2009) The role of school governance efficacy in building an equity context for school reform. IDRA Newsletter (June-July). Texas Intercultural Development Research Association, San Antonio

Semali LM, Kincheloe JL (eds) (1999) What is indigenous knowledge? Voices from the academy. Palmer Press, London

Shizha E (2009) Chara chimwe hachitswanyi inda: indigenizing science education in Zimbabwe. In: Kapoor D, Jordan S (eds) Education, participatory action research, and social change: international perspectives. Palgrave Macmillan, New York, pp 139–154

Shizha E (2013) Reclaiming our indigenous voices: the problem with postcolonial sub-Saharan African school curriculum. J Indig Soc Dev 2(1):1–18

Shizha E (2015) Reclaiming indigenous cultures in African education. In: Jacobs WJ, Cheng SY, Porter MK (eds) Indigenous education: language, culture, and identity. Springer, New York, pp 301–317

Shizha E (2016) African indigenous perspectives on technology. In: Emeagwali G, Shizha E (eds) African indigenous knowledge and the sciences: journeys into the past and present. Sense Publishers, Rotterdam, pp 47–62

Simpson A (2014) Mohawk interruptus: political life across the borders of settler states. Duke University Press, London

Slemon S (1991) Modernism's last post. In: Adam I, Tiffin H (eds) Past the last post: theorizing post-colonialism and post-modernism. Harvester Whearsheaf, Hemel Hempstead, pp 1–11

Soudien C, Sayed Y (2004) A new racial state? Exclusion and inclusion in education policy and practice in South Africa. Perspect Educ 22(4):101–115

Therkildsen O (2000) Comparative studies of relevance to resource mobilisation and democratisation in African countries: a critical review. Paper presented for the conference 'the state under pressure', The Norwegian Association for Development Research, annual conference, 5–6 Oct 2000, Chr. Michelsen Institute, Bergen

United Nations (1993) Draft declaration on the rights of indigenous peoples. United Nations, sub-commission on prevention of discrimination and protection of minorities; report of the working group on indigenous populations, 11th session, U.N. Doc. E/CN.4/Sub.2/1993/29

Viswanathan M et al (2004) Community-based participatory research: assessing the evidence. Evidence report/technology assessment no. 99. AHRQ publication 04-E022-2. Agency for Healthcare Research and Quality, Rockville

Walker S, Berthelsen D (2010) Social inequalities and parent involvement in children's education in the early years of school. In: Green V, Cherrington S (eds) Delving into diversity: an international exploration of issues of diversity in education. Nova Science Publishers, New York, pp 139–149

Watt P (2001) Community support for basic education in sub-Saharan Africa. Africa region human development working paper series. World Bank, Washington, DC

Yeo SS (2003) Bonding and attachment of Australian Aboriginal children. Child Abuse Rev 12(3):292–304

Zhao H, Akiba M (2009) School expectations for parental involvement and student mathematics achievement: a comparative study of middle schools in the United States and South Korea. J Comp Int Educ 39(3):411–428

Zohar D, Marshall I (2004) Spiritual capital: wealth we can live by. Berrett-Koehlar Publishing, San Francisco

Indigenous Governance and Education in Belize: Lessons from the Maya Land Rights Struggle and Indigenous Education Initiatives

14

Filiberto Penados

Contents

Introduction	208
Indigenous Governance: Locating the Alcalde System in the Broader Indigenous Governance Question	209
The Origins of the Alcalde System	210
Belize and the *Alcalde* System	212
The Village Councils	213
The *Alcaldes* in Toledo	214
The *Alcalde* as an Indigenous Form of Governance	215
The Challenges of Education: Belize	218
A Maya Education Initiative: Tumul K'in Center or Learning	221
School Governance as Indigenous Governance	222
Indigenous Governance and Engaging Young People in Education	223
Indigenous Governance and Pedagogy	224
Conclusion: So What Are the Implications of Indigenous Governance for Education?	225
References	227

Abstract

The "dialectic of resistance and colonization" produced the *Alcalde* system, a Maya form of governance allowed the Maya people to maintain a degree of autonomy and was central to both physical and cultural survival during colonial rule. In the last three decades, the Alcalde system has played a critical role in efforts to overcome the effects of colonization and exclusion, to revitalize their communities and to carve a space for a Maya way of knowing and being in Belize. Whether in the struggle to secure Maya land rights that has resulted in a landmark ruling in favor of the Maya at the Caribbean Court of Justice or in efforts to overcome the failings of the education system and dream a more

F. Penados (✉)
Center for Engaged Scholarship Abroad, San Ignacio, Cayo, Belize
e-mail: Fpenados@celabelize.com; fpenados@gmail.com

responsive and decolonized educational practice that has resulted in the Tumul K'in Center of Learning, the principles and practices embodied in the Alcalde system have been instrumental. By examining the history, the principles and practices it embodies and the role it has played in the Maya land-rights struggle and the Tumul K'in education initiative, this chapter considers the limits and possibilities of what Maya governance might contribute to rethinking education.

Keywords
Indigenous governance · Indigenous education · Alcalde system · Belize Maya land rights · Student engagement

Introduction

On May 16, 2016, the police, at the instructions of the chairperson of the Toledo Maya Land Rights Commission, evicted Maya *Alcaldes* from the Commission's premises. The Commission is a government entity established to implement the Caribbean Court of Justice (CCJ) consent order (A consent order is a legally binding order issued by a court as a result of agreement by the concerned parties.) that affirmed Maya land rights. Shortly after the eviction, the chairperson issued a press release explaining her refusal to meet with them by stating that "the role of the Commission was to ensure that the Maya did not become voiceless" and that "the CCJ order did not grant a monopoly on the autonomy of Maya communities to anyone" (Amandala 2016). The *Alcalde* system is an indigenous form of governance. *Alcaldes* are traditional leaders who have been at the center of the Maya Land Rights movement and the court case that resulted in the consent order. They were at the Commission's office to represent Maya communities and communicate Maya disagreement with the way consultations were being carried out by the Commission because such consultations failed to follow Maya consultation protocol; violated international standards such as the International Labor Organization convention 169 (ILO 1989) and the United National Declaration on the Rights of Indigenous Peoples (UN 2008), and divided Maya communities. The "anyone" to whom the Commissioner was referring to was no other than the institution of Maya governance, the *Alcaldes*, the very actors that brought forward the court case that resulted in the consent order which the commission is established to implement. It was therefore perplexing, to say the least, that the Commission on the one hand proposed to guarantee the voice of the Maya people but on the other was refusing to meet with them and sought to delegitimize, the *Alcalde* system.

I begin by telling this story to highlight: the important relationship between indigenous governance and indigenous autonomy; the persistent desire of the state to be in control, and its continuous actions to undermind indigenous governance. At the same time, it serves to signal that in thinking about the relationship between education and indigenous governance, we need to consider not only how indigenous governance can contribute to rethinking education, but also how education can contribute to the vitality of indigenous governance. The colonial history and contemporary role of the Alcalde System in the land rights struggle and indigenous education suggest that indigenous governance offers creative opportunities for rethinking education especially for those in the margins.

But before I proceed, let me introduce myself by telling a story to locate where I am coming from in writing about indigenous governance and education. When my grandfather was in his 90s he told us this story: During the Second World War, a young man from our Yucatec Maya community went to work in the agriculture fields in Europe. After spending a few months away, he came home. To welcome him, his mom served him his favorite drink, *pozole*, a drink made of coarsely ground corn mixed with honey which to enjoy properly one must keep shaking it otherwise the corn and water separate. Upon being served his *pozole*, the young man started shaking his bowl and drinking but strangely, paused and asked his mom: "mom, this is a nice drink, but what is it called?" Shocked, his mom wondered, "what did they do to my son in Europe" he has forgotten the name of his favorite drink. However, at the same moment, she noticed that he was shaking his bowl and relieved, she thought: "he might have forgotten the name, but he remembers how to shake it."

At one level the story is a personal call to his Yucatec grandchildren from a community where many Maya practices were quickly disappearing, to not forget. At another level, it is a call to look for the "shaking," for in the shaking there is hope. It is the starting point for decolonization and for rebuilding indigenous communities. The story of the *Alcaldes* is an example of such "shaking."

Indigenous Governance: Locating the Alcalde System in the Broader Indigenous Governance Question

Central to indigenous struggles is overcoming the destructive legacy of colonialism, rebuilding indigenous society, and carving a space for indigenous ways of knowing and being. This, as Alfred (2009) notes, is a "constant fight" against a process that began with European colonialism, for "even as history's shadow lengthens to mark the passing of the brutal age, the Western compulsion to control remains strong" (Alfred 2009, p. 8). Along these same lines, Quijano (2000) argues that what is called globalization is the culmination of a process that began with the constitution of "colonial/modern European capitalism as a new global power." Quijano is helpful in understanding the underpinnings and operations of the colonial logic. He argues that coloniality operates on two foundational axes: the first is the "codification of the differences between conquerors and conquered in the idea of 'race', ... that placed some in a natural situation of inferiority to the others" (p. 533). The other is a new way of controlling labor, land, resources and products.

> This new structure was an articulation of all historically known previous structures of control of labor, slavery, serfdom, small independent commodity production and reciprocity, together around and upon the basis of capital and the world market. (p. 534)

Indigenous peoples' lands, resources, wellbeing, and ways of knowing and being are often sacrificed in the interest of others at the altar of these two axes. Indigenous struggles for self-determination are ultimately freedom from this control and the creation of a space for indigenous ways of knowing and being. This implies some form of self-government and what should be the focus and nature of indigenous governance?

For Alfred, one of the leading scholars of indigenous governance, "... a government that is not based on the traditional principles of respect and harmonious co-existence will inevitably tend to reflect the cold calculating, and coercive ways of the modern state." (Alfred 2009, p. 1). That is, it will replicate the very colonial discourse that indigenous peoples are trying to overcome. In Alfred's view, indigenous nations cannot be preserved unless action is taken to: restore pride in indigenous traditions, achieve economic self-sufficiency, develop independence of mind, and display courage in defending indigenous land and rights. For Alfred, this can only be achieved if we "recover our strength, our wisdom, and our solidarity by honoring and revitalizing the core of our traditional teaching" (p. 9). He, therefore, advocates for what he calls "self-conscious traditionalism" which he explains as:

> ... an intellectual, social and political movement that will reinvigorate those values, principles and other cultural elements that are best suited to the larger contemporary political and economic reality. (ibid., p. 16)

Within this "self-conscious traditionalism," he argues for an indigenous governance that is based on a ""Native American" political tradition: a commitment to profoundly respectful way of governing based on a world views that values autonomy but also recognizes a universal interdependency and promotes peaceful coexistence among all the elements of creation" (ibid., p. 14).

Placed in the context of the issues raised by Alfred, one can ask in what ways does the experience of the Alcalde System engage the actions that are critical to preserving indigenous nations? In what ways does the *Alcade* system reflect an indigenous political tradition? Furthermore, does it reinvigorate those values, principles, and other cultural elements of Maya that can contribute to the larger contemporary political and economic reality? And finally, in what ways does it offer hope for overcoming the legacy of colonialism?

The Origins of the Alcalde System

Writing about the Maya during the colonial period, Bolland argues that

> The dialectic of colonization and resistance in nineteenth century Belize resulted in the unusual adoption of an institution with Maya and Spanish roots into the British colonial system of local government, an institution that enabled the Maya to preserve a degree of autonomy in the colonial society. (Bolland 1988, p. 131)

The Maya roots of the Alcalde system are probably to be found in the pre-Columbine "town chief" the *batab* (Thompson 1930; Coe 2009). The *batabs* according to Coe (2009) were part of a Maya governance system that included: the *halach uinic,* a regional chief; the *batabs,* town leaders; the *a cuch cab,* a form of town council headed by the *batabs*; and the *ah kulels,* a set of deputies below the council. The *halach uinic,* notes Rugeley (1995), was lost in the Yucatan area as the Spaniards reduced Maya organization to the level of small local communities. The *batabs* along with the *a cuch cab,* those who carry the burden, and the *ah kulels* survived.

As part of their role, the *batabs* "gave audience to petitioners; administered local town upkeep and agricultural activities; acted as magistrate for those civil suits where both parties were of his town; and commanded the warriors of his town on the battlefield" (Coe 2009, p. 103). In other words, the *batab* was an overall leader involved in conflict resolution, justice, community organizing and development, resource management, and war.

The *batab* system was co-opted by the Spanish as a way of indirectly ruling the Maya villages in Yucatan (Farriss 1984). The Spanish never had the human resources to have a presence and completely rule over the Maya and therefore relied on the Maya's own leaders to "maintain order, and keep tribute flowing" (Farriss 1984, p. 87). The Maya leadership became responsible for collecting taxes and organizing labor contribution to colonial projects. For a long period, reports Farriss, the only Spanish presence in Maya villages were the Catholic friars whose mission was both to Christianize and "civilize" the Maya. However, she notes, they lacked the capacity to exercise effective control. They could police and ensure outward compliance but could not control what happened inside Maya homes or heads. Intelligence on the Maya communities and their policing were in the hands of Maya elite and their "commitment to the new ways was grudging or ambivalent at best" (p. 96). Under these circumstances, the Maya in the Yucatan region had a significant degree of autonomy when it came to their own affairs. Resolution of conflict, the management of collective resources, organization of labor, organization of religious and community events, social welfare, and representation on behalf of the community was all in the hands of the local Maya leaders. For all intents and purposes, the Maya in the Yucatan region at the local level governed most of their internal affairs.

The *cajas de comunidad,* one of the institutions established during the early colonial period, illustrates the autonomy of Maya communities and the critical role local leadership played in collective survival. Spanish law established the *cajas de comunidad* as a self-help community fund for instances of epidemics, food scarcity, and for tribute payment to which all Maya had to contribute (Tanck de Estrada 1994). While the Cajas were established under Spanish Rule, Farriss (1984) notes, it was overlaid on Mayan systems that had little resemblance to the Spanish versions. The Maya raised funds through cultivation of community *milpas*, organized community production of goods, and even hired community members out to local haciendas. The local Maya leadership administered these funds reporting annually to the colonial governor. Farriss notes that they usually reported a zero balance of payments and suggests that this was intentional in that they probably did not collect from community members the full tax they were required to do and they simply balanced expenses against revenue. Essentially, for the Mayas the *cajas* "were the portion of community resources used for local needs... which included tribute, church taxes, fiestas, or any other local expenditure" (Farriss 1984, p. 263). In other words, they exercised autonomy in the management of their finances thus contributing to collective survival.

Belize and the *Alcalde* System

Belize, formerly called British Honduras, is part of the Maya region. The Spanish never occupied Belize and the British eventually took possession making it the only English speaking country in Central America. British buccaneers settled in the mouth of the Belize River from where they could easily pirate Spanish ships transporting logwood. Eventually in 1667 when piracy was suppressed they themselves began to cut logwood close to the mouth of the Belize River. This not only meant a more permanent settlement but the importation of African slaves. As the buccaneers moved up-stream and shifted their attention to the extraction of mahogany, they came into greater contact with the Maya.

What form of Maya leadership the British encountered in Belize is not recorded, but it is likely similar to the *batab*. By the 1850s, there is evidence that the British encountered the Alcalde system in their efforts to incorporate the Maya and bring them under colonial control. In 1858 Superintendent Seymour proposed a bill that aimed "to legalize and define the position of Alcalde" which he explained his predecessors had allowed "Yucatec and Indian villages" to elect and present to them for appointment to the position. He proposed to make them something of a police officer, justice of the peace, and magistrate and to have them be nominated by the communities but appointed by the superintendent who would also have the power of suspension. When the legislation was passed, it did not even mention the point that the people would nominate their *Alcaldes* (Bolland 1988). Instead, the bill proposed that the *Alcalde* was to be appointed by the superintendent from individuals he judged to be adequate, and the Alcalde in turn was to appoint village police subject to the approval of the superintendent. In the process of legalizing and defining the *Alcalde*, the colonial administration, as Bolland notes, was imposing on it "British authority and legal concepts" (Bolland 1988, p. 136) and shifting the source of authority from the community to the colonial administration.

Despite Seymour's bill, the reality was that the Maya *Alcaldes* seem to have continued to function as they had. In the 1880s, colonial Secretary Henry Fowler acknowledged the failure of previous policy noting that the Indians were scattered and that "no control was really exercised over them" (Henry Fowler (1887) as quoted in Bolland 1988, p. 146). Fowler proposed a renewal of the *Alcalde* system such that the Maya can be brought under "legitimate influence and control... and be converted from passive and indifferent subjects into loyal and willing settlers" (ibid.). According to Bolland, Fowler makes his intentions clear stating that this is "to exact from them a strict adherence to the legal form of the colony" and "to draw them from their old traditions, and little by little to teach them our more exact methods of justice." (ibid.). That Henry Fowler was still attempting to transform the *Alcalde* system in the late 1800s in order to bring the Maya more effectively under British rule suggest that despite British efforts, the Maya in Belize were about to enter the twentieth century exercising a fair degree of autonomy.

The Village Councils

The *Alcalde* system came under attack again in the 1940s with the introduction of the Village Council which is today regulated by the Village Council's Act (Government of Belize 2000b). The institution of village councils was first introduced by the colonial administration in the late 1940s (Moberg 1992) but established in different villages at different times. It was proposed as a mechanism that would allow community development through self-help – the community would provide labor and the government the financial resources.

The introduction of village councils coincided with the beginning of the independence movement in Belize and the birth of political parties. Moberg (1992) notes that it also coincided with what was happening in other areas of the British Empire emanating from the belief that the existing forms of traditional governance systems were autocratic and incompatible with democratic principles. He suggests "the intent, if not the stated goal, of such alternatives was to undercut established local authorities, creating new village leaders who derived their authority from electoral mandate" (Moberg 1992, p. 13). He concludes that the Village Council system resulted in the destruction of consensual politics and the demise of the *Alcalde* system, except those in the Toledo district of Belize.

The example of Succotz, a Yucatec Maya village in the Cayo District where the *Alcalde* system had been in existence since the 1800s, illustrates how this change from *alcades* to village council occurred. The village council was introduced to Succotz in the 1960s. For a very short period, the *Alcalde* system co-existed with the Village council but was quickly abolished completely. How the abolishment of the *Alcalde* system happened is not clear, but as far as local leaders from around that time recall, it was just something decided by the government with no consultation with the community. The village chairman of 1965 recalls that party politicians (the Minister of Rural Development and area representative at the time) told them that they did not need the *Alcalde* anymore, since they could manage their own communities themselves. He also recalls the slogan that when the Peoples United Party won the struggle for independence, there would be no need to do fajinas. (Fajina is a community collective form of work where all men aged 18 and over maintain village commons.) He recalls that some local politicians went further and suggested villagers ask for payment if they were asked to contribute community work.

The results of the introduction of the Village Council and the abolishment of the *Alcalde* system resulted not only in the destruction of consensual politics, as Moberg argues. It also meant the destruction of collective forms of work to maintain the commons, the loss self-reliance in addressing community works, and the introduction of a dependency on the state. Succotz village leaders of the 1960s, for example, observe that the village council quickly became more a representative of the political parties and not the community. It became a mechanism for mobilizing votes and increased any divisiveness that already may have existed. Today these leaders lament the loss of community, autonomy, and self-reliance.

The *Alcaldes* in Toledo

While the *Alcaldes* ceased to function in the rest of Belize during the 1960s, they continued to operate in Toledo along with the Village councils. Every 2 years, an *Alcalde*, a deputy *Alcalde* (referred to as Second *Alcalde*), and two village police are elected. While the state has attempted to define the *Alcalde's* role and functions under the Inferior Courts Act (Government of Belize 2000a) as a lower court magistrate who along with a deputy are elected by the community and appointed by the attorney general, the Maya have continued to exercise autonomy over the institution of the *Alcalde* (Political Reform Commission Final Report 2000). In 1992, for example, the Maya people established the Toledo Alcalde Association (TAA) which brings together the *Alcaldes* of all the 38 Maya villages in Toledo. The establishment of the TAA has been perhaps one of the most important innovations in the system. Whereas each *Alcalde* in the past had been operating at the level of the local village, the Alcalde Association introduced a regional type of governance that has brought strength to the communities and an ability to engage in broad collective action as in the land rights movement.

In the 1994, the government granted a concession to a Chinese Company to extract timber on Maya lands. This started the contemporary land rights struggle that has spanned over 2.5 decades. The legal struggle has seen the case dragged through local courts, the Interamerican Commission on Human rights, the Belize Supreme Court, and the Caribbean Court of Justice (CCJ). After a series of appeals, the court battle culminated in 2015 with a consent order by the CCJ. Throughout this process, the *Alcalde* system has provided a mechanism for communities to dialogue and make decisions independent of outside forces and maintain a high degree of unity. As noted by Jerry Enriquez (2015):

> Through successive PUP and UDP (PUP stands for the Peoples United Party; UDP stands for the United Democratic Party) administrations, the Maya leadership was also able to keep politics in its place in order to avoid the compromising attachment to one political party or another, ... Such detachment and their internal cohesion were important for the leadership to keep focused and ensure that their investments of time, energies, and other resources are not held hostage to divisive party politics. (Enriquez 2015)

The fact that it is grounded on customary law has also ensured that commitment to collective land rights has been sustained.

The *Alcalde* as an Indigenous Form of Governance

In 2010 the Government of Belize attempted to review the 2000 Inferior Coursts Act. The Toloedo Alcalde Association (TAA) was concerned that the process was constrained and asked for a more consultative process. The TAA's proposal was not accepted and the Government initiative shelved. The TAA went ahead and developed and proposed to the Government their own *Alcaldes* bill. While the government did not adopt the TAA's proposed bill, the TAA has done so itself. The proposed act reveals some key characteristics of the *Alcalde* system evident in the way elections are to be carried out, who is eligible, and on what grounds an *Alcalde* can be removed.

According to the TAA proposed bill (Toledo Alcalde's Association 2010), eligible candidates are village residents who have gone through the ranks of the system. Elections are to be carried out without any campaigning for the position and no postulation on behalf of any political party is to be accepted. In terms of removal from office, a top reason for removal is failure to uphold customary law and other reasons includes failure to do the job, corruption, and drinking. An alclade is expected to be exemplary in honoring and upholding customary law, to consider the advice of elders, and to represent the interests, needs, and concerns of the village to state actors and private entities or individuals.

The foundations of the *Alcalde* system as an indigenous governance, however, live not in the Inferior Court's Act or even the proposed TAA *Alcalde's* bill. Much of the values and wisdom that underlies it is unstated and lives in Maya language, the understandings of elders, leaders, knowledge bearers, and the rest of the Maya community. The name for *Alcalde* in the Q'eqchi language, for example, is Jolomil, K'aleb'aal K'amol b'e. Jolomil refers to head person. K'alebal refers to the village and K'amol b'e refers to leader, guide, speaker. K'utul b'e which means he who teaches or shows the way is offered as a synonym by the Proyecto Linguistico Francisco Marroquin Q'eqchi dictionary (Proyecto Linguistico Francisco Marroquin 2003, p.161). In essence Jolomil Kalebal K'amolb'e refers to the head of the community. The one who shows, teaches, and guides or leads along the path.

The coordinator of the Toledo Alcalde Association explains that Maya governance is essentially about the management of relations between members of the community, between the community and their surrounding environment, and between the community and those from outside the community (Personal communication 9 June 2016). He explains that maintaining right relations is central to the *Alcalde's* role, that it is about making sure that community members are getting along perfectly well, and that they remain as brothers and sisters, are looking after the interests of each other, are not trying to impose on others, and are not trying to hinder others.

This understanding of governance Pablo Mis, is consistent with important Maya principles of interrelatedness and harmonious balance. Greetings in Q'eqchi and Yucatec maya languages remind us of these principles. Victor Cal, the coordinator of the Maya healers Association and teacher at Tumul Kin Center of Learning always explains, along these lines, that the Q'eqchi greeting *Mas sa la cho'ol* is not a simple "how are you?" but is asking: How is your balance or how is your relationship with self, others, environment, and cosmos? A similar explanation is offered of the Yucatec greeting *bixabel* which literally means how is your way or how are you walking? In essence, the goal of indigenous governance is to ensure balanced and harmonious relations; it is about ensuring that as individuals and communities we are staying on the right path.

The *Alclade* must first of all show the way by example, by being a model of right relations. Alfonso Cal (Personal communication 9 June 2016) who has been in the *Alcalde* system for over 30 years and Chairperson of the *Alcalde* association for 6 years explains that the elders of his community asked him to be the scribe of the *Alcalde* when he was 16 because he always attended meetings, always participated in the *fajina*, had never been brought before the *Alcalde*, and had never been fined (Personal communication 9 June 2016). For Mr. Cal, a good *Alcalde* is someone that is not a drunkard, someone that does not get into trouble. In effect a good *Alcalde* is someone who shows the way by being an example of good personal character and upholding customary law. The *Alcalde* also guides along the path of right relations by resolving conflict and counseling in matters that can range from relationships between spouses, parents, and children to business relationships. Finally it fosters and restores right relationships by enforcing customary law.

One of the key responsibilities of the *Alcalde* is to convene the *fajina*. The *fajina* is a practice in which all men aged 18 and above must come out to do community work to maintain the commons reveals much about Maya governance. Participation in the fajina is central to being a member of the community. When an external person wants to become a member of the community, such person must commit to participating in the community meetings and *fajina*. When a person has a home or a farm in the community lands, even if they are not living in the community, they must participate in the *fajina*. The *fajina* is about looking after the collective interests, the interests of each other and about the reciprocal relationships that are necessary in the community. A member of the community cannot simple benefit from the shared resources and the labor of the rest; hence, when a person does not show up for the *fajina* he needs to pay a fine. It is the responsibility of the *alcalde* to convene the *fajina* and to fine people for not participating. In essence it his role to ensure reciprocity.

Another of the primary roles of the *Alcalde* is to organize and facilitate the community meetings which further reveals some key elements of indigenous governance. Mis (Personal communication 9 June 2016) explains that to say I am going the village meeting people say "Xik we chi ab'ink" which literally means "I am going to listen." *Abink* in this sense is referring to the meeting but literally means to listen. The village meeting privileges listening over speaking. Everybody is going to listen, including and particularly the *Alcalde*. The duty of the *Alcalde* is therefore to guarantee deliberation, get people to listen to each other, to work towards a consensus, and to ensure that the people who might be particularly affected or who hold an essential voice speak and are listened to. The *Alcalde's* role is to facilitate the voice of those that live downstream; Mis explains the *Alcalde* will often say "I have listened to Mr. X and Mr. Y but I would encourage Mr. Z to speak." The village meeting is also about making space for the voice of the elders. Often when things become unclear says the coordinator of the TAA, the *Alcalde* will seek the advice of the elders. This very idea is captured in the TAA proposed bill "The *Alcalde* must respect the advice of elders." Similarly, the words of the ancestors have a place – often people will talk about what their grandparents told them about the past. In essence the village meeting is about people listening to each other; it is about looking after each other's and the collective interests by listening to each other, and building consensus. Facilitating all this is the role of the *Alcalde*.

The emphasis of the village meeting is on listening, not on speaking. In order for listening to happen obviously someone must speak. This emphasis on listening means that it must be orderly. The meeting therefore often takes a ceremonial character. It is treated with a degree of sacredness. As the TAA coordinator describes it, it is "ceremony in action." In order for the meeting to happen, everyone must be inside the meeting house, everybody must be silent.

The village meeting, the listening event, has an amazing parallel with the creation story described in the Popul Vuh. The Popul Vuh relates that in the very beginning there is only silence, no animals, birds, or human are there, only the creators are present. This is how the creators came together in a council "...*and then they talked, then they thought, then they worried. They agreed with each other, they joined their words, their thoughts. Then it was clear, then they reached accord in the light and then humanity was clear*" (Tedlock 1996, p. 66). The very creative moment begins with silence, with coming together, with dialogue, with listening and with the putting together of minds and words.

The Popul Vu relates further that the creators first tried making human beings out of clay, but these beings failed to honor and give thanks to their creators – they forgot to show gratitude and so were destroyed. They then tried creating human beings out of wood, but these beings not only failed to honor and show gratitude to their creator but mistreated their implements and the natural environment and so these turned against them and were destroyed. Finally the creators sought the advice of two elders who helped them to create human beings out of corn.

The *abink* of the creators is a creative moment and it is about solving a problem and it is a learning experience. Their *Abink* begins with coming together, with silence, it involves listening, building consensus, failing, and seeking the advice of the elders to finally solve their problem. The community *abink* resonates so strongly with the first *abink* suggesting the deep indigenous roots of Maya governance. If one recalls that the problem the creators are trying to solve is the creation of humans, one can even see the nature and goals of indigenous governance, the silence, the joining of words and thoughts, the seeking of the advice of elders, the consensus, building are processes that speak to becoming more human.

The experience of the *Alcalde's* illustrates what Alfred's (2009) contends are necessary for the preservation of indigenous nations: restoring pride in traditions, achieving economic self-sufficiency, the development of independence of mind, and defending lands and rights. Moreover, it has been able to do so by drawing on traditional values while at the same time adapting to the demands of the contemporary context. Today in particular the *Alcalde* system in Toledo is reinvigorating values, principles, and cultural elements as a protection against cooption and falling victims to the clientelism of the Belizean state. The lessons that can be drawn from the story of the *Alcalde* system as an indigenous governance system are worth enumerating:

1. It illustrates indigenous peoples' continuous struggle to resist and overcome colonialism and its legacy.
2. It illustrates how indigenous governance has been recognized by colonial and state authorities as a lynchpin of autonomy and therefore targeted. However, it also shows the inability of the colonial enterprise to completely erase. Even if it makes indigenous peoples forget the name of the drink, they still remember how to shake it. The survival and revitalization of the *Alcalde* system is evidence of the shaking. It has managed to find cracks in the colonial landscape to put out new shoots whether in Yucatan, Northern Belize, or Toledo, it has been able to take advantage of the these cracks.
3. It illustrates indigenous peoples' capacity to innovate and incorporate non-indigenous practices even when intended to control such as in the redefinition of the cajas comunitarias.
4. It illustrates how indigenous governance embodies many critical indigenous values that can be the basis of new imaginings. The notion of indigenous governance as the facilitation of right relations, the importance of dialogue, community and reciprocity, leadership by example, the importance of facilitating the voices of everyone, and the importance of making space for elders and of honoring tradition are foundational values.
5. It illustrates the importance of indigenous governance to survival and overcoming the legacy of colonialism. The experience in Yucatan, in northern Belize in the 1800s, and the contemporary land rights movement suggests that indigenous forms of governance have been a key to the struggle for both physical and cultural survival.

The indigenous values the *Alcalde* system reveals, its focus on facilitating harmonious relations, its commitment to making space for everyone, the experience of defending autonomy and overcoming the legacy of colonialism, and the story of innovation while honoring tradition, offer important lessons that can be useful in rethinking education.

The Challenges of Education: Belize

The Belize education system like many education systems around the world is characterized by a lack of equity, a growing challenge in meaningfully engaging children and young people, and the absence of democratic governance that might allow for the voices and concerns and aspirations of the most excluded to find a hearing space.

A recent study (Gayle and Mortis 2010) characterized the Belize school system as "a fancy basket that needs to be changed to at least a cheap bucket that can hold water" (p. 108). It reported that the lack of resources, an outdated system, and a human ecology characterized by poverty, vulnerability, and violence are key factors contributing to a failing system (ibid.). This reality is confirmed by Ministry of Education statistics (Dropout rates: Primary school: 8.4% Boys and 6.0% girls; Secondary: 10% boys and 8% Girls. Net enrollment ratio at secondary level 45% (only 45% of children eligible in for secondary school are participating)) that report high repetition rates across the system and alarmingly low participation rate at the secondary level (Ministry of Education 2012).

The low level of young people's participation and engagement in schools is one of the most concerning issues in Belize and perhaps in many other countries; it is one that highlights the failures of the system and the need for rethinking education. The factors that explain school dropouts as the culmination of poor engagement are complex. However, as Clive Harber (2002) argues, the nature of education including meaningless curriculum and oppressive education has much to do with it. Along these lines, Smyth (2006) argues that:

> The reasons students withdraw from school emotionally, educationally, psychologically, and, eventually, physically are multi-faceted and complex, but in the end they boil down to 'political' reasons—that is to say, students refuse to make the emotional and relational investment necessary to become engaged with the social institution of schooling in a manner necessary for learning to occur. (p. 288)

This leads him to argue that

> If we want a more realistic regime of accountability for high schools that is likely to have a chance of success in making a difference in the lives of those most disadvantaged, then it will have to be one that includes the lives, experiences, cultures, family backgrounds, aspirations, and hopes of young people them-selves. (p. 288)

What we are talking about here is the lack of relevance and responsiveness to the reality of disadvantaged children. This is an issue of particular concern to indigenous peoples. Indigenous peoples are concerned about the persisting colonial logic of the education system that prevents the "lives, experiences, cultures, family backgrounds, aspirations, and hopes of young people" and their communities to inform education.

The state and the church have historically dominated the education system of Belize and have done very little to offer a relevant and responsive education to Maya people. A letter of 1914 by Fr. Tenck to the Governor General speaks volumes about how Maya people were perceived and what the purpose of education was:

> I have been told that a delegation of Indians from the neighborhood of San Antonio is now in Belize bothering your Excellency. At present the Indians, whom they are representing, are living in the bush, scattered and isolated like wild animals. We and Your Excellency also, I am sure, are desirous to have them learn at least a few of the most rudimentary sanitary laws and some of the first duties of persons living in a civilized community...
> Do, therefore, what you think but we beg Your Excellency, to keep these subjects of British Honduras in some one place where we will be able to maintain a school for them. In the

> school alone can we place our hope for a brighter future for them. And, would could [sic] compel those ignorant, foolish and selfish parents to send their children to school.... (Tenck, quoted in Wainwright 2009, p. 429)

Tenck reveals how church and colonial authorities perceived the Maya. As he puts it they are "ignorant, foolish and selfish" Indians who are "living like wild animals." The only hope of civilizing them is through education and therefor they must be compelled to send their children. The goal of education, Tenck suggests, is to have the "Maya people learn the first duties of living in a civilized community." Ultimately it is about bringing the Maya more effectively under the control of colonial and church authority. In this task, Wainwright (2009) argues the church and the state are complicit.

This dominance of the church and the state and colonialist tendencies of education for Maya people have persisted. The teaching of Maya history, for example, was not introduced in schools until the year 2000. The language policy continues to view indigenous languages only useful to help children transition from home to school. Language policy reform has consistently been resisted. Efforts to introduce bilingual intercultural education have had to rely on efforts of indigenous organizations with limited support from the state or the church. Clearly culturally responsive education has not been a priority for the church or the state and it is unlikely they will make it a priority.

The church-state system persists in Belize producing, not only, poor levels of accountability between the church and the state but between school managers and parents (Ministry of Education 2012). Gayle and Mortis (2010) reports that throughout the study, teachers, principals, and government personnel complained bitterly about the power relations between the church and the Ministry of Education. Ultimately it is parents and the children that are marginalized. Parent Teacher Associations are largely inexistent and largely dysfunctional where they exist. Parental participation is limited to essentially picking up report cards, receiving complaints about misbehaving children, and fund raising. Within this context, there is limited space for the voices of Maya communities.

The absence of democratic school governance raises a major problem that remains unspoken – the autocratic nature of schools. In 1990 Said Musa Minister of Education and later on Prime Minister noted: "For too long the approach to education in our schools has been *authoritarian*. The teachers have traditionally been the fountains of all wisdom, knowledge and understanding. The student did not dare to disagree." (Musa, quoted in Bennett 2008, p. 133). A telling practice is classroom management which is less about establishing positive relationships and safe spaces and facilitating engaging experiences and more about manipulating students to comply with rules through carrots and sticks. This kind of education is what Paulo Freire (1970) calls "banking" education and one that Shoman (1991) in part attributes to the dominance of the church.

These autocratic dynamics however are not limited to the teacher-student relationship. It also characterizes the relationship between management and teachers in many schools in Belize. It is unlikely that teachers and parents feel any great deal of empowerment to challenge management policy and neither do parents. In effect, these autocratic tendencies tend to "reflect the cold calculating, and coercive ways of the modern state" that Alfred (2009, p. 11) is talking about.

In summary, some of the key challenges that education faces includes the challenge of meaningfully engaging young people and of developing more democratic governance system that might allow the participation of those most affected by the historical and persisting colonial underpinnings. These challenges need to be addressed in rethinking education and the story of the *Alcalde* system and the values and principles it embodies might offer some insights.

A Maya Education Initiative: Tumul K'in Center or Learning

Between 2001 and 2005, I was involved in establishing and directing the Tumul K'in Center of Learning, an initiative that at one level aimed to respond to the challenge of low levels of participation of young Maya people in education. At a higher level, however, Tumul K'in was a decolonizing project, an act of self-determination.

Tumul K'in was established in 2001 by Maya actors and organizations as a response to high levels of poverty (79% in 2002 (National Human Development Advisory Committee 2004, p. 24)) and marginalization among Maya people, limited education opportunities and high "push-out" rates at the secondary level, assimilatory education and social practices, and the exploitation of Maya cultural and natural heritage by others with little benefit to Maya people.

Tumul K'in in the Yucatec and Mopan Maya language refers to a new day, a new time, or a new sun. As such it signaled a new way of thinking about education and development. The notion of "development with identity" was influential in Tumul K'in's efforts. "Development with identity" was an idea emergent in Central and South America that sought to overcome the colonialist underpinnings and negative effects of development thought and practice by creating a space for indigenous ways (Deruyttere 2004; Uquillas and Eltz 2004). It argued that conventional development thought and practice premised on the idea that to develop means a gradual abandonment of indigenous ways – a move from traditional to "modern"; and based on the exploitation of indigenous labor and resources for the benefit of others and the detriment of indigenous peoples themselves is essentially colonialist. Countering that idea, indigenous leaders, activists, and organizations such as Luis Macas, Nina Pacari, the Central American Indigenous council, proposed the notion of "development with identity." "Development with identity" proposed that development ideas are always culturally framed and that each society has the right to define both the speed and direction of development. Indigenous development must therefore be based on indigenous ontology and epistemology; indigenous values, knowledge, and practices need to be at the center.

Tumul Kin refused to pathologize Maya poverty and educational disengagement. It viewed poverty as a result of colonialist development practices and school dropouts as the result of economics, and the inability of schools to provide safe, relevant, and engaging spaces for indigenous children and their communities. In response, Tumul K'in sought to develop an educational practice that was rooted in Maya values and practices and was not only a friendly space for children, teachers, parents, and community but was owned and defined by them. Tumul K'in did not explicitly draw on Maya governance system in its conceptualization. However, the goals and values embodied in indigenous governance were present and contributed to rethinking education in several ways.

School Governance as Indigenous Governance

Given the history of education in Belize, autonomy was critical to Tumul K'in. To address the question of autonomy, school governance became a critical matter. Three underlying concerns influenced the construction of the governing body of Tumul K'in: How can ownership of the school remain in the hands of the Maya community? How can we ensure that the governing body of Tumul K'in remains autonomous from possible coercive forces that have not been responsive to the aspirations of Maya people? How do we ensure that the voice of those that live downstream have a space in shaping and governing the educational institution? These were so important to Tumul K'in that it's governance structure went through several iterations. Finally it settled on a governing body that consisted of representatives from the Toledo Alcalde Association as the traditional leaders, parents, teachers and students as the direct owners and beneficiaries and the Ministry of Education as partner with nonvoting rights.

While the composition of the governing body ensured ownership and control of the school by the Maya communities, to ensure that this body stayed the course, to ensure accountability a Parent, Teacher and Community Association (PTCA) was established to facilitate and promote the engagement of the wider Maya community.

The PTCA became the lynchpin of community and parental participation – aware of the diversity of languages and the need to ensure everybody can listen, it conducted its meetings in three and sometimes four languages (Q'eqchi, Mopan, Spanish, and English) and cognizant that it was not easy to get to Tumul K'in and that parents would have to leave their homes early in the morning without having breakfast, the PTCA fundraised to provide transportation and food for parents when they came to pick up report cards and attend meetings. Recognizing that the formal meetings are intimidating and impersonal, it sought to create spaces for more human relations and more effective participation. It organized overnight sessions at the center for parents to immerse themselves in school and therefore organized overnight stays for parents and elders. These sessions took a more informal nature, a sort of discussions over dinner, in the cornfield, over coffee and started to be known among staff as "dreaming together sessions." These often created spaces where parents and elders could speak from their heart, where they could dream without the formality of a boardroom.

Despite all the PTCA did, there were still parents who sometimes would not come to pick up report cards or attend meetings. Tumul K'in in response established a

Community Liaison officer who along with teachers organized home visits and regional meetings.

There are many other ways in which Tumul K'in sought to generate community participation. A community radio station was established; cultural nights were taken to several communities; students went to learn from community members, and community members came to teach at Tumul K'in; and the institution of Maya Day, an event to celebrate Maya identity and culture that became an annual regional celebration was established.

In summary, guaranteeing the autonomy of Maya people to define the education that best suits their aspirations and ensuring that the voices of those that live downstream were the implicit guiding principles of governance at Tumul K'in. While not explicitly seeking to implement Maya governance principles and values, the fact that these are the practices and values that those involved knew and held they ended up shaping the philosophy and practice of school governance.

Indigenous Governance and Engaging Young People in Education

Tumul K'in adopted the *Alcalde* governance system as its student governance system and this was a critical way in which students participated. Tumul K'in had four classes (years 1–4). Each class elected a first and second *Alcalde* and together eight *Alcaldes* formed the *Alcalde* council of the school and they elected a first and second *Alcalde* as the leaders. Much like the *Alcalde* system in the communities, the class *Alcalde* and the school *Alcalde's* role was to ensure peace and harmony, organize collective work to maintain the commons, and facilitate community meetings.

The school *Alcaldes* organized autonomous student meetings in which they discussed student issues and planned activities for community building. One of the challenges they faced illustrates the significance of these meetings. After their first few meetings, the First Alcalde reported that he was frustrated and did not know what to do. Everybody wanted to speak in his or her own language and this caused tension because not everybody could understand. Our response was that the school valued this linguistic diversity and perhaps they might want to set ground rules. They did. They agreed that anyone could speak in their own language provided someone offered an English translation to ensure everyone understood.

The *Alcaldes* also used these student meetings to organize school cultural nights. Every other week the *Alcaldes* organized a cultural night where students sang, played musical instruments, performed, danced, and shared food. The teachers were also expected to participate and did.

As in every Maya community, the *Alcalde* convened a school community meeting and *fajina*. Every other week they would organize a *fajina* to maintain the school grounds. Everyone including teachers was expected to participate. After the *fajina* a school community meeting was convened and facilitated by the school *Alcaldes*. They developed an agenda that included everything from sharing information about upcoming events, reports, and discussion of concerns.

One of the special roles of the *Alcaldes* was in the question of school discipline. A disciplinary committee was established to support the role of the *Alcaldes* in maintaining peace and harmony. The committee consisted of the two school *Alcaldes*, a PTCA member and the Academic Director. The committee was responsible for situations that went beyond just minor misdemeanors (these were addressed by individual *Alcaldes* and teachers). They investigated matters by talking to the concerned student and those affected, they offered advice and imposed sanctions. These sanctions were generally about restoring peace and harmony – apologizing to a victim, apologizing to the community, carrying out community work, or making repairs to damaged property.

The experience of Tumul K'in's adoption of the *Alcalde* system as its student governance system illustrates how schools can be places for revitalizing and innovating on indigenous governance.

Indigenous Governance and Pedagogy

Tumul K'in aimed to reach and engage all its students and it recognized that to do so it could not be a conventional school nor adopt a conventional pedagogic practice. To this end, Tumul K'in sought to develop a pedagogic practice that rejected pathologizing students, rested on strong, respectful, and positive relations between students and teachers and made use of the assets of the wider community.

Tumul K'in was a live-in program. Because reaching it was difficult, students stayed on campus and went home every 10 days for 4 days during the school year. This provided an opportunity for developing deeper relationships beyond the classroom between students and teachers. They ate, worked, and had fun together. In terms of the latter, the cultural evenings that the student *Alcaldes* organized became one of the most powerful spaces for breaking hierarchies and establishing a relational pedagogy.

The curriculum was organized such that a teacher was made responsible for a group of 10–15 students. These teachers were usually responsible for teaching Agriculture, science, and third related subject, and facilitating a daily 2-h our field-experience. This practice allowed teachers to develop stronger relationships with students, integrate indigenous knowledge, involve traditional knowledge bearers, and break the walls of the school to make the wider community a part of the school.

We thought of Tumul K'in as a community where we *dream together* and a place where *everybody learns and everybody teaches*, where we honored tradition but innovated by *turning things upside down*. We did not consciously sit down to think about the practices and principles of indigenous governance; however, our efforts embodied the concerns and drew from the experience of Maya governance. The dreaming together was ultimately about an education that responds to the needs and aspirations of Maya children and communities and contributes to Maya wellbeing. Tumul K'in was governed and managed for that purpose.

Conclusion: So What Are the Implications of Indigenous Governance for Education?

The implications go in two directions: first, what can education do for indigenous governance given its centrality to the preservation of indigenous nations and the question of indigenous self-determination? and second, how can indigenous governance inform the rethinking of education?

One important concern of the *Alcaldes* is the lack of people with the knowledge, values, character, and commitment to occupy the *Alcalde* position. This is a critical concern for as the coordinator for the Alcalde Association points out, there can be a good indigenous governance system but if there are not people to make it function then it is useless. This concern leads ex-*Alcaldes* in Succotz and Toledo to point out that education has trained people for other purposes, away from indigenous ways and to a disavowal of traditional governance.

During one of the PTCA sessions at Tumul K'in Center of Learning, a community *Alcalde* told the story of a young man to express his concern about the negative impact education was having on indigenous governance. He related a story involving a young man from his community who had graduated from high school who refused to participate in communal work (*fajina*). The young man wrote to him stating that he was no longer going to do *fajina* because he was now a high school graduate. In this *Alcalde's* view, education was eroding customary law, Maya forms of governance, and ultimately community. His story resonates with the story of Succotz and how the *Alcalde* system was undone. More broadly, the story highlights the disconnect between the subjectivity produced by schooling and that desired by indigenous societies. It raises the question regarding the extent to which education disavows indigenous governance or sustains it. The survival of indigenous forms of governance will depend, to a significant degree, on our cognitive commitment to it, and education is a space that can either erode or strengthen that commitment. We are left, therefore, asking the question how can education sustain the values and cognitive commitment to indigenous governance?

In terms of how indigenous governance can contribute to Maya education, one contribution relates to the challenge of reshaping education in a way that honors Maya ways of knowing and being and responds to Maya aspirations. The Belizean education system is a church-state system (Bennett 2008), almost all schools are managed by a church but teachers are paid for by the state. The state and the church, the two principal agents of colonialism, continue to control the education system of Belize (Shoman 1991; Gayle and Mortis 2010). Neither the state nor the church has voluntarily sought to respond to the rights of indigenous peoples to a culturally relevant education. The state has adopted a very passive role that is evident in its language policy. After pressure from indigenous organizations, the policy has shifted from English being the official language to be used in schools, to one where teachers may use native languages to help children learn and indigenous communities may teach their language if they finance it (Ministry of Education 2000, p. 184). The mainstream attitude however is still that the English language should be the dominant language.

As to the church, Shoman (1991) writes that its main concern is religious education and raises doubts about whether it can contribute to offering a decolonized education. The experience of three schools in which Intercultural Bilingual Education (IBE) was introduced in 2009 perhaps reveals the limited commitment there is for cultural responsive education. Of the three schools, two were under a church management and one was under an indigenous organization. In the project review, the teachers from the church-managed schools pointed out that the main threat to the initiative was that teachers trained in IBE were being transferred out of the IBE schools (Penados and Mis 2009). In 2017, all but the indigenous managed school is continuing to sustain IBE.

In the education landscape of Belize where the church-state system lives on, Maya governance that has allowed Maya people to exercise a degree of autonomy might be able to facilitate a space to develop the kind of education Maya people desire. The *Alcalde* system has proven to be effective in securing collective land rights. Securing a space for the kind of education that Maya people deserve and desire might also be possible.

The challenges that Belize's education system faces are complex and it would be simplistic to imagine that there is an easy or even a single solution. Notwithstanding that, indigenous governance can contribute significantly by offering alternative imaginations, new ways of rethinking education and enacting change. Arguably the single most concerning educational challenge in Belize is education's failure to engage children especially at the secondary level. To address this challenge, it might be useful to heed Smyth's (2006) advice quoted earlier, that if we want to make a difference in the lives of the most disadvantaged we must respond and include their experiences, cultures and backgrounds and hopes.

To achieve this, it might be helpful to think of schools as relational organizations and to make them learning communities for young people, parents, teachers, and community. It is precisely here that indigenous governance has much to offer. The *Alcalde* system teaches us that indigenous governance is about the management of relationships. It is about ensuring that people are listening and caring for each other, about making space for the voices of the marginalized, and about restoring harmonious and respectful relations.

The village meeting, the *abink,* as a space to listen, to dialogue, to build consensus, and ultimately to solve community problems teach us much about the importance, and important ways of making space for the voices of young people, parents, and teachers. The village *abink* echoes the creators' *abink* in the Maya creation story from which even deeper teachings can be drawn. It is through the *abink* of the creators that humanity was made possible. Humanity or perhaps humanness seems to require a space in which words and thoughts can be joined together, a space in which it is safe to fail in our first or second attempt, a space where it is proper to seek the wisdom of others. If we want schools to be places where we can become more human, the teachings cannot be clearer.

References

Alfred T (2009) Peace power righteousness: an indigenous manifesto. Oxford University Press, Don Mills
Bennett JA (2008) Education in Belize: a historical perspective. The Angelus Press, Belize City
Bolland NO (1988) Colonialism and resistance in Belize: essays in historical sociology. Cubola Productions, Benque Viejo Del Carmen
Coe MD (2009) A model of ancient community structure in the Maya Lowlands. Southwest J Anthropol 21(2):97–114
Deruyttere A (2004) Indigenous peoples, development with identity and the Inter-American Development Bank: challenges and opportunities. LCR Sustainable Development Working Paper 20, pp 23–31
Enriquez JA (2015, May 15) How the Mayas won: lessons for all Belizeans. Amandala Newspaper, Belize City. Available via Belize in America. http://belizeinamerica.net/how-the-mayas-won-lessons-for-all-belizeans/
Farriss N (1984) Maya society under colonial rule: the collective enterprise of survival. Princeton University Press, Princeton
Freire P (1970) Pedagogy of the oppressed (30th Anniv.). The Continuum International Publishing Group Inc., New York
Gayle H, Mortis N (2010) Male social participation and violence in urban Belize: gangs, gender, God and governance. Ministry of Education, Belize City
Government of Belize (2000a) Inferior Courts Act revised edition. http://www.belizejudiciary.org/web/filebase/?wpfb_s=inferior+courts+act. Accessed 5 June 2017
Government of Belize (2000b) Village Councils Act chapter 88 revised edition 2000. Government of Belize, Belize City
Harber C (2002) Schooling as violence: an exploratory overview. Educ Rev 54(1):7–16
International Labor Organization (1989) Convention concerning indigenous and tribal peoples in independent countries. http://www.ilo.org/dyn/normlex/en/f?p=NORMLEXPUB:12100:0::NO::P12100_ILO_CODE:C169. Accessed 5 June 2017
Maya Land Rights Commission (May 2016) Press Release. http://amandala.com.bz/news/toledo-maya-gob-odds-land-rights-consultations/
Ministry of Education (2000) Handbook of policies and procedures for school services. Ministry of Education, Belmopan
Ministry of Education (2012) Improving access, quality and governance of education in Belize: education strategy 2011–2016. Ministry of Education, Belmopan
Moberg M (1992) Continuity under colonial rule: The Alcalde System and the Garifuna in Belize, 1858–1969. Ethnohistory 39(3):1–19
National Human Development Advisory Committee (2004) Poverty assessment report 2002. Government of Belize, Belmopan
Penados F, Mis P (2009) Safeguarding the rights of indigenous children in the process of development: intercultural bilingual education project review. Prepared for UNICEF Belize, Belize City
Political Reform Commission (2000) Final report of the Political Reform Commission. Political Reform Commission, Belize City
Proyecto Linguistico Francisco Marroquin (2003) Diccionario Q'eqchi'. Proyecto Linguistico Francisco Marroquin, Guatemala City
Quijano A (2000) Coloniality of power and Eurocentrism in Latin America. Int Sociol 15(2):215–232
Rugeley T (1995) The Maya elites of nineteenth-century Yucatán. Ethnohistory 42(3):477–493

Shoman A (1991) Why a national symposium. In: Shoman K (ed) Education in Belize: toward the year 2000. Cubola, Benque Viejo, pp 11–21

Smyth J (2006) "When students have power": student engagement, student voice, and the possibilities for school reform around "dropping out" of school. Int J Leadersh Educ 9(4):285–298

Tanck de Estrada D (1994) Escuelas y cajas de comunidad en Yucatan al final de la colonia. Hist Mex 43(3):195–206

Tedlock D (1996) Popul Vuh: the definitive edition of the Mayan book of the dawn of life and the glories of gods and kings. Touchstone Book, New York

Thompson E (1930) Ethnology of the Mayas of Southern and Central British Honduras. Anthropol Ser 17(2):27–213

Toledo Alcalde's Association (2010) Proposed *Alcaldes* Jurisdiction Bill, 2010. Unpublished, Punta Gorda Town

United Nations (2008) United Nations Declaration on the rights of indigenous peoples. http://www.un.org/esa/socdev/unpfii/documents/DRIPS_en.pdf. Accessed 5 June 2017

Uquillas JE, Eltz MA (2004) The quest and practice of indigenous development. World Bank LCR Development Working Paper 20, pp 9–21

Wainwright J (2009) "The first duties of persons living in a civilized community": the Maya, the Church, and the colonial state in southern Belize. J Hist Geogr 35(3):428–450

Indigenous Leadership: A Complex Consideration

15

Margaret J. Maaka, Kerry Laiana Wong, W. Kekailoa Perry, and Patricia M. G. Johnston

Contents

Introduction 230
Historical Trauma and Indigenous Leadership 232
Well-Executed Leadership 236
Leadership Ascension 239
Leadership Succession 242
A Final Comment 246
References 247

Abstract

Our collaboration on the writing of this chapter reflects the complex nature of Indigenous leadership. We each draw on our experiences as Indigenous educators working within Indigenous and western contexts–Wong and Perry from Hawaiian perspectives, Johnston from a Māori perspective, and Maaka from a Māori perspective in the diaspora of Hawai'i. In keeping with our introduction, our stances on Indigenous leadership are shaped by the contexts in which we live and work, by our missions as educators in higher education, by our efforts to mentor a successor generation, and by our histories as peoples violently dislocated from the fundamental markers of our identities–sovereignty, ancestral lands, language, and cultural knowledge. This dislocation was (and still is) brought by the hands of colonial forces hell bent on forcing geopolitical, economic, and sociopolitical agendas upon us–at our expense. As a result, Māori (with the breached Treaty of

---

M. J. Maaka (✉) · K. L. Wong · W. K. Perry
University of Hawai'i at Mānoa, Honolulu, HI, USA
e-mail: marg@hawaii.edu; kwong@hawaii.edu; wperry@hawaii.edu

P. M. G. Johnston
Te Whare Wānanga o Awanuiārangi, Whakatane, New Zealand
e-mail: trish.johnston@wananga.qc.nz

© Springer Nature Singapore Pte Ltd. 2019
E. A. McKinley, L. T. Smith (eds.), *Handbook of Indigenous Education*,
https://doi.org/10.1007/978-981-10-3899-0_71

Waitangi) and Hawaiians (with the illegal overthrow of a constitutional monarchy) face modern day challenges in recovering all that has been stripped away.

In our writing, then, we choose not to limit our discussion on Indigenous leadership in education to the context of "preschool through university schooling." Since we view "education" as pertaining to anything that leads us out of ignorance, we choose to expand our discussion to the broadest context of Indigenous self-determination that includes the socio-politics of Indigenous knowledge, models, methods, and content within formal and non-formal educational systems. Similarly, our use of the word "community" refers to Indigenous peoples who have been brought up within the geographic boundary of their traditional lands for the purpose of making change. Change makers include individuals from many different arenas including education, health, law, business, politics, and culture and the arts.

While there are many points of interest in an examination of Indigenous leadership, this chapter focuses on historical trauma and Indigenous leadership, well-executed leadership, leadership ascension, and leadership succession. Although our commentaries draw on the Māori and Hawaiian cultures, we believe that they also resonate with other Indigenous peoples. As well, the following commentaries are not to be embraced as received knowledge, rather, they are perspectives designed to invite debate.

Keywords
Indigenous leadership · Historical trauma of Indigenous peoples · Well-executed leadership · Leadership ascension · Leadership succession · Indigenous self-determination

Introduction

In his working definition of Indigenous communities, peoples, and nations, the United Nations' Special Rapporteur Martinez Cobo sets the context in which Indigenous leadership finds itself in modern times:

> Indigenous communities, peoples and nations are those which, having a historical continuity with the pre-invasion and pre-colonial societies that developed on their territories, consider themselves distinct from other sectors of the societies now prevailing in those territories, or parts of them. They form at present non-dominant sectors of society and are determined to preserve, develop and transmit to future generations their ancestral territories, and their ethnic identity, as the basis of their continued existence as peoples, in accordance with their own cultural patterns, social institutions and legal systems. (Martinez Cobo 1986)

This imperative to "preserve, develop and transmit to future generations their ancestral territories, and their ethnic identities" within contexts of nondomination is framed by Linda Tuhiwai Smith's (1999, 34) commentary on the detrimental impact of colonial invasion on Indigenous peoples in our own lands, "It is the story of the powerful and how they became powerful, and then how they use their power to keep them in positions in which they can continue to dominate others." Similarly, Fanon (1963, 210) makes a stark commentary on the brutality of colonialism in his argument that the process, which includes the vehicle of public education, is not simply content to impose its rule upon the present and the future of Indigenous peoples. For him, colonialism "is not satisfied merely with holding a people in its grip and emptying the native's brain of all form and content. By a kind of perverted logic, it turns to the past of the oppressed people, and distorts, disfigures, and destroys it."

It is not surprising, then, that indigenous leadership has evolved as a radical sociopolitical phenomenon. For Indigenous peoples who have been subjugated in our own lands, leadership takes on a complexity that extends far beyond a generic definition of the "skill of motivating a group of people to act towards achieving a common goal" (Ward 2017). Hawaiian scholar activist Haunani Trask's (1993, 5) leadership, a passionate mix of righteous anger, resistance, and call to arms, reflects this sentiment, "And the truth is, that racists are taking everything away from Hawaiians, and they will not be content until Hawai'i has no Hawaiians left. That IS the truth. And I don't care what their names are. That is their intent. Kū'ē! Kū'ē! Kū'ē!" Her rallying cry to kū'ē or resist the dehumanizing impact of colonial oppression heralds the need for Indigenous leadership that champions the sovereign rights of Indigenous peoples. Her sentiment is in keeping with Eruera Stirling's (Stirling and Salmond 1981, 205) stance on the importance of leaders embracing their ancestral pathways:

> The young leaders of today must remain Maori in heart and hold fast to the mana of the ancestors, or they will never find a good pathway for the people and their work will come to nothing.

And her sentiment is in keeping with the revised Coolangatta Statement on Indigenous Peoples' Rights in Education:

> We, the Indigenous peoples of the world, assert our inherent right to self-determination in all matters. Self-determination is about making informed choices and decisions and creating appropriate structures for the transmission of culture, knowledge and wisdom for the benefit of each of our respective cultures. Education for our communities and each individual is central to the preservation of our cultures and for the development of the skills and expertise we need in order to be a vital part of the twenty-first century.

Our collaboration on the writing of this chapter reflects the complex nature of Indigenous leadership. We each draw on our experiences as Indigenous educators working within Indigenous and western contexts – Wong and Perry from Hawaiian perspectives, Johnston from a Māori perspective, and Maaka from a Māori perspective in the diaspora of Hawai'i. In keeping with our introduction, our stances on Indigenous leadership are shaped by the contexts in which we live and work, by our missions as educators in higher education, by our efforts to mentor a successor generation, and by our histories as peoples violently dislocated from the fundamental markers of our identities – sovereignty, ancestral lands, language, and cultural knowledge. This dislocation was (and still is) brought by the hands of colonial forces hell bent on forcing geopolitical, economic, and sociopolitical agendas upon us, at our expense. As a result, Māori (with the breached Treaty of Waitangi) and Hawaiians (with the illegal overthrow of a constitutional monarchy) face modern day challenges in recovering all that has been stripped away.

In our writing, then, we choose not to limit our discussion on Indigenous leadership in education to the context of "preschool through university schooling." Since we view "education" as pertaining to anything that leads us out of ignorance, we choose to expand our discussion to the broadest context of Indigenous self-determination that includes the socio-politics of Indigenous knowledge, models, methods, and content within formal and nonformal educational systems. Similarly, our use of the word "community" refers to Indigenous peoples who have been brought up within the geographic boundary of their traditional lands for the purpose of making change. Change makers include individuals from many different arenas including education, health, law, business, politics, and culture and the arts.

While there are many points of interest in an examination of Indigenous leadership, this chapter focuses on historical trauma and Indigenous leadership, well-executed leadership, leadership ascension, and leadership succession. Although our commentaries draw on the Māori and Hawaiian cultures, we believe that they also resonate with other Indigenous peoples. As well, the following commentaries are not to be embraced as received knowledge, rather, they are perspectives designed to invite debate.

Historical Trauma and Indigenous Leadership

> Born and Raised Hawaiian
> I am a diamond in the rough
> From the land of Zion
> I am the diamond in the rough
> One foot on the sand, one hand Heineken
> Hawaiian I am
> (Napoleon 2012)

> Somewhere in the swirl of
> History we have forgotten
> Your existence
> Good thing our siblings
> Remembered
> Lest we be lost in someone else's story.
> Good thing our siblings remember.
> (Kalahele 2002)

One critique of Indigenous leadership in the native Hawaiian context is that there is none. There is no consistent critical consciousness used in twenty-first-century Indigenous communities. Native Hawaiian leaders who ascend to levels of responsibility in the community appear to be riding the wave of the Hawaiian renaissance movement of the late 1970s and the sovereignty movements of the 1980s and 1990s. Leaders and communities in these situations are typically doing front line work and rarely find the time to stop and critique their own efforts and actions. Other leaders, who make up the intellectual elite, slide into positions of corporate or governmental power. Once there, the demand for self-preservation renders a healthy critique of those institutions almost negligible. For many Indigenous leaders, the wave ride can be short lived because of the lack of support from or coordination with the community that is served. Once ensconced, leaders are managed by more than just their mentors or predecessors. They are managed by the ongoing struggle to work within a community that is cycling between historical traumas and varying degrees of cultural recovery or oppressive recidivism. This can yield a type of leadership that is unable to recognize its own lack of currency and a community incapable of effectively addressing those concerns. The absence of a strong community structure results in an unimproved and unhealthy legacy of poor leadership.

The overall health of an Indigenous community is difficult to determine and even more difficult to correlate with functional and effective leadership. Reason dictates, however, that the relative health of the community can provide valuable insights into the effectiveness of its leaders. The challenge lies in determining when a community's actions are healthy and when they are not. Some will argue that an Indigenous community's ability to adapt to western society and colonial values demonstrates successful community transitions and health. Beamer and Duarte (2009) and Sai (2008), however, argue that the dichotomy of western approaches versus native/Indigenous approaches limits any relevant analysis of Hawai'i's political status under international law. Beamer (2009, 26) further explains that such a dichotomy is false and "composes the conceptual shackles which preserve European hegemony and often re-inscribe links between the colonizer and the colonized." These authors assert that Hawai'i is an occupied state and any efforts to claim decolonization ignore the legitimacy of Hawai'i's national independence. While their analysis is compelling and their critique difficult to dispute, there is merit in separating out the western model of culture in order to identify the imposition of a colonial-like system that has shaped the behaviors and attitudes of Hawaiians living in a US occupied state. It can be argued that these kinds of "improvements" point to a sinister form of assimilationism rather than to a truly transformative and healthy improvement in conditions.

A reflection on the work of Hawaiian island reggae recording artist Bo Napoleon demonstrates this point. Hawai'i's music industry is harnessing the demand of youthful, local consumers by promoting songs that provide a taste of the local island lifestyle, nationalistic undertones, and popular culture in a reggae-like format. Napoleon's (2012) popular single *Born and Raised* incorporates popular Hawaiian nationalist views and reggae to successfully capitalize on the island music market. The song includes unhealthy views contrary to the Hawaiian principles of living well. A careful review of the lyrics shows that Napoleon's song celebrates nationalism superficially while reinforcing colonial-like concepts of abuse and escapism. For example, the song celebrates US cosmopolitanism by recognizing a brand of alcohol noted for its connection to an elevated socio-economic status. The key chorus of the song illustrates this point: "One foot in the sand, one hand Heineken. Hawaiian I am." The lyrics sadly associate Hawaiian identity with negative stereotypes like drinking, greed and wealth, and partying at the beach. The song seems a grotesque blending of two diametrically opposed ways of being. And yet, this is the unhealthy space in which many Indigenous communities find themselves.

Kalahele (2002) provides an alternative stance. He states that, "Somewhere in the swirl of history we have forgotten [our] existence." For Indigenous peoples, remembering will improve the current state of mental, physical, and socio-political health beginning with the acknowledgment that unhealthy conditions do, in fact, exist. Kalahele warns that unless there is a stronger leadership effort to recall and perpetuate a healthy Indigenous community, Indigenous peoples will be lost in someone else's story. Which story will it be for Indigenous peoples and their leaders? The Heineken? The sand? Or something that promotes a more healthy transformation? The answers, says Kalahele, are in the memories of our "siblings," meaning that each of us must consciously contribute to our knowing and healing. This contribution is critical if we expect communities to guide our leaders and if we expect our leaders to serve our people.

Historical trauma of oppressed and Indigenous peoples is a topic that has generated a growing body of research and highlights the reason why so many Indigenous communities and leaders are both struggling and unhealthy. Historical trauma is the transmission of painful experiences from the past to the present. The suffering of past generations is carried forward and re-experienced emotionally, physically, and psychologically by those in the present even though the present generation did not experience the original trauma directly. Degruys's (2005)) study of Post Traumatic Slave Syndrome (PTSS) found that PTSS causes depression and hopelessness, extreme feelings of suspicion, and a sense of learned helplessness. People suffering from PTSS can develop maladaptive or destructive behaviors tied to negative stereotypes in order to deal with traumatic pain. Pokhrel and Herzog (2014, 420) found that in Hawai'i "thoughts, knowledge, or experience associated with historical trauma may enhance substance use behavior via increased perceived discrimination and may also be protective against substance use, possibly via increased pride in one's cultural heritage." Similarly, DeGruys (2005) found that historical trauma has a profound effect on the holistic well-being of the oppressed groups studied. Both studies also found that consciousness or increased exposure to and regeneration of pride through cultural experiences can help heal the trauma and repair the maladaptive behaviors.

Modern Indigenous leaders and communities often employ dominant trauma-triggering social methods in their advocacy and organizing efforts. These "master's tools" (Lorde 1983) are considered necessary to survival in the present Indigenous colonial-like condition. Indigenous leaders use Western tools – like equal protection laws, racial identity, and federal recognition of Indigenous rights – to advance their community's needs, knowing that the tools do not support the larger goal of Indigenous self-determination. So, what happens when those tools become the primary implements of leaders? If normalized, can the tools become a social trap or crutch for the community? The dominant rationale is that Indigenous peoples will improve their condition once they assimilate. Assimilation, or the "melting pot" approach in Hawai'i, prescribes the adoption of Western pluralistic values to alleviate Indigenous anxieties (Spickard et al. 2002). Assimilation requires an acceptance of the historical traumas that maintain conditions of dominance over Indigenous peoples. For Indigenous peoples, historical trauma creates a circular paradox, wherein an Indigenous leader's (and community's) reliance on oppressive values is maladaptive and counterproductive to healing. Ross (1989, 383), discussing the constitutionality of affirmative action cases in the USA, highlights this irony in his statement that affirmative action "demands the paradoxical solution of first taking account of race in order to get to a world where it is not taken into account." Lopez (2000, 172) states that such choices "are made in a harsh racist social setting that may facilitate but more likely will forestall freedom; and that in our decisions to resist, we may shatter but more probably will inadvertently strengthen the racial structures around us." Thus, Indigenous leaders and communities that embrace assimilation will find themselves judging their actions by the colonial-like structures that dominate them. When Indigenous health is measured by how well the native assimilates, the success of that Indigenous community is at risk. Hau'ofa (1994) explains in *Our Sea of Islands* that assimilationist ideals make Indigenous people believe in a small, belittled worldview of perpetual colonial dependency. He warns:

> Belittlement in whatever guise, if internalized for long, and transmitted across generations, may lead to moral paralysis, to apathy, and to the kind of fatalism that we can see among our fellow human beings who have been herded and confined to reservations and internment camps. People... are in danger of being confined to mental reservations, if not already physical ones. (152)

The Indigenous community's health and wellbeing is tied to how well the Indigenous leader and community work together. A healthy approach will build a sustainable social structure for a conscious people and discerning leaders. Critical distancing and analysis is one such approach. One example is the Black community's analysis of Malcolm X. Many Indigenous communities view him as an icon of resistance because of his ability to speak truth to justice in ways that they can understand. In fact, Indigenous communities around the globe have embraced Malcolm X's (1990) nationalistic voice as a means to explain their own political struggles by any means necessary. Wood (1992) suggests that understanding any leader or leadership style requires a critical, honest, and respectful examination. Such an examination may lead to uncomfortable revelations or understandings but provides long term healing and guidance for the community. Wood, in his discussion of the complexity of Malcolm X's imagery and the social iconization of his Black cultural image, notes that in many ways, icons produce believers who gain a sense of communion and authorship. He warns, however, of the dangers of authorship of an icon that courts an illusion. Meaning, of course, as we elevate Malcolm X's image as a radical Black leader, we simultaneously blind ourselves to the other complex messages that his image portrays including questions of nationalism and sexism.

Angela Davis (1992) explores this idea and interrogates Malcolm X's contemporary legacy. She asserts that Malcolm X has been treated as a commodity and transformed "into a backward and imprisoning memory rather than a forward looking impetus for creative political thinking and organizing" (44–45). Borrowing Davis' analysis, Indigenous communities should challenge rather than excuse problems within their leadership to improve the health of the community. Said (2002) explains that sacrifice will intensify for those who are closer to power. He cautions that the importance of leadership lies in the service and hope that leaders provide to the community. Thus, the price of leadership is submission to the community. Likewise, Indigenous communities must be witnesses and courageously testify to what is happening with their leadership. When asked about critiquing other African American community leaders Malcolm X's (In Perry 1989, 87) explained that, "all of us should be critics of each other. Whenever you can't stand criticism, you can never grow." He concluded his statement by saying, "I don't think that we should be above criticism. I don't think that anyone should be above criticism." To effectuate valuable critiques, Indigenous communities (including educational communities) should maintain a critical distance from the inner circle of leadership. The critical space allows for healthy assessments that will advance and improve the capabilities of leaders to deliver on community needs. Wood and Said both understand that critical distance and analysis is a double-edged sword. The lack of critical distance can obscure the critique and lessen the community's ability to advance or improve. Allowing the leadership to operate without a healthy, regular critique is dangerous. Leaders who operate unchecked can mask their shortcomings and use the community's allegiances "to insulate themselves from their mistakes" (Said 2002, 13). Thus, it is not enough to belong to community organizations. There must also be a willingness and process in the community organizations to reexamine the actions of the leadership and make changes necessary to secure Indigenous health and self-governance. This can come only from the Indigenous community's understanding of its own historical trauma and of its willingness to question the function of its leaders' honesty.

In the words of Mary Kawena Pukui (1983, 27), "'A'ole make ka wa'a i ka 'ale o waho, aia nō i ka 'ale o loko." This proverb warns that a canoe is not swamped by the waves splashing outside the canoe, but by the waves splashing inside. Applied today, the proverb can mean that the strength of an Indigenous leader is only as stable as the health of the community he or she serves.

Well-Executed Leadership

> The leadership style of the Indigenous was based on character, merit, and faith. [The past] highlighted and demonstrated the foremost examples of this leadership. It brought out the most historic and famous leaders; leaders whose sacrifice, dedication, and humility ensured our survival and influenced the reality we live in today. . . ..I feel that leadership is something that cannot be developed or taught. . . ..Leadership is revealed, as greatness is revealed. True greatness comes from the inside. . . ..Greatness has no room for ego so it is important to study the ego, embrace the ego, and let go of the ego. We need *Indigenous Leadership Revelation* programs; so young people can awaken their authenticity, responsibility, and become conduits for greatness. Tootoosis (n.d.)

Tootoosis' sentiment on the important roles that knowledge, mana, and ancestral pathways play in Indigenous life, particularly in roles of leadership, is also captured in the works of renowned scholars Mead, Grove, and Pukui. Their corpuses of wise sayings – Māori pēpeha (Mead and Grove 2001) and Hawaiian 'ōlelo no'eau (Pukui 1983) – provide unique insights into the ways in which the world was, and still is, perceived. Mead and Grove elaborate:

> [these] pēpeha reflect thoughts on many aspects of Māori culture; history, religious life, conduct, ethics, warfare, marriage, death, and weather. They are featured in the formal speeches heard on the marae even today and in the oral literature handed down from past generations. ......Indeed for the modern Māori the pēpeha are not merely historical relics. Rather they constitute a communication with the ancestors. Through the medium of words it is possible to discover how they thought about life and its problems. Their advice is as valuable today as before. Their use of metaphor and their economy of words become a beautiful legacy to pass on to generations yet unborn. (9)

The pēpeha "Ānō me he whare pūngāwerewere. [As though it were a spiderweb. A compliment for a fine piece of work such as weaving or carving.]" (Mead and Grove 2001, 17) calls attention to the artistry and intricacy involved in the production or weaving of a web. This imagery highlights the interwoven and configurational elements of fine silken strands that make up a creation wondrous to behold. Indigenous leadership may be viewed as similarly multifaceted and intricate. The web serves as a metaphor highlighting the interconnectedness of leadership roles for the coordination of various talents within communities. If cultural complexity is added to this mix, Indigenous leadership, if well executed, is a magnificent creation to behold!

Another perspective of this pēpeha could focus on the nature of the spider and its work – hardworking, yet solitary and single-minded. The spider makes a web then waits alone for a hapless bug to fly into it. The vibrations of the silken strands call attention to the feast about to be had. There is no partnering with other spiders and, so, the rewards are for the individual only. This is quite foreign to the Indigenous perspective. In his commentary on Hawaiian self-determination, retired Native Hawaiian elementary school principal Myron Brumaghim (2003, AERA presentation) debunks any idea that self-focused leadership is beneficial to his people. He states,

> We want our Hawaiian people to live their dreams. We want educational opportunities for our people that focus energies and resources on guiding them as they journey towards success in life. We want to ensure that our people receive rich educational opportunities that prepare them for good jobs, to be good people living healthy lives and who raise healthy families. And, most important, we want to be self-determining in this process. We need leaders in education who are able to bring our people together to accomplish this.

Brumaghim's words, while emphasizing the Indigenous mission to self-determine, highlight the importance of people working as a collective for the health and wellbeing of all. His reference "we" emphasizes that the work and the leadership involved are not singular entities.

Interconnectedness, particularly collaborative networking, has always been a critical element in both traditional and contemporary Indigenous systems of governance. Effective leadership is predicated, in part, on (a) a mission that has been determined by the collective, (b) the ability to create and maintain effective networks, (c) the welding together of skills and expertise, (d) a selfless commitment to peoples and communities, (e) clearly delineated locations, shared interests, and work ethics, and (f) cultural ways of knowing and doing. This call for networking can also be seen in the Hawaiian ʻōlelo noʻeau "'Aʻohe hana nui ke alu ʻia." It explains that no task is too big when everyone works together for the common cause (Pukui 1983, 18). Like the fine strands that are woven together to form a sturdy, functional spider's web, successful leaders weave together different peoples, places, and organizations with the same effectiveness. Their networks may either be compositions of small groups or compositions of larger, more sophisticated groups of people with similar interests, missions, resources, capabilities, and commitments working together to support each other.

The idea of moral causality might be another perspective of the pūngāwerewere or spider pēpeha. There is the commonly held notion of the web as a tangled structure of deceit as depicted in Sir Walter Scott's (1880) famous poem, *Marmion*...., "Oh what a tangled web we weave, when first we practice to deceive." Throughout history there are numerous examples of evil, deceitful leadership that have caused significant harm. Thankfully, many of these have disintegrated due to lack of moral fiber. To the contrary, in some of his other works, Scott draws attention to the idea of man's collaboration under strong leadership as the vehicle for noble accomplishment:

> The race of mankind would perish did they cease to aid each other. We cannot exist without mutual help. All therefore that need aid have a right to ask it from their fellow-men; and no one who has the power of granting can refuse it without guilt. (Scott 1880)

His work commands attention because it repeatedly illustrates his belief that every human should have a core of decency regardless of class, religion, politics, or ancestry. But even more interesting is the theme of his Waverley Novels that expresses the need for social progress that does not reject the traditions of the past. Of course, there is a strong probability that Scott was not referring to the traditions of Indigenous peoples!

Leadership, whether good or bad, may be seen as a phenomenon of cause and effect. Like a spider's web, every strand of leadership is inextricably connected, touching one part of a web sets off a series of vibrations that reverberate throughout the whole. Spirkin (1984, 70) explains that certainty in man's relationships with the world rests on acknowledgment of this understanding of how causality works. He states, "Ours is a world of cause and effect or, figuratively speaking, of progenitors and their progeny." Maaka et al. (2011, 28) explain the concept of causality and interconnectivity within Indigenous contexts of space, time, and people:

> Every morally-related action bears a consequence, which bears another, which bears another–a chain reaction of cause, effect, and result. For every "problem" there is a multitude of choices, each with its own unique chain reaction. We believe that research [and

leadership] is a process of moral (or immoral) causality–and so, for every "problem" there is a solution that will offer up the best outcome. Indigenous researchers [and leaders] then, must be driven by the needs of our respective peoples; this is why research, self-determination, [and leadership] are inextricably linked in Indigenous contexts.

and further,

....(human agency) entails the ability to make decisions and enact them in ways that affect the world. The idea that humans have this capacity is one that lies at the heart of the movement to revitalize the languages and cultures of Indigenous peoples worldwide. Of particular interest are the considerations that shape various acts of agency, the consequences of decision-making (whether to act or not), and the assignment of responsibility for the decision made.

It is fitting to conclude this commentary with the position that well-executed leadership is not a product, but a process. It is not contingent upon the acquisition and application of a set of leadership skills and abilities, rather, it is contingent upon the relationships among those who lead and those who are lead. In keeping, Hunter and Milofsky (2007) argue that well-executed leadership arises when leaders need to be reminded (and need to remind themselves) that they are citizens first and leaders second. For them, a healthy society is one that has "leaders and citizens joined together in a community, committed to the common wealth and the common welfare" (159). Indigenous communities expect nothing less of their leaders.

Leadership Ascension

Hawaiian society was structured so that the identity of one segment was dependent on that of the next. This is never truer than in the case of leadership. Pukui's collection of ʻōlelo noʻeau is unique because it provides a glimpse of the worldview of Hawaiian society in a bygone era and, pertinent to this discussion, provides some wisdom on the nature of leadership then and now. The ʻōlelo noʻeau "I aliʻi no ke aliʻi i ke kanaka" (Pukui 1983, 125) explains that a chief held the important position of chief because of the people who served him. In particular, this wise saying illustrates how important it was for a chief to consider his people in his decision making. Therefore, it was integral to the aliʻi's identity to fulfill the needs of the makaʻāinana by ensuring that all the resources necessary for survival, particularly water, flourished on the ʻāina. The reciprocal was true: makaʻāinana identity was tied to fulfilling the needs of the aliʻi. This idea is iterated in the ʻōlelo noʻeau (Pukui, 27) "'Aʻole i ʻenaʻena ka imu i ka māmane me ka ʻūlei, i ʻenaʻena i ka laʻolaʻo." Pukui explains that the imu is not heated by the māmane and ʻūlei wood alone, but also by the kindling – in other words, in order to be powerful, a ruler must have the loyalty of the "common people" as well as the "chiefs." Further, embedded in the role of the makaʻāinana was the empowerment of the chiefs. Through their loyalty and service to their aliʻi, the makaʻāinana gave their aliʻi power, which in and of itself was a form of power. Makaʻāinana were free to leave the rule of an aliʻi if they were not satisfied with his or her leadership. It was by removing themselves and their families (as well as the goods and/or services they provided), that the authority of the aliʻi was made somewhat diffuse.

It may be argued that ascension to leadership today involves the deliberate act of choosing to aspire to a higher level of responsibility and consciousness. It is the path taken by those who consciously choose to step up to a higher level of leadership. Typically, this is a personal choice designed to expand the experiences of the person who is ascending, and it is clear that views of ascension to leadership and the norms surrounding such ascension can vary dramatically.

In whatever system, we examine, then, there are those who are satisfied with the current leadership and those who are not, despite shared cultural values within the populace. Favorable views presuppose an alignment between expectations and actual performance. Variation in this regard can occur within or across systems. Some expect an active approach in which a prospective leader either self-nominates or is somehow complicit in that nomination. This active approach requires intent. It requires the belief of an individual in his or her ability to find the best path forward for all. It also presupposes a hierarchy based on ability that is tacitly accepted by supporters. Conceivably, in a case of bad leadership, the populace could be viewed as complicit in its own subjugation as a result of passive support for the system. Moreover, the normalization of such a system would serve to conceal that subjugation. A popular metaphor for such a scenario involves a shepherd leading a flock of sheep. It is in the sheep's nature to follow. For humans, following another person's direction requires trust and, to some extent, a degree of blind faith. As such, active persuasion is key in attracting followers.

Others see paths to leadership that are less actively pursued, but instead taken passively. Here, an individual is recognized by peers as having leadership qualities and is encouraged to ascend to a position from which to exercise them. Such an individual is often not interested in ascension and more often loathe to self-nominate. Participation in a leadership role must occur as a more passive endeavor. It requires being backed into the role by a preponderance of enthusiasm from supportive peers. This scenario would be better described as sheep looking for a shepherd to follow, rather than a shepherd leading the sheep.

In some systems, ascendancy is predetermined. In a monarchial context, for example, the right to rule is ordained by God or the Gods and determined by birth (most often by order of birth and, quite frequently, by gender at birth). It could be argued that this does not always yield optimal results, and there are numerous examples to support such an argument, particularly in the royal dynasties of Europe. However, within a society such as the one thriving in precontact Hawaiʻi wherein chiefs were believed to be deities, ascension by order of birth was strictly adhered to. There were natural separations based on class boundaries, and such separations were supported by tacit agreement within the populace. The chiefly class had complete control of leadership, which was viewed as a divine right. Those privy only to an external view of such a society were unable to evaluate its viability through experience. In order to appreciate the efficacy of this system, an unlearning of previously acquired values needed to take place.

No one path to leadership is inherently superior to the next as each is built on unique values that are shared within a community. Shared values often lead to harmonious governance. These varied paths to leaderships are all worthy of examination. Ascension by right; ascension by self-nomination and self-promotion; and ascension by default, a passive form of ascension that is promoted by others; these are all compared and contrasted here, but they are not ranked. The various regimes can all claim some advantages, but there are also problems that accompany each.

As stated above, in some societies, particularly those labeled as democratic, the ascent to leadership requires self-nomination. A candidate is expected to throw his or her hat into the ring, that is, to self-nominate and to vie for the position against other candidates of like intent. In this system, positions of leadership are acquired by securing a preponderance of support from the masses, a feat that requires, and often demands, self-promotion. This system is at risk of producing less than optimal results especially for supporters of the losing candidates.

From an Indigenous perspective, self-promotion screams out a warning that despite the promise of an improved state of affairs, there is something unnatural about leadership that comes seeking someone to lead. Such leadership is paternalistic in nature and presumes that it is needed in the first place. In return for the provision of such presumptuous guidance, a vote is expected. A passive ascension, on the other hand, although it requires no convincing, no marketing or slick sales pitch, has its own problems. In particular, it cannot satisfy everyone, especially when such satisfaction is mutually exclusive with regard to varying needs. As mentioned above, each system has its problems, but in each, leadership can be changed and new leadership can take over, either alleviating or exacerbating the problems. Those problems occurring within political systems are highlighted by the inability of leaders to manage them to the benefit of the wider community. New information that can be empirically verified is not factored into the equation if it is in any way disruptive of core beliefs. This is not a problem inherent to democracy. Instead, it is a problem that stems from a corruption of democratic ideals (Lee 2016).

At present in Hawai'i, almost two and a half centuries of the infiltration of western ways have all but normalized ascension to leadership via the self-promotion path. This was exacerbated by the overthrow of the constitutional monarchy of 1893 and the subsequent illegal occupation that continues to this day. But in Hawaiian tradition, ascension to power was a right of birth. There is an interesting case in Hakau, the first-born son of Liloa, paramount chief of the island of Hawai'i. The excerpt below describes Hakau's rule as found in Fornander's (1880) account of the ancient history of the Hawaiian people. It serves to exemplify bad leadership.

After the death of Liloa in 1493, Hakau came to power in accordance with the promise made to him by Liloa. At the same time, Liloa's second son, Umi by Akahiakuleana, a woman of lower rank and not of chiefly status as was Pinea (the mother of Hakau), was given religious authority over the kingdom. Despite his ascension to the status of paramount chief, Hakau was, nonetheless, jealous of Umi and openly demonstrated his scorn by constantly excoriating Umi for his lower rank. In order to alleviate the tension peacefully, Umi eventually left the royal court and resettled anonymously in another district:

> After *Liloa's* death *Hakau* became the Moi and chief ruler of Hawaii. He appears to have been thoroughly wicked, cruel, and capricious. I have found no legend in which he is mentioned that has a single good word to say in his behalf. No doubt much allowance must be made from the fact that nearly all the legends relating to him emanated from and were handed down by his opponents, the family of *Umi* and their descendants. Yet making allowances for the exaggeration of his faults, enough remains to load his memory with odium. He was rapacious and extortionate beyond endurance of either chiefs or people. He had the silly vanity of fancying himself the handsomest man on the island of Hawaii, and could brook no rival in that matter. If he ever heard a man praised for his good looks, he would send for him and have him killed. He dismissed, disrated, and impoverished all the old and faithful counsellors and servants of his father, chiefs, priests, or commoners, and surrounded himself with a crew of sycophants and time-servers as cruel and as treacherous as himself. He missed no opportunity to thwart his brother *Umi*, and openly reviled him for his low birth, insisting that his mother was a woman of low degree. *Umi*, unable to bear the taunts of his brother, and not prepared to come to an open rupture with the tyrant, absented himself from the court of *Hakau*, and quietly left Waipio . . . . (76)

Through the course of Hakau's despotic rule, the land and its people of all ranks endured intense suffering, until he was finally stoned to death, according to a number of accounts, by Umi's men. An account of Hakau's death was found in the Hawaiian language newspaper *Ka Lahui Hawaii*, dated Novembers 1, 1877 (2). It was written as follows: "Ma ia kahua hale no i pepehiia ai o Hakau e na kanaka o Umi; *It was at that house foundation (of Liloa) that Hakau was killed by Umi's men.*" Upon the death of Hakau, Umi became the new ruler. Hakau's ultimate demise offers a prime example of the consequences that befall a bad leader. In the case of Hakau and Umi, leadership was initially dictated by birth order and rank. Although the brutality of Hakau persisted for some 15 years, the pendulum eventually swung back to a balanced or righteous state.

Hakau's leadership style suggests that bad leadership is independent of the path taken to a position of leadership and the system within which it is executed. Moreover, it is not fixed to certain time periods. It is just bad leadership. Intolerance of dissent, vanity, capriciousness, inconsistency, instability, fickleness, and an inability to admit fault are leadership traits that, in the end, proved fatal for Hakau. His demise serves as a modern day warning to those who are similarly despotic in their rule – there are many in the international arena who should take heed.

Leadership Succession

The 'ōlelo no'eau "Ka pouhana" or the main post (Pukui 1983, 167) likens Indigenous leadership to the main post of a dwelling that provides the strongest support for the roof. Pukui explains that strong leadership provides support and guidance for the family and for the community. Alan (2014) argues that central to the imperative of strong leadership, especially in today's world, is the need to harness the collective genius of people, rally them behind the mission and vision, and create the conditions in which everyone contributes to the wellbeing of all. Effective leadership is about "tearing down walls," bringing people together, building trust, transforming attitudes and behaviors, and removing barriers that keep people from engaging. Effective leadership is also about having a well thought out succession plan.

Before continuing the discussion, clarification needs to be made about the difference between ascension to leadership and succession in leadership – they are two different phenomena – each dependent on agency. Agency in ascension rests with the individual who aspires to be a leader; that is, he or she who aspires to be a leader may need to navigate a series of tasks or obstacles in order to reach the desired state of leadership. Succession, on the other hand, involves the act of a leader identifying who should inherit his or her mantle of leadership. The agency, in this case, lies with the leader who is to be succeeded. This can be best described as a legacy of leadership, given that there is a distinct understanding that a legacy is something that is given by one person to another (as opposed to something that is received by one person from another). The difference is subtle, yet important.

The general issue of succession in leadership is universally relevant even though the actual execution adheres to culturally specific norms. There is a primordial mandate that accompanies human mortality and compels us to consider our legacy as evidence of our purpose and whether or not we have been successful in advancing it within our lifetime. A legacy presupposes the existence of a successor or a number of successors to whom it constitutes a benefit, that is, as popularized in Disney's *The Lion King*, the "circle of life." The value of the blood, sweat, and tears we invest in fulfilling our purpose is realized only in the perpetuation of that purpose. The accomplishments of our life's work become meaningful insofar as they are of value to those we leave behind, because, as the cliché goes, "You can't take it with you." Thus, it behooves us to undertake efforts to foster successors to whom we might pass the proverbial torch with a reasonable degree of confidence that our mission will continue. Kamehameha the Great's dying words "E nai wale no oukou, I kuu pono ao'e pau" exhorted his successors to continue the work that he had begun in uniting the Hawaiian Kingdom. In these lines, he makes reference to the fact that the work is incomplete and they will need to complete it on his behalf. Kamehameha's words are captured in the song *Nai Wale No Oukou Ao'e Pau*. The song, attributed to Sam'l K. Kamakaia, was published in *Ke Aloha Aina, Buke III, Helu 34*, Aoao 7. Augate 21, 1897.

In the arena of Indigenous knowledge production and Indigenous development, the intergenerational transfer of that knowledge and the intergenerational transfer of control over that development have been identified as increasingly critical goals. Although we would feel most comfortable if we could simply replace ourselves, such a scenario is unlikely for a number of reasons. We obviously cannot clone ourselves, and even if we could, we cannot clone our experiences and the knowledge amassed therein. We will ultimately realize numerous distinctions between our successors and ourselves. This is not to say that one is superior to the other, rather, it recognizes that there are many variables to consider including the fact that we operate in dynamic contexts that require constant readjustment in the execution of our plans.

One common concern in the movement to advance Indigenous causes is the fact that the successor generation does not share the experience of building the movement from the foundation up. They are perceived as oblivious to the amount of effort already invested in the movement and seem to assume that the current situation has always been as it is. This, of course, is only one perspective, and it stems from the expectation that the next generation shares the same dreams and is interested in dealing with the same issues in the same ways. It is perhaps unreasonable to expect our successors to take up our cause, let alone with the same zeal. They are faced with new and perhaps more pressing issues of their own. We believe that we are "creating spaces" for them yet they have no say in the design of those spaces.

Succession is not as much about replacing ourselves as it is about our successors enlarging the spaces that we currently occupy and planning for their reoccupation by future generations. Whatever trajectory the movement takes after that is really up to our successors. Thus, the question we should consider is whether or not they are adequately prepared to do their own thing. Once they are, we must be willing to relinquish control over the movement we have invested so much of ourselves in and allow whatever preparations we have made to influence the trajectory of the successive movement.

It is important, therefore, to select successors who are at once capable, committed, and willing to take up the larger cause of advancing the state of Indigenous peoples. It is in the choice of successors that we retain a modicum of control. This is where our kuleana ("right," "responsibility," "authority") lies. As much as we have done to advance our cause, we are also indebted to those who have mentored us and entrusted us with their knowledge. It is therefore our responsibility to select and prepare worthy successors, those in whom we can entrust our legacy. Whether or not these successors measure up to our expectations is, at least in part, dependent on our ability to make the right choices and to mentor effectively. After that, we relinquish control whether we wish to or not. It is then up to our successors to perpetuate the cause until it is time for them to select successors of their own.

Even if we are successful in selecting worthy successors, a number of challenges remain. For example, the transmission of knowledge and skill sets does not ensure the transmission of other intangible qualities that are essential for success. Loyalty, integrity, diplomacy, fairness, and tenacity are but a few examples of character traits that are not easily transmitted. We cannot expect, for example, that the respect and trust we have built through successful collaborations and networking will automatically pass on to our successors. They will have to earn those things on their own and build upon them by forming their own allegiances and initiatives.

There is no manual to provide instructions on the appropriate amount of leeway to allow those we mentor. We know that the amount of experience is often directly proportional to the level of competence gained by our mentees and that experience is critically dependent on opportunity. Opportunity, however, can lead to either success or failure. Although we set up opportunities for our mentees that are most likely to yield success, there is always the possibility of failure, and failure weakens both their confidence and the confidence that others might have in them. Moreover, success itself can yield unwanted results when the opinions mentees have of themselves are not in accord with our opinions of them. The tension here can irrevocably disrupt the succession process. As we expand the spaces we occupy to make room for our successors to gain experience, we also expand the latitude for possible deviation from our own goals and dreams. This is not an easy call. On the one hand, there is always the concern over the capability of our successors to manage things without a safety net, while on the other, there is our own affinity to the cause that keeps us involved and makes us reluctant to yield completely to our successors.

On the downside, making the right choice of successors is not as easy as it may sound and many of us who mentor successor generation leaders are able to chalk up some failures. Some of our failures can be attributed to mistakes made in our efforts to mentor. One of the biggest stumbling blocks is not being able to gauge the worth of successors until significant mentoring has been invested (or wasted!). While it is true that weak leadership will eventually reveal itself, it is also true that great frustration comes from wasting much time and energy on those who, in the end, reveal that they have no leadership currency. Cashman (2017) notes that self-focused leaders may accrue successes, or garner adulation, or achieve externalized success, but they also tend to get into all sorts of ethical issues. Problematic Indigenous leadership, then, may take on many forms, but the most concerning involves self-absorbed individuals, with unbridled ambition, who value self-interest above service to their people and who will even unscrupulously turn on their mentors in their efforts to promote themselves. To those who behave in such a manner, Myatt (2013) offers the advice that "leadership is about caring about something beyond yourself, and leading others to a better place–even if it means you take a back seat, or end up with no seat at all. Power often comes with leadership, but it's not what drives real leaders." So what is the remedy? For undeserving, self-promoting individuals who turn on the very people who have mentored them, Pukui (1983, 141) has a portentous warning; "Ka hale weliweli o na aliʻi." She explains that the "dreaded house of the chiefs" meant that the chiefs had many taboos, rules, and regulations in their households and to break any of these meant severe punishment, even death for the transgressor. Like the story of Hakau, this ʻōlelo noʻeau reminds us that, in Indigenous contexts, erroneous claims to leadership by those who lack moral character have dire consequences whether real or metaphorical.

Those of us who have spent many years mentoring our successor generation are in agreement that, overall, this is a rewarding endeavor. We remind ourselves that our effectiveness as mentors is defined by the capacity of our successors to effectively don the mantle of leadership and continue uplifting the health and wellbeing of our respective peoples. In talking about the politics of Māori governance and self-determination, Durie (1998, 240) captures the mission of Indigenous leaders' best:

> Fundamentally it [self-determination] is about the realization of collective Māori aspirations. And despite the many faces of contemporary Māori society and the wide range of views which exist, there is nonetheless a high level of agreement that the central goal of tino rangatiratanga (sovereignty) is for Māori to govern and enjoy their own resources and to participate fully in the life of the country. Māori want to advance, as Māori, and as citizens of the world.

Indigenous advancement, then, is contingent, not only upon effective leadership, but also upon effective succession of that leadership.

A Final Comment

Ko te ao mārama! To be ever enlightened! One glance at the 200+ year old histories of devastation visited on Māori and Hawaiians in our own lands by outsiders puts modern day Indigenous leadership into perspective. Our "violent exclusion" from our traditional lands and resources through confiscation and other shady means, as well as our "violent exclusion" from our traditional knowledge, languages, and practices as a result of our forced assimilation into the broader cultures of New Zealand and Hawai'i, have debilitated us to the extent that any return to self-determination is truly a formidable undertaking. The social indicators of success (or failure) paint a bleak picture for our peoples – Māori and Hawaiian children as groups have rates of school absenteeism and referral for special education services that are far above average. Our teenagers are more likely to drop out of high school without qualifications and have the highest suicide rates in the world. Our adults are overrepresented in prisons, have the poorest health records, and are underrepresented as students and faculty in higher education. Chronic homelessness is a Māori and Hawaiian phenomenon (Farrelly et al. 2006; Marriott and Sim 2014; Office of Hawaiian Affairs 2015). With these statistics in mind, we are left asking; what role does Indigenous leadership play in recovering the fundamental markers of Māori and Hawaiian identities – sovereignty, ancestral lands, language, and cultural knowledge? In his doctoral dissertation on Māori sovereignty, Russell (2017) addresses this question by asking his own: Do Treaty of Waitangi settlements enable rangatira to exercise rangatiratanga? He argues that the traditional structures of leadership have diminished over time and have been replaced by western structures such as corporations. He concludes that "traditional elements of leadership have become 'values' or processes of action, rather than being inherent in the role of exercising rangatiratanga," that is, sovereignty (243).

Our commentary on historical trauma and Indigenous leadership, well-executed leadership, leadership ascension, and leadership succession barely scratches the surface of the larger conversation that demands attention. With this in mind, our commentaries are not designed to present definitive answers to what constitutes effective leadership in Indigenous contexts, rather they are designed to move the discussion beyond viewing leadership as "values or processes of action," to examining the challenges faced in building the effective leadership required by Indigenous peoples to help resolve historic and contemporary forms of oppression.

The need to examine traditional structures of leadership is best captured in Robert Jahnke's (2016) *Ata: A third reflection* exhibition. His combination of neon lights; traditional forms, such as crosses and diamonds; and carefully positioned mirrors creates a multifaceted exploration of the "connections between light and perception, history and retrospection" (Friend 2016, n.p.). Jahnke's *Tukutuku*, in particular, draws the viewer on a genealogical journey that traverses time and space. In our final contemplation of Indigenous leadership, Jahnke's work shores up two central considerations that we have expounded on in this chapter – that effective leadership looks back to the future (in other words, it is shaped by the people, places, and spaces of our past, present, and future) and that, like the reflections in Jahnke's mirror, all experiences in life are subject to the perspectives of the viewer. In any given context, then, there is a multiplicity of views, demands, interests, supports, and resistance that need to be considered.

Indigenous peoples, then, have long held the belief that the traditions pertaining to the ways of knowing and doing of the past are necessarily woven into the fabric of the future. It is fitting, then, that we conclude this chapter with another of Eruera Stirling's commentaries on the importance of Māori traditions in leadership:

> The old men told us, study your descent lines, as numerous as the hairs upon your head. When you have gathered them together as a treasure for your mind, you may wear the three plumes, "te iho makawerau," "te pareraukura," and "te raukura" on your head. The men of learning said, understand the learning of your ancestors, so you can talk in the gatherings of the people. Hold fast to the knowledge of your kinship, and unite in the knot of mankind. (As cited in Salmond 1997, 513.)

References

Alan RK (2014) The leadership imperative. Retrieved from http://www.centerod.com/2014/07/leadership-imperative/

Beamer KB (2009) Ali'i selective appropriation of modernity–examining colonial assumptions in Hawai'i prior to 1893. AlterNative Int J Indigenous People 5:138–155

Beamer KB, Duarte TK (2009) I palapala no ia aina–documenting the Hawaiian Kingdom: a colonial venture? J Hist Geogr 35:66–86

Brumaghim MK (2003) Teacher education as a site of struggle: preparing Indigenous teachers and Indigenous teacher educators in Hawai'i. In: Paper presented at the annual meeting of the AERA, Chicago

Cashman K (2017) Thoughts on leadership with Kevin Cashman. Retrieved from http://cashmanleadership.com/site/wp-content/uploads/2017/04/AESC_04.2017_w.header.pdf

Davis A (1992) Meditations on the legacy of Malcolm X. In: Wood J (ed) Malcolm X: in our own image. Doubleday, New York

Degruys J (2005) Post traumatic slave syndrome: Americans legacy of enduring injury and healing. Uptone Press, Oregon

Durie MH (1998) Te mana, te kāwanatanga: the politics of Māori self-determination. Oxford University Press, Auckland

Fanon F (1963) The wretched of the earth. Grove Press, New York

Farrelly S, Rudegeair T, Rickard S (2006) Trauma and dislocation in Aotearoa (New Zealand): the psyche of a society. J Trauma Pract 4(3–4):202–220

Fornander A (1880) An account of the Polynesian race: its origin and migrations and the ancient history of the Hawaiian people to the time of Kamehameha I. Trubner & Co, London

Friend R (2016) Foreword. Bob Jahnke, ATA: a third reflection. Retrieved from http://www.temanawa.co.nz/wp-content/uploads/2016/11/Bob-Jahnke-ATA-a-third-reflection-catalogue.pdf

Hau'ofa E (1994) Oceania: our sea of islands. Contemp Pac 6(1):148–161

Hunter A, Milofsky C (2007) Pragmatic liberalism. Palgrave Macmillan, New York

Jahnke R (2016) ATA: a third reflection. Retrieved from http://www.temanawa.co.nz/wp-content/uploads/2016/11/Bob-Jahnke-ATA-a-third-reflection-catalogue.pdf

Kalahele I (2002) Kalahele. Kalamaku Press, Honolulu

Lee AK (2016) Democracy and education in America: a promise unfulfilled. Dissertation, University of Hawai'i, Honolulu

Lopez IH (2000) The social construction of race. In: Delgado R (ed) Critical race theory: the cutting edge. Temple University Press, Philadelphia

Lorde A (1983) The master's tools will never dismantle the aster's house. In: Moraga C, Anzaldua G (eds) This bridge called my back: writings by radical women of color. Kitchen Table Press, New York

Maaka MJ, Wong KL, Oliveira K (2011) When the children of their fathers push back!: self-determination and the politics of Indigenous research. In: Davis KA (ed) Critical qualitative research in second language studies: agency and advocacy. In: Osborn T (series ed) Contemporary language education, volume. Information Age Publishing, Greenwich

Malcolm X (1990) By any means necessary: speeches, interviews and a letter by Malcolm X. Pathfinder Press, New York

Malcolm X, Perry B (eds) (1989) Malcolm X: the last speeches. Pathfinder Press, New York

Marriott L, Sim D (2014) Indicators of inequality for Māori and Pacific people. Victoria University Press, Wellington

Martinez Cobo JR (1986) Study of the problem of discrimination against Indigenous populations: Final Report. UN Doc E/CN 4/Sub 2 1986/7/21, Add 4, para 379. UN, Geneva

Mead HM, Grove N (2001) Ngā pēpeha a ngā tīpuna. Victoria Uni Press, Wellington

Myatt M (2013) Why you're not a leader. Retrieved from https://www.forbes.com/sites/mikemyatt/2013/01/23/why-youre-not-a-leader/#3c794ec46fb8/

Napoleon B (2012) Born and raised. Robert Sterling Music Publishing, New York

Office of Hawaiian Affairs (2015) Native Hawaiian data book 2015. Retrieved from www.ohadatabook.com

Pokhrel P, Herzog TA (2014) Historical trauma and substance use among Native Hawaiian college students. Am J Health Behav 38(3):420–429

Pukui MK (1983) 'Ōlelo No'eau: Hawaiian proverbs & poetical sayings. Bishop Museum Press, Honolulu

Ross T (1989) The Richmond narratives. 68. Tex Rev 381:381–385

Russell D (2017) Contemporary rangatiratanga: do treaty settlements enable rangatiratanga to exercise rangatiratanga. Unpublished doctoral dissertation, University of Otago

Sai DK (2008) A slippery path towards Hawaiian indigeneity: an analysis and comparison between Hawaiian state sovereignty and Hawaiian indigeneity and its use and practice in Hawai'i today. J Law and Soc Chall 10:69–133

Said EW (2002) In conversation with Neeladri Bhattacharya, Suvir Kaul, and Ania Loomba. In: Goldberg DT, Quayson A (eds) Relocating post colonialism. Blackwell Pub, New Malden

Salmond A (1997) Between worlds: early exchanges between Māori and Europeans 1773–1815. University of Hawai'i Press, Honolulu

Scott W (1880) Marmion. Canto vi. Stanza 17

Smith LT (1999) Decolonizing methodologies: research and Indigenous peoples. Zed Books, London

Spickard P, Rondilla J, Wright DH (2002) Pacific diaspora: Island peoples in the United States and across the Pacific. UH Press, Honolulu

Spirkin A, Daglish R (translator) (1984) Dialectical materialism. Central Books, London

Stirling E, Salmond A (eds) (1981) Eruera: the teachings of a Maori Elder. Oxford University Press, Auckland

Tootoosis C (n.d.) Indigenous leadership in a westernized world. Retrieved from http://lastrealindians.com/Indigenous-leadership-in-a-westernized-world/

Trask H-K (1993) Speech for the 1993 centennial commemoration of the American overthrow of the Hawaiian Kingdom. Retrieved from http://www.markfoster.net/struc/trask.pdf

Ward S (2017) What is leadership? And can you learn to be a good leader? Retrieved from https://www.thebalance.com/leadership-definition-2948275

Wood J (ed) (1992) Malcolm X, in our own image. St. Martin's Press, New York

Situating Indigenous Knowledges and Governance Within the Academy in Australia

16

Maggie Walter and Wendy Aitken

Contents

Introduction	250
Negotiating the Indigenous Within a Culture of Individualization	251
Color-Blind Racism and the Academy	252
How Indigenous Knowledges Are Done in the Australian Academy	253
Breaking Indigenous Knowledges from Segregation	254
Closing the Pedagogy and Indigenous Knowledges Gap	256
Integrating a Dynamic and Initiating Indigenous Knowledges Presence	258
Moving from Goodwill to Rightful Place: Activating Indigenous Governance	259
Engaging Community As Partners: Top and Bottom	260
Investing in Indigenous Knowledges	261
Conclusion and Future Directions	262
References	264

Abstract

The 2012 *Review of Higher Education Access and Outcomes for Aboriginal and Torres Strait Islander People* (the *Behrendt Report*) set a new direction in Indigenous/academy engagement. In contrast to previous (failed) policies, the report prioritizes fostering Indigenous leadership, embedding Indigenous knowledges within university curricula *and* ways of doing business, incorporating Indigenous governance across the sector as keys to improving Indigenous outcomes. Mediating a secure, sector-wide, normalized space for Indigenous knowledges, however, brings with it hazards as well as potential returns. Achieving a whole-of-university responsibility requires opening up a recognition of the non-Indigenous *culture* already deeply embedded in existing governance structures as a pivotal precursor to a normalized empowered Indigenous presence

M. Walter (✉) · W. Aitken
Social Sciences, University of Tasmania, Hobart, TAS, Australia
e-mail: Margaret.Walter@utas.edu.au; Wendy.Aitken@utas.edu.au

© Springer Nature Singapore Pte Ltd. 2019
E. A. McKinley, L. T. Smith (eds.), *Handbook of Indigenous Education*,
https://doi.org/10.1007/978-981-10-3899-0_30

within sector governance systems. Failure to do so risks revitalizing tokenism and/or co-option. Developed from a 2011 submission to the *Behrendt Report*, updated to reflect changes emanating from that report, this chapter explores the challenges, constraints, and unexpected gains inherent in closing the ontological gap between Indigenous and non-Indigenous understanding of Indigenous governance and knowledges within the academy.

Keywords
Indigenous knowledges · Ontological gap · Color-blind racism

Introduction

The 2012 *Review of the Higher Education Access and Outcomes for Aboriginal and Torres Strait Islander People* (hereafter named as the *Behrendt Report*) set a new framework for how the Australian University sector should engage with Aboriginal and Torres Strait Islander people and knowledges. The report has initiated a raft of changes, big and small, across the sector. However, despite some positive outcomes, the work of shifting Aboriginal and Torres Strait Islander business from the margins of higher education to a normalized space remains a "work in progress."

Efforts to Indigenize the academy from the inside results in challenges, expected and unexpected. We investigate these here using the concepts of Indigenous governance and knowledges. By Indigenous governance, we refer not merely to university government entities such as Council and Senate, although an Indigenous place within these is a core component. Rather, Indigenous governance is about Indigenous power and Indigenous authority to deploy the rights inherent in self-determination. These are many but within the academy center on the capacity and space for Indigenous genuine decision-making. To determine, on our own terms: what are and what are not the aspirations and needs for Indigenous students, staff, communities, and nations; and what is and what is not in the interests of Indigenous students, staff communities, and nations. This use of Indigenous knowledge is broader. The concept, as used here, encompasses Aboriginal and Torres Strait Islander scholarship, pedagogy, the cultural and specific knowledges of the many Aboriginal and Torres Strait Islander nations, as well as the shared epistemological tenets that define and delineate Indigenous knowledges from the Western frame that permeates the sector (Walter 2011).

Repositioning of Indigenous knowledges and the peoples of those knowledges cannot occur without active and accepted Indigenous governance systems. Yet, within many higher education settings, an ontological gap between Indigenous and non-Indigenous understandings of what Indigenous governance and knowledges are and how they should/could be positioned within the academy remains. A particular tension is in negotiating the line between a whole of university responsibility for Aboriginal and Torres Strait Islander engagement and participation, and maintaining Indigenous ownership and perspectives of Indigenous knowledges. The breadth of the question goes beyond simple prescriptive determinations. Our overarching purpose is to validate and legitimate the place of Indigenous governance mechanisms and processes and Indigenous knowledges within the academy. The chapter draws on literature in the field but takes a pragmatic rather than theoretical approach. This is achieved primarily by adding experiential data contributed through ongoing discussions with Indigenous academics, nationally and internationally. These positionalities are pertinent and add an empirical dimension to the discussion.

The question the chapter addresses is how do Indigenous university staff, academic and administrative, mediate the risks and hazards in the pursuance of a secure, sector-wide, normalized space for Indigenous governance and Indigenous knowledge systems? And how can the University be bought on the journey? The chapter's discussion is restricted to Australia, but also recognizes that these barriers, challenges, and, indeed, successes are likely to be pertinent to universities of other first world colonized nations, such as Aotearoa, New Zealand, the United States, and Canada.

Negotiating the Indigenous Within a Culture of Individualization

In the cross-cultural university sector context of Indigenous knowledges, there is a tendency to see the "context" as Western and the "culture" as Indigenous. This ontological position leans toward a concentration on Indigenous difference, with little or no consideration of the cultural and social positionality of the Western "context." A deeply embedded, but largely unrealized positioning, reflected in the ongoing popularity of workshops on Indigenous cultural awareness or Indigenous cultural competence, is that it is Indigenous culture that must become known to the mainstream, normal, non-Indigenous university. Indigenous cultural awareness, it seems will somehow support Indigenous knowledges taking their place within the academy. The fatal flaw in this reasoning is the lack of understanding that we are all, Indigenous and non-Indigenous, "cultural" beings and all institutions, and universities in particular, are strong reflectors and reproducers of the dominant cultural mores and epistemological prioritization in how they go about their everyday business.

In Australia, as well as other Anglo-colonized nations, dominant cultural mores and epistemological prioritization are Western in origin. Moreover, this normalized culture is in a relationship of power with Indigenous cultural mores and epistemological positioning. In critical theory, in relationships of power asymmetry, it is the dominant society and culture that more merits examination and from which the way things "be" might be more clearly explained (Held 1990; Horkheimer 1996). A central argument of this chapter, therefore, is that Indigenizing the academy requires a critical exploration of how Western understandings permeate the sector, and how these operate to limit and constrain Indigenous knowledges and understandings to a restricted permanent "outsider" space.

As has been argued elsewhere, the first step toward an understanding of the *Other* is an understanding of the self (Kruske et al. 2006; Walter et al. 2011). Universities, by and large within Western nations, are White, middle-class institutions. How the core social and cultural attributes of class, but especially race, are understood within them are central explanators of the current positioning of Indigenous knowledges within the academy. Because while purely biological understandings of race have long been discredited, as race theorists argue, in the dominant constructs of race, ideas of biological inferiority have merely been replaced by other rationales for non-White inferiority such as cultural or moral deficit (Bobo 1997; Sears and Kinder 1981; Lipsitz 2006; Bonilla Silva 2010; Walter 2014).

Bonilla-Silva (2010) further argues that racialized ways of thinking are not necessarily akin to racism per se, but built into the way the social world is organized. In his materialist interpretation, individual views on race directly correlate with an individual's systemic raced location. Thus within universities, while significant levels of overt racism are, thankfully, no longer the norm, understanding of race generally and Indigeneity and Indigenous culture more specifically is predominantly understood through the lens of White middle class experience. It is from within these class and racially privileged positions that Indigenous peoples, knowledges, and presence are viewed.

Other sociocultural factors also come into play. The most influential of these has been the rise of neoliberalism as the dominant economic and political discourse of Anglo-Western countries. Neoliberalism is defined by Harvey (2005, pp. 2–3) as the theory and practices that posit that "human well-being can be best advanced by liberating individual entrepreneurial freedoms and skills within an institutional framework characterized by strong private property rights, free markets and free trade." Under this framework, the societal unit is the individual and individuals are seen as individually responsible for their own life project (Beck and Beck-Gernsheim 2002). Within such individualistic thinking, it is hard for non-Indigenous people, whose racially dominant position means they do not have to think about race, or to see themselves as part of a racial group, to understand or fully appreciate the social and cultural effect of racially aligned disadvantage, within and without the university, on Indigenous life chances and educational trajectories (Walter et al. 2012).

Bonilla-Silva (2010) argues forcefully that the social circulation of race as a social, rather than a biological, force is supported by a set of sincere race-related fictions. These are widespread among the dominant racial group, in this case nonIndigenous Australians, especially those from Anglo backgrounds. The first is that if individual social actors do not hold to or practice racism, then they are not involved, personally, in racial inequality. The second is that race no longer matters as all people are equal and should be treated that way by individuals and the social system. It is the combination of these two beliefs that lead to what Bonilla-Silva describes as color-blind racism; being personally nonracist combined with the view that race is no longer important.

Color-Blind Racism and the Academy

Such perspectives, far from supporting equality, lead to very raced consequences. Combined with neoliberal individualism, such thinking brings the process of

"Othering" (Hollinsworth 2006) into focus. As Mapstone (1995, p. 79) argues, those from more powerful groups have the power to claim highly valued qualities (such as merit) as related to their own group and to assign to "out-groups" values intricately tied to their lack of equality (such as lack of endeavor). From this value dichotomizing, it follows that if race doesn't matter anymore and they (the dominant race individual) are nonracist, then the problems of "Other" peoples must be because those people are "different"or "deficit." If they only behaved more like "normal" people, all would be well. For Indigenous peoples, the ongoing influence of colonization and dispossession adds a further layer of complexity, magnifying this deficit perception (Walter 2014, 2015).

This institutional social and cultural positioning as "Other" is where the primary risk to Indigenous students, staff, and knowledges lie. Racial Othering, and especially in colonized nation states, the Othering of the marginalized and already highly disadvantaged Indigenous population leads to racialized, but common attitudinal frames among dominant race individuals and groups. Because they (individual or institution) see themselves as nonracist, then their attitudes toward the Indigenous Others must reflect objectivity, ensuring sound, disinterested judgment. This discursive mechanism allows the racially dominant group to simultaneously protest that they are nonracist while leaving the underlying system of racial privilege and disprivilege undisturbed. Thus, according to Bonilla-Silva (2010), universities can be places of racism despite a lack of overtly racist attitudes.

This Western culture influence in shaping how the Indigene is understood and helps to bring the "context" of Australian universities – as the site of integration of Indigenous knowledges – into focus. But overarching concepts such as "Western Culture" are not really useful in understanding the subtle and not so subtle factors that position Indigenous people at all levels as the "Other" within University systems. The hard work of imagining and, more importantly, engineering a different way of thinking, interacting, and valuing Indigenous peoples, culture, and knowledges requires more nuanced reveal. In the following sections, Western cultural influence is operationalized into its within-academy forms.

How Indigenous Knowledges Are Done in the Australian Academy

Australia has 40 universities, nearly all of which are public institutions. The implementation of the *Behrendt Report* recommendations within Universities, while still very uneven, has resulted in some changes in this terrain, especially a rise in more senior positions. Regardless, the underrepresentation of Aboriginal and Torres Strait Islander peoples within these, as students, staff, and within governance, is a long-standing public issue. In 2013, Aboriginal and Torres Strait Islander students made up just 1.4% of all commencing Australian undergraduate students, a rate about half the proportion of Indigenous people in the population. Underrepresentation rates increase across postgraduate degrees, especially research higher degrees. The proportion of Aboriginal and Torres Strait Islander academics is even lower. In nearly two-thirds of Australian universities, Aboriginal and Torres Strait Islander staff representation is below, often well below, 1% of total staff numbers (Moreton-Robinson et al. 2011). Australian universities still need to triple their Aboriginal or Torres Strait Islander academic representation to achieve population parity. This continuing, across the board, underrepresentation means the spaces and places where Indigenous knowledges have been able to fit, let alone flourish, within the university sector, have been severely constrained for many years.

The Australian university system also reflects and reinforces its broader sociopolitical context with an increasing trend toward corporatization. This direction has strengthened the influence of neoliberal ideology of efficiency, choice (user pays), and competition between and within institutions with changes underpinned by free-market notions of autonomous individuals maximizing their rational self-interest. Such an approach stands in stark contrast to Aboriginal and Torres Strait Islander societies, which, despite the diversity of Indigenous cultures nationally and globally, tend to a more "collectivist or allocentric worldview" (Stewart and Allan 2013). From Indigenous perspectives, knowledge and the power that it brings is dispersed, rather than centralized. Within Indigenous ontologies, or way of being, a shared more of relationality, or "relatedness" (see Martin 2008; Wilson 2008) prevails. There is, therefore, a tension between a system which is leaning toward more Indigenous leadership and Indigenous governance while simultaneously moving ever more strongly in a neoliberal direction. This contradiction provides challenges as well as opportunities for how Indigenous knowledges are currently "done" and future directions.

Breaking Indigenous Knowledges from Segregation

Indigenous knowledges are currently marginalized in a myriad of ways, with distinct and tangible barriers to achieving recognition and equal value within higher education remain firmly in place. Understanding the factors that create and maintain these barriers is a vital step in deconstructing them. While cultural "difference" of Indigenous ways of being and understanding the world has been recognized, the requisite shift by the dominant cultural and knowledge systems to provide an appropriate Indigenous space has not been forthcoming. Accommodation has been limited to creating a space to *be* different. Indigenous knowledges' placement as "apart"'from mainstream university business normalizes their frequent exclusion from decision-making processes.

Equal recognition of Indigenous knowledges is currently inhibited by the common fault line of separate, isolated, placement of Aboriginal and Torres Strait Islander business within institutions. Since the inception of the National Aboriginal Education Policy (NAEP) (1989), the standard strategy of addressing Aboriginal and Torres Strait Islander underrepresentation has been the establishment of support centers within individual universities. Primarily funded by Federal Government monies under programs such as the Indigenous Student Success Program (ISSP), Indigenous Centers are usually situated in a discreet, often purpose built, site within the campus. Centers (The term "Center" is used here to refer to the variable discrete

Aboriginal and Torres Strait Islander units found within the large majority of Australian universities.) vary significantly in size and function but all offer formal support programs such as tutorial assistance and informal services such as pastoral care and the provision of a culturally safe, accessible meeting and study place for students. Most are also the primary place of intersection between the wider Aboriginal and Torres Strait Islander community and the university. A number also offer academic programs, including pretertiary qualifying programs aimed at supporting Aboriginal students into higher education within a culturally safe environment.

The rise of discrete Centers as key Indigenous spaces within Australian universities is compounded by the relative rarity of Aboriginal or Torres Strait Islander academics within mainstream academic units. Data on the spread of Indigenous academics throughout faculties and schools is unavailable, but observer knowledge suggests that the majority of Indigenous academic staff at Australian universities are either employed in their university's Indigenous Centre or within another Indigenous framed enclave, such as a health or education unit. Very, very few are employed in mainstream university positions, despite many years of advocacy for change in this area.

Centers are, therefore, the core Indigenous knowledges resource in Australian universities. And we have seen similar centers at universities in Canada and the United States. Their prominence, as Indigenous Centers, however, has a damaging downside. In a significant proportion of universities, such Centers *are* the Aboriginal and Torres Strait Islander strategy. Responsible for all things, Indigenous Centers can become overburdened with policy, program, management, and other responsibilities for which they were never designed. Centers' ability to articulate Indigenous knowledges is further incapacitated by their figurative, if not physical, placement out of sight and mind of the mainstream discussions or debates of university business.

Indigenous governance is not achievable from within such places. Within University hierarchies, Centers and their staff rank lowly. While sometimes included within University committees and working groups, their capacity and power to effect change is highly constrained. And while there is significant goodwill and interest in Indigenous issues among higher level non-Indigenous university management, Center academics mostly do not have the resources or networks to harness that goodwill. Even if they can manage to effect positive change, such change is often one-offs, a great event or high university engagement in a particular program. Indigenous Center staff lack the power and position to embed these changes as "normal" across the University.

Additionally, Centers by virtue of their multiple and specific roles differ dramatically in form and function to mainstream schools, departments and faculties. Their employment structures tend toward a preponderance of administrative rather than academic staff, a structure that reinforces the power imbalance between Centers and other areas of the University, especially faculties and schools. For those with academic ambitions, employment within a Center is frequently a hindrance, not a support. Low numbers of academic staff, mostly at junior academic levels, creates a propensity for Centers to become isolated hinterlands of scholarly inexperience, removed from the formal and informal academic mentoring and career support processes that occur elsewhere within the university. For example, both authors were originally employed within their University's Indigenous Centre, before they had completed their PhDs. Despite this, both were also charged with building the Centre's research track record and supporting other staff in this regard. While willing to undertake this task, it was obvious to all, including ourselves, that we were fundamentally ill-equipped – experience and track record wise – for the role.

Strategies which recognize (necessarily) the uniqueness of the Indigenous place within the Australian higher education system have, therefore, also tended to segregation. This allows a failure to flourish (and to address unequal outcomes for Indigenous people) to be attributed to the Center and its employees. More damagingly, Indigenous knowledges that do exist within an institution are confined within an all-encompassing Aboriginal and Torres Strait Islander enclave, with limited and restricted interaction with the wider university system. The ramification of this is a – usually unintended but highly effective – incarceration of Indigenous knowledges.

By inverse logic, a normalcy of Indigenous knowledges as separately quartered terrain translates to the university mainstream neither being expected to understand such knowledges or change to accommodate them. Hovering perhaps within the institutions' collective subconscious (rather than explicitly stated) Center responsibility, by definition, exempts the wider university, management, faculties, sections, or service areas from effecting any self-initiated engagement with Indigenous knowledges. More insidiously, this permeating practice segregates the Indigenous from the day-to-day and the critical events of university operations. Unless an issue, policy, program, or priority specifically includes the words "Aboriginal or Torres Strait Islander" or "Indigenous," the production, dissemination, or potential contribution of Indigenous knowledges will be absent from consideration in executive planning, discussion, debates, or decisions. University business, at the macro- and microlevel, is normalized as exclusive of Indigenous governance and knowledges.

Closing the Pedagogy and Indigenous Knowledges Gap

Aboriginal and Torres Strait Islander academics' capacity to be independent disseminators of Indigenous knowledges is also compromised by the unequal and unidirectional nature of current knowledge interactions. Aboriginal staff are frequently called upon to: provide cross-cultural (or more latterly, cultural competence) training to staff and/or students; to source community members for Welcome to Country duties; conduct in-teaching of Aboriginal and Torres Strait Islander content; develop university reconciliation or strategic plans; and many other tasks. The dimensions of the knowledge required, and how, when, and to whom it is to be delivered, is usually predetermined. The ability to independently initiate Indigenous knowledge input is severely curtailed or nonexistent. The argument is not that staff should not be engaged in these activities but to highlight the imbalanced nature of the relationship between Aboriginal staff as service providers, and mainstream areas as knowledge service commissioners. A compliant service resource, supplying commodified knowledges on demand, is not compatible with the goal of equal recognition or partnership.

There are also widely known (but usually unstated) pedagogical tendencies within Australian universities dealing with Indigenous knowledges, with responses falling into one of the three categories. The first is to outsource responsibility to Indigenous members of staff (often without regard to their scholarly expertise). The second is to allocate responsibility to a relatively junior non-Indigenous staff member, with little expertise. The third is to not include Indigenous content at all. The reason frequently given by course coordinators for any of these three responses is that they do not have the confidence to engage with Indigenous knowledge content. They are afraid of doing or saying the "wrong" thing and feel this is an area where they cannot have expertise. As argued by Walter and Butler (2013), these Indigenous content behaviors, while frequently dressed up as Indigenous sensitivity, are actually examples of the curricula practice of Whiteness. It is, not to put too fine a point on it, all about race; that of the Indigenous academics and our responsibilities to remove the burden from non-Indigenous academics to engage with race. This racial situating sees many Indigenous scholars being forever constrained within the "Guest Paradigm," dependent on the continuing "goodwill" of the tertiary sector (Morgan cited in McConville 2002, p. 195). Taking on this role is conceived as an Indigenous obligation. There is often an injured sense of valor when requests are rebuffed (Walter and Butler 2013). No thought seems to be given to the disrespect and disregard of Indigenous staff as scholars that this behavior embodies. Under Butler's (2006) concept of bifurcation, Aboriginal and Torres Strait Islander academics are expected to discuss Aboriginal peoples, and more especially, those who live in remote areas, regardless of disciplines or expertise. They are Aboriginal first, before they are seen (if at all) as scholars.

This reliance on the "one-stop shop" for Indigenous knowledge services is problematic pedagogically. With some occupations now mandating Indigenous coursework content as a prerequisite for registration, Aboriginal and Torres Strait Islander academic staff are increasingly called upon to teach-in the requisite "Aboriginal and Torres Strait Islander bit." Yet, such teaching requires specialist professional knowledge – be it social work, nursing, medicine, or education – and sufficient seniority and expertise to successfully manage the interface between the profession and Aboriginal and Torres Strait Islander Australia. Assuming that Indigenous staff members have the expertise for these tasks, seemingly by virtue of Indigeneity, indicates naivety and a failure in the duty of care. The bigger question here is not who should be doing such teaching, but why outsourcing this particular topic, and not others, is deemed appropriate pedagogic practice? Separating responsibility for Aboriginal content can reduce the value of that content, in the perception of the course's students. The result is that Indigenous content in curriculum is either omitted or treated as different from the scholarly standards of other curriculum content.

An obvious prerequisite for a quality pedagogy of Aboriginal and Torres Strait Islander knowledges, within academic teaching, is the employment of appropriately qualified Indigenous staff. However, achievement of this goal is not something that can be remedied in the very short term (see next sections). Other strategies need to be deployed in the interim. The first is focusing institutions' attention on the importance of quality Indigenous scholarly content. Reducing avoidance behaviors on the part of course coordinators requires a recognition that developing Indigenous content can be challenging for non-Indigenous staff. Rejecting the reluctance to engage with Indigenous scholarship is a legitimate position, but generosity is also required to bring academics, faculties, and courses to a resetting of how it is that the University does Indigenous content, teaching, and pedagogy. Being available to course/unit coordinators, providing open and encouraging service mainstream curriculum support in areas such as: cultural appropriateness; appropriate scholarly materials; and course quality and comprehensiveness can help non-Indigenous academics make the transition into more confident Indigenous scholarship and knowledges competence. Such services, however, need to be recognized, formalized, and placed within task frameworks. Without formal acknowledgement, such roles risk becoming just another Indigenous labor expectation.

Integrating a Dynamic and Initiating Indigenous Knowledges Presence

Strengthening the recognition of Aboriginal and Torres Strait Islander knowledges within higher education is not a straightforward process; there are intrinsic risks in whatever strategies are devised. Marking-up Aboriginal and Torres Strait Islander recognition as a priority area within the sector is crucial to remediation. Yet the very act of singling out can lead to a remarginalization by describing these spaces and interactions as "special." Within this scenario, Indigenous knowledges are restricted to spaces outside mainstream operations. There is a little difference between being patronized as "important but over there" and being ignored. Alternatively, integrating Aboriginal and Torres Strait Islander dimensions into the mainstream business of the university risks a remarginalization on the basis of minority status. Regardless of good intentions, Indigenous knowledges can easily become continually, if not permanently, subsumed under the weight of the always competing dominant knowledge matters. And the very operation of dominant (and dominating) hierarchical structures will automatically take precedence. Choosing between the competing hazards of marking out discrete Indigenous space or an integrated model is, however, framed by the foundational fact that equal recognition is unachievable while Aboriginal and Torres Strait Islander people remain so heavily underrepresented across all levels of the sector. A "Whole of University approach" (Behrendt Report 2012) cannot be achieved until there is an understanding within the sector of the values of Indigenous knowledges and an open examination and acceptance of the limitations in Universities' traditional approach to encompass Indigenous governance.

Moving from Goodwill to Rightful Place: Activating Indigenous Governance

If the ultimate goal is to bring Indigenous engagement and knowledges to the center of the higher education system – the same place that Western knowledges and settler population engagement currently resides – how do we go about it? How can the nurturing of Aboriginal and Torres Strait Islander knowledges *and* an explicit recognition of their equal value and validity become standard higher education operating procedure? Obviously, part of the answer is to broaden the Indigenous space and place within Universities. This shift is not possible for Aboriginal and Torres Strait Islander people – staff, students, and/or community – to achieve alone. Neither can we rely on non-Indigenous goodwill. Reliance on goodwill, especially individually located goodwill, is a perilous position. Gains can be swept away in an instant with a change of personnel or structure. The disheartening return to Indigenous knowledges 101, after we have felt that real progress had been achieved, is familiar to nearly all in the sector.

It is a central contention, therefore, that there cannot and will not be real change in the sector without Indigenous governance. This requires as a first step the embedded presence of Indigenous academic leadership that is fully recognized and incorporated into university leadership and governing bodies. In Australia, *the Behrendt Report* has created a climate in which Indigenous academic leadership is possible. Recommendation 32, which advocates for the creation of Indigenous senior management positions, has provided space for an Indigenous voice in places that have previously been closed. At the time of writing, around a quarter of Australian universities had have adopted at least part of recommendation 32 and now have Aboriginal and Torres Strait Islander academics holding positions at the Pro Vice-Chancellor or equivalent level. These positions combine senior management and senior academic credentials (i.e., a professorship). More critically, this trend looks to be broadening across the sector. These senior positions create opportunities to address the divergent demands of Indigenous and Western governance. But without wider university Indigenous governance, they do little to flatten the hierarchy that makes universities uncomfortable places for those traditionally delegated to the bottom position.

Outside forces can also contribute to an Indigenizing of the academy. For example, in Australia, the National Tertiary Education Union, the labor union for higher education staff, has influenced the landscape. In the previous round of workplace agreements, the union bargained on the Indigenous employment clause *first* (rather than the usual last place). This has resulted in a greater proportion of University's Enterprise Agreements stipulating numerical targets for Aboriginal and Torres Strait Islander employment within the sector. These agreements are legally binding, providing leverage for action rather than what has been up till now a commitment-only space. Commitment is not a currency. Frequently, it does not equate to actual expenditure of resources or energy, but operates as a change-blocking mechanism, functioning to forestall, not facilitate change. This shift from stating intentions to quantifying measurable targets is a positive one. It is also a step that needs to be emulated across the space to engender genuine change. The focus has to be on what we are doing, rather than what should happen, or what we would like to happen. But new positive practices need not only to be introduced, they need to also dislodge the plethora of old barrier-building ones.

Engaging Community As Partners: Top and Bottom

A key plank of Indigenization is the integration of the Indigenous throughout universities. A prime strategy for achieving such integration is an inversion of the standard University/Indigenous community engagement practices. Traditionally, community engagement has been at the bottom end of engagement. Community members are invited to events, primarily in the Indigenous Centre. Our institution (along with many others around the nation) employs Elders to culturally support students, again, usually within Centers, and to perform Welcome to Country obligations. These are important aspects of doing University/Community engagement. But on their own, they are insufficient: they do not disrupt, but rather frequently entrench, the understanding of the Indigenous as the different "Other." What is required is the opening of a cohesive, all areas, Indigenous presence to support knowledge pathways for students and staff across institutions. This requires reenvisioning and then reengineering how Aboriginal communities engage with the individual university and with the sector overall. Moreover, strategies to increase Indigenous community engagement need to operate in both directions: to embrace Indigenous community within the university and to include the university in community relations.

Community engagement at the management end of the university is still a rare occurrence, but it *is* a prerequisite for creating and normalizing Indigenous knowledges. And if you can't bring community to University management, then bring University management, which is those who make the decisions and decide the pathway and culture of the university, to community. For example, the University of Tasmania has established a University Aboriginal Policy Working Group. This Working Group is made up of senior members of university staff, including Deans of Faculties and Heads of Divisions such as Human Resources, representatives of university Aboriginal staff, and a group of external senior Aboriginal community members. In doing so, there is no claim made to the originality of this strategy. Other institutions, nationally and internationally, have long had committees that are inclusive of Indigenous community members. What is noteworthy in this example is how the introduction of this particular version of community voice has changed the dynamics of community engagement at the university. The Working Group, now a formal University committee, represents the first time many University management staff had had direct higher education focused interaction with Aboriginal people. The equal numbers and capacity between Indigenous and non-Indigenous members ensure the Indigenous perspective is both heard and understood.

While the existence of Indigenous led working or other groups/committees/entities can and do initiate solid strategies, for real impact they must be integrated into University management structures. Their presence has to be embedded into how the University (and more widely the sector) does business. The work of such University committees also needs to be formally embedded into the University's policy structure: not as something outside or on the margins but a prominent policy setting to which other University policies must include and align. Enabling such integration and embedding requires Indigenous leadership in positions of genuine influence. It is from this central policy structure that other strategies and actions flow.

Investing in Indigenous Knowledges

Equal recognition of Indigenous knowledges is unachievable without a critical mass of qualified, skilled Aboriginal and Torres Strait Islander scholars engaged in its study, origination, and promulgation. As outlined, the low number of Aboriginal scholars as well as their relative junior status and lack of role model and mentoring opportunities means the Australian higher education sector, is as yet, a long way from this prerequisite. The heavy weighting of success in winning research grants on academic's track record, combined with funding entities' lack of understanding of Indigenous research methodologies, exacerbate the problem. This arises from the lacuna of non-Indigenous supervisors and research offices to recognize a place for, and understanding of, Indigenous research at the university level. The point is that Indigenous knowledges cannot achieve its potential or its place within the higher education sector without change within the organization and significant and targeted investment in its scholars.

Harnessing the power of diverse Indigenous knowledges and a consequent Indigenizing of the academy requires a network of dispersed but linked Indigenous scholars. Broad and unrestricted Indigenous participation in management, curricula, research, research higher degrees is not largesse but an obligation. Yet, a frequent response is that while universities are committed to increasing Aboriginal and Torres Strait Islander staff numbers, they are hamstrung because there are not enough qualified Indigenous academics and professional staff available to fill the gaps. Such reasoning is blame shifting. Advertising for Aboriginal or Torres Strait Islander staff when the university itself has little history in supporting, targeting, nurturing, or direct capacity building of Indigenous staff is both naive and presumptuous. If the sector wants to increase the proportion of qualified and skilled Indigenous people in their workforce, the time to start building that workforce was 10 years ago. If the sector wants to have a qualified, skilled Indigenous workforce in 10 years, the time to start is now. Choosing not to do so is a choice that guarantees failure.

Additionally, there is more than one way to raise the level and number of Indigenous academic and professional staff beyond waiting for some hoped for future pipeline effect. For example, a system of supported academic apprenticeships within departments and faculties would create the space for the many Aboriginal and Torres Strait Islander people with good undergraduate results and an interest in academia to be placed within departments. There, staff can be supported in their development as academics through a combination of hands-on academic experience and research scholarships. Additionally, establishing an internal scholarship system to support Center (and other) staff to complete their postgraduate studies would add a level of seniority for existing staff within just a few years. Ensuring Indigenous knowledges and methodologies are included in the university's institutional research strategy framework is also a necessary. Finally, including responsibility for increasing staff proportions as a key performance indicator (KPI) of Faculty and Division Heads, shares the load and concentrates the management mind on how such increases might be achieved beyond having good will and commitment.

Support systems for Indigenous research students also need to be developed, strengthened, and formalized within the mainstream university postgraduate, not outsourced to the Indigenous center. At the postgraduate level, despite the current massive underrepresentation of Aboriginal and Torres Strait Islander students, very, very few postgraduate programs provide specific recruitment activity or program support for this cohort (Walter and Robertson 2009). The result is that Aboriginal and Torres Strait Islander postgraduates are frequently on their own in navigating the fraught path of postgraduate study, supervision, and examination, a path that is epistemologically and axiologically out of sync with Indigenous knowledges.

Completions suffer as a result. This assertion is confirmed by experience of working with Aboriginal postgraduate students at a national level. These students (who were also often simultaneously Centre staff) continually expressed frustration that the use and development of Indigenous knowledges within their scholarship was not understood by their faculty or supervisors. They felt continually pressured to conform to mainstream epistemological norms, where, for example, collecting qualitative data using in-depth interviews was acceptable, but using yarning, a traditional Aboriginal form of relation building communication, was not. This is not an argument for a lowering of scholarly rigor. Rather, it reflects a dearth of understanding or recognition of Indigenous knowledges within the formal structures of scholarship undermining any real possibility of equal recognition of Indigenous knowledges within the research higher degree space (Walter et al. 2008). Again this is a long-standing sector obligation that has remained low key and low priority.

Conclusion and Future Directions

The changes already implemented from the *Behrendt Report* and the flow on effect of those will substantively change the place of Indigenous knowledges within the Australian academy. How quickly that becomes a reality depends on Aboriginal and Torres Strait Islander sector leadership and the overall sector and individual university leadership's capacity to work in genuine partnership. Yet, there is reason to hope that Indigenous governance and Indigenous knowledges can become a normalized presence within Australian universities, neither the "Other" or even cause for celebration.

There is a danger, however, that – having met many of these challenges – the *responsibility* for integrating Aboriginal and Torres Strait Islander knowledges throughout universities will, over time, revert back to the resulting Aboriginal and Torres Strait Islander workforce. But the integration of Indigenous governance and knowledges is very much a two-way process. It requires a willingness to share power and knowledge and an openness to difference and alternative perspectives. Its success relies on the dual acceptance of very different ontologies and their accompanying knowledge systems. This will require self-knowledge, especially from those from the dominant racial groups. Having recognized and formally acknowledged Indigenous knowledges systems, at an institutional level, it should be difficult for a full reversion to old norms.

Indigenizing the academy requires proportionality, integration, and acceptance. It also requires a transformation of university governance and internal structures. As with all of such changes, the beneficiaries are not just Indigenous peoples but the whole university and sector: we value add. It is also important to recognize that within our, and other universities, there are many, many non-Indigenous people eager to support our efforts to Indigenize the academy. It is the job of Indigenous staff and community to help the sector support Aboriginal and Torres Strait Islander knowledges and presence, empowering all to work in partnership with Aboriginal and Torres Strait Islander staff, students, peoples, organizations, and communities. Indigenizing the academy starts and ends with Indigenous and non-Indigenous generosity and willingness to keep on engaging in ways that are a permanent, not fleeting or fluctuating way that Australian universities do business.

Future directions in efforts to Indigenize the academy within the academy in Australia, and likely in other First Nation states, will require a constant vigilance. It is hard, given the many years that Indigenous academics and others have been trying to facilitate and engender a safe, respectful place of Indigenous peoples at all levels with the academy not to feel/become somewhat disillusioned with the very slow pace of progress. It is also not hard to feel that despite all our efforts that there remains a very central lack of understanding within the academy of what we mean by Indigenous knowledges, and why it is so vital that these have a central place within our academies knowledge systems. The risk of reversion, even when considerable progress has been made, also remains.

How to move forward with optimism? Acceptance that the process of Indigenizing the academy and the place of our knowledges is an on-going and likely long-term project is one key strategy. Continuing to build the published scholarship in the area of Indigenous knowledges, across First Nations peoples and across nation states, also will help maintain momentum and ensure that the lessons learned and strategies enacted in one institution or geographic location can be accessed by those outside of those places, now, and into the future. Finally, we need to recognize that our efforts, while frequently feeling undervalued and/or misunderstood, are worthwhile and will benefit not only the current generation of students and scholars, but those in generations to come.

References

Beck U, Beck-Gernsheim E (2002) Individualization. Sage, London

Behrendt Report (2012) Review of higher education access & outcomes for Aboriginal and Torres Strait Islander people (Behrendt Review). Department of Education, Employment and Workplace Relations, Canberra

Bobo L (1997) Race, public opinion, and the social sphere. Public Opin Q 61(1 special issue on Race (spring)):1–15

Bonilla-Silva E (2010) Racism without racists: colour-blind racism and the persistence of racial inequality in the United States, 3rd edn. Rowman and Littlefield Publishers, Maryland

Butler K (2006) (Re)presenting Indigeneity: the possibilities of Australian sociology. J Sociol 42:369–381

Department of Education and Training (1989) National Aboriginal Education Policy. https://www.education.gov.au/national-aboriginal-and-torres-strait-islander-education-policy-1989. Accessed 27 September 2017

Harvey D (2005) A brief history of neoliberalism. Oxford University Press, Oxford

Held D (1990) Introduction to critical theory: Horkheimer to Habermas. Polity Press, Cambridge

Hollinsworth D (2006) Race and racism in Australia. Thomson, South Melbourne

Horkheimer M (1996) Critique of instrumental reason: lectures and essays since the end of World War II. Continuum, New York

Kinder DR, Sears DO (1981) Prejudice and politics: symbolic racism versus racial threats to the good life. J Pers Soc Psychol 40(3):414–431

Kruske S, Kildea S, Barclay L (2006) Cultural safety and maternity care for aboriginal and Torres Strait Islander Australians. Women and Birth 19(3):73–77

Lipsitz G (2006) The possessive investment in whiteness: how white people profit from identity politics. Temple University Press, Philadelphia

Mapstone E (1995) Rational men and conciliatory women: graduate psychologists construct accounts of argument. Feminism and Psychology 5(1):61–83

Martin K (2008) Please knock before you enter: Aboriginal regulation of outsiders and the implications for researchers. Post Press, Teneriffe, Australia

McConville G (2002) Regional agreements, higher education and representations of Indigenous Australian reality (Why wasn't I taught that in school?), Australian Universities' Review, 45(1):15–24

Moreton-Robinson A, Walter M, Singh D, Kimber M (2011) On stony ground: governance and Aboriginal and Torres Strait Islander participation in Australian universities. In: Report to the review of higher education access and outcomes for Aboriginal and Torres Strait Islander people, Commissioned for the Behrendt Review by the Department of Education, Employment and Workplace Relations, Canberra

Stewart J, Allan J (2013) Building relationships with Aboriginal people: a cultural mapping toolbox. Aust Soc Work 66(1):118–129

Walter M (2011) Embedding Aboriginal and Torres Strait Islander presence: opening knowledge pathways. In: Commissioned for the Behrendt review of Indigenous higher education by the Department of Education, Employment and Workplace Relations, Canberra. May 2011

Walter M (2014) Indigeneity and citizenship in Australia. In: Isin EF, Nyers P (eds) Routledge handbook of global citizenship studies. Routledge, London, pp 557–567

Walter M (2015) The race bind: how the denial of Australian Aboriginal Rights continues. In: Green J (ed) Indigenous human rights. Fernwood Press, Novia Scotia

Walter M, Butler K (2013) Teaching race to teach indigeneity. J Sociol 49(4):397–410

Walter M, Robertson B (2009) Scoping an Indigenous centre of researcher development, Indigenous Higher Education Advisory Council, Department of Education, Employment and Workplace Relations, Canberra

Walter M, Habibis D, Taylor S (2011) How White is Australian social work? Aust Soc Work 64(1):6–19

Walter M, Maynard J, Nakata M, Milroy J (2008) Strengthening Indigenous research. In: Njapartji, Njapartji-Yerra: stronger futures, Report of the 2007. Indigenous Higher Education Council Conference. Adelaide. Commonwealth of Australia, Canberra

Walter M, Taylor S, Habibis D (2012) Australian Social Work is White. In: Bennett B, Green S, Gilbert S, Bessarab D (eds) Our Voices: Aboriginal and Torres Strait Islander Social Work. Palgrave Press, Sydney

Wilson S (2008) Research is ceremony: Indigenous research methods. Fernwood Press, Halifax

"A World in which [Alaska Natives] Make the Important Decisions": Re-examining Institutional Discourses and Governance in Higher Education

17

Olga Paniik Skinner and Beth Ginondidoy Leonard

Contents

Introduction	268
Indigenous Governance in Higher Education: Understanding the "Traditional Forms and Functions of These Systems"	269
A Sacred Learning Landscape: Troth Yeddha'	271
"Emphasizing the North and Its Diverse Peoples": University of Alaska Governance and Public Discourse	273
Service to Rural and Alaska Native Peoples: Institutional Priorities	275
A Cultural Centering Point: Troth Yeddha' Park	276
Student Discourse: Support, Advocacy, and Activism	277
Institutional Practices and Diversity: The Chancellor's Advisory Committee on Native Education	278
Native Ways of Knowing, Indigenous Knowledges, and Governance in Higher Education	279
Alaska Native Self-Determination: The UAF Indigenous Studies PhD Program	281
The Alaska Native Studies Council	282
Engaging the Four "Rs": Recommendations for Governance and Research	283
Working to Achieve Awareness: Self-Determination, Sovereignty, and Governance	284
Conclusion and Future Directions	286
References	288

Abstract

This chapter examines key public discourses at the University of Alaska (UA), with a focus on strategic governance as related to the shaping of physical landscapes and "intellectual thought worlds" for Indigenous peoples. Our work

O. P. Skinner (✉)
University of Alaska Fairbanks, Fairbanks, AK, USA
e-mail: ojskinner@alaska.edu

B. G. Leonard
Department of Alaska Native Studies, University of Alaska Anchorage, Anchorage, AK, USA
e-mail: brleonard@alaska.edu

© Springer Nature Singapore Pte Ltd. 2019
E. A. McKinley, L. T. Smith (eds.), *Handbook of Indigenous Education*,
https://doi.org/10.1007/978-981-10-3899-0_33

is informed by Indigenous higher education scholarship as well as critical and decolonizing methodologies. We begin by discussing the Indigenous origins of the landscape currently occupied and governed by the University of Alaska, *Troth Yeddha'* ("Wild Potato Hill") – a resilient and continuing reclamation discourse. This is followed by an examination of the Alaskan cultural and higher education contexts, including formation of the UA system, current governance structures, and the institution's publicly stated responsibilities to Alaska Native students. We discuss the formation of Alaska Native Studies Council, and the positioning of Alaska Natives in advisory and student support organizations including Rural Student Services, the Chancellor's Advisory Committee on Native Education, and the American Indian Science and Engineering Society (AISES). Our analysis engages global recommendations by UNDRIP as related to Indigenous higher education with a focus on how place, identity, and Alaska Native Ways of Knowing participate [in] and influence governance strategies, programs, and objectives.

Keywords

Indigenous higher education · Indigenous governance · Alaska Native education · Indigenous knowledge · Native ways of knowing

Introduction

Many of us, as Indigenous scholars, are positioned within institutions located on Indigenous lands; therefore, we believe Indigenous cultures occupy "rightful places and spaces within these contexts" (Leonard and Mercier 2016, p. 7). We are aware that Indigenous leadership and governance is limited in many institutions that often research and teach about – rather than with and for – Indigenous peoples. Our relationships and positions within this institution orient our analysis of Indigenous higher education governance, as we are members of Alaska Native tribes, and both graduates and current employees of the University of Alaska (UA). Olga Skinner is Yup'ik, enrolled in the Kwethluk tribe in southwest Alaska, and is a long-time resident of Fairbanks in interior Alaska. She earned a BA in foreign languages (Russian and French) and an MEd in language and literacy through the University of Alaska Fairbanks (UAF). Olga's master's thesis documents the life history of her maternal grandmother Olinka/Olga *Arrsamquq* Michael. She is currently an academic advisor for Rural Student Services (UAF), and a PhD candidate in UAF's Indigenous Studies PhD Program.

Beth Leonard is Deg Xit'an and a member of the Shageluk Tribe of interior Alaska. She earned her PhD from UAF in 2007, and served as a full-time faculty member at UAF's School of Education from 2006 to 2013. From 2013 to 2016, Leonard taught for the UAF Indigenous Studies PhD Program in the Center for Cross-Cultural Studies. She is currently an associate professor and director of Alaska Native Studies with the University of Alaska Anchorage, and continues her affiliation with the Indigenous Studies PhD Program, chairing several PhD committees.

Indigenous Governance in Higher Education: Understanding the "Traditional Forms and Functions of These Systems"

Alaska Native peoples have prioritized higher education for several decades. Recommendations for improving Alaska Native access and engagement in higher education originate from individual tribes and tribal consortia resolutions, conferences and gatherings, and conversations with Alaska Native communities, including elders and students (Barnhardt and Kawagley 2010; Barnhardt and Kawagley 2011). The following quote by Cup'ik Elder Lucy Jones-Sparck emphasizes the need for Alaska Native control of education to promote strong identity and cultural connections.

> If Alaska Natives can educate themselves about the traditional forms and functions of these systems and then go ahead and take control, not within the guidelines, policies, and procedures of the western system, but through adaptations to their own ways, then they will truly walk in their own world, a world of their own making, a world in which they make the important decisions. The children and college students can then be educated to know this culture and be confident in it. Our feet will then be planted firmly in prideful recognition of the self, feeling comfortable with who we are, and seeing others of different cultures as they are. (2010, p. 325)

This chapter examines key public discourses at the University of Alaska (UA), with a focus on strategic governance as related to the shaping of physical landscapes and "intellectual thought worlds" for Indigenous peoples, as articulated by Seneca scholar Arthur Parker (1916, p. 255). Our research is informed by scholarship in Indigenous higher education (Brayboy et al. 2012; Leonard and Mercier 2014; Mercier et al. 2011), and critical and decolonizing methodologies (Battiste 2013; Denzin et al. 2000). Alaska Native peoples have developed complex and diverse knowledge systems with accompanying methods of higher education over millennia. Alaska Native knowledge, as a discipline, is currently confined to ethnic or cultural studies within the academy, limiting full recognition of these intellectual thought worlds as authentic, scientific, interdisciplinary, and holistic systems. Many universities continue to be grounded in expectations that students will assimilate to Western ways of knowing, being, doing, and becoming, without critical examination of the histories, rationale for, and current places and spaces of higher education. Tribal Critical Race Theory (TribalCrit), an extension of critical race theory, clearly implicates imperialism, White supremacy, and desire for material gain in the colonization of American Indian peoples (Brayboy 2005, p. 429). As part of a decolonizing methodology, TribalCrit calls for recentering "tribal philosophies, beliefs, customs, traditions, and visions for the future" (p. 430). Decolonization through Indigenizing the academy (Mihesuah and Wilson 2004) to better serve Alaska Native students requires a critical analysis of higher education governance within the University of Alaska context.

While preparing to write this chapter, we struggled with how Indigenous governance might be conceptualized beyond formal higher education leadership roles. In their review of Australian higher education access and outcomes for Aboriginal and

Torres Strait Islanders, Aileen Moreton-Robinson, Maggie Walter, David Singh, and Megan Kimber (Moreton-Robinson et al. 2011) conceptualize governance as "participation and direct influence on university executive functions" and "regulation...refer[ring] to the strategies, programs and objectives to increase Indigenous outcomes including embedding Indigenous knowledge within the university's operations" (p. 5). There is limited literature on leadership and governance in Alaskan higher education; however, Michael Jennings (1994, 2004) and the late Tlingit scholar Louis Jacquot (1974) address Alaska Native peoples' historical participation, challenges, and influence within the University of Alaska system. Jennings (2004) specifically discusses higher education's attempts to further colonize Indigenous peoples through defining and teaching Indigenous knowledges using Western paradigms. Also relevant to an Indigenous governance discourse is Dena'ina scholar Jessica Bissett Perea's "A Tribalography of Alaska Native Presence in Academia" (Perea 2013) that draws on Howe's (1999) tribalography methodology. Perea posits that Alaska Natives are threatened by "the very real and dangerous double erasure of Native agency; first by historical colonial powers, and second by contemporary "post-racial" discourse" (p. 3), a discourse that renders racism nonexistent due to civil rights legislation Perea's list, building off unpublished research by Ray Barnhardt, and most recently updated by Indigenous Studies PhD candidate Alberta Jones, documents names, tribal affiliations, and fields of study for the approximately 90 Alaska Natives who earned PhDs or EdDs between 1970 and 2017. Perea's and Jones' documentation of Alaska Native PhDs/EdDs highlights the continuing underrepresentation of Alaska Natives in graduate education, a troubling trend that has continuing implications for Indigenous higher education governance. Most recently, Inupiaq scholar Pearl Brower's (2016) dissertation examines Indigenous leadership at tribal colleges and Indigenous-student serving universities, including Iḷisaġvik, Alaska's only tribally-governed college. These key sources provide significant contextual background for examining UA's current governance structures in our case study.

We begin by discussing the Indigenous origins of the landscape currently occupied and governed by the University of Alaska (UA), *Troth Yeddha'* (Wild Potato Hill) – a resilient and continuing reclamation discourse. This is followed by an examination of the Alaskan cultural and higher education contexts, including formation of the UA system, current governance structures, and the University of Alaska's current, publicly stated responsibilities to Alaska Native students. We discuss formation of the Alaska Native Studies Council, and the positioning of Alaska Natives in advisory and student support organizations including Rural Student Services, the Chancellor's Advisory Committee on Native Education, and Alaska Native student organizations. Our analysis engages global recommendations by UNDRIP as related to Indigenous higher education with a focus on how place, identity, and Native Ways of Knowing participate [in] and influence governance strategies, programs, and objectives as defined by Moreton-Robinson et al. (2011).

Throughout this chapter, we explore questions concerning the conceptualization of Indigenous governance in higher education, and possibilities for transforming schools and education in multiple global/transnational contexts. As we considered the contexts and implications of Indigenous governance, additional questions, applicable beyond the University of Alaska system, emerged:

1. How, when, and why do Western universities prioritize Indigenous higher education and knowledge systems?
2. Can Indigenous governance exist in a Western institution with limited Indigenous representation at the executive/administrative, faculty, and staff levels?
3. Who governs Alaska Native serving programs and research involving Alaska Native peoples?
4. How does existing Indigenous governance at the University of Alaska influence Alaska Native presence or "seats at the table" in terms of mission, vision, and policy?

A Sacred Learning Landscape: Troth Yeddha'

Indigenous cultures of Alaska are diverse within a vast landscape of 663,268 square miles/1,717,854 km^2. The State of Alaska 2015 census estimates reveal that roughly 19% of the state's total population of 737,625 self-identify as Alaska Native. Alaska Native is a legal term; however, it is now being used as a racial/ethnic identifier; and this pan term tends to gloss over the diversity of Alaska's Indigenous cultures. Alaska has 20 distinct Indigenous languages recently recognized in 2015 as official languages of the state, and several major Indigenous cultural groups including: Iñupiaq, Yup'ik, Cup'ik, Siberian Yupik, Sugpiaq/Alutiiq, Unangax̂/Aleut, Dene'/Athabascan, Tlingit, Tsimshian, and Haida (Alaska Native Language Center n.d.; Brown 2012, pp. 7–21; Williams 2009, pp. 4–11); 12 Alaska Native controlled corporations (with associated nonprofit associations) formed under the Alaska Native Claims Settlement Act of 1971 (ANCSA) that function as major employers and economic drivers within and beyond the State of Alaska; and 229 tribal governments recognized by the U.S. federal government (Fig. 1).

Jeremy Garcia (Hopi/Tewa) and Valerie Shirley (Diné) (Garcia and Shirley 2012) frame schools as "sacred landscapes" (p. 77), emphasizing the roles of institutions and teachers in nurturing critical consciousness and "origins of place" (p. 78; see Freire 2002 for further discussion of critical pedagogy and conscientization). Engagement with education as a sacred landscape calls for a decolonization process through examining ancestral ties to the land and re-envisioning our understanding of who we are as Indigenous peoples in relation to the land and how we move forward. The learning landscape currently occupied and now governed by the University of Alaska Fairbanks (UAF) – Troth Yeddha'– has likely been an Alaska Native/Dene' space since time immemorial. In describing the origins of Troth Yeddha', the late traditional Chief Peter John of Minto, Alaska claimed an Indigenous pedagogy of place – a hope that good thinking and working together would continue under the governance of the University of Alaska; and that the Dene' grandchildren would be appropriately served by this institution:

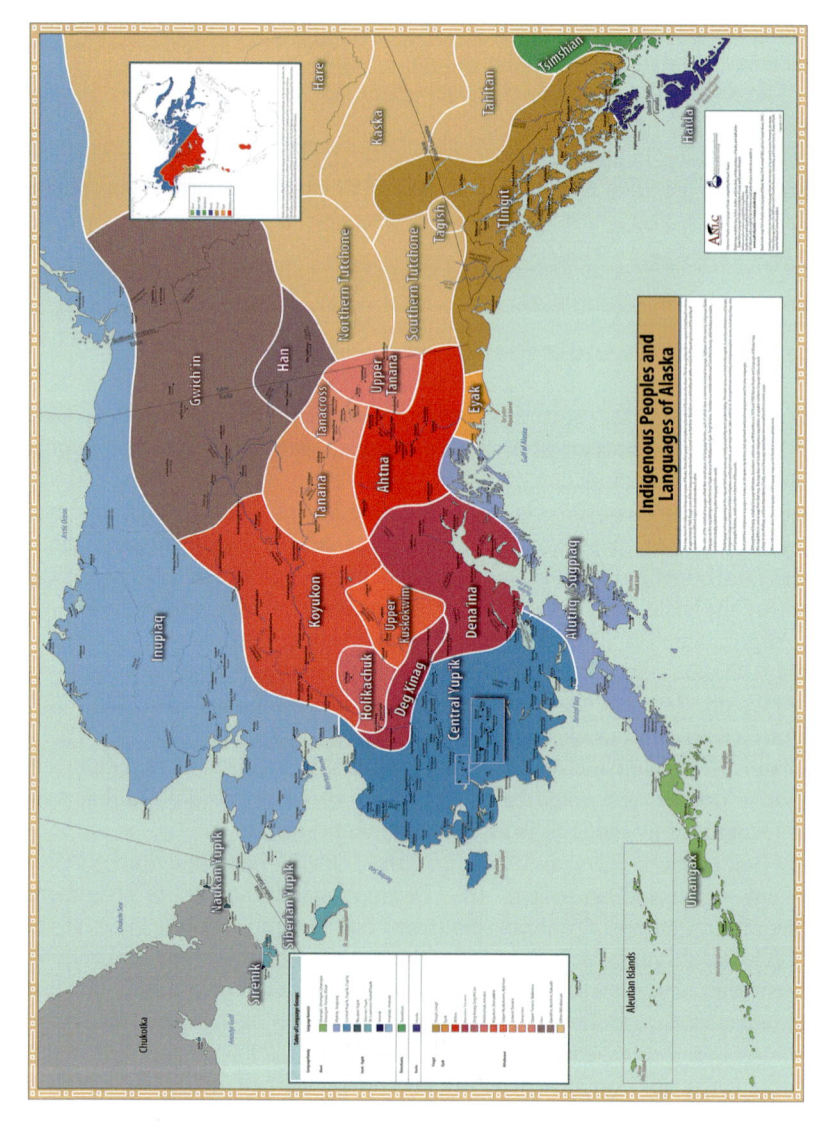

Fig. 1 Indigenous Peoples and Languages of Alaska (Krauss et al. 2011)

> Our people used to come to this hill to pick Troth...Troth Yeddha' was important, a meeting place. The grandfathers used to come to talk and give advice to one another about what they were going to do. When they learned this place would be used for a school, the university, they came here one last time, to decide what they should do. They decided that the school would be good and would carry on a very similar traditional use of this hill – a place where good thinking and working together would happen...They were also giving a blessing to their grandchildren who would be part of the new school.

Initial promotion of this reclamation discourse was largely due to the efforts of former UAF Interior-Aleutians Director Clara (Johnson) Anderson (Koyukon) who created posters of the 1994 speech that were published in 1998. Recognition in UAF's academic catalog followed 7 years after the speech in 2001. Advocates and allies in this effort included the late Vice Chancellor of Rural, Community, and Native Education Bernice Joseph (Koyukon), a number of UAF faculty including James Kari and Gary Holton (both of the Alaska Native Language Center), and Elder Robert Charlie of Minto, Alaska. After some backlash, including claims that there was "insufficient evidence documenting usage of this name" (Holton 2015), in 2013 – some 19 years after Chief John's presentation, the U.S. Board of Geographic Names formally recognized Troth Yeddha' as an official place name.

"Emphasizing the North and Its Diverse Peoples": University of Alaska Governance and Public Discourse

> Mission Statement: The University of Alaska inspires learning, and advances and disseminates knowledge through teaching, research, and public service, emphasizing the North and its diverse peoples.

The University of Alaska began in 1917 as a small land grant college – originally the Alaska Agricultural College and School of Mines. The college later became the University of Alaska Fairbanks (UAF), one of the three main campuses that comprise the University of Alaska system. Public discourse available on UAF's website on the history of the college includes a linear discussion of gold discoveries, the federal Agricultural Experiment Station program, World War II, and formation of various institutes and schools. However, there is no information about Troth Yeddha' in this history. UAF's website includes links to the *Troth Yeddha' Legacy* and there are several informational links available through the Alaska Native Language Center webpage and on the Rural Student Services site. However, there are no links to this information from UAF main webpages – including the "about UAF" link referenced above. There is limited evidence from publicly available information as to the University of Alaska's mission and commitment to its origins of place, the diversity of Alaska Native cultures within the State, nor specifics as to how Alaska Natives and other diverse peoples are being served through higher education.

The University of Alaska Fairbanks' formal governance includes a chancellor who functions as the chief executive officer for the main institution and its affiliated rural campuses; this structure also includes senior level executive positions including vice chancellors, and a provost who oversees academic accreditation. Governance at the college and program levels includes deans and directors who report to the senior positions referenced above. To date, only two Alaska Natives have served at UAF's executive governance level. In 2001, the late Bernice Joseph was appointed executive dean of the College of Rural Alaska (CRA). During her time as executive dean, Ms. Joseph advocated for an Alaska Native position within the senior executive governance level, and in 2006 was appointed to the newly created position – "vice chancellor for rural, community, and Alaska Native education"; she held this position until her retirement in 2013. In 2014, Evon Peter (Gwich'in) was appointed to this vice chancellor post. In this position, Peter oversees UAF's College of Rural and Community Development (CRCD), one of the seven schools and colleges that are part of the University of Alaska Fairbanks. In addition to its Fairbanks-based offices, CRCD includes a number of community campuses, serving 160 communities statewide. The University of Alaska (UA) Board of Regents (BOR) governs the system through setting policy for the statewide campus system. BOR minutes by topic and a list of regents dating back to 1917, are easily located using a Google search, and publicly available via the UA Statewide webpage. Appointments to the University of Alaska's Board of Trustees (later the Board of Regents) by then territorial governors began in 1917 (Alaska became a state in 1959). The first Alaska Native regent – Tlingit Sam Kito, Jr. from Petersburg (#66) – was appointed in 1975 with the first Alaska Native woman regent – Koyukon Mary Jane Fate from Rampart (#107) appointed in 1993. Out of 155 appointments through 2015, 13 (including one student regent) have been Alaska Native – ten men, and three women. The State of Alaska governor is tasked with appointing regents to fill an 11-member board, followed by official confirmation by the Alaska Legislature. Currently, there are three Alaska Natives serving on the UA BOR – all with strong affiliations with ANCSA corporations or major tribal consortia.

The University of Alaska (UA) Statewide office in Fairbanks houses the president who administers the statewide system, serves as the official spokesperson for the university, and reports to the Board of Regents as an executive officer to the board. Chancellors (chief executive officers), provosts (chief academic officers), and vice presidents provide guidance on statewide cross-institutional issues. Faculty, staff, student, and alumni representatives serve on the UA Statewide System Governance Council 2014 as part of a shared governance structure.

In addition to University of Alaska's internal administrative and advisory structures, the State of Alaska serves as part of the larger governance structure, appropriating funding to the UA system annually. Economic concerns often drive legislative priorities and budget appropriations, serving to support, challenge, and/or constrain higher education governance and decision-making in any given year.

To date, only one Alaska Native has served at the University of Alaska Statewide executive level. In 1976, the late Elaine Ramos (Tlingit) was appointed vice president of Rural Educational Affairs (REA), charged with overseeing four rural community colleges and the Alaska Native Language Center (Jennings 1994, p. 123). Alaska Native legislators and the Alaska Federation of Natives

(AFN), a statewide consortium of the 229 federally-recognized Alaska Native tribes, were particularly concerned with the lack of support for rural students. The establishment of REA was largely due to the efforts of Alaska Native legislators, Regent Sam Kito, Jr. and AFN. Ramos' position was controversial as the institution did not view her as qualified to serve without a PhD (despite her previous administrative experience), and university governance questioned the need for REA. This resulted in Ramos' reassignment just months later in that year (Jennings 1994, pp. 128–129). The late Ms. Ramos' appointment to this level, as a "first and only" example is not part of the institution's public history on its website. Considering the University of Alaska's commitments to Alaska Native peoples and diversity, this information is significant to the University of Alaska's public discourse.

We discuss additional examples of institutional priorities and public discourse in the following sections, including accreditation documents, BOR minutes documenting the official naming of Troth Yeddha' Park on the UAF campus, and student activism resulting in programs and initiatives supporting Alaska Native students.

Service to Rural and Alaska Native Peoples: Institutional Priorities

The University of Alaska Fairbanks has a significant percentage of Alaska Native students – 20.1% as of Fall 2016 – and publicly stated responsibilities to Alaska Native peoples. Core themes within UAF's Strategic Plan (2014) include a commitment to "incorporate traditional and local knowledge more fully in appropriate curricula at every level from college preparation to graduate programs" (p. 3) and "double the number of Alaska Native graduate students" (p. 5). UAF's Academic Plan (2007) highlights the institution's pledge to provide "service to rural and Alaska Native peoples…as central to the strategic direction of UAF" (p. 1); as well as fostering "the success of Alaska Native students and research concerning Alaska Native peoples, including documentation and preservation of languages and culture" (p. 2).

University of Alaska's "Shaping Alaska's Future" (SAF) published in 2014 is part of a strategic directions initiative designed to shape policy at each of the major administrative units and affiliated rural campuses. Key statements referencing Alaska Native peoples, cultures, languages, and knowledge include:

- UA recruitment, retention and graduation rates are low, especially for disadvantaged and minority populations and for Alaska Natives. Effect: UA graduates reflect the diversity of Alaska (p. 7).
- Some Alaska Native languages and cultural traditions are endangered. Many communities do not have sufficient resources to safeguard and nurture culture and the arts, so UA plays a vital role in preserving and advancing this knowledge and these traditions. Effect: UA is a major center of culture and the arts in Alaska and is a center of excellence for Alaska Native and indigenous research and scholarship (p. 13).
- Circumpolar communities are experiencing rapid social and economic transformation…these communities need research-based and indigenous knowledge in

order to adapt. UA has the expertise to assist these communities, and to do so must effectively communicate with those who need it. Effect: Alaskans and their communities use research-based information, enriched by traditional knowledge, to successfully adapt to change (p. 13).

There are a number of problematic orientations in the SAF document: these include deficit assumptions regarding Alaska Native people's abilities to maintain their cultures and languages, and the overtly hierarchical separation of research-based and Indigenous knowledge. Engagement of research "enriched by traditional knowledge" also poses challenges in terms of Indigenous ownership of cultural and intellectual property.

Fulfilling commitments articulated in mission, vision, and strategic planning documents continues to be a decolonization challenge in the absence of adequate numbers of Indigenous peoples in governance positions who can shape recruitment, teaching, research, and service policies, with and for Alaska Native communities. As stated previously, the University of Alaska Fairbanks has a significant number of Alaska Native students and this information is easily accessible on UAF's website. However, information on the institution's faculty or staff ethnic diversity is not readily available. Indigenous faculty have never exceeded 5% of total faculty numbers; and faculty numbers are ambiguous since there are several different categories of faculty, including permanent (tenured) faculty, those eligible for a permanent position (tenure-track), and term/temporary employees. Administrative staff contribute in major ways to university governance through participation on staff councils at each MAU, and have significant impacts on student experiences; these impacts include course advising, registration services, and financial aid.

In the next section, we return to the sacred landscape, Troth Yeddha', re-examining the UA Board of Regents' public discourse centering on Alaska Native peoples.

A Cultural Centering Point: Troth Yeddha' Park

In 2008, the University of Alaska Board of Regents (BOR) approved the official naming of Troth Yeddha' Park – located on UAF's West Ridge. BOR minutes describe the park as follows:

> A permanent and culturally expressive place that honors Alaska Native heritage and offers a cultural centering point for all Alaska Native students, staff and faculty on the UAF campus...Troth Yeddha' Park dedicates open space on the UAF campus to Alaska Native history and culture and confirms the University's commitment to incorporating indigenous culture into higher education while also addressing their aspiration to develop a model of how cultural diversity strengthens a university and society. (University of Alaska Board of Regents Official Minutes 2008, p. 13–14)

Through establishing an official park, UAF governance committed to the following goals:

> An increase in Alaska Native student retention and graduation rates; an increase in Alaska Native student perception of cultural sensitivity and awareness at UAF; an increase in knowledge about Alaska Native cultures and history among UAF students, faculty and staff; and, increased preparation among Alaska Native students for entry into both the rural and urban Alaskan workforce. (p. 15)

The Troth Yeddha' Park naming echoes objectives and outcomes in UAF's current strategic and academic plans regarding diversity, and Alaska Native intellectual spaces and places. Individuals and organizations within and outside the UAF governance structure contributed to the Troth Yeddha' reclamation discourse, including the Chancellor's Advisory Committee on Native Education (discussed in a subsequent section) and Doyon, Limited (an ANCSA corporation). As we continued our investigation into institutional priorities and public discourse, we find an ongoing trend of Alaska Native engagement in UAF governance positions, in collaboration with external advocates and allies from corporate, nonprofit, and tribal organizations as noted by Jennings (2004, 1994).

Student Discourse: Support, Advocacy, and Activism

In researching the mission of serving Native students at UAF, Olga Skinner notes a broad deficit discourse regarding Alaska Natives – what she characterizes as an "aversion to serving Alaska Native students historically." Jennings (1994) argues that "the University of Alaska made educational provisions for rural residents [the majority of whom were Alaska Native] only after the intervention of Alaska Native leadership" (p. 92), and elements of this aversion are present in Jennings interview data. However, Jennings overlooks student voice in several initiatives, including the formation of Student Orientation Services.

In 1969, 28 UAF Alaska Native students became major activists in governance while advocating for rural support. The Alaska State Legislature passed House Concurrent Resolution No. 56, which required that the university offer services to support rural students – most of whom are Alaska Native. Student Orientation Services was initially funded by oil companies and employed one counselor and a half-time secretary. In 1985, the name was changed to Rural Student Services (RSS) in response to university restructuring, as well as concern in the Native community that the acronym SOS reinforced deficit assumptions and discourse surrounding Alaska Native students.

In terms of public discourse, RSS recognizes the students involved in the formation of SOS on their website. This activist legacy resulted in a department within the College of Rural and Community Development that serves over 550 students mentored by four academic advisors. RSS offers comprehensive, holistic, student-centered advising to a wide range of prospective and current undergraduate students. Advisors – several of whom are Alaska Native – are informed on Alaska Native peoples and cultures statewide, and carefully attend to students' academic, cultural, and social development, including assisting with the transition from rural sites to Fairbanks, navigating through university governance/bureaucratic systems, and educating on the multiple support systems available to UAF students. In terms of UAF's mission and governance priorities, however, service to rural and Alaska Native peoples, as part of desired Indigenous outcomes (Moreton-Robinson et al. 2011), may be limited due to limited advising staff serving a large rural student body.

Rural Student Services sponsors several Alaska Native student organizations, many of which began as a result of student discourse and advocacy. One such organization is the Alaska Native Education Student Association, which began as a result of a grading controversy described later in this chapter. Other organizations arose out of student interest in Alaska Native dance, the arts, and native games. Some organizations that began out of student interest for science, technology, engineering and mathematics (STEM) and business, have led to connections to larger national and international organizations. In the late 1980s, Alaska Native students interested in the science, technology, engineering and mathematics (STEM) fields began organizing and formally chartered a chapter of the American Indian Science & Engineering Society (AISES) in 1989.

In addressing our earlier questions around institutional priorities and Indigenous governance, much of the research on higher education in Alaska overlooks student governance and activism in initiating and shaping institutional priorities. In the next section, we discuss the formation of the Chancellor's Advisory Committee on Native Education – also initiated through student discourse and activism.

Institutional Practices and Diversity: The Chancellor's Advisory Committee on Native Education

> Mission statement: The Chancellor's Advisory Committee on Native Education [CACNE] shall serve as an advocacy body for the Alaska Native body at the University of Alaska Fairbanks. The committee shall provide guidance and advice to the Chancellor on Native issues and in the planning, monitoring and improvement of educational opportunities at the University of Alaska Fairbanks for Alaska Native students. The body will meet on a regular basis throughout the school year to discuss and make recommendations on issues and problems that affect Alaska Native education.

CACNE was initiated in 1992 by UAF's Alaska Native student body and faculty, in response to disruptive, deficit, and damaging statewide discourse surrounding a faculty member's public allegations of preferential grading standards for Alaska Native students. Perry Gilmore, David Smith and Yup'ik scholar *Apacuar* Larry Kairaiuak (Gilmore et al. 2004) examined this grading controversy in an effort to "raise the level of discourse from one about individuals, specific programs, and groups to one which focuses on a critical examination of institutional practices that consciously and unconsciously undermine diversity and nurture white privilege" (p. 273). The controversy made newspaper headlines statewide over a seven-month period in 1991 and 1992, with students and members of Alaska Native community advocating for a serious inquiry and resolution of the allegation. For Alaska Native students, "grades, diplomas, and academic successes [continue to be]...valued personal accomplishments owned and celebrated by...their extended families and communities" (Gilmore et al. 2004, p. 278).

The UAF chancellor eventually acknowledged that "students, specifically including Native students, earn the grades and credentials they receive...The controversy was unfortunate, and on behalf of the University of Alaska, I apologize to the Native students for any discomfort they may have felt" (Gilmore et al. 2004, p. 276). Gilmore et al. recognize that there have been many changes in the institution's governance structure since 1992 resulting in positive initiatives for Alaska Native students however advocate vigilance "in locating, identifying, and resisting institutional policies and practices that may on the surface look neutral but are actually organized around hierarchical race politics" (p. 280). With the assistance of CACNE and other advocates in Alaska Native higher education, University of Alaska governance has since more publicly committed to Alaska Native students and communities in its mission, vision, and strategic discourses.

CACNE membership includes UAF faculty, students, and Fairbanks community members including community representatives from the Fairbanks Native Association, Tanana Chiefs Conference, and the Fairbanks school district's Alaska Native Education Program Coordinator. CACNE's mission statement and advocacy role are publicly acknowledged on the chancellor's website. As part of the chancellor's governance and advisory structure, the committee meets monthly to discuss issues concerning students, faculty/staff, programmatic, and budget challenges.

In 2015, CACNE mission statement and by-laws were re-examined by the committee, and Beth Leonard noted weaknesses in the current discourse, specifically the section stating the committee "shall provide guidance and advice to the Chancellor on Native issues..." In an email to the committee she asked if the wording might contain a more definitive statement, for example, "the Chancellor will critically attend to the recommendations of CACNE in recognition of the committee members' significant role as advocates and allies in Alaska Native student recruitment, retention and mentoring" (B. Leonard, personal communication, 25 Sep 2015). Revisions to the mission statement and by-laws have yet to be finalized by the committee and current chancellor, and it is unclear as to whether the chancellor may be amenable to a self-determination discourse that affords the committee more power and influence. However, as referenced in the previous discussion of Troth Yeddha' Park, CACNE members are often affiliated with larger power structures, and continue to influence university discourse and governance on multiple levels.

Native Ways of Knowing, Indigenous Knowledges, and Governance in Higher Education

In addressing our question around institutional priorities and Alaska Native peoples, and considering the Moreton-Robinson et al. (2011) criteria around embedding IK in strategies, programs, and objectives (p. 5), in this section, we examine the origins of UAF programs teaching about, with, and/or for Alaska Native peoples.

Alaska Natives have long advocated for authentic programs and coursework, prioritizing these initiatives during and after passage of the 1971 Alaska Native Claims Settlement Act (Jennings 1994, p. 94). In 1970, responding to academic interest in minority and ethnic groups, a unit on Alaska Native history was included in the Seminar in Northern Studies course and formal programming began that year under the first Alaska Native Studies director – the late Tlingit scholar Walter Soboleff who directed the program until 1974. Another Tlingit scholar, Dennis Demmert, continued development of the program. In 1981, the Alaska Native Studies degree was established under Director Michael Gaffney and housed in the College of Liberal Arts.

A broader focus on Native Ways of Knowing/Indigenous Knowledges began in the 1990s, fueled in part by the late Yup'ik scholar *Angayuqaq* Oscar Kawagley, including publication of "A Yupiaq worldview: A pathway to ecology and spirit" (Kawagley 1995). Evolving from a number of earlier projects by Indigenous scholars/educators, and heavily influenced by Kawagley's work, the Alaska Rural Systemic Initiative (AKRSI) began in 1995, funded by the National Science and Annenberg foundations through the Alaska Federation of Natives (AFN). This research initiative was designed to integrate Native Ways of Knowing into classroom content with an overarching goal of improving student achievement in Alaska's precollege classroom systems (Barnhardt 2012). One of AKRSI's legacies is the Alaska Native Knowledge Network (2011), a nationally and internationally recognized database of Indigenous curriculum resources housed at UAF's Center for Cross-Cultural Studies. The ANKN database contributes directly to the university's commitments to diversity, traditional knowledge, and Indigenous/Alaska Native cultures.

In terms of higher education governance and research priorities, Barnhardt's and Kawagley's decision to collaborate with AFN, thereby insuring that the research dollars ($15 million total) were controlled by the tribal consortium, was controversial within the UA system. We can speculate that the reasons for this controversy related to control of resources – both monetary and intellectual – including deficit ideologies around Alaska Native peoples' capabilities to govern complex projects.

Also noteworthy is Kawagley's 1995 pilot videoconference course, Native Ways of Knowing housed in both the education and Alaska Native studies programs. Native Ways of Knowing engaged multiple University of Alaska sites and was televised throughout Alaska. Kawagley's approach allowed an open space for the exploration of how Alaska Native values, oral traditions, pedagogy, subsistence practices, and other cultural aspects generate Alaska Natives' unique systems of knowing being and doing, including how these systems were often traumatically impacted by Western education, disease, displacement, forced removal, and other events (Napoleon 1996).

In 2002, graduate coursework – including Indigenous Knowledge Systems and Documenting Indigenous Knowledge – became core courses in the Cross-Cultural Studies (CCS) master's program. Enrollments include students from diverse disciplines, for example, education, rural development, northern studies, anthropology, natural resources management, psychology, and interdisciplinary studies. The

College of Rural and Community Development and Center for Cross-Cultural Studies now house much of the coursework and programs that focus on Alaska Native peoples at the UAF campus. Coursework regularly taught by Alaska Native scholars includes Cultural Knowledge of Alaska Native Elders, Native Ways of Knowing, Native Ways of Healing, and Indigenous Philosophies. Course enrollments illustrate an inter- and transdisciplinary expansion of institutional places and spaces for IK and Alaska Native Ways of Knowing.

Alaska Native Self-Determination: The UAF Indigenous Studies PhD Program

> …Alaska Native faculty members at all Alaska colleges and universities are in chronically short supply…and, whereas, a strong, cohesive and coherent effort is needed to draw university and other private and public resources together…to prepare a cohort of Alaska Native scholar/leaders with the in-depth knowledge and skills to address the special needs of Alaska, and to link those efforts to the educational developments of other indigenous peoples. (Alaska Federation of Natives 2004)

In her discussion of the Alaska Native Scholars Project, Perea (2013) proposes a "tribalography of presence" (p. 5), a counter-discourse challenging "double absence" (p. 3) that continue to shadow Alaska Native and Indigenous peoples. Perea's documentation of the presence of Alaska Native PhDs in academia (building on unpublished work by Ray Barnhardt n.d.) illustrates a continuing underrepresentation of Alaska Native peoples in higher education faculty and governance positions. This challenge has been an active discussion among Alaska Native governance and leadership, many of whom are networked globally with other Indigenous peoples, and are fully aware of the "Māori 500 PhD initiative" (Villegas 2010).

In 2009, the UA Board of Regents approved the Indigenous Studies PhD Program. International and national networking and advocacy were critical to this initiative, in particular the efforts of Māori scholar Graham Smith and Lumbee scholar Bryan Brayboy. As advocates and allies in Alaska Native higher education in the 2000s, Smith and Brayboy met with executive level administrators in the University of Alaska system including the late Vice-Chancellor Bernice Joseph, former School of Education Dean Eric Madsen, and key faculty including Ray Barnhardt who had been promoting Indigenous studies programming at UAF. As globally recognized scholars, Smith and Brayboy utilized critical quantitative methods in presenting their case to former University of Alaska President Mark Hamilton; that is, as of 2007, UAF had succeeded in graduating only four Alaska Native PhDs in the institution's 80+-year history of granting degrees (1970, 1998, 1999, and 2007). We recall their words to President Hamilton were "we think you [the UA system] can do better."

Smith has a strong history of advocacy in Alaska Native education; he was the keynote speaker for the 2003 and 2010 Alaska Federation of Natives conventions, and the inaugural Alaska Native Studies Conference (ANSC) in 2013. Brayboy served as President's Professor of Alaska Native Education from 2007–2012 and is currently University of Arizona Borderlands Professor of Indigenous Education and Justice. He continues in an advocacy role as well, serving as a committee member for Indigenous Studies PhD students and assisting faculty in research and publications. The Alaska Native Studies Council presented Brayboy with an Excellence in Advocacy and Leadership in Indigenous Higher Education award during the 2016 ANSC hosted by the University of Alaska Anchorage.

As a result of Indigenous Studies and Alaska Native programs and faculty who embed Indigenous knowledge in the institution, the university affords students opportunities to authentically engage Alaska Native Knowledge Systems. These programs privilege Alaska Native ways of knowing and assist students in building identities as Indigenous scholars. Through coursework, students explore previous academic experiences – often overwhelmingly Eurocentric – and engage methods that situate Indigenous knowledge in respectful ways.

Indigenous Knowledges and Alaska Native Ways of Knowing are currently embedded in programmatic coursework and some governance structures due to students, faculty, administrators, allies, and advocates who participate and have direct influence on university executive functions. The UAF College of Rural and Community Development currently employs the largest number of Alaska Native faculty in the University of Alaska system and is governed by a Gwich'in Dene' vice chancellor. The University of Alaska Anchorage (UAA) recently hired six Alaska Native faculty in diverse fields including engineering, biology, medical education, and Alaska Native Studies, and appointed Haida scholar Jeane *Táaw Xíwaa* Breinig as interim associate vice chancellor for Alaska Natives and diversity. The University of Alaska Southeast in Juneau includes three Alaska Native faculty and staff as well as Tlingit scholar Joe Nelson who serves as vice chancellor of enrollment management and student affairs. Institutional academic and strategic plans reflect an improvement in governance and cultural competence discourses from previous decades. However, Alaska Native faculty numbers remain at less than 5% statewide, and questions remain as to if and how the University of Alaska authentically engages IK and Alaska Native Ways of Knowing *outside* of Alaska Native and Indigenous studies programs.

The Alaska Native Studies Council

The Alaska Native Studies Council began as a statewide effort among Alaska Native faculty at each of the University of Alaska campuses. As Alaska Native faculty are underrepresented, the purpose of the Council was to provide support for Alaska Native programs statewide, and assist with efforts to transform K-12 and higher education to better serve Alaska Native students. As an active member, Tlingit scholar and University of Alaska Southeast (UAS) faculty Lance *X'hunei* Twitchell initiated discussions around organization of the Alaska Native Studies Conference in 2012. In 2013, the first conference, organized and governed by University of Alaska faculty including Maria *Shaa Tláa* Williams (Tlingit), Jeane *Táaw Xíwaa* Breinig

(Haida), and Sharon *Chilux* Lind (Aleut), was an international event that drew more than 300 attendees, including executive level leadership. Former University of Alaska Statewide President Patrick Gamble issued the following statement for the conference proceedings:

> The University of Alaska takes great pride in having supported another important milestone in our efforts to uphold the institutional responsibility we owe to the Native citizens of Alaska...The University of Alaska is endowed with a premier cadre of brilliant Indigenous scholars. Now they have organized themselves into a forceful academic voice for promoting the university's many and varied Native Alaskan interests and I expect to see all three major administrative units in the University of Alaska system derive significant overall mission benefits...I fully support their initiative. (Gamble 2014, pp. xi–xii)

In his statement, President Gamble reiterates the general discourse around institutional responsibilities to Native peoples, however also initiates a new discourse that publicly acknowledges the contributions of Alaska Native and Indigenous scholars to the University of Alaska's mission.

Engaging the Four "Rs": Recommendations for Governance and Research

American Indians and Alaska Natives are among the least studied groups within higher education research. Much of the existing research is situated within a positivist paradigm that utilizes the values of middle-class white men and often engages a linear, fragmented view of development (Evans et al. 2010). Significant to the UA's responsibilities to Alaska Natives and diversity discourse is authentic inquiry into the college experiences of Indigenous students, utilizing decolonizing and humanizing methodologies (Paris and Winn 2014) to document student voices and perspectives (Brayboy et al. 2012; Shotton et al. 2013). This approach is endorsed by other Indigenous and non-Indigenous researchers in a range of past scholarly literature, including Cree scholar Verna Kirkness and Ray Barnhardt (Kirkness and Barnhardt 2001) who examined higher education trends in the United States and Canada. Barnhardt and Kirkness found deficit discourses and continuing assimilative policies toward Native students; their recommendations to counter attrition and retention include engagement of the four Rs – respect, relevance, reciprocity, and responsibility. Citing Ron Scollon's (1981) research on Alaska Native students, the authors endorse authentic institutional responsiveness to Alaska Native needs, rather than orientations toward invulnerability that often mark unresponsiveness; this stance resonates in the following quote from Garland and McClellan (2013):

> ...unless the majority of members in an organization understand the unique structural and organizational barriers to full organizational participation by *all* its members, especially those from historically small and marginalized populations, the organization will never achieve the social justice, equity and inclusive ethos it envisions. (p. 159)

Indigenous peoples' experiences in higher education are conceptualized in myriad ways including walking in two worlds (a metaphor challenged by Henze and Vanett 1993), cultural discontinuity (Ortiz and HeavyRunner 2003), biculturalism/bicultural efficacy (LaFramboise et al. 1993), and transculturation (Huffman 2001). Researchers have examined how Indigenous peoples successfully maintain their identities while navigating Western systems, in contrast to those anchored in Indigenous identity but estranged from Western higher education. Aikenhead and Jegede (1999) and other scholars advocate a process of culture-brokering, to facilitate "border crossings...for Aboriginal students by acknowledging students' personal preconceptions and Aboriginal worldviews that have a purpose in, or connection to, students' everyday culture" (p. 6).

Alaska Native leaders continue to advocate for Alaska Native cultures and concerns in higher education. In her keynote speech to the 2005 Alaska Federation of Natives, the late Vice Chancellor Bernice Joseph (2010) described programmatic initiatives that incorporate Indigenous knowledge. She also highlighted examples of Alaska Native science's contributions to Western knowledge, referencing the Inupiat knowledge of bowhead whale populations that positively influenced subsistence policy changes in the 1970s and 1980s (p. 123). Joseph also emphasized the continuing work ahead including the need to grow our own policymakers and collaborative efforts necessary "to keep rural Alaska a viable place to live "(p. 124).

In the following section, we examine an Indigenous governance paradigm that extends previous conceptualizations and paradigms utilizing self-determination (Jones-Sparck 2010, p. 325) and sovereignty discourses; connecting Indigenous governance with IK, human development, identity, and sacred landscapes.

Working to Achieve Awareness: Self-Determination, Sovereignty, and Governance

A common thread that connects Alaska Native cultures is the complex knowledge required to survive and thrive is all of Alaska's diverse landscapes. Though times have changed significantly since contact with European peoples, education remains a priority for Alaska Natives, and Indigenous peoples worldwide look to higher education to assist with self-determination, sovereignty, and cultural survival. Education, however, remains a continuing "site of struggle" (Villegas et al. 2008, pp. 7–8) for Alaska Native peoples as they seek self-determination and sovereignty through collaboration and official roles in higher education governance.

Bryan Brayboy, Amy Fann, Angelina Castagno, and Jessica Solyom (Brayboy et al. 2012) describe sovereignty as "the inherent right of tribal nations to direct their futures and engage the world in ways that are meaningful to them"; while self-determination is defined as the "engagement" or "operationalization" of sovereignty (p. 17). In earlier sections, we referenced the shaping of physical landscapes and intellectual thought worlds juxtaposed with the concept of education as a sacred learning landscape and a cultural centering point (UA Board of Regents 2008). In this section, we propose that our institution recenter Indigenous landscapes and intellectual thought worlds through engaging Alaska Native theories of human development, identity, and place in higher education governance.

Chief Peter John's story of Troth Yeddha' honors Dene' oral traditions and draws attention to the ways in which governance and pedagogy are connected to place, identity through the practice of traditional activities. Worldviews connecting place, identity, knowledge, and wisdom are shared among the diverse Alaska Native cultures, as well as among many Indigenous groups globally. In the introduction of "Being and Place among the Tlingit," fisherman Gabriel George states, "these lands are vital not only to our subsistence, but also to our sense of being as Tlingit people" (Thornton 2008, p. 3). From Indigenous perspectives, land, rather than being viewed as a commodity by western systems, is instead seen as sentient, and bearer of knowledge, wisdom, and identity (see Basso 1996 for additional discussion). Additionally, *T'akteintaan* Elder Ken Grant states, *"Lyee sakoowoo saawx' ch'a tleix ee jeedax goox la haashee koosteeyi,"* "if you don't know the names [of places], your Tlingit way of life will drift away forever" (Thornton 2008, p. 73). These quotes align with Chief John's narrative regarding the importance of Troth Yeddha' as a meeting place where "the grandfathers used to come to talk and give advice to one another…a place where good thinking a working together would happen." Chief John's statements serve to reaffirm Indigenous knowledges regarding connections among place, identity, pedagogy, and governance.

Alaska Native cultures view the world as interconnected; these connections include the spiritual world[s], the physical landscapes, and human behavior. Individual human actions can affect human and nonhuman beings and processes in the environment. The concept of interconnection is present in the Yup'ik base term, *ella-*. Yup'ik scholars *Angayuqaq* Oscar Kawagley (1995, p. 14) and *Arevgaq* Theresa John (2009, pp. 60–61) provide multiple contextual definitions for *"Ella-,"* including "awareness," "consciousness," "weather," "atmosphere," "sky," "world," and "creative force." These terms are related to specific processes, specifically, *ellangellemni*, that is, "when I became aware" and *ellangcarturtua* – "I am working to achieve awareness."

Yup'ik pedagogy includes *qanruyuutet*, "advice," and *qulirat* and *qanemcit*, "stories." Through these methods, *Arevgaq* Theresa John (2009) describes the great power of the mind, the care that individuals need to give their minds, and how to achieve awareness. *Yuuyaraq* – "the way of the human being" – is the proper use of the mind, and path toward achieving balance in surroundings and life. Yup'ik scholar Harold Napoleon (1991) describes *yuuyaraq* as:

> The correct way of thinking and speaking about all living things, especially the great sea and land mammals on which the Yup'ik relied for food, clothing, shelter, tools, kayaks, and other essentials. ... *Yuuyaraq* prescribed the correct method of hunting and fishing and the correct way of handling all fish and game caught by the hunter in order to honor and appease their spirits and maintain a harmonious relationship with them. (p. 5)

Kawagley's tetrahedron (Kawagley 1995, p. 15) shows the relationship of the human realm, the spiritual realm, and the natural realm and the connection to the universe and the circle of life. This diagram also includes *self, family, and mindfulness* illustrating connections to the concept of "awareness" or "consciousness."

Considering institutional discourse that prioritizes diversity, and responsibilities to Alaska Native peoples, cultures, and knowledges, Alaska Native philosophies examining way[s] of the human being and processes of achieving critical awareness have profound implications for Indigenous governance in higher education. A conscientization (Freire 2002) of Indigenous origins of place woven together with pedagogy and identity is underrepresented in University of Alaska's governance systems and course offerings. Alaska Native students pursuing higher education at the University of Alaska continue to encounter barriers as they seek to maintain their origins of place while expanding their knowledge of Western systems. These barriers manifest in myriad ways including lower retention and graduation rates for Alaska Natives than other ethnic groups – although, that being said, student tracking is often restricted to a 6-year timeline that constrains definitions of success for many students who may only have part-time/partial access to higher education.

Conclusion and Future Directions

In this essay, we discuss institutional discourse as related to Indigenous governance practices at the University of Alaska. Our examples highlight institutional responsibilities to Alaska Native peoples, including increased recruitment, retention, and mentoring of Alaska Native students, incorporation of Indigenous culture and knowledge into higher education, and continued documentation and preservation of Alaska Native languages. Our analysis responds to the question of how Indigenous governance is conceptualized and engaged in a Western institution with limited Indigenous representation at the executive, faculty and staff, levels. We apply the Moreton-Robinson et al. (2011) framework in assessing participation and direct influence on university executive functions as well as how Indigenous outcomes are met through embedding Indigenous knowledge within the university's operations. Utilizing this framework, we find that Indigenous participation, places, and intellectual spaces exist within University of Alaska governance systems. Broad statewide, national, and international relationships/networks assist in advocacy efforts that influence institutional priorities and responsibilities toward Alaska Native peoples. Alaska Native seats at the governance table have been building slowly since Alaska Native coursework and programming began in the 1970s.

Brayboy et al. (2014) argue that the unique relationship of tribal nations with the United States extends to institutions of higher education, and that "these relationships are centered on sovereignty and self-determination" (p. 579). Indigenous governance in the University of Alaska system, although present, is constrained by the underrepresentation of Alaska Native faculty, executive and administrative staff, and research oversight positions. And this underrepresentation may further impede Indigenous sovereignty and self-determination for Alaska Native nations and communities. Alaska Native students often pursue higher education for the purposes of community betterment, and Alaska Native nations trust in the University of Alaska system to deliver authentic and effective programming in all fields of study, including Alaska Native and Indigenous studies. The significance of this unique relationship includes the recognition and realization of the tribal nations' desired outcomes, which parallels student goals of community betterment. Higher education is, however, of "little use" if these students are unable to gain "firsthand knowledge and understanding of Native institutions, communities and values" (Brayboy et al. 2014 p. 590). Andersen et al. (2008) emphasize that institutions should view Indigenous higher education as "core university business and not just the responsibility of the Indigenous centres" (p. 4) including placement of Indigenous faculty throughout the institution. Chippewa scholar Duane Champagne (2015) further distinguishes Indigenous studies as "a paradigm distinct from current intellectual disciplines and ethnic studies" adding that "present-day nation-state political theory and institutional capabilities" are incapable of addressing Indigenous peoples' goals of "civil rights...self-government and territory [stewardship]" (p. 106). These multilayered challenges necessitate continued activism and vigilance (Gilmore et al. 2004) as Alaska Natives work toward equitable representation and governance in higher education.

Supporting Jones-Sparck's (2010) call for Alaska Native self-determination and sovereignty – an authentic Indigenous governance at the University of Alaska requires further engagement with the United Nations Declaration on the Rights of Indigenous Peoples (UNDRIP 2008) regarding education, land, and cultural and intellectual property rights. Article 14 calls for local Indigenous control of education and pedagogy "...in a manner appropriate to their cultural methods of teaching and learning" (p. 7). Indigenous control of higher education continues to be challenging. However, collaborative and shared governance between Western institutions and Indigenous communities is progressing with Alaska Native representation on the Board of Regents and in executive level positions. Considering the institution's goals of engaging Indigenous and local knowledges, and supporting language and cultural documentation, attention to UNDRIP Article 11 (p. 6) that addresses traditional and cultural property rights is needed.

Finally, Troth Yeddha' and the traditional names of campus sites as significant origins of place and Indigenous spiritual sites (UNDRIP Article 25, p. 10) – with long histories of occupation and use (UNDRIP Article 26, p. 10) by Alaska's Indigenous peoples – play critical roles in the institution's history and contemporary contexts as related to discourses around service to Alaska Native peoples. Building on these and higher education recommendations from Indigenous scholars referenced in this chapter, recommendations for Alaska Native higher education include access to authentic Indigenous programming and coursework that reinforces connections to culture, knowledge, and place. Access to Indigenous programming should cut across University of Alaska programs, not be limited to the College of Rural and Community Development, Alaska Native Studies or the Indigenous Studies PhD programs. In light of the history of colonization in Alaska and the Americas, and broad recommendations of UNDRIP, the entire student body would benefit from an exploration of Alaska Native worldviews and intellectual thought worlds; including the recentering of Troth Yeddha' and other Indigenous spaces occupied by the University of Alaska Anchorage and the University of Alaska Southeast. Executive administrators, faculty, and staff also need ongoing, critical professional development in order to implement policy in academic and strategic planning documents related to Alaska Native knowledges, cultures, and student access and success.

In this case study, we highlight evidence of Alaska Native governance at the University of Alaska, and broad institutional commitments to recruiting, retaining, and mentoring Alaska Native students and engaging Indigenous Knowledges. As well, we provide specific recommendations for accomplishing institutional goals. We also attend to more broadly to global recommendations around reshaping assimilationist models, for example, Champagne's (2015) recommendations around institutional engagement of "the goals, world views and policy positions of indigenous peoples" (p. 105). In terms of student outcomes, Andersen et al. (2008) maintain that Indigenous "students should emerge from higher education with a stronger sense of their human worth, their specific identity along with their ability to achieve" (p. 4). Re-envisioning and reshaping institutional discourses and governance in higher education is an ongoing challenge; however, many within the UA system recognize the power of Alaska Native communities, especially the influence of the business community, and the potential for constructive collaboration with Alaska Native peoples. With global networking and support systems among Indigenous groups, and strong advocacy and alliances among Alaska Natives statewide, we believe that Alaska Native peoples will continue to transform discourses and governance practices in higher education – actively "walk[in] in their own world" and "making the important decisions" (Jones-Sparck 2010, p. 325).

References

Aikenhead GS, Jegede OJ (1999) Cross-cultural science education: a cognitive explanation of a cultural phenomenon. J Res Sci Teach 36(2):269–287

Alaska Federation of Natives (2004) 2004 Annual Convention: Resolution 04–25

Alaska Native Knowledge Network (2011) http://ankn.uaf.edu. Accessed 14 March 2017

Alaska Native Language Center (n.d.) http://guides.libraries.psu.edu/apaquickguide/intext Accessed 14 March 2017

Alaska Native Language Center: The name Troth Yeddha' (n.d.) https://www.uaf.edu/anlc/troth/ Accessed 16 June 2016

Andersen C, Bunda T, Walter M (2008) Indigenous higher education: the role of universities in releasing the potential. The Australian Journal of Indigenous Education 37:1–8

Barnhardt R (2012) Indigenous education renewal in Alaska. NABE Perspectives (July–August). http://www2.nau.edu/~jar/NABE/BarnhardtCol.pdf. Accessed 28 June 2016

Barnhardt R (n.d.) Rural education development in Alaska: 1970–1988. Unpublished timeline

Barnhardt R, Kawagley O (eds) (2010) Alaska native education: views from within. Alaska Native Knowledge Network, Fairbanks

Barnhardt R, Kawagley O (eds) (2011) Sharing our pathways: native perspectives on education in Alaska. Alaska Native Knowledge Network, Fairbanks

Basso K (1996) Wisdom sits in places: landscape and language among the western apache. University of New Mexico Press, Albuquerque

Battiste M (2013) Decolonizing education: nourishing the learning spirit. Purich Publishing Limited, Saskatoon

Brayboy B (2005) Toward a tribal critical race theory in education. Urban Review 37(5):425–446

Brayboy BMJ, Fann AJ, Castagno AE, Solyom JA (2012) Postsecondary education for American Indian and Alaska natives: higher education for nation building and self-determination. Jossey-Bass, San Francisco

Brayboy BMJ, Castagno AE, Solyom JA (2014) Looking into the hearts of native peoples: nation building as an institutional orientation for graduate education. Am J Educ 120(4):575–596

Brower P (2016) Tumitchiat: iñuqqaat aullarrisiatun iḷisaġviit – A new pathway: Indigenous leadership in higher education. Dissertation, University of Alaska Fairbanks

Brown T (ed) (2012) Native cultures in Alaska: looking forward, looking back. Alaska Northwest Books, Portland

Champagne DW (2015) Indigenous higher education. In: Jacob WJ, Cheng SY, Porter MK (eds) Indigenous education: language, culture, identity. Springer, New York, pp 99–108

Denzin NK, Lincoln YS, Smith LT (eds) (2000) Handbook of critical and indigenous methodologies. UBC Press, Vancouver

Evans NJ, Forney DS, Guido FM, Patton LD, Renn KA (2010) Student development in college: theory, research, and practice. Wiley, San Francisco

Freire P (2002) Pedagogy of the oppressed. Continuum, New York

Gamble P (2014) Statement from University of Alaska leaders. In: Leonard B, Breinig J, Carpluk L, Lind S, Williams M (eds) Transforming the university: Alaska native studies in the 21st century. Two Harbors Press, Minneapolis, pp xi–xii

Garcia J, Shirley V (2012) Performing decolonization: lessons learned from indigenous youth, teachers and leaders' engagement with critical indigenous pedagogy. J Curric Theor 28(2):76–91

Garland JL, McClellan GS (2013) Best practices for national organizations to support the native experience in higher education. In: Shotton HJ, Lowe SC, Waterman SJ (eds) Beyond the asterisk: understanding native students in higher education. Stylus, Sterling, pp 151–164

Gilmore P, Smith DM, Kairaiuak AP (2004) Resisting diversity: an Alaskan case of institutional struggle. In: Fine ME, Weis LE, Powell LC (eds) Off white: readings on race, power, and society. Taylor & Francis/Routledge, Florence, pp 273–283

Henze RC, Vanett L (1993) To walk in two worlds: or more? Challenging a common metaphor of native education. Anthropol Educ Q 24(2):116–134

Holton G (2015) More pushback against Native names. Talking Alaska: Reflections on the Native languages of Alaska. http://talkingalaska.blogspot.com/2015/11/more-pushback-against-native-names.html?view=classic. Accessed 31 May 2016

Howe LA (1999) Tribalography: the power of native stories. J Dramat Theory Crit 14(1):117–125

Huffman T (2001) Resistance theory and the transculturation hypothesis as explanations of college attrition and persistence among culturally traditional American Indian students. J Am Indian Educ 40(3):1–23

Jacquot L (1974) Alaska Natives and higher education, 1960–1972: A descriptive study. Alaska Native Human Resources Development Program, University of Alaska

Jennings M (1994) One university, two universes: The emergence of Alaska Native political leadership and the provision of higher education, 1972–85. Dissertation, University of British Columbia

Jennings M (2004) Alaska native political leadership and higher education: one university, two universes. AltaMira Press, Lanham

John TA (2009) Nutemllarput, our very own: a Yup'ik epistemology. Can J Nativ Educ 32(1):57–72. 129

Jones-Sparck L (2010) Effects of modernization on the Cup'ik of Alaska. In: Barnhardt R, Kawagley AO (eds) Alaska native education: views from within. Alaska Native Knowledge Network, Fairbanks, pp 317–331

Joseph B (2010) Following the lights: native ways of knowing. In: Barnhardt R, Kawagley AO (eds) Alaska native education: views from within. Alaska Native Knowledge Network, Fairbanks, pp 119–124

Kawagley AO (1993) A Yupiaq world view: Implications for cultural, educational, and technological adaptation in a contemporary world. Dissertation, University of British Columbia

Kawagley AO (1995) A Yupiaq worldview: a pathway to ecology and spirit. Waveland Press, Inc., Long Grove

Kirkness VJ, Barnhardt R (2001) First nations and higher education: the four Rs – respect, relevance, reciprocity, responsibility. In: Hayoe R, Pan J (eds) Knowledge across cultures: a contribution to dialogue among civilizations. Comparative Education Research Centre, The University of Hong Kong, Hong Kong, pp 1–21

Krauss M, Holton G, Kerr J, West CT (2011) Indigenous peoples and languages of Alaska. Alaska Native Language Center and UAA Institute of Social and Economic Research, Fairbanks/Anchorage. http://www.uafanlc.arsc.edu/data/Online/G961K2010/anlmap.png. Accessed 31 July 2016

LaFramboise T, Coleman HL, Gerton J (1993) Psychological impact of biculturalism: evidence and theory. Psychol Bull 114(3):395–412

Leonard B, Mercier O (2014) Shaping indigenous spaces in higher education: an international, virtual exchange on indigenous knowledge (Alaska and Aotearoa). Can J Nativ Educ 37(1):218–238

Leonard B, Mercier O (2016) Indigenous struggles within the colonial project: reclaiming indigenous Knowledges in the Western academy. Knowledge Cultures 4(3):99–116

Mercier OR, Asmar C, Page S (2011) An academic occupation: mobilisation, sit-in, speaking out and confrontation in the experiences of Māori academics. Aust J Indig Educ 40(11):81–91

Mihesuah DA, Wilson AC (eds) (2004) Indigenizing the academy: transforming scholarship and empowering communities. Bison Books, Lincoln

Moreton-Robinson A, Walter M, Singh D, Kimber M (2011) On stony ground: governance and aboriginal and Torres Strait islander participation in Australian universities. Report to the review of higher education access and outcomes for aboriginal and Torres Strait islander people. Department of Education, Employment and Workplace Relations, Canberra

Napoleon H (1991) Yuuyaraq: The way of the human being: With commentary. University of Alaska, Fairbanks, College of Rural Alaska, Center for Cross-Cultural Studies.

Napoleon H (1996) Yuuyaraq: the way of the human being. University of Alaska Press, Fairbanks

Ortiz A, HeavyRunner I (2003) Student access, retention, and success: models of support and inclusion. In: Benham M, Stein M (eds) The renaissance of American Indian higher education: capturing the dream. Lawrence Erlbaum Associates, Mahwah

Paris D, Winn MT (eds) (2014) Humanizing research: decolonizing qualitative inquiry with youth and communities. SAGE, Thousand Oaks

Parker AC (1916) The social elements of the Indian problem. Am J Sociol 22(2):252–267

Perea JB (2013) A tribalography of Alaska native presence in academia. Am Indian Culture Res J 37(3):3–27

Regents' Policy: Part I – Mission and General Provisions (2011) University of Alaska. https://www.alaska.edu/bor/policy/01-01.pdf. Accessed 7 June 2016

Rural Student Services (n.d.) http://www.uaf.edu/ruralss/. Accessed 21 June 2016

Scollon R (1981) Narrative, literacy and face in interethnic communication. Ablex Publishing Company, Norwood

Shotton HJ, Lowe SC, Waterman SJ (2013) Beyond the asterisk: understanding native students in higher education. Stylus, Sterling

State of Alaska (2015) 2015 population by borough/census area and economic region. Department of Labor and Workforce Development: Research and Analysis. http://laborstats.alaska.gov/pop/popest.htm. Accessed 8 June 2016

Thornton TF (2008) Being and place among the Tlingit. University of Washington Press, Seattle

UAF Academic Plan (2007) University of Alaska Fairbanks Provost and Executive Vice Chancellor for Academic Affairs. https://www.uaf.edu/provost/general-information-1/academic-plan/. Accessed 2 June 2016

UAF College of Rural and Community Development (n.d.) https://www.uaf.edu/rural/. Accessed 19 March 2017

UAF Facts and Figures (2017) Data as of fall 2016 http://www.uaf.edu/facts/. Accessed 7 March 2017

UAF Office of the Chancellor (2014) Chancellor's Advisory Committee on Native Education: Mission statement. http://www.uaf.edu/chancellor/administration/advisory/cacne/. Accessed 13 June 2016

UAF Office of the Chancellor (2016) Evon Peter. https://www.uaf.edu/chancellor/administration/cabinet/peter/ Accessed 13 June 2016

United Nations (2008) Declaration on the rights of Indigenous peoples. http://www.un.org/esa/socdev/unpfii/documents/DRIPS_en.pdf. Accessed 13 June 2016

University of Alaska (1970) University offers new courses in several ethnic cultures. In: Nanook news: Special new faculty issue. 14, n.p

University of Alaska (1979) Dennis Demmert appointed staff assistant to president. In: Now in the north: A University of Alaska report 9:1, 7

University of Alaska (2014) Shaping Alaska's Future. Unpublished Report. Fairbanks: University of Alaska Office of Academic Affairs and Public Affairs. https://www.alaska.edu/files/shapingalaskasfuture/SAF-FINAL.pdf. Accessed 31 May 2016

University of Alaska (2015) Board of Trustees (1917–1935) & Board of Regents (1935 to present) MASTER LIST. https://www.alaska.edu/files/bor/Board_Member_Master.pdf. Accessed 31 May 2016

University of Alaska Board of Regents (n.d.) https://www.alaska.edu/bor/. Accessed 16 June 2016

University of Alaska Board of Regents Official Minutes (2008) February 6–7, 2008 (Juneau, Alaska). www.alaska.edu/files/bor/minutes/2008/080206minutes.doc. Accessed 14 June 2016

University of Alaska Fairbanks (1981) 1981–1983 catalog. Fairbanks: University of Alaska

University of Alaska Fairbanks (2001) 2001–2002 UAF Catalog. http://www.uaf.edu/catalog/catalog_01-02/troth_yeddh.html. Accessed 31 May 2016

University of Alaska Fairbanks: 2012–13 UAF Catalog. http://archive.is/6gT0. Accessed 31 May 2016

University of Alaska Fairbanks (2013) Home: About UAF – History. http://www.uaf.edu/uaf/about/history/. Accessed 16 May 2016

University of Alaska Fairbanks (2014) UAF Strategic Plan 2012–2019. Unpublished Report. Fairbanks: University Alaska Fairbanks. http://www.uaf.edu/files/provost/UAF-Strategic-Plan-2012-19.pdf. Accessed 31 May 2016

University of Alaska Fairbanks: 2015–16 UAF Catalog. http://www.uaf.edu/catalog/current/overview/troth_yeddha.html. Accessed 31 May 2016

University of Alaska Fairbanks (2017) History. http://www.uaf.edu/uaf/about/history/. Accessed 14 March 2017

University of Alaska Fairbanks Mission Statement (n.d.) http://www.uaf.edu/files/provost/assessment-review/program-review/MissionCoreThemes.pdf. Accessed 31 May 2016

University of Alaska Fairbanks Troth Yeddha' (n.d.) https://uaf.edu/trothyeddha/. Accessed 16 June 2016

University of Alaska System Governance Council Constitution (2014). http://www.alaska.edu/files/governance/SGC-Constitution-Approved-8-7-14.pdf. Accessed 14 June 2016

USGS Geographic Name Information System (2017) Feature detail report for: Troth Yeddha'. https://geonames.usgs.gov/apex/f?p=gnispq:3:0::NO::P3_FID:2745576. Accessed 20 June 2016

Villegas M (2010) 500 Maori Ph.D.s in five years: Insights from a successful indigenous higher education initiative. Dissertation, Harvard University

Villegas M, Neugebauer SR, Venegas KR (eds) (2008) Indigenous knowledge and education: sites of struggle, strength, and survivance. Harvard Educational Review, Cambridge, MA

Williams M (ed) (2009) The Alaska native reader: history, culture, politics. Duke University Press, Durham

African Indigenous Governance from a Spiritual Lens

18

Njoki Wane, Rose Ann Torres, and Dionisio Nyaga

Contents

Introduction	294
Anticolonial Framework	295
Spirituality/ies as a Practice and Pedagogy	295
Definition of Indigenous Governance	299
Nature of Indigenous Governance Through a Spiritual Lens	302
Conclusion	304
References	304

Abstract

This paper is a discussion of spirituality and governance. It seeks to question marketisation, commodification, and corporatization of belief systems. The paper argues that spirituality is fluid, political, contested and unsettled. In line of settlement of spirituality/ies, market rationalities in the name of religion creates neoliberal arrival; which is injurious to governance. The paper seeks to recognise African spiritualities as modelled and created through difference. Rituals and Indigenous practices informs spiritualities. To that end, spiritualities provides freedom of expressions. Commodified spirituality stifles, oppresses, and erases

N. Wane (✉)
Social Justice Education, University of Toronto, Toronto, ON, Canada
e-mail: njoki.wane@utoronto.ca

R. A. Torres
Ontario Institute for Studies in Education, University of Toronto, Toronto, ON, Canada
e-mail: rose.torres@utoronto.ca

D. Nyaga
Social Justice Education/OISE, University of Toronto/School of Social Work, Ryerson University, Toronto, ON, Canada
e-mail: dnyaga.nyaga@mail.utoronto.ca

© Springer Nature Singapore Pte Ltd. 2019
E. A. McKinley, L. T. Smith (eds.), *Handbook of Indigenous Education*,
https://doi.org/10.1007/978-981-10-3899-0_45

bodies under the guise of spiritual freedom. This paper argues corporate spirituality provides manufactured freedom; which stifles democratic governance.

Keywords

Governance · Spirituality/ies · African governance · Power · Market · Rationality · Anti-colonial

> the kind of spirituality that is needed to facilitate full and meaningful participation of citizens requires an overhaul of the democratic project. This renewal journey will eschew the agenda that calls for a primary focus on protecting institutional survival and focus instead on being willing to risk creating space for people to express their felt needs and to find a common path to benefit the common good. (Hewitt 2014, p. 2)

Introduction

We are all spiritual beings and everything we do is mediated through our spiritual practices. Before colonization, our everyday life was interconnected and interwoven with every aspect of our life and this did not come to a halt when imperialism took control of all apparatus of various nations of the world. Different aspects of spiritual practices are engaged in various aspects of resistance. Spirituality therefore acquired another role as an organizing anticolonial praxis among the indigenous communities of the world. That is, Indigenous peoples of the world formed informal and formal resistances which were spiritually led. This led the way in centering their desire amidst colonial damage. Spirituality created possibilities of anticolonial forms of resistance. For instance, in Kenya, people embraced their African spiritualities without naming them. Mau Mau was an anticolonial indigenous government founded on Kenyan spirituality. Mau Mau emphasized freedom, liberty, and collective responsibility through ritualistic practices. Taking the oath for all members in the movement was a form of spiritual connection (Governance) for political emancipation (Mwanzia Koster 2016).

This chapter focuses on spirituality and Indigenous governance through an anticolonial framework. The purpose of this chapter is to explore Indigenous governance through a spiritual lens. This chapter argues that spirituality brings a complex and fluid balance in community governance, discusses the commonalities of Indigenous governance from different Indigenous groups of the world, and examines the importance of incorporating the mind, body, and spirit in Indigenous governance; allowing a celebration of difference and complexities of governance. The first section provides a brief overview of an anticolonial framework while connecting it to the argument of this chapter. The chapter looks at spirituality, its definition, and its applicability as a tool for governance. Later, this chapter examines spirituality and Indigenous governance. In this part, we argue that spirituality is an instrument or a capillary of Indigenous governance.

Anticolonial Framework

An anticolonial framework recognizes spirituality as a foundation of every aspect of Indigenous peoples lives (Dei 2002; Wane 2002). The framework centers spirituality as a form of agency, resiliency, and resistance against colonial project (Wane 2002; Dei and Asgharzadeh 2001). It is a discourse that acknowledges the complex relationship between the mind, the body, and the spirit in decolonization. An anticolonial framework reworks and disturbs knowledges, spiritualities, and cultures towards disrupting power that perpetuate division between Indigenous people. The framework attempts to bring people together to open local, individual, and institutional forms of resistance against colonial processes (Benette 2003). Although some people might argue that we are developing, it ought to be remembered that the process of recolonization still persists. For example, in Africa, the idea of governance and establishment of social conditions conducive for progress erases voices from the grassroots through a military force or through socially constructed poverty. However, a resurgence of Indigenous Spirituality/ies in governance among grassroots, people has challenged the existing ecopolitical status quo. The anticolonial framework acknowledges that Indigenous governance focuses on complex mix of spiritualities.

The authors of this chapter come from colonized communities where they have witnessed the application of spirituality in governance and the subsequent damaging of local governments to create neocolonial governance. This erasure is manifested in education system, health, and many other indigenous ways of living. It is important and responsible to assert our knowing in processes of learning, governance, and teaching. As we engage in these dialogues, it is crucial that our engagement is holistic. Questions needs to be asked such as; What is it we would like to achieve in this chapter; do we want to write a chapter as another academic exercise, another assignment to create currency for our academic careers; do we want to play with words and discourses or do we want to write a counter-discourse on governance that is transformative and steeped in indigenous spiritual practices? Our aim for this chapter is to search for ways of troubling both the visible and invisible structures of governance that perpetuate colonialism and constant recolonization of the mind, body, and spirit. An anticolonial framework allows a genealogical excavation of ourselves and our communities. To that end, anticolonial is critical and reflective. Indigenous spirituality/ies is a tool and an instrument that has been used to map and govern indigenous spaces reflexively. Reflexive process considers politics of space and tools applies in orienting geographies. Anticolonial praxis and theory allows for the validation of emotionally defined knowledges as pivotal in governance.

Spirituality/ies as a Practice and Pedagogy

Spirituality as a component of Indigenous knowledge is complex, personal, and fluid (Carrette 2000; Graham et al. 2012). Spiritualities are political, crossover, nonfoundational, and unstructured (Leon 2014). Indigenous spiritualities cannot be regulated and hence allow personal to become political and free. Nonregulation of spirituality allows resistance. Indigenous spiritualities bring together the differences in beliefs to form a governing practice. On the other hand, governmentality of spirituality erases the personal as political. Spirituality is far broader than religion. Religion is institutionalization of spirituality for the market place (Zwissler 2007). Simply said, religion is the process of packaging and patenting spirituality through simplification for the sake of universalizing a belief system. Commodification of spirituality is colonial. Colonialism creates a hierarchy of beliefs systems as powerful and sellable to the public. Colonialism and science work together towards mapping certain beliefs as rational and others irrational. Religion being a scientific measure of spirituality identifies indigenous spiritualties as dangerous and in need of regulation. Colonialism erased Indigenous peoples' ways of life from the political space (Dei 2002; Wane 2002). This included Indigenous governance, spirituality, education, trading practices, relationships, and land and its relationship to people.

Spirituality as a praxis and pedagogy allows for self-expression (de Souza et al. 2016). It allows for self-determination and definition, which creates multiple expressions (spiritualities) and definitions, which frees the self. A free persona is a free community. As much as spirituality is personal (Koertner 2013; Owen 2012), it is a platform for strengthening the community agency and well-being (Nash and Stewart 2002). In colonial terms, spirituality as a practice belongs to spaces of indignation and outside state policy (Celermajer 2009). Being emotional is followed by regulation of the dangerousness and the damaged (Nyaga and Torres 2017). Such bodies and beliefs so defined as emotional are made public. Being made public is punitive and disciplinary (Foucault 1980). Colonialism is a technology of regulation, definition, and punishment of those spaces and bodies that lie outside the political prism of science/religion. Religion is a colonial and scientific improvement of the deviant and atypical into a universal civilized space of becoming.

The colonial government produced organized religion to the colonized subjects as a regulatory technology and a means of production. A case in point was the introduction of Western religion to the Indigenous peoples of Kenya, where spirituality became a public process of becoming civilized. It commodified and patented spirituality with a profit rational. When spirituality is made public rather than allowing it to become public, it becomes a practice and a tool to control, regulate, and discipline the subjugated bodies (Lewis and Geroy 2000). Religion is a measure of disembodying the self from the maternal and emotional instinct. It is a measure and a panoptic technology of managing bodies, societies, nations, and the land. Religion is what Foucault called governmentality and panoptic system of regulation of bodies, spiritualities, and spaces. Religion historically has been used as civilizational practice and thought (Memmi 1965).

Civilization as a colonial construct is barbaric, antagonistic, and ambivalent (Powell 2011; Razack 2015). Its ambivalence is understood by its barbaric pressure it inserts on the space and bodies it comes into contact. A case in point is the intense economic, cultural, and social pressure Indigenous peoples, women, disabled, radicalized and others face under the guise of civilization. Residential school system in Canada is one among many historical ambivalences of civilizational project. Civilization and law walk hand in hand. They are both order and disorder.

Thielen-Wilson (2014) says that colonization has been the reason why we are divided and broken. Our being is taken away through denial of self-becoming; our spirituality is subsumed to be part of the organized religion. We are giving instructions when or how or what to bring to our ceremonies when we do them in public places. What many of us have failed to notice is that, colonialism as a system and practice works through ordering and simplification. The system believes in identifying through dualistic generalization. Colonialism as a practice and discourse defines normal bodies and spaces as rational and disembodies. Those bodies that are rational are expected to own the public sphere and those that are not are waste and belonging to the private sphere. The body becomes a space of scientific introspection and refinement. Those who cannot become colonially rational and pure are pronounced as deviant and expected to cannibalize themselves. They are falling outside the domain of civilization. They are expended as belonging to the state of nature where law is expendable.

Colonialism affected all aspects of Indigenous peoples' lives – spiritually, socially, culturally, and politically. We follow rules and regulations that continually colonize and damage us. We shelf our desires and envelop damage. Our desire is under colonial measure and erasure. As a practice, colonialism inscribes control and power over bodies and practices defined as emotional and irrational. Foucault (1980) says that power is felt when its illegality is felt on the marginal and local spaces. Under colonial rule, law as power becomes illegal when it is improving the damaged bodies. Aristotelian thought informs us that colonialism reduces the happiness of the human to that of a pig. It is when one cannot act or think as separate being that power becomes a technology of policing, decimation, and regulation. This controlled and measured of human becoming denies personal and "authentic" identity which is core in spirituality. Colonial measure seeks comfort, measurement, an end, and arrival rather than working in complexities. On the other hand, Indigenous spiritualities works even in complexities.

Losing control to self-actualization is alienating and estranging and a denial of human right (Padgett 2007; Wendling 2009). Religion as a colonial technology draws a roadmap that is outside the person and hence it objectifies the human (Fried 2001). By extension and intention, religion denies personal practice and becoming, and as a consequence, we are what Marx and Aristotle would call animals. The human becomes a body with no soul, a reflection of a robot. Religion becomes an opium and a technology to robotize the masses (Boer 2011). Spirituality unmaps religious automation and centers self-validation. To that end, spirituality is anticolonial and a pedagogy for self-government. This should not be seen as self-reclamation but rather a new becoming.

An "authentic" self is beyond and between the panoptic sphere. It is removed from the beam of surveillance that domesticates it under the illusion of freedom. Religion has historically been used as a caging institution for easy disciplinary power and control. Religion is a colonial technology of disciplining the colonized through domestication of their spirituality. According to Foucault, the panoptic prisoners do not intermingle with others. They are in their own individual cubicles physically, spiritually, or emotionally. Religion as a panoptic project imprints its automating power consistently, continuously, and unverifiable on their skin of the colonized. Pastoral programs become a process of colonizing the mind, body, and soul. To that end, religion is a form of governmentality that is institutionalized and scientific. On the other hand, indigenous spiritualities espouses democratic governance by allowing difference, deregulation, and embracing personal spiritual complexities and reconciliation (Bento 2000).

Religion becomes illegal and visible by decimating Indigenous peoples' spiritual practices and by extending indigenous self-governance. Wane (2009) talks about her experiences in a boarding school when religion was introduced to her in grade 5. She was made to fear the unknown. It is what Foucault identifies as fear of the watch tower even when it is empty. That means that even with the absence of the prison warden in the watch tower, the prisoners continue to subject themselves to self-regulation. Wane says that the sound of a bell would automatically make her do the ritual of the sign of the cross. These colonial impositions have a psychological impact on us and our belief system.

Hewitt (2014) says that "Democracy, especially in the west, is accompanied by a lack of confidence and consensus, insecurity, deep introversion, a lack of concern, unwillingness to tackle anything and a lack of a consistent focus to resolve problems that affect the wellbeing of ordinary citizens" (p. 1). Denial to become human leads to dependence on the universal author of our becoming. The being is defined cognitively incompetent, lazy, untrustworthy, and in need of improvement (Memmi 1965). Beings so defined as dependent, internalize the discourse and as such expect to be helped by the rational bodies. Helping become a practice of saving the damaged from self-cannibalization. Religion and charity walk hand in hand. Charity in many instances is a process of harvesting on the pain of the damaged (Razack 2007). This colonial definition of the colonized stagnate a person by making them immobile and consequently regulatable (Memmi 1965). Language, naming, and defining become a technology of situating, pathologizing, and demobilizing the colonized (WaThing'o 1986). Religion as governmentality works along the line of creating pathologies on indigenous spiritualities. This allows the packaging and patenting of the true spirituality for the market even at the detriment and death of other spiritualities. Religion has a colonial and neocolonial rationality of measuring what is to be consumed by the public. Hewitt says that the neoliberal government focuses on serving its own selfish desires, which might run centrally to peoples' desires. Hewitt says that such a government focuses on colonial elevation of Western beliefs system at the pulpit of civilizing. One of the tactics of a colonial government is the claim that we are in a postcolonial era (Young 2001), yet we still see the ravages of residential school system in Aboriginal communities in Canada.

According to Fukuyama (2013), governance is defined as the "...ability to make and enforce rules, and to deliver services, regardless of whether that government is democratic or not" (p. 350). A democratic society has the responsibility to choose its leaders to make and enforce rules. Representational governance seeks to make rules and policies through democratically elected leaders. A political process of voting defines who is going to take the role of the many in determining how the society will be governed. This way of thinking and praxis fails to see the human self-seeking character in the name of servant leadership (Coleman 2008; Strömbäck and Nord 2006). If we violate these rules and regulations, we suffer the consequences. It is about governing the body by a few masquerading as peoples' representatives.

In a colonial thought, the mind takes control and the body is controlled. The body is space to be conquered by the mind, and law necessitates the process of occupation (Clark 2001). The law is masculine and follows the mind. The mind is masculine and body is feminine. The mind is free to move, while the body is camped, domesticated, and controlled. Going by this thought, the indigenous spiritualities are bodies that are emotional, irrational, and social excesses. Since religion is marketable, organized, rational, and profitable, it occupies the mind. Science is used to claim religion as universal, which lead to imposition and fellowshipping by the masses, of the Western scientific spirituality as the truth (Clark 2001). This power is central in colonial governance. Religion becomes the law, the standard, and the measure of what is civilized and uncivilized. Just like the Foucauldian watch tower, the rules are supposed to regulate the body through its imposition and inscription on the skin.

However, in a neoliberal and colonial control, Indigenous spiritualities have been sites of agency and resistance. Spiritualities is an anti-colonial praxis and a thought that organizes and offers a governing rationale that is indigenous and local. Spiritualities have provided a transformative space for the subversion of colonial power and control (Adjei 2007; Shahjahan 2009; Torres and Nyaga 2015, 2016; Wane 2008a, b). Spiritualities allow for the centering of differences. As a praxis, spirituality brings communities together regardless of differences (Sheerattan-Bisnauth 2009). It is reciprocal based, relational, and respectful of other belief systems. Indigenous spiritualities looks at difference as strength and a decolonial asset for the marginalized communities. It accommodates individual difference without necessarily regulating them. Spiritualities are fluid and evolving allowing personal expressions and possibilities, a key necessity of governance. Subsequently, spiritually led governance is fluid and evolves across time and space.

Definition of Indigenous Governance

The centrality of Indigenous governance comes from the belief that everything that exists in the universe is important and has a purpose. Leaders recognize the existence of members of the society they serve. This recognition is embedded in the belief that an individual is a self-determining being with human happiness and right to know and exercise rights and duties (Aristotle 1984). That the personal is mentally, politically, and cognitively powerful. Indigenous governance enhances the strengths and differences among people. It works towards enabling rather than disabling. It centers local desires and works towards realizing individual dreams. Writing in the nature of Indigenous governance in Canada, Reeds (1999) says:

> Most Aboriginal societies valued individual responsibility and independence, but they also believe in the importance of sharing. Cooperation was key and consensus was a central part of decision making. Indigenous leaders should be responsible to the needs and desires of

> their people. Among the Siksika (Blackfoot), leaders gained recognition and authority on the basis of their courage, generosity, honesty, and wisdom. They governed only as long as they had the confidence of their people. (p. 10)

Indigenous governance is community based with all benefits reaching every member of the community. Indigenous governance is seen through the lens of community building (Farrelly 2011). Governance is a community-based art (Gwynn et al. 2015). Indigenous governance never settles and is fluid and temporal. This creates new possibilities and chances for all to inform the art of governance. It means that everyone has a stake in the writing of the story (Marx 1857/58, 1864; Stewart and Warn 2017). This temporality denies the privatization and patenting of governance. Since the artist has no ownership, then the art takes its own course and can be tweaked to fit situations and circumstances without holding the society captive. At every step of the way, the art becomes prone to correction and rewriting. It shows that leaders must accommodate, relate, share, and respect communities in order to govern (Price 2008). Participation of members in governance is crucial. Indigenous governance encourages a shared responsibility and commitment of service. Wangoola (2002) describes African Indigenous governance as:

> For millennia, African communities were guided and driven by a world view and value system at the center of which was a closely intertwined trinity of forces, values, and considerations. The trinity consisted of spirituality, development, and politics with spirituality forming the base and controlling and informing everything that happened in the realm of development politics. In the African world view, social life was dominated by spirituality following which there was some development and a little politics. At the center of African spirituality...according to African spirituality, being is the perpetual flow of energy among animate and inanimate things and between all of these and the gods. (p. 265)

Wangoola succinctly describes African Indigenous governance through spirituality as the foundation of governance in Africa that shapes the society. Development and politics had a spiritual touch. African governance was a capillary between the living, nonliving, and nature. In addition, Basheka (2015) highlights the nature of African Indigenous governance:

> involved strengthened decision-making and control over their organizations, and building on people's skills, personal and collective contributions, and shared commitment to an organization's chosen governance processes, goals and identity. Indigenous governance relates to the variety of skills, teachings, wisdom, ideas, perceptions, experiences, capabilities and insights of people, applied to maintain or improve the governance of society. (p. 470)

Basheka clearly describes the African Indigenous governance as reflexively empowering and transformational. Indigenous governance is based on enhancing and building the capacities of community members through decision-making processes. This makes individuals own the outcome of the deliberation. It does not only serve the few, but it caters for all the needs of the people. It is a government by the people and for the people.

In the Philippines, Tauli-Corpuz (2006), an Igorot scholar states that "at a very early age our parents and elders taught us basic values deemed gawis (good): respect for nature and ancestors, honesty, and love for Mother Earth" (p. 13). Governance is about respect for living and nonliving, and nature. It is about the well-being of the whole community. Aeta Indigenous women healers in the Philippines agreeing with Tauli-Corpuz also state that governance spiritual (Torres 2012). Spirituality to them is about acknowledging the presence of their Creator in their everyday lives. The dead and the living are invited in governance through rituals and cultural performances. Indigenous governance believes in the power of ancestral spirits.

United Nations General Assembly recognizing spirituality among Indigenous peoples of the world states that:

> As much as possible, problems are solved by consensus using procedures that engage all affected parties and exhaust dissent...The recognition and transfer of authority and leadership, whether hereditary or through selection, are also guided by oral history and spiritual and ceremonial traditions. (United Nations General Assembly 2010, p. 12)

Spirituality has a fundamental place in the definition of Indigenous governance. Spirituality is the cord that ties individuals together. Orality is core to governance among the Indigenous peoples. Oral histories bring to the present previous spiritualities through rituals. This connection honors the ancestor and their ingenuity. Governance incorporates both the spiritual and the physical world. This interconnection is necessary and core in decision-making processes. To allow orality to connect the spiritual and the physical world, there are special practices that are undertaken to invite the ancestor in decision-making process. Among the practices are chanting and talking in tongues, mostly done by shamans. The ancestors are invited to partake in healing or prayer. Invitation of the ancestor is ritualized and seeks their help since they can see what we cannot. Makokis (2008) says that "Traditional ceremonies are our spiritual centres and allow us to redefine self-determination in our own ways." (p. 41). To that end, spirituality is political and transformational. In addition, Makokis also explains the importance of spirituality in their lives and community.

> For many nehiyawak, we derive our identity from the family, community, and nation we are born into. How we relate to each other is a fundamental component of how we organize and govern our lives, which inevitably shapes who we are and who we become. By "relate" I am referring to how we relate to "all of our relations" and this includes our human relations, animal relations, spiritual relations, and the intimate relationship we have to Mother Earth who is our lifelong teacher in these unique kinship relations. In relating to each other, nehiyawak in my community will often ask the younger generation questions such as: where are you from? Who are your parents? And, who is your extended family? When I was younger I never quite understood the significance behind these personal questions but as I began to learn more about nehiyawak governance and social organization, I realized that we (nehiyawak) organize ourselves around our relationships to each other, to our families and how this becomes interconnected with our community. By relating to each other in this way we are able to establish a unique governance system based on kinship relations whereby each person holds a unique piece of our community governance lodge together. (Makokis 2008, p. 44)

Spirituality as relational connects human being in governance. Among Indigenous communities of the world, relationship building is an important aspect of governance. Such a spiritual oriented governance recognizes a self-determination while simultaneously inviting them to the common (Mayes 2001; Palmer 2003). For example, when one is asked where they come from, they identify their family names. The family picks names that have saliency from a past. Therefore, when asking someone a question it is about connecting the living and the ancestors. It is a way of making the dead come alive. Asking a name is a resurrection of the ancestors. It is a way of recognizing those who have gone before us and their role in governance. It is calling their names to claim land and bodies walking on them. Indigenous governance is thus holistic, self-determining, relational, and evolving.

Among the Indigenous peoples, spirituality is an epistemology of governance (Wane 2011, 2015). Iroquois scholar Oren Lyons quoted by Makokis (2008) explains the distinctiveness of Indigenous governance and the role of spirituality.

> The central fire, of course, was the spiritual fire. The primary law of Indian government is the spiritual law. Spirituality is the highest form of politics, and our spirituality is directly involved in government. As chiefs we are told that our first and most important duty is to see that the spiritual ceremonies are carried out. Without the ceremonies, one does not have a basis on which to conduct a government for the welfare of the people. This is not only for our people but for the good of all living things in general. (p. 40)

Lyons powerfully explains the significance, centrality, and role of spirituality in governance. Lyons argues that if spirituality is not included in a nation's political action, governance results improper management of the community resources.

Nature of Indigenous Governance Through a Spiritual Lens

Indigenous governance has historically walked through a spiritual prism or continuum. Indigenous governance is a fluid concept, complex and transitional (Arthur 2011). It changes through time and space. The changes are based on the transitional movement of governance through the different spiritualities presented by members of the society (Strelein and Tran 2013). A case in point is the Mau Mau rebellion where rituals were used to create political resistance. Everyone took part in inventing an indigenous governing project against colonialism. To that end, Indigenous governance is ritualistic and culturally oriented. As discussed earlier, there are five qualities of spiritually led Indigenous governance. First, there is a greater "authenticity" to and evolving self and to others. Second is the respect for nature and diversity. Third is recognition of difference as strength. Fourth, there is a clear but complex path to equity and quality. Finally, there is a real demonstration of love and compassion through self to others and vice-versa.

A spiritually centered Indigenous governance provides credibility to leadership. Leadership is a talent to be shared for the well-being of the society. Leaders are given the role to govern a community as a trustee. The leader is chosen by community members and is expected to work with members towards fulfillment of a need. Leadership is not charitable or servant oriented but rather works with the people towards meeting aims, desires, and aspirations. Under a spiritually led Indigenous governance, the power comes from the community (Centre for Indigenous Environmental Resources (CIER) 1996). The community is an asset of social changes. The leader is a facilitator since community members are the experts. Women, nature, ancestors, youth, disabled, seniors, and men perform reciprocal role. There is no division of labor but a goal that needs to be accomplished for the community to succeed (Wane 2002, 2015). Sterling (2002) says:

> The grandmothers are natural teachers because they care for children. In the narratives they laughed and worked and told stories to little children and rode up into the mountains, were kind, were strict, made twine out of plants, cut willow switches to make the children behave, rocked the babies to sleep. Their creation stories and narratives show the children their unique place in their nation's history and contribute to a positive self-image by validating First Nations experiences. Like the grandmothers before us we can create lessons built on experience and storytelling to transmit knowledge and skills, cultural pride, and self-confidence. (p. 5)

Indigenous governance recognizes equity, fairness, and distribution of resources (Wane and Neegan 2007). This is key as Indigenous governance is reciprocal and respectful. It demonstrates love and compassion through working with community members. Case in point is the healing process of an ill member where every member of the society is expected to be present to send good energies. There is a spiritual connection between individual and the community. When a member is sick, the community is sick and by extension ungovernable. New forms of governing come out of the healing and ritualism. The healing is part of Indigenous governance and focuses on the mind, body, and spirit. Sickness is a conflict and a challenge that need community members to come together to solve it. According to the Indigenous women healers in the Philippines that conflict alienates us from ourselves and other (Torres 2012). Rang-ay states:

> Healing other people is a joy for me. I do not ask for money in exchange for my services. I heal because of my "ayat" or love for my people. I do not want my people to suffer. I try my best to help them. There are moments that I get very tired, but I know that if I do not carry out my responsibility to my community and to my people, I will not feel good. Healing is a gift from my Creator and therefore I have to use it for the benefit of my community. (Torres 2012, p. 132)

Grandmother in Kenya have taken up the role of raising their grandchildren who are victims of HIV/Aids. For grandmothers in Kenya, taking care of their grandchildren is a joy and a commitment and not a burden. Being able to raise their grandchildren indicate their support to governance. This is because such children will become future leaders of the community. One of the grandmother said that:

I am very grateful to be part of my community. We love and support each other. We may not be rich in worldly material but we are happy, contented, and supportive of one another. There are times that I get tired; however, seeing my grandchildren growing healthy, strong and respectful is a joy that I cannot even explain. They remind me of my daughter who passed away that life is full of love and beauty. These things cannot be bought by any amount of money. (Wane interview 2007)

Conclusion

Governance without a spiritual focus can be disastrous. Spirituality must be the center of everything that we do in our lives and in our community. This chapter highlighted the role of spirituality in Indigenous governance. Indigenous and non-Indigenous scholars spoke candidly on Indigenous governance and spirituality. Spirituality embraces the connection of mind, body, and spirit. Indigenous governance is relational in nature and does not privilege or discriminate. This chapter featured the nature of governance through a spiritual lens. These features were: greater authenticity to oneself and to others; a clear respect to diversity, nature, and difference; and love and compassion through self and others. This chapter shed light on recognizing the importance of spirituality in our lives and in our community. Let us continue working for a community that serves the benefit of everybody and unmap those practices that hinder us to attain our spiritual goals.

References

Adjei PB (2007) Decolonising knowledge production: the pedagogic relevance of Gandhian satyagraha to schooling and education in Ghana. Can J Educ 30(4):1046–1067
Aristotle (1984) The complete works of Aristotle: the revised Oxford translations. In: Barnes J (ed). Princeton University Press, Princeton
Arthur P (2011) Identities in transition: challenges for transitional justice in divided societies. Cambridge University Press, Cambridge/New York
Basheka B (2015) Indigenous Africa's governance architecture: a need for African public administration theory? J Public Adm 50(3):466–484
Benette JB (2003) Academic life: hospitality, ethics, and spirituality. Anker, Bolton
Bento RF (2000) The little inn at the crossroads: a spiritual approach to the design of a leadership course. J Manag Educ 24(5):650–661
Boer R (2011) Opium, idols and revolution: Marx and Engels on religion. Religion Compass 5(11):698–707
Campbell LH (2003) The spiritual lives of artists/teachers. Paper presented at the annual meeting of the American Educational Research Association, Chicago, 21–25 April 2003
Carrette JR (2000) Foucault and religion: spiritual corporality and political spirituality. Routledge, London
Celermajer D (2009) The sins of the nation and the ritual of apologies. Cambridge University Press, Cambridge
Centre for Indigenous Environmental Resources (CIER) (1996) Discussion paper presenting a First Nation environmental vision statement and self-government implementation strategy
Clark RT (2001) In the law and spirituality: how the law supports and limits expression of spirituality on the college campus. In: Jablonski MA (ed) The implications of student spirituality

for student affairs practice. New directions for student services, no. 95. Jossey-Bass, San Francisco, pp 37–46

Coleman S (2008) The depiction of politicians and politics in british soaps. Telev New Media 9(3):197–219

de Souza M, Bone J, Watson J (2016) Spirituality across disciplines: research and practice. Springer International Publishing, Dordrecht

Dei G (2002) African development: the relevance and implications of "indigenousness". In: Dei G, Hall B, Rosenberg D (eds) Indigenous knowledges in global context: multiple readings of our world. University of Toronto Press, Toronto, pp 70–86

Dei G, Asgharzadeh A (2001) The power of social theory: the anti-colonial discursive framework. J Educ Thought 35(3):297–323

Deloria V, Wildcat DR (2001) Power and place: Indian education in America. Fulcrum Resources, Denver

Farrelly TA (2011) Indigenous and democratic decision-making: issues from community-based ecotourism in the Boumā National Heritage Park, Fiji. J Sustain Tour 19(7):817

Foucault M (1980) Power/knowledge: selected interviews and other writings, 1972–1977. Pantheon, New York

Fried J (2001) Civility and spirituality. In: Miller VM, Ryan MM (eds) Transforming campus life: reflections on spirituality and religious pluralism. Lang, New York

Fukuyama F (2013) What is governance? Governance 26(3):347–368. https://doi.org/10.1111/gove.12035

Graham JR, Coholic D, Groen J (2012) Spirituality in social work and education: theory, practice, and pedagogies. Wilfrid Laurier University Press, Waterloo

Greenstreet WM (1999) Teaching spirituality in nursing: a literature review. Nurse Educ Today 19:649–658

Gwynn J, Lock M, Turner N, Dennison R, Coleman C, Kelly B, Wiggers J (2015) Aboriginal and Torres Strait Islander community governance of health research: turning principles into practice. Aust J Rural Health 23(4):235–242

Hewitt RR (2014) Spirituality for democracy: spiritual resources for democratic participation in the 21st century. Verbum et Ecclesia 35(3):7. https://doi.org/10.4102/ve.v35i3.1345

Koertner UHJ (2013) Syncretism and the construction of a personal spirituality. Theol Today 70(3):295–310

León LD (2014) The political spirituality of Cesar Chavez: crossing religious borders. University of California Press, Berkeley

Lewis JS, Geroy GD (2000) Employee spirituality in the workplace: a cross-cultural view for the management of spiritual employees. J Manag Educ 24(5):682–694

Makokis JA (2008) Nehiyaw iskwew kiskinowâtasinahikewina – paminisowin namôya tipeyimisowin: learning self determination through the sacred. Can Woman Stud 26 (3, 4):39–51

Marx K (1857–58) Economic manuscripts of 1857–1858. In: Marx-Engels, Collected works, vols 28 and 29. Lawrence and Wishart, London

Marx K (1864) Inaugural address of the working men's international association. In: Marx-Engels, Collected works, vol 20. Lawrence and Wishart, London

Marx K [1867]1986 Capital, vol I. Penguin Books, Harmondsworth

Massoudi M (2003) Can scientific writing be creative? J Sci Educ Technol 12(2):115–128

Mayes C (2001) Cultivating spiritual reflectivity in teachers. Teach Educ Q 28(2):5–22

Memmi A (1965) Colonizer and the colonized. Orion Press, New York

Mwanzia Koster M (2016) The power of the oath: Mau Mau nationalism in Kenya, 1952–1960. University of Rochester Press, Rochester

Nash M, Stewart B (2002) Spirituality and social care: contributing to personal and community well-being. Jessica Kingsley Publishers, London

Nyaga D, Torres RA (2017) Gendered citizenship: a case study of paid Filipino male live-in caregivers in Toronto. Int J Asia Pac Stud 13(1):51–71

Owen M (2012) Spirituality is personal and cannot be forced on others. Nurs Stand 26(44):32–32

Padgett B (2007) Marx and alienation in contemporary society. Continuum, London

Palmer PJ (2003) Teaching with heart and soul: reflections on spirituality in teacher education. J Teach Educ 54(5):376–385

Powell CJ (2011) Barbaric civilization: a critical sociology of genocide. McGill-Queen's University Press, Montréal

Price J (2008) Living Inuit governance in Nunavut. In: Simpson L (ed) Lighting the eighth fire: the liberation, resurgence, and protection of indigenous nations. Arbeiter Ring Publishing, Winnipeg, pp 127–138

Razack SH (2007) Stealing the pain of others: reflections on canadian humanitarian responses. Rev Educ Pedagogy Cult Stud 29(4):375–394

Razack S (2015) Dying from improvement: inquests and inquiries into indigenous deaths in custody. University of Toronto Press, Toronto

Reeds K (1999) Aboriginal peoples building for the future. Oxford University Press, Don Mills

Shahjahan RA (2009) The role of spirituality in the anti-oppressive higher-education classroom. Teach High Educ 14(2):121–131

Sheerattan-Bisnauth P (2009) Power to resist and courage to hope: Caribbean churches living out the Accra Confession. World Alliance of Reformed Churches, Geneva

Sterling S (2002) Yetko and Sophie: Nlakapamux cultural professors. Can J Nativ Educ 26(1):4–10

Stewart J, Warn J (2017) Between two worlds: indigenous leaders exercising influence and working across boundaries. Aust Public Adm 76(1):3–17

Strelein L, Tran T (2013) Building indigenous governance from native title: moving away from 'fitting in' to creating a decolonized space. Rev Const Stud 18(1):19

Strömbäck J, Nord LW (2006) Mismanagement, mistrust and missed opportunities: a study of the 2004 tsunami and swedish political communication. Media Cult Soc 28(5):789–800

Tauli-Corpuz V (2006) Our rights remain separate and distinct. In: Tauli-Corpuz V, Mander J (eds) Paradigm wars. Sierra Club Books, San Francisco, pp 13–21

Thielen-Wilson L (2014) Troubling the path to decolonization: Indian residential school case law, genocide, and settler illegitimacy. Can J Law Soc 29(2):181–197

Torres R (2012) Aeta indigenous women healers: lesson and implications. Ph.D. Dissertation, Ontario Institute for Studies in Education. University of Toronto

Torres R, Nyaga D (2015) The politics of cultural representation. Soc Stud 5(9):744–758

Torres R, Nyaga D (2016) Discussion of power through the eyes of the margins: praxis of postcolonial aeta indigenous women healers in the Philippines. Int J Asia Pac Stud 12(2):31–56

Tully J (1995) Strange multiplicity: constitutionalism in an age of diversity. Cambridge University Press, Cambridge

Turner NJ, Ignace MB, Ignace R (2000) Traditional ecological knowledge and wisdom of aboriginal peoples in British Columbia. Ecol Appl 10(5):1275–1287

United Nation General Assembly (2010) Report of the United Nations High Commissioners for Human Rights on the violation of human rights in Honduras since the coup d'etat on 28 June 2009 (3 March 2010), UNDOC A/HRC/13/66

WaThing'o N (1986) Decolonizing the mind: the politics of language in African literature. Heinemann, Portsmouth

Waaijman K (2007) What is spirituality? Acta Theol 27(2):1–18

Wane N (2002) African women and spirituality: connections between thought and action. In: O'Sullivan E, Morrell A, O'Conner M (eds) Expanding the boundaries of transformative learning: essays on theory and praxis. Palgrave Macmillan, New York, pp 135–150

Wane (2007) Grandmothers out for retirement. Interview. Kianjokoma

Wane NN (2008a) Mapping the field of indigenous knowledges in anti-colonial discourse: a transformative journey in education. Race Ethn Educ 11(2):183–197

Wane N (2008b) Primary education for girls: mis/interpretation of education for all in Kenya. In: Lund DE, Carr PR (eds.) Doing democracy: striving for political literacy and social justice. Sage Publication, p 115–230

Wane N (2009) Indigenous education & cultural resistance: a decolonizing project, an essay review of: Donna Deyhle, Karen swisher, Tracy Stevens & Ruth Trinidad Galvan: Indigenous resistance and renewal; Kathryn M. Anderson-Levitt: Globalization & curriculum; Joseph P. Farrell: Community education in developing countries: the quiet revolution in schooling. Curric Inq 39(1):159–178

Wane N (2011) Spirituality: a philosophy and a research tool. In: Wane N, Manyimo Ritskes E (eds) Spirituality, education & society: an integrated approach. Sense Publication, Rotterdam

Wane N (2015) What is spiritual leadership? In: Portelli J (ed) Case studies in leadership. Sage Publication, Thousand Oaks

Wane N, Neegan E (2007) African women's indigenous spirituality: bringing it all home. In: Massaquoi N, Wane N (eds) Theorizing empowerment: black Canadian feminist thought. Innana Publishers, Toronto, pp 27–46

Wangoola P (2002) Mpanbo the African multiversity: a philosophy to rekindle the African spirit. In: Dei G, Hall B, Rosenberg D (eds) Indigenous knowledges in the global contexts: multiple readings of the world. University of Toronto Press, Toronto, pp 265–277

Wendling AE (2009) Karl Marx on technology and alienation. Palgrave Macmillan, Basingstoke

Young R (2001) Post-colonialism: a historical introduction. Blackwell Publishers, Oxford

Zwissler L (2007) Spiritual, but religious: 'spirituality' among religiously motivated feminist activists. Cult Relig 8(1):51–69

Mi'kmaw Kina'matnewey and Mi'kmaw Control over Mi'kmaw Education: Using the Master's Tools to Dismantle the Master's House?

19

John Jerome Paul, Lisa Lunney Borden, Jeff Orr, Thomas Orr, and Joanne Tompkins

Contents

Background and Context	311
Enter Mi'kmaw Kinametnewey and the Mi'kmaw Education Agreement	312
Self-Governance and Self-Determination	313
Community Capacity for Community Control	318
Decolonizing Education Through the Centering of Mi'kmaw Language and Culture	320
Stones of Wisdom from the MK Experience	325
Conclusion	325
References	326

Abstract

In 2010, the Assembly of First Nations (AFN) renewed the call for First Nations Control of First Nations Education, a vision they first laid out nearly 40 years before. While many Indigenous communities and community organizations in Canada are still working toward this ideal, Mi'kmaw Kina'matnewey (MK), a collective of Mi'kmaw communities in Nova Scotia, stands out as a unique example of the vision fulfilled. With high school graduation rates that range from 85% to 90% annually – more than double the graduation rate for Aboriginal students in the rest of the country – MK is undoubtedly the most successful Aboriginal Education system in Canada. In this chapter, we will describe the

---

J. J. Paul
Mi'kmaw Kina'matnewey, Membertou, Canada
e-mail: sanpaul@kinu.ca

L. Lunney Borden (✉) · J. Orr · J. Tompkins
St. Francis Xavier University, Antigonish, NS, Canada
e-mail: lborden@stfx.ca; jorr@stfx.ca; jtompkin@stfx.ca

T. Orr
Antigonish, Canada
e-mail: tom_orr22@hotmail.com

© Springer Nature Singapore Pte Ltd. 2019
E. A. McKinley, L. T. Smith (eds.), *Handbook of Indigenous Education*,
https://doi.org/10.1007/978-981-10-3899-0_32

governance model for MK that includes a board of directors from all 12 member-communities who work collaboratively to guide education from pre-school to post-secondary. We will describe the beginning days of MK and show how it has grown into the organization it is today through a relentless pursuit to cultivate the capacity within Mi'kmaw communities to ensure Mi'kmaw people are working in all levels of Mi'kmaw education. We will show how preparation of pre-service and in-service teachers and administrators from the communities has been an essential component in the decolonization of MK education. We will explain how this work has been supported through partnerships, in particular, through an over 20-year partnership with the Faculty of Education at St. Francis Xavier University. Finally, we will share examples of program achievements in Mi'kmaw language revitalization, numeracy and literacy, and other student achievement measures while also striving toward a decolonized approach to education.

Keywords

Decolonizing Education · Indigenous Education · Self-Governance · Mi'kmaw · Mi'kmaq

[Survival] is learning how to take our differences and make them strengths. For *the master's tools will never dismantle the master's house*. They may allow us temporarily to beat him at his own game, but they will never enable us to bring about genuine change. [Italics added]
– Audre Lorde (1984, p. 111)

We are a unified team of chiefs, staff, parents and educators who advocate on behalf of and represent the educational interests of our communities, and *we protect the educational and Mi'kmaw language rights of the Mi'kmaq people*. [Italics added] (Mi'kmaw Kina'matnewey 2017)

The tension between these epigraphs is palpable. Audre Lorde has argued passionately and articulately that "the master's tools," meaning cogs in the patriarchal and colonial apparatus can never dismantle "the master's house," or the oppressive global system, in its entirety. Lorde was largely focused on criticizing the racism, classism, and homophobia in the feminist movement as antithetical to challenging colonial-patriarchal power structures during the 1980s. However, her statement can be transplanted to the present, as a criticism of efforts to transmogrify the Eurocentric school system, a facet of the broader colonial construct, and use it in the empowerment of colonized peoples.

In this chapter we analyze this criticism through an examination of the governance model and subsequent achievements of Mi'kmaw Kina'matnewey (MK), a community-based organization that provides intermediary educational services and organizational representation to Nova Scotian Mi'kmaw communities seeking to exercise enhanced self-governance in education. In struggles to transform the assimilationist and Eurocentric school system into a decolonizing force in these communities, we argue that MK stands as an example of how to dismantle the master's house using the master's tools. The MK self-governance agreement has enabled capacity building within MK communities that has provided the opportunity to decolonize education at the local level while allowing Mi'kmaw culture, language, and identity to thrive. Despite significant challenges, MK and its member communities have worked hard to further the mission of Indigenous control of Indigenous education and have achieved significant success in these endeavors.

Background and Context

The formal school system, consciously and unconsciously, has long served as a tool of oppression, assimilation, division, and ultimately colonization in Canada. By far the most notorious example of this is the culturally genocidal Indian Residential School (IRS) system, which was jointly established and operated by the federal government and various churches across the country from the 1880s until the last school closed in 1996 (Truth and Reconciliation Commission of Canada 2015). The Truth and Reconciliation Commission of Canada (TRC) has found these schools to have committed acts of "cultural genocide" (2015, p. 1) through their attempts to force assimilation, break down the family unit, and eliminate Aboriginal languages and cultures as a way to terminate the federal government's treaty obligations by fully assimilating Indigenous youth into mainstream Canadian society. All across the country children were taken into residential schools "not to educate them, but primarily to break their link to their culture and identity" (2015, p. 2). Duncan Campbell Scott, the Minister of Indian Affairs responsible for implementing the IRS policy in the 1920s, was very explicit about this goal.

> I want to get rid of the Indian problem ... Our objective is to continue until there is not a single Indian in Canada that has not been absorbed into the body politic and there is no Indian question, and no Indian Department, that is the whole object of this Bill. (As cited in Leslie 1978, p. 114)

Without consultation, the IRS system removed children from their homes to take them to the residential schools, often by force, banned Indigenous cultural practices, and foisted a Euro-Canadian curriculum upon students. For over a century, approximately 150,000 children were taken to residential schools where they suffered from physical, sexual, emotional, and cultural abuse, and many of the survivors have been scarred for life by the predations that they suffered (TRC 2015). Many children did not survive in residential schools. The TRC (2015) reported that children died of diseases at alarmingly high rates in residential schools compared with the general population, and this is based only on data that was recorded; many of the deaths were never reported.

The IRS system was built upon the "assumption that European civilizations and Christian religions were superior to Aboriginal culture" (TRC 2015, p. 4), an ideology that has left a damaging legacy that did not end with those who attended these schools. The impacts of these policies are being felt by survivors, their families, and communities still today.

The IRS system is far from the only example of the use of the Canadian education system to further oppressive colonial processes affecting Indigenous peoples. In provincial schools, institutionalized discrimination remains a fact of life for many Indigenous youth (Neegan 2005; Orr and Cameron 2004). Furthermore, through a process that Battiste (1998) referred to as "cognitive imperialism," the "formal" education system has come to embody the belief that Western epistemologies are the only valid sources of knowledge. This has also entailed the discrediting of other (especially Indigenous) ways of knowing; as such, Indigenous languages, historiographies, and other aspects of Indigenous epistemologies continue to be underemphasized, if not completely absent, in the curriculum of provincial schools. For instance, a survey of Canadian secondary provincial school graduates revealed that almost 80% of respondents felt their schooling did not help them understand Aboriginal issues (Coalition for the Advancement of Aboriginal Studies 2002).

Based on these and other structural obstacles, it is hardly surprising that 36.4% of Aboriginal people in Nova Scotia aged 15 years and older had less than a high school diploma in 2006 (Statistics Canada 2007a), compared to 26.8% among the broader provincial population (Statistics Canada 2007b). Furthermore, the colonial pressures generated by the provincial school system have likely played a major role in the loss of Indigenous languages and cultures. Indeed, only 20.6% of Aboriginal people in Nova Scotia had knowledge of an "Aboriginal language" in 2006 (Statistics Canada 2007a). Evidently, the experience of many Indigenous peoples in Canada with the mainstream school system was, and to a significant extent continues to be, one of colonization and oppression.

Enter Mi'kmaw Kinametnewey and the Mi'kmaw Education Agreement

The vision of a "formal" education system that is empowering instead of disempowering, and which fosters local Indigenous educational control instead of furthering oppression, was perhaps first articulated in a policy format in the National Indian Brotherhood's *Indian Control of Indian Education* policy paper (National Indian Brotherhood 1973). In Nova Scotia, this vision of education was later manifested in the Mi'kmaq Education Act (1998), the product of the Mi'kmaw Education Agreement between the federal government and nine Nova Scotian Mi'kmaw chiefs, which aimed to "enable communities to exercise jurisdiction in relation to education." The act gives signatory communities the power to make laws applicable to primary, elementary, and secondary education and to provide primary, elementary, and secondary educational programs and services to residents. The nine communities that originally signed onto the Mi'kmaq Education Act were Acadia, Annapolis Valley, Potlotek (Chapel Island), Eskasoni, Membertou, Pictou Landing, Sipe'kne'katik (Indian Brook), Wagmatcook, and We'koqma'q. Paq'tnkek, Bear River, and Glooscap also signed the act at later dates. Of these communities, Eskasoni, Membertou, Potlotek, Sipe'kne'katik, Wagmatcook, We'koqma'q, and Pictou Landing run band-operated schools. Millbrook remains as the only Mi'kmaw community in Nova Scotia that has not signed on to this agreement. While the 1972 National Indian Brotherhood manifesto had served as a catalyst for several Mi'kmaw communities to assert their right to establish and control their own schools prior to the formation of 1998 Act, the Mi'kmaq Education Act was an important political watershed.

The Mi'kmaq Education Act (1998) also gave birth to a revamped MK as a "corporation without share capital" to support the delivery of educational programs and services in signatory communities. MK is based in Membertou and run by the Chiefs of these 12 communities, who serve as its board of directors. Most staff members are Mi'kmaw professionals, and community input from annual symposiums informs MK's strategies and policies. The impetus behind its creation was partly derived from a federal desire for an accountable organization. However, this and Mi'kmaw Kina'masuti before it, and the Mi'kmaw Education Authority before that, were also driven by community desire to build capacity, share resources, have their educational interests represented, and foster unity (McCarthy 2001). MK's main roles are to provide intermediary services (similar to those offered by a provincial school board), such as assistance with professional development of staff and needs assessment; as well as to provide a forum to represent the educational interests of its member communities, both in internal decision-making and in negotiations with the Euro-Canadian governments. It does this through a variety of programs and bodies, such as the First Nations School Success Program (FNSSP) and other intermediary services such as Mi'kmaw language resource development, support for students with special needs, and physical education collaborations amongst schools.

Self-Governance and Self-Determination

The National Indian Brotherhood's vision in 1972 of expanding "Indian control of Indian education" (ICIE) was inextricably linked to broader demands for greater powers of self-determination among Indigenous peoples in Canada. The relationship also exists between the Mi'kmaq Education Agreement/MK and struggles for self-governance. The Assembly of First Nations released an updated version of the ICIE document in 2010, calling once again for *First Nations Control of First Nations Education* in which they argued that consecutive federal governments have consistently failed to meet the expectations laid out in ICIE and they argued that the principles of this document were still relevant in 2010. Aboriginal communities are still fighting for the right to govern the education of their children. MK is often held up as an example of this vision coming to fruition.

Self-governance of education has been a structural way to advance Indigenous control of Indigenous education. However, governance without concerted attention to the end goal of decolonizing a system to enable and support individuals and communities to act in self-determining ways risks falling into re-colonizing ways. There are examples both within Canada (Rasmussen 2009) and beyond (Major and

Mulvihill 2009) that illustrate that movements towards self-governance have failed to create self-determination. Colonization has stripped away both governance and determination in Indigenous communities. Within the MK communities, some educational leadership capacity existed through earlier teacher training initiatives post ICIE. In the early 1990s, as the Federal government began moving away from federal schools and transferring control to each Mi'kmaq band, these groups of educators were well positioned to lead with both cultural rootedness and an awareness of the largely colonial education system. With this initial capacity already present, the opportunity to self-govern empowered communities to decolonize the system which then supported greater self-determination and that self-determination then shaped the governance structure to be able to be truly responsive to the community it serves. This was in keeping with the RCAP vision for Aboriginal self-government, with its core purpose of affirming Aboriginal identities, through "the entrenchment of the Aboriginal right of doing things differently" (Dussault et al. 1996, p. 665). This was a radical departure from the usual colonial approach of governing education so that it aligned "with pre-determined Canadian norms of how people should govern themselves" (p. 665). All of this allowed Mi'kmaw communities to realize that 1972 ICIE vision.

One of the key elements of the MK agreement was that the chiefs meet collectively several times per year to take up discussions and make decisions about educational matters affecting the collective. Decisions are made through consensus building. Because of the capacity that has been built within MK communities with respect to education, many professional educators find themselves in positions of leadership on councils, as chiefs, or on education committees and in positions of senior educational leadership within MK and the communities. In many ways, this ensures that the board of directors made up of the chiefs of communities has the educational knowledge and community rootedness to make these important decisions in ways that benefit all communities.

The capacity building brought cultural ways of knowing, being, and doing to what could have potentially become a very colonizing structure. The structure, though at first glance may resemble a typical school board, has been able to work in ways that emerge from community and cultural practices. The value of the collective embedded in a Mi'kmaw worldview mitigates communities pitting themselves against each other as might happen in some mainstream school boards. One unique feature of MK is the annual symposium where each community reports its accomplishments from the past year and sets out aspirations for the upcoming year. This symposium has cultivated a collective learning community and supportive environment that inspires and motivates all communities to continue the work of decolonization. Communities are represented by not only education professionals but also community members that represent multi-generations including elders, youth, and other adult community leaders. There has consistently been a focus on what is best for the advancement of all communities rather than for individual communities. This approach has shaped a communitarian identity, supported by consensus decision-making, as depicted in Orr and Cameron's (2004) *We are Mi'kmaw Kina'matnewey* report.

Although Schouls (2003) has argued that culture is an inadequate reason for claims of self-determination due to his view that many groups have experienced assimilation to the point that they are no longer distinguishable from the mainstream, this is not the case with the Mi'kmaq of Nova Scotia. Mi'kmaw culture is deeply rooted in Mi'kmaw ways of knowing, being, and doing, and transcends usual markers of material culture so often used to identify and discount Indigenous peoples. While it is true that some Mi'kmaw communities have experienced more assimilation and are therefore less connected to language and traditional knowledges, the overall group identity of the collective empowers these communities to decolonize as well. In fact, MK provides resources and supports to these communities to reclaim language and culture in ways that would not have been possible by acting alone. The strength of the whole is greater than any of the parts. Kimlicka (1989) would describe MK as an example of communitarian pluralism because of its efforts to protect Mi'kmaw communities from the dominant colonial agenda.

In educational governance terms, MK is coming to be known as one of Canada's foremost First Nation Education Organizations (National Panel on First Nation Elementary and Secondary Education for Students on Reserve, 2012), or FNEOs. Through the Mi'kmaq Education Agreement, many of MK's member communities have, to varying degrees, taken over the "first level" of educational service (i.e., actual education provision) through band-operated schools, which is another layer of self-governance in education. MK and its ilk serve to provide First Nations' control over the delivery of "second level" or intermediary services, which essentially replace the services provided by provincial school boards.

The MK agreement has been quite appropriately critiqued as failing to provide resources for second level services (McHue 2006; Paquette and Fallon 2010). Since 2008, these services have been provided through funding obtained through FNSSP which is a proposal driven funding program that requires demonstration of data to show student achievement is improving. As Walton et al. (2016) note

> MK worried that mainstream school improvement models might be incongruent with notions of school success held by Aboriginal educators (Toney, 2012). Therefore, *A Framework for School Improvement for Schools* (Orr & McCormick, 2007) was developed, allowing more cultural relevance in terms of knowledge and measures of success. In this framework, MK schools develop school success plans that focus on literacy, numeracy, Mi'kmaw language, and student retention. The effect of including a language goal cannot be overstated as it validates the importance of language and culture in MK schools. Student learning assessments support the school success plan and the performance measures established to access and accelerate both student and school performance. FNSSP allocates funding for a variety of supports that allow access to mentors and consultants who travel to support Mi'kmaq teachers and principals. Prior to FNSSP, educators in MK had little access to these second level services that are common in public schools. The principal now has the range of supports to assist her school with continuous improvement. (p. 113)

While MK continues to argue that core funding for second level services should be part of their agreement, they work with the FNSSP funding to ensure that second level services are provided in a manner that is consistent with a decolonizing approach to education.

The Mi'kmaq of Nova Scotia, and all Indigenous peoples in Canada, does not currently have in place any organization controlling education provision at the "third level." This would include the ability to create educational curriculum – although the MK member communities can modify the existing curriculum to an extent – and oversee schools and second-level service providers. The third level of services is the equivalent of a provincial department of education.

This governance arrangement has been criticized on a number of fronts. Battiste (1998) argues that the limitations placed by the Mi'kmaq Education Agreement on the Mi'kmaq's ability to create their own curriculum is problematic, as it means that curriculum will continue to be created from an outside, colonial context and will thereby continue the aforementioned process of "cognitive imperialism." A more policy-oriented version of this line of reasoning builds on the recommendations of the 1996 Royal Commission on Aboriginal Peoples. It contends that, due to the limited capabilities and resources of FNEOs like MK and of individual schools, an ideal direction to move towards in improving Indigenous education is the creation of a nationwide system of regional education authorities. These regional authorities would oversee a number of FNEOs and provide third-level services, especially curriculum development, thereby avoiding the intrusion of the provincial bureaucracy (McCue and Harvey2006; Mendelson 2008). From this perspective, FNEOs like MK are not a bad thing; they are a necessary step in the right direction and a prerequisite for self-governance in education, but they are not the final step in the journey of self-governance.

The argument that some sort of larger regional body should supersede MK and provide leadership and third-level services has merit. At a purely abstract level, the argument that the Mi'kmaq should have full control over Mi'kmaw education, especially in the area of curriculum development, is in keeping with a decolonizing agenda. However, from a very pragmatic viewpoint, the implementation and administration of a regional FNEO would be a monumental task. It would require agreements with numerous governments at the federal, provincial, and band council levels.

Furthermore, there are many elements of community-based cultural knowledge that are embedded in the way that intermediary services are delivered, not just in who is controlling third-level services. For instance, significant efforts are being made to support the pedagogical development of Mi'kmaw language teachers across MK schools. Literacy, numeracy, and early childhood supports are also helping to embed cultural-practical knowledge of Mi'kmaw worldview into these subject areas. Preliminary findings suggest that these intermediary services are changing the ways that curriculum is enacted in schools. Additionally, to focus exclusively on a higher level of governance authority misses out on the reality that the decisions made by teachers "on the ground" in schools (classroom governance) have the biggest impact on processes and outcomes (Marzano 2003). MK has acknowledged this and is working hard to foster the certification of more Mi'kmaw teachers to teach in Mi'kmaw schools and to support these teachers to be role models and provide cultural-practical knowledge (Orr et al. 2002) to students, thereby enhancing the "formal" education capacity of its member communities (Mi'kmaw Kina'matnewey 2011). This being said, control over third-level services does matter in the education that Mi'kmaw students receive, and thus future efforts to expand self-governance in this direction are worthy of study and perhaps support.

In recent years, MK has formed a more significant working relationship with the provincial Department of Education and Early Childhood Development (EECD) that has ensured greater inclusion of MK representation in decision-making processes. Second level services staff are included in provincial team meetings with representatives of public school boards and MK teacher delegates sit on committees relating to curriculum development, assessment design, and other related committees. Some specific documents, such as the Mi'kmaw Studies 11 courses and the Mi'kmaw Language Framework, have been collaboratively developed by MK and the EECD. The signing of a memorandum of understanding between the Province of Nova Scotia and the Mi'kmaw Nation on Treaty Day, October 1, 2015, that will ensure treaty education is taught at all levels in all subjects serves as a further mechanism for increased collaboration around curriculum development that honors Mi'kmaw knowledge and history. While this is not providing those third level services, it demonstrates how MK capacity that has developed since its inception enables greater influence over the provincial curriucula, programs, and services that are being developed for public schools and implemented in MK schools.

Corntassel (2008) points out another critique of the MK type agreement citing that there are inherent dangers in basing self-governance efforts on a rights-based discourse. For instance, a rights-based approach may tend to deemphasize cultural responsibilities and relationships between communities and with the natural world. This suggests that these dangers might be relevant to MK and its member communities, as their role and powers are supposedly defined by the state-centric and Western-legalistic Mi'kmaq Education Act.

Paquette and Fallon (2010) also critique the nature of the local jurisdictional control and the positioning of MK as a "support service provider" (p. 190) which results in MK having "no meaningful *control* over anything of educational significance" (p. 190) and also results in fragmentation across the collective. We would argue that local jurisdictional control is one of the strengths of MK as collaboration and consensus building ensure greater community voice and accountability. The sharing of capital resources to ensure community schools are built in a timely manner is one example of how collaboration amongst the member communities strengthens all MK communities.

Orr and Cameron's (2006) policy work with MK determined that the organization's purpose is, in reality, driven by the following five key cultural principles:

1. MK respects and affirms its own people and believes they are the key to its success.
2. MK has shaped and is shaped by a collective Mi'kmaw consciousness, which advances issues of common interest and concern to the wider Mi'kmaw nation.
3. MK exists to support community-based aspirations, initiatives, and needs.
4. MK operates through a working group decision-making model, which is multi-layered, circular, and continuous.

5. Appropriate second level services [to be delivered by MK] are determined through the four principles of community, circularity, collectivity, and respect for the Mi'kmaw people.

Orr and Cameron (2006) provide numerous examples of how MK incorporates these principles into its programming and practices. Thus, contrary to the concerns of Corntassel (2008) and Paquette and Fallon (2010), the collective identity fostered by MK and its culturally oriented assertion of rights breeds confidence and trust amongst member communities, which leads MK to be accountable to these communities through the support it provides them – a fundamental shift from a top-down to bottom-up system of authority. Therefore, MK schools and communities are encouraged through an organization with the central purpose of culturally and academically supporting their success.

Evidently, despite its de jure origins in a legal discourse, MK's true beginnings and current governance mandate lie with Mi'kmaw people who are its members and their ways of being, knowing, and doing. The decision of MK in 2015 to enter into a third 3-year agreement with Canada to use funding to enhance intermediary service provides an opportunity to continue to advance the decolonization of the Mi'kmaw education system while also meeting accountability measures established by Canada. As such, it can be said that despite the potential ontological dangers stemming from MK's connections to a rational-legal discourse, it has shown its agency and made major strides towards using the powers that this system has available for decolonizing ends – or, to be more poetic, towards using the master's tools to dismantle the master's house.

Community Capacity for Community Control

As described above, one of the most significant factors contributing to the decolonization of education in MK communities is the capacity development that has happened within the member communities, largely through partnerships with institutions like Cape Breton University and St. Francis Xavier University. When community members are employed in positions at all levels of the education system, Mi'kmaw voice and vision can take center stage. This capacity development was a significant part of the vision for MK from the beginning.

In 1995, a province wide review of teacher education was conducted in Nova Scotia. At roughly the same time the BLAC Report (Black Learners Advisory Council 1996) and the Marshall Inquiry (1996) confirmed that Mi'kmaw and the African Nova Scotia communities continued to be underserved in the public schools in Nova Scotia with institutional and systemic racism in the education system cited as major factors. Teacher education needed to be changed in the province. A Memorandum of Understanding (1995) between the Mi'kmaw community and St. Francis Xavier University committed the School (now Faculty) of Education to include in its mandate the training and preparation of Mi'kmaw educators to teach in band and provincial schools. That mandate and the Faculty of Education's own policies and practices related to addressing the underrepresentation of these groups has enabled the Faculty of Education to graduate 133 BEd students and 40 MEd students with numbers continuing to grow since 1996.

Additional universities have also run cohort programs at the graduate level as well to support MK capacity building. For example, in 2015 there were 13 graduates who received an MEd in Curriculum Supporting Diverse Learners from Mount Saint Vincent University. At the undergraduate level, Cape Breton University (CBU) has played a significant role over the past 20 years in attracting Mi'kmaw students and supporting them to complete Bachelor level degrees, often offering part-time and community-based programs. Cape Breton University has the largest population of Mi'kmaw students in Eastern Canada and produces the highest number of Mi'kmaw graduates. The Mi'kmaq College Institute at CBU has "made it possible for Mi'kmaq students, educators, scholars, and researchers of Mi'kmaq cosmology to establish a curriculum and research agenda which contribute to the achievement of the educational and community goals set by Mi'kmaq communities" (retrieved from CBU website, 2008). The BA in Community Studies program, in particular, allows many Mi'kmaw students to pursue Mi'kmaq Studies for which their lived experiences, cultural knowledge, and interest form a great deal of the curriculum. Having such a robust pool of Mi'kmaw students graduating from CBU has allowed the St. Francis Xavier University Faculty of Education to attract many well-qualified Mi'kmaw candidates into teacher education.

The restructuring of the teacher education program at St. Francis Xavier University in 1995 provided an important starting place for a refocusing of teacher education and considering the place of Indigeneity in it. The Memorandum of Understanding with Mi'kmaw communities marked a clear commitment to address the historical and contemporary imbalance in power relations between Mi'kmaw and non-Mi'kmaw communities and hence school achievement within the Nova Scotia schools. Social justice and equity became key program strands that have been threaded through the entire 2-year experience. This public articulation represented an important commitment by the Faculty of Education to acknowledge issues of power, privilege, exclusion, and marginalization in schools, the university, and the larger society.

As a result of having so many MK community teacher education graduates, MK schools have large numbers of Mi'kmaw teachers and administrators. As a result of this capacity development, more recent teacher education candidates have a high likelihood of being mentored by Mi'kmaw teachers in schools with Mi'kmaw administrators, continuing the project of decolonization through teacher education. Furthermore, Mi'kmaw people hold the majority of positions at the MK office and many Mi'kmaw educators serve as directors of education, members of community council, and at the time of writing this chapter two of the 13 chiefs hold Bachelor of Education degrees, including the chief who serves as the director for the MK board. When well-qualified community members are holding key decision-making positions at all levels of MK, community control can truly emerge.

Walton et al. (2016) recently compared two Indigenous schools, one Inuit and one Mi'kmaw, set in very different geographic, political, cultural, and linguistic contexts but who are both aiming to shed the colonial legacy of Eurocentric schooling. Each community experiences the economic and social effects of colonization and its accompanying intergenerational trauma, yet also has a corresponding degree of resilience, persistence, and hopefulness. Both are headed by Indigenous women from the local community. However, the researchers noted dramatically different success, as defined by graduation rates, experienced in the two school contexts. A closer look at the two contexts suggested that two factors appeared to build school leadership capacity. The first, as previously mentioned, was the long-term partnership developed with St. Francis Xavier University which provided extensive and comprehensive pre-service and in-service education for Mi'kmaw educators thus populating the school with certified Mi'kmaw teachers. The second key factor that surfaced was the presence of MK as a governance structure supporting Mi'kmaw schools. In particular, they highlighted the second level services provided through the FNSSP as noted previously.

Secondly MK itself was an incubator for Mi'kmaw leadership development so that Mi'kmaw students and teachers saw themselves reflected throughout the MK system. MK provided both a leadership incubator for Mi'kmaw educators who took on leadership roles at the systems level and provided Mi'kmaw role models for those educators. Many educators deepened and broadened their skill set and confidence as they rotated through MK positions. Importantly they were supported and mentored by fellow Mi'kmaw educators. The same conditions were not apparent in Nunavut as community teacher education programs (TEP), so much a part of developing Inuit teacher leadership pre-Nunavut greatly diminished in the post-Nunavut period. While the intention for the creation was that Inuit people would be included at all level of governance, they are currently absent in significant numbers at the Ministry of Education levels. This partially explains the difference in the two systems and highlights the significance of the capacity building that MK has enabled.

Decolonizing Education Through the Centering of Mi'kmaw Language and Culture

Band-operated schools provide education at the primary, elementary, and secondary levels in many MK member communities. These schools have come under fire from Mi'kmaq community members and politicians, policy analysts, and academics. According to Poliandri (2011), members of Millbrook First Nation cited the existence of a band-operated school in Indian Brook as a factor in the community's social problems. Furthermore, former Millbrook Chief Lawrence Paul cited the benefits of "integration" from sending the band's children to a provincial school – an assessment with which Poliandri appears to wholeheartedly agree. This analysis fails to acknowledge the role that the Social Determinants of Health (Mikkonen and Raphael 2010) play in educational achievement. It also clearly demonstrates that the deficit view of Indigenous knowledges and the ideology of cultural superiority that was at the heart of the assimilationist policies of the IRS days are still entrenched in research and even community discourse today. From Poliandri's perspective, in order to thrive in the "modern" world, Mi'kmaw children need to be "exposed" to mainstream Canadian society through schools, to learn how to interact and be successful in it. According to this logic, the band-run school's practice of keeping children in their community throughout their "formal" education runs contrary to the necessity of "integration" in mainstream society. The band-operated schools have also been criticized by some community members and students as being unable to teach English literacy skills effectively, due to their emphasis on teaching the Mi'kmaq language in the Mi'kmaq immersion programs (Tompkins et al. 2011), and lacking the necessary resources to create an adequate environment for learning (Orr and Cameron 2004).

There is a fairly limited amount of "hard" qualitative and quantitative data that assesses the band-operated schools, supported by MK, in terms of assessment outputs before and after the creation of MK over a long period of time. It is important to note that although one may not agree with a heavily quantitative and standardized approach to student learning assessment by MK and its schools – indeed, we believe that such data only tells a small part of the story – the quantifiable, accessible nature of the results that it can generate is integral to providing outcomes that will elicit support from communities, chiefs, and especially Indigenous Affairs.

In previous work, Orr and Cameron (2004) provided some valuable information regarding the academic success of band-operated schools. They explained that between 1991 and 2001, the percentage of persons 15 years of age and older without high school certificates decreased by 17.9 points, compared to a 10% decrease for all Registered Indians living on reserve (p. 36). Furthermore, over the same time period MK communities saw a decrease in their unemployment rate by 4.8%, compared to 3.3% among all Registered Indians on reserve (p. 45); and labor force participation in MK communities increased by 15.2 percentage points, versus a 5% increase among all on-reserve Registered Indians (p. 44). Additionally, MK and its member communities have seen a 9.7% increase in the number of persons who have completed a post-secondary education, compared to a 7.6% increase among all Registered Indians living on reserve (p. 42). More recent data of a quantitative nature indicates that Mi'kmaw students in Nova Scotian provincial schools, on average, have fared well below their Euro-Canadian counterparts in literacy and numeracy on provincial assessments in grades 3, 6, and 9 (Thiessen 2009). This helps to contest the mythology that Mi'kmaw students fare better in provincial than band operated schools.

Paul-Gould (2012), Sock (2012), and Tompkins et al. (2011) offer some useful data specific to the success of the Eskasoni Mi'kmaq K-3 immersion program. According to one Elder that they interviewed, there is a link between speaking Mi'kmaq and being able to absorb knowledge: "If you speak your language, then you open up your heart. Once you open your heart, the more knowledge you are able to absorb. You are able to express yourself better rather than it being lost in translation" (May 5, 2010, as cited in Tompkins et al. 2011, p. 57). The researchers found that the Mi'kmaw immersion program at Eskasoni had major positive impacts on students' leadership qualities, self-esteem, and Mi'kmaw identities. Their Mi'kmaw fluency was also impressive, although fluency sometimes declined over the years once students exited the program. Immersion students typically had the highest English reading levels after leaving Grade 3, the last grade of the immersion program. This idea is born out in the classroom, as interviews with immersion teachers of the students during and after they completed the immersion program consistently cited the success of immersion students in a variety of subject areas, as well as their proclivity for extracurricular engagement. For instance, a reading test of the Grade 7 students at Eskasoni suggested that all 16 of the former immersion students were amongst the top 25 learners in terms of literacy levels (out of 81 students overall), and of the 14 students at the highest reading level, all but one were from the immersion program (see Fig. 1).

This information begins to make a strong case that even in the field of "formal" education, MK and its member communities are making important strides to improve outcomes – something that is integral to the success of the Mi'kmaq of Nova Scotia and the furtherance of a decolonizing agenda. Indeed, it appears that MK's focus on greater local control of "formal" education is likely to provide more in the way of educational success than the "integration" approach, in terms of mainstream educational indicators – not to mention the benefits of fostering culturally appropriate education.

As the original immersion students are now graduating from high school and pursuing post-secondary opportunities, the community has moved the immersion program into its own building where students not only speak Mi'kmaq in class but in the hallways, in the gymnasium, and on the playground.

Protecting and growing Mi'kmaw culture and especially language, in order to foster the creation of stronger Mi'kmaw identities among students, has been a major focus of MK and its member communities. Initiatives undertaken with this aim include the creation and sustained support of the Mi'kmaq immersion programs in some schools, MK's hiring of Mi'kmaq language specialists to support program delivery and development, and MK's efforts to support the development of

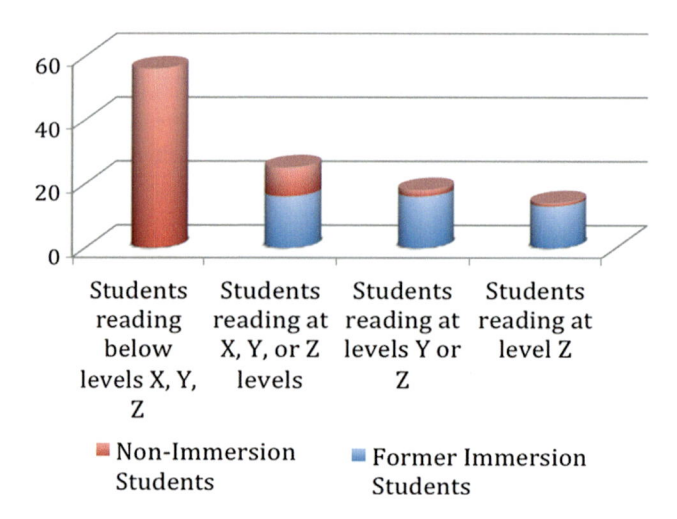

Fig. 1 Eskasoni grade 7 reading levels – immersion and non-immersion students (Source: Paul-Gould 2012, p. 62)

technological (e.g., internet) components of language programs through the First Nations Help Desk (Mi'kmaw Kina'matnewey 2011). MK is also making strides to develop language resources for all communities with the development of language apps and curriculum materials for all MK schools. MK has acquired the rights to translate several Robert Munsch books into Mi'kmaq and these and other Mi'kmaw books are readily available in MK schools. Many books have been made into iPad apps that enable students to read along as they hear the language being spoken. The support for second level services at the MK office has made these initiatives possible.

MK's commitment to Mi'kmaw language revitalization is not only supported by Indigenous elders and scholars but is also in keeping with a deep understanding of the research on bilingual education. Tompkins and Murray Orr (2013) in a review of the literature on bilingual education, and more specifically Aboriginal immersion programs, found that there is strong and robust growing evidence of the success of these programs to deepen identity, improve fluency, and increase academic achievement for Aboriginal children. Furthermore, Barac and Bialystok (2012), in their review of over 50 years of research into bilingual education, reported that "Bilingualism turns out to be an experience that benefits many aspects of children's development" (p. 36). Neuroscience research is also beginning to show the many benefits of bilingualism on brain development, particularly when it is learned in early childhood (Society for Neuroscience 2013).

Language is the heart of a culture and Indigenous people's knowledge of their cultures is integral to their wellbeing. Cairns and Flanagan (2001) disagree, arguing that assimilation of Aboriginal Canadians has largely already taken place, except for relatively minor "subcultural" characteristics, and that the future of these groups lies in further integrating into mainstream Canadian society and embracing the modern economy. Yet Battiste (1998) refutes this neocolonial argument, pointing out that Indigenous knowledge(s) is fundamental for the continuing survival and flourishing of Indigenous peoples. One need to look no further than the intergenerational trauma inflicted upon students through the cultural (not to mention physical and sexual) abuses of the IRS system to realize that assimilation has, and will continue to have, disastrous effects on Indigenous peoples in Canada (Frideres 2011). Battiste supports this position with numerous testimonies by Indigenous peoples surveyed by the Assembly of First Nations, citing the vital importance of preserving Indigenous languages and cultures. She also contends that Aboriginal languages are "beyond dispute" (p. 17) the most integral of all facets of Aboriginal culture(s), as language contains vital traditions and customs:

> The complementary modes of knowing in the tribal world form the essence of tribal epistemology, and have been continually transmitted through the oral tradition. Without Aboriginal languages, the lessons and knowledge would be lost to the people, and their way of life gravely affected. (Battiste 1998, p. 18)

These languages, and their associated epistemologies and attached ways of being and doing, are languishing in the Canadian education system. Even in band-operated schools, structural challenges remain, as the prevalence of the English language and non-Indigenous cultural practices, not to mention a lack of resources, can make learning the Mi'kmaq language and appropriate cultural practices challenging (for example, see Orr and Cameron 2004; Tompkins et al. 2011).

Culturally appropriate education extends beyond the language classroom in MK schools. Dedicated science teachers have encouraged students to build science fair projects every year that draw upon the idea of "two-eyed seeing" (Hatcher et al. 2009) and each year MK sends students to the Canada-wide science fair. Literacy initiatives have focused on bringing professional learning opportunities and classroom resources to teachers in MK schools with a focus on culturally relevant approaches and materials. The *Show Me Your Math* program (Lunney Borden et al. forthcoming) has encouraged thousands of Mi'kmaw students to engage in intergenerational conversations with Elders and other community members as they explore ways of mathematical reasoning inherent in community knowledge and practices. The *Show Me Your Math* program and related inquiry projects have helped center community knowledge as a starting point for mathematics learning which provides an example of how to decolonize mathematics (Lunney Borden and Wiseman 2016). Through all of these efforts, MK is bringing community knowledge into a central role while striving to meet provincial outcomes.

While many school systems across the country struggle to increase the graduation rates for Indigenous students, MK meets or exceeds the graduation rates for all provincial systems in the country. Data from 2009 to 2016 shows that graduation rates in MK schools ranged from 87% to 90% annually (Mi'kmaw Kina'matnewey 2016). Furthermore, attendance rates range from 86% to 91% indicating that students are attending regularly and completing school. Additionally, MK-generated data shows that students are increasingly graduating on time, with an average age of grade 12 students in 2014 being 18.34 years, down from 20.24 in 2009. With nearly 600 MK post-secondary students, the success of MK graduation rate creates new challenges as post-secondary funding is simply inadequate to support all of the students who are seeking post-secondary opportunities.

Furthermore, Orr and Cameron (2004) cite an INAC study conducted with Mi'kmaw students that suggests that only 15% of students in band-operated schools saw major barriers to post-secondary educational success as related to discrimination and lack of cultural programming, compared to 44% in provincial schools (p. 30). More recent comparative data collected in 2011 and 2012 corroborates this earlier finding (Orr et al. 2017).

This information shows that Mi'kmaw language, culture, and identity are inseparable from the wellbeing and future success of the Mi'kmaq. Furthermore, despite lacking resources and operating within a system that was once used to disempower the Mi'kmaq, MK and its member communities that operate their own schools have made major breakthroughs in fostering Mi'kmaq language, improving youth cultural knowledge and capacity, and nurturing Mi'kmaw pride and identity. These outcomes continue to be vital for the collective future of the Mi'kmaw nation.

Stones of Wisdom from the MK Experience

While context matters for MK and the complexity of this collective cannot be transplanted into other contexts easily, there are stones of wisdom that can be gleaned from the MK experience. With everything we have described, one key theme that emerges is that there is a collective community ownership within MK. It is within this ownership that MK finds its roots. The strength of MK is that its people are its most important asset, and there is a collective belief that its future is its people. There has been a consistent focus on the ongoing development of capacity within communities and within people. There are partnerships and organizations that provide the leadership development opportunities and spaces. There are regularized practices such as the annual symposium, the Mi'kmaw language, conference and other educational conferences, the chief's meetings, the education working group meetings for directors and MK leadership, the monthly principal meetings, the student focused experiences like speech festivals and math fairs, and so on that continually bring community members together to celebrate and support the on-going project of decolonizing education. These practices are how decolonization is enacted and they transcend any political shifts in local or school governance because they have become entrenched in the MK life cycle. These moments of coming together provide a public space to demonstrate the actualization of Mi'kmaw education. The conscious recognition of what colonization has done has mobilized the collective to follow a clear path to live out a more Mi'kmaw vision of education. Other Indigenous communities seeking to develop an authentic indigenous education system may learn from the MK's attention to collective ownership, capacity development, and relentless focus on bringing its people together to ensure what happens in classrooms for MK children is always linked to a shared vision. This means that MK has found ways to dismantle the master's house and reconstruct it in ways that are Mi'kmaq.

Conclusion

Colonial practices have been at play since contact and related government policies like residential schools, centralization, and so on have been shattering Indigenous community's ways of knowing, being, and doing for centuries and continue to do so today. MK's decolonizing approach to education is beginning to pull the shattered pieces back together to rebuild and reclaim a Mi'kmaw system of education. MK's vision clearly articulated, and shared by many, keeps language and culture as a central component in children's education:

> Our people have a common opportunity that provides the best possible educational experience such that our students achieve the highest standards in Canada in the broadest sense, and they are comprehensively prepared for their chosen next steps after high school.

The education is provided in a way that our language, culture, and traditions are fostered in their lives thereafter and embedded in their character. We will achieve these goals in both our community as well as in provincial schools. (Retrieved from kinu.ca/introducing-mikmaw-kinamatnewey)

Such a formidable task requires collaboration and partnerships at many levels. This review of MK shows the multiple and complex ways in which communities, educators, institutions, and governments are working to do things in a new way that is rooted in old ways. MK is using the master's tools to dismantle the master's house and then rebuild a new dwelling rooted in Mi'kmaw language, culture, and values.

References

Battiste M (1998) Enabling the autumn seed: toward a decolonized approach to Aboriginal knowledge, language, and education. Can J Nativ Educ 22(1):16–27
Barac, R., & Bialystok, E. (2012). Bilingual Effects on Cognitive and Linguistic Development: Role of Language, Cultural Background, and Education. Child Development, 83(2), 413–422. http://doi.org/10.1111/j.1467-8624.2011.01707.x.
Cairns A, Flanagan T (2001) Aboriginal choices: an exchange. Inroads 10:103–123
Coalition for the Advancement of Aboriginal Studies (2002) Learning about walking in beauty: placing Aboriginal perspectives in Canadian classrooms. Canadian Race Relations Foundation, Toronto
Corntassel J (2008) Toward sustainable self-determination: rethinking the contemporary Indigenous-rights discourse. Alternatives 33:105–132
Dussault, R., Erasmus, Georges, Canada. Indian Northern Affairs Canada & Canadian Electronic Library (1996) Report of the royal commission on aboriginal peoples. Gathering strength (DesLibris. Documents collection). Ottawa, Ont.: Indian and Northern Affairs Canada 3.
Frideres J (2011) First Nations in the twenty-first century. Oxford University Press, Toronto
Hatcher A, Bartlett C, Marshall A, Marshall M (2009) Two-eyed seeing in the classroom environment: concepts, approaches, and challenges. Can J Sci Math Technol Educ 9(3):141–153
Kimlicka W (1989) Liberalism, community, and culture. Clarendon Press, Toronto
Leslie J (1978) The historical development of the Indian Act, 2nd edn. Department of Indian Affairs and Northern Development, Treaties and Historical Research Branch, Ottawa
Lorde A (1984) Sister outsider. Crossing Press, Berkeley
Lunney Borden L, Wiseman D (2016) Considerations from places where Indigenous and Western ways of knowing, being, and doing circulate together: STEM as artifact of teaching and learning. Can J Sci Math Technol Educ 16(2):140–152
Lunney Borden L, Wagner D, Johnson N (2017) Show me your math: Mi'kmaw community members explore mathematics. In: Nicol C, Dawson S, Archibald J, Glandfield F (eds) Living culturally responsive mathematics curriculum and pedagogy: making a difference with/in Indigenous communities. Sense Publishers, Rotterdam
Major T, Mulvihill T (2009) Julius Nyerere (1922–1999), an African philosopher re-envisions teacher education to escape colonialism. New Propos J Marx Interdiscip Inq 3(1):15–22
Marzano R (2003) What works in schools: translating research into action. ASCD, Alexandria
McCarthy J (2001) Mi'kmaq Kina'matnewey: a case study in aggregation. Institute on Governance paper
McCue H (2006). First Nations 2nd and 3rd Level Education Services: a discussion paper for the joint working group INAC – AFN. http://www.afn.ca/uploads/files/education/9._2006_april_harvey_mccue_first_nations_2nd_&_3rd_level_services_paper.pdf
Mendelson M (2008) Improving education on reserves: a First Nations education authority act. Caledon Institute of Social Policy paper

Mi'kmaq Education Act (1998) Retrieved from http://laws-lois.justice.gc.ca/eng/acts/M-7.6/page-2.html#docCont

Mi'kmaw Kina'matnewey (2011) Annual report: 2010–2011. Mi'kmaw Kinamatnewey, Membertou, NS

Mi'kmaw Kina'matnewey (2016) Annual Report: 2015-2016 Retrieved online http://kinu.ca/sites/default/files/doc/2014/Feb/mk_annual_report_2016.pdf

Mi'kmaw Kina'matnewey (2017). Introducing Mi'kmaw Kina'matnewey. Retrieved from: http://kinu.ca/introducing-mikmaw-kinamatnewey

Mikkonen J, Raphael D (2010) Social determinants of health: the Canadian facts. York University School of Health Policy and Management, Toronto

Murray-Orr A, Sock S, Paul-Gould S, Tompkins J (2013) An inquiry into an established Indigenous language immersion program: a case study of a Mi'kmaw immersion program. In: Austin J, Newhouse D (eds) Aboriginal knowledge, language and culture and Aboriginal economic development, vol 1. Atlantic Aboriginal Economic Development Integrated Research Program Publication Series, Halifax, pp. 25–64

National Indian Brotherhood. (1973). Indian control of Indian education. Policy paper presented to the Minister of Indian Affairs and Northern Development Canada

Neegan E (2005) Excuse me: who are the first peoples of Canada? A historical analysis of education in Canada then and now. Int J Incl Educ 9(1):3–15

Orr J, Cameron C (2004) "We are Mi'kmaw Kina'matnewey": an assessment of the impact of the Mi'kmaw Kina'matnewey Self Government Agreement on the improvement of education for participating Mi'kmaw communities. Mi'kmaw Kina'matnewey and AANDC policy report

Orr J, Cameron C (2006) Research regarding K-12 education second level services administration and delivery by First Nations organizations. Indian Affairs Canada research report

Orr J, Paul J, Paul S (2002) Decolonizing Mi'kmaw education through cultural practical knowledge. McGill J Educ 37(3):331–354

Orr J, Robinson D, Lunney Borden L, Tinkham J (2017). There is a difference: Mi'kmaw students' perceptions and experiences in a public school and in a band-operated school, *Journal of American Indian Education*, 56(1):55–80.

Paquette J, Fallon G (2010) First Nations education policy in Canada: progress or gridlock? University of Toronto Press, Toronto

Paul-Gould S (2012) Student achievement, fluency and identity: an in-depth study of the Mi'kmaq immersion program in one community. Unpublished masters thesis, St. Francis Xavier University

Poliandri S (2011) First Nations, identity, and reserve life: the Mi'kmaq of Nova Scotia. University of Nebraska Press, Lincoln

Rasmussen D (2011) Forty years of struggle and still no right to Inuit education in Nunavut. Interchange 19(1):46–52

Schouls TA (2003) Shifting boundaries: Aboriginal identity, pluralist theory, and the politics of self-government. UBC Press, Vancouver

Society for Neuroscience (2013) The bilingual brain. Retrieved from http://www.brainfacts.org/sensing-thinking-behaving/language/articles/2008/the-bilingual-brain/

Sock S (2012) An inquiry into the Mi'kmaq immersion program in one community: student identity, fluency and achievement. Unpublished masters thesis, St. Francis Xavier University

Statistics Canada (2007a) Amherst, nova scotia (Code1211011) (table). Aboriginal population profile. 2006 census. Statistics Canada catalogue no. 92–594-XWE. Ottawa. Released January 15, 2008. http://www12.statcan.ca/census-recensement/2006/dp-pd/prof/92-594/index.cfm?Lang=E (accessed October 6, 2017)

Statistics Canada (2007b) Nova scotia (Code12) (table). 2006 community profiles. 2006 census. statistics Canada catalogue no. 92–591-XWE. Ottawa. Released March 13, 2007. http://www12.statcan.ca/census-recensement/2006/dp-pd/prof/92-591/index.cfm?Lang=E (accessed October 6, 2017).

Thiessen V (2009) Identity, equity, and performance: mathematics and reading literacy in Nova Scotia public schools. Nova Scotia Department of Education, Halifax

Tompkins J, Murray Orr A (2013) Successes and challenges in Mi'kmaw and Wolastoqi Latuwewakon language immersion programs. In: Newhouse D, Orr J (eds) Aboriginal knowledge for economic development. Fernwood Press, Halifax, pp 2–24

Tompkins J, Murray-Orr A, Clark R, Pirie D, Sock S, Paul-Gould S (2011) Best practices and challenges in Mi'kmaq and Maliseet/Wolastoqi language immersion programs. Atlantic Aboriginal Economic Development Integrated Research Program policy paper

Truth and Reconciliation Commission of Canada (TRC) (2015) Honouring the truth, reconciling with future: summary of the final report of the Truth and Reconciliation Commission of Canada. Truth and Reconciliation Commission of Canada, Winnipeg. Retrieved from http://www.trc.ca/websites/trcinstitution/index.php?p=890

Walton F, Tompkins J, Hainnu J, Toney D (2016) School leadership in Inuit and Mi'kmaw context in Canada. In: Clark S, O'Donoghue T (eds) School leadership in diverse contexts. Routledge Taylor and Francis, London, pp 95–114

Part III

Language and Culture

Margie Hohepa and Carl Mika

Language-Culture-Education: Problem and Potential – An Introduction

20

Margie Hohepa and Carl Mika

Contents

An Introduction 332
References 337

Abstract

Education plays an enormous role in the regeneration and reconstruction of Indigenous language, culture, and knowledge. Examples span the globe of Indigenous peoples recreating "traditional" Indigenous education institutions of teaching and learning to support the continuation of their respective languages, cultures, and knowledges. Similarly, there are many and varied examples of Indigenous individuals and groups coopting colonial education institutions to establish education initiatives in support of language and culture regeneration. While originally aimed at dismantling and destroying Indigenous language and culture, colonially imposed education systems at early childhood, compulsory schooling, and tertiary levels have become significant sites for their regeneration and reconstruction. It is on the problem and potential of these systems that many writers in this section focus to develop rich and layered examinations of what we refer to in this introduction as the triad of language, culture, and education.

As section editors, along with section authors, we are ourselves very much implicated in the problem and potential across many dimensions of our respective identities. Along with all the authors, we find ourselves continuously engaging with conceptual shifts that are necessary for language and culture, which have been impacted negatively by colonization, to survive within educational spaces and systems that have invariably been set up with a primary goal

M. Hohepa (✉) · C. Mika
The University of Waikato, Hamilton, New Zealand
e-mail: margie.hohepa@waikato.ac.nz; carl.mika@waikato.ac.nz

© Springer Nature Singapore Pte Ltd. 2019
E. A. McKinley, L. T. Smith (eds.), *Handbook of Indigenous Education*,
https://doi.org/10.1007/978-981-10-3899-0_68

of their destruction. We are both on a personal journey of language and culture regeneration – for Margie, this now includes three generations to her children and children's children; for Carl, it is the subjective endeavor of theorizing a Maori philosophy of language. We are Indigenous educators who have taught in Indigenous education initiatives that span schooling (Margie) and higher education (Carl). We are now both Indigenous scholars in the "Western academy." As Indigenous writers we are, in all respects, formed and spurred on by the limits and potential of both colonization and counter-colonial approaches to language and culture. The concern that the Indigenous writer has for these issues overrides any pretense at objectivity that the Western academic convention strives for.

Keywords

Culture · Language Regeneration · Pedagogy · Curriculum · Indigenous Philosophy

An Introduction

The triad of language, culture, and education that sits at the base of much Indigenous concern is so broad that it can be addressed in several ways. That those three aspects can cohabit so intimately should signal to the reader that, for Indigenous peoples, the problem of colonization is far from over and that this colonization ironically opens up possibilities for further approaches. It is our approach in this special section to consider the unlimited ways in which Indigenous peoples are called to describe a problem arising since colonization, but one that addresses elements that have their integrity in precolonial times. How Indigenous peoples are moved to oscillate between these two registers is not necessarily the focus of the authors that follow, but it is inevitable that any Indigenous writer on the theme(s) of language and culture will have at their backs the problem of colonization even as they discuss the liberating potential of language and cultural regeneration.

The inclusion of education moves the problem of colonization into a more direct line of vision. While research has been identified as "probably one of the dirtiest words in the indigenous world's vocabulary" (Smith 2012, p.1), it could be equally argued that "education" is considered so. Colonially imposed "education" systems were established with a fundamental aim of dismantling and destroying Indigenous language, culture, and knowledge systems (Fournier and Crey 1997; Simon 1998; Smith 2012). The ensuing present-day education systems at early childhood, compulsory schooling, and tertiary levels are sites that can either drive and support, or divert and subvert, Indigenous peoples' efforts to sustain and strengthen their respective language, culture, and knowledge systems.

Acutely aware of the problem even if not explicitly articulating it, the writers who have contributed so expansively to this section are from communities that are affected by a language-culture-education problem or potential. On their own, any of these separate elements of language, culture, and education complicate a theoretical description of life; in pairs, they produce even more inconsistencies and complexities. It will be obvious to many Indigenous readers that language and culture together, for instance, capture so much because they are deeply intertwined. Factor in education – and thus complete the triad – and we see the issues plummet to even greater depths. To attempt to signal the intricacy of this relationship, we can deal with language, culture, and education – to some extent – on their own accounts but always as located within the other elements' worlds. To start with "language," which is the central theme of most of the authors' concerns it is complex, from an Indigenous perspective, and some of the authors allude to its tension with Western views on language. This nuanced complicating of language immediately opens up a set of expectations that cannot be understood by the conventional Western canon: Indigenous peoples are not simply regenerating language as an *item*, a medium of communication, but as a related, coextensive, vibrant entity that constitutes Indigenous selves, is formative, and in its own right educational (Mika 2017). Language can grasp the world according to the view of the Indigenous group, and it is thus a cultural concern. "Culture," in turn, cannot be reduced to some notion of a social grouping that is preferred by the West, because it abstractly signposts the existence of all things in the world and how they allow one to express anything (and hence we return to the issue of "language").

Of course, any attempt to neatly define and then make links between the three is difficult, but let us continue the process by starting with "education" from an Indigenous vantage point. It is multilayered and, like language and culture, deviates from what is expected. The emergence of Indigenous-initiated education firmly centered in language and culture across the globe, whether inside colonially imposed education systems (Hohepa 2014; Warner 2001) or founded on traditional Indigenous education (Cajete 1994), illustrates this Indigenous perspective which is always fuelled with the imagining of what might be and what should be. Indigenous education has close ties with cultural, spiritual, physical, social, and economic well-being, with belonging to land, water, sky, and each other (including the so-called nonhuman or inanimate "other") and with ethics and justice and must therefore be articulated carefully within the local realities of an Indigenous group. Indigenous education's call to be articulated brings us back to the reality of language as a lived and relational experience and therefore as a cultural concern also. It encompasses language as an instrument of enculturation and socialization – language is called upon to help recreate Indigenous culture just as culture is called upon to help recreate Indigenous language (Hohepa et al. 1992). It becomes clear that the possibilities are endless for describing how the three are related.

Chapters in this section exemplify the density of this triad and include themes engaging with Indigenous language and cultural knowledge in the curriculum, Indigenous pedagogy inside and outside of colonial-developed institutions, policy leverages for language learning opportunities, the place of Indigenous language and culture in teacher and higher education, and the politics and/or philosophies of language use, translation, and expansion. All the authors engage with conceptual shifts that are necessary for language and culture, which have been impacted negatively by colonization, to survive.

Some authors in this section present concrete interventions that involve the pairing of language and culture, in culturally defined educational environments or institutional classroom settings. In ▶ Chap. 21, "Aloha 'Āina-Placed Ho'omoana 'Ōlelo Hawai'i: A Path to Language Revitalization," Kapā (Katrina-Ann) Oliveira does this by highlighting the importance of concretizing interventions to ensure that Indigenous language education reflects the cultural reality of students and draws on traditional Indigenous education institutions. Acknowledging that language cannot be taught in isolation from culture and arguing that Indigenous language learning and teaching should not be confined to "western-style classrooms," she explores the impact of Hawaiian immersion camps run under the auspices of the University of Hawaii. The camps not only immerse learners in language but also in contexts of "ancestral" practice, grooming them to become leaders within their Indigenous communities and the Indigenous Hawaiian nation.

In ▶ Chap. 22, "Materials Development for Indigenous Language Learning and Teaching: Pedagogy, Praxis, and Possibilities," Candace Galla presents a concrete example aimed at meeting the significant resourcing challenges facing many Indigenous language regeneration enterprises. She discusses the extent to which digital technology can work as an ally to support the development of pedagogically, and culturally, relevant and authentic Indigenous language teaching materials. She also examines how digital resources help to take learning and teaching out of the "western-style classroom" and into family and community settings, normalizing Indigenous languages as part of everyday, as well as global, life.

In ▶ Chap. 23, "Still Flourishing: Enacting Indigenizing Language Immersion Pedagogies in the Era of US Common Core State Standards," the focus moves more explicitly to the classroom to examine the impact of the imposition of universalization on Indigenous language immersion schooling in this era of standardization. Mary Hermes and Erin Dyke examine how the so-called progressive common standards and curriculum aimed at the goal of national identity continue to "reinforce the settler state and Indigenous erasure." Providing concrete examples from Ojibwe language immersion schooling, illustrate how standards attempt to divert and subvert the regeneration agenda in order to (although in their words "never successfully) reproduce students and teachers as colonized subjects." The chapter exposes the complicated and contradictory challenges that immersion teachers and students have to confront and resist daily as they work to strengthen and grow the immersion schooling movement.

Colonization is a central theme in any discussion of Indigenous language and culture under threat and/or under regeneration. While all chapters acknowledge colonial impacts, a number of authors put colonization to the forefront of their discussions spanning language-culture-education. In ▶ Chap. 24, "Listen to the Voices: Informing, Reforming, and Transforming Higher Education for First Nations' Peoples in Australia," Jeannie Herbert draws on her lived experience as an Aboriginal woman from the West Kimberley region of Western Australia to reflect on language and culture within the realities of colonizing institutions of higher education. She proposes that to truly comprehend Indigenous higher education in Australia, one must understand Australian education as a colonial construct. First Nations people's attempts to ground their tertiary education journeys in their own languages and cultures while engaging with Western knowledges and languages can be conceived as simultaneously themed by colonizing/colonized and counter-colonial experience.

Language and culture can also be reconceived within specific educational disciplines or curricula. Roberta and Jodie Hunter raise the possibilities of culturally responsive teaching in mathematics in ▶ Chap. 25, "Maintaining a Cultural Identity While Constructing a Mathematical Disposition as a Pāsifika Learner." In their critique of marginalizing practices experienced by Pāsifika students learning mathematics in Aotearoa New Zealand, they also touch on interplaying tensions between Indigenous Pacific identity and the colonial construct of minority immigrant identity in settler societies. They argue that teaching of curriculum can never be "culture-free" and, drawing on voices of Pāsifika students and their teachers, illustrate the potential of pedagogy that is closely linked to students' cultural identities and known worlds.

While also putting colonization to the forefront as a central theme, ▶ Chap. 26, "Efforts and Concerns for Indigenous Language Education in Taiwan" signals a shift in focus from Indigenous efforts to colonial government responses and responsibilities. Joy Lin Chen-Feng, Grace Gao I-An, and Debby Lin Pi-I outline the waves of assimilation experienced by Taiwan's Indigenous peoples and then turn to consider Taiwan's colonial government responses to the preservation of Indigenous languages and dialects. While these are described as "top-down projects" in the chapter, international Indigenous movements provided the initial impetus to Taiwan's Indigenous people's activism that brought about legislative change, which in turn leveraged space for concrete language and cultural regeneration efforts. The chapter overviews the language learning opportunities being provided for Indigenous children and youth and resource development, along with growing grassroots activity that has accompanied an increased level of awareness of Indigenous languages.

In ▶ Chap. 27, "Sámi Language for All: Transformed Futures Through Mediative Education," Erika Sarivaara and Pigga Keskitalo continue the assimilation theme with a historical description of its Sámi legacy. The chapter proposes a mediative role for Sámi education in order for language regeneration to counter that legacy of assimilation and its deleterious impact on Sámi peoples. They tease out the problem and potential of "Sámi education" that transverses colonial and national borders crisscrossing Sámi territory(s). The chapter's premise that language regeneration will support the development of "social harmony in a postcolonial situation" is coupled with warnings against problems of essentialism and ethnocentrism, which may not only engender racism against but also within Indigenous peoples.

While ▶ Chap. 27, "Sámi Language for All: Transformed Futures Through Mediative Education," posits a postcolonial future in which regeneration of Sámi languages plays a pivotal role, Mere Skerrett calls for a sovereign future in ▶ Chap. 28, "Colonialism, Māori Early Childhood, Language, and the Curriculum." She seeks to unsettle perceptions that the visibility of te reo Māori (the Māori language) in Aotearoa New Zealand's education system particularly in curricula such as the early childhood document Te Whāriki, is an indication of its legitimation and a reflection that colonization is over. She reminds us that imperialism and colonialism are not located in the historical but remain ideologically and politically imbued within education via policy curriculum and pedagogy, even in the sites we identify as Indigenous language schooling. In those sites where children are the priority, there is much to gain and much to lose. The regeneration of te reo Māori is more than a resistance to colonial rule, more than a counter to assimilation and injustice, and more than a dimension of decolonization. Mere Skerrett argues that is "the assertion of Māori sovereignty" in "'our place'," providing clear "pathways to liberation and self-determination."

The final three chapters turn to forefront language itself. ▶ Chapter 29, "Elaboration and Intellectualization of Te Reo Māori: The Role of Initial Teacher Education" focuses on the necessity of expanding the scope of an Indigenous language in order to disclose the world that is important at the time. In ▶ Chaps. 30, "Ka unuhi a me ka hoʻokē: A Critique of Translation in a Language Revitalization Context," and ▶ 31, "A Term's Irruption and a Possibility for Response: A Māori Glance at "Epistemology"", the phenomena of language and culture are paired by placing particular emphasis on language as a carrier of tradition and/or colonization.

In ▶ Chap. 29, "Elaboration and Intellectualization of Te Reo Māori: The Role of Initial Teacher Education," Tony Trinick advocates for an acceleration of "language intellectualization" to provide new linguistic resources and to support the ability to operate in deeply cognitive ways in an Indigenous language. This is not only important for language regeneration and language vitality argues that, in particular, this is crucial for preparing teachers to teach (and learn) in Indigenous languages at the high levels of abstraction required in schooling and higher education today. Developing a teaching workforce that can teach effectively through a regenerating Indigenous language presents complex challenges. This chapter examines factors that impact on Indigenous language teacher education programs, illustrating pedagogical and curriculum-related tensions that they face, and discusses implications for language planning for Māori medium initial teacher education.

Laiana Wong and Kekeha Solis address the immediate problem of translation and the sorts of worlds that are transported within translation in ▶ Chap. 30, "Ka unuhi a me ka hoʻokē: A Critique of Translation in a Language Revitalization Context." In this chapter they explain their refusal to translate a weekly publication written in the Hawaiian language to English. They argue that translation of Indigenous language text works against language regeneration efforts. Translation of an Indigenous minority language to the colonial language of power carries with it implicit messages of dominance and subordination. Given that language expresses and reflects cultural views of the world, translation from Indigenous to non-Indigenous has potential to undermine the Indigenous cultural lens through repackaging the message to reflect dominant cultural understandings inherent to the translated word.

In the final chapter, Carl Mika further explores the nature of language in his examination of how language needs to be paired with the world philosophically. He examines how the understanding of language, analysis of an utterance or evaluation of a term, encompasses layerings of personal and collective experiences, relationships, histories, and contexts. In doing so he articulates in greater depth the proposition we foreshadowed above: that language is a far from straightforward phenomenon in Indigenous thought and has very little to do with dominant Western views of language.

As a final word of introduction when we sent out the invitation for contributions to this special section, in line with the handbook editors' wishes we deliberately kept these separate concepts of language, culture, and education broad so that contributors could outline, examine, and theorize the concerns and solutions, problems, and potential, from specifically local experiences. Yet what this section also reveals is the possibility for further dialogue on the understandings emerging from the different communities. While language and cultural regeneration emerges as an agenda in common, chapters in this section weave a rich and intricate tapestry of the many and diverse ways Indigenous peoples engage with, challenge, and create "education" to advance this shared agenda.

References

Cajete G (1994) Look to the mountain: an ecology of indigenous education. Kivaki Press, Colorado
Fournier S, Crey E (1997) Stolen from our embrace: the abduction of first nations children and the restoration of aboriginal communities. Douglas & McIntyre, Vancouver
Hohepa M (2014) Te reo Māori and schooling. In: Kawharu M (ed) Maranga mai! Te reo and marae in crisis? Auckland University Press, Auckland, pp 103–127
Hohepa M, Smith G, Smith L, McNaughton S (1992) Te Kohanga Reo hei tikanga ako i te reo Maori. Ed Psych 12(3& 4):333–346
Mika C (2017) Indigenous education and the metaphysics of presence: a worlded philosophy. Routledge, Oxon
Simon J (ed) (1998) Ngā Kura Māori: the native schools system 1867–1969. Auckland University Press, Auckland
Smith LT (2012) Decolonizing methodologies: research and indigenous peoples. Otago University Press, Dunedin
Warner SL (2001) The movement to revitalize Hawaiian language and culture. In: Hinton L, Hale K (eds) The green book of language revitalization in practice. Academic, London, pp 133–144

Aloha ʻĀina-Placed Hoʻomoana ʻŌlelo Hawaiʻi: A Path to Language Revitalization

21

Katrina-Ann R. Kapāʻanaokalāokeola Nākoa Oliveira

Contents

Introduction: A Synopsis of the History of ʻŌlelo Hawaiʻi 340
ʻŌlelo Hawaiʻi at the University of Hawaiʻi at Mānoa 341
Total Language Immersion 342
Hoʻomoana ʻŌlelo Hawaiʻi 343
Educational Frameworks from a Kanaka Perspective 346
    Aloha ʻĀina-Placed Learning: Place-Based Perspectives 346
    Importance of Local Knowledge 349
    Experiential Learning 349
    Historical Accounts 350
    Community Engagement 351
The Importance of Aloha ʻĀina-placed Hoʻomoana ʻŌlelo Hawaiʻi 351
Conclusion 353
References 354

Abstract

I ka ʻōlelo ke ola, i ka ʻōlelo ka make (in language there is life, in language there is death). This ʻōlelo noʻeau (wise saying) inextricably links our survival as a people to the survival of our language. Languages convey nuances unique to our own worldviews, cultures, and traditions.

Kawaihuelani Center for Hawaiian Language at the University of Hawaiʻi at Mānoa and the Hawaiian Language program at the University of Hawaiʻi at Maui are cognizant that language is the carrier of culture and worldview. It is further acknowledged that language cannot be taught in isolation or merely within the confines of a western-style classroom. Thus, both programs seek to incorporate various strategies that contribute toward indigenous language education by

---

K.-A. R. K. N. Oliveira (✉)
Kawaihuelani Center for Hawaiian Language, University of Hawaiʻi at Mānoa, Honolulu, HI, USA
e-mail: katrinaa@hawaii.edu

© Springer Nature Singapore Pte Ltd. 2019
E. A. McKinley, L. T. Smith (eds.), *Handbook of Indigenous Education*,
https://doi.org/10.1007/978-981-10-3899-0_15

creating opportunities for students to study the Hawaiian language via learning environments outside of the traditional language classroom setting.

This paper will explore the impact that hoʻomoana ʻōlelo Hawaiʻi (Hawaiian immersion camps) have had on increasing the language proficiency of ʻōlelo Hawaiʻi (Hawaiian language) students, introducing students to ancestral Kanaka practices, and grooming the next generations of Kānaka to become leaders within the lāhui (Hawaiian nation; Hawaiian community). Furthermore, it will demonstrate how the lessons learned from these language immersion camps intersect with the field of education.

Keywords

Language revitalization · Place-based education · Language immersion · Indigenous knowledge

Introduction: A Synopsis of the History of ʻŌlelo Hawaiʻi

Despite the fact that ʻōlelo Hawaiʻi served as the medium of communication in ka pae ʻāina Hawaiʻi (the Hawaiian archipelago) for many centuries, within a single century of foreign occupation, the native tongue of Hawaiʻi became endangered. This is particularly astounding when one considers that Kānaka (Native Hawaiians) successfully transitioned from a solely oral culture to a highly literate culture rapidly (Lucas 2000). As Wong (2017) asserts

> The technology of literacy was recognized immediately for its capacity to convey meaning at a level transcending that of vocalization. It was clearly an enhanced level of communication readily available to everyone. As such, the rush to acquire the ability to expand the dimensions of communication was so profoundly widespread, being supported and encouraged at the highest levels of society, that the Hawaiian population became one of the most highly literate in the world in a relatively short period of time, which is itself indicative of the capability of Hawaiians to adapt to a rapidly changing world.

By 1834, the same year that the first ʻōlelo Hawaiʻi newspaper, *Ka Lama Hawaii*, was published, between 91% and 95% of Kānaka were reported to be literate (Walk 2014). Over the course of 114 years, more than 100 different ʻōlelo Hawaiʻi newspapers were produced totaling approximately 125,000 newspaper length pages of ʻōlelo Hawaiʻi text (Nogelmeier 2010). In spite of these efforts to sustain ʻōlelo Hawaiʻi as a thriving language, by the early 1980s, fewer than 50 native speakers under the age of 18 remained (Kawaiʻaeʻa et al. 2007).

The rapid silencing of the native tongue of ka pae ʻāina Hawaiʻi was the culminating effect of a number of factors including, but not limited to: the collapse of the Kanaka (Native Hawaiian) population due to introduced diseases, the severance of Kānaka from the ʻāina (the land, that which feeds) via land privatization and taxation, and the loss of sovereignty of the Kingdom of Hawaiʻi by means of the illegal overthrow of the monarchy. On the educational front, laws were created to muffle ʻōlelo Hawaiʻi in the classroom. Act 57 of the 1896 Laws of the Republic of Hawaiʻi stipulated,

The English language shall be the medium and basis of instruction in all public and private schools, provided that where it is desired that another language shall be taught in addition to the English language, such instruction may be authorized by the Department, either by its rules, the curriculum of the school, or by direct order in any particular instance. Any schools that shall not conform to the provisions of this Section shall not be recognized by the Department.

This law remained in effect for 90 years. Thus, it was not until 1986 that 'ōlelo Hawai'i immersion schools could legally run without fear of failing to be recognized by the government.

The marginalization of 'ōlelo Hawai'i in a western-centric educational system historically through laws and ordinances has produced not only a monolingual society, but also a monocultural approach to education. This chapter will explore language revitalization efforts by Kanaka academics to challenge these western-centric monocultural educational approaches by repositioning Kanaka ways of knowing and understanding at the forefront. After discussing the historical context that sets the stage for the 'ōlelo Hawai'i revitalization movement, this chapter will delve into the role that aloha 'āina-placed education has played in 'ōlelo Hawai'i regeneration endeavors.

'Ōlelo Hawai'i at the University of Hawai'i at Mānoa

The University of Hawai'i at Mānoa, the flagship and inaugural campus of the University of Hawai'i system, was the first campus to offer 'ōlelo Hawai'i instruction at the college level. In 1921, the University of Hawai'i Board of Regents declared, "The University should become the center for the study of Hawaiian and a strong effort made to preserve the language in its purity" (Johnson 1998, p.138). To fulfill the University's obligation to ensure the survival of 'ōlelo Hawai'i in perpetuity, kumu 'ōlelo Hawai'i (Hawaiian language teachers) developed a variety of courses and teaching strategies over the years to reverse the language shift (Fishman 1991; Adley-SantaMaria 1997). In 1922, Frederick W. Beckley, the first instructor of 'ōlelo Hawai'i, taught a beginner's course (Johnson 1998). Later, Beckley and his successor, John Henry Wise, relied on religious writings for the basis of their curricula. Succeeding instructors developed their own textbooks or adopted Kanaka ancestral mo'olelo (historical accounts) as their texts.

During the Hawaiian Renaissance of the 1970s, interest in 'ōlelo Hawai'i increased dramatically; several hundred students enrolled in 'ōlelo Hawai'i at the University of Hawai'i at Mānoa alone. Kānaka sought to revitalize 'ōlelo Hawai'i as a living thriving language. Therefore, two measures pertaining to 'ōlelo Hawai'i were added to the Hawai'i Constitution through the Hawai'i Constitutional Convention. First, 'ōlelo Hawai'i was re-established as an official language of ka pae 'āina Hawai'i. Second, the Constitutional Convention (1978) acknowledged the state's responsibility to "provide for a Hawaiian education program consisting of language, culture and history in the public schools" (Article X, Section 4). While the

Constitution was amended to declare that English and Hawaiian were the official languages of Hawai'i, in reality, 'ōlelo Hawai'i was only "required for public acts and transactions only as provided by law" (Article XV, Section 4).

By the early 1980s, 'ōlelo Hawai'i revitalization pioneers, many of whom were 'ōlelo Hawai'i instructors at the University of Hawai'i at Mānoa, recognized the need to grow new generations of 'ōlelo Hawai'i speaking children in order to ensure the survival of the language. They formed the 'Aha Pūnana Leo, Inc. In 1984, the first 'ōlelo Hawai'i immersion preschool, Pūnana Leo, opened in Kekaha, Kaua'i. Modeled after Māori Kohanga Reo in Aotearoa, these "language nests" sought to feed 'ōlelo Hawai'i to the next generations. As previously mentioned, after 90 years, in 1986, Act 57 of the 1896 Laws of the Republic of Hawai'i which forbade the use of 'ōlelo Hawai'i as the sole medium of education was finally repealed, thus paving the way for 'ōlelo Hawai'i to be legally reintroduced in the 'ōlelo Hawai'i immersion classroom. The next year, the Board of Education approved Ka Papahana Kaiapuni Hawai'i (the Hawaiian Immersion Program) as a 2-year pilot project. In 1990, permanent status was granted to Ka Papahana Kaiapuni Hawai'i as a K-12 public school program (Warner 2013).

Total Language Immersion

Total language immersion has proven to be an effective tool for language acquisition and intergenerational language revitalization (Reyhner 1997). The most ideal setting for a second language learner to engage in total immersion is among a community of native speakers. Unfortunately, for second language learners of 'ōlelo Hawai'i, the mother tongue of the Hawaiian archipelago, very few people speak 'ōlelo Hawai'i as their first language today. Native speakers, defined here as 'ōlelo Hawai'i speakers who not only have learned 'ōlelo Hawai'i as their own first language, but who have also learned 'ōlelo Hawai'i from a continuous unbroken line of 'ōlelo Hawai'i first language speakers, fall into two categories: the Ni'ihau community and the very elderly.

As time passes, it is becoming increasingly more difficult to find 'ōlelo Hawai'i native speakers. Ilei Beniamina, a former resident of Ni'ihau, estimated that in 2008, less than 75 people remained in the 'ōlelo Hawai'i native speaking population of Ni'ihau (Kimura et al. 2009). As a result, gaining access into the last 'ōlelo Hawai'i speaking community can be a daunting task for those eager to immerse themselves in the language. The geographical isolation that has enabled the Ni'ihau community to maintain their mother tongue – in spite of laws and other efforts to silence Hawai'i's indigenous language in governmental and educational arenas – has also served as a nearly impenetrable barrier for language enthusiasts. Access to the privately owned island of Ni'ihau is extremely exclusive. Few people outside of the Robinson family who owns the island and the native population that have been residing on Ni'ihau continuously since precontact times have ever set foot on the island. Although a portion of the Ni'ihau community currently resides on the neighboring island of Kaua'i, access is generally limited to those who have previously established personal relationships with members of the recluse community. Thus, total language immersion within a ʻōlelo Hawaiʻi native speaking community is extremely difficult to achieve.

When one compares the number of native speakers of ʻōlelo Hawaiʻi to the number of native speakers of various world languages, it becomes clear why so many indigenous mother tongues are on the verge of extinction. Unlike second language learners of world languages who may gain access to robust communities of native speakers, for second language learners of less commonly spoken languages such as ʻōlelo Hawaiʻi, access to these speech communities is not as readily available. As Adley-SantaMaria (1997) asserts,

> Speakers of Chinese, Spanish, or other so-called "world languages" have non-speakers who can always find a speech community even into the future that will be available to them if they want to learn their languages, but indigenous languages are unique speech communities. Once our native speakers are gone and the younger generations become completely monolingual in English, the loss of our languages is permanent. (p. 136)

Anyone eager to learn a world language need not have a previously established personal relationship or an approved research agenda with members of that speech community in order to be immersed in their target language and culture. Rather, they may simply take a trip to that region of the world; instantaneously, they are immersed in the language and culture of that place. For languages on the verge of extinction, however, access to these scarce speech communities often require an intimate relationship with someone who is either a member of the speech community or is known and trusted by at least one member of that target community.

While total immersion in a thriving speech community is ideal, it is important to note that more than one type of language immersion experience exists. Ken Hale identifies five categories he refers to as "degrees of immersion." The first and most desirable degree is where children learn a language within the home setting. The second degree of immersion is where young children attend a preschool or kindergarten where the target language is the only language utilized. The third degree of immersion is one where a native speaker and a second language speaker spend a great deal of time together speaking solely in the target language. The fourth degree of immersion is where the target language is used as the medium of instruction of a content course (e.g., geography, history, science). The fifth and final degree is the monolingual language course in which the target language is utilized in conversational settings (Hale 2013). The primary focus of this paper, hoʻomoana ʻōlelo Hawaiʻi, falls within the parameters of the fifth degree of immersion.

Hoʻomoana ʻŌlelo Hawaiʻi

To fill the void of an existing robust ʻōlelo Hawaiʻi speech community, kumu ʻōlelo Hawaiʻi have been utilizing hoʻomoana ʻōlelo Hawaiʻi for student and faculty development for several decades. The main objectives of these camps are to achieve increased language proficiency and cultural competency. Many kumu have created weekend-long camps with their students either as a solo venture or collaborative effort with other kumu. Some kumu have organized well-established programs that have spanned more than a decade.

Mauiakama is an example of a ʻōlelo Hawaiʻi immersion aloha ʻāina-placed (a program that places a love and respect for the land at the core of the curriculum) experiential learning initiative. For the purposes of this chapter, the term "aloha ʻāina-placed" is utilized rather than the more mainstream terms, "placed-based" or "ʻāina-based" because "ʻāina-based" simply Hawaiianizes the "place-based" pedagogy by translating "place" to "ʻāina." Aloha ʻāina-placed education is more than simply learning that occurs outside of the classroom. Aloha ʻāina-placed education is a recognition that Kanaka are genealogically related to the ʻāina and the ʻāina is our ancestor. The ʻāina is not only the source of our physical nourishment, but it also feeds us spiritually and mentally. Aloha ʻāina-placed education reinforces the notion that Kanaka have a birthright to reside on the ʻāina and by virtue of this birthright we also have a kuleana (responsibility, burden) to care for and protect the ʻāina.

The Mauiakama summer program, co-organized by kumu ʻōlelo Hawaiʻi from the Maui College and Mānoa campuses of the University of Hawaiʻi system, was created in 2008 to revitalize ʻōlelo Hawaiʻi by providing participants with an opportunity to speak solely in ʻōlelo Hawaiʻi for a week while engaging in hands-on ancestral Kanaka cultural practices with expert practitioners and native speakers of ʻōlelo Hawaiʻi. Participants are taught about the history and significance of the places visited. They also engage in hands-on land management practices such as restoring traditional wetland loʻi (ponded taro gardens), cleaning and maintaining ancient irrigation ditches, clearing invasive plants, and rebuilding traditional fishpond walls. In transit around the island, participants listen to audio recordings of native speakers related to the history of the places visited and the cultural practices that those places are known for. What makes this hoʻomoana ʻōlelo Hawaiʻi unique is its focus on engaging in various mālama ʻāina (sustainability) practices.

Mauiakama consists of two distinct components for which participants may receive up to six upper division university Hawaiian language credits. The first component, worth three credits, is a week of coursework at the University of Hawaiʻi at Mānoa on the island of Oʻahu. Participants engage in a variety of Kanaka cultural practices including, but not limited to: speaking solely in ʻōlelo Hawaiʻi for a week with students, faculty, and native speakers; carving out papa kuʻi ʻai (poi boards); creating pōhaku kuʻi ʻai (poi pounders); producing educational digital stories; fashioning ʻapu ʻawa (coconut bowls); working in a variety of different loʻi; gathering ancestral foods; cooking foods using ancestral methods; learning historical accounts and traditions about the places visited; memorizing ancestral songs and chants; listening to audio tapes of native speakers and lifelong residents of the places visited; learning about the art of haku mele (song and poetry composition); visiting wahi pana (storied places); planting, cultivating, and harvesting taro; and identifying and classifying more than 30 varieties of taro. The second component of the program, worth an additional three university credits, is the weeklong hoʻomoana ʻōlelo Hawaiʻi on the island of Maui. All participants reside together with expert

Kanaka cultural practitioners and native speakers of ʻōlelo Hawaiʻi for the duration of the week at various locations on Maui. Since the kumu conducting Mauiakama are direct lineal descendants of the very families who have called these particular rural places home for centuries, participants have a unique opportunity to learn about the places, people, and practices of the communities they visit in ways that very few ever will.

The long-term, overarching goal of Mauiakama is to revitalize the mother tongue of Hawaiʻi by creating an educational setting integrating ancestral practices along with outdoor experiential learning techniques. The short-term goals of Mauiakama are to increase individual participants' ʻōlelo Hawaiʻi proficiency; foster a love and respect for the natural environment; introduce participants to ancestral Kanaka cultural sustainability practices (e.g., fishing, farming, food preparation); provide participants with a rare opportunity to engage in conversations with native speakers of ʻōlelo Hawaiʻi; increase the visibility of Kawaihuelani Center for Hawaiian Language (Kawaihuelani) at the University of Hawaiʻi at Mānoa to community college campuses; recruit students from community colleges to attend Kawaihuelani by establishing a link between community college students and Kawaihuelani faculty; and educate participants about significant Kanaka cultural sites.

The indicators of success used to measure the progress toward achieving the program's objectives include: conducting written and verbal pre-tests and post-tests to evaluate participants' ʻōlelo Hawaiʻi proficiency levels before and after participation in Mauiakama; creating a video documentary to record participants engaging in ancestral Kanaka cultural sustainability practices, conversing with native speakers of ʻōlelo Hawaiʻi and learning about significant Kanaka cultural sites throughout the island of Maui; and compiling a portfolio for each participant to measure and document his/her own growth.

Over the years, numerous kumu ʻōlelo Hawaiʻi have offered their own hoʻomoana ʻōlelo Hawaiʻi (e.g., Ola Nā Iwi, Huakaʻi i Kahoʻolawe, Kaulakahi Aloha). The location and duration of these immersion camps have varied as have the cultural activities that participants engaged in. However, the goals and objectives of these initiatives remained constant: to increase students' ʻōlelo Hawaiʻi abilities; expose students to hands-on activities incorporating ʻōlelo Hawaiʻi, culture, and history; and to provide opportunities for students to converse solely in ʻōlelo Hawaiʻi for extended periods of time.

While most of the immersion camps created by kumu at the University of Hawaiʻi at Mānoa target students, Annette Kuuipolani Wong, a ʻōlelo Hawaiʻi native speaker from Niʻihau and faculty member of Kawaihuelani, established a faculty development program known as Kaulakahi Aloha in 2002. The purpose of Kaulakahi Aloha was to strengthen the language skills of Kawaihuelani's ʻōlelo Hawaiʻi faculty by immersing them into the Niʻihau community. For 1 week, faculty members resided together on the island of Kauaʻi along with native speakers from Niʻihau. Faculty and native speakers spoke entirely in ʻōlelo Hawaiʻi for the duration of the program, engaged in various Kanaka cultural practices, visited historical sites on the islands of Kauaʻi and Niʻihau, and discussed some of the intricacies of the Niʻihau dialect including vocabulary, jokes, slang, and other expressions unique to the Niʻihau community. Although it only ran for 3 years, Kaulakahi Aloha remains one of the most beneficial professional development initiatives of all time for Kawaihuelani. Faculty members were able to strengthen their own 'ōlelo Hawai'i skills via language immersion with native speakers. The lessons learned and knowledge gained on these immersion trips inspired many faculty members to rethink and revamp their own teaching styles and strategies to include more practical applications of 'ōlelo Hawai'i in their lessons.

Educational Frameworks from a Kanaka Perspective

Hoʻomoana 'ōlelo Hawai'i are rooted in ancestral knowledge systems and ways of knowing. Ancestral knowledge applied in a modern context is what Ledward refers to as "new old wisdom at work" (Ledward 2013, p.35). Indigenous scholars often recognize that many of the so-called "new approaches" and educational teaching philosophies currently utilized in the field of education actually intersect with ancient indigenous epistemologies.

The progress made by Kanaka scholars, who are disenchanted by western pedagogies that fail to value traditional ways of knowing, sheds light on the brilliance of holistic ancestral knowledge bases. Through these collective efforts, great strides are being made to infiltrate the academic arena and legitimize ancestral ways of knowing. Kānaka are demonstrating that their 'ike kupuna (ancestral knowledge), rich in science, mathematics, engineering, and mālama 'āina lessons, are just as relevant today as they were centuries ago.

Gaining recognition for this vast ancestral knowledge is not a struggle that Kānaka face alone. As Adley-SantaMaria (1997) contends,

> In their traditional societies, indigenous people educated the youth in holistic ways teaching them that all of life is interconnected. Those teachings fell on the wayside along with many of our cultures and languages a tragedy of our times. The more we revive and understand the traditional skills, knowledge, and beliefs needed to succeed in an interdependent world, the more one sees the error of thinking that we can focus exclusively on the dominant societal education system and ignore our indigenous ways of teaching of the past. (p.134)

When one considers the massive shift in the intergenerational transmission of knowledge that has occurred over the last century and a half, it comes as no surprise that Kānaka struggle in today's educational system, receiving the lowest scores on standardized tests in comparison to any ethnic group in Hawai'i.

Aloha 'Āina-Placed Learning: Place-Based Perspectives

Learning from the natural landscape and the local community through "place-based education" is not a new phenomenon (Smith 2002). Learning from the environment outside in the elements was commonplace in ancestral times. Educational approaches of this nature, as C. Kanoelani Nāone (2008) asserts, helped children build brain connections necessary for higher level thinking skills, empowered families culturally, passed on cultural ʻike (knowledge) for further perpetuation, reified the importance of listening to the stories of kūpuna (ancestors) and oral tradition, built community relationships, fostered family relationships, nurtured the land, helped to ensure that native plants that are endangered in their natural environment will have a chance to survive and physically connected families to that specific place (p. 192).

Gruenewald and Smith (2008) insist, "All education prior to the invention of the common school was place-based. It is education as practiced in modern societies that has cut ties to the local" (p. 1). Returning to this more traditional way of teaching allows for adapting the curriculum to suit the unique needs of the particular students being taught by taking into consideration where they are from and how their places inform their worldviews.

The connection between Kānaka and ʻāina in aloha ʻāina-based pedagogies cannot be overstated. According to Kanaka historical accounts, the ʻāina is the older sibling of the Kanaka. As the younger sibling, the Kanaka has a duty to respect and honor the ʻāina as its elder sibling. In turn, the ʻāina provides sustenance for the Kanaka. Kānaka are connected to each other and to the natural environment by a common moʻokūʻauhau (genealogy) (Kameʻeleihiwa 1992). Moreover, the ʻāina is viewed as a chief while the Kanaka is a servant in the ʻōlelo noʻeau (proverb), "He aliʻi ka ʻāina, he kauwā ke kanaka" (Pukui 1983, p. 62).

Kanaka connection to places is further reinforced by their experiences and interactions with the ʻāina. According to Kanahele (1986),

In the case of the traditional Hawaiian, for example, almost every significant activity of his life was fixed to a place. No genealogical chant was possible without the mention of personal geography; no myth could be conceived without reference to a place of some kind; no family could have any standing in the community unless it had a place; no place of any significance, even the smallest, went without a name; and no history could have been made or preserved without reference, directly or indirectly, to a place. So, place had enormous meaning for Hawaiians of old. (p. 175)

Aloha ʻāina-placed education grounds students in experiential learning tied to their own places. Aloha ʻāina-based programs encourage a reconnection with one's ancestral homelands, cultural practices, as well as one's communities (Young 1998; McGregor 2007; hoʻomanawanui 2008; Naone 2008; Beamer 2014; Oliveira 2014; Oliveira and Wright 2016).

Aloha ʻāina-placed initiatives that blend the natural environment with Kanaka worldviews are fundamental to revitalizing ʻōlelo Hawaiʻi in a manner that is authentic. Warner (1999) insists,

Language—the words people use to describe their environment, thoughts, emotions—as an expression of worldview is a medium through which people transmit culture and history. Language, separated from the environment it evolved to describe, and the thoughts and emotions that grew in that environment, becomes something new and different. That Hawaiian language taught and learned out of context, distinct from the culture (i.e., its people), becomes a new language that evolved from the original. (p.77)

This approach allows students to connect and relate their academic lessons to their own lives and local environment, not just to the sterile objects and situations conjured up in the confines of a traditional classroom setting. Similarly, Stiles (1997) contends, "Teaching a language in a sterile environment outside the companion culture dooms the language to only academic application" (p. 256). A more effective method of teaching a language is to immerse second language learners in second language rich environments such as those created by hoʻomoana ʻōlelo Hawaiʻi (Reyhner 1997).

Mauiakama and Kaulakahialoha are aloha ʻāina-placed programs built on the premise that Kanaka epistemologies are holistic knowledge systems that incorporate language, place, culture, identity, and personal experience. Thus, these programs seek to increase participants' language production, place-based knowledge, and cultural competency through hands-on experiential learning within the Kanaka community to better understand the worldview of native speakers. Aloha ʻāina-placed educational programs such as these embrace the ʻāina as a kumu (source of knowledge; teacher). The ʻāina grounds the language, culture, worldview, and identity of Kānaka to our kulāiwi (ancestral homeland).

Since the ʻāina is revered as an educator, the western educational notions of "teacher" and "student" are somewhat abstruse. While the kumu kula (school teacher) may be the primary source of knowledge in a traditional western classroom, from an aloha ʻāina-placed perspective, the kumu kula is perhaps better described as a facilitator or catalyst of knowledge seeking. In an aloha ʻāina-placed program, kumu kula openly acknowledge that students and teachers alike may learn a great deal by observing and interacting with the ʻāina. Manulani Aluli Meyer (2003) writes, "Learn from land and not simply about land. Land educates us ... We must all begin, again, to learn from ʻāina. We have places and people who can teach us how" (p.8).

ʻĀina-based collaborative community initiatives, included under the umbrella of aloha ʻāina-placed initiatives, are gaining popularity and becoming established throughout ka pae ʻāina (Ledward 2013). Aloha ʻāina-placed pedagogies are transforming the educational system by normalizing ʻāina-centric teaching strategies. No longer are aloha ʻāina-placed programs seen merely as kīpuka or isolated sites of resistance to the dominant educational system. Rather, aloha ʻāina-placed models are catalysts for systemic societal change (Goodyear-Kaʻōpua 2013).

Numerous Kanaka scholars have highlighted the positive impact of ʻāina-based pedagogies on learners (hoʻomanawanui 2008; Naone 2008; Goodyear-Kaʻōpua 2013; Ledward 2013; Maunakea 2016; Oliveira and Wright 2016). Today, aloha ʻāina-placed programs provide alternative teaching strategies that may appeal to some students who do not thrive in a typical classroom setting. In aloha ʻāina-placed programs, students are often encouraged to work together as a community of scholars to find solutions for the common good of all. Rather than creating a competitive environment where students are pitted against one another, in an aloha ʻāina-placed model, external forces such as climate change and pollution are often the polarizing forces that unite students to work together (Adley-SantaMaria, 1997).

Through aloha 'āina-placed pedagogies, students learn the 'ike ku'una (ancestral wisdom) residing on the 'āina or as Kanaka scholar, ku'ulaloha ho'omananui (2008) refers to it as "'ike 'āina" (ancestral knowledge about land and place). According to emerging Kanaka scholar Summer Maunakea (2016), 'āina-based pedagogies are, "processes of learning and teaching from the natural landscapes and oceanscapes of Hawai'i's environment utilizing 'ike kupuna (ancestral knowledge, language, and customary practices) to frame curricula for all learners. 'Āina-based pedagogies help learners develop a sense of connection to place and instill values of responsibility and interdependence" (p. 3).

Importance of Local Knowledge

The realization that people worldwide have their own socially accepted lens through which they perceive and interpret the world is key to acknowledging the importance of local knowledge. Such a consciousness honors and legitimizes the varied systems of wisdom that exist both locally and globally. It further acknowledges that people relate to the world in ways that are unique to their own life experiences and interactions with their places. All too often, people assume that the Kanaka society is homogenous; Kanaka traditions, practices, and experiences are identical throughout ka pae 'āina Hawai'i.

Through an aloha 'āina-placed curriculum, immersion students learn firsthand from cultural practitioners of various places who approach the same cultural activity (e.g., fishing, farming, weaving, kapa making) differently depending on the lay of the land and sea as well as the resources available to their communities. By engaging in the same cultural practice in different locations, students observe for themselves how cultural practices are performed in ways that are unique to particular communities (Smith 2002).

Local knowledge often reveals itself in a performative nature through cultural practices. David Turnbull (2000) asserts "performative links" are key to understanding places and that a universal aspect of all knowledge systems is their "localness." Performance is a vital means of reinforcing people's identities, giving credence to their social experiences, and constructing a framework by which a society can be understood (Blunt 2003).

Experiential Learning

Kānaka heavily rely on experiences and sensual information to better understand their world. By seeing, hearing, touching, tasting, and smelling, Kānaka draw insight from their environment (Meyer 2001). Therefore, Kānaka are encouraged to "nānā ka maka, ho'olohe ka pepeiao, pa'a ka waha" (watch with your eyes, listen with your ears, and close your mouth) (Pukui 1983, p. 248). Close observation of knowledgeable people coupled with lived experience leads to enlightenment. "Ma ka hana ka 'ike" is a proverbial saying asserting that one learns by actively participating (Pukui

1983, p. 227). "'Ike" has the dual meanings of being able "to see" and "to know." Those who actively participate in various activities can literally "see" how something works and are better able to understand it intimately. Thus, experiential learning is a key component of Mauiakama and other hoʻomoana ʻōlelo Hawaiʻi. As Cajete (2000) suggests, "True knowing is based on experiencing nature directly. 'Doing' and playing are integral parts of Native learning; apprenticeship is a form of directed learning" (p. 66).

Historical Accounts

As previously stated, Kanaka ways of transmitting knowledge were primarily oral in nature in ancestral times. Thus, contextual clues about Kanaka worldviews, culture, and relationship to the ʻāina are embedded in language. Mele (songs) and ʻōlelo noʻeau (proverbs), for example, are prime sources of this type of knowledge. Through songs, composers make references to people, places, and other aspects of their culture. Ancient stories are revealed and remembered through the lyrics of songs. Similarly, proverbs provide a deeper understanding of the culture from which it is derived as well as the traditions and beliefs of the society.

Aloha ʻāina-based programs also provide opportunities for Kānaka to reconnect with the ʻāina by learning the history of events that occurred at these places by studying some of the mele, ʻōlelo noʻeau, and moʻolelo. By singing mele, reciting ʻōlelo noʻeau, and retelling ancestral moʻolelo, the land and kūpuna are given a voice. The ʻāina serves as a textbook on ʻike kupuna (Peralto 2014). The ʻāina is a source by which Kānaka learn about their kūpuna, their struggles, and their successes. By virtue of the fact that Kānaka share the same land base that their ancestors once called home, much of their wisdom is still situated in these places. In *I Am This Land, and This Land is Me*, hula master and Kanaka philosopher Pua Kanahele (2005) exclaims, "We have to pay attention to our Hawaiian native intelligence and experiences. We should be able to look for them, define them—because nothing is lost. In fact, we still have a lot of knowledge that was left to us by our ancestors. It's still there, we just have to go and look for it" (p. 21).

As numerous Kanaka scholars note, ka lāhui Hawaiʻi (the Hawaiian nation) has a long history of being displaced from their ancestral homelands (Young 1998; Warner 1999, 2013; Lucas 2000; Kanahele 2005; McGregor 2007; hoʻomanawanui 2008; Naone 2008; Goodyear-Kaʻōpua 2013; Ledward 2013; Beamer 2014; Goodyear-Kaʻōpua et al. 2014; Oliveira 2014; Peralto 2014; Maunakea 2016; Oliveira and Wright 2016). Hawaiian Studies Professor Jonathan Osorio (2014) asserts,

> The alienation of ʻāina from Kānaka so accelerated and intensified over the nineteenth and twentieth centuries that there has been few of us today who consciously recognize the enormous harm that has been done to us physically, emotionally, and spiritually by that separation. But the evidence of harm is everywhere: crippled and dysfunctional families, rampant drug and alcohol abuse, disproportionately high incidences of arrest and incarceration, and alarming health and mortality statistics, some of which may be traced to diet and lifestyle, which themselves are traceable to our separation from ʻāina (p. ix).

Aloha 'āina-placed initiatives seek to rebuild relationships with kulāiwi and local communities and to create a heightened appreciation for the history of each place.

Community Engagement

The aloha 'āina-placed educational framework values learning via a focus on collaborative community action (Naone 2008; Goodyear-Ka'ōpua 2013; Beamer 2014). Through grassroots efforts, students learn the value of working with others to achieve a common goal that is mutually beneficial. On ho'omoana 'ōlelo Hawai'i, for example, participants often engage in a variety of mālama 'āina activities. The communities visited relish the opportunity for the ho'omoana 'ōlelo Hawai'i participants to work with them because the group is able to accomplish a great deal in a short period of time. With the collective effort of 30–40 people, Mauiakama participants have been known to clear large lo'i in a single day – a task that would take individuals an entire month to accomplish. They have cleared an acre of land of trees and shrubs in a day or two. Participants are reminded of the ancestral proverb, "'a'ohe hana nui ke alu 'ia" (no task is too big when many work together) (Pukui 1983, p. 18). Through experiences like these, they are doing more than just caring for the land, they are building strong communities and lasting connections to the places they visit. They are developing a sense of kuleana to care for one another as well as the 'āina that sustains everyone.

Once a deep and personal relationship with the 'āina is made, magic happens. Students tend to be more receptive to learning the stories and historical accounts about the places they have visited. They develop a lasting bond with the 'āina – even places that they have not been to before. Through aloha 'āina-placed education, students are eager to learn because they are learning about themselves, their ancestors, and their ancestral places; they have a vested interest in the knowledge that they are learning. Students tend to develop an appreciation for language as a link to the past – a way of quoting the kūpuna that came before. Therefore, there is a deep sense of kuleana that they should be good keepers of this knowledge so that they may one day pass this knowledge onto succeeding generations. Through various aloha 'āina-placed educational approaches, including ho'omoana 'ōlelo Hawai'i such as Mauiakama and Kaulakahi Aloha, students are taught the importance of place.

The Importance of Aloha 'Āina-placed Ho'omoana 'Ōlelo Hawai'i

Aloha 'āina-placed ho'omoana 'ōlelo Hawai'i at the university level have been instrumental in the 'ōlelo Hawai'i revitalization movement in many ways. When aloha 'āina-placed programs are coupled with second language acquisition instruction, a strong emphasis is placed on students as agents of their own knowledge production. By utilizing a place-based approach, second language learners are able to adapt their language production to real-life situations within their own lived communities. Through immersion in ʻōlelo Hawaiʻi and experiential learning strategies, students are not simply consumers of others' knowledge, but agents of their own knowledge creation (Smith 2002). The thoughts they construct in ʻōlelo Hawaiʻi, in spoken and written form, have a direct applicability to their own lives. Unlike classroom assignments where students may be asked to translate sentences void of context and cohesive meaning, when students engage in authentic language production, they seek ways to best express their own thoughts and ideas.

Aloha ʻāina-placed hoʻomoana ʻōlelo Hawaiʻi aid in increasing the language proficiency of participants by creating an environment where they feel safe to speak. Through an activity-based approach rather than a grammar-based approach to ground the language to the ʻāina, these hoʻomoana ʻōlelo Hawaiʻi seek to increase the language proficiency of students via sustained periods of language immersion. By being immersed in a ʻōlelo Hawaiʻi speaking community for an extended period of time, participants have no recourse but to communicate in ʻōlelo Hawaiʻi. Without exception, all 246 second language participants of Mauiakama have consistently increased their ʻōlelo Hawaiʻi proficiency through their participation in the program. Posttests conducted at the end of the programs are unswervingly higher than the scores received on pretests conducted prior to the commencement of the hoʻomoana ʻōlelo Hawaiʻi. The students themselves comment on the positive impact that these immersion opportunities have had on their speaking proficiency and listening comprehension skills.

These programs also build a community of scholars who share the common interests of perpetuating the native tongue of ka pae ʻāina Hawaiʻi and reviving Kanaka cultural practices. The fact that people shopping in a grocery store are still amazed to hear families speaking to one another in ʻōlelo Hawaiʻi is a sobering reminder that those of us in the ʻōlelo Hawaiʻi movement still have a lot of work ahead – ʻōlelo Hawaiʻi usage is not yet normalized in ka pae ʻāina Hawaiʻi. Therefore, it is important for ʻōlelo Hawaiʻi practitioners to create speech communities to improve their language proficiencies and to pass their knowledge down to succeeding generations.

Aloha ʻāina-placed hoʻomoana ʻōlelo Hawaiʻi also instill a sense of kuleana in their participants, thereby developing future community leaders. By nature, hoʻomoana ʻōlelo Hawaiʻi attract self-starters and leaders – people who are willing and able to put themselves in vulnerable situations in exchange for the opportunity to strengthen their language skills. Not all college students have the self-confidence to voluntarily expose themselves to a situation where they anticipate feeling somewhat uncomfortable – especially if that experience lasts a week or longer. Time and time again, as former participants of hoʻomoana ʻōlelo Hawaiʻi graduate from the university and seek employment, many of these students enter the workforce poised to make a positive impact on their communities. As they gain more and more work and life experiences, they often become notable figures within the Kanaka community-at-large. Many become activists advocating for the betterment of the Kanaka people and the protection the natural resources of ka pae ʻāina Hawaiʻi. Others become high-ranking officials who have the best interests of their Kanaka community at heart. Still others become educators eager to impart the ʻike kuʻuna that they have learned for the benefit of the next generation. The kumu of these aloha 'āina-placed 'ōlelo Hawai'i immersion programs have the kuleana to prepare the next generation to be the leaders of the not so distant future.

Aloha 'āina-placed ho'omoana 'ōlelo Hawai'i also create alternative learning places for students to thrive. While a great deal of instructional time is still spent within the confines of a classroom, kumu kula who value place-based teaching strategies often incorporate 'āina-based pedagogies into the classroom in the form of mo'olelo, 'ōlelo no'eau, and mele to name a few. For those students who thrive in the classroom setting, the incorporation of mo'olelo, 'ōlelo no'eau, and mele into the curriculum links them to the 'āina. Aloha 'āina-placed programs also provide alternative teaching strategies that may appeal to those students who do not thrive in a typical classroom setting. Beamer (2014) suggests, 'āina-based learning has the power to "create culturally grounded and civically responsible learners who can achieve their full potential" (p.60).

Aloha 'āina-placed ho'omoana 'ōlelo Hawai'i likewise instill a sense of pride for 'ike ku'una. By introducing students to ancestral Kanaka cultural practices through the medium of 'ōlelo Hawai'i, kumu reinforce the notion that not only is 'ōlelo Hawai'i a living language suitable for use in the twenty-first century, but so too are the ancestral cultural practices of their kūpuna. Aloha 'āina-placed learning allows kumu to couple the realities of today with the 'ike ku'una of the past to reinvent Kānaka to meet their current needs. Ultimately, aloha 'āina pedagogies perpetuate ancestral knowledge as links to the past and pathways for the future.

Finally, aloha 'āina-placed ho'omoana 'ōlelo Hawai'i reconnects Kanaka and 'āina. It imparts a sense of respect for the interconnectedness of all living things. Aloha 'āina-based programs reinforce the kuleana of the Kanaka to the 'āina, their 'ohana (families), and the community-at-large (Naone 2008; Goodyear-Ka'ōpua 2013; Oliveira 2014; Osorio 2014; Oliveira and Wright 2016).

Conclusion

I ka 'ōlelo ke ola, i ka 'ōlelo ka make (in language there is life, in language there is death). This 'ōlelo no'eau inextricably links the survival of Kanaka as a people to the survival of their language. Numerous studies support the impact that language immersion has on increasing language proficiency. According to Larry Kimura et al. (2009), a leading scholar in the 'ōlelo Hawai'i revitalization movement, "indigenous language medium education for both the native speaker and non-native speaker can provide a stronger knowledge of the workings and history of the aboriginal language as compared to learning it through a non-indigenous medium of education" (p. 125). Hinton supports the "notion that people can learn second languages similarly to the way in which they learn first languages, through being immersed in an environment where the language is the dominant one being used" (Hinton (1994); quoted in Adley-SantaMaria (1997)). (p. 140)

Ho'omoana 'ōlelo Hawai'i require a huge commitment in terms of planning and funding; nevertheless, Kanaka educators that are committed to the advancement of their people, language, and traditions often value these precious opportunities to immerse second language learners of 'ōlelo Hawai'i in the Kanaka culture and language. After all, if language is to survive and thrive, so too must one's culture; language and culture are inseparable (Warner 1999, 2013). As Ahlers suggests, "There is almost a metonymic relationship between a language and its culture" (Ahlers (1999, p. 137; quoted in King (2009), p. 101). The worldview and identity of native speakers are inextricably linked to their cultures and ancestors (Warner 1999, 2013; King 2009).

A return to Kanaka pedagogies is a return to ancestral knowledge systems that link contemporary Kānaka to their ancestors, land, language, and culture. Aloha 'āina-placed 'ōlelo Hawai'i immersion education is important to the field of education because it provides a venue for indigenous students to thrive and succeed. For too long, Kānaka have been marginalized in their homeland by educational systems that seek to assimilate them to ways of knowing that are foreign to them. Since 'ōlelo Hawai'i aloha 'āina-placed immersion programs are a radical departure from mainstream western educational approaches, teachers who choose to participate in this style of education are by nature usually very receptive to alternative teaching strategies, especially those that honor ancestral ways of thinking and formulating knowledge as well as "anchoring the truth of the discourse in culture" (Gegeo 2001, p. 58).

In as much as the native speaking 'ōlelo Hawai'i community has dwindled, current second language learners still have the privilege and honor of conversing with native speakers and learning their heritage language – a privilege and honor that is not guaranteed for future generations. Therefore, the challenge posed to indigenous language teachers is to consistently and intentionally infiltrate the academy by incorporating innovative teaching approaches that honor ancestral ways of knowing such as place-based, culture-based, and oral knowledge transmission strategies.

References

Adley-SantaMaria B (1997) White Mountain Apache language: issues in language shift: textbook development, and native speaker-university collaboration. In: Reyhner JA (ed) Teaching indigenous languages. Northern Arizona University, Center for Excellence in Education, Flagstaff.
Ahlers J (1999) Proposal for the use of cognitive linguistics in Hupa language revitalization. University of California, Berkeley
Beamer K (2014) No mākou ka mana: liberating the nation. Kamehameha Publishing, Honolulu
Blunt A (2003) Concept box: performance/performativity. In: Blunt A (ed) Cultural geography in practice. Oxford University Press, London, pp 232–233
Cajete G (2000) Native science: natural laws of interdependence, 1st edn. Clear Light Publishers, Santa Fe, NM
Fishman JA (1991) Reversing language shift: theoretical and empirical foundations of assistance to threatened languages. Multilingual Matters, Clevedon
Gegeo DW (2001) Cultural rupture and indigeneity: the challenge of (re)visioning "place" in the Pacific. Special issue. Contemp Pac 13(2):491–507
Goodyear-Ka'ōpua N (2013) The seeds we planted: portraits of a native Hawaiian charter school. University of Minnesota Press, Minneapolis

Goodyear-Kaʻōpua N, Hussey I, Wright EK et al (2014) A nation rising: Hawaiian movements for life, land, and sovereignty. Duke University Press, Durham

Gruenewald DA, Smith GA (eds) (2008) Place-based education in the global age: local diversity. Lawrence Erlbaum Associates, New York

Hale KL (2013) Linguistic aspects of language teaching and learning in immersion contexts. In: Hinton L, Hale KL (eds) The green book of language revitalization in practice. Brill, Leiden, Boston, pp 227–236

Hinton L (1994) Preserving the future: a progress report on the master-apprentice language learning program. News Native Calif 8:14–20

hoʻomanawanui k (2008) ʻIke ʻāina: native Hawaiian cultural based indigenous literacy. Hūlili: Multidisciplinary research on Hawaiian well-being 5:203–244

Johnson R (1998) The Hawaiian language and Hawaiian studies. In: Kamins RM, Potter RE (eds) Mālamalama: a history of the university of Hawaiʻi. University of Hawaiʻi Press, Honolulu

Kameʻeleihiwa L (1992) Native land and foreign desires: how shall we live in harmony?: Ko Hawaiʻi ʻāina a me nā koi puʻumake a ka poʻe haole: pehea lā e pono ai? Bishop Museum Press, Honolulu

Kanahele GS (1986) Kū kanaka, stand tall: a search for Hawaiian values. University of Hawaii Press, Waiaha Foundation, Honolulu

Kanahele P (2005) I am this land and this land is me. Hūlili: Multidisciplinary research on Hawaiian well-being 2(1):21–31

Kawaiʻaeʻa KK, Housman AK, Alencastre M (2007) Pūʻā i ka ʻōlelo, ola ka ʻohana: three generations of Hawaiian language revitalization. Hūlili: Multidisciplinary research on Hawaiian well-being 4(1):183–237

Kimura L, Hawaiian Lexicon Committee, Counceller A (2009) Indigenous new words creation: perspectives from Alaska and Hawaiʻi. In: Reyhner JA, Lockard L (eds) Indigenous language revitalization: encouragement, guidance & lessons learned. Northern Arizona University, Flagstaff, pp 121–139

King J (2009) Language is life: the worldview of second language speakers of Māori. In: Reyhner JA, Lockard L (eds) Indigenous language revitalization: encouragement, guidance & lessons learned. Northern Arizona University, Flagstaff, pp 97–108

Ledward BC (2013) ʻĀina-based learning is new old wisdom at work. Hūlili: Multidisciplinary research on Hawaiian well-being 9(1):35–48

Lucas PFN (2000) E ola mau kākou i ka ʻōlelo makuahine: Hawaiian language policy and the courts

Maunakea SP (2016) ʻĀina-based pedagogies: Cultivating societal, ecological, and educational responsibility within learners

McGregor D (2007) Nā kuaʻāina: living Hawaiian culture. University of Hawaiʻi Press, Honolulu

Meyer MA (2001) Our own liberation: reflections on Hawaiian epistemology. Contemp Pac 13(1):123–198

Meyer MA (2003) Hoʻoulu: our time of becoming : collected early writings of Manulani Meyer, 1st edn. ʻAi Pōhaku Press, Honolulu

Naone CK (2008) The pilina of kanaka and ʻāina: Place, language and community as sites of reclamation for indigenous education the Hawaiian case. Ph.D., University of Hawaiʻi at Manoa

Nogelmeier P (2010) Mai paʻa i ka leo: historical voice in Hawaiian primary materials: looking forward and listening back. Bishop Museum Press, Honolulu

Oliveira KRKN (2014) Ancestral places: understanding kanaka geographies. Oregon State University Press, Corvallis

Oliveira KRKN, Wright EK (eds) (2016) Kanaka ʻōiwi methodologies: Moʻolelo and metaphor. University of Hawaiʻi Press, Honolulu

Osorio JK (ed) (2014) I ulu i ka ʻāina: land. Hawaiinuiakea School of Hawaiian Knowledge, University of Hawaii Press, Honolulu

Peralto LN (2014) ʻO Koholālele, he ʻāina, he kanaka, he iʻa nui nona ka lā: re-membering knowledge of place in Koholālele, Hāmākua, Hawaiʻi. In: Osorio JK (ed) I ulu i ka ʻāina =: Land. Hawaiʻinuiākea School of Hawaiian Knowledge, University of Hawaiʻi Press, Honolulu

Pukui MK (1983) 'Ōlelo no'eau: Hawaiian proverbs & poetical sayings. Bishop Museum Press, Honolulu
Reyhner JA (ed) (1997) Nurturing native languages. Northern Arizona University, Flagstaff
Smith GA (2002) Place-based education: learning to be where we are. Phi Delta Kappan 83:584–594
Stiles DB (1997) Four successful Indigenous language programs. In: Reyhner JA (ed) Teaching indigenous languages. Northern Arizona University, Center for Excellence in Education, Flagstaff
Turnbull D (2000) Masons, tricksters and cartographers: comparative studies in the sociology of scientific and indigenous knowledge. Harwood Academic, Amsterdam
Walk K (2014) King Liholiho led the Hawaiians' amazing rise to literacy in the 1820s. Ka'iwakīloumoku Hawaiian Cultural Center, Honolulu. https://apps.ksbe.edu/kaiwakiloumoku/node/606. Accessed 31 Jul 2016
Warner SLN (1999) "Kuleana": the right, responsibility, and authority of indigenous peoples to speak and make decisions for themselves in language and cultural revitalization. Anthropol Educ Q 30:68–93
Warner SLN (2013) The movement to revitalize Hawaiian language and culture. In: Hinton L, Hale KL (eds) The green book of language revitalization in practice. Brill, Boston, pp 133–146
Wong KL (2017) Personal Communication with K. Laiana Wong
Young KGT (1998) Rethinking the native Hawaiian past. Garland Pub, New York
(1978) Hawai'i constitutional convention and election, Article XV, Section 4
(1896) Laws of the Republic of Hawai'i, Act 57

Materials Development for Indigenous Language Learning and Teaching: Pedagogy, Praxis, and Possibilities

22

Candace Kaleimamoowahinekapu Galla

Contents

Introduction	358
Positionality	359
Materials Development for Indigenous Language Learning and Teaching	360
UBC Course: Materials Development for Indigenous Language Learning and Teaching	362
Technacy Framework for Language Revitalization	362
Multimedia Technology Training & Praxis Model	363
Course Outcomes	367
Course Findings	368
Course Implications	371
Conclusion	372
References	373

Abstract

With an increase in awareness of Indigenous languages on a global scale and with local, grass roots revitalization efforts and initiatives underway, a significant challenge that exists for language learning and teaching is the formulation and availability of language materials. Based on a university course, developed and taught in various iterations at the University of British Columbia, this chapter will discuss pedagogy, praxis, and possibilities for materials development using digital technology in contemporary university settings for Indigenous language learning and teaching. This course has reach beyond students enrolled in the course and in fact has consequences for language speakers and learners of endangered language communities, students

C. K. Galla (✉)
University of British Columbia, Vancouver, BC, Canada
e-mail: candace.galla@ubc.ca

© Springer Nature Singapore Pte Ltd. 2019
E. A. McKinley, L. T. Smith (eds.), *Handbook of Indigenous Education*,
https://doi.org/10.1007/978-981-10-3899-0_12

in K-12 schools, post-secondary institutions, Indigenous communities, families, and so forth that are recipients, readers, and users of the newly developed materials – print or digital resources.

Keywords

Indigenous language revitalization · Indigenous language learning and teaching · Materials development · Multimedia technology · Digital technology · Training and praxis

Introduction

In the nineteenth century, an assimilationist movement swept across the United States and Canada in an effort to erase linguistic and cultural evidence from the first inhabitants - Indigenous peoples that include American Indians, Alaska Natives, Native Hawaiians, First Nations, Métis and Inuit. Migration, urbanization, wage labor, extractive industries, and schooling have shaped Indigenous communities current cultural and linguistic landscape (Luykx 2016) in North America and beyond. Residential schools, language policies, colonial and post-colonial institutions, created long lasting impacts on these populations, resulting in a language shift from Indigenous languages towards English. Despite drastic measures by colonizing powers, "the imposition of European languages and the dislocation of myriad indigenous societies did not halt the dynamic interactions among indigenous speech communities themselves" (p. 1). Indigenous languages, cultures, and people still exist. With an increase in awareness of Indigenous languages on a global scale and with local, grass roots revitalization efforts and initiatives embarked upon in community, a significant challenge that exists for language educators, practitioners, and the community is the limited amount of language materials that are available. While some communities have established orthographic systems, written and audio documentation by early Indigenous community scholars, linguists, missionaries, or published materials in the form of dictionaries, grammars, newspapers, books, digital media, and so forth, other communities continue to rely on oral forms of communication. Further, commercially printed materials used for school curricula have historically excluded Indigenous peoples' histories, knowledge systems, stories, language, and culture, and these are often misrepresented and told from the perspective and voice of cultural outsiders. Over the last decade there has been increased attention by academic researchers and Indigenous scholars on providing critical perspectives and analyses of Indigenous peoples in children's and young adult books as well as a concerted effort by Indigenous authors, illustrators, and publishers to represent Indigenous peoples in a culturally sustaining, authentic, and relevant way (see Harde 2016; Hoffman 2010; Jackson 2016; Reese 2006; Sheahan-Bright 2011). Digital technology addresses some of the disparities that endangered Indigenous languages face, providing a means for Indigenous peoples to develop language materials and resources. The adoption and adaptation of digital technology has been especially evident, for example, in the Hawaiian language educational settings since the 1990s (see Kaʻawa and Hawkins 1997; Hartle-Schutte and Naeʻole-Wong 1998; Warschauer and Donaghy 1997). Indigenous youth have increasingly become active users of digital technology and producers of digital media in an effort to archive, promote, document, and learn their Indigenous languages (see Carew et al. 2015; Cru 2015; Kral 2010, 2011, 2012; Rice et al. 2016; Wyman et al. 2013, 2016).

Drawing on my combined reaching and teaching experiences to date as an Indigenous language and technology teacher and scholar to date, I will outline a university course on materials development and discuss its relevance to Indigenous language education, broadly defined, to reflect pedagogy, praxis, and possibilities while adopting or adapting digital technology. I continue with two frameworks – technacy framework for language revitalization, which proposes contextual factors to consider when considering digital technology for Indigenous language learning and teaching, and multimedia technology training and praxis model, which conceptualizes how multiliteracies are realized in a materials development course for Indigenous language education. The chapter continues with a discussion of course outcomes, findings, and implications. This course has reach beyond students enrolled in the course and in fact impacts language speakers and learners of endangered language communities, students in K-12 schools, post-secondary institutions, Indigenous communities, families, and so forth that are recipients, readers, and users of the newly developed materials – print or digital resources.

Positionality

As a Kanaka Maoli (Native Hawaiʻian), my introduction to materials development began during my graduate studies at the University of Arizona when I attended the American Indian Language Development Institute (AILDI) – an internationally renowned institute, cited by the US Department of Education as one of the ten outstanding programs for minority teacher preparation in the nation (Leighton et al. 1995). AILDI has been a bridge to connect academic institutions with Indigenous communities. Since its inception, AILDI has engaged Indigenous and non-Indigenous allies from a myriad of professions, backgrounds, and communities from across the USA, Mexico, Canada, Australia, South America, and beyond, making significant contributions to Indigenous language learning, teaching, revitalization, documentation, research, and policy.

One of the courses at AILDI that inspired my research included "Computer Applications for Indigenous Communities" taught by Susan Penfield and Phil Cash Cash (Cayuse and Nez Perce) in 2004. The course assignments allowed students to explore the potential of digital technology for language learning and teaching. I created a multimedia language lesson in Hawaiʻian with the intention to share my "work-in-progress" with a Hawaiʻian language preschool teacher, who also happened to be a friend of mine. In spite of Hawaiʻian having a standard orthography, a history of published print material, and more recent success with Hawaiʻian immersion programs and Hawaiʻian medium schools, Hawaiʻian language teachers and educators were working with limited language materials and culturally relevant resources to support and enhance Hawaiian language development (Hartle-Schutte and Naeʻole-Wong 1998; Warschauer and Donaghy 1997) – a hurdle that extends across Indigenous communities working towards language revitalization.

Following the course, I reached out to my teacher-friend in Hawaiʻi but learned that she left her position. Though my project was not shared beyond my peers at AILDI, I used my experience to further my understanding of materials development. In 2005, I had the opportunity to co-teach the AILDI course with Susan Penfield and Tracy Williams (Oneida). Later in the fall, I attended a digital storytelling workshop hosted by the Indigenous Language Institute (ILI) with the then AILDI Program Coordinator Regina Siquieros in Pojoaque, New Mexico. We were tasked to write a story with the hope that we would leave with a printed book by the end of the three-day workshop. I created an original story using pencil drawings and Hawaiian language text, knowing that I would need a proficient Hawaiian language speaker to review my work (though born and raised in Hawaiʻi and brought up in a hula – Hawaiian performative arts – family, Hawaiian was not my first language. I formally learned Hawaiian from grade seven through grade twelve when I attended Kamehameha Schools). I left the workshop with my printed, hard copy, work-in-progress book and was elated to know that materials development for endangered and Indigenous language communities can be created, produced, and published in-house with control over all aspects of the story, text, language, images, and so forth.

My growing interest in Indigenous language learning, digital technology, and materials development provided me the opportunity to join the ILI training team, which traveled to various Native American communities offering digital storytelling workshops. This interest led me to a research study (Galla 2010) involving the aforementioned AILDI course to determine how Indigenous peoples are using digital technology for language documentation, conservation, revitalization, education, and promotion. In addition, three case studies of students were provided to examine whether the digital technologies that were introduced in the 4-week university course to the students were applicable upon return to their respective Indigenous communities. Reflecting on my combined experiences, I have used my knowledge and research to develop a similar course at the University of British Columbia titled "Materials Development for Indigenous Language Learning and Teaching" which has been offered in various iterations since 2012 to the time of this writing.

Materials Development for Indigenous Language Learning and Teaching

Materials development is a recent field of academic study that investigates the principles and procedures of the design, writing, adaptation, production, implementation, exploitation, evaluation, and analysis of language materials, whilst exploring theory and praxis (Tomlinson 2012). Language materials can refer to any resource that is used by language teachers and learners to facilitate language learning. For Indigenous communities, these material products can be in the form of documentation field notes, newspapers, grammars, dictionaries, textbooks, children's books, audio and video recordings (analog and digital), computer and video games, social media, and so forth. The sampling of materials that comprise bits and pieces of the language are instrumental resources for endangered and Indigenous languages that are working towards building language capacity within and for the community. Although these materials are not commercially produced – as we would expect for English language learners, for example – and may not be instructional in nature, the materials nonetheless are relevant and pertinent to Indigenous language learning. Materials development for Indigenous language learning and teaching faces a stark reality than that for languages with billions and/or millions of speakers, especially at a time where many proficient speakers are in the later stages of their life.

During the initial stages of the Hawaiian language revitalization movement, the language programs and classrooms were constrained by the lack of textbooks, pedagogical materials, and other resources in Hawaiian language to support language learning. Hawaiian language parents, extended family, and community members were invited to create pedagogical materials by cutting and pasting Hawaiian translations over original English texts and textbooks (Hartle-Schutte and Naeʻole-Wong 1998; Warschauer and Donaghy 1997). Laiana Wong (as cited in Warschauer and Donaghy 1997), a Hawaiian language instructor, expressed that materials that were created in this manner imposed perspectives from outside the Hawaiian Islands: "We need to develop original materials in Hawaiian that can reflect our own culture, perspective, and reality" (p. 352).

The shortage of pedagogical, culturally relevant, and authentic materials depicting Indigenous language and culture in an appropriate way is a significant challenge that language teachers face worldwide, especially in communities that do not have a standard orthography or a tradition of literacy. Community-based materials development has the power and ability to

> instruct and delight its audience by teaching them histories (and her-stories), enabling them to hear voices that are too often silenced, entertaining them, and allowing them to find their way to understanding even the most complex situations. (Harde 2016, p. 7)

The adoption and adaption of digital technology soon thereafter became critical to revitalizing the language, developing curricula and materials, disseminating materials throughout Hawaii, expanding the domains of communication, and raising the profile of Hawaiian language juxtaposed with English (Galla 2009; Hartle-Schutte and Naeʻole-Wong 1998; Warschauer 1998). Where, since colonization, language, cultural, and historical resources have been published and disseminated about Indigenous communities from the perspectives of non-Natives (Ingle 2003), now Indigenous people and voices can be heard locally, nationally, and globally through the medium of digital technology.

It is critical now more than ever with a reconciliatory movement – specifically in Canada – that books and resources published about and for Indigenous children, youth, and adults are "depicted in positive and human ways in a variety of settings, urban, rural, and reserve" (Harde 2016, p. 5). Children and youth especially need to have books available at their disposal that are representative of themselves and their communities, in various mediums and in the media as well – something which Indigenous people yearn for. Materials development are at the "heart of Native survivance, self-determination, recovery, and development" (p. 7); approaches to them must reflect Indigenous values of relationality (Carjuzza and Fenimore-Smith 2010), respect, responsibility, relevance, reciprocity, (Kirkness and Barnhardt 1991), and resiliency (Galla et al. 2014).

UBC Course: Materials Development for Indigenous Language Learning and Teaching

As mentioned previously, through my cumulative experiences over the last decade, I developed a course at UBC to reflect my theoretical and applied research in the area of Indigenous language learning, teaching and digital materials development. Since 2012 until the time of this writing in Spring 2017, I have offered the course four times and have learned significantly from my Indigenous and non-Indigenous students who represent diverse ages, backgrounds, and professions. Their feedback as language teachers, language learners, and educators has helped me to refine and adapt the course to meet the needs of Indigenous language learners. The following two sections include frameworks that I use to efforts and the consideration of digital technology, whereas the subsequent framework is used as a technology training and praxis model to guide students through levels of progressions during the class.

Technacy Framework for Language Revitalization

Technacy, proposed by the Australian Science, Technology and Engineering Council, is the "ability to understand, communicate and exploit the characteristics of technology to discern how human technological practice is necessarily a holistic engagement with the world that involves people, tools, and the consumed environment, driven by purpose and contextual considerations" (Seeman 2009, pp. 117–118). The framework, as described by Seemann and Talbot (Seeman and Talbot 1995) aims to create "technate individuals" who understand the interrelationship between contextual factors. In a later study on multimedia technology and Indigenous language revitalization (Galla 2010), the framework was reconceptualized as the techacy framework for language revitalization (TFLR) (Galla 2016) to includes five factors – linguistic and cultural, social, technological, environmental, and economic – that are deemed critical in determining the appropriateness of digital technology use for Indigenous language revitalization and education. Each element requires consideration of the other four factors to help decide the appropriateness of technology based upon local context, language endangerment, resources, and individual or community linguistic and cultural goals. Since digital technology may be considered a contentious matter in Indigenous communities due to varying complexities, the TFLR is offered as an introduction to discuss and determine whether digital technology is a practical solution and option that will lead to achieving language goals.

Over the last decade, digital technologies have proliferated to support teaching and learning, and opportunities to interact with languages in non-traditional domains have been created and developed, Additionally, some of these technologies have claimed to "save" endangered and Indigenous languages. The integration of such technologies for endangered and Indigenous communities must place an emphasis on building capacity for language learning and teaching leading towards language proficiency and fluency. Once a language goal is determined, consideration of each of the TFLR factors is encouraged to determine if digital technology is a necessary tool and method to achieve the target objective (Fig. 1). Students are asked to reflect on their unique contexts and explore how each of these factors contributes to or impedes certain language activity within their community. This exercise helps students understand the resources (or lack of resources) they are working with as they work towards revitalizing their respective languages.

This framework and the factors involved offer a reference for individuals and communities who are considering using digital technology for language initiatives. The following questions for each TFLR factor reveal the uniqueness of each community, and by doing so define what types of initiatives (digital and non-digital) are possible. The conversation and discussion that result from these initial questions are foundational in determining what factors inhibit, contribute to, or support the proposed language goal, and whether digital technology is a necessary tool. Table 1 provides a sampling of questions associated with each factor to begin the process of understanding the unique language context we face when working towards Indigenous language revitalization.

This framework seeks to "develop skilled, holistic thinkers and doers who can select, evaluate, transform, and use appropriate technologies that are responsive to local contexts and human needs" (Seeman 2000, p. 2). This holistic approach is based upon factors that influence digital technology use. Indigenous peoples, since contact, have adapted to their changing landscape and environment, using new tools to adjust to changing tides.

Through this exercise, students are able to understand the contextual importance of Indigenous language learning and the resources that are available to help support language development and proficiency. Each student reveals a distinctive situation that they in a sense work from, as the resources will vary tremendously between language, community, and so forth. Students immediately learn that what works for one community may not work for the next, despite our continuing exposure to digital technology.

Multimedia Technology Training & Praxis Model

In 1994, the New London Group coined the term multiliteracies – the "multiplicity of communications channels and media, and the increasing saliency of cultural and

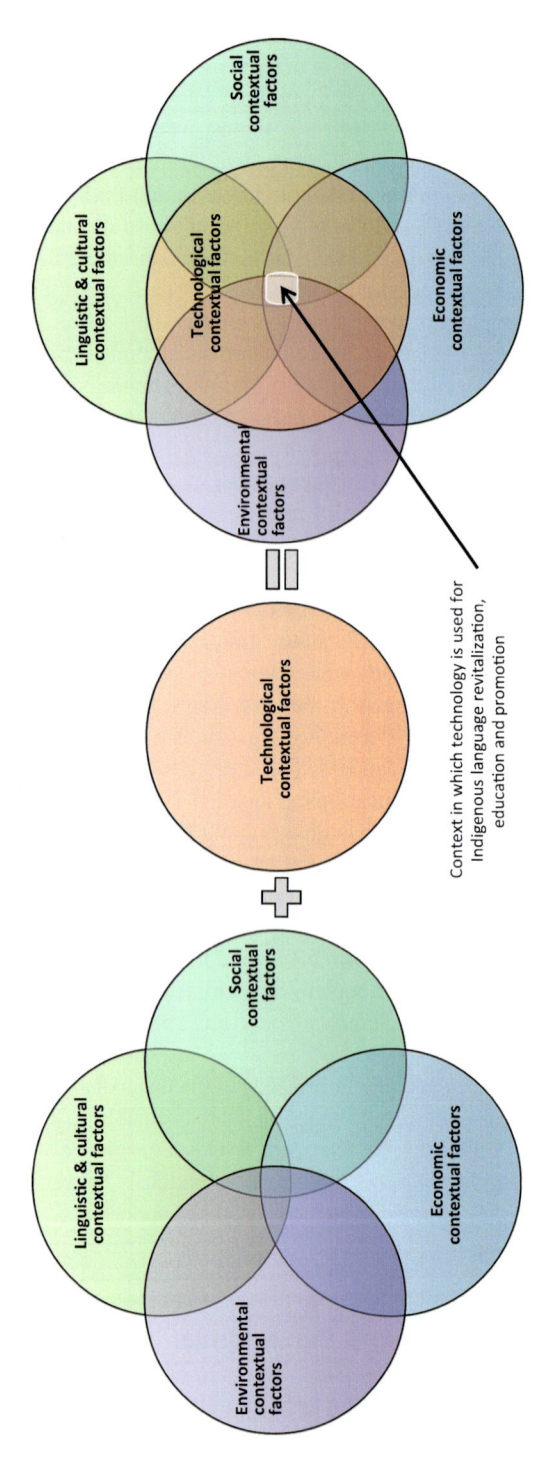

Fig. 1 Technacy framework for language revitalization (Galla 2016)

Table 1 Technacy framework for language revitalization factors (Galla 2016)

TFLR Factors	Questions
Linguistic and cultural factors	What is the vitality of the language (i.e., speaker population, age group)? What are the language ideologies, traditions, values, and cultural beliefs of the individual or community? What are the oral and literacy practices (associated with the language) of the language?
Social factors	In what domains are the language used (home, school, church, community, university government, media, workplace, etc.)? What contexts, activities, and/or gatherings does the oral language appear in (i.e., radio, news, prayer, ceremonies, graduation, parties, etc.)? What literary and/or communicative contexts does the written language appear in (i.e., books, newspapers, magazines, website, blog, e-mail, social media, elections, etc.)? With whom is the language used? (i.e., friends, family, elders, teachers, government officials, etc.)?
Economic factors	What types of financial resources are available to support language revitalization and education efforts? What human resources are available to support language revitalization and education efforts? What additional resources are available to support language revitalization and education efforts? How much time and/or resources can be allocated toward language revitalization and education efforts?
Environmental factors	Where are these language speakers geographically situated (i.e., on traditional land base, urban, suburban, rural, etc.)? Is the language accessible outside of the traditional or home territory (i.e., specific cities/ states/ provinces/ countries where speakers are located)? What terrestrial biome is the language situated in (i.e., polar, temperate, (sub)tropical, dry, wet)? What landforms contribute to the landscape of the traditional or home territory (i.e., mountains, plateaus, canyons, valleys, bay, ocean, volcanoes, etc.)? What natural elements minimize the amount of face-to-face interaction for an extended period of time (i.e., hurricane, flood, drought, blizzard, tornado, landslide, avalanche, etc.)?
Technological factors	What types of infrastructure are in place to support the use of technology? What types of technology are available (to support language learning and teaching)? What types of technology training and information technology support are available?

linguistic diversity" (New London Group 1996, p. 63) – to address the evolution of new media and new literacy practices. Multiliteracies is a pedagogical approach that includes: situated practice, which draws on the experience of meaning-making in lifeworlds, the public realm, and workplaces; overt instruction, through which

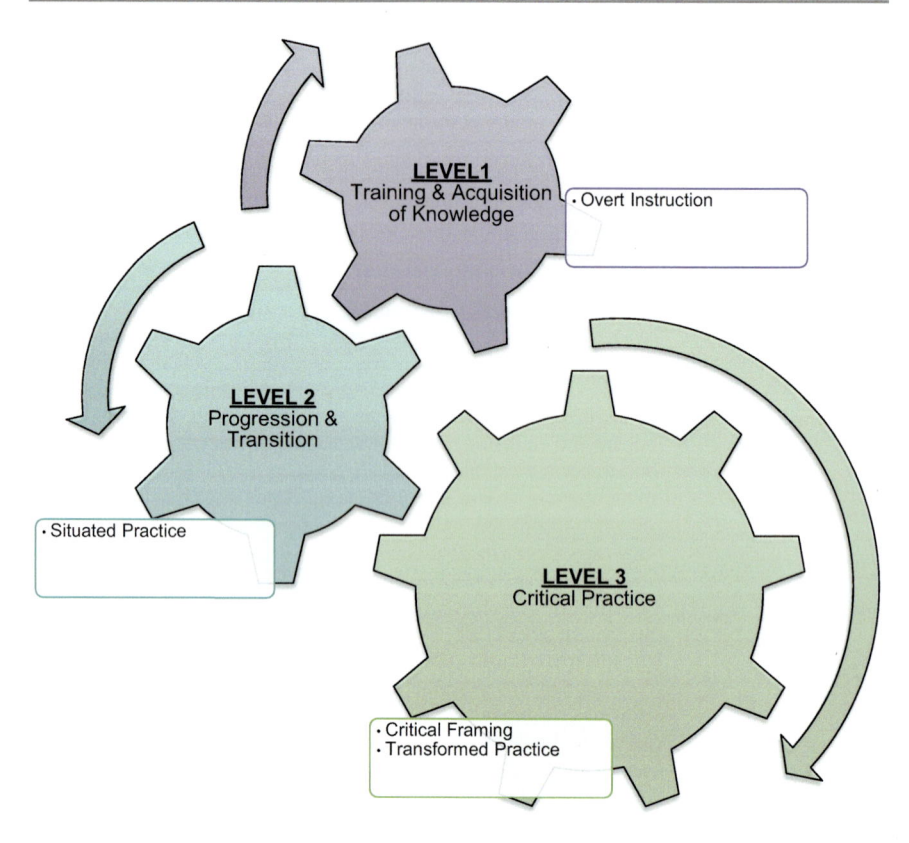

Fig. 2 Multimedia technology training & praxis model

students develop an explicit metalanguage of design; critical framing, which interprets the social context and purpose of designs of meaning; and transformed practice, in which students, as meaning-makers, become designers of social futures.

The multiliteracies framework and its four components are used to guide the training and praxis when developing materials for Indigenous language learning and teaching. I indicate the primary components that transpire in the three levels of this training model in Fig. 2; however, each of the segments may "occur simultaneously, while at different times one or the other will predominate, and all of them are repeatedly revisited at different levels" (New London Group 1996, p. 85). Applying this pedagogy to the university course, in Level 1, students are (re)introduced to common software and learn different built-in features they may not be familiar with. Technical knowledge and skills are acquired through direct instruction and hands-on training. This teaching and training includes

> active interventions on the part of the teacher and other experts that scaffold learning activities, that focus the learner on the important features of their experiences and activities within the community of learners, and that allow the learner to gain explicit information at

times when it can most usefully organize and guide practice, building on and recruiting what the learner already knows and has accomplished. (New London Group 1996, p. 86)

With overt instruction, students are able to "accomplish a task more complex than they can accomplish on their own, and ... they come to conscious awareness of the teacher's representation and interpretation of that task and its relations to other aspects of what is being learned" (p. 86). The diversity of students enrolled will vary tremendously each time the course is offered; thus, this community of learners will require different types of technological assistance – some more complex than others. In Level 2, depending on their familiarity with the digital technology introduced, willingness to explore on their own, and motivation, students use their prior knowledge, as well as overt instruction and hands-on training, to consciously practice what is acquired – they find ways to connect what they have learned to their particular interest and/or needs. With guidance from the instructor or more capable others (e.g., assistants, other peers in the classroom), students can apply their knowledge of what was acquired in Level 1, so as to become more comfortable and make the skill intuitive. In Level 3, a critical awareness, understanding of knowledge, and growing mastery of skills are applied to their practice, taking into consideration various contextual factors mentioned in the TFLR. At this stage, "theory becomes reflective practice" (p. 87), in which students are creating and developing materials for real purposes. Through this process, students determine the various resources they have in their community (e.g., school, library, home, and community center) that can contribute towards materials development and Indigenous language revitalization. Depending on the resources, students transfer meaning from one context (e.g., university) to another (e.g., their community) and can decide what digital technology can be used to best support their resource development and language learning and teaching efforts.

Course Outcomes

Universities are entitled and privileged spaces that are afforded a wealth of resources (e.g., computers, language labs, new high-end technology, IT staff and support, language education specialists) and often house archived language materials from Indigenous communities in various mediums (e.g., wax cylinders, reel-to-reel, field notes, and records documented by linguists and anthropologists). To build on earlier research (Galla 2010) and iterations of the course, it was important to use, (re)introduce, software and digital technology that is commonly found in most homes, offices, workplaces, schools, libraries, and community centers.

The tools chosen for this course are based on three levels of technology initiatives: low-, mid-, and high-technology (Galla 2009). These initiatives scaffold students' learning with digital technology as well as interaction with language. Low-technology or unisensory initiatives "emphasize one sensory mode, allowing the learner to receive the Indigenous language through sight or hearing. More specifically, the user visually sees the language either in printed material (e.g., books) or on a screen (e.g., subtitles), or audibly via a speaker or sound system" (p. 173). Mid-technology or bisensory initiatives allow "the learner to receive the Indigenous language through sight and hearing and/or require the use of a keyboard and mouse (point and click), and access to the Internet" (p. 174). High-technology or multisensory initiatives include "asynchronous communication, synchronous communication, or multimodal interactivity between the user and the technology. In this category, input and output of the Indigenous language are key factors" (p. 175).

The project-based outcome is also scaffolded so that students build on earlier initiatives. Depending on the audience, the materials that are developed for the course will vary tremendously from the medium, context, lesson, and language. For example, using the publishing layout format in MS Word (on a Mac) or MS Publisher (on a PC), students create original text for their low-technology initiative (LTI) to include in a printed material (i.e., storybook, manual, workbook). Images, photos, graphics, and tables can be included to support the language. To continue with this example, the next level – mid-technology (MTI) – uses the LTI as base to then record audio that accompanies the text (i.e., audiobook, ebook, digital story). Students can use Audacity – a free audio editing software – to record audio that is exported to a CD, or record audio in PowerPoint to support the language text in a multimodal environment. To produce a high-technology initiative (HTI) emanating from the aforementioned examples, students are tasked with creating a multimodal lesson that provides an interactive experience incorporating text, images, audio, hyperlinks, and so forth, which allows the learners to evaluate their learning at their own pace. Listed in Table 2 are additional examples of low-, mid-, and technology initiatives.

The funds of knowledge that students bring into this course, as well as their linguistic and cultural diversity, shape how they each develop original material and for whom the materials are intended (e.g., early learners, adult learners, family members, language teachers). Students are also asked to consider the types of technology they use in the course, since university settings oftentimes offer more resources than their community, schools, and organizations they are working with. At the end of the course (approximately 40 contact hours), students develop three materials that they can use independently or collectively, while (re)learning new features of existing technology and building and developing ICT skills.

Course Findings

The course title "Materials Development for Indigenous Language Learning and Teaching" attracts both Indigenous and non-Indigenous students who are speakers and/or learners of an Indigenous language. Students that enroll in the course who are not familiar with Indigenous languages are generally interested in learning how to apply principles of materials development to their language teaching and practice (e.g., ELL, EAL, heritage languages), as well as learning about Indigeneity. On the first day of class, it is always revealing to hear about the language diversity of each of

Table 2 Representative media and products of low-, mid-, and high-technology initiatives

Levels	Media	Examples of Products
Low	Desktop publishing/printing press	Books, fliers, newspapers, newsletters, calendars, posters, banners, advertisements
	Radio	News, headlines, language lessons, songs, commercials, public service announcements
	Audio recordings, digital storybooks, lessons	Wax cylinders, 8-track tape, LPs, cassette tapes, CDs, DVDs, audio podcasts, mp3, digital audio files, presentation software, e-books
	Videos/movies	Tape reels, Betamax, VHS, DVDs, video podcasts, digital movie files (mp4, mov)
	Television	News, headlines, language classes, cultural events, commercials, public service announcements
Mid	Audio media accompanied by texts	Audio recordings in the Indigenous language (IL) accompanied by a transcript in the IL, audio/digital storybooks in the IL accompanied by the story in the IL, video/movie in the IL with subtitles in the IL, television programs in the IL with subtitles in the IL
	Web-based media	Wikis, electronic libraries, search engines, on-line dictionaries (with or without audio), web sites, social media platforms
High	Asynchronous communication	Blogs, discussion boards, e-mail, course management systems
	Synchronous communication	Telephone, chat, webcam, audio/video conference, VoIP
	Interactive multimedia	Digital/computer/video games, electronic bulletin board system, language learning software, virtual reality

the students. Due to the heterogeneity of the students, a multitude of languages and professions are represented in any given course. Since the course requires students to apply what they are learning and the materials they are developing to their learning and teaching environments, there is great motivation to create high-quality language resources that can be used in their practice.

In addition to theory, practice, and hands-on-training, some class time is made available for students to work on their projects, as well as to seek help from the instructor and/or peers. Students spend a significant amount of time outside of class meetings to storyboard, gather resources, test out software, consult with speakers, write text, and record audio. Knowing that not all students in the class speak, learn, and/or have obtained permission to develop materials for an Indigenous community, students are encouraged to create language resources in their heritage language.

Due to the nature of the course and its intensive schedule, students continue to revise their materials when the course has been completed, seeking additional language resources (e.g., archived documents, curriculum material) and consultation from proficient speakers and language authorities (e.g., grammar, nuances), graphic designers (e.g., culturally relevant and appropriate images), and community (e.g., authentic representation of Indigenous knowledge). This is a critical component of materials development, especially when working with and for Indigenous communities who are continuously finding ways to bring their languages back to fruition. For materials that embed Indigenous knowledge into language resources, it is recommended that a protocol be established (if not currently in place) to provide a framework that guides the process. For example, students may work with language speakers in their family; however, if materials will be provided to the larger community, there may be a Language Authority and/or Language Council that would need to review and authenticate the materials before the resources are made available (e.g., community, schools, public) and published in print and digital form. Materials that contain Indigenous knowledge must be treated with ultimate respect and care since recent colonial history, from an outsider perspective, still often misrepresents Indigenous peoples in images, books, film, and media.

For some students, the technology initiatives have reconnected them with their linguistic and cultural heritage, sparking opportunities to inquire with family members about ancestry, language, history, identity, travels, and photographs. A bond develops, as many students have not had the opportunity to learn their Indigenous language or heritage language through intergenerational language transmission. Colonial languages have had detrimental effects on students' well-being and ancestral knowledge, severing the direct connection between children, parents, grandparents, and the many generations that have come before. Parents are thrilled with the opportunity to teach their adult children their Indigenous or heritage language, thus creating a language bond that brings generations closer together. For others, new relationships with language speakers and learners are established.

The project-based outcome compelled many students to inquire about their unique cultural heritage, which made them cognizant of language ability. Students were exposed to language diversity and came to appreciate their own linguistic heritage and experiences. For some, this prompted discussions with family members to learn about their genealogical and linguistic history, while other conversations focused on writing, pronunciation, and so forth. This resulted in retracing their family's journey, having open dialogue about language attitudes (i.e., reasons for choosing to speak the "dominant" language instead of their heritage or Indigenous language), reminiscing about past and current events, and revisiting family photos. These experiences, some of which were painful, helped to shape and form some of the students' very personal projects.

Theoretical discussions were complemented with practical hands-on technology training, which provided speakers, learners, and educators with opportunities to create and develop materials for language education. In addition to learning the foundational theories and concepts of Indigeneity, multimodality, multiliteracies, new literacies, and the adapted technacy framework, their learning went far beyond the course goals and requirements. Embedded in the classroom environment were notions of funds of knowledge (Gonzalez et al. 2005), democratic merit (Brayboy 2014), community of practice (Lave and Wenger 1991), and identity (Esteban-Guitart and Moll 2014a, b).

In a short period of time, each student successfully created several language materials, which included a printed resource (LTI), audio recording to accompany the printed resource (MTI), and a multimedia interactive language lesson (HTI). Additionally, students demonstrated how their materials would be implemented in a language learning and teaching environment. Though each student varied in their language ability, digital technology skills, and academic background, their enthusiasm and success came from the need to create language-learning environments for their family, community, students, and themselves. This space acknowledged Indigenous "'funds of knowledge' (Moll et al. 1992) as valid and relevant pedagogy and scholarship" (Galla et al. 2014, p. 203), allowing students to draw from their linguistic and culture knowledge and ways to bridge academia and community.

Course Implications

The course objectives have guided the project-based outcomes, drawing critical attention to implementation, schedule, and training opportunities. Theory, practice, and daily readings are discussed to reflect students' careers, professions, and personal interests. For some students (particularly non-Indigenous students), this is the first course that draws from an Indigenous perspective. Though the content of the course is based on language learning and materials development, the discussions in essence reveal many forms of colonization that have been imposed on Indigenous peoples, and knowledge systems that have not been widely acknowledged or accepted by academe. This requires foundational grounding in Indigeneity from the start of class and having open dialogue about the various terminologies that is used in practice – some forms of which may be more appropriate than others depending on situational context (e.g., Indigenous, Aboriginal, First Nations, Inuit, Metis, Native American, and American Indian).

Offering the course in condensed timeframe (2.5 hours per day for 3 weeks – usually a summer session) provides students with an "immersive" experience in a sense, because we are meeting on a daily basis and (re)learning skills, which are then applied to their material resources – to be used in their practice. There is no downtime but rather an accelerated momentum that requires students to create original text and then add different elements to develop their low-, mid-, and high-technology initiatives – their project-based outcome. The products that they finally create can be used independently or collaboratively. To combat the potential anxiety of what is expected in the class, examples from the instructor as well as former students' work are shared to formulate some ideas.

Since time is limited, it is beneficial for the instructor to conduct a short questionnaire beforehand to determine the language background, technology skills, and particular interest in the course for each of the students to determine what their overall needs may be. In an effort to connect with the students prior to the beginning of the course, this will help them to identify, gather, and/or contact relevant resources (e.g., language materials, speakers) that may be necessary for their materials development for language learning and teaching. Collaboration is also key as students find that they do not possess all the tools necessary to successfully develop materials. Consultation is required with their peers and other language speakers so that they can receive feedback on their initiatives. Class time is primarily allocated to the daily theme inclusive of required readings, local and global examples of materials, hands-on training, and some lab time, in addition to a few guest speakers. It is imperative that students be provided in-class time to "test" out software and have multiple opportunities to ask questions specific to their project.

Finally, in an effort to see how their technology initiatives will be used in a language-learning environment, a microteaching immersive language lesson is presented at the end of the class. This provides students a chance to showcase their newly developed materials, but more importantly it gives students an opportunity to evaluate the effectiveness, usability, appropriateness, and relevancy of their technology initiatives in practice with a group of motivated adult learners – their peers in the course. Creating these technology initiatives encourages self-reflection and self-assessment (Hartle-Schutte and Naeʻole-Wong 1998) as materials are developed for under-resourced languages. For Indigenous communities, the process is "as much about personal integrity as [it is] about collective responsibility and as much about research as [it is] about education and other forms of engagement" (Smith 2012, p. 125). Materials that are developed and created are "cultural artifacts with epistemological orientations" (Harde 2016, p. 7) that help readers, learners, and users mediate Indigenous knowledges.

Conclusion

Indigenous peoples have the right to "revitalize, use, develop and transmit to future generations" their own Indigenous languages (Article 13.1), "establish and control their educational systems and institutions providing education in their own languages" (Article 14.1), "establish their own media in their own languages and to access to all forms of non-Indigenous media" (Article 16.1), and "practise and revitalize their cultural traditions and customs" which includes "the right to maintain, protect and develop the past, present and future manifestations of their cultures, such as ... technologies and ... and literature" (Article 11.21) (UN 2008). With the United Nations Declaration on the Rights of Indigenous Peoples, language policies, funding opportunities, and activism Indigenous communities have moved forward on language programming and schooling initiatives in an effort to restore the language in homes, schools, community, and beyond. Language resources are at the crux of this revitalization movement to support language speakers, learners, and teachers towards proficiency and fluency. By engaging in materials development, language educators can help themselves "to understand and apply theories for language learning" and "to achieve personal and professional development" (Tomlinson 2001, p. 67).

Digital technology has presented opportunities for communities to develop language materials and resources in-house, which has the potential for newly created materials to be disseminated and distributed locally, nationally, and/or globally; to expand the environment in which the language is used; to provide relevance, significance, and purpose; and to document, archive, and revitalize Indigenous languages (Galla 2009). Though this course is offered at a university, the ideal situation would be to teach these courses in community at a local facility (e.g., computer lab, school, language center) using their existing technologies to determine what is possible with their current resources based on their language goals.

The ability to generate culturally sustaining, relevant, place-based, and authentic materials in-house allows for complete control, ownership, and rights of the creation, development, production, publication, and distribution of resources. With appropriate software, communities are no longer dependent on large-scale publishing companies to print, to distribute language materials, and to oversee what type of content, text, and images would "sell" or appeal to a general audience. Materials development costs for printed books typically would be relatively inexpensive and would cover a laser printer (capable of duplex printing in color), toner, paper, cardstock, extended stapler, and staples. In addition to printed resources, an equally suitable format is a digital file that can be selectively available to community members, language speakers, language learners, and/or made publicly available to the general public for download or viewing. This energy efficient format eliminates paper altogether, which may allow for greater distribution for language materials to reach those who are living away from the traditional homelands where the Indigenous language is spoken. The digital file may also be saved as a pdf file, as well as in a booklet (and duplex) format so that these resources, in particular a folded book sized 8.5 inches by 5.5 inches, can be printed in homes, schools, work, community centers, and libraries as needed.

As Indigenous peoples around the world are finding ways to revitalize their languages, digital technologies can be recognized as an ally that supports language learning and teaching efforts, initiatives, programming, and education. Developing and learning new skills to assist with language revitalization builds capacity within Indigenous communities to grow the number of in-house material and curriculum developers, as well as language speakers. Digital technology for materials development and digital technology as resources requires appropriate planning to ensure that technology-based initiatives enhance language learning (Jones 2008) "in a manner that is appropriate to their cultural and linguistic realities" (Villa 2002, p. 92). Materials and resources – linguistic and cultural – published in Indigenous languages allow the languages to "co-exist with other, more dominant, languages. It helps the languages feel more "normal," more a part of daily life" (as cited in Galla 2016, p. 9) – a goal that endangered language communities are striving for.

References

Brayboy B (2014) Looking into hearts of native peoples: nation building as an institutional orientation for graduate education. Presentation at University of British Columbia

Carew M, Green J, Kral I, Nordlinger R, Singer R (2015) Getting in touch: language and digital inclusion in Australian Indigenous communities. Lang Doc Conserv 9:307–323

Carjuzza J, Fenimore-Smith K (2010) The give away spirit: reaching a shared vision of ethical Indigenous research relationships. J Educ Controv 5(2):1–12. http://www.wce.wwu.edu/Resources/CEP/eJournal/v005n002/a004.shtml. Accessed 20 Jan 2014

Cru J (2015) Language revitalisation from the ground up: promoting Yucatec Maya on Facebook. J Multiling Multicult Dev 36(3):284–296

Esteban-Guitart M, Moll LC (2014a) Funds of identity: a new concept based on the Funds of Knowledge approach. Cult Psychol 20(1):31–48

Esteban-Guitart M, Moll LC (2014b) Lived experience, funds of identity and education. Cult Psychol 20(1):70–81

Galla CK (2009) Indigenous language revitalization and technology: from traditional to contemporary domains. In: Reyhner J, Lockard L (eds) Indigenous language revitalization: encouragement, guidance & lessons learned. Northern Arizona University, Flagstaff, pp 167–182

Galla CK (2010) Multimedia technology and Indigenous language revitalization: practical educational tools and applications used within Native communities. Dissertation, University of Arizona

Galla CK (2016) Indigenous language revitalization, promotion, and education: function of digital technology. Comput Assist Lang Learn 29(7):1137–1151. https://doi.org/10.1080/09588221.2016.1166137

Galla CK, Kawai'ae'a K, Nicholas SE (2014) Carrying the torch forward: Indigenous academics building capacity through an international collaborative model. Can J Nativ Educ 37(1):193–217

Gonzalez N, Moll LC, Amanti C (eds) (2005) Funds of knowledge: theorizing practices in households, communities, and classrooms. Erlbaum, Mahwah

Harde R (2016) Putting first nations texts at the center. Bookbird 54(1):4–9

Hartle-Schutte D, Nae'ole-Wong K (1998) Technology and the revival of the Hawaiian language. Reading Online. http://www.readingonline.org/electronic/hawaii/. Accessed 23 Jul 2009

Hoffman A (2010) Stories that matter: native American fifth graders' responses to culturally authentic text. Dissertation, University of Arizona

Ingle HT (2003) Connections across culture, demography, and new technologies. In: Solomon G, Allen N, Resta P (eds) Toward digital equity: bridging the digital divide in education. Allyn and Bacon, Boston, pp 75–87

Jackson A (2016) "Openly searching, inventive and welcoming": Oceania and children's literature. Bookbird 54(3):4–9

Jones LC (2008) Listening comprehension technology: building the bridge from analog to digital. CALICO J 25(3):400–419

Ka'awa M, Hawkins E (1997) Incorporating technology into a Hawaiian language curriculum. In: Reyhner J (ed) Teaching Indigenous languages. Northern Arizona University, Flagstaff, pp 151–157

Kirkness VJ, Barnhardt R (1991) First Nations and higher education: The Four Rs – respect, relevance, reciprocity, responsibility. J Am Indian Educ 30(3):1–15

Kral I (2010) Plugged in: remote Australian Indigenous youth and digital culture. Center for Aboriginal Economic Policy Research, Australian National University. http://caepr.anu.edu.au/sites/default/files/Publications/WP/WP69_0.pdf. Accessed 10 Jan 2017

Kral I (2011) Youth media as cultural practice: remote Indigenous youth speaking out loud. J Aust Inst Aborig Torres Strait Islander Stud 1:4–16

Kral I (2012) Text, talk, and technology. Multiling Matters, Bristol

Lave J, Wenger E (1991) Situated learning: legitimate peripheral participation. Cambridge University Press, New York

Leighton MS, Hightower AM, Wrigley PG (1995) Model strategies in bilingual education: professional development. Policy Study Associates and U.S. Department of Education, Office of Bilingual Education and Minority Languages Affairs, Washington, DC

Luykx A (2016) Introduction: Indigenous American languages in contact and in context. Int J Sociol Lang (240):1–7. https://doi.org/10.1515/ijsl-2016-0012

Moll LC, Amanti C, Neff D, Gonzalez N (1992) Funds of knowledge for teaching: using a qualitative approach to connect homes and classrooms. Theory Pract 31(1):132–141

New London Group (1996) A pedagogy of multiliteracies: designing social futures. Harvard Educational Review 66(1):60–92

Reese D (2006) American Indians in children's literature. https://americanindiansinchildrensliterature.blogspot.com. Accessed 1 Feb 2017

Rice E, Haynes E, Royce P, Thompson S (2016) Social media and digital technology use among Indigenous young people in Australia: a literature review. Int J Equity Health. http://www.ncbi.nlm.nih.gov/pmc/articles/PMC4881203/. 15 Accessed 1 Jun 2016

Seeman KW (2000) Technacy education: towards holistic pedagogy and epistemology in general and Indigenous/cross-cultural technology education. Paper presented at the technology education research conference

Seeman KW (2009) Technacy education: understanding cross-cultural technological practice. In: Fien J, Maclean R, Park M (eds) Work, learning and sustainable development. Springer, Dordrecht, pp 117–131

Seeman KW, Talbot R (1995) Technacy: towards a holistic understanding of technology teaching and learning among Aboriginal Australians. Prospects 25(4):761–775

Sheahan-Bright R (2011) Red, Yellow, and Black: Australian Indigenous publishing for young people. Bookbird 49(3):1–17

Smith L (2012) Decolonizing methodologies: research and Indigenous peoples, 2nd edn. Zed Books Ltd., New York

Tomlinson B (2001) Materials development. In: Carter R, Nunan D (eds) Teaching English to speakers of other languages. Cambridge University Press, Cambridge, pp 66–72

Tomlinson B (2012) Materials development for language learning and teaching. Lang Teach 45(2):143–179. https://doi.org/10.1017/S0261444811000528

United Nations (2008) United Nations declaration on the rights of Indigenous peoples. UN General Assembly. http://www.un.org/esa/socdev/unpfii/documents/DRIPS_en.pdf. Accessed 1 July 2010

Villa DJ (2002) Integrating technology into minority language preservation and teaching efforts: An inside job. Lang Learn Technol 6(2):92–101

Warschauer M (1998) Technology and Indigenous language revitalization: analyzing the experience of Hawai'i. Can Modern Lang Rev 55(1):139–159

Warschauer M, Donaghy K (1997) Leokī: a powerful voice of Hawaiian language revitalization. Comput Assist Lang Learn 10(4):349–361

Wyman LT, McCarty TL, Nicholas SE (2013) Indigenous youth and multilingualism: language identity, ideology, and practice in dynamic cultural worlds. Routledge, New York

Wyman L, Galla CK, Jimenez-Quispe L (2016) Indigenous youth language resources, educational sovereignty, and praxis-oriented research: Connecting a new body of language planning research to the work of Richard Ruiz. In: Hornberger N (ed) Honoring Richard Ruiz and his work on language planning and bilingual education. Multilingual Matters, Bristol, pp 395–429

Still Flourishing: Enacting Indigenizing Language Immersion Pedagogies in the Era of US Common Core State Standards

23

Mary Hermes and Erin Dyke

Contents

Introduction	378
A Note on Coauthorship, Settler Accomplices, and Strategic Essentialism	380
Overview of Ojibwe Language Revitalization and Education	381
Resurgences of Ways of Knowing and (in Spite of) State Standards	383
Examples of Curricular Tensions within an Ojibwe Immersion School	388
The Significance of the Change, the Significance of the Name	388
Example 2: "Measuring Text Complexity" and the Naturalization of Settler Ideologies	390
Example 3: What Western Curricular Cycles Mask	393
Conclusion and Future Directions	395
References	397

Abstract

Since the common schools movement, the struggle for the American curriculum is the struggle for the means of (re)producing national identity. For Indigenous peoples, state-sanctioned standards and curricula, no matter how progressive, have always served to naturalize and reinforce the settler-state and Indigenous erasure. Yet, language immersion schools have become widely popular tools in efforts to revitalize Indigenous lifeways in North America and beyond. In this chapter, we discuss the controversial relationship between education and revitalization within the context of North American, and specifically Ojibwe efforts to reclaim school spaces for the enactment of Indigenous ways of knowing

---

M. Hermes (✉)
College of Education and Human Development, University of Minnesota, Minneapolis, MN, USA
e-mail: mhermes@umn.edu

E. Dyke
Oklahoma State University, Stillwater, OK, USA
e-mail: erin.dyke@okstate.edu

© Springer Nature Singapore Pte Ltd. 2019
E. A. McKinley, L. T. Smith (eds.), *Handbook of Indigenous Education*,
https://doi.org/10.1007/978-981-10-3899-0_21

(epistemologies). We describe common tensions that arise in designing curricula that aim to simultaneously revitalize an Ojibwe land-based and relational epistemology *and* meet local and national standards in Wisconsin, USA. We recount examples from a Prekindergarten-5th grade Ojibwe language immersion school in order to illuminate the ways standards attempt to (but never successfully) reproduce students and teachers as colonized subjects, pulling them into a complex of state rules, unstated expectations, and discourses. Through our examples, we illustrate the ways immersion teachers and students must resist daily the universalization of Western epistemologies within the standards and, correspondingly, students' and teachers' own erasure. We conclude by offering considerations and future directions for research and practice that can help us to better understand the contradictions and complexities of working within education institutions that aim to revitalize Indigenous lifeways.

Keywords
Common Core State Standards; Indigenizing pedagogy; Indigenous education; Indigenous language revitalization; Ojibwe

Introduction

Since the common schools movement during the late nineteenth century, the struggle for the American curriculum is the struggle for the means to (re)produce a national identity, including narratives that legitimize the nation's existence (Kliebard 2004). Kliebard writes that state power over the curriculum was, and continues to be, wielded as a tool to manage moments of crisis and contingency that threaten the state's hegemony (p. 1–5, also see Grumet 1988; Grande 2004). As Coulthard (2014) and many others have noted, the state's investment in reproducing a dominant narrative of "democracy," and contemporarily, "liberal pluralism," serves to mask the histories of the nation's origins in Indigenous genocide, slavery, and the plundering of the land's natural resources. The (re)production of a national identity via curricular standards has always been premised on the erasure and sentimentalization of the land's Indigenous peoples and their diverse lifeways and worldviews.

Against attempts to stabilize (and accumulate capital via stabilizing) a naturalized settler American subject via standardization, Indigenous and other oppressed peoples in what is now called the USA continue the long struggle for cultural self-determination. Today, people are rising up against colonial erasure – from Black Lives Matter to immigrant rights and labor movements to Indigenous-led movements against extractive capitalism, including the ongoing (as of writing) Standing Rock Sioux-led multination coalition fighting to protect their (and many North Americans') water against the Dakota Access oil pipeline. (Water protectors argue the pipeline would seriously impact the Missouri River and its many tributaries (Woolf 2016).) The popular visibility of decolonial and abolitionist social movements is fracturing the foundations of America's master narrative on multiple fronts, including the intersecting movements against police brutality, mass incarceration and deportation, and the slow death of Black, Brown, and Indigenous bodies and ecologies. Such movements illuminate the failures of and "cracks" within efforts to standardize and control what young people can know or study within and beyond school. The official curriculum is never neatly transferred between teacher and student: classroom spaces are often sites of struggle, possibility, rebellion, and tension.

We write from within the transnational movement to revitalize Indigenous languages, and, more specifically, the movement for Ojibwe language revitalization. As McCarty and Nicholas (2014) write, despite our current era of intensified "language policing" via federal policies that mandate high stakes testing and standards, schools have been targeted by many Indigenous communities as sites of linguistic and cultural reclamation. The Indigenous language revitalization (and interrelated) decolonial movements have existed as long as state education has been working to "kill the Indian and save the man," attempting to force Indigenous and other peoples to abandon their languages and ways of life in favor of European "civilization" (Grinde 2004). However, with immersion schooling emerging as a tool for revitalization, today Indigenous education is a complex terrain of interests and social trajectories. In this chapter, we focus on contemporary tensions that play out within sites of language immersion education, using the context of Ojibwemowin (Ojibwe language) education in the USA as example.

We first contextualize movements to revitalize Indigenous languages in North America, and within that, the state of Ojibwe revitalization. Next, we consider the US Common Core State Standards (CCSS) and attempt to "[unveil] the epistemic silences of Western epistemology" (Mignolo 2009, p. 162) encoded within what many have argued are relatively progressive standards. Drawing on specific moments within a Pre-K-5th grade Ojibwe immersion school in Wisconsin, USA, we describe the ways that schools are simultaneously, and often contradictorily, state technologies that perpetuate colonization *and* gathering places for the subversive enactment of decolonial resistance and self-determination. Through these examples, we highlight tensions that arise from immersion educators' engagement in efforts to revitalize Ojibwe language and culture *while simultaneously* being forced to prove to the state that they are teaching according Wisconsin's Common Core Standards (WCSS, or Wisconsin's version of CCSS). We argue that while state-enforced curriculum structures attempt to constrain the content knowledges and structures that are emerging from the language and culture of the Ojibwe people, immersion classrooms can offer possibilities for students and teachers to question, resist, and critique the perpetuation of Indigenous erasure.

We conclude by arguing that Indigenous knowledges represent a very different way of perceiving the world, or a different epistemological stance, than those found in WCCS and state-sponsored standards more broadly. Along the lines of McCarty and Nicholas (2014), we suggest that language revitalization efforts *within* state education are limited yet strategically important, and that they be understood in relation to and in collaboration with Indigenous institutions *beyond* education and the state that serve to reproduce Indigenous lifeways, i.e., kinship relations, ceremonies, and sites of organized resistance (i.e., the Standing Rock Camp of the Sacred Stone). Indigenous knowledges are not lost, forgotten, or dying, as many official textbooks imply. They thrive best where our Indigenous languages also thrive. It is through recognizing and better understanding the contradictory state and decolonial interests at play within Indigenous immersion education that we can further develop strategies and practices for "affirming the epistemic rights of the racially devalued" (Mignolo 2009, p. 162), creating more resilient indigenizing pedagogies in and through Indigenous languages and cultural ways.

A Note on Coauthorship, Settler Accomplices, and Strategic Essentialism

Mary/Waabishkimiigwan is of mixed Native American (Dakota), white (mostly Irish), and Chinese (Toysan) heritage. She is a longtime community member at Lac Courte Oreilles Ojibwe reservation and speaks Ojibwe. She does not qualify for "enrollment" or citizenship under the current constitutional rules – in some sense she is an "undocumented immigrant" to the Ojibwe nation. In 2000, she collaborated with Ojibwe language activists to found the Waadookodaading Ojibwe Language Institute (Waadookodaading), a Pre-K through 5th grade immersion school, where she served as director for its first 5 years. For the past 20 years, Mary has simultaneously balanced her community language efforts with her bill-paying efforts, and so has enjoyed being a professor at the University of Minnesota. We coauthors met at the University of Minnesota when Erin took an Ojibwemowin revitalization course with Mary and became coconspirators in all things political and meaningful.

Erin's ancestors, in an attempt to escape poverty, migrated from Poland to Chicago, Illinois (unceded Miami territory) during a wave of Eastern European immigration to the USA in the late nineteenth and early twentieth centuries. Her ancestors' language and cultural ways were quickly lost (forsaken) upon arrival as they became White, learned to speak English, and passed as "American." She is just one of many settler and Indigenous graduate students that Mary has expertly recruited to revitalization.

Our approach to movement work draws inspiration from the North American-based Indigenous Action Network's (2015) concept "accomplices not allies." They write: "An accomplice as academic would seek ways to leverage resources and material support and/or betray their institution to further liberation struggles. An intellectual accomplice would strategize with, not for and not be afraid to pick up a hammer" (n.p.). It recognizes that universities continue to coerce Indigenous communities into violent, paternalistic relationships (cf. Smith 1999), and that Indigenous language revitalization is necessarily entwined with movements against the university as such.

We locate the origins of many of the tensions that we identify in immersion education in the forceful ways education and the academy become so easily and quickly dehistoricized and disconnected from their mutual constitution with settler-colonialism. In our coauthorship, as we write across our differences in histories, settler and Indigenous identities, and racialization, we pay close attention to these differences in power and perspective and the ways in which they inform or create controversy within our coproduction of knowledge and representation.

Overview of Ojibwe Language Revitalization and Education

Historically and contemporarily, First Nations and Native American peoples have a distinct perspective that exists in conflict with those of the US and Canadian settler-colonial nation-states. This difference in view is marked first by the reciprocal relationships to land and other beings, as opposed to the capitalist accumulation mentality. And second, it is starkly marked by the collective experience of genocide, dispossession, and forced migration. Indigenous communities fight to protect and nurture this perspective in spite of American cultural hegemony. Yet, Indigenous people in North America are not uniform in worldview, politics, or visions for the future. They are made up of multiple identities, and speak many different, and sometimes opposing, discourses. They move between and hybridize cultural practices that vary according to the vast differences in the politics of place across North America, creating anew every day what it means to be Indigenous here. Like other nations, they comprise people who make infinite and unpredictable decisions about who they are as individuals in today's world while maintaining membership in their own tribal communities and fighting for their communities' self-determination. It is this struggle against the forces of Eurocultural domination and capitalism that produces a uniquely Indigenous/Indigenizing and enduring oppositional perspective against official Eurotraditional worldviews privileged in many US and Canadian textbooks, tests, and standards.

A traditional Indigenous way of identifying differences while maintaining the fluidity and complexities of "difference" has been through our Indigenous languages. Like many Indigenous people all over this Mother Earth, we (Mary) listen to the particular sounds animals make to know where they are from and what our relationship to them might be, knowing that they do not need us to survive as we do them. Our word for language itself is the same for all animals' sounds: "inwe" or "she makes a characteristic call" (Ojibwe People's Dictionary). These sounds can be recreated, additional languages learned or appropriated and exchanged with other groups. With endless creative variation, along with a stable (enough) way to identify a place of origin, language is remarkable in its ability to be fluid and anchored in the same moment.

Historically, speaking many languages or even distinct varieties of Ojibwe served as a way to identify the particular place and group or groups a person originated from. Ojibwe country comprises a vast area of land in North America. Imagine a halo that emanates from the Great Lakes, encircling a wide swath of territory within the central part of the continent. Ojibwe people travelled these lakes and rivers all the way to the east coast, including the St. Lawrence seaway. All over the core of North America, the Ojibwe traded, traveled, and shared language and culture via small dispersed (not centrally organized) communities. The so-called "dialects" of Algonquian, or even specifically of Ojibwe, are like infinite variations on a flowering vine – beautiful, distinct, and affected by its particular place yet recognizable across many places. Today ("Language table" is a commonly used term to describe relatively informal community language initiatives that gather people, often around a table of food, to speak and socialize in their Indigenous language.):

Ojibwe (or Chippewa or Anishinaabem) has an estimated 50,000 speakers across the United States and Canada. With an estimated 500–700 first speakers of Southwestern Ojibwe, the most endangered dialect of Ojibwe, currently there is a strong grassroots push for revitalization. Encouraged by language tables, 2 language immersion camps, widespread second language or heritage Ojibwe classes, and recently, Ojibwe immersion schools, second language learners of Ojibwe are struggling to find effective ways to learn a language that they rarely, if ever, hear spoken in everyday conversations. (Hermes and King 2013, p. 126–127)

To date, there are six Ojibwemowin immersion schools in the Minnesota/ Wisconsin area. Waadookodaading Ojibwe Language Institute (Waadookodaading), where our examples derive, was one of the first (Niigane Ojibwe Immersion School within the Leech Lake Band of Ojibwe started during the same year). Although we cannot report on immersion schools on the Canadian side, Mary has heard of at least seven more by word of mouth. There exist even more language programs within public and tribal schools, with Ojibwe being one of the most widely institutionally taught Indigenous languages in the United States. These programs are gravely affected by the fluency/teaching skills of the teachers. At the same time, they fight to thrive despite limited funding sources, assimilative teacher preparation programs, and certification requirements. Further, there is little curriculum already produced using Ojibwemowin as the medium of instruction. These challenging work conditions are also operating under racist structures of American schooling – for example, under the weight of (White) fellow public or tribal school educators' perceptions that they are "just doing their Indian voodoo thing," as one Ojibwe immersion teacher described (Dyke 2016).

Waadookodaading teaches in and through Southwestern Ojibwe. It is attempting to create infrastructure that allows us to decide and prioritize the knowledge and skills we want our young people to have. Mary has been involved in revitalization for 16 years, marked by assisting with the start-up of Waadookodaading (Hermes 2004). But actually, it is not quite accurate to call the start of an immersion school the start of revitalization. All of those Elders, all of those children of speakers who learned and many more who did not learn, still kept the love for our language alive. *There is no "beginning" of a revitalization effort, we are ones in a long line of sentries. Bearing witness, remembering, keeping alive with love, our languages.*

McCarty and Nicholas (2014), in their review of school-based reclamation in the USA and Canada, describe the reason why such efforts have become so important to the broader revitalization movement:

> Despite the fact that schools are "extremely contentious places" (Rockwell and Gomes 2009, p. 105), the reality is that in settings around the world, schools – the single place where children spend much of their waking hours – are looked to as prime sites for language reclamation. As stated by the Hopi linguist, educator, jurist, and activist Emory Sekaquaptewa, "Someone must take the responsibility for language preservation, and the logical place is the school" (quoted in Nicholas 2005, p. 34). We now have more than 25 years – fully a generation – of data on such efforts. It is time to take stock and to reconsider: What roles have schools played in reclaiming and revitalizing threatened Indigenous mother tongues? (p. 108)

Their complex answer to this question: "School-based programs are not the only means to reclaim a threatened language, nor are they necessarily the most efficacious" (p. 130). Yet, they argue, schools are a critical and strategic tool in the movement. Like McCarty and Nicholas (2014), so many others have long pointed to historical and contemporary iterations of state policies shaping education standards and federal language policies that serve as barriers to decolonizing the US educational system (Hermes 2005a, b; Richardson 2011; Lomawaima and McCarty 2002). Most recently, Native American and allied scholars have argued that the recuperation of multiculturalism in education has made popular the insidious notion that one can "add" culture into curriculum founded in White epistemologies (Hermes 2005a) (CITE).

Mary's foray into language revitalization began when elders critiqued the ways that culture was being taught in tribal schools. They argued that, for example, just adding in a pipe ceremony to the normal school day did not constitute a culture-based curriculum. As one parent and elder described it:

> To me, it's a way of life-you have to live it. Just talking about it or reading about it, that's not enough. I see that academics could be taught differently at the school but I don't know exactly how. My kids ... have a hard time. I know they have to learn that stuff [academics], but I believe there is definitely a different way to teach it. I mean math and science, reading. They could integrate it with culture. (Hermes 2005a, p. 49)

In her visits to tribal schools and conversations with elders and administrators, Mary found that elders viewed culture as a verb, an everyday practice (versus a noun or static set of aesthetics), and that, as a tribal school administrator stated, "the Ojibwe language is where it all comes from, it's all based out of that" (p. 49).

When static representations of cultures are added to existing structures of thought in US schools (structures that are premised on Indigenous erasure), the curricula's conceptual frameworks act as a container. On the one hand, the represented culture fulfills the teachers' "duty" to be culturally responsive in our era of cultural pluralism. On the other hand, such a framework of "inclusion" serves to contain the knowledge-building power of non-White peoples. As we illuminate in the following, attempts to reclaim education as sites of Indigenous language and culture revitalization are in deep tension with the epistemologies that have historically and continue to undergird the American curriculum. We argue that both cannot exist alongside one another in harmony but are always already in conflict. Indigenous immersion education is a continuous struggle to center epistemologies to which Western education has historically constructed itself in opposition (Tuck and Gatzambide-Fernández 2013; Meiners 2002).

Resurgences of Ways of Knowing and (in Spite of) State Standards

I (Mary) know that all of the many layers of identity within myself are real; there is not one "real" indigenous self buried under all the rest. And, I (Erin) know that my whiteness was historically wielded as a tool to control and exploit the labor of my working class Eastern European ancestors, who brought with them their own traditions and ways of knowing rooted to their homeplaces. They/we were conscripted into the project of colonization and nation-building via the psychological wage of whiteness (cf. Roedigger). And so we struggle in writing this piece to keep that at the forefront, even as we use these imperfect categories of "Indigenous knowledges" or "White knowledges". We try, where we can, to interrupt this thinking and to acknowledge and theorize the polyphony of voices, identities, and discourses that live in these terms and across our own co-authorship. Just as we attempt to hold the complexity of differences that exist within 'Indigenous epistemologies', we cannot act as if there is a unified 'European epistemology'. For now, we name this as a theoretical problematic, and, at times, employ a tactic of strategic essentialism (Spivak 1990), using temporarily unified categories that enable us to describe the tensions between state standards and Ojibwe ways of knowing. At the same time, we recognize and signal the importance for historical and geo- and body-political situated specificity (Mignolo 2011) in discussions surrounding epistemology.

As of January 2016, 42 out of 50 US states have adopted the Common Core State Standards (CCSS), a public-private venture to standardize curricula across the USA (Au 2013, pp 1–4), the most recent iteration of the (highly profitable) struggle for the American curriculum. States that have not adopted CCSS tend to have their own similar version of these standards (i.e., Oklahoma State Standards). CCSS encompasses kindergarten-12th grade English/language arts skills (including literature, informational text, foundational skills, writing, speaking and listening, language; and it defines texts according to their range, quality, and complexity). It also encompasses and defines level-appropriate literacy in history/social studies, science, technical subjects, and a range of mathematics (CCSS Website). In states where the standards are in place, school administrators must demonstrate the alignment of their curricula, and often purchase standardized curricula that make this process more efficient. States that have adopted CCSS or similar standards hold schools accountable via regular state testing. Often these tests are high stakes (e.g., in Oklahoma, 3rd graders who do not pass their reading test are disallowed from moving up to 4th grade). In Wisconsin, the main geographic focus of our paper, through a state test system called Wisconsin Forward, students are tested in English language arts every year in grades 3–8; grades 4 and 8 in Science; and 4, 8, and 10 in Social Studies. The Wisconsin High School Assessments are comprised of a series of tests in English, reading, math, science, and writing in grades 9–11 (Wisconsin Department of Public Instruction Website).

Today's era of standardization and high stakes testing, a massive billion-dollar industry, is increasingly subsuming most aspects of education under capitalist market logics that reinforce Western values of individuality, competition, meritocracy, and modernity (Brown 2015). For example, now, most teacher candidates in the USA are required to be evaluated by the multinational corporation Pearson Education and their Teacher Performance Assessment (edTPA) prior to certification. Interrelated moves to standardize, universalize, and metricize a discrete set of knowledge – what students (and teachers) "need" to know for today's world – are the latest in a long line of attempts to, among other things, discipline the space-times of and decolonial possibilities for Indigenous education.

One of the more potent myths of American democracy – that education is a ladder to upward social and economic mobility – is swaying. The new millennium ushered in massive political and economic shifts that have seriously impacted local and global landscapes in education. Weis and Fine (2012) note that in the last decade:

> Educational segregation and stratification have become more normative; the testing industry now dominates public schools; mass incarceration of Black and Brown bodies is well recognized as a national problem; "college for all" is the mantra while the tertiary-level sector itself becomes increasingly stratified; [and] unemployment rates and student loan debt skyrocket. (p. 177)

This new educational era is most notably marked by aggressive federal policies, like the 2001 No Child Left Behind Act and its subsequent reiterations, that served to privatize large portions of the education system (Lipman 2011) and police Indigenous languages (McCarty and Nicholas 2014).

Many Indigenous cultures have long been aware of the assimilative effects of American public education, yet understood education as a means for surviving the violences of our settler colonial reality (See Grinde 2004; Grande 2004; Lomawaima and McCarty 2002). Yet given the recent transformations in the political economy of education, popular belief in educational "achievement" as a means for climbing out of poverty is waning, even among middle class communities for whom success in education previously ensured class security. We would argue that such a belief has never really had much hold on many Indigenous or working class communities (cf. MacLeod 1996; Willis 1977). Study of decolonial social movements from the 1970s and on illuminates that interest and participation in education, especially higher education, among Indigenous communities has grown largely in response to Indigenous-led efforts *to reclaim these institutions*.

As a result of the gains made by the American Indian Movement and Indigenous-led efforts toward tribal sovereignty (Smith and Warrior 1996), the number of American Indians in public and private degree-granting institutions more than doubled between the years of 1976 and 2006 (Lomawaima and McCarty 2002). More and more Indigenous people are completing degrees in higher education in no small part due to the resurgence of Indigenous intellectual traditions within these institutions (e.g., the creation of Native American Studies departments and research centers) and the creation of Indigenous-led tribal colleges. The collective memory of the violence of boarding and public schools has produced in Indigenous communities a resilience and resistance to schooling alongside strategies for reappropriating space and resources within it.

Today, a major barrier to the language revitalization movement's appropriation and subversion of school spaces is state surveillance of the curriculum via CCSS. Some proponents (and even some skeptics) of CCSS have argued that the standards are at least better than previous attempts to contain and prioritize what (certain people believe) students must know because they are ostensibly "focused on developing critical learning skills instead of mastering fragmented bits of knowledge" (Au 2013, n.p.). For example, the Wisconsin Common Core Standards (WCCS), the US state where our story takes place, are said to "help educators in Wisconsin build a ladder of skills and dispositions that lead to accelerated achievement across disciplines" (WDPI 2011a, p. 23). According to the Wisconsin Department of Public Instruction (WDPI), the skills and dispositions acquired as a result of implementing CCSS will better prepare students for postsecondary education as well as the workforce by means of disciplinary literacy (read: English) acquisition:

> In Wisconsin, disciplinary literacy is defined as the confluence of content knowledge, experiences, and skills merged with the ability to read, write, listen, speak, think critically, and perform in a way that is meaningful within the context of a given field. (WDPI 2011a, p. 1)

And further, a brochure from the state superintendent states that English Language Arts standards are meant to "build an understanding of the *human* experience" and produce students as "thinking and feeling *world citizens*" (Evers 2011, p. 1, emphasis added). Unifying terms such as "the human experience," "every student," and "world citizens" serve to mask the uneven power and relations of coloniality between (especially White) settler and many Indigenous students or English and Ojibwemowin. Why is "every student in Wisconsin" expected to become a "world citizen" when some students are actively prohibited from belonging to their own sovereign nations? How is it that Indigenous students in Wisconsin are expected to study "the world" and the "human experience" when they are actively frustrated by the state from learning their own communities' languages and cultural ways? Whose experience or world are they studying?

WCCS's epistemic silences are further exemplified in the language they use to describe and place value on "literacy." Its default language is English despite the fact that myriad languages, Indigenous and otherwise, are spoken widely in Wisconsin and the USA more broadly. According to the WDPI, English is synonymous with reading, writing, speaking, and listening. Nowhere in the WCCS, or the CCSS more broadly, exists the notion that there may be vast differences in the ways "literacy" is understood in other, particularly oral, cultures, and languages. Evidence of this lies most visibly in WCCS's assumption that one can dissociate the "skills" of literacy from "content." The relative freedom with which teachers can choose content is used as an example of its supposedly progressive aspects. As we illuminate in our examples from the immersion school below, this dissociation is impossible within complex, oral, and verb-based storytelling and relational languages like Ojibwemowin. The standards articulate an "education for every child," where "every child" subtly (or not so subtly) implies "every English-speaking white child."

In WCCS, while English serves as an umbrella term, "culture" functions to distinguish content that is (O)ther than English or normative conceptions of an American student (white, suburban, and middle-class). In the efforts to ensure that every child within the US graduates prepared for college and careers, "schools need to provide high quality instruction, balanced assessment and collaboration reflective of culturally responsive practices" (WDPI Website). To understand precisely where and how there is a conflict, we must ask from what epistemological viewpoint do these standards originate? What does it mean for the state to espouse values of cultural responsivity while mandating these particular standards without Indigenous communities' input or participation?

Throughout the WCCS and CCSS, culture is referred to as something that can be added in, as something that is not in conflict with the universalized, generic skills supposedly necessary for developing successful learners. For example, WDPI states that "WCCS provide the foundation for learning for every student in Wisconsin, regardless of their unique learning needs" (WDPI 2011a, p. 14). It goes on to state that "students in Wisconsin [shall] come to understand *other* perspectives and cultures" (p. 24, emphasis added). WCCS claims that, first, the standards are for every student, and, second, that "other" cultural perspectives can be understood via the set of scaffolded skills WCCS universalizes as the "foundation" of learning. The overlay of a Western indexicality silences Indigenous ways of knowing that cannot (nor should) be parsed into skills versus content.

Western discourses are positioned as the neutral location from where knowledge is produced, what Walter Mignolo (2011) describes as the zero-point epistemology. Belief in the zero-point is a belief that what one knows is not situated, partial, or limited by one's relations. The construction of "culture" is interrelated with this Enlightenment-era stance. Duranti (1997) writes, "In the nineteenth century culture was a concept used by Europeans to explain the customs of the people in the territories they came to conquer and populate" (p. 23). "Culture" is the "object" of study, distinct from the researcher, who is objective and untainted by the "other." Producing knowledge about "culture" from the zero-point not only enabled colonialist government administrators and military to more effectively discipline and manage the colonized; the stance also legitimized a supposed European moral and religious superiority. The zero-point epistemology and its perpetuation today in the academy has been heavily critiqued by many postcolonial and postmodern feminist scholars (see for example: Said 1979; Haraway 1988; Harding 1986).

As Richardson (2011) writes, the legacy of the zero-point continues to undergird state-mandated standards and curriculum in schools:

> The theoretical and philosophical foundations of curriculum act as forces which continuously eclipse the conceptual, theoretical and philosophical forces of Aboriginal intellectual traditions. (p. 333)

The bifurcation of "skills" from "content" in WCCS exemplifies the kind of supposed neutrality and universality of "knowing" espoused by those who (fail to) locate themselves at the zero-point. The study of Indigenous languages in a variety of fields illuminates, however, that language itself orients us in deeply different ways (Hermes 2005a). While the zero-point epistemology, and its reproduction within the field of education and education policy, orients teachers to make certain pedagogical choices appear to be normal, "best practice," or "common sense," immersion educators' attempts to teach Ojibwemowin *and* meet state standards are painfully aware that the "zero-point" is a historically European epistemic stance that exists in tension with Ojibwe ways of knowing.

Examples of Curricular Tensions within an Ojibwe Immersion School

One of the things I (Mary) love about ceremony is the distribution of knowledge. At first it appeared to me that there was clearly a hierarchy, as I started to understand the ceremony through the Ojibwe language I realized, that everyone was just "sitting in" for someone – some spirit – anyway. The idea of hierarchy and expert unraveled from there. An expert is someone that knows more, perhaps in a certain context, knows the most, and that is the one who is on top of the pile. The smartest, the best, the most powerful. But when different people, sitting in for different manidoo (spirits), all know something slightly different, and from a different point of view, well then, this idea of expert goes out the window. We all know parts, and we all sit in a different place. And this is how we share, teach and reinvigorate that conversation, in the ceremony. The structure holds us in this way. The idea of a "standard" then – something written by an expert (the first kind), the individual with "the most" knowledge is foreign to this Indigenous learning structure, actually has no place in this particular social context. Standards are generated by experts within disciplines, all of these structures are from Western academics, which are also based on individual knowledge, and in this US colonial context, that translates to power.

In our examples, the immersion teacher's move to subvert the standard is an opportunity to resist and appropriate space in the classroom for decolonial study. Many Ojibwe immersion teachers, and likely other Indigenous teachers as well, have become masters at this epistemic disobedience. As one Ojibwe immersion teacher recounted to Mary during a language pedagogy workshop, "I can take a speck of dust, make a lesson that meets five standards *and* has a cultural teaching in it." Such a statement illuminates the pressures and constraints that standards place on immersion teachers' work. Appropriating and subverting the language of the standards, rearticulating the skills from the WCCS under a framework of Indigenous knowledge and values, or ignoring the standards altogether at times to make space and time for Indigenous epistemology is the work teachers grounded in Indigenous languages, but situated in settler-colonial places, must do.

The Significance of the Change, the Significance of the Name

In Bimijiwanikwe's (Bimijiwanikwe (Michelle) Haskins was a kindergarten immersion teacher for 9 years. She is our colleague, friend, and sister. We refer to her here as Bimijiwanikwe and many of these examples are published in her masters thesis and in Hermes and Haskins (2018). She currently works at Lac Courte Oreilles Tribal Community College.) Kindergarten classroom at Waadookodaading Ojibwe Language Institute (Waadookodaading), many parents are hoping that their children are "ready for first grade" by the end of the year. Bimijiwanikwe is a talented veteran immersion teacher. Depending on the year, she often has the class reading in Ojibwe and English by mid-year. One of the most telling examples of a clash of expectations is in a seemingly simple name-writing activity. Writing one's name is a part of the

Wisconsin's state standards (WDPI 2011a) and a normative preschool and kindergarten activity. It's often presented to children and families as a matter of safety – children need to be able to provide their names to authorities and adults in cases of emergency. It is also one of the first writing skills that Kindergarteners are expected to learn in order to indicate whose worksheets or assignments belong to whom, a kind of individualizing surveillance wrapped up in the individualized system of testing, evaluation, and promotion predominant in most schools.

In the immersion school however, Ojibwe names are usually much longer and typically have more syllables than English names. Some children are learning to say their name in Ojibwe for the first time. They struggle to speak it, let alone to write it. Take, for example, the Anishinaabe name, Niiyaandiwed (Nee-yawn-di-wade), typical in its level of difficulty. Writing all 12 letters requires a significant amount of time and fine motor skills. One immersion teacher recalls a little boy saying, "I wish my name was Makwa [bear]," as he was writing his 15-letter-long name (Hermes and Haskins 2018).

Beyond this difference, at Waadookodaading, the skill of name-writing is intimately entwined with the work of providing space and guidance for students to make sense of and re-value their own Indigenous identities and histories. Ojibwe cultural values are transmitted orally, often through storytelling, and Ojibwe spiritual names are deeply rooted in culture and identity. Kindergarten students at the Ojibwe immersion school spend the first 6 weeks of school participating in cross-curriculum activities to assert their identities are valid and powerful. For example, Bimijiwanikwe (2015) describes in her masters thesis how she supported students' lack of motivation to engage in learning activities where they were required to first write their name on a worksheet or piece of paper:

> In my heartbreak and determination to find a better way to help my students to meet the outcomes of WCCS of early literacy, reduce anxiety, and foster cultural identity, I created tracing-name strips to glue onto their work. This adaptation was made for all students so that no student was made to feel singled out [because while some students had as few as six letters, some had upwards of twenty three]. Having a choice is empowering for all mankind. Additionally, a discussion on the importance of our Anishinaabe spiritual names, how it came to be that Ojibwe people have them, and how we take care of our names, even in print, occurred. This conversation was a review of content learned earlier about the Ojibwe naming ceremony, which is retold in the Ojibwe Creation Story. The Ojibwe Creation Story is transferred generationally by the means of oral tradition, a natural learning facet for Anishinaabe people. (p. 42)

Here, Bimijiwanikwe describes the ways in which teaching and encouraging students to persevere in writing their names is entwined with the developing of their understanding of where they come from, who they are in the world, and linking the skill of printing one's name with "how we take care of our names," and, thus, our identities and cultural traditions.

Alternatively, in WCCS name-writing is treated as a basic skill detached from the cultural significance of naming: for WCCS, the name is merely a unique identifier, a way for children to associate themselves with their individual writing assignment or worksheet. However, in Ojibwe culture, one's spiritual name is provided during a naming ceremony. It signifies who one is to this world and to the spirit world, it connects a person to a group of namesakes, and it leads one through many ceremonies and steps of life. One's Ojibwe name is a source of pride for Anishinaabe people, and one of the strongest ceremonial traditions in practice today.

Further, Ojibwe traditions of learning are collaborative and relational. Alternatively, in normative school practice, a student's name at the top of the page signifies that s/he "owns" this work, it is his/hers to receive credit for, and plagiarism is often met with strict discipline. This form of knowledge ownership does not translate well in Ojibwe intellectual traditions, which emphasize such values as honoring the wisdom of elders and collaboration, and which are predicated on a trusting relationship between one who seeks knowledge and one who can offer guidance. It is important to note here that "Waadookodaading" in Ojibwe means "the place where we help each other," a phrase with a categorically different and less hierarchical associations than "school," "teacher," or "student."

Within Indigenous oral traditions, one initiates learning by offering tobacco to a person one believes can guide them (Archibald 2008). The learner knows whom to ask a priori or discovers this via his/her kinship relations. The asker already exists in a network of relationships with the elder or guide. In fact, it is through this network that the asker would know who to even ask for the teaching. A common way of greeting an unfamiliar face is by asking questions that place an individual within a network of relations: questions like, "where are you from? What is your clan? Who is your mother? Are you related to so and so?" There is no need to say one's name because there is almost always a relationship that exists between the two, and this relationship is what enables one to ask for guidance in the first place.

Example 2: "Measuring Text Complexity" and the Naturalization of Settler Ideologies

Within WCCS literacy standards, the state rationalizes the importance of literacy almost solely along the lines of how such literacy skills will prepare students for the worlds of college and work. The research used to support this rationalization deemphasizes critical thinking (although pays it lip service) and focuses on research that argues that vocabulary in K12 texts is becoming simpler, while colleges and workplaces are requiring students and workers read more complex vocabulary. For example, the WDPI cites a 2006 study conducted by ACT, Inc. (a major transnational testing corporation) that studied "which skills differentiated those students who equaled or exceeded the benchmark score (21 out of 36) in the reading section of the ACT college admissions test from those who did not" (p. 2). This study built on a previous ACT, Inc. study that correlated reading scores on its test to a college student's probability of earning a C or higher in an introductory U.S. history or psychology course. WDPI asserts that this research supports their definition of measuring text complexity, which is largely based on Lexile scores, or a system that measures the difficulty level of individual words. WDPI states:

> The most important implication of this [ACT, Inc.] study was that a pedagogy focused only on "higher-order" or "critical" thinking was insufficient to ensure that students were ready for college and careers: what students could read, in terms of its complexity, was at least as important as what they could do with what they read. (WDPI 2011b, p. 2)

The significance of student growth in understanding big words and "doing something with them" is described by WDPI along the lines of participation in college, careers, and citizenship.

Within the tripart system of evaluation (below), the only allusion to text ideology or epistemology exists within the qualitative evaluation of the text: "knowledge demands," or do students have enough background knowledge to comprehend the text?

Standard 10: Range, Quality, and Complexity of Student Reading K-5

Measuring Text Complexity: Three Factors

Qualitative evaluation of the text:	Levels of meaning, structure, language conventionality and clarity, and knowledge demands
Quantitative evaluation of the text:	Readability measures and other scores of text complexity
Matching reader to text and tasic:	Reader variables (such as motivation, knowledge, and experiences) and task variables (such as purpose and the complexity geerated by the task assigned and the questions posed)

Note: More detailed information on text complexity and how it is measured is contained in Appendix A.

The quantitative evaluation factor gestures toward the studies cited by WDPI that argue that K12 texts and literacy pedagogy must keep up with the level of difficulty of vocabulary demanded in colleges and workplaces. The third factor "matching reader to text and task" is tied deeply to what WDPI describe as the ways in which K12 schools fail to hold students "accountable for what they read on their own," citing the need for students to be able to engage in independent reading in college and for their careers (WDPI 2011b, p. 2). The standard, taken as a whole, illustrates the WCCS's zero-point epistemology: its preoccupation with producing "good" students and workers, the devaluation of critical analysis, and the lack of recognition that texts are not authorities but rooted in place, history, and perspective.

The following in-class example describes Bimijiwanikwe's's (2015) kindergarten class discussion of *The Three Little Pigs*. Her facilitation of a classroom discussion of the text illuminates the tensions between the intentions of the WCCS literacy standards and the aims of Waadookodaading to foster Ojibwe self-determination in learning and living with the land. For Bimijiwanikwe and her class, the discussion and comprehension of a common fable becomes deeply entwined with understanding and critically analyzing the origins of the fable in relation to an Ojibwe relational worldview. In Bimijiwanikwe's recounting of her class discussion, it is clear that their collective engagement with the story is not legible within the framework that WCCS outlines for the purposes and measures of literacy skills. We quote her here (Haskins 2015) at length.

We read the story of The Three Little Pigs, a story retold to ensure that the fear and hatred toward wolves lives for generations through Euro-American fairytales because early settlers feared the loss of livestock brought to North America (PBS 2008). Students were asked to reflect on whether or not wolves are bad and were asked why they thought these stories were being told? S4 raises his hand and waits to be called upon and said, *"Mii wenji nishkaadizid ma'iingan* [Because the wolf is angry]". S5 raised her hand shaking with enthusiasm. I call on her. S5 said, *"Eya' mii wenji bakade* [Yes because he is hungry]". S10 didn't raise his hand but I wanted to know what his thoughts were. S10 said, "prolly because he's bad". S6 chimes in without being called on and said, *"Gaawiin, gimikwendaan ina Bimijiwanikwe gii-ikido awesiiyag omaa ayaawaad dabwaa niinawind* [No, remember when the teacher said the animals were here before we were]?" Although the construct of S6's Ojibwemowin was not grammatically correct, I accepted S6's response. I was looking for deeper meanings and interpretive knowledge on why the students thought the story was written. I did not make corrections in speech nor did I recast in this activity.

S8 raised her hand and waited to be called on. When S8 was given an opportunity to speak, she said, *"Ma'iingan wa'aw Bimijiwanikwe's doodem* [Wolf is the teacher's clan]". I responded by saying, *"Ma'iingan ogikendaan gichi-niibowa, gichi-gikendaasod* [Wolf knows a lot, as he is really smart]. *Wenipanad da-amwaadwaa gookooshag miinawaa bizhiikiwag, agiw miigaazosigwaa Chi-mookomaanag awesiiyag* [It's easy to eat pigs and cows as those European animals have no way of fighting]." S7 said, "Oh yeah! *Nimikwendaan gii-piidoonaawaag bizhiikiwag* on those *gichi-jiimaanings mewinzha* [I remember they brought the cows on ships a long time ago]." I said, *"Mii gwayak, ishwaaso daso-giizisag booziwag da-bi-izhaawaad omaa Anishinaabe akiing* [It took several moons/months to get to America on a boat]". S1 said, *"Ma'iingan nindinawemaagan* [Wolf is my relative]". I reinforced S1's statement by saying, *"Gidebwe, Ma'iingan gindinawemaaganaanig* [You speak the truth, the Wolf is our relative]". I asked the students again, *"Aaniin dash awiiya gaa-tibaajimowaad yo'o Niswi-gookooshag* [Why was the story of the Three Pigs told]?" S9 said, *"Ganabaj…Aaniin ge-ikidoyangiban* to make people be scared of *Ma'iingan* [Maybe…How do we say, to make people scared of the Wolf]?"

The students did not see wolves as being bad, and they did indeed need to be respected for their intellect and wolf's role in our Creation Story. Students also identified how the wolf helps to keep balance among the lifecycle and should be especially respected as brother of the Anishinaabeg. (Haskins 2015, p. 36–37)

Bimijiwanikwe revalues the Ojibwe Creation Story as a strategy for interpreting the fable. Yet, according to WCCS, oral stories such as the Ojibwe Creation Story are not considered complex texts for use in teaching literacy skills (WDPI Website, K-5 Literacy Standards). Yet Bimijiwanikwe's classroom discussion illuminates that the Ojibwe oral tradition is a critical resource for unmasking the settler colonial underpinnings of pervasive fables, like *The Three Little Pigs*.

For Bimijiwanikwe, the practice of "reading" the fable was less about facilitating students' comprehension of some predefined authoritative interpretation, and more about assessing and developing students' cultural knowledge. She writes that her lesson on the fable had to do "both/and":

These students emerging cultural knowledge was revealed through further classroom discussion and completion of the Story Maps where the students wrote the name of the story, the author, and drew pictures to illustrate the story setting, characters, and the sequential events that took place in the story. (p. 38)

While she engaged students in a critical discussion of the fable in order to situate it within an Indigenous history (the fable was a tool for the reproduction of settler identities), she also engaged students in practicing normative literacy skills, such as naming parts of the story and understanding sequencing. Bimijiwanikwe's example illuminates the tensions between the standards and Ojibwe epistemology – while the standards find the latter skills sufficient to produce good workers, students, and citizens (of the USA), Waadookodaading as a decolonial education project struggles to provide space for students to understand the ways in which this production (of workers, students, and citizens) is premised on their own Indigenous erasure.

Example 3: What Western Curricular Cycles Mask

Our final example illuminates the space-time differences in CCSS/WCCS and Ojibwe lifeways. While the WCCS uses and naturalizes as universal the Gregorian standard (12-month) calendar, Indigenous communities (especially those that heavily rely on subsistence hunting, growing, and gathering) respond to cyclical transformation in the land and weather (i.e., harvest cycles). It is in following the natural progression of the seasonal gifts of harvest that the Anishinaabe have survived by first having spiritual acknowledgement of "Who" the Creator is and that we are related to all living beings. Paying homage to our Creator and our ancestors is done through ceremonial rites of passage and other cultural practices that are determined by the universe. Ojibwe people respond to the universe by migrating, gathering, and cultivating Indigenous knowledge from season to season as a way of life, rather than adopt Euro-models of industrial agriculture or resource extraction (i.e., iron ore mining) – modes of living that currently dominate Ojibwe ancestral lands.

One staff member from Waadookodaading stated the overarching curriculum goal as: "We respond to the food cycles of the season." While Waadookodaading follows a Gregorian calendar, they also have an entirely different way of viewing time – one that is not determined by a square on a page, but by what is happening in the environment. While many school calendars also were historically created to respond to planting and harvest seasons, the school calendar was determined largely by settler agrarian practices, and, in many places, other nonagrarian rationales like physical comfort in buildings without or before air-conditioning technology or, in urban areas, the labor needs of industrialism (Fischel 2006). Alternatively, the immersion school schedule is determined by when the fish are spawning, the sap is running, and the rice is ready to harvest. The ability to "read" the environment is important. Responding to the Earth, gathering foods that are ready, means that the overarching school structure is shaped by these activities *and* literacy, math, or any other academic skills that can be covered while also carrying out these activities.

For an example of such a land-based pedagogy, Keller Paap, a Waadookodaading teacher, describes Waadookodaading's responsiveness to the land and the relationship between land-based knowledge and language:

> Language, I think with any cultural practice, it has a specific vocabulary and teaching in that activity within that practice. So, for instance, all the words about boiling sap, the way that it boils, have specific terms that describe it very very accurately that allow you to develop a deep comprehension of the activity and why you do it and how you do it. (Finn 2016)

He describes the ways in which the cultural practice of the sugarbush harvest, or the spring season where maple syrup is harvested from trees, is encoded in the language in ways that enunciate the actual work and skills of harvesting sap. In the forest-as-classroom, the hoses, buckets, fire-tending, and various complex tools needed for the sugarbush give the appearance of an outdoor science classroom. Students are working alongside teachers and elders, working the taps, tending the fire, and tasting the sap. Here, science, culture, history, tradition, and language are all intimately entwined (versus discrete disciplines and subject areas within WCCS).

He goes on to describe the ways in which this land-based knowledge is a critical tool for "reading" the world, including the social, political, and the global (which, from an Ojibwe perspective, are inseparable from the "natural"):

> Ultimately it's prepping them and building an intellectual framework that they'll be able to apply to and adapt to. No matter where they are in the world, that will help them. And I think they're prepared with knowledge and ability that they feel proud of, that they feel connected to their ancestry in a deeper way. They have a much broader and deeper understanding of Ojibwe perspective in relation to the local community, the local environment, and the world. (Finn 2016)

Paap highlights the importance of preparing students with "knowledge and ability they feel proud of" and that connects them "to their ancestry in a deeper way." This rootedness in place, history, and identity are all, according to Paap, assets in surviving within and understanding their fraught relationship to settler-colonialism (e.g., the politics of their mostly White, rural surrounding community). As many scholars studying the value of ethnic studies programs and culturally relevant pedagogy in US schools have noted, such culture-based schooling – while not necessarily legible within the framework of the standards or testing – has had the overall effect of supporting minoritized students to complete high school and attend college at much higher rates (cf. Sleeter 2011). This body of research supports Paap's assertion that students learning in and through an Ojibwe perspective (versus the universalized perspective of WCCS) can be just as, if not more, "successful" in navigating settler colonial institutions and life than their peers without access to the kind of learning and relationships that Waadookodaading offers.

Such a land-based structure and pedagogy exemplifies a reciprocal relationship to the environment that is at odds with WCCS social studies standards that privilege and naturalize a political economy of scarcity. For example, in the grade two standards:

> Students [...] continue to build their foundational understanding in the social studies disciplines of citizenship and government, economics, geography and history. They learn about the need for fair voting processes, and the importance of constitutions and obeying rules. They *study indigenous people and the influence of a variety of cultures on our society,*

gaining an understanding of the United States' common heritage and diverse roots. Students begin to understand how resources and physical features influence the distribution of people around the world, and use maps and other geographic tools to explain the characteristics of places. They use *calendars and timelines to track the passage of time and chronicle events.* By describing the trade-offs of a decision, *students learn the concept of opportunity cost and its connection to scarcity of resources.* (WDPI Website, Social Studies Standards, emphasis added)

Analysis of the standard reveals the tensions between Waadookodaading's land-based approach and the naturalization of a White settler "we/our." The language used ("Indigenous people" and "a variety of cultures" have influenced "our" society) implies that Indigenous and "other" (nonwhite) cultures are not included within "our." The language ignores the social constructedness of space-time and naturalizes "scarcity of resources" as if it is not something that was artificially created via the export of capitalist accumulation via colonialism and the extraction and plundering of natural resources – the foundation of the wealth of the nation.

Ojibwe people in the Great Lakes region lived for hundreds of years with an abundance of wild life (fish, moose, caribou, deer, elk, porcupine, beaver, partridge, goose, duck, bear, squirrels, muskrat), wild rice, edible plants (including every wild delicious berry, plum, and tuber under the sun), and medicinal plants too numerous to mention here. Ojibwe people would harvest this abundance in addition to summer gardens, where harvests were shared among relations. In and through a land-based Ojibwe perspective, students are made aware of multiple orientations and are learning flexibility and adaptability. Although the standards are meant to create an umbrella containing all "other" cultures underneath it, Ojibwe ways of knowing and living on the land directly contradict the foundational premises of concepts such as scarcity and of the fixedness of time and space. Waadookodaading attempts a form of learning that both acknowledges and works within these dominant ideologies (e.g., the Gregorian calendar), yet it also practices what Medin and Bang (2014) describes as adaptive reorganization within a complex system. The immersion school teaches through yet resists compliance with a system that is incongruent with Ojibwe heritage, all the while in and through an endangered language that most are still learning. This is the daily work of Indigenous immersion teachers.

Conclusion and Future Directions

When I (Mary) arrived in Thunder Bay, in the ceremony that wasn't for me, but really was for me, I spoke only in Ojibwemowin. Ron commented "It's the change! It's coming!" as he did a silent happy dance. Ron travels, as Mashkikiiwinini do, and he talks to all kinds of folks. I have noticed more and more that others share his perspective. Now the conversation is shifting: We are no longer talking about how we need to "save the language." We (the ones who are learning) are talking about health and wellness and we can already see the change. The conversation has shifted from a focus only on policy and immersion schools to health, wholeness, and to spirituality – where it has always been. My move, and maybe other people see this too, is to grow language in families, *grow health in families (and I mean the Ojibwe version of "families" that recognizes all kinds of complex kinship relations we are situated within in daily life (not the Western, heteronormative version). We are starting this fall. We let the word spread through the families we see at ceremony because they are the ones using the language. Many but not all, are the ones whose children attend the immersion school too. The immersion school is the smallest of concentric circles. We need to keep reaching out, beyond who we know or who we see is making an effort. We need to widen the circles and make sure there is room for everyone.*

The examples we share illuminate the complex ways that immersion schools are both sites that reproduce the settler state *and* places that resist, reproduce, and create a new Ojibwe lifeways. The education system in North America was historically created and implemented as a means to construct a national identity. Within an interlocking web of ruling relations, schools continue to be manipulated by federal and state policies that harm language revitalization efforts and discipline Indigenous teachers and students via standards that devalue and invisibilize Indigenous ways of knowing. As the examples from Waadookodaading illuminate, Indigenous language activists and educators have managed to subvert the aims of the state through appropriating school spaces through Indigenizing pedagogies. Immersion teachers teach students to write their name, not as a simple skill to master so the teacher can identify a student's work, but as a practice of caring for and forming a deeper connection to one's spirit name. Literacy is a decolonial practice, not merely a skill to socialize "good" students, workers, and (US) citizens. And, Waadookodaading maneuvers and negotiates its curriculum within the normative school calendar to ensure students are learning how to "read" and respond to the land.

The struggles that Waadookodaading immersion teachers face as they attempt to prepare children for a world that privileges and naturalizes Western ways of knowing are struggles that many immersion schools face in North America (McCarty and Nicholas 2014). Within many Indigenous communities, parents and young people face "mixed messages" about the value of their heritage language. "Within "the hierarchical positioning of Native languages and English," Lee (2009) states, there is a continuous negotiation "to determine the place of Native languages in relation to the privileged position of English" (p. 310, as cited in McCarty and Nicholas 2014, p. 128). Yet, despite these challenges, McCarty and Nicholas (2014), in their extensive review of the roles and responsibilities of immersion schools, illuminate the ways in which the appropriation and reclamation of school spaces for revitalization has significantly increased the number of Indigenous speakers in North American communities where these efforts exist.

While Indigenous immersion schools have produced more speakers, it is critical that we learn from these efforts, including paying attention to their limitations. Within immersion school efforts, it is critical we ask questions such as: How do the relatively small projects of immersion schools (relative to the communities they seek to include) coupled with the hierarchical and prohibitive associations that many working class people have with education institutions impact accessibility to such projects? How do the historical tensions that exist between education institutions and parenting/families, community, and alternative spaces of learning impact the Indigenous language revitalization movement? While we must strategically build from within the system (i.e., appropriating immersion schools, creating immersion programs within tribal schools), we must also build within (and create anew) our own institutions (e.g., ceremonies, families, reservations, and tribal governments) (see also McCarty and Nicholas 2014).

These are major questions for revitalization workers within immersion schools generally; however, academic researchers can do much to strengthen immersion school efforts in ways that can support the growth of the movement more broadly. Immersion school efforts are just getting off the ground in many places – McCarty and Nicholas (2014) write that the immersion school movement is just 25 years old. As one immersion teacher stated to Erin, Waadookodaading is one of the oldest Ojibwemowin immersion schools at 16, "but it is still just a baby." We ask of academic researchers studying immersion schools and other school-based Indigenous language revitalization efforts (including ourselves): How can researchers further study and build institutional knowledge of immersion teachers' strategies and "adaptive" practices across other Indigenous immersion sites? How can researchers (including the authors) support immersion schools and programs to productively share knowledge and resources across such efforts in ways that are practically minded and not merely subsumed into relatively closed academic circuits of knowledge?

Ojibwe lifeways are here, they have always been. We spend millions of dollars searching for something we have lost, looking outside of ourselves. And it is all right here, under our noses. We are drawn in by the grants, the systems that threaten our existence, teacher educators who appear to have something we are lacking. Of course we can learn from teacher education, we can learn from experienced curriculum makers, we can learn about language acquisition from linguists and language pedagogues. But learning is not a one-way street. We do not need to forget what we know to become teachers or to grow the movement within, against, and beyond state education. We need only to believe in it, to dig deeper and to look to those in our communities perpetually excluded from the academy who have been doing this work all their lives. Digging medicine, watching where the beavers make houses, and knowing the difference between what makes us sick and makes us well – this knowledge continues to be relevant and have always been here.

References

Archibald JA (2008) Indigenous storywork. UBC Press, Vancouver
Au W (2013) Coring social studies within corporate education reform. Crit Educ 4(5):1–4.
Haskins M/Bimijiwanikwe (2015) Ojibwe immersion early literacy. Capstone project, University of Minnesota-Duluth
Brown W (2015) Undoing the demos. MIT Press, Boston
Coulthard GS (2014) Red skin, white masks. University of Minnesota Press, Minneapolis
Duranti A (1997) Linguistic anthropology. Blackwell, London

Dyke E (2016) The fight for the right to teach. Dissertation, University of Minnesota

Evers T (2011) WI common core state standards for English language arts. In: Wisconsin department of public instruction website. Available via http://dpi.wi.gov/sites/default/files/imce/common-core/pdf/ela-stds-app-a-revision.pdf. Accessed 1 Sept 2016

Finn R (2016) Waadookodaading: Ojibwe language immersion school (film). In: The ways. Retrieved from: http://theways.org/story/waadookodaading. Accessed 1 Sept 2016

Fischel WA (2006) "Will I see you in September?" An economic explanation for the standard school calendar. J Urban Econ 59(2):236–251. https://doi.org/10.1016/j.jue.2005.03.006

Grande S (2004) Red pedagogy. Rowman & Littlefield, New York

Grinde DA Jr (2004) Taking the Indian out of the Indian: U.S. policies of ethnocide through education. Wicazo Sa Rev 19(2):25–32. Colonization/decolonization, I (Autumn 2004). Available via http://www.jstor.org/stable/1409496

Grumet MR (1988) Bitter milk. University of Massachusetts Press, Boston

Haraway D (1988) Situated knowledges. Fem Stud 14(3):575–599

Harding SG (1986) The science question in feminism. Cornell University Press, Ithaca

Hermes M (2004) Waadookodaading Indigenous language immersion: personal reflections on the gut-wrenching start-up years. In: Ibáñez-Carrasco JF, Meiners, E (eds) Public acts: disruptive readings on making knowledge public. Routledge, New York, pp 57–72

Hermes M (2005a) Ma'iingan is just a misspelling of the word wolf. Anthropol Educ Q 36(1):43–56

Hermes M (2005b) Complicating discontinuity. Curric Inq 35(1):9–26

Hermes M, Haskins M (2018) Unbecoming standards through Ojibwe immersion: the wolf meets ma'iingan. In: Wigglesworth G, Simpson J, Vaughan J (eds) Language practices of indigenous children and youth: the transition from home to school. Palgrave Macmillan, London

Hermes M, King KA (2013) Ojibwe language revitalization, multimedia technology, and family language learning. Lang Learn Technol 17(1):125

Indigenous Action Network (2015) Accomplices not allies: abolishing the ally industrial complex. Available via http://www.indigenousaction.org/accomplices-not-allies-abolishing-the-ally-industrial-complex/. Accessed 1 Sept 2016

Kliebard HM (2004) The struggle for the American curriculum. Psychology Press, London

Lipman P (2011) The new political economy of urban education. Taylor & Francis, New York

Lomawaima KT, McCarty T (2002) When tribal sovereignty challenges democracy. Am Educ Res J 39(2):279–305

McCarty TL, Nicholas SE (2014) Reclaiming Indigenous languages. Rev Res Educ 38(1):106–136

MacLeod J (1996) Ain't no makin' it. Westview Press, Philadelphia

Meiners E (2002) Disengaging from the legacy of lady bountiful in teacher education classroom. Gend Educ 14(1):85–94

Mignolo W (2009) Epistemic disobedience, independent thought and de-colonial freedom. Theory Cult Soc 26(7–8):159–181

Mignolo W (2011) The darker side of western modernity: global futures, decolonial options. Duke University Press, Durham

Nicholas S (2005) Negotiating for the Hopi way of life through literacy and schooling. In: McCarty TL (ed) Language, literacy, and power in schooling. Erlbaum, Mahwah, pp 29–46

Public Broadcasting System (2008) The wolf that changed America. Wolf wars: America's campaign to eradicate the wolf. http://www.pbs.org/wnet/nature/the-wolf-that-changed-america-wolf-wars-americas-campaign-to-eradicate-the-wolf/4312/

Richardson T (2011) Navigating the problem of inclusion as enclosure in native culture-based education. Curric Inq 41(3):332–349

Rockwell E, Gomes AMR (2009) Introduction to the special issue: rethinking Indigenous education from a Latin American perspective. Anthro Ed Quart 40(2):97–109. https://doi.org/10.1111/j.1548-1492.2009.01030.x

Said E (1979) Orientalism. Vintage Books, New York

Sleeter C (2011) The academic and social value of ethnic studies. In: National Education Association. Available via http://www.nea.org/assets/docs/NBI-2010-3-value-of-ethnic-studies.pdf. Accessed 1 Sept 2016

Smith PC, Warrior RA (1996) Like a hurricane: the American Indian movement from Alcatraz to wounded knee. New Press, New York

Smith L (1999) Decolonizing methodologies: research and Indigenous peoples. Zed Books, London

Tuck E, Gatzambide-Fernández R (2013) Curriculum, replacement, and settler futurity. J Curric Theor 29(1):72–89

Weis L, Fine M (2012) Critical bifocality and circuits of privilege. Harv Educ Rev 82(2):173–201

Willis P (1977) Learning to labor. Columbia University Press, New York

Wisconsin Department of Public Instruction (2011a) Wisconsin model early learning standards, 3rd ed. Available via http://www.collaboratingpartners.com/documents/SectionC54-64final_000.pdf. Accessed 1 Sept 2016

Wisconsin Department of Public Instruction (2011b) Common Core State Standards for English language arts & literacy in history/social studies, science, and technical subjects. Appendix A. Available via http://www.corestandards.org/assets/Appendix_A.pdf. Accessed 1 Sept 2016

Woolf N (2016) North Dakota oil pipeline protesters stand their ground. In: The guardian. Available via https://www.theguardian.com/us-news/2016/aug/29/north-dakota-oil-pipeline-protest-standing-rock-sioux. Accessed 1 Sept 2016

Listen to the Voices: Informing, Reforming, and Transforming Higher Education for First Nations' Peoples in Australia

24

Jeannie Herbert

Contents

Introduction	402
Beginning with a Personal History	402
Our Histories: Levers to Decolonize and Heal?	404
Impact of the Untold History Begins to Emerge	404
Reading the Evidence of the Emerging Literature	405
Acknowledging the Truth and Preparing to Heal the Wounds	406
Positioning the University to Engage in the Healing Process	406
Transforming Universities into Places that Meet Our Learning Needs	407
Changing History	407
Positive Shift in Education Service Delivery for Indigenous Students	408
Establishing Aboriginal and Torres Strait Islander Presence Within Schools	408
Making Our Voices Heard	409
Transforming Universities	410
Indigenizing the Academy	411
Contextualizing the Indigenous "Presence" Within Contemporary Australian Universities	412
Sociocultural Change that Has Influenced the Capacity of Indigenous Peoples to "Engage," to Make Their Voices Heard, Within the Academy	413
Stories of Success	413
Listen to Indigenous Voices: Narratives of Success	418
Conclusion	420
References	421

Abstract

This chapter will provide insights into the value of tertiary education journeys that are grounded within First Nations peoples' own cultures and languages. This practice provides a structure that enables the learner to navigate through what could be argued

---

J. Herbert (✉)
Charles Sturt University, Dubbo, NSW, Australia
e-mail: jherbert@csu.edu.au

© Springer Nature Singapore Pte Ltd. 2019
E. A. McKinley, L. T. Smith (eds.), *Handbook of Indigenous Education*,
https://doi.org/10.1007/978-981-10-3899-0_13

to be an alien learning environment where learners are bombarded by language and/or epistemologies that serve to confuse and often exclude them from engaging in the learning activity. In Australia, First Nations people are relative newcomers to the university; hence, their engagement with the Western knowledges and epistemologies, which underpin higher education offerings in this country, has not been easy. Doubtless, this reality could be argued as reflecting the evolution of higher education in Australia. But equally, it could be argued that it is impossible to comprehend the contemporary realities of Indigenous higher education in Australia, without having some appreciation of how it has evolved within the wider framework of what Australian Education really is – an essentially colonial construct. In this chapter the author draws upon her own lived experience, as an Aboriginal woman and long-time educator, to critically reflect upon the impact of Australia's colonial history and the increasing need for change that will enable First Nations students to engage in the process of empowering themselves through their education. Based upon her own experiences, she discusses some of the positive pathways that have begun to emerge in recent years. In exploring some realities of Aboriginal and Torres Strait Islander student learning journeys she seeks to highlight experiences that have had a positive impact upon the individual's capacity to take up the challenge.

Keywords
Act of cultural remembering · Cultural knowledge · De-colonisation · Education as a colonial construct · Education as tool of empowerment · First Nations · First Nations reclaiming spaces · Higher Education · Indigenize the Academy · Indigenizing the Academy · Indigenous Australians · Narratives of success · Universities as sites of transformation

Introduction

As an Aboriginal educator, I would argue that a critical aspect of appreciating the tertiary education journeys of contemporary Aboriginal and Torres Strait Islander peoples is to have some knowledge of what has gone before and some insights into the way in which this country's First Peoples were positioned within the formal education structures that are claimed to enable people to access the knowledge and skills they need to live full and rewarding lives. This is where we come up against the first hurdle – actually obtaining information that will inform our understanding: in other words, listening to the stories of people who were a part of that history.

Beginning with a Personal History

I believe that education was the natural career choice for me. My mother had an abiding belief that a good education was the means to enable individuals to build a "good life" for themselves and their families. My grandmother, a Nykinya woman from the West Kimberley region of Western Australia, saw education as the key to people being able to make their own decisions concerning the work choices they could make in order to earn a living. Being prepared for life as a servant, she had, from a very young age, lived within the confines of a station homestead, an aftermath of the spread of pastoralism into the Kimberley during the late 1800s. My grandmother received no formal schooling, hence was illiterate in terms of being able to read and write English. However, being dumped by the station owners as a young pregnant teenager in the town of Derby and left to fend for herself, she became very literate in terms of reading the society in which she lived. In due course, however, her three daughters, then aged 8, 6 and 4 years, were taken, bundled onto a ship with other Aboriginal children, similarly summarily removed from their families, and sent over 1550 nautical miles south to be institutionalized in Perth. My mother, in recounting the story of her childhood many years later, told me they had received a very basic education over about 3 years and were then removed from the classroom and placed in training within that same home. Each girl was trained in every aspect of domestic service – cleaning, housekeeping, cooking – so that by 14 years of age, they could be put out to work as domestics. This was no escape into a "normal life." Each girl was released into service under an agreement that rendered her totally under the control of her employer, working very long hours for little, if any, reward. As time-off or payment for labor depended entirely upon the whim of their employer, it took my mother 10 years to save enough to pay her boat fare back to Derby in an effort to find her mother and brothers. In retrospect, I quite understand why both women had such total belief in the value of education and why, in my mother's case, in the continuing absence of any secondary schools north of Geraldton, she was determined to send every one of her eight children south to receive a secondary education. The oldest child, I was dispatched to Geraldton High School in 1956.

I decided to begin this chapter with a personal family history as a means of providing "an insider" view of what has happened to many layers of our First Nation's families, over the years it has taken for the process of colonization to play out across the continent. These stories may never have been recorded in any publication but they were nevertheless the very real life experiences of my mother, my aunts, and my grandmother, and, without doubt, these "family" stories have had a profound influence upon me, my siblings, my cousins ... but I also appreciate that we are not alone. Many have suffered similar or worse experiences – dreadful, demeaning intergenerational histories that continue to oppress many. This approach is not intended to imply that the written records of the process that left people without their country, their means of survival, and destroyed their family structures and cultures are not valuable. But, unless they also reflect the knowledge, the memories of those who were actually subjected to the "lived experience," then one could question the validity of the opinions offered, the conclusions drawn. Such thinking, concerning the importance of the Indigenous "experience" could be argued as aligning with Smith's (2009) arguments concerning the importance of "Indigenous educational leadership" in achieving improvement in Indigenous educational outcomes, in which he indicates "major change is possible in a relatively short time in terms of indigenous educational underdevelopment" (2009, p. 1).

Our Histories: Levers to Decolonize and Heal?

Reflecting upon the historical framework, I would argue that before we can hope to redress the "high and disproportionate levels of educational underdevelopment" (Smith 2009, p. 1) that also accrued to First Nations learners in Australia, we need to better inform ourselves of the possible underlying causes and the apparent persistence of such underdevelopment. Hence, it is critical that we find a way of filling the gaps in the written history of Aboriginal education prior to 1967. "Working Together: Aboriginal and Torres Strait Islander Mental Health and Wellbeing Principles and Practices" (2010), a ground-breaking publication presenting the outcomes of a study into the state of Indigenous mental health, was designed to address community concerns regarding the increasing level of Indigenous youth suicides across the country. I would recommend it become mandatory reading for all contemporary, and intending, educators. Specifically, in chapter "The Social, Cultural and Historical Context of Aboriginal and Torres Strait Islander Australians," Dudgeon et al. identify the direct outcomes of passing the so-called "Aboriginal Protection Acts," within each of the Australian states and territories, as being an increase in racism and legislation that virtually ensured the "pauperization of Aboriginal peoples" (Milnes 2001, p. 32). Significantly, having revealed the Western Australian Aborigines Act 1905 as "a gross erosion of rights" marking the beginning of a "period of formidable surveillance and oppression of Aboriginal people." Dudgeon et al. further argued that, if the "1905 Act is symbolic of Indigenous oppression ... the 1967 National Referendum, when Aboriginal rights were won back, is symbolic of emancipation" (2010, p. 30).

Through in-depth examination of the historical records in my own study (Herbert 2003), I came to understand the way in which education had been used as the tool of the colonizer. Initially it had served to exclude Aboriginal children from schools and an education that would have enabled them to be valued members of communities. Ultimately, it was this lack of education that served to exclude Aboriginal people from the wider society. It is as a result of that personal journey into the educational archives that I came to understand my own responsibility, as an Aboriginal educator, to engage with our communities and the wider Australian society in an examination of that history. Such a process enables people to develop a deeper understanding of the realities of our colonial history and its possible impact upon different people and/or groups (Herbert 2003). I would argue such active engagement constitutes critical practice in developing our capacity, as individuals and groups, to comprehend and ultimately speak back, as our means of overcoming the continuing damage of that history.

Impact of the Untold History Begins to Emerge

In general, following the 1967 referendum, it could be argued that there was no real comprehension of the magnitude of the issues that were beginning to emerge as serious Indigenous health and education detriments. Around the country, however, and especially in First Nation's communities, critical connections were becoming evident concerning the possibility of long-term devastating impacts in the aftermath of the "colonial era." The reality of such an impact became increasingly obvious following the release of reports from some of the massive enquiries that have been undertaken in the decades following that referendum. Two critical enquiries included the:

1. Royal Commission to investigate the causes of deaths of Aboriginal people while held in State and Territory gaols. The Royal Commission, which was implemented in August 1987, was established in response to a growing public concern that deaths in custody of Aboriginal people were too common and poorly explained. Following various interim reports (Johnson 1991), the final report, signed on 15 April 1991, made 339 recommendations, mainly concerned with procedures for persons in custody, liaison with Aboriginal groups, police education, and improved accessibility to information (accessed 5 July, 2016). http://www.naa.gov.au/collection/fact-sheets/fs112.aspx
2. Human Rights and Equal Opportunity Commission National Inquiry into the Separation of Children from their Families was conducted between 1995 and 1997 with the report of the inquiry, The Bringing Them Home Report (Human Rights and Equal Opportunity Commission 1997), being tabled in the Commonwealth Parliament in 1997 (accessed 5 July, 2016). https://www.humanrights.gov.au/sites/default/files/content/pdf/social_justice/submissions_un_hr_committee/6_stolen_generations.pdf
    The "Stolen Generations" is the name given to Aboriginal children who were forcibly removed or taken under duress from their families by police or welfare officers between the years 1910 and 1970 – estimated to be at least 100,000. The *Bringing Them Home* Report details this investigation (accessed 5 July, 2016). http://www.sbs.com.au/news/article/2012/05/25/timeline-stolen-generations

Reading the Evidence of the Emerging Literature

As evidence of what was done to Aboriginal and Torres Strait Islander families and children has been published, there has been growing awareness in the wider population, not only of the dreadful suffering that was inflicted on people because of their race but also of the awful legacy that allows the oppression to continue in many places – places where people remain isolated though not always by distance. In a study entitled, "Factors that impact upon the attendance, suspension and exclusion of Indigenous students in secondary schools," Herbert used data gathered in remote, rural and urban settings in New South Wales and Northern Territory schools, to highlight ways in which teachers might become more effective teachers of Indigenous students. Significantly, those teachers conducting the research argued that many of the emerging issues were common across all levels of education, throughout the country. Most critically, however, across all research sites the evidence clearly highlighted the importance of schools engaging more closely with their Aboriginal communities in order to better understand and value the cultures these students, and their families, were bringing into the school community (Herbert et al. 1999).

Education institutions across all sectors have been relatively slow to respond in ways that would better prepare Aboriginal and Torres Strait Islander people to acquire the knowledge and skills they need to recover their lives and empower themselves in ways that will enable them to take control of their own futures. First Nations peoples who have managed to obtain qualifications enabling them to be employed within various levels of educational service delivery are not only few in number but also, too often, experience considerable difficulties in making their voices heard. Elsewhere in the wider community, the impact of almost 200 years of colonial history continues to ensure the virtual invisibility of too many First Nations peoples.

Acknowledging the Truth and Preparing to Heal the Wounds

This is a critical moment for higher education. Based upon the findings of my PhD study, I would argue that it is time that the truth regarding the role of education as a tool of the colonizer (Herbert 2003) was acknowledged and responsibility taken for effecting the change that is much needed in our society. Leaders in the education community do have the capacity, the knowledge, and the power to transform the nation through a process of building the human currency needed not only to heal the wounds but also to build the relationships that will enable us, as a nation, to recognize, accept, and value our differences as the first step in uniting and moving into the future as one nation. Universities must accept the challenge of being the incubators of this national change process.

Positioning the University to Engage in the Healing Process

Through my personal experience as a teacher, counsellor, researcher, and educational manager, I would argue that a critical prerequisite for understanding the contemporary realities of Indigenous higher education in Australia is to have some insight into how it has evolved within the wider framework of what Australian Education really is – an essentially colonial construct. This is an important factor, for the journey of evolution has not only provided the means but also in a sense been the catalyst for where Indigenous higher education is currently located – a legacy of Australia's colonial past. The question we must ask ourselves is "What is the difference between past and present?" for this is a critical truth when considered with the context of Altamirano-Jimenez' argument:

> If we think of universities as social spaces actively participating in the process of knowledge production (Lefebvre 2000), they have been implicated in the reproduction of hegemonic narratives that have erased and silenced the existence of Indigenous people and epistemologies. Universities are also a representation of society at large. (2014, p. 38)

These are truths we must accept in reflecting upon our own purpose within the academy. It is critical that we address the past by naming and accepting the truth of what was done as the first step in healing the wounds, in making the connections that will enable us all to experience that sense of "belonging" that allows us to get on with our lives. According to Altamirano-Jimenez, there is such diversity in our knowledges that we need our universities:

> to provide a range of politically, intellectually, and practical courses meant to serve the needs of Indigenous people and their communities because", citing de Sousa Santos, Arriscado-Nunes & Meneses (2008) "social transformation cannot be achieved without cognitive justice. From this perspective, indigenizing the academy means that we work to transform universities into places that are open to the diversity of knowledge systems and that 'we decolonise knowledge' itself." (2014, p. 42)

Through my on-going journey with Aboriginal and Torres Strait Islander students and communities over many decades, I have developed a deep awareness of peoples' expectations of education including, more recently, higher education. It is from within that shared space of being – imagining, reflecting, understanding, appreciating, and valuing – that I have come to realize that wresting control of education, a previous tool of the colonizer, to make it what we want it to become, is the only way we can ensure it does become a powerful tool of empowerment for ourselves, and, ultimately, all of our people. The underlying question, however, is "Once we have that autonomy, that self-determination, what will we do differently?"

Transforming Universities into Places that Meet Our Learning Needs

Having embarked upon my personal research career by the end of the 1980s and commencing my PhD investigation into Indigenous success in education by the mid-1990s, I was continually confronted with the paucity of the written record. In considering possible causes for this situation, I decided it could have been a reflection of the fact that there was virtually no Indigenous student present within the Australian university until the late 1990s. But, having been a classroom teacher for over 20 years before specializing in Indigenous education in the early 1980s, it had been my personal experience that there was some resistance to the notion that Indigenous peoples had the same rights to a good education as other Australians – an education that would enable them to achieve employment and life outcomes similar to those of other Australians. Yet Indigenous pedagogies and epistemologies were not a consideration. First Nations students were expected to acquire and use Western ways of knowing and being, in order to engage with the world. While the source of such thinking became obvious in undertaking the literature review for my PhD study, it was strongly reinforced during interviews with my informants (Herbert 2003).

Changing History

Following the 1967 referendum, there was a concentrated effort around effecting desperately needed change that would bring some hope for the future into Aboriginal lives. One of the key areas of focus for such change was education and, with the

Australian Government now controlling Indigenous Affairs, the Aboriginal and Torres Strait Islander Education Policy Taskforce was established in 1988 and the National Aboriginal and Torres Strait Islander Education Policy (NATSIEP) was implemented in schools at the beginning of 1990.

Positive Shift in Education Service Delivery for Indigenous Students

The implementation of the National Aboriginal and Torres Strait Islander Education Policy (NATSIEP) marked the beginning of a major shift in educational service delivery for Indigenous Australian students across all sectors of education. The 21 long-term goals set out in this Policy were designed to (i) increase Aboriginal and Torres Strait Islander involvement in educational decision-making; (ii) provide equality of access for Aboriginal and Torres Strait Islander people to educational services; (iii) increase equity of Aboriginal and Torres Strait Islander participation in education; and (iv) to achieve equitable and appropriate educational outcomes for Aboriginal and Torres Strait Islander people. Such outcomes would be achieved through enhanced co-operation and collaboration between the Australian Government and its various states and territories. Most importantly, however, a key element of the policy was the requirement that educational providers across the country would submit annual written reports detailing the enrolment, participation, retention, and completion rates of their Indigenous students. Making education providers in all States and Territories finally accountable for what was happening, or not happening, to Indigenous students across all levels of education, gave many Indigenous educators cause for hope that Indigenous education was about to undergo much needed positive change. I personally recall the sense of euphoria many of us experienced with the implementation of this policy, especially in response to the very welcome changes designed to increase engagement between schools and their parent and community groups.

Establishing Aboriginal and Torres Strait Islander Presence Within Schools

Obviously, the achievement of these goals would be dependent upon the capacity of individual schools to build positive relationships with the parents and communities of Indigenous students enrolled within their schools. This was never going to be easy due to the long history of Indigenous exclusion from Australian schools. Given the growing sense of urgency around addressing issues associated with improving Indigenous educational outcomes, many schools turned their attention to identifying existing activities or structures that could provide an initial point of engagement. One example of an event that was especially visible in 1990–1991 was NADOC (National Aborigines Day Observance Committee) which was changing to become NAIDOC due to the growing awareness of the two different and distinct cultural histories of Aboriginal and Torres Strait Islander peoples. This was a timely change because in the process NAIDOC moved from being a one day celebration to become a week-long commemoration, hence increasing the number of very informative and educational events available to school communities. This act of cultural remembering continues although, while local committees continue to organize local events, a National NAIDOC Committee now makes key decisions concerning events that constitute a national celebration.

More recently the continuing celebration of our cultures is beginning to reflect an increased diversity of activities such as more schools offering students the opportunity to learn their own Aboriginal language at school and an increasing number of young adults, mainly men, offering sessions to enable young children, in their local community, to engage in cultural activities. The ultimate focus within such groups is re-connecting with their culture. Teaching such "cultural knowledge" to young children is intended to re-establish individual and group responsibilities associated with caring for country and culture. According to community feedback, it is also increasing the number of young Indigenous teachers, both male and female, who are becoming highly competent teaching professionals. These teachers are using their teaching skills to deeply engage their students – both Aboriginal and non-Aboriginal – in a diversity of cultural activities designed to enable all students to "come into the culture" – their own or one they have created – in order to better understand their environment and the community in which they live today. Such reflective practice on the part of these young teachers is reminiscent of the behaviors Yazzie-Mintz (2007) discusses as a result of her research into teacher conceptions of culturally appropriate curriculum. In her observations of what informs the practice of three Navaho teachers, she seeks to answer the question, "What does a teacher have to know and what actions must be taken in order to create content and culturally relevant learning opportunity for students?" (2007, p. 73).

Making Our Voices Heard

Many Aboriginal and Torres Strait Islander people, having made the move into the space commonly known as "the uni," either as teachers or learners, in the 1990s/2000s, soon discovered that occupying a space does not necessarily equate to being welcome, or for that matter, welcomed! In fact, the space could be likened to Nakata's "cultural interface" (1998), "the academy ... (is where) ... we come to learn 'about' "Indigenous knowledge in similar ways to how we came to learn 'about' Indigenous cultures and issues via the established disciplines" (Nakata 2007, p. 9). While such a reality will without doubt create a dilemma for some in terms of how to deal with the issue of feeling "unwanted," it seems to me that there is an alternative viewpoint.

Having researched the issue of Indigenous student empowerment through education over the past two decades, I would argue that, having gained entry, it is time to stake our claims. While we might be labeled "latecomers" as a result of having come but lately to the university, we need to acknowledge that we are also the "trailblazers." It is our responsibility to build the pathways that will enable other members of our families and communities to join us. We may need to show the way by mapping the terrain or sharing stories about what happens in this space, so that when those who follow do arrive they will know how to find their way to what they are seeking. One of the ways in which we can achieve this is by writing about our own experiences so that we might contribute to publications such as this. It is important that we fulfil the physical act of sharing our stories, of ensuring the oral histories of First Nations' peoples are included in that act of spreading the word, of informing others so that the wider public, the global communities, are not only armed with the knowledge of what was done but that the act of acquiring such knowledge might also enable them to be better prepared to prevent future colonization. Within this context, I would argue that in publications such as this the inclusion of First Nations' stories, oral histories of real family's experiences, are just as valid, or at least equally as important as those academic publications that have been re-constructed from written records. This aligns with the argument put forward by Arbon and Rose, in their introduction to the sixth journal published by The World Indigenous Nations Education Consortium (WINHEC) and themed "Indigenous Voices, Indigenous Research." They argue the importance of publications where Indigenous authors get the opportunity "to not only deconstruct the hegemony of Western knowledge but, radically draw on ancient local knowledge of Indigeneity (sic) to in turn articulate powerfully Indigenous voices and research" (2010, p. i).

Lester-Irabinna Rigney, in a paper considering issues impacting Indigenous Australian intellectual sovereignty, states that: "Higher education is fundamental for preparing Indigenous peoples with the necessary skills not only to reclaim, protect and nurture Indigenous cultures but also to prepare the next generation for an ever-changing modern society" (2001, p. 2). While few would disagree with this argument, it would have been useful if Rigney had also provided some practical examples of the skills needed and how they might be obtained. This is due to the fact that, over a decade later, the Australian Government in support of its claim that a "strong higher education system benefits everyone" reveals that, while "[u]nder-represented groups such as those from low socio-economic backgrounds, Indigenous Australians, and students from regional areas have increased their participation in recent years" (Australian Government 2016, p. 3), it appears Indigenous higher education participation remains below parity. Furthermore, the Aboriginal and Torres Strait Islander Higher Education Advisory Council has highlighted "the need to increase Indigenous participation in STEM and business fields, where Indigenous Australians remain significantly under-represented" (2016, p. 11).

Transforming Universities

It is obvious, from what has been discussed to this point, that Australian education systems have not yet succeeded in making the transformation from their colonial beginnings. There is no disputing that there has been considerable progress since the implementation of the NATSIEP in 1990, but the continuing failure to achieve parity for Indigenous Australian students in relation to their access, participation, and successful completion of higher education programs reveals continuing dysfunction in the system. This is not an issue that will be addressed without genuine commitment on the part of all Australian Governments and Educational providers although there are some promising developments providing a glimmer of hope for improved futures for First Nations people, around the country. Equally, however, for First Nations peoples desiring to overcome the impact of colonialism over the past quarter of a century, the time has come where they must assume control of their own liberation (Freire and Macedo 1998, p. 54) and build their own strong futures. Within this context, it could be argued that initiatives emerging from Indigenous staff, students, or community groups could hold the greatest promise of future empowerment. Providing opportunities for Indigenous Australians to take control of their own futures so they might develop a deep sense of "belonging" would appear critical to ensuring they will not only "come in" to the university but, more importantly, that they will "stay, engage and ultimately graduate."

Indigenizing the Academy

A critical focus in many contemporary Australian universities is a move to Indigenize the academy as a critical process in enabling First Nations' peoples to feel they do have a place in the university, hence begin to experience a sense of belonging and of being valued. Implicit within this objective of Indigenization is the goal of raising the visibility and engagement of First peoples in all areas of the university while simultaneously establishing processes and practices that demonstrate a genuine valuing of their knowledges within the academic structures of the university. It could be argued that a vital element in achieving such outcomes is contingent upon finding ways of enabling the Indigenous voice to establish a space from which to speak, a space in which First Nations' peoples will have the capacity to develop their personal sense of belonging. An emergent element in achieving such a vital outcome is argued as the need to Indigenize university curricula.

Within this context, the work of Mackinlay and Barney (2012) – in particular their curriculum renewal project investigating Indigenous Australian Studies as a means of delivering university education that is empowering to the student – is valuable. In their Australian Learning and Teaching Council funded project entitled "Exploring Problem-Based Learning and Transformative Education in Indigenous Australian Studies," they examined the teaching and learning processes being used in the teaching of Indigenous Studies across five Australian universities. The researchers decided to use Problem-Based Learning (PBL) approaches in undertaking their study. They soon realized, however, that the persistent stigma attached to the historical practice of framing Indigenous people as a "problem" had effectively rendered the terminology they were using as not " ... politically or pedagogically appropriate" (2012, p. 5). In the process of redefining what they wanted to achieve they identified the need to change the terminology they were using; hence, PBL became "PEARL" (2012, p. 5). This new term was intended "to encompass the political, embodied, active, and reflective aspects of this learning approach" (2012, p. 12). The way in which a pearl is created and grows was perceived as having alignment with the pedagogical processes in Indigenous Australian Studies. Hence, "PEARL" was perceived as creating space for "education as an inherently political process linked intimately to the interrogation and deconstruction of colonialism"; thus, it "could be described as both a critical pedagogy and a critical race agenda" (2012, p. 14). The authors argue that this process of using critical race theory to reveal the power of whiteness as a legacy of colonialism demonstrates the reality that PEARL can represent a transformative process. It is this deep engagement in activities that should lie at the heart of any Indigenous Australian studies program (2012, p. 15).

Contextualizing the Indigenous "Presence" Within Contemporary Australian Universities

Darlaston-Jones et al. in reflecting upon their research into the relevance of contemporary psychology curricula for Indigenous students remind us that "The fabric of cultural understanding, values, beliefs and behaviours that characterise a particular society is woven through multiple mechanisms, including the education system" (2014, p. 87). Significantly, however, they indicate that, within our universities:

> ... the add-on approach of inclusion of Aboriginal and Torres Strait Islander content might increase the knowledge of non-Indigenous psychology students to the history of colonization and the contemporary legacy of harm that ensued, but it does not identify the unearned privilege associated with being part of the dominant group. (2014, p. 87)

Yet it is this sense of privilege that needs to be challenged, for it is the assumptions of right and dominance that flow from such attitudes that have ensured this nation's First Peoples remain powerless and effectively "silenced" within our educational institutions. This was a critical focus of my own PhD study which "was designed to open up a space in which Indigenous Australian respondents might speak back to non-Indigenous educators, thus becoming a part of the process that is needed to change the discourse about Indigenous Australian student achievement in higher education" (Herbert 2003, p. 89). However, I also acknowledged this was not going to be easy, being mindful of Nakata's warning against complacency in assuming progress is being made in creating a space from which Indigenous scholars might begin to speak back:

> ... I cannot dispute that changing ways of thinking have led to the improvement of the conditions of many Indigenous people. I would argue, however, that for an indigenous scholarship to develop, the argument does not rest there. The issue for indigenous scholars is one of how to speak back to the knowledges that have formed around what is perceived to be the Indigenous positions in the Western 'order of things' (Foucault 1970). This is a crucial point that I have always found difficult to articulate. (Nakata 1998, p. 2)

Yet, almost 20 years after Nakata voiced his concerns regarding the inability of Indigenous scholars to have their voices heard, Darlaston-Jones et al. argue that "the power of Whiteness" remains the dominant force in Australian society, thus ensuring "structural discrimination continues unabated" (2014, p. 87). Furthermore they assert that, until we destabilize "the iterative nature of these dominant reinforcing processes" (2014, p. 87), effective and sustainable change will not be possible within our education settings.

Sociocultural Change that Has Influenced the Capacity of Indigenous Peoples to "Engage," to Make Their Voices Heard, Within the Academy

In identifying the critical need for Indigenous agency in overcoming their own past oppression, it is important that we also acknowledge the recency of the university experience for First Nations peoples in Australia. There was virtually no "presence" until 1990, and it is significant that the NATSIEP Review of 1995 revealed considerable concern on the part of Indigenous respondents regarding the issue of "equity" and, in particular, within the context of higher education, called for "a more contextualized view of equity as 'equality of regard'" (DEET 1995, p. 17) that recognizes the specific learning needs of individuals and groups.

Darlaston-Jones et al. argue that the complexities of multicultural educational contexts need "to be created in a deliberate and formative manner that provides the opportunity for all players to participate in the reflexive critique necessary to facilitate such reconstitution" (2014, p. 88). Yet they argue that, to date, the literature seems to be suggesting that, despite this focus on Indigenization, many Indigenous students continue to be denied access to curriculum that actually does "critique or question the dominant discourses in terms of power and privilege that are the legacy of non-indigenous Australians" (2014, p. 88). While this viewpoint may be somewhat depressing, I know, from my own work in four universities over the past 20 years, that our people are moving forward in terms of seeking to empower themselves through their engagement in higher education.

Stories of Success

In this brief summary, I will endeavor to outline behaviors that I consider encapsulate successful learning outcomes for Indigenous students. While my descriptions may not reflect what some would consider "educational success," they are based upon my personal observations and engagement as an educator over many decades. I draw directly upon my personal experiences within the Australian higher education institutions in which I have worked.

In my lecturing role at James Cook University in North Queensland, I developed and delivered an undergraduate subject designed to provide all participants with an opportunity to engage in Indigenous learning experiences being taught by Indigenous people. While the focus of the course was intended to open up communication around Indigenous lifestyles – traditional and contemporary, cultural and spiritual worlds, language or lifeworlds – course content in different locations could vary considerably depending upon the most important influences upon peoples' lives. Hence, some communities chose to: (i) focus on the impact of history – both pre and post-colonial – upon the lives of those who lived there; (ii) demonstrate how their lifestyles were deeply entwined with the environment as main food source, calling for a need to care for country; (iii) emphasize the importance of their culture – language, ceremony, responsibilities; or (iv) potentially focus on a specific discipline, such as art, environment, land use, environmental science, or land management.

I would work with the community leaders to negotiate course content and issues around teachers, routines, payment, teaching materials, or quality assurance. All details would be agreed before any field trip was advertised to students. These subjects were generally delivered in field trip mode so coach companies would take care of all logistics such as camping gear, provision of meals, travel to and from the site and, provide any additional transport we might require during the field trip We preferred to camp in the bush – somewhere in the vicinity of the community but not in it – so there was time for group reflection each evening. This subject was offered every semester and, because it was a cultural experience, it did not sit in particular year levels, rather, students enrolled in an experience in which they personally had an interest. There was one written assessment task that was due for submission within 2 weeks of returning from the trip. I supervised and designed all other assessment tasks. Some tasks were collaborative group tasks where small groups would then report back to the whole group regarding some aspect of their learning and their perceptions around the value of such knowledge. This was intended to open up critical discussion that would encourage students to think critically about what they were learning – to reflect, to challenge each other. Another assessment task involved individuals delivering an oral presentation (no written paper) of the learning they had taken from whatever activity they had been asked to report upon. They delivered this report in front of the whole student group and me as audience. Critical discussion would follow. This was a highly successful subject. Sometimes there might be complaints about the lack of "creature comforts" as a result of camping out but I never received complaints about course content or the manner in which the content was delivered – most students were totally engaged with whatever was happening. Significantly, Indigenous students, regardless of their previous educational levels, and many international students scored highly in the oral evaluations whereas non-Indigenous Australian students handled the written assessment more competently.

As Director and later Vice-Chancellor of Bachelor Institute of Indigenous Education (BIITE), I spent a considerable amount of my time travelling, including to many of the remote communities we serviced in both "the Centre" and "the Top End." BIITE, a specialist tertiary education institution, has delivered education and training to Aboriginal people from rural and remote locations for over 35 years. In recent years, it has increased enrolments of Indigenous Australians from throughout the country. While valuing the diversity of its student body has been a particular strength of this unique educational environment, its capacity to cater for increasing diversity has been possibly its greatest challenge in recent years. The statistical evidence suggests many of the students enrolling at BIITE have not been adequately prepared for tertiary education and/or BIITE accepts many students who would not gain access to tertiary education elsewhere in the country.

BIITE caters for a multiplicity of learning needs due to the fact that:

- Students coming from rural and very remote locations are often disadvantaged by the long-term impact of previous educational disadvantage and limited life experiences caused by the extreme isolation of their lives.
- Students from urban backgrounds may have had higher levels of previous education and different life experiences due to coming from mainstream urban environments, but come to BIITE to strengthen their own sense of identity as an Aboriginal or Torres Strait Islander person by participating in an Indigenous educational experience.

The Institute provides a "both-ways" philosophical context, locating its practice in a space that acknowledges Aboriginal and Torres Strait Islander epistemologies as its foundation and its framework for delivering a culturally sustainable education within an Indigenous Australian knowledge environment. It is this act of valuing Aboriginal and Torres Strait Islander knowledges that challenges the status quo of mainstream education. Locating BIITE students in more meaningful learning structures enables them to engage in more empowering learning experiences.

For a more in-depth explanation of this student-centered method of delivery, I would recommend the work of Robyn Ober & Melodie Bat on Both-ways education (Ober and Bat 2008).

Teaching materials, service delivery, staffing, and student support services must respond directly to identified student and community needs within a diversity of remote, regional, and urban locations. Travel is a way of life for both students and staff; it ensures an equitable spread of services while delivering learning opportunities that will enable students to expand their own life and learning experiences across a diversity of geographic locations. The sheer remoteness of many Indigenous communities serviced by BIITE, unreliable connectivity and lack of facilities, mean there can be little reliance on technology in relation to online enrolments and course delivery.

While the high costs associated with delivering this unique educational service throughout the NT are a major issue, the rewards for students include:

- Diversity of language-related programs, which enables students to produce resources written in their own language with accompanying English language translations. Art classes are conducted in conjunction with writing programs that enable the acquisition of skills needed to illustrate texts. Such programs are also designed to provide people with skills needed to set up business enterprises around writing and producing texts and other materials in their home communities.
- Art courses, including Artists in Residence Programs, which provide opportunities for students to engage in activities that enable them to acquire the skills and knowledge they may need to become an artist. Courses focus on developing sensitivity and responsibility around protocols regarding representations and displays in art field – vital knowledge for those seeking to work in this industry.

- Diploma courses which provide people with the skills they need to obtain work, within their community, in fields such as health, education, caring for the environment, etc.
- Media training programs which equip students with skills associated with operating equipment and technology and delivering programs in remote and urban locations.
- A large range of resource materials, including books (written and audio), CDs, and movie DVDs that reflect Aboriginal and Torres Strait Islander interests in traditional stories, bush foods and medicines, regional issues and language publications are designed, developed, and produced through collaborations with individuals and communities. It is this focus on the importance of collaborative engagement at the community level that ensures BIITE's capacity to use a both-ways approach to all aspects of design, development, and publication.
- A large range of resource materials that are designed, developed, and produced through collaborations with individuals and communities, including books – written and audio – and CDs and movie DVDs that reflect Aboriginal and Torres Strait Islander interests around traditional stories, bush foods and medicines, regional issues, and language publications. Such publications/productions, being so collaborative with specific communities, engage with a process that ensures a both-ways approach to all aspects of design, development, and publication.

Significantly, however, in acknowledging the value of the learning experience Indigenous students might experience within the Bachelor environment it is worth reflecting upon the challenges associated with differing worldviews around the notion of "costs." Without doubt there could be a considerably richer higher educational experience offered to the Indigenous students "coming into" Bachelor Institute from a diversity of educational and cultural backgrounds – language, culture, and heritage – in order to ensure they, too, are prepared "to reclaim, protect and nurture . . . Indigenous cultures" while also being prepared to engage in an "ever-changing modern society" (Rigney 2001, p. 2). But as long as funding allocations are determined by those unable to appreciate the challenges associated with different worldviews of "costs" the power imbalances within Australian society will continue. The human costs of failing to hear the Indigenous voice, of continuing to deny the real needs in terms of fiscal costs, will ensure our First Nations people continue to be denied an equitable education. Such failure will ensure maintenance of the current power imbalance and without doubt perpetuation of the "status quo" – a persistent symbol of the Invasion which cost the First Australians greatly.

In reflecting upon the time I spent at BIITE, I remember a vibrant, challenging learning environment where students and staff engaged in an on-going, often joyous, collaborative interaction of learning together. It was this "togetherness" that enabled them to address issues, no matter how difficult, and produce a rewarding learning experience and satisfactory outcomes for all concerned.

Currently, I am Foundation Chair of Indigenous Studies and Pro-Vice Chancellor – Indigenous Education at Charles Sturt University, a regional university in New South Wales. A key responsibility of my roles is to engage with the diversity of communities serviced by CSU. The dual roles necessitate many meetings, so considerable travel, both within and beyond university campuses, is a key factor. My considerable experience in education, including within this sector, has highlighted the importance of getting out and "engaging with" community groups as opposed to simply "attending meetings" where there is a tendency for considerable formality in discussing agenda items. It has been my experience that many community participants are silenced by the requirements of "the process" in meetings conducted within a "formal" mode. Undertaking effective community engagement is a core focus of my roles; hence, I need a process that not only enables me to meet a diversity of groups but also ensures we are able to effectively communicate with each other. It was this need that led to the development of "Collaborative Conversations."

Collaborative Conversations provide a process that enables me to engage in the deep conversations that enable me to gain insights into what people think higher education is all about and how the service we provide might meet their particular needs. To ensure the process works, I begin with a definition of the meaning of "collaborative" so those present realize that this is not an activity where they are going to sit and passively listen to someone "telling them" what they should do. They are urged to participate in the conversation that focuses on their expectations – what they want to get out of "going to university," their hopes and fears, their strengths and weaknesses, and their vision for better futures for themselves and their communities. Since developing and trialing the process in 2014, I have used it to engage with secondary school students and community groups and to obtain feedback about effectiveness of CSU services/programs for Indigenous students from various staff, students, and an Elders group.

More recently, I found it to be a useful tool in working with students enrolled in the Wiradjuri Language, Culture and Heritage Graduate Certificate (WLCH GC). This unique course is a direct outcome of the work of the CSU Wiradjuri Language, Culture and Heritage Program Committee that was established some years ago to enable Wiradjuri people to have a voice in the university. Wiradjuri communities provided guidance and advice relative to how specific programs or initiatives would ensure Wiradjuri knowledge was recognized and valued, thus enabling Wiradjuri students to feel they had their own place within the university. While the Committee continues to be jointly chaired by the DVC Academic and Aunty Flo Grant, an important Elder in the local community, the development of WLCH GC was inspired by Uncle Stan Grant Snr (HonDLitt). It was a long project given the many obstacles, such as no written materials or texts and no pool of potential students with the pre-requisite basic Wiradjuri language skills to enroll. These hurdles took time to overcome.

The course is structured so that students commence with the Wiradjuri Language subject before progressing through subjects considering issues of culture and heritage and ways of rebuilding Indigenous Nations. Within this framework of understanding, they then undertake a professional study of a Wiradjuri Community Development activity. Such a process could be argued as central to recovering Wiradjuri language, culture, and heritage within the context of rebuilding the Wiradjuri Nation.

The WLCH GC was implemented in 2014 and was an immediate success. It is conducted as an on-line course with students coming in to the university to participate in four residential schools during their course. This enables them to have face-to-face contact with Uncle Stan and their lecturers. In June 2016, I attended a residential and invited students and staff to talk with me about the course. I used the Collaborative Conversations process to guide the discussions. The response to my request and the information that was shared with me through that process was not only enlightening but also, at times, extremely emotional. The following is a brief overview of some insights I gained through that unique engagement.

Listen to Indigenous Voices: Narratives of Success

The Collaborative Conversations delivered such a wealth of information, so many different opinions that all I can do in this paper is provide a brief insight into some student responses. I endeavored to select opinions that were representative of all responses concerning the course. In seeking to identify what might be termed a general consensus, I believe most students would agree with these words of a student:

> This course delivers whatever you want it to deliver – it is different for every individual.

The following selection of comments seek to provide an insight into what individuals consider they, personally, are achieving through their unique learning journey.

> It's about family – discovering who and where and what I want to be –was critical that I had my son here beside me learning exactly the same thing. We're both here – at "uni" – learning some of the most important stuff of his life. He's having an incredible journey at the moment ... it's where he needs to be. We're here with family, yeah. It's been an awesome experience. This Higher Education course is really important for me – I can pass it on to my kids – the value of what I've learnt here. That's really important to me as I pushed those values onto them in the first place. It wasn't just because they wanted to do it. I didn't force them, but, they saw what education had done for me in my life.
> I'm in this course because I have a deep respect for the Wiradjuri concept of Yindyamarra and I wanted to show my respect for Wiradjuri people who never had the opportunity to live their culture, speak their language.
> I have always had a deep sense of longing related to needing knowledge about my culture, my heritage.
> I enrolled in this course because I wanted to better myself. But, you know what, I never expected ... I can't explain what happened to me ... (Pause) ... all I can say is this ... (begins thumping his chest above his heart) ... It hit me right here – just like that – suddenly I KNEW this was what had been missing in my life – this was what I had been WAITING for! (He is silent for a time ... then turns back to look me straight in the eye while tapping the front part of his head) ... now I KNOW what I am going to do with my life. When I have finished this course I'm going to go away and get things sorted out. Then I'm coming back here – back to CSU – and I am going to enrol in whatever course I have decided I want to do and after I graduate, I'm going to go out there and work in that profession. You know why I am going to do that? (I shake my head.) Because up until now I have never thought someone

like me could go to "uni." I never knew what went on in here – all I knew was I wouldn't be able to do it! But I'm here now – I had to come in here to do this course and that has changed me. I know this place – this university – now. I know what goes on in here and it doesn't scare me anymore. I am going to walk out of this place very soon with a Wiradjuri Language, Culture and Heritage Grad. Cert. I'm very proud about that. I like that feeling so I'll be back next year to do the next course I want to do. I know who I am now so I hold the power – I am in control of me and that makes me feel real good.

All of those participating in these Collaborative Conversations spent some time reflecting upon how it felt to be really engaged in the learning experiences offered through this course with comments such as: "*It was really hard at first but there came a point where ... suddenly you could do it! You could SAY the words – you could join the right bits together.*" While this might be "*awesome*" or "*unbelievable*" for some, there were others who could find no words to describe the feeling – all they knew was they just felt "*so happy.*" One student encapsulated the experience as: "*It's suddenly like you feel WHOLE – that's when you realize there's been something missing, something deep inside you, you couldn't speak about it because you didn't have the words – we didn't have our own language, our Wiradjuri language.*"

Through their engagement, students were discovering they had varying levels of language skills but that was no major concern – all that mattered was that they were in a place now where they could learn their language.

Some had specific agendas such as needing knowledge of their language to fulfill requirements of their Native Title claims. The majority were enrolled simply because they believed learning their language was an essential first step in recovering their culture and coming to appreciate their own heritage.

Some students spoke of experiencing concern about how they might reconcile their feelings of deep joy within the context of their relationships within the other side of their ancestry. In acknowledging the need to enable non-Wiradjuri family connections to appreciate what they were going through in "*discovering that my Wiradjuri side is still alive*" some were thinking they might teach these families "to speak Wiradjuri and understand the beliefs" as a means of enabling everybody to be part of the space, all in there "together" improving the quality of their lives.

> Immersion in the language enables you to keep hearing it in your head until sometime you just start saying words – you keep doing that till you finally get the pronunciation. Then you've got to start talking to others – spreading the word. After a while others, who also lost their language, will start repeating what you are saying. That way, we hope to get more people wanting to enrol in this course, especially people who work in education or health. It seems like there's two parts to this model. It just sort of grows and breeds its own. So you can go to the residentials, you learn the pronunciation but it takes a while before you can let it come out. Then one day, you're sitting in a public forum somewhere and you use language to "acknowledge country." That's a deep statement because, in using that language, you're declaring that this is Aboriginal land in a really deep way. Non-Aboriginal people doing this are demonstrating their respect, not only for that place but also for the owners of that place. They are also acknowledging that they know, deep inside themselves, that they can only ever be 'visitors' to that place.

Learning the language is one way of demonstrating that respect and understanding – a really essential way. We should be teaching this language to every student at this university so they can begin to understand their own place on this land. But there are protocols around that and we don't control those. It's a matter of who gives permission for the language to be taught or for different people to learn the language. Those are questions we still need to find answers to.

Conclusion

The use of a personal family history provides a powerful introduction to this chapter, revealing how what was done to individual members within many families became, over time, a highly effective weapon in the intergenerational destruction of the First Nations of this country. In exposing the continuing denial of access to even the most basic education that has taken place over generations, this chapter highlights the reality that it was the longevity of that colonial experience that caused such overwhelming damage. It is this reality that continues to confront all who seek to overcome their colonial legacy. But in acknowledging that progress may have been tragically slow, this chapter also reveals there is hope for the future. Possibly the most significant lesson to emerge across the diversity of learning sites was the reality that, if individuals wish to build effective pathways into better futures for themselves and their families, they must recognize the need to take responsibility for their own journeys. The increasing acceptance, in recent years, of the importance of social and emotional health and well-being as the means of enabling individuals to take control of their own lives and futures, has served to highlight the desperate need for education services that do deliver "tools" for self-empowerment. What is on offer must be meaningful to the learner and must fulfil some individual need so that engagement in the learning contains an inherent reward for the learner. The emerging strength of educating for empowerment becomes obvious in the outcomes emerging from research initiatives such as the highly effective National Empowerment Project led by a team of health and educational researchers including people such as Professor Pat Dudgeon from the University of Western Australia. But this chapter also reflects the value of tertiary education journeys that are grounded within First Nations peoples' own cultures and languages. Significantly, the practice appears to create a structure that learners can relate to, where they can experience that "sense of belonging" that ensures they become critically engaged in the learning process. Delivering education in the individual's own language enables the learner to explore and expand the new knowledge, language, and skills within a framework of familiarity where the "new" can be interpreted and assimilated into the learners' own knowledge structures and understandings. The use of such practice, within educational institutions, ensures First Nations learners engaging in cross-cultural learning environments and/or situations are provided with a learning experience that is not only empowering for the learner but also enables a quality of learning engagement that is equally satisfying for the teacher and fellow-learners. These are critical elements in developing the respectful relationships that result in the "deep engagement" that enables transformational learning. It is this reality that highlights the importance of establishing a place for Indigenous knowledges – language, culture, heritage – in contemporary universities. The conversations I have shared clearly reveal that higher education can provide the critical tools that do enable our First Nations peoples to recover from the trauma of colonization and discover their capacity to construct new futures for themselves and their families. They will achieve this in the new space where side-by-side Western knowledges and Indigenous knowledges are becoming critical components in inspirational new learning collaborations.

References

Altamirano-Jimenez I (2014) Neo-liberal education, indigenizing universities? Can J Nativ Educ 37(1):28–45. Indigenizing the International Academy

Arbon V, Rose M (2010) Indigenous voices indigenous research. In Arbon (ed) World Indigenous Nations Higher Education Consortium Journal, Grovedale, vol 2010(6). pp i–iii

Australian Government (2016) Driving innovation, fairness and excellence in Australian higher education. Higher Education Group, Canberra

Darlaston-Jones D, Herbert J, Ryan K, Darlaston-Jones W, Harris J, Dudgeon P (2014) Are we asking the right questions? Why we should have a decolonizing discourse based on conscientization rather than indigenizing the curriculum. Can J Nativ Educ 37(1):86–104

DEET (1995) National review of education for Aboriginal and Torres Strait Islander peoples – final report. AGPS, Canberra

Dudgeon P, Wright M, Paradies Y, Garvey D, Walker I (2010) The social, cultural and historical context of Aboriginal and Torres Strait Islander Australians. In: Purdie N, Dudgeon P, Walker R (eds) Working together: Aboriginal and Torres Strait Islander mental health and wellbeing principles and practices, Grovedale, pp 25–42

Freire AMA, Macedo D (eds) (1998) The Paulo Freire reader. The Continuum Publishing Company, New York

Herbert HJ (2003) Is success a matter of choice? Exploring Indigenous Australian notions of success within the context of the Australian university. PhD Thesis, Royal Melbourne Institute of Technology

Herbert J, Anderson L, Price D, Stehbens C (1999) If they learn us right: a study of the factors affecting the attendance, suspension and exclusion of Aboriginal students in secondary schools. Australian Centre for Equity through Education, Erskinsville

Human Rights and Equal Opportunity Commission (1997) Bringing them home. Commonwealth of Australia, Sydney, p 250. https://www.humanrights.gov.au/sites/default/files/content/pdf/social_justice/submissions_un_hr_committee/6_stolen_generations.pdf. Accessed 5 July 2016. http://www.sbs.com.au/news/article/2012/05/25/timeline-stolen-generations. Accessed 5 July 2016

Johnson E (1991) Royal Commission into Aboriginal deaths in custody. National report, vol 2. Australian Government Publishing Service, Canberra. http://www.naa.gov.au/collection/fact-sheets/fs112.aspx. Accessed 5 July 2016

Mackinlay E, Barney K (2012) Introduction. Aust J Indig Educ 41(1):10–17.

Milnes PD (2001) From myths to policy: Aboriginal legislation in Western Australia. Metamorphic Media, Perth

Nakata M (1998) Anthropological texts and Indigenous standpoints. http://www.ion.unisa.edu.au/conf/virutalconf/weaving/papers/martin.html

Nakata M (2007) The cultural interface. Aust J Indig Educ 36(Suppl):7–14

Ober R, Bat M (2008) Paper 2: both-ways: philosophy to practice. Ngoonjook 32:56–79

Rigney L (2001) A first perspective of Indigenous Australian participation in science: Framing Indigenous research towards Indigenous Australian intellectual sovereignty. Kaurna High Educ J 7:1–13

Smith GH (2009) Transforming leadership: a discussion paper. Keynote paper presented at the Simon Fraser University Summer Institute Lecture Series "Leading Change in Education," July 6, Surrey

Yazzie-Mintz T (2007) From a place deep inside: culturally appropriate curriculum as the embodiment of Navajo-ness in classroom pedagogy. J Am Indian Educ 46(3 Special Issue):72–93

Maintaining a Cultural Identity While Constructing a Mathematical Disposition as a Pāsifika Learner

25

Roberta Hunter and Jodie Hunter

Contents

Introduction	424
The Context of Developing Mathematical Inquiry Communities	425
Causes and Effects of Deficit Theorizing	426
The Components of Developing Mathematical Inquiry Communities	429
Pāsifika Values and Their Role in Shaping Classroom Social Norms	432
Connecting Mathematical Problems to the World of the Students	433
Language and Cultural Identity	434
High Expectations and Ethics of Care	436
Conclusion	437
References	439

Abstract

Many Pāsifika students enter New Zealand schools fluent in their own language and with a rich background of knowledge and experiences. But, within a short period of schooling they join the disproportionately high numbers of Pāsifika students who are failing subjects such as mathematics within our current education system. The reasons are diverse but many can be attributed directly to the structural inequities they encounter which cause a disconnect (and dismissal) of their Indigenous cultural values, understandings, and experiences.

In this chapter, we examine and explore the different practices which have marginalized Pāsifika students in our schools and more specifically in mathematics classrooms. We explain how some of the "taken-as-granted" practices in mathematics classrooms match the cultural capital of the dominant middle-class students but position Pāsifika students in ways which cause them cultural dissonance. What we clearly show is that the teaching and learning of mathematics

---

R. Hunter (✉) · J. Hunter
Massey University, Auckland, New Zealand
e-mail: R.Hunter@massey.ac.nz; J.Hunter1@massey.ac.nz

© Springer Nature Singapore Pte Ltd. 2019
E. A. McKinley, L. T. Smith (eds.), *Handbook of Indigenous Education*,
https://doi.org/10.1007/978-981-10-3899-0_14

cannot ignore the student's culture despite the beliefs held by many that mathematics is "culture-free." In contrast, we illustrate that the teaching and learning of mathematics is wholly cultural and is closely tied to the cultural identity of the learner. We provide many examples over 15 years that illustrate that when teachers use pedagogy situated within the known world of their Pāsifika students and which premise student choice over their spoken language their sense of belonging within schools is affirmed. We draw on the voices of the Pāsifika students to show how Pāsifika-focused culturally responsive teaching has the potential to address issues of equity and social justice which supports them retaining their cultural identity while constructing a positive mathematical disposition.

Keywords

Culturally responsive teaching · Cultural identity · Mathematical disposition · Equity · Social justice

Introduction

Within New Zealand's polyethnic society, Pāsifika peoples hold an important place. Pāsifika as a term has come to describe Indigenous peoples from other Pacific Island nations who live in Aotearoa New Zealand. In the post–second world war industrial era and into more recent times, their contributions, both economically and politically, have helped shape New Zealand as we know it today. Equally important are the Pāsifika ancestral links with Māori, the Indigenous people of New Zealand. In addition, the rich and colorful elements Pāsifika peoples bring to New Zealand add to the cultural landscape of this country. Currently, there are less than 10% of students of Pāsifika ethnic origin attending New Zealand schools. Wylie (2003) indicates a doubling of these numbers by the year 2051, and Brown and colleagues (2007) signal that Pāsifika students are the fastest growing population in New Zealand schools. However, appropriate institutional and policy-driven responses have been slow to acknowledge, respect, and incorporate core Pāsifika goals and values. One of the major consequences of this, as many researchers (Alton-Lee 2003; Bills and Hunter 2015; Nakhid 2003; Wendt-Samu 2006; Young-Loveridge 2009) have documented, is the disproportionate number of Pāsifika students who perform well below the desired levels in comparison to their Pākehā (Māori term commonly used to refer to European New Zealanders) and Asian counterparts in mathematics and literacy. Our aim in this chapter is to explore how Pāsifika students are able to develop a strong mathematical identity as they simultaneously engage in mathematical activity which values and draws on their Indigenous cultural practices.

Unless the structural inequities and hegemonic practice Pāsifika students encounter in New Zealand schools are addressed, serious social and political consequences are signaled when considering the projected demographics. Vale et al. (2016) highlight how the connection between "educational achievement including aspirations and socio-economic context are predictably consistent" (p. 100). These researchers draw on the work of Jorgensen and her colleagues (2012, 2014) who argue that contributing factors to underachievement include "student mix, student family background, parental connection(s) to school, teacher quality, student language skill(s), curriculum alienation and so on" (p. 100); all factors we see in our work with Pāsifika students. These students are predominantly found in schools within high poverty areas and where socioeconomic disadvantages are the greatest.

Throughout this chapter, we engage with issues of equity and social justice and illustrate how particular practices used in New Zealand schools have marginalized Pāsifika learners and caused many to be disenfranchised from school mathematics, as a consequence delimiting study and career opportunities. We draw on Nieto's (2002) framing of culture. Within this framework, the culture of the Pāsifika learner can be seen as one which is comprised of dynamic and ever-evolving traditions, social and political relationships, and a world view constructed, shared, and transformed by a group of people who are joined together by a number of factors which include common values, a common history (for example, originating from and being Indigenous to a Pācific Island nation and being immigrants or children of immigrants to another Pacific Island nation – New Zealand), geographic location, language, social class, and religion. In this chapter at the heart of what we describe is a mathematics program which we argue has the potential to be transformative in addressing social justice issues. Through working within the *Developing Mathematical Inquiry Communities (DMIC)*, teachers are able to engage in Pāsifika-focused culturally responsive teaching to support their students to construct a positive and strong mathematical and cultural identity as mathematical learners and doers in New Zealand classrooms.

In the next section, we will outline the development of *Developing Mathematical Inquiry Communities (DMIC)* program. Throughout the chapter, we will draw on its components to explore and examine the way in which the different parts of *DMIC* support Pāsifika students to learn and do mathematics which provide equitable outcomes.

The Context of Developing Mathematical Inquiry Communities

The innovative *DMIC* program was initially developed more than 15 years ago through collaboration with a group of teachers in a school in a high-poverty urban area in Auckland with predominantly Māori and Pāsifika students. Subsequently, a gradual roll out of schools involved in *DMIC* has resulted in the current involvement of 52 schools (35 schools in West and South Auckland, 8 schools in Porirua, Wellington, 4 schools in Tauranga, 1 in Rotorua and Palmerston North and 4 schools in Christchurch). Altogether, approximately 950 teachers are formally included in the project although throughout New Zealand many other schools have informally joined. The data used in this chapter was drawn from teacher reflections and interviews collected regularly over each school year by independent researchers throughout the past 15 years. The quotes used in this chapter were selected because they reflect views that have been consistently voiced over the duration of the project by teachers involved in the program.

DMIC was designed to address the persistent underachievement of Māori and Pāsifika students, caused by the many structural inequities they had encountered in previous mathematics programs in New Zealand. This included the recent New Zealand Numeracy Development Project (NZNDP) (Ministry of Education 2004) intervention that, though well intentioned, made minimal difference to mathematics education disparities. Within the NZNDP project, all students progressed but Asian and Pākeha students' achievement was more accelerated, and so the achievement gap widened significantly for Māori and Pāsifika students (Young-Loveridge 2009). While the NZNDP project promoted some good pedagogical practices, it also reflected the taken-for-granted cultural tapestry embedded in New Zealand schooling structures grounded in the dominant middle class Pākeha or "white" culture (Milne 2013). These schooling structures, we will show have allowed deficit theorizing to be maintained towards many Pāsifika learners.

In the next section, we describe the effect of deficit theorizing and how it has contributed to negative teacher and student perceptions of Pāsifika students as mathematical learners.

Causes and Effects of Deficit Theorizing

Consistently over time, the lower educational performance of groups of diverse students, such as Pāsifika peoples within the New Zealand context, has been attributed to the learners themselves or to their impoverished circumstances (Nieto 2002). Deficit theorizing which is applied to those marginalized within the mathematics classroom is immediately evident in teacher reflections when we begin to enact *DMIC* classrooms within schools with Pāsifika students. Frequently, our initial work with teachers is framed by comments from teachers such as "you don't understand, these students come to school with no mathematics." A reflection from a Principal after a year of their school being involved in *DMIC* noted the influence of deficit theorizing on their expectations:

> All of those things that we probably thought that our kids couldn't do but we weren't giving them the opportunity to do that.

In this statement the Principal has recognized that learning is enabled or constrained by the opportunities provided to students.

Pāsifika students are similarly influenced by their experiences in New Zealand classrooms. Quotes from them prior to beginning in *DMIC* classrooms illustrate the deficit views they hold of their own culture in relation to mathematics. When asked "how does it feel to be ____ (here we are exploring their cultural identity) in the mathematics classroom" approximately 20% of student responses indicate a negative view. One perception, often presented, is a view that the cultural or ethnic group they identify with do not engage with mathematics:

Sometimes it makes me feel different because Tokelauans don't do maths.

Other students indicate a belief that to be successful in mathematics you must enter what Milne (2013) described as "white-space." This is a space in an educational setting which represents the dominant middle class Pākeha or "white" cultural group:

> It feels like I'm a different person from a Samoan person… because whenever I'm learning maths I think I'm a Palagi (White) person… because whenever I'm doing maths I can't remember I'm Samoan. I don't like about maths when I get up to the hard part I can't do it I don't feel like a white person anymore I feel like myself again and I'm nervous.

In contrast, after a year in *DMIC* classrooms all students could make connections between both mathematics in their classrooms and mathematics within their Indigenous culture. Moreover, they indicated the relevance of mathematics in their lives. They could also provide a counter to a common perception about who is considered capable in mathematics based on their observations of teacher behavior:

> It feels good that your teacher likes (you) cause like sometimes teachers think that like white people and Asian people will get the answer correct but it's good that our teacher believes in all of us. Like she believes in all of us in the same way and yeah it's really good.

Many of the common deficit views held by New Zealand teachers and the students themselves can be attributed to the way in which streaming by ability is a common practice in New Zealand schools. Ability grouping has a long history as a popular pedagogical strategy used in mathematics in New Zealand classrooms and its use was further popularized by the New Zealand Numeracy Development Project (Ministry of Education 2004) as a prescribed part of the Project in the form of strategy-based teaching groups (Ministry of Education 2004) and continues to be used in the current Accelerated Learning in Mathematics (ALiM) program. Given that only 11% of Year 8 Pāsifika students are at or above curriculum standards (Education Assessment Research Unit and New Zealand Council for Educational Research 2015), it can be assumed that most Pāsifika learners find themselves in the lower ability groups. We have suggested in previous articles (Civil and Hunter 2015; Hunter and Anthony 2011) that the widespread use of ability grouping as a practice may be another cause for Pāsifika students' disaffection with mathematics. In the next section, we will elaborate on possible reasons.

Grouping by ability in mathematics classrooms is a contested pedagogical practice. Many supporters of ability grouping argue that it is a means to cater with wide student diversity in classrooms. Although some researchers (e.g., Kulik and Kulik 1992) argue that particularly the gifted and talented students benefit when ability grouped, other researchers (e.g., Braddock and Slavin 1995; Boaler and Wiliam 2001) contend that grouping by ability neither caters for all students nor raises achievement. This was confirmed in a recent PISA study (Scheicher 2014) which indicated that the degree of a school system's vertical stratification was negatively related to equity of education outcomes, while there was no clear relationship with excellence. The researchers outline limited positive effects on student learning while comparing these with the many negative outcomes (Scheicher 2014). These include development of low self-esteem and disengagement from learning. More importantly, as is the case for our Pāsifika learners, Zevenbergen (2003) outlines how students from the dominant cultural groups often occupy the upper ability groups while students from marginalized groups (for example, low SES, Indigenous, immigrant, and culturally diverse) are most often found in the lower ability groups. Zevenbergen (2003) theorizes that the different ability groupings of students are more a reflection of social constructs than intelligence or ability. What Zevenbergen (2003) suggests and we can confirm happens in New Zealand is that when ability groups are used where different groups of students are positioned is not a random occurrence, rather it is closely linked to student backgrounds and whether their cultural capital (Bourdieu and Passeron 1973) is privileged in the context of the classroom.

Previously (Civil and Hunter 2015; Hunter 2008; Hunter and Anthony 2011) we illustrated the way in which as a group of learners Pāsifika students are often more reticent to talk and are also less likely to ask questions or to challenge. We suggest that this particular cultural behavior is often assumed by teachers to be an indicator of lack of understanding, thus leading erroneously to Pāsifika students being disproportionately represented in the "lower" ability groups in classrooms. Not only does this cultural disconnect lead to poor judgments on behalf of the teacher but also the use of ability-based teaching groups in themselves is contrary to the values and ethos of Pāsifika learners and whānau (the extended family or community who live together in the same area). The use of streamed groups encourages undesirable competitiveness and places an importance on individual success. An emphasis or focus on the individual is in direct contrast to the Pāsifika notions of the value of communalism and collectivism. Within a Pāsifika view, the success of individual group members is judged by the success of the collective as a whole. Within this frame, the role of the individual includes being of service to others and within the mathematics context the focus is on ensuring that the knowledge is constructed and shared collectively. Integrating Pāsifika values into the *DMIC* environment is also reflected in how the Pāsifika students view what doing mathematics encompasses. They integrate being successful as a mathematical learner within a positive cultural identity. This is illustrated by a student in a *DMIC* classroom who compared her former experience in a high-ability group in a previous classroom with her current experience in a mixed ability group in a *DMIC* classroom:

> At the start of the year I would have said being a successful mathematician meant being in the top group and getting the answers right. Now, I think it is being a good person. Not being the person who is always right but helping others as well. That makes you good at maths.

A number of researchers (e.g., Boaler et al. 2000; Marks 2012; Zevenbergen 2001) describe the qualitatively different experiences learners have from each other in the ability-grouped classrooms, and the way in which teacher expectations of different groups of mathematical learners widened the gap between them rather than affording all students the same learning and growth opportunities. This can be explained when you consider that there is a tendency for students in higher ability groups to receive rich and challenging learning experiences while the students in the lower groups are most often likely to receive more procedural teaching shaped around lower expectations (Boaler 2014). A common reflection we hear from teachers after their initial introduction to *DMIC* is illustrated in this teacher's statement:

> I am really surprised when I hear some of the kids I thought were lowies asking good questions or sharing their thinking, really good thinking...I really thought they knew nothing and so I just used to tell them what to do.

Her beliefs about the perceived ability of the students in the lower groups had formed the basis of her deficit thinking and shaped her expectations for what they could say or do. In contrast towards the end of the year we see shifts in beliefs, and many teachers voice similar thoughts to the teacher here:

> Hmm- I never thought my children couldn't do mathematics but I'm enjoying exposing **all** children to bigger number, decimals etc. I have had some surprises when listening to children share strategies, very exciting when you would never have heard it in the past. When the passive, quiet ones speak it is a magical moment.

A consistent theme across the different teachers is a level of surprise and excitement at what happens when **all** children are provided with learning opportunities that are challenging and culturally meaningful to them. However, what the students are getting is access to learning opportunities that similarly develop a positive mathematics identity afforded to other students in New Zealand classrooms.

In the next section we will outline the components central to *DMIC* and to developing students with a strong and positive mathematical identity.

The Components of Developing Mathematical Inquiry Communities

DMIC incorporates the best pedagogical practices of what has been termed variously as inquiry or reform (Wood et al. 2006) or ambitious mathematics teaching (Kazemi et al. 2009) within culturally responsive teaching (Gay 2010). The focus of *DMIC* is on development of in-school and across-schools collaboration in building classroom communities of mathematical inquiry. A key part of the *DMIC* mathematics program are the participation and communication patterns that support students to construct and use proficient and reasoned mathematical practices (Hunter 2008). Central to the *DMIC* work is a Communication and Participation Framework (Hunter 2008); a tool used to scaffold teachers to engage students in mathematical practices within communities of mathematical inquiry. An important component of the

Communication and Participation Framework is the ways in which teachers can use it adaptively, flexibly, and in culturally responsive ways.

The development of proficient mathematical practices is closely aligned to construction of a positive mathematical identity. Although there are inconsistencies in the use of the term identity in mathematics education, some researchers (e.g., English et al. 2008; Gutiérrez 2013; Sfard and Prusak 2005) draw our attention to the way in which mathematical identities are developed through engagement and participation in mathematical activity. For example, identity has been referred to by Sfard and Prusak (2005) as the "missing link" in the "complex dialectic between learning and its sociocultural context" (p. 15). Other researchers draw our attention to the way in which identity is related to issues of power (Gutiérrez 2013) and access (English et al. 2008) and therefore to equity concerns. Considering mathematical identity as developed within mathematical activity in turn highlights the importance of *all* students being provided with opportunities to participate in mathematical practices.

Mathematical practices evolve through socially constructed interactive discourse. They are specific to, and encapsulated within, the practice of mathematics (Ball and Bass 2003). Mathematical practices include the mathematical know-how which extends beyond constructing mathematical knowledge to include specific actions and ways of learning and using mathematics. There are many examples of mathematical practices which proficient problem solvers use and do and these include explaining, representing, and "justifying claims, using symbolic notation efficiently, defining terms precisely, and making generalizations [or] the way in which skilled mathematics users are able to model a situation to make it easier to understand and to solve problems related to it" (RAND 2003, p. xviii). Inherent in the development and use of mathematical practices are specific ways of talking and reasoning, ways of asking questions, and challenging others.

To engage students in mathematical practices can be challenging for a number of reasons. As noted, not all students are comfortable asking questions or explaining their reasoning beyond talking to a friend. The challenges were illustrated through interviews at the beginning of the school year when the students had just begun in *DMIC* classrooms. In the early interviews, a substantial number (46%) of the students gave negative responses when asked about engaging in mathematical practices (for example, explaining and justifying mathematical explanations, representing reasoning, and responding to challenge). Their initial responses were often linked to emotional aspects (e.g., being scared, or feeling nervous, or frightened). The responses were also commonly associated with negative behavior from peers such as being laughed at or ridiculed. For example, one student stated:

> What I don't like about math is about how when you make a mistake people make a big joke out of it and then that can be really embarrassing.

Similarly, another student when asked about explaining their ideas said:

> I feel kind of nervous because sometimes other people might say no that's wrong and it freaks me out... because it feels like I've done everything wrong.

At the end of the year, after the students had been in the *DMIC* classrooms, there was a noticeable shift in the student attitudinal/emotional responses; considerably fewer students (13%) provided a negative response. Interestingly, the negative responses were no longer linked to derogatory responses from peers; rather they were personal characteristics linked to self-descriptions of themselves as shy or quiet:

> (I don't like) Getting up and showing my work because I'm nervous around people... I'm a quiet kid.

Developing a classroom in which students use a range of mathematical practices within a community of inquiry is challenging for many teachers, whether working with students from the dominant middle class Pākeha or more diverse groups (Hunter 2010). The complexities are many, including who talks when and how, and what mathematics is talked about (Hunter 2008). In this program, teachers are required to reposition themselves as facilitators and members of the learning community (Hunter 2013) and engage students in constructing and presenting mathematical explanations and justification. Providing equitable access for all students to participate in the mathematics discourse of the learning experience substantially increases the demand on teachers to understand the culture of their students. This is illustrated in reflections made by teachers when they have just begun to engage in the *DMIC* program. For example, one teacher wrote the following statement:

> Challenged by establishing the idea of our learning waka [canoe]; a culture of learning together to succeed, I was surprised at how little I knew about my students. I have had to really talk to the children like what they do on weekends and special times and ask the Pāsifika teachers about food they eat.

Nevertheless, many teachers are open to change when they explore the possibilities. As an example one teacher stated:

> Cultural-cognitive link opens up a raft of issues that stereotype Pāsifika as a disadvantaged segment of society. The new maths strategy will enable real growth to be made, with the greatest benefactor being me!

When teachers take into account Pāsifika languages, cultures, and identities, the mathematics teaching pedagogy in the schooling context changes, and the students are more readily able to engage in mathematical practices. This is consistent with what we have learnt from Paulo Freire (2000) about transformative education. Freire argues that through engaging people who have been marginalized and dehumanized by drawing on what they already know, education is able to transform oppressive structures in equitable ways. Within *DMIC* classrooms, careful consideration is given to increasing student voice and autonomy to question and challenge in culturally appropriate ways. In a previous article Hunter and Anthony (2011), drawing on findings from a *DMIC* classroom, illustrated that when the teacher attended to classroom social and discourse norms, more students were able to engage and contribute at higher cognitive levels. In particular, what was highlighted was how participation increased in mathematical practices and activities when the teacher considered his or her Pāsifika students' strengths and employed pedagogical strategies constructed around the Pāsifika values, and when they provided space which was "culturally, as well as academically and socially responsive" (MacFarlane 2004, p. 61).

Other aspects of the *DMIC* program include a demand for teachers to have high expectations and use challenging contextualized tasks, which are more likely to lead to rich conceptual understandings. The problems and tasks are set within the known and lived social and cultural reality of the students. Careful consideration is given to how the students view their ways of participating and communicating. The intent is that they are able to maintain their cultural identity while simultaneously building a positive mathematical identity. Social norms which shape classroom work and interactions are built around core Pāsifika values in order to ensure that our Pāsifika students are able to participate fully in mathematical practices.

Pāsifika Values and Their Role in Shaping Classroom Social Norms

Given the increased emphasis over the past two decades placed on the students communicating their mathematical reasoning, equitable participation in the mathematical discourse is of prime importance and Pāsifika values play a central role (Hunter 2007). Although the Pāsifika students in *DMIC* classrooms are composed of a diverse group of Pācific Nations people, together they have a set of cultural commonalities. These are within a set of core Pāsifika values which include such values as reciprocity, respect, service, inclusion, family, relationships, spirituality, leadership, collectivism, love, and belonging (Anae et al. 2001). Pāsifika students in the classrooms may be first generation to New Zealand or they may be second, third, or even fourth generation New Zealand born and may be variously influenced by the majority cultural norms. Nevertheless, the core Pāsifika values of their whānau continue to have a major impact on how they interact and behave within their home and affect how they participate and communicate in the school context.

Core Pāsifika values can cause dissonance for some Pāsifika students because they do not align with those commonly used in New Zealand classrooms. Bok (2010) suggests educational systems tend to privilege the beliefs and values of the dominant middle class. This dissonance was illustrated by Hunter and Anthony (2011) where they found that the Pāsifika students on entry to a *DMIC* classroom indicated that they considered they learnt through listening to the teacher as an appropriate mode of learning. Notions of listening (rather than active participation and inquiry) links to the Pāsifika value of respect where teachers as elders are considered to hold knowledge which is always correct and unquestionable. Similarly, they illustrated the discomfort Pāsifika students initially felt when required to question and challenge the teacher and other students, because they were concerned that it might be considered disrespectful and could cause a loss of face. Learning mathematics is about learning the codes of the discipline of mathematics including how to engage in a range of mathematical practices including argumentation. Clearly if, as Gutiérrez (2002) argues, we need to consider the importance of participation and achievement (as learning) we need to think about how the Pāsifika values can be placed at the center of teachers' practices to support students to engage in mathematics.

School mathematics is not just about learning mathematics knowledge; it is also about learning to engage in particular behavior and act like a mathematician. As part of challenging the hegemonic European practices commonly found in many New Zealand classrooms, within the *DMIC* program we enact what Atweh and Ala'i (2012) term a "socially response-able approach to mathematics education" (p. 98). Rather than using direct instruction, the teachers use more open and flexible pedagogy which incorporates the core Pāsifika values to shape the social norms of the classroom. The students work in small groups to construct shared problem solutions. Clear expectations are placed on them that they have both an individual responsibility to understand and a collective responsibility that they make sure their peers understand also. As part of the interactions in the classroom, notions of working as a family are emphasized because family, particularly the extended family, encompasses all the Pāsifika values. As one teacher explained:

> Family is big, it's everything. The way our classes are set up now everyone has a chance to share ideas, and like a family everyone helps out, and nobody is left out because everybody has a job to do and that's the Pāsifika way and the Māori way. We talk about that a lot as a class, like if you are doing the housework everybody helps or if you are making an umu or hangi (earth oven) everybody has a job to do. It might be dig the hole or peel the spuds but you have a job... and like with a vaka (canoe) everybody has got to paddle in the same direction, in time if you are going to move and the kids can relate to that because that's their world.

In turn, the students talk about their place in these classrooms in ways which reveal their sense of relationships, family, and belonging. It is evident that drawing on the common values of the different cultural groups represented in Pāsifika peoples, being responsive to "students' cultural ways of being" (Civil and Hunter 2015, p. 296) and using these to shape the social norms support the students to construct a positive mathematical and cultural identity.

Connecting Mathematical Problems to the World of the Students

Central to growing our Pāsifika students' mathematical understandings as rich conceptual knowledge is the use of group-worthy (Featherstone et al. 2011), mathematically complex and challenging problems or problematic activity. A requirement in the construction of the problems is the need for connections to be made with the cultural and social contexts of the students' daily lives. This undoubtedly poses challenges for teachers as this teacher explains:

> The challenge is making things culturally relevant when I don't have the cultural knowledge myself so I find myself tending to write problems about school life, fruit, sport, gear, etc.

The emphasis in the writing of the problems is on the world the students currently inhabit in their beyond school world where they locate themselves. This allows for the students to recognize and value mathematics in their social and cultural world and gain access to the mathematics in the problem. In New Zealand, the school mathematics problems, activities, and pedagogy have most often better reflected the cultural capital of the dominant middle class Pākeha cultural groups. In this chapter, the term cultural capital used by Bourdieu and Passeron (1973) is defined by McLaren (1994) as being the general cultural background, knowledge, disposition, and skills that are passed on from one generation to another. As we use it, cultural capital represents "ways of talking, acting, and socialising, as well as language practices, values, and types of dress and behaviour" (McLaren 1994, p. 219). The act of teachers writing specific problems around the world of Pāsifika students repositions them as having valid cultural capital in their own mathematics classrooms as is evident in the following student statements:

> The maths is about us, about the community. The problems relate to our cultures and celebrations which makes it more understandable.
> It makes it easier for us to learn…like the ula lole (lolly necklace) problem because most of us have made it before and we can see it and have a picture in our minds so we can see how it's proportions and ratios like one chocolate to three fruit burst or minties.

Their responses illustrate their recognition that the activities that they engage in at home involve mathematics and that it is valued. Moreover, having the problems set within contexts they can relate to makes the mathematics more accessible. As Freire (2000) argues, to gain equitable outcomes, it is important to situate educational activity in the lived experience of the learners.

Language and Cultural Identity

In New Zealand we have had a long history in education of "English language only" policies, both overt and covert. Although government policy changed more than 30 years ago with the renaissance of Māori in the 1970s, many teachers still hold implicit beliefs that students should speak in English at school and English remains the language of instruction (Meaney 2013). Many Pāsifika students enter New Zealand schools fluent in their own language and with a rich background of knowledge and experiences, but within a short period of schooling they join the disproportionately high numbers of Pāsifika students who are failing within our current education system. Language-based equity issues are a constraining factor. Within DMIC classrooms, teachers are asked to support students to shift between their first home language and English when discussing, explaining, and justifying their mathematical understandings. This acknowledges the difficulties Pāsifika students encounter when learning mathematics including when equivalent words or concepts are not readily available in their first language. The word problems used in *DMIC* classrooms require that the students read and make sense of the problem contexts. The ability to code-switch from one language to another to support student understandings thus provides equitable access. Initially some teachers voice concerns that they do not know what the students are saying when they encourage students to use both languages; however, they come to realize it is an important consideration in the empowerment of the students. For example, two different teachers explained why it was needed:

> I am Samoan so I understand what they are saying as well but if they were Cook Island I would just get some of the Cook Islanders to talk in their language and translate for me or represent in a different way so I would get them to draw it and I would understand what they are drawing so it doesn't matter what nationality they are.
> It's really powerful if they can use their own language because sometimes it might just be that they don't understand the question or even the ones that speak English there might not be a word in English that represents what they are talking about or they might be more confident speaking Samoan or Tongan and then others can translate. Without that, like in the past those kids didn't have a voice and you would just think they couldn't do it. It really helps transfer the power as well, as I don't always understand and they have to translate for me and their understanding really improves when they do this.

Clearly, the teacher had recognized that speaking in a language the student chooses supported the development of student voice and agency. In student interviews, the students also acknowledged how speaking in their first language provided opportunities for their peers. At the same time, it normalized their use of their first language within the school environment and added to their cultural identity (and mathematical identity):

> Sometimes it helps to explain things in Tongan because some of the Tongans in our class are new and their English isn't that good but they can understand the maths in Tongan which is cool because before you didn't really speak Tongan in class.

Language is closely interwoven with culture and identity for Pāsifika students. Clearly evident in the *DMIC* classrooms is the way in which the use of the student's first language supports them as learners to draw on the Pāsifika values in ways which they feel comfortable. Other studies in *DMIC* classrooms (e.g., Bills and Hunter 2015; Civil and Hunter 2015; Hunter and Anthony 2011) show that when teachers use pedagogy situated within the known world of their Pāsifika students, and which premise student choice over the spoken language they use, achievement results are reversed, and positive cultural identities and mathematical dispositions are constructed. Evident in these studies is recognition that mathematics education is a sociocultural activity embedded in sociopolitical contexts with the teaching and learning of mathematics as "situational, contextual and personal processes" (Taylor and Sobel 2011, p. ix).

High Expectations and Ethics of Care

While teachers in our program commonly state that they think all children can do mathematics, the way they phrase these statements belies the spoken words and indicates that they hold fixed mind sets (Dweck 2008). Fixed mind sets are exemplified when teachers are continuously influenced by theories which relate to grouping and teaching by ability and which support deficit thinking which we will explore later in this chapter. Dweck (2008) argues a need for teachers to hold a growth mind set: one in which ability is not fixed but able to be grown and changed. Within a growth mind set, mathematical ability is grown through persistence, effort and hard work, challenges and struggle are celebrated, and mistakes are considered learning opportunities. Dissonance supports the development of a growth mind set as is evident in the following teacher statement:

> This is all hard learning for me. I am implementing more effectively the justification status, intellectual contribution ideas. I believe this is instrumental in not only improving learning across all areas for all students, but also in solving problems I am having with a group of boys. I think they are having mind-set difficulties and won't take risks because their maths knowledge they think is low.

Closely tied to a growth mind set is that of notions of ethics of care. An ethic of care is an important component of the mathematics classroom (Noddings 2005). A lot of importance is placed on how to enact ethics of care in ways which enable rather than disable students. At times, an ethic of care may be misinterpreted by teachers. For example, rather than encouraging students to risk-take and celebrate mistakes, at times teachers think that they should keep the students safe from mathematical practices because they may make them feel uncomfortable. As noted, we reported earlier about the reluctance of some Pāsifika students to talk or ask questions during classroom lessons. Some teachers respond by allowing the behavior, misunderstanding and interpreting it as a Pāsifika trait. However, as a key equitable action, the teachers need to interpret and work with the behavior within an ethic of care. Within this frame they need to draw on the Pāsifika values to scaffold students to engage in the mathematical discourse. Such actions indicate that they care enough to facilitate a student to engage in essential mathematical practices within culturally responsive environments. Drawing on ethics of care can be challenging for teachers and so, initially, they have to explore ways to enact it. But once the teachers realize its importance, it becomes a feature of their practice and a way to increase their expectations of all students. As an example, here is a quote from a teacher who realized the power of using an ethic of care in a culturally responsive way:

> I challenged the children to explain their thinking so I could see what they were capable of, and what a difference it made. I saw how well the children responded too and how much they enjoyed the challenging questions they were asked.

Pāsifika students can also step in and "save" their peers as part of them enacting the Pāsifika values. Nevertheless, teachers need to consciously support them to work within an ethic of care and support students in a different way. For example, one teacher described a boy from her classroom as easily missed during small group work because he never spoke and did not participate. She observed that the other students in his group would "save" him by providing an answer for him. She went on to describe her actions during small group-work:

> I just said "Oh no, remember we care about Tane enough that we want to hear what he has to say. If he doesn't know then he knows what he needs to do to ask. You know that he needs to ask a question."

She then went on to describe how after a long period of waiting, the student asked a question. He then responded and the pride which resulted from his participation was evident for all to see.

Conclusion

Notions of equity are a complex and challenging concept within mathematics education. To some, equity in mathematics education is equated as equal opportunities for all to learn through accessing both a common mathematics curriculum and qualified teachers; others equate equity with equality of mathematical achievement outcomes across student groups (Foote and Lambert 2011). However, Gutiérrez and Dixon-Román (2011) argue the need to look beyond taking what they term interchangeably as either "gap gazing" or an "achievement gap perspective" (p. 23). They call attention to the problems which emerge because this lens supports an assimilationist approach in which the aim is to close the gap between students from the dominant culture (in New Zealand the middle class Pākeha students represented in the hegemonic European practices) and the marginalized students, in contrast to questioning the validity of the measurement tools or even the focus on achievement. This assimilationist approach is represented in the New Zealand Ministry of Education requirements which focus mainly on our reporting of lifts in achievement according to the national standards. Although, lifts in student achievement have been part of the success of *DMIC,* the more important focus has been on other valued outcomes including an increase in student voice and agency, increased pro-social skills, enhanced mathematical dispositions, and the valuing of the mathematics within the home and cultural context. For example, when interviewed a number of students made reference to their increased autonomy:

> In this maths we have more power. He [teacher] gives us the problem but the problem is about us. . . .. Our reality and we have to figure it out, we are responsible for our own learning and others' learning too, we have control.

Other students talked about how being taught mathematics in a *DMIC* classroom normalized them and their culture within the school setting:

> When the maths is about us and our culture, it makes me feel normal, and my culture is normal.
> Yeah like it is normal to be Samoan or Tongan.

However, these important outcomes are not positioned within the New Zealand education system as being valued outcomes and as a result "gap gazing" prevails.

We argue that the achievement gap discourse diverts attention away from the structural inequities Pāsifika students encounter in many mathematics classrooms and by failing to question these, the prevailing discourse of "gap gazing" puts the problem back with the Pāsifika community. In this way, the disengagement of Pāsifika students from mathematics can be attributed to constructs other than the teacher and is attributed to factors including personal and psychological, home environments and poverty. Other researchers (e.g., Delpit 1988; Flores 2007; Ladson-Billings 2006; Martin 2007; Milne 2013) frame equity issues around various alternative gaps. These include the power gap, the opportunity gap, the education debt, and the white spaces created when the hegemonic European practices dominate the curriculum. These have all been evident in the different sections of this chapter.

Bok (2010) draws our attention to the way in which educational systems are significant in the reproduction of unequal access to, and results from, education systems for such students from high poverty areas. In contrast to those more economically privileged, they do not have the requisite social and cultural capital (Bourdieu and Passeron 1973) that positions them for success in school and beyond. Vale et al. (2016) point out the ways in which schools reflect certain pedagogical practices. They describe how mathematics teaching is particularly "susceptible to routinized practice" (p. 100) in which teacher voice dominates. Unfortunately, this leads to issues of social justice because evidence shows that teachers adjust their teaching approaches and expectations to their perceptions of what they consider students are capable of (Atweh et al. 2014). Issues of social justice were evident throughout the chapter.

In this chapter we have drawn on 15 years of on-going research in New Zealand mathematics classrooms. We have illustrated that the teaching and learning of mathematics cannot be decontextualized based on the pervasive public belief that mathematics is "culture-free"; a view which supports the cultural deficit or "cultural blindness" (Gay 2010, p. 21) paradigm taken by many New Zealand educationalists. Our focus has been placed on the many different components of Pāsifika-focused culturally responsive teaching and the journey teachers in schools with predominantly Pāsifika students take to enact it. While the journey to develop a mathematics learning environment in which Pāsifika students are able to construct both a strong and positive cultural and mathematical identity is challenging, the words of a teacher say it all:

> The Project is using the strengths of our Pāsifika whānau and children to improve their maths and to achieve.

References

Alton-Lee A (2003) Quality teaching for diverse students in schooling: best evidence synthesis. Ministry of Education, Wellington

Anae M, Coxon E, Mara D, Wendt-Samu T, Finau C (2001) Pāsifika education research guidelines. Ministry of Education, Wellington

Atweh B, Ala'I K (2012) Socially response-able mathematics education: lessons from three teachers. In: Dindyal J, Cheng LP, Ng SF (eds) Mathematics education: expanding horizons. Proceedings of the 35th annual conference of the Mathematics Education Research Group of Australasia, vol 1. MERGA, Singapore, pp 99–105

Atweh B, Bose A, Graven M, Subramanian J, Venkat H (2014) Teaching numeracy in numeracy and early grades in low income countries. Gmbn Deutsche. Available via https://www.giz.de/expertise/downloads/giz2014-en-studie-teaching-numeracy-preschool-early-grades-numeracy.pdf. Accessed 20 Nov 2016

Ball D, Bass H (2003) Making mathematics reasonable in school. In: Kilpatrick J, Martin J, Schifter D (eds) A research companion to the principles and standards for school mathematics. National Council of Teachers of Mathematics, Reston, pp 27–45

Bills T, Hunter R (2015) The role of cultural capital in creating equity for Pāsifika learners in mathematics. In: Marshman M, Geiger V, Bennison A (eds) Mathematics education in the margins. Proceedings of the 38th annual conference of the Mathematics Education Research Group of Australasia. MERGA, Sunshine Coast, pp 109–116

Boaler J (2014) Ability grouping in mathematics classrooms. In: Lerman S (ed) Encyclopedia of mathematics education. Springer, Dordrecht, pp 1–5

Boaler J, Wiliam D (2001) 'We've still got to learn'. Students' perspectives on ability grouping and mathematics achievement. In: Gates P (ed) Issues in mathematics teaching. RoutledgeFalmer, London, pp 77–92

Boaler J, Wiliam D, Brown M (2000) Students' experiences of ability grouping – disaffection, polarisation and the construction of failure. Br Educ Res J 26(5):631–648

Bok J (2010) The capacity to aspire to higher education: "it's like making them do a play without a script". Crit Stud Educ 5(2):163–178

Bourdieu P, Passeron JC (1973) Cultural reproduction and social reproduction. In: Brown RK (ed) Knowledge, education and cultural change. Tavistock, London

Braddock J, Slavin R (1995) Why ability grouping must end: achieving excellence and equity in American education. In: Pool H, Page J (eds) Beyond tracking: finding success in inclusive schools. Phi Delta Kappa Educational Foundation, Bloomington, pp 7–20

Brown T, Devine N, Leslie E, Paiti M, Sila'ila'i E, Umaki S, Williams J (2007) Reflective engagement in cultural history: A Lacanian perspective on Pāsifika teachers in Aotearoa New Zealand. Pedagog Cult Soc 15(1):107–118

Civil M, Hunter R (2015) Participation of non-dominant students in argumentation in the mathematics classroom. Intercult J 26(4):296–312

Delpit LD (1988) The silenced dialogue: power and pedagogy in educating other people's children. Harv Educ Rev 58(3):280–298

Dweck C (2008) Mindset and math/science achievement. Teaching & leadership: managing for effective teachers and leaders. www.opportunityequation.org

Education Assessment Research Unit and New Zealand Council for Educational Research (2015) Wānangatia te Putanga Tauira National monitoring study of student achievement: mathematics and statistics 2013. Ministry of Education, Wellington

English LD, Jones GA, Bartolini Bussi M, Lesh RA, Tirosh D, Sriraman B (2008) Moving forward in international mathematics education research. In: English LD (ed) Handbook of international research in mathematics education, 2nd edn. Routledge, New York, pp. 872–905

Featherstone H, Crespo S, Jilk L, Oslund J, Parks A, Wood M (2011) Smarter together! Collaboration and equity in the elementary math classroom. NCTM, Reston

Flores A (2007) Examining disparities in mathematics education: achievement gap or opportunity gap? High Sch J 91(1):29–42

Foote MQ, Lambert R (2011) I have a solution to share: learning through equitable participation in a mathematics classroom. Can J Sci Math Technol Educ 11(3):247–260

Freire P (2000) Pedagogy of the oppressed. Continuum, New York

Gay G (2010) Culturally responsive teaching: theory, research and practice. Teacher's College Press, New York

Gutiérrez R (2002) Enabling the practice of mathematics teachers in context: toward a new equity research agenda. Math Think Learn 4(2/3):145–187

Gutiérrez R (2013) The sociopolitical turn in mathematics education. J Res Math Educ 44(1):37

Gutiérrez R, Dixon-Román E (2011) Beyond gap gazing: how can thinking about education comprehensively help us (re)envision mathematics education? Springer, Dordrecht

Hunter R (2007) Teachers developing communities of mathematical inquiries. Unpublished doctoral thesis, Massey University, Palmerston North

Hunter R (2008) Facilitating communities of mathematical inquiry. In: Goos M, Brown R, Makar K (eds) Navigating currents and charting directions. Proceedings of the 31st annual conference of the Mathematics Education Research Group of Australasia, vol 1. MERGA, Brisbane, pp 31–39

Hunter R (2010) Changing roles and identities in the construction of a community of mathematical inquiry. J Math Teach Educ 13(5):397–409

Hunter R (2013) Developing equitable opportunities for Pasifika students to engage in mathematical practices. In: Lindmeier AM, Heinze A (eds) Proceedings of the 37th international group for the psychology of mathematics education, vol 3. PME, Kiel, pp 397–406

Hunter R, Anthony G (2011) Forging mathematical relationships in inquiry-based classrooms with Pasifika students. J Urban Math Educ 4(1):98–119

Jorgensen R (2012) Exploring scholastic mortality among working class and Indigenous students: a perspective from Australia. In: Herbel-Eisenmann B, Choppin J, Wagner D, Pimm D (eds) Equity in discourse for mathematics education: theories, practices and policies. Springer, Dordrecht, pp 35–49

Jorgensen R, Gates P, Roper V (2014) Structural exclusion through school mathematics. Educ Stud Math 87(2):1–19

Kazemi E, Franke M, Lampert M (2009) Developing pedagogies in teacher education to support novice teachers' ability to enact ambitious instruction. In: Hunter R, Bicknell B, Burgess T (eds) Crossing divides, proceedings of the 32nd annual conference of the Mathematics Education Research Group of Australasia. MERGA, Wellington, pp 11–29

Kulik J, Kulik C (1992) Meta-analytic findings on grouping programmes. Gift Child Q 36(2):73–76

Ladson-Billings G (2006) From the achievement gap to the education debt: understanding achievement in U.S. schools. Educ Res 35(7):3–12

Lampert M, Beasley H, Ghousseini H, Kazemi E, Franke M (2010) Using designed instructional activities to enable novices to manage ambitious mathematics teaching. In: Stein MK, Kucan L (eds) Instructional explanations in the disciplines. Springer, Pittsburgh, pp 129–141

MacFarlane A (2004) Kia hiwa ra! Listen to culture. New Zealand Council for Educational Research, Wellington

Marks R (2012) How do children experience setting in primary classrooms? Math Teach 230:5–8

Martin D (2007) Mathematics learning and participation in African American context: the co-construction of identity in two intersecting realms of experience. In: Nasir N, Cobb P (eds) Diversity, equity, and access to mathematical ideas. Teachers College Press, New York, pp 146–158

McLaren P (1994) Life in schools: an introduction to critical pedagogy in the foundations of education. Longman, New York

Meaney T (2013) The privileging of English in mathematics education research, just a necessary evil? In: Berger M, Brodie K, Frith V, Le Roux K (eds) Proceedings of the seventh international mathematics and society conference, vol 1. MES7, Cape Town, pp 65–84

Milne A (2013) Colouring in the white spaces: reclaiming cultural identity in whitespace schools. An unpublished doctoral thesis, Waikato University

Ministry of Education (2004) Book 3: getting started. Learning Media, Wellington

Nakhid C (2003) "Intercultural" perceptions, academic achievement, and the identifying process of Pācific Islands students in New Zealand schools. J Negro Educ 72(3):297–317

Nieto S (2002) Language, culture, and teaching: critical perspectives for a new century. Lawrence Erlbaum, Mahwah

Noddings N (2005) The challenge to care in schools. Teachers College Press, New York

RAND Mathematics Study Panel (2003) Mathematical proficiency for all students: towards a strategic research and development program in mathematics education. RAND, Santa Monica

Scheicher A (2014) Equity, excellence & inclusiveness in education: policy lessons from around the world. International summit on the teaching profession. OECD Publishing. Available via https://doi.org/10.787/978964214033-en. Accessed 2 Nov 2016

Sfard A, Prusak A (2005) Telling identities: in search of an analytic tool for investigating learning as a culturally shaped activity. Educ Res 34(4):14–22

Taylor SV, Sobel DM (2011) Culturally responsive pedagogy: teaching like our students' lives matter. Emerald Group Publishing, Bingley

Vale C, Atweh B, Averill R, Skourdoumbis A (2016) Equity, social justice and ethics in mathematics education. In: Makar K, Dole S, Visnovska J, Goos M, Bennison A, Fry K (eds) Review of Australasian mathematics education research 2012–2015. Sense Publishers, Singapore, pp 97–118

Wendt-Samu T (2006) The 'Pāsifika umbrella' and quality teaching: understanding and responding to the diverse realities within. Waikato J Educ 12:35–49

Wood T, Williams G, McNeal B (2006) Children's mathematical thinking in different classroom cultures. J Res Math Educ 37(3):222–255

Wylie C (2003) Status of educational research in New Zealand: New Zealand country report. New Zealand Council for Educational Research, Wellington

Young-Loveridge J (2009) Patterns of performance and progress of NDP students in 2008. In: Findings for the New Zealand numeracy development project 2008. Ministry of Education, Wellington, pp 12–26

Zevenbergen R (2001) Is streaming an equitable practice? Students' experiences of streaming in the middle years of schooling. In: Bobis J, Perry B, Mitchelmore M (eds) Numeracy and beyond. Proceedings of the 24th annual conferences of Mathematics Research Group of Australasia. MERGA, Sydney, pp 563–570

Zevenbergen R (2003) Ability grouping in mathematics classrooms: a Bourdieuian analysis. Learn Math 23(3):5

Efforts and Concerns for Indigenous Language Education in Taiwan

26

Chen-Feng Joy Lin, I-An Grace Gao, and Pi-I Debby Lin

Contents

Introduction	444
Historical Background	446
Legislative and Policy Support for Indigenous Language Education	448
Current Condition of Indigenous Languages in Taiwan	450
Students' Attitudes Toward Learning Indigenous Languages	452
Indigenous Language Education Policy and Projects in Taiwan	454
Council of Indigenous Peoples	455
Six-Year Indigenous Cultural Revitalization and Development Project	455
Six-Year Indigenous Language Revitalization Project	455
Indigenous Language Proficiency Certificate	457
Training of Indigenous Language Teachers	457
Online Learning Materials	458
Indigenous Language Research and Development Center	458
Ministry of Education	459
Local Governments	460
Future Project	460
Challenges on Indigenous Language Education	461
Conclusion	463
References	464

C.-F. J. Lin (✉)
National Pingtung University, Pingtung, Taiwan
e-mail: joylin@mail.nptu.edu.tw

I.-A. G. Gao
University of Helsinki, Helsinki, Finland
e-mail: an.gao@helsinki.fi

P.-I. D. Lin
Department of Environmental Health, Harvard T.H. Chan School of Public Health, Boston, MA, USA
e-mail: pil864@mail.harvard.edu

© Springer Nature Singapore Pte Ltd. 2019
E. A. McKinley, L. T. Smith (eds.), *Handbook of Indigenous Education*,
https://doi.org/10.1007/978-981-10-3899-0_11

Abstract

Taiwan has over 16 tribes of Indigenous peoples, consisting of 42 local dialects from 3 major Austronesia language systems. Indigenous peoples in Taiwan have for centuries been assimilated into the surrounding Chinese Han culture. Following the international Indigenous people's rights movements in the 1980s, Indigenous peoples in Taiwan started a cultural and social movement, which resulted in the legislation of the Indigenous Peoples' Basic Law. The Basic Law leveraged room for negotiations to enact concrete efforts for Indigenous cultural revitalization. Language education is one of the most urgent priorities of this revitalization. The central government initiated a nationwide effort to preserve Indigenous languages. Two terms of the Six-Year Indigenous Language Revitalization Project have already been implemented by the government, which has laid the foundation for expanding Indigenous language education, including training Indigenous language teachers and developing an Indigenous Language Proficiency Certification. Many local governments are also involved in providing language learning opportunities for Indigenous children and youth, such as establishing Indigenous immersion kindergartens and incorporating Indigenous language curricula in elementary schools. Resources for online learning have also been designed, providing opportunities for learning Indigenous languages using computer and mobile technology. These top-down projects give rise to an increase of grassroots actions and awareness to preserve Indigenous languages has been intensified. This chapter provides an overview on works relevant to Indigenous language education in Taiwan and the challenges this project faces. Recommendations are given at the end to provide direction for future efforts on Indigenous language revitalization in Taiwan.

Keywords

Indigenous education · Indigenous language · Taiwan · Indigenous language revitalization plan · Austronesian languages

Introduction

Indigenous peoples make up about 2% of the total population of Taiwan, totaling 549,127 people as of May, 2016 (RIS 2016). The Council of Indigenous Peoples currently recognizes 16 Indigenous tribes. They are the Amis, Atayal, Paiwan, Bunun, Tsou, Rukai, Puyuma, Saisiyat, Yami, Thao, Kavalan, Truku, Sakizaya, Sediq, Hla'alua, and Kanakanava (Fig. 1).

Indigenous peoples in Taiwan speak languages belonging to the Austronesian family that encompasses 386 million people spreading from Easter Island in the east to Madagascar in the west, and from New Zealand in the south to Taiwan in the north (Bellwood 1991). Taiwan is believed to be the Austronesian homeland from a linguistic perspective (Blust 1984). About 24 Indigenous languages were found to be spoken in Taiwan up to the twentieth century, including Ketagalan, Taokas,

Fig. 1 Distribution of Indigenous tribes in Taiwan (Figure adapted from Taiwan Indigenous People's Knowledge Economic Development Association (2016))

Papora, Babuza, Favorlang, Hoanya, Siraya, Makattao, Taivoan, Kavalan, Pazeh, Thao, Atayal, Saisiyat, Bunun, Tsou, Saaroa, Kanakanavu, Rukai, Paiwan, Puyuma, Amis, Seediq, and Yami. However, nine of the 24 languages (Keta[n]galan, Taokas, Papora, Babuza, Favorlang, Hoanya, Siraya, Makattao, and Taivoan) are already extinct (Zeitoun et al. 2003). Among the 16 officially recognized tribes, 42 local dialects have been recorded. The linguistic history of Taiwan is complex, demonstrating the diversity of the region.

A language is not only a tool for cultural exchange and communication but is also an important medium for passing on history, wisdom and cultural practices. Language provides evidence of an established society. However, with societal change, migration, and lack of support in the everyday environment, some languages face threats of extinction. What often eventuates is the emergence of a numerical or politically powerful majority that influences the minority by forcing them to learn the dominant culture and language. Indigenous peoples have encountered Dutch traders, Spanish naval invasions, colonization by the Qing dynasty, and the national language education policy to assimilate them into the dominant society imposed by the Japanese and Han Chinese (Nationalist Party). These outside influences negatively influenced Indigenous people's identities and their aspiration to self-govern. Additionally, Indigenous languages were expected to go extinct under the unified language education policy. As the world started to realize the importance of endangered languages, the Indigenous peoples in Taiwan also became aware of the risks of losing their identity to assimilation with a larger group of people. Fortunately, Indigenous people still have their languages precariously preserved, some being frequently spoken in everyday life and some in the observance of religious practices. The progressive efforts of communities and government working together in recent years have led to the implementation of policies to preserve Indigenous languages. This chapter provides an analysis of the different policies, approaches, and their outcomes. The analysis hopes to make better policy recommendations for the future.

Historical Background

To understand fully to state of Indigenous languages in Taiwan, it is essential to first understand the history. Based on archaeological evidence, Indigenous peoples of Taiwan have inhabited the land for thousands of years. Puyuma heritage artifacts date Indigenous people's existence on the island back to at least 7000 years ago (Digital Museum of Taiwan Indigenous Peoples 2016).

Studies of Indigenous languages of Taiwan can be traced back to the nineteenth century (Lee 2004). Analysis and historic comparisons of Indigenous languages have been documented even before these linguistics studies. For example, in 1822 J. H. Klaproth published "Sur la langue des indigènes de l'île de Formose" (On the indigenous languages of the Island of Formosa) in the Asia *Polyglotta*, which first confirmed the native languages of Taiwan to belong to the Austronesian family. In 1859, H.C. von der Gabelentz's article, "Über die formosanische Sprache und ihre Stellung in demmalaiischen Sprachstamm" (About the Formosan language and its position in the Malaysian language family), discussed the relationship of Taiwanese Indigenous languages to various Austronesian languages.

Dutch colonizers in Taiwan learned Indigenous languages during occupation (Li 2007). They translated and taught the Bible to Indigenous Peoples in their own Indigenous languages. In contrast, the Qing dynasty completely ignored the existence of Indigenous languages and attempted to eliminate them. Because there were different dialects used by the Han Chinese immigrants on the island at that time, the government allowed the Han Chinese to speak in their mother tongues to study Confucian teachings; however, Indigenous peoples were restricted to use their own mother tongues. The Japanese colonial period initially respected the Indigenous languages, but slowly used this as lure to manipulate a new educational policy that assimilated Taiwanese culture into Japanese culture. By the end of the Japanese colonial period, there were strong restrictions on Indigenous language usage.

The Chinese Nationalist party, which reclaimed Taiwan in 1949, was the first colonial regime that brings Indigenous education into the modern education system. Since the retrocession of Taiwan by the Nationalist Party, five major language education policies have been proposed (Chao 2014). The first is the Retrocession of Taiwan in 1945–1949, during which Mandarin Chinese was recognized along with Indigenous languages. Starting in 1945, the Chinese Nationalist Party implemented an assimilation policy on Indigenous peoples and began the removal of Japanese influences. At this point, Mandarin Chinese was used in classroom to transition from Japanese, although Indigenous languages were still permitted in schools. The second era was the time from 1949 to 1987, when the government of the Republic of China relocated to Taiwan and enforced strict, Mandarin-only policies while prohibiting all other languages. This period is also marked by the most intense persecution of Indigenous people. In 1949, the government announced the "Mountain Education Policy" which promoted the speaking of Mandarin and prohibited any Indigenous people from speaking or teaching their Indigenous languages. The third policy was enacted after the lifting of Martial Law in 1987 and ran until 1998. This period saw the initiation of a revival of Indigenous languages and education. However, most of the focus were on other local dialects spoken in Taiwan and most teachers still delivered lesson content in Mandarin and no strong emphasis was placed on Indigenous language education. More challenges surfaced as many of the elders fluent in Indigenous languages passed away. The fourth period involves the implementation of the Education Act for Indigenous Peoples in 1998–2005. Policies and legal standards for Indigenous language education started when the Draft for the Indigenous Peoples Basic Law was announced in 1998. The Education Fundamental Act, which passed in 1999, gave provisions for special support for the Education Act for Indigenous Peoples (1998). The final stage began with the passage of the Indigenous People's Basic Law in 2005. The Ministry of Education and the Council of Indigenous Peoples modified the Education Act for Indigenous Peoples after the Indigenous People's Basic Law was enacted. This change included Indigenous languages under the purview of Indigenous education. A proficiency requirement for Indigenous languages was added to the Affirmative Action of Indigenous Education in 2007 to encourage students to learn their Indigenous language.

This historical overview shows that even though Taiwan is the home of many Indigenous peoples, much of Indigenous people's cultural heritage was destroyed by political, social, cultural, and educational threats imposed over four centuries of colonization by the Dutch, Spanish, Qing, and Japanese (Chen 2004).

The destruction of language in the process of social change is an important catalyst to establish protective policies to revitalize Indigenous languages. Indigenous peoples of Taiwan have also come to a greater self-realization after years of unequal treatment that it is time to claim equal rights and to practice and maintain Indigenous culture and lifestyle, including their language. In the drafting of the Indigenous Language Development Act of 2015, it was noted that Indigenous peoples of Taiwan suffered great losses from the enforcement of the Mandarin speaking policy, and the first step toward cultural revitalization was to preserve the language. From a political perspective, appropriate action and methods should be taken to communicate the importance of Indigenous languages not only in Indigenous communities but also in all communities in Taiwan.

Legislative and Policy Support for Indigenous Language Education

In this section we provide an in-depth review of the legislative and policy efforts in Indigenous language education at different stages that have supported the raising of Indigenous cultural awareness and cultural identity. Three interrelated parts are discussed in this section. First, we delineate the institutional basis of Indigenous language education in both the Constitution and the Indigenous Peoples Basic Law. Institutional underpinning is examined to show the environment of Indigenous language education on the legal level. Second, we discuss the critical roles of the Council of Indigenous Peoples and the Ministry of Education in upholding Indigenous language education. Finally, an up-to-date account of the development of the Indigenous Language Development Act is provided to demonstrate the historical contingency of Indigenous language education in Taiwan.

The rights for Indigenous language education first appeared in national law in 1997. The highest law in Taiwan, the Constitution of the Republic of China, included an additional article to embrace cultural pluralism. Paragraph 11 of the Additional Article 10 promulgated July 21, 1997, states, "the State affirms cultural pluralism and shall actively preserve and foster the development of Indigenous languages and cultures." This provision initiated the legal foundation to establish more detailed laws to reform Indigenous language education. The Additional Article of the Constitution affirmed the importance of Indigenous languages.

The Council of Indigenous People (formally Council of Indigenous Peoples, Executive Yuan) is the central institution that governs Indigenous affairs in Taiwan. At its inception in 1996, the Department of Education and Culture ranked Indigenous language research, preservation, and heritage as the top priorities (Palemeq and Muzuer 2015). The Council of Indigenous People referenced various international legal instruments to protect the rights of Indigenous peoples to use, preserve, and develop Indigenous languages. The Indigenous Peoples Basic Law, promulgated in 2005, specifically states the rights for Indigenous languages in Articles 9, 12, and 30. The Basic Act states that development of Indigenous languages shall be stipulated by law. Article 9 lays out the plan for a research agency on Indigenous languages, a language proficiency evaluation system, and preferential measures for Indigenous peoples who have proficiency in Indigenous languages. Article 12 provides foundations for Indigenous language broadcast media and institutions, and Article 30 provides for Indigenous language interpretation. Beyond the general provisions stipulating that the government shall respect

Indigenous languages (Article 30), the Basic Law did not explicitly discuss the right for Indigenous language education.

The Ministry of Education is another primary administrator of Indigenous education matters. The Ministry first compiled primary school curricula for Indigenous language education in 1995. The Education Act for Indigenous Peoples of 1998 incorporates Indigenous languages in sections on school education (Article 10), curricula (Article 21), qualified teachers (Article 24 and 26), and social education (Article 28 and 30). The Education Act for Indigenous Peoples specifically calls *"to ensure young Indigenous children have the opportunities to learn their own Indigenous language, history and culture"* (Article 10) within the public education system. With regards to curricula, Article 21 states "governments at all levels shall provide Indigenous students at preschool, elementary school and junior high school level with opportunities to learn their respective ethnic languages, histories and cultures." The Education Act for Indigenous Peoples also adds the requirement of a language proficiency test for qualified teachers (Article 24). Articles in the Act clearly state the methods for Indigenous language preservation. Projects and additional actions have also been generated based on these articles and the Basic Law, reflecting the will of the government to preserve languages with tangible plans and programs.

The Taiwanese government worked on establishing the Indigenous Language Development Act to have a legal base for Indigenous language development after the promulgation of the Indigenous Peoples Basic Law in 2005. Support for Indigenous languages is most strongly evident in Article 9 of the Basic Law, which calls for the creation of a dedicated agency on Indigenous language. Article 9 states,

> The government shall establish a special unit responsible for Indigenous language researches and for an Indigenous language proficiency evaluation system in order to actively engage in the promotion of Indigenous language development.
> The government shall provide preferential measures for Indigenous peoples or hold special civil service examinations designed for Indigenous peoples where, under the relevant laws and regulations, it may require beneficiaries or candidates to pass the afore-mentioned evaluation or have proficiency in Indigenous language.
> The development of Indigenous language shall be stipulated by law. (Indigenous Peoples Basic Law)

In May 2017, the Indigenous Language Development Act passed its third reading and took effect. Indigenous languages are symbols of identity, culture, and validity for Indigenous peoples. Indigenous language education has been implemented in Taiwan for more than a decade, and significant progress has been made in laying the legal foundation for Indigenous language education. Nevertheless, even with the Indigenous Language Development Act, the situation for the endangered languages remains dire and many scholars and educators have expressed concerns over the effectiveness of the current policies on revitalizing Indigenous languages (Chao 2014). The next section of the chapter will explore the current condition of Indigenous education and discuss the challenges encountered during the implementation of Indigenous language education and revitalization projects.

Current Condition of Indigenous Languages in Taiwan

Indigenous language classes are available in formal and informal educational systems. In the formal education system, 20 Indigenous language immersion kindergartens are currently available; one 40-min Indigenous language class per week is required from first grade to sixth grade and is offered as an elective from seventh grade to ninth grade. College level courses are available in several universities, including National Chengchi University, National Donghwa University, National Taiwan University, and National Hsinchu University of Education. In informal educational systems, there are language nest classes (available in the evenings and on the weekends), language classes in tribal and community colleges, and intensive summer Indigenous language classes (Huang 2015). Indigenous language classes are crucial in the process of revitalization. The language vitality surveys conducted by the Council of Indigenous Peoples provide additional information on how best to engage with Indigenous speakers.

These two national surveys aimed to understand the current situation of Indigenous language usage. The surveys included an Indigenous language situation questionnaire and an Indigenous language ability questionnaire. The first survey was conducted in 2012 targeting the Kuvalan, Thao, Tsou, Kanakanavu, and Hla'alua tribes in Taiwan. Out of 8,494 Indigenous persons from the five tribes, 2,112 participated in the study. The survey showed that among the five tribes, the percentage of participants who spoke their Indigenous language was the lowest among the Hla'alua tribe (Table 1). The majority of these speakers were over 61 years old. The Tsou tribe had the highest percentage of middle schoolers (seventh grade to ninth grade) who can speak their mother tongue and the highest percentage of speakers who feel their Indigenous language abilities are fluent. Among the other four tribes, only 1.0–5.0% of the participants reported fluency in their Indigenous language.

In the second survey (Table 2) conducted in 2013 by the Council of Indigenous Peoples, the targeted groups included: Amis, Bunun, Puyuma, Saisiyat, Tao, and

Table 1 Indigenous language usage among participants of the first Indigenous language survey (Data adopted from the Council of Indigenous People's Indigenous Language Report (2016a))

Name of tribe	Number of participants	Percentage of Indigenous language speakers (%)	Percentage of participants >61 years old who can speak an Indigenous language (%)	Percentage of middle school students (grades 7–9) who can speak an Indigenous language (%)	Percentage of the speakers who feel their Indigenous language is fluent (%)
Kuvalan	384	47.0	85.5	17.8	2.0
Thao	239	26.2	43.5	11.0	3.0
Tsou	1028	61.4	86.0	34.3	25.7
Kanakanavu	207	32.0	75.0	19.5	5.0
Hla'alua	254	10.6	47.6	4.6	1.0

Table 2 Indigenous language usages among participants of the second Indigenous language survey (Data adopted from the Council of Indigenous People's Indigenous Language Report (2016a))

Name of tribe	Dialect	Number of participants	Percentage of Indigenous language speakers (%)	Percentage of participants >61 years old who can speak an Indigenous language (%)	Percentage of middle school students (grades 7–9) who can speak an Indigenous language (%)	Percentage of the speakers who feel their Indigenous language is fluent (percent varied across age group) (%)
Amis	Northern Amis	819	48.1	84.6	16.7	2–14
Amis	Central Amis	1353	53.0	86.0	22.0	2–14
Amis	Costal Amis	2455	55.8	86.9	33.3	2–17
Amis	Malan Amis	884	61.9	93.6	9.7	2–26
Amis	Hengchun Amis	341	49.6	87.5	19.6	1–18
Bunun	Takituduh	276	46.0	85.0	9.7	1–18
Bunun	Takibakha	364	68.7	100	50.0	0–11
Bunun	Takivatan	243	64.6	84.3	32.5	3–15
Bunun	Takbanuaz	573	58.8	90.5	32.4	1–15
Puyuma	Nanwang	284	35.6	84.8	3.2	1–15
Puyuma	Katratripul	227	21.1	54.2	5.4	0–6
Puyuma	Ulivelivek	321	28.7	77.1	1.9	2–19
Puyuma	Kasavakan	179	33.0	81.3	5.9	2–19
Saisiyat		1143	31.9	81.8	13.9	2–19
Tao		1002	74.9	92.2	59.4	1–28
Sakizaya		295	69.8	95.5	46.2	2–4

Sakizaya. Different dialects within each tribe were also surveyed, among which, the Amis and Bunun tribes had five different dialects each, and the Puyuma had four different dialects, while the remaining three languages have only a single dialect, for a total of 17 Indigenous dialects surveyed. The total population from these six tribes is 280,736 Indigenous persons, and 12,177 of them were randomly sampled to participate in the study. A high proportion of subjects surveyed from the Tao, Sakizaya, Bunun, and Amis tribes still speak their traditional dialect. However, most of the speakers were elders aged 61 years or older. The percentage of young people who can speak their traditional dialects was relatively low and a smaller portion of people felt their Indigenous language was fluent.

These data suggested that Indigenous languages are losing their vitality. Differences were found across regions, dialects, and age groups in regards to the use of Indigenous languages. Overall, the loss of Indigenous languages was more severe in nontraditional territories compared to traditional territories. Most Indigenous language speakers were elders, and major loss of Indigenous language was observed among the group aged 30–40. Most of the participants reported speaking Indigenous languages with family, during traditional ceremonies, or in tribal gatherings. Although Indigenous languages are less used among Indigenous peoples, most participants did report positive attitudes toward the revitalization of Indigenous languages, suggesting that the effort to promote and revitalize Indigenous languages has some positive effects.

Students' Attitudes Toward Learning Indigenous Languages

The Council of Indigenous Peoples has been publishing annual reports on Indigenous Education since 1998. In 2014, they assessed Indigenous students' attitudes toward learning Indigenous languages. The survey was conducted with seventh grade Indigenous students in both regular middle schools and Indigenous middle schools. According to Article 3 of the Education Act of Indigenous Peoples, Indigenous middle schools are schools where the student population consists of more than one-third Indigenous students. The survey found the number of students who understand their mother tongue was low based on the students' self-reported listening ability. Only 4.24% reported to be at expert level, meaning they fully understand the spoken language (Table 3). In regards to speaking ability, the majority of the students reported having novice levels (Table 4). A higher percentage of Indigenous middle school students reported understanding the language compared to those students who study at regular middle schools. This suggests that environment is an important factor affecting students' ability to speak in their mother tongue and that the mainstream education curricula may have suppressed students' ability to learn Indigenous languages.

Singing is a type of verbal expression that can help students understand their mother tongues. Traditional songs can especially help with sentence retention, remembering traditional stories, and other historical content. Indigenous peoples in Taiwan historically used songs and rituals to communicate with nature and with each other. Sawtoy (2016) pointed out that songs and dances are central to the traditional Amis culture. During religious rituals, celebrations, work, and leisure time, Amis people sing and dance to express their feelings and emotions. Indigenous elders use chanting to pass down oral history from one generation to another. It has been said by Indigenous peoples that, "songs make up our being" (Sawtoy 2016). Students' Indigenous language ability has also been evaluated by their ability to sing traditional melodies and folk songs. The survey on students' ability to sing Indigenous songs shows that more than half of the students knew at least a few songs. Similar to their language ability, a higher percentage of students from Indigenous Middle

Table 3 Self-reported Indigenous language listening ability among seventh grade Indigenous students (Data adopted from the Council of Indigenous Peoples (2014))

School	Total (N)	Expert (%)	Intermediate (%)	Novice-intermediate (%)	Novice-low (%)	Cannot understand (%)	Did not respond (%)
Indigenous middle schools	1748	6.12	31.92	17.62	37.53	5.78	1.03
Regular middle schools	3985	3.41	19.15	13.90	46.35	16.51	0.68
Total	5733	4.24	23.04	15.04	43.66	13.24	0.78

Table 4 Self-reported Indigenous language speaking ability among seventh grade Indigenous students (Data adopted from the Council of Indigenous Peoples (2014))

School	Total (N)	Expert (%)	Intermediate (%)	Novice-intermediate (%)	Novice-low (%)	Do not speak (%)	No response (%)
Indigenous middle schools	1629	2.95	5.77	55.37	30.69	4.54	0.68
Regular middle schools	3300	1.64	4.03	43.79	42.73	7.15	0.67
Total	4929	2.07	4.61	47.62	38.75	6.29	0.67

Schools indicated familiarity with Indigenous songs (Council of Indigenous Peoples 2014a).

One of the biggest challenges for Indigenous language revitalization is that younger Indigenous people do not communicate daily in their mother tongues anymore. The 2014 survey showed that only 6.83% of students reported using their mother tongue every day. The low rate of Indigenous language communication among young Indigenous students makes revitalization work even more challenging. Student motivation and attitude are important concerns for promoting Indigenous language education. When asked about students' perception of Indigenous languages in society, more than half of the students reported few people speak their Indigenous language as the first language. When students hold this kind of perception, they may feel there are not enough people with whom they can communicate using their Indigenous language. This saps motivation for them to speak or to learn Indigenous languages. However, most students do hold a positive attitude about using Indigenous languages. The survey also indicated that the majority of the students agreed that speaking their Indigenous language is the responsibility of all Indigenous people, and that parents should teach their children Indigenous languages. Students agreed that speaking Indigenous languages is a means for cultural inheritance and were proud of their

Indigenous culture and languages. When asking students the reason preventing them from speaking Indigenous languages, most students reported, "using Indigenous language is not very convenient to communicate with others" (38.64%). Other reasons reported included, "not being able to speak Indigenous languages even though my parents can speak the mother tongue" (26.13%), "people around me do not speak Indigenous language" (21.16%), "personal psychological factors" (15.09%), "Indigenous languages were not taught in school" (8.75%), and "parents do not speak Indigenous languages" (6.50%). The reasons reported by students enrolled in regular school and Indigenous middle schools were comparable.

Despite the fact that Indigenous languages are not widely used in daily conversation, most Indigenous students in seventh grade were willing to learn Indigenous languages. More than 50% of seventh grade Indigenous students in regular middle schools reported high interest in learning Indigenous languages and only 1.95% reported no interest at all.

As most Indigenous parents lose the ability to communicate with their children in Indigenous languages, the role of Indigenous language teachers becomes crucial. The responsibility to pass on Indigenous languages is being placed on schools and Indigenous teachers. Stakeholders often challenge this approach to language revitalization. 79.87% of the Indigenous middle schools and 80.01% of the Indigenous elementary schools reported difficulties in teaching Indigenous languages (Council of Indigenous Peoples 2014). Reasons for the hardship were threefold. First, the school reported that students did not express a high interest in learning Indigenous languages. Second, students came from different tribes, resulting in a small student body for each language, thus making it hard to allocate enough resources for each language. Third, schools reported difficulty in finding Indigenous language teachers. In elementary schools, similar problems were noted. In addition, a lack of supportive environment to learn Indigenous languages at home and in local communities was reported. Funding and Indigenous language curricula, in contrast, were of less of concern.

The above revelations indicate that fewer and fewer Indigenous students are using Indigenous languages in daily life. The force of assimilation of the Han Chinese mainstream dialect is silent yet powerful. Indigenous languages in Taiwan now face endangerment. Fortunately, most Indigenous students showed positive cultural identity and high interest in learning Indigenous languages. Another major difficulty in current Indigenous language education is the small teaching force. More Indigenous language teachers are desperately needed in order to revitalize the language for the next generation (Council of Indigenous Peoples 2014). In the next section of the article, policy efforts on revitalizing Indigenous language will be presented.

Indigenous Language Education Policy and Projects in Taiwan

The discussion on Indigenous language education policy and projects can be divided into national and local levels. Council of Indigenous Peoples and Ministry of Education are the two primary national level governmental agencies charged with administering Indigenous language education.

Major projects from the Council of Indigenous Peoples will be presented first, including the Six-Year Indigenous Cultural Revitalization and Development Project, Six-Year Indigenous Language Revitalization Project, Indigenous Language Proficiency Certification, and training of Indigenous language teachers, followed by discussions on the efforts made by the Ministry of Education. At the end of this section, example projects carried out by local governments will be presented.

Council of Indigenous Peoples

Six-Year Indigenous Cultural Revitalization and Development Project

Indigenous language research, preservation, and heritage were one of the mandated areas for the Council of Indigenous Peoples at its establishment in 1996. Starting in 1999, the Six-Year Indigenous Cultural Revitalization and Development Project encompassed Indigenous language revitalizations (The first 6- Year Indigenous Language Revitalization Project 2008). The main goals of the first Six-Year Indigenous Cultural Revitalization and Development Project (1999–2004) included (1) reconstruction of tribal history, (2) establishment of Indigenous academy to promote cultural education, (3) construction of Indigenous museums, (4) promotion of cultural development among Indigenous teenagers, (5) training and empowerment of Indigenous persons and groups, and (6) Indigenous language revitalization.

After the completion of the first Six-Year project, a second Six-Year Indigenous Cultural Revitalization and Development Project (2008–2013) was proposed, with a total budget of approximately USD$ 3.3 million (The second 6-Year Indigenous cultural revitalization and development project 2008; The Second 6-Year Indigenous Language Revitalization Project 2014). Its aims were (1) training of Indigenous professionals in history, culture, and art (including Indigenous Youth Cultural Enrichment Program); (2) research on Indigenous history, culture, and art; (3) enrichment of Indigenous museums; (4) creating environments to develop Indigenous music and dance; (5) subsidies for Indigenous communities to host traditional rituals and ceremonies; (6) promotion of all forms of artistic events; and (7) setting up offices for Indigenous cultural revitalization.

Compared to the first Six-Year project, the second placed more emphasis on art and culture. Due to the large scope of Indigenous language revitalization, a separate program was proposed that focused specifically on language revitalization efforts.

Six-Year Indigenous Language Revitalization Project

Indigenous languages education was included in the first Cultural Revitalization and Development Project, but the results were inconclusive. Due to the large scope and efforts required for language revitalization, a new project specifically focused on Indigenous languages was initiated in 2008. The funding for this project came from the central government, with a total budget of approximately USD$ 23.6 million. This is the most important project for Indigenous language education, as it is the biggest nationwide project to target Indigenous languages specifically. The project had ten primary goals: (1) strengthen Indigenous language legislation; (2) establish Indigenous language organizations; (3) develop dictionaries for Indigenous languages and Indigenous language curricula; (4) promote research on Indigenous languages and development; (5) cultivate Indigenous language revitalization staff; (6) promote family-, tribal-, and community-based learning of Indigenous languages; (7) utilize multimedia and digital technology for teaching Indigenous languages; (8) implement Indigenous Language Proficiency Certification; (9) collect traditional and modern Indigenous songs; and (10) train specialists to translate policy, law, and regulations into Indigenous languages. The ultimate goals of the project are to preserve Indigenous languages as living languages in hope that, 1 day, Indigenous languages can be incorporated as official languages of Taiwan.

After the implementation of the First Six-Year Indigenous Language Revitalization Project, several problems were identified, including the slow progress on language revitalization, the rise of diverse learning media, the hardship of promoting the Indigenous Writing System, the urgency of saving endangered languages, and the lack of Indigenous language specialists. In addition, the numerous dialects and their complexity made the language revitalization process even more challenging. In the Second Six-Year Indigenous Language Revitalization Project (2014–2019), six main goals were set out to address these challenges. The first goal is to strengthen the connection between Indigenous languages and families where languages are used. There it is vital to create a family learning environment. It is evident that reviving the connection is essential to ensure successful languages revitalization. To build on the experience of the first 6-year program, the second 6-year program will continue to work on making "speaking and learning Indigenous languages" the trend in the Indigenous society.

The second goal is to build a comprehensive learning system from the cradle to the grave. The emphasis is placed in developing a systematic learning process, starting with Indigenous language immersion in preschool to adult education. In addition, digital technology is employed to make learning Indigenous languages more efficiently. Apart from the abovementioned enabling environmental factors to revitalize Indigenous languages, the role of specialists should not be overlooked. Therefore, the third goal of the project is to train Indigenous language revitalization specialist. To ensure specialists being sustainable, a comprehensive training system for Indigenous language revitalization specialists is warranted, including four levels of training (basic, beginner, advanced, and professional). Collaboration is urgently needed with higher education institutions that provide master and PhD programs in Indigenous language studies. Funding for short-term study abroad and for attending international conferences to facilitate experience sharing from other countries is also necessary. Of course, the presence of the specialists alone cannot guarantee the success of revitalization because what is being taught matters. This brings us to the fourth goal: the curricula. The Indigenous language learning curricula has to be diversified. Three sets of curricula had been developed in the first Six-Year Project

("Words," "Daily Conversation," and "Reading and Writing"). Advanced-level curricula (such as "Cultural and Creative Work") and other diverse curricula will be developed, such as children's books, translated books, Indigenous literature, and grammar books. An online database on Indigenous language resources and e-learning website will be established under this project. Diversifying the Indigenous language curricula is the first step to fully recognize the language rights of the Indigenous peoples, which brings us to the fifth goal: language rights.

The meaning of language rights may be context-dependent. Language is a right to freedom, which shall be freely used by the people without interference by the State. At the same time, it is a social right that a State shall be obligated to promote. For Indigenous peoples, it is also a form of collective right, linked with the sustainability of its nation. Therefore, the key factor of whether this project can be successful depends on whether the state is honoring its constitutional obligation.

Lastly, the project also takes note in eliminating discrimination based on sex and promotes gender equality. The concept of gender identity and gender sensitivity shall be incorporated when implementing the Indigenous language revitalization at all stages.

Indigenous Language Proficiency Certificate

The Indigenous Language Proficiency Certificate was proposed in 2001. The Certificate provides four levels of proficiency ranking, including basic, intermediate, advance, and professional. No restriction was set on applicants' nationality, age, ethnicity, or education level. In 2014, the Indigenous language proficiency test required for the Affirmative Action for Indigenous Students was incorporated into the Indigenous Language Proficiency Certificate program. Currently, certifications are available for 16 language groups and 42 dialects and are given in 16 test sites. According to a survey conducted by the Council of Indigenous Peoples (2014a), most of the Certificates were granted for Amis, Paiwan, and Bunun languages. Between 2001 and 2011, a total of 17,165 people had applied for the certificate and 8321 people passed the test. The development of a test bank and practices tests was initiated in 2008.

Training of Indigenous Language Teachers

No formal educational training is required for Indigenous language teachers at this point. The Council of Indigenous Peoples hosted training workshops to prepare fluent speakers who had obtained the Indigenous Language Proficiency Certificate to become teachers. By 2011, more than 4000 people had attended the workshops (Council of Indigenous Peoples 2014). Opportunity for observational learning was provided based on different curricula. A database of qualified Indigenous language specialists was built in 2008. More than 5000 people who had obtained the Indigenous Language Proficiency Certificate or had attended the training workshop were registered in the database (Council of Indigenous Peoples 2014).

Online Learning Materials

The Council of Indigenous Peoples developed online learning materials to meet the growing demand of online learning in the forms of online dictionaries, e-Books, and an e-learning platform.

Indigenous Language Online Dictionary (2016e) began its development in 2007. Sixteen online dictionaries are currently available, one for each of the 16 officially recognized tribes. The dictionary provides search functions from and to Mandarin Chinese. The dictionaries can be downloaded for offline use. Other learning materials on the website include downloadable vocabulary flashcards, vocabulary games and assessments. The website has on average 15,000 viewers per day, and a total of 9.8 million views up to June 2016 (Indigenous Language Online Dictionary 2016e).

Indigenous Language E-Park is the central platform for Indigenous languages learning, it provides downloadable textbooks, multimedia materials (videos and interactive children's books), online games, teaching materials and resources for teachers, and links relevant to Indigenous languages (Council of Indigenous Peoples 2016a). Another online e-learning platform is the Indigenous e-Learning website, which provides downloadable textbooks and teaching materials, video courses, and online courses (Indigenous e-Learning 2014b). Courses in vocabulary, songs, and stories are available for 14 Indigenous languages. There are currently a total of 42 courses available on the website now. An Android App "Indigenous Language Genius" is also available (Council of Indigenous Peoples 2016a). It provides the learning curricula for grade 9–12. However, no statistics are yet available on the utilization frequency of these e-learning materials.

Taiwan Indigenous eBooks, which is available in both website and mobile App format, provides 355 eBooks in 16 different Indigenous languages. More than 7,000 reads had been recorded at the end of June 2016 (Taiwan Indigenous eBooks 2016c).

Indigenous Language Research and Development Center

Funded in 2013, the Indigenous Language Research and Development Center was established on the basis of Article 9 of the Indigenous Peoples Basic Law, which states "the government shall establish (a) special unit responsible for indigenous language researches and (an) indigenous language proficiency evaluation system in order to actively engage in the promotion of indigenous language development." The five mandated goals for the center included: (1) research on loanwords and new words; (2) research on the Indigenous Language Proficiency Certification test and the construction of a test bank; (3) research on Indigenous language teaching methods, including curricula assessment and development; (4) research on grammar and word formulation; and (5) research on Indigenous language revitalization (Indigenous Language Research and Development Center 2016f).

Some examples of the work accomplished by the center include hosting international conferences on Indigenous languages, translation of western literature texts into 16 Indigenous languages (Palemeq 2016) and publishing research findings on loanwords, new words, and the language revitalization process (Indigenous Language Research and Development Center 2016f). The center is also very active in disseminating information on social media to engage with a broader audience.

Ministry of Education

Prior to the establishment of the Council of Indigenous Peoples, the Ministry of Education had started to develop and compile Indigenous language curricula as part of its Indigenous Education Development and Improvement Projects. In 2006, the Ministry initiated the Indigenous Education Development Five-Year Midterm Case Project (2006–2010) to encompass Indigenous language teaching into the Local Dialect classes required for primary schools. The Ministry also developed learning assessment methods and a training system for Indigenous teachers. In higher education institutions, the Ministry of Education set up programs for Indigenous studies, task forces for Indigenous language teaching, and Indigenous Research and Development Centers.

To establish an Indigenous writing system, the Ministry first commissioned Professor Paul Jen-Kuei Li to develop the Austronesian Language Symbol System (1994). The system was later replaced by the Indigenous Language Writing System to ensure consistency (Council of Indigenous Peoples and Ministry of Education 2005).

Progress concerning indigenous education can be observed from the White Paper for Indigenous Education Policy (2011) published by the Ministry of Education. In the white paper, Indigenous languages education was pointed out as one of the key issues in Indigenous education (Ministry of Education 2011). Instead of having a ministry-wide program, small projects were implemented to promote Indigenous language education across different sectors in the Ministry. The Ministry of Education's annual educational report provides detailed examples of the programs that had been implemented in promoting Indigenous languages. To sum up, two measures can be delineated when it comes to promote indigenous languages: institutional reform and the development of language tools.

First, institutional reform took place within the educational system at both elementary and tertiary level. Indigenous language teaching was implemented at kindergarten level during 2014–2015, and grants were provided for local government to institute educational programs for this type of mother tongue language education. On the other hand, nine universities formed associations to train elementary school teachers and set up local language educational centers in schools. These centers are responsible for the development and promotion of local language programs.

Second, language tools were developed to facilitate an indigenous language-friendly environment. The tools include "Taiwan Indigenous Language and History Encyclopedia," "Indigenous Language Wikipedia," Fifth Edition of the Basic Indigenous Language Teaching Materials, "Neologism for Indigenous Language," and "Indigenous Language Writing System." Awards and seminars were created to consolidate people's motivation to use these tools. These tools are further strengthened through programs and activities, including National Indigenous Reading and Speech Contest, Mother Tongue Language Contribution Award, and stipend provided to local organizations promoting Indigenous languages based on the Local Language Education Aid Policy.

Local Governments

Local governments refer to the 13 county governments and 6 municipal city governments in Taiwan. Every year the Council of Indigenous Peoples allocated budgets to collaborate with local governments and civil society organizations to establish "language nests" or "tribal classrooms," Indigenous language classes, and Indigenous cultural experience camps (Chao 2014). Successful implementation required strong will and collaboration effort from the local governments. Some local government also initiated efforts on Indigenous language educations in addition to the aids from the central governments. For example, Taipei City Government began the "Indigenous language nest" program in 2001, which provided 2 h of class each week for 11 Indigenous languages. In 2010, a total of 35 language nests teaching 10 languages had been established. On average, 378 people attended the language nests each month, but only 10.64% of them were under 18 years of age (Hsieh 2010). Other programs initiated by the Taipei City Government included holding training camps for Indigenous language teachers, editing Indigenous language textbook, hosting Indigenous cultural events, and broadcasting Indigenous language and culture education on the radio (Indigenous Peoples Commission of Taipei City Government 2003). Similar language nest programs were implemented by New Taipei City, Taoyuan City, Kaohsiung City, Hsinchu City, Tainan City, Taidong, Pingtung, Hualien, and Yilian. Other examples for promoting Indigenous language included hosting drama contests, vocabulary contests, and speech contests in Indigenous languages to raise learning incentives.

In 2016, the Pingtung County Government held an International Austronesian Language Education Forum for the first time. More than 250 Indigenous language education practitioners participated in the Forum. The Forum invited three international experts in Maori (New Zealand), Ainu (Japan), and Sami (Norway) languages to share their experiences on the language revitalization. The Forum not only generated tangible recommendations but also prompted local people to action. The impact of this local event was nationwide. The Forum engaged local Indigenous elders with scholars. This type of bottom-up effort showed that the awareness for Indigenous language revitalization is growing in Taiwan.

Future Project

In 2016, the Council of Indigenous People and the Ministry of Education joined efforts to develop an Indigenous Education Five-Year Midterm Development Project (2016–2020). The Project places an emphasis on "self-determination, equality, respect, diversity, and honor," with a center focus on "cultivating the next Indigenous generation and equipping them with competitiveness, cultural awareness, and self-determination" and to "regain basic rights, affirm fundamental learning, initiate cultural education, and practice multicultural goals." Language revitalization and promotion were not stated directly in the project (Council of Indigenous Peoples and Ministry of Education 2015). To achieve a true practice of cultural education, a solid plan of Indigenous language revitalization must be established. The Project, which laid out 12 strategies, 35 execution items, and 148 specific actions, lacked of tangible focus on Indigenous languages. A detailed plan for language reconstruction for Indigenous education is highly recommended by the authors of this chapter. Other observation based on the direction and actions of the 2016–2020 Five-Year Project included:

1. The trend to self-learning has begun even with limited policy endorsement and funding. With time and more policy endorsements, it will become a common norm.
2. Through years of discussion, concrete policies and legal bases have been established for Indigenous education. More funding is also available. Indigenous peoples' opinions have been more accepted by mainstream society.
3. Though the overall condition of Indigenous peoples is improving, there are still traces of discrimination toward this minority population. It is a long road with many challenges waiting for Indigenous education toward sustainability and maturation.
4. Many of the languages for the smaller tribes are nearly impossible to revitalize. However, digital recording can help keep records of these languages, in hopes that these endangered languages could be preserved for future revitalization efforts.

Challenges on Indigenous Language Education

Despite efforts, Indigenous language development in Taiwan continues to face challenges. In identifying these challenges, it enables us to see where we can further progress. First, one of the biggest challenges has been a lack of coherent policy direction taken by the Ministry of Education and the Council of Indigenous Peoples. These two government agencies have carried out parallel and duplicate efforts on Indigenous language education. The inadequate collaboration results in wasted resources and time. For instance, the Ministry of Education previously spent millions of Taiwanese dollars on developing local dialect curricula for 13 different Indigenous languages, but they were later shelved (Chao 2014). The lack of consensus on the Indigenous Writing Systems in the beginning also staggered the revitalization progress. Horizontal communications between central governmental agencies and vertical communications between central governmental agencies, schools, and local governments were laborious, and very little attention was paid to assessing project outcomes (Hung 2014). This problem has been noted and addressed in the most current Indigenous Education Five-Year Midterm Development Project, which is a joint project by the Ministry of Education and the Council of Indigenous Peoples. Effective communication between the Ministry of Education and the Council of Indigenous Peoples is central to creating sustainable collaboration.

Second, not having an independent system to train Indigenous language teachers is a severe challenge to sustain indigenous language education. The initial approach by the Ministry of Education was to train Indigenous schoolteachers who already held valid teaching licenses to become Indigenous language teachers. Short-term training workshops on Indigenous languages were available to the teachers. However, most of the Indigenous schoolteachers did not have the ability to speak Indigenous languages fluently; thus, most of the teaching was accomplished by Indigenous language specialists who did not have any formal education training (The Education and Culture Committee of the Control Yuan 2003). Indigenous schoolteachers were not required to attend the language workshops to teach Indigenous languages, and there exists no assessment of their language proficiency. For Indigenous language specialists who do not hold a teaching license, they must obtain Indigenous Language Proficiency Certification in order to teach in public schools. The Indigenous language specialists responsible for the actual teaching expressed that Indigenous language education does not have a clear place in the school system and most schools lack Indigenous cultural sensitivity (Huang 2004). The Ministry of Education has made some progress to incorporate Indigenous language in higher education institutions, such as the institution of local language educational centers in universities (Ministry of Education 2015). A formal education program for Indigenous languages teachers can help them gain more respect in the schools and facilitate the promotion of Indigenous languages in the formal education system. Because there is no independent training system, Indigenous language teachers gain their qualifications by cobbling together fragmented policies. Consequently, teaching indigenous languages is still largely ignored by the formal education system. For this reason, it is necessary that Indigenous peoples need to have our own independent training system.

Third, Indigenous peoples' language revitalization cannot be realized without an increase in designated teaching hours coupled with additional resources. Currently, only one class (40 min) is allocated for Indigenous language per week in public schools (first grade to ninth grade). The effect of a single hour of language learning per week is minimal. Most schools schedule the class during nonofficial class hours (early mornings or weekends). Some schools mix students from different grades or different languages in the same class. The lack of classroom space forces some teachers to teach in the gym or in the hallway. Indigenous language specialists who assist in teaching primary schools usually did not have enough support or respect from school officials. Many of them need to travel from school to school in order to maintain full-time employment status (Hung 2014). These conditions discourage passionate teachers and create new obstacles to guaranteeing Indigenous peoples' rights to a sustainable language education.

Fourth, a proper legislative framework is urgently needed to promote indigenous languages at the preschool level. The critical window for learning language is between 5 and 7 years old. Indigenous language immersion preschool can lay the foundation for Indigenous language learning (Pawan 2006). There are currently 20 experimental Indigenous language-immersion kindergartens (Council of Indigenous Peoples 2016b). The lack of legislative framework leads to insufficient funds and resources for the preschool level.

Following are tentative recommendations to meet the challenges delineated above. The following aspects are important for the future work of promoting indigenous language education. Firstly, identify those who are still able to speak indigenous languages fluently. These people are key to revitalize indigenous languages and preserve indigenous language-friendly environments. More awareness for language rights in schools and other public sectors needs to be generated. In addition, the revitalization process will benefit from the self-initiating wills from each tribe. Each tribe should be given the resources and power to manage and revitalize its own language and create a safe and convenient environment to practice these languages. Furthermore, family is the foundation to establish good learning environment for Indigenous languages. Increasing the number of children who start learning Indigenous languages from an early age is the most sustainable way to save endangered languages. Secondly, an adequate allocation of resources from the central government to local governments and institutions is necessary. Empowering those people who work closely with their own culture and language will help maximize the effects of revitalization. Retired Indigenous persons would prove an enormous asset to help educate the new generation to speak Indigenous languages. Third, creation of a platform for experience exchanges can allow experts and scholars to work collectively toward language preservation and revitalization that attracts new talent. For example, international conferences on Indigenous language education are an effective means to highlight the importance of practicing Indigenous languages in daily life. The platform can also document the efforts for long-term assessment and evaluation.

Finally but importantly, the journey of language revitalization should be conceptualized in a long-term scale where new ideas and innovations are constantly being incorporated. Many Indigenous languages are slowly being replaced by mainstream languages; new ideas are currently needed for language revitalization, especially for those languages that are on the brink of extinction. Revitalization is possible with the help of the government, academia, and NGOs. Endangered languages require more attention and specially dedicated research teams to persist long term in helping local tribes maintain their linguistic identities by creating a lively learning environment.

Conclusion

Recent international trends and new policies brought new opportunities and acceptances for Indigenous languages in Taiwan. Indigenous languages are vital to Indigenous peoples' identities and community development, but the extent of achieving revitalization is linked to Indigenous peoples' social status. Many Indigenous peoples have not yet realized the importance of language revitalization because they are under great social and economic pressure. In addition, the lack of Indigenous language specialists is the biggest concern for Indigenous language development in Taiwan. Indigenous people need to utilize these given revitalization resources and work toward a common goal. This chapter aims to serve as a reference for the international Indigenous language education community and also act as a starting point for future language revitalization for Indigenous peoples in Taiwan.

References

Bellwood P (1991) The Austronesian dispersal and the origin of languages. Sci Am 265:88–93. https://doi.org/10.1038/scientificamerican0791-88

Blust R (1984) The Austronesian homeland: a linguistic perspective. Asian Perspect 26(1):45–67

Chao S-C (2014) Táiwān yuán zhù mínzú yǔ jiàoyù zhèngcè zhī pīpàn lùnshù fēnxī (The critical discourse analysis of Taiwan Indigenous language education policy). Kèchéngyánjiū (J Curric Stud) 9(2):053–078. https://doi.org/10.3966/181653382014090902003

Chen L-Y (2004) Táiwān yuán zhùmín yùndòng yǔ yuán zhùmín jiàoyù zhèngcè guānxì zhī tàntǎo (The relationship between policy and Indigenous movements for Indigenous education in Taiwan). Yuán zhùmín jiàoyù jikān 34:27–46

Council of Indigenous Peoples (2014a) Yuán zhù mínzú jiàoyù diàochá tǒngjì (Indigenous education survey). http://www.ns.org.tw/download.asp. Accessed 22 June 2017

Council of Indigenous Peoples (2014b) Indigenous e-Learning. http://e-learning.apc.gov.tw/default.aspx. Accessed 24 June 2016

Council of Indigenous Peoples (2016a) Indigenous language network. http://web.klokah.tw. Accessed 24 June 2016

Council of Indigenous Peoples (2016b) Jìntòu shì zú yǔ jiàoxué yòu'éryuán (Immersion Indigenous language Kindergarten). http://kindergarten.klokah.tw. Accessed 22 June 2017

Council of Indigenous Peoples (2016c) Taiwan Indigenous eBooks. http://alilin.apc.gov.tw/tw. Accessed 24 June 2016

Council of Indigenous Peoples (2016d) Yuán zhù mínzú yǔyán diàochá yánjiū sān nián shíshī jì huà (3 year project on Indigenous language survey). http://alilin.apc.gov.tw/files/ebook/30617674756c2e9fc961d7/_SWF_Window.html. Accessed 22 June 2017

Council of Indigenous Peoples (2016e) Indigenous language online dictionary. http://e-dictionary.apc.gov.tw/Index.htm. Accessed 24 June 2016

Council of Indigenous Peoples (2016f) Indigenous Language Research and Development Center. http://ilrdc.tw/. Accessed 24 June 2016

Council of Indigenous Peoples and Ministry of Education (2005) Yuán zhù mínzú yǔyán shūxiě xìtǒng (Indigenous language writing system). http://dore.tacp.gov.tw/tacp/ebook/apc110003_bbog_oth20090813031/index.html. Accessed 22 June 2017

Council of Indigenous Peoples and Ministry of Education (2015). Fāzhǎn yuán zhù mínzú jiàoyù wǔ nián zhōng chéng jì huà 105–109 (Five-year Indigenous education development midterm project, 2016–2020). Taipei

Digital Museum of Taiwan Indigenous Peoples (2016) Yuán zhùmín wénhuà nián biǎo (Indigenous culture chronology). http://www.dmtip.gov.tw/Museum/Article.aspx?CategoryID=15. Accessed 22 June 2017

Education Act for Indigenous Peoples (1998). Ministry of Education, Republic of China (Taiwan)

Hsieh J-L (2010) Xuéxí shèqū huà huóluò dūshì yuán zhù mínzú yǔ (Community learning of Indigenous languages in urban areas) Táiběi yuányě diànzǐ bào, 20. http://epaper.taipei.gov.tw/public/epaperHTML/08251232871/04.htm?id=n04. Accessed 22 June 2017

Huang LM-J (2004) Táiwān yuán zhù mínzú yǔ jiàoyù xiànkuàng jí zhǎnwàng – zú yǔ zǒngtǐ xuéxí huánjìng zhī yíngzào (Current situation and prospect of Indigenous language education in

Taiwan – create comprehensive learning environment of the Indigenous language). In: Ethnic and cultural development conference, Taipei

Huang LM-J (2015) Development and future prospective on Indigenous languages Indigenous. Language Research and Development Center 2015 annual report round table discussion, 15 Dec 2015, Taipei

Hung Y-Y "Sukudi" (2014) Yuán zhù mínzú zú yǔ jiàoxué zhī wǒ jiàn (My view on Indigenous language education). Xīn shìjì zhìkù lùntán 65:48–51

Indigenous Peoples Commission of Taipei City Government (2003) A special report of Indigenous language nest in Taipei. Indigenous Peoples Commission of Taipei City Government, Taipei

Lee H-H (2004) Táiwān lìshǐ gè shíqí yǔyán zhèngcè zhī fēnxī bǐjiào (Comparison of language policy in each historic period in Taiwan). In: Yǔyán rénquán yǔ yǔyán fù zhèn xuéshù yántǎo huì lùnwén jí. Department of Language Education at Taidong Univeristy, Taidong

Li PJ-K (1994) Zhōngguó yǔwén táiwān nándǎo yǔyán de yǔyīn fúhào xìtǒng (Chinese language Taiwan Austronesian language symbol system). Ministry of Education, Republic of China (Taiwan), Taipei

Li T-Y (2007) Táiwān yuán zhù mínzú yǔyán yánjiū shǐ jí qí pínggū (The history of the research on Taiwanese Aboriginal languages and the evaluation of the research history). Zhèngdà mínzú xuébào 26:165–190

Lim S-T (2003) Yuán zhù mínzú de zú yǔ jiàoyù gàikuàng (Overview of Indigenous language education). Yánxí zīxùn 20(1):35–40

Ministry of Education (2011) White book on Indigenous education. Ministry of Education, Republic of China (Taiwan), Taipei

Ministry of Education (2015) 104 Yuán zhùmín jiàoyù tuīdòng chéngxiào gàikuàng bàogào (Annual progress report on the promotion of Indigenous education in Taiwan). https://indigenous.moe.gov.tw/EducationAborigines/Article/Details/3059. Accessed 24 June 2016

Palemeq Y (2016) Connect with the world through translation: a case with Taiwanese Indigenous languages. The development of Taiwanese Indigenous media and languages on 31th May, 2016 at Festival of Pacific Arts, Guam

Palemeq Y, Muzuer A (2015) Relevant regulations on Indigenous languages in Taiwan. Indigenous Language Research and Development Center. http://ilrdc.tw/research/policy/law.php. Accessed 24 June 2016

Pawan C (2006) Cóng niǔ xī lán máolì zú de yǔyán cháo kàn táiwān de yuán zhùmín mǔyǔ jiàoxué (From Maori language nest to reflect Indigenous language education in Taiwan). Taiwan Int Stud Q 2(1):163–184

RIS (2016) Tái mǐn xiàn shìyuán zhù mínzú rén☐☐kǒu (Census on Indigenous population). Ministry of the Interior, R.O.C (Taiwan), Taipei

Sawtoy S (2016) Oral folklore and literature of love. The development of Taiwanese Indigenous media and languages on 31th May, 2016 at Festival of Pacific Arts, Guam

Taiwan Indigenous People's Knowledge Economic Development Association (2016) Distribution of Indigenous peoples in Taiwan. http://www.twedance.org/aboriginal00.aspx. Accessed 24 June 2016

The Education and Culture Committee of the Control Yuan (2003) An investigation study on the problems of native language instruction in the elementary school. The Control Yuan, Taipei

The First 6-Year Indigenous Cultural Revitalization and Development Project (1999) Council of Indigenous Peoples, Republic of China (Taiwan), Taipei

The First 6-Year Indigenous Language Revitalization Project (2008) Council of Indigenous Peoples, Republic of China (Taiwan), Taipei

The Second 6-Year Indigenous Cultural Revitalization and Development Project (2008) Council of Indigenous Peoples, Republic of China (Taiwan), Taipei

The Second 6-Year Indigenous Language Revitalization Project (2014) Council of Indigenous Peoples, Republic of China (Taiwan), Taipei

Zeitoun E, Yu CH, Weng CX (2003) The Formosan language archive: development of a multimedia tool to salvage the languages and oral traditions of the indigenous tribes of Taiwan. Ocean Linguist 42(1):218–232

27 Sámi Language for All: Transformed Futures Through Mediative Education

Erika Katjaana Sarivaara and Pigga Keskitalo

Contents

Introduction	468
The Legacy of Assimilation in Sápmi	470
What Is Sámi Education?	472
Mediating Sámi Education	474
Mediating Structures in Sámi Language Revitalization	476
Conclusion	478
References	479

Abstract

This chapter deals with the mediative role of Sámi education in Sámi language revitalization. Education, in the form of mediative structures, provides the tools necessary to effect language revitalization to counter the legacy of assimilation, which has deleteriously affected Sámi people on most social measures. Mediative education is significant because it creates transformation in Indigenous communities, helping arbitration, peacemaking, resolution, and negotiation practices to flourish. This chapter focuses on mediative contexts and their instances, as well as on the implementation of mediating pedagogy in the field of Sámi education research. The chapter is theoretically constructed on the authors' respective research in Sámi education, assimilation and revitalization; it turns on the premise that language revitalization builds social harmony in a postcolonial situation, and

---

E. K. Sarivaara (✉)
Faculty of Education, University of Lapland, Rovaniemi, Finland
e-mail: erika.sarivaara@ulapland.fi; erika.sarivaara@gmail.com

P. Keskitalo
Duodji and Teacher Education, Sámi University of Applied Sciences, Kautokeino, Norway

University of Lapland, Rovaniemi, Finland
e-mail: pigga.keskitalo@samiskhs.no

© Springer Nature Singapore Pte Ltd. 2019
E. A. McKinley, L. T. Smith (eds.), *Handbook of Indigenous Education*,
https://doi.org/10.1007/978-981-10-3899-0_16

that there are certain key tasks that need to be fulfilled to recover endangered languages. The revitalization process of the Sámi languages and moreover strengthening language domains are core aims in Sámi education in Northern Europe. Crucially, attempts to nurture these languages draw on broader practices of education and human rights.

Keywords

Sámi language · Revitalization · Indigenous education · Sámi education · Mediating structures

Introduction

Relying on previous studies as well as new research, our article presents a collaborative model of language recovery, which facilitates an increase in the number of language speakers and also supports language domains. A mediating language revitalization model aims to create peace for Indigenous societies in a postcolonial situation (see Hylland Eriksen 1992; Olthuis et al. 2013). Recent research literature has focused on the present situation of the Sámi languages and aspirations for language revitalization (Lehtola 2015; Linkola 2014; Olthuis et al. 2013; Outakoski 2015; Pasanen 2015; Rasmussen 2013; Sarivaara 2016; Seurujärvi-Kari 2012; Äärelä 2015). This chapter emphasizes key tasks involved in the recovery of endangered languages. Sámi people, like many Indigenous peoples in the world, have experienced and continue to experience inequitable practices, and moreover, these have caused major societal changes and suffering in communities. Unpacking these unfair and oppressive practices has fuelled and sustained our desire to explain situation and context. How we identify the issues starts with the title "Sámi for all." We consider whether it is feasible to share the Sámi language with others, when the survival of the language is threatened.

We share a common interest in developing Sámi education and revitalizing language, and are mothers, primary school teachers, educators, Indigenous scholars, and language revitalizers. We find all these roles significant and supportive of each other, because sharing experiences within Indigenous communities empowers individuals and eventually promotes communities. Our worldviews are holistic, and our vision is characterized by passion: it is caring, joyful, loving, meaningful, cooperative, and mediating. Our interest extends to Sámi educational issues because of our common role as teacher educators. We became colleagues at the Sámi University of Applied Sciences (former Sámi University College) when Erika assumed the role of assistant professor of education in teacher training. Pigga had already commenced working there in 1999, first as an assistant professor and then as a doctoral scholarship holder in 2005. She completed her PhD in 2010. Erika completed her PhD in 2012 as a doctoral scholarship holder. Together, we desire to work toward the rethinking of linguistics, power, and policy. We concentrate on Sámi education from a critical viewpoint on Indigenous education. As a starting point, critical Sámi research aims to raise significant questions and promote Sámi issues in society (see also Sarivaara et al. 2014). Sámi are living in four countries under four school systems, school laws, and curricula. The Sámi Indigenous peoples live in the Nordic countries of central and northern Sweden, Norway, northern Finland, and on Russia's Kola Peninsula, and have long held connections to other populations. As education researchers we have wanted to write from a critical orientation about these circumstances, especially since sovereignty is limited.

This chapter is based on separate PhD doctoral and postdoctoral research projects, which are being jointly further developed. We have wanted to write together in order to learn from each other, and to share and discuss our experiences and knowledge with each other and with others. Joint projects and extended cooperation may result in broader views, which we are interested in constructing and testing. Indigenous peoples themselves need to rethink their pedagogical practices, and society also needs to be appraised of Indigenous people's issues and problems. Suoranta and Ryynänen (2014) have contributed the concept of "rebellious research" to the field of critical research. According to them, the aim of rebellious research is to change society so that it is more equal, and in which researchers take risks other than in terms of academic competition. In this respect, the roles of Indigenous scholars are often both activist and researcher. We have made it our aim to be transformative in our own research and to translate its rebelliousness into writing. In this chapter, we concentrate on the Finnish Sámi situation, although we also examine practices across the four countries Sámi live in, in order to compare different contexts. We were both born and live in Finland, although Pigga is now working in Norway in the Sámi University of Applied Sciences and Erika is in Finland at the University of Lapland.

The starting point lies in historical inequity. The current situation of Sámi necessitates looking back at the long path of assimilation, which Sámi to an extent continue to experience. Demolishing such assimilationist processes is necessary to improve the future of the Sámi language. In Finland, assimilation began with the so-called Age of Enlightenment in the 1600s (see Keskitalo et al. 2016; Rasmussen 2013). Assimilation has coincided with cultural colonization (Keskitalo et al. 2016), which has been realized in Finland through church activities since the 1600s, border establishment, Finnish nationhood building, nation schools of the 1800s (Keskitalo et al. 2014), and through increasingly replacing Sámihood with Finnish language and culture (see Paksuniemi 2009). Before the 1980s, there was hardly any support for Indigenous or minority cultures and languages in the national school system of Finland.

According to The Sámi Parliament Act, the Sámi Homeland Area covers the northern Finland municipalities Utsjoki, Inari, Enontekiö, and northern Sodankylä (traditionally, the Sámi Area was much larger). In the Sámi Homeland Area, education is divided into Finnish and Sámi speaking classes according to need. Generally, attendance at Sámi speaking classes has been for those whose mother tongue is Sámi and for those with a parent registered on a Finnish Sámi Parliament electoral roll, which acts as formal proof of Sámihood by giving a person Sámi status. One may also study the Sámi language as a foreign language for approximately 2 h per week, but currently over 75% of Sámi speaking children live outside of the Sámi Home Land area and their recourse to the study of the language is greatly limited. The Finnish Board of Education policy dictates that they can study Sámi language for only 2 h in a club teaching immigrants and Sámi people. This policy's tokenism seriously threatens the future of Sámi languages. One more proactive answer could have been the establishment of revitalization schools; however, the first was only opened in 2015 in Utsjoki.

There are currently three Sámi languages spoken in Finland. While North Sámi is the strongest language with approximately 25,000 speakers in three countries, in Finland, however, there are only about 1350 North Sámi speakers left, according to the official national statistics. Inari Sámi language has around 500 speakers and is only spoken in the municipality of Inari in Finland. Skolt Sámi language has around 500 speakers. All of the Sámi languages are considered to be seriously threatened (Rasmussen 2013). It is projected that speakers will halve in the near future if radical measures are not taken (Hylland Eriksen 1992).

The area inhabited by the Sámi is called Sápmi in Sámi language. There are approximately 100,000 Sámi living in these countries, although data collection processes are found to be inadequate, and there is hence a lack of clear demographic information about Sámi people. What can be asserted quite categorically is that the Sámi – as with many other Indigenous peoples – comprise a minority. They are recognized and protected under international conventions and declarations on the rights of Indigenous peoples and national laws and acts. Sámi livelihoods have historically been connected to the land and water. Sámi originate from hunter-gathering tribes, and traditional livelihoods are fishing, hunting, reindeer herding, and later small-scale farming. According to linguistic studies, Sámi language emerged during the second millennium BC at the latest, which also generated Sámi culture (Aikio 2004, 2006, 2012). The Sámi languages are Finno-Ugric languages; they are therefore related, for example, to the Finnish language. The primordial Finnish and Sámi are assumed to have separated at the end of Stone Age. The history of the Sámi shows various changes, notable ones including: a move from collecting culture to reindeer herding (from 1400–1600); and the disruption of their traditional ways through the arrival of settlers, together with the introduction of epidemics and the church.

The Legacy of Assimilation in Sápmi

Centuries of assimilation policies and sociolinguistic reasons have endangered Sámi languages (see Aikio 1988). Currently, Sámi are part of the globalizing world with various cultural flows and blends, and have more or less embraced urbanization (Seurujärvi-Kari 2012) and living in multiple and diverse contexts in postmodern societies. Empowerment, revitalization, education, and research are core components of the transformation and future for Indigenous peoples, each having their own set of challenges. A deliberate focus of the Sámi people, in particular, is now on recovery and language revitalization through Indigenous education, which, taken as a whole, calls for societal activism.

The assimilation processes foisted on Sámi have varied from country to country. Assimilation processes in Finland occurred rather invisibly when compared to, for example, the situation in Norway, where forced Norwegianism was enshrined in official documents. In Norway, the assimilation policy was formally implemented so that the Sámi had to be "Norwegianized." This period of enforced Norwegianism continued from approximately the 1850s to the 1980s, crucially aiming to extirpate the Sámi language and the Sámi identity (Minde 2005).

Differences within assimilation processes can make it challenging to recognize and distinguish assimilation strategies and measures. In Finland, the aim of the nationalist policy was to strengthen the position of the Finnish language and the Finnish identity. The government prioritized the ideology of nation building, in particular through a folk school system. The needs of minorities were ignored until the 1960s, when the Indigenous movement began. Sweden, meanwhile, exercised passive segregation measures, namely the *lapp-ska-vara-lapp* policy (The Lapp Should Stay Lapp policy), whereby Sámi children were sent to segregated hut schools (Henrysson 1992). Sámi in Russia have experienced limited schooling since World War II. Additionally, forced relocations stretched the capacity of the Russian Sámi (Afanasyeva 2013). Political relationships between nations over which Sápmi lies add further complexity. Historically, Finland was under Swedish Kingdom since 1100–1200 until 1809. After that, Sweden was in union with Norway. During 1809–1917, Finland was under Russia.

Border issues have indeed played a significant role in the assimilation of Sámi, often with ongoing implications. Taxes levied from Sámi people acted as a basis for shaping national borders of Lapland in Sweden, Norway, and Russia (originally Novgorod). European nationalism since 1850s also affected assimilation, and it strengthened during and after World War II. The Sámi were assumed to be a conquered people, who could only live as human by giving up old traditions and embracing a more sophisticated, settled way of life. It would not be until the first Sámi conference held in 1953 (Seurujärvi-Kari et al. 2011) that a Sámi ethnic wakening would be signaled, but formal "nation-state" boundaries had well and truly disrupted the lifestyles of Sámi in many ways – for example, nomad Sámi reindeer herding was threatened in Finland, leading to the founding of the Reindeer Herders association. Resulting controversial challenges and issues have included debates about who is a Sámi, who is allowed to herd reindeer, land usage, economics and funding, and other organizational matters.

In countries where Sámi people are living now there may be nine or ten different Sámi languages, where historically there were even more. While it is unclear whether these were all separate languages or dialects, the differences between the remaining nine or ten Sámi languages suggest that these are indeed different Sámi languages, some with different dialects. Six of these languages are written, originally developed through church activities. Before 1978 in North Sámi, there were 13 different orthographies. In Finland, the Lapland Education Society set out to create the North Sámi orthography (Jones 2012). Cooperation between the languages is now formalized in Sámi Parliaments in Finland, Sweden, and Norway.

According to our studies and perceptions, assimilation has thus, among other things, to a certain degree weakened the Sámi cultural identity and set in train a process of language shift. The process has resulted in a complex situation that has also impacted on Sámi education. Revitalization has been ongoing since the 1990s following lengthy periods of assimilation, with variable degrees of success. Quite clearly, the Sámi language and Sámi identity have become popular themes of study, particularly due to their improved situation. Some of the Sámi have established resilient forms of cultural identity as well as cohesive Indigenous communities, especially within areas where there is a strong presence of Sámi language and culture. However, some Sámi have been disadvantaged for example due to their backgrounds and locations, and so assimilation has had much more of a marked impact.

Sámi identity was placed under close scrutiny when assimilated Sámi first moved to revitalize their languages and when interest in their own roots and backgrounds was revived. At the same time, debate has arisen regarding who should determine the mode of revitalization and who should be allowed to participate in it. Thus, any discussion of the process of revitalization, according to our critical observation, needs to consider the vexed question of who counts as a Sámi member of the Sámi community (Keskitalo and Sarivaara 2014; Sarivaara and Keskitalo 2015, 2016). Throughout the world, there are different understandings around Indigenous membership. In Finland, linguistic capability has been a key determiner of Sámi identity (Sarivaara 2012). In contrast, New Zealand Māori identity in its strictest genealogical sense requires a blood link to a Māori ancestor (Kidman 2007, 60).

Erika Sarivaara (2012) presents a picture of today's Sáminess, which is characterized by diversity and fragmentation. Her research raises internal tensions, and particularly the Sámi identity conflict within Sámi society in Finland, and moreover discloses the complex consequences of Sámi history (see also Lukin 2014). Further, Sarivaara explores themes arising from her research interviews, such as cultural continuity and the issue of cultural identity over generations. In addition, interviews reflected experience that might be understood through the concept of ethnostress (see Kuokkanen 1995). This refers to a situation when one feels unable to fulfill the claims of Indigenous identity, and moreover is afraid to express the Sámi identity in public.

What Is Sámi Education?

A Sámi education paradigm has been in train since the nineteen nineties and is connected to the Sámi University of Applied Sciences (see e.g., Aikio 2007, 2010; Balto 1997, 2005, 2008; Hirvonen 2004; Jannok Nutti 2014; Keskitalo 2009, 2010). Many areas in need of development exist in Sámi education, such as educational philosophy development for the Sámi in order to solve the heritage of cultural colonization, learning materials, and qualified teachers, as well as Sámi educational achievement and equality. Sámi education remains unsystematized (see Aikio-Puoskari 2001; Hirvonen 2004; Keskitalo 2009, 2010; Linkola 2014). Even if solutions to educational problems are found, the Sámi education development process itself is still ongoing. For example, in Norway a Sámi curriculum, and a school system called Sámi School, has been in place since 1997. However, according to research literature, the Sámi school is organized pursuant to the mainstream school system (Hirvonen 2004; Keskitalo 2009, 2010). Developmental work that is premised on Sámi content matter needs to continue. Meanwhile, Indigenous peoples in general wrestle with similar issues (see e.g., Babaci-Wilhite 2015; Grande 2004; King and Schielmann 2004; McConaghy 2000; Lipka et al. 1998; Smith 1999, 2003, 2005; Ventsel and Dudeck 1995).

Traditional modes of Sámi education appear to be vastly different to those of the dominant West, but they may be quite familiar to other Indigenous peoples. Paavo Päivänsalo's (1953) review cited historical literature and sources concerned with "Traditional child-rearing practices of the Sámi." He stresses that traditional Sámi child-rearing aimed to create an individual who was physically durable and possessed the abilities to excel at traditional livelihoods such as reindeer herding, forestry, fishing, and further homemaking. Furthermore, it sought to embed moral obligations toward other people and to following religious practices of traditional Sámi life, and to give them the physical strength and resistance they needed in their lives. Päivänsalo wrote his text just after World War II when modernization had started in earnest among the Sámi people. More recently, Asta Balto (1997) has defined Sámi traditional child-rearing as holistic and a nonauthoritative culture-based practice which makes its own logic. Balto (2005) has pointed out the main goal of traditional child-rearing seems to be preparing an individual for life – to be able to survive different environments, to develop good self-esteem, and a base for life and joy. She stresses that the Sámi child-rearing strategies are often indirect and avoid confrontations between the children and adults involved. This model of raising the child is possible with the support of an extended network of adults around the child who are involved in raising him or her. The network offers the child care and mental security, and helps the child to establish attachments to adults outside the nuclear family. Moreover, naming is significant, with the namesake relationship providing an opportunity to expand the child's social network. Sámi adults use advanced methods to achieve the desired impact regarding their child-rearing efforts, such as storytelling, *nárrideapmi*, diverting strategies, and practices implicit in the Sámi language (Balto 2005).

Sámi education now draws on the wider intention of Indigenous education. Lately, the need for a critical research tradition in Indigenous education research has become apparent. Denzin and Lincoln (2008) emphasizes *hope, love*, and *shared community*, which are considered as the basic values of pedagogy for mediating Indigenous education research. Scholars in pedagogical fields are interested in all human activities and experiences. This kind of research orientation emphasizes the human voice, so that it is possible to *experience* knowledge to improve practices, and also highlights the need for diverse approaches. Extended collaboration benefits the purposes of inclusion and mediates the sharing of information. Research conducted from this point of view also strengthens learning processes among research networks (Denzin and Lincoln 2008).

Like Indigenous education (see, e.g., May and Aikman 2003), Sámi education specifically focuses on teaching traditional knowledge, models, methods, and content within formal or nonformal educational systems. We argue that Sámi education, through pedagogical research and schooling, can also help to resolve and/or mediate the legacy of assimilation. In particular, it seeks to reverse the ongoing language shift that results in an open wound among the Sámi people. Sámi language ability in a person's recent family history has been the basis of an official membership in Sámihood. In Finland, Sámihood has been concretized through the membership of Sámi Parliament electoral roll membership. Crucially, the knowledge of Sámi language is part of entry into Indigenous status among the Sámi in Finland (Sarivaara 2012). This has led to decades of more or less embittered debate about who is Sámi and who is not. While powerful assimilation processes have been continuing for centuries, aiming to remove linguistic and cultural knowledge, there is now also a legal requirement for Sámi language knowledge in the family (via the individual, parents, or grandparents). Controversial debate of these issues continues. At the same time, individual Sámi rights are dependent on the membership of the Sámi Parliament electoral roll in Finland which, as we have noted, requires linguistic capacity. Another competing discourse supports a principle of *cultural* capacity. Both scenarios are problematic in a so-called postassimilationist era.

Mediating Sámi Education

Problems of assimilation and agency – including who may count as Sámi – ground any discussion about mediative pedagogy and its structures. Here we focus on contexts, accounts, and implementation of the mediating pedagogy in the field of Sámi education research, while continuing to cast a critical eye over the ineffectiveness of State intervention thus far. Mediation encompasses inclusion and caring, and it asks for participatory and concrete outcomes. From this perspective, mediation is a versatile concept. This section draws on earlier theories about mediating education (e.g., Berger and Neuhaus 1970; Denzin and Lincoln 2008; Nurmi and Kontiainen 1995) and, in accordance with this chapter's title, calls for more active and innovative efforts to revitalize the Sámi language. Sámi language revitalization in Finland has been partly based on formal Sámihood and connection to the Sámi Parliament Electoral Roll; we suggest, however, that these measurements are narrow and ineffective. We want to increase Sámi language usage through radical multicultural ideology that is inclusive and actually expands the number of language speakers. These kinds of measures are in use in New Zealand (see Nicholson 2003) and Inari Sámis (Olthuis et al. 2013).

Mediation can be thought of as both a broad and specifically educational phenomenon. According to the Oxford American Writer's Thesaurus (Auburn et al. 2012), the concept mediate is synonymous with arbitrate, make peace, resolve, and negotiate. Peter Berger (1979, 169) defines the concept of mediating structures as "those institutions which stand between the individual in his (sic) private sphere and the large institutions of the public sphere." According to Brad Lowell Stone (2012), these ideas can be traced to Edmund Burke (1790), Alexis de Tockueville (1988), John Stuart Mill (1999), and Pierre-Joseph Proudhon (Hyams 1979), as well as to efforts to preserve the corporate rights of social groups. Mediating structures are moreover a tool for multicultural education contexts. The concept of bundling mediating structures was proposed by Berger and Neuhaus (1970), who proposed that family culture and school culture should be merged in order to empower pupils.

Further, Nurmi and Kontiainen (1995, 68) applied the model so that mediating structures could successfully operate in educational intercultural contexts. Therefore, we emphasize that mediating structures aim to remedy cultural conflict that may appear within a multicultural situation.

In other words, mediating structures are intercultural educational tools. Mediating education appoints objectives of the research for transmission by a caring, loving, and inclusive sense, as well as allows for the creation of models in conflict resolution. Generally, the intercultural context may create a base for cultural conflict. For example, in multilingual and intercultural educational practices, cultural conflicts can arise due to asymmetric power relations (Keskitalo 2010). Mediating structures intersects between the past, the present, and the future circumferentially, so that tendencies to essentialize other cultures are lessened.

These therapeutic qualities manifest at various points within theory. Vivian R. Johnson (1994) concretizes mediating structures to mean the counteracting of poverty and discrimination. She mentions families, neighborhood groups, religious groups, and voluntary associations as mediating structures. She points out that, for example, for each child the institution of the family is a mediating structure between him or her and the school. Nonetheless, Bourdieu (1977) suggests that the ability of the family to mediate between the child and the school is a function of the amount of cultural capital or skills, disposition, background, and knowledge the family possesses. Low-income and minority families are less likely to successfully mediate for their children because they have less cultural capital that schools value and reward than do high-income and mainstream families (Johnson 1994). Bourdieu's ideas about cultural capital are also relevant to language revitalization: the amount of cultural capital may affect the ability to revitalize, participate with activities of revitalization, or demand revitalization for one's own children. Johnson's and Bourdieu's ideas, which concentrate on societal problems, can be expanded to be meaningful for mediating structures needed in Indigenous language revitalization. It is quite likely, in the context of Indigenous revitalization that any resulting actions will occur at both personal and group levels and include practical and attitudinal aspects. Additionally, any writing and discussion on the topic needs to be opened up *as* both personal and political, and concrete and abstract acts, thus reflecting the reality that language revitalization is formidably difficult.

A Sámi educational research paradigm should therefore be closely based on a sophisticated awareness of collective Sámi assimilation. Sámi education that is based on an inclusive mediating perspective plays a significant role in order to revitalize Indigenous languages and culture. The revitalization process of the Sámi languages and strengthening activities for language domains are core educational means for the postassimilation phase in Sápmi, Northern Europe. Sámi education questions how education and schooling can dismantle skewed, unequal setups in society. Further, how through educational research, we can mediate the strengthening of inclusive Indigenous integrity. In this sense, and sharing the experiences of other Indigenous peoples (see Denzin et al. 2008), Sámi education is performing then as constructive and capable of dissolving conflicts and ensuring proactive activity.

Mediating structures creates bridges between the past, present, and future, and their variability helps us to avoid cultural mystification and essentialism. Among other things, they bring into concern the reality of multilingual and multicultural contexts. Keskitalo (2010) highlights that through *mediating structures* it is possible to achieve balance in Sámi school, and moreover resolve a school's culture, and possible cultural conflicts. Colonial history and asymmetrical power relations have obstructed the Sámi from forming their own school culture. Mediating structures enables the establishment of a school culture that includes the Sámi view (Keskitalo 2010). The starting point of the research is a sense of pedagogical care and inclusive activities. As a result, mediating Sámi research aims to create suitable models for the resolution of conflicts.

Mediating Sámi education includes many different approaches and theoretical perspectives with an interest in critical knowledge and multiple emancipation. With culturally relevant and potent research activities, we strive to improve Sámi society. The aim is to promote Sámi self-government and to proceed with the aspiration of unraveling colonial structures, adaptations, and stereotypes. Furthermore, similar critical issues have become more urgent in the field of Indigenous research (McLaren and Kincheloe 2007). Contributing to solidarity recognizing human rights, liberty, and self-government are the basic objectives that mediating Sámi education aims for. What is needed to make it a concrete reality? For Indigenous people, communication and dialogue, ethical and human management, emancipatory and empowering pedagogy, cultural welfare, and collective responsibility ascend more and more into importance. Enacting supportive and practical measures helps to change the circumstances. Collaborative interaction and active dialogue between all other people in general is significant to the survival of the Indigenous people. These kinds of human encounters are meant to rebuild Indigenous communities and nations in accordance with their ecologies, so that the Indigenous peoples are able to maintain, remember, share, and consider their roles and thus rename, collaborate, protect, and democratize their everyday life (Smith 1999).

Mediating Structures in Sámi Language Revitalization

Mediating structures for language revitalization necessitates an awareness of sociopolitical and socioeconomic issues as well as attempts to actively resolve these rather than let them be. Linguistic domains such as schools, family, society, media, friends, and also leisure facilities are significant factors when revitalizing languages (Baker 2011). Schools may achieve effective revitalization results, if other support are pursued. Eventually efficient language revitalization includes the following characteristics:

1. Educating new speakers to the language, crucially involving the home domain and intergenerational transmission (King 2009; Spolsky 1989).
2. Adding new functions by introducing the language into domains where it was previously unused or relatively underused (Ó Laoire 2006).

3. Identifying the language being revived by both established speakers and neo-speakers (Huss et al. 2003).
4. Involvement and activity on behalf of individuals and the speech community as well as awareness that positive attitudes, action, commitment, strong acts of will, and sacrifice may be necessary to save and revitalize the language (Ó Laoire 2006).

The objective of mediating structures is to reinforce cultural identity and indigeneity, however avoiding ethnocentrism. Exclusionary practices may lead to ethnocentric perspectives and, crucially, do not build a society that values pluralism and cultural diversity. Mediating Sámi educational research aspires to solve assimilation so that it enables assimilated Sámi to confirm their inherent cultural identity and indigeneity. More precisely, Indigenous education is about raising Indigenous individuals for Indigenous citizenship and life in Indigenous and mainstream communities. Sámi education seeks to act as a reverse circuit to assimilation and as the reinforcer of Sámi awareness. Mediating Sámi research can promote functional way of approaching these main challenges and provide practical tools for developing Sámi education that supports the revitalization and holistic flourishing of the Sámi people and culture.

Mediation of Sámi education is focusing on practices that can disassemble oblique and unequal relationships in Sámi communities. Secondly, the other significant task is to strengthen the pedagogical research concerning mediating and inclusive Indigenous identities.

A concrete objective that deserves priority is to constructively solve internal conflicts and oppression within Sámi society. For example, defaulting interaction and poor management of internal conflict are part of the process of lateral violence, which can be viewed as an expression of internalized colonialism. Internalized colonialism can be harmful for Indigenous communities as it causes negative attitudes and, further, oppressed people to stand against each other. Richard Frankland states that:

> [T]he organised, harmful behaviours that we do to each other collectively as part of an oppressed group: within our families; within our organisations and; within our communities. When we are consistently oppressed we live with great fear and great anger and we often turn on those who are closest to us. (Australian Human Rights Commission 2011, 8)

Mediating structures should create synergic connections within the revitalization process. Basically, it means to increase the synergy between different groups and societal institutions. Such synergy forms as a result of extended collaboration. However, it crucially requires tolerance, solidarity, and the development of cultural identities. We emphasize that language revitalization in mediating education enables individuals to construct and strengthen their cultural identity and language skills within a community characterized by a positive atmosphere and spirit. These circumstances enables individuals to develop and flourish. Furthermore, practical language-related activities should be implemented in communities such as language nests for kindergarten children, primary school revitalization language classes, or adult revitalization teaching. Societal support for such plans and goals creates the concrete framework but an individual's own attitudes toward the revitalization process plays the most important role.

Conclusion

The goal of Indigenous education is to help Indigenous individuals to grow to be members of their community and society. Today's Sámi pupils are the members of a global, changing society. From a Sámi educational point of view, it is urgent to examine what kind of skills future Sámi society requires, together with the values and problems that respectively support and challenge it. Empowerment, revitalization, and the aspirations possible through education and research are important factors and goals for Indigenous people's futures. For this reason, it is important to be reflective concerning what kind of future Sámi society we are creating, what kind of values are important for us, and what kind of things ask to be reversed or to changed.

It is clear that ethnocentrism does not empower Indigenous peoples, but rather maintains essentialist attitudes and paradigms. In addition, an ethnocentric perspective may trap individuals in the victim role, which in a collective context means that the group remains hindered by past discrimination. The victim role means that the person feels unable to change unsatisfactory circumstances. It may bring negative discourses into communities and, moreover, it involves negative emotions such as scapegoating and seeing a future without hope. Simplistically stressing the Indigenous cultural background to enhance feelings of power and a sense of superiority does not acknowledge Indigenous people but rather merely enacts aspects of essentialism and ethnocentrism, which export racism within and against the Indigenous peoples.

The victim role does tend to be one phase within Indigenous people's awareness raising and revitalization processes. Traumatic experiences of the past should be grieved over and openly discussed within communities so that people are finally able to move on from them. However, the victim role may constitute a problematic base for discourse within Indigenous people's communities. Also, essentialism and ethnocentrism may generate negative attitudes toward Indigenous peoples. In that sense Indigenous critical education as a research field plays a core role in preventing further assimilation.

We have suggested that mediating Sámi education necessarily adopts Sámi identity research and can serve as a means to explain the multiple, fragmented, conflicted, diverse situations. Mediating Sámi research is a tool to examine and explain the multicultural educational context. Mediating education points out the value of an inclusive, caring, and participatory approach. Within this context, mediating Sámi education is multifaceted. The objective of mediating education is to identify oppressive issues, and also to try and solve them (see Suoranta and Ryynänen 2014). In addition, mediating structures corroborate human rights, which aim to include all peoples and involve them in the development of society. Minorities would benefit from constructing strategies that enhance their minority position. Therefore, mediating structures are tools that aim to dismantle asymmetric power structures.

Language revitalization benefits from mediating structures, since it enforces the individual's language learning and hence increases language domains. Mediating structures also aim to tackle – at societal, practical macro and micro, and individual levels – the complicated practical and psychological issues that may help or hinder language revitalization. Research in this area would benefit from practical work with language revitalization; moreover, scholars and educators should work together to help it to progress.

Crucially, there is an emergent need for Sámi language revitalization classes without formally sanctioned ethnic boundaries, such as Sámi language nests for kindergarten age children. This we call a radical multicultural inclusive model that is already in use in Norway and more or less in New Zealand. These models offer a way to increase the linguistic vitality of Indigenous languages. In Finland, it is policy to keep the Sámi language revitalization mostly for official Sámi – the Sámi and their children who have voting rights in the Sámi Parliament Electoral Roll – the situation is politically difficult as there are voices that want to keep the voting group tight and small and predictable. We wanted to point out this demanding situation which may stymie the potential for language revitalization.

Further, there is a constant need for law, acts, measurements, efforts, implementations, politicians, officials, and activists who care about language revitalization and people putting those efforts into reality. We suggest that researchers should actively take part in acts of revitalization in societies. As Banks (2006) suggests, we should teach our children to know, care, and act in order to achieve sustainable well-being in our Indigenous communities, to know our history, culture, customs, and worldview, and to care about Us, but also about the Other, in order to create empathy toward humanity. And finally, to act in order to reclaim and maintain our language and customs. We do not need simple typologies but rather we must critically evaluate pedagogical actions in order to enhance or change them and to assemble the best practices from Indigenous education and general pedagogy, and crucially recognize language sharing as a mediative education act by sharing the language for all – as language is shared humanity.

References

Äärelä R (2015) Saamenkielisen kielikylvyn toteutus kielipesissä (The Sámi language immersion practices at language nests). Agon 1–2. http://agon.fi/article/saamenkielisen-kielikylvyn-toteutus-kielipesissa/. Accessed 15 June 2016

Afanasyeva A (2013) Forced relocations of the Kola Sámi people: background and consequences. University of Tromsø. Faculty of Humanities, Social Sciences and Education. Master of Philosophy in Indigenous Studies

Aikio M (1988) Saamelaiset kielenvaihdon kierteessä. Kielisosiologinen tutkimus viiden saamelaiskylän kielenvaihdosta 1910–1980 (The Sámi in language shift. Language sociological research about five Sámi village language shift). SKS, Helsinki

Aikio A (2004) An essay on substrate studies and the origin of Saami. In: Hyvärinen I, Kallio P, Korhonen J (eds) Etymologie, Entlehnungen und Entwicklungen: Festschrift für Jorma Koivulehto zum 70. Geburstag. Finno-Ugric Association, Helsinki, pp 5–34

Aikio A (2006) On Germanic-Saami contacts and Saami prehistory. J de la Société Finno-Ougrienne 91:9–55

Aikio, A (2007) Saamelainen elämänpolitiikka (The Sámi life policy). University of Lapland. Faculty of Education. Licentiate thesis

Aikio A (2010) Olmmošhan gal birge – áššit mat ovddidit birgema (Mankind prospers certainly – things that promote success). ČálliidLágádus, Kárášjohka

Aikio A (2012) An essay on Saami ethnolinguistic prehistory. In: Grünthal R, Kallio P (eds) A linguistic map of prehistoric Northern Europe. Finno-Ugric Association, Helsinki, pp 69–117

Aikio-Puoskari U (2001) Saamen kielen ja saamenkielinen opetus Pohjoismaissa: tutkimus saamelaisten kielellisistä ihmisoikeuksista Pohjoismaiden kouluissa (The instruction of and in Sámi language in Nordic countries: research about the Sámi people lingual rights at Nordic countries' schools), vol 25. University of Lapland. Publications of the Northern Institute for Environmental and Minority Law. Juridica Lapponica

Auburn D et al (eds) (2012) Oxford American writer's thesaurus, 3rd edn. Oxford University Press, Oxford, NY

Australian Human Rights Commission (2011) Social justice report 2011. Australian Human Rights Commission, Sydney

Babaci-Wilhite Z (2015) Local languages as a human right in education. Sense Publishers, Rotterdam

Baker C (2011) Foundations of bilingual education and bilingualism. Multilingual Matters, Clevedon

Balto A (1997) Sámi mánáid bajásgeassin nuppástuvvá [Sámi child-rearing in change]. Ad Notam Gyldendal, Oslo

Balto A (2005) Traditional Sámi child-rearing in transition: shaping a new pedagogical platform. AlterNative 1(1):85–105

Balto A (2008) Vitalizing Sámi cultural knowledge in everyday school-life. Action research and the capacity building of Sámi teachers. J Aust Indigenous Issues 11(4):25–35

Banks JA (2006) Cultural diversity and education. Foundations, curriculum, and teaching, 5th edn. Pearson Education Inc, Boston

Berger PL (1979) In praise of particularism: the concept of mediating structures. In: Facing up to modernity – excursions in society, politics and religion. Penguin Books, Middlesex

Berger PL, Neuhaus RJ (1970) Movement and revolution. Doubleday, Garden City

Bourdieu P (1977) Outline of a theory of practice. Cambridge University Press, Cambridge

Burke E (1790) Reflections on the revolution in France. James Dodsley, London

Denzin NK, Lincoln YS (2008) Introduction. In: Denzin NK, Lincoln YS, Smith LT (eds) Handbook of critical and indigenous methodologies. SAGE, Thousand Oaks, pp 1–20

Denzin NK, Lincoln YS, Smith LT (eds) (2008) Handbook of critical and indigenous methodologies. SAGE, Thousand Oaks

Grande S (2004) Red pedagogy: native American social and political thought. Rowman & Littlefield Publishers, Lanham

Henrysson S (1992) Saami education in Sweden in the 1900's. In: Kvisti R (ed) Reading in Saami history, culture and language, III. Umeå University, Umeå, pp 103–110

Hirvonen V (2004) Sámi culture and the school. Reflections by the Sámi Teachers and the realization of the Sámi school: an evaluation study of Reform 97. Saami University college, Karasjok

Huss L, Grima AC, Kind KA (eds) (2003) Transcending monolingualism: linguistic revitalization in education. Swets and Zeitlinger, Lisse

Hyams E (1979) Pierre-Joseph Proudhon: his revolutionary life, mind & works. J Murray, London

Hylland Eriksen T (1992) Linguistic hegemony and minority resistance. J Peace Res 29(3):313–332

Jannok Nutti Y (2014) Sámi teachers' experiences of indigenous school transformation: culturally based preschool and school mathematics lessons. Alternatives 9(1):16–29

Johnson VR (1994) Connecting families and schools through mediating structures. Sch Community J 4(1):311–318

Jones P (2012) Bálgáš. Lapin sivistysseura pohjoissaamen ortografian kehittäjänä vuosina 1932–1951 (Small path. Lapland education association as a developer of North Sámi orthography during 1932–1951). Seminar of history. University of Tampere

Keskitalo JH (2009) Sámi máhttu ja sámi skuvlamáhttu: teorehtalaš geahčastat (The Sámi knowledge and Sámi school knowledge – theoretical review). Sámi dieđalaš áigečála 1–2:62–75

Keskitalo P (2010) Saamelaiskoulun kulttuurisensitiivisyyttä etsimässä kasvatusantropologian keinoin (Cultural sensitivity in the Sámi school through educational anthropology). Dissertation, University of Lapland. Dieđut 1/2010. Sámi allaskuvla, Guovdageaidnu

Keskitalo P, Sarivaara E (2014) Välittävän saamentutkimuksen merkitys (The meaning of mediating Sámi research). In: Määttä K, Uusiautti S (eds) Voimaa välittävästä tutkimuksesta (The basics of caring research). Lapin yliopistopaino, Rovaniemi, pp 55–64

Keskitalo P, Lehtola VP, Paksuniemi M (eds) (2014) Saamelaisten kansanopetuksen ja koulunkäynnin historia Suomessa (Sámi people education and school history in Finland). Siirtolaisuusinstituutti, Turku

Keskitalo P, Nyyssönen J, Paksuniemi M, Turunen T, Linkola I-A, McIntosh L (2016) Saamelaisten ja Australian alkuperäiskansojen kouluhistorian erityispiirteet (The special features school history of Sámi and Australia indigenous peoples), Ennen ja nyt. http://www.ennenjanyt.net/2016/09/saamelaisten-ja-australian-alkuperaiskansojen-kouluhistorian-erityispiirteet/. Accessed 30 Jun 2017

Kidman J (2007) Engaging with Māori communities: an exploration of some tensions in the mediation of social sciences research. He Pārekereke. Victoria University of Wellington

King J (2009) Language is life. In: Reyhner J, Lockard L (eds) Indigenous language revitalization: encouragement, guidance & lessons learned. Northern Arizona University, Flagstaff, pp 97–108

King L, Schielmann S (2004) The challenge of indigenous education: practice and perpectives. Unesco, Paris

Kuokkanen R (1999) Etnostressistä sillanrakennukseen. Saamelaisen nykykirjallisuuden minäkuvat. (From Ethnostress into building bridges. The Self-Images of Contemporary Saami Literature) In M. Tuominen, S. Tuulentie, V.-P. Lehtola, & M. Autti (eds) Pohjoiset identiteetit ja mentaliteetit, osa I: Outamaalta tunturiin (Northern Identities and Mentalities, part I: From Forest land into Mountain areas) Rovaniemi, University of Lapland, pp 95–112

Lehtola VP (2015) Sámi histories, colonialism, and Finland. Arctic Anthropol 52:22–36

Linkola IA (2014) Saamelaisen koulun kielimaisema – etnografinen tutkimus saamen kielestä toisen asteen oppilaitoksessa (The Sámi School's linguistic landscape – an ethnograpical study on the Sámi language at an upper-secondary education institution). Dissertation, University of Lapland. Dieđut 2/2014. Sámi allaskuvla, Guovdageaidnu

Lipka J, Mohatt GV, Ciulustet G (eds) (1998) Transforming the culture of schools. Yup'ik Eskimo Examples. Lawrence Erlbaum Associates Publishers, Mahwah

Lukin K (2014) Eteläistä saamentutkimusta (The Southern Sámi Research) Elore, vol 21–1/2014. Suomen Kansantietouden Tutkijain Seura ry. http://www.elore.fi/arkisto/1_14/lukin.pdf. Accessed 27 Dec 2017

May S, Aikman S (2003) Indigenous education: addressing current issues and developments. Comp Educ 39(2, Special Number (27)):139–145. Indigenous education: new possibilities, ongoing constraints

McConaghy C (2000) Rethinking indigenous education: culturalism, colonialism and the politics of knowing. Post Pressed, Flaxton

McLaren P, Kincheloe JL (2007) Critical pedagogy: where are we now? Peter Lang, Pieterlen

Mill JS (1999) On liberty. Broadview Press, Peterborough

Minde H (2005) Sámiid dáruiduhttin – Manin, mo ja makkár váikkuhusat? (Assimilation of the Sami – implementation and consequences). In: Lund S, Boine E, Broch Johansen S (eds) Sámi skuvlahistorjá 1. Davvi girji, Kárášjohka. http://skuvla.info/skolehist/minde-s.htm. Accessed 30 Nov 2016

Nicholson R (2003) Marketing the Maori language. In: Reyhner J (ed) Teaching indigenous languages. Northern Arizona University, Flagstaff, pp 206–212. http://jan.ucc.nau.edu/jar/TIL_16.html. Accessed 15 Oct 2016

Nurmi KE, Kontiainen S (1995) A framework for adult learning in cultural context: mediating cultural encounters. In: Kauppi A, Kontiainen S, Nurmi KE, Tuomisto J, Vaherva T (eds) Adult learning in a cultural context. University of Helsinki. Lahti Research and Training Centre. Adult Education Research Society in Finland, Lahti, pp 65–71

Ó Laoire M (2006) Language education for language revival. In: Brown K (ed) Encyclopedia of language and linguistics, vol 6. Elsevier, Oxford, p 407

Olthuis ML, Kivelä S, Skutnabb-Kangas T (2013) Revitalising indigenous languages: how to recreate a lost generation. Multilingual matters, Bristol

Outakoski H (2015) Multilingual literacy among young learners of North Sámi. Contexts, complexity and writing in Sápmi, vol 27. Umeå University. Department of Language Studies. Umeå Studies in Language and Literature

Päivänsalo P (1953) Lappalaisten lastenhoito- ja kasvatustavoista (Lappish child care and childrearing practices). Suomen kasvatus-sosiologinen yhdistys, Helsinki

Paksuniemi M (2009) Tornion alakansakoulunopettajaseminaarin opettajakuva lukuvuosina 1921–1945 rajautuen oppilasvalintoihin, oppikirjoihin ja oheistoimintaan. Acta Universitatis Lapponiensis 161, University of Lapland, Rovaniemi

Pasanen A (2015) Kuávsui já peeivičuová. 'Sarastus ja päivänvalo' – Inarinsaamen kielen revitalisaatio (Kuávsui já peeivičuová. 'The dawn and the daylight' – revitalization of Inari Saami language). Dissertation, University of Helsinki. Uralica Helsingiensia, 9. Suomalais – Ugrilainen Seura, Helsinki

Rasmussen T (2013) "Go ealáska, de lea váttis dápmat". Davvisámegiela etnoligvisttalaš ceavzinnávccaid guorahallan guovtti gránnjágielddas Deanus ja Ohcejogas 2000–logu álggus (When recovering, it is hard to tame. North Sámi ethnolinguistic vitality research in two neighbour countries). Dissertation, Arctic University of Norway. Sámi allaskuvla, Guovdageaidnu

Sarivaara EK (2012) Statuksettomat saamelaiset. Paikantumisia saamelaisuuden rajoilla (Non-status Sámi. Locations within Sámi borderlands). Dissertation, University of Lapland. Dieđut 2/2012. Sámi allaskuvla, Guovdageaidnu

Sarivaara EK (2016) Emergent Sámi identities: from assimilation towards revitalization. In: Toivanen R, Saarikivi J (eds) New and old language diversities. Multilingual Matters, Bristol

Sarivaara E, Keskitalo P (2015) Fátmmasteaddji giellaealáskahttin (The mediating language revitalization). Agon (1–2):18–26. http://agon.fi/article/fatmmasteaddji-giellaealaskahttin/. Accessed 12 June 2016

Sarivaara E, Keskitalo P (2016) The definition and task of mediating Sámi research. Int J Res Stud Educ 5(4). http://www.consortiacademia.org/index.php/ijrse/article/view/1367. Accessed 24 Jan 2017

Sarivaara E, Uusiautti S, Määttä K (2014) Critical Sámi research as the means of finding ways of seeing. Int J Soc Sci Res 2(1). http://www.macrothink.org/journal/index.php/ijssr/article/view/4521. Accessed 25 Jan 2017

Seurujärvi-Kari I (2012) Ale jaskkot eatnigiella. Alkuperäiskansaliikkeen ja saamen kielen merkitys saamelaisten identiteetille (Don't turn it down mother-tongue. The significance of the indigenous movement at the Sámi language and the Sámi identity). SKS, Helsinki

Seurujärvi-Kari I, Halinen P, Pulkkinen R (eds) (2011) Saamentutkimus tänään (Sámi Research Today). Suomalaisen Kirjallisuuden Seura, Helsinki

Smith LT (1999) Decolonizing indigenous methodologies. Zed Books, New York

Smith GH (2003) Kaupapa Maori theory: theorizing indigenous transformation of education & schooling. The University of Auckland & Te Whare Wananga o Awanuiarangi: tribal-university, New Zealand. http://www.aare.edu.au/03pap/pih03342.pdf. Accessed 25 Jan 2017

Smith GH (2005) Mai i te Maramatanga, ki te Putanga Mai o te Tahuritanga: from Conscientization to transformation educational perspectives. College of education, vol 37(1). University of Hawai'i at Manoa. http://www.hawaii.edu/edper/pdf/Vol37/Mai.pdf. Accessed 30 Jan 2017

Spolsky B (1989) Conditions for second language learning. Oxford University Press, Oxford

Stone B (2012) Mediating structures. First principles. ISI Web J. http://www.firstprinciplesjournal.com/articles.aspx?article=348&loc=r. Accessed 27 Jan 2017

Suoranta J, Ryynänen S (2014) Taisteleva tutkimus (Rebellious research). Into Kustannus Oy, Helsinki

Tocqueville de A (1988) Det gamle regime og revolusjonen. (trans: Ørbo B). Aschehoug, Oslo

Ventsel A, Dudeck S (1995) Do the Khanty need a Khanty curriculum? Indigenous concepts of school education. Siberian Studies. www.siberian-studies.org/publications/PDF/beventseldudeck.pdf. Accessed 28 Jan 2017

Colonialism, Māori Early Childhood, Language, and the Curriculum

28

Mere Skerrett

Contents

Introduction: Colonial Pursuits	484
Colonial Architecture	485
Historical Developments Underpinning Language Policy in Education Settings	486
The Power of Veto of Māori Language in Education Continues	487
Legal and Political Developments: The Old Māori Language Act 1987	488
The New Māori Language Act 2016	489
Kōhanga Reo	490
Structural Reform and Government Policies: The Meade Report	490
Before Five Policy Statement	491
Glacial Policy Responses to the waiMāori Stream	491
Te Whāriki: An Ideological Conundrum	492
Māori Language as Resistance	497
Te Rangatiratanga o te Reo (Language as Liberating)	500
Conclusions	501
Glossary	501
References	502

Abstract

This Chapter unsettles Māori language in education generally, and in the early childhood curriculum particularly, its historical antecedents, and government leaden-footed policies (Waitangi Tribunal, Pre-publication Waitangi Tribunal report 2336: Matua Rautia: the report on the Kōhanga Reo claim. Waitangi Tribunal, Wellington, 2012) in a colony which still is colonizing. It troubles some of the norms of *Te Whāriki: He whāriki mātauranga mō ngā mokopuna o Aotearoa: Early childhood curriculum* (Ministry of Education, Te Whāriki: he whāriki mātauranga mō ngā mokopuna o Aotearoa: early childhood curriculum.

M. Skerrett (✉)
Victoria University of Wellington, Wellington, New Zealand
e-mail: mere.skerrett@vuw.ac.nz

© Springer Nature Singapore Pte Ltd. 2019
E. A. McKinley, L. T. Smith (eds.), *Handbook of Indigenous Education*,
https://doi.org/10.1007/978-981-10-3899-0_17

Learning Media, Wellington, 1996; Ministry of Education, Te Whāriki: he whāriki mātauranga mō ngā mokopuna o Aotearoa: early childhood curriculum. Ministry of Education, Wellington, 2017) (Te Whāriki) and provides further ideological clarification around what has come to be known as kaupapa Māori (praxis, pedagogy, power and curriculum). It provides a challenge to curriculum in the early years, a challenge to the hegemonic norm, countering dominant discourses and contesting universalization, raising questions about the relationality of language to the curriculum. It promotes a re-framing of the curriculum through a Māori (see Glossary) pedagogical frame as a resistance to the displacement/replacement theory brought about through colonization. It argues that *te rangatiratanga o te reo* (the sovereignty of the Māori language to Māori culture) is not just about resistance to injustice and the inversion of colonial rule, but the assertion of Māori sovereignty through Māori language in "our place," all of it and everywhere. It is a reassertion of the legitimation and authority of te reo Māori and the rights of children to live te reo Māori, to live its history, its future, its identity, its world-views, its values, its symbolism, and its spirit. This chapter remains interested in the politics and policy environment while concentrating on our Māori children – our greatest allies in the Māori language revitalization endeavor.

Keywords
Early Years · Curriculum · Māori language · Kōhanga Reo · Kaupapa Māori · Colonization · Māori sovereignty · Identity politics · Language revitalization · Bilingualism · Te Whāriki

Introduction: Colonial Pursuits

Imperialism, through its colonial outpost in Aotearoa/New Zealand (Smith 2012), was anchored via the Treaty of Waitangi signed in 1840 by representatives of the Queen of England and the incumbent Hapū (smaller tribal groups). This was a colonial instrument aimed at peaceful settlement by the British, rather than the cession of sovereignty as is often claimed, mainly to justify land confiscations and political hegemony, particularly once British numerical dominance was achieved (Mikaere 2011; Mutu 2010; Walker 2004). Mythologizing discourses really began to take hold in the minds of the settler people once political and numerical dominance was accomplished (Ballara 1986; Bevan-Smith 2012). As Ballara (1986) succinctly put it "…in the end, in spite of the treaty, it was to be the concept of the wandering savage who had no rights to land that was adopted and recognised by the settler governments once self-government was attained" (p. 36). The imperialist project continues to reinvent itself in Aotearoa in order to strengthen its compartmentalizing structure of silencing Indigenous (with a capital I) tongues, daily. Colonial science terminally incorporates Indigenous spatiality into colonial rule, forcing the subalterns into the hinterlands (Shilliam 2016) in pursuit of the insatiable desire to "accumulate."

Colonial Architecture

In Aotearoa, education pathways were mapped out *for* Māori *in* English, in a context of contempt. Governor Grey diverted missionary education from what is now considered sound *additive* bilingual pedagogical practice (Walker 2004) to deficit *subtractive* pedagogical practice (Where one language is subtracted creating one dominant language system.) commencing with the 1847 Education Ordinance, where instruction was to be totally in English. Clause 3 supported the giving of public funds to schools, *provided* that instruction was given in the English language (New Zealand Legislative Council Ordinances 1841–1853). Successive pieces of legislation further compartmentalized and hierarchized Māori language (as disposable), land (as survey-able), and people (as subservient to British settler interests), all in the interests of colonial architecture and colonial science (referenced through the English language). While education policy as text mandated English in the curriculum, the corollary, the policy as discourse became one of deficit theorizing for Māori, through an anglicizing curriculum. Māori children continue to experience harm as they endure forced assimilation into a whitestream (Common parlance for a monoculturally "western" British education system.) system and inculcation into the current stratified social order.

The 1938 education edict by the then Labour Prime Minister Peter Fraser (written by Clarence Beeby) asserted that "…every person, whatever his level of academic ability, whether he be rich or poor, whether he live in town or country, has a right, as a citizen, to a free education of the kind for which he is best fitted, and to the fullest extent of his powers" (Alcorn 1999, p. 38). It cemented the enforcement with a "free, secular, and compulsory" directive. This came at great cost to Māori children growing up in the "system." When you analyze it, the much revered and celebrated Beeby dictum was not far from the 1848 mantra of the evangelicals and their godly ordered world reflected in the third verse of the Anglican hymn endorsing the Georgian hierarchical system, *All things Bright and Beautiful*. The line "*The rich man in his castle, The poor man at his gate, God made them high and lowly, And ordered their estate,*" is a particularly poignant piece of propaganda. The British school system then came under the control of the clergy. The philosophical underpinnings of classification and categorization were imported into Aotearoa, ostensibly reinvented in the Beeby dictum through the operative words "for which he is best fitted." For many Māori "being fitted" meant little more than "being marginalized" in education.

This chapter scrutinizes contexts, political developments, policy documents, and curriculum. It commences with an overview of Māori language in education highlighting the contexts, prevailing ideologies, and undercurrents of policy culminating in a critique of the Māori Language Acts. The context and politics of Kōhanga Reo (language nests) is followed by an analysis of government policies. New Zealand's curriculum *Te whāriki: He whāriki mātauranga mō ngā mokopuna o Aotearoa: Early childhood curriculum* (Ministry of Education 1996) (*Te Whāriki*) is examined through the lens that prevailing colonial archaeology remains political and productive. According to Duhn (2012), curriculum reflects the socio-historical conditions and context of the times. It is a highly contestable, cultural construct. "It represents desires, aspirations and ambitions for the child as future contributor to society from the viewpoint of powerful adults" (p. 84). It makes statements about what kind of subject New Zealand, as a nation, wants. *Te Whāriki* is nation building. What kind of child, and nation, is in the imagination of *Te Whāriki*? What kind of child, and home-land, is in the imagination of Māori? The contexts and discussion overview shifts from Māori language seen as a disposable "problem" under the nation-state regime; to language as a "right" and a "resource" in the latter half of the twentieth century. It is argued that the undercurrents of imperialist projects steeped in 200 years of paternalistic colonial mind-sets continue their efforts to silence Māori Indigeneity through policy in text and policy in practice. The juxta-positioning of decolonizing Indigenous frameworks of *rangatiratanga* (sovereignty or self-determination) and *te rangatiratanga o te reo* (the prestige and determination of Indigenous languages) illustrates the power of Indigenous languages to liberate minds through language.

Historical Developments Underpinning Language Policy in Education Settings

In the context of Māori language education, it is argued that te reo Māori is the terralingua of Aotearoa New Zealand. Māori interests in the language are not the same as the interests of any other minority group in New Zealand society in its own language (Waitangi Tribunal 2010). Why not? Because the Māori language is Indigenous to Aotearoa. Māori language is the language of this land and belongs to the people who live here. Māori culture is a millennium culture (Walker 2004). Its history should be spoken through the language in which the culture developed. But after over a thousand years of development in Aotearoa, the culture (and language) was swiftly disrupted with British colonization.

The *Waitangi Tribunal* (A commission which has been established to examine Māori claims for restitution for breaches of the 1840 Tiriti o Waitangi.) *Māori Language Report* of 1986 (Waitangi Tribunal 1986) provides a broad overview of Māori language in the 1900s in three 25-year periods. In the first 25-year period, Māori children went to school as monolingual Māori-speaking children and the main educational effort was to teach them English, at the expense of Māori. Māori language "had to be left at the school gates" (p. 8). Many children were punished for speaking the Māori language. In the second 25-year period, largely because of their school experiences, those children brought up their own children to speak English from infancy. They did not want the next generation to suffer the disadvantages (and punishments) they themselves had to endure. While many were, to a greater or lesser extent, bilingual, their first language was English. In the third quarter of the century, the process of language shift accelerated, with the move to English monolingualism in Māori children. So effective was the process that by the early 1960s when Māori people were actively engaged in early childhood education programs, they too stressed the need for their young children to be instructed solely in English. I started school in 1962. My generation was 99% English speaking Māori children, with a few Māori/English bilinguals (MEBs) and even fewer Māori language monolingual speaking children. Many witnesses in the 1986 Waitangi Tribunal hearing gave evidence of the injustices of the monocultural system, resulting in negative racist attitudes, towards both Māori children and Māori language, and the lack of provision across the whole of the education system.

The Power of Veto of Māori Language in Education Continues

Approximately 30 years later, I was made aware of experiences with a school Principal and senior language staff strikingly similar to that in the 1980s. Enquiries were made into appropriate Māori language provision at enrolment into a secondary school for a young person who had been in Māori immersion up until that time. To cut a long story short, there was none. Leave was then sought to enroll her into a university-level Māori language class, requiring her to attend university lectures twice a week. That request was denied. After ongoing discussions and email correspondence, all attempts to address the matter were thwarted, with often-lame excuses like "we have parents wanting leave to enroll their children in cycling club – what's the difference?" and so on. The value of te reo Māori and what it meant educationally, psychologically, and spiritually, for that student (and her whānau) in terms of the relationship of language to culture and identity, were not even remotely considered. The issue was taken to the National Office of the Ministry of Education (MOE) in Wellington. The Ministry of Education replied, highlighting the need to consider the learning needs of the student with reference to the Treaty principles and the strong expectation that *all schools* should be working towards offering students te reo Māori and tikanga Māori as part of the curriculum. So it seems school policy was out of touch with government policy (and law) in the way they planned and prioritized curriculum matters. Like so many schools around the country, particularly secondary schools, this school was in conflict with the Treaty. The Beeby in/out-clause had kicked in. The expectation was that Māori children were to fit into a very narrow prescription of a predetermined education pathway that they are "best fitted" for – and that did not include a Māori language pathway.

The pace of change is indeed slow. In the case of the evidence to the Waitangi Tribunal in 1986 and the example given 30 years later, it is crystal clear this kind of veto and erasure remains. Colonial attitudes and subtractive language practices are entrenched in education. The Tribunal noted

> ...something has gone wrong...We suspect that somewhere at some influential level in the Department, there remains an attitude—it may be in planning or in education boards, or at the level of principals or head teachers, we cannot say—a vestige of the attitude expressed by a former Director of Education who wrote in the middle of the first half of this [20th] century: "... The natural abandonment of the native tongue involves no loss on the Māori ..." [See Māori and Education, ed, P M Jackson 1931 at p 193]. We have no reason to think that such an opinion is held in the topmost levels of the administration in the Education

Department today, but whether it does exist at other strategic points in the system is a matter of concern. (p. 37)

The Tribunal rejected the backward view in terms of the impact of language loss. The 1986 Waitangi Tribunal not only agreed that state policies had jeopardized the Māori language, but went beyond that to allocate responsibility for widespread Māori educational "failure" as residing within the education "system," concluding that the system was operating in breach of the Treaty of Waitangi. That fact-finding was historical. For example, since 1955 the Department had been aware that an understanding of Māori language and culture was necessary for both the full personal development of Māori children and to assist Pākehā children "...to fully appreciate the history, achievements and character of Māori society" (cited at p. 35). By 1955, there was a strong and growing demand for the Māori language to be taught more extensively in the schools. The Tribunal noted the resolution of the 1955 Committee on Māori Education that supported the teaching of the Māori language and its recommendation that everything possible be done to implement it. Sir Apirana Ngata had been lobbying for that to happen a decade prior to that (Ramsden 1948). Since the Tribunal hearing there have been some legal and political developments, but how far have we come?

Legal and Political Developments: The Old Māori Language Act 1987

In the wake of the Waitangi Tribunal (1986) deliberation on the question of whether te reo Māori is a language of the state, it concluded that the Māori language could be regarded as a "taonga" (treasured possession) and in July the following year the Māori Language Act (1987) was passed into legislation. The Act declared te reo Māori to be a "taonga" (in terms of the Treaty of Waitangi, to be protected and promoted) and an official language of New Zealand.

Te reo Māori is one of New Zealand's two official languages. Its official status, however, has yet to be recognized and reflected "in practice" in educational settings in spite of its legal and political recognition. In the face of all the evidence, the government Māori education strategy documents *Ka Hikitia* and related policies acknowledge that the "system" should "step up" to meet the needs of the people. But a strange irony, in those policies Māori are positioned as a "priority" group (Ministry of Education 2008, 2012). Although this suggests that change is imminent, nothing changes. It simply reinforces a longstanding myth that Māori, as a "priority" group, are accorded special "privileges," re-centering the focus of resource allocation for "all children." In this Pākehā dominance (power and privilege) is maintained, and Māori continue to struggle for linguistic, social, cultural, and spiritual survival. The positioning of Māori in a special place in whitestream education creates a pedagogy of duplicity as Māori children remain objectified as a "problem" to be fixed, yet somehow, inexplicably, "privileged." This discourse of "privilege" being afforded to Māori often leads to practices of contempt which sustain the colonial underpinnings of racism and linguicism.

The New Māori Language Act 2016

In the lead up to the passage of the new Māori Language Act, the Bill referred to *Te Reo Mauriora* as focusing on one aspect or context for development, iwi (or tribes) with, remarkably, less focus on education. The *Te Reo Mauriora* (Te Puni Kōkiri (Ministry of Māori Development) 2011) review used a UNESCO 2009 framework for determining the state of a language in terms of its vitality, and drawing on relevant statistics the panel considered te reo Māori to fit somewhere between "definitely endangered" (Definitely endangered: children no longer learn the language as a mother tongue in the home.) and "severely endangered (The language is spoken by older generations; while the parent generation may understand it, they do not speak it to the children or among themselves.)" according to intergenerational transmission measures (p. 17). It considered socio-historical linguistic sustainability requires the merging of the current educational focus with a focus on growing the language in homes. Even though a central theme was improving the quality of language used by teachers, the notion of te reo Māori being a core part of the national curriculum was felt to be premature.

On 14 April 2016, *Te Ture mō Te Reo Māori 2016: Māori Language Act* (2016) was passed into legislation with the date of assent being 29 April 2016, subsequently repealing the old Act. Its stated purpose is

(a) To affirm the status of the Māori language as
  (i) The Indigenous language of New Zealand
  (ii) A taonga of iwi and Māori
  (iii) A language valued by the nation
  (iv) An official language of New Zealand
(b) To provide means to support and revitalize the Māori language (p. 29).

The Act provides for the establishment of an entity named *Te Mātāwai* which, together with the Crown, is to develop Māori language strategies to support the promotion and revitalization of te reo Māori. But it raises questions. What does clause (ii) that the Māori language is "a taonga of iwi and Māori" mean given the juxtaposition of the words "iwi and Māori," when iwi are Māori? Or is the "iwi" referred here referring to all "iwi" – iwi Pākehā and Māori? All of the speeches made in Parliament on April 14, 2016, when the Bill was passed into law referred to the notion that te reo Māori was for all New Zealanders. If that is indeed the case, what does it mean for the nation to "value" a language? Does it have to be spoken to be valued? Can one value a language when it is not spoken? It can easily be said "I value Latin" but is that enough to bring a dead language back to life? If it is a national language, an official language, valued by all, and for all New Zealanders, does that mean all New Zealanders should have access to it to enable them to speak it? How than can that be achieved? What does it mean for education and the language/s of curricula?

Kōhanga Reo

In the wake of the reo Māori lobbying of the 1970s, the Māori language march and a nation-wide kaumātua (elder) hui of the 1980s, and the restructuring of New Zealand in the neoliberal advance of the 1980s and 1990s, Te Kōhanga Reo (TKR) was born. The intention at the beginning of the TKR movement was to stay the decline of te reo Māori and to address issues of sociocultural and identity disruption due to colonization (Skerrett-White 2003). By bridging the sociolinguistic gap between generations, some of the sociocultural disruption associated with language loss would be alleviated, also contributing to a socioculturally rejuvenated iwi Māori (Māori tribal peoples). The first kōhanga reo opened in 1982. Within 3 years the number had risen dramatically, driven by Māori communities with a sense of urgency in acting to protect and promote te reo me ngā tikanga Māori (the Māori language and culture).

Between 1982 and 1993, the number of kōhanga reo rose by around 80 per year and their enrolments by more than 1,400 a year, to reach 809 and 14,514, respectively, in 1993 when kōhanga reo provided for just under a *half* of all mokopuna in early childhood care and education (ECCE) (ECCE and ECE are used interchangeably to represent the same early childhood sector.) (Waitangi Tribunal 2012). However, that year was the zenith for Kōhanga Reo. The movement started to decline largely due to what has been referred to as "glacial" (Walker 2004) and leaden-footed (Waitangi Tribunal 2012) policy responses to Māori language protection and promotion. It did not help that public policy was introduced which deliberately undermined the philosophy, goals, and practices of Te Kōhanga Reo. The subsidy cuts (Parents had to be in either full time work, or training, to access a subsidy for their child to attend Te Kōhanga Reo.) in 1994 made it difficult for parents to remain involved in Kōhanga Reo to help to bridge the intergenerational language gap. Many of us working in Kōhanga Reo at that time marched down the main street of Hamilton in protest because of the impact of the government drive towards marketization in education and the cutbacks.

The subsidy cuts were seen by government as a way of maximizing workforce potential through upskilling parents into training or seeing Kōhanga as a childcare facility to free up young mothers particularly for the labor market. Kōhanga Reo was not seen as a platform for upholding and growing Indigenous knowledge. From that point on development was impeded, Kōhanga Reo is now only providing for under a *quarter* of all Māori mokopuna in early childhood care and education.

Structural Reform and Government Policies: The Meade Report

In 1988, early childhood education (ECE) came fully under the Education Department (now the Ministry of Education). The Working Group Report (known as the Meade Report) (Meade 1988) promised much in terms of equity across the ECE sector (quality provision, more parental choice, adequate funding) but which did not translate into appropriate policy (see *Before Five*, 1988).

The Meade Report noted the place of te reo Māori and tikanga Māori as concerns of Māoridom and as central tenets of quality ECE provision and the terms of reference included Treaty recognition. Skerrett-White (2001), however, argued that an unintended outcome of the Report was that it locked TKR settings into a pattern of decline and stated "The writing was on the wall that TKR would not only be shifted to 'education' [portfolio], but that it would be subjected to the same educational reforms of marketization and regulation as other educational providers..." (p. 14). In other words, TKR came under the regulatory framework meant for the whitestream sector.

Before Five Policy Statement

The policy statement *Before Five*, issued in December 1988 by government, reneged on earlier promises of equity in the Meade Report. It opted for an independent reviewing regime, from an essentially "developmental" epistemological frame, as well as assuring a compliance regime in a regulatory structure (Waitangi Tribunal 2012) from an English oriented ontological frame. The developmental frame was based on the arbiters of "correct" or "normal" development and colonizing theories of child development. The ontological frame forced the TKR movement into compliance where Pākehā norms and behaviors became the benchmark.

Since the early heady days of Kōhanga Reo expansion, the challenges for bilingual provision have intensified, especially because of the lack of well-educated, proficient speakers and teachers of Māori. The glaringly obvious policy gaps led to predictable outcomes. Of the shift of TKR from Māori Affairs to the Ministry of Education in 1989, it was argued "While many working in the early childhood sector hailed the *Before Five* reforms, many working in TKR felt a sense of foreboding" (cited in Skerrett-White 2001, p. 16). Early on in the establishment of TKR, Te Rangihau, a much-esteemed Māori elder, warned;

> We have come a long way in a very short time with Te Koohanga (Some tribal dialects prefer the written double vowel to a macron, as in Koohanga and Kōhanga.) Reo and already I am seeing the signs of professionals in many fields homing in to take advantage of those aspects that can be documented for personal gain or for political purpose. If this trend was to continue and we were to take this to its extreme conclusion, my fear is that we would no longer have a people's movement, let alone a Maaori people's movement. (TKR Trust Incorporated 1984, cited in Skerrett-White 2001)

Wider iwi-Māori (tribal groupings) were gravely concerned. Political developments in the intervening years have proven those concerns predictably valid.

Glacial Policy Responses to the waiMāori Stream

The Waitangi Tribunal Reports (2010, 2012) found that te reo Māori is in renewed decline, occurring at both the young and old ends of the spectrum. The Tribunal asserts that Kōhanga Reo were established not because of the Department, but *in*

Table 1 Māori enrolments in ECE. Adapted from Education Counts (2016) Statistics

Year	2010	2011	2012	2013	2014~	2015~
No. of Māori enrolments in centers using te reo Māori for 81–100% of the time	9,152	9,375	9,154	9,001	8,454	8,384
Total number of Māori enrolments in ECE	35,885	37,808	38,644	40,909	45,648	45,128

spite of it and that "... the extraordinary success of TKR is clear evidence that the Māori community sees that Māori language and culture are a necessary element for the self-esteem, dignity and mana of Māori people" (p. xi). The outcome is bilingual, bicultural children and a strengthened whānau. It is argued that the reo "movement" has been "...weakened more by the governmental failure to give it adequate oxygen and support than by any Māori rejection of their language" (Waitangi Tribunal 2012, p. xi). Further, that if trends continued over the next 15–20 years, the Māori language speaking proportion of the population would decline further. That trend has continued (see Table 1).

The decline is occurring in the context of a growing Māori population. Since 2000 the pattern of decline in the percentage of Māori ECE enrolments at Kōhanga Reo has been an average of 1% per annum from 36.6% in 2000 to the latest statistic collected by the Annual Census of ECE Services of 18.6% in 2015.

The *Wai262* Report argues that the bureaucracy's efforts to put in place measures to deal with and encourage the Māori language renaissance have been "[d]ecidedly leaden-footed" (p. 58) and that the explosion in the numbers attending kōhanga reo in the early 1980s should have instantly signaled supply and demand issues. Failure to meet the demands of quality immersion/bilingual education has accounted for the eventual decline in student numbers and not the failure of the language movement.

Te Whāriki: An Ideological Conundrum

Te Whāriki, He Whāriki Mātauranga mo ngā Mokopuna o Aotearoa (Ministry of Education 1996) (*Te Whāriki*) the early childhood curriculum for Aotearoa/NZ was developed from 1991 to 1996. Following extensive consultation with diverse groups *Te Whāriki: Draft guidelines for developmentally appropriate programmes in early childhood services* was published in 1993. Several pilot projects were established, but it was not until the end of 1995 that the Ministry of Education finally funded a round of English medium teacher development contracts offering widespread support specifically for its implementation (Nuttall 2005). Even though TKR came under the umbrella of the MOE no such support was accessible to those of us working there. While the whitestream focused on achieving regulatory compliance, and learning about assessment practices (in the context of neoliberal reform) for many of us working in the waiMāori (Wai Māori is a Māori term used for freshwater. I use this term because for many Māori in the whitestream the pathways are muddied with poor language policy and differing educational outcomes. In the waiMāori stream the additive bilingual outcomes are ideologically clarified for Māori English bilingualism to be the result.) stream committed to Māori language revernacularization, it was more a matter of "who has got a garage and is it warm" – so inequitable was the access to resource. Whereas curriculum matters were being discussed in residential professional development in-service courses funded by government for the whitestream (Nuttall 2005), the paradigmatic shift that took place in the waiMāori stream came about by the groundswell of whānau Māori belief in the idea of, and excitement in hearing, very young children speaking Māori. That phenomenon was foreign to the baby boomer generations. But the groundswell soon flattened.

Te Whāriki was eventually published in 1996 (Ministry of Education 1996). (It has recently been updated – *Te Whāriki, He Whāriki Mātauranga mo ngā Mokopuna o Aotearoa* (Ministry of Education 2017).) The regulatory framework for early childhood services was reviewed in the mid-2000s and new regulations were gazetted or officially notified by the Government in 2008. All early childhood services including the Māori medium sector are required to meet the *Curriculum Standard: general* as part of those regulations. The regulatory framework was consolidated and, unwittingly, the TKR movement was swept away on the wave of regulatory reform.

Under the heading, "*The Educationalisation of Early Childhood*" (Early childhood education was and still is outside the compulsory sector.) Duhn (2012) asserts the education sector reforms coincided with major social reforms in Aotearoa, making it a "text-book case" for the neoliberal project. The moves constituted the political will towards the educationalization (and standardization) of early childhood. *Te Whāriki* explicitly emphasizes that learning is a life-long process that "begins at the very start of life" (Ministry of Education 1996, p. 7). The catch phrase of the day was "from the cradle to the grave." The curriculum provides links to the primary sector curriculum, *The New Zealand Curriculum Framework*. Although ECE is positioned outside the compulsory sector, the baby and young child is now part of a *grid* that produces the norms, locked in. This movement pushes the preschool aged child who remains at home into the increasingly "not normal"/at risk margin, the space already occupied by Māori. Before long Māori (and Pasifika) children (and families) became the targets for increased participation into whitestream provision, not the fast dwindling waiMāori stream.

Duhn (2012) argues that *Te Whāriki* functions as a technology of neoliberal government. It is publicized as being the first bicultural curriculum statement developed in New Zealand and puts up a strong case for all children in New Zealand to being bicultural, stating:

> This is a curriculum for early childhood care and education in New Zealand. In early childhood education settings, all children should be given the opportunity to develop knowledge and an understanding of the cultural heritages of both partners to Te Tiriti o Waitangi. The curriculum reflects this partnership in text and structure. (p. 9)

However, ERO (2013) found that the practices are far from "bicultural." Many services only referred to the Treaty and Treaty partnerships in their philosophy statements, not in practice. Too few ECCE centers were actually working in partnership with whānau Māori and through a bicultural curriculum which was responsive to Māori community. The report suggested that *Te Whāriki* was not well understood or implemented. ERO proposed that there was insufficient guidance, highlighting the common practice being very few services (only 10%) working in-depth with *Te Whāriki*, with most centers evaluated (80%) only making *some* use of it by having it documented (in their philosophy statement and planning). ERO noted that *practice* was often far removed from *intent* and highlighted some concerns relating to the *broad* nature of *Te Whāriki* framework. It stated that the framework "does not provide the sector with clear standards of practice for high quality curriculum implementation" (p. 2). It is argued here that the relationship between *biculturalism* and *bilingualism* is not ideologically (and therefore pedagogically) clarified as part of the determinants of "quality" and that one cannot be bicultural, if one is monolingual.

Duhn (2012) discusses the conundrum of *Te Whāriki* when she argues that New Zealand culture remains *assumed* rather than explicit and that "...the lack of definition of the 'centre' re-produces power relations by re-producing the Same/Other binary. By defining New Zealand culture different, to say British culture, solely on the basis of the presence of Māori people and to a lesser extent Pasifika people, New Zealand culture becomes part of the powerful centre that is western culture" (pp. 89–90). Further, the assumption of "sameness" is constructed against the backdrop of all *that is not the same*, and where important symbols and concepts like mātauranga (Māori knowledge) and whanaungatanga (Māori preferred practices of family-ness) are positioned in a colonial linguistic master/servant relationship, open to definition and interpretation according to the unspecified "center." Such appropriation simply provides a veneer of inclusivity.

Similarly, it is argued that along with the culture (essentially western British) being assumed, there is an assumption that the language of that culture, the "center," is English and therefore that all children must "speak English." The way *Te Whāriki* frames this is evident in the following learning outcomes.

Children develop:

- An increasing knowledge and skill, in both syntax and meaning, in *at least one* language
- An *appreciation of te reo* as a living and relevant language
- Confidence that their first language is valued (MOE 1996, p. 76, emphasis added)

English is the dominant language in Aotearoa, and the one compulsory language of the curriculum in all schools (the compulsory sector). Coupled with the idea that *Te Whāriki* in part is about the schoolification of the early childhood sector, the first outcome then is to develop the "national *Whāriki* child" knowledgeable (semantically and syntactically) in and of *English*, but with an *appreciation* of the "*other*" reo – Māori language. While there is a lack of specificity as to the language of the "center," that it is *English* becomes obvious when it sits alongside the specificity of the "appreciation" outcome linked to te reo Māori. It simply re-produces the "Same/Other binary" that Duhn discusses and is clearly a case of linguafaction, the systematic language, and cultural destruction associated with the colonization of Aotearoa, facilitating the fragmentation of land/s, dismantling Māori social structures of whānau, hapū, and iwi, and disrupting sociolinguistic practices through assimilation (see Skerrett 2014, 2016). Having an "appreciation" clause does little to promote bilingualism with very young children in any event. That is at the heart of the "dilemma of *Te Whāriki*." While these are reframed as evidence of learning and development in the current update, they are essentially the same:

- Confidence that their first language is valued and increasing ability in the use of at least one language
- An appreciation of te reo Māori as a living and relevant language (MOE 2017, p. 42)

To complicate the issue, Duhn argues that this is happening at a time when New Zealand is deeply entangled in discourses and movements of globalization with the growing flow of people across national borders as Aotearoa becomes increasingly more cosmopolitan. She says that *Te Whāriki* shies away from addressing the complexities of multiculturalism quoting Lady Tilly Reedy's keynote speech where she asked, "Why pretend to be multicultural, if bicultural doesn't work?" (cited in Duhn 2012, p. 90).

It is important to understand that bicultural education *is* multicultural education because it deals with more than one culture. Nancy Hornberger (2009) provides further ideological clarification to the issue when she talks about intercultural and multilingual education. On the issue of multilingualism, at its best it is:

1. Multilingual in that it uses and values *more than one* language in teaching and learning
2. Intercultural in that it recognizes and values understanding and dialogue across diverse lived experiences and cultural worldviews
3. Education that draws out the knowledge/s students bring to the educational setting. (p. 198)

In line with Nancy Hornberger, the Māori language stream of education is multilingual/multicultural as its aims are, at the least, to use *more than one* language in teaching and learning. English-medium settings have historically employed subtractive approaches to Māori language learning and teaching with assimilatory into "New Zealand" (Pākehā/British) culture. Further, *Te Whāriki* shies away from addressing the complexities of biculturalism because of lack of analysis around what it means to be bicultural, and the relationship of language/s to biculturalism. The curriculum framework translates, in practice, into a common implicit (western) curriculum through a common implicit (western) language by design. Therein lies the dilemma of *Te Whāriki;* how do you implement *bicultural* curriculum *mono-lingually*?

That is not the intention of *Te Whāriki*. Lady Tilly Reedy, one of the architects of *Te Whariki*, said that she felt the burden of responsibility of "...thinking in Māori and laying down a philosophical framework in Māori that would survive the challenge of an education system which had had 200 years of implementing a system that was different to Māori and ignorant of Māori" (Reedy 2013, p. 2). She added "Unfortunately in the final analysis when the opportunity came to implement in the multi society we often boast about, the Ministry of Education and governments of the day could not throw off its colonial cloak entirely" (p. 2). Why? It is argued here that the real gem of *Te Whāriki* lies in the untapped knowledge, untouched potential that is in Part B which is written in te reo Māori. Whilst page 10 of *Te Whāriki* states "The English and Māori texts parallel and complement each other" (MOE 1996), they do not. Part B is unique, stemming from a Māori world view. Duhn (2012) argues that the parallel/complementing analysis has more of a closer association with the colonial loom than traditional weaving of a whāriki. She goes on to describe the loom and its association with European industrialization and one of the symbols of capitalism at its most inhumane, stating

> Weaving was one of the first industries of the emerging capitalist order. The weaver was literally tied to his or her loom. Survival depended on his/her ability to skilfully guide raw material between the grids of the industrial loom. The transformation from yarn to linen occurred to pre-set patterns. Weavers were required to aim for flawless, uniform weaving. Weavers were exploited to the extreme. (p. 97)

Duhn then goes on to discuss traditional weaving from process and structural perspectives.

> Throughout the process of weaving, the product retains some of the pliable qualities of the raw material. The weaver is not tied to a particular location – she can weave anywhere. Furthermore, the absence of a structural device, other than the weaver's imagination of what she wants to weave, allows for all kinds of shapes to emerge.

What is important in the traditional process is the very first line of the weave, called *Te Aho Matua,* literally the foremost thread. That first interlay sets the firm foundations of the weave, with and through the mediation of the spiritual domain, Indigenous knowledge, skills, values, and desires; all laid out in the casting of *Te Aho Matua*. The foundation then guides the creative endeavor. It provides the blueprint but very differently to the loom that restricts and constrains. Once *Te Aho Matua* is laid down, there can be lines of flight at any moment, with the utilization of any resource; it is all dependent on where the weaver wants to go. However, there is always a connection back to *Te Aho Matua*. That is the creativity embodied in the traditional style of weaving. Care, deliberation, and skill within the scaffold of the cultural context with its own values and knowledge ensure the success of the endeavor. That is why the metaphor of *Te Aho Matua* lays the philosophical foundations of kaupapa Māori education. According to Tuki Nepe:

> *Te Aho Matua* is a philosophical doctrine that incorporates the knowledge, skills, attitudes and values of Maori society that have emanated from a purely Kaupapa Maori metaphysical base. (1991, p. 41)

The parallel gridlock in the weft/warp construct locks te reo Māori into a separate frame. The structure creates blind spots, where children who are caught in the blind spots remain invisibilized. It is a fine example of the linguafaction that happens with many Indigenous languages which are objectified and where there is no space to crossover in an interface.

The messages of *Te Whāriki* are indeed mixed and confused. So too are many of the people working out in the field charged with its implementation. Duhn (2012) goes on to discuss the *Whāriki* framework in terms of the *Whāriki* child woven into the warp and the weft of the frame. She discusses how the centers working within this frame can do one of two things: use the curriculum to challenge existing power relations (within communities and the wider society) or carry on business as usual (maintaining the status quo and existing power relations). It is argued here the latter is the default mechanism where the business as usual has its roots firmly entrenched in the colonial architecture of New Zealand. Within the weft/warp frame, there are then distinct visions of the Whāriki children emerging who are monoglots. According to the policy document, *Tau Mai te Reo* Māori language in education provision (MOE 2013) consists of two streams. The streams are Māori medium education and Māori language in English medium education. The streams are distinct and likely to deliver varying language outcomes for learners; many learners transition in and out of these pathways throughout their education journey (p. 19). *Te Whāriki*, building on the relationship of biculturalism to bilingualism, needs to decide what stream it is swimming in. There are implications for teachers and community.

Māori Language as Resistance

This chapter has been both a documentation of injustice and a resistance to the subjugation of Māori knowledge and language in the creation of space for the Māori voices to be "heard," to be "listened to," to "be known," to "be lived." It challenges racism, linguicism, colonialism, and all the other isms and schisms. It explores relevant policy documents influencing Māori education in general (early years' bilingual/immersion education specifically) commencing with the colonial backdrop of Treaty signing and the treachery involved in turning it into an instrument of invasion, land confiscation, and duplicity through the colonial courts. It overviewed the impact colonization and Treaty jurisprudence on Māori education and the Kōhanga Reo movement. A succession of settler government legislative acts largely determining land tenure and establishing all of the socio-political structures (councils, hospitals, prisons, churches, asylums, and schools) meant the imposition of a foreign system as far as Māori were concerned. Political developments and public policies ushered in systematically undermined the Treaty as enforced assimilation was on the educational agenda for Māori. Māori rights went unprotected. Māori socio-cultural disruption is the result. Māori language shift occurred at the same rate as land confiscations and relocations. Māori resistance has been constant. Māori are resurgence inevitable.

The 1985/1986 legal decision concerning the recognition and role of the Māori language as a taonga meant a guaranteed right to protection under the Act. But in spite of subsequent legal and political developments, our language and culture is still threatened. The power of veto and harmful practices that have been going on in schools for a very long time are explored through the Waitangi Tribunal hearings of 1986 and my own recent experiences as a Māori parent. They highlight the significance of the number one issue in education for Maori learners and that of keeping them safe from harm, psychologically, pedagogically, culturally, and linguistically. According to the Office of the Children's Commissioner (2016):

> For mokopuna Māori, culture is a key element of identity that can influence their sense of belonging either positively or negatively. When children's cultural needs are met, their sense of belonging is enhanced. When they are disconnected from their culture, the opposite is true. Therefore, Māori cultural competence is crucial in a child-centred system... This sense of identity and belonging is fundamental to children and young people's psychological wellbeing. (p. 21)

That there are strategic points in the education system where there remain attitudes of it being acceptable to harm Māori children and their whānau through the myriad of microaggressions is clear. The new Māori Language Act 2016 afforded the opportunity to tackle the obvious problem of a monolingual, mono-cultural racist, linguicist education system. Instead, it steered away from the issue of providing for Māori language in the system, the whole system. The discussion of the slow Crown response to initiatives forwarded in the Kōhanga Reo movement demonstrated how it has stymied advancements, making many of the difficulties associated with Kōhanga Reo and the stream of Māori language education politically constructed problems. Kōhanga Reo is constantly resisting the hegemonic politics of neoliberal capture and control as educational policies, and the law remains out of kilter with the needs of the Māori language movement. While it may be a truism that no language can reside exclusively within an education system or school, it is widely acknowledged that the state education system played a major role bringing the Māori language to near language death through the shift from Māori to English. It should therefore play a pivotal role in helping to reverse that language shift, but it does not. It does the reverse. It programs Māori children to disengage with their heritage language.

Kōhanga Reo was established to stay the impact of language loss and socio cultural dislocation experienced in Māori communities. It has been the leading light in bilingual education in Aotearoa/New Zealand and internationally. It is a whole-of-whānau approach to language regeneration, through the intergenerational transmission of te reo Māori while also returning to the mana (authority, esteem, integrity) of the whānau (the smallest unit of Māori tribal structures) the care and education of the very young. However, it has been shown how the movement has been swept away in the tsunami of strategic policy developed for an English-language sector, leaving a weakened "parent-led" or "whānau (family) –led" (TKR) movement and a reinforced teacher-led (monolingual English) sector creating a "parent-led, teacher-led" divide. The divide created the moribund context for TKR (with a "nonquality" categorization under the *Pathways to the Future* policy) (MOE 2002) and a burgeoning mainstream ECCE context (categorized as "quality" under the *Pathways* policy). While the intention may have been the professionalization of the teaching profession in the early childhood sector, the nascent Kōhanga Reo movement was particularly vulnerable as there were no "officially sanctioned" teacher education programs. Funding went the way of the professional "teachers." The Māori "parent-led" stream suffered losses in enrolments and a decline in funding. The follow-on inequities, entrenched at the structural level, became evident with accelerated growth in English-medium; and a forced shift for many Māori parents and their children into the English sector as options became limited. This also contributed to the rapidly declining numbers and resources in the Māori-medium sector. The linguicist colonial apparatus of the state, powerfully authoritative and menacing, constantly eroded the Māori language goals of the Māori-medium sector. The gross inequities are evident today.

The dominant ideology in educational policy and practice positions Māori children as deficit, passive objects within a system of one-size-fits-all; the "one-size" being fashioned around dominant Pākehā settler children and their language. This gives the dominant group the power base. The dominant language, knowledge, and values foisted upon Māori via a narrow (foreign) curriculum by racist teachers are harmful to Māori children. Skutnabb-Kangas' (2015) construct of *linguicism* already referred to above is helpful. She argues that while the state (via whitestream teachers) may not "intend to harm children" (p. 5) teachers are harmful because the educational structures within which they operate are harmful. Māori language and knowledge noticeably absent in the dominant whitestream schools. Unfortunately, that is where the majority of Māori children are positioned, largely through lack of provision.

It is argued in this chapter that the relationship between biculturalism and bilingualism is not ideologically (and therefore pedagogically) clarified as part of the determinants of "quality," in the early childhood sector. There is also the corollary argument that one cannot be bicultural, if one is monolingual. These relationality ideas extend the policy discussion on the cuts to Kōhanga Reo, seen through the "productivity" lens rather than a "platform for upholding and growing Indigenous knowledge." That is, they are more than just a vestige of colonialist imposition but an example of the ongoing binary positioning of Indigenous languages (and knowledges) as expendable, to be relegated to the periphery, while centering and expanding the colonial language at the center. This is a good example of the insidiousness of colonizer power colonizing. Moreover, the policy frameworks, in highlighting "inclusivity" through "biculturalism," are working to target Māori children for increased participation into whitestream provision, not the fast-dwindling waiMāori stream. Double language is double power, which possibly gives a clue to an unspoken, though characteristic, fear of "other" (and another colonial strategy). This troubles the theme of *Te Whāriki* as a bi/multicultural framework by continuing Māori as deficit (to be fixed, fit for purpose) and then by promoting a duplicitous facade. On the face (and language) of the framework, it is Indigenous weavers who are doing the weaving, or at least are involved in the project. However, the weaving process and the weavers sit within a binary of often-conflicting relationships driven by contradictory British and Māori values, languages, philosophies, and epistemologies. This elucidates why "participation" has continued to be both "assimilatory" and "illusionary" for Māori. Equally, it remains "colonizing" and "perplexing" for Pākehā. Therein lies the conundrum that is clearly a fault in the cognitively dissonant design, resulting in a deception. It is worthwhile reiterating that the status quo of education, steeped in 200 years of paternalistic colonial mindsets, remains at the center of policy and practice in New Zealand.

Te Rangatiratanga o te Reo (Language as Liberating)

Rangatiratanga (often translated as sovereignty or self-determination) is about the ability to control the way the world enters into our minds, bodies, and daily lives and the ability to think critically and respond collectively in order to mediate external influences and the rate of change, which affects our lives and resources. Smith (2012) argues that what is slightly different between notions of struggle "in the margins" is that when attached to a political idea such as *rangatiratanga* not just the margins but all space in New Zealand can be regarded as Māori space. Importantly, this takes the struggle out of specifically "Māori contexts" which can be narrowly defined, even somewhat gridlocked as in the case of *Te Whāriki* and "...into the spaces once regarded as the domain of the 'settler' or Pākehā community, such as large institutions like universities where Māori really are a small minority" (p. 202). Further, that rather than just seeing ourselves as merely "existing" in the margins we see ourselves, as our ancestors did, all over this land. Our ancestral houses are mapped on to the land, from Cape to Bluff, to Wharekauri and beyond. As Smith puts it "Aotearoa, New Zealand is 'our place', all of it, and that there is little difference, except in the mind, between, for example a Te Kōhanga Reo where Māori are the majority but the state is there, and a university, where Māori are the minority and the state is there" (p. 202). Further, a *rangatiratanga* frame addresses injustice. It contests the positioning of Māori children as subservient objects for subjugation. It challenges the notion of whitestream teachers as "authority and authoritative," rejecting the construct of linguistic hierarchies, exposing linguafaction and challenging linguicism. All languages are powerful. All children have the right to move beyond the master/servant relationships of colonization.

Te rangatiratanga o te reo (translated here as the sovereignty of language) then is not just about resistance to injustice and the inversion of colonial rule, but the assertion of Māori sovereignty through Māori language in "our place," all of it and everywhere. It is a reassertion of the legitimation and authority of te reo Māori and the rights of children to live te reo Māori, to live its history, its future, its identity, its world-views, its values, its symbolism, and its spirit. It is a drive to invert the prevailing colonial ideologies of hierarchizing languages. No, the world is not English, or Spanish or French or whatever the colonial language happens to be. Indigenous languages enable the liberation from the gridlock of colonial curriculum and the blind spots of erasure they create. The liberatory power of the Māori language to free the Māori mind from the language and thinking of the colonizer is what is inherent in *te rangatiratanga o te reo, kia Māori*. Māori language is central to the freedom thinking needed to dismantle colonial architecture, disrupt colonial rule, and disturb colonial expansion. Freedom thinking is needed to break the illogic of coloniality in order to reoccupy spaces beyond the margins, beyond the hinterlands.

Conclusions

> Everyone who says that they're a New Zealander the language is for all of us. Both the Māori language and the Pākehā language. (The late Te Oraiti Calcott; Waka Huia 2016)

Our treasured Māori language is our life force; it nourishes our souls and feeds our minds. If we think of language as a taonga and a valued resource, then the growth of Māori/English bilingual children in Aotearoa will greatly enhance the nation's mana and wealth in a system in which both the official spoken and written languages are equally sanctioned, equally valued, equally loved, and equally honored, as was envisioned in the Treaty of Waitangi. If we do not, then we pass up the most vitally significant way of unravelling and understanding the dominant discourses of myth making. We have no other way of inversion – or turning things around. Our language is our last defense. It houses our stories, our world-views, and our knowledge/s; it is our cultural archive and our national treasure and sustains our tūrangawaewae – our place to stand. It is that simple. Māori language shapes the Māori mind, leaving no space for the illogic of colonialism to infiltrate. You cannot speak with a Māori mind if you do not have it. It is time to throw off the colonial cloak completely.

Te reo Māori defines what it means to be a "kiwi," the sentiment that underpins the quote drawn on at the outset of this chapter by Aperahama Taonui. In 1840 at the signing of the Treaty of Waitangi, he put out a resounding warning not to lay a shroud on the Treaty of Waitangi but to cloak the Treaty with our unique, kiwi-feathered, cloak. The warning was prophetic and solemn in its sense of foreboding. Aotearoa has been shrouded for a time, but the *rangatiratanga* framework provides us with clear pathways; *te rangatiratanga o te reo* provides us with the epistemological tools to pursue those pathways to liberation and self-determination.

Glossary

Aotearoa Land of the Long White Cloud/New Zealand
Hapū Smaller tribal groups/Sub-tribe/pregnant
Hui Meeting, gathering
Iwi Tribe, people, bones
Kaupapa Māori education A distinctly Māori, philosophically and linguistically enriched, education system
Kōhanga reo Māori language nest (Early Years Educational Setting)
Marae Formal Māori gathering place
Mātauranga Māori Māori knowledge systems

Pākēhā Non-Māori New Zealanders
Papatūānuku Mother earth
Rangatiratanga Sovereignty/Self-determination
Tamariki Children
Taonga Treasure, anything prized
Te The
Te Aho Matua The central thread
Te ao Māori Māori worldviews
Te ao Pākehā Pākehā worldviews
Te Puni Kōkiri Ministry of Māori Development
Te reo The language
Te reo mauriora The flourishing language
Te Taura Whiri Māori Language Commission
Tikanga Custom
Tino Rangatiratanga Right to exercise authority, chiefly autonomy, self-determination
Tūrangawaewae A place to stand
waiMāori Fresh water/Māori stream in education
Waka Canoe
Wānanga Institution of higher learning, discuss in depth
Whakairo Carving
Whānau Family (including extended)
Whare House
Whāriki Flax woven mat

References

Alcorn N (1999) To the fullest extent of his powers: C.E. Beeby's life in education. Victoria University Press, Wellington
Ballara A (1986) Proud to be white? A survey of pākehā prejudice in New Zealand. Heinemann Publishers, Auckland
Bevan-Smith J (2012) The new cannibal club: deconstructing history in Aotearoa New Zealand. Unpublished doctoral thesis, University of Auckland
Duhn I (2012) Globalising childhood: assembling the bicultural child in the New Zealand early childhood curriculum, Te Whāriki. Int Crit Child Policy Stud J 1(1):82–105
Education Counts (2016) Māori Education. Retrieved from: https://www.educationcounts.govt.nz/home
Education Review Office (2013) Working with Te Whāriki. Education Review Office, Wellington. Retrieved from http://www.ero.govt.nz/assets/Uploads/Working-with-Te-Whariki-May-2013-web.pdf
Hornberger N (2009) Multilingual education policy and practice: Ten certainties (grounded in Indigenous experience). Language Teaching 42(2):197–211. https://doi.org/10.1017/S0261444 808005491
Māori Language Act 1987 (1987) New Zealand legislation. Retrieved from http://www.legislation.govt.nz/act/public/1987/0176/latest/DLM124116.html

Meade A (1988) Education to be more. Report of the Early Childhood Care and Education Working Group. Government Printer, Wellington

Mikaere A (2011) Colonising myths Māori realities: He rukuruku whakaaro. The Wānanga o Raukawa, Huia Publishers, Wellington

Ministry of Education (1996) Te Whāriki: he whāriki mātauranga mō ngā mokopuna o Aotearoa: early childhood curriculum. Learning Media, Wellington

Ministry of Education (2002) Pathways to the future: Ngā huarahi arataki. Learning Media, Wellington

Ministry of Education (2008) Ka hikitia – managing for success: Māori education strategy 2008–2012. Ministry of Education, Wellington

Ministry of Education (2012) Me Kōrero – let's talk! Ka hikitia – accelerating success: 2013–2017. Ministry of Education, Wellington

Ministry of Education (2013) Tau mai te reo: the Māori language in education strategy 2013–2017. Ministry of Education, Wellington

Ministry of Education (2017) Te Whāriki: he whāriki mātauranga mō ngā mokopuna o Aotearoa: early childhood curriculum. Ministry of Education, Wellington

Mutu M (2010) Constitutional intentions: the Treaty of Waitangi texts. In: Mulholland M, Tawhai V (eds) Weeping waters: the Treaty of Waitangi and constitutional change. Huia Publishers, Wellington

Nepe TM (1991) E hao nei e tenei reanga. Te toi huarewa tipuna: Kaupapa Māori – An educational intervention system. Unpublished MA Thesis, NZ: University of Auckland

New Zealand Legislative Council Ordinances (1841–1853) Public ordinance no. X. Government Printer, Wellington, pp 73–74

Nuttall J (2005) Looking back, looking forward: three decades of early childhood curriculum development in Aotearoa New Zealand. Curric Matters 1:12–29

Office of the Children's Commissioner (2016) State of care 2016. Retrieved from http://www.occ.org.nz/assets/Publications/OCC-State-of-Care-2016FINAL.pdf

Ramsden E (1948) Sir Apirana Ngata and Māori culture. A.H. & A.W. Reed, Wellington

Reedy T (2013) Te Whāriki: a tapestry for life. Keynote presented at the New Zealand Conference on Early Childhood Education and Care in co-operation with the Ministry of Education and the OECD ECEC Network, Wellington

Shilliam R (2016) Colonial architecture or relatable hinterlands? Locke, Nandy, Fanon, and the Bandung spirit. Constellations 23(3):425–435. Wiley

Skerrett M (2014) Dismantling colonial myths: centralising Māori language in education. In: Ritchie J, Skerrett M (eds) Early childhood education in Aotearoa New Zealand: history, pedagogy, and liberation. Palgrave Macmillan, New York, pp 10–34. https://doi.org/10.1057/9781137375797.0004

Skerrett M (2016) The determinants of 'quality' in Aotearoa/New Zealand: Māori perspectives. In: Cannella GS, Pérez MS, Lee IF (eds) Critical examinations of quality in childhood education and care: regulation, disqualification, and erasure. Peter Lang, New York, pp 59–82

Skerrett-White MN (2001) The rise and decline of te kohanga reo: the impact of government policy. In: Ritchie J, Parsonson A, Karetu T, Te Uira N, Lanning G (eds) Te Taarere aa Tawhaki. Waikato University College, Hamilton, pp 11–22

Skerrett-White MN (2003) Kia mate rā anō a tama-nui-te-rā: reversing language shift in kōhanga reo. Unpublished doctoral thesis, Waikato University, Hamilton

Skutnabb-Kangas T (2015) Linguicism. In The encyclopedia of applied linguistics. Malden, MA: Blackwell, pp 1–6

Smith L (2012) Decolonising methodologies: research and Indigenous peoples, 2nd edn. Zed Books, London

Te Puni Kōkiri (2011) Te Reo Mauriora: Te arotakenga o te rangai reo Māori me te rautaki reo Māori. Review of the Māori language sector and the Māori language strategy, Apr 2011. Retrieved from http://www.tpk.govt.nz/_documents/te-reo-mauriora.pdf

Te Ture mō Te Reo Māori 2016: Māori Language Act 2016 (2016) New Zealand legislation. Retrieved from http://www.legislation.govt.nz/act/public/2016/0017/latest/DLM6174509.html?search=ts_act_Maori+language_resel_25_a&p=1

Waitangi Tribunal (1986) Report of the Waitangi Tribunal on the te reo Māori claim. Waitangi Tribunal, Wellington

Waitangi Tribunal (2010) Pre-publication Waitangi Tribunal report 262: Te Reo Māori. Waitangi Tribunal, Wellington

Waitangi Tribunal (2012) Pre-publication Waitangi Tribunal report 2336: Matua Rautia: the report on the Kōhanga Reo claim. Waitangi Tribunal, Wellington

Walker R (2004) Ka Whawhai Tonu Matou. Struggle without end, revised edn. Penguin, Auckland

Elaboration and Intellectualization of Te Reo Māori: The Role of Initial Teacher Education

29

Tony Trinick

Contents

Introduction	506
Methodology: Theories of Language Planning	508
Dimensions of Language Planning	510
Language Intellectualization	512
Language Elaboration and Intellectualization: Pedagogical Implications	513
Language Elaboration and Intellectualization: Language Revitalization Implications	514
The Use of the Term Intellectualization	514
Te Reo Māori in Education Planning	515
The Development of Te Reo Māori in Schooling: Post 1980s	515
Te Reo Māori Elaboration: Schooling	517
Initial Teacher Education: The Māori Medium Experience	518
Language Planning: Māori-Medium Initial Teacher Education	519
Language Elaboration and Intellectualization in Māori-Medium ITE	520
Conclusion and Future Directions	521
References	523

Abstract

There is a growing consensus among language planning scholars that in marginalized indigenous languages contexts, such as Māori, there is a need for deliberate efforts to accelerate the process of language intellectualization in the higher domains of education, and there are questions as to whether this is occurring systematically in Māori-medium initial teacher education (ITE). Intellectualization of a language involves the development of new linguistic resources to support teaching and learning in the medium of that language. The intellectualization of a language associated with education is considered desirable for both sociolinguistic

T. Trinick (✉)
Te Puna Wānanga, Faculty of Education and Social Work, University of Auckland, Auckland, New Zealand
e-mail: t.trinick@auckland.ac.nz

and educational reasons. By expanding the domains where the language is spoken into tertiary education, it supports the prestige of the language – an important consideration in reversing indigenous language shift. An intellectualized variety of the language is required at the higher levels of Māori-medium ITE, in order to develop the professional competence of the teachers to teach in Māori-medium schools. Drawing on theories of language planning, this chapter examines the development of Māori-medium ITE, noting it has been similarly impacted on by many of the sociopolitical forces facing the Māori-medium schooling sector. This chapter examines the major pedagogical and language revitalization implications for Māori-medium education, primarily concerned with the intellectualization of the Māori language that needs to be urgently addressed.

Keywords
Language intellectualization · Initial teacher education · Indigenous languages

Introduction

In order for Māori-medium learners to achieve success and Māori-medium schooling to survive and flourish and remain an indispensable component of te reo Māori (Māori language) revitalization, a continued supply of teachers with the necessary competencies, skills, and disposition is required (Hohepa et al. 2014). While there is ongoing debate about what this range of skills and dispositions ought to be, this chapter argues teachers require the following skill – the ability to discuss and disseminate conceptual material at high levels of abstraction in te reo Māori. Although this is only one dimension of being an effective teacher, it does have significant implications for the teaching and learning of the various subjects for schooling and for te reo Māori revitalization itself. Drawing on language planning (LP) theories, this chapter will discuss why the ability to discuss concepts at high levels of abstraction or in language planning terms "to elaborate and intellectualize the language" is important sociolinguistically (language revival) and educationally (teaching and learning).

Language planning as it is considered today in the literature generally consists of three interrelated dimensions, namely status, corpus, and language-in-education planning (Kaplan and Baldauf 2005). Status planning generally involves decisions a society or group must make about language selection and implementation, particularly within the official domains of language use in government and education, such as the English only policy in schooling in Aotearoa/NZ for over 100 years. Status planning has played a significant part in language shift in the Māori community to English and continues to do so today – despite te reo Māori being an official language in the modern era.

Corpus planning, on the other hand, focuses on changes by deliberate planning to the actual corpus or shape of a language itself, and involves the development of a standard orthography, creation of terminology and registers (Ferguson 2006). Planned corpus activities have usually been undertaken by language experts, such as Te Taura Whiri (Māori Language Commission), resulting in the production of new terms, dictionaries, writing styles, and pronunciation guides. Corpus planning is important for minority languages, such as te reo Māori, because the language was excluded from important domains such as schooling and tertiary education for over 100 years, and thus lacked the specialist terminology and register for teaching subjects such as mathematics. Corpus planning is also related to the standardization (codification) and elaboration (functional development) of a language. Ironically, in the New Zealand context, this process has not always been supported by the older Māori speaking community, as the corollary of language standardization is language change – an anathema to the older generation endeavoring among other things to preserve their dialects. However, the elaboration of a language is important and desirable in education because it focuses on the functional development of that language to enable it to operate in new domains such as Māori-medium schooling. This chapter will discuss briefly the elaboration process of te reo Māori in education in the modern era to support Māori-medium education in the period 1980–2016 and will examine whether this development has similarly occurred at the initial teacher education (ITE) level.

Related to language elaboration is the idea of language intellectualization. The intellectualization of a language involves the development of new linguistic resources for discussing and disseminating conceptual material at high levels of abstraction (Liddicoat and Bryant 2002). Language intellectualization is not confined to tertiary education, but can be found at all levels of education and takes place in a variety of other Māori language domains outside of formal schooling such as the debates that frequently occur on the marae (meeting house). It is a dynamic process and is characteristic of most languages, particularly so for indigenous languages such as te reo Māori who have thrown off the yoke of language suppression and are having to develop an expanded range of functions in domains such as education very quickly.

The third dimension of LP, language-in-education planning, substantially involves the state educational sector (Kaplan and Baldauf 1997). According to Cooper (1989), acquisition planning is "directed toward increasing the number of users, speakers, writers, listeners, or readers of a language" (p. 33). Acquisition planning concerns the teaching and learning of languages, whether national languages or minority indigenous languages such as te reo Māori, and is often situated in schooling (Bakmand 2000). Kaplan and Baldauf (1997) contended that the school has become one of the most critical sites for reversing language shift and for language revitalisation in endangered language contexts. Schools can become agents of positive language change, raising language loss or language use issues with students and the language community, thereby influencing the linguistic beliefs and practices of the language community (Skutnabb-Kangas 2000). In order for a language to function as the medium of instruction in schooling, it should also be used in some domains outside the schooling system, including in tertiary education.

This chapter will briefly examine LP in Māori-medium schooling to provide a context to examine LP efforts in Māori-medium ITE, particularly in regard to language elaboration and intellectualization, drawing on various ITE reports that have been commissioned (i.e., Murphy et al. 2008). This chapter will also examine why the intellectualization of a language at the tertiary level associated with education is important. For example, Liddicoat and Bryant (2002) argue that it has been important to introduce an intellectualized variety of the language at the higher levels of education including teacher education, in order to develop the professional competence of the teachers who will implement an intellectualized variety at the primary and secondary levels of education. There is where teacher education can play a key role.

In many countries, the role of intellectualizing a language is frequently the responsibility of ITE institutions and/or education faculties (Gonzalez 2002). It is questionable whether this is occurring for te reo Māori (Māori language) in education at the ITE level (Murphy et al. 2008). While several ITE institutions have emerged since the 1990s in response to the demands of the Māori-medium schooling sector, in the absence of qualified and experienced Māori-medium lecturers to teach the programs, many components of the programs are taught in English (Murphy et al. 2008). In defense of this pedagogy, one of the common arguments is that the knowledge and skills learned in English by the graduates are transferable to Māori-medium schooling contexts. The second connected issue-facing Māori-medium ITEs is that most student teachers are second language learners of the Māori language (Murphy et al. 2008). Researchers such as Cummins (2000) whose theories have had a significant influence on bilingual education in countries such as New Zealand advocate drawing on the learner's first language resources to support the acquisition of the second – in the case of most students in Māori-medium ITE this is English. This raises the issue of where and when do student teachers learn the specialized language to teach such subjects as mathematics in the medium of Māori. Clearly then there is a major tension between the learning of the specialized Māori language and learning the pedagogical content knowledge of subjects. This chapter argues that there are major pedagogical and language revitalization implications in this tension for Māori-medium education – primarily to do with the development of the academic register, the intellectualization of te reo Māori, and the status of the language itself.

Language planning, including the elaboration and intellectualization of te reo Māori in education at the tertiary level, has not been a priority area of education research nationally. Moreover, there appears to be minimal international and national literature on indigenous language ITE in terms of its role in revitalizing endangered languages in education.

Methodology: Theories of Language Planning

This research is located in an area where research from two interrelated disciplines is useful. Education and sociolinguistics (in particular, LP) have much in common. The processes of learning and communication are closely interrelated and are situated in fluid and evolving sociopolitical contexts. The histories of the two disciplines have common features. Traditionally, both utilized mostly quantitative, scientific methods, and, in particular, statistically based research techniques to investigate research questions. Over time, critical theories have emerged in reaction to the limitations of the positivist paradigm and have sought to explain both education and LP in light of the cultural, political, historical, and economic influences that shape them. Sociolinguistic and education interests overlap, particularly when the language concerned is an endangered indigenous language. A brief overview follows of the development of LP theory.

Initially, LP was seen as purely a technical exercise carried out by language experts supposedly working objectively to solve language problems (Nekvapil 2006). The problem could be transforming an oral language into a written one by the development of a standard orthography, grammar, and dictionaries (corpus planning). However, much of the focus during the early period of LP research in the 1960s was on the "rationalizing" of languages to select a national language for the purposes of modernization and related nation building (status planning), rather than just corpus planning per se. Ricento (2000) suggested that a widely held view among Westernized sociolinguists at that time was that linguistic diversity – bilingualism and/or multilingualism, presented obstacles for national development, while linguistic homogeneity was associated with modernization and westernization. While LP was a new research discipline in the 1960s, this particular linguistic hegemony was not new to many contexts, including schooling. For example, one of the imperatives that underpinned the 1867 Native Schools Act in New Zealand which decreed that English should be the only language used in the education of children was based on similar linguistic hegemonies of "rationalizing" languages so as to select a national language for the purposes of nation building (Simon 1998).

Criticisms of early approaches to LP include the argument that early LP failed to adequately analyze the impact of national plans and policies on local contexts and the use of language planning by dominant groups to maintain their economic and political advantage (May 2005; Ricento 2000). The latter went unseen because there was little reference initially to the role of ideology in language policy (Tollefson 2002).

By the 1970s, postmodern theories had emerged in reaction to the positivist outlook of early LP work. Work in critical linguistics (Fowler et al. 1979; Halliday 1978, 1985) and sociolinguistics (Hymes 1972) increasingly challenged positivist linguistic paradigms. These developments, referred to as "critical theory" approaches (Ricento and Hornberger 1996, p. 406), sought to explain LP in light of cultural, political, historical, and economic influences, influencing the field of language planning. In contrast to previous LP work, scholars such as Wolfsan and Manes (1985) eventually focused on the social, economic, and political effects of language planning. Additionally, Spolsky (1995), whose work and views have significantly influenced Māori language revitalization efforts, highlighted that LP exists within a complex set of social, political, economic, religious, demographic, educational, and cultural factors. That is, language needs to be looked at in its widest context and not treated as a closed universe that focused just on terminology creation.

The third stage in LP research started about the mid-1980s and continues to the present day. At this stage, research turned to the topic of language ecology, with a focus on multilingualism and the state of endangered languages. Hornberger (2002) considered the language ecology metaphor "as a set of ideological underpinnings for a multilingual language policy" (p. 35). In particular, Hornberger pointed to how languages exist and evolve in an ecosystem along with other languages, and how their speakers "interact with their sociopolitical, economic and cultural environments" (2002, p. 35). This metaphor also applies to how the linguistic situation should be considered in relation to Māori-medium ITE – a component of the wider macro-level language revival efforts.

From the 1990s, academics such as Skutnabb-Kangas (2000), Phillipson (1997), and May (2001, 2005) have provided a language rights (LR) and/or human rights perspective on language ecology. One of the principal concerns of LR is that the establishment of minority/majority language hierarchies is neither a natural process, nor primarily a linguistic one (May 2012). Rather, "it is a historically, socially and politically construed process, and one that is deeply imbued in wider (unequal) power relationships" (May 2012, p. 2). The LR paradigm argues that minority languages such as te reo Māori, and their speakers, should be accorded the same rights and protections that majority languages already enjoy (Skutnabb-Kangas 2000). A number of researchers have focused on linguistic discrimination in education – a practice that many would argue has been a characteristic of the Aotearoa/NZ education system. Paulson and Heidemann (2006) cited several examples in the education of linguistic minorities to this end. The aim of their research was to "contextualize the relations of power and inequality that characterize the landscape of language planning within education, in order to (re) emphasize that language policy is never simply and only about language" (Paulson and Heidemann 2006, p. 305). Barwell (2003) suggested that the language used in schools, as in wider society, is closely bound up with issues of "access, power and dominance" (p. 37). Consequently, minority languages may be devalued, and speakers of such languages potentially disadvantaged. Therefore, an education system that assumes students from minority groups should be taught subjects only through a majority or dominant language is an example of linguistic discrimination (Barwell 2003).

Dimensions of Language Planning

As noted in the introduction, initially researchers in LP differentiated two distinct kinds of language planning activities: those concerned with attempts to modernize the language (corpus planning), and those concerned with modifying the environment in which a language is used (status planning). Although status planning and corpus planning involve different activities, the relationship between these two types of planning processes can be considered complementary (Clyne 1997). Cooper (1989) added a third focus: acquisition planning. Some researchers, for example,

Kaplan and Baldauf (2005), have adopted this latter focus in models of language planning in the form of language-in-education.

While language elaboration is considered a component of corpus planning, its outcomes quite clearly have an impact on the status of te reo Māori and te reo Māori in education. The elaboration of a language focuses on the functional development of that language to enable it to operate in new domains (Kaplan and Baldauf 1997) such as Māori-medium education. According to Haugen (1983), once a language has been codified, there is a need to continue "the implementation of the norm to meet the functions of a modern world" (p. 373). While social te reo Māori has been codified for some time, the language of schooling was excluded for over 100 years. However, elaboration is not merely a matter of increasing the richness of the vocabulary – more is required (Kaplan and Baldauf 1997). Kaplan and Baldauf (1997, 2003) maintained that the government and its agencies must encourage the use of the language in every possible sector, so that internalization of the language occurs across the population at a rate much greater than that just through the education sector.

The idea that state agencies must encourage usage of the elaborated language in a wide range of domains, including television, employment, printed material, and so on, is promoted by recent reports into the state of te reo Māori (see Paepae Motuhake 2011; Waitangi Tribunal 1986, 2010). May (2005) makes a key distinction in his work between legitimation (the formal recognition of a language, i.e., Māori Language Act) and institutionalization (establishing normal use of languages in various language domains). He argued that the latter is the key indicator as to whether a minority language successfully re-enters the public domain or not (May 2005). Questions remain as to whether this is in fact occurring with te reo Māori in education – at least beyond the realm/domain of schooling.

Kaplan and Baldauf (1997) contended that language elaboration is a complex and ongoing process, and all languages have some mechanism for elaboration. Languages change in the general community as new technologies emerge or old technologies are abandoned, and in education, as new pedagogical theories emerge. Kaplan and Baldauf (1997) advance the idea that language communities need various mechanisms to modernize their language so that it continues to meet their needs. In the Aotearoa/NZ te reo Māori context, one of the mechanisms to modernize the language is the work of the Māori Language Commission (Te Taura Whiri i te reo Māori) in standardizing the language (see Harlow 1993 for further discussion).

A component of language elaboration is terminology modernization and, according to Kaplan and Baldauf (1997), it is the area that has generated the most discussion in corpus planning (see Trinick and May 2013, including terminology development for Māori-medium schooling). In culturally, socially, technologically, and economically changing conditions around the world, many new words are generated each year. Terminology development is a major preoccupation of language agencies and academics in countries that have language agencies such as Aotearoa/ NZ (Kaplan and Baldauf 1997), as well as the work of specialist organizations, such as the Ministry of Education in Aotearoa/NZ who support schooling. This raises the question of who carries out this work at the tertiary level to support Māori-medium ITE.

Language Intellectualization

Related to language elaboration in LP is the idea of language intellectualization. The intellectualization of a language involves the development of new linguistic resources for discussing and disseminating conceptual material at high levels of abstraction (Liddicoat and Bryant 2002). As noted, the intellectualization of a language associated with schooling is considered desirable for a number of reasons. For example, Bull (2002) argues that intellectualization in education is an important element of language maintenance, because education is central to expanding the range of domains in which a language is used and for transmitting forms of language beyond those used in home domains. This also supports the prestige or status of a language (Liddicoat and Bryant 2002) as the prestige of a language is an important consideration in reversing indigenous language shift in languages such as te reo Māori. The greater the prestige, the more likely language shift will occur in support of that language and vice versa.

Liddicoat and Bryant (2002) also argue that it is important to introduce an intellectualized variety of the language at higher levels of education including teacher education, in order to develop the professional competence of the teachers who will implement an intellectualized variety at the primary and secondary levels of education. This is where teacher education can play a key role. Finlayson and Madiba (2002) suggested that the development of academic discourse or registers is a characteristic of most languages that are developing an expanded range of functions in their societies. According to Garvin (1973), intellectualization is an important dimension of language development because it is a way of providing "more accurate and detailed means of expression, especially in the domains of modern life, that is, in the spheres of science and technology, of government and politics, of higher education, of contemporary culture, etc." (p. 43).

However, Schiffman (1996) expressed skepticism about the intellectualization process by citing examples of the lack of progress in the languages of India, where the indigenous languages were expected to replace English as a means of modern communication. Schiffman (1996) strongly argued that it is not possible to develop registers in a language through a conscious effort. He believed that registers should develop naturally in the language through use and over time, as was the case in English (Schiffman 1996). Despite Schiffman's skepticism, Finlayson and Madiba (2002) highlighted research conducted in a number of countries in which it is argued that good progress has been made in planned intellectualization. Although language intellectualization may occur naturally, there is a growing consensus among LP scholars that, in developing languages such as te reo Māori, there is a need for conscious and deliberate efforts to accelerate the process and to make it more effective (Finlayson and Madiba 2002; Trinick 2015). This chapter will examine whether or not planned intellectualization is occurring in ITE programs that identify themselves as Māori-medium schooling.

Language Elaboration and Intellectualization: Pedagogical Implications

Without getting into too much discussion on what the following linguistic terms mean, this section discusses the pedagogical implications of the teachers' language skills and proficiency etc., and the effect of their language ability on student learning. This issue will be discussed further in the section on Māori-medium ITE.

Broadly, it is argued that the language proficiency of the teacher in terms of the specialized language of schooling affects the language proficiency of students which in turn affects the learning of the student generally (Skerrett 2011). Skerrett (2011) further argues that a synthesis of research into immersion/bilingual education points to the contention that effective teachers need both the Basic Interpersonal Communication Skills (BICS refers to language skills needed in social situations) and Cognitive Academic Language Proficiency (CALP refers to formal academic learning). CALP includes listening, speaking, reading, and writing about subject area content material. Most of the research into the relationship between BICS and CALP has focused on the learner, particularly students' learning in their second or third language (Cummins 1991, 2000). This paper focuses on the student teacher in primary school teacher education who will be required to teach subjects such as mathematics. Mathematics has been chosen to illustrate the pedagogical issues because mathematics is a high status subject in the Aotearoa/NZ schooling context. Mathematics is abstract by nature and consists of specialized terms, grammar, and representations, that collectively make up the mathematics register. Children learn the register so they can understand and use mathematics (Cocking and Mestre 1988; Mousley and Marks 1991; Pimm 1987). Teachers, on the other hand, are learning the mathematics register so that they can teach children. This is a different function for the learning of the mathematics register. Research has highlighted a range of linguistic features of the mathematics register that are challenging to learners, and thus have considerable pedagogical implications for both the teaching (the teacher) and learning (the student) of mathematics (see Pimm 1987).

As Pimm (1987) argues, to extract meaning from mathematical statements, and to convey that meaning in spoken or written discourse requires teachers (and students) to have a functional grasp of the mathematics register. Meaney et al. (2012) argue this implies students in Māori-medium need to be explicitly taught the register. Research also highlights the key role of teachers in modeling the language that is needed to support students' acquisition of the mathematics language (see Bickmore-Brand and Gawned 1990; Meaney and Irwin 2005). It is argued that perhaps more than any other subject, the construction of knowledge about mathematics depends on the oral language explanations and interactions of the teacher (see Schleppegrell 2007; Veel 1999), especially where the medium of instruction is the student's weaker academic language as is the case for many students in Māori-medium (Rau 2004).

Mathematical language is not shaped so as to promote interpersonal communication, but rather to provide a picture of mathematical knowledge/concepts and to support the application of algorithms. This links to the role of bridging language in mathematics classrooms as the link between conversational language and the formal language of the mathematics register (Herbel-Eisenmann 2002), and the even greater need for teachers to provide bridging language for second language speakers because of the need to build up conversational language at the same time as the mathematics register (Meaney et al. 2012). The shift from everyday conversational language to communicating mathematically using the specialized register is perhaps the most concrete way of describing the process of intellectualization (Gonzalez 2002) and applies to all subjects in the Māori-medium curricula. Collectively, this research points to several key language considerations for Māori-medium education. This includes the contention that teachers require a functional grasp of the language of the various school subjects, including the register. This raises the issue of where do teachers in the Māori-medium education context learn this language and register and how to intellectualize it? This will be discussed further on in this paper.

Language Elaboration and Intellectualization: Language Revitalization Implications

Language choices are influenced, consciously and unconsciously, by social changes that disrupt the community in numerous ways, and include external pressures or "dislocations" (Fishman 1991). Dislocations can be divided into different categories, including economic, social, and demographic (Fishman 1991). The social status of a language, that is, its prestige value, is closely related to the economic status of the language, and is also a powerful factor in language vitality and, conversely, in promoting linguistic assimilation to the dominant language (Baker 2011). In the Aotearoa/NZ context, when a majority language such as English is seen as giving higher social status and more political power, the shift to English from Māori is exacerbated. In the social arena, intellectualization serves to raise the prestige of indigenous languages such as te reo Māori, since it is competing with the dominant language, English, in terms of its functional use in a range of fields and disciplines. While it is only one way of promoting te reo Māori, LP research shows that indigenous groups such as Māori are more likely to speak Māori and encourage their whānau (family) do so if it is used in many different domains including higher education (Spolsky 2005).

The Use of the Term Intellectualization

The use of the term "intellectualization" may be problematic to some readers, particularly for those not familiar with the linguistic terms describing language development. Any talk of "intellectualization" may be patronizing to some, because it can be argued that Māori have long practiced higher order cognitive activity or thinking. These activities are occurring in many domains including the marae (the open area in front of the meeting house, where formal greetings and discussions take place). The use of the term does not imply te reo Māori is inferior somehow, to supposedly more advanced languages such as English. The problem for te reo Māori is that it was excluded from schooling and tertiary education for over 100 years. It now can be argued that the intellectualization of te reo Māori at the level of schooling to teach such subjects, such as, mathematics has been established. The quality of teaching is another argument. A corpus of standardized specialized terms has been created, and various iterations of papakupu (dictionary) and curriculum have been developed to support teaching to the upper levels of secondary school. Te reo Māori is the language of instruction, subjects are taught at a high level of abstraction, there is academic literature in te reo Māori and so on. These are all indicators of the intellectualization of language in the schooling domain (Gonzalez 2002). The question is whether this is similarly occurring at the tertiary level of ITE to support the Māori-medium schooling domain?

Te Reo Māori in Education Planning

Te reo Māori in education is situated in the third dimension of LP, that is, language-in-education. However, it is important to acknowledge that the other two major dimensions of LP, status and corpus planning also occurred in education in Aotearoa/NZ, albeit almost exclusively in the modern era, that is, from the 1980s onward. School has become one of the most critical sites for causing or ironically reversing language shift and for language revitalization in endangered language contexts. One of the reasons for this is that education is most often controlled by the state which is the case in Aotearoa/NZ, and thus can be readily used as an agency of state LP. Second, education is also the site where the sociopolitical and ideological values of the language community are transmitted and reflected – the very values that may support language revival. Schools can, therefore, become agents of positive language change, raising language loss or language use issues with students and the language community, thereby influencing the linguistic beliefs and practices of the language community (Skutnabb-Kangas 2000).

Comprehensive critical analyses can be found in a range of research literature on the impact of colonial linguistic hegemony from the late nineteenth century on te reo Māori in education (see Simon 1992) and contemporary Māori education policies, both overt and covert, in regard to Māori education generally (see Penetito 2010; Smith 1996). Thus, the following section focuses primarily on the emergence of Māori-medium schooling in the late 1970s and early 1980s in response to the parlous state of the language.

The Development of Te Reo Māori in Schooling: Post 1980s

The change in the status of te reo Māori, from an initially high-status language of early colonial communication to a low-status language in Aotearoa/NZ, had contributed considerably to language shift to English in the Māori community, to the extent that by the 1970s te reo Māori was considered an endangered language (Spolsky 2005). It was against this background of rapid and significant language loss that the Māori community initiated bilingual education in Aotearoa/NZ (May and Hill 2005). At the point of the reintroduction ((re)vernacularization) of te reo Māori in the form of bilingual education in the late 1970s and early 1980s, there was no national language plan and no formal language policy for te reo Māori use and implementation in Aotearoa/NZ (Peddie 2003). In 1976, in response to the increasingly parlous state of the language, a range of rural and urban communities were able, through the strength of their own convictions and the use of data from the seminal Benton (1981) study into the health of te reo Māori, to persuade both the Minister of Education and officials of the Education Department that a bilingual school should be set up (Benton 1984). Subsequently, in 1980, additional schools, including the former Māori (native) schools in predominately rural areas, were also given official bilingual status. These schools, with support from their elders and local whānau, were trying to save te reo Māori from extinction in their particular communities (Benton 1984). By 1988, 12 years after this change of status for schools such as Ruatoki where Maori language was still the dominant language of the community, 20 bilingual schools had been established in predominantly Māori communities, including in urban areas. In addition, 67 primary schools and 18 secondary schools operated with some bilingual classes (May 2001).

These early bilingual schools were required to follow the English-medium syllabus for schools. There was no formal Māori-medium curriculum, and limited te reo Māori resource materials to support learning and teaching. Their development reflected a wider trend at that time – much of the school curriculum, resource development, and long- and short-term Māori language-in-education planning was highly localized, responsibility having fallen to principals, staff, and whānau of individual schools (Benton 1984). Consequently, the implementation of a bilingual-school-based curriculum varied widely from community to community (Benton 1984).

Following on from these early bilingual education reforms, kōhanga reo (early childhood language nests) were launched in 1982, initially run independently by parents as an important part of the "Māori renaissance," motivated by widespread Māori recognition of the urgent need to revitalize te reo Māori by that time (King 2001). As many commentators on this renaissance have noted, kōhanga reo (early childhood language nest) were probably the most influential development in the language revitalization movement in Aotearoa/NZ (Penetito 2010; Walker 1990, 1996).

Outside of the few bilingual schools noted previously, most of the compulsory state education sector remained ambivalent toward, or actively resisted, Māori community language aspirations (McMurchy-Pilkington and Trinick 2008). Linguistic human rights had not yet emerged as an influential paradigm in resisting language shift and language death, and the Māori Language Act was not yet a reality (May 2003). Graduates from kōhanga reo were entering the state school primary-level system into questionable or, in most cases, nonexistent te reo Māori programs and, as a consequence, concerns emerged about their language loss after a short period of time in these schools (Smith 1997). The poor response by state schools to these initial te reo Māori revitalization efforts prompted groups of Māori to establish primary-level kura kaupapa Māori (primary school teaching all subjects in the medium of Māori) from 1985, outside the state education system (Smith 1997).

Somewhat belatedly, and after considerable lobbying from te reo Māori education groups, the Education Amendment Act was passed in 1989, and it was to have far-reaching implications, albeit at different time scales, for te reo Māori in schooling. The Education Act 1989 did, nonetheless, crucially endorse Māori-medium schools, kura kaupapa Māori, at primary (and secondary) level as a legitimate state-funded schooling alternative within the state education system (May 1999), serving those students who had been in kōhanga reo (early childhood language next). While state support of kura kaupapa Māori has since proved something of a double-edged sword, requiring kura kaupapa Māori to implement state-mandated curricula and assessment practices developed from essentially Eurocentric interests, the 1989 Education Act at least provided the opportunity for kura kaupapa Māori to gain financial and operational support in the further expansion of Māori-medium education (McMurchy-Pilkington and Trinick 2008).

The demand from Māori for secondary Māori-medium education did not cease with the 1989 Education Act, and the 1990 Education Amendment Act, kōhanga reo and kura kaupapa Māori. As noted by May and Hill (2005), there was a domino effect throughout the education system. There was increasing demand for Māori-medium secondary schooling options, in order to meet the educational needs of fluent Māori-speaking students graduating, in turn, from kura kaupapa Māori (May and Hill 2005).

The first state-funded wharekura (secondary school teaching in the medium of Māori) opened in 1993 with Year 9 and 10 students at Hoani Waititi Marae, in West Auckland (Campbell and Stewart 2009). Wharekura are the secondary school (years 9–13) prototype of Māori-medium immersion, as distinct from kura kaupapa Māori, that focus on the primary level (years 1–8). Since that time, a number of wharekura have emerged, generally attached to kura, with common governance and management (Ministry of Education 2008).

Te Reo Māori Elaboration: Schooling

When te reo Māori was reintroduced into schooling in the 1980s, as the language of instruction for all subjects, considerable development was required and continues to be required as new ideas and initiatives are introduced into Māori-medium education. While substantial lexication occurred for all subjects, no two subjects have followed an identical development path. For example, the elaboration of the language of mathematics and literacy received much more Ministry of Education support because of their perceived high-status, while others less so. See Stewart (2010) and Heaton (2016) for discussions on the elaboration of the language of pūtaiao (science) and hauora (health) respectively.

Following is a brief description of the process of elaboration of the language to teach schooling subjects (see Trinick 2015 for a more comprehensive discussion). While it has taken several 100 years to develop the English-medium subject registers, the Māori-medium lexicon and register has had to be developed in a short space of time to parallel what is expected in English-medium education. A feature of the initial development of the lexicon was the informal approach taken, involving kaumātua (elders), teachers, and community working together to establish a corpus of appropriate terms, rather than any formal LP approach (Trinick 2015).

The initial strategy for 150 years of creating or adopting new words for subjects was generally through the use of loanwords and borrowing terms. Expanding the language into new domains in this way came to an abrupt halt in the 1980s, with the establishment of the state LP agency, Te Taura Whiri, with an emphasis on linguistic purism and not borrowing terms as the basis for corpus development. This is because, over time, Māori attitudes (including those of members of Te Taura Whiri) to loanwords have varied as different ideologies gained ascendency and the status of te reo Māori changed. In the 1980s, when Te Taura Whiri was created, te reo Māori was no longer in a position of dominance in the community – as it had been prior to the 1940s. Accordingly, there was much greater reluctance to continue the use of transliteration (to give loanwords a Māori language phonology), given the perceived threat at that time to ongoing te reo Māori use (Trinick 2015).

Due to limitations in resources and expertise, Te Taura Whiri eventually withdrew from the process of developing the specialized lexicon for schooling. In the current absence of a centrally agreed body with authority to define and plan codification and elaboration of te reo Māori for teaching and learning, responsibility has defaulted to the Ministry of Education and, by extension, to their contractors and the development teams responsible for each individual Māori-medium education initiative.

Initial Teacher Education: The Māori Medium Experience

As noted, it is important to introduce an intellectualized variety of the language at the higher levels of education including Māori-medium teacher education, in order to develop the professional competence of the teachers who will implement an intellectualized variety at the primary and secondary levels of Māori-medium education. This section will examine LP efforts in Māori-medium ITE, drawing on various reports with a particular focus on the elaboration and intellectualization of the language.

Initial teacher institutes have existed in one form or another since 1862 in Aotearoa/NZ (Openshaw and Ball 2006) as English-medium only, but this was to eventually change, if somewhat diffident to the challenges of the Māori-medium schooling sector. The impact of research in the 1970s (i.e., Benton 1979) that showed te reo Māori in a precarious state and the subsequent demands by communities and activists to revitalize the language, saw a rapid growth in students learning the language (Walker 1984). It was not until 1974 when there was a response to the issue of te reo Māori teacher supply by providers of ITE in the form of such programs as Te Atakura, which fast-tracked native speakers of the language into a teaching qualification (Shaw 2006). However, these programs focused on meeting the demand for secondary teachers of te reo Māori and did not address the chronic shortage of Māori-medium teachers caused by the rapid growth of Māori-medium schooling in the 1980s. ITE followed similar patterns of ambivalence to te reo Māori as the state schools showed to the needs of kōhanga reo graduates in the 1980s. By the early 1990s, various ITEs, under pressure from the schooling sector, responded by developing bilingual type programs. While based on good intentions, these programs followed patterns similar to those of Taha Māori (Māori language enrichment) programs in schools, whereby Māori culture was acknowledged and even given some emphasis, but was not aimed at developing te reo Māori proficiency to the level required to teach in Māori-medium schools (Stewart et al. 2016). Eventually programs were developed in response to the crisis in Māori-medium teacher supply in various institutions, whereby in 2008, 12 programs defined themselves as Māori-medium (see Hohepa et al. 2014, for a critical review of the history of the development of Māori-medium ITE).

Language Planning: Māori-Medium Initial Teacher Education

At the point of the reintroduction ((re) vernacularization) of te reo Māori in education in the early 1980s, there was no national language plan and no formal language policy for te reo Māori use and implementation in Aotearoa/NZ (Trinick 2015). In the absence of any official Māori-medium education plan, the development of Māori-medium curricula (Te Tāhuhu o te Mātauranga 1996, 2008) became de facto LP for the Māori-medium schooling sector. However, there has not been any national LP for Māori medium ITE, either de facto or de jure. The 12 ITE programs that have defined themselves as Māori-medium do have language policies of sorts that generally reflect the level of autonomy they have (Hohepa et al. 2014). For example, the two tertiary ITE programmes that identify as teaching totally in the medium of Māori and not using such techniques as code switching are either a wānanga (a tertiary institution that provides education in a Māori cultural context) or Private Training Establishment (PTE) and thus have much more autonomy then programs located in the larger mainstream Universities (Murphy et al. 2008). This raises the issue of what is the ideal percentage of the program taught in te reo Māori.

There are researchers who maintain that clear, sustained separation of languages in immersion instruction advocated by policy such as that in the two ITE programs is a valid pedagogical approach (Cloud et al. 2000; Tarone and Swain 1995). One of the most compelling reasons for separating the languages of instruction and not allowing language learning approaches such as code switching or front loading in L1 is the concern that encouraging the use of both languages to teach a subject such as mathematics education will favor the more proficient language, typically, the home language or L1. This is especially so in the Aotearoa/NZ context when the home language of the student teacher is most often English, the language of the majority in the community and the language of power in the larger society (Tarone and Swain 1995).

The additional challenge for ITEs preparing teachers to teach in Maori-medium schools is the fact that te reo Māori is the second language of most of the student teachers (Murphy et al. 2008). Many of these student teachers have had all their learning of mathematics in the medium of English (Trinick 2015). Some scholars argue that there is a place for "judicious" use of the L1 to support L2 learning in bilingual programmes (Cummins 2000; McMillan and Turnbull 2009; Swain and Lapkin 2000). Cummins (2007) questioned the "rigid" separation of languages in bilingual programmes and argued that research evidence provides minimal support for these assumptions. Additionally, researchers argue strongly that bilingualism and biliteracy cannot be achieved through monolingual philosophy or methodology, and that using the students' total language resources is more effective (Baker 2006; Cummins 2007).

Although there has been research on students who do not have the language of instruction as their first language in the mathematics classroom, there has been much less on the issues faced by student teachers who are not learning in their first language. Moreover, there is no evidence currently, that the monolingual te reo Māori ITE programs are any more effective at producing competent Māori-medium teachers overall than say those ITE programs that allow teaching in both languages.

Language Elaboration and Intellectualization in Māori-Medium ITE

The reports into the state of Māori-medium ITE (Hohepa et al. 2014; Murphy et al. 2008; Skerrett 2011) note that students and lecturers alike struggle with language demands required to teach particular learning areas – pāngarau (mathematics) and pūtaiao (science), through the medium of Māori, especially those areas where new vocabulary is constantly being coined. This points to the contention that students are not encountering these terms in their schooling (Trinick et al. 2014) and ITEs lack the range of curriculum experts whereby it can be assumed that the lecturers would know these terms (Murphy et al. 2008).

Unlike the compulsory schooling sector, which is controlled by the Ministry of Education, and Teachers Council, there was no agency that regulated or has assumed responsibility for corpus and status planning of te reo Māori at higher education levels. For the most part, each institution has created its own corpus of terms to support the teaching of the various disciplines that make up their programs. This situation is reminiscent of the early corpus development of terms for the various subjects for Māori-medium schooling in the late 1990s and early 1980s where schools created terms for their immediate needs. As noted, this terminology work eventually became more systematic for the schooling sector because of the intervention of two state agencies – Te Taura Whiri (Māori Language Commision) and the Ministry of Education. Tertiary education has been able to draw on this work in different ways, albeit still somewhat limited to meet the needs of the tertiary sector.

It now can be argued that the intellectualization of te reo Māori at the level of schooling to teach such subjects, such as, mathematics has been established. The quality of teaching is another argument. A corpus of standardized specialized terms has been created which tertiary institutions can refer to including papakupu (dictionary). Second, there have been a range of professional development projects for teachers, particularly mathematics and literacy (Christensen 2003; Trinick and Stephenson 2010). Collectively, a range of literature and resources have also been created to support these professional development projects for Māori-medium teachers. However, it cannot be assumed that every ITE has the capacity to draw on this resource created for Māori-medium schooling, because as noted a number of these ITEs lack the range of curriculum experts (Murphy et al. 2008) and while ITEs can draw on the curriculum specific vocabulary, language intellectualization is more than vocabulary development. It is the ability to articulate, discuss, and represent the underlying mathematical concepts in te reo Māori that is important for the teaching and learning of mathematics. If as research suggest, learning the register is important to learn mathematics, then so is the teachers ability to present the register flexibly in response to the different learning situations and to meet the differing learning needs of students (Ball and Bass 2000).

This flexibility is also connected to Herbel-Eisenmann's (2002) discussion of the role of bridging language in mathematics classrooms as the link between conversational language and the formal language of the mathematics register. This is also connected to the issue raised earlier in relation to Basic Interpersonal Communication Skills (BICS) and Cognitive Academic Language Proficieny (CALP). While Herbel-Eisenmann (2002) was working in an English-medium situation where the students and the teachers were native speakers, it could be argued that there is an even greater need for teachers to provide bridging language for second language speakers because of the need to build up conversational language at the same time as the mathematics register.

According to Veel (1999), perhaps more than any other discipline, the construction of knowledge about mathematics depends on the oral language explanations and interactions of the teacher. Veel (1999) reports although that teacher's spoken language predominates in maths classes, the teacher's words are needed to interpret the meanings of the visual and symbolic representations and therefore are powerful agent in learning process. Several studies have found that children mirror the teacher's language (Khisty and Chval 2002; Raiker 2002). This means that the language that the teacher uses is an important factor in determining the quality of language the children speak. Murphy et al. (2008) argue that poor teacher language proficiency may lead to poor student language proficiency. Similarly they argue that teachers lack of understanding of the technical language and concepts may impinge on student learning (Murphy et al. 2008).

Conclusion and Future Directions

All this discussion leads to the conclusion that there is considerable pedagogical tension between learning te reo Māori and learning mathematics education in the Māori-medium ITE context. Clearly some ITEs are reverting to teaching mathematics education in the medium of English because it is the first language of most of the students, but this then restricts their ability to learn the specialized registers eventually needed to teach children. For many student teachers, the time spent in the ITE is critical for developing their Māori language proficiency because it will be the last domain they can develop their proficiency before becoming practicing teachers. However, learning mathematics education in their second language may well impinge on their mathematical education understanding. This is not an easy tension to resolve.

However, in order to function as the language of instruction, that is to intellectualize te reo Māori in ITE, clearly it has to be read, spoken, and written. Murphy et al. (2008) and Hohepa et al. (2015) note the percentage of the programs who self identify as Māori-medium (12 programs) vary in terms of the percentage of content taught in the medium of Māori. It ranged from two programmes that taught all courses in the medium of Māori, to five programs that stated they delivered all courses in the medium of te reo Māori about 80% of the time, to two programs that delivered less than 30% of the program in te reo Māori. Because models for ITE are revised in six to 10 year cycles, and there is a paucity of research in this area, it is thus difficult to determine which pedagogic models best support teaching and learning in Māori-medium. As noted by Skerrett (2011, p. 133), the terms "competency" and "bilingual"/"bilingualism" are difficult to define and are highly controversial in pedagogical terms. While it is unclear what aspects such as the language threshold ought to be, it is clear that graduates from English-medium programs or minimum levels of instruction in te reo Māori that teach in Māori-medium will need to learn the specialized registers on the job.

The entry requirements in regard to te reo proficiency levels ranged from "being able to demonstrate a high level of fluency to very little" (Murphy et al. 2008; Hohepa et al. 2015). Similarly, there were a range of language outcomes and expectations of student graduates in these Māori-medium ITE programs. The issue of entry criteria is very contentious as academic institutions such as universities and wānanga in New Zealand are very sensitive to external accreditation requirements that may impinge on their academic freedom and autonomy (Hohepa et al. 2014; Trinick 2015). These issues are compounded by the probability that standardized language proficiency requirements will cause major problems in obtaining qualified teachers in Māori-medium where there are already teacher shortages and a small pool of Māori speakers wishing to enter the teaching profession (Kane 2005; Hohepa et al. 2015; Murphy et al. 2008; Skerrett 2010, 2011). The Education Council, an institute that accredits Māori-medium ITEs, has acknowledged the issue of te reo Māori entry requirement for students and the issue of language intellectualization by developing a linguistic framework, TātaiReo (see Murphy et al. 2008), but at this point it is optional. Essentially, the framework sets out a range of language competence students in ITEs should reach as they progress through their programs and the sorts of linguistic knowledge they should know, such as how children acquire a language (Murphy et al. 2008). This framework is a good first step in developing some consistency across programs and ensuring graduates have the range of linguistic proficiencies to support learners. Teachers require specific language skills in order to successfully facilitate ākonga (student) learning in Māori-medium settings. As noted, the type of language needed to do well in an education context differs from the language used for everyday communication (Murphy et al. 2008).

In the absence of any language plan or regulation for Māori-medium teacher education, intellectualization of te reo Māori has been difficult to implement and develop consistently. Additionally, the difficulties can be attributed to the fact that with so few programs, the discipline lacks a critical mass of academics with an interest and expertise in the various subject areas and te reo Māori (Hohepa et al. 2015). It is also expected that academics participate in various national and international discourse communities as per the requirements of New Zealand's Performance Based Research Funding (PBRF). In other words, publish in international journals that are much more highly rated than local, and present in international academic forums in English, thus further privileging English (Trinick 2015).

While there are several unresolved tensions and issues in Māori-medium ITE as a collective, it must be acknowledged that there are very good Māori-medium graduates entering the profession and effective Māori-medium ITE programs. The aim of this chapter is not to cast dispersions on all and sundry. However, it is the belief of the author, that with a clear national language plan for Māori-medium ITE, simultaneously acknowledging the mana motuhake (independence), language intellectualization for te reo Māori will be more robust than the current process. Thus, the substantial variability that currently exists between and in programmes in respect of the languages requirements identified in the various reports commissioned into the state of Māori-medium ITE would be reduced (i.e., Murphy et al. 2008; Hohepa et al. 2014). The Murphy et al. (2008) and Hohepa et al. (2014) reports offer a constructive way forward, albeit not sufficient enough to address all the issues – that is Māori-medium ITE educators need to be much more proactive as a collective in sharing their experiences and solutions, and learning about new developments in curriculum and language acquisition. Substantial research is also needed to identify what the required te reo Māori thresholds might be for entry and the teaching of the Māori-medium ITE program to produce affective teachers. Research is also required into the challenges student teachers in ITEs face learning such subjects as mathematics education in their second language.

References

Ball D, Bass H (2000) Interweaving content and pedagogy in teaching and learning to teach: knowing and using mathematics. In: Boaler J (ed) Multiple perspectives on the teaching and learning of mathematics. Ablex, Westport, pp 83–104

Barwell R (2003) Linguistic discrimination: issues for research in mathematics education. For the learning of mathematics. Int J 23(2):37–43

Baker C (2006) Foundations of bilingual education and bilingualism. Clevedon: Multilingual Matters

Baker C (2011) Foundations of bilingual education and bilingualism (5). Bristol: Multilingual Matters

Benton R (1981) The flight of the Amokura: oceanic languages and formal education in the Pacific. Wellington: New Zealand Council for Educational Research

Bakmand B (2000) National language planning, why (not)? J Int Commun 3. Retrieved from http://www.immi.se/intercultural/

Benton R (1979) Who speaks Māori in New Zealand? New Zealand Council for Educational Research, Wellington

Benton R (1984) Bilingual education and the survival of the Māori language. J Polynesian Soc 93(3):247–266

Bickmore-Brand J, Gawned S (1990) Scaffolding for improved mathematical understanding. In: Bickmore-Brand J (ed) Language in mathematics. Heinemann, Portsmouth, pp 43–58

Bull T (2002) The Sámi language(s), maintenance and intellectualisation. Curr Issues Lang Plann 3(1):28–39

Campbell R, Stewart G (2009) Ngā wawata o ngā whānau wharekura: aspirations of whānau in Māori-medium secondary schools. New Zealand Council for Educational Research, Wellington

Christensen I (2003) An evaluation of Te Poutama Tau 2002: exploring issues in mathematical education. Ministry of Education, Wellington

Cloud N, Genesee F, Hamayan E (2000) Teaching content. In: Cloud N, Genesee F, Hamayan E (eds) Dual language instruction: a handbook for enriched education. Heinle & Heinle, Boston, pp 113–138

Clyne M (ed) (1997) Undoing and redoing corpus planning. Mouton de Gruyter, Berlin

Cocking R, Mestre JP (1988) Linguistic and cultural influences on learning mathematics. Lawrence Erlbaum, Hillsdale

Cooper RL (1989) Language planning and social change. Cambridge University Press, Cambridge

Cummins J (1991) Language development and academic learning. In: Malave L, Duquette G (eds) Language, culture and cognition. Multilingual Matters, Clevedon

Cummins J (2000) Language, power and pedgogy: bilingual children in the crossfire. Multilingual Matters, Clevedon

Cummins J (2007) Rethinking monolingual instructional strategies in multilingual classrooms. Canadian J Appl Linguist 10(2):221–240

Ferguson G (2006) Language planning and education. Edinburgh University Press, Edinburgh

Finlayson R, Madiba M (2002) The intellectualisation of the indigenous languages of South Africa: challenges and prospects. Curr Issues Lang Plann 3(1):40–61

Fishman J (1991) Reversing language shift: theoretical and empirical foundations of assistance to threatened languages. Clevedon: Multilingual Matters

Fowler R, Hodge B, Kress G et al (1979) Language and control. Routledge & Kegan Paul, London

Garvin PL (1973) Some comments on language planning. In: Rubin J, Shuy R (eds) Language planning: current issues and research. Georgetown University, Washington, DC, pp 24–33

Gonzalez A (2002) Language planning and intellectualization. Curr Issues Lang Plann 3(1):5–27

Halliday M (1978) Language as social semiotic: the social interpretation of language and meaning. University Park Press, Baltimore

Halliday M (1985) Introduction to functional grammar. Edward Arnold, London

Harlow R (1993) A science and mathematics terminology for Māori. In: McKinley E, Waiti P (eds) SAMEpapers. University of Waikato, Hamilton, pp 124–137

Haugen E (1983) The implementation of corpus planning: theory and practice. In: Cobarrubias J, Fishman J (eds) Progress in language planning. International perspectives, Contributions to the sociology of language. Mouton, Berlin, pp 269–289

Heaton S (2016) The juxtaposition of Māori words with English concepts. 'Hauora, well-being' as philosophy. Educ Philos Theory. https://doi.org/10.1080/00131857.2016.1167583

Herbel-Eisenmann BA (2002) Using student contributions and multiple representations to develop mathematical language. Math Teach Middle Sch 8(2):100–105

Hohepa M, Hāwera N, Tamatea K (2014) Strengthening the preparation, capability and retention of Māori medium teacher trainees. Ministry of Education, Wellington

Hohepa M, Hawera N, Tamatea K, Heaton S (2015) Te Puni Rumaki: Strengthening the preparation, capability and retention of Māori medium teacher trainees. Report commissioned by the Ministry of Education. Wilf Malcolm Institute of Educational Research and the University of Waikato, Wellington

Hornberger N (2002) Multilingual language policies and the continua of biliteracy: an ecological approach. Lang Policy 1(1):27–51

Hymes D (1972) Models of the interaction of language and social life. In: Gumperz JJ, Hymes D (eds) Directions in sociolinguistics: the ethnography of communication. Holt, Rinehart & Winston, New York, pp 35–71

Kane RG (2005) Initial teacher education policy and practice: final report. Ministry of Education, Wellington

Kaplan R, Baldauf R (1997) Language planning from practice to theory. Multilingual Matters, Clevedon

Kaplan R, Baldauf R (2003) Language and language-in-education planning in the Pacific Basin. Dordrecht: Kluwer Academic

Kaplan R, Baldauf R (2005) Language-in-education policy and planning. In: Hinkel E (ed) Handbook of research in second language teaching and learning. Lawrence Erlbaum, Mahwah, pp 1013–1034

Khisty L, Chval K (2002) Pedagogic discourse and equity in mathematics: when teachers' talk matters. Math Educ Res J 14(3):154–168

King J (2001) Te Kōhanga Reo: Māori language revitalisation. In: Hinton L, Hale K (eds) The green book of language revitalisation in practice. Academic, San Diego, pp 118–128

Liddicoat A, Bryant P (2002) Intellectualisation. A current issue in language planning 3(1):1–4

May S (1999) Indigenous community-based education. Multilingual Matters, Clevedon

May S (2001) Language and minority rights: ethnicity, nationalism and the politics of language. Longman, London

May S (2003) Re-articulating the case for minority language rights. Curr Issues Lang Plann 4(2): 95–125

May S (2005) Language rights: moving the debate forward. J Socioling 9(3):319–347

May S (2012) Language and minority rights: ethnicity, nationalism and politics of language, 2nd edn. Routledge, New York

May S, Hill R (2005) Māori medium education: current issues and challenges. Int J Biling Educ Biling 8(5):377–403

McMillan B, Turnbull M (2009) Teachers' use of the L1 in French immersion: revisiting a core principle. In: Turnbull M, Dailey-O'Cain J (eds) First language use in second and foreign language learning: intersection of theory, practice, curriculum and policy (pp. 15–34). Clevedon: Multilingual Matters

McMurchy-Pilkington C, Trinick T (2008) Potential & possibilities. In: Carpenter V, Jesson J, Roberts P, Stephenson M (eds) Ngā kaupapa here: connections and contradictions in education. Cengage Learning, South Melbourne, pp 133–144

Meaney T, Irwin KC (2005) Language used by students in mathematics for quantitative and numerical comparisons: NEMP probe study report. University of Otago, Dunedin

Meaney T, Trinick T, Fairhall U (2012) Collaborating to meet languages challenges in indigenous mathematics classrooms. Springer, Dordrecht

Ministry of Education (2008) Ka Hikitia: managing for success: the Māori education strategy, 2008–2012. Ministry of Education, Wellington

Motuhake P (2011) Te Reo Mauriora – Review report. Te Puni Kōkiri, Wellington

Mousley J, Marks G (1991) Discourses in mathematics. Deakin University Press, Geelong

Murphy H, McKinley S, Bright N (2008) Whakamanahia te reo Māori. He Tirohanga Hotaka – an exploration of issues and influences that affect te reo Māori competences of graduates from Māori-medium programmes. New Zealand Teachers Council, Wellington

Nekvapil J (2006) From language planning to language management. Sociolinguistica 20:92–104

Openshaw R, Ball T (2006) New Zealand teacher education: progression or prescription? Educ Res Perspect 33(2):102–123

Paulson CB, Heidemann K (2006) The education of linguistic minorities. In: Ricento T (ed) An introduction to language policy: theory and method. Blackwell, Oxford, pp 292–310

Peddie R (2003) Languages in New Zealand: population, politics and policy. In: Barnard R, Glynn T (eds) Bilingual children's language and literacy development: case studies from Aotearoa/New Zealand. Multilingual Matters, Clevedon, pp 8–35

Penetito W (2010) What's Māori about Māori education? Victoria University Press, Wellington

Phillipson R (1997) Realities and myths of linguistic imperialism. J Multiling Multicult Dev 18(3): 238–247

Pimm D (1987) Speaking mathematically: communication in mathematics classroom. Routledge Keegan Paul, London

Raiker S (2002) Spoken language and mathematics. Camb J Educ 32(1):45–60

Rau C (2004) A snapshot of the literacy achievement in 1995 and 2002–2003 as an indicator of Māori language acquisition for year 2 students in 80%–100% Māori immersion programmes. Language Acquisition Research. Ministry of Education, Wellington, pp 61–82

Ricento T (2000) Historical and theoretical perspectives in language policy planning. In: Ricento T (ed) Ideology, politics and language policies: focus on English. John Benjamins, Amsterdam, pp 9–24

Ricento T, Hornberger N (1996) Unpeeling the onion: language planning and policy and the ELT professional. TESOL Q 30(3):401–427

Schiffman H (1996) Linguistic culture and language policy. Routledge, London

Schleppegrell M (2007) The linguistic challenges of mathematics teaching and learning: a research review. Read Writ Q 23(2):139–159

Shaw L (2006) Making a difference: a history of the Auckland College of Education, 1881–2004. Auckland University Press, Auckland

Simon J (1992) Social studies: the cultivation of social amnesia. In: McCulloch G (ed) The school curriculum in New Zealand: theory policy and practice (pp. 253–271). Palmerston North: Dunmore Press

Simon J (1998) Ngā kura Māori: the native schools system 1867–1969. Auckland University Press, Auckland

Skerrett M (2010) A critique of the best evidence synthesis with relevance for Māori leadership in education. J Educ Leadersh Policy Prac 25(1):41–50

Skerrett M (2011) Whakamanahia te reo Māori: he tirohanga rangahau – a review of literature on the instructional and contextual factors likely to influence te reo Māori proficiency of graduates from Māori medium ITE programmes. New Zealand Teachers Council, Wellington

Skutnabb-Kangas T (2000) Linguistic genocide in education, or worldwide diversity and human rights? Lawrence Erlbaum, Mahwah

Smith L (1996) Ngā aho o te kakahu matauranga: the multiple layers of struggle by Māori in education. Dissertation, University of Auckland

Smith GH (1997) The development of kaupapa Māori: theory and praxis. Dissertation, University of Auckland

Spolsky B (1995) Conditions for language revitalization: a comparison of the cases of Hebrew & Māori. Curr Issues Lang Soc 2(3):177–201

Spolsky B (2005) Māori lost and regained. In: Bell A, Harlow R, Starks D (eds) Languages of New Zealand. Victoria. University Press, Wellington, pp 67–85

Stewart G (2010) Language issues in Māori chemistry education. AlterNative 6(1):66–71

Stewart G, Trinick T, Dale H (2016) Huarahi Māori: two decades of indigenous teacher education at the University of Auckland. In: Whitinui P, Rodríguez de France C, McIvor O (eds) Promising practices in indigenous teacher education. Springer Education, New York

Swain M, Lapkin S (2000) Task-based second language learning: the uses of the first language. Lang Teach Res 4(3):251–274

Tarone E, Swain M (1995) A sociolinguistic perspective on second language use in immersion classrooms. Mod Lang J 79(2):166–177

Te Tāhuhu o te Mātauranga (1996) Pāngarau i roto i Te Marautanga o Aotearoa. Te Pou Taki Korero, Wellington

Te Tāhuhu o te Mātauranga (2008) Te Marautanga o Aotearoa. Learning Media, Wellington

Tollefson J (2002) Limitations of language policy and planning. In: Kaplan R (ed) The Oxford handbook of applied linguistics. Oxford University Press, New York, pp 415–423

Tribunal W (1986) Report of the Waitangi tribunal on the te reo Māori claim (Wai 11). Waitangi Tribunal, Wellington

Tribunal W (2010) Te reo Māori. Waitangi Tribunal Report 2010 (Wai 262). Waitangi Tribunal, Wellington

Trinick T (2015) Te reo Tātai: the development of a mathematics register for Māori-medium schooling. Dissertation, University of Waikato

Trinick T, May S (2013) Developing a Māori language mathematics lexicon: challenges for corpus planning in indigenous language contexts. Curr Issues Lang Plann 14(3–4):457–473

Trinick T, Stephenson B (2010) Evaluation of Te Poutama Tau: Māori-medium, numeracy project, 2003–2009. In: Holton D, Irwin K, Linsell C (eds) Findings from the New Zealand numeracy projects. Learning Media, Wellington, pp 72–87

Trinick T, Meaney T, Fairhall U. (2014). Teachers learning the mathematics register in another language: an exploratory study. In: Craig T, Morgan C, Schuette M,, Wagner D (eds). Special issue: language and communication in mathematics education ZDM: International Journal on Mathematics Education 46 (6), 953–965

Veel R (1999) Language, knowledge and authority in school mathematics. In: Christie F (ed) Pedagogy and the shaping of consciousness: linguistic and social processes. Continuum, London, pp 185–216

Walker R (1984) The Maori response to education in New Zealand. In: Paper presented at the Nga tumanako: Māori educational development conference, Turangawaewae Marae. 23–25 Mar 1994

Walker R (1990) Ka whawhai tonu mātou: struggle without end. Penguin, Auckland

Walker R (1996) Māori resistance to state domination. In: Peters M, Hope W, Marshall J, Webster S (eds) Critical theory, poststructuralism and the social context. The Dunmore Press, Palmerston North, pp 257–268

Wolfsan N, Manes J (1985) Language of inequality. Mouton, Berlin

Ka unuhi a me ka hoʻokē: A Critique of Translation in a Language Revitalization Context

30

Kerry Laiana Wong and Ron D. Kekeha Solis

Contents

Community Language Background 530
Negotiating Public Access 531
Suppression of the Minority 533
Protecting the Official Fish 535
To Translate or Not to Translate: Lexical Issues 537
To Translate or Not to Translate: Beyond Lexicon 540
Another Compromise on Translation 542
Conclusion 543
References 543

Abstract

In 2002, an agreement was reached with the Honolulu StarBulletin, one of two daily newspapers published in Honolulu at the time (The two have since merged to become the Honolulu StarAdvertiser.), which provided for the weekly publication of a column written in the Hawaiian language. There was only one stipulation: a short "synopsis" written in English would accompany each article. It was also agreed, after lengthy negotiations, that outside of this synopsis, no translation would be provided to the general public. The column, entitled Kauakūkalahale, is still running today, although the initial no-translation agreement has recently been renegotiated.

This chapter deals with the theoretical, political, and educational issues that underpin the decision not to provide English translations to the public, despite

---

This title is borrowed from an early Kauakūkalahale article in which a case was made in opposition to the translation of traditional Hawaiian language publications into English (Wong 2003). The Hawaiian phrase reflects that position.

K. L. Wong (✉) · R. D. K. Solis
University of Hawaiʻi at Mānoa, Honolulu, HI, USA
e-mail: kwong@hawaii.edu; rsolis@hawaii.edu

© Springer Nature Singapore Pte Ltd. 2019
E. A. McKinley, L. T. Smith (eds.), *Handbook of Indigenous Education*,
https://doi.org/10.1007/978-981-10-3899-0_19

numerous requests. In particular, and in spite of wider pedestrian beliefs to the contrary, it is argued that translation is counterproductive to the goals of language revitalization and, if provided, would effectively support the continued subordination of Hawaiian to English. The fact that English dominates the linguistic interactions of the inhabitants of Hawaiʻi, as well as Hawaiʻi's linguistic landscape (This term refers to the "visibility and salience of languages on public and commercial signs in a given territory or region" (Landry and Bourhis 1997, p 23)), and that the subconscious inclination of second language learners is to understand the world in terms of a habitual linguistic template provided by English (Benjamin Lee Whorf recognized the existence of "habitual everyday concepts wherein speakers take (i.e., appropriate) language patterns as guides to the nature of reality." See Lucy 1992, p 46.), suggests that the revitalization of Hawaiian is heavily dependent on a continued connection to English. Grammatical structures and the lexical corpus have been deeply infiltrated as well, albeit with minimal resistance, and the ongoing conflation of the two languages with respect to worldview, even if it rises to the level of consciousness, goes largely unaddressed. The authors feel that translation supports the continued domination of English and hampers the efforts to retain the independence and uniqueness of Hawaiian linguistic expression.

Keywords
Language revitalization · Translation · Language subjugation

Community Language Background

For the past three decades, beginning with the establishment of the Pūnana Leo Hawaiian language medium preschools and the Hawaiian Language Immersion Program in the State of Hawaiʻi Department of Education (See Warner 2001, also Wilson and Kamanā 2001 for further information on the establishment of these programs.), the number of first language speakers of Hawaiian whose primary caregivers are native speakers of Hawaiian has decreased dramatically. The intergenerational transfer (This term is borrowed from Fishman 2001.) of this form of Hawaiian has been severely retarded as speakers of the more traditional Hawaiian are replaced by an increasing number of "NEO" speakers (NeSmith 2003 recognizes a split between TRAD speakers (i.e., speakers of more traditional forms of Hawaiian) and NEO speakers who are more susceptible to influence from English.) who are either second language learners or have been raised bilingually, with their Hawaiian language experiences provided primarily by other second language learners. This might have occurred through direct language instruction, subject matter instruction conducted in Hawaiian, or the minimal ambient speech to which emerging speakers are exposed in their communicative environments. Second language speakers and children raised by second language speakers currently comprise a prohibitive majority of the Hawaiian language speaking community. Of issue is the fact that their language use experiences rarely involve interaction with the few remaining native speakers who have been raised by other native speakers of Hawaiian. They are instead, heavily influenced by second language speakers. As such, current circumstances facilitate the speaking of a hybrid language (i.e., NEO-Hawaiian) that maps Hawaiian over more familiar English ways of thinking and speaking.

The authors of this chapter see translation as detrimental to the expressed goals of the Hawaiian language revitalization movement. We argue that translation from Hawaiian to English merely approximates the intended meaning of the author. Yet, the translation is represented more broadly as a legitimate clone of the original, and is accepted as such. In actuality, it is merely some individual's interpretation of the original text. Although this interpretation can provide a window through which nonspeakers of Hawaiian might make sense of the original, it only does so because of a fabricated connection between the two languages. It is the familiarity of English that provides insight into the meaning while the Hawaiian remains somewhat cryptic. Translation effectively blocks the receiver from experiencing an unadulterated Hawaiian expression.

Clearly, languages change over time as new ways of speaking are introduced. Contact with external ideas generally yields linguistic change. In the present context, wherein English serves as the lingua franca of the community, that change has been responsive to preexisting, and somewhat calcified, language use patterns of English. As such, the character of the emergent Hawaiian is eerily reflective of English. This path has led Hawaiian into a state of flux, forcing it to seek guidance from English in the remaking of itself. Instead of doing the research to revitalize traditional ways of speaking and applying the results to our present language use needs, we are satisfied with a level of communication that is successful for the very fact that it is familiar. We ultimately find ourselves speaking English in Hawaiian (This idea is attributed to colleagues of the famous linguist, Roman Jacobsen. They wrote jokingly in his obituary that he was able to speak Russian in six different languages. We have revised this idea in order to characterize speakers of Hawaiian whose first language is English. See New York Times (July 22, 1982).). Translation, although it can provide a semblance of access to intended meaning, supports the innate tendency we have to make sense of the world based on how we already see it. We, in effect, perpetuate a fraud upon ourselves when we view translation as adequately representative of its counterpart. Silva argues, "Much of the translation is unsatisfactory, however, because it is impossible to convey all of the cultural coding that English strips away, and equally impossible to avoid the Western cultural coding that English adds (2004, p 12)." We agree with this claim, and we hold it to be true of translation from English to Hawaiian as well.

Negotiating Public Access

As mentioned above, the advent of the Kauakūkalahale Hawaiian language column in the Honolulu StarBulletin was preceded by some fairly extensive negotiations with representatives of the paper. Their major concerns dealt with public access to the ideas presented within the articles and the possible exposure of the paper to litigation, primarily for libel. The access issue centered on the accommodation of a predominantly English-speaking readership. We refer to this as the economic argument. The newspaper, although it provides a valuable public service, is ultimately a private business venture that survives on sales. The paper itself can be sold either online or in hard copy, and advertising space can be sold to other businesses in order to cover costs. As for its exposure to liability, this is obviously a major concern. In response to this concern, however, we raised the following question. In what language would a charge of libel be adjudicated? If it were to be adjudicated in English, the libel would have to be determined based on translation. If it were to be conducted in Hawaiian, it would be necessary to translate the applicable U.S. laws into Hawaiian in order to facilitate relevant application. It would also require the establishment of legal precedents to guide decisions on legality. During the negotiations, we told the newspaper's representatives that a libel suit would actually work in favor of our goals. It would force the courts to establish guidelines for delineating the boundaries of appropriate editorial comment in Hawaiian. Moreover, it would require an adjudication of the legal standing of translated documents. Interestingly, it would also call into question the right of a U.S. court to adjudicate such a case in Hawai'i, which some people consider to be a sovereign state, and not under the jurisdiction of U.S. laws.

Looking again at economic concerns, the newspaper is a medium that has struggled to survive as younger people shift to social media in order to stay abreast of current issues and events. A fine line can be drawn between profit margins and journalistic integrity. That is, journalistic integrity must, at times, contend with journalistic popularity and, as such, compromises must be made. The StarBulletin's initial position was that the Hawaiian language articles be accompanied by English translations wherein the two would appear side by side, thus increasing the potential readership. This issue was clearly driven by an understandable mandate to maximize profits. Given this economic focus, the value of publishing Hawaiian language articles in a public forum was obviously being viewed from a vastly different perspective to our own. The newspaper was in the business of making money by conveying information, a feature not readily achievable solely through Hawaiian. We, on the other hand, were in the business of presenting Hawaiian as a legitimate form of communication, independent of English and focused more on survival than profit.

Interestingly, we had initially approached the Honolulu Advertiser back in 2002 with the idea of a Hawaiian language column. Their response fell on the other side of the spectrum to that of the StarBulletin. The Advertiser treated our offer to provide a weekly Hawaiian language column as tantamount to a request for advertising space. They offered us the "opportunity" to promote the official language of the State on the condition that we pay a mere $10,000.00 per page. On top of this, they required an English translation for all text written in Hawaiian (thus requiring the use of more space). It was as though the publication of editorials in Hawaiian was no different than the publication of an advertisement designed to market some consumable product. In all fairness, we were in fact attempting to promote the image of Hawaiian in the public psyche. It was, in a sense, a marketable product. The main difference, however, was the absence of a profit motive. Nonetheless, we were being challenged to view the publication of Hawaiian in their terms. It was simply put up or shut up. Given that the survival of the Advertiser was inextricably tied to the maximization of profit, it is perhaps unfair to criticize their attitude. These were simply two separate viewpoints each blind to the other's vision. The Honolulu Advertiser was, after all, holding true to its name.

As we grew to realize, this was a clear indication of the standing of the Hawaiian language at the time. It was not viewed as having economic value, at least by the Advertiser. After rejecting their offer, we approached the editors of the StarBulletin whom we found to be much more sympathetic to our cause. They were willing to treat Hawaiian as a legitimate medium through which to disseminate news and editorial comment, as well as stories of public interest. They were interested in publishing our articles in the Today section, which featured stories primarily local in scope. We suspect that, in their view, the printing of Hawaiian language articles would increase sales. Be that as it may, both parties viewed the publication of Hawaiian as mutually beneficial. Nonetheless, we were not in the least interested in providing English translations.

During that initial negotiation, we had argued that a required translation would adversely affect the Hawaiian-ness of the Hawaiian. It would effectively pull Hawaiian in the direction of English and, as such, run counter to our revitalization goals. An increased connection to English was the last thing we wanted. Instead, it was important to minimize the suffocating influence of English, an influence that has been so pervasive throughout the world that English has been referred to as a "killer language" (Skutnabb-Kangas 2002, p 181). This sentiment is echoed by Ngugi wa Thiong'o who characterized the growth of dominant languages at the expense of weaker languages as "linguistic Darwinism" (Ngugi 2011, p 244). Since the vast majority of Hawaiian language speakers today are first language speakers of English, there is a strong tendency to approach the explication of thought through that lens. In other words, even without the requirement of translation, we would be challenged to divorce ourselves completely from the tendency to make sense of our world through our first language. Our first language habits operate at the subconscious level. Moreover, our subconscious subscription to the ideology of English (Grace 1981) would prevent us from viewing this as problematic. This is a major issue for people involved in language revitalization efforts. Reversing language shift requires the mass acceptance of a counter narrative to the ideology of English.

Suppression of the Minority

The numbers game is not an uncommon practice for locating power in democratic societies. Arguments can be won simply by citing a preponderance of support for the "winning" position, the relative merits of such a position being of little consequence. In this view, we find a classic example in which the tyranny of the majority (This phrase is attributed to John Adams who used it in 1788.) allows for the acceptance of weak arguments as valid. We agree with Fanon's position that "(t)he desire to attach oneself to tradition or bring abandoned tradition to life again does not only mean going against the current of history but also opposing one's own people (Fanon 1963, p 224)." One reader found it difficult to believe that we would choose not to offer translations for the articles. He characterized our position as "counterintuitive" (Kauakūkalahale articles are accompanied by contact information for the two editors. We respond to all inquiries either in English or Hawaiian depending on the language in which they are received.), the assumption being that a majority of sensible writers would seek to reach the widest possible audience. Surely we were sacrificing an opportunity to reach a wider readership in order to protect an exclusionary position. There were arguments that failure to provide translation would widen an already noticeable rift between Hawaiian language "haves" and "have nots" (Kuwada 2009). But our reasons for not providing translations had little to do with an inexplicable desire to limit readership, or even to privilege an exclusive group of insiders. We were much more concerned with generating an overall increase in the number of people capable of reading Hawaiian. Not unlike the negotiation with the newspaper, this reader was assuming that the primary goal of our effort was to disseminate information and opinion. Our position was one he was not inclined to accept, that is, the article is symbolic of the legitimacy of Hawaiian as a language suitable for mass communication. It was imperative that it be allowed to speak for itself and not depend on English in order to convey meaning. Moreover, counter to arguments that providing translations would yield a net increase in the number of readers capable of accessing Hawaiian, we foresaw a very different outcome. The increase would be realized only in access to the English version of the Hawaiian. Translations would actually preclude readers from ever learning enough Hawaiian to access the ideas directly. The provision of translations would effectively negate one of the primary motivations for learning Hawaiian. As for reaching a broader audience, our hope is to do so in Hawaiian, without an intermediary. Pandering to the majority ultimately supports the ideology of English.

Again, this would work at cross-purposes with our stated goal, the revitalization of Hawaiian. Language shift and language loss are extremely common consequences that minority languages face when confronted with the pervasiveness of dominant languages (See Dorian 1989, whose edited book offers valuable insight into the consequences of language loss.). For those concerned with the ramifications of these consequences, particularly the erosion of heritage, it is difficult to convey the gravity of such loss to those who are not. We decided that one way to explicate our position was to turn the argument around. That is, we would acquiesce to requests for English translations of the Hawaiian if the same were required of English. That is, if all English articles were translated into Hawaiian and the two were printed side by side, our concerns would be mitigated. When this compromise position was suggested, however, the individual remained incredulous. Why would anyone choose to write in a language that is inaccessible to an overwhelming majority of potential readers? Why on earth would we not want to disseminate our ideas to the broadest possible audience? After all, that is the ostensible purpose of any form of mass media (We say "ostensible" here after heavy exposure to CNN and Fox News political commentaries that cater to polarized audiences.). Even when it was pointed out to him that there is a social imperative to rectify the unjust historical events that lead to the subordination of the Hawaiian language to English, he remained unconvinced. Our position seemed to make little sense to him. According to his logic, everyone speaks English and very few people speak Hawaiian; therefore, failure to provide English translations for articles written in Hawaiian represents a counterintuitive position. His intuition, however, suggests that we follow the same path, i.e., providing translations, which brought us to the present need for translation.

The fact that extensive colonization had enabled English to supplant Hawaiian as the lingua franca of the community was not one this reader was prepared to consider relevant. He was not inclined to focus on an injustice visited upon a group of people whose linguistic connection to reality had been usurped. Rather, he was more interested in the rights of individuals to access a service that is meant for public benefit. Our reasons did not align with his view of equal access, and that is not an uncommon experience for those who espouse minority viewpoints. We happen to believe that it would be more intuitive to address the inequity suffered by a group of people, manifested in the Hawaiian case by the loss of our language of heritage, than to complain about insufficient access of individuals to ideas presented in that language. Some of the responsibility for gaining that access ultimately reverts to the individual. After all, there are numerous opportunities publicly available to those individuals wishing to learn Hawaiian. Of course, this path requires some effort.

Protecting the Official Fish

Although both Hawaiian and English enjoy "official" language status under the laws of the State of Hawai'i (This became law at the State of Hawai'i Constitutional Convention of 1978.), the progress of Hawaiian is not completely dependent on legal status. It is still necessary for speakers to elect to use it. In fact, the wording in the law allows for the perpetuation of a hegemonic relationship between the two languages. It states, "Whenever there is found to exist any radical and irreconcilable difference between the English and Hawaiian versions of any of the laws of the State, the English version shall be held binding" (State of Hawai'i 1978). Ironically, this codicil effectively renders the official language status of Hawaiian vacuous with regard to the law, in that it is officially subordinated to English. It offers only limited status in the legal domain, and, in the broader context, offers no substantive support for revitalization efforts. That can only be achieved by expanding the domains of use available to Hawaiian, along with its communicative efficacy within those domains. It does, however, symbolically represent Hawaiian as something of value, something worth nurturing and protecting. This symbolic negation (or semblance thereof) of the de facto hierarchy is of critical importance in increasing the capital available to Hawaiian (This idea is borrowed from Bourdieu 1991.). And yet, despite the symbolism, not all supporters of Hawaiian share this view. There are some who have criticized the official language status as being about as valuable as having an official fish (For the State of Hawai'i, that would be the humuhumunukunukuāpua'a, a type of triggerfish.). Dr. Sam L. No'eau Warner (Personal communication.), upon being apprised of this concern, responded simply by stating, "At least they can't kill the official fish." In line with this view, it should be noted that the law does, in fact, offer Hawaiian some legitimacy with regard to its use as a language of wider currency.

The de jure legitimacy of Hawaiian opens up the possibility for Hawaiian to stand on its own, without translation, in public spheres. This right also makes it possible to reform the linguistic landscape by offering a choice in terms of linguistic expression even in private domains. It does not present a threat to the existence of English, only to the level of its dominance. With regard to perception, of course, monolingual speakers of English would be effectively excluded from access to some of the ambient language in the community. However, with regard to production, it is inconceivable (at present) that they would ever be compelled to use Hawaiian in place of English. It merely allows for people to opt for one or the other. This is perhaps the nexus of the dispute. There is more at stake here than the protection of an official fish. The legitimization of Hawaiian could conceivably cut into the linguistic market share currently controlled by English. In order to maintain their range of communicative viability, monolingual speakers of English would have to learn Hawaiian. Also, a proliferation of Hawaiian language use would likely lead to an increase in economic opportunities available to Hawaiian language speakers, a reversal of fortune of sorts, placing English monolinguals at a disadvantage. They would then have to learn Hawaiian in order to "get ahead in life."

The above argument is reflective of the one formerly invoked at the advent of the Pūnana Leo Hawaiian language immersion preschools. The idea of Hawaiian language immersion education met with some skepticism even among Hawaiians. It was believed that there was an opportunity cost associated with sending children to such schools. By doing so, parents were effectively neglecting their children's English language development. Some even went so far to characterize it as "retarding" the children. At that time, the ideology of English was firmly entrenched in the psyche of the Hawaiian community, and the idea that it was necessary for children to speak English in order to get ahead in life was pervasively accepted. We are provided a glimpse of this attitude in a short story written by Sarah Nākoa in her collection of short stories called "Lei momi o 'Ewa." In one autobiographical piece, Mrs. Nākoa describes her grandmother's words as she (Sarah) is sent off to her first day of primary school (in compliance with the laws at the time), advising her to focus on learning English, "E paʻa pono i ka ʻōlelo a ka Haole. Mai kālele i kā kākou ʻōlelo. ʻAʻohe he pono i laila. Aia ke ola o ka noho ʻana ma kēia mua aku i ka ʻike pono i ka ʻōlelo a ka poʻe Haole" (Nākoa 1979).

Her grandmother was buying into the majority view of the community at the time. Like many others, she believed that English would provide her granddaughter with the linguistic tools to make her successful in life. This constituted the gist of an economic argument used to make a case against Hawaiian language immersion education, the same argument used to question the value of majoring in Hawaiian at the tertiary level. It also supports the argument of the reader mentioned above who found our position to be "counterintuitive." Although there has been some movement away from this ideology of linguistic inequality, it remains psychologically real for many people, especially those who are unfamiliar with the field of language study (Wong 2011a). This ideology remains so deeply ingrained in the psyche of the community that only a small number of people can claim conversational fluency in Hawaiian today.

In our view, equitable treatment of the two languages would do little to decrease the prominence English enjoys worldwide. It would, however, do much to elevate the status of Hawaiian in the opinion of the public and increase its chances for survival among that segment of the population for which it is the language of heritage. An elevation in actual value would eventually be realized with the inevitable expansion of its practical domains of use. Hawaiian would no longer rely on the limited power of its official language status in order to garner respect. Of course, motivation for choosing Hawaiian as a medium of communication must, at least initially, transcend the promise of economic gain. The real value of speaking Hawaiian is located in both its capacity to mark identity and its unique worldview. The dissemination of thought through various avenues of mass media is a critical component in the restoration of our language of heritage.

To Translate or Not to Translate: Lexical Issues

The question of accuracy was raised in the preceding arguments. Our position aligns with that of Hymes who suggested that no matter how well the translation is performed, it cannot perfectly represent the meaning of the source language as realized by a native speaker of that language (Hymes 1981). This is compounded by the fact that languages change over time and so do meanings (Fishman 2001). We have maintained that, although translation can suggest a semblance of equivalence between meanings, it can never accurately represent meaning cross-linguistically or cross-temporally. Too many degrees of separation are possible. Differences in dialect, context, and perspective could contribute to significant variation among multiple interpretations of a single piece. One translator's interpretation might be substantially different from that of the next, simply based on the difference in the type of translation employed. Hymes has spoken of the incongruous relationship between "literal" and "literary" translations, noting that literary translations are often superior (Hymes 1981, p 42), i.e., more accurate in their representations of meaning. This clearly suggests that translation is an inexact endeavor. Divergence also occurs, perhaps even more prominently, between the translation and its original. Each language has its own peculiar features that defy efforts to create equivalencies designed to offer monolinguals accurate access to a second language.

Vocabulary items in one language never really match up perfectly with their reflexes in another. That is, there is never a true one to one correspondence. Even words that are created specifically to account for a foreign concept (borrowings) can exhibit differences from their intended counterparts (In an effort to modify the lexicon, numerous words have been coined in order to account for novel concepts. These have been compiled in a supplementary dictionary called Māmaka Kaiao (Kōmike Huaʻōlelo 2003), and are also available online.). The English word "church," for example, does not match a single Hawaiian counterpart. It refers to two different concepts represented by two distinct meanings. One indicates a physical structure and is referred to as a hale pule or "house of prayer" in Hawaiian. The other indicates a type of organization referred to as a ʻekalesia, a borrowed word with Greek roots. There are numerous examples of one word in English having multiple reflexes in Hawaiian. There are also numerous examples of Hawaiian words with multiple reflexes in English. For example, the word "pule" is glossed as follows:

> pule. 1. nvt. Prayer, magic spell, incantation, blessing, grace, church service, church; to pray, worship, say grace, ask a blessing, cast a spell. (Probable derivatives are *pulepule*, *pupule*, and *ʻōpulepule*.) ... 2. n. Week. ... 3. Same as *ʻōpule 1*. (Pukui and Elbert 1986, p 353)

Here we can see other semantic connections generated by this word. The connection to casting a spell is one that English speakers do not normally associate with praying. There are other disconnections as well. The third meaning points to the word ʻōpule as being synonymous with ʻōpulepule, which is glossed below:

> ʻōpulepule. 1. vs. Moronic, somewhat crazy, psychotic. (Pukui and Elbert 1986, p 353)

Pule thus transcends the concept of prayer, taking us in a different direction altogether, one that some might find sacrilegious or even heathen. As we can see, the range of Hawaiian meanings for pule does not exactly map over the range of meanings for pray in English. Moreover, the word church generally refers to a Christian organization or Christian house of worship and does not encompass other deities or forms of religious ritual.

Given the relatively small phoneme inventory of Hawaiian, a number of words borrowed from English match existing Hawaiian forms with traditional meanings. They are transliterated into Hawaiian by adjusting their pronunciation to comply with the phonotactics of Hawaiian. For example, Hawaiian does not allow consonant clusters. English words with consonant clusters must undergo adjustment when they are borrowed into Hawaiian. For example, in order to transliterate the word truck, it is necessary to break up the consonant cluster in the onset of the syllable. It is also necessary to add a vowel at the end in order to avoid having a closed syllable, i.e., one ending in a consonant. Consonantal substitutions are also made as necessary. This yields the borrowed word kalaka.

These transliterations, although they can account for their English source meanings, fail to match up exactly with other synonyms in Hawaiian. The word "pia," for example, has a number of traditional Hawaiian meanings that are unconnected to English. But it is also the transliteration of beer and, as one might imagine, is frequently used in that capacity. In fact, this meaning is more commonly recognized than any of its other traditional meanings, e.g., arrowroot, starch (as made from arrowroot), pale yellow in color, a variety of taro, a variety of sweet potato, a stone used to fashion adzes, and a stork. We see this focus on English as an unfortunate consequence of borrowing and an unfortunate consequence of language shift. Although it is a necessary evil in the modernization of Hawaiian, it also draws

Hawaiian closer to English. And as columnists focused on maximizing separation between the two languages, we see minimizing the use of borrowed concepts, wherever possible, as a useful strategy. We find the dependence on translation and transliteration as strategies for borrowing to be reflective of English dominance. They illustrate our dependence on English and our inclination to see the world through that lens. The fact that there is a dearth of examples in which English has borrowed Hawaiian concepts into its lexicon makes the imbalance painfully salient. Instead of these strategies, we find circumlocution (The American Heritage Dictionary offers glosses that cast circumlocution in a slightly negative light (1992). The result is considered unnecessarily wordy, evasive, and roundabout. Wong has argued that indirect speech represents the norm in communicative exchanges (Wong 2011b).) to be a favorable option. Its adverse effects in terms of English influence are far less pronounced. It constitutes a retelling of the information in a way that privileges Hawaiian ways of speaking while protecting against undue influence from English.

Looking at terminology in the Hawaiian family system, we find another salient example of the overpowering effect English has had on our language. Certain specific terms either transliterated from English or constructed from Hawaiian roots to accommodate the English worldview, have dominated the speech community. Here the influence cuts deeper than the mere borrowing of words. It materially affects the Hawaiian family system and the responsibilities that are vested in each position on the genealogical matrix. We examine three such words here, i.e., palala, tita, and hoahānau.

Palala and tita are transliterated from the English words brother and sister. Although they accommodate the expression of family relationships to which English speakers are accustomed, they fail to represent the Hawaiian view of these relationships. The following words represent a more traditional way of indicating those relationships in Hawaiian:

kaikua'ana – elder brothers of male/elder sisters of female
kaikaina – younger brothers of male/younger sisters of female
kaikuahine – sister of male
kaikunāne – brother of female

As we can see, the familial references are segregated by gender in two obvious ways. Firstly, within the same gender, birth order determines the appropriate term, and the same term is used for both genders in order to mark that relationship. In English, a modifying term is necessary for drawing a distinction in birth order. The words older and younger are used to make birth order distinctions. Secondly, separate terms are used in order to mark cross-gendered relationships depending on focus. In English, a single term is used to mark both intra- and inter-gender relationships. That is, males and females can both have brothers and sisters.

The above examples illustrate important worldview distinctions between the two languages that cannot be sustained through linguistic borrowing. The borrowed term conjures up a view of the world that fails to match that of its borrowed source. The range of meanings available to the source word transcends the range available to its translated counterpart. For example, palala accounts only for the English meanings that brother evokes in the family system. There are other meanings of brother that are not evoked by palala. For example, if we use the word brother to describe a fellow member of some organization such as a church, palala would not be appropriate. These relationships would require the word hoahānau. It is a compound made up of two words, hoa (friend) and hānau (birth) (The fact that these two words have been compounded and spelled as a single word suggests a desire to express this new concept. Schütz suggests that this indicates an attraction to the prestige value offered by English (Schütz 1994).). This same word is also commonly used to refer to the relationship between cousins, even though the four words listed above were used traditionally to describe relationships amongst cousins (Handy and Pukui 1998).

This compound word is clearly not a transliteration of the English word cousin and, despite its Hawaiian roots, might very well be a neologism that entered the vocabulary after the arrival of English speaking explorers. In support of this claim, we point to the fact that it fails to account for the gender and birth order factors that exemplify Hawaiian worldview in this area. Again, one of the consequences of translation is the stripping away of some important aspects of familial relationships that mark Hawaiian as a unique linguistic system. The use of hoahānau is far more prevalent than the use of kaikuaʻana, kaikaina, kaikunāne, and kaikuahine, and foreshadows the leveling of these uniquely Hawaiian distinctions, and perhaps eventually, their complete eradication.

To Translate or Not to Translate: Beyond Lexicon

Grammatical structures can also differ between languages and lead to disparities in focus, agency (See Wong (2011b) for an extended discussion of agency and the cross-linguistic differences between Hawaiian and English.), or even referential meaning. On top of that, context, tone, genre, perspective, gender, and a number of other factors can contribute to the disparity in meanings between the interpretation and its source. This is not surprising. Even in the same language, the hearer cannot claim to have accessed the exact meaning intended by the speaker. Cross-linguistically, there is much greater opportunity for misinterpretation, especially between second language learners and native speakers of the language in question. Second language learners are liable to construct their statements, and understand the statements of others, based on heavily ingrained thought patterns from their first language. According to Sapir, "We see and hear and otherwise experience very largely as we do because the language habits of our community predispose certain choices of interpretation" (as cited in Carroll 1995, p 134) (Carroll presents selected works of Whorf, in which this quote from Sapir initiates a chapter.). Those choices are guided by habit and are quite difficult to avoid (Lucy 1992) (Lucy also credits Whorf for recognizing that language behaviors are habitually conditioned.), even when their existence rises to the level of conscious thought. Lucy also recognized the existence of substantial variation across languages that "even when there is apparent similarity, there may be differences in semantic implication that can make exact translation equivalence difficult" (Lucy 1992, p 194).

A salient example of the difference between English and Hawaiian is found in the way one concept is compared to another. One might utilize the preposition "from" in order to indicate that one concept differs from the other, or the preposition "between" in order to indicate the nexus of the disconnect. Thus, "the taro is different from the breadfruit" or "the difference between the taro and the breadfruit" both rely on this disconnect, ultimately depending on the existence of the other as a point of reference. Hawaiian handles this idea quite differently. Instead of depending on a relationship that negatively links one item to the other (i.e., the taro is not like the breadfruit), Hawaiian treats the two items as though they are completely independent of each other. The phrase "ua ʻokoʻa ke kalo a ʻokoʻa ka ʻulu" literally indicates the independence of the two items. There is nothing "between" them and one is not in any way derived "from" the other. English speakers learning Hawaiian are likely to construct their speech based on that which is familiar, in which case they end up calquing the English way of expressing this disconnect (i.e., ua ʻokoʻa ke kalo mai ka ʻulu or "the taro is different from the breadfruit"). In recognition of this pervasive tendency among immersion school children, as well as numerous adult speakers of Hawaiian, Warner wrote a children's book designed to counter this type of English influence. The book, entitled *ʻOkoʻa ka palaoa, ʻokoʻa ke koholā*, illustrates numerous physiological features not shared by the two creatures while offering immersion students a more traditionally Hawaiian way of conceptualizing the independence of each (Warner 2009) (This particular analysis was raised by our colleague, Dr. Margaret Maaka. Her background in cognitive development enabled her to recognize the independence of two items as an inadvertent lesson about Hawaiian ways of speaking and knowing.).

There are numerous other examples of English worldview dominating the construction of thought in Hawaiian. One fairly common example can be found in the pervasive use of interrogative words as integral pieces in the production of statements. This represents a form of what Odlin called transfer, a type of interference by one language on another in the mind of the speaker, that materially alters the basic function of such statements, assigning to them properties of the speaker's native language (Odlin 1989). An example of this can be found in the use of the Hawaiian word "pehea," an interrogative term that can be glossed as "how" in English. The fact that this word can be used in English both as an interrogative marker as well as the object of a verb of cognition suggests to the second language learner of Hawaiian that the same holds true in Hawaiian. In other words, in English it is possible to use "how" in order to say both of the following:

How does Kale pound taro?   Pehea e kuʻi aiʻo Kale i ke kalo?

I know how Kale pounds taro.   *Uaʻike au pehea e kuʻi aiʻo Kale i ke kalo.

*Although this type of construction is quite common amongst today's speakers of Hawaiian, it is not a usage found in more traditional samples of Hawaiian language use. Its prevalence today is clearly linked to a tendency for native speakers of English to assume that a Hawaiian word can be utilized with equal range as its counterpart in English. We submit that this phenomenon is supported by an unfounded belief in the legitimacy of translation.

There are numerous other examples that can illustrate the shortcomings of translation, including the metaphorical meanings that apply to certain ways of speaking. In particular, Hawaiian prominently features what are referred to as ʻōlelo noʻeau, or proverbial expressions that offer insight into Hawaiian worldview and provide guidance for behavior that conforms to that worldview. In Pukui's collection of ʻōlelo noʻeau (Pukui 1983), we can see two levels of translation that are designed to privilege the English speaker interested in Hawaiian worldview. At one level, a fairly literal translation is provided. In many cases, however, this translation provides only lexical equivalencies adjusted to align with English grammatical patterns, but are of little value in pursuing the intended meaning (or meanings). Most offer a second, more figurative translation designed to allow closer access to intended meaning. The maintenance of ʻōlelo noʻeau is recognized as a critical piece in the reconstruction of the Hawaiian language (Solis 2009). One feature of the ʻōlelo noʻeau is that, similarly to double entendres, it provides an indirect path for proposing a particular position, thus allowing for a choice of interpretations. In other words, a statement can be made without causing an affront to the interlocutor, who is thus allowed to save face. This type of diplomacy supports the maintenance of solidarity between speakers and harmony within the community (Wong 2011b).

Another Compromise on Translation

At the end of 2015, we entered into a renegotiation with the StarAdvertiser over translation. We had sent in an article that was critical of a top University of Hawaiʻi administrator. The article was critical of this administrator's actions, compensation, and some issues of conflict regarding very lucrative contractual agreements with the private sector that unduly influenced the direction of research in that administrator's particular college. The editors were asking for a full translation of the article as a requirement for its publication. After operating for over 12 years relatively translation free, this new requirement caught us off guard. We argued that this was not part of the original agreement and that translation would compromise our revitalization goals. For a plethora of reasons, including the arguments laid out above, translation does not provide an accurate representation of the original piece. The editors were adamant, however, explaining that the original agreement was ill advised and that it would be irresponsible for them to publish ideas to which they had no access.

After raising many of the same arguments we had depended on the first time around, we found ourselves increasingly sympathetic to the editors' dilemma. No matter how we spun it, it was their responsibility to oversee the professionalism of their product. Both their concerns and ours had merit. Our arguments were taken into consideration and a new compromise position was reached. We would not be required to provide a narrow translation of the column but, instead, would rewrite the main ideas in English. And, this rewrite would not be made available to the public. Its use would be reserved strictly for internal purposes. In the end, we were effectively maintaining our no-translation policy, and the only cost to us was realized in the additional work.

Conclusion

The connection between Hawaiian words or phrases and their translations in English can be widely disparate and a number of factors can be designated as contributors to that disparity. Ways of speaking can differ dramatically from language to language leaving translations ill equipped to represent accurately the intended meanings of their original counterparts. Although it is true that translation offers an educated guess at intended meanings, it cannot be counted on as equivalent. The receiver of linguistic input merely utilizes any and all available communicative resources to approximate its meaning, thus assuming a right to access that meaning. However, the purposes for using language cannot, as many have claimed, be purely communicative. It cannot be assumed to require a complete and unadulterated transmission of ideas from a producer to a receiver. In some cases, language can be used for the purpose of confounding meaning, or even denying its access to certain parties. In our context, Hawaiian is being used to indicate its legitimacy within an English dominated context. Translation of the Hawaiian into English not only allows for misinterpretation, it allows for the continued domination of an English worldview, thus undermining our primary purpose for maintaining the column. Moreover, it suggests that Hawaiian is only valuable when it can be accessible to monolingual speakers of English. Although translation could yield an overall increase in the number of individuals capable of accessing meaning, it does not guarantee the accuracy of that meaning. If left unquestioned, translation is allowed to promote itself as an accurate representation of intended meaning. We find this to be counterproductive to language revitalization efforts.

References

Bourdieu P (1991) Language & symbolic power. Harvard University Press, Cambridge
Carroll JB (ed) (1995) Language, thought, and reality: selected writings of Benjamin Lee Whorf. MIT Press, Cambridge
Dorian N (ed) (1989) Investigating obsolescence: studies in language contraction and death. Cambridge University Press, Cambridge
Fanon F (1963) The wretched of the earth. Grove Press, New York
Fishman JA (2001) Why is it so hard to save a threatened language? In: Fishman JA (ed) Can threatened languages be saved? Multilingual Matters, Clevedon, pp 1–22
Grace GW (1981) An essay on language. Hornbeam Press, Columbia
Handy ESC, Pukui MK (1998) The Polynesian family system in Ka'ū. Mutual Publishing, Honolulu

Huaʻōlelo K (2003) Māmaka Kaiao: A modern Hawaiian vocabulary. University of Hawaiʻi Press, Honolulu

Hymes D (1981) "In vain I tried to tell you": essays in native American ethnopoetics. University of Pennsylvania Press, Philadelphia

Kuwada B (2009) To translate or not to translate: revisiting the translation of Hawaiian language texts. Biography 32(1):54–65

Landry R, Bourhis R (1997) Linguistic landscape and ethnolinguistic vitality an empirical study. J Lang Soc Psych 16(1):23–49

Lucy JA (1992) Language diversity and thought: a reformulation of the linguistic relativity hypothesis. Cambridge University Press, New York

Nākoa SK (1979) Nā ʻōlelo aʻo o ka wā kamaliʻi. In: Wilson W (ed) Lei momi o ʻEwa. Ke Kumu Lama. ʻAhahui ʻŌlelo Hawaiʻi, Honolulu, pp 18–19

NeSmith K (2003) Tūtū's Hawaiian and the emergence of a neo-Hawaiian language. ʻŌiwi: A Nat Hawn J 3:68–77

Ngugi wT (2011) Linguistic feudalism and linguistic Darwinism: the struggle of the indigenous from the margins of power. In: Romero-Little ME, Ortiz SJ, McCarty TL, Chen R (eds) Indigenous languages across the generations – strengthening families and communities. Arizona State University Center for Indian Education, Tempe, pp 241–246

Odlin T (1989) Language transfer: cross-linguistic influence in language learning. Cambridge University Press, New York

Pukui MK (1983) ʻŌlelo noʻeau: Hawaiian proverbs and poetical sayings. Bishop Museum Press, Honolulu

Pukui MK, Elbert SH (1986) Hawaiian dictionary. University of Hawaiʻi Press, Honolulu

Schütz AJ (1994) The voices of Eden: a history of Hawaiian language studies. University of Hawaiʻi Press, Honolulu

Silva NK (2004) Aloha betrayed: native Hawaiian resistance to American colonization. Duke University Press, Durham

Skutnabb-Kangas T (2002) Marvelous human rights rhetoric and grim realities: language rights in education. J Lang Ident Educ 1(3):179–205

Solis RDK (2009) A kau aku i nā mamo. AlterNative 5(2):174–187

State of Hawaiʻi (1978) Hawaiʻi state constitution, official languages, article XV, section 4. State of Hawaiʻi, Honolulu, p 1

Warner SLN (2001) The movement to revitalize Hawaiian language and culture. In: Hinton L, Hale K (eds) The green book of language revitalization in practice. Academic Press, San Diego, pp 133–144

Warner SLN (2009) ʻOkoʻa ka palaoa, ʻokoʻa ke koholā. Ka Lau ʻUlu, Honolulu

Wilson WH, Kamanā K (2001) Mai loko mai o ka ʻiʻini: procceding from a dream. In: Hinton L, Hale K (eds) The green book of language revitalization in practice. Academic Press, San Diego, pp 147–178

Wong KL (2003, April 13) Ka unuhi a me ka hoʻokē. Honolulu StarBulletin Kauakūkalahale column

Wong KL (2011a) Language, fruits, and vegetables. In: Romero-Little ME, Ortiz S, McCarty TL, Chen R (eds) Indigenous languages across the generations – strengthening families and communities. Arizona State University, Arizona, pp 3–16

Wong KL (2011b) Hawaiian methodologies of indirection: point-less vs. pointless. In: Davis KA (ed) Critical qualitative research in second language studies: agency and advocacy. Information Age Publishing, Charlotte, pp 151–170

A Term's Irruption and a Possibility for Response: A Māori Glance at "Epistemology"

31

Carl Mika

Contents

Introduction	546
A Māori Term Analysis and the Language of Things	548
The Self within the Object and its Name	548
My Dislike of "Epistemology"	552
Referring to the Original Sense of "Epistemology"	555
Consequences of "Epistemology" for the Māori User	559
Glossary	561
References	561

Abstract

Language for Māori (Indigenous people/s of Aotearoa New Zealand) is complicated because it seems to emerge from, and indeed merge with, both the human and nonhuman worlds, from an idea and yet from the materiality of things, and from colonized and traditional realms. Analyzing a term has to take place within the full nature of language and also its objects and, in turn, those objects' worlds. In this chapter, I consider the term "epistemology," which tends to grab my attention as an emissary of certainty, calling me to address it. The term is equally as far-reaching as language as a whole, and rather than referring to it as if it is a human-derived phenomenon, I look to its autonomy for guidance. This approach, I argue, sits better with a Māori philosophy of language than that which underpins more dominant discourse analysis. The evaluation of a term must also be carried out as if it is a personal matter, and asks for the Māori writer to look to his or her own experiences and background and to have special regard for both tribal and

---

C. Mika (✉)
The University of Waikato, Hamilton, New Zealand
e-mail: mika@waikato.ac.nz

© Springer Nature Singapore Pte Ltd. 2019
E. A. McKinley, L. T. Smith (eds.), *Handbook of Indigenous Education*,
https://doi.org/10.1007/978-981-10-3899-0_20

individual idiosyncrasies. These aspects are necessarily unique to individuals within their colonized and tribal contexts, and they draw the Māori writer or student to the term and signal how one should analyze it. The approach I have adopted is my own and is educational to the extent that it shows one way of engaging with the world of a term. I am therefore more interested in the power of language to educate the indigenous self while we use it (or it uses us), than I am in teaching and learning in more orthodox Western senses. I conclude by likening this inability to get to the static properties of language to my tribal origins and events.

Keywords
Māori · Epistemology · Reo · Language · Mātauranga · Papatūānuku · Philosophy

Introduction

Many of us as Māori writers suspect that language is a different phenomenon for us than it is for the West, and the depth and expanse of that difference is immense. Language for Māori is complicated because it seems to emerge from, and indeed merge with, both the human and nonhuman worlds, from an idea and yet from the materiality of things, and from colonized and traditional realms (Mika 2016b). That language is so complex should come as no surprise to us, given that our worldviews are equally as convoluted and, at times, paradoxical. Where Western philosophical approaches wish to iron out those twists and turns that characterize Māori thought (see for instance: Ahenakew et al. 2014; Cooper 2008), making it logical and rational, instead Māori thought about language and its world insists that we stay within a convoluted landscape of the "at-once": language is *at once* dense and free-floating, settling upon as well as already immediately within the world to which it refers. It is hence at once world and a describer of the world. It is this dual nature of language which makes it hard to describe. After all, how can any of us step outside of the world and then describe language, given we are using language ourselves to try and represent it? Or given that language is connected to the world that we are part of? It would seem that stepping outside of the world to then be able to analyze language, while using language to review language and the world we have just transcended, is impossible.

In this chapter, I seek to meld the personal with the educational. I consider a Māori philosophy of language through my reaction to a term that irrupts into my thinking – "epistemology" – and discuss that term as an aspect of language. My aim is hence to speak about language through its most granular item – a term – while conveying my dislike for that particular term. When referring to "language" I may just as well be referring to the relationship of all objects with the world, because language, when discussed, seems to slip back into the realm of all things. If we relinquish the Western idea's grandeur that language is simply an envelope that transmits ideas, then we soon come up against this difficulty. In that Western tradition, the division between secular and supernatural has led to the depiction of language as a shell. "Epistemology," viewed in that sense, is simply an arbitrary sign for a concept. But it is the more worlded aspects of language that ask for my attention through the constant interruption and sway of that term, epistemology. To deal with the theme somewhat negatively: there are some elements of the discussion I want to exclude (Please see glossary towards end of chapter for definitions of Māori terms.). I do not wish to refer to the beauty of a particular language such as te reo Māori in my discussion, even though the beauty (or otherwise) of a language can be a philosophical issue. The *sound* of language as it originates from humans, or whether it is euphonic or not, is therefore not my concern, but I do note that silence is equally important, philosophically speaking. I also do not seek to refer to the use of a particularly spiritual octave of language in ceremonies, but instead my thinking emerges from the possibility that language, thought of in a particular way, is also a metaphysical concern in everyday usage. My problematizing of language additionally deviates from the issue of identity and knowledge of te reo Māori: there are indeed certain features of the Māori terms that distinguish it from English equivalents, although whether these are entirely absent from English or simply whether they are overtaken by the strictness of thought that modernity encourages (Ahenakew et al. 2014) is uncertain. I *do* want to include that a term, whether in the colonial language of English or in the traditional register of Māori, can open onto a world's density that is either oppressive or liberating, but even here I note that this requires the attention of the thinker, who is him- or herself already constructed by what the world has revealed to him or her. Also, the term "epistemology" contains two main components – "epistemi" and "-ology." For the sake of keeping within the limits of a book chapter, I deal only with the first but briefly acknowledge here that "logos" – which "ology" derives from – has its own sophisticated genealogy in Western philosophy that, in its current form as "logic" (Gonzalez 2009), actually sits well with the problems I raise about "epistemi."

The chapter is hopefully educational at the same time, because I attempt to provide an example of how a term can be critiqued through a Māori regard toward language as I have outlined it above. It is not particularly worried with the meta-discipline of education as such, and I do note at this point that education is not simply about teaching and learning, as it is also congruent with the epistemically uncertain yet constant guidance from the world, or "tohu" as Royal (2005) calls it. A further educational act takes place in the retelling of that experience and in its potential use for others. This communicative act is not the one that seeks a symmetrical response from its recipients (Biesta 2010). As a set of "sentences that push" (Mika 2013), it encourages the reader to propose their own reaction to a term and determine their own subsequent way in relation to it. Further, and more conventionally for education as a process of edification, an analysis of a term is indeed related to education as a discipline to the extent that it is often reverted to at tertiary level (especially in graduate work), and this chapter might therefore be educationally pragmatic because it offers one way of dealing with a term from a Māori philosophical perspective. It seems that there are some fundamental shortcomings within a poststructuralist approach to, for instance, a term, and I urge that a Māori analysis of a term stems from a personal reaction – another facet of Royal's "tohu." While this personal aspect of analysis is not always fully passed over in mainstream discourse critique, it takes on a particularly important hue for the Māori writer, and it must be expanded on for different reasons – not the least of which is that language has always claimed us and called to us to address it.

A key method I propose in the analysis is to look to the most basic tenet of a word – its etymology – and evaluate that against a Māori philosophy that the individual Māori writer may also have speculated on. The etymology of a term, I suggest, carries its "sense" or its very first ontological regard for the world. Further, the Māori writer can think deeply about where to place his or her material in the text. I do not discuss this organization in the body of the chapter but make the following observations: that material can be divided roughly into the writer's speculative thinking on the one hand, and already established knowledge or text on the other; that, in order to emphasize the writer's personal reactions to a term and their own thinking on it, it is sometimes politically and philosophically expedient to divide their speculative thinking from that other well-known body of work; and that there is really no set method that can be established to dictate what should be included where. I have called this form of aside "subtext" in relevant parts of the chapter. Subtext informs my decisions to write, may indeed dictate from afar what I write, and occasionally may dictate quite closely what I write. Of course, this right to speculate on discrete and extensive matters of existence is the right of all Māori, and it is up to us to demarcate that thinking from already frequently occurring knowledge.

Although I have some keenly felt problems with the term "epistemology," I end by noting that this attitude is not so clear-cut. If language is a worlded phenomenon, as I argue, and I am constituted by it and its objects, then my relationship with it must be more indeterminate than I thought. Ultimately, any conclusion that a Māori critic of terms will arrive at will be based on the nature of the philosophy of language and world that they have identified. My summary is less a conclusion than an acknowledgement that it is not up to me to dispense with the term "epistemology": it has too thoroughly captivated me for that.

A Māori Term Analysis and the Language of Things

The Self within the Object and its Name

We have to contest dominant beliefs of language if we are to analyze terms because, like other activities – such as research, for which it is now widely accepted that a critique of dominant propositions must occur – a philosophy of language must also operate from a starting point that is agreeable to Māori. One of the problems with poststructuralist approaches to the analysis of terms is that proponents often resist the notion of essence (Newman 2001; see also Gordon 2012); the ontological prior or "wairua" (entrenched but changing spirit) of language is then undermined. The underpinning of poststructuralist ideas has been to approach language and knowledge as if they are socially constructed, not really *immediately* colonizing or uplifting, instead intertwined with the playing out of power within the human world. While there have been good reasons for that denial – these reasons stem largely from valid hang-ups that the West must deal with because their dominant thinking rests on identifying unchanging properties of things – *we* cannot immediately reject the notion of essence to a thing. To do so would be to reject the infusion of the world within an object and its name. Essence is linked to the spiritual realm (Royal 2012), is different to the West's version (see for instance: Mika 2015a) and language from a Māori philosophy is both completely dense and densified. It is immediately dense, because it always already has to it the world, and it becomes ever more worlded as the things that comprise the world reorganize themselves constantly even in a term. The ways of describing this dual world in language are scarce in English, but the overall concept exists throughout Māori metaphysics and therefore, one would assume, within all stages that follow. In that sense, language is our master because it encourages us to step away from it but, of course, as I have suggested, we never can.

The "what is language?" question is nearly as clichéd as its well-worn counterpart "what is a table?" Both questions in fact have as much relevance for Māori as they do for any other group, particularly in the face of a colonizing approach that tends to make both language and its object straightforward. Both have implications for how one views the world through language. But in some vital senses, asking the "what is" question in either case is futile, for while the true nature of a thing ("the table") can be approximated through language, and although language itself is a phenomenon that in some cases can be veered toward, language as an issue for both inquiries remains ultimately elusive. Language certainly interjects historically and spatially on its users, and it is therefore related to the human world, but, like the world it conjoins, it retains its own obscurity. It is thus one point at which being and the human self actively meet (Chauvet 2001), and for Māori the stakes are higher because the object that contains to it the whole world decides language as much as the human self. Moreover, language in its wider sense may be the complete text of the world; this text could obscurely be referred to as "Papatūānuku." It would then be the complete array of possibilities that the world displays to itself; key here is the word "display," for things in the world reveal themselves in a sort of language. This "worlded" (Mika 2016b) register of language then structures our own ability to talk about those things. As the human dimension to the world, we are one element that has its own way of revelation to the rest of the world, which then responds. This view of language is disturbing because it means that we – the apparent originators of language – are in its thrall.

At the basis of language is a term which, despite its molecular size, is equally as powerful as the full gamut of language. Therefore, there are some basic premises that I must adhere to when considering the full influence of a term from a Māori philosophical standpoint. First, I am being speculative, not knowledgeable. I cannot state with much certainty what the sense of a term is, for instance, nor can I make grand claims to its essence, or to the way in which the world infuses it. It would be possible to analyze a set of utterances or sentences with these issues of language in mind; however, my approach in this chapter is to consider a single term as a worlded, textural phenomenon that calls for a *tentative* assessment of its impact on its (Māori) users. Here, I should reiterate that the approach asks for us to think of ourselves *within* or as part of the term (our wellbeing is constructed by the term, which has a potency that draws upon particular historical and metaphysical assumptions). Moreover, there is certainly a place for the social constructivism of critical discourse analysis, but we should remember that the ability of a term to order things in the world for our perception means that the term is dealing with our *ideas*, which are in fact our whanaunga. The social for Māori is hence not confined to the world of humans and manmade political institutions. The social (in the Western vein) idea of a word is also part of the term to the extent that a term contains *at once* all other times. We can, therefore, interpret the social as always-already containing to it all other apparently social epochs that the West would argue only elapse over time (Mika and Tiakiwai 2016). There are others who have argued the fact of our existence within language or text (see for instance: Heidegger 2001; Derrida 1998), but I emphasize that a Māori view of language asks us to think about how language animatedly engages with us on its own terms.

Subtext: Precision and Reductionism

Involved though this view of language may seem, the dominant suggestion that it is a parse set of rules, the microscopic study of which can yield meaning, is insufficient for a Māori worldview, and needs to actively be taken to task. The reductionism that characterizes the Western view of the world, at least from an indigenous viewpoint, has popularly been attributed to Descartes (Capra 1982). Seeking the pure meaning of a sentence and considering its usefulness from that point on does suggest a Cartesian influence, but the Western philosophical enterprise of reducing the nature of language in such a way has a sophisticated history. Philosophers of empiricism such as Locke reduced language so that it simply conveyed an idea of an object (Dawson 2007). The Verificationists, having emerged from the logical positivists in the 1930s, imbued language with meaningfulness if it could impact on experience. The sentence being uttered must make a difference to future experience (Lycan 2000; Mika 2007). Despite these few, extremely popular views, it is true that Western philosophy has frequently challenged its own dominant explanations for language, mainly through the vehicle of Continental philosophy, with such thinkers as Merleau Ponty, Hölderlin, Martin Heidegger, and Foucault arguing in their own ways that most approaches to language in the West have been deficient. With its phenomenological articulation of the being of language and its struggle to explicate an existence beyond the metaphysics of man, Continental philosophy could be seen as the champion of other views of language.

For Western humanity, however, language's significance would be that it gives expression to a correct idea of a thing. The dominant approach to language in the West has indeed been to find a ground of absolute truth for an utterance, and this attempt at finding the truth through an analysis of an object's correspondence with an idea may strike a Māori readership as implausible because it so evidently disdains the realms of hiddenness and unverifiability that reside within both object and idea. Further, the leading view of language as a precise signifier of an object tightens a

Māori view of the world, and so it becomes necessary to address how we discuss language itself while we draw on its power and, indeed, while it and its objects form us. Reflecting instead on how opaque it is, is no easy task because it immediately throws the interlocutor him- or herself into a state of uncertainty (Mika 2015b). To begin with, saying that "language *is* opaque" deals a stinging blow to the asserter, as he or she must then regress to another step to then deal with the certainty of *that* utterance. There then follow subsequent, infinite regresses that call for disclaimers. The steps into the unknown of language and its worlded objects proceed for me in this way:

> Language is unknowable
> I have made this statement of certainty; therefore, I have used language, an apparently unknowable phenomenon, as if I know it
> There must therefore be some sort of deep, unseen field within which I work that subverts what I am trying to say about language: after all, I have made a statement of certainty about language, despite noting its unknowability
> But then, in identifying that field, I am again using language as a pointer towards it, with clarity in mind – I am saying that it "is," I have stated that "there must *be* some sort of deep, unseen field"
> What "is" the nature of this "is"?
> But then, how can I get at the nature of the "is" when I am referring to it with the "is"? Especially when, at the backdrop of my thinking, the "is" does not exist as a linguistic particle in Māori thought. (Mika 2016b)

Well then, I will do away with the "is." But if I instead formulate the question as "how does language arise?", I am still singling language out for my concern, distancing it from its relations in this and other worlds, and therefore even preferring the same notion of time that the West (and the "is") encourages, because I am attempting to explain a sequential process through the academic mode of writing (language does *this* and then *this* and then *this* – this is the "how" of language).

And so on.

However, what is it about language that does this – that pushes us while forever claiming us? It is perhaps this question above all that demonstrates this contradiction of language, for I am asking a question *about* the properties of language while naturally residing *within* language (resorting to it). Indeed, the "what is" question belongs to Aristotle; it is the first step in a move away from language because it makes language a priority as it sets about describing the nature of a thing. If, for instance, I ask "what is Māori knowledge?", then I am obsessed with detaching from language in order to look down on it (Mika 2016b), to seek terms that will adequately outline Māori knowledge. It is really language and terms that I am concerned with expressing in the "what is," not so much Māori knowledge. The problem with the "what is," is that it assumes that we were never part of language apart from in some conceptual sense. In that Western reading of language, language has never really owned us but we have owned language.

Incidentally, as Māori writers we are all confronted by these unseen characteristics of language. But the Māori philosopher of language is especially responsible for inquiring into this interminable process, because it is meant to be the role of Māori philosophy to consider the flux of ideas. He or she, however, is caught up in the lure of language and becomes aware of its relationship to its worldedness because language cannot be "gotten around." It is the very text upon which he or she operates. Language sums up the world and is simultaneously the revelation of things in the world, and these things are immediately worlded (Mika 2016b) and imbued with an original text which we cannot distil to a single principle. We soon realize that there is a more profound set of assumptions that cohere terms that are ontologically prior to the linguistic sign. Our immersion within language, or the fact that we are – somewhat dramatically speaking – at its mercy or at least bound by it, also attests to our need to speculate on language on our terms. While help for this can come from poststructuralism, for instance, it soon becomes obvious that this mode of critique is inadequate for its neglect of essence. Language for Māori, as I have suggested, is inherently imbued with the fullness of the world. New materialism offers some similarities to a Māori philosophy of language but places less emphasis on the already-constituted nature of one thing by all others as the very text that materially forms the self; language thus does not have "too much power" (Barad 2007, p. 132) if we view it less as an invention of humanity – as poststructuralism does – and more as the full landscape within which one is immersed.

My Dislike of "Epistemology"

With this texturality of a term in mind, our process begins from the outset, when one starts to become aware of a feeling toward a term. Is there some particular word that irks a writer or student? It can be either a Māori or English term, or any other. Our attention to a term is not neutral; it accord with or chafes against us for a reason. Is it overused? Does it seem to stand in for a very complex set of phenomena that need to be explored but that are too readily rushed over in the course of academic writing? Is there a certain person who utters it too readily? Does it feel plausible or is it too gushy? These questions bring into relief the peculiarity of a writer and thinker, and one person cannot cite the exact same reasons as another for choosing the same term because it is likely resonant with an individual's whakapapa (genealogical relationship), and their experience inside language, among other things. We may or may not be able to articulate the precise motive for alighting on a term as there may be several forces at work for an object and its term as they select us. But we can acknowledge that an object has drawn us to itself. At this stage we encounter one of the first possibilities for our existence within the term, because it has already claimed us in a way that we cannot readily deal with.

The term "epistemology" shares close quarters with its more accessible counterpart "knowledge," with the two often being used interchangeably. "Epistemology" attracts me to it for two main identifiable reasons: first, it is used so frequently that it feels overused in much literature (as does its equivalent, knowledge); and, second, it asserts a particular view of an object and its relationship to all others. The first problem constitutes a human-related issue, the second points to the ontology of the term itself, quite apart from its potential overuse. It vexes me, and unlike much academic approach to analyzing a term or discourse, I am compelled to acknowledge that fact as a Māori writer, because to do so reflects a greater honesty than moving straight to a view of the term as separate from the self. This latter problem, where I would deceive myself as an *objective* thinker, is considered by Sartre (1984) to be "bad faith," because I have simply ignored "the real" (Flynn 2013). We can see a certain attempt to evade emotion in the work of such authors as Elizabeth Rata (2006) who may have been better off signaling that she had a subjective problem with kaupapa Māori (formalized Māori approach) (see: Pihama 2010), and that this pique was actually the basic compulsion for her to begin her assault on it. This quick jump to the objective also occurs with many of us as Māori writers, with harsh consequences: for the Māori writer, to elude the issue of language's irritation is to pretend that the world is indeed compartmentalized, with emotion on the outer when it comes to the self's relationship with an object or idea and its term. Most likely, no term is so neutral, and it becomes even less so when it is used frequently. A term has the ability to snap us to immediate attention, and on reflection it seems that the term "epistemology" has, for some time, swiveled itself into view for me, demanding a response.

My problem with the term "epistemology" may well derive from its frequency in academic texts, but sharing equally with it is "knowledge," which is overwhelmingly calculative in a period of modernity (Heidegger 1977). I noted this instrumentalism when reading a report to the Waitangi Tribunal, which is a forum to hear Māori claims of grievance against the Crown, that was dealing with a claim around cultural and intellectual property. In this report (Williams 2001), "mātauranga Māori" was discussed according to its positive knowledge of a practice, object, or idea, but never did I get any glimpse into its sustained possibilities for thought on the dark matter of those same phenomena. That is, mātauranga Māori, as it was dominantly conceived there, appeared to make proclamations of certainty about things (and that tendency matches the overall nature of "evidence" which does seek certainty about an object). Stewart (2007) notes what I believe is a variation on that idea when she states "another important point is that mātauranga is holistic, without the compartmentalization of Western conceptions of knowledge" (p. 139). The frequently used phrase "how do we know what we know?" therefore sits well with that version, whereas I am more a proponent of "how is it that we don't know?" My preference for the latter quite possibly comes from a love of, and fixation with, language and its relationship with ideas. For as long as I can remember, I have consciously latched on to words as the building blocks of thought, but I became acutely aware of how much more potent an object is than our ability to attach a word to it. This constant speculation on the thought and a word only increased their elusiveness, and I do recall concluding many years ago that it was simply meant to be so. Thought, language, and object were left to exist beyond my knowledge. I also remember being impatient with the way in which a word was proposed as a one-dimensional entity in mainstream schooling, as if it had no particular "aura" or after-effect. The repetition of a term in one's mind, its playfulness, and the malapropism that can come from one term's imposition into our utterance – these fundamentally unknowable textures of language were almost entirely ignored.

Although this narrative merely represents my own experience, it is material, like everyone else's experience, and a Māori interpreter of a term probably needs to pay closer attention to it than his/her Western counterpart. In Western academic practice, one tends to launch into an analysis of the term without acknowledging that initial "prickle" of a term and its origins. The academic trained in Western thought launches at it from a Kantian viewpoint as if its totality, while certainly "there," cannot be known and thus is not worth any further attention. However, the term is a relation of ours, as is an idea, and it somehow tugs persistently at our focus, and needs to be addressed on that basis. For me, the process and conclusion I arrived at were highly informative – not simply in a conceptual sense, but materially also because they displayed for me my own vulnerability towards an object and any term to relate with it. Thus, seeking to *know* is particularly vexing for me, especially when we seek to know at the expense of thinking for its own sake. "Epistemology" is, of course, the study of that drive to know, and so it is hardly surprising that it should become a concern. It is also like many other terms in academia that appear to have lost their verve. I do not take issue with whether the use of the term is correct (after all, there are various interpretations of it) – merely that it is resorted to in order to explain a complex Māori ground of experience that it cannot do justice to. Like "knowledge," epistemology is *the* way of describing the fundamentally separate entity. At this stage, though, I am explaining that just through my orientation toward the term, which I have surmised has come about within a context of uncertainty. I now turn to the etymology of the term, to explore how it might either support or derogate from my initial misgiving about it.

Subtext: The Lure of Language for the Māori Subject

Various other Māori writers have identified that language is essentially a nonhuman event and that it draws the human world to it. Mildon (2011) cites Delamere, who suggests that nature and language are thoroughly interrelated:

> In the grander scheme of things, traditional Te Reo are the voices of nature; the jolt of an earthquake, the song of a bird, the rustling of leaves, the rumbling of thunder before a storm, the piercing bolt of lightning in the night sky, the rushing waves of a tsunami, the cry of a whale, the fresh smell of rain on the earth. (p. 10)

These forms of language are perhaps less about their audibility than their tacit influence on the self and on the rest of the world. They relate to the intrinsic relatedness of the world's phenomena as much as they do to a sensed phenomenon, even if at times they are perceptible. Māori writers who do venture into the first principles of thought allow that language has (for went of a better word) *spiritual* qualities, but they attribute these characteristics to language in different ways. Language may be linked with "wairua" or spirit (Browne 2005), for instance, in order to explain its "sense" that precedes simple meaning of terms. This primordiality of language can be drawn on to guide teaching and learning, and it thus becomes important in the everyday domain. Browne avers that language is a personally invigorating phenomenon that, with its correspondence with "wairua," emotionally charges the individual learner. The Māori language, when uttered by humans, is sometimes said to be an expression of the relationship that the world has with us (Jeffries and Kennedy 2008). An assertion of another can then have profound consequences on both the natural world and other humans, as the utterance can present other worlds, even in such banal and colonial settings as courtrooms, classrooms, and clinics. Royal reflects that it was Maori Marsden's "emphatic expression of [his] statements that, at first, influenced the process of my entry into Māoritanga" (cited in Mika 2013, p. 214 fn. 85). It can be assumed that language had a quality beyond being simply directional in Royal's instance; indeed, Marsden's statements themselves open up realms for further thinking in a material sense. Language may therefore be related to a signifier as it is commonly posited, but beneath the apparent symbol of its words lies a reality that may well be likened to an infinitude which will occasionally see fit to point its human object in one direction or another.

Referring to the Original Sense of "Epistemology"

Terms are thus not innocent, and they have a deep influence on all other things in the world. The term carries out a material function on the world at large (it is not merely a conceptual stand-in for a grand idea, but corresponds with a fundamentally unknowable, textual non foundational foundation). The responsibility of the Māori term analyst here is to discern the term as if it opens onto a material sphere. That is, a term contains a world at its inception and then opens up onto realms that are either colonizing or rejuvenating for Māori. I am arguing for an evaluation of its nature at its outset, through its etymology, and suggest that the origins of a term display its orientation to the world. This "appeal to essence, and, indeed, related conceptual tools such as eidos, totality, type, or quotient, needn't collapse into the foreclosed ascription of essential*ism*" (Gordon 2012, p. 3). The "sense" that we obtain about a term's essence is somewhat different from its dictionary meaning, although the latter can also help us in our speculative approach. We relatedly keep in mind throughout this largely abstract exercise that a term contains a life-force, and that it orders things in the world in ways that are either convivial with, or antithetical to, our philosophies.

How should we know "epistemology" apart from the fact that it is a linguistic unit? What does it do to the world, including its users? Although I am still thinking of epistemology as a term, I am more intent on regarding it as a performative entity that can organize things in the world in various ways. I suspect that this play of language-as-world occurs in various forums, and I first articulated it for myself when I was representing clients as a lawyer, appearing at the Waitangi Tribunal. In these contexts, the Crown permits hearings to take place in the Māori language, yet the Māori claimants often remain distressed at something that often cannot be identified. I surmised that, although the language used in the hearings was sometimes te reo Māori, the Tribunal still silently insisted on a particular ontology for it (Mika 2007). It would be something that would need to be human-derived, because the Māori witness would have to answer questions that required a direct answer; it would have to refer to one object at a time; in referring to that object, it would have to illuminate that object fully to be admissible; and the human speaker would have to step outside of language and become its master. All this took place while the Māori language was being used. Stewart (2016) notes in relation to this problem that there is a "loss of meaning when these words are extracted from their original philosophical context" (p. 96). In fact, the Māori register did little to solve the problem that the deep colonization of language and its object posed, apart from allowing those who were familiar with the language to speak more comfortably. This experience was yet another that I feel compelled to recount, because it highlighted that language (in the sense that dominant Western philosophy intends it) is not really the problem, but instead it is language and its weddedness to the world that is at the heart of the matter.

Within and without these settings, things become the object of precision through language (see Andreotti et al. 2011). The aim is to get at the "is" of a thing. In a Māori philosophy of language and metaphysics, it may be more useful to substitute the "what is" with the more speculative "perhaps an object engages in such a way, either through or as a part of language." Firstly, the term "material" – which "what is" tries to ascertain – does not really suffice, as it seems to suggest that physical space is being taken up. If I state that a term contains to it all the world (and I do understand language from a Māori philosophical viewpoint in this sense), then I mean that the term is material but in a different way to how the West understands it as a discrete object containing to it its own distinctive properties that allow it to retain its own space. Instead, I mean that all things exist in their full nature as they collapse with each other within language. Senghor (2010) notes that "for the African, matter in the sense the Europeans understand it, is only a system of signs which translates the single reality of the universe: being, which is spirit, which is life force" (p. 479). We could think of this notion of matter as constituting a "textured" or "worlded" nature of language, although it is important to remember that these terms are meant in the sense just described, not in more free-flowing ways that insist that it is the human self alone who textures or "worlds" language. We can see here that there is a form of resistance in expressing a Māori worldview on language, for we have to account for what it probably is *not* as much as what it likely *is*. Expressing the textured nature of language is itself a counter-colonial enterprise, not solely a traditional one. Words such as *not* or *instead* are hence hugely useful as they allow us to immediately deviate from whatever we have just been forced to encounter while we make a proactive statement about a Māori philosophy of language.

So what exactly is it about the West's view of an object – and thereafter the infiltration of that assumption into the substance of our own philosophy – that privileges precision, asserts an understanding that an object is only important insofar as it is "sensed," moved between one human to another? Here we move directly to the term "epistemology," because it is one that silently upholds a view of solidity and objectivity. This complex issue, as I have suggested, moves toward a general worlded ontology. In this metaphysics, "episteme" understands the self's relationship to things in the following way:

> In ancient times the basic view was set forth that cognition [*episteme, sciential*] can be achieved only when our statements [*logos*] "stand" upon a firm foundation [*epistemi*]. (Grassi 1980, p. 68)

From a Māori perspective, an object becomes stuck in space and time, there for the strong subject to draw on it at will. A ground is suggested that is separate from other things in the world; one prevails upon this foundation to propose about another thing, rather than within the relationship of that thing to the self. Incidentally, the attempts of Western linguistics to separate the phenomenon of "land" from "Placenta" (which are one and the same in the Māori term "whenua"), through separate concepts of each and thereafter distinct meanings through language, could well originate from this self-evident ground upon which the Māori self is made to position him- or herself. "Land" as "ground" then threatens to become the ascendant idea in "whenua"; it is solid and tangible, and since contact it has become something *onto which* one is encouraged to place an economic value.

Indeed, the idea of "ground" is not so straightforward for Māori, because Papatūānuku, who governs ground, is prior to, but inclusive of, the ability to conceptualize. She is moreover material primordiality (Mika 2016a), resulting in thought and materiality being one. Standing *upon* the ground is akin to saying that one claims Papatūānuku of one's own making, rather than being claimed by her. In the dominant Western view, one also makes her a product of one's ideas, rather than acknowledging being constituted by her or reflecting on the possibility that language is the fullness of the world. However, Papatūānuku constitutes all things and presents a mode of expressing that saturation of things throughout the world. I draw at this point on the word "textural" to highlight the *text* of Earth that constitutes us. For Derrida (1998), the notion of "text" is somewhat similar in that it captures the totality of what can be uttered; with "Papatūānuku," who is a primordial entity that also gives rise to perception of objects and ideas, modes of expression are fully delivered to us as co-constitutive entities in the world, *not* as masters of either language or things in the world. Entities are hence not sufficiently described through poststructural descriptions of language, as things contain to them an essence that is conveyed through Papatūānuku and that we must, I suggest, acknowledge at all steps of our discussions about language. With the text that Papatūānuku designates, language is historically disruptive; that is, events continue to live through it and materially *constitute* utterances of all sorts. Everything therefore takes place within the sovereignty of Papatūānuku as an act of text, including not only discussions about colonization but also colonized utterances. Colonized utterances are everywhere, even as part of apparently traditionally pure discourses; vine-like, they entangle the latter and are not absent simply because they are not acknowledged. Conversely, a colonizing utterance is only able to be given voice because of its other. A racist expression, then, is forever constituted by the absent; its utterers are possibly always irked by the lurking "nativeness" of what they are attempting to deal with through the racist remark. A Māori constitutive grounding of text lies in the idea that Papatūānuku is simultaneous primordial Being but formed by all other things. A Māori notion of text is therefore more entity-derived and thing-driven than Derrida's version, even though, as Derrida would have it, we are also constrained by the fact that one thing always signifies another.

Subtext: Philosophical Infiltration for Māori

The belief that one could find a solid conceptual foundation has its origins in Parmenides, who averred that reality could be founded as constant. Language itself would suffer the same fate, and the stage was set for its radicalization under Plato who exalted *ousia* or permanent essence (Sweeney 2015). Plato imputed extraordinary importance to the Form, which all concepts of objects are derived from, and this rationalism would be decisive for both language and its object. Unlike Māori, who would place language within an object and its complete relationship with the world, Plato encouraged a view of language that would prefer what lies beyond the object, and language would then be unanchored from the world as Māori perceive it. An object would then have to be based on a solid conceptual foundation and its term would similarly be certain only when relating to that Form. Things in the world would be primarily static. After Plato, Aristotle placed essence within the object, not supernatural to it (Tarnas 1991). The way had then been paved for a general reductionist approach to the significance of an object. These propositions by hugely influential philosophers contextualize "epistemology"; they add to the solidity of the ground that epistemology reveals through its etymology. An object becomes meaningful only insofar as one can utter with certainty about it, or come to grips with it through a solid stance upon a foundational conceptual ground.

Māori have been consistently influenced by the notion that language can obtain a final conceptual ground upon which one can stand, and Māori academics are not immune. Many of us, myself included, can acknowledge that language is an unknowable "phenomenon," yet we declare this in a self-assured way. Language is then made a vehicle of certainty despite its reference to its own uncertainty. Western concepts of presence and categorization have already asked for me to declare something at least about language as a self-evident truth! We have forced it back on itself, to look on itself as a displaced entity, have urged it to contradict itself in a way that does not sit well with a Māori view of paradox. This perversion of the self, object, and its language has an historical context, some of which can be adumbrated here. Certainty through language has imposed itself as a colonizing horizon of Māori thought, and it has threatened Māori worldviews since contact with Pākehā. In New Zealand, there is a history in policy and education of making an object something separate from everything else, including the person talking about it. Thus, from early contact onward, language was posed as a representational tool, not one that reflects what Whitt et al. call a presentational worldview (Whitt et al. 2001). It is relatively well known, for instance, that the Māori language was described in education policy as inferior (Stewart 2014), and less academic or important than the English language (see for instance: Waitangi Tribunal 1986): as early as 1867, Carleton asserted that the Māori language was one that "was imperfect as a medium of thought" (p. 863). Alongside devaluing the *Māori* language, the vitality of language itself as a presenter of objects was threatened through the subsequent implementation of this sentiment, and it was becoming a tool of the human speaker, simply there to convey an exact idea. Later on, te reo Māori was introduced as an auxiliary language, being able to step the Māori student up to a higher level of precise and correct expression in the form of the English language (Mika 2013). At these early stages, Māori students and their families would have been subtly introduced to a warped notion of what language itself is. The inspector of Māori schools believed in 1931 that Māori students were incapable of expressing themselves 'properly' in English (Barrington 1966), thus promoting an idea of an object's and its term's clarity.

None of this, of course, is to say that language for Māori needed to be thought of as a vehicle either of precision or its opposite, simply that its exactness may not have been the primary focus. The issue may well have been more complex than that of precision, because although "traditional Maori education placed great emphasis on linguistic proficiency" (Benton 1989, p. 7), seeking exactness through language could itself have been reliant on a number of factors – the relationship of the self to the idea or object being discussed, how "shadowed" the idea or object was, and even the genealogical link of the speaker to the entire place and time that the object was located in at that particular time. But even then, language could have simply worked so thoroughly in synchronicity with the voidness ("kore") of an idea or object that it preferred to work within an imprecise mode (Mika 2016b), not merely as a tool for pointing definitively to an idea or an object. Language itself therefore became an idea based on a ground of truth.

Consequences of "Epistemology" for the Māori User

Certainty through "epistemology" is influential for its ability to train our minds. We are talking about its ontological maneuver as much as the linguistic sign. Indeed, it does things with our view of language itself (and thus we have doubled up on language as a concern through one of its emissaries, a term which happens to be "epistemology"). It urges us to control language as if the latter can move across objects seamlessly, describing them and allowing us to draw on those objects at will in an economical way. We are now constantly and silently challenged to think of things in the world so that they can be transmitted through language in the form of a concept. Epistemology is one word that threatens a Māori conception of both language and its objects, and in order to clarify what is the issue here, we must think about this gigantic yet unseen mode of colonization from a cultural context. Although "epistemology" appears straightforward and not needing to be thought about now – apart from within the context of knowledge revival and transmission – its impact as a material entity is consequential. "Epistemology," is behind the overuse of Māori terms in policy, for instance, because it proposes that translation is simply a linguistic concern, not a metaphysical one. The Māori terms are subjected to "high visibility"; they are made to conform to a sense of the world that prefers the single appearance of a thing, rather than a thing as an emissary of all others. They are disciplined, trained, and understood in advance as plain, simple, and human-derived. One current prolific example is the term "whānau," which seems to flourish everywhere in government policy. The Māori reader may be left perplexed at the fact that almost everything apart from the nonhuman world now is a "whānau" or family as far as any government is concerned. Policy does not acknowledge that within the human family there exist its nonhuman counterparts, including ancestors, mountains, rocks, plants, and even unseen phenomena. Indeed, there are "whānau" that appear to have nothing to do with humans, although they also link to the human world in some form or other. "Whānau" in these contexts indicates nothing more than its English equivalent "family"; if it did, it would transcend the policy document. But any such transcending is strictly forbidden. Instead, a government is seen to be performing equitably by including the precise operation of the terms even though the terms now open onto a colonizing world.

Subtext: Rupture

To reiterate: language, object, and term derive from the inescapability of Papatūānuku. Papatūānuku, incidentally, cannot be addressed through dominant forms of Western philosophy, which tends to act like science in trying to smooth out paradoxes and inconsistencies. While Papatūānuku gives rise to all things, she is simultaneously constituted by them all, and dominant Western philosophy cannot gain an entrance point to an understanding of her because its major architects and usual suspects, including in particular Aristotle, Hume, and, to a certain extent, Kant, are incapable of accepting that very first possibility. Moreover, we are therefore bound by her texturality. Secondly and relatedly: if all things are constituted by Papatūānuku, then within any one, simple utterance there exist all other things, although they may not be perceptible. Certain things reveal themselves at times to us, and we then express them, but Papatūānuku and all her elements are responsible for that expression and continue to live through it. If language is textural then it is dense with things that are instantaneous with, and are irruptive from, Papatūānuku. By "irruptive" I mean that they might seem to burst through the All of the text and appear to be fragmentary, but they are actually still governed by the interplay of everything else. When I think of language as the most misunderstood and yet most fundamental of all forms of expression, its obscurity – involving our lack of finality on what forms language, what language sets about forming, and indeed how language forms us even as we thereafter utter it – becomes its most decisive feature. A philosophy of language that is caught up with the upheaval of a material and conceptual ground calls for me to approach terms as if they are animate entities, as fundamentally unknowable as they are real, shedding their dictionary meaning and instead instructing me to reflect on their enigmatic nature.

For all Māori writers and students, the correspondence between their origins and the presentation of their ideas will be unique, and may not be based on the solid ground that the West silently and relentlessly insinuates is within our reach, although they may have a completely different way of articulating it than I do. "Rupture," "irrupt," and "erupt" for me are all useful English terms gesturing toward a restless, co-existing earthy, and conceptual ground. The history of my own iwi, Tuhourangi, would urge me to resist a final conclusion, and dissuade me from even pretending to sum up on the issue of language and its relationship with objects and with the troublesome nature of "epistemology." By my strong affiliations to the peculiar coinstantaneous history of Tuhourangi, I am instead taught uncertainty, through the abyssal nature of my "ground" there. In 1886, the mountain that we reference, Tarawera, erupted, killing many and affecting everyone from that area. The uncertainty of that event, creating a fissure as it undoubtedly did within the minds of the tribal members as much as in the earth itself, sets in place a template for proposing that a thing in the world is in fact *beyond* epistemology at every turn. Concluding is to privilege *epistemi*, and it tries to cordon off a certain section of the material world as well, bringing it into absolute clarity by dispensing with it as a summary. But the seemingly traumatic eruption sets in motion the distinct possibility that I can simply underscore a proposition with the same schism that affected my tribal territory. With that in mind, even "epistemology" must contain something about it that appeals to me, because it so vehemently motions to me, summoning me to attend to it, and I have responded. I cannot therefore completely abandon it out of sight; it is too complicatedly enmeshed in my own regard for that to happen. Leaving my concern breached by the mystery that language brings to it therefore reinforces the currency of where I come from.

Glossary

Iwi Tribe
Kaupapa Māori Formalized Māori approach
Kore Voidness
Māoritanga The essence of being Māori
Mātauranga Knowledge
Ousia Essence
Pākehā European New Zealander
Papatūānuku Earth Mother; infinite substance; originating text of life; that which languages
Te reo Māori The Māori language
Tohu Sign
Wairua Spirit
Whakapapa Genealogical relationship
Whānau Family
Whanaunga Relations
Whenua Land/Placenta

References

Ahenakew C, Andreotti V, Cooper G, Hireme H (2014) Beyond epistemic provincialism: de-provincializing indigenous resistance. AlterNative 10(3):216–231

Andreotti V, Ahenakew C, Cooper G (2011) Epistemological pluralism: ethical and pedagogical challenges in higher education. AlterNative 7(1):40–50

Barad K (2007) Meeting the universe halfway: quantum physics and the entanglement of matter and meaning. Duke University Press, London

Barrington J (1966) Maori scholastic achievement: a review of policies and provisions. N Z J Educ Stud 1(1):1–14
Benton R (1989) Maori and Pacific Island languages in New Zealand education. Renaiss Pac 4(8–10):7–12. Survival International, Paris
Biesta G (2010) Witnessing deconstruction in education: why quasi-transcendentalism matters. In: Ruitenberg C (ed) What do philosophers of education do? (and how do they do it?). Blackwell Publishing, West Sussex, pp 73–86
Browne M (2005) Wairua and the relationship it has with learning te reo Māori within Te Ataarangi. Unpublished Master of Educational Administration thesis. Massey University, Palmerston North
Capra F (1982) The turning point: science, society and the rising culture. Simon & Schuster, New York
Carleton H (1867) Maori schools bill (second reading). N Z Parliam Debates 1(Pt. 2):862–868
Chauvet L (2001) The sacraments: the word of god at the mercy of the body. The Liturgical Press, Collegeville
Cooper G (2008) Tawhaki and Māui: critical literacy in indigenous epistemologies. Crit Lit 2(1): 37–42
Dawson H (2007) Locke, language and early-modern philosophy. Cambridge University Press, Cambridge
Derrida J (1998) Of grammatology. Johns Hopkins University Press, Baltimore
Flynn T (2013) Jean-Paul Sartre. Available at: The stanford encyclopedia of philosophy. https://plato.stanford.edu/archives/fall2013/entries/sartre/
Gonzalez F (2009) Plato and Heidegger: a question of dialogue. The Pennsylvania State University, University Park
Gordon L (2012) Essentialist anti-essentialism, with considerations from other sides of modernity. Quaderna 1:1–12
Grassi E (1980) Rhetoric as philosophy: the humanist tradition (trans: Krois J, Azodi A). Southern Illinois University Press, Edwardsville
Heidegger M (1977) The question concerning technology and other essays (trans: Lovitt W). Harper, New York
Heidegger M (2001) Poetry, language, thought. Perennial Classics, New York
Jeffries R, Kennedy N (2008) Māori outcome evaluation: a Kaupapa Māori outcomes and indicators framework and methodology. The University of Waikato, Hamilton
Lycan W (2000) Philosophy of language. Routledge, London
Mika C (2007) The utterance, the body and the law: seeking an approach to concretizing the sacredness of Māori language. SITES 4(2):181–205
Mika C (2013) Reclaiming mystery: a Māori philosophy of being, in light of Novalis' ontology. Unpublished PhD dissertation, The University of Waikato, Hamilton
Mika C (2015a) The co-existence of self and thing through 'ira': a Māori phenomenology. J Aesthetics Phenomenol 2(1):93–112
Mika C (2015b) Thereness: implications for Heidegger's 'presence' for Māori. AlterNative 11(1):3–13
Mika C (2016a) 'Papatūānuku/Papa': some thoughts on the oppositional grounds of the doctoral experience. Knowledge Cult 4(1):43–55
Mika C (2016b) Worlded object and its presentation: a Māori philosophy of language. AlterNative 12(2):165–176
Mika C, Tiakiwai S (2016) Tawhiao's unstated heteroglossia: conversations with Bakhtin. Educ Philos Theory. https://doi.org/10.1080/00131857.2015.1135409
Mildon C (2011) Te romiromi o tohungatanga. www.aiohealing.com. Accessed 10 July 2013
Newman S (2001) From Bakunin to Lacan: anti-authoritarianism and the dislocation of power. Lexington Books, New York
Pihama L (2010) Kaupapa Māori theory: transforming theory in Aotearoa. He Pukenga Kōrero: A J Māori Stud 9(2):5–14

Rata E (2006) Ethnic ideologies in New Zealand education: What's wrong with kaupapa Māori. Delta 58(1):29–41

Royal T (2005) Exploring indigenous knowledge. In: Paper presented at the the indigenous knowledges conference – reconciling academic priorities with indigenous realities. Victoria University, Wellington

Royal T (2012) Te Ao Mārama – the natural world – mana, tapu and mauri. In: Te Ara – the encyclopedia of New Zealand. http://www.teara.govt.nz/en/te-ao-marama-the- natural-world/page-5. Accessed 16 June 2016

Sartre J-P (1984) Being and nothingness: a phenomenological essay on ontology. Washington Square Press, London

Senghor L (2010) Negritude: a humanism of the twentieth century. In: Grinker R, Lubkemann S, Steiner C (eds) Perspectives on Africa: a reader in culture, history, and representation. Wiley-Blackwell, Malden, pp 477–483

Stewart G (2007) Kaupapa Māori science. Unpublished doctoral dissertation, The University of Waikato, Hamilton

Stewart G (2014) Te reo Māori in classrooms: current policy, future practice. SET 3:3–7

Stewart G (2016) Indigenous knowledge and education policy for teachers of Māori learners. Knowl Cult 4(3):84–98

Sweeney C (2015) Sacramental presence after Heidegger: onto-theology, sacraments, and the mother's smile. Cascade Books, Eugene

Tarnas R (1991) The passion of the western mind: understanding the ideas that have shaped our world view. Ballantine Books, New York

Tribunal W (1986) Te reo Maori claim. In: Waitangi Tribunal website. www.waitangi-tribunal.govt.nz/. Accessed 16 June 2016

Whitt L, Roberts M, Norman W, Grieves V (2001) Belonging to land: indigenous knowledge systems and the natural world. Oklahoma City Univ Law Rev 26:701–743

Williams D (2001) Matauranga Maori and taonga. The nature and extent of treaty rights held by iwi and hapū in indigenous flora and fauna cultural heritage objects and valued traditional knowledge: Matauranga Maori. In: Waitangi tribunal website. http://www.justice.govt.nz/tribunals/waitangi-tribunal. Accessed 16 June 2016

Part IV

Societal Issues

Bryan McKinley Jones Brayboy and Megan Bang

Societal Issues Facing Indigenous Education: Introduction

32

Bryan McKinley Jones Brayboy and Megan Bang

Contents

Introduction 568
Conclusion 573
References 574

Abstract

Wider societal issues can impact significantly on the education of Indigenous Peoples, although sometimes the connections are not obvious to everyone. This section presents the reader with a wide range of current, and ongoing, challenges across a variety of Indigenous contexts. The chapters include exploring the school-prison-community trajectory of Indigenous Peoples in the USA and Aotearoa New Zealand, human rights violations in South America, environmental education in the USA and the Pacific, and the engagement and support of Indigenous students and their families. Along with further chapters in other Indigenous contexts, they all relate to the reimagining of the role of Indigenous knowledges in education and identity formation processes.

We have forwarded in this introduction a framework (referred to as the five E's) around which to conceptualize the narrative that informs this section (Brayboy et al., RISE: a study of indigenous boys and men. Paper prepared for RISE: boys and men of color, Philadelphia, 2017). The five E's are empowerment, enactment,

---

B. M. J. Brayboy (✉)
Arizona State University, Tempe, AZ, USA
e-mail: Bryan.Brayboy@asu.edu

M. Bang
Northwestern University, Evanston, IL, USA
e-mail: Megan.Bang@northwestern.edu

© Springer Nature Singapore Pte Ltd. 2019
E. A. McKinley, L. T. Smith (eds.), *Handbook of Indigenous Education*,
https://doi.org/10.1007/978-981-10-3899-0_76

engagement, envision, and enhancement. Empowerment is how Indigenous communities come to unlock and utilize their own inherent power to change their communities and lives. Enactment is the intentional practice that communities use to teach their children to be part of the group. Engagement centers on relationships between people and place, rooted in mutual respect and sustenance. Envision is guided by creating a purpose-driven framework which, we argue, relates to community self-determination. And lastly, enhancement is a recognition that there is room for both institutional and tribal support to address the envisioning process. These important concepts, we argue, do not place us as "victims" regarding the impact of wider societal structures but provide a sense of agency (both individual and community) and hope about how to recapture, reestablish, and re-instantiate our nations of peoples. We believe that the chapters in this section highlight both the perils and the possibilities of the futures of Indigenous Peoples.

Keywords
Societal issues · Nation building · Cultural reflexivity · Community empowerment

Introduction

The consideration of wider societal issues as it relates to questions of Indigeneity and Indigenous education is important. We want to frame our thoughts in this section around the five E's developed elsewhere (Brayboy et al. 2017). The five E's are empower, enact, engage, envision, and enhance. These E's, as we hope to demonstrate in this introduction, and we believe are illustrated throughout this section, are crucial to Indigenous education and the schooling of Indigenous students. If Indigenous children and the communities and individuals that serve, nurture, and steward them understand larger questions of sovereignty, both as an individual issue and as a community one, they are more inclined to educate – and school – their children in ways that will strengthen communities and build long-term capacity.

We (Bryan and Megan) have, over the years, debated the notion of empowerment, because like Deloria (1970) we believe that power can neither be given nor received. Instead we take up the term to think about the process by which individuals and communities come to unlock and utilize their inherent powers. This might be the engagement of sovereignty (comprising self-determination – both individually and communally), or it might be a program that focuses on language movements. This is what some have called a nation building (Brayboy et al. 2012) approach; it is crucial for communities to engage in strengthening and building their own capacity to engage in creating futures of their own making.

There is an important element to empowerment in communities that is intertwined with Indigenous Peoples understanding of our knowledge systems. Comprised in this is how communities come to, and engage in, the process of knowing. Western philosophers might refer to this as epistemologies; empowerment is rooted in how communities come to know. But knowing is not enough; communities and their members must do things. The doing is reflective of the knowing; it is also reflective of the realities of the communities and its members. Some philosophers have referred to the process of doing and explaining the realities as ontology. The realities of Peoples are different; and, yet, they are profoundly impacted by what people know. Those knowledges, and their concomitant actions, are rooted in particular values. These values might revolve around connections to land, or to other people, or living things. The spiritual components of these values must be considered as one considers how we think about both knowing and doing; these do not occur in a vacuum. This axiological thread is crucial to consideration of the inherent power in people and peoples. Finally, the engagement of power is both taught and learned. Being clear on the process of teaching and learning (what philosophers might call pedagogy) is crucial to succession planning; communities are primarily interested in their survival and creating thriving lives for their children and grandchildren; they are also engaged in honoring their ancestors. Pedagogical practices inform how we think about knowledge, its enactment, and the values surrounding both knowing and doing.

These systems, rooted in relationships, are formed in the intersections of ideas. As Elizabeth Sumida Huaman (▶ Chap. 39, "Yachayninchis (Our Knowledge): Environment, Cultural Practices, and Human Rights Education in the Peruvian Andes") notes:

> Based on the Andean cycle of life, Quechua knowledge systems are organized and purposeful towards a good and balanced life for all beings. There are clearly defined responsibilities for human beings and protocols for engagement with all elements in the universe – from the sun and moon, heavens, and stars, to the rivers and trees and animals, to the ancestors.

Relatedly, Whyte (▶ Chap. 40, "Reflections on the Purpose of Indigenous Environmental Education") writes, "When I thought more about our traditions, I realized that their importance is not that they are 'ancient' or 'the way it's always been.' Rather, they are stories or guides for understanding the moral fabric of our peoples that is woven with these qualities of trust, empathy, consent, and many others." The intersections between what people know and how they believe are crucial to the education and schooling of Indigenous children.

The second E, enact, is the ability to practice particular teachings that engage and implement identity development. While we note the importance of pedagogy above, we want to highlight the crucial aspect of tying particular practices to how people become Peoples. That is, what does it mean for individuals to become parts of groups? Is there a secret code involved? A password that parents pass down to their children? Are there particular genetic traits that individuals have? We argue that there are deliberate, intentional practices that communities have relied on for millennia to teach their children to be part of their community. These lessons, these practices, coalesce around larger questions of community survival. In this instance, we do not mean survival as simply staying alive; it is more complex. As Vaioleti and Morrison

(▶ Chap. 36, "The Value of Indigenous Knowledge to Education for Sustainable Development and Climate Change Education in the Pacific") remind us in relation to the Pacific:

> Pacific culture and knowledge has always been traditionally conceived, produced, applied, and critiqued by Pacific peoples, and therefore there exists a long-standing tradition of developing complex yet self-sustaining systems. The respect, reciprocity, and the enduring endeavor to maintain the vā (relational space between people and the environment), in turn, will continue to be an immensely significant and invaluable component of the cultural capital of the Pacific.

Survival necessitates staying alive, but there is a level of thriving embedded in the enactment. Perhaps we should call it "thrivival" in order to fully explain the wealth and goodness inherent in identity development for people and peoples.

Bang and colleagues (▶ Chap. 41, "Indigenous Family Engagement: Strong Families, Strong Nations") note, "we suggest the everydayness of Indigenous families' lives are perhaps the sites in which the most radical and hopeful possibilities for Indigenous resurgence and futures can and do unfold." Enactment is future facing; it is hopeful and resurgent. And, it is both specific and has broad implications. Prasit and Meixi (▶ Chap. 38, "Indigenous Educational Movements in Thailand") write:

> Indigenous people in Thailand have always been engaged in the process of self-definition and in 2007, a transIndigenous movement in Thailand solidified. The global flow of ideas and connections to international Indigenous alliances promoted leaders to form the Network of Indigenous Peoples in Thailand (NIPT) to give voice to Indigenous issues in Thailand.

Enactment is also about amplifying the voices of peoples so that they, in the words of Ojibwe scholar Scott Lyons (2000), set the terms of the debate. The terms of the debate are local; they are also international. The shared experiences of Indigenous Peoples as it relates to education and schooling are crucial to understand the power of this volume in relation to enactment.

Our intent here is to recognize that while enactment happens by and through individuals, it also circles around communities and their collective members. The identity development is both singular and plural in that it happens in both individuals and collectives. So, while some might refer to the enactment as informal practices – denoting that this happens outside of schools and the schooling process – we argue that anything that addresses the future of a community must be engaged with a seriousness that calling it "informal" diminishes.

The third E, engage, centers relationships between people and place. For Indigenous Peoples, place matters. The relationships between us and the land are rooted in mutual respect and sustenance. For human beings, we are fed by the land, whether it is through the four-leggeds, vegetables and fruits that grow on it, the waters that provide us with hydration and fish and vegetables, and the air, which provides birds, water, and sunlight. The relationship calls on humans to care for the lands, water, and air. Elliott and Fryberg (▶ Chap. 35, ""A Future Denied" for Young Indigenous People: From Social Disruption to Possible Futures") argue, "it is vastly important that Indigenous communities strengthen their connection with their traditional territories; this can be done through land–/place-based teaching and learning, land restoration projects, and food and medicine harvesting practices." Lands feed us physically; they also teach us.

Indeed, humans serve as stewards of the land in multiple senses. We are responsible for the land's well-being in our hunting, gathering, farming, fishing, and other extraction practices. And humans are – as noted above – responsible for leaving the land, air, and water better than we received it for the generations to follow. This goes beyond more traditional forms of sustainability in which human beings are expected to leave lands and places as they found them.

These relationships, as they relate to education, are going beyond lands and peoples, however. We must engage relationships between people and knowledges. Some knowledge is embedded in the course content. Much of it, however, is the content of the places in which people live, the teachings passed down through generations, and the knowledges shared between people orally and through example. These different knowledges come from different sources and serve different ends. Taken together, however, they can be used to assist individuals and communities toward some higher end. And, it is the idea of a purposeful framework that we now turn.

The fourth E, envision, is guided by creating a purpose-driven framework. This framework is largely guided by the concept of nation building that we referenced earlier. There is an important connection between education and, in many cases, schooling – as it relates to nation building. By this, we do not mean the kinds of nation building that imperial powers engage in when they hope to "spread democracy" by over-running sovereign nation states with different ideological leanings. Instead, we mean the ways that tribal communities and nations create futures of their own making. Chin et al. (▶ Chap. 34, "Systems of Support: What Institutions of Higher Education Can Do for Indigenous Communities") define the importance of nation building in the following way:

> Nation building in education means preparing and training Native teachers, principals, and counselors who understand students' cultures, knowledges, and contexts. It also means preparing and training physicians, engineers, business entrepreneurs, social and public health practitioners, and legal thinkers who can provide direction and act in the capacity of community leaders for health and well-being, infrastructure, economic development, law and governance, and so forth. A nation building agenda identifies areas of improvement or needs that community members should focus on and emerges when tribal leaders, elders, and community members come together to identify an asset-based outlook for the future community.

There is a purpose to community-driven work. It is about the perpetuation of that community; it is also about the evolution and envisioning of what is to come. Again Bang and her colleagues (▶ Chap. 41, "Indigenous Family Engagement: Strong Families, Strong Nations") show they understand the complexities of a nation-building approach writing, "A challenge for us is always to both dream and contribute to birthing resurgences and Indigenous futures — an elsewhere to the current settler-colonial forms and systems of education — as well as to account for the here-and-now enclosures." These enclosures, they help us understand, "include racism, invisibility, tokenism and forced compliance." They go on to argue that the enclosures "are remedied through practices and acts of resurgence (which include learning from and with lands and waters, multi-generational learning, new partnerships between Native and non-Native peoples, and collaborations between schools and families)." The relationships between the possibilities and the enclosures require that the education and schooling of Indigenous children must be engaged with care and love.

In the future-making process, Indigenous Peoples and communities envision their futures and engage sovereignty. By sovereignty, we mean the inherent rights of Peoples to govern themselves. As an inherent right, we believe that sovereignty manifest itself and is operationalized in self-determination. In spite of the fact that the reference is self-determination, the emphasis here is not on individuals, but on community self-determination. When communities govern themselves and build and strengthen capacity, they are creating a purpose-driven framework.

Nation building, of course, is not the only way this happens. It is one example. Others might be when communities focus on language policy and planning, or reframing and controlling particular narratives about their own health or well-being, or resisting national compulsory education. The point here is that when tribal nations and communities are driven by particular purposes – strengthening themselves and moving toward a successful future (determined by the community), they have engaged in the process of envisioning.

The final E, enhance, is a recognition that there is room for both institutional and tribal support to address the envisioning process. Interestingly, some argue that we must have a return to tradition and believe that there is some form of purity in this return. We believe that there are particular principles rooted in traditions including a recognition of the importance relationships to land, the role of survival and stewardship that honors ancestors and creates opportunities for youth, a recognition of the role of imperialism and colonization, and the honoring of particular knowledge systems. There should, however, also be some recognition that Indigenous Peoples have always adapted and adjusted. It is how we have survived. The notion that being static is the pathway forward is nonsensical. What role do institutions, which have traditionally been colonizing forces, have in enhancing the present and futures of our citizens and communities? Solyom et al. (▶ Chap. 33, "Carceral Colonialisms: Schools, Prisons, and Indigenous Youth in the United States") help us understand the intersections between the "traditional" and the "institutional," with a full understanding that tribes can be institutional, when they write:

> Thus culturally relevant curriculum must become a process that reshapes schools' institutional functions, changing schools as sites of assimilation in to facilitators of self-determination through education—regardless of location. Access to educational spaces which provide students with the benefit of cultural reflexivity are a means to allay and eventually counteract the negative legacy of assimilationist colonial education policies.

As it turns out, cultural reflexivity is an acknowledgment of the flexibility (and its concomitant wisdom) of Indigenous Peoples to educate and school our children.

At the same time, Smith et al. (▶ Chap. 37, "Reclaiming Our People Following Imprisonment") argue that a key to turning around the imprisonment rates of Māori in New Zealand requires the work of the State and Māori. They state:

> ...while the prison system remains in its current form, providing the right type of support post release is critical [...]. That support needs to be consistent and long term, with people who have a strong and positive effect in their lives. This project met those two needs by providing iwi-based (tribal) health and social service support, combined with key hapu (extended family) facilitators. Both these supports mean that tangata ora (people who are healing) have potential lifetime support that goes beyond the life of a service contract. Both these supports provide culturally solid, potential lifetime support which do enrich the lives of the tangata ora.

Conclusion

Taken together, this collection of essays begs the question: What does this mean for the education and schooling of Indigenous children? The essays ask us to reimagine the role of knowledge and knowledges in the education and schooling process. How might we reimagine what counts as knowledge that is sanctioned by the state as something worth knowing? These chapters force us to acknowledge what we, as Indigenous Peoples, have known since time immemorial. Our knowledge is good knowledge. It is smart, is interesting, and serves as a foundation not only for personhood, survival, and engagement with the natural world and others, but it is also illuminating for life and education/schooling for the twenty-first century. There must be calls for reimagining and rethinking curricula and evaluation of what kinds of knowledges should count. They call for a reimagining of how we teach and learn and what we teach. And, importantly, there is a call in these chapters to acknowledge the centrality of relationships (both negative and positive) between people, knowledges, school and schooling, each other, and place. There is hope in the essays about how to recapture, reestablish, and re-instantiate our nations of peoples. Our hope is that they serve as guideposts for not only Indigenous Peoples and educators but for non-Indigenous Peoples on ways to rethink schooling for our children. Those children deserve the very best we can give them.

In the twenty-first century, Indigenous Peoples remain poised to lead in education, schooling, the environment, knowledge production and reproduction, health, relationships to land, and other related areas. In order to do so, we draw on lessons cumulatively attained and learned over millennia and adaptations to surrounding technologies. The leadership of these goals can be enhanced by the places in which many of us work – the schools, universities, and other educational institutions – but the enhancement must be done with care, concern, caution, and collaboration. We believe that the chapters in this section address the five E's and highlight both the perils and the possibilities of the futures of Indigenous Peoples.

References

Brayboy BMJ, Fann A, Castagno AE, Solyom JA (2012) Postsecondary education for American Indian and Alaska Natives: higher education for nation building and self-determination. Jossey-Bass, San Francisco

Brayboy BMJ, Solyom JA, Chin J, Tachine A, Bang M, Bustamante N, Ben C, Myles C, Poleviyuma A, Tom M, Abuwandi S, Richmond A (2017) RISE: a study of indigenous boys and men. Paper prepared for RISE: boys and men of color, Philadelphia

Deloria V (1970) We talk you listen: new tribes new turf. Bison Books, Lincoln

Lyons SR (2000) Rhetorical sovereignty: what do American Indians want from writing? Coll Compos Commun 51(3):447–468

Carceral Colonialisms: Schools, Prisons, and Indigenous Youth in the United States

33

Jeremiah A. Chin, Bryan McKinley Jones Brayboy, and Nicholas Bustamante

Contents

Introduction	576
From Boarding Schools to Prisons	578
Colonial Schooling	579
Punishing Native Students	580
Disciplining Native Students in Arizona	582
Sampling Arizona	582
Defining Key Variables	584
Changing the Institution Through Self-Determination	597
Conclusion and Future Directions	600
References	602

Abstract

In this chapter, we attempt to open conversations on the school-prison nexus and indigenous youth by tracing the history of colonization from boarding schools to the modern school to prison pipeline, focusing on a statistical analysis of school discipline in Arizona schools. The attempted assimilation and colonization of Indigenous youth in the United States has moved from boarding school policy to the modern network of zero tolerance and school discipline policies that form the "school to prison pipeline" as students are pushed out of classrooms and in to mass incarceration. Although the school to prison pipeline has been documented and analyzed in many communities of color, the extent and effect of the school-prison nexus for Indigenous youth in the United States has been under-explored. We found that schools with a predominantly non-white student population, particularly predominantly American Indian and Alaska Native schools, reported higher rates of school discipline. Furthermore, reports of Indigenous students

---

J. A. Chin · B. M. J. Brayboy (✉) · N. Bustamante
Arizona State University, Tempe, AZ, USA
e-mail: jeremiah.chin@asu.edu; Bryan.Brayboy@asu.edu; Nicholas.Bustamante@asu.edu

being disciplined for purported dress code violations when wearing traditional Indigenous hair styles signifies the ways in which colonization permeates the educational system in the United States. These destructive, disruptive, and colonial educational practices must be stopped.

Keywords

School to Prison Pipeline · School-prison nexus · Mass Incarceration · Indigenous Youth · American Indian/Alaska Native schooling

Introduction

On August 23, 2017, a 4-year-old American Indian boy, named Jabez Oates was sent home from school because his long hair violated school district policy on appropriate dress (Fonrouge 2017). Oates' mother, Jessica Oates, a member of the Cocopah tribe, noted that she had documentation from the tribe about the cultural significance of long hair for males. She said, "It's a symbol of strength." Ms. Oates worked to conform to the district's rules by sending Jabez to school with his hair in a bun. Apparently, having Jabez's hair in a bun violated district policy, being called "an 'inappropriate hair accessory'." In a later interview, the superintendent of the district noted, "Parents have a right to seek an appropriate educational setting for their child, just as Ms. Oates has the right to place her child in a district that reflects her personal expectations for standards of appearance." The superintendent takes an important cultural marker for a male's body and turns it into an issue of *school choice*; disregarding the lack of realistic choices for Ms. Oates, a single mother looking for a second job to support her family.

By framing discipline as choice, the superintendent ignores the cultural and historical components of an "individual choice" and reframes the debate as the district's interest in maintaining "standards." To wit, his statement notes, "There are procedures in place for addressing concerns over policy if it is Ms. Oates' desire to have her son educated in Barbers Hill ISD. But we would and should justifiably be criticized if our district lessened its expectations or longstanding policies simply to appease." In this case, the idea of "appeasing" a cultural decision and using policy as a way to discipline difference is one way that institutions begin to institutionalize "expectations" against Indigenous peoples. An accommodation that would facilitate learning and inclusion is made to appear as a violation of policy, placing blame for punishment and rejection of a 4-year-old who honors his culture on the shoulders of his mother, who may have no practical choices about where to live, work, or send her child to school. Jabez Oates will only ever have one first day of school, and it will – forever – be marred by a principal and his superintendent's perceptions and a policy for appropriateness that demonizes Jabez's (and by extension his mother's and their tribe's) culture. Stories like Jabez's are disappointingly common, making almost annual appearances in news and education circles. Jabez's story is a reminder that schools begin the disciplining process early and often for Indigenous children. This is not a new phenomenon.

Schools are institutions of learning and conditioning – formally educating students in subjects like math or science, while also instilling cultural norms and values. In the United States, learning has become interwoven with discipline, creating controlled environments where students are taught to obey authority and act in conformity with white norms and policies. These range from in-class norms of interaction, or, as Jabez story shows, dress and physical appearance. Failure to conform to policy results in punishments ranging from lowered citizenship grades, to zero tolerance policies that tie behavior to suspension or expulsion, and serve to push students out of school (Noguera 2003). These policies disproportionately effect students of color and students with disabilities to create a "school to prison pipeline" that pushes youth from education to incarceration (Christle et al. 2005; Tuzzolo and Hewitt 2006; Kim 2009; Winn and Behizadeh 2011; Vaught 2011, 2017; Nance 2014; Laura 2014; Redfield and Nance 2016; Morris 2016).

The school to prison pipeline encompasesses inequitable educational outcomes and experiences for students of color, emphasizing the impact of structural discrimination on low income and racialized youth and their families experience in relation to the school system (Noguera 2003; Vaught 2011; Morris 2016). Studies highlight the way disciplinary practices (Kim 2009; Losen 2011; Noguera 2003), school resources and teachers (Christle et al. 2007; Tuzzolo and Hewitt 2006) and the presence of school resource/police officers (Nance 2014), negatively affect the educational opportunities of youth of color generally, and Black, Latina/o, and American Indian/Alaska Native students specifically.

Studies focusing specifically on Black and Latino boys and raise important issues in interrupting the criminalization of Black and Brown boys, but scholarly analyses of the school to prison pipeline rarely focus on the school-based criminalization of Black and Latina girls (Morris 2016) or Indigenous youths, particularly those in rural areas (Healey 2013). Thus, discussions on the racialization and criminalization of youth in schools fail to account for the ways race and gender contribute to negative educational outcomes for girls of color or Native youth. As Monique Morris points out, "the narrative arc of the school-to-prison pipeline has largely failed to interrogate how punitive discipline policies and other school-related decision-making affect the well-being of girls" (2016, p. 11). Black and Brown girls or Indigenous youths do appear in national studies on school discipline and the school-to-prison pipeline and reveal disproportionate, and statistically significant, disparate disciplinary practices for Black, Brown, and Indigenous youths in comparison to white youths (NCAI 2015; Redfield and Nance 2016; U.S. Dept. of Ed. 2014; Wallace et al. 2008). However, the inclusion of Indigenous youth is largely as a comparison group, and they remain absent from statistical and anecdotal narratives of the school to prison pipeline. This cursory inclusion is symptomatic of statistical analyses that expose systemic issues but render the experiences of American Indian students invisible because of a lack of a statistically significant sample size (Shotton et al. 2013). In this chapter, we use the terms American Indian, Alaska Native, Native Hawaiian, Native, and Indigenous to refer to the original inhabitants of the lands that now make up the United States, including Alaska and Hawaii, and their descendants. We are specific where possible in identifying which Indigenous peoples or nation we are speaking directly about. We alternate between these terms because we recognize that grouping people in this way is a social construct rooted in a shared history of oppression from colonial forces from Europe and their descendants in the United States. Just as there is no essential or definitional experience that defines Indigenous peoples, there is no term that all Indigenous peoples will agree on.

Discussions of the school-to-prison pipeline are growing in academic literature on education, law, and policing – critiquing the disproportionate impact of zero tolerance policies, current events, and effects that have increased discipline and policing (Morris 2016; Nance 2014; Vaught 2011, 2017). Fewer studies situate this in the historical context, building on the histories of racialization and white supremacy in the United States that associate blackness, otherness, or indigeneity with criminality and valorize whiteness to create racial disparities that continue to grow (Morris 2016;Vaught 2011, 2017). The school to prison pipeline is nothing new, but unfortunately also shows few signs of rust or disrepair. As the story of Jabez that opened this chapter shows the criminalization of youth has been well maintained.

The school-to-prison pipeline for Indigenous peoples in the United States is rooted in the history of colonization and assimilation through boarding schools. Schools, as institutions, are sites and extensions of colonial power in the application of social policy to the bodies and ways of knowing of indigenous youth. The next section situates the school-to-prison pipeline rooted in ideologies of discipline behind the boarding school movement, identifying how colonization has shifted from forced assimilation through removal to a removal from schooling for failure to properly assimilate. This shift is an important adaptation made by schools. We then turn to focus specifically on how disciplinary practices are enacted in Arizona, based on recent data accumulated by the United States Department of Education. Contrasting historical accounts and modern qualitative data helps to begin conceptualizing and reframing the way schooling, and school discipline, are enacted for American Indian Youth. We conclude by reflecting on the school as a colonial institution and turn towards Critical Indigenous Research Methodologies (Brayboy et al. 2012) to consider how culturally relevant institutions can disrupt the school to prison pipeline.

From Boarding Schools to Prisons

Schools serve multiple purposes; they educate children in particular subjects, they lift certain elements and expectation that society's power-brokers deem desirable and appropriate. Boarding schools were a violent assimilationist effort to cultivate ideal Native Americans citizens; to transform indigenous peoples and knowledges into white, Anglo norms. Indigenous youth who did not fit Eurocentric norms found themselves unfit for inclusion into US civil society, but even those whose ways of being and knowing were colonized by schools were still marginalized (Lomawaima and McCarty 2006). The modern prison industrial complex similarly functions within a state of white supremacy, as school safety and disciplinary policies are often used to demarcate students of color for amplified punishments that too often introduce and link minority youth to the carceral state, either as inmates or guards (Gilmore 2007; Jung et al. 2011; Noguera 2003). Moreover, the school to prison pipeline is complicated by the role of private prisons, whose influence in state legislatures across the country directly contribute to legislation that both underfunds public instruction and increases the presence of for-profit prisons (Jung et al. 2011). The modern school to prison pipeline underscores and reinforces normative behaviors, views, and knowledges associated with ideal (white supremacist) citizenship, functioning as a filtration system for capitalism, sorting out those who may participate or those subject to the warehousing, labor, and disenfranchisement of people through mass incarceration.

Colonial Schooling

Schools that serve as a mechanism of social control over non-white populations by the removal and cultural demonization of children are nothing new. As K. Tsianina Lomawaima and Teresa McCarty explain, "the education of American Indian children has been at the very center of the battleground between federal and tribal powers" (2005, p. 5). Beginning in the late nineteenth century and continuing well through the twentieth, the Indian boarding school system was a means of social, academic, cultural, and physical control – regulating Tribal governance and culture by removing youth and forcing education only in white ways of speaking, behaving, and learning (Adams 1995; Ellis 1996; Lomawaima and McCarty 2006). Richard Pratt, founder of the infamous Carlisle Indian School, plainly stated the assimilationist mission of boarding schools was to "kill the Indian in him and save the man" by removing Native youth from their home communities to off reservation boarding schools (Adams 1995, p. 52). This assimilation was not with the intent of integration; rather the intent was to create docile, differentiated bodies for labor and exploitation:

> Native individuals, as well as particular cultural traits or practices, were being fitted into an American 'safety zone' of obedient citizenry and innocent cultural difference. Parameters of the safety zone corresponded to relations of power: Safe citizens were part of a subservient proletariat, and safe cultural differences were controlled by non-Native federal, Christian, and social agencies that could proclaim themselves benefactors dedicated to 'preserving' native life. (Lomawaima and McCarty 2006, p. 49)

By assimilating Native youth and marking them as other, boarding schools ensured marginalization that would eliminate connections with their home community, while racial marginalization and low-level schooling would guard against social advancement in White spaces. The modern carceral state is thus modeled on the boarding school system's ideological process of marking particular bodies as deviant others, removing them from their homes and communities, and then forcing discipline or docility.

Punishing Native Students

Current policies of discipline that push students out of the classroom are the colonial legacy of boarding schools. Punitive zero tolerance policies continue the assimilation and marginalization for American Indian students by marking characteristics of student dress, look, or behavior as criminal with harsh consequences. Jabez Oates' story is not an isolated incident – schools across the United States continue to sweep Native youth into punitive school discipline simply for upholding cultural traditions. For instance in 2014, a 5-year-old Navajo boy named Malachai Wilson was sent home from his first day of kindergarten because his long hair violated the school's dress code. Texas' Seminole school district policy requires "[b]oys' hair shall be cut neatly and often enough to ensure good grooming" with special exemptions on religious or cultural grounds so long as the school is given prior notice and an administrator approves (Moya-Smith 2014). A year later at Arrowhead Elementary School in 2015, Jakobe Sanden, a Seneca boy, was sent to the Principal's office for being a distraction. His crime? A mohawk haircut that honored his ancestors. The principal worried that his hair may have violated policy and sent him home without a second thought (Bever 2015; DeMille 2015; Wood 2015). Policing what characteristics constitute "good grooming" for boys are indicative of larger, implicitly biased school policies that seek to punish non-white student behavior as deviant. Though Malachi and Jakobe would return to school without having to cut their hair, with apologies from administrators, Malachi will never have another first day of school, and Jakobe will always know that his hairstyle – and that of his ancestors – will remain suspect at Arrowhead Elementary.

Cultural conflict in the education of youth of color is part of a long history of colonization and white supremacy in the United States. For Indigenous youth in particular, indigenous education can be, according to Creek scholar K. Tsianina Lomawaima (2000), summarized in three simple words: "battle for power" (p. 2). Education scholars have thoroughly identified the disconnect between white schooling and Indigenous youth, highlighting the history of assimilation in US schools and simultaneous resistance by Native students and communities (Brayboy 2005; Lomawaima and McCarty 2006). Even as schooling has become less overtly assimilationist, Native students are still excluded and alienated from educational processes, prompting calls for culturally responsive schooling and culturally relevant/sustaining/revitalizing pedagogies to foster, enhance, and promote Indigenous achievement (Brayboy and Castagno 2009; Brayboy and Maaka 2015; Castagno 2012; Castagno and Brayboy 2008; McCarty and Lee 2014).

These principles take on added significance in school discipline, as demonstrated in the lawsuit against the Winner School District in South Dakota. In 2004, the US Office for Civil Rights of the Department of Education (OCR) targeted Winner for compliance review based on community reports of racism and disciplinary discrimination against Native students (Kim 2010, p. 967). Parents reported that students left the district because of harassment and unfair discipline, but for the local Rosebud Sioux community, the only alternative was an on-reservation boarding school, which "poses a hardship for the families and the students who would otherwise be able to live at home" (ibid. at 967 n. 68), while others would drop out, or even wind up in a juvenile correctional facility (ibid. at 969). After a group of parents sued the school district, the parties entered into a mediation process between three parents, two tribal representatives, three district administrators, and three members of the district's Board of Education – ending with a consent decree agreeing to increase graduation rates, decrease suspensions and police referrals, with various attendance and participation requirements (ibid.).

In this case, the lawsuit over disproportionate disciplinary policies and local harassment lead to a mediation that resembles the type of community involvement that culturally relevant schooling seeks to achieve. Critically, this process demonstrates how even schools that are under tribal control may become burdensome to Native students and families, as those who live off-reservation would have to send their children to live in dormitories away from their home. Even though the students are on their Indigenous homelands, they are not with their parents and families on a daily basis. Still, Winner School District litigation is exceptional mostly in that parents were able to directly show discrimination and racism recognized by courts. As Jabez, Malachi, or Jakobe's stories illustrate, school policies also hinge on cultural norms that can ostracize and discipline Indigenous students for traditional practices, connected to indigenous ways of being and knowing, which are labeled as abnormal or deviant.

The control, management, and suppression of knowledge production over Indigenous and persons of color is central to United States colonization. To this end, education was used to suppress Indigenous axiologies, ontologies, pedagogies, and epistemologies and replace them with eurocentric ways of learning and being (Brayboy 2005; Lomawaima and McCarty 2006; Smith 2012). Education is a sociohistorical process used to model colonial structures of power and further codify relationships of power, particularly white supremacy (Brayboy 2005; Ladson-Billings 1998; Vaught 2011). Peruvian decolonial scholar Anibal Quijano (2000) explains the interdependence between education, identity, and colonization of the Americas as the "constitution of Europe as a new *id*-entity needed the elaboration of a Eurocentric perspective of knowledge, a theoretical perspective of the idea of race as a naturalization of colonial relations between European and non-Europeans" (p. 534). Creating a distinct European identity through colonization necessitated naturalizing Indigenous inferiority through race and white supremacy. The delineations between peoples and knowledge systems became constitutive elements in Western education environments, where the classroom and dominant institutions of education became sites of colonialism. Students who did not embody the cultural norms and European normative values associated were labeled as deviants, needing discipline.

Epistemological and physical abuses of the boarding school system have not died, but instead evolved into discretionary disciplines of the modern school-to-prison pipeline. Punishment of youth of color is made to appear as an outlier, hidden behind neutrally worded general policies that upholding the rules of the education system to make for a more cohesive, or white, educational environment. The stories of Jabez Oates, Jakobe Sanden, and Malachi Wilson reflect the ways in which discipline is meted out against Native children; punishing the children to undermine the parents', and thereby community's, adherence to traditional appearance, at least with respect to hair. School discipline and the school-to-prison pipeline extend the rationale of the boarding school by making student behaviors, thoughts, and actions the problem, rather than focusing on the institutional and systemic barriers in schooling. We believe this connection is exposed by quantitatively identifying if, where, and how Indigenous youth are disciplined. It is to this work that we now turn.

Disciplining Native Students in Arizona

In order to define how discipline is meted out, we turn to the Civil Rights Data Collection (CRDC) housed in the Office of Civil Rights of the Department of Education. The Civil Rights Data Collection (CRDC) is a biennial mandatory survey required by the United States Department of Education, collecting data on education and civil rights issues to analyze equity and opportunity. As a part of federal funding, schools are required to self-report on a variety of categories, from student enrollment to teacher salaries and budget to use of school discipline. The unit of analysis in this data is institutional, as schools will report the aggregate number of students in a given school, for example identifying the total number of American Indian students. To create our dataset, we took the excel files provided by the CRDC, merged and cleaned the data using Stata statistical software to focus specifically on Arizona. We then cleaned the data to identify key variables and perform multivariate regression analyses, described below.

Sampling Arizona

We chose the 2012 CRDC dataset because at the time we requested data, it was the most current dataset with robust and complete data on Arizona. We focus on Arizona for three reasons. First, it is where we currently reside, making it more relevant to our personal experiences. Second, Arizona is home to 22 federally recognized tribal nations and communities, with the third largest American Indian population in the United States. This means a greater proportion of Native students in the total population to avoid statistically insignificant representations of Native youth in our sample. Third, because of the large Native population and number of reservation communities in Arizona, we believed we were more likely to find diversity in schooling environments for Native youth, with a greater likelihood of predominantly American Indian schools in urban and rural settings, as well as larger proportions of American Indian students in urban and rural public, private, and charter schools. The advantage of CRDC data is that it collects public, magnet, charter, and other non-private schools throughout the state of Arizona, leaving us with 1920 schools in our dataset (see Table 1). Unfortunately, the disadvantage of the CRDC data is that all the numbers are self-reported leaving some frequent missing responses, particularly in measures of school discipline. The demographics for our total sample

Table 1 School sample ($n = 1917$)

Variable	%	Mean (SD)
School type		
Public school	71.06	
Magnet, alternative or charter	28.94	
Title I schools	61.35	
Grades taught		
PreK	0.89	
K – 6 (elementary school)	17.29	
7 & 8 (middle school)	12.24	
K – 8	19.79	
Mix of grades (K – 8)	17.86	
7–12	3.65	
9–12 (high school)	20.52	
K – 12 (all grades)	2.92	
Ungraded (Juv. Justice/online)	4.84	
School size		
Small (2–315 students)	33.44	
Medium (315–662 students)	33.23	
Large(662 + students)	33.33	
Phoenix/Tucson	54.79	
Total school spending (dollars)		3,767,312 (2.95×10^7)
Average teacher salary		42,248.36 (34,458.24)
Per-student spending		6877.66 (24,525.82)
Total FTE of classroom teachers		28.95 (22.65)

includes all 1920 schools reported in the original data; however, the final analysis reduces our total to 1874 schools that reported all disciplinary measures, and of those schools most reported few to no instances of discipline.

As Table 1 demonstrates, the sample is predominantly public schools, with 28.94% of schools identifying as magnet, alternative, or charter schools. The CRDC defines magnet, alternative, and charter school as distinct schools, but notes this includes programs that are located within other schools – i.e., a magnet program housed in a public school. For our purposes, we wanted to show the divide between schools based on differences in funding from the district – magnet, alternative, and charter schools are more narrowly focused at specific issues, populations, or subjects, and receive different types of funding. Title I schools are defined by federal funding provided by Title I of the Elementary and Secondary Education Act, which provides additional federal funding to schools where more than 40% of the student population are identified as low-income. We use the grades taught variable to show the distribution of the different types of school and ages of students within that school in our sample. We split our data into thirds by the number of students enrolled, thus creating small, medium, and large schools within the sample so we could see if the size of the school affected school discipline. Furthermore, we used the zip codes available within the dataset to divide our data by whether the school is located in a zip code in the Phoenix or Tucson Metropolitan Statistical Areas, to try and see if there are differences in the discipline meted out by urban and rural schools. Finally, we used fiscal variables to capture school funding, looking at total school spending, that was subdivided into the average teacher salary and per-student spending which synthesizes school size and spending. However, as shown in Table 1, each fiscal measure has a large standard deviation, especially in per-student spending where the standard deviation of 24,525.82 is nearly four times as large as the mean of 6877.66, showing large variance in the spending reported by schools. This indicates a broad range spending among the schools in the sample, with no consistent average across the sample. Finally, we also wanted to look at the Total FTE of teachers employed by the schools, to indicate student-teacher ratios and employment.

Defining Key Variables

Race

Looking at the effects of discipline within the school-to-prison pipeline for Native students requires identifying key variables: school discipline, sex, and race. The CRDC defines race along seven racial categories, adopted in 2007, using a two part question to identify racial and ethnic data. First students are identified as Hispanic/Latino of any race, then they are identified as American Indian or Alaska Native (AI/AN), Asian, Black or African American, Native Hawaiian, or other Pacific Islander, White, or Two or More Races. If students are identified as Hispanic/Latino, they are tabulated as Latino, even if other categories are selected.

The CRDC data misses important racial subtleties, marking Afro-Latinos simply as Latino, or, as particularly relevant to Arizona, Latinos with Native heritage. Thus a student who is Navajo and Mexican would only be identified as Latino in the CRDC data. Furthermore if a student identifies with multiple racial categories, i.e., Black and AI/AN, they would be tabulated in the two or more races category automatically, even if they did not identify under this broader multiracial category. This means that data for Black, American Indian/ Alaska Native, Latina/o, and Asian American students likely underestimate the representation of these groups within the sample, and the lack of nuance clustering students as multiracial underrepresents the varied effects of different socioeconomic and geographic factors for students at the margins of these narrowly defined categories. While there are theoretical and practical issues with the way identity is treated by these data, the standardization of data on race in the CRDC helps to identify discrete racial groups, particularly AI/AN, which are most relevant for our analysis. However, we believe it may also underestimate the effects on Indigenous youth by overly narrow conceptions of race and indigeneity. Again, since we are dealing with school level data, the school's categorization (or miscategorization) of students could speak to the way students are conceptualized as part of the student body, thus, with these caveats, we use the schools categorization of students to see if a relationship exists between school demographics and discipline.

Table 2 School demographics ($n = 1917$)

Variable	Mean (SD)
Student enrollment	572.98 (543.31)
By race	
American Indian/Alaska Native	29.42 (80.78)
Asian American	16.38 (32.29)
Black	30.53 (47.04)
Hawaiian/Pacific Islander	2.25 (5.27)
Latino	240.34 (295.34)
White	244.63 (336.83)
Multiracial	9. 41 (32.38)
By sex	
Male	294.28 (272.32)
Female	278.70 (273.10)

School racial demographics in Arizona are identified in Table 2, showing the mean racial and sex demographics for Arizona within the sample. We created variables representing the mean number of students by race, by sex, and by race *and* sex. The proportions and means of students by race and sex are nearly identical to the general racial demographics, but we use the race and gender interaction variables in our final regression models.

The mean racial demographics in Arizona schools within the sample differ dramatically from the United States census. American Indian and Alaska Natives are 7.89% of the students in Arizona schools in our sample, compared to 1.6% of the national population (Census 2016). Similarly Latinos represent 41.06% of the student population of sampled schools, more than double the 17.8% in recent U.S. Census data (2016). White (41.53%) and Black (5.05%) are underrepresented in the sample in contrast with the national census data (61.3% and 13.3% respectively). However, the size and racial composition of schools varies greatly across the sample, demonstrated by the large standard deviations in Table 2. Although the mean Black and American Indian populations are both near 30 students, the large standard deviations (47.04 and 80.78 respectively) exemplify how school racial demographics are not consistent across the sample, and the data contains many outliers.

Part of this is due to large high schools and online schools; there are 13 schools in Arizona with more than 3000 students, three of which are online schools with more than 5000 students. In Arizona, online schools provide virtual classroom environments for students to learn and submit work, but also still involve student and teacher interaction, all through digital environments. Students are still subject to disciplinary measures from their respective schools, but the physical classroom environment differs, even between online schools. Some online schools are magnet programs, housed within physical school campuses, others are purely virtual environments. Furthermore, the CRDC data includes no distinctions between online an in person programs, meaning data would have to be manually researched and recoded to distinguish all online schools from in-person charter, magnet, or alternative schools.

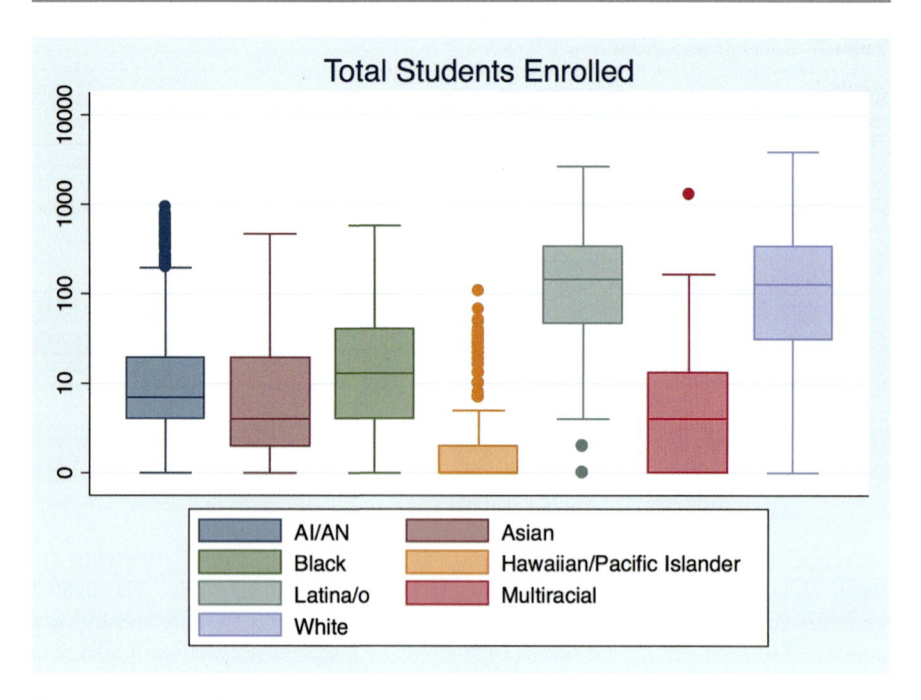

Fig. 1 Enrolled Student Demographics

In future studies, we would like to distinguish this information, but for our purposes in this analysis, we do not believe the online in-person distinction was sufficient for its own analysis, other than noting the ways they contribute to the population gaps.

These 13 online schools have 4.5% of the students in the 1920 schools in the sample. Additionally, there are 262 charter, online, and public schools in our sample that have less than 100 total students enrolled. Schools with 100 students or less thus make up about 13.65% of the schools in our sample, but only about 1.21% of the sample. Figure 1 shows a box and whisker plot to visualize the outliers in our sample, considering the large number of schools with a small student body, and the few schools with a large student body. These large schools necessitated the box and whisker plots to be shown logarithmically to show the medians and quintiles for each variable, meaning each tick is exponentially larger than the previous. Box plots in Fig. 1 demonstrate that, particularly for American Indians, Alaska Natives, Native Hawaiians, and Pacific Islanders, the mean student population obscures the numerous outlier schools with large Indigenous populations.

This inspired us to highlight the predominant racial groups at various schools, to give better perspective of how these variations in the mean student populations represent the racial diversity or segregation at Arizona schools. In Table 3, we start by looking to two key features of segregation, majority minority schools and intensely segregated schools.

Most Arizona schools are majority minority schools meaning there are more non-white students than white students (55.78%), while a small but significant

Table 3 School segregation ($n = 1917$)

Variable	%
Majority minority school	55.78
Intensely segregated (>90% white)	1.41
Intensely segregated (>90% AI/AN)	4.17
Intensely segregated (>90% Latino)	7.29

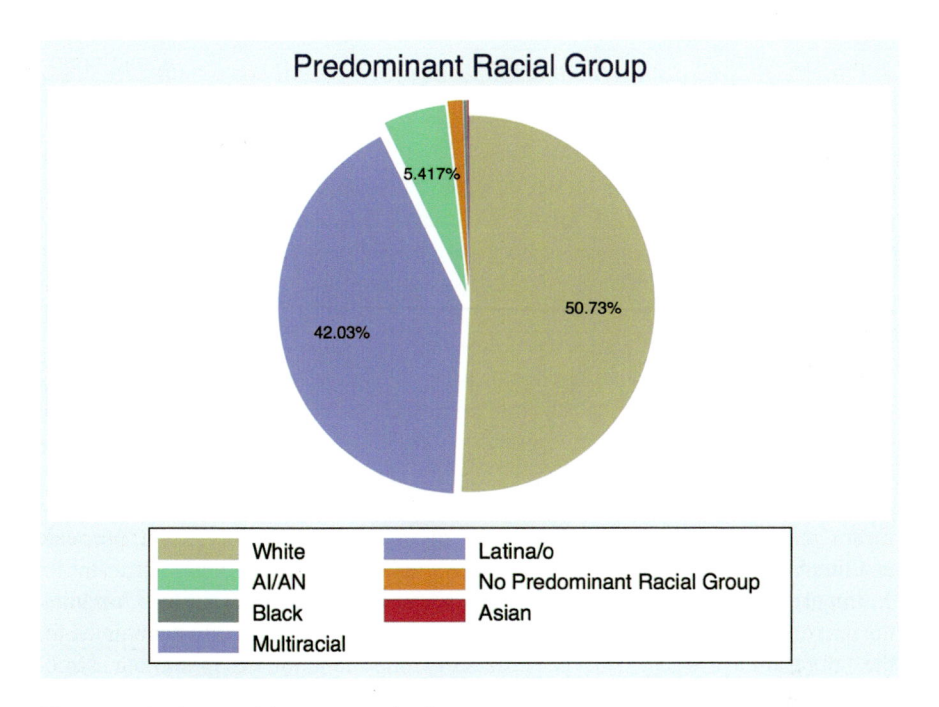

Fig. 2 Predominant racial group at a school

amount of schools are intensely segregated, is defined as schools where more than 90% of the student population was one racial group (Orfield et al. 1994). Table 3 shows that a majority of schools in our sample are majority minority (55.78%), with some schools intensely segregated by race for Latinos, Whites, and Natives (7.29%, 1.41%, and 4.17% respectively).

However, even though most schools in the sample are majority minority, Fig. 2 shows that most schools are still predominantly White (50.73%), meaning that White students are the largest racial group at the school. The remaining schools are predominantly Latina/o (42.03%), with some predominantly Native schools (5.42%); less than ten schools are predominantly Black, Asian, or Multiracial (0.10%, 0.31%, and 0.10%, respectively); and 25 schools have no predominant racial group (1.30%). Interestingly, the percentage of intensely segregated Native schools (4.17%) being so close to the percentage of predominantly Native schools (5.42%) emphasizes that most predominantly Native schools are intensely segregated.

Table 4 School discipline summary ($n = 1917$)

Variable	Mean (SD)
Total discipline	81.06 (134.30)
Law enforcement	2.98 (9.86)
Corporal punishment	0.33 (5.58)
Mechanical restraint	0.02 (0.48)
In-school suspensions	37.34 (82.64)
Out-of-school suspensions	38.19 (58.35)
Expulsions	0.71 (3.74)

School Discipline

Based on our review of the literature, a central feature of study for the school to prison pipeline is school discipline. We created a composite "school discipline" variable by combining the varied forms of discipline within the dataset: manual restraint, corporal punishment, in school suspension, out of school, arrests, expulsions, and referrals to law enforcement. Table 4 shows the mean number of reported instances of each type of school discipline that we focused on.

The large standard deviations demonstrate the spread of this sample – meaning that while many schools reported no discipline, or zero instances of a type of discipline, some schools reported extremely high numbers particularly in both in- and out-of-school suspensions. In 2012, Arizona schools in our sample range from zero in-school suspensions, all the way up to 1206 in-school-suspensions. This means that even though suspensions are the most common discipline, the scale and number of disciplinary measures varies greatly between schools.

Importantly, we want to emphasize that because our data is institutional, meaning the unit of analysis is at the school level, it means that all of our data is aggregated for the entire student body. This is particularly important for discipline and demographics of the school since the CRDC data reports raw aggregate numbers based a school's reported data. The number of disciplinary actions are not tied to the number of students but reflect a general count of actions taken against students, so it is impossible to tell if, for example, one student has been suspended four times and expelled, or four students have been suspended and another has been expelled. However, we believe that this institutional data allows us to look at the ways in which schools take disciplinary action by analyzing how those disciplinary measures are distributed by race and gender, giving us a way of highlighting structural problems but unable to correlate individual actions or behaviors to school responses. We can say from this data that schools may discipline specific populations disproportionately to their representation in the student body or relative to other groups in the sample, but we cannot say why or how those students are being targeted.

Therefore, to account for the variations in school size and racial demographics across different schools, we created a per-student discipline variable, which we disaggregated by race, demonstrated in Fig. 3 and in Table 5.

This per-student discipline variable simply reflects the number of disciplinary actions reported against a student of that group, created by dividing disciplinary

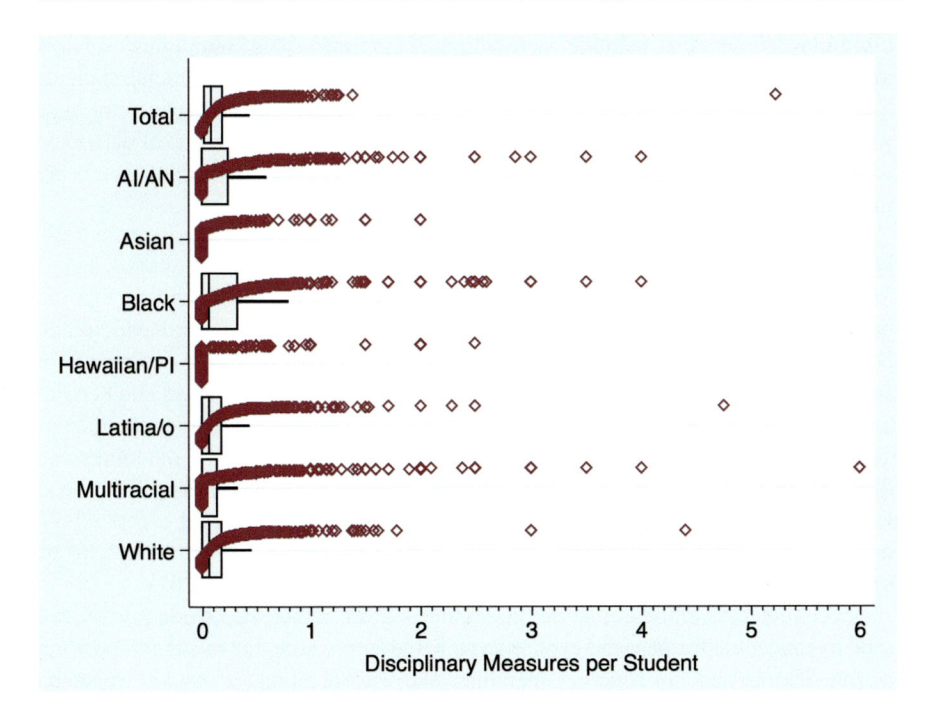

Fig. 3 Disciplinary measures per student, by race

Table 5 Per student school discipline, by race ($n = 1917$)

Variable	Mean (SD)
Per student	**0.1428 (0.2142)**
American Indian/Alaska Native	0.1759 (0.3398)
Asian American	0.0572 (0.1728)
Black	0.2210 (0.3785)
Hawaiian/Pacific Islander	0.0611 (0.2431)
Latino	0.1373 (0.2424)
White	0.1405 (0.2359)
Multiracial	0.1578 (0.4218)

measures reported for each group by the total number of enrolled students of that group ($\frac{number\ of\ disciplinary\ measures\ by\ race}{number\ of\ enrolled\ students\ by\ race}$). Therefore the disciplinary measures demonstrated in Fig. 3 and described in Table 5 represents that for every American Indian and Alaska Native students in a school in Arizona, on average, 0.1758 disciplinary actions were reported per enrolled American Indian and Alaska Native Student. Figure 3 demonstrates the many outliers, particularly for students of color, with some schools reporting more than two disciplinary actions taken for every student of color enrolled in a school. Black, Native, and Multiracial students all show rates of discipline above the average across racial groups. This highlights schools implementing disciplinary actions against Black, Native, and Multiracial students disproportionate to their representation in the student body. Again, because we have school-level data and not student-level data, we can only speak in terms of discipline relative to school demographics, rather than assessing whether particular students are more or less likely to be disciplined.

Disproportionate Discipline

School-to-prison literature often focuses on disparities by race or funding that are particularly significant (Orfield et al. 1994; Nance 2014; Laura 2014; Redfield and Nance 2016). The lack of adequate school funding limits access to resources for students and has the compounded effect of students falling behind peers and becoming disengaged from education in general (Nance 2015). Too often, students of color are the pool of students being bearing the costs of lower education outcomes and disparate rates of punishment associated with school funding (Darling-Hammond 2015; Morris 2016). Pedro Noguera notes, in the majority of United States school districts, low academic achievers and Black and Latino males are most likely to be over represented in suspension, detention, and expulsion practices (2003).

Since this dataset focuses at the institutional level, rather than student level, we tried to conceptualize race and economic status by contrasting the racial composition of the schools and the school's spending. We use spending as our key financial variable, as this is the only assessment of funding within the dataset. Overall spending helps to look at some of the disparities between the potential for resources to be made available to students, which is particularly important for understanding what students are being left behind or becoming disengaged from the classroom experience. To allow for easier comparison, we created an ordinal spending variable that divided schools into three equal groups (low, medium and high) based on the amount of money spent per-student, which is then contrasted by race, shown in Table 6.

Across all seven racial groups, Black and American Indian/Alaska Native students have the highest rates of per-student discipline, regardless of per-student spending. For schools in the low and mid tiers of per-student spending, mean per-student discipline for Black students ($\bar{x} = 0.2357$ and $\bar{x} = 0.2544$ respectively) is noticeably higher than the overall mean for per-student discipline or mean per-student discipline for Black students ($\bar{x} = 0.2210$), yet schools in the highest tier drop off dramatically ($\bar{x} = 0.1746$). Per-student discipline of Latina/os and Whites, however, appear to consistently increase with higher funding, though still below any of the means for Black or Native students. For us this was a startling display that per-student discipline, for Whites, Latinos, and overall, appear to increase with spending, as most studies show that schools that are underfunded face the largest disciplinary issues. Per-student discipline for American Indian and Alaska Native students, however, seems to fluctuate based on spending, but without noticeable increases or decreases overall or by spending. Table 6 highlights that not only is school discipline varied by race, but school finance may play an important factor in the distribution of discipline in schools.

Table 6 Per-student discipline by race & per-student spending ($n = 1875$)

Disciplinary measures (per student)	Mean (SD)	Per-student spending (3 categories)		
		Low ($ 0–3005)	Mid ($3016–4617)	High ($4626+)
Total	**0.1428 (0.2142)**	**0.1212 (0.1451)**	**0.1330 (0.1590)**	**0.1735 (0.2980)**
AI/AN	0.1759 (0.3398)	0.1719 (0.2789)	0.1800 (0.3425)	0.1759 (0.3889)
Asian	0.0572 (0.1728)	0.0593 (0.1427)	0.0679 (0.1823)	0.0448 (0.1892)
Black	0.2210 (0.3785)	0.2357 (0.3281)	0.2544 (0.4281)	0.1746 (0.3702)
Hawaiian/PI	0.0611 (0.2431)	0.0695 (0.2529)	0.0775 (0.2643)	0.0364 (0.2066)
Latino	0.1373 (0.2424)	0.1213 (0.1706)	0.1275 (0.1668)	0.1626 (0.3418)
White	0.1405 (0.2359)	0.1253 (0.1638)	0.1390 (0.2192)	0.1570 (0.3016)
Multiracial	0.1578 (0.4218)	0.2272 (0.5514)	0.1621 (0.3479)	0.0855 (0.3139)

Therefore we created a set of variables try to focus strictly on the proportionality of discipline within schools, indicating if the proportion of disciplinary measures was less than or equal to the proportion of the student population $\left(\frac{school\ discipline\ by\ race}{total\ school\ discipline} \leq \frac{students\ by\ race}{total\ students} \right)$.

Black and Native students in Arizona are, on average, disciplined at higher rates than other students, as demonstrated in Table 6. However, as Table 7 shows, they are also more likely to be disproportionately disciplined at a school level. The proportionality demonstrated in Table 7 is calculated by looking at whether each racialized group's disciplinary measures is proportional to their representation in the student body. The first row in Table 7 is the percentage of schools which reported disciplinary measures equal to or less than the number of enrolled students of color, i.e., if a school is 40% White, and White students make up 20% of school discipline incidents, then they are classified as less than or equal to percent of the population. However, Table 7 demonstrates that schools were more likely to disproportionately discipline Black and American Indian students than White and Latino students, emphasizing the racialized disparities previously indicated by the sample. Still, the majority of schools across these four racial groups indicated schools punished proportionally to a group's percentage of the student population.

Distributions of Discipline

Because of the racially disproportionate means in Arizona schools' rates of discipline, we want to ensure that these disparities are statistically relevant and try to eliminate the possibility they are simply due to chance or random error. In our sample, data on disciplinary measures are positively skewed, meaning most of the schools report less than one disciplinary measures per student (median $= 0.08$, skewness $= 8.57$), and a long tail of outliers, going up to 5.23 disciplinary measures per enrolled student (kurtosis $= 175.24$). As shown in a histogram of per-student discipline in Fig. 4, the distribution of school discipline is not a normal, symmetrical distribution around the mean.

However, because we did not want to ignore the outliers and transforming the data to simulate a normal curve is more difficult considering the large number of

Table 7 Proportionality of discipline by race ($n = 1920$)

Proportionality	Percentage of sample			
	AI/AN	Black	Latino	White
Less than or equal to % population	64.32	51.30	84.84	80.31
Greater than % of student population	35.68	48.70	15.16	19.69

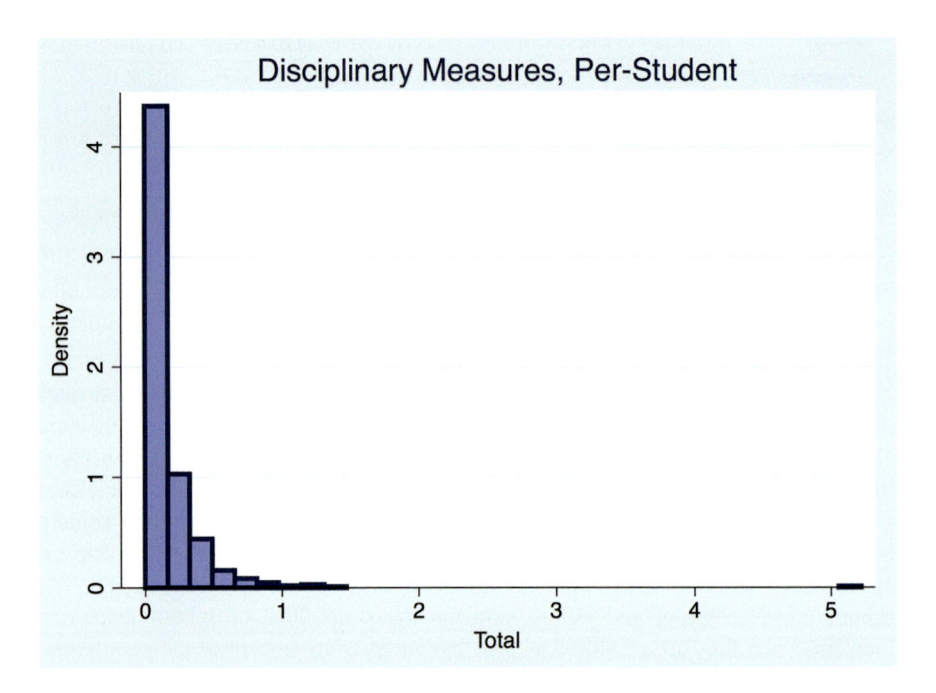

Fig. 4 Histogram of disciplinary measures, per-student

schools reporting zero discipline, we used the Wilcoxon-Mann-Whitney two-sample rank-sum test (WMW test) to compare distributions of data between two non-parametric groups. Rather than focus on the means or plotting a line of best fit along the distribution of the data, the WMW test sorts and ranks the data in two groups, then calculates and compares the sum of ranks for each group and the sum expected by chance (Longest 2012). Put simply, this test checks to see whether the distribution of data between two independent groups is significantly different, and not due to random chance. For our purposes, we used the per-student discipline variable and compared the distributions of discipline by race, focusing on the demographics of the school using our variables for majority minority schools, predominant racial groups, and intensely segregated schools.

These data displayed in Table 8 show that there are statistically significant differences in schools' per-student discipline rates based on the predominant racial group of the school. In schools where White students make up less than 50% of the

Table 8 Wilcoxon Rank-Sum Test: per-student discipline ($n = 1875$)

Variable	Obs.	Mean(SD)	Median	z-score	p-value
Majority minority schools					
White $\geq 50\%$	807	0.12 (0.24)	0.06	−4.703	<0.001
White $<50\%$	1068	0.16 (0.19)	0.10		
Predominant racial group					
AI/AN					
Non-AI/AN	1772	0.14 (0.21)	0.08	−3.954	<0.001
AI/AN	103	0.26 (0.29)	0.17		
Latina/o					
Non-Latina/o	1070	0.14 (0.24)	0.07	−2.997	0.003
Latina/o	805	0.15 (0.17)	0.09		
White					
Non-white	943	0.16 (0.19)	0.10	3.732	<0.001
White	932	0.13 (0.24)	0.07		
Intensely segregated					
AI/AN					
$<90\%$ AI/AN	1796	0.14 (0.21)	0.08	−3.939	<0.001
$\geq 90\%$ AI/AN	79	0.27 (0.30)	0.18		
Latina/o					
$<90\%$ Latina/o	1735	0.15 (0.22)	0.08	3.753	<0.001
$\geq 90\%$ Latina/o	140	0.10 (0.17)	0.05		
White					
$<90\%$ white	1848	0.14 (0.21)	0.08	1.32	0.009
$\geq 90\%$ white	27	0.09 (0.15)	0.03		

student population, WMW test indicates that rates of per-student discipline were statistically significantly greater than the rates of per-student discipline majority White schools ($z = -4.703, p < 0.001$). Similarly, for schools were American Indian and Alaska Native students were the predominant racial group, or where the student body was more than 90% Native, the rates of per-student discipline were statistically significantly greater ($z = -3.954, p < 0.001$ and $z = -3.939, p < 0.001$, respectively). However, in schools where Whites were the predominant racial group, intensely segregated Latina/o schools, and intensely segregated White schools, the rates of per-student discipline were statistically significantly *lower* than non-predominantly White or nonintensely segregated White or Latina/o schools ($z = 3.732, z = 1.32,$ and $z = 3.753$, respectively). What these WMW tests reveal is a relationship between per-student school discipline and school demographics, particularly when there schools have a high concentration of American Indian and Alaska Native students in the student body. Per-student discipline does not disaggregate the severity or distribution of discipline in the student body but does indicate that these schools are more likely to have higher rates of discipline, making students at these schools more vulnerable to punishment and tracking into the school prison pipeline we have described.

In order to further illuminate the structural relationship between schooling, race, and discipline, we repeated the WMW tests, this time using per-student discipline variables for American Indian Alaska Native, Black, Latina/o, and White students. Again, each of these focuses per-student discipline on the number of disciplinary measures recorded for students of that race, meaning only schools that report enrollment of Native, Black, Latina/o, and White students would be included in each group's per-student discipline variable.

The distribution of per-Native student discipline mirrors the trends we saw with the overall per-student discipline in Table 8. Looking specifically at discipline per-Native student, the distribution of discipline was statistically significantly higher in majority minority schools, predominantly non-White schools, and intensely segregated Native schools ($z = -5.258$, $z = 4.833$, $z = -5.617$, respectively). Across other racialized groups, we see that in both Black and White per-student disciplinary measures, there are similar, statistically significant, higher rates of per-student discipline in majority minority schools, predominantly Latina/o schools, and predominantly non-White Schools. This signals a general institutional problem, since the various WMW tests in Table 9 indicate that predominantly non-white schools have statistically significant differences in the rates of per-student discipline. Put simply, students in predominantly non-White schools are generally disciplined at higher rates, regardless of the race of the student being disciplined.

But of course, this comes with exceptions in intensely segregated schools, i.e., schools where the student body is more than 90% one race. For Native, Black, and Latina/o per-student discipline, our WMW tests showed median per-student discipline was statistically significantly lower in intensely segregated Latina/o schools ($z = 2.095$, $z = 1.979$, and $z = 2.546$ respectively, $p < 0.05$) . Only Latina/o per-student discipline had a median greater than zero (median $= 0.04$). In intensely segregated Native schools, median per-discipline rates for Black, Latina/o, and White students were statistically significantly lower, all with medians of 0.00 ($z = 3.848$, $z = 4.313$, and $z = 5.744$, respectively, $p < 0.001$). Yet for Native students in intensely segregated Native Schools, median per-student discipline was statistically significantly higher, with a median of 0.18 compared to the median of 0.00 in non-intensely segregated Native schools ($z = -5.617, p < 0.001$). American Indian and Alaska Natives are the only racial group in our WMW tests to have more schools with higher median rates of per-student discipline in intensely segregated schools where they are the largest student group. Latina/o and White per-student discipline in intensely segregated Latina/o and White schools are statistically significantly lower, than in non-intensely segregated schools.

Overall, our WMW tests reveal that race is a statistically significant factor in the rates of per-student discipline. Both in the composition of the student body and in the per-student discipline by race, schools serving a larger proportion of Native students reported higher rates of discipline. For us, this signals a systemic issue, particularly in looking at the school to prison pipeline, by highlighting the structural inequalities that exist at the school level. Again, because all of the CRDC data we use in this study is at the school level, rather than at the individual level, it is more difficult to be precise in how race is effecting the rates of school discipline, and what confounding

Table 9 Wilcoxon Rank-Sum Test: per-student discipline, by race

Variable	AI/AN ($n = 1667$)			Black ($n = 1591$)			Latina/o ($n = 1807$)			White ($n = 1811$)		
	Obs.	Med.	z-score	Obs.	Med.	z-score	Obs.	Med.	z-score	Obs.	Med.	z-score
Majority minority												
White ≥50%	688	0.00		692	0.09	−5.258***	795	0.06	−3.514***	807	0.06	−4.097***
White <50%	979	0.05		899	0.15		1012	0.07		1004	0.10	
Predominant group												
AI/AN	1564	0.00		1554	0.14	−6.007***	1759	0.07	1.432	1748	0.07	4.529***
Non-AI/AN	103	0.17		37	0.00		48	0.00		63	0.00	
Latina/o	941	0.00		874	0.09	−2.717*	1002	0.06	−4.401***	1030	0.05	−6.159***
Non-Latina/o	726	0.02		717	0.18		805	0.07		781	0.11	
White	855	0.05		776	0.16	4.833***	887	0.07	3.224**	879	0.10	3.264**
Non-white	812	0.00		815	0.10		920	0.07		932	0.06	

(continued)

Table 9 (continued)

Variable	AI/AN (n = 1667)		Black (n = 1591)	Latina/o (n = 1807)	White (n = 1811)								
	Obs.	Med.	Med.	z-score	Obs.	Med.	z-score	Obs.	Med.	z-score	Obs.	Med.	z-score
Intensely segregated													
AI/AN													
<90% AI/AN	1588	0.00	0.00	−5.617***	1574	0.14	3.848***	1783	0.07	4.313***	1771	0.07	5.744***
≥90% AI/AN	79	0.18			17	0.00		24	0.00		40	0.00	
Latina/o													
<90% Latina/o	1573	0.00	0.00	2.095*	1498	0.14	1.979*	1667	0.07	2.546*	1689	0.07	1.873
≥90% Latina/o	94	0.00	0.00		93	0.00		140	0.04		122	0.00	
White													
<90% white	1654	0.00	0.00	0.977	1583	0.13	1.475	1786	0.07	3.445***	1784	0.07	2.228*
≥90% white	13	0.00	0.00		8	0.00		21	0.04		27	0.02	

*p < 0.05; **p < 0.005; ***p < 0.001

factors may exist. Yet from the disparities in mean and median rates of discipline, and from our Wilcoxon-Mann-Whitney tests, we can see that school demographics play a statistically significant factor in the rates of discipline. Particularly for Native youth, these data reveal potential disparities and structural issues that need further investigation and analysis.

Limitations

The relationships we look at in our statistical analyses are unfortunately very narrow and do not have a robust structure to look at the many confounding or moderating variables that could affect discipline rates, at the individual and institutional level. Unfortunately, the limitations of this sample and dataset are that they rely on self-reported institutional level observations rather than student level results. Additionally, these data do not include variables that we believe are relevant to interrogating how and why discipline is disproportionately applied, and no aggregated data on actions or instances that the school deems sufficient for discipline – a student suspended for harassing another student and a student suspended for coming to school with a non-conforming hairstyle are represented simply as suspensions in the data. Additional important information should include the racial/sex demographics of teachers and staff, additional indicators of which disciplinary measures are discretionary or compulsory, and most importantly whether there is overlap in discipline (i.e., are the same few students being expelled, suspended, and physically punished multiple times, or are these one-time instances spread across the student body?). In future research and data, collection factors associated with administrative and institutional demographics are needed, as well as quantitative and/or qualitative comparative case studies on schools that to gain insight into the disciplinary experiences of students at the individual level, particularly for AI/AN youth who have been largely excluded from quantitative data in school-to-prison research.

Changing the Institution Through Self-Determination

We have spent this chapter focusing on how data may misrepresent, misunderstand, or completely overlook the experiences of American Indian and Alaska Native students to emphasize how American Indian Students are racialized and disproportionately punished, but even these data are just the tip of the iceberg in how educational institutions continue to fail American Indian students. Stories of Indigenous students and communities highlight the ways in which colonial, white supremacist states have attempted to erase people socially, culturally, spiritually, and physically from their homelands. Statistics tell their own story of how these different examples are connected to larger systems and structures of power – how the story of Jabez, Jakobe, and Micah are part of a systemic disenfranchisement of students of color, which exploits cultural perseverance as a reason for discipline rather than celebration. Rather than take a deficit-oriented perspective, we emphasize racialized disparities to highlight the inadequacies in US educational institutions serving Indigenous students.

Statistics, on the surface, present a grim state of affairs for American Indian student achievement and are misinterpreted as the individual fault or problem of American Indian students, placing the burden of performance on students rather than on the schools failing them. Just as Jabez Oates' principal blamed his mother and culture rather than reconsidering the exclusionary school policy, this lens not only fails students but enhances white supremacy. Under this lens, it is simpler to categorize American Indian students as problems, incompatible within education settings. However, delving deeper into the statistical analyses as we have sought to do in this article, the numbers reveal narratives of how institutions of education have failed Indigenous students, and students of color generally. This necessitates questioning the pedagogical environment and curriculum in which Indigenous learners are being instructed, and also how Indigenous students see themselves within education settings. Fundamental to the success of Indigenous students and more broadly students of color are curriculums that are grounded in community, reciprocity, cultural reflexivity, and self-determination.

American Indian and Alaska Native students are guaranteed education through treaties, statutes, administrative policies, and executive statements. Historically, this has meant assimilation through education that enforces white supremacist, eurocentric ways of learning and knowing. In the 43 years since *Morton v. Mancari* (1974), United States policy has embraced the liminal status of Native peoples in the United States – recognizing American Indians and Alaska Natives both as racialized people and people who possess a unique political status derived from history, treaties, Tribal citizenship, and federal laws and policies (Brayboy 2005). Yet even in this era of self-determination, the liminal status recognized by courts of law holds little weight in combating classroom discipline and the school to prison pipeline. Intervention from federal authorities can provide some relief, like when the Office of Civil Rights intervened in Winner School District, mentioned earlier in the article, but this is an exceptional case for a systemic issue. American Indian and Alaska Native's political status that guarantees education is instead negated by wake of racialized, colonial policies from dress codes to zero tolerance that push American Indian, Alaska Native, Native Hawaiian, Black, Latino, and other students of color out of schools and into prisons. The problem comes from the fact that the institution of schools themselves may in fact be too rooted in a colonial, white supremacist agenda to facilitate the inclusion of all students of color, or enable the success of all students. This pushes us to consider how and in what ways Indigenous students should be better served through educational environments that valuate Indigenous ways of being and learning – what we would call culturally relevant institutions.

Creating culturally relevant institutions means incorporating culturally relevant schooling and pedagogy to rework institutions from their foundations. A teacher dedicated to culturally responsive schooling can do wonders for a classroom of Indigenous students, but if this is done within a school that sends students home for having the wrong haircut, or speaking out at the wrong time, or some other form of discipline, these important efforts of pedagogy and schooling are negated by institutional constraints. We suggest that culturally relevant institutions come from principles found in Critical Indigenous Research Methodologies ("CIRM"), grounding research and curriculum, as well as institutional structure, in indigenous knowledge systems, with emancipatory and anti-colonial focuses concentrating on the needs of communities in which the research is being engaged.

The overarching principles of CIRM are rooted in the four "r's": relationships, responsibility, respect, and reciprocity and accountability (Brayboy et al. 2012). These principles focus research on the strengths and needs of a community, as identified by the community. Within this framework, the community is not the *object* of inquiry but rather a research partner that instills Indigenous values, knowledges, and guidance into the research process. CIRM is an emancipatory method of inquiry as it pushes Indigenous communities "to reclaim research and knowledge-making practices that are driven by indigenous peoples," (2012, p. 425). This reclamation of what knowledge making processes constitute implicates how Indigenous students learn and are perceived within education settings. Institutionally reforming how the subjugated knowledges, histories, and practices of Indigenous peoples is instrumental in confronting and counterbalancing education models that over punish, under value, and under serve Indigenous students. Maori Scholar Linda Smith stresses the importance of engaging in work that is self-reflexive and that also points to the knowledges and needs of the communities in which scholars work. Smith's *Decolonizing Methodologies* (2012) encourages research to be grounded in community's ways of being and knowing, and in partnership with those communities. The same principle of reflexivity in the production of knowledge via research is true in the classroom, in the curriculum, and must also be true for the institution of schooling itself. Lumbee scholar Bryan Brayboy notes, the concepts of culture, knowledge, and power take on new meaning when examined through an Indigenous lens. Governmental and educational policies constructed schools as institutions with the goal of assimilation and colonization. As Brayboy (2005) explains, "colonization has been so complete that even many American Indians fail to recognize that we are taking up colonialist ideas when we fail to express ourselves in ways that may challenge dominant society's ideas about who and what we are supposed to be, how we are supposed to behave, and what we are supposed to be within the larger population" (p. 431). Pedagogically and administratively, colonial models of education have negatively influenced how American Indian students have come to be seen within education settings. In this light, American Indian students cultures, like Jabez, Micah, and Jakobe's hair, are branded as negative, distracting behaviors in need of institutional intervention, and correction through discipline. The right of Indigenous communities and students to actively participate and manage what practices are administered in learning is integral in decolonizing educational institutions.

Chicana scholar Gloria Anzaldua underscores the destructive effects of colonial ideologies and practices have had on colonized peoples; she notes "[b]y taking away our self-determination, it has made us weak and empty." (1999, p. 108). Culturally responsive curriculum brings self-determination back to the educational setting by forefronting students' unique cultural experiences and students actively take part in producing new academic knowledges (Belgarde et al. 2003, p. 42). Within the context of the education of American Indian students, sovereignty and self-determination are paramount in developing culturally relevant curriculums that augment the success of American Indian students (Castagno and Brayboy 2008). However, gaining access to culturally relevant curriculum is not simple, even when such programs exist. As was evident in the Winner School District suit, American Indian students had an on-reservation alternative, but it presented additional difficulties and burdens in travel and living away from families. Thus culturally relevant curriculum must become a process that reshapes schools' institutional functions, changing schools as sites of assimilation in to facilitators of self-determination through education – regardless of location. Access to educational spaces which provide students with the benefit of cultural reflexivity are a means to allay and eventually counteract the negative legacy of assimilationist colonial education policies. In these spaces, as opposed to traditional spaces of education, the bodies and epistemologies of Indigenous students are not the subjects of scrutiny, contestation, or punitive discipline. Rather, their experiences and ways of being are sources of strength and repositories of knowledge.

Conclusion and Future Directions

In 1916, Seneca scholar Arthur C. Parker wrote:

> Human beings have a primary right to an intellectual life, but civilization has swept down upon groups of Indians and, by destroying their relationships to nature, blighted or banished their intellectual life, and left a group of people mentally confused....The Indians must have a thought-world given back. Their intellectual world must have direct relation to their world of responsible acts and spontaneous experiences. (p. 258)

The stories, history, and data provided in this chapter underscore the extent to which American Indian, Black, and Latino students disproportionately disciplined and punished in schools, particularly in Arizona where the punishment of Black and American Indian youth exceeds their representation in the student population. Though our data and analysis highlight the negative consequences of discipline, they also highlight the dearth of what is known about the day to day experiences of individual students, particularly Indigenous students that are directly affected by disproportionate rates of punishment and negative educational outcomes. Anecdotal evidence like the stories of Jabez Oates, Malachi Wilson, and Jakobe Sanden allow us to peek behind the curtain of data and see how neutrally worded policies come with disciplinary consequences, particularly for Indigenous students attempting to live the traditions and culture of their peoples, and how instructors and administrators brand them as outsiders asking for something more than an education. The referrals to the principal's office, phone calls from administrators, and referrals home because their physical appearances disrupted the learning environment of their peers highlight how native bodies are marked in the education system. It is a remnant of a colonial past that coercively disciplined and attempted to assimilate indigenous peoples into Western representative models of students and pupils.

However, we also know that programs promoting culturally responsive curriculum have a record of successfully funneling students into higher education, transforming the institutional pipeline from prison to community engagement. In Tucson, Arizona, for example, ethnic studies programs were integrated into the Tuscon Unified School District, offering courses for African American, American Indian, and Mexican American studies that used culturally relevant pedagogies and teaching practices to transform how students interact with the education system. These programs were initiated within the public schools at all levels to redress low graduation rates, poor performance rates on standardized examinations, and overall poor academic achievement among their students (Hawley 2012). Mexican American Studies (MAS) and American Indian Studies in particular emphasized the indigenous traditions of peoples of the southwest and Central and South America, though because of the white supremacist and anti-immigration political climate, Mexican American Studies was targeted by local politicians as a source of hostility that they sought to eliminate all of the ethnic studies programs in TUSD and the state.

Programmatically, MAS advances both indigenous knowledge values emanating from Mexico and also provided history lessons that included Mexican history of the southwestern United States into class discussions. The program became the subject of scorn by local legislators and was effectively banned for purportedly promoting curriculum that advocated for an ethnic group, against an ethnic group, or the overthrow of the US government. In truth, the ethnic studies program was initiated to advance the success of its students by using culturally relevant and reflective curriculum, Tucson MAS curriculum was derived from Indigenous knowledge bases by making use of the Mexican Indigenous cultural concepts of Nahui Ollin (Our Age) that encompass notions of Tezcatlipoca (self-reflection), Quetzalcoatl (precious and beautiful knowledge), Huitzilopochtli (the will to act), and Xipe Totec (transformation) and the Mayan principle of In Lak Ech (you are my other me) (Villanueva 2013). The curriculum included the use of creation stories, decolonial pedagogies, self-reflection, Chicano history.

The culturally responsive curriculum grounded in community, which included Indigenous and cultural history salient to the Mexican American and Latino students with backgrounds from Central America proved to be an effective pedagogical tool in navigating a hostile educational institution. Over time, the program was successful and resulted in graduation rates, specifically in 2008 MAS students were 18% more likely to pass AIMs testing. Arizona's Instrument to Measure Standards (AIMS) Test is a standardized test used to examine academic achievement in math, reading, writing, and in science from public school students in grades 3–12. In 2010, the students were 64% more likely to pass aims testing. Moreover, MAS students were shown to be 162% more likely to pass than students who did participate in MAS courses. These increased rates of academic performance ultimately contributed to students successfully transitioning out of high-school via graduation as opposed to exiting the education system via expulsion or drop out. Students who participated in MAS courses were between 51% and 108% more likely to graduate from high school than non-MAS students. The positive effect of Tucson MAS curriculum on students is exemplary of how programs grounded in culturally relevant pedagogies and practices and intentionally designed for students to engage their histories, epistemologies, can have on successful education outcomes for marginalized populations. With students being taught in styles of instruction that engaged and valued Indigenous pedagogies and epistemologies, the relations of power within the classroom shifted. The instruction and classroom environment did not hinge on obedience and discipline management rather the classroom space was liberatory and promoted the self-expression of students in ways relevant to their respective histories and communities.

We believe that taking away culture, forcing assimilation, and removing an Indigenous *thought world* in curriculum leads to damaging effects in education outcomes, a manifestation of which are disparate rates of punishment. Indigenous students, through education models that result in disparate rates of punishment, and subsequent egresses from spaces of learning, are deprived of a right to education. Moreover, maintaining a system that alienates Indigenous children from the time they enter school leads, invariably, to deleterious effects, including the overrepresentation of Indigenous peoples in prisons. History and present show that the state of education for students of color, particularly American Indian students, is interwoven with state managed discipline. Discipline in schools is a continuation of education's colonial legacy. Boarding schools attempted to erase Indigenous values and supplant cultural knowledges with European and American ways of being. Institutional commitments to culturally relevant curriculums and teacher practices are a step towards amending fraught experiences of Indigenous students in education.

References

Adams D (1995) Education for extinction: American Indians and the boarding school experience. University Press of Kansas, Lawrence, pp 1875–1928

Anzaldúa G (1999) La Frontera/Borderlands: The New Mestiza (2nd Ed.). Aunt Lute Books, San Francisco

Belgarde MJ, Mitchell R, Arquero A (2003) "What do we have to do to create culturally-responsive programs?: the challenge of transforming American Indian teacher education," indigenous perspectives of teacher education: beyond perceived border. Action Teach Educ XXIV(2):42–54

Bever L (2015) Native American boy pulled from class over Mohawk haircut. The Washington Post. Retrieved From: https://www.washingtonpost.com/news/morning-mix/wp/2015/09/19/native-american-boy-pulled-from-class-over-mohawk-haircut/?utm_term=.3118557b6b0d

Brayboy BMcKJ (2005) Towards a tribal critical race theory in education. Urban Review, 37(5), 425–446

Brayboy BMcKJ, Castagno AE (2009) Self-determination through self-education: Culturally responsive schooling for Indigenous students in the USA. Teaching Education, 20(1), 31–53

Brayboy BMcKJ, Maaka MJ (2015) K–12 achievement for indigenous students. J American Indian Education, 54(1), 63–98

Brayboy BMJ, Gough HR, Leonard R, Roehl RF, Solyom JA (2012) Reclaiming scholarship: critical indigenous research methodologies. In: Handbook of qualitative research. Jossey-Bass, San Francisco, CA, pp 423–450

Castagno AE (2012) "They prepared me to be a teacher, but not a culturally responsive navajo teacher for navajo kids": A Tribal Critical Race Theory Analysis of an Indigenous Teacher Preparation Program. J American Indian Education, 51(1), 3–21

Castagno AE, Brayboy BMcKJ (2008) Culturally responsive schooling for Indigenous youth: A review of the literature. Review of Educational Research, 78(4), 941–993

Christle CA, Jolivette K, Nelson CM (2005) Breaking the school to prison pipeline: Identifying school risk and protective factors for youth delinquency. Exceptionality, 13(2), 69–88

Christle CA, Jolivette K, Nelson CM (2007) School characteristics related to high school dropout rates. Remedial and Special education, 28(6), 325–339

Darling-Hammond L (2015) The flat world and education: How America's commitment to equity will determine our future. Teachers College Press, New York

DeMille D (2015) Native American child sent home over traditional Mohawk. USA Today/St. George Spectrum. Retrieved from http://www.usatoday.com

Ellis C (1996) To change them forever: Indian education at the Rainy Mountain Boarding School, 1893–1920. University of Oklahoma Press, Norman

Fonrouge G (2017) American-Indian boy banned from school for having long hair. New York Post. Retrieved from https://nypost.com/2017/08/24/american-indian-boy-banned-from-school-for-having-long-hair/

Gilmore RW (2007) Golden gulag: prisons, surplus, crisis, and opposition in globalizing California. Univ of California Press, Berkeley

Hawley WD (2012) An empirical analysis of the effects of Mexican American studies participation on student achievement within Tucson Unified School District. Doctoral dissertation, The University of Arizona

Healey MA (2013) The school-to-prison pipeline tragedy on Montana's American Indian reservations. N Y Univ Rev Law Soc Change 37:670–726

Heitzeg NA (2009) Education or incarceration: zero tolerance policies and the school to prison pipeline (Forum on Public Policy Online). Retrieved from http://www.eric.ed.gov/PDFS/EJ870076.pdf

Jung MK, Vargas JC, Bonilla-Silva E (2011) State of white supremacy: racism, governance, and the United States. Stanford University Press, Palo Alto

Kim CY (2009/2010) Procedures for public law remediation in school-to-prison pipeline litigation: lessons learned from Antoine v. Winner School District. N Y Law School Law Rev 54:956–974

Ladson-Billings G (1998) Just what is critical race theory and what's it doing in a nice field like education? International journal of qualitative studies in education, 11(1), 7–24

Laura CT (2014) Being bad: My baby brother and the school-to-prison pipeline. New York, NY: Teachers College Press

Lomawaima KT (2000) Tribal sovereigns: Reframing research in American Indian education. Harvard Educational Review, 70(1), 1–23

Lomawaima KT, McCarty TL (2006) "To remain an Indian": lessons in democracy from a century of native American education. Teachers College Press, New York

Longest KC (2012) Using Stata for quantitative analysis. SAGE Publications, New York

Losen D (2011) Discipline policies, successful schools, and racial justice. The civil rights project/Proyecto Derechos Civiles. Available at http://escholarship.org/uc/item/4151361g

McCarty T, Lee T (2014) Critical culturally sustaining/revitalizing pedagogy and Indigenous education sovereignty. Harvard Educational Review, 84(1), 101–124

Morris MW (2016) Pushout: the criminalization of black girls in schools. The New Press, New York

Morton v. Mancari (1974) 417 U.S. 535

Moya-Smith S (2014) Navajo kindergartner sent home from school, Ordered to Cut His Hair. Indian Country Today. Retrieved From: https://newsmaven.io/indiancountrytoday/archive/navajo-kindergartner-sent-home-from-school-ordered-to-cut-his-hair-Q6N9lYjFWESBNQlS39YHmw/

Nance JP (2014) Students, police, and the school-to-prison pipeline. Wash Univ Law Rev 93(4):919–987

Nance JP (2015) Students, police, and the school-to-prison pipeline. Wash Univ Law Rev 93, 919–987

National Congress of the American Indian (NCAI) (2015) Are native youth being pushed into prison? Retrieved from http://www.ncai.org/policy-research-center/research-data/prc-publications/School-to-Prison_Pipeline_Infographic.pdf

Noguera PA (2003) Schools, prisons, and social implications of punishment: rethinking disciplinary practices. Theory Pract 42(4):341–350

Norris T, Vines PL, Hoeffel EM (2012) The American Indian and Alaska native population: 2010 census briefs. United States Census Bureau. Retrieved from: https://www.census.gov/prod/cen2010/briefs/c2010br-10.pdf

Orfield G, Schley S, Glass D, Reardon S (1994) The growth of segregation in American schools: Changing patterns of separation and poverty since 1968. Equity & Excellence in Education, 27 (1), 5–8

Quijano A (2000) Coloniality of power, Eurocentrism and Latin America. Nepantla: Views from South 1(3):533–580

Redfield SE, Nance JP (2016) School-to-prison pipeline: preliminary report. American Bar Association, School to prison pipeline task force. Available at https://www.americanbar.org/content/dam/aba/administrative/diversity_pipeline/stp_preliminary_report_final.authcheckdam.pdf

Smith LT (2012) Decolonizing methodologies: Research and indigenous peoples. Zed Books Ltd., New York

Shotton HJ, Lowe SC, Waterman SJ (eds) (2013) Beyond the asterisk: understanding native students in higher education. Stylus Publishing, LLC, Sterling

Tuzzolo E, Hewitt DT (2006) Rebuilding inequity: the re-emergence of the school-to-prison pipeline in New Orleans. High Sch J 90:59–68

United States Department of Education (2014) Data snapshot:school discipline. Issue brief no.1 Office for Civil Rights. Accessed online at http://ocrdata.ed.gov/Downloads/CRDC-School-Discipline-Snapshot.pdf

US Census Bureau (2016) Table B02001 race, American community survey. Retrieved from https://factfinder.census.gov/faces/tableservices/jsf/pages/productview.xhtml?pid=ACS_17_1YR_B02001&prodType=table

Vaught SE (2011) Racism, public schooling, and the entrenchment of white supremacy: a critical race ethnography. State University of New York Press, Albany

Vaught SE (2017) Compulsory: Education and the dispossession of youth in a prison school. University of Minnesota Press, Minneapolis

Villanueva S (2013) Teaching as a healing craft: decolonizing the classroom and creating spaces of hopeful resistance through Chicano-indigenous pedagogical praxis. Urban Rev 45:23–40

Wallace Jr JM, Goodkind S, Wallace CM, Bachman JG (2008) Racial, ethnic, and gender differences in school discipline among US high school students: 1991–2005. The Negro educational review 59(1–2), 47–62

Winn MT, Behizadeh N (2011) The right to be literate: literacy, education, and the school-to-prison pipeline. Rev Res Educ 35:147–173

Wood B (2015) American Indian student at Utah's arrowhead elementary told to cut his Mohawk or leave. Salt Lake Tribune. Retrieved from http://www.sltrib.com

Systems of Support: What Institutions of Higher Education Can Do for Indigenous Communities

34

Jessica A. Solyom, Jeremiah A. Chin, Bryan McKinley Jones Brayboy, Amber Poleviyuma, Sarah Abuwandi, Alexus Richmond, Amanda Tachine, Colin Ben, and Megan Bang

Contents

Introduction	607
The Education Debt: Colonization Through Education	610
Building Nations and Local Capacity Through Education	613
"Make Men of Them": Programs Serving Indigenous Boys and Men	614
The Hale Mua Initiative	616
American Indian Summer Bridge Program	618
State of Programming for Native Men and Boys	619

J. A. Solyom · C. Ben
Arizona State University, School of Social Transformation, Tempe, AZ, USA

J. A. Chin · B. M. J. Brayboy (✉)
Arizona State University, Tempe, AZ, USA
e-mail: Bryan.Brayboy@asu.edu

A. Poleviyuma
Hopi-Tewa Women's Coalition to End Abuse, Second Mesa, AZ, USA

S. Abuwandi
Arizona State University, Phoenix, AZ, USA

A. Richmond
University of Colorado Boulder, Denver, CO, USA

Indian education at Arizona State University, Tempe, AZ, USA

A. Tachine
American Indian College Fund, Denver, CO, USA

M. Bang
Northwestern University, Evanston, IL, USA

© Springer Nature Singapore Pte Ltd. 2019
E. A. McKinley, L. T. Smith (eds.), *Handbook of Indigenous Education*,
https://doi.org/10.1007/978-981-10-3899-0_48

Principles for Successful Indigenous-Serving Programs and Liaisons 620
    Empower: Nurturing Indigenous Ways of Being and Knowing 621
    Enact: Spiritual Practices and Sharing Stories 622
    Engage: Relationships with People and Place Matter 622
    Enlighten: Reciprocal Learning from Engaging with Family,
    Elders, and Mentors 623
    Envision: Purpose-Driven Framework 624
    Enhance: Institutional and Tribal Support 624
Sustaining Systems of Support: Institutional Partnerships with Indigenous Peoples 625
Conclusion 627
References 628

Abstract

The purpose of this chapter is to highlight ways institutions of higher education (IHEs) can support culturally relevant community-driven measures and asset-based research that allows Native students to excel academically and display enhanced well-being, self-efficacy, and self-esteem (McCarty, Teach Educ 20:7–29, 2009). This chapter presents an overview of the challenging social and academic context facing Indigenous boys and men (ages 12–25) in the United States. We argue that Indigenous peoples know how to successfully develop research and engaging learning spaces that advance anti-oppressive education and "permits historical and contemporary perspectives of Indigenous material culture to critically wrestle with dominant discourses" so that Native youth develop a stronger sense of identity and self-confidence (Bequette, Stud Art Educ 55:214–226, 2014, p. 215). Programs that prepare Native boys and men to be academically and culturally successful do so by using asset-based approaches to respond to existing need, placing Native peoples in position as leaders, and understanding that successful mentors and highly qualified teachers are not always one and the same. Furthermore, these programs demonstrate a commitment to capacity- and nation-building efforts and respond to historical trauma and coloniality in Indigenous communities. We introduce two programs as examples, one located in the southwest and one in the pacific that demonstrate support for courses of study, activities, or resources designed by community members and education leaders. Using these programs as examples, we offer six principles that appear to guide successful programs. These principles are intended to serve as the beginning of a conversation with the understanding that more can and should be added.

    Students are more likely to develop healthy identity formation, be more self-directed and politically active, and have a positive influence on their tribal communities when IHEs recognize the challenges facing Indigenous students and work to complement education programing rather than seek to dominate and control it. This understanding is important because even though they are designed to assist or address issues facing Native youth, IHEs may create programs that overtake, superimpose, or otherwise colonize community efforts. We conclude by offering recommendations for how IHEs can form meaningful relationships and partnership with existing or emerging community-based efforts to create systems of support that center Indigenous communities and knowledges as partners rather than subjects or objects.

Keywords

Indigenous education · Community-based programs · Youth · Nation building · Capacity building

Introduction

> But you who are wise must know, that different Nations have different Conceptions of things; and you will therefore not take it amiss, if our Ideas of this Kind of Education happen not to be the same with yours. We have had some Experience of it: Several of our Young People were formerly brought up at the Colleges of the Northern Provinces; they were instructed in all your Sciences; but when they came back to us they were bad Runners, ignorant of every means of living in the Woods, unable to bear either Cold or Hunger, knew neither how to build a Cabin, take a Deer, or kill an Enemy, spoke our Language imperfectly; were therefore neither fit for Hunters, Warriors, or Counsellors; they were totally good for nothing. We are however not the less obliged by your kind Offer, tho' we decline accepting it; and to show our grateful Sense of it, if the Gentlemen of Virginia will send us a dozen of their Sons, we will take great Care of their Education, instruct them in all we know, and make *Men* of them.
>
> *Speaker for the Haudenosaunee (Iroquois Confederacy), as told by Benjamin Franklin,* Remarks Concerning the Savages of North America (1784)

In the last 50 years, US federal education policy has slowly embraced collaboration with Indigenous peoples that recognizes the importance of Indigenous knowledges in formal education. However, formal and long-lasting partnerships between Indigenous peoples and local institutions of higher education (IHEs) remain tenuous. Before we get into the details of why that is, it is critical to understand the foundation of Indian education in the United States. We begin by acknowledging the entirety of the United States exists on Indigenous lands. Nearly all of the 3.7 million square miles of land were taken by force, policies, or treaties, usually in exchange for promises of health, education, protection, and welfare. With over 500 treaties signed, the majority of promises made have not been honored.

Broken treaties and federally driven policies of attempted physical and epistemological genocide have left a wake of significant present-day economic, health, and education disparities for Indigenous youth (Throughout this chapter, we use the terms Indigenous and Native to refer generally to American Indian, Alaska Native, Native Hawaiian, and other Pacific Islander peoples colonized by the United States. Though we recognize this is a geographically dispersed, diverse, and highly different population, our terminology recognizes the history of these peoples as the first inhabitants of the lands taken, colonized, annexed, or otherwise seized by the United States. We try to be as specific as possible talking about different populations and regions). In 2015, the Centers for Disease Control and Prevention reported suicide as the second leading cause of death for American Indian and Alaska Native (AIAN) and Native Hawaiian and Pacific Islander (NHPI) youths ages 15–24. Furthermore, a 2016 analysis of the National Youth Risk Behavior Survey found that US Indigenous youth ages 15–24 were no more likely to consider suicide than other groups yet were 25.5% more likely to attempt suicide (Qiao and Bell 2017).

When we focus on education measures, disparities begin in early childhood. In 2014, the US Department of Education reported that Native kindergartners were twice as likely to be held back as their white peers with boys representing 61% of those held back. As students matriculate through the educational "pipeline," national standardized testing reveals only 21% of AIAN and 28% of NHPI fourth graders (~9 years old), and 22% of AIAN and 24% of NHPI eighth graders (~13 years old) score "proficient" or above in reading (National Center for Education Statistics 2015, Table 221.20). In mathematics, 23% of AIAN and 30% of NHPI fourth graders scored at or above proficient, while 20% of AIAN and 29% of NHPI eighth graders scored above proficient (National Center for Education Statistics 2015, Table 222.20). Compared to their non-Native peers, Native students are more likely to be mislabeled as having learning disabilities and placed in special education classes (NIEA n.d., p. 26). Given these dire statistics, disparities continue through secondary and postsecondary/tertiary education.

In 2013, the national secondary school graduation rate for all AIAN students was 67%, which was 14.2% below the national average (National Center for Education Statistics 2015, Table 219.40) (problematically, US national education data has only begun to report Pacific Islanders as a discrete group since 2011. In this graduation rate data, Pacific Islander populations are bundled into an overbroad "Asian or Pacific Islander" category, making data unspecific to Native Hawaiians and Pacific Islanders). For the nearly 48,000 students enrolled in government-run Bureau of Indian Education schools, the graduation rate in 2014 was 53% (Executive Office of the President 2014). While the enrollment of Indigenous students in IHEs has more than doubled in the past 30 years, only 13% of Natives earned bachelor's degrees, and only 5% earned graduate or professional degrees – less than half of the national average for both bachelors and graduate degrees (NCAI 2012).

For Indigenous boys and men, educational disparities become more stark. In the 2012–2013 academic year, the high school graduation rate for AIAN males was 65%, 5% lower than the 70% graduation rate for Indigenous females (National Center for Education Statistics 2015, Table 219.40). Graduation rates are intimately connected to school discipline. According to the US Department of Education's Office for Civil Rights, in the 2011–2012 school year, Native boys were disciplined at nearly double the rate of their White peers in primary and secondary education. For out-of-school suspensions, more Black and AIAN boys were suspended than all other racial groups combined. Thirteen percent of AIAN boys received an out-of-school suspension in the 2011–2012 school year, compared to 7% of Native Hawaiian/Pacific Islander boys, and more than double the 6% of White boys receiving suspensions (there is a certain level of awkwardness here that is separating out American Indian and Alaska Native children from Native Hawaiian and Pacific Islander children. The authors of this chapter would, under other circumstances, characterize all these children as Indigenous. And, they are. The US system of classification, however, separates the two groups out. For us to try to disaggregate these data in meaningful ways is problematic. Therefore, we are inclined to leave it as is but respectfully acknowledge that the problem of labeling is an important one). AIAN girls were suspended at 7% (half the rate of Native boys) yet at nearly triple the rate of suspensions for White girls (at 2%) (2012). These statistics demonstrate that Indigenous boys and girls are more often being problematized in school settings, which can derail their educational progress.

Disparities between Indigenous men and women persist in college enrollment patterns (importantly, this language of gender and sex in statistical data is largely essentialist and binary. These large samples, particularly in government data, do not account for trans, two spirit, or otherwise gendered or sexed populations and largely depend on colonial, patriarchal, cisgender, heteronormative politics. Keeping this in mind, we present this data in this way to generalize as to the way that Indigenous populations have been constrained and defined according to colonial norms, resulting in the targeting of cisgendered males, under a colonial patriarchal framework). In 1976 AIAN male and female enrollment in undergraduate education was evenly split (49.9% male, 50.1% female), yet in 2015 parity shifted to 40.4% male and 59.6% female among American Indian and Alaska Natives. For NHPI in 2015, males represented 46.57% of enrolled NHPI undergraduate students. However, over the past 30 years, enrollment inverted for AIAN males in graduate education. In 1976 AIAN males represented 58.3% of AIAN graduate students yet dropped to 36% in 2015. Similarly, NHPI males only make up 38.5% of the graduate student population (National Center for Education Statistics 2015, Table 306.10).

These statistics are not intended to downplay the achievements of Native students; our intent is to emphasize the decline and disparities in AIAN and NHPI male enrollment as they represent larger statistical trends that Indigenous boys and men face that are distinct institutional and systemic problems. The numbers speak to a nationwide, systematic failure to fulfill the promises of health, education, protection, and welfare as articulated in treaty negotiations. Rather than speak of an "achievement gap" or "education deficit," language that wrongly frames the problem as individualized failings of Native youth or communities and unjustly burdens Indigenous peoples, we present these disparities in an acknowledgement of what Gloria Ladson-Billings refers to as the "education debt" (2006). Shifting understanding from deficit to debt recognizes that educational inequities are not natural phenomena but by-products of a history of colonization, oppression, and assimilation – creating a debt that must be repaid through acknowledgment, engagement, and opportunities.

As demonstrated by the epigraph at the beginning of this chapter, education provided by IHEs may not always be beneficial to address the multifaceted problems faced by Native communities. Imperial education that forces Euro-Western norms, ideals, and values has not – and will not – improve Indigenous peoples. Too often, formal education may turn young men into "bad Runners" who have acquired a college degree but who are unable to help their communities. A colonial approach fails to understand the critical role of taking a fuller, more rounded approach to learning, being, and living as an Indigenous person, or Indigenous man, while also being aware of the myriad interconnected challenges and advantages that Indigenous people face. We look to Indigenous community perspectives to provide insight that focuses on preparing "good Runners," thereby mending this gap in knowledge between Indigenous communities and IHEs.

In the next sections, we consider ways in which institutions of higher education can help repay the education debt through meaningful partnerships with Indigenous peoples. We look at ways in which Indigenous communities have created programs that center Indigenous peoples as leaders as well as Indigenous ontologies (ways of being) and epistemologies (ways of knowing) in order to repair the harms of coloniality. These programs reimagine the ways in which IHEs can better serve Indigenous peoples (we want to be clear that IHEs, in this model, serve tribal nations and communities. They do not dictate the challenges, questions, or issues addressed or explored by research, initiatives, or programs. Rather, IHEs respond to the requests and desires of communities and tribes). The next section traces the origins of the education debt for Indigenous youth by offering a partial exploration of the history of assimilation in education as a way to understand why these historical injuries have not healed. Next, we explore ideas of nation- and capacity-building to frame what we believe to be the goals for relationships between IHEs and Indigenous communities. Third, we present two key programs that embrace community efforts and culturally meaningful ways of Indigenous learning, being, and knowing. One program focuses on educating Native boys and men on best practices as *citizens of their Indigenous nations*, and the other focuses on the role of formal Western education in increasing graduation and college success for Native boys and men. Both are committed to treating and shaping Native men and boys as future leaders within their communities and respective fields. Drawing on these efforts, we conclude by presenting considerations for how IHEs can forge meaningful connections that support asset-based community programs.

The Education Debt: Colonization Through Education

> One day some white people came among us and called a meeting of the parents... They had come after some boys and girls and wanted to take them a long way off to a place about which we knew nothing. I consented at once, though I could think of nothing else but that these white people wanted to take us far away and kill us... To me it meant death, but bravery was part of my blood, so I did not hesitate. Luther Standing Bear (Lomawaima and McCarty 2006, p. 16)

Throughout the nineteenth and twentieth centuries, the US federal government and Christian missionary organizations actively targeted Native youth for colonization and assimilation into White European standards. This was accomplished under the guise of providing education through boarding schools. The objectives for this assimilationist agenda were largely driven by Carlisle Indian Industrial

School founder Captain Richard H. Pratt who believed education should be used as a strategy to "Kill the Indian, [and] Save the Man." In other words, schooling would become a tool to eliminate the spiritual, cultural, and linguistic orientations of students and replaced with White Eurocentric practices and values. Today numerous testimonials from boarding school students, survivors, and staff remain, which paint vivid pictures of the deplorable actions used by school administrators and personnel to accomplish these objectives – proving that Standing Bear's suspicions about being taken away and killed were well founded.

Countless Native children and youth were ripped from their communities and alienated from their sense of humanity, separated from their families and homelands, in many cases indefinitely. Students were restricted from accessing their personal belongings and traditions including wearing traditional clothing and hairstyles. Moreover, they were stripped from their livelihood, speaking the language of their ancestors, and nurturing the development of their cultural and ancestral knowledges. The result has manifested in a condition known today as "historical trauma." Historical trauma refers to a "cumulative emotional and psychological wounding, over the lifespan and across generations, emanating from massive group trauma experiences" (Brave Heart 2003, p. 7) (although historical trauma research has reached wide acceptance in education and health sciences research, there is another body of scholarship that questions, doubts, and critiques historical trauma frameworks to push historical trauma away from an individual/community problem in order to spotlight current structural actors that continue to perpetuate oppression and trauma. Kirmayer, Gone, and Moses (2014). We argue that recognizing historical trauma as an individual, community, and structural issue is more multifaceted, incorporating past oppressions to highlight ongoing harms from past oppressions and present-day responsibilities of actors who have, and continue to, engage in the misappropriation, colonization, and harm of Indigenous peoples). Restricting use of heritage language and cultural expression, for example, not only facilitated assimilation, it created a silence and change in the learned behaviors of individuals who were forced to suppress emotions and thoughts to themselves (Lomawaima and McCarty 2006). These actions were further compounded by legislation such as the 1819 Civilization Fund Act, which set aside monies for missionaries to establish schools on reservations in Indian Country that promoted the conversion to Christianity and colonization efforts, and the 1892 Thomas J. Morgan "Rules for Indian Courts," which effectively outlawed American Indian spiritual and religious expressions and practices. The psychological pain and spiritual grief resulting from such oppressive conditions led to harms across generations and an overall skepticism of federal and state systems. For some Native peoples, this legacy has led to a deep distrust toward formal education institutions and the US federal government.

While Native communities proceed to address the current impacts and present-day manifestations of historical trauma, Native students continue to experience difficulty with the education system. The cycle of colonialism remains. Native students are likely to face educational contexts with curriculum and pedagogical practices that fail to recognize Indigenous perceptions, values, worldviews, learning styles, and knowledges as legitimate. Furthermore, Native students have to navigate marginalization, racism, and hostile policies. For those Native students who identify strongly with their Native cultural identity, they may be more likely to face cultural discontinuity (Brayboy 2004, 2005) and personhood invalidation (Tachine et al. 2017) between their culture and the culture of educational institutions. Native students' experiences and identities are fluid, complex, and layered with access to context of place and people. Oversimplifications of Native identity miss nuances of experiences and harm perceptions of dynamic peoples.

Empirical research and institutions often overlook this fluidity of identity formation. Low teacher and counselor expectations stunt academic, personal, and professional development opportunities, driving Indigenous scholars to explore asset- and strengths-based factors that enhance Native student persistence. These approaches include factors such as mentoring, role modeling, community support, and culturally responsive education programming (Castagno and Brayboy 2008; Shotton, Lowe, and Waterman 2013; Tachine et al. 2017). Involvement in culture-related activities and relationships with educators who have an understanding of Indigenous cultures and histories leads to positive educational experiences. However, educators and institutions are rarely held accountable for the continued perpetuation and oppression of Native peoples through Eurocentric education practices and contexts.

While the practices and implementation may have changed, US education of Indigenous students remains tied to histories of colonization and assimilation. Native students may no longer be forcibly removed from their homes, yet they remain more likely to be referred to discipline officers or experience "push out" from schools than to be put on-track for college (Solyom 2017). Reports of Native students being sent home or disciplined for having a traditional hairstyle remain common in public schools. Even students who approach graduation are sometimes punished for combining Indigenous symbols and expressions with school graduation regalia like donning hard-earned eagle feathers on their graduation caps. These stories remind us that, although a far cry from mission and boarding schools, institutions of education remain a site of trauma and cultural exclusion for Native students.

Despite ongoing challenges and an unpaid educational debt, Native communities often promote education as a source of hope and strategy for self-determination. According to Lomawaima and McCarty (2006), "Native communities have persistently and courageously fought for their continued existence as *peoples*, defined politically by their government-to-government relationship with the U.S. and culturally by their diverse governments, languages, land bases, religions, economies, education systems, and family organizations" (p. 7). Therefore, Native students are frequently encouraged throughout their academic careers to return to their communities and give back. Historically viewed as the "Indian Problem," the resilient experiences, knowledges, cultures, and ways of being demonstrated by Indigenous students suggest a strong potential to contribute and strengthen not only academia but society at large.

Building Nations and Local Capacity Through Education

In order to ensure the education debt is repaid, educational programs for Indigenous peoples must provide culturally appropriate, responsive, and respectful learning environments and opportunities. With over 570 American Indian tribes, more than 250 Alaska Native villages. Native Hawaiians, and many other Pacific Islanders, Indigenous peoples in the United States may share certain needs and desires – especially commitments to sovereignty and self-determination – but their approaches will vary depending on their unique local histories, languages, customs, and needs. In other words, historical, social, geographic, and political contexts shape Indigenous goals and visions for nation building and partnering with external institutions and governments.

Nation building can be properly understood as the "political, legal, spiritual, educational, and economic processes through which Indigenous people engage in order to build local capacity to address their educational, health, [and] legal...needs" (Brayboy et al. 2012). Nation building is directly tied to sovereignty and self-determination. Sovereignty refers to the "inherent right of [Indigenous] nations to direct their futures and engage the world in ways that are meaningful to them" (Brayboy et al. 2012, p. 17). Self-determination, which is the enactment of sovereignty, "provides greater control to tribal citizens and their government in planning, designing, implementing and controlling the public affairs of their respective tribes." Combined, sovereignty and self-determination are utilized by Indigenous nations and communities to drive nation building visions through defining long-term goals for the community including (re)imagining and (re)invigorating programs, processes, and initiatives to meet those goals.

Nation building serves as a tool for Indigenous communities to outline a set of guiding principles or philosophies for education, economic structures, systems of governance, how they will be controlled, by whom, and how this will be accomplished. A nation-building agenda fosters local leadership and situates Native peoples as leaders. This requires developing a plan for ensuring community members have the education, knowledge, and expertise to fill present and future community needs. This may require establishing a system of education and governance that ensures local processes are community owned, operated, controlled, and guided by the values, beliefs, goals, and practices of the local community. Nation building can exist outside the immediate community as Indigenous peoples foster relationships, partnerships, and programs with external or Indigenous institutions.

Nation building in education means preparing and training Native teachers, principals, and counselors who understand students' cultures, knowledges, and contexts. It also means preparing and training physicians, engineers, business entrepreneurs, social and public health practitioners, and legal thinkers who can provide direction and act in the capacity of community leaders for health and well-being, infrastructure, economic development, law and governance, and so forth. A nation building agenda identifies areas of improvement or needs that community members should focus on and emerges when tribal leaders, elders, and community members come together to identify an asset-based outlook for the future community.

Components of a nation building agenda can be short-term and narrowly focused, like a heritage language after-school program or summer arts camp; or they can be broad, long-term, and multitiered. For instance, students may express personal goals and aspirations to learn in areas of study that can improve their community economically, educationally, politically, or in well-being while keeping their culture intact and not assimilating. Under a nation-building framework, this may spark an education initiative shaped by the Indigenous community aimed at fulfilling those goals. Whatever the vision, nation building through self-education centralizes the entire community – as a people with cultural traditions, language, heritage, and governance – and takes into account both the people and the context in which they live, have lived, and hope to live.

Capacity building is essential to meet goals of nation building. One cannot expect a community or the concomitant traditions associated with a particular group to sustain themselves if the knowledge or skill sets are kept with one person. These knowledges and skills must be passed down and supported by the community so that they can continue to be transferred to generations well into the future. In knowing the history, goals, and experiences of the people, Indigenous communities utilize that knowledge to imagine ways of strengthening their communities. There must be thoughtful succession planning. The enactment of a nation building agenda through capacity building in education should not be confused with individual successes, though these should also be celebrated. The individual success must be put in context, capacity building that goes beyond formal training and role modeling to include programs and agendas that recognize and enhance the needs and roles within the community. The heart of nation building is always driven by the success of the community: to be engaged in addressing the desires, needs, and wants of community via asset-based and culturally relevant and respectful approaches.

Nation building is not a complete rejection of Western education or knowledges. Indigenous communities must sift through Western practices and knowledges to discern what best meets their community, in context. Nation building in education therefore builds on four key components: a commitment to sovereignty and self-determination, an awareness of the local and historical context of tribes, strengths-/asset-based approaches, and capacity building.

"Make Men of Them": Programs Serving Indigenous Boys and Men

To engage a nation building framework focused on capacity building, we began this chapter by considering the historical context of the education debt and presenting statistics on disparities in education. This information contextualizes some of the many issues facing Indigenous peoples, particularly Indigenous boys and men, in the United States. School discipline or declining graduation and enrollment rates for Indigenous boys and men in the United States signal a crucial need that communities are trying to address yet despite this growing need programs and solutions lack significant scholarly discussion or media attention, limiting discourse on and visibility of powerful local efforts and insights currently underway.

Our understanding of Indigenous men and boys is limited, which is antithetical to goals of nation building. Though research has explored ways in which colonization has impacted and reshaped Indigenous gender/sex dynamics by imposing White, Eurocentric norms of patriarchy and masculinity, there remains a dearth of literature specifically addressing Indigenous men or masculinities (Bitsóí 2007; Barker 2017; Perea 2017). A literature review of programs serving Indigenous boys and men in the United States found 609 articles and dissertations that mentioned programs serving Indigenous peoples, but only 48 (7%) of these programs specifically addressed issues, questions, or even disaggregated data facing Indigenous boys and men (Brayboy et al. 2016). Much of the discussions of masculinities and gender for Indigenous boys and men have wrongfully attempted to deter feminist and critical interrogations of patriarchy and masculinities in Indigenous communities or fall into the trap of attempting to "remasculinize Indigenous men... inadvertently reify[ing] heterosexist ideologies that serve conditions of imperial-colonial oppression" (Barker 2017, p. 24). This obstructs the worldviews and perspectives of Indigenous matrilineal societies. Our focus on men and boys is not an attempt to re-center men in conversations, which too frequently overemphasize cisgender male participation and obscure the critical contributions of women and LGBTQ leaders, teachers, activists, organizers, and thinkers. Instead, we focus on men and boys in education to interrogate the ways in which programs can address a holistic education that not only promotes community growth (e.g., nation building) and success by recognizing men and boys as critical sources of strength for their Indigenous nations and also reevaluate toxic, patriarchal masculinities from an Indigenous perspective.

In the next section, we describe two educational programs (the Hale Mua program in Hawai'i and the American Indian Summer Bridge Program in Arizona) that serve Indigenous boys and men and explore how they are working outside of typical academic designs to strengthen communities in distinct ways. We offer an overview of these programs followed by a general discussion of the state of programming for Native men and boys. The following information was drawn from a comprehensive literature review of programs targeting Native men and boys (Brayboy et al. 2016). The review covered 16 years of research (2000–2016) on education programs specifically designed to promote the well-being and achievement of Indigenous boys and men ages 12–25. Data analysis focused on the following three questions: what types of strengths-based education programs or interventions have been offered specific to AI/AN/NH/PI boys and men? Where? And, what successful guiding principles and practices have emerged from these interventions that lead to increased personal and academic achievement?

We present these two programs because they are illustrative of strengths-based and asset-based programs which help to inform beneficial principles and practices for supporting Native men and boys. Strengths-based approaches focus on the promises and possibilities of people, their communities, and their homelands. Such approaches draw on the expertise and knowledges of the collective with an eye toward creating a community of interdependent learners to address challenges

(Brayboy et al. 2016). Programs that use this approach see wisdom in intergenerational exchanges of knowledge that produce culturally and linguistically vibrant communities and respond to present needs and opportunities (Marlow and Siekmann 2013). Similarly, an asset-based approach imagines new possibilities through Native student's capabilities, as partners in learning and knowledge construction. Educators listen to the stories that students share about their families, life experiences, and histories and include elders, parents, and community members as active participants in schooling. Asset-based approaches stress that education must be relevant to the current struggles facing youth and must aid in learning about policies, rights, and status of Indigenous peoples (and their nation) so they can aid in nation building.

Our 2016 review of the literature revealed only nine programs that have been established for the purpose of serving the distinct needs of Native men and boys. Six of the nine programs identified were for youth ranging from 8 to 17 years old. Each program had an emphasis on general Indigenous culture, both in values and in practices. Three of the nine programs were related to education, either administered by IHEs or other local academic partners, and focused on postsecondary readiness or increasing rates of high school completion. Other programs focused on developing relationships and identity. Eight out of the nine programs focused on an individual's place and responsibilities in the home, tribal community, or greater society. Lastly, four of the nine programs emphasized the role of community mentors or role models as an aspect of the program. In general, these programs and their hosting organizations either extended or included the local Indigenous community.

We contacted the nine programs and requested interviews and/or more information. However due to a limited time frame, we were only able to interview two programs: the 'Aha Kāne Foundation (Hale Mua) and Maricopa Community Colleges (American Indian Summer Bridge Program). Both programs are grant-funded and dedicated to educating Indigenous boys and men, stressing the importance of Indigenous cultures. For this chapter, we highlight key aspects of the Hale Mua Initiative in Hawai'i and the American Indian Summer Bridge Program at Maricopa Community Colleges in Arizona (for a more detailed elaboration of the interviews and methodological approach, please refer to Brayboy et al. 2016).

The Hale Mua Initiative

Originating in 2012, the Hale Mua Initiative is a mentoring program designed to reestablish intergenerational connections between Native Hawaiian boys and men through activities, rites, and gatherings rooted in Indigenous ways of being and knowing. Groundwork for Hale Mua began in 2006 at the 'Aha Kāne Native Hawaiian Men's Conference to address issues of health and well-being among Native Hawaiian men. These conferences were designed in the spirit of traditional cultural gatherings (as opposed to European style conferences) and brought together community members to focus on traditional roles of men that had been lost. Participants noted how men had become disconnected from their cultural identity as part of family and community and appeared to be suffering from intergenerational and historic trauma, much the result of colonization. Even as these gatherings focused on the well-being of men, women outnumbered men three to one. Women participants urged male attendees to address both the low male attendance rates at 'Aha Kāne as well as the larger problems facing men on the islands. Several months after the 2012 gathering, nearly a dozen boys attempted suicide, spurring the founders of Hale Mua and the community to hold gatherings and discussions on why this was happening to their youth.

From these internal discussions, founders of Hale Mua submitted a proposal to the Queen Lili'uokalani Trust for seed funding to begin a series of programs that would extend beyond the conference or annual gathering to a more active role in the everyday lives of Native Hawaiian men and boys. The Trust, created in 1909 from lands dedicated by Queen Lili'uokalani to benefit destitute and orphaned Native Hawaiian children, provided 3 years of funding for Hale Mua and was supplemented by funds from the Atherton Family Foundation as well as the Department of Native Hawaiian Health at the John A. Burns School of Medicine. Hale Mua focused on gathering community partners and potential male mentors, ages 18–80, and boys, ages 6–8, as participants who could actively engage the mission of connection and learning in traditional Native Hawaiian ways.

Named after the Hawaiian "men's house," Hale Mua began by visiting three different communities and hosting a series of 3-day weekend retreats to discuss the meaning of mentorship and promote traditionally male activities and discussions across various life stages. In the 1st year, Hale Mua organizers sought nominations for older males identified as "successful" Hawaiian men by their community to serve as mentors who could share their knowledge with young men in traditional Native Hawaiian practices (such as fishing) as well as general knowledges (such as how to successfully interview for a dream job). This process stressed the importance of intergenerational relationships with young men and elders in creating a space and pathways for success. The young men (the mentees) were then tasked with reaching out to young boys in the following year. Over time, this ensured the gatherings would be helpful and productive, rooted in Native Hawaiian ceremonies, rites, and rituals that would ground discussions on what it means to be a Native Hawaiian man.

As an ongoing project, Hale Mua aims to have at least a 2:1 ratio of mentors to youth, to not only temper behaviors of youth but also ensure the relationships between mentors and youth come from multiple perspectives and create a wider network of support. In their own words, Hale Mua is designed around the Indigenous institution

> where Hawaiian men learned the roles and responsibilities of being a successful father, husband, and warrior, and basic occupations like farming and fishing. Elders and master practitioners served as educators. This emphasized moral character development and adherence to kapu (taboos) governing forbidden or inappropriate behavior. The education received in the Hale Mua also encouraged the preservation and maintenance of mana (power). By sustaining one's mana, each kāne fulfilled his kuleana (responsibilities) by honoring his kūpuna (elders). (Hale Mua 2017)

From inception to its ongoing course of programs, Hale Mua represents an Indigenous community-embedded project designed and orchestrated by community members in the service of intergenerational connection and responsibility. Each activity and gathering has purposes rooted in Native Hawaiian ways of being and knowing, providing youth connections to their elders in person, and sustaining the traditions of Native Hawaiian men. Long-term, Hale Mua coordinators hope to receive enough funding to create a permanent space for Hale Mua within the communities they serve – both as a sacred site of gathering and learning and for the kind of intergenerational connections and permanence that are necessary to ongoing community and well-being.

American Indian Summer Bridge Program

Since 2011, the American Indian Summer Bridge Program (AISB) at Maricopa Community Colleges (MCC) in Arizona has focused on creating a network of support for American Indian boys with the hopes of ensuring college success. The AISB is one of many programs created by the MCC to promote achievement and retention in higher education at the ten community colleges within Maricopa County, which includes the greater Phoenix Metropolitan Statistical Area, and shares borders with the Salt River Pima Maricopa Indian Community (Salt River), the Gila River Indian Community (GRIC), and Tohono O'odham Nation. Funded by a grant from Salt River, the AISB recruits a cohort of American Indian eighth grade boys, between 11 and 16 years of age, from different communities in the Phoenix area. Students are given a full scholarship to enroll in one summer college course. The course focuses on strategies for college/academic and life success and is taught by an American Indian faculty member. The program also provides ongoing events and mentoring throughout the year. Students are taken on trips to local universities, the Heard Museum in Phoenix (dedicated to American Indian art and history), the Challenger Space Museum, and other local educational learning facilities.

The "Strategies for Success" course is taught at the Chandler Gilbert Community College. The course focuses on college readiness and teaches strategies that emphasize study skills, time management, finding and utilizing financial resources for higher education, understanding and meeting faculty expectations, and using student support services available at MCC. By reaching out to eighth grade students, typically students entering or preparing to enter secondary education, the program begins the process of college transition early. This ensures that students keep postsecondary education in mind as they move through high school while connecting them with mentors and resources outside of their school or familial networks.

Central to the goals of the AISB is the network of mentors for students, providing them not only with connections and ideas for student success, but role models in higher education. As a part of the MCC Male Empowerment Network, the AISB is designed to provide a support network for males of color throughout the ten community colleges. The AISB represents an outreach program to draw together college students, graduates, and future college students to create an intergenerational support network that will last from eighth grade through college graduation. Importantly, the network goes beyond students and faculty at community colleges and features guest speakers, or men of color who are leaders in their respective fields, and emphasizes American Indian speakers in hopes of providing role models for AISB students.

Although students, mentors, staff, and instructors in the AISB are not from the same community, their shared experiences as Indigenous peoples in Arizona provide a network of support and understanding. The structure and purpose of AISB show the importance of programs, student organizations, services, and groups that focus on Indigenous experiences, particularly in educational settings. By relying on existing staff and support faculty, AISB shows the importance of having Indigenous faculty, support staff, and others who either share or understand the experiences of Indigenous boys and men as a part of the key programmatic functions. For all those involved in AISB, program organizers stress in their curricula and training the importance of respecting social and cultural norms of the different communities the students come from, to properly use instructional tools that draw from Indigenous knowledges and to include the students perspectives from their home communities. Above all, AISB creates familiarity with college campuses and expectations, focusing on a success skills course that begins the transition to higher education early in students' careers.

State of Programming for Native Men and Boys

Mentoring and role modeling are central to capacity building. Both Hale Mua and the AISB are building capacity largely through the use of role models and mentors and by using cultural knowledges. Yet the structure and content of each program is distinct. Hale Mua is grassroots, community built, and community grounded. It emphasizes the importance of relationships, cultural connectedness, ceremony, and place in identity development in specific community sites under a Native Hawaiian framework. The AISB program on the other hand serves a diverse group of Native youth at an IHE. Though AISB may not emphasize a specific traditional ceremony or language in the same way as Hale Mua, it operates with the understanding that role-modeling is key to success for Native men and boys. Similarly, both are primarily community funded, Hale Mua receiving grant through the Queen Lili'uokalani Trust and AISB through Salt River, and have relationships to local colleges and universities.

Institutionalized programs like Summer Bridge Program create important pathways for students to reach higher education. Yet these programs must also consider ways in which support is provided when students hit institutional barriers. Institutionally grounded programs need to be able to respond to institutionally created obstacles – whether that is school discipline and its relationship to the school to prison pipeline, the tracking of Indigenous students into noncollege preparatory programs or special education, or simply the lack of institutional commitment beyond a summer bridge program, noting the temporal limitations that exist. Bridge programs like AISB are crucial, but their focus only on higher education lacks Hale Mua's holistic model that provides mentors and role models while interrogating what it means to be an Indigenous man, in an Indigenous setting, from an Indigenous perspective. As an institutionally created and driven program focused on retention and degree completion, AISB lacks the broad agenda that community-created and community-driven programs like Hale Mua have.

Despite these differences, both asset-based programs respond to vital needs and are dedicated to empowering men with the knowledge and skill sets needed to become leaders in their fields and communities. Hale Mua establishes Native peoples in position as leaders, while Summer Bridge Program encourages Native leadership in professional and academic settings. Interestingly, both models suggest there is a difference between successful mentors and "highly qualified teachers." Both seek to build capacity and Hale Mua additionally focuses on addressing nation building efforts by responding to the effects of historical trauma and coloniality. Both validate and promote Indigenous knowledges, recognize the importance of community embeddedness and languages, and use materials that are informed by those Indigenous knowledges. Lastly, they focus on preparing leaders. In the case of Hale Mua, local leadership is taking charge and only Hale Mua offers a focus on different knowledges needed for different cultural and personal life stages (e.g., boy, man, father, warrior, elder).

Principles for Successful Indigenous-Serving Programs and Liaisons

Our review of the literature and interviews with Hale Mua and AISB suggest that programs which enhance education outcomes for Native men and boys appear to be driven by six promising principles: they *empower, enact, engage, enlighten, envision,* and *enhance.* Empowerment refers to harnessing and accentuating Indigenous knowledges while also acknowledging traumas specific to Native boys and men in order to provide a space for healing; mentors matter and are critical to preparing boys and men to be successful. Enactment is the ability to practice particular teachings about cultural protocol, spiritual practices, and sharing stories. Engaging in relationships with people (e.g., institutional staff, faculty, and family), place (e.g., home and homelands), and ceremony are critically important for Native peoples. This principle stresses the fact that place-based learning and access to culturally significant geographic areas are important. The enlighten principle refers to the reciprocal learning that ensues when engaging with others including family, elders, mentors, and other community members, while envision refers to a purpose-driven framework that strengthens students' motivation to persist in education. This may be tied to a desire to "give back" to their community or to help fulfill a nation building agenda. Lastly, enhancement refers to the ways in which institutions and tribes provide support to Native students (e.g., having Native instructors, curriculum centered on Indigenous pedagogy). Together, these principles contribute positively to Native student persistence and success. We discuss these principles in more detail below.

Empower: Nurturing Indigenous Ways of Being and Knowing

Effective programs that assert empowerment harness and accentuate Indigenous knowledges, create space for peer networks and sharing, and acknowledge traumas specific to Native boys and men in order to provide a space for strength and healing. Programs with an empowerment perspective foster identity in meaningful ways, including teaching Native languages and cultural traditions that reflect Native epistemologies, allowing men and boys to gain the skills to enhance self-determination. Promoting empowerment through the facilitation of cultural knowledges and emphasizing relationships to tribal communities are meaningful ways of redressing historic and present-day institutionalized oppression. We briefly mentioned the fluidity and complexity of identity earlier, which speaks to aspects of polyculturalism. These polycultural aspects show up with mixed race or mixed national peoples, two-spirit and/or transgendered peoples, and those tied to urban, rural, suburban geographies. Learning to navigate different social contexts, while retaining an Indigenous sense of self and resisting assimilation, are important tools that programs serving Indigenous boys and men must nurture and strengthen. Empowerment work underscores the importance in recognizing internalized oppression and historical trauma through by promoting the strengths and positive qualities of Indigenous peoples. Examples of this include strengthening identity formation through identifying personal strengths within themselves and others. By instilling a greater sense of self-confidence, Native students are more equipped to survive and thrive at school settings.

The promotion of cultural knowledges and ways of being serves as sources of strength and motivation for Indigenous peoples in spaces where they are traditionally underrepresented and underserved. What Hale Mua, AISB, and others have found is the reason why Native students are able to successfully navigate institutions of education is because they have a special strength and resilience to adapt to potentially challenging situations and take away value from any experience. Empowering Indigenous students' success means recognizing the array of strengths they draw from their cultural backgrounds and communities to persist. For institutions of higher education and programs seeking to empower Indigenous students, this means incorporating cultural environments with motivation. Consider Hale Mua's social and physical location of the men's house within the community – building on existing cultural strengths to empower youth with existing community strategies, highlighting resources that may have previously gone underutilized or unnoticed. Indigenous students are better served and better equipped to achieve in education settings when culture is empowered – viewed as a resource, fundamental to instruction and educational, personal, and professional success.

Enact: Spiritual Practices and Sharing Stories

Enactment refers to the ability to practice spiritual teachings and share stories. Tradition-based spiritual practices, rooted in Indigenous epistemologies and ontologies, are an integral source for Indigenous peoples. Important to these practices is providing space and opportunities for Native men and boys to dialogue about their spirituality and life experiences. In Hale Mua, this is a central function of the men's house, providing a distinct and unique space for men and boys to teach, understand, and negotiate spirituality, tradition, and life experiences in an intergenerational context. Activities in Hale Mua draw from Native Hawaiian spirituality and community stories, passing these stories down while cooking, crafting, or simply sharing space. We recognize that many Native men and boys practice and believe in different faiths, but how spirituality is defined and practiced is not the purpose of this discussion. Rather, we acknowledge the powerful role that spirituality has on Native men and boys. Like identity complexities, spirituality is equally complex and often tied to a sense of self.

Another important aspect of enactment involves sharing stories with other Natives. A focus on dialogue is important since trauma can be expressed in disillusionment with community leaders and grief about perceived culture loss as well as the complex connections between traumatization at the level of the individual and the community. Stories offer a place for Native men to heal connecting and relating with those who may encounter similar experiences or to provide awareness to boys on situations they may encounter from the perspective of men who have experienced them. Creating safe and culturally relevant spaces for Native boys and men to share their stories, like what Hale Mua has done, is a form of enactment and reeducation that allows them to reconnect to a collective experience, potentially alleviating feelings of individualized shame or isolation.

Engage: Relationships with People and Place Matter

Engaging in relationships with people (e.g., institutional staff, advisors, faculty, peers, and family) and place (e.g., home and homelands) are critically important for Indigenous success. Relationships matter. This means enhancing existing familial or community relationships while building relationships in new spaces – as Native students prepare for higher education, careers, or different transitions and contexts in life. When it comes to making important education and life decisions, it is important to keep in mind, when Native peoples are asked to consider a course of action, they may be hesitant to make an immediate decision as an Indigenous worldview may necessitate discussion with the family prior to committing to something that could impact the family or larger society. Institutions of higher education and programs serving Native boys and men should recognize and seek to facilitate these important relationship networks by providing students opportunities and space to foster and maintain these connections. Policies and practices within education that promulgate the relationality between Native students and tribal communities are crucial to the future success and capacity of Native communities.

Similarly, institutions must also help students to forge new connections and bonds, both with their own communities and with communities within the institution. The strength of programs like AISB is in building these connections between students, by creating an eighth grade cohort with ongoing activities so students have a peer relationship network as they continue through school and into higher education. Furthermore, creating connections with institutional staff and mentors in higher education at an early age means these relationships have time to develop and grow over time. Students are therefore better able to understand the resources available to them and recognize the support that exists not only in their families and communities but in their future educational institutions. Reaching out to youth also allows institutions to form connections with their families and communities, building the trust that is essential to relationships between Indigenous communities and educational institutions to move away from the histories of exploitation and assimilation that have generated trauma.

Enlighten: Reciprocal Learning from Engaging with Family, Elders, and Mentors

Closely linked with the engagement principle is the enlighten principle, which is reciprocal learning (enlightenment) that ensues when engaging with others. Powerful learning is exchanged when Native students connect with family. This principle emphasizes the influential role of *mentorship*. Actively seeking supportive relationships with positive, non-violent elders and mentors in the community enhances success that may be passed down with each successive generation. We mentioned in the previous section that asset- and strengths-based approaches see wisdom in intergenerational exchanges of knowledge, produce culturally and linguistically vibrant communities, and respond to present needs and opportunities. Social support from elders, community members, and faculty/staff mentors is powerful for student success. Mentors, both from an educational and cultural context, are key to aspiring Native students. Peer mentoring programs can also help in the adjustments/demands of college life. Building on established relationships means not only role modeling between Native boys and men but also seeking and providing mentors from different communities, genders, sexualities, and professional lives, to foster the reciprocal learning that helps students remain focused, yet open-minded and engaged with different understandings of what it means to be an Indigenous person, and thereby what it may mean for the student, or their community, to be an Indigenous man.

Envision: Purpose-Driven Framework

The envision principle refers to the purpose-driven framework that strengthens students' motivation to persist in college. A desire to help community can be a guiding force for Native students as it illustrates a "full circle of purpose" (Elliott 2010, p. 177). Both AISB and Hale Mua are focused on persistence of Native boys and men, with two distinct approaches. Hale Mua takes an intergenerational persistence to the core of community and Indigenous ways of being and knowing in the many activities of the men's house, connecting boys with men and elders from their community that they may not have connected with previously. For AISB, the connection to persistence comes from different American Indian men in careers, showing the results of persistence in education with the hopes of role modeling for the eighth grade boys involved while also providing mentorship for these boys to offer assistance in their chosen educational path. For boys becoming men, phrases like "man up" or "grow a pair" wrongfully tie masculinities to an individualized strength that exists in isolation, forcing a false narrative that boys become men on their own and that masculinity is not a community negotiated process. By connecting Native boys and men in this way, Hale Mua and AISB reinforce the reciprocal relationship of community for men who are too often told to bear burdens on their own. Envisioning Native boys and men in a community, and as part of larger Indigenous communities, reassures students with support and thereby encourages long-term persistence, particularly in higher education. In many ways, the notion of envisioning is directly tied to larger conversations around the importance of tribal nation building, mentorship, and relationships (Brayboy et al. 2012, 2014). The nature of being driven by collective purpose is crucial to the success of all Native students and peoples; it is especially true for Indigenous men and boys.

Enhance: Institutional and Tribal Support

Our final principle, enhance, should guide IHEs in providing support to Native students. Within institutions, having Native instructors, access to classes on Native topics, curriculum centered on Indigenous pedagogy, and applying life skills, all contribute positively to Native student persistence and success. Educators should not assume that all students understand European-based stories and their themes. To enhance success, institutions and instructors should focus on community-relevant stories, pedagogies, and epistemologies. This means not only teaching in ways that are relevant to the learning styles of the Indigenous peoples being taught but to incorporate subject matter that is most relevant for the local community and the students being taught. This also means avoiding essentialist notions of Indigeneity and masculinity. The activities, rituals, and conceptions of what it means to be a man in Hale Mua may have connections or similarities to activities in AISB, but this does not mean either model should be imposed or transplanted in other communities. Rather, Hale Mua and AISB show models of building strength and support that are relevant to the local community by building on their Indigenous perspectives, rather than attempting to superimpose an absolutist, essentialist, romanticized, and counterproductive definition of Indigenous manhood. This would simply be reifying colonial practices with a pseudo-Indigenous face. Rather, by focusing on enhancing existing community programs and networks of support as Hale Mua and AISB strive to do, institutions can build on existing networks with funding, structural support, and connections that foster important programs and strategies for success.

Institutions seeking to enhance communities rather than colonize should focus on consultation and partnership with communities. This means not only hiring faculty, staff, and administrators who understand local issues and are even from local Indigenous communities but ensuring retention of students, faculty, and staff by collaborating with local Indigenous communities. Programs like AISB and Hale Mua do not exist in a vacuum, but both have funding partnerships with local colleges and universities, which enable their success without attempting to impose a model of success. We argue that the key to enhancing institutions and communities comes in partnership that recognizes the importance and salience of local Indigenous knowledges in serving Indigenous peoples, rather than attempting to impose formulaic programs that would defeat the purpose of the partnership.

Sustaining Systems of Support: Institutional Partnerships with Indigenous Peoples

Programs and institutions addressing the needs and experiences of Indigenous boys and men recognize the importance of education and schooling but must be mindful of histories of colonization and assimilation. Therefore, student success must be rooted in forming systems of support – connecting historically colonial institutions of higher education to Indigenous communities and culture through partnership and collaboration that values and centers Indigenous epistemologies and ontologies. Engaging Indigenous students through culture-affirming approaches and helping to facilitate relationships within their community can effectively counter disparate educational outcomes. Moreover, this necessitates a recognition that education goes beyond the formal and Westernized notion of schooling to include learning *within* Indigenous communities. Such learning is often family-, community-, and environmental-based, connecting boys and men to their homelands, defining or redefining Indigenous masculinities, and allowing for important ceremonies and sacred and spiritual practices to take place.

Programs serving Native boys and men emphasize the importance of cultural knowledges and how Indigenous peoples strategically apply those knowledges for survival and success. Moreover, peer support and mentoring are vital to redress challenges and inequitable education outcomes. Mentors, role models, and bonding activities provide culturally effective spaces and reflective relationships to acknowledge and discuss critical issues of importance to Native boys and men. Brave Heart et al. (2012) describe alternative ways of thinking about interventions for men by focusing on the impacts of historical trauma that have resulted in "male separation from the traditional self, internalization of oppression, and identification with the aggressor – an intrinsically devalued true self" (p. 179). Thematically, Hale Mua and AISB shift from a deficit approach to a repayment of the education debt discussed earlier by engaging Native men in culturally relevant and relational-oriented approaches that each emphasize relationships to family, community, identity, and culture – mending bonds that have been damaged by colonization while strengthening connections between generations.

We believe Native communities best understand the challenges facing them and may have their own solutions in place or new ideas for resolving problems facing boys and men but may lack resources, funding, or support. Ultimately, our goal in this chapter is not to necessarily reshape educational institutions or the community, but rather reshape the relationship between the two, thereby strengthening Indigenous peoples. In other words, we are not suggesting that communities need institutions of higher education to design and operate their programs; they need their support as partners in understanding that Native peoples are the ones who provide relevance to the community. So how can IHEs help support the nation building goals of tribal communities and enhance Native student development and success?

Overall, IHEs must recognize there is no one-size-fits-all model for Indigenous communities. American Indian, Alaska Native, Native Hawaiian, and Pacific Islander communities are diverse and distinct, connected by the colonial power of the United States. Each community has different needs, protocols, contexts, and desires. Each community may have differing ideas of the health and education needs of their youth. Building on our six principles, there are some basic tenets to keep in mind when working with and for tribal communities and their students:

1. Research design and collaboration must be rooted in context that honors and engages protocol that varies from community to community – this encompasses interpersonal interaction, ways of speaking, types of questions that are considered respectful or rude, or standards for eye contact, among many various ways of communicating. The simplest solution to understanding and engaging in respectful protocol is to hire or work with members of that community, who can not only serve as a connection between IHEs and Indigenous communities but can ensure that best practices match Indigenous community expectations.
2. Relatedly, research needs to examine non-Western forms of education as strengths-based forms of instruction. Indigenous knowledges should be used in the classroom for instruction and understanding for Indigenous peoples, not just as the subjects of study by White researchers or as topics of conversation in predominantly white institutions.
3. Research and programs must build capacity, primarily through mentorship. In other words, IHEs must recognize that capacity is built by preparing Indigenous

boys to be Indigenous men, serve in ceremony and understand their role, and place in relation to being in mutually rewarding (inter)dependent (inter)relationships with other men, women, and all others.
4. IHEs can encourage funders to take seriously the invisibility and erasure of Native peoples more generally and Native boys and men more explicitly. There is a clear need for funders to take the issue of the current state of Indigenous boys and men – and their communities – seriously. To this end, new funding streams need to be opened that will allow researchers opportunities to explore the current state of education, health (both mental and physical), culture and linguistic, justice-related, suicidality, labor, nutrition, and housing for Indigenous peoples more generally and Indigenous boys and men more specifically. These opportunities should take both topic-specific and intersectional analyses. It is difficult to fully address the nature of the challenges in front of us without fully understanding what the challenges – and resources to respond – truly are.
5. Creating Native cultural centers on college campuses allow young men there to both have a refuge from the daily stressors of being on campuses that are often hostile to them and to engage in community building. Coordinating a physical space to provide emotional and psychological support is also crucial. We recommend that institutions implement student support groups and encouraging culture-specific student groups. Combining the physical with the psychosocial elements is crucial in assisting Indigenous men in making the transition into higher education.

Conclusion

Educational institutions have a fraught relationship with Indigenous communities, to put it lightly. Histories of assimilation and colonization have deprived Indigenous peoples of educational systems that embrace Indigenous knowledges, culture, and people. Particularly for Indigenous boys and men, this has meant assimilation, tracking into criminal justice systems, or imposed and unresolved trauma. Academic research on Indigenous boys and men are more likely to use "at-risk" descriptors and frame discussions of Indigenous boys and men as dysfunctional, deficit, or unfit for schooling while noting feelings of isolation, loss of cultural identity, depression, and other symptoms of trauma. Yet, Indigenous communities and people are resilient and have created solutions to problems felt in their communities, often lacking support from institutions of education to enrich Indigenous communities. Rather than take people and resources from the community, we advocate for ways in which institutions of education can support and partner with Indigenous communities to their mutual benefit.

With the dearth of research on strengths- or asset-based educational programs and institutions serving Indigenous men and boys, our analysis of Hale Mua and AISB suggests six guiding principles to improve education outcomes beyond typical curriculum, discussions, or practices. We suggest that Indigenous peoples know how to successfully develop research and engaging learning spaces that advance anti-oppressive education and "permits historical and contemporary perspectives of Indigenous material culture to critically wrestle with dominant discourses" so that Native youth develop a stronger sense of identity and self-confidence (Bequette 2014, p. 215). By focusing on empowering, enacting, engaging, enlightening, envisioning, and enhancing programs serving Indigenous boys and men, institutions of higher education become better able to support existing community involvement while ensuring space for future community and institutional developments.

Indigenous communities are more than gatherings of people; they are nations with the sovereign right to govern themselves and shape their lives in ways they see fit. Self-determination includes the creation and modification of laws to support Indigenous nation building, even when US Federal laws may provide funding, guidance, or even impose boundaries on governance. In education, this means ensuring systems of support for Indigenous education initiatives by creating and maintaining Indigenous education departments and funding Indigenous institutions from primary schools to universities and general policies to fund, support, and strengthen Indigenous communities through educational partnerships. Education on Indigenous terms is often difficult, as US institutions – courts, administrative bodies, and academia – have a hard time understanding Indigenous epistemologies, ontologies, and sovereignty in education because education has historically been rooted in assimilation to Western standards of learning instead of adapting to the cultural needs of Native students and faculty. Nation building in education thus recognizes Indigenous peoples' dual citizenship as US citizens and tribal citizens. Education is more than ensuring people can contribute to the US or individual successes but also to their own communities and continue to teach the generations after them.

References

Barker J (ed) (2017) Critically sovereign: indigenous gender, sexuality, and feminist studies. Duke University Press, Durham

Bequette JW (2014) Culture-based arts education that teaches against the grain: a model for place-specific material culture studies. Stud Art Educ 55(3):214–226

Bitsóí LL (2007) Native leaders in the new millenium-an examination of success factors of native American males at Harvard College. University of Pennsylvania, Dissertations & Theses Global. (304821805), Philadelphia

Brave Heart MY (2003) The historical trauma response among natives and its relationship with substance abuse: a Lakota illustration. J Psychoactive Drugs 35(1):7–13

Brave Heart MY, Elkins J, Tafoya G, Bird D, Salvador M (2012) Wicasa Was'aka: restoring the traditional strength of American Indian boys and men. Am J Public Health 102(5):S177–S183. https://doi.org/10.2105/ajph.2011.300511

Brayboy BMKJ (2004) Hiding in the Ivy: American Indian students and visibility in elite educational settings. Harv Educ Rev 74(2):125–152

Brayboy BMKJ (2005) Transformational resistance and social justice: American Indians in Ivy League universities. Anthropol Educ Q 36(3):193–211

Brayboy BMKJ, Fann AJ, Castagno AE, Solyom JA (2012) Postsecondary education for American Indian and Alaska natives: higher education for nation building and self-determination. ASHE High Educ Rep 37(5):1–154. John Wiley & Sons

Brayboy BMKJ, Solyom JA, Castagno AE (2014) Looking into the hearts of native peoples: nation building as an institutional orientation for graduate education. Am J Educ 120(4):575–596

Brayboy BMKJ, Solyom J, Chin J, Tachine A, Bang M, Bustamante N, Ben C, Myles C, Poleviyuma A (2016) RISE: a study of indigenous men and boys. Report prepared for the center for the study of race & equity in education, graduate school of education. University of Pennsylvania, Philadelphia

Castagno AE, Brayboy BMJ (2008) Culturally responsive schooling for indigenous youth: a review of the literature. Rev Educ Res 78(4):941–993

Centers for Disease Control and Prevention, National Center for Injury Prevention and Control (2015) Web-based injury statistics query and reporting system (WISQARS). Available from www.cdc.gov/injury/wisqars. 04 Jan 2018

Elliott SA (2010) Walking the worlds: the experience of native psychologists in their doctoral training and practice (Ph.D.). Available from ProQuest Dissertations & Theses Global. (763614385)

Executive Office of the President (2014) 2014 Native youth report. Retrieved from https://www.whitehouse.gov/sites/default/files/docs/20141129nativeyouthreport_final.pdf

Hale Mua (2017) Hale Mua Initiative. Available at https://www.ahakane.org/events/hale_mua_initiative

Kirmayer LJ, Gone JP, Moses J (2014) Rethinking historical trauma. Transcultura Psych 51(3):299–319

Lomawaima T, McCarty T (2006) To remain an Indian: lessons in democracy from a century of native American education. Teachers College Press, New York

Marlow PE, Siekmann S (eds) (2013) Communities of practice: an Alaskan Native model for language teaching and learning. University of Arizona Press, Tucson

McCarty TL (2009) The impact of high-stakes accountability policies on native American learners: evidence from research. Teach Educ 20(1):7–29. London: Taylor & Francis Online

National Congress of American Indians (2012) Demographic profile of Indian country. NCAI Research Policy Center, Washington, DC Retrieved from http://www.ncai.org/policy-research-center/research-data/bb_2012_november_demographic_profile.pdf

National Indian Education Association (n.d.) Native nations and American schools: the history of natives in the American education system. National Education Association. Retrieved from http://www.niea.org/our-story/history/native-101/

Perea JB (2017) Audiovisualizing Iñupiaq men and masculinities *On the Ice*. In: Barker J (ed) Critically sovereign: indigenous gender, sexuality, and feminist studies. Duke University Press, Durham

Qiao N, Bell T (2017) Indigenous Adolescents' suicidal behaviors and risk factors: evidence from the National Youth Risk Behavior Survey. J Immigr Minor Health 19(3):590–597

Shotton HJ, Lowe SC, and Waterman SJ (2013) Beyond the asterisk: understanding Native students in higher Education. Stylus, Sterling

Tachine A, Cabrera NL, Yellow Bird E (2017) Home away from home: native American students' sense of belonging during their first year in college. J High Educ 88(5):785–807. https://doi.org/10.1080/00221546.2016.1257322

U.S. Department of Education, National Center for Education Statistics (2015) Digest of education statistics (2015 ed.). Retrieved from https://nces.ed.gov/programs/digest/current_tables.asp

U.S. Department of Education, Office for Civil Rights (2012) Civil rights data collection. Available at https://www2.ed.gov/about/offices/list/ocr/data.html?src=rt

U.S. Department of Education Office for Civil Rights (2014) Civil rigths data collection: data snapshot: early childhood education. Available from https://www2.ed.gov/about/offices/list/ocr/docs/crdc-early-learning-snapshot.pdf

"A Future Denied" for Young Indigenous People: From Social Disruption to Possible Futures

35

Emma Elliott-Groves and Stephanie A. Fryberg

Contents

Disruptions of Collective Capacities of Indigenous Populations	633
Possible Self-Concepts: Me or Not Me?	635
Real-World Consequences of Erasure	638
Conclusion	644
References	647

Abstract

Representations of contemporary Indigenous people in the USA and Canada are poorly reflected in public institutions. Portrayals are rare and generally inaccurate, highlighting the erasure of Indigenous people from current discourse. Such erasure is an inevitable result of settler colonialism, a process that aims to replace the Indigenous inhabitants of a given region with settlers. Settler colonialism is predicated on the notion that land can be owned as private property, and that Indigenous people have no special claim to their traditional territories. The US government and its legal system have supported its ends, which have disrupted the web of relationships necessary for Indigenous identity development. These relationships include prescriptions for what it means to be an Indigenous person and how to conduct one's life in a good way. In conjunction with representational erasure, their disruption prevents young Indigenous people from developing positive concepts of self. In the face of cultural invisibility and widespread

---

E. Elliott-Groves (✉)
Initiative for Research and Education to Advance Community Health (IREACH), Partnerships for Native Health (P4NH), Washington State University, Seattle, WA, USA
e-mail: Emma.elliott@wsu.edu

S. A. Fryberg
American Indian Studies and Psychology, University of Washington, Seattle, WA, USA
e-mail: fryberg@uw.edu

© Springer Nature Singapore Pte Ltd. 2019
E. A. McKinley, L. T. Smith (eds.), *Handbook of Indigenous Education*,
https://doi.org/10.1007/978-981-10-3899-0_50

negative stereotypes, the attempts of young people to build healthy identities for themselves can be compromised or completely thwarted. They cannot find ways to connect the narrative thread of their past and present with their possible futures, which are effectively foreclosed. Thus, representational erasure places young Indigenous people at great psychological risk, culminating far too often in suicide. To mitigate these effects, we recommend raising social awareness of settler colonialism and reimagining public education in ways that will affirm rather than deny Indigenous values.

Keywords

Indigenous erasure · Settler colonialism · Collective capacities · Possible selves · Identity development · Social representation

When young Indigenous people look out into the world, they seldom see themselves or members of their group represented. The issue is not a total absence of representation; rather, young people are exposed to a predominance of eighteenth- and nineteenth-century images instead of contemporary representations in which they might recognize themselves (Shear et al. 2015). This absence is true across a variety of consequential domains, such as education, media, health, and law. The representational erasure of contemporary Indigenous people in the USA and Canada is largely a reflection of settler colonial discourse. Although there are many settler colonial states, including the USA, Canada, Australia, and New Zealand, this paper will draw from the North American context. Used broadly, the term "Indigenous" here refers to the first people of the land, and at the core of Indigenous identity is relational responsibility, as constituted by history, ceremony and spirituality, language, and land (Alfred and Corntassel 2005). By drawing on theories of social psychology and engaging a settler colonial theoretical framework, this paper theorizes the consequences of representational erasure on identity development and wellbeing for young Indigenous people in the USA and Canada.

With the intention of acquiring land, settler colonialism aims to erase Indigenous populations from their homelands and replace them with settler societies (Lefevre 2015). In addition to land dispossession, settler colonialism seeks to remove Indigenous political authority (Coulthard 2014). Ultimately, settler colonialism is about Indigenous erasure for the purpose of land acquisition made possible through an unequal distribution of power between the nation state and its first people. Through representational erasure, the presence of Indigenous people and their cultural practices are altered, appropriated, or erased, ultimately threatening the process of identity development for young Indigenous people.

Actively writing Indigenous people out of the domain of contemporary representation is tantamount to an erasure of entire ethnic groups and has devastating psychological consequences for young Indigenous people. The lack of contemporary Indigenous representation in mainstream media and across US or Canadian institutions is pervasive despite the rich and lasting contributions of Indigenous people to North American societies. Native Americans in the USA and First Nations and Inuit people in Canada have made significant contributions in areas such as economic development, military service, conservation, and environmental protection, yet many of these contributions lack visible representation. The result is Indigenous erasure. This representational and contextual reality begs the question, "How can young Indigenous people develop a contemporary self when their people have been metaphorically frozen in the past and contemporarily written out of the present and the future?" The answer to this question importantly depends upon the content of the social representations and narratives that are available to young people. In the absence of positive social representation (e.g., role models from ethnic, gender, or class population), young Indigenous people are tasked with their own identity development in the context where their social representation is not acknowledged or represented accurately. The lack of widespread misrepresentation or lack of visible representation of Indigenous people presents obstacles to identity making and impedes young people's efforts to figure out who they are and what they will become in the future. As a result, they experience greater psychological risk than their non-Indigenous peers who are represented more widely and more favorably, leading to stress, depression, anxiety, and suicidal ideation.

Put forth in this paper are three key implications of Indigenous erasure: first, it disrupts Indigenous social and cultural formations; secondly, it limits the possible selves available to young Indigenous people for identity development; and thirdly, it elevates psychological risk for many young Indigenous people. Settler colonial theory is presented as a frame for this discussion, referring specifically to historical and contemporary disruptions of Indigenous collective capacities (Whyte 2015). Next, thoughts on how such disruption limits the available representations necessary for Indigenous identity development are discussed followed by real-world, social, and cultural outcomes of Indigenous erasure. Finally, culturally specific suggestions for educators and mental health practitioners to alleviate the impact of Indigenous erasure on identity development are offered, with the larger objective of expanding Indigenous possible selves and decreasing the risks associated with an absence of representation.

Disruptions of Collective Capacities of Indigenous Populations

The study of how colonization has disrupted Indigenous social and cultural formations is not new. Various studies have discussed the impact of these disruptions on Indigenous communities (Chandler et al. 2003; Whyte 2015). The social and cultural formations, or collective capacities, of a community refer to the interacting systems of humans, nonhumans, entities, and landscapes that support its capacity to self-determine and to adapt to changing circumstances, such as colonization (Whyte 2015). For example, Indigenous collective capacities include relationships with the land and other living entities, religious and cultural narratives, social and cultural ways of life, and political and economic systems (Whyte 2015). The central component of collective capacities are the interacting relationships embedded within each system, which have been conceptualized specifically to enhance community members' quality of life and increase their ability to determine their own futures. For young Indigenous people, a large part of identity development depends on one's role in community and the practices embedded within the culture, as well as one's responsibility to the collective (Cajete 1994). In other words, young people learn what it means to be "a human, one of the People" through their community relations (Cajete 1994, p. 41). When the collective capacities of the community are disrupted, the necessary relationships and representations available for identity development are limited or absent, which presents the psychological consequence of erasure. The capacity to sustain a thriving community is predicated on the collective's ability to establish and maintain strong social and cultural formations (Trosper 2009), including educational and child welfare systems. In settler colonial states, however, the process of colonization has encroached on Indigenous institutions and relationships.

Settler colonialism is a complex and continuous social process aimed at eliminating Indigenous people through the disruption of their collective capacities (Whyte 2015; Wolfe 2006). The principal endeavor is the creation of a homeland for settlers, a goal typically achieved by the acquisition of Indigenous land and the subsequent establishment and management of permanent settler structures (Allen 1986; LaDuke 1999; Maracle 1996; Veracini 2010; Wolfe2006). This process disrupts Indigenous social and cultural formations and degrades quality of life by creating food insecurity, lowering standards of public health, and compromising cultural integrity, thereby hindering community members' efforts to determine their own futures (Whyte 2015). Without the ability to plan, prepare for, and adapt to changing circumstances, Indigenous people experience many psychological and material consequences, including limited or foreclosed possible selves.

In the USA, settler colonialism was facilitated by specific actions of the federal government, including the forced relocation of American Indian children to boarding schools in the nineteenth and twentieth centuries; the Dawes Act of 1887, which attempted to privatize tribal lands for individual ownership and sale; and the termination and relocation policies of the 1940s through 1960s (Adams 1995; Ellis 1996; Lomawaima and McCarty 2006). In Canada, settler colonialism operated through similar federal policies including the Crown Lands Protection Act of 1839, which empowered the federal government as guardians of all Crown lands; the 1867 British North America Act, under which Indians and Indian land became federal responsibility; and the Indian Act of 1876 which defined and racialized Indian identity, supported the removal of Indian children from their family homes, and mandated the removal and forced sedentarization through the reservation system (Haig-Brown 1988; Johnston 1995; Kirmayer and Valaskakis 2009).

In contemporary society, the disruption of Indigenous collective capacities continues with the disproportionate representation of Native American children in foster care (Cross 2008), the disproportionate police violence against young Native American adults (Center on Juvenile and Criminal Justice 2014), and the scarcity of tribally run and tribally determined schools. Child removal, for example, ensures that Indigenous knowledge systems atrophy. When parents and elders are prevented from nurturing and educating subsequent generations in the social and cultural practices that ensure collective well-being, the entire collective is placed at risk.

Another factor associated with the psychological consequences of erasure is temporal persistence, which refers to the ability of individuals and cultures to connect the narrative thread of the past with their own present and future (Chandler et al. 2003). Temporal persistence involves understanding shared social and cultural practices and experiencing oneself and one's culture as continuous through time. In the context of identity development, however, the notion of temporal persistence highlights a paradox of human existence: we must continually change, yet we necessarily remain the same (Chandler et al. 2003). Young people who face this paradox must draw on their collective capacities to facilitate their development as human beings. In the case of Indigenous young people, however, collective capacities have often become so fractured, and self-images so compromised, that it is difficult for them to link past, present, and future.

Chandler and colleagues argue that cultural continuity, manifesting as community control over health, education, policing, land claims, government, and cultural spaces, can serve as a protective buffer against suicide in First Nations' communities in British Columbia. In one of their studies, suicide rates were directly correlated with the degree of cultural continuity in each community, such that Firsts Nations' communities striving to preserve and promote their own social and cultural practices experienced less suicide (Chandler and Lalonde 1998). In another study, they found that 85% of actively suicidal young people had difficulty understanding their own or others' persistence across time (Chandler et al. 2003). At the individual as well as the collective level, an inability to connect the past with the present and future exacerbates suicide risk (Chandler et al. 2003). Disruptions of collectives' social and cultural formations are indeed a matter of life and death.

By jeopardizing collective abilities to adapt to changing needs, the obstruction of social and cultural formations in Indigenous communities places the entire collective at greater psychological and material risk than their non-Indigenous counterparts. The same obstruction limits the availability of representations that could help Indigenous young people understand what it means to be a good, right, or moral person. Representations that reflect cultural invisibility, negative stereotypes, and widespread cultural mismatch leave these young people in a constant state of psychic disequilibrium (Rich 1994). To understand and potentially reverse these destructive processes, the next section examines the dependency of an individual's possible selves on available cultural representations.

Possible Self-Concepts: Me or Not Me?

As social beings, we all engage with a vast network of other people's ideas about who and what we are supposed to be. Within this network, everyone must develop a sense of self, which includes imagining our "possible selves," or who we might like to become in the future (Markus and Nurius 1986). Possible selves, either positive or negative, are cognitive manifestations of our hopes, fears, threats, and goals (Markus and Nurius 1986). They are self-concepts that are dynamically constructed through everyday interactions (Oyserman and Fryberg 2006), including prevalent attitudes, values, and social practices. Positive possible selves, which are associated with goals, and negative possible selves, which are associated with fears, serve as motivational and regulatory guides for behavior, providing a crucial cognitive link between present and future (Oyserman and Fryberg 2006). Research demonstrates that students whose possible selves include a good balance of desired ("I want to be a good student") and feared selves ("I fear being a bad student") perform better in school. In the process of identity development, thoughts about who we once were, who we currently are, and who we might become emerge directly from the social representational landscape. Because possible selves are dynamic constructs, the possible futures available to young people can be expanded or foreclosed, depending on the representational landscape. For Indigenous young people, the representational landscape is imbued with stereotypes and historical misrepresentations that shape and too often limit their self-concepts in relation to temporal persistence.

Therefore, the question of possible selves for Indigenous young people is not simply about what is going on in their minds, but about what is depicted in the world. This includes the systems of relationships in which they are engaged, as well as the ways in which those systems are affected by the representational landscape. When faced with a representational landscape that disregards or erases their perceived or actual self or social group, Indigenous young people are placed at a greater disadvantage during the process of identity development. Although American Indian, Alaska Native, and First Nations people have demonstrated significant resiliency in the face of widespread change, the focus here is on the risks and challenges associated with settler colonization in North America. The simultaneous prevalence of negative representations and absence of positive representations have adverse psychological consequences for young Indigenous people as they try to develop positive possible selves. For Indigenous populations, widely available representations often falsify or exclude positive reflections of Indigenous identity, resulting in a form of Indigenous erasure. Like all young people, they must engage with and ultimately shape their self-understanding on the basis of available social representations (Fryberg and Townsend 2008). Yet not all social representational landscapes are created equal.

The social representational landscape comprises the ideas and images accessible in a given social context that help people orient themselves and communicate with one another (Moscovici 2001). Social representations serve two functions. First, they provide a way to define, categorize, and develop generalized knowledge about people and objects to assist us in interpreting the world. Second, they are directive: they tell us how to think, interpret, feel, and act in the context of social and cultural norms. Thus, what a young person considers possible is a direct reflection of the representations available in the broader social world, including home and school. Young people negotiate their own identity development by drawing on these preformed and widely available ideas about the identity of their social group. They then determine whether the possible futures that emerge from these ideas represent "me or not me."

When available representations are limited, negative, or absent, young people may realize that these ideas and images simply do not reflect their own self-concepts, creating internal conflict (Fryberg and Townsend 2008). In contrast, this inequity across social groups in the availability of positive representations presents some young people access to multiple possible selves that reflect a positive version of "me." To illustrate this inequity, we introduce Sans, an 18-year-old high school senior who is a member of the Cowichan Tribes in Canada; he was interviewed as part of a study conducted by one of the authors of this paper (Elliott 2016) aimed at understanding suicidal behavior from the perspective of community members. One part of the interview, directed specifically at young people, focused on possible selves. When asked if he had considered any job opportunities after graduation, Sans replied, "I can't imagine there's that many jobs in this town for Native people. I heard most are heading out of British Columbia for worthy jobs. I guess I'll have to leave." He proceeded to describe significantly racist attitudes toward Native people in his hometown, which he associated with the lack of job opportunities for himself and others like him. Clearly, his observations of the social representational landscape had helped him to develop generalized knowledge about what was available to him and to others in his social group. In turn, this acquired knowledge served a directive function. Like many of his peers, Sans seemed resigned to the necessity of moving out of the province in order to find his livelihood. Although he did not want to leave his family or community, he felt hopeless about his own prospects for employment. Sans had seen few social representations of First Nations men who acquired "worthy jobs" in his community after high school graduation. Because of this representational erasure, his possible selves were severely constrained.

This example highlights the fact that social contexts are not "equal-opportunity self-schema afforders" (Fryberg and Townsend 2008, p. 174). In other words, the availability of positive and inclusive social representations varies widely, depending on one's social identity (a construct informed by race, gender, ethnicity, sexuality, and similar categories). Every society is organized around particular social identities, such that members of different social groups encounter varying representations and unequal social identity contingencies. These contingencies are predicated on specific social positions and can be positive or negative; in particular, social identity contingencies include all "possible judgments, stereotypes, opportunities, restrictions, and treatments that are tied to one's social identity in a given setting" (Purdie-Vaughns et al. 2008, p. 615). For oppressed populations, these identity-based contingencies often reflect and result in physical and psychological risks. In the example above, Sans associated his identity as a First Nations man with the contingency of unemployment in his own community. While those in the social mainstream might encounter positive, inclusive opportunities and treatment from others, Indigenous people like Sans more often contend with restricted opportunity and negative treatment (Fryberg and Townsend 2008).

This research demonstrates that cultural narratives and associated representations deeply embedded in the contemporary social representational landscape influence the possible selves available to young people for identity development. In the process of identity development, young people draw from this landscape to determine what it means to be a person and what is possible for themselves. The disruption of Indigenous social and cultural formations on a collective level has degraded the social representational landscape of Indigenous young people, and thus their everyday experiences and possible futures. Many of the cultural narratives and associated representations linked with Indigenous people are negative, false, or obsolete. As such, they limit the possible selves available to young Indigenous people, with deep implications for their psychological well-being. Without appropriate social representations to guide their self-understanding, young people face a type of erasure that influences their identity development. In this case, young people are vulnerable to such conclusions as "who I am doesn't fit" or "who I am is not good enough." Too often, the consequences are psychological distress and disequilibrium. To deeply understand how settler colonialism and the disruption to Indigenous collective capacities influence the development of possible selves, the next section provides real-world examples and consequences of Indigenous erasure. First, the theory of invisibility is presented including the concepts of absolute and relative invisibility. Next, negative stereotyping and cultural mismatch of Indigenous populations are offered as two forms of relative invisibility. Lastly, to demonstrate real-world, social, and cultural outcomes for Indigenous populations, Indigenous suicide is discussed as the ultimate result of erasure through colonization.

Real-World Consequences of Erasure

To understand the real-world consequences of absent or inaccurate representations, Fryberg and Townsend (2008) offer the theory of invisibility. Their approach illustrates the ways in which possible selves for oppressed populations can be undermined. Invisibility or erasure operates in many obvious ways, including overtly destructive stereotypes, to limit or deny possible selves. However, various tacit or taken-for-granted factors also legitimate certain people while discounting others; for example, these factors are brought to bear in situations of cultural mismatch or of institutional racism that privileges white people. Depending on the social representations available, underrepresented young people often contend with a context in which their social reality or worldview does not match the social representational landscape or is omitted entirely; despite the pervasive cultural mismatch, this situation goes unnoticed or is taken for granted. Social identities, including what it means to be a person or how to be good or righteous, are formed through bidirectional or mutual interaction with the social environment. The possible ways to develop a sense of self are observed and mediated through an array of social representations, whose availability varies widely according to social group identity. The psychology of invisibility refers to the psychological impact of engaging a social environment in which one's likeness or representation is absent or misrepresented. Fryberg and Townsend (2008) present two types of invisibility with deep psychological implications for underrepresented populations: absolute and relative.

Absolute invisibility is characterized by a total absence of positive or negative representations (Fryberg and Townsend 2008). Young people who confront such a landscape must develop their identities without any road map for how to be a good person in the world. North American Indigenous people are invisibilized in many public spaces, including mass media, education, and professional fields. For example, although they comprise about 2% of the US population, Native Americans are virtually absent from primetime television and feature films (Leavitt et al. 2015). In Canada, media representations of Aboriginal people function to safeguard dominant interests by depicting Aboriginal people as a threat (Harding 2006). Furthermore, among postsecondary degrees conferred in 2012–2013, only 0.54% were awarded to Native Americans (Kena et al. 2016). Similarly, in Canada, Aboriginal people are more likely to have a trades and college certificates than a university degree, indicating the disparate rates of representation in higher education institutions (Statistics Canada 2015). In degree-granting institutions in the USA, less than 1% of faculty are Native Americans, demonstrating the near absence of Native professional role models in academia (National Center for Education Statistics 2016). As a result, Native people feel the effects of representational invisibility during every interaction in their private and public lives.

Relative invisibility. The persistent misrepresentation (including stigmatizing and stereotyping) or limited positive representation of certain groups is known as relative invisibility (Fryberg and Townsend 2008). The misrepresentation of social group identity is evidenced through stereotypes or generalizations about entire social groups. Couched within misrepresentation are identity contingencies, or circumstances associated with belonging to a particular social group, that either afford or constrain opportunity based upon social location (Purdie-Vaughns et al. 2008). Limited positive representation of social identity can be observed through the concept of cultural mismatch. The theory of cultural mismatch states that inequality is produced when the dominant cultural patterns do not match the cultural patterns of underrepresented populations (Stephens et al. 2012b). Seen through the lens of stereotyping and cultural mismatch, relative invisibility denies Native people their full humanity.

For Indigenous people, social misrepresentations are embodied structurally in everyday institutions, including schools, churches, families, government facilities, and healthcare centers. In the following sections, practical examples of negative stereotyping and cultural mismatch are provided to illustrate the consequences of invisibility on underrepresented populations. First, examples of negative stereotyping are offered, with particular emphasis on the psychological and physical repercussions of this type of erasure. Next, independent concepts of personhood are contrasted with interdependent concepts of personhood to illustrate the cultural mismatch that Indigenous populations experience in mainstream US society. The pervasiveness of these misrepresentations results in relative invisibility, a status that is especially harmful to populations experiencing overt or covert oppression. When social group identities are misrepresented, young people must build their identities in a landscape of stereotypes.

Negative stereotyping. In contemporary US society, Native Americans are portrayed largely in a homogeneous and outdated manner as "frozen in time" (Leavitt et al. 2015). This portrayal confers relative invisibility on Native Americans, because mainstream groups are unlikely to recognize people who look modern as authentically Indigenous. The negative force of such culturally sustained ignorance is encapsulated in a common stereotype: "All the real Indians died off" (Dunbar-Ortiz and Gilio-Whitaker 2016). This myth of nonexistence plays out in contemporary institutions and influences the daily experiences of Native people. For example, a study aimed at understanding the frequency and quality of Native American representation in the K-12 system in the USA concluded that 87% of state educational standards present Native people in a pre-1900 context (Shear et al. 2015). Such historicized stereotyping of Native Americans lowers the self-esteem of Native students, deters their academic achievement, and undermines their beliefs in community efficacy.

Other destructive stereotypes include notions that Native Americans are "savage and warlike" or "dumb Indians." These constructs have been embedded in legal principles, court rulings, and educational guidelines – indeed, in the underlying philosophies of virtually all social and cultural institutions in the USA – to justify the large-scale extermination of people and cultures by settler colonists (Dunbar-Ortiz and Gilio-Whitaker 2016). Equally harmful are stereotypes that all Native people are poor, prone to alcoholism or addiction, and uneducated. If contemporary Native Americans diverge too far from these false representations, they become invisible. Conversely, the absolute invisibility of Native Americans in a given consequential domain, such as education or health, undermines Native engagement with those domains.

Identity contingencies. Both the absence of representation and persistent misrepresentation are contingencies that limit identity development and reduce quality of life for oppressed and marginalized populations. These contingencies are reflected in judgments and stereotypes about certain social groups, as well as in differential opportunities and restrictions that affect these groups (Purdie-Vaughns et al. 2008). Such identity contingencies pose psychological as well as physical threats. Under the rubric of "stereotype threat," these factors have received scholarly attention in the context of African American experience (Purdie-Vaughns et al. 2008). Stereotype threat refers to the fear that the judgment of others, or one's own actions, will confirm a negative stereotype about the group with which one identifies (Steele 1997). The perceived danger of confirming such harmful biases depresses intellectual functioning and identity development (Steele 1997).

The history of police violence against black and brown people in the USA illustrates the identity contingencies associated with relative invisibility. Many members of these populations actively fear US law enforcement. Given the nationwide currency of false assumptions and racial stereotypes, parents in African American, Native American, and Latino families are proactive in teaching their children, especially males, how to interact with police officers. Fear of police brutality, incarceration, and death drives the need for "the talk," in which parents explain what their children must do and must not do if they are to avoid harm from the police. Both having and heeding "the talk" are a condition of safety for these populations. Notably, parents of White children do not have to consider this identity contingency, and might not even be aware of the relative privilege they enjoy.

Police violence against African Americans is a major topic of national conversation and a central concern of the "Black lives matter" movement. Yet media reports of the death of Native Americans during police encounters are essentially invisible. When broken down by race and age, Native Americans comprise three of the top five groups most likely to be killed by police officers (Center on Juvenile and Criminal Justice 2014). Nonetheless, few non-Native people are aware that Native Americans experience police violence at rates comparable to, if not higher than, African Americans. The impact of losing a loved one is devastating, and the trauma is compounded by the sense of injustice associated with police violence. For Native Americans, this loss is further intensified by the invisible nature of their experience. Parents suffer the psychological pain of having to teach their children that the larger society views them as "less than," while young people are left trying to navigate their own self-worth in a context where their life, their worldview, and their safety is not valued. In many cases, repeated experiences with police officers result in a settled perspective that this injustice is "just the way it is." Once they adopt such a perspective, Native people expect unjust interactions with police officers and have difficulty imagining a world in which their possible selves are not placed at risk. The absence of public acknowledgement of police violence against Native people is a contingency that they must negotiate in order to remain physically and psychologically safe.

Cultural mismatch. Populations that experience a mix of absolute and relative invisibility, as well as the negative stereotypes associated with the latter, are likely to find that their cultural expectations are out of sync with the dominant narrative. The theory of cultural mismatch suggests that placement in an incongruous cultural environment can elicit psychological distress that alters biological functioning (Stephens et al. 2012a). For example, Stephens and colleagues found that first-generation university students experienced greater difficulties adjusting to university life than did students whose parents also participated in higher education. They attributed this finding to a cultural mismatch between academia's institutionalized norms, which reflect individualized notions of self, and the interdependent norms of many first-generation students from working-class backgrounds. In another example, Fryberg et al. (2013b) demonstrated that Aboriginal students in a culturally matched environment reported higher levels of belongingness and more potential for success. Conversely, students tasked with operating in an environment where values and norms did not match their own risked an attenuated sense of belonging and a reduction in their perceived potential for success (Fryberg et al. 2013b). In most public US educational settings, the environment is conceptualized, designed, and implemented to highlight individuality, autonomy, and achievement. Thus, students with an interdependent orientation, such as Native Americans, are at a disadvantage in such settings.

The concept of personhood and the values of individualism that are most prevalent in the USA and Canada are based on European American society and are not shared by most other cultures in the world (Sampson 1988). Markus and Kitayama propose that independent versus interdependent views of self, which are associated with Western versus Asian cultures, respectively, are actually contrasting theoretical perspectives (1991). In the independent view of self, each person is unique, autonomous, and self-contained, motivated by the need for individual achievement and self-consistency (Markus and Kitayama 1991). Other scholars have described this view as egocentric or individualistic (Kirmayer 2007). In the interdependent view, by contrast, each person is defined in relation to multiple others (e.g., family or community) and is motivated by the need for collectivism, respect for others, and cooperation (Kirmayer 2007; Markus and Kitayama 1991). This perspective is also described as sociocentric. Related variations on interdependent views of self have been characterized as ecocentric (self in relation to the environment) and cosmocentric (self in relation with the cosmos or ancestral world) (Kirmayer 2007). Concepts of self influence people's sense of who they used to be, who they are now, and who they might become, thereby providing a framework for being in the world. When a person's model of self does not match the model endorsed by others in the same environment, psychological discord will ensue as that person tries to determine how his or her self fits into the broader social world – if at all.

Indigenous concepts of personhood. Emerging from a largely interdependent standpoint, Indigenous people view themselves as a reflection of the multiplicity of reciprocal relationships (with each other and with ancestors, plants, animals, and the cosmos) that inform their past, present, and future selves. Indigenous conceptions of reality are typically based on an understanding of mutual reciprocity (Cajete 1994; Kawagley 1993). This principle refers to the Indigenous orientation of self in sustainable, bidirectional relations with others and the physical world (Cajete 1994). Indigenous ethics and moral guides, or what it means to "walk in a good way," are shaped by mutual reciprocity, and are thus informed by responsibilities to family, community, nature, and spirit (Cajete 1994; Kawagley 1993).

For interdependent societies, such as Native American tribes or First Nations' bands, the link between culture and psychological well-being is tied to membership in the tribal community. This interdependence is reflected in the deep sense of reciprocity that characterizes all social relations. However, an interdependent orientation in the context of an independent society poses a severe cultural mismatch. Indigenous collectives often find themselves in social contexts where their values, norms, and worldviews are not adequately acknowledged, leaving young Indigenous people in particular with the challenge of navigating a world of misrepresentation as they attempt to develop their identities. In the absence of positive social representations, and lacking deep connections to each other, to plants and animals, and to the ancestral world, members of Indigenous collectives face an existential threat: they may not know who they are.

Cultural mismatch in everyday interactions and individual experiences is one of the subtler outcomes of contemporary settler colonization. The prominent messages of independence, achievement, and autonomy embedded in North American institutions exclude Indigenous people by rendering their worldview irrelevant, wrong, or obsolete. Indigenous students will continue to be colonized through the institution of education as long as they are relegated to classrooms where their interdependent perspectives are wholly absent, and where they are responsible for fitting themselves into alien cultural models. Such environments falsify the assumption that North

American classrooms are neutral spaces that afford every student the same chance to belong and succeed.

Frantz Fanon argued that the colonial process involves turning the social fabric inside out by both denigrating and denying the humanity of the colonized person (Fanon and Philcox 2007). Ultimately, colonized people can either accept new identities that are consistent with their colonizers' stereotyped perceptions, or they can revolt against these characterizations (Memmi 2013). A key step in pushing back against colonization is to identify the processes of erasure and invisibilization that prevail in everyday institutions. In the context of settler colonialism, the need for positive resistance to the physical and existential threats embodied in these institutions is underscored by an all-too-frequent outcome of such threats: Indigenous suicide.

Indigenous suicide, an ultimate reflection of settler colonial erasure. Suicide is a profoundly disturbing occurrence that challenges our assumptions about life and human existence and leaves an overwhelming sense of agony and confusion among the survivors of suicide loss. The grief of losing a loved one is devastating, and the loss is compounded by the sudden and unexpected nature of their death. Suicide disproportionately affects Indigenous populations in Canada, the USA, New Zealand, and Australia (Hunter and Harvey 2002). In the USA, American Indian and Alaska Native young people are at especially high risk: the suicide rate among people aged 15–34 years is 1.5 times higher among Native Americans than in the all-races population (Center for Disease Control 2015), with substantial variation across Native communities. In Canada, suicide and self-inflicted injuries are the leading causes of death for First Nations young people under the age of 44 years, with First Nations men (15–24 years) particularly at risk (Centre for Suicide Prevention & Canadian Mental Health Association 2013). Despite widespread concern about suicide in all Indigenous people, the root causes of suicidal behavior on a collective level remain uncertain. Those left behind wonder what makes some people relinquish their own futures and decide to take their own lives. However, suicide is not a reflection of any single factor in isolation; rather, it is a final expression of interactions among numerous mechanisms at the personal and social levels.

Suicide has been theorized largely from an individualistic standpoint in mainstream psychological research. That is, models of suicide describe suicidal behavior in terms of individual predicaments, which are typically understood in the context of a mental health condition. Individual-level risk factors for suicide are no different for Indigenous people than for people in other populations. At the level of the Indigenous collective or community, however, risk factors must be understood as the products of colonization, subjugation, and ultimately, the erasure or disruption of Indigenous collective capacities. A study conducted by one of the authors with the Cowichan Tribes in British Columbia sought to understand the perspective of multiple community members on the meanings of and explanations for suicide in their collective (Elliott 2016). She conducted 20 interviews and one focus group, each with an emphasis on understanding the lived experiences of each participant in relation to suicidal behavior. Participants were asked about the reasons for suicide, their characterizations of suicidal behavior, and appropriate healing and helping practices. Their explanations for suicidal behavior were based on their shared experience of colonization and its impact on the interdependent nature of Cowichan society and culture (Elliott-Groves 2017). Their stories about suicide were rooted in the social and cultural disruptions to collective capacities that prevented Cowichan individuals, as well as the collective as a whole, from planning and preparing for the future. They highlighted the unequal distribution of power that Cowichan members experienced in the context of education, politics, economy, food systems, and land loss. All these explanations can be understood through settler colonial theory and are a reflection of the erasure of Indigenous social and cultural formations.

Embedded in their stories was a worldview that centered on the collective orientation of the Cowichan community and the responsibilities inherent in each relationship that linked tribal members. When asked, "Why do you think our young people are dying by suicide?" a Cowichan elder named Kyle responded, "You see, our ancestors wanted us to understand and value the sacredness of life. Some of our kids are losing their way because they are losing connection with our ancestors and our ceremonies." From his standpoint, suicidal behavior was a reflection of fractured relations with ancestors and cultural practices. Cowichan people's understanding of personhood is directly related to multiple mutual relations, including ancestors. These relationships are imbued with deep responsibilities that span human, animal, plant, ancestral, and cosmic entities. Kyle's response acknowledges the relational responsibility that Cowichan people have to ancestors. The act of honoring ancestors is embedded within multiple cultural practices and is believed to bring spiritual strength and protection. The process of settler colonization has in many ways disrupted social and cultural practices including ceremonial acknowledgments. With a disruption to collective capacities, including spiritual practices, Cowichan young people are placed at risk for suicide. By acknowledging the multiplicity of relations, as Kyle implies, young people can demonstrate the importance of interconnectedness, which informs their purpose in life as members of the Cowichan Tribes. Further, a worldview that embraces the sacredness of life is very different from the dominant paradigm in current approaches to suicide, called the "prevention account" – the need to ensure that people do not kill themselves. Kyle's response suggests that the interview question, which was framed in terms of a deficit, was not a cultural match for his strengths-based, relational worldview. More so, his answer points to the importance of engaging culturally specific models of self, especially interdependent models, when theorizing suicide or designing interventions.

Conclusion

To understand Indigenous identity development, the broad question addressed is how young Indigenous people can arrive at a positive sense of identity in the context of widespread erasure and invisibility. Using settler colonial theory as a starting point, the discussion centered on the ways in which disruption of Indigenous collective capacities informs the contemporary social representational landscape where young Indigenous people must learn what it means to be a person. With land acquisition as the primary motivation, settler colonialism aims to erase Indigenous people and their collective capacities in order to establish settler structures on the land. The permanent establishment of settler colonization inscribes the land with a vast array of social, cultural, political, and economic meanings that empower settlers to adapt to the colonized environment while inhibiting the ability of Indigenous communities to plan and prepare for their own futures. The fracturing of the Indigenous relationship with land and traditional lifeways, as perpetrated through various assimilative processes, impedes the organizing structures that facilitate collective livelihood. With the disruption of these collective capacities, the continuity of Indigenous communities is threatened, leaving young Indigenous people in a social representational landscape that does not reflect their actual or perceived concepts of self. The result is psychological disequilibrium and a foreclosure of possible selves.

Because they provide a crucial link between present and future, possible selves are influenced by everyday experiences and environments. Across the life span, an individual person entertains multiple self-representations informed by social and cultural constructs. Young people in particular must engage with the ideas and practices of their everyday lives and shape their own self-understanding on this basis. Since lived experiences vary across individuals, families, communities, and cultural groups, the possible selves available to young people are socially constrained. Concepts of self are constructed through interaction with the social representational landscape, and thus figure among the most important regulators of future behavior, with the potential to expand or limit possible selves.

Social invisibility, both absolute and relative, erodes the availability of positive social representations. The result is a society in which some people must deal with identity contingencies based on their affiliation with a marginalized group. Everyday institutions such as schools and health systems are deeply imbued with implicit models of self, which might not match those sought by young Indigenous people. When they look at the world and fail to see themselves reflected, their risk of adverse psychological effects is elevated, because they cannot find the "original instructions" that would tell them what it means to be a person (Nelson 2008). They are left to negotiate a world in which their concept of self is neither affirmed nor validated. The erasure of Indigenous representation is accomplished by a variety of mechanisms, including negative stereotyping, stereotype threat, and cultural mismatch. These mechanisms have deleterious psychological and biological effects on oppressed populations, and for Indigenous young people in particular, they can depress educational achievement and lead to psychological distress, culminating far too often in suicide.

Recommendations. To counteract the effects of colonization on Indigenous populations, including American Indians, Alaska Natives, First Nations, Inuit, and Canadian Métis, broad recommendations for researchers, educators, and mental health professionals are provided. These recommendations are by no means comprehensive; rather, offered here is a broad multidimensional approach to decolonization, which may facilitate the expansion of possible futures for Indigenous people.

Interested parties are encouraged to consider how they can reach beyond the deeply embedded structures of inequality to offer positive representations and experiences to the people most affected by existing structures.

First, an understanding of the role of settler colonialism in Indigenous erasure and invisibility calls for a reconsideration of existing disparities in education and mental health, which are presented here as predominant symptoms of structural inequality. Second, the repercussions of settler colonization are far more than theoretical. The mechanisms of erasure activated by this phenomenon continue to compromise the educational and psychological well-being of young Indigenous people across multiple social contexts.

In educational settings, persistently mediocre achievement scores among secondary students in general, and Indigenous students in particular, call for a reimagining of what can be accomplished by formal and informal learning environments. To mitigate the effects of invisibility on Indigenous students, interdependent approaches to learning must be engaged (Fryberg et al. 2013a). In specific terms, relationships must be cultivated in all social spaces and projects to foreground interdependent values such as community engagement, collaboration, and collective responsibility. In this way, identity-safe learning environments can be created for marginalized groups. These environments should engage cultural practices that explain what it means to be a person, including Indigenous storytelling, teaching and learning practices, and social and cultural ways of knowing. Educational institutions can foster positive Indigenous identities by emphasizing the intergenerational social structures of Indigenous people, by hiring teachers and staff that represent the Indigenous student body, and by providing a variety of positive Indigenous role models and representations.

Cultural matching studies demonstrate the importance of including educators of diverse cultural backgrounds in the design of curricula and instructional practices. Cohen et al. (2006) argue that affirming the identity of a threatened social group has the greatest positive impact at the start of transition periods, such as the beginning of a school year or the launch of a major assignment. Similarly, Stephens et al. (2012b) demonstrate that affirming social group identity has positive effects on students' performance. In an educational study with working-class students, they reframed college welcome letters to highlight interdependent models of self, yielding positive effects on performance in subsequent activities for these students. In contrast, when they used welcome letters framed from an independent standpoint, working-class students performed worse on subsequent tasks and experienced higher levels of stress. Educators are therefore advised to launch activities and frame assignments in ways that match the cultural ways of knowing and cultural models of self of their Indigenous students.

At the level of community, Chandler and colleagues (Chandler and Lalonde 1998; Chandler et al. 2003) argue that the loss of cultural continuity between past and future is related to the above-average suicide rates recorded in First Nations communities (Chandler et al. 2003; Wexler 2006), while communal striving for cultural continuity is a primary protective factor against suicide. Strengthening community-level control over health, education, policing, treaty and land claims, and food systems is an important way to mitigate the effects of erasure and invisibility on Indigenous young people. Indeed, the fact that Indigenous people in North America continue to grow and flourish demonstrates that communal striving can succeed, and that Indigenous groups as well as colonizers can take effective action to ameliorate and ultimately halt the ongoing psychological colonization of Indigenous communities.

In order to understand the lived experience of community members from their own perspective, there is a fundamental need to attend to relational responsibilities in collective communities. For many Indigenous people, a relationship with ancestral lands enables access to ontological ways of knowing and a vast body of local wisdom, while removal from those lands threatens their understanding of human life and poses an existential threat. When possible futures are degraded or cut off, psychological distress follows. Thus, it is vastly important that Indigenous communities strengthen their connection with their traditional territories; this can be done through land–/place-based teaching and learning, land restoration projects, and food and medicine harvesting practices, for example.

Recommendations are offered as a guide for the work of researchers, educators, and healthcare providers. Professionals are asked to reflect on how their practices and institutions might be contributing to Indigenous erasure instead of reversing its harmful effects. To expand sociological and ecological futures, and to create a just democracy for all people, it is necessary to understand the holistic and multidimensional needs of community members on the level of their daily lives. All participants in a democracy are subject to this imperative. After all, responsible relations with others and with the natural world sustain human existence and link us all together in a vast web of life.

References

Adams DW (1995) Education for extinction: American Indians and the boarding school experience, 1875–1928: ERIC. University Press of Kansas, Lawrence

Alfred T, Corntassel J (2005) Being indigenous: resurgences against contemporary colonialism. Gov Oppos 40(4):597–614

Allen G (1986) The sacred hoop. Beacon Press, Boston

Cajete G (1994) Look to the mountain: an ecology of indigenous education: ERIC. Kivaki Press, Durango

Center for Disease Control (2015) Suicide: facts at a glance. Retrieved from http://www.cdc.gov/violenceprevention/pub/suicide_datasheet.html

Center on Juvenile and Criminal Justice (2014) Who are police killing? Groups most likely to be killed by law enforcement. Retrieved 1 Mar 2017, from http://www.cjcj.org/news/8113

Centre for Suicide Prevention, Canadian Mental Health Association (Producer) (2013) Suicide prevention resource toolkit. Retrieved from http://www.suicideifo.ca

Chandler M, Lalonde C (1998) Cultural continuity as a hedge against suicide in Canada's first nations. Transcult Psychiatry 35(2):191–219

Chandler M, Lalonde C, Sokol B, Hallett D, Marcia J (2003) Personal persistence, identity development, and suicide: a study of native and non-native north American adolescents. Monogr Soc Res Child Dev 68(2):1–138

Cohen GL, Garcia J, Apfel N, Master A (2006) Reducing the racial achievement gap: a social-psychological intervention. Science 313(5791):1307–1310

Coulthard GS (2014) Red skin, white masks: rejecting the colonial politics of recognition. University of Minnesota Press, Minneapolis

Cross T (2008) Disproportionality in child welfare. Child Welfare 87(2):11–20

Dunbar-Ortiz R, Gilio-Whitaker D (2016) All the real Indians died off: and 20 other myths about native Americans. Beacon Press, Boston

Elliott-Groves E (2017) Insights from Cowichan: a hybrid approach to understanding suicide in one first nations' collective. Suicide Life Threat Behav. https://doi.org/10.1111/sltb.12364

Elliott ER (2016) New thinking for intervention: towards a culturally responsive model of understanding indigenous suicide. University of Washington Libraries, Seattle

Ellis C (1996) To change them forever: Indian education at the Rainy Mountain boarding school, 1893–1920. University of Oklahoma Press, Norman

Fanon F, Philcox R (2007) The wretched of the earth: Frantz fanon; translated from the French by Richard Philcox; with commentary by Jean-Paul Sartre and Homi K. Recording for Blind & Dyslexic, Bhabha

Fryberg S, Covarrubias R, Burack JA (2013a) Cultural models of education and academic performance for native American and European American students. School Psychol Int 34(4): 439–452

Fryberg S, Townsend SS (2008) The psychology of invisibility. In: Adams G, Biernat M, Branscombe N, Crandall C, Wrightsman L (eds) Commemorating Brown: the social psychology of racism and discrimination. American Psychological Association, Washington, DC

Fryberg S, Troop-Gordon W, D'Arrisso A, Flores H, Ponizovskiy V, Ranney JD et al (2013b) Cultural mismatch and the education of aboriginal youths: the interplay of cultural identities and teacher ratings. Dev Psychol 49(1):72

Haig-Brown C (1988) Resistance and renewal: surviving the Indian residential school. Tillacum Library, Vancouver

Harding R (2006) Historical representations of aboriginal people in the Canadian news media. Discourse & Society 17(2):205–235

Hunter E, Harvey D (2002) Indigenous suicide in Australia, New Zealand, Canada and the United States. Emerg Med 14(1):14–23

Johnston BH (1995) Indian school days. University of Oklahoma Press, Norman

Kawagley AO (1993) A Yupiaq world view: implications for cultural, educational, and technological adaptation in a contemporary world (T). Retrieved from https://open.library.ubc.ca/cIRcle/collections/831/items/1.0098864

Kena G, Hussar W, McFarland J, de Brey C, Musu-Gillette L, Wang X, . . . Diliberti M (2016) The condition of education 2016. NCES 2016–144. National Center for Education Statistics, Jessup

Kirmayer L (2007) Psychotherapy and the cultural concept of the person. Transcult Psychiatry 44(2):232–257

Kirmayer L, Valaskakis GG (2009) Healing traditions: the mental health of aboriginal people in Canada. UBC Press, Vancouver

LaDuke W (1999) All our relations: native struggles for land and life. South End Press, Cambridge, MA

Leavitt PA, Covarrubias R, Perez YA, Fryberg S (2015) "Frozen in time": the impact of native American media representations on identity and self-understanding. J Soc Issues 71(1):39–53

Lefevre TA (2015) Settler colonialism. In: Oxford bibliographies in anthropology. Oxford University Press, Oxford

Lomawaima KT, McCarty TL (2006) To remain an Indian: lessons in democracy from a century of native American education. Teachers College Press, New York

Maracle L (1996) I am woman: a native perspective on sociology and feminism. Press Gang Publishers, Vancouver, British Columbia

Markus HR, Kitayama S (1991) Culture and the self: implications for cognition, emotion, and motivation. Psychol Rev 98(2):224

Markus HR, Nurius P (1986) Possible selves. Am Psychol 41(9):954

Memmi A (2013) The colonizer and the colonized. Routledge, Abingdon

Moscovici S (2001) Social representations: essays in social psychology. New York University Press, New York

National Center for Education Statistics (2016) Race/ethnicity of college faculty. Retrieved from NCES, degrees conferred by race, 2016

Nelson M (2008) Original instructions: Indigenous teachings for a sustainable future. Rochester, Vt.: Bear & Company

Oyserman D, Fryberg S (2006) The possible selves of diverse adolescents: content and function across gender, race and national origin. In: Possible selves: theory, research, and applications. Nova Science Publishers, New York, pp 17–39

Purdie-Vaughns V, Steele CM, Davies PG, Ditlmann R, Crosby JR (2008) Social identity contingencies: how diversity cues signal threat or safety for African Americans in mainstream institutions. J Pers Soc Psychol 94(4):615

Rich A (1994) Blood, bread, and poetry: selected prose 1979–1985. WW Norton & Company, New York

Sampson EE (1988) The debate on individualism: indigenous psychologies of the individual and their role in personal and societal functioning. Am Psychol 43(1):15

Shear SB, Knowles RT, Soden GJ, Castro AJ (2015) Manifesting destiny: re/presentations of indigenous people in K–12 U.S. history standards. Theory & Research in Social Education 43(1):68–101. https://doi.org/10.1080/00933104.2014.999849

Statistics Canada (2015, November 11) Aboriginal people are more likely to have trades and college certificates. Retrieved 23 Mar 2017, from http://www.statcan.gc.ca/pub/89-645-x/2010001/education-eng.htm

Steele CM (1997) A threat in the air: how stereotypes shape intellectual identity and performance. Am Psychol 52(6):613

Stephens NM, Fryberg S, Markus HR, Johnson CS, Covarrubias R (2012a) Unseen disadvantage: how American universities' focus on independence undermines the academic performance of first-generation college students. J Pers Soc Psychol 102(6):1178

Stephens NM, Townsend SS, Markus HR, Phillips LT (2012b) A cultural mismatch: independent cultural norms produce greater increases in cortisol and more negative emotions among first-generation college students. J Exp Soc Psychol 48(6):1389–1393

Trosper R (2009) Resilience, reciprocity and ecological economics: northwest coast sustainability. Routledge, London; New York

Veracini L (2010) Settler colonialism: a theoretical overview. Palgrave Macmillan, Houndmills/New York

Wexler LM (2006) Inupiat youth suicide and culture loss: changing community conversations for prevention. Social Science Medicine 63(11):2938–2948

Whyte KP (2015) Indigenous food systems, environmental justice, and settler-industrial states. In: Rawlinson M, Ward C (eds) Global food, global justice. Cambridge Scholars Publishing, Newcastle upon Tyne, p 177

Wolfe P (2006) Settler colonialism and the elimination of the native. Journal of Genocide Research 8(4):387

The Value of Indigenous Knowledge to Education for Sustainable Development and Climate Change Education in the Pacific

Timote Masima Vaioleti and Sandra L. Morrison

Contents

Introduction	652
Global Contexts	653
Education for Sustainable Development (ESD), Climate Change (CC), and Pacific Indigenous Knowledge	654
Kiribati MOE and Climate Change Curriculum Framework (CCCF)	655
H.O.P.E Framework as a Methodology	656
H for Holistic	657
O for Ownership	658
P for Partnership	658
E for Empowerment	658
Mapping of the Current Curriculum	659
Distribution of CC Theme Topics in the Current Curriculum	659
Distribution of Four Climate Change Topics in the Curriculum	659
Possibility for the Future of I-Kiribati in Other Nations	659
Samoa and METI Taiala Program	661
METI: A Case Study	663
The Taiala Program	664
Looking to the Future	667
Conclusion	668
References	669

T. M. Vaioleti (✉)
Faculty of Education, University of Waikato, Hamilton, New Zealand
e-mail: tmvaioleti@gmail.com; vaioleti@waikato.ac.nz

S. L. Morrison
School of Māori and Indigenous Studies, University of Waikato, Hamilton, New Zealand
e-mail: samorr@waikato.ac.nz

© Springer Nature Singapore Pte Ltd. 2019
E. A. McKinley, L. T. Smith (eds.), *Handbook of Indigenous Education*,
https://doi.org/10.1007/978-981-10-3899-0_8

Abstract

Pacific knowledge systems have always had to deal with change. Living in the vastness of the Pacific and exposed to environmental challenges has resulted in communities that are constantly needing to adapt to improve their conditions. Climate change (CC) is a more recent and indeed urgent phenomenon to which to respond. The Education for Sustainable Development (ESD) agenda established by the United Nations Educational Scientific and Cultural Organisation (UNESCO) is an attempt to encourage communities to set in place educational responses and strategies and to make informed choices regarding sustainable issues now and in the future.

The authors have worked on educational responses to ESD and CC in the Pacific over many years. Central to their approach has been the acknowledgment that both ESD and CC require a broad based, interdisciplinary, and holistic approach and any approach must uphold culture as its underpinning driver. Being critically sharpened by experiences of living in the colonized reality of Aotearoa/New Zealand and familiar with old Polynesian values, the authors are able to work alongside communities to coconstruct innovative solutions to assist in fulfilling the ESD agendas in the Pacific. Such experiences can be made relevant to other contexts.

This article will review approaches to ESD and CC education in two case studies in which Indigenous concepts were made central. Firstly in Kiribati, where the research was undertaken in partnership with Ministries, UNESCO Apia, and NGOs to firstly map the current school curriculum to include and strengthen climate change education (CCE) by creating a CCE framework which is culturally and contextually relevant.

Secondly, in the nonformal sector, the authors led work with an NGO in Samoa to train "Taiala" (pathbreakers) to incorporate the principles of ESD and CC adaptation into their villages through a leadership training workshop.

On both occasions, the approaches allowed for an innovative mix of Indigenous models to form an integral part of finding solutions to the ESD and CC challenges and to also ensure that the application was appropriate and allowed for successful educational outcomes as determined by the communities themselves and also for themselves.

Keywords

Indigenous knowledge (IK) · Education for sustainable development (ESD) · Climate change education (CCE) · Pacific development · Fonua · Tofi

Introduction

This chapter examines the application of Indigenous notions and approaches to two case studies in which sustainable development was emerging as a challenge. It discusses firstly the efforts by a State actor, the Ministry of Education (MOE) in the Micronesian nation of Kiribati to include CC in its curriculum. The next case study focuses on an NGO (nongovernment organization), Matuaileo'o Environment Trust (METI) from the Polynesian nation of Samoa, whose aim was to incorporate the principles of education for sustainable development in the routines of village life in 50 villages through an education and leadership development endeavor in response to local needs.

Both cases emerged through a series of strategic and collaborative partnerships. The actors in the first case were UNESCO Pacific, Ministry of Education (MOE) Kiribati, Indigenous Māori and Pacific Adult Education Charitable Trust (IMPAECT*) a New Zealand NGO, and the University of Waikato. They were tasked to develop a Climate Change Curriculum Framework (CCCF) for Kiribati that is appropriate to their current realities. Further, in both case studies, Indigenous knowledge systems were a strong contributor to empowering the communities to transform themselves to meet their own cultural, spiritual, and economic aspirations in the face of an uncertain world.

From a global level, both cases were also guided by international policy commitments: The Millennium Development Goals (MDG), Education For All (EFA), and more recently the Sustainable Development Goals (SDGs) which were sanctioned by the United Nations in September 2015.

Global Contexts

The developing nations of the South Pacific generally have high regard for international global policy on education. Over past years, these nations have worked closely with development partners on initiatives to address shared education challenges in the region (UNESCO 2015). Through the transition from EFA and MDG to the SDGs, there have been valuable lessons and experiences to inform the way forward. At the core of the 2030 Agenda for Sustainable Development is the notion of inclusion (United Nations 2017).

Education is a codified stand-alone goal. Goal 4 of the SDGs states "ensure inclusive and equitable quality education and promote lifelong learning opportunities for all" by 2030. At a high-level UNESCO meeting in Paris in November 2015, there was also agreement on the Education 2030 Framework for Action (United Nations 2017). Equally important for the Pacific region was the December 2015 gathering of world leaders at the United Nations CC Conference (COP 21), where global agreements on global warming and tackling climate change were adopted. Integral to the success of the COP21 plan are education and training, to raise awareness and to assist people in making informed decisions while promoting changes in lifestyles, attitudes, and behaviors.

Given the comparative slowness of progressing the United Nations intentions, the realities for the small, isolated, and low-lying Pacific nations is that they are being negatively impacted by CC and other global issues now and increasingly in multiple rates.

Education for Sustainable Development (ESD), Climate Change (CC), and Pacific Indigenous Knowledge

Thaman (2009) presents an argument for Pacific nations to hold on to their cultures through educational platforms especially in terms of developing resilience strategies. She suggests a total transformation in the way Pacific nations approach education, as some practices in both industrial countries and the Pacific are moving in a direction of unsustainability. As it is for all nations, ESD for the Pacific nations is essential given the environmental pressures, the pervasive individualism, and systemic selfishness that underpins capitalism and its education systems (Teaero 2003; Thaman 2009; Vaioleti 2011; Vaioleti et al. 2012).

Sustainable development is not a new idea for the Pacific nations (Teaero 2010; Vaioleti 2011). For some, living in isolated islands with limited land mass and high dependence on the ocean and weather for their survival, their education systems have traditionally taught them how to live with nature, support each other, and respect their environment as active and codependant members of a coherent system. Their Indigenous education was about learning one's tofi (or tofi'a: role and responsibility) which was a way of life or living that maintained balance and harmony with each other, nature, and the god/s (fonua). This is a way of being, otherwise referred to as fakafonua, which refers to the practices or ways of the land. Faka or fa'a in Samoan and vaka in Fijian means "way of" and fonua (Tongan) is a notion that in its physical form means the land and all that is contained within, including the water bodies in its environment. In its intellectual form, it can mean language, thought, and political system; it can mean its cultural social systems or religious systems that all add up to the knowledge particular to an area or a group. *Fonua* is the Tongan spelling with the same concept expressed as *fanua* in Samoan, *whenua* in Māori, *vanua* in Fiji, and *enua* in the Cook Islands. Fakafonua includes the practices of the fonua of Tonga; fa'asamoa and fa'afanua are the Samoan practices.

Pacific Indigenous thought systems and knowledge are relational, functional, and contextualized. Their basic ontology is conducive to reciprocity and respect that leads to balance and harmonious existence, a holistic type of sustainability. ESD advocates a spirit of preservation that Pacific peoples identify and align with in their ecologically anchored social/cultural practices such as fakatonga or fakasamoa (Teaero 2009; Thaman 2009; Vaioleti et al. 2012).

The emergence of sustainable development that underpinned the climate change research in Kiribati and that involved the community in Samoa had to be contextualized respectively to the fonua therefore aligning with the three pillars for ESD: society, environment, and economy. The addition of culture as the fourth pillar is vital for Pacific nations. Culture influences the work with which the authors are involved including those discussed in this chapter. The authors' work with Indigenous communities in Samoa, Tonga, Fiji, Kiribati, the Solomon Islands, and Vanuatu were underpinned by their local perspectives and respective cultures (Vaioleti et al. 2002; Vaioleti 2011).

Kiribati MOE and Climate Change Curriculum Framework (CCCF)

The former Secretary-General of the United Nations, Ban Ki-Moon, stated that climate change is "the defining issue of our era" (United Nations 2008). Nowhere is this more pertinent than in Small Island Developing States (SIDS) where some of the most vulnerable peoples live. In the Republic of Kiribati, climate change is already being experienced and urgent attention is being led by the Office of the President.

At the UN level, the Republic of Kiribati has been using many global frameworks to raise these issues. It has been working extensively with the many agreements that acknowledge the challenges that Small Island Developing States (SIDS) face in the effort towards achieving sustainable development. These include the United Nations Framework Convention on CC, Barbados Program of Action, Millennium Development Goals the United Nations Framework Convention on Climate Change (UNFCC), the Sustainable Development Goals, as well as the Kyoto Protocol.

Midway through 2011 and in the ensuing 2 years, the authors led a team of researchers to develop a Climate Change Curriculum Framework (CCCF) for Kiribati which was based on the principles of Education for Sustainable Development (ESD). This group of researchers worked in partnership with the Pacific branch of UNESCO based in Samoa. The tasks were to:

- Map the existing curriculum across all the school subjects to assess the extent to which CC-related areas were being taught
- To find appropriate points of intervention to include CC in the curriculum where it was not being taught

The Republic of Kiribati is comprised of 33 small fragmented remote low-lying islands spread over four million square kilometers, yet its total land area is only 726 km^2. The main administrative centre of Kiribati is South Tarawa which is undergoing rapid and intensive urbanization. The Kiribati 2009 Demographic and Health Survey shows that the total population in mid-2010 was 103,466 (92,533 at the time of the 2005 census), and 50,010 of the total (just under 50%) were living in South Tarawa. Half of the Kiribati population is under the age of 21 and 36% of the total is under the age of 15 years (Kiribati Demographic and Health Survey 2009). With a heavy youth population, there are serious implications for future planning in an already resource constrained environment, especially when an increase in population is predicted (Bedford and Hugo 2011).

The impacts of CC are expected to be severe and, as reported in a World Bank Report, will have serious impacts on coastal land and infrastructure, water resources, agriculture, human health, ecosystems, and fisheries (as cited in Logan 2009). These impacts for Kiribati are already evident in Tarawa where the research team for this project observed rising sea level against low-lying lands, the impact of sea acidification on seafood sources, intrusion of sea water into wells, other water supplies, food fields, and increased severity and regularity of natural disasters. On top of these, the challenges are magnified by physical isolation, heavy reliance on others for sea and air connections, and lack of a close relationship with other developed countries, financial and other resources.

For Kiribati, there are many urgent crises looming, including rising sea levels, the rapid decline in sea-based food supply for the local population and the economy due to acidification, decreased water quality, and dwindling water sources. Internal migration from outer islands to Tarawa for a better life through education and employment multiply the infrastructural challenges that are common to most smaller and poor Pacific nations. In addition, CC challenges experienced by such low-lying nations such as Kiribati further exacerbate these pressures at unsustainable levels.

The expansion of human activities and importation of foreign materials, services, and food associated with population growth also threatens the limited environmental resources, the islands' traditional subsistence economy, traditional knowledge systems, and culture. Yet despite these challenges, the communities endeavor to make a life from the limited resources they have, which is an important ESD lesson from which schools could learn. The research team observed an example of this propensity to adapt to changing environments, by young people using the land vacated by the sea at low tide for organized football and other games until the tide returned. These tendencies to rise above disasters are strengths that are associated with I-Kiribati. (I-Kiribati is a term which refers to the Indigenous people of Kiribati.) It is claimed that more than any other Micronesian country, Kiribati has held on to its traditional values and customs (Teaero 2009).

The Kiribati 2010 National Framework for CC and Climate Change Adaptation asserts that culture and identity as I-Kiribati is imperative and must be at the forefront of discussions (Office of Te Beretitenti Republic of Kiribati 2010). The intention of the Climate Change Framework was to encourage the use of local culture in tandem with scientific knowledge to preserve and grow cultural and traditional knowledge and to build a holistic capability to cope with CC and its challenges. This was seen as important to keep up with the twenty-first-century knowledge and community membership while maintaining identity, pride, and global citizenship obligations.

This framework then is a Kiribati scientific and cultural response to the climate change discourses. It recognizes the central role that the community plays in giving effect to such transformation. Cultural values and relationships between people and their lands and seas inform our deliberations in the formation of the framework. The work undertaken by Logan (2009, pp. 18–19) which notes "the degree to which Kiribati values influence adaptation to climate change" and that "cultural traditions are still very strong and relevant at all levels of governance" reinforces this position.

H.O.P.E Framework as a Methodology

The H.O.P.E Framework was applied and referenced from the Tokyo Declaration of HOPE 2009 and had significant input from Professor Konai Thaman, reputed Tongan scholar, poet, and philosopher. In that document, "Holistic," "Ownership-based," "Participatory," and "Empowering" were characteristics that have both informed and surfaced from ESD practice and have synergy with Pacific research values. The H.O.P.E acronym provides a list of the characteristics; the arrows indicate that it is not just a set of descriptions but an intricate interrelationship between the characteristics that deepens ESD practice. Talanoa, which is a term used for consultations, exchanges, and is guided by Pacific protocols (Vaioleti 2006, 2011, 2013) as well as being the base of culturally relevant Pacific research methodology, was used to guide the consultation and conversation with stakeholders. The combination of these two localized and international frameworks advocated and guided this ESD and CC endeavor. The structure of H.O.P.E is as below (Fig. 1).

The following commentary discusses the application of the H.O.P.E elements in the Kiribati CCCF development.

H for Holistic

Teaero (2009) suggests that, for I-Kiribati, the wholeness of a person is based on three significant values encompassed in te mauri (traditional blessings), te raoi (peace), and ao te tabomoa (prosperity), and that the teaching of appropriate cultural values and their application will help on all matters and aspects of life. These values informed all the research and development team's considerations throughout the development and relationships with the Kiribati stakeholders.

The research team, however, realized that CC education and ESD are important transformative agents and it needed to move people to adopt behaviors and practices to live full and worthwhile lives by combining holistic as well as scientific approaches. It was necessary for the team to reconceptualize CC in ways that will encourage educators, planners, and learners to engage CCE and ESD in a systemic and holistic way. To allow for ease of planning, teaching, and learning the project was guided by the following four themes:

- Awareness: Creating and raising awareness through education and public information
- Adaptation: Coconstructing strategies with partners, some of which may come from traditional practices to adapt to CC
- Mitigation: Coconstructing responses with partners to reduce the impact of CC
- Related issues: The responses to issues brought about by CC or loss of identity, environment degradation, poverty, and marginalization as a result of unequal

Fig. 1 Structure of H.O.P.E framework (As adopted from Asia-Pacific Centre for Culture for UNESCO 2009, p. 8)

development which may include urbanization, loss of leadership due to the migration of leaders, or professional classes (young and old) to global markets

O for Ownership

It was vital that the research team worked with the local community to ensure that the curriculum was sourced in their culture or fakafonua. This allowed a sense of ownership of their learning and the goals for their school curriculum by the community. That insight drove the authors and the research and development team to ensure that local learning concepts, values, and language were included in the CC framework. Views of the teachers, teacher training institutions, NGOs, and churches were included in both constructions to enhance the communities' sense of ownership. In many ways the authors realized that communities and individuals already had an intrinsic awareness of the concept of tofi although it was locally named because of the kinship units of mwenga (household), utu (extended family), and kainga (kin relationships). The village systems thrived on everyone knowing their role.

P for Partnership

Partnering with community including youth, institutional experts locally and internationally, was vital for ensuring that the Framework was at the cutting edge of the CCE field, yet easily delivered and relevant to the educational needs of Kiribati in the twenty-first century and beyond.

There is a popular Kiribati saying which says that in discussions with the community you have to "sit on their mat." Therefore finding out whose mat to sit on then building relationships which allowed for the shared sitting involved having community partners with which to work. Partnerships were essential to the ongoing success of the project and the development needs of the country, a point made by Corcoran (2016) in his PhD thesis on the implications of climate change for the livelihoods of urban dwellers in Kiribati.

The research for the CCCF was reviewed by experts on ESD and Education for All (EFA), including UNESCO (Paris ESD team), South Pacific Regional Environmental Programmes (SPREP) Samoa, and the Universities of Washington and Hawai'i.

E for Empowerment

The authors met on two occasions with several village leaders, public servants, school leaders and students to listen to what they identified as being important factors to include in the CC and ESD elements of the school curriculum. This was important to ensure the inclusion of community voices, affirm community aspirations, and to ensure the decision making (present and future) would be led by the community.

Mapping of the Current Curriculum

The CCCF maps the curriculum to locate and assess CC-related topic coverage within and across the subjects. There were three ways that the CCCF team used to identify their findings and to suggest where it may be possible to insert CC topics into each subject. A tick was used to signal that an existing topic was definitely CC-related. The letter "p" (for possible) indicated a topic that could be CC-related in the different subjects. An "o" (for opportunity) was given to a point in a subject that could be an entry point for a CC-related topic. We have not discussed the mapping chart that revealed the "p" finding in this discussion as it has less significance to the topic of this chapter. The following represents the occurrence of CC topics accumulated for each existing subject area.

Distribution of CC Theme Topics in the Current Curriculum

It was found that the topics that may be related to CC were taught in environmental science only. Given that the pillars of ESD are economy, society, and culture as well as environment there was very little CC topics in developmental studies and social science which represent the ESD pillar of "Society"; very low CC topics in Agriculture, Science, Biology, Developmental science could represent the ESD pillar of "Economy." Therefore there was a significant imbalance in the Kiribati curriculum if it was examined to assess its ESD and CC strength as seen in the following graph (Fig. 2).

Distribution of Four Climate Change Topics in the Curriculum

Using data from the mapping charts, the current CC-related topics in the curriculum were analyzed against the four Climate Change themes of Knowledge and Understanding, Adaptation, Mitigation, and Related issues. The following graph in Fig. 3 is the result.

What is very obvious from the above graph is the little attention that has been given to "Adaptation," an area that is vital for the continuity and sustainability of the communities in Kiribati. It is an area that potentially could provide meaningful employment for the community. Under the theme of Related Issues, addressing migration and revitalization of culture that can lead to improved self-esteem and other sociopolitical benefits was also a strong consideration.

Possibility for the Future of I-Kiribati in Other Nations

A strong element of the many talanoa the CCCF team had with teachers, principals, parents, and young people was around the loss of tradition and culture due to urbanization and disconnection from home island or village. Anticipating that most of the current students may migrate to other nations in the near future, it

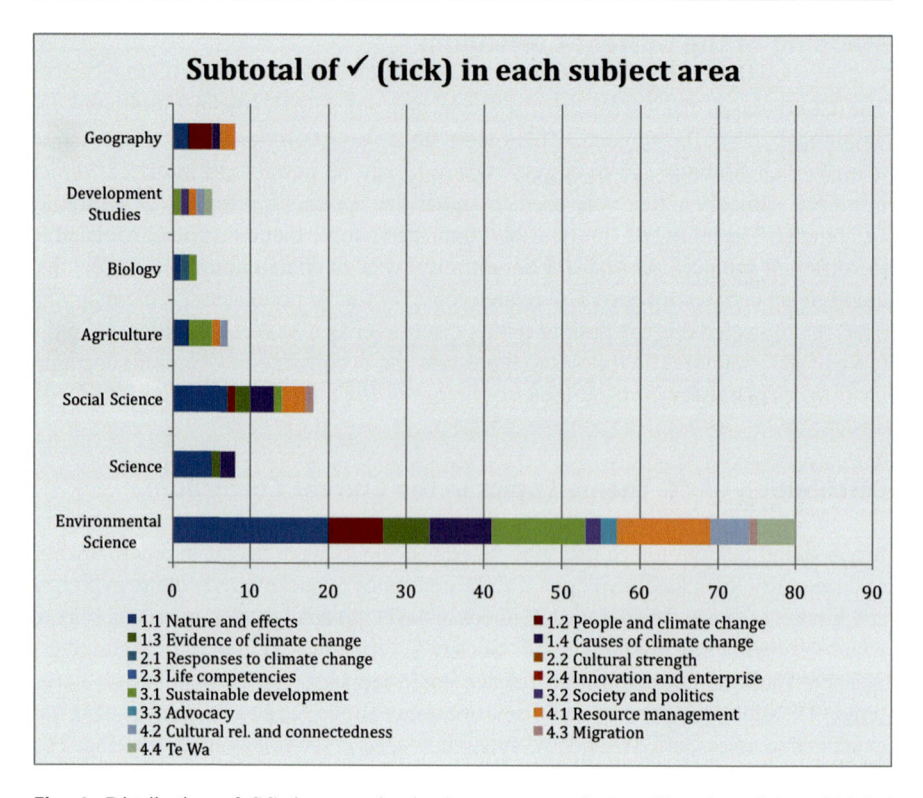

Fig. 2 Distribution of CC theme topics in the current curriculum (As adopted from Vaioleti et al. 2011, p. 42)

would be important to increase CCE across the four themes but mainly in the Related Issues theme to specifically reinforce students' cultural fortitude to ensure identity and community continuity.

Entry points were identified as "o" for opportunity to include CCE topics into different subjects. These "o" points of entry were sought by CCCF team to create a CCE system that is spread across the four themes to make the curriculum more balanced, more relevant, stronger, and more culturally robust than it currently was. The following graph in Fig. 4 is the visual representation of these efforts.

The Kiribati President, Anote Tong, says that for many I-Kiribati communities, migration is a strong probability (Chapman 2012, p. 1). The school curriculum then must help prepare the community for international citizenship and the foundation for such success is in cultural continuity. Kiribati is a Pacific nation that is endeavoring to fortify itself against many challenges such as the erosion of its language, identity, urbanization, and the global threat of CC. One of the approaches it has taken is through introducing CC formally into its schools. Other Pacific nations are preparing for similar issues at different levels.

The next part of this chapter discusses such a case in Samoa, only this case study and approach has a more informal education and community approach.

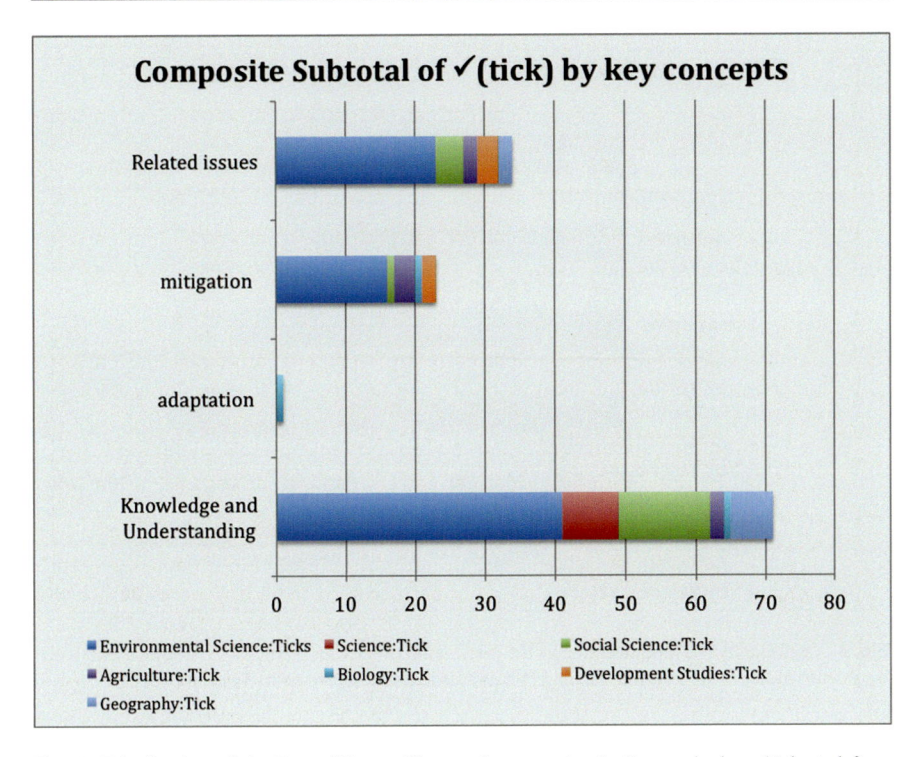

Fig. 3 Distribution of the Four Climate Change theme topics in the curriculum (Adopted from Vaioleti et al. 2011, p. 43)

Samoa and METI Taiala Program

A UNICEF report on the state of youth in the Pacific (2011, p. 11) shows that "young men not-in-education or work may be contributing little to their community. The issue is particularly serious in Kiribati, Marshall Islands and Samoa, where around half or more of young men aged 20–24 years are not engaged in productive activity (58 per cent of males 20–24 years in Kiribati, 44 per cent in Marshall Islands and 46 per cent in Samoa)."

In Samoa, over a quarter of the total population are in the wider youth-age group of 15–30 years (Curtain and Vakaoti 2011). Given high unemployment and underemployment (including in Kiribati), the particular challenges which young people in the Pacific area face include limited opportunities of decent and meaningful work. Meaningful work has a deep cultural and spiritual importance to the Indigenous cultures of the Pacific given their focus on being a subsistence economy.

Vaioleti (2011) wrote on the significance of a Tonga saying "Ko e faka'ilonga 'oe tangata ko 'ene ngaue" (the mark of a person is his/her work), contributing to the wellness of the group for the harmonious wellbeing of community living and existence in Tonga. His study also revealed that the aim of education for Tongan

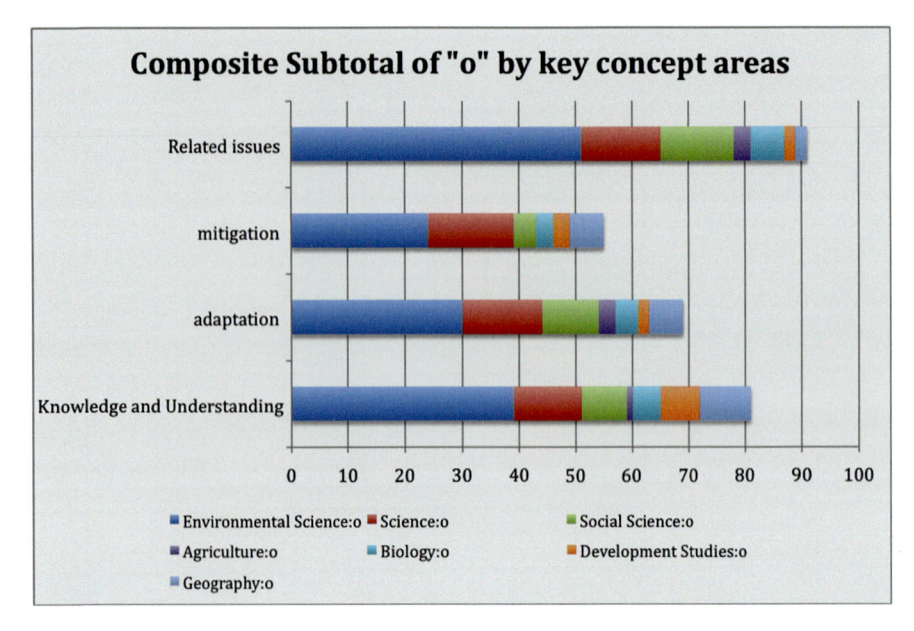

Fig. 4 Opportunity ("o") points of entry for distribution of the four themes for CC topics and to also be an entry point to allow for enhancing cultural fortitude (Adopted from Vaioleti et al 2011, p.46)

people was to enable them to carry out their tofi'a (tofi, fatongia, roles) to their sisters, own families, and to the fonua in order to achieve and maintain harmony with each other and their god/s (ibid., pp. 184–186). One of the iconic poems to have come from the Pacific written by the paramount chief and current Head of State of Samoa Tuiatua Tamasese alluded to the importance of fatongia, tofi, or tofi'a (role, obligation, duty) of appropriate/meaningful work for the psychological, spiritual, and economic wellness of a Pacific person as below:

> I am not an individual
> I share divinity with my ancestors, the land, the seas and the skies.
> I am not an individual, because I share a *tofi* with my family, my village and my nation.
> I belong to my family and my family belongs to me.
> I belong to my village and my village belongs to me.
> I belong to my nation and my nation belongs to me.
> This is the essence of my belonging. (Tui Atua 2009, p. 1)

One's tofi is not only vital for the wellness of one's family, village, and nation but it provides identity and self-worth to individuals. Meaningful work contributes to the cohesion of small villages where every person's effective contribution is vital for the sustainability of their community, be it physical, economic, intellectual, emotional, or spiritual.

Given the consistent high unemployment in the Pacific, the Prime Minister of Samoa, the Hon. Tuilaepa Malielegaoi in his opening speech of the Pacific Region

Commonwealth Youth Ministers Meeting that Samoa hosted in 2015, declared that "we cannot keep doing the same things we did yesterday and hope for a different outcome" (Samoa Government 2015, p. 1). This statement then calls for different and innovative approaches and for both the formal sector and the informal and nonformal sectors to work collaboratively and in mutually beneficial ways to assist with meaningful work for the benefit of the fonua.

METI: A Case Study

Consonant with this thinking, METI, a well-established NGO, had already been aware of critical education gaps, of out-of-school youth, of health and educational issues that have a severe impact on the quality of livelihoods of the people with whom they were working in the villages. Thus, they were able to identify policy gaps and to provide education in order to effectively implement responses in the communities and villages of Samoa.

In 2002, METI worked with the authors to facilitate the training of trainers within a European Union-funded research and development project. This 2-week project was run in Fiji as well as in Samoa; it helped to establish METI's capability of working in a participatory mode with grassroots communities, and it allowed METI's staff to become familiar with adult education techniques. The authors promoted the application of Indigenous knowledge systems to crucial problems and for sustainability.

METI has as its mission "to provide a service to the people of Samoa that promotes simultaneously the preservation of their environment and the sustainable development of their natural resources and in addition helps them to develop into individuals living in harmony with nature" (METI 2016). Its vision continues along the same philosophy, namely "to provide participatory non-formal training of the necessary management skills and promote capacity building to achieve sustainable living in Samoa through self-reliance, particular of grassroots communities" (METI 2016).

When METI realized that the Government had identified major obstacles to sustainable development and poverty reduction at the community level, such as lack of education, of awareness, and of capacity on the part of the communities, and realized the need to collaborate, METI started to address these issues (Talanoa 2015). Over the years, METI has developed a wide-ranging project portfolio and has acquired a lot of expertise. Its current programs include the METI's Noncommunicable Diseases Programme (2013–2014), funded by a grant from the US Embassy; the grant allowed METI to expand its programs of health promotion (situated at the Samoa Sleep Clinic/Healthy Living Clinic in Apia) and to use its existing multisectoral outreach program (the Taiala programme) for conducting health surveys in ten villages around Samoa, raising awareness about obesity and a variety of noncommunicable diseases, their prevention and control.

METI has been accepted by the Samoa Qualifications Authority (SQA) as a "Non-Formal Learning Provider" and in 2013, its "Life Skills" training course was officially certified by the SQA. METI has now been invited to formally apply for recognition as a "Post-Secondary Education Training (PSET) Provider" and to have its courses certified and credited, including "Permaculture Training," "Basic English for Development," and training courses for "Life Skills" coaches. In this way, graduates will receive credits that may help them to access additional courses at the Technical Colleges or the National University of Samoa.

METI also provides "Healthy Living" seminars on whole-food plant-based (WFPB) diet to reverse the effects of chronic diseases, and it offers health monitoring for those individuals who are willing to adopt the WFPB nutrition program. These seminars are changing the way Samoans think about food and nutrition, in addition to reversing the effects of chronic diseases like diabetes, high blood pressure, and obesity.

The release of the 2007 report of the Intergovernmental Panel on Climate Change (IPCC) came as a "wake-up call" to METI. It realized that the climate change is destined to have a far more destructive and far earlier impact than previously estimated; significant rises of global temperatures could well be experienced by the end of this century, bringing irreversible and devastating changes to the planet. As a result, METI decided to mainstream climate change action in all its projects and programs, and to deepen its involvement at the local level, in the villages, in the effort to promote improved and sustainable livelihoods for villagers, through climate change education (CCE) and education for sustainable development (ESD), as well as through the promotion of good health.

The Taiala Program

In 2010 METI officially created its Taiala program. This had been a mutual vision of the cofounder of METI, the late senior matai (chief) Matatumua Vermeulen and of the current director Dr. Walter Vermeulen. In a way the designation "Pathbreaker" signifies that the environment and social systems that have led to so much destruction and to the marginalization of so many (including women and youth) must be discontinued.

METI's request – in the year 2000 – for assistance with Taiala training gained seeding funding from the Samoan Government. As a pilot scheme, a basic Life Skills Course (LSC) development program was held in 13 villages around Samoa. From among the 182 graduates of this course, 24 individuals were chosen for additional training that would lay the foundation of METI's Taiala Programme.

The Taiala needed to be chosen from villages where the chiefs had a long-standing relationship and trust in the work of METI. The chosen village member would be expected to work collaboratively and cooperatively as members of a larger collective. Responsibility, reciprocity, as well as leadership skills were key values in their selection.

Those who were selected were ordinary men and women; some were chiefs (male and female) or orators, others married and single men and women, retired public servants, others were trusted taulelea or untitled men. What they all had in common is that they were sons and daughters of the villages in which they lived and worked.

Thanks to the respect and trust they command, the Taiala are individuals whom the other villagers will listen to and from whom they learn. The Taiala remain living in their respective villages and are the front-line health workers, education workers, and workers for sustainable development. Their experience has its source in their village communities and is shaped by their village; their acquired skills are then returned to the village. This is in line with the "aiga" (kinship) responsibility that is innate to them.

On 1 May 2015, having successfully obtained funding, METI's 3-year Climate Change Action project started with the Taiala. The action, through a two-tier arrangement, consists of METI's Central Training Team providing training, monitoring, and mentoring to the Taiala, who, in turn, implement several streams of interlinked activities in the target villages. The overall objective of the action is to attain – for a significant proportion of the adult population in 50 villages around Samoa, via culture sensitive participatory training and development – balanced, self-directed behavior, a more ecologically attuned world view, and the wisdom to engage in cooperative action. These are essential components of the spirit of collective and individual self-reliance which is needed for the communities' sustainable wellbeing.

In June 2014, the authors conducted a weeklong "Facilitators and Leadership Training for the Taiala." The format of the workshop was similar to the format successfully facilitated in 2002 under the CROPPRO, and drew on its success. The workshop had the following objectives:

1. To nurture a culture of harmony in homes and communities
2. To firmly embrace sustainable development
3. To engage with the meaningful mitigation of climate change and in actions of adaptation
4. To raise the Taiala's level of awareness of the task to promote a spirit of self-reliance
5. To increase the capacity of the Taiala to engage with ease in the cultural, socioeconomic, and political lives of villages, of the country, and the world community

The theoretical basis of the workshop drew on the work of Rahman, who believes in grassroots mobilization for the promotion of the collective intellectual capacities of people (Rahman 1993): People conduct their own inquiries into their living conditions and their environment, and arrive at their own solutions. Moreover, the work of Freire, specifically his "problem-posing education" through the creation of "teacher-students" and "student-teachers" (Freire 1972), was regarded as an important tool in working towards empowerment.

The facilitators (also the authors) referenced the Pacific concept of "ako" (Vaioleti 2011, 2013) to guide their learning relationship with the Taiala. Intrinsic to ako is the importance of learning Indigenous concepts such as compassion, respect, serving others and aiga (kainga or extended kin) important to maintaining harmonious living. One of the pillars of "ako" is empowerment. This is particularly vital, given the highly stratified societies of the Pacific, such as the societies of Tonga and Samoa (Vaioleti 2011).

In the "ako" approach, the participants became teachers, helping the facilitators to conceptualize the relational structures of their villages and the needs of their clients, raising the facilitators to a level where they were able to align their own teaching with that of the participants; as a result, learning from the sessions became more relevant as discussed by Vaioleti (2011) as the "founga ako." The building of relationships and sharing of power are integral to the philosophy of METI and are important factors for the success of "ako."

The training strategy was to conduct a theoretical and practical workshop on integrated participatory actions; the topics of the workshop included methods and principles of adult learning and teaching, capacity-building and leadership-development, building resilience in order to achieve self-reliance, awareness of climate change and its impacts, and the concepts of sustainable development. METI's leadership team were present during the workshop, enriching the approaches used. Through this partnership, the Taiala were able to bring in their traditional knowledge and customs, and to make sense of their wisdom at the interface of current ESD and scientific and academic discourses thus taking the learning back to their respective communities.

Given the considerable level of skill which METI had already started to develop in past training programs by working at ground or village level, the Taiala concept was considered by many of the participants capable of developing into an even more dynamic and successful initiative, as well as able to provide the leadership required for positive village transformations. While this would be subject to appropriate resources and ongoing training opportunities, it was noted also that ongoing mentoring was important as well as maintaining the relationships in the village, particularly with village chiefs.

Paramount in the minds of Samoans is "vā," which is a broad Polynesian notion of the relational space between people and the environment, between people and their god/s (Thaman 2003, 2009; Vaioleti 2011). The needs connected to these basic coordinates dominate the thinking of the peoples of the Pacific, especially of the peoples of Samoa and Tonga, because, if those needs are satisfied, this leads to good relationships between people, and to good relationships between people and their environment and their god/s.

The workshop evaluation was testimony to the fact that the Taiala were willing and appreciative learners, wishing to immediately apply their new skills in the villages in which they worked. By the end of the workshops and professional development, the Taiala were each able to:

1. Display three examples of how they will contribute to harmonious relationships within family, community, and the global family
2. Communicate three practical applications of an ecologically attuned world view
3. Share one example of a political, economic, or cultural issue in the village they will engage in, in order to make things better
4. Display three examples of how they can use learning from the workshops to promote self-reliance and sustainability (for example, regarding food security)

5. Display three examples of cooperative action and how it can be adapted to different villages and communities and possibly be made a part of national policy
6. Show three examples of action adaptive to climate change in their villages (involving awareness, relocation, planting, with an eye on economic, nutritional, and health security)
7. Demonstrate three examples of behavior mitigating climate change in their villages and country (involving internal and international policies, as well as technical procedures)

However, the importance of the Taiala programme extends beyond a successful activity and a short period of training. The building of capacities focussed primarily on developing the skills of, and imparting the required knowledge to, the Taiala trainees in order to make them effective internal animators. This must be embedded in further developments, in order to continue their beneficial effects even after the project period and in order to strengthen METI's role in promoting lifelong learning.

The innovativeness of METI's approach to creating self-reliant communities which are capable of mitigating climate change and adapting to it consists in the integrated use of a variety of approaches. METI also displays a clear gender focus by ensuring that women are integral to its sustainable development activities. METI sees a real opportunity for a new role of the women's committee, a traditional institution in the Samoan village, especially as the crucial driving force for the acceptance, by the households, of WFPB nutrition as an antidote to obesity and NCD. Efforts will be made for a close working relationship between the women's committees and the cooperatives in the target villages. Within the METI Health programme, health seminars are now being held in village settings, using the Taiala. For the convenience of the public, these seminars are offered both during the day and in the evening.

In order to increase further peer support for sustainable development action, METI has encouraged individuals who have completed the nonformal trainings to set up cooperatives for farmers and producers in their respective villages. From a social point of view, cooperatives foster participation in decision-making: decisions are made inclusively and democratically. In this way the cooperatives offer their members peer support for continued permaculture (planting and food production using the patterns observed in the Samoan natural ecosystems) practice and sustainable development initiatives. The Taiala are also being trained to facilitate training workshops for farmers who wish to become eligible to join the participatory guarantee scheme of organic certification; this scheme is promoted by the Secretariat of the Pacific Community (SPC).

Looking to the Future

The Prime Minister of Samoa stated that education is the key to sustainable development.

As a consequence, the Government is committed to ensuring that Samoa achieves the UN Education Goal through the strategies outlined in the UNESCO's Framework for Action Education 2030 (Samoa Government 2015). METI is operating within a favorable political climate of sympathy towards the SDGs. The Government has a clear policy, encouraging "a new partnership" between the public sector and the private, and also between these sectors and the academic sector; it has welcomed METI's efforts in life skills training and permaculture promotion. Hopefully, this political goodwill is going to be strengthened when the results of the ongoing and intended actions become manifest.

With the implementation of the Taiala program in the target villages – introducing the Taiala as internal animators and active participants in cooperative activities – it is expected that the Taiala will make sure that "ownership" of decision-making remains at the level of the cooperatives, which will guarantee the sustainability of sustainable development action to underpin the mitigation of CC and the adaptation to climate change.

It is anticipated that a more enlightened village leadership will emerge following the sustained efforts at the village level to promote a new mind-set which reflects a more peaceful, inquisitive, and ecologically attuned world view. These efforts, it is expected, will lead to an increase in the ability of village leaders to make rational decisions and lead to vibrant communities, capable of carrying out self-reliant initiatives which will bolster their resilience.

Conclusion

Two case studies have been reviewed in this paper which focus on educational responses to ESD and CC in the Pacific. One case study occurs in the formal sector and the second case study occurs in the nonformal sector. Underpinning the educational response is the importance and the role of Indigenous knowledge systems which while contextual relate to the importance of fakafonua, the practices or ways of the land and through the concept of tofi or tofi'a to maintain balance and harmony with each other, nature, and the god/s (fonua). This then forms a Pacific Indigenous baseline for ESD and CC education, a philosophy that underpinned both the Kiribati CC curriculum development and Taiala program.

Pacific culture and knowledge has always been traditionally conceived, produced, applied, and critiqued by Pacific peoples, and therefore there exists a long-standing tradition of developing complex yet self-sustaining systems. The respect, reciprocity, and the enduring endeavor to maintain the vā, in turn, will continue to be an immensely significant and invaluable component of the cultural capital of the Pacific. However, as the boundaries of many Pacific nations have been challenged with growing globalization and the cash economy assuming greater centrality in the lives of Pacific peoples, the traditional skills and Indigenous knowledge are being gradually sidelined to the peripheries. Cultural concepts have a role in developing relevant skills, values, attitudes, identity, a sense of self-worth, a sense of belonging, knowledge, empathy all necessary to develop people's ability to engage effectively and productively in everyday life even if they leave their home nations to seek opportunity elsewhere. Such a contribution is vital as the world seeks to explore solutions to the imposing problems of environmental challenges and climate change. Every person's contribution is vital for the sustainability of their community, be it physical, economic, intellectual, emotional, or spiritual; this all adds to a strong sense of belonging to a village, a community, a nation, and a global community whose survival depends on a collective momentum forward.

References

Asia Pacific Cultural Centre for UNESCO, ESD Journey of Hope. Final report of the Asia-Pacific Forum for ESD educators and facilitators, Tokyo, 22–24 Aug 2009

Bedford R, Hugo G (2011) Population movement in the Pacific: a perspective on future prospects. Report commissioned by the Department of Labour (New Zealand) and the Department of Citizenship and Immigration (Australia)

Chapman P (2012) Entire nation of Kiribati to be relocated over rising sea level threat. http://www.telegraph.co.uk/news/worldnews/australiaandthepacific/kiribati/9127576/Entire-nation-of-Kiribati-to-be-relocated-over-rising-sea-level-threat.html. 23 Aug 16

Corcoran J (2016) Implications of climate change for the livelihoods of urban dwellers in Kiribati. Thesis, Doctor of Philosophy (PhD), University of Waikato, Hamilton. Retrieved from http://hdl.handle.net/10289/10442

Curtain R, Vakaoti P (2011) The state of Pacific youth 2011: opportunities (2007) and obstacles. Suva. http://www.unicef.org/pacificislands/State_of_the_Pacific_Youth_Report_web.pdf. 12 May 2016

Freire P (1972) Pedagogy of the oppressed. Harmondsworth, Middlesex: Penguin

Kiribati Demographic and Health Survey (2009) Kiribati National Statistics Office, Secretariat of the Pacific Community (SPC)

Logan T (2009) Education for sustainable development in the Pacific – a mapping analysis of Kiribati. Report prepared for UNESCO Apia Office, Cluster Office for the Pacific States

METI (2016) Our mission and vision. https://metisamoa.wordpress.com/about-us/our-mission. 13 Nov 2016

Office of Te Beretitenti, Republic of Kiribati (2010) The Kiribati 2010 National framework for climate change and climate change adaptation

Rahman A (1993) People's self-development: perspectives on participatory action research: a journey through experience. London: Zed Books

Samoan Government (ed) (2015) Prime Minister opens Pacific Region Commonwealth Youth Ministers meeting. http://www.samoagovt.ws/2015/09/speech-prime-ministeropens-pacific-region-commonwealth-youth-ministers-meeting/. 13 Aug 2016

Teaero T (2003) Indigenous education in Kiribati. In: Thaman KH (ed) Education ideas from Oceania: selected readings. Institute of Education, The University of the South Pacific, Suva, pp 106–115

Teaero T (2009) Curriculum policies and framework in the context of Pacific values: a view from Kiribati. In: Sanga K, Thaman KH (eds) Re-thinking education curricula in the Pacific: challenges and prospects. Institute for Research and Development in Māori and Pacific Education, Victoria University, Wellington, pp 159–172

Teaero T (2010) Weaving a living from living cultures: challenges and opportunities. In: Nabobo-Baba U, Koya CF, Teaero T (eds) Education for sustainable development. Continuity and survival in the Pacific. School of Education, University of the South Pacific/Asia-Pacific Cultural Centre for UNESCO, Suva/Tokyo, pp 149–166

Thaman KH (2003) Educational ideas from Oceania: selected readings. The University of the South Pacific & UNESCO, Suva

Thaman KH (2009) Making the good things last: a vision of education for peace and sustainable development in the Asia Pacific region. http://www.accu.or.jp/esd/forum_esd_2009/speakers.html. 13 Sept 2016

Tui Atua TTE (2009) More on meaning, nuance and metaphor. In: Suaalii-Sauni T, Tuagalu I, Kirifi-Alai TN, Fuamatu N (eds) Su'esu'e Manogi; In search of Fragrance, Tui Atua Tupua Tamasese Ta'isi and the Samoan Indigenous Reference. National University of Samoa, Apia

UNESCO (2015) Pacific education for all. 2015 review

UNICEF (2011) The state of youth in the Pacific. https://www.unicef.org/pacificislands/State_of_the_Pacific_Youth_Report_web.pdf. 23 Sept 16

United Nations (2008) Acting on climate change. The UN system delivering as one. United Nations Headquarters, New York

United Nations (2017) Sustainable development: knowledge platform. Retrieved from https://sustainabledevelopment.un.org

Vaioleti TM (2006) Talanoa research methodology: a developing position on Pacific research. Waikato J Educ 12:20–34

Vaioleti TM (2011) Talanoa, Manulua and Founga Ako: frameworks for using enduring Tongan educational ideas for education in Aotearoa/New Zealand. Unpublished doctoral thesis, University of Waikato, Hamilton

Vaioleti T (2013) Talanoa: differentiating the talanoa research methodology from phenomenology, narrative, Kaupapa Maori and feminist methodologies. Te Reo 56:191

Vaioleti TM, Morrison SL, Vermeulen W (2002) Training for trainers in participatory learning in Samoa: commissioned report for the European Commission. METI, Apia

Vaioleti TM, Morrison SL, Corcoran J, Edwards R (2011) Framework for key educational concepts/learning objectives on climate change for curricula in the Kiribati. Report to UNESCO, University of Waikato, Hamilton, pp 1–68

Vaioleti LMM, Morrison SL, Vaioleti T (2012) Education on sustainable development and climate change in Aotearoa New Zealand: scoping on the state of climate change education in Asia and the Pacific. Final report. Report to Climate Asia Pacific, Climate Asia Pacific, pp 1–53

Reclaiming Our People Following Imprisonment

Cherryl Waerea-i-te-rangi Smith, Helena Rattray, and Leanne Romana

Contents

Introduction	672
Kaupapa Maori Research	673
Why Are our People in Prison	674
Early Prisons, a Military History	676
Introduction to the Project	677
Recognizing the Differences Between Hapu and Iwi	678
Iwi Resurgence	679
The Practical Reality of Reconnecting People to their Ancestry	679
Preliminary Interviews	680
What Tangata Ora Told us from their Preliminary Interviews	681
Wananga	684
This Town Is our Tribe	685
Second Wananga	687
Tangata Ora Voices	688
How Tangata Ora Responded to Wananga	688
Effectiveness of Tangata Ora Project and Wananga in Reconnecting Tangata Ora with their Hapu	689
Impact of Increased Knowledge Regarding Hapu on Rates of Reimprisonment	689
Conclusion	690
Glossary	691
References	692

Abstract

Mass incarceration needs to be seen as part of the complex historical picture of the development of settler states, a picture that is located within the dispossession of land and identities. Most analysis locates mass incarceration as a school to prison pipeline, a poverty to prison pipeline, and a victimization to prison

---

C. W. Smith (✉) · H. Rattray · L. Romana
Te Atawhai o te Ao, Whanganui, New Zealand
e-mail: cherryl@clear.net.nz; helena@teatawhai.maori.nz

© Springer Nature Singapore Pte Ltd. 2019
E. A. McKinley, L. T. Smith (eds.), *Handbook of Indigenous Education*,
https://doi.org/10.1007/978-981-10-3899-0_54

pipeline. These factors while extremely significant and relevant fail to grapple with the Indigenous factor. The Indigenous factor means that if you are Indigenous in colonized countries, you are likely to be among the most highly imprisoned peoples in the world. For Maori in Aotearoa (New Zealand), despite being 17% of the population, women make up 60% of the prison population and Maori men make up over 50%. Current analyses fail to grapple fully with the disproportionately high rate of Indigenous incarceration in settler states. Very often these factors are examined in isolation to the mass dispossession of Indigenous identity, lands, language, and culture over relatively few generations.

Maori community workers have long recognized that a key to turning around the imprisonment rates of Maori is twofold, it is a battle to change state systems which have shaped and enacted historical and contemporary injustice, and it is simultaneously a battle waged in restoring the hearts and minds of those impacted by imprisonment. Our researchers worked with Maori community workers and a group of 35 Maori men and women coming out of prison. Over 2 years we interviewed them and we attempted to reconnect them to their iwi history and iwi support. The initiative that we ran with iwi support was enormously successful. We worked with 35 Maori men and Maori women post release and although statistically 18 should have returned to prison within the first year, only four returned to prison. This article will look at what Maori researchers alongside of community workers and researchers did that enabled Maori men and women to successfully strengthen their lives, increase their understanding of their world, build support systems, and stay out of prison.

Keywords
Maori · Prison · Iwi · Hapu · Historical trauma · Imprisonment · Indigenous · Intergenerational trauma · Indigenous models of intervention · Whanganui · Waikato

Introduction

Mass incarceration needs to be seen as part of the complex historical picture of the development of settler states, a picture that is located within the dispossession of land and identities. Most analysis locates mass incarceration as a school to prison pipeline (Pane and Rocco 2014), a poverty to prison pipeline (Jenkins 2017), a victimization to prison pipeline (Rook and Sexsmith 2017). These factors, while extremely significant and relevant, fail to grapple with the Indigenous factor. The Indigenous factor means that if you are Indigenous in colonized countries, you are likely to be among the most highly imprisoned peoples in the world. For Maori in Aotearoa, despite being 17% of the population, Maori women make up 60% of the prison population and Maori men make up over 50% (Department of Corrections [Corrections] 2016). Current analyses (Ministry of Justice 2000; Newbold 2007; Department of Corrections 2008a; Sensible Sentencing Trust 2011) fail to grapple fully with the disproportionately high rate of Indigenous incarceration in settler states.

Very often these factors are examined in isolation to the mass dispossession of Indigenous identity, lands, language, and culture over relatively few generations (Jackson 1988; Durie 2007; Quince 2007; Bull 2009; Mulholland and McIntosh 2011; Workman 2011; JustSpeak 2012; Tauri and Webb 2012; Mihaere 2015). In the last few years within New Zealand the prison population has gone from 6,000 to over 10,000 (Corrections 2016). The percentages of Maori have continued to increase in that time.

Maori community workers have long recognized that a key to turning around the imprisonment rates of Maori is twofold, it is a battle to change state systems which have shaped and enacted historical and contemporary injustice, and it is simultaneously a battle waged in restoring the hearts and minds of those impacted by imprisonment. Our researchers worked with Maori community workers and a group of 35 Maori men and women coming out of prison. Over 2 years we interviewed them and we attempted to reconnect them to their iwi (tribal) history and iwi support. The initiative that we ran with iwi support was enormously successful. We worked with 35 Maori men and Maori women post release and although statistically 18 should have returned to prison within the first year, only four returned to prison. This article will look at what Maori researchers alongside of community workers and researchers did that enabled Maori men and women to successfully strengthen their lives, increase their understanding of their world, build support systems, and stay out of prison.

Kaupapa Maori Research

Te Atawhai o te Ao is a Whanganui-based Kaupapa Maori Research Institute. The research we undertook was undertaken from people from iwi that we belonged to. We are a Research Institute that is based within our own iwi (tribal) region, in our case within the Whanganui city. Within the broader district there are three main iwi groups with dozens of hapu or sub-iwi. These three main iwi groupings can, at times, work collaboratively. Staff within the Institute come from these three iwi groupings.

Kaupapa Maori research is centered in Maori views and understandings of the world. Maori values underpin all aspects of the research approach and links to the importance that Indigenous peoples place on relationships, reciprocity, and trust. Kaupapa Maori research is political research as it analyzes relations of power and seeks to benefit Maori communities.

For this project we worked with iwi-based community researchers both in the Whanganui district and in Waikato. This gave the research a particular kaupapa Maori (Kaupapa Maori is a Maori approach, a Maori way of doing something.) lens. Community researchers were highly knowledgeable about the different families, connections, tensions and at times could negotiate complex situations that could be completely overlooked by outsiders. They were also highly mobile and diverse in their contacts and able to work innovatively with often few resources but very good connections.

Underpinning the research was the question, what could we do to intervene in the current picture from our place in the world? When it comes to the question of prisons and imprisonment, unlike policy makers that tend to read the criminal justice system as being about bad people from bad families, we were seeing our own families, cousins, siblings, uncles, and aunties who in the ordinary world are for most of their lives doing good but who commit crimes. We are also seeing our relations being failed when their health needs such as addictions and mental health are not being adequately or appropriately dealt with. At times we are also seeing relations go to prison because of lack of support in the legal system and racial profiling. Where the crimes are extreme they are being disconnected from whanau (family) or are isolating themselves, but this group is relatively small. Clearly there are also allied issues that we are seeing such as literacy, addictions, mental health issues, early life and historical trauma (Walters et al. 2011; Wirihana and Smith 2014) that need to be addressed. As a result of the dislocation from iwi connections there are many families living in towns who have lost the connection to their own hapu (Hapu is a sub-tribe.). The participants discussed that freely in their discussions.

Why Are our People in Prison

There is an extensive literature that seeks to explain who goes to prison and why. The literature falls into two broad categories and it is important to understand the focus of this literature. One area examines the pathology of the individual and examines areas such as attachment theory, adverse childhood experiences literature, genetics, brain and development research, childhood trauma research, fetal alcohol research, and traumatic brain injury. This literature looks at the individual's life chances and tends to look at a lifeline of exposures to victimization and research that helps to address this. There is also literature that seeks to explain the social, economic, and environmental factors that impact on who goes to prison and why. This includes poverty research, state systems research such as state child care and protection research, victimization research, sexuality research, criminal justice system research, racism and inequalities research, and industrial complex research.

Indigenous research has intersected with all of the above because none of that research explains fully why the highest rates of imprisonment are for Indigenous Peoples. Indigenous researchers and writers are currently attempting to analyze the above writing as well as to emphasize the critical role of history in shaping Maori imprisonment rates and outcomes. Maori researchers have been focused on examining the criminal justice system, the reconstruction and institutionalization of whanau, the inequities and inequalities, constitutional and Treaty issues, and racism, particularly institutional racism. Institutional racism has long been challenged by Maori across many sectors (Jackson 1988). Ministry of Justice figures in 2015 show that when it comes to assault, 26.3% of Maori will be sentenced to imprisonment while only 13% of Europeans will be imprisoned for the same crime. Racial profiling of youth has been acknowledged even by Police Commissioner Mike Bush through the acceptance of "unconscious bias" as a problem that needs to be addressed by police (2015).

Researchers have also made the links to the high numbers of Maori who have been abused in state institutions as children. Between the 1950s and 1980s over 100,000 New Zealand children were removed from families and placed into state care, and most of them were Maori. Many of them suffered abuse (Mulholland and McIntosh 2011). What is clearly shown in Indigenous critique is that Indigenous peoples are being criminalized in particular ways, that particular way is tied to the development of settler states.

The current population in the country shows that Maori make up 17% of the total population, 712,000 identify themselves as Maori (Statistics NZ 2015). One in three are under 15 years old. The Maori youth rate is growing and the numbers of Maori youth can be up to 50% in some primary schools. In 2015 only 69.8% of Maori remained in school to the age of 17 compared to 83.9% of the overall school population (Ministry of Education 2017).

Within New Zealand the Treaty of Waitangi signed with Maori tribes in 1840 has placed clear obligations in New Zealand to honor "tino rangatiratanga" (Maori sovereignty or chieftainship). Under current legislation Ministries are compelled to respond to Maori inequities. Because of the alarmingly high Maori incarceration rate a Treaty claim was taken to the judicial body, the Waitangi Tribunal, in 2016. The Treaty of Waitangi Tribunal claim led by Tom Hemopo, a former Maori probation officer collectively with three iwi, brought together the key Maori prison researchers in 2016 to present evidence against the Crown regarding inaction by governments to reduce the disproportionate number of Maori returning to prison. In 2017 the Tribunal released its findings:

> We have therefore found that the Crown has breached the principle of active protection by not sufficiently prioritising the protection of Māori interests in the context of persistently disproportionate Māori reoffending rates.
> ... We have also found that the Crown has breached the principle of equity by not sufficiently prioritising the reduction of Māori reoffending rates.
> ... We have found that the Crown has not, at this point, breached the principle of partnership. ... We have found, however, that if the Crown does not live up to its stated commitment to develop these partnerships, it risks breaching its partnership obligations.

In the meantime, recent research by non-governmental social organizations show clear patterns of an entrenchment of poverty, which again Maori are highly represented in. Patterns of inadequate resourcing across critical support services creates a falling tower impact. Without adequate basic state benefit incomes, without adequate resourcing for children with physical health problems, without adequate resourcing for all mental health services, without adequate services for women's shelters and domestic violence services, without adequate funding for schools to deal with high energy children or critical learning assistance or adequate training, with high class number sizes, with assessment regimes taking over teachers' lives, without critical supports available for victims of sexual violence and many other key areas, key supports get taken away and pressure goes on families. In Aotearoa these services have been hit hard in the last 5 years. Pressure on state services that daily deal with those in poverty are noting a rise in anger among their clients and in recent years, security guards are highly visible and regulate entry into government social security offices.

Higher rates of imprisonment are all known to be linked to changes in these sectors. This is set against a withdrawal of funding and adequate funding of services across many fronts, for example, counselling supports in schools, learning and behavioral supports in schools, pastoral care supports in schools, employment training opportunities, employment, adult literacy support, addiction support, mental health identification and support, crisis intervention support, and a multiple range of ways that supports need to happen. Furthermore, while services may be available, are they Maori services that can make the cultural connect to our people and their histories? There is advancement of whanau ora programs, developed and advocated for Maori that work with whole families proactively, and provide critical Maori community support services, but these services are underfunded.

There is also a massive literature on the failure of prisons. The people we interviewed were clear that prisons are a school for learning how to be a better criminal and they provide people with criminal networks. There are some rehabilitation type programs in prisons but the focus remains on punishment not restoration. Mental health problems are not treated in prisons except to contain and ensure safety. Prisons are not equipped to deal with the problems. We found high rates of Traumatic Brain Injury with resultant behaviors and emotional behaviors among the tangata ora but no treatment had ever happened. We also found high rates of sexual violence victimization, again with no treatment or support provided. Addictions research clearly points to underlying trauma as key to working with addictions, another issue that is only sparsely considered in prisons.

Early Prisons, a Military History

Public records do not acknowledge the history of the justice systems in settler states. Early prisons in Aotearoa were established predominantly for Maori. The first prisons were inside military stockades during land wars of the nineteenth century. Mass incarceration of Maori and photos of Maori prisoners were published throughout the country. As Maori subjection to the Crown and the removal of land progressed so too did the growth of prisons.

Incarceration of Maori is an area of history that is being revived through Treaty settlements. As each tribe compiles their own historical records, there is a reminder of the significant leaders and people who were captured and transported away from iwi regions. The first capital punishments, death by hanging, were Maori and these were public deaths, born of the need to publically punish, humiliate, and to subdue Maori who fought against the alienation of lands and the attempts to maintain self-rule. In iwi considered to be in rebellion, there are cases where Maori filled up the jails and were interred in caves, exiled on islands, and transported to other areas.

These early disparities on who was locked up in prison has not changed throughout time.

Maori lives and experiences are diverse and historically and inter-generationally the majority have been displaced from traditional lives, living, and knowledge. Historical trauma research shows that significant impacts accrue when you have a history of land dispossession, wars and its aftermath, being exiled, becoming refugees, widespread death through epidemics, language dispossession, racist treatment by institutions and for Maori families that has been sustained within the relatively short period of about six generations. The agency, resilience, coping strategies, fighting back, and the determination of Maori to survive as distinct people has also been ongoing.

The work of decolonizing and telling histories that account for Maori lives and ancestry will continue to be struggled over for many decades. Many Maori and Pakeha allies are challenging the ways that histories are told also but this is ongoing work to decolonize official telling and honoring of history.

While large numbers of Maori have had their connections to their lands disrupted, we have retained both knowledge of traditional lands and have retained our stake in iwi areas particularly through marae. We have remembered and do retell our own stories and basis of our beliefs through many forms of cultural expression such as kapa haka and art. But we also tell of the destruction and consequences on the people through the generations. If Maori have a hidden curriculum it has been sustained, fostered, and celebrated in the Maori language and in all forms of Maori expression, sometimes coded, sometimes overt for example in activism.

Introduction to the Project

This research project focused on the question, if you reconnected Maori men and women coming out of prison with their intergenerational connection to hapu (extended families) knowledge, the land, and the people, would that stop them returning to prison? We knew that once Maori are imprisoned, 60% are currently returning. So prison is a deterrent for only 40% (Department of Corrections 2008b).

Early on in the project we discussed naming our participants. We did not want to use the reductionist term "ex-prisoners." We wanted an identity that affirmed them. Instead we used the name that a local health provider, Te Oranganui, was using – "tangata ora" which means people who are well or who are healing. The name recognized both humanness and their health. As we proceeded with the project we had to retrain others to relinquish the other terms they were using also such as "clients," "ex-offenders."

The Tangata Ora project informed a wider program of research, He Kokonga Whare which was funded by the Health Research Council of New Zealand, and examined Maori intergenerational trauma and wellbeing. In the Tangata Ora project we had gathered brief intergenerational biographies. We also sought to determine whether reconnecting tangata ora with their hapu through a series of interviews and wananga would reduce the likelihood that they would return to prison, and although the small sample size used in this research means it is not possible to generalize the findings of this study to wider populations, there does appear to be a connection between tangata ora participation in the project and an absence of their return to prison. Where no connection existed, the project sought to establish whether reconnecting them with their Iwi roots could serve as a cultural protective factor in preventing their return to prison.

Using structured interviews and a series of wananga (gatherings) that included an exercise in visual ethnography, the research team initially interviewed 35 tangata ora and then conducted a series of wananga called hapu wananga. When a participant was identified a meeting was held with them to establish their circumstances, to talk to them about the research, to identify any issues with interviewing. For example, where it should take place, transport issues, timing, and other logistical issues. Early on in the contact we identified whether the person was connected to health and social services and if they were not we gave them the opportunity to receive that support.

We sought to identify those who had been released from prison who were from iwi in the central and lower North Island. We worked with hapu specifically because hapu is where the generational and land-based knowledge still resides, especially if your whanau is disconnected from the tribe. The reason for this was that on previous research projects we had found that it was common for there to be a breakdown in trust and communications with certain members of whanau. Restoring these relationships was important work that was long term and best done by local community workers. To that end we identified key health and social workers who would support the tangata ora long term at the beginning of the project.

Our goal was to connect the tangata ora with key hapu knowledge holders who would know the family name and could provide the generational and land history of the person. This was done through wananga and visits to different sites. Tangata ora would be able to share what they learnt with their whanau.

Recognizing the Differences Between Hapu and Iwi

Hapu are the land-based connected groupings that involve a collection of families. The Treaty of Waitangi was signed with the collective hapu of Aotearoa. Hapu are where marae and land interests and shared histories meet. The knowledge of sacred sites, the care of these sites, the care of marae and rivers and land sites, food gathering, and major decision-making about caring for land and the people occurs at hapu. It is hapu that keep the home fires burning, it is hapu that do the work to maintain customary history, knowledge, and daily practise. It is hapu and whanau that maintain marae.

Iwi are traditional entities that operated in a different way to hapu. Generally, they are the larger confederations, which shared dialect, iwi boundaries, and origins and knowledge. Jointly sharing iwi boundaries, iwi identifiers and in times of conflict iwi would become predominant for collective action. The Treaty of Waitangi settlement process has prioritized iwi governance entities. As a result this has brought together hapu to work as iwi, whose work focuses on ensuring iwi rights and responding to the state.

Through Treaty of Waitangi claims within the country, most iwi are either currently fighting for land claim settlements or have moved through this process. Claims and settlements are currently engaging a great deal of iwi governance time and energy. Claims have completely changed iwi landscapes through reclamation of some lands, compensations, and knowledge bases. However the Claims process remains controversial because they cannot address the width and breadth of social and historical injustice. The parameters for settlement have been set by political expediency and perceived affordability.

Iwi Resurgence

Most research with Maori ignores iwi identification. We worked in three iwi districts. All three of these districts are in post settlement except for Whanganui. Iwi are increasingly pushing to get tribe-specific data from government agencies across a range of sectors. We were unable to get permission to work with the Department of Corrections in the research project and were unable to identify who was being released from prison that was connected to our particular tribe. We are not the only Maori researchers denied permission for research by Corrections. Corrections do not identify iwi affiliation, but Maori staff working inside the prisons commonly do ascertain this information. Although many iwi have Treaty of Waitangi settlement arrangements that entitle iwi to particular rights with Ministries and government departments, very few iwi have currently established clear relationships with Corrections. Within the regions that we worked, we found that iwi were struggling to have any sort of relationship with the local prisons or the relationship only extended to the occasional program being run by a iwi health or social service provider. This changed later in Waikato with the appointment of a iwi liaison worker.

The Practical Reality of Reconnecting People to their Ancestry

Within Aotearoa, we have knowledgeable people within each hapu and tribe who know the main families and descent lines of those families. If a person knows the names of their grandparents, from our hapu knowledge base we can often track and connect people. Some iwi, for example, Ngai Tahu, have gathered extensive records on their iwi people and assist people to find their ancestral links. Mostly this reconnecting is done through contacting key people within hapu. Maori services often work with these key hapu people but it is a very under-recognized network. In urban centers there can be several generations of disconnection. Many urban and iwi services assist clients to identify their tribe and hapu, if they are able to. Many services already recognize that whakapapa, where it can be tracked, is an important component to healing.

It took us over a year to find, meet, and recruit tangata ora into the project. We had to find a group who generally were lying low in the community and even within wider whanau it was not always known that they had been in prison. But further to this we had to identify and only recruit people who had particular iwi affiliations. Our community researchers used their extensive knowledge of networks, families, services, and a wide range of creative ways to identify and recruit participants into the study. Social media networks, gang networks, iwi radio, community workers were all activated to assist us to encourage people to contact us if they would be interested in participating in the study. If we did not have our community research networks this study could not have happened. In the end we had 35 that fitted the criteria. We worked for 2–3 years with each tangata ora.

Preliminary Interviews

In order to work with tangata ora we had to build trust, which took not just an initial meeting but several meetings and discussions with the community researchers. Community researchers remained flexible to be able to meet in homes, finding spaces for children, and organizing food so that they did not drain family resources. First interviews were over one and a half hours long and covered a range of topics. Interviews provided a rich and descriptive narrative of tangata ora lives; their connection to their history, culture, and language; their pathways into prison; and what they thought would improve their lives.

During these interviews we identified their knowledge of iwi connections. We also used screening tools for early life trauma and traumatic brain injury and a microaggression screen. We also had key health or social workers available to us throughout all stages of connecting with tangata ora so that we could ensure they had support and any follow-up that was needed. The screening tools were particularly revealing in identifying early and lifetime trauma. In the open-ended questioning of interviews, the women and men tended to normalize or underplay their own victimization experiences but the screening tools which asked for estimates of the numbers of times that they had been knocked unconscious, for example, and asked more specific questions, gave us more accurate information of the victimization rates. The screening often even surprised interviewees themselves when they had to count the number of incidents they had been exposed to. Most of the tangata ora that we interviewed scored highly on the traumatic brain injury screening tool that we used. As a result we gave copies of the results to the tangata ora and worked in collaboration with health workers to assist in any follow-up.

These interviews were particularly hard on the community researchers as they listened to tough stories. Although our community researchers were often knowledgeable community workers, they were hit hard by the stories they were told. The tangata ora whose early lives and treatment was poor as children was particularly difficult for the researchers. The exposures to physical and sexual violence at young ages and the attempts by children to cope and be resilient, only to have critical supports taken away, was heart-breaking to listen to. Stories abounded of children who just wanted a safe home, who just wanted to stop being moved around and used as pawns, who just wanted to remain with that one loving person, who just wanted to stay with that one school teacher. We debriefed and reflected often.

What Tangata Ora Told us from their Preliminary Interviews

For all of the tangata ora, coming out of prison was a difficult transition unless there was supportive family waiting for them and a job that had been kept for them. Following release from prison, the majority of tangata ora were one step away from crisis. They struggled to make ends meet financially and could accumulate debt, they struggled to find housing or had tenuous housing, they had conditions that were difficult to fulfil with community probation or state benefits, they could be surrounded with unstable and volatile relationships. All of these types of issues left tangata ora living precariously, with the real possibility of a quick return to prison.

For the majority they came out of prison and went into a type of seclusion. With little money coming in and waiting for state benefits, they struggled. Daily life for many tangata ora after their release from prison consisted of long hours of being at home, fulfilling probation requirements, domestic duties, socializing, and other various activities to keep themselves occupied. Many reported difficulties in securing gainful and sustainable employment, and there was a sense of diminished worthiness arising from their inability to provide financially and materially for their families.

Some enjoyed the domestic routines, but almost all said they would have preferred to be in employment, making financial contributions to the running of their homes, and meeting the needs and desires of their partners and family.

They said prisons just helped them to be better criminals. Most tangata ora held their position that prison did not deter crime, and reiterated comments regarding prison as a "holiday camp" for some prisoners. Having said that however, when asked about violence in prison, they said that they were exposed and subjected to violence and in some cases needed to form alliances to stay safe. Also they commonly said they could access drugs and alcohol which enabled them to continue addictions. Most tangata ora told us that imprisonment did not help them to stop offending. Instead they said that while in prison, opportunities were there to be able to build criminal networks, and gather criminal intelligence for utilization in further offending when released from prison.

The importance of the right type of support. Tangata ora also told us that what helped them most upon release was support that remained consistent and long term, particularly supportive partners and family members. When it came to talking about what they thought would help them, they did say that spending time with people who had a stronger and more positive effect on deterring criminal offending made more sense.

They also felt they needed more connection and understanding of themselves as well as their cultural and ancestral roots. They needed good quality and culturally competent and considerate programs and services.

Barriers to their successful reintegration included the challenges of relearning how to maintain routine in their daily lives, discrimination, abstaining from negative influences, and the difficulty of changing old habits and associations. Some were also unable to identify and desist from poor decision-making that often led to criminal behavior, nor had the ability to make alternative decisions. These factors prevailed as a result of a lack of learning to make better choices and behave in socially acceptable ways when younger. Tangata ora also told us that the barriers to successful reintegration included lack of connection to their inner selves and their cultural and ancestral roots, the challenges they faced in meeting their release conditions, or their attitudes to doing so.

How they saw their identity. From the initial interview, we found that there was a range of connectedness to their Maori identity. We asked them how much they knew about their grandparents and further back in their own history. We also asked them about fluency in Maori language.

Several tangata ora were confidently able to recall back several generations of their family on both their mother's and father's side, but over half were only able to recall back as far as their grandparents, and sometimes only on one side of their family, as highlighted by this tangata ora:

> Q: Just going back to your grandparents, do you know or did you hear anything about the generation before your grandparents.
> A: Nah not really. See Mum's a South Island Maori, so she's from the South Island. The old man he was born in Taihape and they met down south, the old man was a Pakeha.

For some tangata ora they could not access information through their own immediate family:

> In our family, you don't ask.

There were clearly areas of the past that tangata ora also preferred to cover over, and to not speak about or pass on to the next generations:

> In my whanau, asking about the past is not ok.

This meant that they would have to actively go against their family in order to find out information and seek it from other sources.

Maori language connectedness. The responses provided by tangata ora illuminated significant diversity in cultural and ancestral knowledge and experience. There were those who reported growing up on marae and around fluent speakers of te reo, and who had been taught about their iwi ancestry from a very early age.

There were others who had very little knowledge:

> Q: Have you learned any Maori language or do you know much about your Tribe?
> A: Oh I picked it up. A little at a time. The Maori language you know, but I can't speak it fluently, I can't really translate it either, but I understand the basics. I know my tribe and my hapu.

There were also those who were interested in furthering their knowledge of their history:

Q: Do you have any interest or desire to engage with your tribe or do something for them?
A: I sure do. I want to take my boy back and yeah. ...
Q: What does that mean to take your boy back?
A: To take him and show him around. I want to learn it first, so that I can take him and pass it down.

Did they have a connection to hapu? Only one tangata ora reported an active connection with their hapu and marae. The other tangata ora had little knowledge regarding their tribe, hapu, and marae connections, nor had they pursued further learning in te reo Maori. For some they signaled that it was a matter of confidence and knowledge:

Q: Have you made attempts to learn about your iwi (tribe)?
A: I have but not really.
Q: What would it mean to you if you did, or why haven't you?
A: I haven't just 'cos, I know where to start, it's just the means of getting there and the transport and time and who to go to, it could make a difference and you could meet whanau that I hadn't met before you know, some story that might resolve something.

What they told us about schooling. While many of those we spoke to had high rates of adverse childhood experiences, schools tended to operate imposing further punitive approaches. Schools lacked the ability to recognize or support these children whose home lives were fraught. When they did encounter a teacher who they felt they could relate to, they got moved on. Services were seen as punitive and blunt, in other words – the answer was removal of children, from classroom activities, from classes, from schools. Schools were unable to see the learning difficulties that some of these children had.

An allied survey that we undertook in the research looked at traumatic brain injury which for these children could be common, as could other learning challenges. Bright children tried to apply themselves in schools but failed through lack of support and consistency, through inability to get basic support to keep them afloat. Girls who withdrew into themselves were ignored, and boys were identified as discipline problems and were treated accordingly. Teachers did not inquire into the background of children, so hunger, the care of other siblings, lack of adequate clothing, stress, and other contributing factors that lead to inattention in class were ignored.

What they told us about racism and discrimination. Tangata ora reported discrimination as a daily impact. They reported common occurrences of being followed in shops, being targeted by police. Evidence released by police reports (Ministry of Justice 2011) shows the disproportionate numbers of Maori that are apprehended, disproportionate numbers on remand, charged and higher numbers receiving a sentence of imprisonment. Maori are more likely to be reliant on legal aid and to go to court with no lawyer. They are more likely to plead guilty to just get it over with. They are less likely to have the literacy to deal with accumulated debt or fines. They also told us that they can struggle to fulfil complex bail, home detention, curfew, and probation conditions. They are considered to be less likely to "show remorse" in the court in the ways that non-Maori judges assume they should.

Wananga

Following the initial interviews, we worked to identify key hapu knowledge holders within the iwi that we were working with. That sentence sounds so easy but this was a big effort that could only be undertaken because we were already located inside iwi and knew how to do such a thing. We had to firstly identify the primary iwi and hapu that we were dealing with and activate our own networks to find the key people to talk to. This really involved knowing the people whose knowledge extended back through all the generations of a sub-tribe and in some cases to a whole tribe. Community researchers were invaluable in carrying out this work and the Institute used a wide and varied iwi knowledge base. All community researchers are involved within their own whanau, hapu groupings and several have held senior iwi positions so they were able to activate their own kumara vines.

Within the project, the hapu knowledge holders would need to have two meetings with researchers and hold two wananga for the tangata ora. Lastly the tangata ora were interviewed to ascertain their thoughts on whether reconnecting them with their hapu was an effective intervention in preventing their return to prison, their experiences of the Tangata Ora Project, their treatment by the research team, and any suggestions on what they think might improve future iterations of the project.

In the initial meeting we had with hapu knowledge holders we outlined the purposes of the project and also outlined the work they would be required to do. All of them were very keen to work with the tangata ora. We emphasized the need to pass on whakapapa (genealogical) knowledge as well as their own connectedness. None of the hapu workers that we identified were commonly working with these particular whanau, although in some areas they are.

The primary role of hapu facilitators was to think about men and women coming out of prison to consider how they would reconnect them to their hapu knowledge. Because they were often facilitating reconnection in informal ways, we left it up to the hapu facilitators to decide how they would do this. We asked the hapu facilitators to identify the key historical events for the tribe and for the hapu before meeting with tangata ora. What was discussed was the ways in which the tangata ora connected to the hapu and what key historical events that happened within their hapu, and also stories connected to the land and people.

Unfortunately two of the tangata ora were returned to prison before they had gotten to the workshop.

The activities with the hapu facilitators definitely caused tangata ora to reframe their world. Hapu facilitators in wananga tended to seat people in a circle and always did karakia or whakamoemiti (prayer), mihi whakatau (welcome), waiata tautoko (song) to set the scene for the wananga. The wananga focused on connection and reducing isolation by filling in knowledge of connectedness to the lands, rivers, and places they lived on as well as specifically showing them where they fitted in a much bigger and proud history. It also highlighted connection to each other and encouraged participation with marae and tribe, which was not there at the beginning of the wananga. Hapu facilitators could choose how they imparted knowledge, in some cases site visits and in others discussion, use of whakapapa charts, and a range of tools. Tikanga processes (correct iwi protocols) and hui (meeting) processes emphasize connection, sanctity, and a bigger picture to peoples lives which the hapu facilitators knew how to deal with. The ways in which the hapu facilitators gave information was diverse, from one to one games, to site visits, to more formal type discussions and meetings.

Wananga had a deep impact at a number of levels:

> During wananga they were exposed to their deeper history, generations of connection to the seen and unseen connections to the lands, mountains, rivers all around them. Hapu facilitators gave them the understanding that their tupuna (ancestors) that they didn't know existed gave them the right to stand as tangata whenua tuturu not just as the self proclaimed urban-hard (Hapu facilitator).

Food was supplied in abundance at all wananga and leftovers were packaged for tangata ora to take home. In the aftermath of wananga during the cleanup time, the health worker was able to talk and offer support on a range of needs. It was at this more personal time that issues arose about seeking help and counselling.

We also found that hapu facilitators were often clarifying derogatory stories that tangata ora had heard about their own people, as well as clarifying the names of the places and stories of the ancestors.

This Town Is our Tribe

At the beginning of wananga, tangata ora were seeing themselves as strongly connected to towns or streets, "This town is our tribe."

As researchers, who were largely aware of their own iwi affiliations, we tended to view iwi identity quite simply, you are either Maori with a good knowledge of your tribe or you are not. This simplistic approach was challenged by our tangata ora. We assumed that they had "lost" knowledge of their hapu and they were living more as Pakeha. But we underestimated their existing knowledge. As one of the hapu facilitators noted after one wananga:

> There was no doubt in my mind that they were more knowledgeable about Maori and connections than first appeared with their discourse on belonging and their application of tikanga in regards to that. A random discussion on the origin of carving was posed, with a contribution from all bar one to that discussion, demonstrating their knowledge of iwi variations to the origin (Hapu facilitator).

The difference in their knowledge was that it was not connected to their place of origin, their tribe. It brought a new found appreciation for those of us who are connected to seeing the strength of our own people to hold on to our ways of being and snippets of knowledge under external pressure. As one hapu facilitator noted:

> Self-descriptions were Maori but not tribe or hapu connected. The tangata ora stated themselves as 'insert name of town – hard'. This meant that they knew their town, their relationship with the people in the town and how they fitted in their behaviour with each other. They had no doubts that they were born and bred from their town. They strongly asserted their Maori identity but in a form that they created. They held tangihanga (traditional funerals) in homes; they would lay down hangi (traditional cooking) for important occasions, operating semi marae in garages and at their homes (Hapu facilitator).

They were also clear that there were some things they were not going to change and hapu facilitators did not challenge that aspect of their identities but rather built on their knowledge and corrected misinformation:

> They were clear that no one was going to take away from them the modern sense of their belonging. But they would learn missing layers of history that they should think about as being there too as an expression of belonging now that they know (Hapu facilitator).

Within towns they could be all meeting at tangihanga (funerals), for example, and not understanding that they were related or how. Maori families created support networks in town but also did not know they were actually related, even when they were living within their own traditional iwi areas.

The biggest impression was made on tangata ora when site visits were made to places of historical significance, and they could hear the stories of their ancestors at those places. Several disclosed having visited these places before, and were not aware of their cultural connection to the sites visited:

> A: Yeah up to the maunga (mountain); yeah that's the first time. In my childhood we used to go up to that hill every day because it was the school bus run. But the mountain I have never known and never seen it because we had never gone that far. It was only like only another 500 metres away.
> Q: From where you went every day?
> A: Yeah and so the historical significance of that area, now that I'm 40 it's like. . . and look what I can see with my eyes; you saw everything – east, north, south and west. It was a buzz.
>
> Another tangata ora:
> Yes. That was the first time I've ever been there and heard about that kaupapa and about that rangatira (chief). Then you're looking over and then 'churrrr'. Mean!
> Q: So you're saying you would travel along that road and not even be aware of the history until then?
> A: Yeah, cause I always go out there to fish. Plus my brother died up the road from there.

Tangata ora also felt that the topics discussed during the wananga provided new insights to their culture and ancestral roots for those with little or none prior, and for others, built upon knowledge they already had, with this increase in knowledge manifesting as improved self-esteem and confidence, gained through knowing more about who they were, and where they came from (Quince 2007).

Most tangata ora reported that they had found the wananga useful as it improved knowledge of cultural and ancestral origins and they felt it would be helpful for others coming out of prison to learn. They also felt that hapu and marae would provide tangata ora with more support upon release and a wider network of support.

Wananga issues that arose. The holding of wananga with tangata ora was not without challenges. While Maori protocols and environments can mediate potential conflict, we knew that some tangata ora had affiliations to opposing gangs. Processes were undertaken prior to the wananga to ensure that these matters were not the primary issue on the day. In some cases, mediation was done prior to the wananga or addressed openly in the wananga and explanations given of what the kaupapa was. What did happen, however, was that new understanding of connections emerged across the lines, that while gang affiliations and rivalry might be there, a deeper longer connection was revealed in the wananga, of many generations and a common shared history. Tangata ora set aside most of their differences when participating in the project, and some still talk since the project has ended. This is an extremely positive development arising from this research, and demonstrates the possibility that when it comes to culture, gang affiliations do not need to inhibit progress (Desmond 2011). Also one of the hapu facilitators found out that her home had been burgled by one of the tangata ora of the wananga. This was known prior to the wananga, and was addressed in a Maori way by discussing clearly what the learning space was about. The tangata ora and the hapu facilitator mediated, and this cleared the way for the wananga to proceed.

Second Wananga

At Wananga two, reconnection went to another level as tangata ora were each individually shown their own connections through whakapapa charts and discussions about their whanau. One participant spent most of his time reading a Manawhenua report (http://www.ngatiapa.iwi.nz/downloads/manawhenua/Ngati%20Apa%20Manawhenua%20Report%201998.pdf), and as a result he was gifted the report. This report had his whanau names in it, and this was his first time discovering his whakapapa.

Their hapu was identified and all but one were connected to the land they were currently living on. They were given the hapu name and shown how through whakapapa they connected so well:

You are on your land, here through this hapu, you are a descendant of this hapu.

This land is my land.

You belong here in a modern sense.

You belong here in an ancient sense.

In ancient times we lived here, and we still live here. You are the Ahi Kaa.

Marae aren't in here in this town any-more, but our stories are (Hapu facilitator).

Hapu facilitators emphasized ancestry, but also the sanctity and importance of people. The sanctity of women as connecters to the land, and men as connectors to the sky. They explained how these ancient stories give us guides for living today, and that this pathway for correct living was created for them and is ancestrally created.

Tangata ora enjoyed meeting others from their hapu, some of whom they had known previously, but had not realized they were connected through hapu as well. There were also reports regarding the positive benefits of participating and sharing in the hapu wananga as a group, indicating the group-based nature of the hapu wananga made the experience much easier to engage in and, for most, more enjoyable. In the main, most tangata ora reported participating in the Tangata Ora Project because they were asked to, but two tangata ora reported participating as they felt they had knowledge and experiences to share that they hoped would benefit the project.

Tangata Ora Voices

Q: What went well for you during that wananga?
A: They pulled out all of the whakapapa and put it on the table. Because I hadn't really tried to delve into my father's side of whakapapa. I know my dad and his dad and then my koro's dad, and then my koro's dad's dad. I know as far back as there.

Introduced into this Wananga was photovoice. Each tangata ora was given a camera to record their perspectives and observations of hapu. They were asked to bring 10 photos that they had taken to the next gathering. They could choose any topic they liked.

How Tangata Ora Responded to Wananga

Most tangata ora reported that working in groups during the wananga was helpful, as some were not confident engaging with or speaking in front of others, so being a part of a group helped them build their confidence watching others engage and speak, until they were ready to do so themselves. One tangata ora spoke of how the project connected her with people she would have never spoken to in the past, and how she had continued to speak with those people after the wananga.

Most tangata ora expressed appreciation for opportunities to talk about and share their experiences and stories with others, with one reporting how liberating talking about her past had been for her, and was helping her come to terms with a few things, and begin to move on from them. They also expressed appreciation for the koha they received from the project team for their participation in the project.

Some tangata ora felt that their priorities had changed since participating in the project, with one disclosing a significant reduction in domestic violence in her home, and others reporting they considered their families as treasures, with one spending more time with her children, and another dedicating all their spare time to working on regaining custody of their children who were in the care of others.

Effectiveness of Tangata Ora Project and Wananga in Reconnecting Tangata Ora with their Hapu

There is obviously an interest in learning about one's cultural self, perhaps this is something that should be considered by hapu themselves to develop and deliver, as it is them after all, who are the rightful teachers of this knowledge (Bishop 1998).

Impact of Increased Knowledge Regarding Hapu on Rates of Reimprisonment

Since participating in the project and the Wananga, none of the tangata ora involved in the post-wananga interviews had returned to prison. When queried about why they thought this was, some tangata ora felt that their involvement in the project had made them stop and think about the way they were living their lives, and the things that were really important to them, with some deciding crime and going to jail again was not important, but being around for their children, grandchildren, and families was.

> Q: So do you think you will go back to jail?
> A: Nah
> Q: What do you think the main reason for that would be?
> A: Knowing there's someone there I can turn to and treasure my family more and my grandson; cause we got him before and I didn't know who to turn to or who to talk to. I was just like in four walls, and either you take it or I didn't know what to do. I'd been going to jail since 2009 till last year and I haven't been back

And this from another tangata ora:

> Q: Why do you think it's not useful to learn about your ancestral roots?
> A: You should learn; you should learn it actually, your ancestral roots so you can pass it on to your kids and to their kids

Despite the significant advances made regarding a sense of connection to their tribe and hapu, and despite the reported effect their involvement in the Tangata Ora Project had on their views of themselves and the things in their lives that were worth staying out of prison for, some tangata ora remained uncertain about their ability to desist offending in future, and others were even less certain about their possible reimprisonment, as reported by this tangata ora:

> Q: Do you think you will go back to jail?
> A: That's the million dollar question. I don't want to go back and I have said this like a million times that I don't want to go back. I have changed my thinking and I have changed

some of my lifestyle options. I have stopped addictions and some bad behaviours, so I have got a very high chance of not going back to jail

All of the tangata ora disclosed aspirations not to return to prison, but the sense this was not always in their control remained.

Conclusion

This project focused on the wisdom that exists within our own communities. What do our people say helps to strengthen our own people? Whether we are teachers, health workers, probation officers, prison workers, social workers, business owners, we are often engaged in connecting and reconnecting our people. Does that notion help to intervene in the growing tide of Maori imprisonment? This project worked with those people who had the knowledge base and could reconnect tangata ora with a deeper sense of themselves and their place in the world. At a practical level it gave the potential for new support systems to be there for tangata ora as well.

While we found a population that was one step away from crisis on a daily basis, the project did change these men's and women's expected outcomes. The parallel work of providing hapu, iwi health, and social services support alongside of wananga about hapu worked in this situation.

From an iwi perspective, iwi are attempting to increase participation by their own people. But sometimes this work needs to be actively facilitated. We also found that disconnection from iwi can happen within the traditional iwi land areas, but this disconnection can also be remedied if groups who are bound by shared history and connection are brought together.

When it comes to health and social services delivery, policy makers need to understand that reconnecting to a service that is tribe- or hapu-based is a lifelong connection that is made, not a connection for the term of a contract. Iwi membership is bigger than a service provider and will endure and continue.

We also learnt that our strength and resilience to hold on to identity is fought for fiercely in urban contexts and this creates new identities. New formations for Maori identity are created, and these need to be understood from the iwi perspective in order for connections to remain.

For tangata ora the hapu facilitators reminded them of the importance of knowledge and that they were all a part of a large and powerful interconnected network of iwi tangata, with strong family bonds to each other, and to the land from which their people came. Their involvement in the Tangata Ora Project reconnected them to each other and gave them an opportunity to reflect on what was really important to them, in ways many of them may not have had the opportunity to do so for some time. It was very clear by the end of the project, what was important was their families and their culture, demonstrated both through the absence of a return to prison for those tangata ora interviewed, and their reports of positive and useful experiences from their involvement in the project.

This project reaffirms that while the prison system remains in its current form, providing the right type of support post release is critical and can intervene in recidivism. That support needs to be consistent and long term, with people who have a strong and positive effect in their lives. This project met those two needs by providing iwi-based health and social service support, combined with key hapu facilitators. Both these supports mean that tangata ora have potential lifetime support that goes beyond the life of a service contract. Both these supports provide culturally solid, potential lifetime support which do enrich the lives of the tangata ora.

This project caused changes not only for tangata ora but to everyone involved. Everyone on the project was related to one another, these relationships have just been reactivated and remain a potential lifetime network. We remain deeply indebted to all those who agreed to participate in the project. You will never be forgotten.

Glossary

Aotearoa New Zealand, Māori term for New Zealand.
Hangi Earth oven to cook food with steam and heat from heated stones.
Hapu Kinship group, clan, tribe, sub-tribe, section of a large kinship group and the primary political unit in traditional Māori society. It consisted of a number of *whānau* sharing descent from a common ancestor, usually being named after the ancestor, but sometimes from an important event in the group's history. A number of related *hapu* usually shared adjacent territories forming a looser tribal federation (*iwi*).
Iwi Extended kinship group, tribe, nation, people, nationality, race, often refers to a large group of people descended from a common ancestor and associated with a distinct territory.
Kai Food, to eat, to consume, feed (oneself), partakes, devour.
Kapahaka Māori Performing Arts, performance, Māori song/dance.
Karakia/Whakamoemiti Prayer, to recite, or chant.
Kaupapa Topic, policy, matter for discussion, plan, purpose, scheme, proposal, agenda, subject, program, theme, issue, initiative.
Koha Gift, present, offering, donation, contribution, especially one maintaining social relationships and has connotations of reciprocity.
Koro Elderly man, grandfather, grandad, grandpa, term of address to an older man.
Kumara vines Maori lines of networking.
Manawhenua Report This report has been commissioned by Te Rūnanga o Ngāti Apa as part of their preparation for presentation of Wai 265, the Ngāti Apa land claim before the Waitangi Tribunal. The purpose of this report is to provide a definition of the nature and extent of Ngāti Apa manawhenua. This report is a component of the overall research and reporting project currently underway as part of Wai 265.
Māori Indigenous New Zealander, indigenous person of Aotearoa/New Zealand.

Marae Village, communal village, courtyard. The open area in front of the *wharenui*, where formal greetings and discussions take place. Often also used to include the complex of buildings around the *marae*.
Maunga Mountain, mount, peak, sacred hill.
Mihi Whakatau Speech of greeting, official welcome speech, speech acknowledging those present at a gathering.
Ngai Tahu A tribal group in the South Island of New Zealand.
Pakeha New Zealander of European descent, English, foreign.
Rangatira High ranking, chiefly, noble, esteemed.
Taihape A town located near the middle of the North Island of New Zealand.
Tangata Ora People of wellness (literal translation). People who are well or who are healing. Term used for men and women who have been released from prison.
Tangata Whenua Tuturu Original People of the Land.
Tangihanga Traditional Māori Funeral.
Te Reo The Māori language.
Tikanga Māori traditions and protocols, correct procedures, customs.
Treaty of Waitangi A treaty first signed on 6 February 1840 by representatives of the British Crown and various Māori chiefs from the North Island of New Zealand.
Treaty Settlements The settlement of historical Treaty of Waitangi claims.
Tūpuna Ancestors, grandparent(s).
Waikato Region in the upper North Island of New Zealand.
Wānanga To meet and discuss, deliberate, consider, seminar, conference, or forum.
Whakapapa Genealogy, genealogical table, lineage, descent.
Whānau Family, extended family, family group.
Whānau Ora (Programmes) A key cross-government work program jointly implemented by the Ministry of Health, Te Puni Kōkiri, and the Ministry of Social Development.
Whanganui City in the lower North Island of New Zealand.

References

Bishop AR (1998) Examples of culturally specific research practices: a response to Tillman and Löpez. Int J Qual Stud Educ 11(3):419–434

Bull S (2009) Changing the broken record: new theory and data on Māori offending. In: Paper presented at addressing the underlying causes of offending; what is the evidence? Institute of Policy Studies, Victoria University Wellington, Wellington

Bush M (2015) Police working on unconscious bias towards Māori. Retrieved 10 Feb 2017, from https://www.maoritelevision.com/news/national/police-working-on-unconscious-bias-towards-maori

Department of Corrections (2008a) Over-representation of Māori in the criminal justice system. Retrieved 28 Mar 2016, from http://www.corrections.govt.nz/resources/over-representation-of-māori-in-the-criminal-justice-system.html

Department of Corrections (2008b) Reconviction patterns of released prisoners: a 48 months folow-up analysis. Retrieved 28 Mar 2016, from http://www.corrections.govt.nz/resources/reconvict

ion-patterns-of-released-prisoners-a-48-months-follow-up-analysis/re-imprisonment-rates-first-timers-and-recidivists.html
Department of Corrections [Corrections] (2016) Prison facts and statistics – December 2016. Retrieved 10 Feb 2017, from http://www.corrections.govt.nz/resources/research_and_statistics/quarterly_prison_statistics/prison_stats_december_2016.html
Desmond P (2011) Trust: a true story of women and gangs. Penguin Random House, Auckland
Durie ET (2007) The study of Maori offending. In: Based upon an address to the New Zealand Parole Board Conference. Te Papa, Wellington, 23 July 2007
Jackson M (1988) He Whaipaanga Hou: the Māori and the criminal justice system – a new perspective, New Zealand Department of Justice Policy and Research Division, Wellington
Jenkins M (2017) Poverty is the new crime. DePaul J Soc Justice 10(1):1–7. http://via.library.depaul.edu/cgi/viewcontent.cgi?article=1133&context=jsj
JustSpeak (2012) Māori and the criminal justice system. A youth perspective. Retrieved from http://docplayer.net/3181058-Maori-and-the-criminal-justice-system-a-youth-perspective-a-position-paper-prepared-by-justspeak.html#show_full_text
Mihaere R (2015) A kaupapa māori analysis of the use of māori cultural identity in the prison system. Doctoral thesis. Victoria University of Wellington. Retrieved from http://researcharchive.vuw.ac.nz/xmlui/bitstream/handle/10063/4185/thesis.pdf?sequence=2
Ministry of Education (2017) Education counts: retention of senior students in secondary schools 2015. Retrieved 10 Feb 2017, from https://www.educationcounts.govt.nz/statistics/indicators/main/student-engagement-participation/retention_of_students_in_senior_secondary_schools
Ministry of Justice (2000) Māori responsiveness in police and justice sector. Ministry of Justice, Wellington
Ministry of Justice (2011) Maori responsiveness in police and justice sector. Ministry of Justice, Wellington
Mulholland M, McIntosh T (2011) Māori and social issues. Ngā Pae o te Māramatanga, Huia Publishers, Auckland
Newbold G (2007) The problem of prisons: corrections reform in New Zealand since 1840. Dunmore Publishing Ltd., Auckland
Pane DM, Rocco TS (2014) Transforming the school to prison pipeline. Sense Publishers, Rotterdam
Quince K (2007) Maori and the criminal justice system in New Zealand. In: Tolmie J, Brookbanks W (eds) The criminal justice system in New Zealand. LexisNexis Butterworths, Wellington, pp 333–359
Rook J, Sexsmith S (2017) The criminalization of poverty. In: Winterdyk J (ed) Crime prevention: international perspectives, issues and trends. Taylor & Francis Group, Boca Raton, pp 318–341
Sensible Sentencing Trust (2011) Sensible sentencing trust poll. Sensible Sentencing Trust, Napier. Retrieved 10 Feb 2017, from http://sst.org.nz/wp-content/uploads/2015/02/SST_Research_ColmarReport_2011.pdf
Statistics New Zealand [NZ] (2015) How is our Maori population changing? Retrieved 10 Feb 2017, from http://www.stats.govt.nz/browse_for_stats/people_and_communities/maori/maori-population-article-2015.aspx
Tauri JM, Webb R (2012) A critical appraisal of responses to Máori offending. Int Indigenous Policy J 3(4):5. Retrieved from http://search.proquest.com/docview/1400225547?accountid=33567
Walters KL, Mohammed SA, Evans-Campbell T, Beltrán RE, Chae DH, Duran B (2011) Bodies don't just tell stories, they tell histories: embodiment of historical trauma among American Indians and Alaska natives. Du Bois Rev 8(1):179–189. https://doi.org/10.1017/S1742058X1100018X
Wirihana R, Smith C (2014) Historical trauma, healing and well-being of Māori communities. MAI J 3(3):197–210. Retrieved from http://www.journal.mai.ac.nz/sites/default/files/MAI_Jrnl_3%283%29_Wirihana02.pdf
Workman K (2011) Māori over-representation in the criminal justice system – does structural discrimination have anything to do with it? Retrieved from http://www.rethinking.org.nz/assets/Newsletter_PDF/Issue_105/01_Structural_Discrimination_in_the_CJS.pdf

Indigenous Educational Movements in Thailand

38

Prasit Leepreecha and Meixi

Contents

Introduction	696
PART I: Ethnic Diversity of the Indigenous Peoples in Thailand	697
Who Are the Indigenous People of Thailand?: Names and Meanings	697
Ethnic Diversity in Thailand	698
Indigenous Movements in Thailand	702
PART II State Education to Build a Nation – The Impact of Thai Government Policy Toward Indigenous Youth and Communities	703
Mapping, Borders, and Indigenous Identity as a Threat to Nation Building	704
Education for Indigenous Highland Communities as Complex and Contradictory	707
Cold War Pressures: Assimilative Education Policies	708
Global Pressures: Testing and Other Global Trends in Education	709
Long-Term Impacts of State-Led Educational Initiatives for Indigenous People	710
PART III Building Coherent Communities – Movements Toward Expanding Indigenous Identity Through Education	712
Education as a Community Right	712
Moves to Resurgence I: Collaborations for Mother Tongue Education in Highland Communities	713
Moves to Resurgence II: Designing Pathways Home from Urban Indigenous Schools	715
Moves to Resurgence III: Expanding New Terms and Identities to Build Indigenous Power	718
Conclusion Building a Fire: Bridges of Power Toward a "Both–And"	720
References	721

P. Leepreecha (✉)
Department of Social Science and Development, Faculty of Social Sciences, Chiang Mai University, Chiang Mai, Thailand
e-mail: prasit.lee@cmu.ac.th

Meixi
College of Education, University of Washington, Seattle, WA, USA
e-mail: meixi@uw.edu

© Springer Nature Singapore Pte Ltd. 2019
E. A. McKinley, L. T. Smith (eds.), *Handbook of Indigenous Education*,
https://doi.org/10.1007/978-981-10-3899-0_55

Abstract

This chapter celebrates Indigenous education movements in Thailand. Despite state attempts to homogenize its citizenry historically and today, Indigenous communities in Thailand have always been active in strengthening their family, cultural, and linguistic practices. Through connections to other Indigenous movements regionally and globally, Indigenous educators in Thailand are organizing what we call "moves to resurgence" in communities, in schools, and particularly in the in-between spaces across schools and their local communities. In this chapter, we provide an overview of (1) the history and construction of indigeneity and ethnicity in Asia that complicates a "white-other" binary, (2) the long-term impacts of schooling for Indigenous youth as it relates to the formation of nation-states in Southeast Asia, and (3) how Indigenous communities in Thailand have skillfully navigated across worlds to create coherent identities for themselves. We provide three cases that intentionally build innovative "both-and" constructions of identity and resist binary state narratives that attempt to place Indigeneity in contradiction to statehood. To resist the continued erasure of Indigenous peoples in Asia, we highlight case examples of Indigenous resurgence and celebrate Indigeneity in Thailand.

Keywords

Thailand · Education · Indigeneity · Indigenous movements · Indigenous identity · Indigeneity in Asia

Introduction

Distinct linguistic and cultural groups in Thailand have existed long before the formation of the nation-state. Since the 2000s, these communities have been advocating for the rights to play a larger role in the education of their children and mediate long-term impacts of national compulsory education. Until recently, Indigenous highland communities have not been allowed to engage in a process of self-identification and self-determination. This was exacerbated by a system of national compulsory education that left little room to value and celebrate non-Thai practices, languages, and identities. The long-term impact of schooling initiatives that are implemented in the rural mountain villages or initiatives to bring highland youth to lowland schools continue to be felt today through the devaluation of Indigenous practices and the loss of their own culture and languages. While schooling has "reshaped local worlds" (Keyes 1991), this often ignores the agency of Indigenous people who have been setting up systems of learning to shape their own worlds.

This chapter explores how Indigenous communities are moving beyond state constructions of identity, ethnicity, and borderlands to build networks of learning movements for Indigenous education in Thailand. For those that call Thailand's borderlands home, highland communities have built and led movements of Indigenous people that are purposely collaborative and necessarily transborder. Despite not being officially recognized as Indigenous by the Thai government, highland leaders have been engaging in a process of self-definition to recognize themselves and their national movement as Indigenous peoples of Thailand. As scholars who have been active in these movements, our chapter outlines first, the political nature of self-definition in relation to state policies. Second, we explore the long-term impacts that schools have had on Indigenous highland identity and knowledge systems; participation in national compulsory education has often resulted in the erasure and devaluation of Indigenous knowledge and identity. Finally, we focus on Indigenous moves to resurgence and how Indigenous people have been acting to promote their own systems of knowledge and languages that bridge the formal school system and the larger community.

The concept of indigeneity is only just being recognized in Asia and is thus complex for schools and communities (Erni 2008; Baird et al. 2017). This chapter highlights how Indigenous communities navigate this complexity to build coherent identities for themselves despite ongoing state efforts to essentialize and place national and Indigenous identities in opposition to each other. We provide cases of Indigenous resurgence that creatively connect and advance state and community learning systems to build Indigenous power in the context of state nationalism in an increasingly globalized world. This chapter expands current notions of indigeneity by resisting the erasure of Indigenous communities in Thailand and highlighting interracial, national, and global dynamics that are common to Indigenous communities in Asia.

PART I: Ethnic Diversity of the Indigenous Peoples in Thailand

Who Are the Indigenous People of Thailand?: Names and Meanings

Unlike the new settlement and former colonized countries, Thailand had never been colonized by European forces. However, as a modern nation-state, the geo-body of Thailand was created by the influence of European colonies and the modern technology of cartography (Thongchai 1994). Initially, the country's name was "Siam" and this was changed to "Thailand" in 1939, due to the mainstream of Tai speaking groups. Other non-Tai speaking groups who are Indigenous groups in Thailand then became ethnic minorities, or the "others within" (Thongchai 2000a). Among those were more than 60 dialect groups throughout the country and 10 highland ethnic groups were labeled "hill tribes" or ชาวเขา (*chao khao*) in Thai, the Karen, Lua, Hmong, Mien, Lisu, Lahu, Akha, Khamu, Htin, and Mlabri (McCaskill et al. 2008). In a survey by Mahidol University's Institute of Languages and Culture for Rural Development that continued from 1993 to 2001, 62 languages were identified throughout the country – 24 Tai languages, 22 Austroasiatic languages, 11 Sino-Tibetan languages, 3 Austronesian dialects, and 2 Mien-Hmong (Leepreecha in press). The state government then set up specific socioeconomic development projects directly toward developing these "hill tribes" (McCaskill and Kampe 1997); the mountain borderlands of Thailand were problematic, a site of intervention

(McKinnon 2004). Since the mid-2000s, young leaders from these groups joined the international movement of Indigenous peoples in other continents and set up the Network of Indigenous Peoples in Thailand (NIPT). Despite there were national movement and adoption of United Nation Declaration on Rights of Indigenous Peoples (UNDRIP) in 2008, the term "Indigenous people" has been rejected by the Thai government who state that the highland people of Thailand are "not considered to be minorities or Indigenous peoples but as Thais who are able to enjoy fundamental rights and are protected by the laws of the Kingdom as any other Thai citizen" (Erni 2008, p. 444).

In the Thai context, labels are often ascribed to Indigenous highland communities without them having much say in their own identity or the process of self-definition. These ethnic groups are referred to by many other names instead. Most commonly, the highland communities are labeled hill tribes or ชาวเขา (*chao khao*) – literally translating to people of the hills (Laungaramsri 2003). The label "hill tribe" did not come from a process of self-definition, but from a way for the Thai officials and foreigners to contrast those who lived at 10,000 ft over sea level to those commonly classified "Thai" or lowlanders (Theerawhekhin 1978, p. 68, as cited by Laungaramsri 2003). *Chao khao* can also mean "the other people" as opposed to ชาวเรา (*chao rao*) or "the us-people" referring to the central Thai people as "us" (Laungaramsri 2003). The term "ethnic minority" ชนกลุ่มน้อย (*chon gloom noi*) is another label used to distinguish this group in opposition to the Thai majority in the country (Burutphat 2518). Another term is "ethnic group" กลุ่มชาติพันธุ์ (*gloom chat ti phan*), which has been used by scholars to refer to groups of people who are not part of the mainstream. This term is broader and has more positive associations than the "hill tribe" or *chao khao* label, since it includes every cultural group throughout the country, regardless of the length of time they have settled in Thailand.

Ethnic Diversity in Thailand

The Indigenous community has been classified by linguists, historians, and anthropologists (See Fig. 1a, b for maps of Southeast Asia). However, according to the National Council of Indigenous Peoples in Thailand, there are 42 different non-Tai Indigenous groups with a total population of 4,282,702 people have united under this movement (Samnakngan Chonphao Phuenmuang Haeng Prathet Thai 2558, as cited in Leepreecha in press). In addition to the Thai speaking groups, other native groups in Thailand include the Mon, Karen, Lua, Shan, Lao, Kui, Khmere, Chong, Munni, Malayu, etc. Ancestors of these groups have lived in Thailand for generations. Meanwhile, there are many groups whose ancestors moved into Thailand before the emergence of the modern Thai state between late nineteenth to early twentieth centuries. These include the Chinese, Phuan, Lue, Laos (from Laos), Hmong, Mien, Khamu, etc. There are also groups who have migrated into Thailand a couple of decades ago – the Lisu, Lahu, Akha, Dara-ang, Vietnamese,

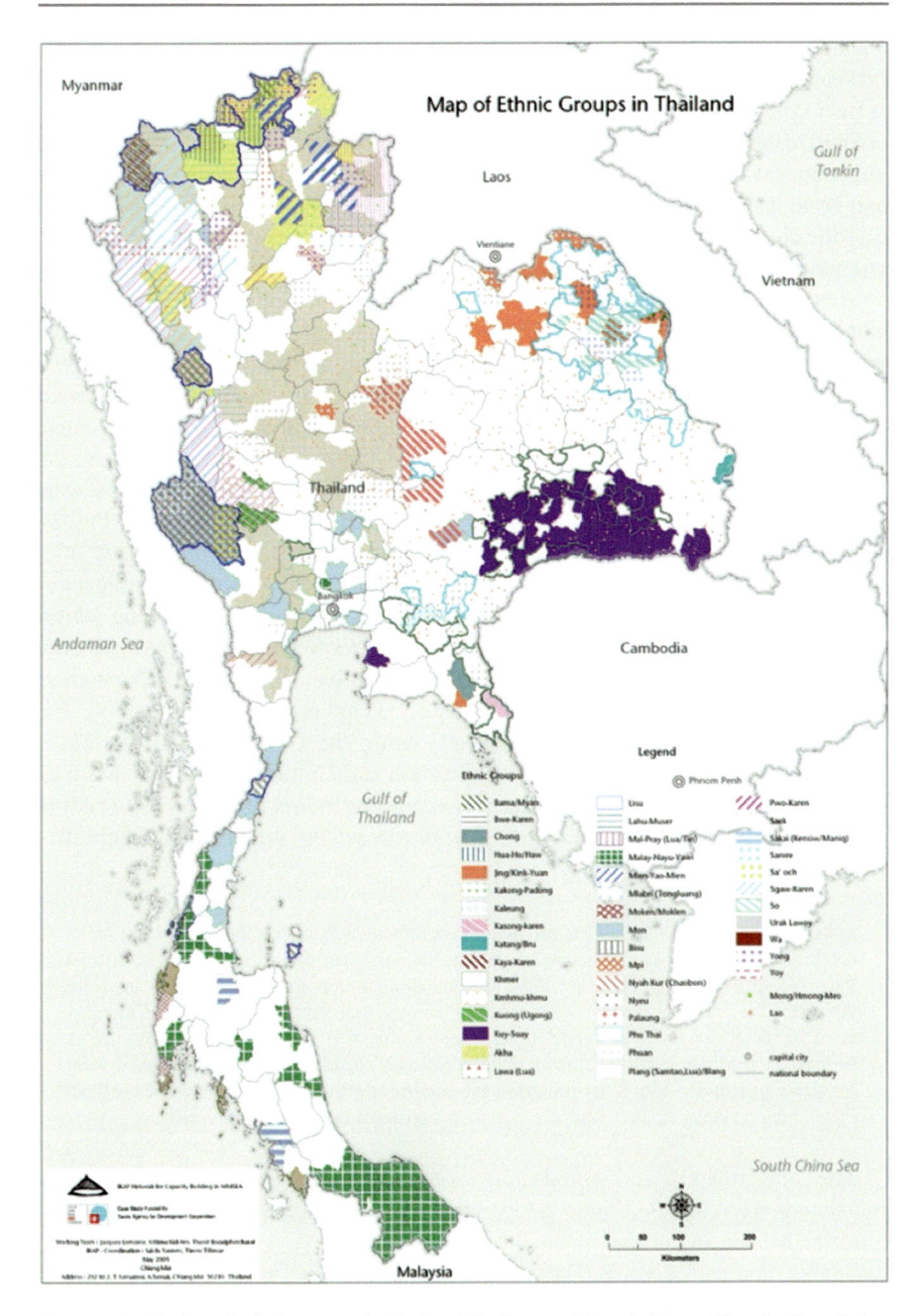

Fig. 1 Distribution of ethnic groups in Thailand (Indigenous Knowledge and Peoples Foundation (IKAP), Chiang Mai)

among others. There is a variety of ethnic groups who have settled in Thailand from different time periods. However, unlike other neighboring countries, the Thai government never surveyed or recognized these ethnic groups but only attempted to assimilate them and make them become Thai. Only in the past decades did the state government register and classify peoples who lacked Thai citizenship into 19 groups and issue different temporary colored cards for them (Laungaramsri 2014). These classifications, however, were based on citizenship concerns and ethnic diversity was never seen as part of the Thai state.

Among those ethnic groups, the "hill tribes" which comprises of ten highland ethnic groups in Northern Thailand became the prominent, due to increasing national security fears that the Thai government believed the "hill tribes" caused. This fear oriented, around 1.2 million peoples much of the government's policies toward highland groups during 1960–2000s. As stated above, while some groups are native to the land, and while others settled in Thailand for one to two centuries, and yet other groups have migrated into Thailand decades ago, these 10 groups were categorized "hill tribes" and portrayed as recent immigrants (Young 1961) (Fig. 2).

Despite these labels, through the creation of Indigenous networks and after external and internal debates, this group has chosen to call themselves Indigenous people, ชนพื้นเมือง (*chon pheun mueang*) or ชนเผ่าพื้นเมือง (*chon pao pheun mueang*) or literally "people of the land." The term *chon pao phuen muang* (ชนเผ่าพื้นเมือง) was agreed upon and adopted by the committee members of the National Council of Indigenous Peoples in Thailand (NCIPT, สภาชนเผ่าพื้นเมืองในประเทศไทย in Thai) during the October 31, 2558 (2015) workshop at Inter-Mountains Peoples Education and Culture in Thailand Association (IMPECT) in Chiang Mai, Thailand (Leepreecha in press). The NCIPT states in a proposal that was submitted together with the act for the National Legislative Assembly, that,

> Indigenous communities, peoples, and nations are those which, having a historical and social continuity before the establishment of present nation-states, consider themselves distinct from the main society. They are not the dominating group in the nation-state and are determined to preserve, develop and transmit their ancestral territories, their ethnic identity, and their language for future generations. These are basic of their continued existence as peoples, in accordance with their own cultural patterns, social institutions, and legal system for living peacefully with other groups in the nation-state society (Samnakngan Chonphao Phuenmuang Haeng Prathet Thai 2558, p. 1, as translated by Prasit Leepreecha)

This shift in words and who decides its terms of use is central to contemporary Indigenous movements. Ethnic categorization and identification in Thailand have historically been an outsider's one. Indigenous leaders thus responded to the need to self-define and self-identify. They began a transition from using the label of "hill tribe," which has been a term used by outsiders during the 1950–2000s, to "Indigenous peoples" (Leepreecha in press; Morton and Baird in press). Choosing to claim Indigenous status for themselves allowed Indigenous leaders in Thailand to connect with Indigenous people's movements globally and find solidarity with other communities who share similar struggles (Morton and Baird in press). Laungaramsri

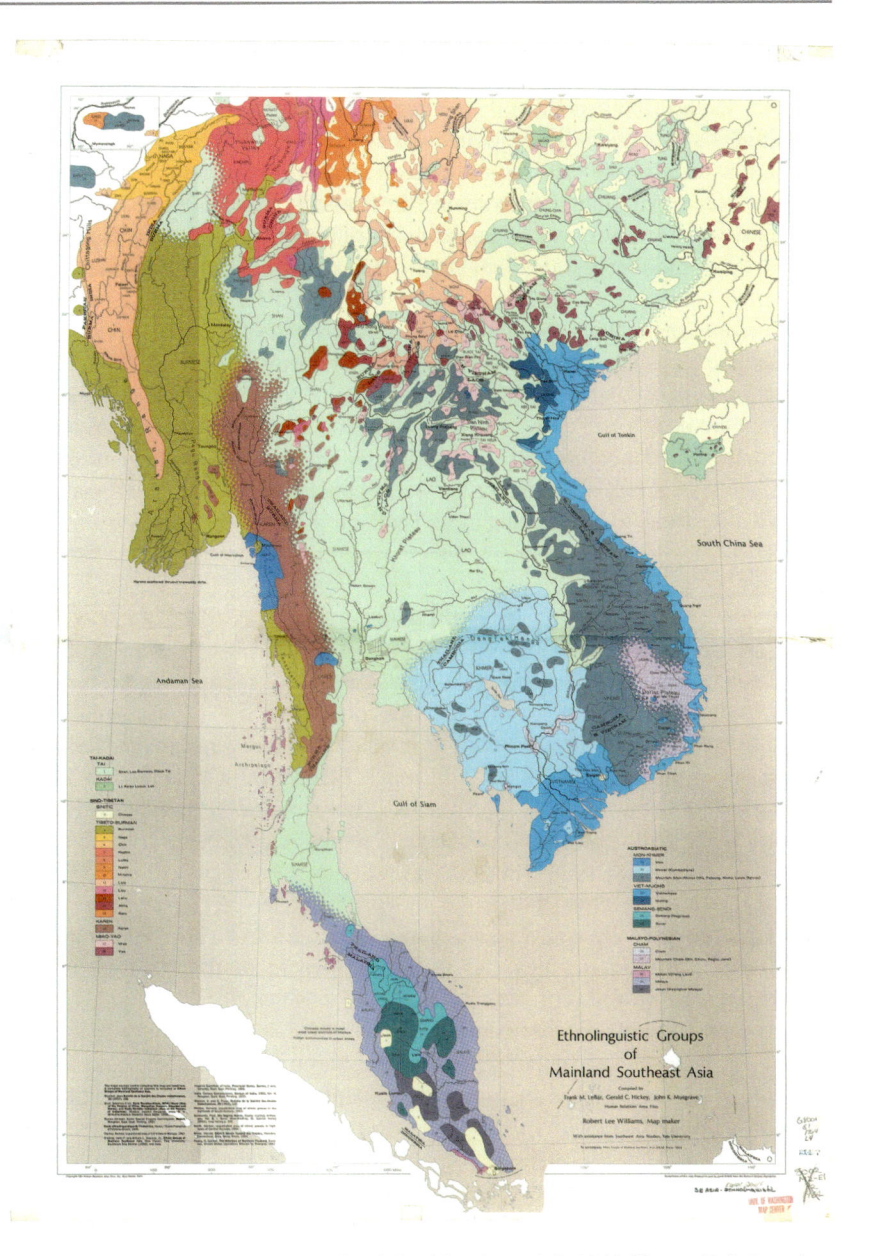

Fig. 2 Map of Ethnolinguistic Groups of Mainland Southeast Asia 1964, Human Relations Area Files

(2003) writes that "Ethnic categories in the modern Thai nation are, therefore, not simply constituted by shared/common identity but represent a powerful instrument or confinement and control by the modern state. At the same time, ethnicity is by no means an immediate given but is constantly achieved/ created through a process of negotiation" (p. 157). This process of negotiation is at the center of debates over Indigenous rights in Thailand.

Even though Indigenous communities in Thailand have participated in Indigenous rights movements internationally, they are not allowed to claim Indigenous status, nor have claimed to such a status translated to authentic meaning for their peoples (Network of Indigenous Peoples in Thailand 2010). Central Thais also claim indigeneity to Thailand, and the positionality of the Indigenous peoples in relation to Thai society is still contested (Erni 2008). The use of the label "Indigenous peoples" lies at the heart of the politicized citizenship debate for highland communities in Thailand and their rights to control their educational experience.

Thailand boasts of its distinct linguistic and cultural groups, but outside of tourism, diversity is often seen as a threat to a monocultural Thai national identity and thus the unity of the country. This next section explores how highland leaders created an Indigenous network to garner strength as a "community of becoming" (Leepreecha in press) – a community that is constantly making and remaking itself and what it means to be Indigenous in Thailand today.

Indigenous Movements in Thailand

Indigenous people in Thailand have always been engaged in the process of self-definition and in 2007, a transIndigenous movement in Thailand solidified. The global flow of ideas and connections to international Indigenous alliances promoted leaders to form the Network of Indigenous Peoples in Thailand (NIPT) to give voice to Indigenous issues in Thailand (Leepreecha in press). Through this network, Thailand celebrated Indigenous Peoples' Day for the first time in 2007 (Rattanakrajangsri 2014) and this public event has been organized every year since. From 18 groups in its inception, the network now has 35–57 active groups from across the country (Leepreecha in press). This network (originally made up of mainly highland communities) has steadily grown in strength to include lowland minority groups as well. The Network of Indigenous People in Thailand is organized loosely with an internal coordinating body, IMPECT, as its secretary office to serve as a liaison between Indigenous representatives throughout Thailand, and an external arm, the National Council of Indigenous Peoples of Thailand (NCIPT) that was founded in 2010 to aid with external coordination to NGOs, government offices, and international organizations (Leepreecha in press). NIPT has led legal reform initiatives in the National Legislative Assembly and also the nation's participation in the UN permanent forum on Indigenous issues (Leepreecha in press). NIPT is slowly gaining voice and power in civic society. The NIPT has created media, statements, books, and increased public awareness of Indigenous issues in broader Southeast Asia.

However, representations of Indigenous highland people as dangerous or in conflict with the nation-state continue to make it hard for many to be fully participating members of Thai civil society or for Indigenous communities to control their own education (Hyun 2014; Keyes 2008). Even though Thailand voted in favor of and ratified the United Nations Declaration on the Rights of Indigenous Peoples in 2008, they argue that every group in Thailand, including the Thai, is Indigenous. Today, there is still no clear policy regarding Indigenous people in Thailand or definition of Indigenous people, and it is mostly the work of scholars and nongovernmental organization (NGOs) that try to define the terms and meanings. The Network of Indigenous Peoples in Thailand has joined and now alliances such as the Asia Indigenous Peoples' Pact, Network of Indigenous Peoples in Thailand, and the International Working Group for Indigenous Affairs have come together to advocate for the rights of Indigenous peoples across borders. Comprising villagers, elders, Indigenous scholars, and NGOs, the NIPT works on the issues of Indigenous rights to land through community land titles, access to forests homelands and natural resources for food sovereignty, and protest the lack of citizenship for undocumented Indigenous people who were not counted as part of the national census in the early twentieth century and remain stateless. According to a 2008 UNESCO survey, 38% or 380,000 highland Indigenous people still lacked citizenship and only had a "hill tribe" status card (Calderbank 2008).

Initiatives to actively build and strengthen Indigenous identity and knowledge systems through education have also been at the forefront of NIPT and IMPECT's work. Groups such as the Indigenous Education Network, Pestalozzi Children's Foundation, IMPECT, Ton Kla Youth Network (TKN) and Foundation for Applied Linguistics have organized events and projects to protect Indigenous languages. For example, Foundation for Applied Linguistics is embarking on a 4-year project from 2559–2562 (2016–2020), to include of Indigenous studies as part of their strategic plan (Indigenous Education Network, 2559). To engage the public, these groups and scholars also use media and literature to circulate Indigenous perspectives on identity that shift public opinion on highland communities.

Educational initiatives that safeguard Indigenous identity are deeply political in nature as the purposes and practices of schooling for highland communities in Thailand have often limited the ways that Indigenous youth can define themselves. Schools are tangible and powerful forces that have often devalued and erased Indigenous identity through the state-disseminated texts and assessments (Keyes 2008; Goodman 2013). We now turn to how colonial mapping and school as a technology for nation-state building have framed how Indigenous youth and communities imagine who they can be.

PART II State Education to Build a Nation – The Impact of Thai Government Policy Toward Indigenous Youth and Communities

In Siam, the negotiation of kingdom boundaries made school an important tool in the formation of the nation-state. The Kingdom of Siam was a multiethnic kingdom where diverse groups lived and worked (Thaweesit and Napaumporn 2011). In order to maintain the sovereignty of their lands during the height of colonialism, central Siamese leaders were pressured by the French and British to map undefined and porous borders of the kingdom in the quest to create a nation (Thongchai 1994).

Furthermore, in an effort to unite the newly imagined geo-body and prevent the fragmentation common to the premodern states, Siamese leaders undertook nation-building projects to demarcate both a territory and a specific population that would belong to the newly forming nation-state (Thongchai 1994).

After the British waged war with the Burmese in the 1850s, they began to negotiate borders with the Siamese to distinguish British and Siamese domains. In response to the threat of colonization, Bangkok troops were tasked with mapping officials under King Chulalongkorn's instructions to "know all the localities under his sovereignty" (Thongchai 1994, p. 121). For the Siamese leaders, modern geography was "the only language the West would hear and only a modern map could make an argument" that would establish the geo-body of Siam. For the first time ever in Southeast Asia, mapping was used as the technology to establish this new geo-body. As Thongchai says, "the geo-body of Siam was being created literally on paper" (p. 127).

Socioeconomic projects to "civilize" highland communities along the Thai border rapidly intensified during the Cold War (Hyun 2014; Keyes 2008). The international conflict played out in larger Southeast Asia as other nations (Myanmar, Laos, Vietnam) were gaining independence around Thailand (Keyes 1997). Large-scale state educational initiatives for highland communities thus began when Thailand's porous borders were of heightened state interest and highland communities were in the government spotlight (Vaddhanaphuti 2005). During this period, Indigenous highland people began to be stereotyped as dangerous and problematic to the security of the Thai state. National media and textbooks showed Indigenous communities as communist sympathizers and forest destroyers (Hongladarom 1999; Vandergeest 2003); there was a "hill tribe problem" along the borders of Thailand that needed to be dealt with (Keyes 1997; Laungaramsri 2003). The creation of this "other within" served to justify the political and social control of the borders and people into the twentieth century (Thongchai 1994; Hyun 2014). Schooling was thus a tool to ensure central state legitimacy, cultural assimilation, and ideological control of people and the ground the central state had claimed through the process of mapping (Vaddanaphuti 1991, 2005).

Mapping, Borders, and Indigenous Identity as a Threat to Nation Building

According to Thongchai (1994), before European colonialism, the Kingdom of Siam, Burma, and Vietnam were all overlords of the region, with overlapping kingdom limits. The Siamese kingdom was centered around Bangkok (See Fig. 1 above for a map). Smaller kingdoms (e.g., Lanna, Luang Phrabang, and Vientiane) and tinier chiefdoms (Karen, Lao, Phuan, Phuthai, and other ethnic groups) were interspersed along most of Siam's frontiers. These smaller kingdoms paid submission to multiple overlords for protection, where the chiefdom's limits of control also overlapped with others. Chiefdoms were more fragmented but had autonomy in the ruling of their community. As the British and French began establishing their colonies around Siam, the Siamese were forced to modernize in order to maintain its sovereignty and prevent further losses of territory through the European technology of mapping. By the end of European expansion in 1909, the Siamese geo-body included various kingdoms that were culturally distinct from those living in Bangkok (about 30–35% of people of the Siamese empire) and that also recently had belonged to other political entities (Keyes 1997).

Mapping led to a territorialization of state power; it defined and organized people and place (Vaddhanaphuti 2005). First, the creation of fixed national boundaries prompted the establishment of state departments such as the Royal Forestry Department and the Ministry of Education. These institutions responsible for natural and human resources such as "unoccupied" forests and "unschooled" communities led to a "paradigm shift in the relationship between the Thai state and resources, people, and space insofar as the state had for the first time accepted responsibility to use all resources for the purposes of national development" (Vaddhanaphuti 2005, p. 153). In *Seeing Like A State* (Scott 1998), "contemporary development schemes... require the creation of state spaces where the government can reconfigure the society and economy of those who are to be 'developed'" (p. 187). Thus there was a need to "transform peripheral nonstate spaces into state spaces," which was often traumatic and racialized for the inhabitants of highland forest communities (Scott 1998, p. 187, also cited in Vaddhanaphuti 2005).

Second, boundaries constructed ethnospatial taxonomies of the "Other Within" as opposed to the We-Self of "Thainess" (Thongchai 1994, 2000a). Since the border of "Thainess" was more limited than the geo-body of the nation state, the Siamese elite embarked on a project to define the "Others within" that "reaffirmed their superiority, hence justifying their rule, over the rest of the country within the emerging territorial state" (Thongchai 2000a, p. 41). To be civilized, was to thus be "Thai," and to be modern was to be the West (See Fig. 3 below). This taxonomy of "civility" was a product of both nationalism and globalization and drove Siamese elite to embark on projects along this ethno-spatial-temporal trajectory.

Compulsory state education was a tool to assimilate all ethnic groups under the blanket of "Thai-ness" or ความเป็นไทย (*kwarm pen tai*) (Keyes 1991). "Thai-ness" is a collective identity that also reflects the importance of ethnic homogenization as fundamental to nation-building and modernization, where conversely, heterogeneity is a threat to national security and nationhood (Laungaramsri 2003). "Thai-ness" was defined as three things: (1) *chat* or nation (where speaking Tai is a symbol of

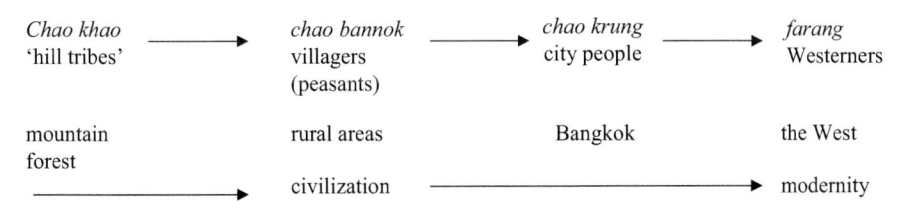

Chao khao 'hill tribes'	→	*chao bannok* villagers (peasants)	→	*chao krung* city people	→	*farang* Westerners
mountain forest ──────────────→		rural areas civilization		Bangkok ─────────────────→		the West modernity

Fig. 3 Table adapted from Thongchai (2000a), The others within: travel and ethnospatial differentiation of Siamese subjects 1885–1910

membership), (2) *satsana* or religion (being Thai is also to be Buddhist), and (3) *phra mahakrasat* or the King (which implied loyalty to the monarchy) (Keyes 1997; Laungaramsri 2003), and schooling was a way to make Thai citizens.

Under King Vajiravudh (King Rama VI), the Compulsory Education Act was created in 1921 to provide "equal" education for all. This act allowed the central government to dominate and control education in Thailand instead of letting ethnic minority groups like the Muslim and Chinese communities run their own schools. Central Tai became the language of instruction; until 2010, teaching languages other than Thai was forbidden in schools (Coalition on Racial Discrimination Watch 2012). In 2010 former Prime Minister Aphisit Vejajiva approved the National Language Policy to allow the teaching of other mother tongue languages and bilingual education in schools for non-Thai speaking children (Coalition on Racial Discrimination Watch, 2012). However, till this day, native languages are still prohibited at all times in highland schools run by the Border Patrol Police to continue to inculcate the idea of "Thai-ness" and loyalty (Hyun 2014). Curriculum and textbooks were also standardized to teach central Thai history, and teacher education programs mandated that all teachers are to be trained by government teachers' college before they can teach in any school, including religious and private schools (Fig. 4).

Increasing centralized control at the height of Thai nationalism under King Vajiravudh fed emerging ethnic conflict in Thailand, strengthening regional identities (Keyes 1997). The 1930s and 1940s saw the rise of ethnoregionalism in north and especially in the northeast region of Isan (Keyes 1997). Central Thai leaders deemed ethnoregionalism a variation of "Tai-ness" based on geography and language. For these regional groups, Thai leaders began an "inclusivist" national integration policy to "accommodate diversity within a national community" (Keyes 2008, p. 14).

Herein lies the important distinction between "ethnoregional" identities and "ethnic minorities" classification, where "ethnoregional" groups refer to those within the nation's borders are differences "taken to be characteristic of a particular part of the country rather of a distinctive people" (Keyes 1997, p. 213). Highland communities are seen to never be "Thai enough" and thus a problematic people (Morton and Baird in press). The "ชาวเขา (*chao khao*)" term highlights and accentuates a hill-valley dichotomy at odds with the *chao rao*, the us-people (Laungaramsri 2003). Highland dwellers, who once had an interdependent relationship with lowland dwellers, were now seen as dangerous and non-Thai. They were stigmatized, labelled as intruders to Thai territory, destroyers of the forests, opium cultivators, and a threat to national security (Laungaramsri 2003; Keyes 2008; Thongchai 2000a).

Thailand prides itself on never being formally colonized, but Siam's escape from Western colonialism was legitimized and maintained ironically by their quest for modernity based on drawing knowledge and skills from the West, so much so that scholars have labelled Thailand as having undergone a process internal colonialism or "autocolonizing quest for *siwilai* (civilization)" (Thongchai 2000b; Loos 2006; Harrison and Jackson 2010, p. 18). As a response to growing pressures from EuroAmerican imperial forces during the colonial and postcolonial periods, the Siamese elite's internal colonization as they built the nation-state makes Thailand

Fig. 4 Photo of highland ethnic students lining up in front of their school and listening to their teacher after singing the Thai national anthem, chanting in Buddhism, and paying respects to Thai national flag (Cover of textbook on Thai Peoples), highland village of Northern Thailand, in early 1980s (Non-formal Education Center, Lampang, 1985)

"semicolonial" or "cryptocolonial" (Harrison and Jackson 2010). Education was thus an important tool for the consolidation of state power driven by EuroAmerican frames of modernity. For with it, political and national purposes could be realized.

Education for Indigenous Highland Communities as Complex and Contradictory

It is difficult to identify a single comprehensive policy for the education for Indigenous communities in Thailand. Often, there were many organizations with overlapping or even conflicting agendas (McNabb 1993). The first state government schools in the highland community were in 1935 in Tak Province. Then in the 1950s, Border Patrol Police schools and Chao Pho Luang Uppatham (His Majesty the King's Patronage) schools were set up in Chiang Mai and Chiang Rai Provinces. Later on, schools under regular and specific educational agencies were built in highland villages.

Today, there are a few key players providing education to highland communities. First, the Office of Basic Education Commission is responsible for all schools. This office sets up school branches in highland villages. Second, the Non-Formal Education Office is in charge of setting up learning centers and bilingual programs in villages where schools could not be set up. A third player is the Special Education Administrative Office, and its two branches, the Welfare Education Schools and the Royal-People Welfare School, build schools in mainly remote areas for children "at-risk." Fourth, the Border Patrol Police Command Office is also a key player in highland Indigenous education and has set up schools-cum-surveillance centers supported by Thai Royal projects. Finally, the National Buddhism Office also educates ordained highland boys and provides vocational education to girls (Buadaeng and Leepreecha 2009).

These governmental programs ranged from defense concerns to deal with the "hill tribe" problem, tourist development, opium crop replacement initiatives, nation-state objectives, and even unresolved issues such as land ownership and citizenship debates. Educational policies also tend to stretch a monocultural-multicultural continuum, with debates surrounding what "level of cultural diversity is appropriate in the curriculum, the amount of resources that can be allocated to minority schools, and the extent to which higher educational achievement should be encouraged" (McNabb 1993, p. 18). Mobility for Indigenous youth is thus often "one piece of a larger, more complex set of relations, strategies, and negotiation" (McNabb 1993, p. 25).

Indigenous education policies are not only complex but also often contradictory and based on a kind of "selective integration" (Vaddhanaphuti 2005). On the one hand, Indigenous communities are seen to live in harmony with nature and are often used as a symbol of Thailand's diversity. Indigenous art and culture is often appropriated for tourism and marketed as part of Thailand's exotic attractions. At the same time, Indigenous communities are seen as uncivilized protestors that oppose the government's forest policies, fighting for the right to solve their own challenges (Vaddhanaphuti 2005).

Cold War Pressures: Assimilative Education Policies

For the state, schools are important "technologies of power" that are part of ongoing efforts to create, modernize, and secure the Thai nation (Foucault 1977 as cited in Keyes 2008, Jukping 2008; Kampe 1997). Schools were designed to instill a "development orientation" in villagers so that they will "come to accept the domination of the Thai state as an unquestioned given in their social life" (Keyes 1991, p. 89). For the "hill tribes" in northern Thailand, it is clearly stated

> Education for tribal people should be implemented in a distinctive way, which differs from general lowland primary schools. Specific educational curriculum should be developed. Teachers [who will be sent to teach tribal children] should be trained in an extraordinary course. It is not only for tribal people to be able to read and write, but also to have them loyal to the government." (Kachadpai 2518 [1975], p. 226, translated by Prasit Leepreecha)

The first large-scale state educational initiative for Indigenous children began with the creation of Border Patrol Police schools-cum-surveillance centers in highland villages (Hyun 2014). This included the training and deployment of Border Patrol Police to teach central Thai language and history to highland communities. During the Cold War era (1956–early 1980), 721 Border Patrol Police schools were set up to build a "'human border" along the territorial border" (Hyun 2014, p. 344) so that the border of "Thainess" would coincide with the defined geo-body boundary of Thailand (Hyun 2014). There are currently about 61 Border Patrol Police schools in northern Thailand with about 507 teachers and 30% being heritage teachers – teachers who had previously attended Border Patrol Police schools and came back to teach (Hyun 2014). National security was equated to strong Thai nationalism and the Border Patrol Police schools administered government presence and ideological control to fashion Thai citizens (Gillogly 2004). Second, government programs and Christian missionaries also brought Indigenous youth to city centers to study (Keyes 1997; McNabb 1993). Buddhist missionaries then followed suit to begin similar assimilation projects (Keyes 1997). This practice is especially common for students who want to continue onto secondary school in villages without one.

In school, the teaching of nation-state traditions, symbols, and songs, along with the use of official calendars, state-sanctioned textbooks, and learning materials based in the Thai language and history "re-shaped local worlds" (Keyes 1991) and also created imaginary ones. Through school, disperse populations would thus feel like part of an "imagined community" based on Thainess (Anderson 1983/2006). Schools enacted a "spatial culture" with a temporal order where uncultured, rural citizens learn how to appropriately interact with government officials and organizations (Keyes 1991, p. 90). Teachers are "cultural brokers" (Keyes 1991) that "ha [ve] leaned less toward brokering knowledge relevant to the villagers' world than to establishing the authority of a particular form of knowledge" (Keyes 1991, p. 109) – in this case, the superiority of Thai knowledge and the Thai way of being.

Moreover, textbooks and curriculum produced and distributed in Bangkok seldom mention ethnic minorities, unless in ways that characterize highland Indigenous people as problematic. Schools perpetuate ethnic stereotypes through such deeply troubling practices while Indigenous history, knowledge, or traditions of highland communities are not represented in state-disseminated educational materials. Such projects to "civilize the margins" that were based on "ethnocide" and "cultural imperialism" (Duncan 2004, p. 108). In fact, these assimilation and erasure projects were deemed so effective that the Tribal Research Institute focused closed in 2004 stating that "there was no need for the further study of the hill tribes as they were now considered to have become Thai" (The Nation April 15, 2004; Buadaeng 2006).

Global Pressures: Testing and Other Global Trends in Education

Moreover, in standardized testing, Thailand's Ordinary National Educational Test or (O-Net) reveals the "myth of meritocracy" by using testing as an evaluation tool (Goodman 2013). Goodman (2013) argues O-Net promotes a kind of "policing" and a "normalizing gaze" of the Thai education system (citing Foucault 1977). This normalizing gaze "molds society in nearly invisible ways and encourages self-censorship" so that students are "methodically socialized" to accept the true knowledge of the test and not question the central knowledge of the O-Net exam. For example, a multiple choice question (See below) asks "The kind of terrain in which humans chose to settle from ancient times until today is: (a) river basins, (b) plateaus, (c) mountains, or (d) valleys" (Goodman 2013, p. 11).

Question on the O-Net Thai National Test (Goodman 2013, p. 11)
The kind of terrain in which humans chose to settle from ancient times until today is:

1. River basins
2. Plateaus
3. Mountains
4. Valleys

The question privileges lowland communities over highland ones as they are the "humans" that chose to settle in river basins (only one answer is allowed) – as real humans live in the river basin, not the mountains. Similar questions privilege urban knowledge over rural knowledge and the use of central Thai as the official language. As this test that can deny or admit students to university, O-Net seems to privilege only knowledge from the center and is another tool to consolidate central power for nationalistic purposes. Goodman's (2013) analysis of the Thai standardized test shows the educational hegemony that has begun to shape education initiatives and to determine the lived opportunities for students in Thailand. Thus the longer Indigenous students participate in the dominant national state schools, the more often they accept Thai hegemony and their second-class status in Thailand.

Nondominant communities that do not align with these goals, nor perform according to this one measure are then deemed deficient and are seen in need of remediation. An added layer of pressures includes global education reform movements that promote only one "ideal" way of being – one congruent with human capital theory that supports consumption, individualistic competition, and economic production (Tatto 2006; Tabulawa 2003; Meyer and Benavot 2013). In the 1990s, with increasing globalization, Thai education systems were worried about building a "knowledge economy" (Baron-Gutty and Chupradit 2009). For example, "global languages" like English and Chinese are offered in every school and are valued more highly than local languages. The interconnectedness of the globe and by extension, education systems, has had an unprecedented effect on teachers and their work and lives (Paine and Zeichner 2012).

Long-Term Impacts of State-Led Educational Initiatives for Indigenous People

In a study of Indigenous students studying at university or vocational schools, McNabb (1993) still questions the effects of educational "achievement" on Indigenous families and communities – mobility at what costs? While the Thai government is mainly designed to socialize Indigenous youth as inferior to their Thai counterparts, the government, along with NGOs and missionary groups, has provided financial resources to support Indigenous youth to pursue higher education (McNabb 1993). Even so, the "development" of "hill tribe" communities has often come at the expense of "environmental degradation, loss of cultural identity, and the enhancement of conflict between the hill tribes [sic] on the one hand and the state agencies and lowland farmers on the other" (Vaddhanaphuti 2005, p. 164).

Still today, Indigenous youth in urban areas are constantly framed as being deficient in contrast to norms of Thai-ness. Similar to how the label "English-language learners" often reinforces "deficit-oriented, uncomplicated, and uneven narratives about students" from non-dominant communities (Gutiérrez and Orellana 2006, p. 503), Indigenous youth are "Thai-language learners" that need to be "made Thai" in order survive function in Thai society (Kampe 1997). Furthermore, such a label essentializes such a group trait and with it, comes assumptions about academic deficits or disadvantages (Moll 2000; Nasir et al. 2006; Rogoff 2003). Often in Indigenous education, instead of seeing multiple cultural practices within the school as an asset to the construction of a rich learning environment, heterogeneity or "otherness" is often seen as a deviation from the established dominant norm.

Furthermore, due to the lack of representation of highland communities in state-disseminated curricula, Indigenous youth often regard local languages, traditions, ways of knowing, and even the elders themselves to be "backward" or "old-fashioned" (Chandraprasert 1997). They often aspire to be like the *khon muang*, the "city people" (Wallace and Athamesara 2004). This is particularly true for urban Indigenous populations that frequently interact with Thais. They aspire to speak Thai without an accent and may try to hide their tribal identity when operating in lowland Thai society. Thai identities are assumed over tribal ones, and ethnic inferiority and erasure are systematically organized in younger generations (McCaskill 1997; Chandraprasert 1997; Chotichaipiboon 1997; Hyun 2014).

While some highland youth can speak Thai fluently, they often experience conflict between their cultural identity and their Thai national identity. For example, in the Border Patrol Police schools that currently exist in the highlands, there has been a *heritage teachers* program to encourage those from the various Indigenous groups to return to their villages and teach. These heritage teachers who return to the village were proud to assist in their village's development but simultaneously also felt that they were outsiders to their own village. They did not feel respected by the villagers because as Thai government officials, they were perceived to have "become fully Thai" (Hyun 2014, p. 349). At the same time, these teachers are often never "Thai enough" when participating in Thai society. They *both* want to send their children to Thai schools for a chance at a "better life" and even move into the dominant spaces to acquire membership in that group (Toyota 2005, as cited in Hyun 2014) *and* also want to be able to teach their own language and traditions to their children.

While the state has set up an Indigenous and Thai identity to be in conflict with each other, we now turn to how Indigenous youth and communities have in fact dextrally navigated through seemingly opposing home-school worlds to build coherent identities for themselves and their communities. In the next section, we outline moves to resurgence as youth and communities participate in the protection and expansion of Indigenous identity in Thailand today.

PART III Building Coherent Communities – Movements Toward Expanding Indigenous Identity Through Education

Indigenous people of the Greater Mekong Subregion have always "challenged the limits" of such control and asserted their identity and culture (Leepreecha et al. 2008a). This movement has become even stronger since 2007 with the creation of community and youth networks of Indigenous activists to ensure the well-being and educational justice of local communities in Thailand. Moreover, there have also been more transnational efforts that purposely work to refuse national boundaries as limits to collaboration. In this third section, we explore why education is a community right for Indigenous communities. We do so by outlining three moves to Indigenous resurgence. First, we provide a case study of how families in highland villages are collaborating to design local curriculum and implement Mother Tongue education in their schools. Second, we highlight an urban Indigenous school and how they have designed pathways home by deeply engaging students in a learning network that builds from family knowledge. Last, we explore other ways that Indigenous communities are reinventing what it means to be Indigenous within and beyond Thailand today. They are expanding ideas of literacy and development and creatively leveraging globalization and technology to strengthen Indigenous identity in their own communities locally and across borders (McCaskill et al. 2008).

Education as a Community Right

In 2005, the Thai government passed the Education for All Cabinet Resolution that mandated public education be expanded to all children regardless of nationality and legal status up to Grade 12. However, despite state efforts and pressures to broaden access to education, a central question here is education by whom and for whom?

One guiding basis of movements in Indigenous education in Thailand today is that families and communities have the right to play a part in the education of their children. While rights frameworks often still follow nationalist agendas and EuroAmerican frameworks, it also affords a certain kind of consciousness about ones' rights to culture and education (Barry 2013). In the 1990s, grassroots organizations, like Prawase Wasi and the Assembly of the Poor, criticized the centralized military-based administration, particularly the Ministry of Education, calling for more power to be given to local communities in order to mitigate corruption (Baron-Gutty and Chupradit 2009). During the revision of the constitution of 2540 (1997), villagers throughout the country contributed their thoughts and perspectives to what would be called, the "Constitution of the People" (Baron-Gutty and Chupradit 2009). Community rights in this new constitution included rights to natural resources management, rights to protect their own culture and local wisdom, and rights to education – that is, the right to teach about their own knowledge for their children in the regular state-sponsored school system (Barry 2013).

In line with the 2540 (1997) Constitution, the National Education Act (NEA) of 2542 (1999) was passed as the largest education reform to promote the decentralization of national curriculum. This act mandated that 30% of all school content should be provided and developed by the local community, driven by local participation in the education of their children, while the remaining 70% of courses taught in K-12 education would come from the national curriculum (NEA 1999 Section 23; Minister of Education 2003 as cited in Baron-Gutty and Chupradit 2009). Legally, each community has not only right to, but obliged to decide what knowledge and practices their children should learn at school.

This 30–70 composition of the local-national curriculum is not actualized in most urban and rural schools. Teachers and school administrations continue to teach without collaborative community participation. They do not invite local community leaders to design and teach local wisdom or languages. Indigenous networks and NGOs have tried to mediate the school-community relationship by working with school leaders and teachers first, to open up space their curriculum for local knowledge systems, and second, train the local experts in the development their own courses that can be taught in local schools.

Indigenous communities have become increasingly aware of the need to build coherent narratives and make meaning of seemingly separate modern knowledge and local wisdom systems (Fujioka 2002). One important example of this is school-village collaboration in Mother Tongue education, particularly for preschool and elementary students. The most successful cases are when local elders and teachers collaborate to create mother tongue and local curriculum that are cotaught during the school day. Furthermore, due to increasing numbers of students leaving their home villages to study in the cities, there also have been initiatives to work with welfare schools in the cities with high populations of Indigenous youth. To illustrate how Indigenous resurgence has begun in across rural and urban schools, we provide two case studies of Indigenous education movements in the following sections. These two examples offer varied ways of how families and communities are centering their dreams and claiming their right to shape the educational experiences of their children (Fig. 5).

Moves to Resurgence I: Collaborations for Mother Tongue Education in Highland Communities

Thai language is intimately linked to Thai nationalism and nation building. The teaching and use of Indigenous languages in public schools is still deemed suspect and contrary to national interests. We provide a case study from the Inter-Mountain Peoples Education and Culture in Thailand Association (IMPECT) and their longstanding work in protecting Indigenous mother tongue languages. This case is important because of the nature of collaboration between various actors – elders, families, and local Thai school teachers – to create locally designed curriculum and

Fig. 5 Indigenous students demonstrate their ability on reading and telling story in both indigenous and Thai languages at the annual mother-tongue conference in Chiang Mai Province of Northern Thailand (Taken by Prasit Leepreecha in 2015)

mother tongue language instruction. We discuss their work in a primary school in the Mowakhi village in Chiang Mai to show that when community participation is truly valued and sustained, education with community members actually helps to build a bridge to students' sociocultural heritage, while also advancing local and modern knowledge (IMPECT 2012).

The multigenerational Mowakhi school involves local leaders, parents, and teachers intimately in the village to design materials and course content for their children (IMPECT 2012). The school curriculum emphasizes learning both Thai and the Pgazk' Nyau systems of knowledge as essential to prepare their children for civic and economic participation both in Thai society and village life. For over 20 years, this school has been kept alive by its community, just as it, too, advances local ways of knowing and being. This has even sparked a growing movement in neighboring villages to also celebrate and uphold their people, language, and ways of knowing. This is similar to Wallace and Athamesara's (2004) work that provides a case study of a community-centered curriculum that involved and honored local community member's histories and knowledge in a rural highland community.

Through this school, the Pgazk' Nyau have prepared their children and their community to expand their identity through a connection to community stories and practices, and in so doing, strengthen their agency for active civic participation in Pgazk' Nyau community life and larger Thai society (IMPECT 2012). In the Mowakhi community, community members are deeply involved as teachers, curriculum designers, and key decision-makers at school. It is only with this heterogeneous expertise based in multiple epistemologies and practices that communities move closer to self-determination in Thailand (IMPECT 2012; Wallace and Athamesara 2004).

This kind of village-school collaboration is difficult to sustain at times. For example, the Hmong village of Mae Sa Mai in Chiang Mai highlights some of the challenges in implementing locally designed curriculum. Even though there were a variety of program offerings that ranged from local plant medicines, working with silverware and tree plantation and reforestation, cooperation between teachers and elders was unclear (Buadaeng and Leepreecha 2009). Furthermore, teachers' definition of local knowledge often narrowly focuses on vocational skills training and the sale of products, not so much for the learning of school-based subjects (Baron-Gutty and Chupradit 2009). Indigenous home practices and knowledge systems are still largely ignored and not considered productive nor important for school. In other instances, local teachers might be reluctant to collaborate with villagers or are too focused on completing the national syllabus, viewing integrating local knowledge systems as less important. Integration of curriculum might require fellow native educators and NGOs allies to negotiate strategies to make local curriculum an enacted everyday practice in the formal school systems in the villages (Buadaeng and Leepreecha 2009). Since developing local curriculum is not funded by the state, lack of funding for communities to design and teach this curriculum to the youth make might such a project fall through.

However, knowing that cases like the Mowakhi school are possible, more communities are exercising their agency to embark on similar collaboration efforts projects that leverage the National Education Act of 2542 to teach their Indigenous languages and knowledge systems. In 2007, various schools came together to share their locally developed curriculum "Education Systems and the Preservation of Local Wisdom and Ethnic Culture" research program at Chiang Mai University (Buadaeng 2008b). Elders and teachers continue to work through such challenges so that imagining education for self-determination does not have to be a distant reality. In the next section, we highlight another way to create connections between home and school knowledge, and how this might be possible for more communities.

Moves to Resurgence II: Designing Pathways Home from Urban Indigenous Schools

Told that the city offers "better" educational opportunities for their children and that advancement means children must leave behind their community and family in the mountain and adopt urban nation-state forms of life, there is an increasing trend of parents sending their children to stay and study in boarding schools in the city (Morton and Baird in press; Buadaeng and Leepreecha 2009). Furthermore, some village schools only go up to Grade 6 and attending secondary school means that students must leave their home villages to study in the lowland cities. This is also driven by financial incentives from a variety of donors and missionaries to provide free room and board for Indigenous highland students while they study (Buadaeng 2008a). While this may create layers of complications between the goals of the donors and state schooling, continuing education after the elementary grades in schools in the city have opened pathways to higher education, but students who have migrated to lowland areas also often lose connection to their homelands and feel inferior to their Thai counterparts (McNabb 1993).

Recently, the largest urban government-supported welfare school in Chiang Rai has undertaken strategies to create connections between school and home. Founded by two Karen educators, Sahasatsuksa school has a student population of over 2700 students from 12–15 different tribes. Almost all their students live in hostel facilities run by Christian or Buddhist missionaries or other international aid groups. While most of the teachers are not Indigenous, there are a significant number of Indigenous teachers who have graduated from Sahasat, then returned to teach there. Sahasat teachers already visit the villages of their students each year to meet with families and here we present initiatives from this urban Indigenous school to describe a new effort to design pathways home for the increasing number of students coming to live and study in the city.

In February 2015, Sahasat began designing learning in tutorial relationships (Tutoría), where students learn to engage in dialogue with their teachers and with each other as a way to learn. Originating from México, Tutoría attempts to transform alienating vertical relationships of power between teachers and students to build a horizontal learning network where students are part of the teaching community in class (Cámara 2003). This was a way to deeply engage heterogeneity in the classroom as this learning network called for student and family participation in a teaching and learning network and more youth and family designed curriculum (Meixi 2017). The data in this paper comes from a community-based design research study that initially involved school leadership, teachers, and students in 2015, and then expanded to include families in 2017 (Bang et al. 2010). In the following section, we highlight some reflections from students, teachers, and families from this work to design pathways home from school.

The first shift that we saw in Sahasat was that students felt that they had value and could contribute to the work of teaching and learning at school. This also resulted in changes in the way students also advocated for new forms of teaching and learning. Using a collection of 40 student reflections, we highlighted typical student responses after they have participated in the Tutoría learning network.

Student 1: I have fun. I can learn in an easy going way and I can have my own thinking because it's easy going activity and I have fun. I dare to think and take action.
Student 2: I am glad that I have learned new things and I have become brave because I have brought what I have known to teach my friends. Normally, I am not a brave one. After I have taught others, I have become brave.

The idea of "dare" was coded on 15 student responses. These students use the Thai word "กล้า," meaning "to have courage" or "overcome fear to do something." Importantly, it was the relational nature of learning that made it "fun" and "easy going" so that students felt the responsibility and desire to contribute to the learning network. One other student wrote, "Everyone can help teaching, every classroom should be equal." This student recognized an individual's own abilities to be a part of teaching, but also saw that the classroom was full of other actors too.

Classroom is often governed by fear and students in small ways are finding their voice and gaining confidence that their opinion matters, that they could own and be agents of learning at school. Students understood their new role as assets to the class and now considered themselves mediators and designers of learning where normatively, teachers are seen as the main mediators of learning in the classroom.

Furthermore, as more students "dared" to be brave and take up agency in learning, teachers also began to question their own perceptions about students' ability to participate in the work of teaching and learning at school. In a collective reflection session a teacher, Teacher O recognized she was engaging in the suppression of the use of the Akha language in her students in contrast to Thai, which is constantly insisted on as the language of use in school. Akha is an Indigenous language, spoken by around 1000 Akha students in Sahasat school and is one of the commonly spoken languages at school. She said, "I told them, you can't use Akha to explain it to each other because tomorrow morning, students from (another school) are coming and you can't use Akha with them! But actually now that I think about it, they actually should speak any language, like Akha."

Indigenous youth are often asked to not use their language in order to integrate and interact with their Thai counterparts. Speaking Thai is to orient oneself outward, for communicability and translation. While this is true, native languages are often subordinated to the use of Thai. Teacher O makes public her shift from a curriculum-centered framing to a child-centered frame; she began to orient in, toward the child, not what the curriculum externally demanded of her. This is a powerful move of resistance to the required subordination and it is also a standing up to common notions of what is valued by the state. Ultimately it worked against the devaluation of Indigenous peoples and their ways of knowing, speaking, and being.

Furthermore, during our family interviews at students' home villages, families shared skills and practices that were important to their family and community. While there was a shyness about the knowledge that the family held, there was also pride in intergenerational knowledge of bamboo for the creation of their home and in the expertise in recognizing patterns when harvesting mangoes. In one family, a student, Beu heard about the practice of his grandmother who was an expert at spinning cotton into thread but also that his mother could not do so anymore. When asked what learning he wanted to design at school, Beu spoke of his desire to learn the practice of cotton spinning and prevent its potential loss of such a valuable family practice. When asked why he wanted to focus his curriculum on this practice, Beu said, "I want to create lessons on practices that we had before but are not really seen in everyday life today... what people did in the past, like how we can turn cotton into thread." Beu is currently working with his grandmother to create and teach this practice to his teachers and classmates at Sahasat. Indigenous youth in urban areas can be conduits that actively build school-village connections for continued family involvement in the practices of school.

These are some examples of how urban Indigenous youth and their school are opening up spaces to design pathways back home to strengthen relations between knowledge systems that schools and society has otherwise have tried to erase. This, however, just involved 6 students out of the 2700 at Sahasat and more work needs to be done to open up these spaces at school. Designing participation structures and curriculum at school was a potential pathway to a resurgence of these community practices and as Beu shared, for such practices to take on contemporary forms.

Instead of allowing the state to run and determine educational pathways for their children, Indigenous peoples have solidified and expanded their role to set goals, negotiate curriculum, and participate in school, both in highland villages and in the lowland areas where they send their children to school. In light of the history of state education as a means to remediate deficits, designing for legitimate student and family participation in the work of learning and teaching at school opens up new possibilities for strengthening both school and home practices by creating coherence between them.

Moves to Resurgence III: Expanding New Terms and Identities to Build Indigenous Power

Until today, Indigenous peoples have developed a variety of strategies to defend their rights to define "development," define "language," and to define who they are. Particularly when their world is highly globalized and international borders are increasingly porous, "nation-states continue to exercise substantial control over Indigenous people and their territories" (Leepreecha et al. 2008b, p. 2). However as schooling attempted to forget who we are to reshape local worlds, Indigenous communities have always been shaping their own worlds and reconstituting space and possibility. Indigenous communities are always in processes of "internalizing aspects of globalization and nationalism, while at the same time attempting to externalize aspects of their Indigenous cultural beliefs and practices" (Leepreecha et al. 2008b, p. 2). In the book *Challenging the Limits* (2008a), Leepreecha et al. synthesize five strategic response of various Indigenous groups in the Greater Mekong Subregion to the forces of globalization and nationalism. The first tactic is direct mobilization and organization in the case of the Karen in Burma. Second, groups have been taking control to defining their own identities as a way to counter dominant negative stereotypes and gain recognition and influence in the social, economic, and political spheres. Third, Indigenous groups have been reconstructing social relations and traditional knowledge in order to maximize influence and benefits from existing government structures. Fourth, other groups have taken a more subversive stance involving nonconfrontation but the "rejection/withdrawal/escape/hiding" in response to expanding power and control by government and nongovernment authorities (Leepreecha et al. 2008b, p. 7). Last, others have challenged the notion of boundaries to form cross-border projects through "the use of available social and cultural spaces" to take advantage of the opening of more economic and diplomatic relations between states. These movements take place in a context of collaboration and learning and building upon the tactics and strategies of each other.

For example, Hmong communities have collaborated to create a transnational identity with the aid of technology (Leepreecha 2008). Nationalism and globalization which were meant to shape and erode Hmong ethnic identity can and has been reappropriated. In a study of Hmong identity, Leepreecha examines how Hmong communities in Thailand and the USA transcend state borders to create artifacts of globalization for a shrinking world. These include audiovisual media, publications, and cultural artifacts such as story cloths for circulation. Hmong communities have also expanded global networks of kinship to cyberspace, churches, and businesses for increased connections across time-space to strengthen and reproduce Hmong identity (Leepreecha 2008).

Similarly, Lahu communities work between a tension of opposing forces of homogenization, erasing difference among various practices that exist in an imaginary space, and heterogenization, maintaining and creating difference at local levels (Pine 2008, citing Appadurai). Using the case of literacy, Pine (2008) examines how the Lahu have been "desettling" ideas of literacy through being aliterate. While writing is a technology of power, "the possession of writing identifies the group in question as modern, while the absence of writing is an important aspect of a "traditional" identity," as in the case of the Lahu (Pine 2008, p. 220). While the highland-lowland divide has categorized hill tribe peoples as being uncivilized and less developed because they possess no writing system, Pine offers that the Lahu challenges common notions of literacy that supposedly is at the pinnacle of a "civilized" culture and the classification of "developed" people based on orthography. Instead, being Lahu is a practice and *speaking* Lahu is at the heart of it. Lahu "loss-of-writing myths" problematizes literacy as a homogenous discourse today and the ways which we understand development and civilizing projects (Pine 2008). In a world where being with-writing grants access to the "civilized" and "global currents intent on eliminating difference" (p. 232), Lahu people are negotiating what it would be to be with-writing, just as those with-writing cannot place Lahu and other minoritized groups at the margins of literacy practices.

Finally, while the Karen were more readily accepted into Thai society, they too undergo the "dual process of defining one's own group and being defined by others to establish meaningful ethnic group boundaries" (Leepreecha et al. 2008b, p. 2). Their strategy has been a "process of converting modernity into tradition and inscribing part of their knowledge tradition into modernity" (Gravers 2008, p. 150). They have participated in official governmental capacities across borders, while mobilizing their own communities, protecting their Indigenous knowledge systems and cosmology, and using "communalization within/against nationalization and globalization" (Gravers 2008, p. 174).

Compulsory state schooling steeped in Thai nationalism and global orientations to education mandate that Indigenous youth constantly negotiate being essentialized in their individual and collective processes of becoming. In this section, we have tried to show various ways the expansion of connections between school and home can help Indigenous youth navigate and move between the worlds of home and school to find coherence in the making of who they are. In response to efforts to define, reduce, and simplify, Indigenous identity in Thailand, youth and families hold the complexity of what it means to be Indigenous today. They hold onto their histories, languages, practices, and culture while simultaneously invent and expand the definitions of what it means to be Indigenous. They have creatively used globalization to strengthen their own movements and identities (Leepreecha in press; Leepreecha 2008). They have used the school to facilitate increased connections to their language, practices, and culture, *and* learned the skills and tools to allow them to navigate Thai society with incredible dexterity. The move to see themselves as "both" "and" are Indigenous moves to resurgence.

Conclusion Building a Fire: Bridges of Power Toward a "Both–And"

šɨ̂ʔ mâ à-mī hɛ̂, chɔ mâ ɔ̀-g̈â ɨ̄.

When there is lots of wood the fire is strong; when there are many people their strength is great.
– Lahu Proverb
(Using transcription by Matisoff 2011)

In the years ahead, the Network of Indigenous Peoples in Thailand continues to build a stronger network to negotiate pathways to Indigenous education with the state government so that parents and community leaders can determine the learning of their young. We are collectively creating bridges of power that both ground our young people in their own language and culture and provide them the skills to participate in Thai society. Unlike Indigenous movements in the Americas, Indigenous people in Thailand often have to prove they are "Thai enough" to have their claims translate into actual provisions and rights (Morton and Baird in press). Like in the Lahu proverb above, this makes a transIndigenous, transborder network is key to sustaining its development and strength to understand and grow from how others navigated the complexity of state policies and provisions.

For Thai educators and policy makers, they should understand that Indigenous identity is not in conflict with a national one; youth should not need to choose between being Thai or "not Thai enough." Schools must support Indigenous youth to be proud of *both* their history and culture *and* also be "Thai-enough." Indigenous youth and peoples always have and continue to build a complex yet coherent identity of what it means to operate and thrive in the space in-between school and home, from highland to lowland, from home wisdom to Thai ones. They do so with amazing resourcefulness and grace. Our schools need to allow for and accept the navigation of complex, multilayered identities that our Indigenous youth bring to school.

Finally, there is much more research to be done in the academy to highlight and the ongoing strength and struggles of Indigenous people in Thailand and in Asia. This will help people understand and resist the erasure of Indigenous communities in Asia and expand the conversation of settler-colonialism that is conflated with inter-race dynamics. The concept of indigeneity is beginning to be recognized in Asia and has been officially adopted by governments in Japan, Taiwan, Nepal, the Philippines, and Cambodia (Erni 2008). Many Asian governments, however, continue to reject the concept of "indigeneity" (Erni 2008). Increased research in this area will help shift and expand public opinion and policy on indigeneity in Asia where much more work and research need to be done to resist the continued erasure of Indigenous people in the region. Being Indigenous in Asia is deeply political and the more voices we have centering Indigenous voices on this complex issue, the stronger our fire.

References

Anderson B (1983/2006) Imagined communities: reflections on the origin and spread of nationalism (Rev. Ed edn). Verso Books, London/Newyork

Baird IG, Leepreecha P, Yangcheepsutjarit U (2017) Who should be considered "Indigenous"? A survey of ethnic groups in northern Thailand. Asian Ethn 18(4):543–62

Bang M, Medin D, Washinawatok K, Chapman S (2010) Innovations in culturally based science education through partnerships and community. In: Khine M, Saleh I (eds) New science of learning: Cognition, computers and collaboration in education. Springer, New York, pp 569–592

Baron-Gutty A, Chupradit S (2009) Reinforcing Thai wisdom with local curriculum at school. In: Baron-Gutty A, Chupradit S (eds) Education, economy and identity: ten years of educational reform in Thailand. IRASEC – Research Institute on Contemporary Southeast Asia, Chiang Mai, pp 23–36

Barry CM (ed) (2013) Rights to culture: heritage, language, and community in Thailand. Bangkok/Chiang Mai: Princess Maha Chakri Sirindhorn Anthropoly Centre/Silkworm Books, Silkworm

Buadaeng K (2006) The rise and fall of the tribal research institute (TRI): "Hill tribe" policy and studies in Thailand. Southeast Asian Stud 44(3):362

Buadaeng K (2008a) Ongkornphatanaekchonkabkan song sermkansuksakaeklum chat phan bon phuenthi sung (Non-governmental organisations and the promotion of education among highland ethnic groups). Research report of Social Research Institute, Chiang Mai University, Chiang Mai

Buadaeng K (2008b) Kan phathana rabob kan suksa phue anurak watthanatham lae phasa chatphan (Developing educational systems for the conservation of culture and language). Research report of Social Research Institute, Chiang Mai University, Chiang Mai

Buadaeng K, Leepreecha P (2009) Modern education systems and impact on ethnic minorities. In: Baron-Gutty A, Chupradit S (eds) Education, economy and identity: ten years of educational reform in Thailand. IRASEC – Research Institute on Contemporary Southeast Asia, Chiang Mai, pp 37–53

Burutphat K (2518) Chon Kloom Noi nai Thai. Phrae Phittaya, Krungthep

Calderbank D (2008) Plight of the hill tribes: education needed in struggle to empower hill tribe communities. Bangkok Post, 12 Aug 2008, p E3

Cámara G (2003) Learning for life in Mexican rural communities: The Conafe post-primary centers. CONAFE, México City

Chandraprasert E (1997) The impact of development on the Hilltribes of Thailand. In: McCaskill D, Kempe K (eds) Development or domestication? Indigenous peoples of Southeast Asia. Silkworm Books, Chiang Mai, pp 83–96

Chotichaipiboon T (1997) Socio-cultural and environmental impact on economic development on Hill tribes. In: McCaskill D, Kempe K (eds) Development or domestication? Indigenous peoples of Southeast Asia. Silkworm Books, Chiang Mai, pp 98–116

Duncan CR (ed) (2004) Civilizing the margins: southeast Asian government policies for the development of minorities, 1st edn. Cornell University Press, Ithaca

Erni C (2008) The concept of Indigenous peoples in Asia: a resource book. IWGIA, Copenhagen

Foucault M (1977) Discipline and punish: the birth of the prison. Vintage Books, New York

Fujioka R (2002) Case study on educational opportunities for hill tribes in Thailand: implications for sustainable rural development. Food and Agriculture Organization of the United Nations Regional Office for Asia and the Pacific, Bangkok

Gillogly K (2004) Developing the "hill tribes" of northern Thailand. In: Duncan CR (ed) Civilizing the margins: southeast Asian government policies for the development of minorities. NUS Press, Singapore, pp 116–149

Goodman J (2013) The meritocracy myth: national exams and the depoliticization of Thai education. J Soc Issues Southeast Asia 28(1):101–131

Gravers M (2008) Moving from the edge: Karen strategies of modernizing. In: Leepreecha P, Kwanchewan B, McCaskill D (eds) Challenging the limits: Indigenous peoples of the Mekong region. Silkworm Books, Chiang Mai, pp 13–54

Gutiérrez KD, Orellana M (2006) The problem of English learners: constructing genres of difference. Res Teach Engl 40:502–507

Harrison RV, Jackson PA (2010) The ambiguous allure of the west: traces of the colonial in Thailand. Hong Kong University Press, Hong Kong

Hongladarom K (1999) Competing discourses on Hill tribes: media representation of ethnic minorities in Thailand. In: Presented at the Presented at the 7th international conference on Thai Studies, University of Amsterdam, Amsterdam

Hyun S (2014) Building a human border: the Thai border patrol police school project in the post–cold war era. J Soc Issues Southeast Asia 29(2):323–363

IMPECT (2012) Mowakhi. Retrieved from http://www.forestpeoples.org/topics/environmental-governance/video/2012/08/new-video-impect-mowakhi

Jukping S (2008) Mae khru khong chaat: a study of women teachers of Thai Hill tribe children. Doctoral dissertation, University of Iowa, Iowa City. Retrieved from The University of Hong Kong Libraries

Kampe K (1997) The culture of development in developing Indigenous peoples. In: McCaskill D, Kempe K (eds) Development or domestication? Indigenous peoples of Southeast Asia. Silkworm Books, Chiang Mai, pp 132–182

Keyes C (1991) The proposed world of the school: Thai villagers entry into a bureaucratic state system. In: Keyes CF, Keyes EJ, Donnelly N (eds) Reshaping local worlds: rural education and cultural change in Southeast Asia. Yale University Southeast Asian Studies, New Haven, pp 87–138

Keyes C (1997) Cultural diversity and National Identity in Thailand. In: Brown ME, Ganguly S (eds) Government policies and ethnic relations in Asia and Pacific. MIT Press, Cambridge, MA, pp 197–232

Keyes C (2008) Ethnicity and the nation-states of Thailand and Vietnam. In: Leepreecha P, Kwanchewan B, McCaskill D (eds) Challenging the limits: Indigenous peoples of the Mekong region. Silkworm Books, Chiang Mai, pp 13–54

Laungaramsri P (2003) Ethnicity and the politics of ethnic classification. In: McKerras C (ed) Ethnicity in Asia. Routledge, London/New York, pp 157–173

Laungaramsri P (2014) Contested citizenship: cards, colors, and the culture of identification. In: Maston J (ed) Ethnicity, borders, and the grassroots Interface with the state: studies on Southeast Asia in honor of Charles F. Keyes. Silkworm Books, Chiang Mai, pp 143–162

Leepreecha P (2008) The role of media technology in reproducing Hmong ethnic identity. In: McCaskill D, Leepreecha P, Shaoying H (eds) Living in a globalized world: ethnic minorities in the Greater Mekong Subregion. Mekong Press, Chiang Mai, pp 89–114

Leepreecha P (in press) Becoming Indigenous peoples in Thailand. J Southeast Asian Stud

Leepreecha P, McCaskill D, Buadaeng K (eds) (2008a) Challenging the limits: Indigenous peoples of the Mekong region. Silkworm Books, Chiang Mai

Leepreecha P, McCaskill D, Buadaeng K (2008b) Introduction. In: Leepreecha P, Kwanchewan B, McCaskill D (eds) Challenging the limits: Indigenous peoples of the Mekong region. Silkworm Books, Chiang Mai, pp 13–54

Leepreecha P, Kwanchewan B, McCaskill D (2008c) In: Leepreecha P, Kwanchewan B, McCaskill D (eds) Integration, marginalization and resistance: ethnic minorities of the Greater Mekong Subregion. Silkworm Books, Chiang Mai

Loos T (2006) Subject Siam: family, law, and colonial modernity in Thailand. Cornell University Press, Ithaca

Matisoff JA (2011) "Stung by a bee, you fear a fly": areal and universal aspects of Lahu proverbial wisdom. Bull Sch Orient Afr Stud Univ Lond 74(2):275–304

McCaskill D (1997) From tribal peoples to ethnic minorities: the transformation of Indigenous peoples: a theoretical discussion. In: McCaskill D, Kempe K (eds) Development or domestication? Indigenous peoples of Southeast Asia. Silkworm Books, Chiang Mai, pp 26–60

McCaskill D, Kampe K (eds) (1997) Development or domestication? Indigenous peoples of Southeast Asia. Silkworm Books, Chiang Mai

McCaskill D, Leepreecha P, Shaoying H (2008) Globalization, nationalism, regionalism, and ethnic minorities in the Greater Mekong Subregion: a comparative analysis. In: McCaskill D, Leepreecha P, Shaoying H (eds) Living in a globalized world: ethnic minorities in the Greater Mekong Subregion. Mekong Press, Chiang Mai, pp 89–114

McKinnon K (2004) Locating post-development subjects: discourse of intervention and identification in the highlands of Northern Thailand. PhD dissertation, Australian National University, Canberra

McNabb S (1993) Tribal education in northern Thailand: policy implications of current mobility patterns. Asian Thought Soc Int Rev 18(52):18–29

Meixi (2017) Shifting power at school: Youth participation in teacher professional learning settings as educational innovation. International Journal of Innovation in Education, 4(2/3: Special Issue on Re-configuring Learner Experiences: Opportunities and Systemic Challenges), 107–125

Meyer HD, Benavot A (2013) PISA and the globalization of educational governance: some puzzles and problems. In: PISA, power and policy: the emergence of global educational governance. Symposium Books, Oxford, UK, pp 7–26

Minister of Education (2003) Announcement from the Ministry of Education. Details on 2001 basic education curriculum [in Thai]. Ministry of Education (year 2546), Bangkok

Moll LC (2000) Inspired by Vygotsky: ethnographic experiments in education. In: Lee CD, Smagorinsky P (eds) Vygotskian perspectives on literacy research: constructing meaning through collaborative inquiry. Cambridge University Press, Cambridge, UK

Morton MF, Baird IG (in press) From hill tribes to Indigenous peoples. J Southeast Asia Stud

Nasir NS, Rosebery AS, Warren B, Lee CD (2006) Learning as a cultural process: achieving equity through diversity. In: The Cambridge handbook of learning sciences, 1st edn. Cambridge University Press, New York, pp 489–504

Network of Indigenous Peoples in Thailand (2010) Report on the situation of human rights and fundamental rights of Indigenous peoples in Thailand. Chiang Mai

Office of the National Education Commission, & Office of the Prime Minister, Thailand (1999) National Education Act of B.E. 2542 (1999). Retrieved from http://planipolis.iiep.unesco.org/upload/Thailand/Thailand_Education_Act_1999.pdf

Office of the National Education Commission, Thailand (1999) National Education act: an education reform act for future development of the Thai people. Office of the National Education Commission, Thailand. Retrieved from http://www.edthai.com/act/index.htm

Paine L, Zeichner K (2012) The local and global in reforming teaching and teacher education. Comp Educ Rev 56(4):569–583

Pine JM (2008) Landscapes of literacy: the view from a Lahu village. In: Leepreecha P, Kwanchewan B, McCaskill D (eds) Integration, marginalization and resistance: ethnic minorities of the Greater Mekong Subregion. Silkworm Books, Chiang Mai, pp 219–235

Rattanakrajangsri K (2014) Thailand (The Indigenous world 2014). The International Work Group for Indigenous Affairs, Copenhagen, pp 284–290. Retrieved from http://www.iwgia.org/iwgia_files_publications_files/0671_I2014eb.pdf

Rogoff B (2003) Orientating concepts. In: The cultural nature of human development. Oxford University Press, Oxford, UK/New York, pp 3–36

Scott JC (1998) Seeing like a state: how certain schemes to improve the human condition have failed. Yale University Press, New Haven

Tabulawa R (2003) International aid agencies, learner-centered pedagogy and political democratization: a critique. Comp Educ 39(1):7–26

Tatto MT (2006) Education reform and the global regulation of teachers' education, development, and work: a cross-cultural analysis. Int J Educ Res 45:231–241

Thaweesit S, Napaumporn B (2011) Integration of minorities in Thailand. In: Thailand migration report 2011 – migration for development in Thailand: overview and tools for policymakers. International Organization for Migration, Bangkok, pp 131–142

Thongchai W (1994) Siam mapped: a history of the geo-body of a nation. University of Hawaii Press, Honolulu
Thongchai W (2000a) The others within: travel and ethno-spatial differentiation of Siamese subjects 1885–1910. In: Turton A (ed) Civility and savagery: social identity in tai states, 1st edn. Curzon Press, London, pp 38–62
Thongchai W (2000b) The quest for "Siwilai": a geographical discourse of civilizational thinking in the LateNineteenth and early twentieth-century Siam. J Asian Stud 59(3):528–549
Toyota M (2005) Subjects of the nation without citizenship: the case of "hill tribes" in Thailand. In: Kymlicka W, He B (eds) Multiculturalism in Asia. Oxford University Press, Oxford, pp 110–135
Vaddhanaphuti C (1991) Social and ideological reproduction in rural northern Thai schools. In: Keyes C (ed) Reshaping local worlds: formal education and cultural change in rural Southeast Asia. Yale University Southeast Asian Studies, New Haven
Vaddhanaphuti C (2005) The Thai state and ethnic minorities: from assimilation to selective integration. In: Snitwongse K, Thompson SW (eds) Ethnic conflicts in Southeast Asia. Institute of Southeast Asian Studies, Singapore
Vandergeest P (2003) Racialization and citizenship in Thai Forest politics. Soc Nat Resour 16(1):19–37. https://doi.org/10.1080/08941920309172
Wallace M, Athamesara R (2004) The Thai community curriculum as a model for multicultural education. Int Educ J 5(1):50–64
Young OG (1961) The Hill tribes of Northern Thailand: a socio-ethnological report. Thai-American Audiovisual Service, Bangkok

Yachayninchis (Our Knowledge): Environment, Cultural Practices, and Human Rights Education in the Peruvian Andes

39

Elizabeth Sumida Huaman

Contents

Introduction	726
The Remaking of the Andean World: Colonial Dominion Over Quechua Place, Body, and Thought	728
The Spanish Invasion of Peru	729
Conquest of Indigenous Places	730
Conquest of Indigenous Bodies	731
Conquest of Indigenous Thought	732
The Dominant Pathway to Development	734
Indigenismo: Movements Towards Social Justice	735
Persistent Structural Inequalities	738
Dominant Theories of Economic Growth	741
Violent Turns	742
Exogenous Projects of Development and the Creation of Poverty	743
Hawallaqtamanta (From the Rural Community): Land, Memory, and Quechua Education	746
Dominant Education and Quechua Education	747
Pachamama ñuñunchis (Mother Earth Breast Feeds Us): Quechua Land, Knowledge, and Ways of Knowing	748
The Fall of a God	755
Indigenous Rights Education (IRE)	759
Conclusion	761
References	762

Abstract

Increasingly, over the past decade, environmental problems have forced Indigenous farmers to rethink broader impacts to their self-reliance where exogenous environmental destruction represents another shift for Andean Indigenous

---

E. Sumida Huaman (✉)
Comparative International Development Education, University of Minnesota, Minneapolis, MN, USA
e-mail: eshuaman@umn.edu

ontologies – demanding multiple and innovative interventions and strategies. This chapter argues that conceptions, practices, and spaces of Indigenous education based in Indigenous knowledge systems constitute the central arena from which to consider these problems. Thus, in order to advance notions and practices of Quechua education, this chapter first traces ideologies of conquest to projects of development and their social, cultural, economic, and political impacts in the highlands of Peru. This chapter then draws from archival and Quechua narratives in order to highlight Indigenous epistemologies, specifically Quechua knowledge systems that situate the Andean world as an ecology of balance and struggle. Lastly, international discourses of environmental rights and human rights education in Indigenous educational design and practice are discussed.

Keywords

Quechua and Indigenous knowledge systems · Quechua land, language, and education · Indigenous rights and environmental education

Introduction

At first, everything was empty and dark. The creator Con Ticsi Viracocha created the sky, the earth, and the first beings that would inhabit the earth.
The earth was populated with immense animals and people who lived in disorder and without harmony in the darkness. Because of this, they say that from the lake of Collasuyu swelled once again Con Ticsi Viracocha accompanied by other deities. Because the people he had created at first had acted poorly, he turned them to large stones. Suddenly, he made the Sun and the Day and commanded that the Sun walk the course that he takes. Then he formed the Stars and the Moon. From the same stones, he forged certain people: a leader to govern and rule and pregnant women and others with children. He said to his companions: "These people will be called such and will emerge from such spring, in such province; there they will populate and there they will grow; these others will emerge from such cave, they will be called this, and they will populate these provinces; and like this, according to these models, they will emerge from springs, rivers, caves, and other places that I say." (Taken from Quechua oral tradition by Gutierrez Verastegui 1986, translated by the author)

Despite the expansion of European empires through vicious colonial strategies that left lasting imprints on Indigenous homelands across the globe, extant Indigenous epistemologies and cultural practices have been exceptionally resilient. From vibrant origin stories to local Indigenous scientific knowledge, many Indigenous communities worldwide maintain connections between peoples and with their environments, evident through daily practices and special ceremonial observances. Quechua peoples encompass thousands of Andean highland communities, and their stories, language (Quechua and its many local varieties), and agricultural ways of life exemplify this indelible spirit. Quechua children are taught through lectures and stories like the one translated by Gutierrez Verastegui (1986) that this life is a rich full life, sumaq kawsay, to be lived honoring the beings that facilitate all life on earth, like Tayta Inti (Father Sun), Mama Killa (Grandmother Moon), and the Apus (deities). (In this chapter, I do not italicize Quechua words in order to make the statement through the writing that these words are on par with English. This was taught to me by Maori colleagues Huia Jahnke-Tomlins and Margaret Forster in 2015 through a writing collaboration project.). Quechua community members are also taught values associated with life – that things in creation must be appreciated, taken care of, and most importantly, respected, admired, and loved (Bolin 2006; Ames 2013a; Sumida Huaman 2014). These values cultivated by a life in the chakra, the farm fields, of the Andes are exercised through respectful interaction and acknowledgment through prayers and regard for the life force that flows through everything, pacha. Such ancestral protocols are key elements of Indigenous knowledge systems and Indigenous ways of knowing, which embody the philosophies and values-based actions that define the relationships that Indigenous peoples hold to their worlds (local environment, living and nonliving beings), the universe (beyond the local environment, stars, planets, constellations), and to each other (human interactions within community and with other, even distant peoples) (Barnhardt and Kawagley 2005; Alfred and Corntassel 2005; Sumida Huaman 2014). Moreover, these Indigenous systems are innovative; that is, they are based in ancestral beliefs and practices, as well as considering other useful forms of knowledge, including Western knowledge.

At the same time, despite value to the sociocultural identity development of Quechua children and the ideals of harmonious balance of the Andean world, Quechua knowledge systems, if acknowledged at all, were negated starting in the sixteenth-century colonial period as demonstrated by Spanish accounts (Cieza de Leon 2011). Today, Quechua knowledges and associated cultural practices are actively demeaned in mainstream Peruvian discourse as either deterrents to national goals of modernization – especially when related to natural resource extraction on Indigenous lands – or as irrelevant and insignificant towards "real" or valid advancement in science, technology, and education in the name of national progress (Sumida Huaman and Valdiviezo 2012). Complicating the dominant construction of Quechua peoples and the valuation of their knowledges are specific and increasing environmental shifts and events, some beyond Quechua and local community control, which produce consequences for those living an already publicly disparaged rural or agricultural lifestyle (Ames 2013b). For example, in 2016, local media reports emerged from various regions around Peru linking extensive damage to agricultural harvests with environmental issues, including climate change. In some regions, over 90% of Indigenous crops were lost due to new forceful weather patterns, forcing regional governments to declare states of emergency and Indigenous farmers to rethink broader impacts to their self-reliance.

As the impacts of development and globalization are debated in Peru and more widely in Latin American, how Indigenous communities will envision and drive their own futures are critical questions, and central to this discussion is the role of education at all levels, which is perhaps the most important arena from which to consider Peru's most persistent environmental, social, political, and economic strengths and weaknesses. Indigenous education (conceptions, practices, and spaces) based in Indigenous knowledge systems and efforts to explore the richness of Quechua knowledge systems and what yachayninchis (our knowledge) has to contribute to local and global solutions are at the heart of this chapter. At the same time, due to tenacious processes of colonization in the Americas beginning in the late 1400s and subsequent projects of development that have created environmental, social, political, and economic turmoil, this chapter is also concerned with power and the impacts of colonial subjugation of Indigenous peoples and its current manifestations evident in various forms in the twenty-first century. Thus, this chapter first traces ideologies of conquest, imperialism, and development and their social, cultural, economic, and political impacts in the Peruvian highlands. The chapter then draws from archival and Quechua narratives in order to highlight Indigenous epistemologies, specifically in Quechua knowledge systems, that situate the Andean world as ecology of balance and struggle. Lastly, international discourses of environmental rights and human rights education in Indigenous education design and practice are discussed.

Due to increasing environmental problems, more evident than ever is the fact that human action is not isolated within the global ecosystem. While Indigenous populations in Peru are disproportionately impacted by exogenous-driven environmental exploits because of the ongoing colonialist desire for natural resources in their homelands, there are resounding effects on all populations – for example, climate change is diminishing subtropical glaciers, threatening water sources for agricultural production that feeds local and national populations. As a result, the links between development, environment and land, local peoples and epistemologies, and education and social justice could be explored towards solutions. This chapter addresses this in three sections: *I. The remaking of the Andean world: Colonial dominion over Quechua place, body, and thought* – focusing on ideologies of conquest, European-Catholic supremacy, and its persistence in current dominant Peruvian political discourse, which directly impacts how the identities of Indigenous peoples have been constructed by the European other for explicit purposes; *II. The dominant pathway to development* – discussing responses to Indigenous subjugation and marginalization through the language of social justice and Indigenous participation; and outlining Peru's participation in the development project and its discourses of modernization and progress, which require control over decision-making regarding Indigenous lands; and *III. Hawallaqtamanta (from the rural community): Land, memory, and Quechua education* – highlighting Quechua knowledge systems that originate from the rural community and that are complemented by Indigenous social movements, the language of Indigenous rights, environmental rights, and human rights education. Critical of colonial European ideologies and development spurred by *el occidente* (the West) and thrust upon Indigenous populations, the ultimate goal of this chapter is to demonstrate hope through distinct interpretations of Indigenous knowledges as vital undercurrents in education.

The Remaking of the Andean World: Colonial Dominion Over Quechua Place, Body, and Thought

Indigenous peoples in Peru remain the most historically marginalized, isolated, and exploited populations in the country. Further, Indigenous lands are threatened by discourses of progress, translated on the ground as development. As a result, understanding Indigenous oppression is a unique task, especially if education-as-intervention is linked with social justice imperatives – meaning, understanding the current status of Indigenous peoples in Peru requires a deep interrogation of historical and colonial processes and current policies. Such analysis is a critical undertaking to any authentic dialogue of contemporary Indigenous peoples and education. Thus, this section examines three primary themes of colonial dominion in Peru, beginning with context on the Spanish invasion, followed by discussion of attempted conquest over Quechua place, body, and thought.

The Spanish Invasion of Peru

Prior to the Spanish invasion of Peru in 1532, the Inca Empire governed the Andes, spanning the Tawantinsuyu, Land of the Four Quarters – Chinchasuyu to the northwest, Antisuyu to the northeast, Cuntisuyu to the southwest, and Collasuyu to the southeast, areas today known as Colombia, Ecuador, Peru, Bolivia, Chile, and Argentina. Quechua was the language of the Incas spoken throughout these regions and remains a majority Indigenous language with an estimated ten million speakers, roughly over four million in Peru alone (Hornberger and King 2001; Hornberger and Coronel-Molina 2004).

When the Spanish military and clergy, financed by the Catholic church and Spanish Crown, arrived in Peru, they encountered established civilizations with existing political, social, cultural, religious, and economic systems already in place. However, meaningful acknowledgment of this is rejected in Peruvian society other than in anthropological books and in the tourist industry where Indigenous peoples, histories, edifices, customs, and attires remain rigidly fixed in a stunning yet vanquished past. For centuries, Quechua and Indigenous peoples in Peru have been characterized by others: the "problem of the Indian" outlined in government language from the colonial era to the present has boxed Indigenous peoples into static caricatures of a primitive past who are deterrents to progress (Sumida Huaman and Valdiviezo 2012). However, Indigenous scholars and allies have long since responded by reframing this so-called problem as a social justice challenge for all members of society to rebuild a more equitable and humane world (Valdiviezo 2014).

Part of rebuilding the colonial "world turned upside down," as Indigenous chronicler Guaman Poma de Ayala wrote, is accomplishing what he strived to do in 1615 – creating dialogue regarding injustices against Indigenous peoples (1980). Recognizing how deeply entrenched these injustices are is an important step towards deconstructing the conditions of Indigenous peoples in Peru. Through narratives written by Spanish and Indigenous chroniclers during the colonial era, testimonies of the horrific treatment of Indigenous peoples by the Spanish exhibit the beginnings of Peru's unequal socioeconomic and political system, both as a viceroyalty and later, as an independent nation. Colonial subjugation of Indigenous peoples linked with abuses and corruption by Spanish administrators and church clergy figures prominently in texts written in the 1500s by Bartolome de las Casas and Guaman Poma de Ayala who sent their work to Spain. Based on their work, this era can be detailed by at least three distinct realms of violent military and political conquest: conquest of Indigenous places, conquest of Indigenous bodies, and conquest of Indigenous thought.

Conquest of Indigenous Places

Conquest of Indigenous places was an essential task towards establishment of enduring Spanish power over land as territory and personal possession versus Quechua conceptualizations of land and its fruits as "that which gives to the people" (translated from Quechua). Starting with the *encomienda* system, large swaths of arable land and Indigenous peoples on that land were given to Spanish elites. Later, these land grants became *haciendas*, where Quechua people labored ironically on their ancestral homelands to serve the *hacendado*, the Spanish landowner and master. This system of Spanish extraction continued into the 1960s until the Peruvian agrarian reform movement under the Velasco administration. However, justification for the stripping of land and forced labor was already deeply rooted through the issuance of Papal Bulls starting in the 1400s, like the Dum Diversas of 1455 and Inter Caetera of 1493, which validated the expansion of European empires through the Catholic church. Linked with the Catholic fervor of the Spanish Inquisition and justification of the church's persecution of other faiths (Griffiths 1996), "discovery" of the new territories of the Americas prompted further justifications, permissions, and mandates for acquisition of all territories, people, and resources by the Spanish and Portuguese. Such documents represent some of the earliest records of land-grabbing, natural resource extraction, and slavery policies in the Americas. As a powerful entity bound to and more influential than the Spanish Crown (because of its believed direct pipeline to God), the Catholic church had the power to justify Spanish conquest and encourage expansion of empire as a God-given directive. Translated into current realities, dominion over places has manifested into projects of development based on dominant notions of civilization, modernization, and Westernization.

In addition to seizing of Indigenous lands and extraction of gold and silver, for example, Spanish supremacy was also established through urbanization. Because of the preexisting cities of the great Indigenous civilizations of Mexico and Peru, the Spanish constructed their conquest and evangelization through urbanization (Spitta 2007). In Peru, colonial urbanization required the dismantling of grand Indigenous architectural structures, the rebuilding and new construction of Spanish structures over Indigenous foundations, and the negation of Indigenous abilities to have yielded "truly civilized" and advanced architectural and urban planning. Peruvian comparative literature scholar, Silvia Spitta also illustrated that the number of Spanish cities – 225 by 1580, 331 by 1680, and by the end of the seventeenth century, almost all of the urban sectors now in existence – "highlights the extent to which the conquistadors immediately understood colonization as a conquest of place and urbanization of history" (p. 294). She argued that the Spanish quickly became urban settlers within an "inflexibly reproducible grid" that placed elite Spanish administrators at the center of cities and relegated the Indigenous people to the margins, so accelerating race, class, and geographic placement.

Spitta also drew from the work of Sebastian Salazar Bondy, a Peruvian journalist who critiqued the descendants of the Spanish now the Peruvian elite oligarchy. He argued that these *Limeños* had created a superficial culture and livelihood based on exploitation and marginalization of Peru's Indigenous peoples, and he wrote scathingly of Peru's urbanites and those who wished to belong to this "high society" at the expense of their own dignity (1964). His class-consciousness arguments focused on the lasting effects of colonization on place and cultural production, where Spitta pointed out his observations of Lima inextricably linked past injustices with the present:

> in this telltale spatialization of race and power even the dead are assigned a place—buried above ground in rectangular buildings, each coffin in an individual slot. Significantly, then, the pre-Columbian past that underlies the city has long been paved over and is conveniently forgotten in the national imaginary. Bones do not mix with bones; colonial and postcolonial remains do not lie next to pre-Columbian indigenous remains. Even the dead have to be segregated so that the past can be smuggled out of the present. (2007, p. 295)

The results of Spanish colonization through urbanization and the development of elite upper-class Spanish and *Limeño* urban identities as the superior class in Peru remain visible. Asserting or claiming *serrano* (highlander), *cholo* (Indian) or *nativo* (Native) identity can be tremendously challenging for Indigenous people, particularly youth who receive messages largely from mainstream media and institutions, including school, that glorify urban and "professional" lifestyles in comparison with dominant Peruvian society characterizations of rural life as poor, backwards, and generally lacking and uneducated Indigenous farming livelihoods (Crivello 2011; Sumida Huaman 2015).

Conquest of Indigenous Bodies

> They forced their way into native settlements, slaughtering everyone they found there, including small children, old men, pregnant women, and even women who had just given birth. They hacked them to pieces, slicing open their bellies with their swords as though they were so many sheep herded into a pen. They even laid wagers on whether the could manage to slice a man in two at a stroke, or cut an individual's head from his body, or disembowel him with a single blow of their axes. They grabbed suckling infants by the feet, and ripping them from their mother's breasts, dashed them headlong against the rocks. Others, laughing and joking all the while, threw them over their shoulders into a river, shouting, 'Wriggle, you little perisher.' (Bartolome de las Casas 1992, p. 15)

The violence of the Spanish conquest played out most horrifically in Latin America through the conquest of Indigenous bodies – literally the killing of men, women, and children, and the forced marriage, rape, and abuse of Indigenous women by Spanish colonizers. At the physical level, Indigenous bodies were reduced to "things" (Freire 1970), viewed as labor commodities and slaves. Spanish

Dominican priest and chronicler, Bartolome de las Casas, accompanied the Spanish during their invasion of the Americas and witnessed firsthand the methods by which the Spanish brutalized Indigenous communities. Chronicling the devastation in the early colonial period in his *Short Account of the Destruction of the Indies* in 1542 and sent to Phillip II, he advocated for humane treatment of Indigenous peoples. Based on de las Casas' belief that rationality bound all men of the world, he argued for the peaceful conversion of Indigenous peoples whom he believed were made in the image of God and held understanding, individual will, free choice.

Of the widespread European colonization on the African continent, Kikuyu postcolonial scholar, Ngũgĩ wa Thiong'o proposed *dismemberment* (2009). He argued that multiple colonial acts, from defacing Indigenous cultural symbols and demeaning sacred sites to literal beheadings and mutilations of African bodies, were acts of colonial triumph intended to humiliate colonial subjects. Beyond conquest and humiliation though, lay the enactment of dismemberment as "the central character of colonial practice" (p. 5), a forced and violent separation of African personhood, continent, and diaspora through slavery, removal of Indigenous peoples from their lands, and European parceling up of African lands most evident through colonial demarcation and mapping of African homelands. Furthermore, he argued that dismemberment as an "act of absolute social engineering" had a clear capitalist modernization agenda from which Europe only benefitted. In Peru, dismemberment is triumph and humiliation over Andean bodies, the severing of Indigenous access and stewardship of ancestral lands and natural resources, and the denial of Indigenous capabilities to live self-sufficiently with dignity, to nurture their Indigenous knowledge systems, and to know themselves as indispensable cultural beings connected to social memory valuable to them and others.

Conquest of Indigenous Thought

> So tell me, how is it you have put your hopes in a stone as if it were the true God, do you not see that this stone cannot understand what you ask of it?...If it could speak it would tell you, Indian, you are mad and blind...Do you not see that I am a stone, that the birds and foxes dirty themselves upon me, if I am a stone as you can see, how can I be God? (de Avedaño in 1649 quoted in Griffiths 1996, p. 185)

That there exists any question of Indigenous thought or intellect as valid and essential to national development, particularly through education, is telltale of the dominant social and political climate in which Indigenous people find themselves. Crucial to acknowledge is that such attitudes are endemic to Peruvian dominant society. The words of Diego de Avedaño, a Spanish Jesuit in colonial Peru, exemplified not only incredulity regarding Quechua beliefs about the Andean world, but also currently serve to diminish those beliefs as impossible or ludicrous. Writing in reference to Quechua beliefs that stone, *rumi*, and standing stone, *wanka*, were living beings, relatives, and could be sacred deities enshrined and adored by Quechua people who placed offerings for them, he argued that these things could not speak, could not reason, were inanimate objects and therefore could not be deities. What sets such Spanish colonial assertions apart is not theological difference but rather the purposeful and resolute insistence of Quechua minds as voids, consistently and forever lacking – lack of religion, lack of morality, lack of intellectual capacity, and sense believed essential to civilization. Postcolonial responses have since worked to debunk as lore colonial narratives that propagate Indigenous ineptitude as inherent undeniable characteristics and that justify colonial control and establishment of society.

> the oppressors attempt to destroy in the oppressed their quality as "considerers" of the world. Since the oppressors cannot totally achieve this destruction, they must *mythicize* the world. In order to present for the consideration of the oppressed and subjugated a world of deceit designed to increase their alienation and passivity, the oppressors develop a series of methods precluding any presentation of the world as a problem and showing rather as a fixed entity, as something given—something to which people, as mere spectators, must adapt. (Freire 1970, p. 139, Freire's emphasis)

In order to make sense of dominant assertions regarding Quechua thought or intellect, Freire's theorization of conquest is useful: conquest is antidialogical action, and antidialogical action is always present in conquest. In order to know the Andean world as a place of dialogical relationships, understanding how they have been disrupted is an important part of maintaining and reclaiming Quechua knowledge systems. Dismembering Indigenous connections to their stories, cultural practices, and values – their knowledge systems – is a necessary act of conquest in order for the colonizer to legitimize power. In order to maintain this power, and because those connections cannot be totally destroyed, the colonizer must then mythicize the world. This "world of deceit" – one that Salazar Bondy (1964) argued was invented by the Peruvian oligarchy employing Indigenous marginalization – must remain fixed in order to shift the identities of the colonized from considerers of their own worlds and bearers of their own imaginations to spectators who, at best, must adapt.

While this process is in reality nonlinear and there is much to be said of Indigenous agency, the repercussions of Spanish and dominant national political mythicization of the Andean world are evident, notably in the construction of formal education for Quechua children. In the colonial period, Spanish education embodied an agenda of transculturation, designed to transform Quechua people by instructing nonassociation where Indigenous identity was separated from markers of high (Spanish) civilization (Wood 1986). Since that era, defining characteristics of formal education for Indigenous peoples in Peru have been acculturation, citizenship, and the production and maintenance of "good workers" (Carnoy 1974).

Collectively, what conquest of Quechua places, bodies, and thought represent is the endemic quality of ideologies of imperialism that are founded in European-Christian superiority (Miller 2011) and antidialogical worldview (Freire 1970). These ideologies were enacted and expressed through colonial strategies of dismemberment (wa Thiong'o 2009), which resulted in the remaking of the Andean world – Quechua land became Spanish-owned territories defined by Spanish maps; Quechua bodies became things to exterminate, humiliate, and exploit; and Quechua minds

Ideologies and practices of conquest:
Spanish-Catholic Supremacy, antidialogical action, and dismemberment

Conquest of Indigenous place:
Land becomes *territory*--Spanish land grants and elite urbanization

Conquest of Indigenous body:
Indigenous bodies become *things*--violence enacted on bodies, natural slavery, and commodification of human labor

Conquest of Indigenous thought:
Indigenous minds are *voids*--intellect as nonexistent, invalid, and lacking

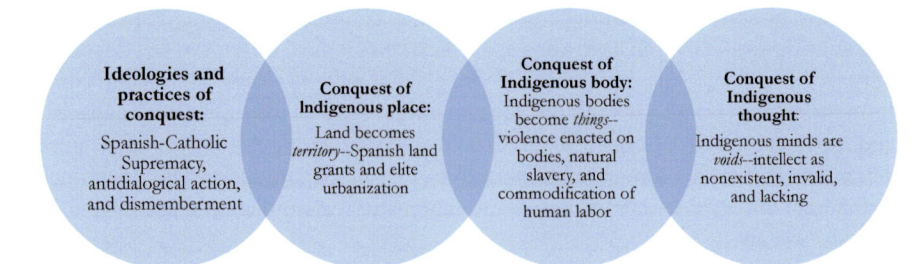

Fig. 1 Ideologies and practices of conquest

were reduced in colonial discourse to nothing more than simple, fillable vessels (see Fig. 1). As wa Thiong'o wrote, "Dismembered from the land, from labor, from power, and from memory, the result is the destruction of the base from which people launch themselves into the world" (p. 28). In the Andes, the attempted destruction of that base, which is at once sociocultural, political, economic, environmental, spiritual, physical, and intellectual, is not forgotten – and is evident at multiple levels, most obviously in public and political discourse and fixated on economic development.

The Dominant Pathway to Development

Peru's colonial trajectory is not completed, and one of the underlying themes of this extension is the persistence of uneven power relations and dominant political reliance on exploitation of Indigenous lands and labor. One of the most seductive expressions of this dynamic is the discourse of national progress through development projects and towards modernization. However, because progress is largely defined by those in political power and the economic elite, modernization is seen as taking a singular path and projects of development as necessary, positive, and for the common good – ideas widely debated and globally refuted (McMichael 2010). Because Indigenous peoples have been historically fixed within a hierarchical social, racial, class, and economic structure in Peru, the need to deconstruct these discourses is long overdue, especially given that ideas of nationhood, progress, development, and modernization are never rigidly exercised.

This section attempts to contribute to dialogue by providing historical context of different perspectives of these ideas stemming from alternative imaginations (Chhetri and Chhetri 2015). Beginning with notions of resistance from the colonial period, *indigenismo* and its movements towards defining and achieving social justice are mentioned. Then, despite symbolic and intellectual shifts in resistance, persistent structural inequalities and dominant theories of economic growth are explored, followed by an example of a violent turn in recent Peruvian history. Lastly, exogenous projects of development through extractive industry and other environmental impacts are linked with the creation of poverty before leading into the third section of this chapter, which explores why environmental devastation represents great loss for the world.

Indigenismo: Movements Towards Social Justice

Although injustice was widespread during colonization, there was resistance. Among the most visible was the armed Indigenous resistance in the eighteenth century through the military campaign of José Gabriel Condorcanqui, known as Túpac Amaru II, translated from Quechua as Fighting Serpent. In the Andes, the serpent is a deity representing Uqhu Pacha, the Inside World, and is responsible for cycles of creation and destruction. Starting in 1780, Túpac Amaru and his wife, Micaela Bastidas, led an Indigenous uprising against Spanish colonizers throughout the Andes. They encouraged Quechua people to take up arms against the Spanish and to fight for the return of their lands. Although he was captured and quartered in the Plaza of Cusco in 1781, the story of his resistance grew well into the twentieth century, and he has since become an iconic figure of rebellion against Spanish dominion, of the struggle for justice by the silenced and subjugated, and a symbol of Quechua political resistance.

Scholars have also offered that *indigenismo*, a Latin American political ideology, is the most recent in a spectrum of anticolonial resistances beginning in the colonial period. Indigenous peoples are at the center of a philosophical movement to value Indigenous ways of life and articulate their hopes for the future, to renounce exploitation of Indigenous peoples, to advocate for Indigenous rights, and to incorporate Indigenous peoples fully and fairly into national life economically, socially, and politically (Chang-Rodriguez 1984). Some of the most renowned proponents of twentieth century *indigenismo* were Peruvian journalists, novelists, and scholars. They were descendants of the Spanish elite who rejected class and racial discrimination, of mixed Indigenous-Spanish ancestry, from rural and urban roots, and primarily educated in some of the most elite universities, including the Universidad Nacional Mayor de San Marcos in Lima. Outspoken critics of racial and economic injustices against Quechua peoples, they publicly denounced descendants of the Spanish conquistadores and European immigrants who formed the capitalist elite class in Peru. Writing poetry on the Quechua peoples beginning in 1918 was César Vallejo; José Carlos Mariátegui wrote *Seven Interpretive Essays on Peruvian Reality* (1997) in the 1920s prior to his death at 35; and perhaps most moving was José María Arguedas, whose literary work in the 1930s until his suicide in 1969 focused on Quechua language and livelihood and their intersections with dominant society. Of those promoters of *indigenismo*, Arguedas's work not only provides some of the most compelling Quechua cultural elements using Quechua language (Arguedas 1972), but his work also has some of the clearest implications for education.

Arguedas produced some of Peru's greatest literary contributions in essays, novels, and poetry, including *Agua* (Water) in 1935; *Yawar Fiesta* (Blood Celebration) in 1941; *Los Ríos Profundos* (Deep Rivers) in 1958; *Todas las Sangres* (All the Blood) in 1964; and *El Zorro de Arriba y el Zorro de Abajo* (The Fox Above and the

Fox Below) published posthumously in 1971. Raised by Quechua, his writing is viewed by scholars as a hybrid of autobiography and class and racial commentary providing thick description of Quechua communities, people, language, and cultural practices. As a Quechua language speaker, his Quechua language phrases and poetry demonstrated his affiliation with Quechua people, admiration for the language, internalized pain at their oppressed social condition, and his belief in Quechua autonomy. He used his writing to describe Quechua isolation, resistance, and beauty in the Andes, and his work made clear that isolation on one's own terms and for the purposes of maintaining one's dignity represented possibilities in a dominant Peruvian society rigidly confined by its own unjust construction of the world. This construction had disrupted the Andean world to society's detriment through the denial and destruction of the cultural wealth of its original communities.

Arguedas was also a staunch proponent of recognizing Quechua peoples and lands as comprising Indigenous nationhood, which he believed had been subdued but not defeated due to their cultural wealth through folklore – Quechua songs and stories perpetuated in each Andean village. He advocated for appreciation of distinction of nations, which he believed could only benefit Peru. Based on his literary accomplishments recognized worldwide, before his death he was awarded the national Peruvian prize named for el Inca Garcilaso de la Vega, and in 1968, he accepted this award for contributions to the cultural arts. In his acceptance speech, he famously described his worldview with the hope that the "great nation of Andean lands" and the "humanized part of the oppressors" could unify:

> And the path had no reason to exist, nor was it possible for it only to exist as an empire of victor plunderers; or that; the defeated nation relinquishes its soul, although not in appearance, formally, and takes from the victors, that is to say it acculturates. I am not acculturated; I am a Peruvian who proudly, like a happy demon speaks in Christian and in Indian, in Spanish and in Quechua. (Jose Maria Arguedas's "Inca Garcilaso de la Vega Award" acceptance speech, 1968)

"I am not acculturated; I am a Peruvian who proudly, like a happy demon speaks in Christian and in Indian, in Spanish and in Quechua" has been cited by those who support coexistence of Quechua and Spanish language and identities. The idea that one can strive to elevate the status of Quechua language and knowledge is one of Arguedas's most important contributions to education. Though lesser known, his work in education remains significant as philosophical inspiration and pedagogical motivation for Peruvian educational scholars and practitioners. As a teacher and teacher advocate, traveling through Andean communities in the 1920s, he observed national curricula in Quechua communities and its severe impacts on Quechua children in formal schools. In the 1930s, he worked with the Peruvian Ministry of Education as an expert on Peruvian folklore, which he argued was based in local knowledge and central to the education of Quechua children.

> This isolated village, illiterate, however creates a very coherent conception of how actual man appeared and to explain who made the great works that exist in the pre-hispanic ruins, creates a different humanity...These people illiterate like this, isolated like this, humbled

like this, have an extraordinary capacity to make for themselves an image of this world, of its origin, and of its destiny...The teachers in each and every place where they are [should] inform themselves of all of these beliefs, because those beliefs are going to give them an approximate idea of what each individual of the community in which they work, of what each individual believes is this world, how it was created, for what it was created, and where it will end. (José María Arguedas, "The Importance of folklore in education," author translation)

Arguedas argued that education should not remain the same oppressive system, which he believed demonstrated dominant society's ignorance of Indigenous cultures, furthering the silencing of Indigenous peoples while preventing quality and effective schooling for Indigenous children. His ideas about education have since influenced scholars involved in rethinking culture and education in Peru, primarily by learning to valuing local folklore.

In terms of policy, through the 1940s and 1950s, attention was hoisted onto Indigenous communities, mainly Quechua villages where education became the focal point for greater inclusion of Quechua peoples into mainstream society. In 1945, Bolivia and Peru launched a joint country educational initiative, the Convening Project on Indigenous Education between the Governments of Bolivia and Peru. This was a plan to "incorporate the Indian into nationality as an active factor of production and consumption" and due to the urgent necessity for "immediate and complete cultural and moral rehabilitation" through education that would afford Indigenous people "the same opportunities in each country and recognize their equal rights and equal participation in civic responsibilities" (Giesecke Sara-Lafosse 2007, p. 180). Like subsequent national educational plans for Indigenous communities in Peru, the primary driver for formal education remained citizenship development and the production of workers and consumers to participate in the national economy and to ensure financial stability, which policymakers believed would prevent Indigenous civil unrest (Carnoy 1974). In addition, using *indigenista* recommendations to appreciate the cultural value of Quechua peoples, policies in formal education began to reflect suggestions for folklore in curriculum development (Giesecke Sara-Lafosse 2007). However, while recognition of Indigenous peoples through folklore was well intentioned, folklore was defined by evident cultural practices – Quechua songs, which contain themes about nature and values like love; Quechua stories, which tell of the origin of man, local places, and local elements; and Quechua dances, which are ceremonial and social and related to the seasons, the earth's cycles, and agricultural practices like farming and herding. Because of the way in which Quechua culture was interpreted by those in charge of designing educational policies and practices for Indigenous peoples, and because Quechua culture was essentially distilled to folklore, deeper understanding and value attached to the Quechua knowledge system could not permeate entrenched ideas of what constitutes knowledge, who Quechua people are, and what Quechua knowledge has to offer *within and beyond* songs, stories, and dances. Although Quechua songs, stories, and dances offer profound observations honed over millennia regarding the natural world and its cycles, because of their relegation to "mere folklore," the centrality of Quechua cultural practices and knowledge to formal education has since become difficult to justify to educational policymakers and Quechua parents alike. Both groups ask why Peruvian children should go to school to learn stories and sing songs or to speak a language that has little value to a secure financial future in dominant society, which requires fluency in Spanish (and now English language acquisition) and rote learning to gain university entrance and preferably, an urban white-collar job (Valdiviezo 2009; Crivello 2011; Sumida Huaman 2015).

Persistent Structural Inequalities

Although *indigenismo* remains inspirational by addressing Indigenous equal participation and rights in Peru, cycles of domination are persistent. The example of folklore represents one of the most aesthetically pleasing aspects of Quechua cultural practice, yet incorporation of a song or story in a lesson is neither substantial nor significant recognition of the potential contributions of Quechua knowledges. In their work on American Indian boarding schools in the United States, K. Tsianina Lomawaima and Teresa McCarty developed the "safety-zone" theory (2006). Boarding schools for American Indians represented a federal government mandate for assimilation and civilization of Indian children, and while these schools did work towards these ends, they also allowed some tribal cultural practices and symbols to be incorporated into curricula and play. Lomawaima and McCarty argued that the federal government oscillated its policies towards Indian tribes, between restrictionism and permissiveness, reflecting deliberate mechanisms for control of Indian people: Some cultural practices are deemed "safe" to the mainstream, and some are not, and who decides is telling. Similarly, in Peruvian formal education policy, Quechua songs, stories, and dances are "safe" inasmuch as they maintain their aesthetic as markers of a quaint and colorful culture and nothing more. Quechua language is also "safe" as long as it is contained within superficial parameters, like names of streets or archaeological sites, which are useful to the Peruvian tourist industry. Quechua cultural practices and knowledges are safe as long as they remain symbols of an ancient past and a vivid present that can be used to promote authenticity and heritage to the world. Knowledge and cultural practices also remain safe as long as they do not threaten dominant mythicization of the world; that is, Quechua culture must not upset existing social and class hierarchies, and knowledge must not challenge dominant assumptions about the nature of the world and its resources as crafted by Western modern science, for example, and in the service of capitalism.

Resistance and dissention emerging from Quechua and Indigenous peoples in Peru has long since been a dominant national fear, particularly because those who comprise the ruling and European descendant classes in Peru are a population minority. Indigenous peoples and *mestizos*, the term for people of mixed Indigenous-Spanish ancestry, are estimated to form upwards of 80% of the national population. However, what should be noted regarding the classification of peoples in Peru is that the array of racial identities can be complex. The term *mestizo*, invented during the Spanish colonial era, is a widely accepted yet contentious categorization.

This is because Spanish domination of all things Indigenous was such a common trait of colonization in Peru that triumph over race represented an important victory for the Spanish colonizers – and they could claim that intermarriage with Quechua peoples was responsible for fathering an entirely new race. However, *mestizo* and the multiplicity of other racial categories that resulted from Spanish construction led to bipolarity of identity where a Quechua individual striving for upward social mobility might publicly claim more Spanish and European heritage, weighing the costs of Quechua ancestry, language expertise, family and community affiliation, and geography. Misconstrued as internalized shame towards heritage language, culture, people, and homeland, identity choices reflect racial discrimination and deep class and social stratification in Peru (Hornberger 1988).

The population of Quechua people throughout the Andean nations is so large that in fact, the need to cultivate diplomacy through cultivation of democratic principles in order to maintain national security and stability in Peru is also promoted by the United States federal government. Foreign Language Area Studies (FLAS) fellowships are provided to university students in the USA in order to study a less-commonly taught language that is spoken in regions of the world where the Department of State has interest. Quechua is a FLAS-funded language. Because of these agendas – national and foreign – Peru's oscillation of education and language policies towards Indigenous peoples can be tracked, and for Indigenous peoples, there is little expectation that justice should be given by others. Also, the very nature of *indigenismo* and more contemporary calls for Indigenous justice are based on societal recognition of past injustices in order to collectively rectify wrongs and build a world of distinct nations who respect and need each other.

There was a brief historical period in Peru where manifestations of social justice did appear through top-down approaches. In 1968, General Juan Velasco Alvarado, a Peruvian military general, orchestrated a bloodless coup overthrowing then-President Belaúnde and taking power as the President of the New Revolutionary Government. Velasco remained in power until 1975 when he was overthrown by another military coup. Because of the laws and reforms he introduced, there are many critics of the Velasco administration, from the right wing to Velasco's own left wing. However, at least three major laws he introduced created stirrings in dominant Peruvian society due to their intent to address inequalities towards Indigenous peoples: The first was land reform, which effectively ended *hacendado* rule over Indigenous lands and redistributed lands seized by the colonizers to Indigenous people; the second was bilingual education (which has since evolved into IBE, intercultural bilingual education) for Indigenous children; and the third was attempting to raise the status of Quechua through a law that made Quechua an official language of Peru.

Velasco's political rhetoric appeared to usher in an era of reforms that would correct injustices of the colonial past. In his June 24, 1969, speech, he declared that from that time forward, the Peruvian peasant (i.e., Indigenous farm worker) would "truly be a free citizen, part of a nation that would recognize his right to the fruits of the earth that he works...no more as he has been until now...a man to be exploited by another man" (author translation). Through what he called his revolutionary government, he instituted the Law of Agrarian Reform (Decree Law No. 17716), which re-appropriated some 15,000 properties totaling nine million hectares to Indigenous peoples. When he introduced the law, he appealed to a concept of national unity and spoke of the agrarian reform in defense of the humble peasants of the nation whose roots occupied shared national history and "whose image of justice emerges from our own and immemorial past."

> This is our greatest desire: To labor for our community and for its youth social legislation where man can live with dignity, knowing that he lives in a land that is his and in a nation where he is the owner of his destiny...This is our greatest guarantee of true and just social peace in the future of our nation...*To the man of the earth we can now say in the immortal and liberatory voice of Túpac Amaru: "Peasant, the master will no longer eat from your poverty!"* (excerpt from President Velasco's Law of Agrarian Reform speech, Lima, 1969, author's emphasis)

Velasco's government, though short-lived, offered some critical ideas to Peruvian politics – that national development required justice for Indigenous peoples and that shared vision and actions towards social justice constitute nationhood. Such definitions of national development and nationhood linked with direct legislation and clear enactment are not evident in Peruvian public political discourse today.

There are also "realities" of the Velasco reforms that scholars have pointed out as failures of his administration. Critiques of the revolutionary government question whether or not its leaders, including Velasco, had a firmly defined vision of the future as well as a clear plan and strategies to achieve that future. Much of Velasco's attention was focused on dismantling the Peruvian oligarchy and challenging those who would continue to exploit Peru's natural resources and people. He gained the attention of the United States and foreign corporate interests by confiscating extractive industries and confronting multinational corporations (Walker 2014); he also drew from the imagery of Túpac Amaru in order to rally his movement around the symbolism of Indigenous resistance; and he produced political discourse that redefined concepts that had previously been used against Indigenous peoples by those in power. National development, modernization, and progress became goals that actually required the incorporation and direction of Indigenous peoples in society and to avoid further social injustice that Velasco believed would lead to civil unrest (Walker 2014). However, some scholars viewed a fatal flaw as the lack of unified vision within leadership that could sustain a socialist government beyond overthrowing the oligarchy (McClintock 1981). Participatory social democracy would easily be pitted against corporatism and capitalism, and this tension remains today.

The longevity of Peru's oligarchy was not resolved during the Velasco administration. There remained strong critics of the land reform movement, and the emergence of research has helped to illuminate some of the tensions during this time period. Enrique Mayer's work (2009) included, among other narratives, those of former *hacendados*. These and other explorations have acknowledged their research limitations while seeking to demonstrate the need for multiple stories to emerge from government-enforced policies. From a social research perspective, upper class elite stories representative of Peru's oligarchy, which Velasco sought to overthrow, are a valid reminder to view policy and its immediate and historical impacts from different angles. However, the wealth inherited from Spanish colonialism and connections to current elitist ideologies and lifestyles must be made clear. At the same time, the lack of Indigenous perspectives and gendered and generational explorations regarding this time period is disturbing. Thus, as researchers we are cautious and aware that the history and legacies of Spanish colonialism told by Indigenous voices are made mutable when dominant narratives take center stage. The stories of Indigenous Andeans living in the *hacienda* system since the colonial period and well into the decade leading up to the Velasco administration are deserving of study and place in the greater social memory of all Peruvians. Further, in terms of driving research, the stories of *hacendados* and alternatively, the lack of Indigenous accounts, particularly using Quechua language and its varieties and based on participation and research direction from Indigenous community members offer us the question of how our inheritance defines our experiences. Whether we have inherited colonial wealth, status, and opportunity or poverty and denial of access born of foreign exploitation remind us that we alone do not create our destinies despite our best capacities or dreams.

Dominant Theories of Economic Growth

In Peru there remain significant tensions between those who believe that national development requires addressing inequalities and establishing social justice and those who believe that national development is based on capital gained through exploitation. The latter is aligned with Western ideas of economic growth and society, most notably W.W. Rostow's theory of economic "take-off." Take-off theory originated in the 1960s when Rostow proposed his economic growth model, since becoming development dogma. He argued that economic growth took place in stages: the first stage begins with what he referred to as a "traditional" society, typically agrarian (which he pitted against Western modernity) – "A traditional society is one whose structure is developed within limited production functions, based on pre-Newtonian science and technology, and on pre-Newtonian attitudes towards the physical world" (p. 4). The second stage requires preconditions for "take-off" where societies embrace the possibility of economic growth – an attitude that in many cases is exogenous through "intrusion by more advanced societies. These invasions—literal or figurative…set in motion ideas and sentiments which initiated the process by which a modern alternative to the traditional society was constructed out of the old culture" (p. 6) and where economic progress is qualified as good. Rostow viewed "take-off," as a watershed in modern human history – "The forces making for economic progress…expand and come to dominate the society. Growth becomes its normal condition. Compound interest becomes built, as it were, into its habits and institutional structure." (p. 7). During "take-off," investment and savings skyrocket. After take-off, there is a drive towards maturity and further self-sustained growth (p. 9), after which, the stages are completed through mass consumption beyond necessities. As a caveat, Rostow noted that final stage of economic growth was not confined to static descriptors but contained deeper questions and choices that societies themselves would face. Reflecting on his theory 30 years later, he acknowledged that the stages of economic growth were not without global consequences, particularly with regards to strain on natural resources and pollution of the environment (1990).

While advocating for increased attention by governments towards international and public policy cooperation, Rostow nonetheless maintained his theory of a linear economic trajectory and definitions of societies therein. He believed some societies remained "trapped" in precondition stages that were neither traditional – due to the vast reach of technology in the modern age – nor capable of "take-off" without significant foreign intervention. These "late-comers," as he referred to them, appeared to represent resistance/problems to economic development. Such rigid definitions of science and technology and compartmentalization of peoples without consideration of endogenous goals are problematic and limit possibilities of open and genuinely curious dialogue *with* Indigenous communities for whom science and technology may have different definitions, purposes, and applications.

Violent Turns

Beginning in the 1960s, *Sendero Luminoso*, Shining Path, propelled by Maoism planted seeds for what would become a violent guerrilla movement that escalated through the 1970s, 1980s, and 1990s (Stern 1998). Leaders of *Sendero* claimed to be waging war against capitalism and the marginalization and resulting poverty of Indigenous and other Peruvians due to foreign and domestic corporate and government greed and increased Peruvian dependency. Civil conflict ensued with Peruvian police and military clashing with *Sendero* soldiers and civilians and leaving approximately 70,000 dead or missing according to Peru's 2003 Truth and Reconciliation Commission. Universities became battlegrounds as antigovernment sentiment through student and faculty protest or mobilization resulted in torture, killing, or disappearances during what has become known as "the time of fear." Amnesty granted to military personnel left the Peruvian public and human rights watchers around the world questioning accountability for the lost lives, many of which were Indigenous. *Sendero* was also viewed as problematic based on their methods of communist indoctrination in Andean villages involving public executions and abuses of girls and women that resulted in multiple traumas from which Andean Indigenous communities are in recovery (Degregori 2012).

In some ways, the rise of this violent movement represented profound frustration of Peru's most economically impoverished communities. Consistently among the poorest regions in Peru, Ayacucho, where *Sendero* was cultivated by university intellectuals, was like many other regions in the Andes, seemingly desolate and forgotten. Although there is no doubt that Peruvian citizens, including Indigenous peoples, are engaged in rebuilding and building nationhood, Indigenous voices are consistently muted by those in power. Maintaining a peaceful society then is also at risk: Despite the efforts of those in the Velasco administration to build a definition of nationhood that upheld social justice through full inclusion of Indigenous peoples in Peruvian society, Western-based economic ideologies appear victorious.

Exogenous Projects of Development and the Creation of Poverty

In Peru today, power is most clearly articulated through economic gain on a large-scale and global level in extractive industry and exploitation of natural resources. Moreover, because economic growth is touted as beneficial for *all* Peruvians, any consideration of Indigeneity or unique cultural or linguistic knowledge will be challenged with regards to its relevancy to progress for *all*. In this political climate, the transition of conquest into development is unflinching and strengthened by international, multinational, and private interests.

Starting in the late 1960s, anthropologist June Nash began studying the participation of Indigenous peoples in tin mining in the Bolivian Andes. Her work was among the earliest depictions of the intersection of Indigenous identities and their reformations with participation in industry. She was concerned with the relationship between interpretation of experience and creation of action through the ideology of miners. Nash viewed Indigenous peoples as in great transition, referring to this as "cholification" or "Indianization," using derogatory terms for Quechua peoples that were being repurposed by Quechua themselves. She argued that "Indianization" revealed both resistance and selective acceptance of aspects of the dominant culture. As far as resistance and self-determination were concerned, she believed that at their core was Indigenous epistemology, primarily the notion of pacha – space and time, and the energy that flows through all things. She argued that unlike workers in other industrial centers, deeply entrenched precolumbian roots, exercised through articulation of beliefs and rituals, gave Quechua a distinct and strong identity that served as the basis for their self-determination in creating a "new class definition of their national status" (1993, pp. 2–3).

Like other theorists questioning dependency and extraction in Latin America (Escobar 1995; Esteva 2010), Nash was also critical of ideologies of development reliant upon capitalism, which she argued were unsustainable. She was also a proponent of Indigenous-based inquiry regarding development on Indigenous lands, where Indigenous peoples were at the center of decision-making despite exogenous influence: "Only a redefinition of the aim of the development process which will put people at the center of planning and reject the exploitation of natural riches for short-run gains will reverse the situation" (1993, p. 16). Since her fieldwork, there have been some political changes in Bolivia not necessarily representative of other Andean nations. However, explorations like these provide important cases and comparative lessons regarding how an area once unified under the Inca, the *Tawantinsuyu*, which remains geographically and culturally linked, is dealt with by the states that govern them today.

Writing of Indigenous mobilization and social movement linked with land development in Argentina, vom Hau and Wilde (2010) not only critiqued dominant notions of development as did Nash decades earlier, but also provided Indigenous perspectives on the construction of poverty that have been emerging from Indigenous mobilization and activism. Due to displacement from ownership of Indigenous lands – leaving Indigenous people in their own words, living on "captive lands" – and colonial political and economic control, Indigenous peoples had become the most economically disadvantaged population. But as vom Hau and Wilde also argued, because of their activism and promotion of rights, the very origins of poverty, its definitions, and its metrics were being addressed by Indigenous peoples: "The focus on the nexus between territorial rights, resource governance and indigenous wellbeing points to the poverty-creating processes of recent capitalist transformations" (p. 1298). They criticized research on "Indigenous poverty" as containing significant gaps due to lack of analysis on Indigenous agency and political subjectivities, the narrow focus on poverty as income-based, and perhaps most importantly, the ignored tensions between dominant definitions of poverty and how Indigenous peoples view their own well-being (p. 1287). Instead, they proposed that poverty is not endogenous to Indigenous ways of life, but rather is a relational condition created by economic injustice due to colonial and corporate control over land that is further exacerbated by "adverse incorporation of local communities into...new land and labour markets that threatens their subsistence strategies and economic security" (p. 1298).

Bebbington's work on extractive industry in the Andes forms much of the basis for deeper explorations of the causes of poverty and alternately, endogenous and Indigenous definitions of wealth (2010). He argued that poverty is an outcome of particular relations of power and that although social movements emerge in response to these relations, their scope is not limited to issues of poverty when poverty is defined (by others) as lacking something; instead, social movements, "emerge to challenge dominant ideas as to how society should be organized, to draw attention to needs not currently attended to under existing social arrangements, to argue that existing arrangements need protecting and deepening, and to make visible identities rendered invisible or abnormal by prevailing relationships of power" (2010, p. 1). Because of their rootedness in Indigenous identities and ability to reconsider power relationships and inequalities and to articulate visions of how and by whom society should be rebuilt, one of the greatest accomplishments of Indigenous social movements is their power to shift the nature of public debate. Through social movement, which is a mechanism of ideological production – identities, discourses, visions, strategies, and change – Indigenous peoples create their own opportunities to articulate new ways of thinking about problems. Part of the problem with public political discourse, aside from its fixation with progress through development, is the faulting of Indigenous peoples for what is viewed as a homogenous and traditional state of being, which includes primitiveness and poverty.

If we are to challenge the constructs of poverty, we will need to define how capital is measured (Bebbington 1999), by whom, and for what purposes. We will also need to challenge what McMichael (2010) referred to as the "epistemic privilege of the market calculus" whereby the market is the dominant lens for understanding development, resulting in casualties that persecute, marginalize, and silence Indigenous "misfits." When local Indigenous communities mobilize around their own questions, they defy and transcend their categorization, and there is incredible potential for Indigenous social movements to draw attention to how nationhood and progress are defined and lived, including rethinking poverty and Indigeneity.

Such mobilization has yet to dissolve unequal power relations that involve development on Indigenous lands in the name of national progress. In recent years, Indigenous-state tensions escalated, most publicly through what became known as the Bagua standoff between Indigenous peoples in the Amazon region of Peru and Peruvian police and military in 2009. Leading up to this confrontation were a series of decrees set forth by then-President Alan Garcia and directly related to the 2006 US Peru Free Trade Agreement (FTA), which would open up protected Indigenous lands to foreign investment in development that the national government considered to be under-utilized by Indigenous peoples. On June 5, 2009, at the *Curva del Diablo* (Devil's Curve), road near the town of Bagua, Awajun, and Wampis Indigenous peoples clashed with government forces. For the USA, special concessions for investment through exploitation of natural resources in other regions around the world provide benefit for corporate and government interests; as a result, accountability regarding who is impacted and what ultimately happens in other places is not a factor if any intended gain is compromised. For Peru, manifestations of conquest over Indigenous lands remain a reality and not just historical cases. Then-President García argued that land that could be used for national profit was laid to waste by Indigenous peoples – and for him, what was "national" and who stood to gain never included Indigenous consultations.

> There are millions of hectares of idle timber, other millions of hectares that the communities and associations have not cultivated nor will they cultivate, in addition hundreds of mineral deposits that cannot be worked...The rivers that go down from each side of the mountain range are a fortune that go to the ocean without producing electric energy. There are, in addition, millions of workers that do not exist, even though they do labor, well their work does not serve them to have social security or a future pension, because they do not contribute what they could contribute multiplying the national savings. So, there are many unused resources that are non-returnable, that do not receive investment and that do not generate jobs. And all because of the taboo of surpassed ideologies, for idleness, for insolence or because of the "law of the dog of the garden" who recites: "If I do not do it, no one can do it." (Alan García, *El Comercio*, October 28, 2007, author translation)

La ley del perro del hortelano, or the "law of the gardener's dog," is a saying that refers to a dog who guards a garden: The dog does not eat the products of the garden, nor does he let anyone else eat of the garden. García applied this comparison to Indigenous peoples living communally in their protected homelands – like the dog, they would neither use nor allow anyone else to use the natural resources. Aside from the racist nature of García's discourse or his apparent lack of concern regarding any long-term social or environmental consequences of natural resource extraction and exploitation, what is clear from his commentaries is the belief that Indigenous lands are primed for the taking – not unlike the language of the early European colonizers who saw "virgin" and "abundant" land occupied by ignorant people.

In addition, no matter how compelling the idea that the entire Peruvian population (regardless of their socioeconomic class and ethnic identities) could benefit from development, distribution of "benefits" and most importantly, prior consultation regarding development on Indigenous lands and how Indigenous peoples view its implications remains unclear:

> Value is taken from certain spaces and distributed to others. The spaces that bear the brunt of the externalities generated by extraction are in the vicinity of the wells, mines, pipelines and smelters, and in none of these three countries are environmental safeguards and regulations handled with the seriousness necessary to offset the risk that today's sites of extraction will be tomorrow's sites of contamination and reduced viability. Meanwhile benefits and opportunities accrue in other spaces – in departmental and national capitals and more generally in areas of demographic concentration. This seems to be exactly the same whether we are talking of the north of La Paz in Bolivia, Yasuní in Ecuador, or Rio Corrientes in Peru. And once again, these are spaces that are occupied by indigenous groups who have been systematically and repeatedly disadvantaged by national development models. That pattern shows no sign of changing, whether under neoliberal or post-neoliberal regimes. (Bebbington and Humphreys Bebbington 2011, pp. 141–142)

Andean countries hold significant natural resources highly coveted by corporations and nations around the world. In their commentary on extractive industry in Ecuador, Peru, and Bolivia, Bebbington and Humphreys Bebbington (2011) noted some important similarities: All three countries hold the expansion of extractive industry as the "pillar of macroeconomic strategy," and government intolerance to resistance of this expansion is only increasing in ways that limit dissenting citizen voices through legislative reforms and criminalization of protest (p. 140). At the local level, the Peruvian example demonstrates that if expansion continues, conflicts may emerge from localities demanding greater shares of extractive industry revenue, thereby leading to inter-Indigenous community conflict (p. 141). Given possible health and environmental repercussions with long-term impacts on human populations at the epicenters of extractive industry, such trade-offs are not unexpected – and there are numerous cases of these in the Andes already. Furthermore, because the emphasis on these development dynamics is on Indigenous participation and negotiation, *Indigenous ownership and Indigenous management* of development is subjected to the cycle that Bebbington and Humphreys Bebbington referred to – value taken from Indigenous places for distribution to others. In order for Indigenous peoples to reshape this dynamic as more than spectators or minor recipients, shifting the nature of how the environment is viewed and usage of environmental resources through local and wider debate is a critical step that must be driven and maintained by, within, and among Indigenous communities who have the ability to demonstrate real and applicable ways that their knowledge systems and sociocultural identities matter in Peru and elsewhere.

Hawallaqtamanta (From the Rural Community): Land, Memory, and Quechua Education

Quechua communities base their ways of life on the Andean calendar, which is an Indigenous cycle of ceremonies and environmentally based activities. Every August marks the new year for the Andean calendar, and ceremonies conducted in Quechua communities and in the Quechua language acknowledge the change of season and provide offerings to the Apus. Like many other occasions throughout the Andean calendar, this is a time of direct conversation between Quechua people and their environment for the purpose of mutually sustaining all life – trees and plants, lakes, water, rivers, animals large and small.

In the Quechua worldview, the link between environment, language, cultural practices, and Indigenous pedagogies is clear: Environmental resources *are* educational resources, as Steve Smith, Ojibwe STEM (science, technology, engineering, and mathematics) instructor asserted (Personal communication, 30 June 2016). Indigenous scholars and educators around the world have validated these connections through development of theoretical frameworks on Indigenous pedagogies, Indigenous research, and curriculum development with Indigenous communities that priorities Indigenous knowledge systems but also includes access to other knowledges (May 1999; Smith 2000; Pihama et al. 2004; Kawagley 2006; McKinley 2005; Aikenhead and Mitchell 2011; Battiste 2002, 2013). As the Andean world has been made and remade, and the destiny of Quechua peoples and our environment is debated in public political discourse using economic metrics, how Indigenous peoples will engage and using what tools is unprecedented. Building on the preceding sections that outlined limitations imposed upon Indigenous communities, this section highlights major themes and strengths in Quechua knowledge systems and their relationship to education; in other words, addressing what Quechua people are fighting to protect and why this struggle matters.

This section begins with general characteristics of dominant and Quechua education, followed by description of Quechua lands and pedagogies as educational resources where our knowledge, yachayninchis, is education in situ. Because Quechua educational resources are threatened by projects of development, this section is therefore also concerned with environmental deterioration and neglect. By describing the impending loss of an Andean god, impacts on the perpetuation of Quechua knowledge for future generations are examined. Lastly, international discourses of environmental rights and human rights education and their usefulness in Quechua education design and practice through *Indigenous rights education* (IRE) are discussed.

Dominant Education and Quechua Education

Since Spanish colonization, the role of education as cultural imperialism (Carnoy 1974) has been to subordinate Indigenous peoples through strategies of European indoctrination and assimilation that have served to invalidate Indigenous knowledge. Because education is a powerful method of instilling nationhood and citizenship (defined by others), schools have assumed a central role in the production of Indigenous children for the purposes of the state. Formal education, like progress or development, is often singularly defined, executed, and assessed. As a result, deconstructing schooling for Quechua children requires steady interrogation of the purposes of formal education. Today, Quechua knowledges do not factor significantly in state-sponsored formal education of Quechua children, which can be argued is indicative of the colonial inheritance that all Peruvians have received – the notion that first, Indigenous people do not know anything of worth, and second, that what they do know is superstition and a marker of their ignorance.

Valdiviezo's research (2014) demonstrated key trends in public and political discourse in Peru that she argued persistently characterize Indigenous peoples to the detriment of actual support of Indigenous knowledges in Peruvian education: Indigenous people's beliefs are absurd and backward (including language, knowledge, and cultural practices); Indigenous people are an obstacle to development (and deterrents to national unification, for example); Indigenous people are less than citizens (despite the 1993 Constitution that establishes Indigenous peoples as citizenship, "real" Peruvian citizenship is a privilege based on socioeconomic status, race, and ethnicity, and not a right); the purpose of formal education is to defeat or fix Indigenous peoples (a tool of civilization to correct Indigenous people of their absurd beliefs and to bestow culture upon them). At the same time, the allure of formal education for Indigenous peoples is undeniable as schooling promises a means to better oneself through increased social mobility and white-collar employment (Valdiviezo 2009; Sumida Huaman 2015).

Some of the most compelling research on learning and teaching in Quechua communities focuses on the role of the community as the primary teacher of Quechua children within Quechua spaces. Since the seventeenth century through the writings of Inca Garcilaso de la Vega who detailed Quechua ways of life and beliefs, to Arguedas's advocacy for folklore as legitimate knowledge and pedagogy, to contemporary in-depth educational research on Quechua children in Andean communities (Gutierrez-Verastegui 1986; Cerron-Palomino 1989; Calero Pérez 1996; Bolin 2006; Sumida Huaman and Valdiviezo 2012; Ames 2013a; Valdiviezo 2013; Sumida Huaman 2014), the fact that Quechua community members impart distinct local environmental-cultural knowledge to their children has been well established. Yet the interdisciplinary rigor of Quechua knowledges, in-depth explorations of how knowledge is exchanged, and why Quechua is significant beyond the local are not priorities in the construction of formal education for Quechua children. More often than not, the intellectualism, values, and problem-solving capabilities of Quechua peoples are undermined, which has fit well in the colonial trajectory. Today especially, marginalizing Indigenous epistemologies conveniently erases any notion that the earth is sacred, a worldview that contradicts widespread exploitation of the environment and expansion of extractive industry across the Peruvian Andes and into the Peruvian Amazon. Furthermore, if we consider that Quechua education has functioned for generations according to seasonal cycles and engagement with the environment through cultural activities that serve sumaq kawsay, a beautiful life for all, disrupting reciprocity for human gain alone is a strange proposition.

Pachamama ñuñunchis (Mother Earth Breast Feeds Us): Quechua Land, Knowledge, and Ways of Knowing

Throughout the Andes, agriculture is based on recognition of Andean seasonal cycles detailed by daily and ceremonial events: the preparation of the earth for the planting (July and August), planting season (September and October), maintenance of the emerging and growing crops (November through April), and the harvest and new seed selection (May-June). Each stage of the life of plants is accompanied by ceremonial organization and participation of farmers and their families and communities. During the preparation of the earth for planting, new village leadership will be selected to oversee the entire agricultural year and to ensure the collaboration of community members with each other and the natural world through the ceremonies that are conducted. In the Mantaro Valley of Junín, for example, the season begins with offerings to the Apus and the planting of the fields of the deity protectors of the community. This is a tradition that though altered, endured the conquest when Catholic saints replaced Quechua curacas, spiritual heads, as the caretakers of those fields. This ritual planting, across the Quechua highlands, continues according to the belief that no one but the Apus has benevolence over these lands and that what ayllpanchis, the land, gives is a blessing (Photo 1).

Quechua farmlands, like those found in the Mantaro Valley of Peru, are rich in varieties of corn, potatoes and tubers, quinoa, and other grains. The early Spanish found that there were almost as many plants cultivated in the Andes by the Quechua as there were in all of Europe and Asia combined, and today the Andes remains one of the continuously cultivated original Indigenous agricultural centers in the world where the majority of Andean plants have been cared for by Quechua people for over 8,000 years (Valladolid and Apfeel-Marglin 2001, p. 652). Writing about the history of Peru's El Proyecto Andino de Tecnologías Campesinas (The Andean Project of Peasant Technologies, PRATEC), Valladolid and Apfeel-Marglin further argued that

Photo 1 Corn harvested in the Huaman Carhuamaca family chakra in the Mantaro Valley (Image by Elizabeth Sumida Huaman)

Quechua cosmovision is directly linked with Indigenous scientific knowledge that has yielded the crops we see today.

Family- and community-scale farms averaging several hectares or more provide for Quechua subsistence, as well as for local and other markets. These farms (chakra in the Quechua language) are considered the means to a good life in the Andes and represent their own ecosystems within the Andean world. Quechua believe that the Andean world can be understood according to hanaq pacha, kay pacha, and ukhu pacha – the upper world (of the skies and heavens), this world (of living plants, animals, elements, and humans), and the inside world (the world of our ancestors). These interconnected worlds are watched and cared for by deities, and they are also mediated by human beings who have a responsibility to acknowledge the beings in each world and to care for what has been given. Complementing this familiarity with the Andean world is the fact that the central Andean regions have the greatest ecological density in the world and that eight of the eleven world climates can be found here – making weather in distinct zones variable, to which Andean farmers have long since understood how to mitigate and accommodate culturally and scientifically (Valladolid and Apfeel-Marglin 2001, pp. 653–654).

Like other significant places in Andean communities, the chakra and its sustainability as a provider is a place where exercise of Andean cosmology is required, and is therefore more than just a space that produces the foods that people and animals consume. In the chakra, one encounters rich soil, surrounding fruit trees, worms, and insects. With the sun, moon, stars, clouds, and rains overhead, seeds are planted, nurtured, and grow. Entering the chakra, recognition is given to these elements, as well as to the ancestors who set their bare feet upon this soil to cultivate this land generation after generation. Offerings are made prior to planting and throughout the agricultural year, and it is not uncommon to see farmers offering coca to the elements or to see a newly planted field with beautiful fresh flowers placed upon the earth – communicating the hope to the earth, ancestors, and other community members that this chakra yields beauty. The physical and spiritual labor that is dedicated to the chakra is demonstrated by many acts throughout the Andean cycle of life – daily work and special times like harvesting are complemented with offerings, prayers of hope and prayers of gratitude, and any losses of crops are considered loss of life, seen as deaths in the community.

On the one hand, agricultural losses represent stark economic problems for Indigenous family livelihoods and for the overall Peruvian economy and Gross Domestic Product; on the other hand, exogenous environmental destruction represents yet another shift for Andean Indigenous ontologies – demanding multiple and innovative interventions and strategies. Because Andean communities have been reliant on small family- and community-scale subsistence farming for thousands of years, Quechua livelihoods are dependent upon ancestral practices of cooperation and reciprocity, like the ayni, kinship sharing reflected through collaboration in work. These are not individualistic ways of being, and Quechua ways of knowing assert the power and promise of the collective – people caring for people, the environment caring for people, and people caring for the environment (Photo 2).

Photo 2 Lifelong Wanka farmer, Mama Victoria, husking corn that will be selected for seed and used for food, Hatun Shunqo, Peru (Image by Elizabeth Sumida Huaman)

In addition to organizing the agricultural life of a Quechua community and the ceremonies associated with each stage of the life of the plants, the greater context of the Andean calendar is the Quechua understanding of the universe and the role of runakuna, people, in the universe. Runakuna are part of creation, living beings who like every other living entity and contain the life force of the universe within them, and in order to honor this life, ceremonies are carefully planned and carried out throughout the Andean year and are inextricable from the Quechua agricultural cycle, the Quechua pastoral cycle, and so forth. Figuring centrally in these ceremonies are the deities and elements associated with hanan pacha, kay pacha, and ukhu pacha. However, because the term Pachamama is often interpreted in popular culture according to its literal translation to English from Quechua – pacha for earth and mama for mother – the deeper philosophies within the Quechua language and the Andean world are often misunderstood or oversimplified. That Pachamama is Earth Mother and feminine does not actually do justice to the complexity and centrality of pacha in the Quechua knowledge system. While Pachamama can be applied in one sense in reference to the earth, pacha is space and time and refers to the dynamic changing nature and energy of the universe. Although Western anthropologists have written extensively about pacha in Andean cosmology, if Indigenous peoples are the bearers, perpetuators, shapers, and innovators of their own knowledge systems, the ways in which they understand their own philosophies and how they wish to represent that knowledge needs to be much more richly explored. Space needs to be created, expanded, and defended in order for this to happen.

Although Quechua peoples have rich oral traditions, their reliance on orality as a method of transmitting cultural teachings does not preclude them from sharing knowledge that they decide to share in written form. Since the colonial period, Quechua scholars have been demonstrating their ability to utilize Quechua and Spanish languages, orality and literacy, Quechua cultural practices and resources, and Spanish resources and tools. Scholars like Don Diego de Castro Titu Cusi Yupanqui wrote his own narrative account of the conquest based on oral history with Inca peoples in 1570; published in 1609, Garcilaso de la Vega wrote a detailed account of Inca life, landscape, and religion prior to the conquest; and in 1613, Don Juan de Santa Cruz Pachacuti Yamqui Salcamaygua wrote a detailed account of Inca life. All of these works focus on Quechua people, ways of life, and beliefs associated with rituals. In addition to what can be collected through oral histories in direct participation with Quechua peoples living in Andean communities, these works constitute yuyayninchis, our shared social memory. Yuyayninchis, our memory, and yachayninchis, our knowledge, are inextricably linked in Quechua knowledge systems, based in pacha.

Quechua knowledge systems (I refer to Quechua knowledge systems as plural since there are vast Quechua landscapes, communities, and language varieties. The argument here is to offer and protect opportunities for local peoples to explore their own knowledge systems while recognizing some potential shared elements outlined in this section of the chapter.) are rich, detailed, complex, and dynamic. These systems and Quechua ways of knowing – exercise, practice, conservation, and vitality of what is known – are still in existence in the highland Andes today and constitute the learning that Quechua children experience outside of formal schools. Research by Indigenous and non-Indigenous scholars over the past two decades has demonstrated this in different ways: From the work of Rosina Valcárcel who wrote in the 1980s of the prominence of Quechua myths as resistance to colonial domination (1988), to Patricia Ames whose work focuses on out-of-school learning processes and transitions in the lives of Quechua children and tensions with formal schooling injustices (2012, 2013c). In an attempt to contribute to this conversation on not only how Quechua knowledge systems can be identified, but more importantly, how these constitute Quechua learning within Andean communities, some major themes are identified here.

1. **Quechua knowledge systems are organized systems of knowledge for living in the natural world** – Pacha Mamamanchispi lluy kawsaqkuna: sach'akuna, qochakuna, unukuna, mayukuna, uywakuna hathunraq, huch'uyraq (Note that I use the Quechua Collao variety in this chapter, and the sentences in Quechua are not intended to be translations of the English phrases. Rather, they are assertions of what is stated using Quechua daily language.): Within Quechua knowledge systems, all elements are interdependent. Language is inextricable from philosophy, and philosophy is inextricable from values. Based on the Andean cycle of life, Quechua knowledge systems are organized and purposeful towards a good and balanced life for all beings. There are clearly defined responsibilities for human beings and protocols for engagement with all elements in the universe – from the sun and moon, heavens, and stars, to the rivers and trees and animals, to the ancestors.
2. **Quechua knowledge systems are local paradigms of place concerned with universal thriving** – Lluy runakunapas munayta ñawpaqman puririnanchispaq: Quechua knowledge systems constitute Andean ways of viewing the world through living within a particular context. However, the universe is broad, and local worldview is matched with conscientiousness of life in other places and is

deeply concerned with far-reaching impact as understood through pacha; space and time are not limited.

3. **Quechua knowledge systems are flexible and adaptable** – Chay tomaqakuna Español nisqa runakuna llaqtanchisman chayamusqankumanta pachan, kay Pacha Mamanchistaqa qhellicharanku, "idolatría" nispa manaña Pacha Mamanchisman Haywarikuyta qorankuñachu, inkakunata soq'ayuspa qonqachiyta munaranku, ichaqa Inkakunaqa manan kawsayninkuta qonqayta atirankuchu chayrayku pakallapi ruwaqku, Pacha Mamanchismanqa Haywarikullasqakupuni, ichaqa españolkuna mana chaypi iñisqakuchu, chayrayku Pacha Mamanchis kunan wañunayashan: Because knowledge is not bound by space and time, Quechua knowledge systems are based on fluidity and equilibrium. While the Spanish conquest and European notions of superiority continue to influence Quechua ways of life and people, knowledge from other cultures and their practices can be gained if deemed useful and respectful of the Andean world. Additionally, the visceral and real impacts of the conquest and current environmental threats to the Andean world are processed within Quechua knowledge systems and become part of what is known, yachayninchis, and what is remembered, yuyayninchis. Within what is known and what is remembered, what is learned and experienced, solutions to current problems can be explored.

4. **Quechua knowledge systems are vital dialogue and exchange** – Pacha mamanchiswanqa rimananchispuni sapa púnchay, Pacha Mama: qori montera, qolqe pullera, qanmi ñuñuwankiku, qanmi uywawankiku, qan patapin noqayku wawaykikuna kawsayku, noqaykutaqmi "español" runakuna chayamusqankumanta pacha usa hina kawsashayku yawarniykita soq'ospa, manataq qanta allintachu qhawarishaykiku: Quechua knowledge systems are concerned with sustaining all life in the Andean world and maintaining balance with the universe. These systems exist alongside other knowledge systems and are therefore vital. Pedagogies are intricately involved and rooted in the practice of relationship through conversation with the universe – that humans and other living beings, including plant life and animals, maintain a relationship with each other through communication and reciprocity. Not only are ceremonies acts of conversation between humans and the universe, but also there are stories that teach the value of conversation, such as the exchanges between corn plant and yuyu, an edible herb, that grows among the corn (see Photo 3).

5. **Quechua knowledge systems nurture individuals and community through learning and teaching** – Allinta yachananchis, umanchispi allinata hap'inanchis: Experiences within Quechua knowledge systems are facilitated by community members of all ages who direct, facilitate, learn, and participate in its practices; from the community healer to the youth learning to irrigate a field for the first time, each community member is recognized for particular talents, characteristics, and for their abilities to share these within the Andean world.

6. **Quechua knowledge systems are concerned with values towards harmony and justice** – Kamachi simikuna: More profound than socialization or construction of nationhood, Quechua knowledge systems are concerned with the cultivation of values of justice in each Quechua person throughout their entire lifetime. The ideal

Photo 3 Chakra with plants and flowers conversing with the corn in a southern valley of Cusco (Image by Elizabeth Sumida Huaman)

Quechua is often described as umayoq, sonqolloq, kallpayoq (possessing a good mind, possessing a good heart, and possessing strength). Within the chakra, teaching and reinforcement of other values during every stage of the growth of plants – respect, love, humility, thankfulness, and sharing – are shown to the elements, crops, and other community members through daily and ceremonial practices.

7. **Quechua knowledge systems are Quechua illumination and innovation** – Ñawpaqman puririy, t'ikariy: The Quechua knowledge system is interdisciplinary and holds principles of science, technology, engineering, art, mathematics, history, and social studies. Western discourses of knowledge separate these, but to Quechua, they are inextricable from each other and the natural world. Innovating and creating new approaches for sustaining Quechua ways of life and bringing solutions to problems is inherently the work of the Quechua knowledge system (see Photo 3): science in the form of agricultural cultivation and astronomy, technology in the form of advanced irrigation, engineering in the design of hydraulics, art in the form of sculpture and goldwork, and mathematics in the form of textile and architectural design (Photo 4).

This is not a classification of Quechua knowledge, but rather an offering of some observable patterns and continuities. Moreover, because knowledge has been

Photo 4 Inca hydraulic engineering work of Tipón (Image by Elizabeth Sumida Huaman)

commodified in the mainstream (May 1999; Valladolid and Apfeel-Marglin 2001), the purposes of knowledge are important to explore; in this process of inquiry, we can begin to distinguish Quechua knowledge as a way of living in the world from a body of thought whose metrics are based primarily on acquisition for human gain.

The Fall of a God

The Quechua knowledge system is vast and rich. As a structured and organized system of knowing the Andean world and maintaining a relationship with the universe, this system is also crucial to the sociocultural identities of Quechua children. For the past few decades, scholars working with Indigenous communities in Peru have amassed arguments regarding the local, national, and global benefits of these distinct identities (Zúñiga et al. 1987; Valcárcel 1988; Hornberger 1988; Aikman 1995, 1999; López 1996; Sumida Huaman and Valdiviezo 2012). No Quechua individual should have to justify or seek validation from dominant society regarding the worth of their identity. However, because of the longitudinal power inequalities resulting in silencing, marginalization, outright hostility, and negation of

Quechua as intellectual or anything other than primitive at worst, aesthetic only at best, there is a need to establish a baseline of respect for Indigenous knowledges – that Quechua knowledge systems and Quechua people contribute to world knowledges in ways that are productive to the survival of our own and other species. The threats to life today are unprecedented, and although not of Quechua making, when their knowledge is threatened and undermined, so is their human potential to repair the world.

> Waytapallana, they say, is a man and woman. He is not alone…All of the flowers that the people are starting to bring now grow on Waytapallana—the flowers for Tayta Shanti—the woman protects the flowers the people go to pick. Look, if you have a noble heart, if you are pure and peaceful and enter to pick flowers, nothing will happen to you. You can cut the flowers peacefully. However many you want, you can bring. But if you go to the place, our Tayta Apu on Pachamama, they say when you enter Pachamama, she knows who you are. They say that maybe you are easily entering to pick flowers, but you become lost little by little, being tempted by prettier and prettier flowers—Just like that! You can disappear into the mountain. Pachamama knows all the feelings you carry, who you are. She studies the people. (Mama Yolanda, Fieldnotes 1997, author translation)

In 2004, Mama Yolanda, a Quechua Wanka speaker and community member living in the Mantaro Valley of central Peru passed away leaving her own legacy of Quechua stories told through the oral tradition and intimate knowledge of every section of her homelands that she passed on through daily interaction to her family members. She spoke of local shrines, wari or sacred places, farm fields that all carry Quechua names, the stories behind ceremonies, and of the mountains and their deities. Waytapallana, a glacier visible from her family house in the small Andean community in which she was born, is one of the special places she described (see Photo 5). Known in Quechua stories as related to the deity, Huallallo Carhuancho, the mountain glacier is affectionately called Waytapallana, the place where the flowers are picked, and this glacier is a landmark in the region that is central to ceremonies in the Andean calendar. Surrounded by glacial lakes, flowers that are used in ceremonies are ritualistically gathered from this place. As Mama Yolanda explained, this deity is not alone, but part of a family of mountains and peaks. Furthermore, she described the relationship that people have with this place and the earth and what type of *heart* it takes in order to even walk in the area. Her understanding of this place and her emphasis on human responsibility are vital elements in Quechua knowledge – that places are not removed from human emotion and intention.

In addition to its cultural significance, Waytapallana is also significant as a water source for this region and for the nearby capital city of the region of Junín, Huancayo. Western modern science views the Mantaro basin as distinct in Peru due to its biodiversity, natural reserves, and its glaciers like Waytapallana – which is arguably the most important glacier in the basin (Lagos 2007). With an elevation ranging from 4800 to 5768 m, Waytapallana is part of the Cordillera Oriental of the central Andes and located approximately 32 km from Huancayo (Quispe Palomino 2010, p. 15). As Mama

Photo 5 Waytapallana glacier (Image by Elizabeth Sumida Huaman)

Yolanda also acknowledged, Waytapallana is part of a complex of other mountain peaks including Yanaucsha, Lasuntay Grande, Lasuntay Norte, Cochas, Chuspi, Chulla, Ichu, Yanacancha, Tello, Rangra, Talves, Putacocha, Anchigrande, Chonta, Palpacocha, Champacoto, Pacaco, and Panchamayo; collectively, these form approximately 25 black, green, blue, and turquoise glacial lakes, which feed into various rivers that are connected to villages across the region (Quispe Palomino 2010, p. 16).

In the Mantaro region, not only is food grown locally by Quechua farmers for family and community subsistence, but also for commerce and trade (i.e., crops are routinely sent to Lima). However, this region is also under severe environmental threat due to sources with deep histories of colonial domination and neoliberalism – soil and water contamination through use of pesticides since the US introduction of DDT to the region post-World War II, water contamination of the Mantaro River due to regional mining projects, and perhaps most visibly to Waytapallana, climate change – which scientists believe is not likely to improve (Mark et al. 2010). Since the 1980s, Waytapallana's icecaps have been melting, and over 50% of the surface area of the glacier is estimated to have been lost. This loss represents cultural challenges coupled with inevitable complications for water consumption and agricultural sustainability.

Carefully crafted documentation of significant places in the Mantaro region paired with local narratives and commentary was provided by Father Jaime Quispe Palomino of Huancayo in 2010. He described his work as addressing the urgency of growing the consciousness of human ecology to understand and curb the destruction of the environment. He divided his work into three areas: the deterioration of the environment through contamination and its death and destruction; the current state of local animals also Indigenous to the region; and an exaltation of the land, the animals, and the universe. As in Father Quispe Palomino's work, reports emerging from the region have are conveying compelling testimony regarding environmental loss: Increasingly since 2011, news media has reported on the recession of Waytapallana and its projected impacts both locally and nationally. *El Diaro del Comercio* began tracking local government efforts in Huancayo to conserve the region and protect Waytapallana from further losses. On December 7, 2014, *La República* described the loss of Waytapallana as "the fall of a giant" and described scientific projections based on the current rate of recession that Waytapallana will disappear by 2050. *La República* also reported that La Comunidad Andina de Naciones (The Andean Community of Nations) warned that as a result of glacier loss across the Andes, 2020 would see problems with access to water for human consumption, agricultural use, and hydroelectric energy, impacting an estimated 40 million people. Culturally speaking, the loss of Waytapallana is unimaginable, and there are no Western scientific projections to describe such an impact on Quechua knowledge and memory:

> The legend of the origin of Huaytapallana tells of the confrontation between the gods Huallallo Carhuincho and Pariacaca, due to the daughter of the first, a beautiful girl called Huaytapallana. The son of Pariacaca tricked her and in reprisal, Huallallo Carhuincho killed him. Pariacaca took revenge, in turn, drowning the girl in the lake Carhuacocha. The war between the two gods was bloody and only ended when Wiracocha intervened, and he converted them into the snows on top of the mountains of Huancayo and Huarochiri. The legend says that on the day that the snows melt, the gods will return to govern the land of the Huancas. It seems like that day grows closer. (Miranda 2014)

Given the widespread impact of environmental damage both caused in Peru and elsewhere that has resounding effects throughout the globe, the loss of Waytapallana appears imminent. While local and national governments using international research support seek to address the vast loss of these resources in Peru, local community members throughout the Andes consider the direct impacts to their lives. There is increasing attention towards the intersection of physical risk associated with the direct impacts of glacier recession and vulnerability – from susceptibility to resiliency as response to environmental degradation – most critically appearing in studies of political ecology (Trigoso Rubio 2007). What we see is an epistemological clash – between Quechua knowledge and environmental exploitation based on progress exemplified through neoliberalism, and where direct impacts are immediately observable on local people who contend with the future in unprecedented ways. Respecting and caring for local environment, loving the chakra and earth, and being humbled by and gracious with what has been given are in opposition to dominant economically driven ideologies of natural resources. In light of explicit losses due to environmental degradation, we also see that Quechua values and stories do have critical relevance to science and ecological planning after all.

Indigenous Rights Education (IRE)

While Quechua are aware that their knowledge systems are beneficial for human behavior and understanding towards peaceable living with the universe, the fight in contemporary political discourse to demonstrate how and why this matters has been underway for decades. Framed as a reflection of collective conscience, critical Indigenous stories take on political power distinct from that which has been misappropriated by dominant Peruvian society as merely rural beliefs or folklore. While acknowledging modes of Andean resistance, Andean communities and scholars are transcending resistance; they are building new discourses and responses that position Quechua knowledges at the center of the conversation on progress, development, and nationalism. Education, both out of school learning processes and formal schooling, is paramount in such endeavors as state control over spaces where learning occurs is increasingly confronted by Indigenous peoples.

Questions around how education in both spaces can be constructed for the benefit of Indigenous peoples are clear. Quechua knowledge systems and discourses of human rights (HR) and earth rights have been useful in framing positions of Quechua knowledge in human and environmental interaction. However, in Indigenous terms, there are important critiques of the language of rights as state-sponsored, endorsed, or recognized. Tsalagi scholar Jeff Corntassel's work offers critical insights in this regard by rejecting state-recognized discourses that are distracting to Indigenous empowerment – where Indigenous peoples reframe rights as *our inherent responsibilities*, reconciliation as *resurgence*, and resources as *relationships* (2012). I do not dispute this, and the hope would be that local Quechua peoples and Indigenous peoples engaged in monumental and persistent environmental and educational battles would reframe the language of rights using Indigenous philosophies and languages. In Quechua, this might be along the lines of chanin, or justice in English, and its accompanying stories and cultural practices. However, for the time being, the discourse of rights is employed by Indigenous community members asserting Indigenous presence in national and international arenas. Furthermore, in light of ever-growing projects of development and environmental consequences in Peru and across the Andes, the how-and-why-Quechua-knowledge-matters justification is now more apparent than ever: In order to equip generations with the language and tools to lead and manage their own natural resource interests with local and global accountability to people and places, international discourses of rights (re)framed locally create and hold space for Indigenous peoples to place themselves in conversation from which they have been excluded, if they so choose.

Indigenous rights education (IRE) is a tool to expand Indigenous epistemologies in connection with community-driven educational goals that must interact with the state. IRE is founded in local Indigenous knowledge systems, including what and how local Indigenous peoples determine is vital to their ability and the ability of the beings and places in which they live to thrive (Sumida Huaman 2017). An example of this is collectively exhibited in the United Nations Declaration on Indigenous Rights (UNDRIP). Stemming from local Indigenous knowledge systems, IRE is linked with Indigenous rights, human rights (HR), and place/earth rights.

Post-World War II and as a response to the atrocities committed in Europe, human rights emerged as a critical discourse for framing the rights of individuals and societies. In this time period, delineations regarding rights and international crimes against humanity were drafted through the 1945 London Charter of the International Military Tribunal (Nuremberg Charter), the 1948 Convention on the Prevention and Punishment of the Crime of Genocide, and the Universal Declaration of Human Rights (UDHR) adopted by the United Nations in 1948 (see: http://www.un.org/es/universal-declaration-human-rights/). Since its adoption, the UDHR has served to provide one frame for considering rights viewed as universal and incontrovertible, and ideas regarding human rights and their consideration and application have since been expanded. O'Byrne (2013) argued that HR also involved necessarily regarding theories of human nature and the role of the individual, theories of society and the social context of HR violations, theories of ethics and condemnation of HR violations by civil society, theories of politics and the role of the state, and logic of modernity where progress is mythologized and a better world is imagined.

Because this chapter is concerned with not only how HR can be framed by Indigenous peoples but also how HR is taught, the work of Monisha Bajaj is apt. Drawing from Amnesty International's prepositions that link education and HR, she centralized her inquiry about the expansiveness and potentials of human rights education (HRE) through the lenses of education *about* human rights, education *through* human rights, and education *for* human rights (2011, p. 483, Bajaj's emphasis). Each of these targets the design, structure, and content of HRE in a way that demonstrates the potential of HR frameworks in practice. In terms of education and according to the 2006 UN World Programme for Human Rights Education, Bajaj highlighted one definition of HRE as "education, training and information aiming at building a universal culture of human rights through the sharing of knowledge, imparting of skills and moulding of attitudes directed to: a) the strengthening of respect for human rights and fundamental freedoms; b) the full development of the human personality and the sense of its dignity; c) the promotion of understanding, tolerance, gender equality and friendship among all nations, indigenous peoples and racial, national, ethnic, religious and linguistic groups," among others (p. 484). Bajaj pointed out that the UN's definition of HRE was aimed at seeking commitment from member states and using a top-down approach focused on national policymakers. Drawing from models of HRE produced by international organizations and national efforts in India, she argued that ideological variation was a strength in producing HRE initiatives – that is, not only does the very idea of HRE engender interest, but also the ability of organizations and peoples to use their own worldviews to inform what HRE is and how it can be practiced on the ground are important markers for what HRE can become.

Because of the innovative capacity of Quechua knowledge, ideas and practices regarding HRE can supplement proposals for Quechua education *about*, *through*, and *for* human rights from Quechua worldviews concerned with both local and global issues. Central to any Quechua proposal is connectivity to land – the severing and disruptions of which were addressed in the first and second parts of this chapter. Issuing proposals for Quechua education will include several challenges: First, how can Quechua communities reframe the language of HR and HRE according to their own principles, values, and desires? Second, how can Indigenous lands and natural resources be reclaimed, revitalized, managed, and protected through Quechua education using principles that first recognize Indigenous ties to land as more than abstract and based in customary international law (Anaya and Williams 2001)? Third, drawing from and transforming discourses of HRE, how can Quechua education frame environmental degradation and climate change and produce educational interventions that combat dominant and public political discourse around progress and projects of development in the Andes region? Last, how can Quechua educational practices and realities speak back or contribute to the discourse of HR and HRE in ways that maintain the integrity of Quechua knowledge while also producing shared knowledge that benefits all life on this earth?

Over the past decade, we have seen prospects for solutions, such as discourse on the rights of Mother Earth that reflect Indigenous ideals of human-environmental relationships and political and social activism. Bolivia's Proposal for a Law of Mother Earth (2010) is a self-described framework that acknowledges people, society, and place in transition through the industrial era and is the result of a critique of neoliberalism and capitalism: "We urgently need alternatives to the capitalist development model that destroys the environment and has caused the financial, energy and food crises, as well as climate change and deep inequalities within and between societies" (p. 5). Aligned with Quechua epistemology that prioritizes balance with the universe, the objectives of this framework were described as "to guarantee the co-existence and preservation of life," which involve a philosophy of humans as a part of nature where Mother Earth is a subject entitled to her own protections – the violations of which are punishable as crimes. Outlining the role of individuals and the role of the state, descriptions of the rights of Mother Earth, along with policy recommendations, were outlined in this document, which has been scrutinized within the Bolivian plurinational state and by critics and supporters of Bolivia's political evolution worldwide. Unclear is how Indigenous peoples and allies will confront structural inequalities that preclude Indigenous participation in these discourses and in setting the agenda for these discussions of power, land, and education.

Conclusion

> From our breath to Pachamama, we know how to conserve the land and the waters, which are the blood of Pachamama. We make offerings, as did our ancestors before us. (Mama Ines, personal communication, Cusco, 27 June 2016, author translation)

In this chapter, Quechua knowledge system characteristics have been highlighted in relation to the Andean world and over time, including historical impositions that have resulted in the remaking of the Andean world. Environment and natural resources have been subjected to colonial imposition and overtaking, as well as globalization and climate change, and exogenous and neoliberal projects of development. Newer examinations and propositions mindful of past resistances and current hopes to transcend resistance towards the creation of new ideas and solutions that honor the past are discussed. As a result of these confluences, yachayninchis (Quechua knowledge) and yuyayninchis (Quechua social memory) are fluid and require consideration of Indigenous epistemologies, which can also be described as Indigenous wisdom fluencies, lending themselves to transitions on Quechua lands throughout the Andes that Quechua peoples confront. As an exclusive and largely destructive tool of the discourse of progress and the promises of modernity towards socioeconomic betterment, projects of development remain extensions of imperialism and its colonial trajectory. A singular pathway of development undermines Indigenous conceptualizations of human life on this planet, where discourses of progress equal participation in the global capitalistic market focused solely on economic gain and where quality of life is measured through financial indicators and interaction and access to Western technology. Quechua knowledges offer solutions towards repairing this world, and equipped with the language of the past two decades of Indigenous rights, place/earth rights, and human rights education, there is an opportunity to create space for meaningful and productive dialogue that unseats dominant colonial and neoliberal narratives of what humanity is and which pathways we might take in this world.

References

Aikenhead G, Mitchell H (2011) Bridging cultures: Indigenous and scientific ways of knowing. Pearson, Cambridge
Aikman S (1995) Language, literacy and bilingual education: an Amazon people's strategies for cultural maintenance. Int J Educ Dev 15:411–422
Aikman S (1999) Schooling and development: eroding Amazon women's knowledge and diversity. In: Heward C, Bunwaree S (eds) Education, gender and development: beyond access to empowerment. Zed Books, London, pp 65–81
Alfred T, Corntassel J (2005) Being Indigenous: resurgences against contemporary colonialism. In: Bellamy R (ed) The politics of identity-IX. Government and Opposition, Ltd, Oxford, pp 597–614
Ames P (2012) Language, culture, and identity in the transition to primary school: challenges to Indigenous children's rights to education in Peru. Int J Educ Dev 32:454–462
Ames P (2013a) Niños y niñas andinas en el Perú: Crecer en un mundo de relaciones y responsabilidades. [Andean boys and girls in Peru: growing up in a world of relationships and responsibilities]. Bulletin de l'Institut Français d'Études Andines 42:389–409
Ames P (2013b) ¿Construyendo nuevas identidades? Género y educación en los proyectos de vida de las jóvenes rurales de Perú. [Constructing new identities? Gender and education in the projects of the life of rural youth in Peru]. Instituto de Estudios Peruanos, Lima
Ames P (2013c) Learning to be responsible: young children transitions outside school. Learn Cult Soc Interact 2:143–154
Anaya J, Williams R (2001) The protection of Indigenous peoples' rights over land and natural resources under the Inter-American human rights system. Harv Hum Rights J 14:33–86
Arguedas JM (1972) Katatay y otros poemas/Huc Jayllicunapas. [Trembling and other poems]. Instituto Nacional de Cultura, Lima
Bajaj M (2011) Human rights education: ideology, location, and approaches. Hum Rights Q 33:481–508

Barnhardt R, Kawagley OA (2005) Indigenous knowledge systems and Alaska ways of knowing. Anthropol Educ Q 6:8–23

Battiste M (2002) Indigenous knowledge and pedagogy in First Nations education: a literature review with recommendations. Indian and Northern Affairs Canada, Ottawa

Battiste M (2013) Decolonizing education: nourishing the learning spirit. Purich, Saskatoon

Bebbington A (1999) Capitals and capabilities: a framework for analyzing peasant viability, rural livelihoods and poverty. World Dev 27:2021–2044

Bebbington A (2010) Poverty reduction and policy regimes thematic paper: social movements and poverty in developing countries. Civil society and social movements, programme paper number 32, Oct 2010. United Nations Research Institute for Social Development

Bebbington A, Humphreys Bebbington D (2011) An Andean avatar: post-neoliberal and neoliberal strategies for securing the unobtainable. New Polit Econ 16:131–145

Bolin I (2006) Growing up in a culture of respect: child rearing in highland Peru. University of Texas, Austin

Calero Pérez M (1996) Nación Huanca. [Huanca nation]. Editorial "San Marcos", Peru

Carnoy M (1974) Education as cultural imperialism. David McKay Company, New York

Cerron-Palomino R (1989) Lengua y sociedad en el valle del Mantaro. [Language and society in the Mantaro Valley]. Instituto de Estudios Peruanos, Lima

Chang-Rodriguez E (1984) El indigenismo Peruano y Mariategui. [Peruvian indigenism and Mariategui]. Rev Iberoam 50:367–394

Chhetri N, Chhetri N (2015) Alternative imaginations: examining complementarities across knowledge systems. In: Sumida Huaman E, Sriraman B (eds) Indigenous innovation: universalities and peculiarities. Sense, Rotterdam, pp 11–24

Cieza de Leon P (2011) The Kingdom of the Incas. Editorial Piki, Cusco

Corntassel J (2012) Re-envisioning resurgence: Indigenous pathways to decolonization and sustainable self-determination. Decolonization 1:86–101

Crivello G (2011) 'Becoming somebody': youth transitions through education and migration in Peru. J Youth Stud 14:395–411

de Ayala GP (1980) Nueva cronica y buen gobierno, reprint. [The new chronicle and good government]. Biblioteca Ayacucho, Ayacucho

de la Vega G (1966) Royal Commentaries of the Incas and general history of Peru. University of Texas, Austin

de las Casas B (1992) A short account of the destruction of the Indies, translated by Nigel Griffin. Penguin, London

Degregori, CI (2012) How difficult it is to be God: shining path's politics of war in Peru, 1980–1999. Critical human rights series edited by Steve Stern. University of Wisconsin, Madison

Escobar A (1995) Encountering development: the making and unmaking of the Third World. Princeton University, Princeton

Esteva G (2010) Development. In: Sachs W (ed) The development dictionary, 2nd edn. Zed, London, pp 1–21

Freire P (1970) Pedagogy of the oppressed. Continuum, New York

Giesecke Sara-Lafosse M (2007) Los fundamentos del folklore y su vínculo con la educación. [The fundamentals of folklore and its link with education]. Rev Antropol 5:163–197

Griffiths N (1996) The cross and the serpent: religious repression and resurgence in colonial Peru. University of Oklahoma, Norman

Gutierrez Verastegui B (1986) Lecturas Huancas. [Huanca lessons]. Tierra Adentro Ediciones, Lima

Hornberger N (1988) Bilingual education and language maintenance; a Southern Peruvian Quechua case. Foris Publications, Dordrecht

Hornberger NH, Coronel-Molina SM (2004) Quechua language shift, maintenance, and revitalization in the Andes: the case for language planning. Int J Sociol Lang 167:9–67

Hornberger NH, King KA (2001) Reversing Quechua language shift in South America. In: Fishman J (ed) Can threatened languages be saved? Reversing language shift, revisited: a 21st century perspective. Multilingual Matters, Clevedon, pp 166–194

Kawagley AO (2006) A Yupiaq worldview: pathway to ecology and spirit, 2nd edn. Waveland, Long Grove

Lagos P (2007) Peru's approach to climate change in the Andes mountain region. Mt Res Dev 27:28–31

López LE (1996) Donde el zapato aprieta: Tendencias y desafíos de la educación bilingüe en el Perú. [Where the shoe is tight: tendencies and challenges of bilingual education in Peru]. Revista Andina 2:295–336

Mariátegui JC (1997) Seven interpretive essays on Peruvian reality. University of Texas, Austin

Mark BG et al (2010) Climate change and tropical Andean glacier recession: evaluating hydrolic changes and livelihood vulnerability in the Cordillera Blanca, Peru. Ann Assoc Am Geogr 100:794–805

May S (ed) (1999) Indigenous community-based education. Multilingual Matters, Clevedon

Mayer E (2009) Ugly stories of the Peruvian agrarian reform. Duke University, Durham

McClintock C (1981) Peasant cooperatives and political change in Peru. Princeton University, Princeton

McKinley E (2005) Locating the global: Culture, language and science education for indigenous students. International Journal of Science Education 27:227–241. https://doi.org/10.1080/09500690420003258861

McMichael P (2010) Changing the subject of development. In: McMichael P (ed) Contesting development: critical struggles for social change. Routledge, New York, pp 1–14

Miller R (2011) American Indians, the doctrine of discovery, and manifest destiny. Wyoming Law Review 11:329–349

Miranda O (2014, December 7) La caída de un gigante: el nevado Huaytapallana. [The fall of a giant: the Huaytapallana glacier]. La República

Nash J (1993) We eat the mines and the mines eat us: dependency and exploitation in Bolivian tin mines. Columbia University, New York

O'Byrne DJ (2013) Human rights: an introduction. Routledge, New York

Pihama L, Smith K, Taki M, Lee J (2004) A literature review on Kaupapa Maori and Maori education pedagogy. The International Research Institute for Maori and Indigenous Education, Auckland

Plurinational State of Bolivia (2010) Proposal for a law of Mother Earth. Proposal of Bolivian social movements and civil society, La Paz

Quispe Palomino J (2010) Visión Ecológica de la región Junín, 2da edición. [Ecological vision of the Junin region]. Bisagra Editores, Huancayo

Rostow WW (1990) The stages of economic growth: a non-communist manifesto, 3rd edn. Cambridge University, Cambridge

Salazar Bondy S (1964) Lima la horrible. [Lima the horrible]. Biblioteca ERA, Ciudad de México

Smith G (2000) Maori education: revolution and transformative action. Can J Nativ Educ 24:57–72

Spitta S (2007) Lima the horrible: the cultural politics of theft. Mod Lang Assoc 122:294–300

Stern S (ed) (1998) Shining and other paths: war and society in Peru, 1980–1995. Duke University, Durham

Sumida Huaman E (2014) Tuki ayllpanchik [our beautiful land]: Indigenous ecological education in the Peruvian highlands. Cult Stud Sci Educ 9:1–19

Sumida Huaman E (2015) "Why can't we admire our own?": Indigenous youth, farming, and education in the Peruvian Andes. In: Sumida Huaman E, Sriraman B (eds) Indigenous innovation: universalities and peculiarities. Sense, Rotterdam, pp 129–148

Sumida Huaman E (2017) Indigenous rights education: Indigenous knowledge systems and transformative human rights in the Peruvian Andes. Int J Hum Rights Educ 1:1–34

Sumida Huaman E, Valdiviezo LA (2012) Indigenous knowledge and education from the Quechua community to school: beyond the formal/non-formal dichotomy. Int J Qual Stud Educ iFirst:1–23

Trigoso Rubio E (2007) Climate change impacts and adaptation in Peru: the case of Puno and Piura. UNDP human development report 2007/2008, Fighting climate change: human solidarity in a divided world. Human Development Report Office Occasional Paper

Valcárcel R (1988) Mitos: Dominacion y resistencia Andina. [Myths: domination and Andean resistance]. Universidad Nacional Mayor de San Marcos, Lima

Valdiviezo LA (2009) 'Don't you want your child to be better than you?': Enacting ideologies and contesting intercultural policy in Peru. In: Vavrus F, Bartlett L (eds) Critical approaches to comparative education: vertical case studies from Africa, Europe, the Middle East, and the Americas. Palgrave Macmillan, New York, pp 147–162

Valdiviezo LA (2013) Cosmovisiones indígenas y construcciones sobre la interculturalidad en la educación bilingüe. [Indigenous cosmovision and constructions about interculturality in bilingual Peru]. Rev Peru Investig Educ 5:99–123

Valdiviezo LA (2014) Political discourse and school practice in multilingual Peru. In: Cortina R (ed) The education of Indigenous citizens in Latin America. Multilingual Matters, Bristol, pp 187–209

Valladolid J, Apfeel-Marglin F (2001) Andean cosmovision and the nurturing of biodiversity. In: Grim JA (ed) Indigenous traditions and ecology: the interbeing of cosmology and community. Harvard University, Cambridge, pp 639–670

vom Hau M, Wilde G (2010) 'We have always lived here': Indigenous movements, citizenship, and poverty in Argentina. J Dev Stud 46:1283–1303

wa Thiong'o N (2009) Something torn and new: an African renaissance. BasicCivitas, New York

Walker C (2014) Reflections of Tupac Amaru. Berkeley Rev Lat Am Stud Fall:59–60

Wood R (1986) Teach them good customs: colonial Indian education and acculturation in the Andes. Labyrinthos, Lancaster

Zúñiga M, Ansion J, Cueva L (eds) (1987) Educación en poblaciones indígenas: políticas y estrategias en América Latina. UNESCO OREALC, Santiago de Chile

Reflections on the Purpose of Indigenous Environmental Education

40

Kyle Powys Whyte

Contents

Introduction	768
Indigenous Environmentalism	768
Indigenous Environmental Education	771
Indigenous Climate Change Planning	774
Indigenous Traditional Environmental Education	777
Collective Continuance	780
Education for Collective Continuance	783
References	785

Abstract

The essay offers reflections on the purpose of Indigenous environmental education. Indigenous peoples engage in wide-ranging approaches to environmental education that are significant aspects of how they exercise self-determination. Yet often such educational practices are just seen as trying to genuinely teach certain historic traditions or scientific skill-sets. Through reviewing the author's experiences and diverse scholarly and practitioner perspectives, the essay discusses how Indigenous environmental education is best when it aims at cultivating qualities of moral responsibilities including trust, consent and accountability within Indigenous communities. The concept of collective continuance is one way of thinking about how moral responsibilities play significant roles in contributing to social resilience. Understanding education in this way can be used to address some of the major issues affecting Indigenous peoples everywhere, including environmental justice, gender justice and the resurgence of traditions.

K. P. Whyte (✉)
Michigan State University, East Lansing, MI, USA
e-mail: kwhyte@msu.edu

Keywords

Environmental justice · Indigenous knowledge · land education · place-based education · Indigenous ecology

Introduction

I'm going to share some of my personal reflections on the purpose of Indigenous environmental education from my perspective as a Potawatomi person, relative, scholar, and activist currently living in the Great Lakes region in Turtle Island/North America. This essay is an expression of my perspective and exercise of my rather recent memories and not a research essay. I write from the concern that much is at stake in Indigenous environmental education since so many of our peoples face rampant pollution, food insecurity, biodiversity loss, reckless land and energy development, "natural" disasters, and risky climate change impacts. Brigitte Evering and Dan Longboat claim these environmental issues "disrupt relationships with land" and "community sustainability" (Evering and Longboat 2013, 242), threatening Indigenous health, cultural integrity, political sovereignty, economic vitality, and overall wellness. Some of my reflections will take the form of brief anecdotes from my professional and nonprofessional experiences, though the details will be anonymized since I'm giving opinions on my personal memories instead of aspiring to generalizable knowledge claims from research. The anecdotes are supposed to be illustrative, and I hope they are helpful to the readers. My sense is that people who also work in related contexts will recognize the issues I'm trying to highlight.

I'll begin in this essay with a broad discussion of Indigenous environmentalism and then move on to reflect on education more closely.

Indigenous Environmentalism

Indigenous peoples in North America lead some of the most profound environmental movements in the world. As part of its long engagement in anti-colonial resistance, the Standing Rock Sioux Tribe led a major mass movement to attempt to stop the construction of the Dakota Access pipeline. Diverse Indigenous conservationists, such as Sophia Rabliauskas of the Poplar River First Nation or the late Isidro Baldenegro Lopez of the Tarahumara people, have worked to protect millions of acres of critical forest ecosystems from risks including logging and hydropower. The Village of Kivalina filed a lawsuit in the US against the energy industry, including ExxonMobil Corp., for climate change damages. The Black Mesa Water Coalition has worked for years on environmental justice issues related to water quality, drinking water, and mining in the Navajo and Hopi Nations and has advocated for transitioning to clean, renewable energy. The voices and actions of Indigenous advocates in the Americas have impacted environmental issues globally, including the voices Winona LaDuke, Rodrigo Tot, Ailton Krenak, Gail Small, the late Berta

Caceres, Tarcila Rivera Zea, Sheila Watt-Cloutier, and Tom Goldtooth, among many others.

It's not surprising that Indigenous peoples are compelled to address environmental problems. North American Indigenous peoples often have living intellectual traditions and heritages that center what many people today now refer to as resilience and sustainability. Mayan and Aztec peoples have ancient institutions of astronomy, calendars, and historical record keeping that seek to guide societal preparation to anticipate and respond to seasonal change and interannual trends (Kidwell 2004). Diverse Anishinaabe and Algonquin peoples, among many other North American groups, have long legacies of seasonal round economies, cultures, and political organizations, where societal institutions are designed to best suit the changing dynamics of ecosystems (Benton-Banai 2008; Witgen 2011; Child 2012). Pacific Coast groups, including Nuu-cha-Nulth peoples, have ceremonies such as give-aways (potlatch ceremonies) that motivate nonselfish behavior for the sake of environmental conservation and food security/sovereignty (Trosper 2002; Atleo 2006; Atleo 2002). Yet, in the last five centuries, Indigenous peoples in North America have suffered the advancement of capitalism, industrialization, and colonialism sanctioned by nations like Canada, Mexico, and the US. These forms of domination have rendered many groups vulnerable to new environmental problems caused by military invasion and technology use, extractive industries (including monocrop agriculture and forestry), land and water dispossession and forced geographic displacement, and laws and policies that banned ceremonies and divested Indigenous children of their languages and knowledges. Heather Davis and Zoe Todd call the impact of colonialism, industrialization, and capitalism ecologically "seismic" (Davis and Todd 2017); Larry Gross calls it "apocalyptic" (Gross 2016).

I seek to do what I can to exercise my responsibilities to support Indigenous planning, research, and advocacy on environmental issues. A lot of what I try to do involves collaborating with Indigenous leaders, communities, scholars, scientists, and governments to achieve two outcomes: addressing environmental harms and risks arising at the interface of colonialism, capitalism, and ecological change; strengthening the role of living Indigenous traditions and heritages of sustainability and resilience in guiding and framing our actions. I've worked especially in the Great Lakes on both US and Canada sides, but also, though less intensively, beyond the region. Most people who are involved in similar endeavors can likely attest to the diversity of activities, including development of Tribal planning processes, historical research on environmental traditions and practices, participation in ceremony, support for frontline advocacy, reform of law and policy, and communication through writing, tweeting, Facebooking, and engaging other media. In my job as a professor, I've tried to build awareness of Indigenous intellectual traditions of resilience and sustainability in higher education, Indigenous expectations for good collaboration and allyship in environmental and research initiatives, and Indigenous philosophical contributions to the meaning of environmental justice and food sovereignty.

In my own reflections, I've thought of different ways in which to discuss some of the concepts within the broad and highly diverse orbit of Indigenous intellectual traditions and environmental movements. One concept I've thought a lot about is *collective continuance*, which I will tie to Indigenous environmental education at the end of this essay. Collective continuance is the idea that some of the gifts of Indigenous traditions are entire systems of how societies can be organized to be most responsive to different types of change – whether the changes are extreme weather events, intergenerational traumas, seasonal cycles, or military invasions by other societies. Collective continuance is certainly a lot like resilience or sustainability. Yet, Indigenous traditions of collective continuance often focus on how *moral relationships* are significant factors in facilitating how members of a society self-determine their responses to various changes arising from the dynamics of social and ecological systems. Broadly, moral relationships refer to particular types of bonds or affinities. These bonds connect diverse members of a society together, human and nonhuman, through establishing mutual (but not always equal) expectations about how each member ought to treat one another. One of the most important moral relationships in collective continuance is *responsibility*.

Responsibilities can be laden with qualities such as trust, consent, accountability, and reliability. One example of how these qualities work within collective continuance that I'll discuss later is the relationship between Anishinaabe/Neshnabé people and wild rice (Manoomin or Mnomen) that is involved in the seasonal round tradition (I sometimes put the different spellings in English of Ojibwe, Odawa, and Potawatomi languages just to reference *some* of the diversity of accents and English dictionaries.). It's a mutual responsibility in which people and rice are expected do what is in each of their powers to enhance the conditions required for one another to contribute uniquely to the overall wellness of their shared community. The contributions to community wellness are diverse. At one level, they include human and nonhuman nutrition, habitat protection, and safety (such as for fish or birds or for shortages in other food sources). At another level, rice is entangled with stories, educational processes, knowledge keeping practices, giveaway traditions, ceremonial protocols, the vetting of leadership, economic systems, and diplomatic ties that are the fabric of society. So – just focusing on a single slice – someone who is responsible for monitoring rice health must go through an educational process created by their community that can vouch for their trustworthiness as a caretaker; they must also, through ceremonies or giveaways, demonstrate publically their accountability to all their relatives. As knowledge changes over time, the staff of Tribes that use newer scientific instruments to monitor and protect rice, for example, are nonetheless expected to be vetted by elders, work with traditional caretakers, receive guidance from the larger community, and demonstrate their accountability for doing their part to protect the plant's future. Here, what starts as just the idea of humans having responsibility for rice for the sake of nutrition, opens up into an entire universe of qualities of the moral relationship, including trust, accountability, and many more qualities if I were to keep discussing. And I've not even talked about rice's responsibilities to humans – or discussed the many other relationships beyond just rice!

These qualities of the mutual responsibility between humans and rice are, at the same time, aimed at avoiding preventable harms, such as malnutrition or ecological degradation, and promoting the underlying community conditions required for all beings to pursue their life aspirations, including being able to have meaningful spiritual and cultural lives. Concepts of collective continuance, then, are similar to concepts of resilience or even environmental sustainability because of their emphasis on conservation and adaptive capacity. Yet concepts of collective continuance are unique for their emphasis on looking at moral relationships as a vector through which to examine the interrelationships between human and ecological systems. Studies of collective continuance focus on topics such as knowledge systems that privilege accountability between keepers and learners of knowledge, ceremonies that concretize nonselfish norms, consensus-based decision-making processes that uphold consent, empathetic types of consciousness relating to nonhuman beings (e.g., plants) or entities (e.g., water, ecosystems) as having animacy or agency, respecting diversity in areas such as gender identities and leadership attributes, and protecting the support systems needed for people to engage in civil disobedience when circumstances require it. In this way, collective continuance is about the intensified integration of morality with sustainability and resilience.

The reflection I'll focus on most in this essay concerns the connection between collective continuance and the purpose of Indigenous environmental education, though I won't get to that exact topic until the very end.

Indigenous Environmental Education

Environmental education is a significant topic when I think about Indigenous environmental movements, living intellectual traditions and heritages, and concepts I use a lot, like collective continuance. By "environmental education," I simply mean learning activities that focus on deepening the relationships between humans and nonhuman neighbors and systems, which include plants, animals, fishes, insects, ecosystems and habitats, ecological flows, and entities such as water or air, and the earth system. Environmental education is nothing new for us. Related to what I described earlier, Indigenous peoples have diverse and ancient traditions of how teaching and learning are significant for sustaining critical ecological relationships and supporting resilience in response to seasonal and interannual environmental changes. In many traditions, English words such as "human," "nonhuman" and "more-than-human" are unsatisfying translations that, unfortunately, we have to rely on in many contexts. For many Indigenous peoples see humans and nonhumans as kin or relatives to one another who are bound together through reciprocal responsibilities – akin to family – that support their mutual wellness. Some Indigenous persons identify themselves more with nonhuman ancestors, clans, or other beings than with some special human category. In these ways, Indigenous peoples are often less likely to have some privileged category for "human" that denotes a uniquely rational, wise, knowledgeable, or free being or species.

Indigenous scholars who I read have articulated different reasons for why environmental education is critical for us. Leanne Simpson discusses how "...few communities are equipped with the necessary resources to effectively deal with the over-whelming number of environmental issues facing their people and their lands."

Simpson claims that education provides "knowledge [Indigenous persons] can apply to the situations they face in their communities... skills to ensure the cultural survival of their people...[and to] become environmental problem solvers within Aboriginal communities, and Aboriginal political or urban organizations" (Simpson 2002, 14). *Land Education*, a recent book edited by Kate McCoy, Eve Tuck, and Marcia McKenzie, features scholars such as Delores Calderon and Megan Bang, among others. Calderon describes how "Land education requires us to consider Indigenous agency and resistance tied to Indigenous cosmologies" and to "destabilize" colonial ideologies that erase Indigenous relationships to their territories (Calderon 2014, 27). Bang et al. discuss, in their work in Chicago, how Indigenous environmental education works to cultivate "longer views of our communities and our homelands not enclosed by colonial timeframes. . ." and seeks to "center Indigenous epistemologies and ontologies by (re)storying our relationships to Chicago as altered, impacted, yet still, always, Indigenous lands..." (Bang et al. 2014, 3). All of these scholars privilege both a sobering, critical account of the current situations of Indigenous peoples and a call for the important and varied roles Indigenous intellectual traditions can play in response to contemporary challenges.

Indigenous peoples are developing and maintaining diverse types of environmental education. In my own orbit, the Tribe I belong to, the Citizen Potawatomi Nation in Oklahoma, and other related Anishinaabe/Neshnabé peoples in the Great Lakes region, have taken great efforts to create and practice educational programs that maintain or revive our traditional relationships to the environment, including relationships to waters, lands, plants, animals, fishes, insects, and ecosystems taken in their entirety (e.g., wetland regions). These environmental educational programs focus on a range of topics, from birch bark canoe building, to wild rice harvesting, to hunting skills, to corn cultivation, to the respectful harvesting of medicines. The *Match-E-Be-Nash-She-Wish* (Gun Lake) Band of Pottawatomi Indians started the *Jijak* Foundation. The foundation revitalized a summer camp in their territory to support educational programs ranging from maple sugar harvesting to Indigenous food sovereignty gatherings. Sylvia Plain created the Great Lakes Canoe Journey, "a project that envisions bringing together the citizens of the Great Lakes Basin... to celebrate our relationship to the waterways, to each other, and to learn about Anishinaabe canoe culture and canoe building" (Plain 2017).

In Indigenous environmental education, "program" is not really the right term if we take it to suggest some discreet starting and ending point for learning. For much Indigenous education, in my experience, occurs within family, clan, and other kinship networks over many generations. In my earlier work as part of a project Nick Reo developed on Ojibwe subsistence hunting, we found that education in the ethics, skills, and ceremonies of hunting at the Lac du Flambeau Band of Lake Superior Chippewa Indians occurs across family, clan, and other kinship relationships through each hunter's lifetime. Learning and teaching never ended. Over the course of their lifetimes, people invested in education to continually learn how to become better relatives to the animals they hunted and to the family and community members they are responsible for sharing harvests with. One hunter expressed how bad it feels to know that humans can't give their lives to deer – revealing a powerful aspiration toward reciprocity and a sense that human gratitude for deer is never satisfied (Reo and Whyte 2012). When I was showing Reo what I just wrote here, he also told me briefly a related story. In one of his collaborations on Indigenous water ethics, his partners told him it was awkward to hear him refer to their work together as a "project." For "project" seemed to fail to acknowledge the ongoing-ness, long-term relationship-building, and personal commitments that really mattered to his collaborators and motivated them to continue on.

At the same time, most Indigenous communities also feature diverse arrays of "programs" in environmental education that work on timelines similar to classes (3 months long, weekly meetings, and so on). I know many friends who are proficient speakers of Ojibwe, Odawa, or Potawatomi accents or who are skilled black ash basket makers because they attended a combination of classes. Though in many cases, these friends took extra time and effort to learn from elders outside of class settings, relying on community and family relationships to make that learning opportunity possible. These friends will continue to become educators themselves in these areas as a part of their lifetime learning.

Indigenous governments and intergovernmental organizations have invested in other types of environmental education that are aimed at supporting Indigenous persons' advancement in dominant US and Canadian institutions. Tribal colleges and scholarships to nonTribal institutions of higher education often serve to make available training in scientific, legal, policy, and other fields that pertain to careers that address environmental issues. Often graduates of these programs work for their own or other Indigenous governments in departments, offices, or divisions of natural resources and environmental quality. In many cases, Tribal professionals seek guidance from the intellectual and governance traditions of the Tribes they work for (which could be the Tribes they belong to). Jamie Donatuto and Larry Campbell of the Swinomish Tribe, in their roles as staff and Tribal members, have drawn on the Tribe's culture and traditions to understand and educate about community environmental health (Donatuto 2008; Donatuto 2016). Or the College of Menominee Nation developed its Sustainable Development Institute in 1993. The institute came out of the commitment that sustainability has always been part of Menominee life, including "respect for the land, water, and air; partnership with other creatures of earth; and a way of living and working that achieves a balance between use and replenishment of all resources" (Morris 2017).

Indigenous environmental education importantly includes the traditions of collective action that work to achieve social, political, and cultural transformation. Indigenous mobilization to protect water is an example, including the multiple treaty initiatives such as Treaty Rights at Risk (Tribes of Western Washington), the Mother Earth Water Walk, and the NoDAPL (Dakota Access Pipeline) movement (Dhillon and Estes 2016; Treaty Indian Tribes in Western Washington 2011; McGregor 2005). Participants in these mobilizations often don't use "activism" or "protest" to describe what they are doing; rather, they describe themselves as water protectors, water walkers, relatives of water, among other identities and kinship relationships tied to reciprocal responsibilities. They often describe their actions as ceremonies. Melanie Yazzie's work speaks to Indigenous environmental justice activism pertaining to water as the "social life of water," which expresses and enacts a "radical politics of relationality" (Kearns 2017). In the NoDAPL efforts, many Indigenous persons, both from the Standing Rock Sioux Tribe and others, designed camps, performed ceremonies, and engaged in diverse protocols that are uniquely Indigenous traditions of collective action. Indigenous organizations and peoples have longstanding traditions of education in how people can learn to orchestrate and participate in collective action *as* ceremony and protocol and observe norms about who (human or non-human) has responsibilities to communicate (e.g., speak), listen, advise, and represent.

Though I'm not trained, either through Indigenous, US, or other institutions, as an education scholar or specialist, I've endeavored to work in Indigenous environmental education as best I can. So in this essay I can share experiences, but I don't have the depth in the educational literature that a scholar trained in the field would, and hence I can't cite widely from educational scholarship. I've codesigned with dynamic colleagues experiences such as the Indigenous Planning Summer Institute at the College of Menominee Nation Sustainable Development Institute, the Tribal Climate Camp with the Affiliated Tribes of Northwest Indians (hosted by a different Tribe each year), and numerous climate change planning workshops for Tribes in the Great Lakes. I've also trained many hundreds of scientists in Indigenous approaches to collaboration with Tribes on environmental issues. In my practices as an educator, I've engaged traditional education as pertains to climate change, Tribal climate change planning, and the advancement of Indigenous pedagogy in the sciences for promoting ethical intercultural collaboration (though these labels for typecasting Indigenous education are provisional given they can imply false demarcations across highly integrated approaches to educational practices).

In my personal experiences witnessing, being a student in, or organizing Indigenous environmental education, I've come to wonder about what purposes Indigenous environmental education serves.

Indigenous Climate Change Planning

I engage with Indigenous environmental education most often through climate change planning with a number of Tribes in the Great Lakes region. In one part of my work in this area, a collaborator, Mike Dockry, and I, discussed the idea of trying to Indigenize futures planning through facilitating Tribal scenario development on how best to prepare for climate change. We expanded this work with collaborators Chris Caldwell and Marie Schaefer in projects organized by the Sustainable Development Institute at the College of Menominee Nation. Scenario planning involves people imagining plausible and possible futures tied to certain issues they are concerned about, both as individuals and as members of self-governing communities and nations. Scenarios express visions of the future that suggest ideas for how people living today can prepare themselves for the sake of maintaining their capacity to honor their ancestors and support the wellness of their own and future generations. Scenario planning is as much an educational process as it's about planning and governance. People can see scenario planning as a way to raise greater awareness of and increase the practice of the community's own traditional ways of talking about the climate, such as their seasonal round system. Fulfilling this goal involves creating opportunities for bringing different knowledge keepers and learners together at appropriate times and places. People also often want to learn what others, outside of the Tribe, are saying or know about climate change, especially other Indigenous peoples, as both a global phenomenon and a local issue. So scenario planning often involves inviting educators and creating opportunities to learn from the experiences and tools of other Indigenous peoples, universities and non-profits, inter-Tribal organizations, and US or Canadian national or state/provincial agencies. Sometimes people who are members of or work for a particular Tribe may feel like they don't have a venue for sharing their knowledge about climate change or may not see how they can take leadership in climate preparedness that pertains to their duties as members/citizens or employees. In the planning institutes I'm part of that I referenced earlier, a lot of what we discuss collaboratively are the best ways that scenario planning can be used to energize community events, persuade Tribal council, and energize people of all generations to address climate change.

In scenario planning, climate change is a highly integrated topic. Climate change issues, from increasingly severe droughts to warming waters, are at once issues of politics and economics (e.g., treaty rights), health (e.g., dietary changes), culture (maintenance of traditions), and environmental management (e.g., choices about what species to conserve and restore), among many more dimensions. So scenario planning requires addressing all these dimensions together. Yet in the educational work required for scenario planning, what I often find is a central challenge: Tribal staff are really separated from each other, even in rather small communities or nations. So the educational aspect of scenario planning often becomes an exercise in empowering relationships – which goes beyond simply providing information about climate change or providing opportunities to express visions of the future that can persuade Tribal leadership. It's not uncommon, for example, that in different Tribes there are no working relationships across people specializing in areas such as language maintenance/revitalization, health, and environmental management. Each of these areas are divided up into departments or offices that are "silo'd" or "stove-piped" off from each other, so to speak. Working in these offices involves devoting time to meeting specific objectives that are the ones designed by the US government or Tribal program that supports and funds the office. These objectives are often associated with very pressing Tribal needs, such as recording an elderly fluent speaker or addressing diabetes prevention.

At the same time, I find people in each line of work will cite problems due to a lack of integration once we start talking about organizing educational activities for scenario planning. People in Tribal environmental offices sometimes are concerned that they don't get enough community engagement in their work because there is little linguistic, storytelling, or cultural content to public events or meetings or internships they put on; language teachers sometimes say it's hard to teach language without access to the lands, waters, and environmental skillsets that inspired the language in the first place. Or I know of situations where Tribal health professionals and Tribal environmental professionals rarely collaborate, which is ironic given the connections between environmental quality, diet and exercise, and health outcomes, as the body of work of Alice Tarbell and Mary Arquette demonstrates directly (Tarbell and Arquette 2000). I think the mutual solutions are rather clear in theory. The problem, of course, is that US federally recognized Tribes have come to operate using organizational structures heavily influenced by US and Western political traditions, which divvy up issues like health, culture, food, and the environment to separate sectors or departments – reducing them to being matters of "resources," "rights" or "jobs." These traditions are quite different from the organizational traditions derived from Indigenous calendars or seasonal rounds where government integrated together the issues with clear connections, such as language, health, economics, spirituality, politics, and the environment. In these contexts, the scenario planning process is often about how to reestablish integration and find ways to restore qualities of accountability, inclusivity, and reciprocity across people and offices that are unnecessarily kept separate. So the key outcome of the educational part of scenario planning often turns out to be the effort to engender greater qualities, such as accountability, across stove-piped offices that make it possible to address climate change in an integrated fashion. This outcome may seem very far removed from climate change preparedness. But is it that far removed (a rhetorical question)?

The importance of qualities of reciprocity, inclusivity, and accountability are part of other aspects of the educational process in scenario planning. I remember one scenario process in particular as illustrating this point. It was a scenario visioning workshop involving many people involved in subsistence/sustenance hunting and fishing. In this case, many Tribal members who attended placed a lot of emphasis on US recognized treaty rights as protecting their responsibilities to support their families and communities through harvesting relationships with different plants and animals. My collaborators and I thought we had come up with a really good scenario idea to discuss with the attendees: What if 50 years from now the US negates all treaty rights? Given climate change impacts on animal and fish habitats, what would this scenario be like? What would the Tribe do? After we posed the scenario, no one really looked very surprised. Then, someone finally chimed in and said that the Tribe would probably be fine because everyone would just go back to "poaching." For readers not familiar with this context, "poaching" doesn't really refer to illegal harvesting as a solution to climate change. Rather, it turned out that in the many years before the Tribe had relitigated their treaty with the US, people engaged in secretive harvesting. This harvesting was made possible thanks to dense moral relationships with qualities like reciprocity, accountability, and inclusivity across different families and communities.

In a not so far-off era when it was "illegal" to be Indian and exercise treaty rights, these qualities of moral relationships allowed many people to collectively monitor environmental change to stay on top of harvesting trends, train young people, and maintain an orderly network of communication so that harvesters could share with those who needed food the most. The relationships needed for "poaching" are very much ones that could be useful for addressing climate change, and US recognized treaty rights were not, at the time, necessary for people to have and maintain these relationships. Some participants thought that the legal and bureaucratic aspects of US recognized treaty rights have actually led some people to disengage from or forget about the importance of these qualities of moral relationships. The participants then suggested that the scenario planning and educational process should be about recognizing and reempowering these family/community qualities for improving people's knowledge of environmental change (and hence responsiveness to climate change) and creating a sense of environmental stewardship in young people. Again, this scenario workshop seemed to go far afield from the topic of imagining climate change futures. But that's just one way of looking it, as I would argue that the workshop actually got far closer to the heart of climate change than perhaps what was originally intended when we posed the abnegation of treaty rights as a scenario.

In this work on Tribal climate change planning, it has seemed to be that the purpose of Indigenous environmental education is really about empowering qualities of moral relationships.

Indigenous Traditional Environmental Education

Tribal traditions in the Great Lakes related to wild rice, sturgeon, bees, and deer are the types of curricular topics many Tribal members are interested in working on, especially as they are connected to Indigenous languages. For these species' life cycles and peoples' linguistic expressions for them are connected considerably to seasonal and interannual environmental changes. At the same time, the distinctness of traditions is central to many Indigenous peoples' identities in the Great Lakes region and tied to treaty rights, cultural and moral responsibilities, and nutrition and exercise. Plants like wild rice or fish like sturgeon, for example, are charismatic for many Native persons, which make them ideal for attracting people to invest their time to participate and learn about a range of topics, from language to climate change. I've also witnessed or participated in many different traditional educational programs related to environmental skill-building through visiting many different Tribes as part of my climate change and conservation work as well as my everyday desires as a Tribal member wanting to learn more about our history and culture.

In my experience, I see a lot of "traditional" environmental education programs that attempt to faithfully or genuinely maintain or revive traditions. Yet often my experiences are punctuated by my having extremely critical and negative reactions to the ways in which some traditional education activities are designed and implemented. Gender is one of the examples that concerns me most. I've seen in some cases traditional educational activities that privilege male leadership, men's knowledge, and masculine perspectives on the significance of certain traditions and their histories. I have been told that these male roles are unquestionably part of Tribal heritage dating to time immemorial. Often, however, I found through research or talking in depth with elders that such interpretations of history were largely inaccurate or based on hasty reconstructive analyses of the already problematic work of nonIndigenous anthropologists. These experiences remind me of Jennifer Denetdale's body of research on situations in the Navajo Nation. In these situations, she challenges the cogency and accuracy of how "tradition" is used to justify marriage inequality, the exclusion of women from leadership, and other moral issues (Denetdale 2006, 2009).

At times, when I've discussed matters of differing historical interpretation, I was told that even if my view was correct, there was still another reason to organize traditional education this way. I was told that it was important to accommodate what I might call here "hyper or overly-emphasized masculinity" in traditional environmental education to reinvigorate men's sense of having relevant roles in their societies, given the oppression Indigenous men have faced. One example I hear a lot is that historically hunters had to have aggression to effectively carry out that responsibility, so masculine aggression should be accommodated as an outlet for Indigenous men today. Yet, in my interactions with multiple harvesting communities, I don't find male hunters, for example, as needing to invest in a hyper or toxic masculinity or patriarchal mindset or to see aggression as a necessary ingredient for success. In fact, relational qualities – including community accountability and empathy – seemed more to motivate successful hunting, leaving men and boys who are susceptible to adopting patriarchy with many viable alternatives. The alternatives arise from both Indigenous traditions of community-based reciprocal responsibilities but also from practices modeled by men today who practice ethical, liberatory gender identities and norms.

Many Indigenous peoples also see their traditions as involving nonbinary gender systems. In historical work and my discussions with many Anishinaabe/Neshnabé persons, it's the case that persons of diverse genders and ages have long traditions of hunting too, whether performing the actual harvesting or participating collectively in all the activities associated with hunting (e.g., butchering, cleaning, etc.) (See Norrgard 2014; Buffalohead 1983; Child 2012; Sinclair 2016). Even in cases of a few Tribes I know where some members are convinced that something sounding like patriarchy (not just patrilineality) is accurately part of their history, I'm not sure why its maintenance and the normalization of exclusion are morally acceptable aspirations. I couldn't help thinking that there must be a way to maintain and valorize our traditions and ceremonies through education without sanctioning privilege and exclusion. Historically, Indigenous traditions seem to be more about building and maintaining interpersonal trust, high standards of consent, and respect for diversity. In my mind, such cohesion makes it more possible to discuss and address patriarchal and other forms of domination that affect everyone, albeit differently – such as how Indigenous girls and boys are trafficked sexually in areas with extractive industries (e.g., the Bakken) (Deer and Nagle 2017) or the state-sanctioned violence that Indigenous persons experience distinctively in relation to their gender, such as murder, going missing, domestic abuse, police assault, and exploitation.

I've contrasted some of the problems I saw in some cases with traditional education I felt particularly appreciative of. I saw educational programs teaching traditions and ceremonies that claimed that the traditions embraced inclusiveness, trust, consent, empathy, and diversity. I have discussed with collaborator and friend Deborah McGregor how in some of the Great Lakes water walks inspired by the Mother Earth Water Walk, for example, the walkers valorized certain conceptions of

Anishinaabe women's responsibilities to water; at the same time, the walkers were open to all interpretations of environmental responsibilities inclusive of all genders. In my recent work with Sherry Copenace, we have discussed how she teaches coming of age ceremonies in Winnipeg, Manitoba and Kenora, Ontario that allow persons to choose whether to participate in ones oriented toward boys or girls. Someone can choose to do both too (Copenace 2017a). So, for example, learning to be "Anishinaabe" in one's environmental relationships meant learning about a morality that didn't sanction exclusion and privilege, even in cases where some of the teachings may have an initial binary gender orientation for various reasons. Some friends and scholars also point out that these initial binary gender orientations in some traditions are more reflective of a failure of translation from Anishinaabe language and culture to English language and US and Canadian settler culture. Margaret Noodin writes that "Anishinaabe language and culture acknowledge gender difference, but in a way that relies on choice and context rather than fixed and predictable rules" (Noodin 2014, 12). My experiences, and Noodin's sentence quoted here, suggest an important morality that needs to be the focus of traditional environmental education.

In the examples I have given, it's qualities like trust or accountability that are most important as a way of learning about relationships to nonhumans, such as water in the Mother Earth Water Walk. I have followed Tribal sturgeon restoration in the Great Lakes region for some time now. I find many restoration projects to be very powerful expressions of Indigenous traditions. Sturgeon, who have ancient relationships with many Tribes, have been greatly harmed by US and Canadian settlement, from overfishing to dams. But the purpose of Tribal sturgeon restoration is rarely, in my opinion, just about making it possible to add sturgeon back to our regular diets or to be able to practice certain sturgeon ceremonies or customs exactly as our ancestors did. The Little River Band or Ottawa Indians and the Menominee Nation created public ceremonies and community feasts to commemorate the centrality of sturgeon in certain moral relationships. Sturgeon is a trusted and reliable *relative* of people, often called a "grandparent" owing partly to the fish's wisdom and long life. That sturgeon would, as Jay Sam says, "sacrifice" itself for humans, should motivate humans to become aware of how they can be trustworthy and accountable environmental stewards so that sturgeon (an anadromous) fish will return each year (Holtgren et al. 2014). Little River's sturgeon-release ceremony invites the public to attend when juvenile sturgeon are released into the river each fall, exposing many non-Natives to Indigenous histories, culture, and traditional knowledge of sturgeon, as well as sturgeon biology and life cycles and environmental challenges. The Menominee sturgeon feast each spring is also public, bringing Menominee and non-Menominee together for educational and cultural immersion in sturgeon-related history, values, and practices, including dance.

When I talk to Odawa and Menominee attendees, some tell me that they see the ceremony and feasts, which attract hundreds of people, as a chance to commemorate accountability to the fish, to create intercultural conversations about sturgeon science, to heal relationships with settlers through a public discussion of environmental degradation, and to engender responsibilities in future generations. At the Odawa ceremony, many children of all heritages personally release a juvenile sturgeon into the river. The ceremonies and feasts bring people together to strengthen moral qualities, in this case accountability, but also trust, consent, and reciprocity. They seek to not only rebuild the social fabric of Indigenous peoples, but also to repair the conflicting relationships with settler and other non-Indigenous populations in the region. Winona LaDuke, writing on the restoration of sturgeon at White Earth, has expressed hope that "Maybe the fish will help a diverse set of people work together to make something right. . … The fish help us remember all of those relations, and in their own way, help us recover ourselves" (LaDuke 1999). To me, in sturgeon restoration, Indigenous environmental education is not really about *the* human and *the* fish; rather, it is about invigorating in today's times and for the future moral relationships through which all beings respect one another based on their interlocking responsibilities and their unique contributions and agencies (Whyte 2018).

Here, again, this time with Indigenous traditional environmental education, it seems the purpose has to do with empowering qualities of our mutual responsibilities to one another.

Collective Continuance

In my experiences with education, when I contrasted examples that I appreciated with ones I was uncomfortable with, I began forming conclusions that the difference involved the presence or absence of certain qualities of our mutual responsibilities to other humans, nonhumans, and the environment. Qualities here refer to properties of relationships that make it possible for the discharge of the contributions associated with the relationships to have wide societal and environmental impacts - whether impacts are understood as outcomes (e.g. clean water) or protection of ethical norms (e.g. self-determination). So, for example, the responsibility (i.e. the particular type of relationship) to teach others how to harvest appropriately (a responsibility both to other humans and to plants and animals) will have an important impact if teachers are trustworthy, if they are inclusive of difference and refrain from exclusionary practices, if students can consent to their own learning by being able to ask questions and engage in dialogue, and if learning involves practices that build a sense of community accountability among diverse humans and nonhumans – among other examples of qualities. When I thought more about our traditions, I realized that their importance is not that they are "ancient" or "the way it's always been." Rather, they are stories or guides for understanding the moral fabric of our peoples that is woven with these qualities of trust, empathy, consent, and many others. Consider a tradition like wild ricing, now in more detail.

Many Anishinaabe/Neshnabé peoples have spiritual connections to wild ricing going back to their origin stories that involve a migration in which a white shell instructed them to stop at the place where food grows on water. Education about wild ricing can be about learning the exact techniques for monitoring rice beds, harvesting rice, parching, organizing ceremonies that feature wild rice in different ways, and so on. At another level, wild rice traditions involve much more. They are about how to design and organize societal institutions to be consensual, accountable, reciprocal, trustworthy, empathic, and respectful of secrecy (what I call diplomacy). Wild rice is not actually important just because of its historic connection to Anishinaabe people. If we look more closely at different practices of wild ricing, historically and across different communities today, we see that over time ricing facilitated critical qualities of responsibilities.

One quality is trust. Community members trusted the persons and clans vested with authority and knowledge. Consent is another quality. Anishinaabe ricing involves the opportunity to consent to the leadership through ceremonial and vetting processes that people had to pass through to be acknowledged as leaders or experts. These leaders or experts were accountable to the communities. Trust and consent worked to solidify gender equality and fluidity. Resilience (or redundancy) is another quality. Ricing developed as a highly redundant practice as people are motivated to monitor many rice lakes, making ricing resilient in cases of environmental change. The harvesting camps and protocols facilitate the creation of many knowers of rice habitats, not just a few people who end up being overtaxed with working on behalf of entire communities. Diplomacy is another quality, where it refers to the desire to engage with people without divulging secrets. Families, clans, and Tribal groups formed close relationships to avoid trespass but also to ensure restorative justice occurred when someone wrongfully or accidentally used the rice bed that another family depended on. Societies with high degrees of trust, consent, diplomacy, and redundancy, among many other qualities, have the moral fabric to work together in good times and bad times and the relationships across humans and nonhumans that support the developing and maintenance of important environmental knowledge. For at least these reasons, I would speculate that societies with high degrees of these qualities of responsibilities can best respond to environmental and social changes.

A range of scholars point out that there was a period in early twentieth century history in which Ojibwe men began to participate more in wild ricing, berry harvesting, and other activities that previously were led by women. Evidence indicates that this gender shift occurred as the plant was commodified for sale to nonnative consumers and access to land dwindled due to US colonialism (Vennum 1988; Norrgard 2014; Child 2012). Critically, there are at least two interpretations of this type of change. The first interpretation is that this may have been an instance of undermining women's leadership, respect, and expertise, which is a historic and ongoing violence of US colonialism. The US deliberately undermined women's roles as diplomats and knowledge holders (Sleeper-Smith 2005). A second interpretation, which also bears out in some accounts of the transition, is that the ancestors who made these decisions perhaps felt strongly that gender roles could shift fluidly at different times because trust and consent flourished to a sufficient degree. So the shifts wouldn't have facilitated, at least at that time, the emergence of patriarchy. While, depending on the particular community or time period, this interpretation could simply not be true, I invoke it here to illustrate the importance of how a society – in the case that strong moral relationships and qualities of responsibilities are maintained in the face of adversity – can allow certain shifts in traditions to occur ethically for the sake of protecting the wellness of future generations. If the shift worked in this way, it would keep open the possibility that women would be able to return to the involvement with rice that they once had and be acknowledged for their continued leadership in ricing, often behind the scenes, while under great duress and hardship.

My analysis here is not just backward looking. Indeed, it's the moral relationships with rice that have supported Anishinaabe leadership in responding to pressing environmental issues in the Great Lakes, including mining, commercial agriculture and genetic modification of plants, irresponsible recreational activities, oil and gas pipelines, and fracking. The Chippewa Tribe of Minnesota, with sponsoring partners such as the University of Minnesota, hosts a biannual conference called the *Nibi & Manoomin Symposium* that works to educate non-Indigenous persons, the state, academic institutions, and corporations about the moral qualities of wild rice. Last year's conference was titled "Accountable Relationships." The work of the Indigenous Environmental Network, the Great Lakes Indian Fish and Wildlife Commission, the Mother Earth Water Walk, Honor the Earth, and many Tribal governments have stood up against threats to water quality and wild rice habitats in the name of the moral relationships bound up with water and rice. The current Indigenous resistance to the Enbridge Line 3 pipeline is an example of how the significance of moral relationships today supports direct action against environmental hazards. While today Tribes use new types of science and new governance instruments (e.g., US treaties, state laws, federal programs, Tribal economic revenues) to protect rice and the environment, it is again those ancient qualities of responsibilities to wild rice that continue to motivate these major conservation and environmental justice endeavors.

When I reflect on wild rice and many other examples, like sturgeon or "poaching," I get the sense that the fabric of our societies are woven of qualities of responsibilities that protect our potential to live good lives, allow us the options to change without compromising trust and consent, and motivate us to resist domination. Sherry Copenace has discussed with me how *bimaadiziwin*, or the good life, really refers to the capacity of a society or Tribal nation to do the best within the circumstances its members happen to be facing (Copenace 2017b). I have tried to approximate this way of thinking in my reflections on *collective continuance*, which I discussed at the beginning. Again, collective continuance is the idea that certain qualities of moral relationships, like consent or trust, are crucial for supporting our societies' capacities to respond and adapt to changes we face. When we think of our traditions, each of these clans, committees, decision-making processes, ceremonies, and so on ensured that people trusted those vested with authority, consented to leadership, protected valuable knowledge, and promoted inclusivity and diversity. Traditions are not techniques only in the sense of a skill or even a hobby. They are moral relationships that guide how society is organized socially, culturally, politically, and ecologically. The moral relationships are valuable historically for at least two reasons when thinking more specifically about human interactions with the environment. First, they represented systems that were attuned to, and had reciprocal feedback loops, for particular types of ecosystems. Second, they also facilitated adaptation to more extreme changes, such as US colonialism, making it possible for many Native people to have survived some of the worst domination any group of people can endure. Both reasons can be actualized today too and into the future, though the forms and practices are and will be different. An entire legacy of philosophy and practice that connects moral relationships to institutional orders is perhaps one of the greatest gifts our ancestors gave us. They gifted us an entire intellectual tradition unfolding over many hundreds of years, where we can study and discuss how moral relationships with qualities of accountability, trust, consent, reciprocity, respectful diplomacy, and many others are built into our societies' political organizations, cultures, religions, social norms, and economies.

Education for Collective Continuance

Anishinaabe studies scholars often write about many examples of what I am calling collective continuance, including concepts of transmotion, migration, seasonality, and transformation. I interpret this in the diverse work by Brenda Child, Gerald Vizenor, Heidi Stark, Niigaan Sinclair, Scott Lyons, Deborah McGregor, John Borrows, Megan Bang, Kim Blaeser, Mike Dockry, Robin Kimmerer, among many others. I read a lot of this work as showing, in varied ways, how it's qualities of mutual responsibilities that ought to be the focus of what we do as Anishinaabe peoples today. Education, say, on how to harvest and distribute wild rice, should be just as much about the techniques as it's about, say, how to organize a wild rice committee that is trustworthy, inclusive, mutually accountable, and consensual. Reading a recent introduction by Joanne Barker to the book she edited, *Critically Sovereign*, she quotes Leanne Simpson to make important connections between "ethical values" and how we interpret traditional teaching or education. In *Dancing on Our Turtle's Back*, Simpson challenges static concepts of traditions based on "rigidity and fundamentalism," arguing instead for the importance of "self-actualization, the suspension of judgement, fluidity, emergence, careful deliberation, and an embodied respect for diversity" (Barker 2017, 25; Simpson 2011, 25). For me, reading this, I see these moral relationships as ones that can create better learning environments that support philosophies of ethical and just institutional design and philosophies that motivate direct action to address forms of domination that can tear our peoples part, including patriarchy, economic exploitation, and the US and Canadian desires to erase our cultures, histories, diversity, and political self-determination.

Indigenous studies scholars have widely identified moral relationships as significant for guiding how Indigenous peoples respond to power and domination. Sarah Deer shows how the renewal of traditional restorative justice as a response to sexual violence in Indigenous communities must protect against the tendency for Indigenous men to internalize settler hetero-patriarchal values that distance them from being accountable to their communities (Deer 2009). Mishuana Goeman discusses how diverse Indigenous persons appealed to their ethics of community accountability, even outside of their traditional forms, when they reorganized themselves in urban centers in response to the US twentieth century Indian relocation policy

(Goeman 2009). Dian Million supports the quality of inclusivity as a significant ethic of Indigenous women's social justice work and activism (Million 2013). Megan Bang's work on science education shows how it's precisely reciprocal responsibilities rich in moral qualities between human and nonhuman worlds that are missing in STEM education for children (Bang 2018). Each of these scholars offers qualities of responsibilities – including accountability, consent, trust, reciprocal responsibly, and others – as guiding solutions for the continuance of our diverse peoples, at the same time they trenchantly critique sexism, racism, classism, and other forms of domination.

For my own referential purposes, I think of this orbit of thought as offering diverse concepts of collective continuance. Concepts of collective continuance highlight how particular qualities of moral relationships are valuable to us for how they are organized systematically to support the capacity of our peoples to respond effectively to changes that we can't control. Adaptive capacity, of course, is *not* – at least to me – about turning the other cheek to the on-the-ground violence imposed by systems of structural domination, such as settler colonialism. The adaptive capacity of collective continuance does not require us to sacrifice the importance of anti-violent activism, public ceremony, and radical critique of settler colonial domination for the sake of institution building or the need to make internal reforms within our communities. For example, I heard widely from different persons how the *Mni Wiconi* (*water is life*) philosophy expressed by Standing Rock Tribal members and embraced by Indigenous peoples globally has a number of values. It honors Lakota and Dakota traditions of ethical relationships with water *as a relative*, motivates radical resistance to extractive industries, and recommends alternative designs for institution building that protect genuine consent, build trustworthiness, and embrace gender equality and fluidity. While the philosophy articulates these goals, *Mni Wiconi* is importantly about environmental sustainability, resilience, and conservation too (see Dhillon and Estes 2016 for many of the views I have heard).

In Indigenous studies, I read much scholarship as enriching our understanding of morality and continuance: "Survivance" (Gerald Vizenor), "*naw'qinwixw*" (Jeanette Armstrong), "muskrat theories" (Megan Bang), "fish pluralities" (Zoe Todd), "Native feminism's spatial practice" (Mishuana Goeman), "grounded normativity" (Glen Coulthard), "land education" (Eve Tuck, Marcia McKenzie, Kate McCoy), "radical politics of relationality" (Melanie Yazzie), "resurgence" (Leanne Simpson), "polity of the Indigenous" (Joanne Barker), "Indigenous legal orders" (John Borrows and Val Napoleon), "an open sense of place" (Soren Larsen and Jay Johnson), and many others too numerous to cite here (Vizenor 2008; Armstrong 2007; Bang et al. 2014; Todd 2014; Goeman 2009; Coulthard 2014; Tuck et al. 2014; Kearns 2017; Simpson 2016; Barker 2017; Napoleon 2013; Borrows 2002; Larsen and Johnson 2012). While I tend to interpret these forms of scholarship as concepts of collective continuance, their contributions arise from their own intellectual and community orbits beyond what I can discuss or further analyze here. Indigenous environmental education *for* collective continuance refers to education designed to immerse us in our traditions of qualities *of moral relationships across generations*. From trustworthiness to inclusivity, these moral relationships are critical to the flourishing of our societies in the face of conditions of constant domination. The moral relationships that make up collective continuance support our capacity to grow connections to particular places *and* to adjust ethically and critically when our lives migrate to different places or when we encounter less familiar circumstances. Concepts of collective continuance honor our histories and the resurgence of our traditions. At the same time, these concepts support what is – on my view – perhaps the best tradition of Anishinaabe and other Indigenous peoples: critical reflection and thoughtfully designed institution building. The collective continuance of our peoples must involve the coordination of a diverse range of actions, including radical activism and the politics of refusal (Simpson 2014) against settler colonialism, but also Indigenous planning, diplomacy, internal reform of our governments and self-criticism.

For Indigenous environmental education, then, one purpose is learning – in diverse, inclusive and generationally appropriate ways – about how to maintain and transform moral relationships within and across our peoples for the sake of our collective continuance. Indigenous environmental education must be at the forefront of pedagogy that makes crucial connections across moral qualities and environmental issues that matter to our peoples. It must be able to connect concepts and issues together, *such as* consent, patriarchy, *water is life* and environmental justice, *or* community accountability and trust, gender politics, hunting, and treaty rights – among many more necessary connections.

References

Armstrong J (2007) Native perspectives on sustainability: Jeannette Armstrong (Syilx) [Interview transcript]. Native Perspectives on Sustainability. www.nativeperspectives.net

Atleo ER (2002) Discourses in and about the clayoquot sound: a first nations perspective. In: Magnusson W, Shaw K (eds) A political space: reading the global through clayoquot sound. Montreal, MQUP

Atleo MR (2006) The ancient Nuu-chah-nulth strategy of hahuulthi: education for indigenous cultural survivance. Int J Environ Cult Econ Soc Sustain 2(1):153–162

Bang M, Curley L, Kessel A, Marin A, Suzukovich ES III, Strack G (2014) Muskrat theories, tobacco in the streets, and living Chicago as indigenous land. Environ Educ Res 20(1):37–55

Bang, M (2018) Faculty Website, University of Washington. https://education.uw.edu/people/faculty/mbang 3 Accessed 4-22-2018

Barker J (2017) Critically sovereign: indigenous gender, sexuality, and feminist studies. Duke University Press, Durham

Benton-Banai E (2008) Anishinaabe almanac: living through the seasons. Kenjgewin Teg Educational Institute, Ontario

Borrows J (2002) Recovering Canada: the resurgence of indigenous law. University of Toronto Press

Buffalohead PK (1983) Farmers warriors traders: a fresh look at Ojibway women. Minn Hist 48(6):236–244

Calderon D (2014) Speaking back to manifest destinies: a land education-based approach to critical curriculum inquiry. Environ Educ Res 20(1):24–36

Child BJ (2012) Holding our world together: Ojibwe women and the survival of community. Penguin, New York

Copenace S (2017a) Ayaangwaamiziwin. In: Paper presented at the panel & conversation on religion, philosophy, theology & the anthropocene at Michigan State, East Lansing, MI, October 18

Copenace S (2017b) Personal discussion, July 7, 2017

Coulthard GS (2014) Red skin, white masks: rejecting the colonial politics of recognition. University of Minnesota Press, Minneapolis

Davis H, Todd Z (2017) On the importance of a date, or, decolonizing the anthropocene. ACME 16(4):761–780

Deer S (2009) Decolonizing rape law: a native feminist synthesis of safety and sovereignty. Wicazo Sa Review 24(2):149–167

Deer S, Nagle MK (2017) The rapidly increasing extraction of oil, and native women, in north Dakota. The Federal Lawyer, pp 35–37

Denetdale J (2006) Chairmen, presidents, and princesses: the Navajo Nation, gender, and the politics of tradition. Wicazo Sa Review 21(1):9–28

Denetdale J (2009) Securing Navajo national boundaries: war, patriotism, tradition, and the Diné Marriage Act of 2005. Wicazo Sa Review 24(2):131–148

Dhillon J, Estes N (2016) Introduction: standing rock, #NoDAPL, and Mni Wiconi. Hot Spots, Cultural Anthropology, https://culanth.org/fieldsights/1007-introduction-standing-rock-nodapl-and-mni-wiconi

Donatuto J (2008) When seafood feeds the spirit yet poisons the body: developing health indicators for risk assessment in a native American fishing community. University of British Columbia, Vancouver

Donatuto, Jamie, Larry Campbell, Robin Gregory (2016) Developing responsive indicators of indigenous community health. Int J Environ Res Public Health 3(9):899–915

Evering B, Longboat DR (2013) An introduction to indigenous environmental studies. In: Contemporary studies in environmental and indigenous pedagogies. Springer, New York, NY, USA pp 241–257

Goeman M (2009) Notes toward a native feminism's spatial practice. Wicazo Sa Review 24(2):169–187

Gross LW (2016) Anishinaabe ways of knowing and being. Routledge, New York

Holtgren M, Ogren S, Whyte KP (2014) Renewing relatives: nmé stewardship in a shared watershed. In: Tales of hope and caution in environmental justice https://hfe-observatories.org/stories/. Accessed March 10, 2018

Kearns F (2017) Water is life, relationality, and tribal sovereignty: an interview with Melanie Yazzie. In: The Confluence, vol 2017. University of California, Riverside

Kidwell CS (2004) Native American systems of knowledge. In: A companion to American Indian history. Blackwell, Malden, pp 87–102

LaDuke W (1999) Return of the sturgeon: namewag bi-azhegiiwewaad. News from Indian Country, August 31

Larsen SC, Johnson JT (2012) Toward an open sense of place: phenomenology, affinity, and the question of being. Ann Assoc Am Geogr 102.3:632–646

McGregor D (2005) Traditional ecological knowledge: an anishnabe woman's perspective. Atlantis 29(2):103–109

Million D (2013) Therapeutic nations: healing in an age of indigenous human rights. University of Arizona Press, Tucson

Morris D (2017) Letter from the President. http://www.menominee.edu/About_CMN.aspx?id=1233. Accessed 1 Dec 2017

Napoleon V (2013) Thinking about Indigenous legal orders. In: Dialogues on human rights and legal pluralism. Springer, Dordrecht, pp 229–245

Noodin M (2014) Bawaajimo: a dialect of dreams in Anishinaabe language and literature. Michigan State University Press, East Lansing

Norrgard C (2014) Seasons of change: labor, treaty rights, and Ojibwe nationhood. UNC Press Books, Chapel Hill

Plain S (2017) Great Lakes Canoe Journey https://www.youtube.com/watch?v=Ewmc_4cMo_U. Accessed 23 Jan 2018

Reo N, Whyte K (2012) Hunting and morality as elements of traditional ecological knowledge. Hum Ecol 40(1):15–27. https://doi.org/10.1007/s10745-011-9448-1

Simpson L (2002) Indigenous environmental education for cultural survival. Canadian Journal of Environmental Education (CJEE) 7.1:13–25

Simpson L (2011) Dancing on our turtle's back: stories of Nishnaabeg re-creation, resurgence and a new emergence. Arbeiter Ring Publishing, Winnipeg

Simpson, Audra (2014) Mohawk interruptus: Political life across the borders of settler states. Durham, NC, USA. Duke University Press, Durham, NC, USA

Simpson L (2016) Indigenous resurgence and co-resistance. Critical Ethnic Studies 2(2):19–34

Sinclair N (2016) Returning to ourselves: two-spirit futures and the now. In Nicholson H (ed), Love beyond the body, space & time: an indigenous LGBT sci-fi anthology. Bedside Press, Winnipeg, ON, Canada, pp 12–19

Sleeper-Smith S (2005) [A]n unpleasant transaction on this frontier: challenging female autonomy and authority at Michilimackinac. J Early Republic 25(3):417–443

Tarbell A, Arquette M (2000) Akwesasne: a native American community's resistance to cultural and environmental damage. In: Hofrichter R (ed) Reclaiming the environmental debate: the politics of health in a toxic culture. MIT Press, Cambridge

Todd Z (2014) Fish pluralities: human-animal relations and sites of engagement in Paulatuuq, Arctic Canada. Etudes/Inuit/Studies 38(1–2):217–238

Treaty Indian Tribes in Western Washington (2011) Treaty rights at risk: ongoing habitat loss, the decline of the salmon resource, and recommendations for change. Northwest Indian Fisheries Commission (NWIFC), Olympia

Trosper RL (2002) Northwest coast indigenous institutions that supported resilience and sustainability. Ecol Econ 41:329–344

Vennum T (1988) Wild rice and the Ojibway people. Minnesota Historical Society Press, St Paul

Vizenor G (ed) (2008) Survivance: narratives of native presence. University of Nebraska Press, Lincoln

Whyte KP (2018) Critical investigations of resilience: a brief introduction to indigenous environmental studies & sciences. *Daedalus: Journal of the American Academy of Arts and Sciences 147*(2):136–147

Witgen M (2011) An infinity of nations: how the native new world shaped early North America. University of Pennsylvania Press, Philadelphia

Indigenous Family Engagement: Strong Families, Strong Nations

41

Megan Bang, C. Montaño Nolan, and N. McDaid-Morgan

Contents

Introduction	790
Historical Overview of Family Engagement Research	792
The Rise of Family Engagement Policy	793
Refusing Settler-Colonial Enclosure	794
Racism, Invisibility, and Exclusion	794
Tokenism and Inclusion	796
False Decision-Making: Railroading and Rubber Stamping	797
Resurgence in the Everydayness of Families	798
Renewing and Remembering Roles, Relations, and Responsibilities with Lands, Waters, and More-than-Humans	799
Renewing and Remembering Relationships Across the Life Span	800
Reimagining Relationships with Non-Indigenous Educators and Systems	804
Impacts of Indigenous Family Engagement on Academic Outcomes	804
Implications and Conclusions	806
References	807

Abstract

In this chapter we argue for amplifying and renewing Indigenous family leadership and engagement in systems of education that aim to support Indigenous communities' resurgence. Families are the heart of Indigenous nations and communities. For many Indigenous people and communities, families include all of our relations – reflecting multiple generations, extended family, other community members, more-than-humans, and the lands and waters of our

---

M. Bang (✉)
Northwestern University, Evanston, IL, USA
e-mail: mbang3@uw.edu; mbang3@u.washington.edu

C. Montaño Nolan · N. McDaid-Morgan
College of Education, University of Washington, Seattle, WA, USA
e-mail: nolanc3@uw.edu; nikkimcm@uw.edu

© Springer Nature Singapore Pte Ltd. 2019
E. A. McKinley, L. T. Smith (eds.), *Handbook of Indigenous Education*,
https://doi.org/10.1007/978-981-10-3899-0_74

homes. While forms of everyday resistance and resurgence are enacted by Indigenous families and communities, systems of education for Indigenous children and youth often remain sites of trauma, assault, and aims of Indigenous erasures. Much work has been done by Indigenous scholars and allies to challenge hegemonic and settler colonial agendas in education and to assert Indigenous families and communities as changemakers reshaping education toward thriving Indigenous futures. This chapter synthesizes across literature on Indigenous family engagement to argue for (1) the need for continued assertions of Indigenous families' and communities' ways of knowing and being; (2) engaging Indigenous families and communities as dreamers, nation-builders, and future elders; and (3) engaging promising strategies for reimagining and cultivating family-community-school relationships.

Keywords
Indigenous education · Indigenous families · Family engagement · School-community partnerships · Settler-colonialism · Indigenous resurgence

Introduction

Families are the heart of Indigenous nations and communities. For many Indigenous people and communities, families include all of our relations – reflecting multiple generations, extended family, other community members, more-than-humans, and the lands and waters of our homes. Indigenous familial relationships have a wide geography and reflect Indigenous knowledge systems as they unfold in everydayness (Corntassel and Scow 2017). Families are the archetype for Indigenous nations and often reflect a complex web of interdependence between all things. Families are the primary contexts in which Indigenous children learn who they are, Indigenous ways of knowing, and what is expected of them as they become adults and eventually become good elders. In this way, the strength and well-being of Indigenous families are fundamental to the strength and well-being of Indigenous nations. Given this perspective, we suggest the everydayness of Indigenous families' lives is perhaps the sites in which the most radical and hopeful possibilities for Indigenous resurgence and futures can and do unfold (Simpson 2011; Corntassel and Scow 2017).

While the centrality of Indigenous families to Indigenous nationhood may seem straightforward enough, it also is the reason that settler-colonial nation-states have routinely created and enacted policies across generations intended to dismantle, disrupt, or assimilate Indigenous peoples through forced changes in familial structures and relations (e.g., Muir and Bohr 2014; Sarche and Whitesell 2012). Although the well-known insidious strategies like forced attendance to boarding schools have subsided, policies intended to intervene in and reshape familial relationships continue to be widespread. Examples include compulsory attendance laws, high rates of foster care, legal guardianship instead of kinship, and age segregation in classrooms, among others. Additionally, forced removal from traditional homelands, policies that restrict access to land and water to engage in traditional harvesting and hunting practices, or legislation preventing Indigenous spiritual practices have intended to sever human relationships with land, waters, and more-than-humans – relations central to Indigenous families. These impacts on movement and activity are further entrenched by the curricular aims of much of schooling. Mainstream curriculum and pedagogy contributes to and perpetuates settler-colonial narratives of Indigenous erasure, conquest, and dispossession (e.g., Calderon 2014; Grande 2004; Shear et al. 2015; Tuck and Gaztambide-Fernández 2013).

Evolving from this history, Indigenous family engagement and leadership in schools is again a focus in policy and practice wherein family engagement in schools is being mandated, measured, and resourced to reflect particular stances and goals. While this is true across the globe to a great extent, in this piece we will primarily focus on dynamics connected to the United States in which family engagement paradigms largely remain a one-size-fits-all assimilative demand modeled after White, middle-class forms of engagement and practices. However, there has been a swell of research on Indigenous family engagement from Indigenous peoples across the earth that can provide important resistance to and redirection of dominant family engagement strategies that perpetuate settler-colonial aims and histories. Our goal in this piece is to articulate a framework – rooted in a critical review of the literature – for Indigenous family leadership in systems of education that cultivate cultural and intellectual vibrancy and contribute to Indigenous collective well-being. As Indigenous and mixed-race mothers of children in US schools, former classroom educators in pre K-12 settings, and as scholars of education, we [authors] recognize that our histories and experiences shape our analysis of the literature and our hopes and dreams for our family and community well-being and the kinds of roles we might play in family leadership and educational transformation. A challenge for us is always to both dream and contribute to birthing resurgences and Indigenous futures – an elsewhere to the current settler-colonial forms and systems of education – as well as to account for the here-and-now enclosures. It is our hope that the stories, analyses, and recommendations here resonate with Indigenous families globally and contribute to heterogeneous and locally nuanced forms of family leadership and engagement that contribute to Indigenous well-being and educational justice.

We begin our review by situating mainstream family engagement as a research-policy-practice field within a broader settler-colonial agenda. Here we unpack mainstream constructions of family engagement and how it impacts Indigenous families today. Secondly, we explicate several dimensions of enclosure that Indigenous families face when attempting to transform schools and systems. This section is divided into three main findings: (1) racism, invisibility, and exclusion of Indigenous families in school, (2) tokenism and inclusion toward Whiteness in transactional family engagement paradigms, and (3) inauthentic decision-making processes based on onboarding to school agendas and fostering compliance. By explicitly naming these enclosures, we hope to highlight the difference between assimilative forms of family engagement and the promising forms of Indigenous resurgence enacted by families in the everyday. In the third section, we explicitly focus on promising practices and everyday resurgence in families and beyond. In this section we highlight four main facets of family engagement that contribute to Indigenous resurgence: (1) learning from and with our lands, waters, and more-than-humans is integral to Indigenous family engagement, (2) multigenerational and lifelong learning are integral to Indigenous education and therefore foundational for Indigenous family engagement, (3) relationships and collaboration with non-Indigenous educators and systems need new forms of partnership that recognize and cultivate everyday Indigenous resurgence; and (4) equitable and transformative collaboration with families leads to rigorous academics and higher achievement for Indigenous students. Broadly, our findings call for the need for continued assertions of Indigenous families' and communities' ways of knowing and being to combat colonial enclosures. Beyond these forms of resistance, we also find the need to open imaginative and creative spaces in which Indigenous families and communities are engaged as dreamers, nation-builders, and future elders. Finally we suggest schools and other educational institutions need to develop new forms of family-community-school partnerships.

Historical Overview of Family Engagement Research

Since the 1960s, parent involvement and family engagement have been explicitly articulated as broad sweeping reform efforts to improve education (Ishimaru et al. 2016). Normative parent involvement literature suggests that increasing parent engagement increases the educational attainment of students (e.g., Epstein 1987; Epstein and Sheldon 2002; Henderson and Mapp 2002). Much of this research, however, focuses on particular practices that are normative to White, middle-class families. These include volunteerism, fundraising, and practicing "school" at home by reading or helping with homework, among others. Power, race, language, and gender are implicated in much of this work but are often silent. In the late 1990s and early 2000s, the rhetoric and policy impacts of parent involvement and family engagement began to address the particular "challenges" of engaging racially and ethnically distinct populations. For example, handbooks on parent involvement were published with chapters pertaining to different racial groups, including "Native" parents (e.g., Berger 2000; Butterfield and Pepper 1991; Redding et al. 2011).

Specific to Indigenous families, the Indian Nations at Risk Task Force (INART), a division of the Department of Education in Washington, D.C., published a landmark report in 1991 on the state of US parent involvement in education and appropriate strategies for ensuring American Indian and Alaska Native (AI/AN) parental participation in schools (Butterfield and Pepper 1991). This report reviewed 100 citations relevant to parent involvement and AI/AN education, including hearings and public testimonies. Like many reports of the time, it included a set of barriers to participation including unwelcoming school climates, differences between home and school cultures, and parental behaviors that may hinder participation such as alcohol abuse, dysfunction, and violence. Unlike many parent involvement handbooks of the time, the INART report critically examined the role schools played in harming Indigenous communities through boarding schools and removal of children from families and recognized how this history contributes both to the skepticism of AI/AN parents toward educational systems and to systemic health and economic disparities (Butterfield and Pepper 1991). Recommendations from this report tended to propose culturally responsive adaptations to normative practices for AI/AN families but had not yet started to address differences in knowledge systems or to question purposes of family engagement in education.

Within the broader field of parent involvement and family engagement, critical race scholars were also calling attention to deficit constructions and assimilative demands, as well as their consequences, of parent involvement paradigms (e.g., Delgado and Stefancic 2000; Howard and Navarro 2016; Ladson-Billings and Tate 1995; Solorzano 1998). For example, in a persuasive handbook chapter, Baquedano-López et al. (2013) detail the deleterious ways that parents of color are forced to either assimilate to normative schooling *and child-rearing* practices or be labeled as deficient parents. The consequences of these choices on parents of color impact not only educational opportunities for children and youth but often impact familial and community abilities to organize themselves in culturally appropriate and sustaining ways. Furthermore, while critical race scholars have paid careful attention to the classed, gendered, and racialized rhetoric and practices that figure centrally in parent involvement and family engagement, they do not consider the ways that settler-colonialism and the dispossession of Indigenous peoples from their homelands also figures centrally into education and family engagement. Indigenous families and communities continue to be positioned into having to choose between either participating as compliance officers for schools enacting settler-colonial agendas or being positioned as deficient, deviant, or uncaring. Indeed this choice is reflective of a long-standing paradigm in which generations of Indigenous children were removed from their families and placed in foster care. While the Indian Child Welfare Act is designed to stop the removal of Native children from Native families, Native children remain significantly overrepresented in the foster care system reflecting the ongoing disruption to thriving Indigenous families (e.g., White 2017). The characterizations and perceptions of school systems with respect to child-rearing are a critical factor in this ongoing dynamic.

The Rise of Family Engagement Policy

Family engagement is becoming increasingly scaled and mandated through legislation in North America. For example, within the United States, the Every Student Succeeds Act [ESSA] requires Title 1 schools (those serving low-income students), including Bureau of Indian Education (BIE) schools, to have a *written* family engagement policy and to enact it (NCLB 2002; Henderson 2016). This includes funding for family engagement outreach and programs of at least 1% of Title 1 funds received by the district. Schools are required to seek family input on how those funds will be used to support family engagement and evaluate the efficacy of those programs and practices.

These policies arise amid a preponderance of "gap gazing" (Gutiérrez 2008) research that focuses on the disparities and barriers facing students and families of color, including Indigenous families. Couched in this ever-increasing demand for high-stakes accountability and measures to combat the "achievement gap" is a push for normalizing White and middle-class epistemologies as the standard upon which to measure Indigenous students (Gutiérrez 2008; Villegas 2009) and families. These standards promote individuality, meritocracy, capitalism, and consumerism as desirable outcomes of education that perpetuate settler-colonial logics of land as a material resource and assimilation as progress (Villegas 2009). Federal policy and school adoption of family engagement has been shaped by settler notions of family, success, and education; however, because decisions about family engagement and funding are left to individual schools, we think there is potential to shape everyday implementation toward Indigenous futurity.

Through our analysis of the literature, we argue that Indigenous family leadership in schools requires attending to the political dimensions of how family engagement is framed, legislated, funded, and enacted as well as to the everyday resurgence of Indigenous families that contribute to the lived experiences and wellness of our families, communities, and nations. So far we have attended to the political enclosures and opportunities happening at national scales. In the next section, we highlight the enclosures faced by Indigenous families routinely in and by schools.

Refusing Settler-Colonial Enclosure

Equitable and transformative partnerships between schools, families, and communities require collaboration and shared decision-making practices. This means enacting reciprocal relationships between stakeholders where families and community members are seen as teachers with perspectives that matter (Murphy and Pushor 2004). Unfortunately, the literature we reviewed was rife with examples where settler paradigms slipped into and enclosed (Richardson 2011) even the most well-intentioned family engagement models (e.g., Lipka 1986). In this section we explicate some of the enclosures typical across the literature including racism, tokenism, and railroading.

Racism, Invisibility, and Exclusion

Racism and stereotypes about Indigenous families are common challenges found in the literature we reviewed that spanned across time and places (e.g., Butterfield and Pepper 1991; Coleman-Dimon 2000; Davis 1988; Herzog et al. 2016; Kaomea 2012). In interactions with non-Indigenous educators and school systems, Indigenous families and students face low expectations (Kaomea 2012), stereotypes about cultural practices and beliefs (Kaomea 2012; Lea et al. 2011; Robinson-Zañartu and Majel-Dixon 1996), and systemic barriers to participation in schools (Friedel 1999). In one of the very few large-scale quantitative studies with

Indigenous families, 234 families representing 55 tribes were surveyed about their satisfaction with and perceived efficacy of public, BIE, and tribal schools in the United States. Resoundingly, families expressed their frustration with public and BIE schools, citing disrespect of Indigenous families and a deep concern over the lack of presence of Indigenous cultures in their children's formal educational experiences (Robinson-Zañartu and Majel-Dixon 1996). Tribal schools were viewed more favorably except in the area of special education. When this study was replicated 10 years later, results had not changed (Herzog et al. 2016). Many of the participants made comments that the administrators or teachers did not, in fact, want Native parent involvement (Herzog et al. 2016; Robinson-Zañartu and Majel-Dixon 1996). This form of exclusion occurs regularly for Indigenous families, particularly when they do not participate in school-sanctioned ways (e.g., compliance). Friedel (1999) writes:

> Public schools, like residential schools, tend to remain closed to Native parents; they continue to exist as isolated 'islands' outside the community. Where residential schools might be viewed as cultural invasion, perhaps public schools can be seen as 'cultural occupation.' In both cases parents remain on the outside looking in. (p. 142)

In addition to overt racism and exclusion, Indigenous families and students face invisibility within schooling curricula and pedagogy (Hare 2012; Garcia 2014; Kaomea 2012). This invisibility perpetuates non-Indigenous educator perceptions of Indigenous parents as having deficient parenting skills and a lack of interest in children's education. However, there has been excellent research that examines and contrasts family and community-based practices with those of schools to demonstrate the problem is not about deficiency or interest but one of visibility. For example, Hare (2012) studied the family literacy practices in five Anishinaabe Head Start centers in Canada and compared them to school literacy practices. She notes that oral history, being on the land, and engaging in ceremony all contribute to the developing literacy practices of Indigenous children that shape how they see and make sense of the world. In particular, Hare argues that reading and renewing relationships with land are important literacy practices of Indigenous communities that are most often overlooked when schools assess the capabilities of Indigenous students and families. She writes:

> Young indigenous children learn to interpret their environment and understand the significance of place, territory and landscape through land-based pedagogies, which emphasize stories, specific teachings, observation and experiential learning. They are 'reading their world' and, in doing so, learning their histories, ideologies and identities. (p. 407)

In this compelling example, family practices and land-based education practices that support Indigenous children's learning and identity development are both missing and invisible in formal schooling practices. Further, we suggest that these practices and forms of learning are reflective of Indigenous knowledge systems. While educators may not explicitly subscribe to western supremacy and assimilation, dynamics of erasure and invisibility are nonetheless reflective of these historicized dynamics and create school contexts that enact forms of ontological and epistemological violence (e.g., Moreton-Robinson 2011; Marker 2006). However, it is also critical to note that these dynamics do not lead to practices and solutions defined by unexamined forms of multicultural inclusion.

Tokenism and Inclusion

Overwhelmingly, the literature demonstrated that non-Indigenous educators and administrators often lack an understanding of the history of schooling with respect to Indigenous communities or the ways in which schools continue to be shaped by and reflect settler-colonial agendas. Further, much of the literature demonstrated that educators are rarely adequately prepared to engage Indigenous learners in culturally responsive ways (e.g., Castagno and Brayboy 2008). This phenomena has been explored broadly but also with respect to Indigenous knowledge systems (e.g., Barnhardt and Kawagley 2005; Battiste 2002; Deloria and Wildcat 2001), Indigenous science (e.g., Cajete 2000), and literacy education (e.g., Archibald 2008; Freire 1970) among other specific foci. This is uniquely consequential in urban areas where not only are educators ill-prepared to support Indigenous students but Indigenous students may also find themselves socially isolated in dominant-majority classrooms and communities left to navigate racialized dynamics without a peer group (e.g., Johnston-Goodstar and VeLure Roholt 2017).

To remedy this, many schools are turning to community partners to aid in the cultural education of students by establishing cultural nights or bringing in speakers for school-wide assemblies or classroom activities. Sometimes families are brought in for focus groups or listening sessions where they are asked to share their experiences and opinions with administrators or educators (Friedel 1999). While these might be genuine efforts to include families in schools, cultural knowledge and practices are still positioned as extracurricular or peripheral to daily teaching and learning and have not had significant impact on increasing familial belonging nor do they reflect a foundational shift in paradigms which are in service of Indigenous thriving. Indeed Bequette (2009) and Friedel (1999) caution against asking elders, artisans, and other knowledge holders to volunteer their time and expertise, particularly if it is done so as a one-time participation without the intent of sustained or long-lasting partnership as this form of ad hoc, flat, representational inclusion can be deleterious to developing true collaboration. Further, these one-off inclusions tokenize Indigenous families and ways of knowing as non-Indigenous educators "position Indigenous knowledge holders (e.g., Elders, storytellers) as 'special guests' rather than foundational" and "non-Indigenous teachers are [then] tasked to rework the curriculum to make it more relevant to Indigenous students' cultures" (Madden et al. 2013 p. 219). These forms of inclusion are typically framed by unexamined multicultural perspectives that are largely shaped in response to Whiteness and often fail to move the ground from assumptions of western epistemic supremacy and tokenized representational discourses toward epistemic heterogeneity (Richardson and Villenas 2000). Such forms of inclusion often do not open spaces to create relevant and sustaining learning environments with Indigenous families and community members as leading and empowered decision-makers, thus as Indigenous scholars have long argued are ultimately counterproductive for Indigenous sovereignty and futurities (e.g., Deloria 1971; Vizenor 1989).

False Decision-Making: Railroading and Rubber Stamping

Unfortunately, many family engagement strategies reinforce power and decision-making with school officials and educators rather than engage in broader community deliberation and decision-making that transforms historically saturated power structures (López et al. 2016). Frequently schools will elevate and tokenize individual families to "rubber stamp" initiatives that schools deem important – initiatives that are frequently driven by the imperatives of Whiteness and settler-colonialism (Richardson and Villenas 2000). While there have been some increased efforts for schools to listen to the stories and experiences of Indigenous families, decisions about if and how to utilize those stories and knowledges remain with schools (Murphy and Pushor 2004; Coleman-Dimon 2000). Even when decision-making processes are in place, they are often politically charged spaces where power and privilege manifest and can contribute to within community tensions (e.g., Young 2011). Sharing her own experiences as a parent in a Native program in Alberta and as a researcher, Friedel (1999) describes how non-Aboriginal staff and administrators in the district continually undermined and prevented the decision-making and implementation of the Aboriginal parent advisory group that oversaw the Native program. She writes:

> Instead of being involved in planning and executing the educational program at Sprucewood School as was outlined in the recommendations that were approved by school board trustees, parents are kept busy trying to cope with everyday problems at the school. And they continue to deal with these alone instead of with the help of the Aboriginal community as was proposed in the recommendations. (p. 151)

Collaborating with Indigenous families in order to center and honor Indigenous knowledges and practices in schools is paramount to the educational success of students; however, doing so without first acknowledging the historical legacy of settler-colonial education on Indigenous communities allows for erasure of such history and enclosure of decolonial possibilities (Lipka 1986). Further, engaging Indigenous families in western forms of decision-making processes (e.g., hierarchical decision-making that reinforces the status quo) will not contribute to extensive transformations. Indigenous forms of deliberation, diplomacy, and decision-making as collective processes that attend to here-and-now urgency as well as being accountable to past and future possibilities and enclosures (e.g., Corntassel and Scow 2017; Whyte 2017) offer new pathways for family leadership and engagement.

Resurgence in the Everydayness of Families

Everyday enactments of Indigeneity and processes of decolonization and renewal matter for the wellness and strength of Indigenous nations, and they are pragmatic and empowering for families. In spite of the clear racism, tokenism, and assimilative imperatives inflicted on Indigenous families, there are also promising new practices and models for family engagement that *begin with* Indigenous families as the foundation for healing and education. Importantly, as we reviewed literature, we noted that there was a marked shift in scholarship which focused on family well-being and cultural resurgence. This scholarship also tended to have a marked difference in the methodological approach and sensibilities – more specifically it utilized Indigenous methodologies (e.g., Smith 2013). Increasingly scholars seem to be recognizing historicity in approaches to Indigenous family engagement and working to engage Indigenous families as nation-builders and changemakers in educational reform. In short, they often articulated pathways of Indigenous resurgence that begins and continues with families. While protecting and evolving treaty rights and other legal expressions of Indigenous sovereignty will remain critical, an important emergent edge in this work is to focus, support, and understand resurgence in the everyday forms of practice in family life (Corntassel and Scow 2017). From this perspective, the vitality and growth of everyday resurgence in Indigenous families across our communities is what will continue to grow our sovereignty and nationhood.

Focusing on everydayness through analysis of family roles, relations, and responsibilities is a promising strategy. Corntassel and Scow (2017) did just this through an analysis of Indigenous fatherhood and articulated four dimensions of everydayness to attend to including relationality, convergences of time and place, politics of intimate settings, and gender relationships. Corntassel and Scow (2017) argue that much of the resurgence literature takes up the political and legislative stances of nationhood and sovereignty, and also importantly there is opportunity to explore the processes of resurgence in intimate settings. They argue that "the processes that Indigenous peoples assert for self-determination are just as important as the results of that struggle" (p. 56). Central to resurgence is living relationality which they define as the web of interconnected human and more-than-human relations and responsibilities that define us as Indigenous peoples. In connecting relationality to Indigenous resurgence, they write: "by examining lived relational aspects of being and becoming Indigenous, we effectively subvert universal generalizations and localize struggles for family resurgence and personal decolonization" (p. 58). For example, the authors turn to their own roles, relationships, and responsibilities as fathers and "other-fathers" to examine the intimate acts of fathering that contribute to the well-being and wholeness of children, families, and through this nations. Reflecting on these roles also demands attention to decolonizing gender constructions and gendered relationships. Corntassel and Scow's (2017) suggest many of the gendered roles and politics expected of families are based on colonial forms of gendered binaries that do not often reflect or respect traditional practices, particularly for two-spirit, queer, and trans identifying Indigenous peoples. As the authors put it, "After all, community 'traditions' are constantly changing and evolving. Even our community notions of complementarity in terms of gender roles need to be rethought and considered from queer or two-spirited perspectives" (p. 63). As mothers, daughters, aunties, cousins, and women, we are continually working through our desires and expectations of roles, relations, and responsibilities as well and those projected on to us. Further, we are always also working to renew our relations across roles which can and often do include resisting and refusing powered dynamics defined by colonialism.

Working from our own felt theories (Million 2009) – that is the things we know and feel that we may not always have the words for but sometimes the songs for – we are learning to move and act in our everyday lives with relentless critical awareness (e.g., Mignolo and Tlostanova 2006; Mignolo 2011) and decolonization on the one hand and on the other an unwavering reach for well-being, love, fierce grace, and strength that enflesh Indigenous ways of knowing and being in the here-and-now. Through focusing on the everyday, we can more intentionally refuse (e.g., Tuck and Yang 2014) the ways in which ongoing colonization and neoliberalism invade and try to restructure our daily lives but also refuse living in the negation or shadow of settler-colonialism. Many Indigenous scholars have long called for not only a focus on the content of our practices but perhaps even more importantly on enacting the processes by which our knowledges and ways of being have come to be. Deloria (2001) in discussing Indigenous learning states "we should be concerned with re-creating the conditions within which this learning occurred, not merely the content of the practice itself (pp. 58–59)." From this perspective, the everydayness of our families is critical site of re-creating the conditions for learning for children and families but also those that propel our resurgence.

Corntassel and Scow (2017) identify renewal and remembering as two key daily acts that are subtle yet powerful in their ability to transform relationships and potentially systems. Renewal refers to the daily interactions that strengthen our relationships and model how we are to be as Indigenous peoples: "They help us focus on the things that matter" (p. 62). Remembering refers to intentional acts of knowing the histories and relationalities of our peoples, lands, and waters in order to "enact our deepest love" (p. 63). One of the authors, Mick Scow, says that for him remembering includes returning with his family to their homelands and relations, but it also means building new relations with people and lands and waters where he now lives. These moments in everydayness and the ways they unfold can also be important convergences of time and place. They argue that attending to everydayness allows us to see and (re)act to the here-and-now as well as keep in view the past and present manifestations of possibility and enclosure. We suggest this longer-term and nonlinear view of time and place opens up new landscapes for decolonization and refusal of settler paradigms of child-rearing and separation from land.

Renewing and Remembering Roles, Relations, and Responsibilities with Lands, Waters, and More-than-Humans

Renewing and remembering includes our relations with lands and waters and is critically missing from family engagement policy and practice in the United States.

Reading the land has always demanded complexity and attention to time scales beyond human scales and forms of deliberation that support complex ecological decision-making (e.g., Whyte 2018). However, learning to read the land is itself a complex and lifelong teaching and learning process that happens in Indigenous families' and communities' daily interactions (e.g., Marin and Bang accepted; Bang et al. 2014; Hare 2012). While a review of land-based education (e.g., Simpson 2014; Tuck et al. 2014), which is focused on Indigenous learning as emergent from our relations and practices with lands, waters, and more-than-human relatives, is beyond the scope of this paper, we would be profoundly remiss to not acknowledge that this growing body of work has important implications for family engagement. In our review, we found very little literature explicitly articulating this nexus between land-based education and family engagement – at least with respect to schooling contexts. This absence is loud and in our view reflective of the dominant paradigm of centering schools and the west – not renewing and remembering our roles, relations, and responsibilities in the everyday. Increasing work that engages land-based perspectives and Indigenous family engagement could be an important area of development.

Renewing and Remembering Relationships Across the Life Span

Educational institutions have evolved to be predicated on age segregation. While this is in part because of the way neoliberalism constructs labor markets, it is also reflective of a particular view of learning and child development. These forces restructure roles, relationships, and how we enact our responsibilities to one another. These changes in interaction have had significant impacts not only at macroscales but also at micro-interactional levels that have shifted how children learn and participate in everyday activities (e.g., Rogoff 2014; Alcalá et al. 2014; Mejia-Arauz et al. 2018). An important aspect of everyday resurgence is working to remember and renew relationships across the life span and engagement in intergenerational learning. Such forms of learning carry significant implications for the ways in which institutions are structured. While we think there is room for significantly more work in this area, there are two areas of research that we highlight below.

Caregiving relationships in the early years are fundamental to raising and socializing Indigenous children into Indigenous ways of knowing and being. Many scholars contend that the early years of a child's life are foundational for the development of their identities as Indigenous peoples and prepare them to be leaders and members of their nations (e.g., Fleer 2006; Romero-Little 2010; Muir and Bohr 2014). As such, participation in cultural activities in the intimate and public spheres of their lives is essential. For example, Garcia (2014) begins his paper on reimagining school-community relationships with a story of the ceremonies that renew relationships between young people and the community in order to reimagine what formal K-12 school-community partnerships could look like. He writes:

> In [Hopi naming ceremonies] my daughters were shielded from Dawa (sun) for 20 days upon which they were properly introduced after my family — primarily members of the Hoaspoa (roadrunner) clan — came to wash their hair with their Tutsmingwu (white ear of corn representing her mother) and offered a Hopi name. This is one of many initial phases that reaffirms a sense of commitment and a formal acknowledgement of our collective roles and responsibilities as a clan and as an extended family to our children. Though we may perceive this ceremony as one in which we formally introduce our children to the world with many blessings, in many respects it speaks to a larger expectation— that requires each of us to live into the roles of supporting and nurturing our children throughout their lifetime. (p. 61)

Ultimately, Garcia (2014) calls for partnerships with schools that build upon the relationality central to Indigenous families and communities. This means expanding current conceptions of "family" to include the multitude of relationships that make up children's support systems, not just "parents." But it also means providing time and space for Indigenous and non-Indigenous families and educators to (1) recognize and unpack histories of oppression, resilience, and resurgence, (2) collectively identify barriers and opportunities for community-defined wellness, and (3) develop new practices that support cross-generational collaboration. Intentionally planning for time and place to be present in the healing and developing of new relations is necessary for Indigenous resurgence.

These early years also prepare children to enter into formal schooling as learners and thinkers (McWilliams et al. 2011; Romero-Little 2010; Lawrenchuck 1998). While there is a plethora of research that posits early childhood centers are assimilative and colonizing spaces for Indigenous children (e.g., Pérez and Saavedra 2017), there is also a demand for high quality and culturally sustaining care for children whose parents choose to work outside of the home. While, these centers need to prepare children to navigate mainstream educational systems as they enter K-12 schooling (Romero-Little 2010), a key need is for the development of learning environments in which this preparation is not detrimental to children learning their own ways. Positioning children to learn and develop expertise in Indigenous ways of knowing and being in opposition to academic success on western terms is a social construction shaped by historicized conquest narratives and claims to singular epistemic paradigms. Human beings have the capacity to speak multiple languages, make meaning in multiple ways, and navigate across multiple contexts. Developing learning environments that can accomplish such forms of life will require collaboration between Indigenous families and early childhood centers (both Indigenous and non-Indigenous) to collectively design and implement pedagogy and practices that support young children's development as whole and healthy Indigenous people. This is no small task, yet there are now multiple models for integrating Indigenous family leadership in the design and implementation of early childhood programming (e.g., Hubbs-Tait et al. 2005).

For example, Romero-Little (2010), in studying Cochiti Pueblo and Jemez Pueblo resurgence, contends that families are actively combating colonial pressures of assimilation through ownership of Head Start centers on the reservations. These communities are laying the grounds for both renewing and remembering traditional socialization practices and preparing young children for western forms of education by being a part of the planning and implementation of learning in the Head Start centers. This includes daily commitments to speaking the language in homes and creating language nests in early childhood learning centers where children spend most of their day.

Recognizing the need to address high rates of poverty and mental and physical health issues, many models of early childhood learning also integrate other social services to support families (Kaomea 2012; Lawrenchuck 1998; McWilliams et al. 2011). These often include training for families on effective and culturally appropriate child-rearing strategies. As Muir and Bohr (2014) put it, "Colonialism, residential schools, racism, and poverty have marked family relationships in a multitude of destructive ways that are only beginning to be understood" (p. 68). A key challenge for many social programs, including early childcare, will be to reimagine programs so that they offer safe spaces for intergenerational healing and learning of traditional practices rather than enclosing family trainings that definitize and assimilate Indigenous families into Whiteness. Furthermore, there is a need for more explicit attention to gender norms, roles, and expectations within the current literature.

Multigenerational and community learnings are key aspects to Indigenous pedagogy and ways of knowing and being. Indigenous children learn from not only those in their family but also from elders and other adults and children in community. We also recognize that the burgeoning field of Indigenous studies affords us intellectual relationships with Indigenous knowledge holders globally through scholarship and research. In addition to caregiving as a multigenerational learning and teaching process, we also found two distinct ways of connecting youth and elders within communities reflected in the literature: through youth-driven community engagement and school-based collaboration with elders and artisans to develop and implement curriculum and pedagogy.

> Indigenous youth will be at the forefront in sustaining our Indigenous communities and they will no doubt be faced with the responsibility of navigating socio-cultural, environmental, political and economic issues while simultaneously preserving their Indigenous knowledge systems. (Shirley 2017, p. 164)

As expressed in the quote above, many scholars recognize the importance of Indigenous youth leadership in education and research (e.g., Shirley 2017; Tuck 2015). And many programs now exist that allow for youth-driven design and implementation of Indigenous-specific programming. Castagno and Brayboy (2008) provide a synthesis of key principles for culturally responsive schooling for Indigenous youth. One of these principles is that "schooling must be connected to student lives, engaging, and collaborative to be effective and culturally responsive for Indigenous youth" (p. 979). This requires explicit connections between learning opportunities and community wellness such that youth can visibly see the impact of their learning and leadership within their communities (Castagno and Brayboy 2008; Lee 2007). This also requires long-term collaborations between elders, artisans, and community members to collectively design and implement culturally responsive curricula and pedagogy (e.g., Bequette 2009; Lipka et al. 2005, Madden et al. 2013; Murphy and Pushor 2004; Zeegers 2011).

Community-based education models (CBEM) are one way Indigenous communities are addressing this need for holistic and meaningful learning for Indigenous students (e.g., May 1999). For example, Lee (2007) provides a case study of a New Mexican CBEM secondary school aiming to transform western educational systems to be more culturally relevant to their community by utilizing field-based, hands-on, and Indigenous pedagogies. As part of the program, math, science, and tribal governance lessons occurred in the afternoons in Pueblo communities. Lee (2007) describes:

> [S]tudents had immediate and in-depth interaction with community members and environmental issues that affected the communities over the course of an academic year. Thus the community sites became the learning environments through the involvement of community members as partners and mentors and resulted in lasting benefits for both students and communities. (p. 201)

Integral to the success of this program was the weaving together of multiple forms of pedagogy and knowledge. Teachers in the school worked intimately with Pueblo environmental administrators and leadership to generate important themes for curricular design. "The school developed the specifics of the curriculum organized around these thematic issues so that the field experiences and classroom learning supported and complemented one another" (Lee 2007, p. 202). Students also took leadership in their own learning to seek out knowledge holders about treaty rights impacting water and land relations in the community. This collaboration between teachers, Pueblo administrators, community members, and youth demonstrates that multiple forms of expertise, experience, and activity are necessary to develop rich and meaningful learning opportunities that engage real-world problems. Beyond programming *for* Indigenous youth, providing opportunities for youth to meaningfully engage in and make decisions about their own education is paramount to cultivating their leadership and analytic skills, both of which are critical for addressing twenty-first century demands.

Extending these findings, we argue that collaboration between schools, families, and community also builds resilience and adaptive capacity, thereby contributing to Indigenous collective continuance (Whyte 2018). Resilience and adaptive capacity here refer to the ability of a community to "maintain its members' cultural integrity, health, economic vitality, and political order into the future and avoid having its members experience preventable harms" (p. 355). We believe that explicit attention to onto-epistemic navigation practices that prepare youth for living in increasingly diverse and mobile communities also support collective continuance (e.g., Bang and Medin 2010; Shirley 2017). Onto-epistemic navigation is necessary to work through current local and global problems while maintaining Indigenous knowledges and ways of knowing. For Shirley (2017) this requires not only teaching students their histories from Indigenous perspectives but also helping them navigate the emotions that come up through the learning process. Teachers have to engage both the heart and the mind to help Indigenous youth heal as they examine the ongoing traumas

Indigenous people experience through helping them make change in the present and future. In order to contribute to everyday resurgences, collaborations between schools and families will likely require a commitment to everyday forms of Indigenous learning, predicated on the relationality between multiple generations of community members.

Reimagining Relationships with Non-Indigenous Educators and Systems

Respectful and reciprocal relationships are foundational for cultivating the types of long-term collaborations necessary for Indigenous resurgence. There needs to be increased efforts at preparing Indigenous educators to work with Indigenous and non-Indigenous learners. However, currently most Indigenous children will encounter predominately White women in formal schooling. The views of these educators about Indigenous children, families, and communities shape not only their practice and interaction with students but also the success of any collaborative effort. When non-Indigenous educators lack historicity and hold deficit views, Indigenous families are more likely to refuse engagement (Lipka 1986), instead opting for protective and proactive strategies at home. However, we also see possibility in the construction of new forms of engagement that work toward Indigenous resurgence. Many authors recognize the need to build non-Indigenous educator capacity to work with Indigenous families as well as their ethical commitments to Indigenous communities' well-being. Building trusting and collaborative relationships requires critical reflection and ongoing renewal of relationships. For example, racism, exclusion, and railroading are still common barriers faced by Indigenous families in school contexts. Explicitly and intentionally addressing deficit assumptions about Indigenous families is required before partnerships can be formed (Kaomea 2012). This includes recognizing and honoring the history of colonialism and resurgence of Indigenous peoples globally as well as the particular histories of the families non-Indigenous educators are working with. Another way to address deficit assumptions is home-visiting, where educators engage families in their homes and in community events to learn more about the students and families they work with (Lowe and Bubb-Conner 2014; Murphy and Pushor 2004). This flips the family engagement paradigm so that it is non-Indigenous educators who go to community, rather than families going to school. Further, it disallows a view of Indigenous families as unengaged or uncaring.

Impacts of Indigenous Family Engagement on Academic Outcomes

Academic outcomes based in western knowledge systems do not need to be antithetical to Indigenous futurity. Indeed navigation of international diplomacy and resisting problematic policy means that our peoples will need forms of expertise in knowledge systems outside of our own. Within the family engagement literature we reviewed, there was a simultaneous denouncement of the rise of standardization and accountability to Whiteness and also the commitment to academically rigorous learning and achievement. It is clear from our review that educational attainment should be considered successful when Indigenous children and communities are healthy and thriving (Akee and Yazzie-Mintz 2011). As we saw in the above findings, this includes meaningful learning opportunities that also contribute to Indigenous community well-being and continuance of knowledge and language.

There is now robust research to demonstrate that young people who are deeply connected to their peoples, lands, and waters are also more likely to be resilient in formal education (LaFramboise et al. 2006; McMahon et al. 2013) and more likely to pursue and persist in higher education (Akee and Yazzie-Mintz 2011; Guillory and Wolverton 2008). In an examination of the disparity between US White and Indigenous attainment of higher education, Akee and Yazzie-Mintz (2011) surveyed the experiences of 62 college graduates, representing 44 tribal nations. Specifically, they asked graduates for the familial and cultural experiences that most hindered or contributed to the completion of their degree. Authors found that all respondents had some exposure to Indigenous history and culture in their schooling and most engaged routinely in Indigenous practices and ceremony. For example, authors found that 30% of respondents learned their Native language in school, and 75% spent time with elders. Akee and Yazzie-Mintz contend that these experiences contributed to the success of Indigenous scholars. They write:

> Our results... indicate that individuals who were more exposed to indigenous cultural activities were less likely to take a break between high school and college. Additionally, we found that the more exposure a student had to Native cultural activities as a child, the more likely they were to attend a large Research I university. (p. 136)

Creating opportunities for young people to engage regularly with Indigenous cultural practices and in their language supports academic achievement, rather than hinders it. When young people have regular opportunities to recognize their own histories, practices, and languages within school-based education, they are more likely to develop discipline-specific identities that contribute to their resilience and creativity in schools.

In conclusion, Indigenous family and community engagement practices should consider four principles highlighted throughout the chapter: (1) learning from and with our lands, waters, and more-than-humans is integral to Indigenous family engagement, (2) multigenerational and lifelong learning are integral to Indigenous education and therefore foundational for Indigenous family engagement, (3) relationships and collaboration with non-Indigenous educators and systems need new forms of partnership that recognize and cultivate everyday Indigenous resurgence, and (4) equitable and transformative collaboration with families leads to rigorous academics and higher achievement for Indigenous students. In practice, this requires that educators, administrators, and policy-makers collaborate with Indigenous families in ways that support the inclusion of Indigenous ways of knowing and being in curricula and resist settler-colonial enclosures toward Indigenous resurgence.

Implications and Conclusions

We have argued that attending to and intentionally engaging the everyday in Indigenous families contributes to Indigenous well-being, resurgence, and nationhood. Importantly according to Corntassel and Scow (2017), it is important to resist romanticization of traditional responsibilities and practices. The process of renewal will take many forms, particularly across urban and intertribal contexts as Indigenous peoples envision and enact solidarities that work toward collective and individual determination and wellness. However there are several key sensibilities in Indigenous family engagement efforts that we rearticulate.

Critical historicity is a necessary foundation for collaboration and education with Indigenous families. Recognizing the global historical legacy of settler-colonialism as well as the local ways schools and Indigenous families have interacted is necessary research for all formal and informal educators working with Indigenous families. This could include talking with local elders and knowledge holders, visiting cultural centers, and online research. It is important to seek out not only the history of colonialism and oppression but to search for resistance and resurgence in your local communities.

Partnerships require reciprocity, respect, and the development of politicized trust. Trust, reciprocity, and respect are foundational aspects of long-term partnerships (e.g., Vakil et al. 2016). Generative partnerships with Indigenous families and communities require explicit recognition that multicultural forms of inclusion blind to Indigenous sovereignty perpetuate colonialism. Indigenous family and community engagement policies were not created to lead to any revolutionary change. In fact, some would posit that they merely shift the blame from structural inequities that governments and societies maintain to Indigenous parents and families. Educators, administrators, and policy-makers must critically consider whom family and community engagement policies and practices are meant to benefit and whether or not these actions are fulfilling their purpose and toward what ends. Indigenous family and community engagement should support Indigenous peoples' self-determination and nation-building. They should build adaptive capacities, visibilize Indigenous resilience, and bolster Indigenous resurgence. The opportunity is to contribute to Indigenous resurgence by contributing to multiple forms of activity and participation.

Non-Indigenous educators and administrators must self-reflect on stereotypical, racist, and privileged assumptions about Indigenous families and how these assumptions have and continue to impact their relationships and interactions with Indigenous students and families. While continuing to challenge assumptions and stereotypes, educators must begin the process of reaching out and serving Indigenous communities in order to build trust. This could take the form of attending cultural events, meeting families on and off campus, visiting homes if families are comfortable with it, and inviting family and community members into the classroom as teachers, collaborators, and decision-makers.

When working with Indigenous families, ensure that your engagement processes and practices reflect a commitment to long-term and sustained collaborations with multiple families and community members. Utilizing a single family or organization repeatedly contributes to tokenism of Indigenous families and perpetuates asymmetrical power relations. Collaboration should position Indigenous families and community members as meaningful decision-makers in order to create culturally resurgent learning experiences throughout the school year.

References

Akee RQ, Yazzie-Mintz T (2011) "Counting experience" among the least counted: the role of cultural and community engagement on educational outcomes for American Indian, Alaska Native, and Native Hawaiian students. Am Indian Cult Res J 35(3):119–150

Alcalá L, Rogoff B, Mejía-Arauz R, Coppens AD, Dexter AL (2014) Children's initiative in contributions to family work in Indigenous-heritage and cosmopolitan communities in Mexico. Hum Dev 57(2–3):96–115

Archibald JA (2008) Indigenous storywork: educating the heart, mind, body, and spirit. UBC press, Vancouver

Bang M, Medin D (2010) Cultural processes in science education: supporting the navigation of multiple epistemologies. Sci Educ 94(6):1008–1026

Bang M, Curley L, Kessel A, Marin A, Suzukovich ES III, Strack G (2014) Muskrat theories, tobacco in the streets, and living Chicago as Indigenous land. Environ Educ Res 20(1):37–55

Baquedano-López P, Alexander RA, Hernandez SJ (2013) Equity issues in parental and community involvement in schools: what teacher educators need to know. Rev Res Educ 37(1):149–182

Barnhardt R, Kawagley A (2005) Indigenous knowledge system and Alaska Native ways of knowing. Anthropol Educ Q 36(1):8–23

Battiste M (2002) Indigenous knowledge and pedagogy in First Nations education: a literature review with recommendations. Indian and Northern Affairs, Ottawa

Bequette JW (2009) Tapping a postcolonial community's cultural capital: empowering Native artists to engage more fully with traditional culture and their children's art education. Vis Arts Res 35(1):76–90

Berger E (2000) Parents as partners in education: families and schools working together, 5th edn. Merrill, Upper Saddle River

Butterfield R, Pepper F (1991) Improving parental participation in elementary and secondary education for American Indian and Alaska Native students. In Indian Nations at Risk Task Force commissioned papers. Department of Education, Washington, DC

Cajete G (2000) Native science: natural laws of interdependence. Clear Light, Santa Fe

Calderon D (2014) Speaking back to manifest destinies: a land education-based approach to critical curriculum inquiry. Environ Educ Res 20(1):24–36

Castagno AE, Brayboy BM (2008) Culturally responsive schooling for Indigenous youth: a review of the literature. Rev Educ Res 78(4):941–993

Colman-Dimon H (2000) Relationships with the school: listening to the voices of a remote Aboriginal community. Aust J Indigen Educ 28(1):34–47

Corntassel J, Scow M (2017) Everyday acts of resurgence: Indigenous approaches to everydayness in fatherhood. New Divers 19(2):55–68

Davis S (1988) Partners at school: a handbook on how to involve Indian and Metis parents in school activities. Retrieved from https://eric.ed.gov/?id=ED382364

Delgado R, Stefancic J (2000) Critical race theory: the cutting edge, 2nd edn. Temple University Press, Philadelphia

Deloria V (1971) Of utmost good faith. Straight Arrow Books, San Francisco

Deloria V Jr. (2001) Traditional technology. In Deloria V Jr., Wildcat D. (eds). Power and Place: Indian Education in America. Fulcrum Resources, Golden.

Deloria V, Wildcat D (2001) Power and place: Indian education in America. Fulcrum, Golden

Epstein JL (1987) Parent involvement: what research says to administrators. Educ Urban Soc 19(2):119–136

Epstein JL, Sheldon SB (2002) Present and accounted for: improving student attendance through family and community involvement. J Educ Res 95(5):308–318

Fleer M (2006) Troubling cultural fault lines: some Indigenous Australian families' perspectives on the landscape of early childhood education. Mind Cult Act 13(3):191–204

Freire (1970) Pedagogy of the oppressed. Continuum, New York

Friedel TL (1999) The role of Aboriginal parents in public education: barriers to change in an urban setting. Can J Nativ Educ 23(2):139–158

Garcia J (2014) Re-examining Indigenous conceptualizations of family and community involvement. J Fam Divers Educ 1(1):58–74

Grande S (2004) Red pedagogy: Native American social and political thought. Oxford Rowman & Littlefield Publishers, Lanham

Guillory RM, Wolverton M (2008) It's about family: Native American student persistence in higher education. J High Educ 79(1):58–87

Gutiérrez R (2008) A "gap-gazing" fetish in mathematics education? Problematizing research on the achievement gap. J Res Math Educ 39(4):357–364

Hare J (2012) "They tell a story and there's meaning behind that story": Indigenous knowledge and young Indigenous children's literacy learning. J Early Child Lit 12(4):389–414

Henderson A (2016) Quick brief on family engagement in Every Student Succeeds Act (ESSA) of 2015. National Education Association. https://ra.nea.org/wp-content/uploads/2016/06/FCE-in-ESSA-in-Brief.pdf. Accessed 08 Feb 2018

Henderson A, Mapp KL (2002) A new wave of evidence: the impact of school, family, and community connections on student achievement. Annual synthesis. National Center for Family & Community Connections with Schools, Austin

Herzog C, Smith P, McGinnis J (2016) Parent voices revisited: American Indian relationships with schools. ProQuest Dissertations and Theses

Howard TC, Navarro O (2016) Critical race theory 20 years later: where do we go from here? Urban Educ 51(3):253–273

Hubbs-Tait L, Tait DA, Hare C, Huey E (2005) Involvement of Native American families in early childhood education. In Saracho O, Spodek B (eds). Contemporary perspectives on families and communities in early childhood education, 225–246

Ishimaru AM, Torres KE, Salvador JE, Lott J, Williams DMC, Tran C (2016) Reinforcing deficit, journeying toward equity: cultural brokering in family engagement initiatives. Am Educ Res J 53(4):850–882

Johnston-Goodstar K, VeLure Roholt R (2017) "Our kids aren't dropping out: they're being pushed out": Native American students and racial microaggressions in schools. J Ethn Cult Divers Soc Work 26(1–2):30–47

Kaomea J (2012) Reconceptualizing Indigenous parent involvement in early educational settings: lessons from Native Hawaiian preschool families. Int Indigen Policy J 3(4):1–19

Ladson-Billings G, Tate WF IV (1995) Toward a critical race theory of education. Teach Coll Rec 97(1):47–68

LaFromboise TD, Hoyt DR, Oliver L, Whitbeck LB (2006) Family, community, and school influences on resilience among American Indian adolescents in the Upper Midwest. J Community Psychol 34(2):193–209

Lawrenchuk RE (1998) Parent participation in a Cree and Ojibway Head Start program: development of a conceptual framework. Masters thesis, University of Manitoba

Lea T, Thompson H, McRae-Williams E, Wegner A (2011) Policy fuzz and fuzzy logic: researching contemporary Indigenous education and parent-school engagement in North Australia. J Educ Policy 26(3):321–339

Lee T (2007) Connecting academics, Indigenous knowledge, and commitment to community: high school students' perceptions of a community-based education. Can J Nativ Educ 30(2):196–216

Lipka J (1986) School-community partnerships in rural Alaska. Rural Educ 7(3):11–14

Lipka J, Hogan MP, Webster JP, Yanez E, Adams B, Clark S, Lacy D (2005) Math in a cultural context: two case studies of a successful culturally based math project. Anthropol Educ Q 36(4):367–385

López G, Kuttner P, Yanagui A (2016) What does partnership taste like?: reimagining family-school partnerships through participatory design research. Paper presented at the annual meeting of the American Education Research Association (AERA), San Antonio, pp 1–29

Lowe K, Bub-Connor H (2014) Teaching at the cultural interface: establishing a responsive classroom through the authentic engagement of a teacher, Aboriginal students and parents. Paper presented at Joint AARE-NZARE 2014 conference, pp 1–13

Madden B, Higgins M, Korteweg DL (2013) "Role models can't just be on posters": re/membering barriers to Indigenous community engagement. Can J Education/Revue Canadienne de L'éducation 36(2):211–247

Marin A, Bang M (accepted) "Look this is how you know": forest walks and knowledge building about the natural world. Cognition & Instruction

Marker M (2006) After the Makah whale hunt: Indigenous knowledge and limits to multicultural discourse. Urban Educ 41(5):482–505

May S (ed) (1999) Indigenous community-based education. Multilingual Matters, Philadelphia

McMahon TR, Kenyon DB, Carter JS (2013) "My culture, my family, my school, me": identifying strengths and challenges in the lives and communities of American Indian youth. J Child Fam Stud 22(5):694–706

McWilliams MS, Maldonado-Mancebo T, Szczepaniak PS, Jones J (2011) Supporting Native Indian preschoolers and their families: family-school-community partnerships. Young Child 66(6):34–41

Mejía-Arauz R, Rogoff B, Dayton A, Henne-Ochoa R (2018) Collaboration or negotiation: two ways of interacting suggest how shared thinking develops. Curr Opin Psychol 23:117–123

Mignolo W (2011) The darker side of western modernity: global futures, decolonial options. Duke University Press, Durham

Mignolo W, Tlostanova MV (2006) Theorizing from the borders: shifting to geo-and body-politics of knowledge. Eur J Soc Theory 9(2):205–221

Million D (2009) Felt theory: an indigenous feminist approach to affect and history. Wicazo Sa Rev 24(2):53–76

Moreton-Robinson A (2011) Virtuous racial states: the possessive logic of patriarchal white sovereignty and the United Nations Declaration on the Rights of Indigenous peoples. Griffith Law Rev 20(3):641–658

Muir NM, Bohr Y (2014) Contemporary practice of traditional Aboriginal child rearing: a review. First Peoples Child Fam Rev 9(1):66–79

Murphy B, Pushor D (2004) Parent marginalization, marginalized parents: creating a place for parents on the school landscape. Alberta J Educ Res 50(3):221–235

No Child Left Behind Act of 2001 (2002) P.L. 107-110, 20 U.S.C. § 1116

Pérez MS, Saavedra CM (2017) A call for onto-epistemological diversity in early childhood education and care: centering global south conceptualizations of childhood/s. Rev Res Educ 41(1):1–29

Redding S, Murphy M, Sheley P (2011) Handbook on family and community engagement. Information Age Publishing, Charlotte

Richardson T (2011) Navigating the problem of inclusion as enclosure in Native culture-based education: theorizing shadow curriculum. Curric Inq 41(3):332–349

Richardson T, Villenas S (2000) "Other" encounters: dances with whiteness in multicultural education. Edu Theory 50(2):255–273

Robinson-Zañartu C, Majel-Dixon J (1996) Parent voices: American Indian relationships with schools. J Am Indian Educ 36(1):33–54

Rogoff B (2014) Learning by observing and pitching in to family and community endeavors: an orientation. Hum Dev 57(2–3):69–81

Romero-Little ME (2010) How should young Indigenous children be prepared for learning? A vision of early childhood education for Indigenous children. J Am Indian Educ 49(1–2):7–27

Sarche M, Whitesell N (2012) Child development research in North American Native communities – looking back and moving forward: introduction. Child Dev Perspect 6(1):42–48

Shear SB, Knowles RT, Soden GJ, Castro AJ (2015) Manifesting destiny: re/presentations of indigenous peoples in K–12 US history standards. Theory Res Soc Educ 43(1):68–101

Shirley VJ (2017) Indigenous social justice pedagogy: teaching into the risks and cultivating the heart. Crit Quest Educ 8(2):163–177

Simpson LB (2011) Dancing on our turtle's back: stories of Nishnaabeg re-creation, resurgence, and a new emergence. Arbeiter Ring Press, Winnipeg

Simpson LB (2014) Land as pedagogy: Nishnaabeg intelligence and rebellious transformation. Decolon Indigen Educ Soc 3(3):1–25

Smith LT (2013) Decolonizing methodologies: research and indigenous peoples. Zed Books, London

Solorzano D (1998) Critical race theory, race and gender microaggressions, and the experience of Chicana and Chicano scholars. Int J Qual Stud Educ 11(1):121–136

Tuck E (2015) Research with Indigenous youth. Building capacitys and cultivating innovations research Brief 6. Retrieved from http://indigenouseducationtools.org/assets/primaryimages/IET06_ResearchwithIndigenousYouthIssue06.pdf

Tuck E, Gaztambide-Fernández RA (2013) Curriculum, replacement, and settler futurity. J Curric Theor (Online) 29(1):72–89

Tuck E, Yang KW (2014) R-words: refusing research. In: Paris D, Winn MT (eds) Humanizing research: decolonizing qualitative inquiry with youth and communities. SAGE, Thousand Oaks, pp 223–248

Tuck E, McKenzie M, McCoy K (2014) Land education: Indigenous, post-colonial, and decolonizing perspectives on place and environmental education research. Environ Educ Res 20(1):1–23

Vakil S, deRoyston MM, Nasir N, Kirshner B (2016) Rethinking race and power in design-based research: Reflection from the field. Cognition & Instruction 34(2):194–209

Villegas M (2009) This is how we "role": moving toward a cosmogonic paradigm in Alaska Native education. Can J Nativ Educ 32(1):38–56

Vizenor G (1989) Trickster discourse: comic holotropes and language games. In: Narrative chance: postmodern discourse on Native American Indian literatures. University of New Mexico, Albuquerque, pp 187–211

White V (2017) Disproportionality of American Indian children in foster care. Master of Social Work Clinical Research Papers

Whyte K (2017) What do Indigenous knowledges do for Indigenous peoples? In: Nelson MK, Shilling D (eds) Keepers of the green world: traditional ecological knowledge and sustainability. Cambridge University Press

Whyte K (2018) Food sovereignty, justice and indigenous peoples: an essay on settler colonialism and collective continuance. In: Barnhill A, Doggett T, Egan A (eds) Oxford handbook on food ethics. Oxford University Press, Oxford

Young IM (2011) Justice and politics of difference. Princeton University Press, Princeton

Zeegers M (2011) Positioning the school in the landscape: exploring black history with a regional Australian primary school. Discourse Stud Cult Polit Educ 32(3):343–356